1860	1880	1900	1920	1940

1890s:
Sperry and Hutchinson begin a trading stamp company.

C.W. Post creates coupons to promote Grape Nuts cereal.

1920s:
Alfred Sloan of General Motors (GM) segments the auto market.

GM introduces target pricing.

Questionnaire-based research grows.

Cash-and-carry wholesalers begin.

Southland Ice Co. opens the first convenience store in Texas.

1880s:
Macy's China department begins odd pricing.

Borden's, Quaker Oats, Vaseline, Pillsbury's Best, and Ivory Soap brands begin.

Early 1900s:
Variety stores are established.

Dealer (retailer) brands begin.

Wanamaker begins a one-price policy, marking prices on every item.

1930:
King Kullen opens the first supermarket in New York.

1870:
Averill Paint Company is granted the first U.S. trademark.

1931:
Procter & Gamble introduces the product manager system.

1860s:
Macy's, Wanamaker, Stewarts, and Zion's open the first department stores.

1908:
Henry Ford designs the Model T.

1937:
Masters opens the first discount store in a New York loft building.

1911:
Curtis Publishing Co. appoints a manager to conduct marketing research.

Mid 1940s:
Rack jobbers begin to sell nonfood items to supermarkets.

1850s-60s:
Singer Sewing Machine introduces installment sales and franchising.

1948:
The General Agreement on Tariffs and Trade (GATT) is signed.

MARKETING

MARKETING

4th EDITION

Joel R. Evans
Hofstra University

Barry Berman
Hofstra University

MACMILLAN PUBLISHING COMPANY
New York

COLLIER MACMILLAN PUBLISHERS
London

Book Team

Acquisition Editor: *Michele Rhoades*
Developmental Editor: *Madalyn Stone*
Production Supervisor: *J. Edward Neve*
Production Manager: *Pam Kennedy Oborski*
Text Designer: *Patricia Smythe*
Cover illustration: *Jerry McDaniel*
Illustrations: *John Odam Associates*

This book was set in Jamille Book by TSI Graphics,
printed and bound by R. R. Donnelley & Sons Company.
The cover was printed by Lehigh Press.

3 2280 00475 2473

Copyright © 1990 by Macmillan Publishing Company, a division of
Macmillan, Inc.
Printed in the United States of America

Earlier editions, copyright © 1982, 1985, and 1987 by Macmillan
Publishing Company

Macmillan Publishing Company
866 Third Avenue, New York, New York 10022

Collier Macmillan Canada, Inc.

Library of Congress Cataloging in Publication Data

Evans, Joel R.
    Marketing / Joel R. Evans, Barry Berman. — 4th ed.
        p. cm.
    Includes bibliographical references.
    ISBN 0-02-334401-6
    1. Marketing. I. Berman, Barry. II. Title.
  HF5415.E86 1990   89-12886
  658.8 — dc20   CIP

Printing: 1 2 3 4 5 6 7 8   Year: 0 1 2 3 4 5 6 7 8 9

THE MACMILLAN SERIES IN MARKETING

O'Connor
PERSONAL SELLING

Tull and Hawkins
MARKETING RESEARCH, Fifth Edition

Tull and Kahle
MARKETING MANAGEMENT

Weilbacher
ADVERTISING, Second Edition

Weilbacher
CASES IN ADVERTISING

Weilbacher
MARKETING MANAGEMENT CASES, Fourth Edition

Wood and Johnson
CONTEMPORARY TRANSPORTATION, Third Edition

To

Linda, Jennifer, and Stacey
Linda, Glenna, and Lisa

About the Authors

Joel R. Evans (Ph.D. in Business with majors in Marketing and Public Policy) is the Retail Management Institute Distinguished Professor of Business and Professor of Marketing and International Business at Hofstra University. Previously, Dr. Evans was department chairperson for seven years. Before joining Hofstra in 1975, he worked for United Merchants and Manufacturers, owned a retail mail-order business, and taught at Bernard M. Baruch College and New York University. He has also served as a consultant for such diverse companies as PepsiCo and Nynex.

Dr. Evans is the author or editor of numerous books and articles and is active in various professional associations. At Hofstra, he has been honored as a faculty inductee in Beta Gamma Sigma honor society and received two Dean's Awards and the School of Business Faculty Distinguished Service Award. In 1988, Dr. Evans was selected as Teacher of the Year by the Hofstra M.B.A. Association.

Barry Berman (Ph.D. in Business with majors in Marketing and Behavioral Science) is the Walter H. "Bud" Miller Distinguished Professor of Business and Professor of Marketing and International Business at Hofstra University. Previously, Dr. Berman was the associate dean of the Hofstra School of Business for seven years. He has served as a consultant to such organizations as the Singer Company, Associated Dry Goods, the State Education Department of New York, and professional and trade groups.

Dr. Berman is the author or editor of numerous books and articles and is active in various professional associations. He served as the associate editor of the *Marketing Review* for many years. At Hofstra, he has been honored as a faculty inductee in Beta Gamma Sigma honor society and received a Dean's Award. In 1984, Dr. Berman was selected as Teacher of the Year by the Hofstra M.B.A. Association.

Joel R. Evans and Barry Berman have worked together since 1976 and are the co-authors of three best-selling Macmillan texts: *Marketing,* 4th Edition (1990), *Retail Management: A Strategic Approach,* 4th Edition (1989), and *Principles of Marketing,* 2nd Edition (1988). At present, Drs. Evans and Berman are also co-directors of the Hofstra University Retail Management Institute. Both regularly teach undergraduate and graduate marketing courses to a wide range of students.

Preface

We believe that a marketing textbook for the 1990s must incorporate both traditional and contemporary aspects of marketing, carefully consider environmental factors, present the roles of marketing and marketing managers, and show the relevance of marketing for those who interact with or who are affected by marketing activities (such as consumers). We also believe that a textbook should describe marketing concepts to readers in an interesting, comprehensive, and balanced manner. As we indicate at the beginning of Chapter 1, marketing is truly "an exciting, dynamic, and contemporary field."

Although the basic components of marketing (such as consumer behavior, marketing research, and product, distribution, promotion, and price planning) form the foundation of any introductory-level marketing textbook, contemporary techniques and topics also need to be covered in depth. Among the contemporary topics that are examined in full chapter length in *Marketing* are strategic planning and marketing, consumer demographics, consumer life-styles and decision making, organizational consumers (including manufacturers, wholesalers, retailers, government, and nonprofit institutions), international marketing, service and nonprofit marketing, and marketing and society. Environmental effects are noted throughout the book.

Marketing explains all major principles, defines key terms, integrates topics, and demonstrates how marketers make everyday and long-run decisions. Illustrations based on organizations such as American Express, DuPont, Holiday Corporation, Kentucky Fried Chicken, Mr. Goodwrench, Navistar, Nike, Perrier, Premier Industrial, 3M, Upjohn, Sony, the U.S. Postal Service, and Westinghouse appear in each chapter. The illustrations build on the textual material, reveal the exciting and dynamic nature of marketing, cover a wide variety of firms, and involve students in real-life applications of marketing.

We began preparing the fourth edition of *Marketing* after receiving input from professors throughout the country via both a detailed focus group session and a lengthy written questionnaire, talking with a number of students, and obtaining considerable feedback from the Macmillan sales force. Our objectives were to retain the material and features most desired from prior editions and to elicit suggestions for new material and features to be included in the fourth edition, while maintaining the appropriate length of the book.

The Tradition Continues

These general features are retained from prior editions of *Marketing:*

▶ A lively easy-to-read writing style.
▶ A balanced treatment of topics (by size of firm, goods- and service-based firms, profit-oriented and nonprofit firms, final and organizational consumers, etc.).
▶ Comprehensive coverage of important marketing concepts, including three chapters each on product, distribution, promotion, and price planning.
▶ A full-color design throughout the book, including about 150 photos and 140 figures. These illustrations are all keyed to major concepts in the text as well as being visually attractive.
▶ Part openers that provide integrated overviews of the chapters in every part.
▶ Detailed part-ending cases.
▶ An appendix on careers in marketing.
▶ An appendix on marketing mathematics.
▶ A 650-item glossary.
▶ Separate company, name, and subject indexes.

These features are also retained from the third edition and are contained in each chapter:

▶ Chapter objectives that outline the major areas to be investigated.
▶ An opening vignette that introduces the material through a real-world situation.
▶ Descriptive margin notes that highlight major concepts.
▶ Boldface key terms that identify important definitions.
▶ Many flowcharts and current figures and tables that explain how marketing concepts operate and provide up-to-date information.
▶ Numerous footnotes, most from the 1980s (including many from 1988 and 1989), to enable the reader to do further research.
▶ A summary of the material covered.
▶ Review and discussion questions that vary in scope and depth from requiring definitions to requiring complex decisions.
▶ Two cases (except Chapter 1, which has an appendix on hints for analyzing cases) that deal with real companies or situations. There are 46 end-of-chapter cases in all, involving all types of companies.

New to the Fourth Edition

These are some of the many new or added features contained in the fourth edition of *Marketing:*

▶ Part openers are linked to a comprehensive marketing figure, which ties the various parts of the book to one another.
▶ All chapter-opening vignettes are completely new. These vignettes deal with major events that relate to the chapter at hand, such as firms' renewed interest in listening to their customers, AT&T after its breakup, the value of single-source information, the latest revision in the SIC code system, the growth of regional marketing, the use of yield management pricing, Europe in 1992, and the role of ethics.
▶ Each chapter begins with an overview.

▶ Each chapter has new thought-provoking "marketing controversy" and "you're the marketer" boxes. The controversies involve such subjects as the marketing orientation of colleges, mergers and LBOs, reversing a declining product life cycle, service versus inventory levels, advertorials and ambush marketing, and the American Heart Association's seal of approval. You're the marketer boxes involve such topics as the U.S. personal savings rate, new Coke, Acura, $3,000 luggage sets, joint ventures, Whittle's Channel One, and Pillsbury.

▶ Chapter summaries are now keyed to chapter objectives. These summaries are followed by a listing of key terms, with text page references.

▶ End-of-chapter questions are now divided into separate "review" and "discussion" categories.

▶ All chapter-ending cases are completely new. Among the organizations included are Audiovox, Boeing, Canon, Caterpillar, Gerber, Mars, Marriott, MasterCard, McCaw (cellular telephone service), Next, Rubbermaid, Suzuki, and Tandy.

▶ All eight part-ending cases are new. They deal with a startup firm — ACT (Appliance Control Technology), targeting business customers, pioneering versus later product-entry strategies, Wal-Mart's retail strategy, Carnival Cruise Lines' promotion strategy, pricing in the watch industry, Colgate-Palmolive's international marketing approach, and Kodak's plans for the 1990s.

▶ There are major revisions/changes in such chapters as "An Overview of Marketing" (1), "Strategic Planning and Marketing" (3), "Organizational Consumers" (7), "Developing a Target Market Strategy" (8), "An Overview of Product Planning" (9), "Marketing and Society" (23), and "Integrating and Analyzing the Marketing Plan" (24). There is one less chapter in the fourth edition, with the material on marketing in the future now better placed throughout the book.

▶ Many definitions are from the 1988 American Marketing Association's *Dictionary of Marketing Terms,* which is the AMA's first new dictionary since 1960.

▶ There is new or expanded coverage of PIMS, marketing information systems, the latest SIC code classification, planning a target market strategy, the VALS 2 typology, the distinction between goods and services, electronic data interchange in distribution, telemarketing, direct product profitability, ethics, and other topics. There are also more examples involving service and industrial marketing placed throughout the text.

▶ The most current data and examples possible are used.

▶ There is a new Appendix C, which describes the computerized exercises that accompany the text. A computer symbol on the relevant chapter pages keys the exercises to the concepts involved.

How Marketing *Is Organized*

Marketing is divided into eight parts. Part 1 presents an overview of marketing, describes the environment within which it operates, presents strategic planning and marketing, and discusses the marketing research process and marketing information systems. Part 2 provides an understanding of final and organizational consumers. It examines demographic data, life-style factors, consumer decision making, target market strategies, and sales forecasting. Part 3 covers product planning, the product life cycle, new products, mature products, branding, and packaging.

Part 4 deals with distribution planning, channel relations, physical distribution, wholesaling, and retailing. Part 5 examines promotion planning, the channel of communication, advertising, publicity, personal selling, and sales promotion. Part 6 covers price planning, price strategies, and applications of pricing. Part 7 shows how marketing's expanded scope includes international marketing, service and nonprofit marketing, and societal issues. Part 8 integrates marketing planning and looks to the future.

Three student supplements are available to complement *Marketing,* 4th Edition. A comprehensive study guide contains chapter objectives, chapter overviews, key terms and concepts, short-answer questions, discussion questions, long and short application exercises, and part-ending review quizzes. *Computer-Based Marketing Exercises* consists of a microcomputer exercise diskette keyed to Appendix C in the text. These exercises enable students to better experience marketing decision making and better understand text concepts in such areas as market segmentation, product planning, advertising budgeting, and performance ratios. *Paintco III* is a "hands-on" computer simulation, whereby individual students or student teams portray firms in the paint industry.

A complete teaching package is available for instructors. It includes corporate videos, transparencies, separate resource and lecture manuals, a semiannual newsletter, and testing materials.

We are pleased that previous editions of *Marketing* were adopted at hundreds of colleges and universities nationwide. We hope the fourth edition will be satisfying to continuing adopters and meet the needs of new ones. Thanks for your support and encouragement.

Please feel free to send us comments regarding any aspect of *Marketing,* 4th Edition or its package: Joel R. Evans or Barry Berman, Department of Marketing and International Business, Hofstra University, Hempstead, N.Y., 11550. We promise to reply to any correspondence we receive.

J. R. E.

B. B.

About the Computer Supplements That Accompany *Marketing,* 4th Edition

As noted in the preface, *Marketing,* 4th Edition has two computer supplements available for students: *Computer-Based Marketing Exercises* and *Paintco III.* Both of these are microcomputer-based and available for IBM PCs and compatibles. They are extremely user-friendly, do not require prior computer experience, may be used on standard or color monitors, and are not dependent on knowledge of software such as Lotus 1-2-3. All directions are contained on computer screens and are self-prompting.

Computer-Based Marketing Exercises is designed to apply and reinforce specific individual concepts in *Marketing,* 4th Edition in an interactive manner. The exercises are explained in Appendix C at the end of this text; throughout *Marketing,* a computer symbol is used to signify which concepts are related to the exercises. An accompanying master computer diskette (which may be ordered by the instructor) can be used to reproduce student exercise disks. The 14 exercises are as realistic as possible; relate to important marketing concepts; allow students to manipulate marketing factors and see their impact on costs, sales, and profits; are relatively independent of one another; and encourage students to improve computer skills.

Each of the exercises may be handed in as a class assignment or used for student self-review/self-learning. Page references to the relevant concepts in *Marketing,* 4th Edition are provided for each exercise, both on the computer diskette and in Appendix C at the end of this text. Students get to experiment with cross-tabulation tables, bar charts, spreadsheets, graphic scales, matrices, profit-and-loss statements, and ratios. While graphics quality is high, no computer graphics board is needed. These are the exercises:

1. Boston Consulting Group Matrix
2. Questionnaire Analysis
3. End-Use Analysis
4. Segmentation Analysis
5. Product Screening
6. Total-Cost Approach
7. Economic Order Quantity
8. Advertising Budget
9. Price Elasticity
10. Key Cost Concepts
11. Standardizing Marketing Plans
12. Allocating Functional Costs
13. Performance Ratios
14. Optimal Marketing Mix

Paintco III is a "real-world" simulation that enables students or student teams to practice a broad range of marketing decisions on a PC through a student diskette before handing in a decision sheet to the instructor. Each student or student team represents a paint manufacturer who makes marketing decisions with regard to market segments served, product quality, distribution intensity, advertising and personal selling as a percentage of sales, and prices charged. Seasonality must also be taken into account.

After trying out their decisions on the PC via the student diskette, each student or student team hands in a written (or computer-generated) decision sheet to the instructor who enters all the students' decisions on to a master computer diskette (both the student and the instructor master disks must be ordered by the instructor). Then, sales and profit data are generated and printed for every student company, based on industry averages and seasonality factors. The simulation would normally be conducted over six to eight weeks, with each week representing a sales quarter. *Paintco III* has extensive player's and instructor's manuals.

We believe these computer supplements greatly enhance text material, further demonstrate the dynamic and exciting nature of marketing, and are important tools in the emerging ''age of the computer.'' We welcome your feedback on *Computer-Based Marketing Exercises* and *Paintco III.*

J. R. E.

B. B.

Acknowledgments

Throughout our professional lives and during the period that this book was researched and written, a number of people provided us with support, encouragement, and constructive criticism. We would like to publicly acknowledge and thank many of them.

During our years as graduate students, we benefited greatly from the knowledge transmitted from professors Conrad Berenson, Henry Eilbirt, and David Rachman, and colleagues Elaine Bernay, William Dillon, Stanley Garfunkel, Leslie Kanuk, Michael Laric, Kevin McCrohan, Leon Schiffman, and Elmer Waters. We learned a great deal at the American Marketing Association's annual consortium for doctoral students, the capstone of any marketing student's education.

At Hofstra University, colleagues Herman Berliner, Dorothy Cohen, Benny Barak, Andrew Forman, Pradeep Gopalkrishna, William James, Keun Lee, Brian McNeeley, Russell Moore, James Neelankavil, Venkat Mummalaneni, James Parker, Saul Sands, Elaine Sherman, and Ven Sriram, stimulated us by providing the environment needed for a book of this type.

We would especially like to thank the following colleagues who participated in a focus group session or reviewed all or part of the *Marketing* manuscript during preparation of the fourth edition. These reviewers made many helpful comments and significant contributions to revisions in the book:

Lawrence Feick (University of Pittsburgh)
Betsy Gelb (University of Houston)
William Harris, III (Ohio University)
Jon Hawes (University of Akron)
Jerry Ingram (Auburn University)
James Littlefield (Virginia Polytechnic Institute and State University)
H. Lee Meadow (Salisbury State College)
Ronald Michman (Shippensburg State University)
William Pertulla (San Francisco State University)
S. R. Rao (Cleveland State University)
Randall Rose (University of South Carolina)
A. Edward Spitz (Eastern Michigan University)
George Winn (James Madison University)

We would also like to thank these colleagues for their insightful reviews for prior editions of *Marketing* and *Principles of Marketing:*

Julian Andorka (DePaul University)
Harold Babson (Columbus State Community College)
Ken Baker (University of New Mexico)
Stephen Batory (Bloomsburg University)
Richard Behr (Broome Community College)
Kurt Beran (Oregon State University)
John Boos (Ohio Wesleyan University)
Donald B. Bradley, III (University of Central Arkansas)
James Brock (Montana State University)
Harvey Bronstein (Oakland Community College)
Sharon Browning (Northwest Missouri State University)
John Bunnell (Broome Community College)
Jim Burrow (North Carolina State University)
Steven Calcich (Norfolk State University)
Yusef Choudhry (Rochester Institute of Technology)
Linda Jane Coleman (Salem State College)
Richard Cummings (College of Lake County)
Benjamin Cutler (Bronx Community College)
Homer Dalbey (San Francisco State University)
Peter Doukas (Westchester Community College)
Rebecca Elmore-Yalch (University of Washington)
Frank Falcetta (Middlesex Community College)
Stanley Garfunkel (Queensborough Community College)
Donald Gordon (Illinois Central College)
Harrison Grathwohl (California State University at Chico)
Blaine Greenfield (Bucks County Community College)
Thomas Greer (University of Maryland)
Robert Hammond (Lexington Community College)
G. E. Hannem (Mankato State University)
Nancy L. Hansen (University of New Hampshire)
Allen Heffner (Lebanon Valley College)
Thomas Hickey (State University of New York at Oswego)
Nathan Himmelstein (Essex County College)
Laurence Jacobs (University of Hawaii at Manoa)
Mary Joyce (University of Central Florida)
Paul Joice, Sr. (Walla Walla College)
Albert Kagan (University of Northern Iowa)
Ruel Kahler (University of Cincinnati)
Bernard Katz (Oakton Community College)
J. Steven Kelly (DePaul University)
John Kerr (Florida State University)
Bettie King (Central Piedmont Community College)
John Krane (Community College of Denver)
William Layden (Golden West College)
Marilyn Liebrenz-Himes (George Washington University)
Robert Listman (Valparaiso University)
James Littlefield (Virginia Polytechnic Institute and State University)
John Lloyd (Monroe Community College)
William Locander (University of Tennessee)
Keith Lucas (Ferris State College)
Ken McCleary (Central Michigan University)

James McMillan (University of Tennessee)
H. Lee Meadow (Salisbury State College)
John Mentzer (Virginia Polytechnic Institute and State University)
Jim Merrill (Indiana University)
James Meszaros (County College of Morris)
Edward Moore (State University of New York College at Plattsburgh)
John Morgan (West Chester University)
Margaret Myers (Northern Kentucky University)
Donald Nagourney (New York Institute of Technology)
Kenneth Papenfuss (Ricks College)
Dennis Pappas (Columbus State Community College)
Terry Paul (University of Houston)
Michael Peters (Boston College)
Ann Pipinski (Northeast Institute of Education)
Edward Popper (Northeastern University)
William Qualls (University of Michigan)
S. R. Rao (Cleveland State University)
Edward Riordan (Wayne State University)
David Roberts (Virginia Polytechnic Institute and State University)
Donald Robin (Louisiana Tech University)
Barbara Samuel (University of Scranton)
Robert Schaffer (California State Polytechnic University at Pomona)
Stanley Scott (Boise State University)
Mohamad Sepehri (Sheperd College)
Richard Sielaff (University of Minnesota, Duluth)
M. Joseph Sirgy (Virginia Polytechnic Institute and State University)
Richard Skinner (Kent State University)
Michael Smith (Temple University)
Gregory Snere (Ellsworth Community College)
Patricia Sorce (Rochester Institute of Technology)
A. Edward Spitz (Eastern Michigan University)
Jeffrey Stoltman (University of Nebraska, Lincoln)
Robert Swerdlow (Lamar University)
Donna Tillman (California State Polytechnic University at Pomona)
Ed Timmerman (Abilene Christian University)
Frank Titlow (St. Petersburg Junior College)
Charles Treas (University of Mississippi)
William Vincent (Santa Barbara City College)
Gerald Waddle (Clemson University)
Donald Walli (Greenville Technical College)
John Walton (Miami University)
J. Donald Weinrauch (Tennessee Technological University)
Mildred Whitted (St. Louis Community College at Forest Park)
David Wills (Sussex County Community College)
Martin Wise (Harrisburg Area Community College)
Joyce Wood (Northern Virginia Community College)
Gene Wunder (Ball State University)
Richard Yalch (University of Washington)
Anthony Zahorik (Vanderbilt University)
William Ziegler (Seton Hall University)

ACKNOWLEDGMENTS

To the many students at Hofstra who reacted to material in *Marketing,* we owe a special thanks, because they represent the true constituency of any textbook authors.

Our appreciation is extended to the fine people at Macmillan, with whom our relationship dates back to 1976. We especially thank the people on the editorial team for *Marketing,* 4th Edition: Bill Oldsey, Michele Rhoades, David Shafer, and Madalyn Stone. We are also extremely grateful for the design, production, marketing, and other efforts of Johnna Barto, Ann Berlin, Amy Davis, Randi Goldsmith, Lucy Hebard, Laura Ierardi, Leo Malek, Carine Mitchell, Edward Neve, Pamela Kennedy Oborski, Bob Pirrung, and Pat Smythe.

We are pleased to recognize the contributions of Diane Schoenberg, our editorial associate; Julie Conway, our graduate research assistant; Linda Berman for comprehensive indexes; and Linda Evans for proofreading.

To our wives and children, this book is dedicated—out of respect and love.

Joel R. Evans
Barry Berman
Hofstra University

Brief Contents

Contents

xxi

part 1
AN INTRODUCTION
TO MARKETING

In Part 1, we begin our study of marketing and discuss concepts that form the foundation for the rest of the text.

1 **An Overview of Marketing** Here, we show the dynamics of marketing, broadly define the term "marketing," trace its evolution, and explain the marketing concept. We examine the importance and scope of marketing, as well as marketing functions and performers. We also contrast the marketing approaches of Nike and Worlds of Wonder.

2 **The Environment of Marketing** In this chapter, we depict the complex environment within which marketing operates, with emphasis on both the factors that are controllable and those that are uncontrollable to an organization and its marketers. We show that without adequate environmental analysis a firm may function haphazardly or be shortsighted.

3 **Strategic Planning and Marketing** Here, we study different types of marketing plans and the relationships between marketing and other functional areas. We also describe the steps in the strategic planning process in detail and cover the product/market opportunity matrix, Boston Consulting Group matrix, PIMS, General Electric business screen, and Porter generic strategy model.

4 **Information for Marketing Decisions** In this chapter, we explain why marketing decisions should be based on sound information. We describe marketing research and the process for undertaking it. We show that marketing research may involve surveys, observation, experiments, and/or simulation. We also explain the role and importance of the marketing information system —which coordinates marketing research, continuous monitoring, and data storage and provides the basis for decision making.

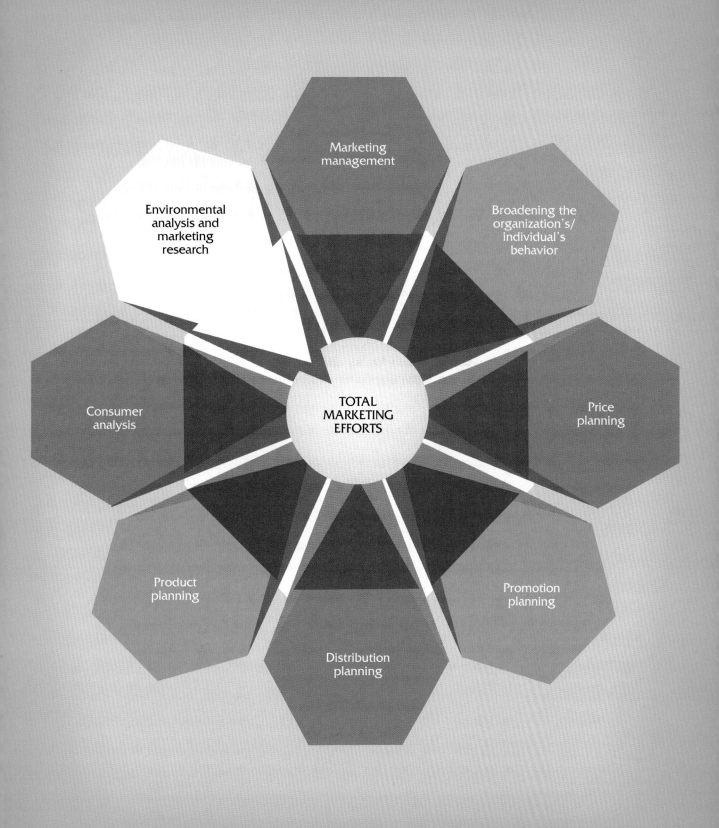

Marketing
management

Broadening the
organization's/
individual's
behavior

Environmental
analysis and
marketing
research

Price
planning

Consumer
analysis

TOTAL
MARKETING
EFFORTS

Promotion
planning

Product
planning

Distribution
planning

CHAPTER *1*
An Overview of Marketing

CHAPTER OBJECTIVES

1. To illustrate the exciting, dynamic, and influential nature of marketing

2. To define marketing and trace its evolution, with emphasis on the marketing concept

3. To show the importance of marketing as a field of study

4. To describe the basic functions of marketing and those that perform these functions

5. To present and compare successful and unsuccessful approaches to marketing

W hat do such classic products as the Pyrex measuring cup (by Corning) and the Samsonite garment bag have in common? After years of popularity, their makers suddenly discovered that many people found their features did not solve their problems. So the companies have redesigned them, and as a reward for paying more attention to buyers' tastes, they have seen the products' sales soar.

From consumer-product companies to industrial manufacturers, corporations are spending more time and money than ever before trying to find out just what it is that consumers want.

For these firms, an important milestone has been reached—they are truly consumer-oriented companies practicing the marketing concept. What does this mean? These firms "talk" to customers to discover their needs and work hard to satisfy them; and they do this in a systematic, goal-oriented manner. As C. Merle Crawford, editor of the *Journal of Product Innovation Management,* noted: "Companies know that if products are not right on target when they come onto the market, people will find products that are." Let us illustrate how this consumer orientation is being applied, by looking at situations involving consumer goods, industrial goods, and service firms.

At Corning, the 50-year-old Pyrex measuring cup was redesigned after the firm received consumer input about features they did not like. Now, the handle is easier to hold, the cup can be stacked, and the cup is deeper (to prevent microwave spillovers).

At Samsonite, consumer research revealed that consumers were dissatisfied because garment bags did not prevent their suits from wrinkling and did not contain adequate pockets for storing shoes and other small items. As a result, a newly designed product (which holds suits so as to prevent wrinkling and has a number of compartments) was introduced. Says Samsonite's president, "Now, we're asking consumers right back at the idea stage what they want."

At Worthington Industries, a Columbus, Ohio, steel processor, every employee carries the company's "golden rule" on a card: "We treat customers, employees, investors, and suppliers as we would like to be treated." Worthington routinely sends its own machinists to meet with the machinists of its corporate customers to clarify communications and make sure that customer needs are understood.

Reprinted by permission.

At Scandinavian Airline Systems (SAS), the company views its most valuable assets as the customers who fly on its airplanes, not the airplanes themselves. Service performance standards exist both for employees directly serving customers and for support personnel, such as baggage handlers. Says SAS' chief executive: "If you're not serving the customer, your job is to serve those who are."

Sometimes, it takes a company too long to become customer-oriented and it pays the price:

For decades, executives of the General Motors Corporation decided among themselves what kinds of cars Americans wanted. But now, with GM's market share down sharply, those days are gone. GM executives genuinely appear to be trying to listen to what customers are saying. Stunned by the company's loss of market share—from 44.5 per cent in 1984 to 35 per cent now—once-arrogant GM executives speak today in humbler tones.[1]

In this chapter, we will learn more about the pivotal role of marketing, see how marketing has evolved over the years, and look at its scope.

[1] William Glaberson, "Listening to the Consumer Again," *New York Times* (April 6, 1988), pp. D1, D6; Ron Zemke, "Scandinavian Management—A Look at Our Future?" *Management Review* (July 1988), pp. 44–47; and John Holusha, "Humbler G.M. Is Now Listening," *New York Times* (January 30, 1988), pp. 33–35.

Overview

Marketing is an exciting, dynamic, and contemporary field. It influences us each day in both our roles as providers of goods and services and as consumers.

In our role as goods and service providers, we make such marketing-related decisions as choosing who our customers are, what goods and services to offer, where to sell our goods and services, what features to emphasize in advertising, and what prices to charge. Marketing-related activities are not confined to industrial firms or to people who are called "marketers." These activities are utilized by all types of companies and individuals. For example, a certified public accounting firm must specify its client base (such as small firms versus large firms versus individuals); the services to offer (such as accounting services only versus accounting plus consulting services); the location(s) of offices (such as at a commercial or residential site); whether to advertise through newspapers, magazines, direct mailings, and so on (and what message to convey in these ads); and the fees to be charged (which could be based on hourly rates or an annual flat rate keyed to the services performed).

In our role as consumers, the marketing practices of goods and service providers impact on many of the decisions made by our parents, spouses, other family members, friends and associates, and/or us. Marketing practices are in play when we are born (what doctor our parents select, the style of baby furniture they buy), while we grow (our parents' purchase of a family car, our choice of a college), while we conduct our everyday lives (our use of a particular brand of toothpaste, the purchase of status-related items), and when we retire (our consideration of travel options, a change in living accommodations). For virtually every good and service we purchase, the marketing process affects the assortment of models and styles offered in the marketplace, where we shop, the availability of knowledgeable sales personnel, the prices we pay, and other factors.

This chapter introduces the field of marketing, shows its dynamic nature, defines the term "marketing," looks at marketing's evolution and scope, outlines the various marketing functions and performers, and contrasts a successful use of marketing with an unsuccessful one.

The Dynamics of Marketing

As formally defined later in the chapter, marketing encompasses all of the activities involved in anticipating, managing, and satisfying demand through the exchange process. Such activities include environmental analysis and marketing research, consumer analysis, product planning, distribution planning, promotion planning, price planning, international marketing, and marketing management. Through the following examples, we will glimpse the dynamic nature of marketing by showing how a variety of firms engage in marketing activities.

Based on its analysis and research of the changing automobile industry, in particular the longer-lasting factory paint jobs and rustproofing for new autos, Maaco Enterprises recently decided to refocus its business. With 450 franchised outlets in the United States and Canada, 500,000 paint jobs a year, and annual sales of $250 million, Maaco has been by far the largest operator of car painting centers; but with the changing environment, Maaco realized that it could not sustain sales growth if it concentrated only on paint jobs. So, Maaco is now aiming to increase its sales via collision-

repair work. See Figure 1-1. Said Maaco's president, Anthony A. Martino, "Part of the attraction for us is that there isn't any major player. It may take five years to get well established, but we think we have a better shot at it than anybody else."[2]

The Consumer Network is a research company providing important consumer information to firms such as Sara Lee, Procter & Gamble, Heinz, and Winn-Dixie, via a $200 per year newsletter. Monthly the Consumer Network surveys up to 5,000 consumers nationally to anticipate buying trends. Through the Consumer Network, firms have learned that many consumers are interested in single-serving sizes, convenience-oriented foods, and resealable cereal bags; that much of bank advertising and marketing is perceived as confusing; and that consumers often find food advertising to be offensive, boring, uninformative, and dishonest.[3]

Every year companies around the world introduce tens of thousands of new products to stimulate consumer interest and stay ahead of competitors. Some of these products succeed and many others fail. According to *Fortune* magazine, these are a few of the "hottest, most-innovative, best-selling items" now on the market:

▶ Sony's Video Walkman, a 2 1/2 pound combination color television (with a three-inch screen) and videocassette recorder.
▶ Upjohn's Rogaine, the first prescription hair-growth medication approved by the Food and Drug Administration. See Figure 1-2.
▶ Max Factor's No Color Mascara, a nonsmudging cosmetic that is one of the most successful new cosmetic products in twenty years.
▶ NEC's UltraLite laptop computer, a thin 4.4 pound product with four times the speed of the IBM XT.[4]

[2] Frank Allen, "Maaco, with Car Paint Jobs Lasting Longer, Turns to Collision Repair," *Wall Street Journal* (December 2, 1988), p. B3.
[3] Laura Loro, "Doyle Keeps Tabs on Spending Trends," *Advertising Age* (September 26, 1988), p. 78.
[4] Edward C. Baig, "Products of the Year," *Fortune* (December 5, 1988), pp. 89–98.

FIGURE 1-2
**Introducing Rogaine by
Upjohn**
Rogaine is the first
prescription drug for
stimulating hair growth on
the crown (vertex) of the
head in individuals with
male pattern baldness
(alopecia androgenetica).
Reprinted by permission.

Holly Farms, a poultry producer that sells its products through various grocery stores, recently discovered the perils of incomplete distribution planning. Holly Farms developed what it thought was the "Cadillac of poultry," its roasted chicken; but the grocers with which it dealt bought far fewer chickens than Holly Farms anticipated. The grocers were dissatisfied with the short shelf life of the product. Because the chicken's quality would erode after 18 days, and it could take up to 9 days to ship the product from Holly Farms' plant to stores, grocers had only about a week to sell each chicken. Holly Farms also acknowledged that "it probably didn't go far enough to tailor its marketing program to each supermarket chain or spend sufficient time educating managers."[5]

As part of its promotion efforts in communicating with consumers, Campbell Soup Co. is one of the fifty leading advertisers in the United States with annual expenditures exceeding $260 million. In 1989, $60 million was allocated to ads for Campbell's red-and-white label soups, the oldest product category carried by the firm that also markets Prego spaghetti sauce, Pepperidge Farm baked goods, Mrs. Paul's frozen seafoods, Vlasic pickles, Godiva chocolate, and several other brands. And, after a decade's absence, Campbell has revived its "M'm m'm good" slogan in soup advertisements: "Research showed the 'M'm m'm good' tag is so closely identified with Campbell that 74 per cent of all adults remember it." The company is also placing renewed advertising emphasis on the Campbell Kids. These efforts are intended to help Campbell maintain its hefty 66 per cent share of the prepared-soup market.[6]

---

[5] Arthur Buckler, "Holly Farms' Marketing Error: The Chicken That Laid an Egg," *Wall Street Journal* (February 9, 1988), p. 44.

[6] Judann Dagnoli, "Campbell Reheats 'M'm M'm Good'," *Advertising Age* (September 26, 1988), p. 4.

Recently, MasterCard International, the second-largest credit-card firm in the United States, with about 145 million cardholders (compared with 165 million cardholders for Visa International), sought to raise the fees that merchants (such as retailers) paid for processing MasterCard transactions. The company proposed to raise interchange fees, the amounts received by the member banks issuing credit cards to customers, by as much as 29 per cent, in order to generate greater revenues and profits for MasterCard International and its member banks. But large merchants quickly complained about the fee increases and said they would encourage shoppers to make purchases with other credit cards, such as Visa. Shortly thereafter, MasterCard International scaled back its proposed increases.[7]

Nordson Corp. is a Westlake, Ohio-based medium-sized manufacturer of specialized machinery used to apply adhesives, sealants, and coatings. The firm concentrates on customized equipment for special market niches. International sales account for more than half of Nordson's $245 million in total annual revenues. Nordson's international prowess is summed up in these comments:

> The companies that succeed in the 1990s will be export-oriented, especially those specializing in equipment used to modernize industry. They will have good foreign distribution and understand how to make their equipment attractive to foreign buyers.

> Nordson represents the manufacturing company of the future. The United States may produce less steel during the 1990s, but there will be more opportunity for companies that apply the latest technology to do some job better and more efficiently.[8]

At IBM, an essential task of marketing management is to utilize the most efficient marketing organization possible. This has led to three major reorganizations since 1982, in response to changing market conditions. Prior to 1982, IBM had separate marketing divisions for large-scale computers, intermediate and smaller computers, and office products (such as typewriters). At that time, to improve efficiency, it set up two basic divisions, one to handle the biggest customers and the other to handle the remaining accounts; each division sold all IBM product lines. In 1985, IBM announced that it would combine the divisions and then separate them into North-Central and South-West sales groups, with each group selling all product lines to all customers in its geographic area to be more responsive to customers. However, in 1988, after disappointing results, IBM substantially decentralized its marketing efforts by shifting responsibilities away from top management to six relatively autonomous product and marketing groups. Said IBM's chief executive, "there's no way that one small set of managers at the top should think they are close enough to the action to make the decisions in all these areas." This represented a major change in IBM's management philosophy.[9]

The formal study of marketing requires an understanding of its definition, importance, scope, and functions, as well as the evolution of marketing and the marketing concept. These principles are discussed in the next three sections.

---

[7] Robert Guenther, "MasterCard Fee to Retailers Is Increased 29%," *Wall Street Journal* (September 19, 1988), p. 2; and Robert Guenther, "MasterCard, in 'Competitive Response,' Scales Back Scheduled Increase in Fees," *Wall Street Journal* (November 21, 1988), p. B10.

[8] Ralph E. Winter, "Nordson Is Poised to Compete in the '90s," *Wall Street Journal* (November 29, 1988), p. A8.

[9] Geoff Lewis, Anne R. Field, John J. Keller, and John W. Verity, "Big Changes at Big Blue," *Business Week* (February 15, 1988), pp. 92–98.

Definitions of Marketing

The definitions of marketing can be grouped into two major categories: classical (narrow) definitions and modern (broad) definitions. In classical terms, marketing is defined as

> the performance of business activities that direct the flow of goods and services from producer to consumer or user.[10]

or

> the process in a society by which the demand structure for economic goods and services is anticipated or enlarged and satisfied through the conception, promotion, and physical distribution of such goods and services.[11]

Classical definitions place too much emphasis on distribution activities and on economic goods.

These classical definitions of marketing are oriented toward the physical movement of economic goods and services. As such, they have several weaknesses. The role of physical distribution and marketing channels is overemphasized. Government and nonprofit institutions, which are now frequently engaged in marketing, are omitted. The importance of exchange between buyers and sellers is overlooked. The strong impact on marketing by many publics — such as employees, unions, stockholders, consumer groups, and government agencies — is not considered.

The modern definition is much broader.

A proper definition of marketing should not be confined to economic goods and services. It should cover organizations (Red Cross), people (political candidates), places (Hawaii), and ideas (the value of seat belts). A consumer orientation must be central to any definition. A company attains its objectives by satisfying consumers. Marketing is not just concerned with enlarging demand; it also attempts to regulate demand to match supply. For example, many electric utilities seek to smooth out demand in summer months by getting business and final consumers to shift usage to times where capacity is not strained. The social nature of marketing, such as ethics and product safety, needs to be included in a definition. The organization needs to ask whether a good or service should be sold, as well as whether that good or service can be sold.

The breadth of marketing was officially recognized by the American Marketing Association (AMA) in 1985 when it replaced the classical definition it had approved in 1960 with this one:

> Marketing is the process of planning and executing the conception, pricing, promotion, and distribution of ideas, goods, and services to create exchanges that satisfy individual and organizational objectives.[12]

As the then president of the AMA indicated, the new definition "shows the wide-ranging dimensions of marketing." The discipline is "not limited to activities in which businesses are involved. It can involve the activities of a nonprofit organization or the marketing of an idea or a service as well as a product."[13]

---

[10] Ralph S. Alexander (Chairman), *Marketing Definitions: A Glossary of Terms* (Chicago: American Marketing Association, 1960), p. 15.

[11] "Statement of the Philosophy of the Marketing Faculty," The Ohio State University, College of Commerce and Administration (Columbus, Ohio: 1964), p. 2. Reprinted in the *Journal of Marketing*, Vol. 29 (January 1965), pp. 43–44.

[12] "AMA Board Approves New Definition," *Marketing News* (March 1, 1985), p. 1.

[13] Ibid.

A broad, integrated definition of marketing forms the basis of this text. While the definition used is quite similar to the one now accepted by the AMA, it is more concise:

> *Marketing* is the anticipation, management, and satisfaction of demand through the exchange process.

Marketing involves goods, services, organizations, people, places, and ideas.

Anticipation of demand requires a firm to do consumer research on a regular basis so that it develops and introduces offerings that are desired by consumers. See Figure 1-3. *Management of demand* includes stimulation, facilitation, and regulation tasks. Stimulation tasks arouse consumers to want the firm's offering through attractive product design, intensive promotion, reasonable prices, and other strategies. Facilitation is the process whereby the firm makes it easy to buy its offering through convenient locations, availability of credit, well-informed salespeople, and other strategies. Regulation is needed when there are peak periods for demand rather than balanced demand throughout the year or when demand is greater than the availability of the

Marketing includes ***anticipating demand, managing demand,*** *and* ***satisfying demand.***

FIGURE 1-3
At 3M, One Idea Leads to Another
Reprinted by permission.

How a dirty old sneaker made living rooms livable.

When 3M first developed fluorochemicals, they did everything we expected... and a bit more. The bonus came when some spilled onto a tennis shoe and tests showed that part of the shoe just *couldn't* be easily soiled. It was the birth of "Scotchgard" Protector...the world's finest soil and stain repellent for carpet and fabrics.

It was another case of 3M people stretching their minds. Sharing technologies, probing, exploring. To make small ideas big ones; to make big ideas better.

It's an environment we encourage at 3M. To promote innovation. To make our people eager and able to respond to your needs. And it works wonders.

Let us demonstrate. Tell us of a business problem you have and watch how quickly we respond. Call Terry Baker at 800-328-3234. In Minnesota call 612-736-6772.

At 3M, one idea leads to another.

3M

FIGURE 1-4
Providing Customer Satisfaction
Reprinted by permission.

offering. Then the goal is to spread demand throughout the year or to demarket a good or service (reduce overall demand). *Satisfaction of demand* involves actual performance, safety, availability of options, after-sale service, and other factors. For consumers to be satisfied, the goods, services, organizations, people, places, and ideas they patronize or support must fulfill their expectations. See Figure 1-4.

Marketing activities can be directed to consumers and to publics. ***Consumer demand*** refers to the characteristics and needs of final consumers, industrial consumers, wholesalers and retailers, government institutions, international markets, and nonprofit institutions. A firm may appeal to one or a combination of these. ***Publics' demand*** refers to the characteristics and needs of employees, unions, stockholders, consumer groups, the general public, government agencies, and other internal and external forces that affect company operations.

Demand is affected by both consumers and publics.

The marketing process is not complete until consumers and publics ***exchange*** their money, their promise to pay, or their support for the offering of the firm, institution, person, place, or idea.

Exchange completes the process.

The Evolution of Marketing

The origins of marketing can be traced to people's earliest use of the exchange process: barter (trading one resource for another — for example, food for animal pelts). To accommodate the exchange process, trading posts, traveling salespeople, general stores, and cities evolved along with a national monetary system.

During the latter 1800s, the Industrial Revolution marked the beginning of the modern system of marketing. Until that time, exchanges were limited because people did not have surplus items to trade. With the onset of mass production, better transportation, and more efficient technology, products could be manufactured in greater quantities and sold at lower prices. People began to turn away from self-sufficiency (such as making all of their own clothes) to purchases (such as buying a new suit or dress). Improved mobility, densely populated cities, and specialization also enabled more people to participate in the exchange process.

During the initial stages of the Industrial Revolution, output was limited and marketing was devoted to the physical distribution of products. Because demand was high and competition was low, companies did not have to conduct consumer research, modify products, or otherwise adapt to consumer needs. Their goal was to increase production to keep up with demand. This was known as the ***production era*** of marketing.

*In the **production era,** output increased to meet demand.*

Once a company was able to maximize its production capabilities, it hired a sales force to sell its inventory. At first, while the company developed its products, consumer tastes or needs received little consideration. At first, while the company developed its products, consumer tastes or needs received little consideration. The role of advertising and the sales force was to make the desires of consumers fit the attributes of the products being manufactured. For example, a shoe manufacturer would produce brown wingtip shoes and use advertising and personal selling to convince consumers to buy them. The manufacturer would not determine consumer tastes before making shoes or adjust output to those tastes. This was known as the ***sales era*** of marketing.

*In the **sales era,** firms sold products without first determining consumers' desires.*

As competition grew, supply began to exceed demand. A firm could not prosper without input from marketing. A marketing department was created. It conducted consumer research and advised management on how to design, price, distribute, and promote products. Unless the firm adapted to consumer needs, competitors might be better able to satisfy consumer demand and leave it with surplus inventory. Although the marketing department participated in company decisions, it remained in a subordinate or conflicting position to production, engineering, and sales departments during this period of evolution in marketing. This was known as the ***marketing department era***.

*The **marketing department era** occurred when research was used to determine consumer needs.*

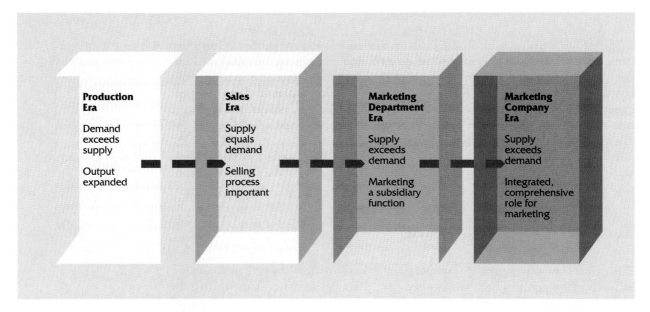

FIGURE 1-5 **How Marketing Evolves**

*The **marketing company era** integrates consumer research and analysis into all company efforts.*

Over the past thirty years, the central role of marketing has been recognized by many firms; and the marketing department has become the equal of others in the company. At these firms, major decisions are made on the basis of thorough consumer analysis. Competition is intense and sophisticated. Consumers must be drawn and kept to the firm's brands. Company efforts are integrated and frequently re-evaluated. This is known as the **marketing company era**. Figure 1-5 shows the key aspects of each era in the evolution of marketing.

The marketing concept and marketing philosophy are the underpinnings of the marketing company era. They are examined here.

The Marketing Concept

*The **marketing concept** is consumer-oriented, integrated, and goal-oriented.*

The **marketing concept** is a consumer-oriented, integrated, goal-oriented philosophy for a firm, institution, or person. See Figure 1-6.

In 1954, Peter Drucker (a leading management professor and consultant) emphasized the role of marketing in the success of a business. His words are just as valid today:

> If we want to know what a business is we must start with its purpose . . . . There is only one valid definition of business purpose: to create a customer. What business thinks it produces is not of first importance — especially not to the future of the business or to its success. What the customer thinks he is buying, what he considers "value" is decisive — it determines what a business is, what it produces, and whether it will prosper.[14]

One of the first formal statements on the marketing concept was made in 1957 by John B. McKitterick, then president of General Electric. McKitterick told a meeting of the American Marketing Association that the marketing concept was a customer-oriented, integrated, profit-oriented philosophy of business.[15]

---

[14] Peter Drucker, *The Practice of Management* (New York: Harper & Row, 1954), p. 37.
[15] John B. McKitterick, "What Is the Marketing Management Concept?" in Frank M. Bass (Editor), *The Frontiers of Marketing Thought and Action* (Chicago: American Marketing Association, 1957), pp. 71–82.

12

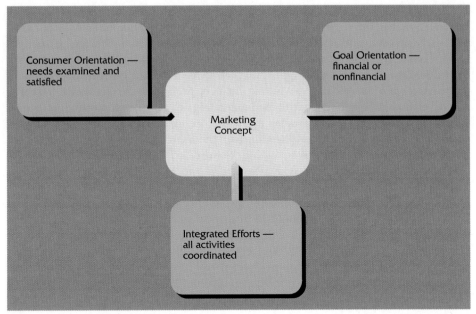

FIGURE 1-6
The Marketing Concept

During the past thirty years, many companies have increased their reliance on marketing, as these illustrations show:

Marketing is the process of defining, anticipating, and creating customer needs and wants and of organizing all the resources of the company to satisfy them at greater total profit to the company and to the customer.[16] (B. F. Goodrich)

Today, the thrust of our merchandising is more varied and complex, to meet the needs and desires of our customers. May [Department Stores] has diversified strategically to broaden and strengthen its position as a leading retailer, by growing through three distinct approaches to the market. Each of these operations serves the tastes, trends, and shopping patterns of significant segments of the consumer market.[17]

American Greetings believes the greeting card industry will continue to offer our company opportunities for growth. Building upon our past success, our commitment is to grow in our core business. Our prospects for long-term growth will be governed by our strengths as a creative and marketing company. Our talented people are attuned to the marketplace. Therefore, we will expand our markets by providing a continuous flow of products which respond to the changing and emerging tastes of consumers.[18]

[To LTV Steel Co.], the customer is the ultimate boss in every respect. Manufacturing systems, "people" programs, process controls, and revolutionary styles of management must have product quality and customer service as their primary focus. And these systems are eminently achievable with existing resources.[19]

These statements demonstrate that, for a variety of firms, the marketing company era has arrived; marketing is now seen as the underlying philosophy of business, around which other decisions are made.

[16] Don C. Miller, "Total Marketing—Management's Point of View," Third Regional Industrial Marketing Conference, American Marketing Association, Columbus, Ohio, March 31, 1960.
[17] *May Company, Annual Report for 1976*, p. 4.
[18] *American Greetings 1985 Annual Report*, p. 4.
[19] "Steel Company's Fortunes Improve When It Becomes Customer-Driven," *Marketing News* (October 10, 1988), p. 10.

The elements of the marketing concept are crucial to the ultimate success of a good, service, organization, person, place, or idea. A customer orientation requires an examination of market needs, not production capability, and development of a plan to satisfy them. Goods and services should be viewed as means to accomplish ends and not the ends themselves. Under an integrated marketing focus, all activities relating to goods and services are coordinated, including finance, production, engineering, research and development, inventory control, and marketing. The firm, organization, or person should be goal-oriented and employ marketing to achieve goals. The goals may be profit, a cure for a disease, increased tourism, the election of a political candidate, an improved corporate image, and so on. Marketing helps achieve goals by orienting the organization toward satisfying consumers and providing desirable goods, services, or ideas.

Marketing goals may be profit, a cure for a disease, or an improved corporate image.

While the marketing concept enables an organization to analyze, maximize, and satisfy consumer demand, it should be realized that the concept is only a guide to planning. The organization must also consider its strengths and weaknesses in such functional areas as production, engineering, finance, and distribution. Marketing plans need to balance goals, customer needs, and resource capabilities. In addition, the impact of competition, government regulations, and other forces external to the firm must be evaluated. These factors are discussed in Chapters 2 and 3.

Selling Versus Marketing Philosophies

Figure 1-7 focuses on the differences between selling and marketing philosophies. The benefits of a marketing, rather than a sales, orientation are many. Marketing stresses consumer analysis and satisfaction, directs the resources of the firm to making the goods and services that consumers want, and is adaptive to changes in consumer characteristics and needs. Under a marketing philosophy, selling is used to communicate with and understand consumers; consumer dissatisfaction leads to changes in policy, not a stronger or different sales pitch. Marketing looks for real differences in consumer tastes and develops offerings to satisfy them. Marketing is oriented to the long run, and marketing goals reflect overall company goals. Finally, marketing views customer needs in a broad (for example, heating) rather than a narrow (for example, fuel oil) manner.

With a marketing orientation, selling is used to communicate with and understand consumers.

The Importance and Scope of Marketing

It is important to study the field of marketing for several reasons. Since marketing stimulates demand, a basic task for it is to generate consumer enthusiasm for goods and services. In the United States, the Gross National Product (GNP) — the total market value of goods and services produced in a country during a year — is about $5 trillion.

Marketing stimulates consumers, costs a large part of sales, employs people, supports industries, affects all consumers, and plays a major role in daily lives.

A large amount of each sales dollar goes to cover the marketing costs associated with such activities as product development, packaging, distribution, advertising and personal selling, price marking, and administering consumer credit programs. Some estimates place the costs of marketing as high as 50 per cent or more of sales in certain industries. Yet, it should not be assumed that the performance of some marketing activities by consumers would automatically lead to lower prices. For example, could a

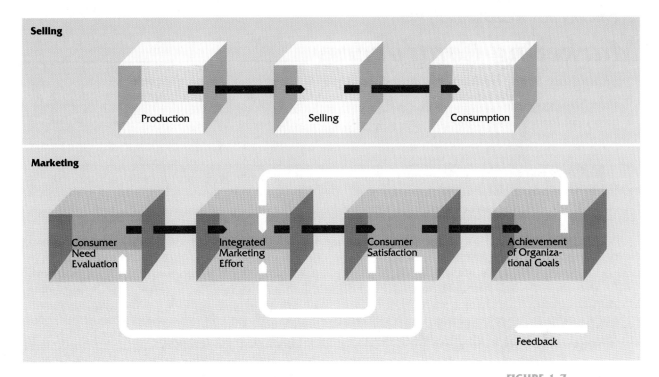

Production → Selling → Consumption

Marketing

Consumer Need Evaluation → Integrated Marketing Effort → Consumer Satisfaction → Achievement of Organizational Goals

Feedback

FIGURE 1-7
The Focus of Selling and Marketing Philosophies

consumer really save money by flying to Detroit to buy a new car directly from the manufacturer rather than a dealer? Would a consumer be willing to buy clothing in bulk in order to reduce a retailer's transportation and storage costs?

Between one-fourth and one-third of the civilian labor force in the United States is engaged in marketing activities. This includes people employed in the retailing, wholesaling, transportation, warehousing, and communications industries and those involved with marketing activities for manufacturing, financial, service, agricultural, mining, and other industries. For instance, about 19 million people work in retailing, 6 million in wholesaling, and 4 million in transportation. And projections indicate that future employment in marketing will remain strong.

Marketing activities support entire industries, such as advertising and marketing research. Total annual U.S. advertising expenditures exceed $125 billion. Many agencies, including Young & Rubicam, Saatchi & Saatchi, Backer Spielvogel Bates, and BBDO, have worldwide billings of $3 billion or more. Approximately $5 billion worldwide is spent yearly on marketing research. Companies such as Nielsen, IMS International, Pergamon/AGB, SAMI/Burke, and Arbitron generate yearly revenues of more than $100 million dollars each.

All people serve as consumers for various goods and services. By understanding the role of marketing, consumers can become better informed, more selective, and more efficient. Effective channels of communication with organizations can also be established and complaints resolved more easily and favorably. Consumer groups have a major impact on firms.

Because resources are scarce, marketing programs and systems must function at their peak. For example, optimization of store hours, inventory movement, advertising expenditures, product assortments, and other areas of marketing will better coordinate resources. Some industries may actually require demarketing (lowering the demand for goods and services). The latter often include oil and gasoline.

15

Marketing Controversy

Should a College Be Marketing-Oriented?

Have you ever been closed out of a class taught by a popular professor and been forced to take another professor's class or delay taking that course for a semester? Have you ever taken a course that you feel has little impact on your career or life-long educational goals?

In theory, a college or university with a total commitment to its students (a pure marketing orientation) would not let the preceding occur. Such a college would:

▶ *Allow students to opt for pass/fail grades in most courses.*

▶ *Give students high flexibility in choosing the courses to complete their degrees.*

▶ *Have no class-size limits for popular faculty members and courses.*

▶ *Give transfer credits for courses at other schools in a liberal manner.*

▶ *Use student course and teacher evaluations as important inputs in annual faculty evaluations.*

▶ *Offer new courses for students based on their suggestions.*

▶ *Specify the name of the faculty member teaching every course prior to registration.*

▶ *Allow student input in important decisions affecting them (such as curriculum development and revision, faculty tenure, and tuition).*

However, although most colleges and universities have some level of marketing orientation, almost none have a pure marketing orientation. Many faculty and administrators believe that there should be rigorous course requirements, that pass/fail grading reduces student motivation, that class-size limits are necessary to foster a good learning environment, that transfer credits should be limited, that students can observe only one aspect of teaching performance—communication skills—and not others (such as subject matter expertise and the level of the presentation), and so on. They also often believe that students may be unable to make the best possible decisions about their education.

What do you think?

Marketing impacts strongly on people's beliefs and life-styles. In fact, marketing has been criticized as developing materialistic attitudes, fads, product obsolescence, a reliance on gadgets, conspicuous consumption (status consciousness), and superficial product differences and wasting resources. Marketers reply that they merely respond to the desires of people and make the best goods and services they can at the prices people will pay.

Marketing has a role to play in improving the quality of life. For example, marketing personnel often encourage firms to make safer products, such as low-tar cigarettes and child-proof bottle caps. They create public service messages on energy conservation, cures for diseases, driver safety, abuses of alcohol, and other topics. They help new goods, ideas, and services (for example, microwave ovens, improved nutrition, and automated banking) to be accepted and assimilated by people.

The scope of marketing is extremely wide. Among the areas in which marketing is involved are pricing, warehousing, packaging, branding, selling, sales force management, credit, transportation, social responsibility, retail site selection, consumer analysis, wholesaling, retailing, vendor appraisal and selection, advertising, public relations, marketing research, product planning, and warranties.

A knowledge of marketing is also valuable for those not directly involved in a marketing job. For example, marketing decisions must be made by doctors (What hours are most desirable to patients?), lawyers (How can new clients be attracted?), management consultants (Should the fees charged be higher, lower, or the same as competitors?), financial analysts (What investment opportunities should be recommended to clients?), research and development personnel (Is there consumer demand for a potential "breakthrough" product?), economists (What impact will the economy have on the ability of various industries to market their offerings?), statisticians (How should firms react to predicted demographic changes?), teachers (How can students learn to be better consumers?), city planners (How can industrial firms be persuaded to relocate to the city?), nonprofit institutions (How can contributions from donors be increased?), and others. Each of these professions and organizations requires an understanding and satisfaction of patient, client, consumer, student, taxpayer, or contributor needs. And more of them than ever before are now undertaking marketing activities such as research, advertising, and so on.

Marketing awareness is valuable for those working in nonmarketing jobs.

Marketing Functions and Performers

There are eight basic ***marketing functions:*** environmental analysis and marketing research, consumer analysis, product planning (which includes goods, services, and ideas), distribution planning, promotion planning, price planning, broadening the organization's/individual's scope, and marketing management. These functions are shown in Figure 1-8, which also notes where these functions are discussed in the text.

*The basic **marketing functions** range from environmental analysis to marketing management.*

Here are brief descriptions of the basic marketing functions:

► Environmental analysis and marketing research—Involves monitoring and adapting to external factors that affect success or failure, such as the economy and competition; and collecting data to resolve specific marketing issues
► Consumer analysis—Involves examining and evaluating consumer characteristics, needs, and purchase processes; and selecting the group(s) of consumers at which to aim marketing efforts
► Product planning (including goods, services, and ideas)—Involves developing and maintaining products, product assortments, product images, brands, packaging, and optional features; and deleting faltering products
► Distribution planning—Involves establishing relations with distribution-channel intermediaries, physical distribution, inventory management, warehousing, transportation, the allocation of goods and services, wholesaling, and retailing
► Promotion planning—Involves communicating with customers, the general public, and others through some form of advertising, publicity, personal selling, and/or sales promotion
► Price planning—Involves determining price levels and ranges, pricing techniques, terms of purchase, price adjustments, and the use of price as an active or passive factor

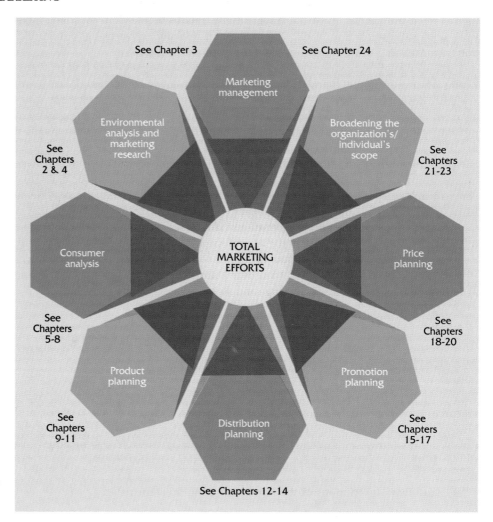

FIGURE 1-8
The Basic Functions of Marketing

▶ Broadening the organization's/individual's scope — Involves deciding on the emphasis to place, as well as the approach to take, on international marketing, service/nonprofit marketing, and societal issues

▶ Marketing management — Involves planning, implementing, and controlling the marketing program (strategy) and individual marketing functions; and appraising the risks and benefits in decision making

Generally a company should first study its environment, gather relevant marketing research data, and analyze its potential customers to determine their needs and select the consumer group(s) on which to focus. Then, the firm should plan its product offerings, make distribution decisions, determine how to communicate with customers and others, and set appropriate prices. These four functions (in combination, known as the marketing mix) should be undertaken in a coordinated manner, based on environmental and consumer analysis. At this point, the company should also decide on its involvement with international marketing, service/nonprofit marketing, and societal

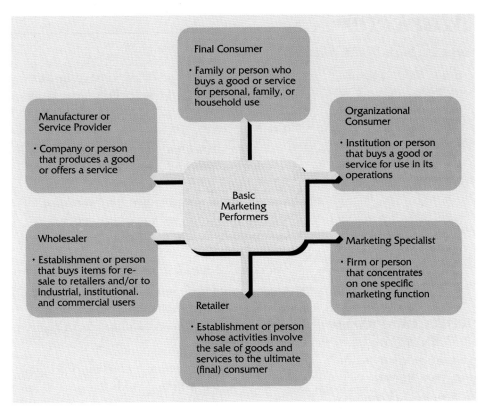

FIGURE 1-9
Who Performs Marketing Functions

issues. Through marketing management, the firm's total marketing program would be planned and carried out in an integrated manner, with fine-tuning as necessary.

Although many marketing transactions require the performance of similar marketing functions, such as consumer analysis, product planning, distribution planning, promotion planning, and price planning, there are a number of ways they can be carried out (such as a manufacturer distributing through full-service retailers versus self-service retailers, or a financial services company relying on telephone contacts by its sales force versus in-office visits to potential small business clients by sales personnel).

Marketing performers are the organizations or individuals that undertake one or more marketing functions. They include manufacturers and service providers, wholesalers, retailers, marketing specialists, and organizational and final consumers. As shown in Figure 1-9, each of these performers has a different role. It is important to note that while the responsibility for fulfilling marketing functions can be shifted and shared in a variety of ways, the basic marketing functions usually must be completed by one performer or another. They cannot be eliminated in many situations.

While in some instances one marketing performer decides to carry out all — or virtually all — marketing functions (such as Tandy Corporation developing its own products under the Realistic, Tandy, and Radio Shack, and other brands; distributing these products in its own trucks to company-owned Radio Shack and other stores; placing its own ads in various media; controlling the prices of its products; and selling overseas), for a number of reasons, one performer usually does not undertake all marketing functions:

*Usually at least one **marketing performer** must undertake each of the basic marketing functions.*

One performer often does not have the resources or ability to undertake all marketing functions.

19

You're the Marketer

How Can Pepsi Increase Its Slice of the Market?

When it was introduced in 1984, PepsiCo's Slice (a lemon-lime flavored soda containing 10 per cent real-fruit juice), was viewed as a major success. It was the first soda to feature fruit juice. By May 1987, Slice had an impressive 3.3 per cent market share of the $40 billion U.S. retail soda market, placing it among the ten best-selling sodas.

Unfortunately, Slice's success was short-lived. Despite adding mandarin orange, apple, and cherry cola (both regular and diet) versions, Slice's market share dropped to less than 2 per cent by the end of 1988.

Here's what happened:

▶ Newer competitors, such as Coke's Minute Maid orange soda and Cadbury Schweppes' Sunkist, have better brand recognition and brand credibility in the juice segment.

▶ Overall, fruit-flavored soda has not captured a large market share. Cola-based beverages still account for about 70 per cent of the soft-drink market; lemon-lime drinks have 10 to 12 per cent and orange drinks between 5 and 8 per cent.

▶ Coca-Cola's research shows that consumers are more concerned about how a product tastes than with its juice content. So, its Minute Maid orange juice now contains 2 per cent juice (down from 10 per cent); Sunkist contains no juice (down from 10 per cent). But Slice's juice content was not reduced to 2 per cent until 1989.

▶ According to one marketing expert, "you have a product characteristic, the addition of juice, in which the consumer doesn't see much benefit."

As the marketing manager responsible for Slice, what would you do?

SOURCE: Based on material in Doron P. Levin, "Slice: Case Study of a Setback," *New York Times* (July 15, 1988), pp. D1, D3; and Patricia Winters, "Pepsi Re-Aims Slice," *Advertising Age* (December 12, 1988), pp. 3, 68.

▶ Many producers do not have the financial resources necessary to sell directly to organizational or final consumers. They need intermediaries to participate in the distribution process.

▶ Marketing directly to customers would often require producers to make complementary products or sell the complementary products of other manufacturers so that the distribution process is carried out efficiently.

▶ A performer may be unable or unwilling to complete certain functions and may seek a marketing specialist to fulfill them.

▶ Many performers are too small to accomplish certain functions efficiently.

▶ For many goods and services, established distribution methods are in force and it is difficult to set up other methods (such as bypassing independent soda distributors in order to sell directly to retail stores).

▶ Some consumers may want to buy in quantity, pick up merchandise, visit self-service outlets, and so on, to save money.

Marketing in Action

In this section, two different approaches to marketing, one successful and one unsuccessful, are presented and contrasted.

Nike: Soaring Through the Air[20]

From its 1972 founding to 1983, Nike (named for the Greek goddess of victory) prospered. Its annual sales from athletic shoes and sports apparel grew to $1 billion and profits reached $58 million. The company capitalized on the U.S. jogging boom and captured one-half of the running-shoe market; it appealed to "self-involved" and brand-conscious consumers. Wisely, Nike foresaw a leveling off of jogging in the United States by the early 1980s (as people diversified their fitness efforts) and broadened its product lines.

Sound marketing principles have been followed by Nike.

Then, from 1984 to 1986, Nike's sales stagnated and its profits dropped sharply. Nike faced strong competition from Reebok and other "glamorous" firms, as its market share fell to 19 per cent (compared to 37 per cent for Reebok). It was late entering the aerobics shoe market. Inventories accumulated, resulting in reduced profit margins and substantial handling costs. It introduced some newer products without adequate testing. Management efforts were poorly focused. As Nike's founder commented: "We grew up when the only competitor was Adidas. We went along so well for so long that everybody thought it was our destiny to succeed."

After studying its problems and environmental factors (such as the economy, competitor strengths and weaknesses, trends in the sports-shoe and apparel industry, and so on), Nike executives enacted a well-conceived marketing plan. On an ongoing basis, they do research to monitor trends and anticipate opportunities.

On the basis of consumer analysis, Nike now places more emphasis on the young adult and nonrunner market segments. Nike knows that 15- to 22-year-olds purchase 30 per cent of all sneakers, about four pairs per person each year, even though they represent only 15 per cent of the U.S. population. And, because of the aging U.S. population and the greater number of women involved in physical fitness activities, Nike has an expanded line of athletic shoes for walkers and aerobics-type shoes. For example, there are about 20 million serious walkers in the United States.

Nike's product-planning efforts stress performance, full product lines, and regular new-product introductions. There is a greater emphasis on the Nike Air cushioning system, now used in a variety of Nike sports shoes. The firm offers shoes in virtually every sports category, including running, walking, aerobics, tennis, basketball, golf, and others. Its extensive apparel line with the Nike logo is also featured. Recent new-product introductions include technological advances, such as the Sock Trainer running shoe and brighter colors and designs (to reach the youth market). There is extensive product testing for all new items.

The company's improved distribution system requires retailers to order well in advance; reorders can be made later if consumer demand for certain models is higher than expected. This system allows Nike to plan inventories better and not overstock warehouses. In 1983, Nike had an average of 22 million shoes in its warehouses; since then, it has reduced that amount by about two-thirds.

In its promotion efforts, Nike capitalizes on the popularity of sports celebrities, particularly basketball star Michael Jordan, who endorses Nike Air Jordan basketball shoes. The company has sold several million pairs of Air Jordan shoes. In 1988, Nike's total U.S. advertising budget exceeded $40 million; and its "Just Do It" campaign,

---

[20] Barbara Buell, "Nike Catches Up With the Trendy Frontrunner," *Business Week* (October 24, 1988), p. 88; G. Christian Hill and Joseph Pereira, "Nike's Profit, Sales Surged in Quarter as Firm Gains Ground on Rival Reebok," *Wall Street Journal* (September 20, 1988), pp. 2, 22; and Pat Sloan, "Reebok Responds to Nike," *Advertising Age* (February 20, 1989), pp. 2, 72.

FIGURE 1-10
Nike's Newest Air Jordan
These shoes are the fourth generation of Nike basketball shoes, with features such as air-sole cushioning and a footframe for greater stability. The suggested retail price is $110.
Reprinted by permission.

showing noncelebrities in serious sports activity, was much more effective than Reebok's confusing "Let U.B.U." campaign.

Because of its high performance image, Nike does very well with people willing to pay $50 or more for a pair of shoes. It attracts customers interested in "price performance" rather than fashion. A very popular model is the new Nike Air Jordan priced at $100 (and up) per pair, shown in Figure 1-10. Nike customers are brand loyal and not very price conscious. This enables the firm to maintain high profit margins.

Nike's international marketing operations are better, especially in Europe where distribution and promotion are much improved. For example, Nike has adapted to European distribution by centering on small, independently owned stores carrying little inventory. Nike's international revenues account for about 40 per cent of total company revenues.

Nike's marketing management is well focused, and there is good coordination among marketing, design, and production. Decisions are regularly reviewed and modified, if necessary. By the end of 1988, Nike's U.S. market share had risen to 32 per cent, and fiscal 1988 profits were $102 million. Nike is well positioned for the future.

Worlds of Wonder: From Toy Superstar to Bankruptcy[21]

Worlds of Wonder has had a number of problems because of poor marketing.

After graduating college, Don Kingsborough sold such items as skin lotion and eight-track stereos. Then, he formed his own firm to distribute several manufacturers' products. His best-seller was Atari's Pong, the first mass-marketed video game. In 1983,

---

[21] Anthony Ramirez, "Top Gun in the Toy Business," *Fortune* (March 2, 1987), pp. 88–94; Carrie Dolan, "Yesterday's Marvel, Worlds of Wonder Inc. Is in Worlds of Trouble," *Wall Street Journal* (October 28, 1987), pp. 1, 18; Richard Brandt, Susan Benway, and Dori Jones Yang, "Worlds of Wonder: From Wall Street Charmer to Chapter 11," *Business Week* (March 21, 1988), pp. 74–78; and Alice Z. Cuneo, "Worlds of Wonder Toys Go Low Tech," *Advertising Age* (February 6, 1989), p. 56.

Don sold his firm to Atari and became head of sales and distribution. When Atari went into a tailspin, he left the firm. In early 1985, an inventor came to Kingsborough with the idea for a high-tech talking toy teddy bear with moving eyes and mouth. Don saw great potential for the bear and signed a licensing agreement that gave him exclusive rights to it in return for a royalty fee. Using his own funds, he set up a new company, Worlds of Wonder. Thus, Teddy Ruxpin began.

A prototype bear was developed and then streamlined into an item retailing for $70 to $80, reaching the market in time for Christmas 1985. In 1986, Worlds of Wonder introduced Lazer Tag (which allowed users to "shoot" each other with light-emitting pistols). These two products quickly became the hottest-selling U.S. toys. For fiscal 1987, ending on March 31, 1987, the firm's sales were $327 million, the highest second-year sales of any firm in U.S. history.

But by the end of 1987, Worlds of Wonder owed creditors $260 million, its October-December loss was $187 million, and it filed for bankruptcy (using Chapter 11 of the federal bankruptcy law) to protect it from creditors. What happened? Worlds of Wonder, in its energetic rush to expand, violated many fundamental marketing principles — and paid the price for doing so.

Worlds of Wonder failed to analyze its environment properly. It did not foresee an overall slowdown in the toy industry, which was unable to generate a big hit along the lines of Cabbage Patch Kids, Pound Puppies, or Teddy Ruxpin in 1987 or 1988. It overestimated the growth potential for high-tech toys and did not recognize the amount of competition that popped up in such a short time.

By offering only expensive, high-tech toys, Worlds of Wonder misread the basic consumer appeal of traditional toys: "My kids make their own animals talk. It's part of their fantasy life." (A parent's comment) "Parents favor more traditional, lower-priced games that provide hours of enjoyment compared with high-tech toys that last three days." (A toy store executive's comment)

Product-planning efforts were too ambitious and disjointed for a young firm with a limited product base. Rather than build on the success of Teddy Ruxpin and Lazer Tag and concentrate on related products, the company had 100 to 150 different new products (such as radio-controlled Muppets, Wondervision videocassette recorders, and Little Boppers dancing dolls) in development in 1987. In almost every case, there were delays in perfecting and introducing the new products, as well as costly overruns. Also, by diffusing efforts so much, Worlds of Wonder reduced its chances for a big hit.

Because of the company's late shipments and questionable quality control, relations with retailers deteriorated. For example, many retailers had to use heavy discounts to clear out Lazer Tag kits that were received after peak holiday shopping seasons. And new products were consistently shipped after the dates promised to retailers. Mechanical problems with Teddy Ruxpin dolls resulted in customer returns equal to 20 per cent of some retailers' sales.

During its heyday, Worlds of Wonder allocated $50 million for advertising, which effectively stimulated consumer demand. However, when the firm ran into cash-flow problems, it cut back drastically on advertising, leaving new products with almost no promotion to back them up. This contributed to consumer indifference and ill will between Worlds of Wonder and its retailers.

With regard to price planning, the firm was too slow to introduce inexpensive toys. Its high-tech items appealed to a small segment of the market; and as one observer noted, "People aren't out there looking for $100 dolls." Each time inventory levels became too high, large price discounts had to be offered. Not until February 1988, after it had already declared bankruptcy, did Worlds of Wonder offer low-priced toys such as $3 silly rubber Germs.

Many delivery delays and mechanical problems with Worlds of Wonder's products were due to an overreliance on foreign suppliers, who just could not keep up with its growth. By early 1988, it owed Hong Kong suppliers $40 million, further slowing down deliveries.

The firm's management efforts were continuously criticized. Company credibility was poor because of overly optimistic sales projections, late new-product introductions, out-of-control growth, and an inventory glut. Marketing activities were not coordinated, and Don Kingsborough asserted too much control over the marketing experts who had been brought into the firm. Finally, in early April 1988, a little over two years after selling the first Teddy Ruxpin, Don Kingsborough was forced to leave the company he had founded. Worlds of Wonder's creditors insisted that a new management team take over and try to bail out the firm. During 1988, sales fell by over 75 per cent from 1987.

Nike Versus Worlds of Wonder

Table 1-1 contrasts the marketing approaches taken by Nike and Worlds of Wonder, based on the information just presented. Most significantly, Nike has been thoroughly involved with sound marketing practices, whereas Worlds of Wonder has not been. Nike has well applied the marketing concept — consumer orientation, integrated effort, and goal orientation; Worlds of Wonder has not.

Format of the Text

This book is divided into eight parts. The balance of Part One concentrates on the marketing environment, developing marketing plans, and the information needed for marketing decisions. These topics set the foundation for examining the specific components of marketing. Part Two deals with marketing's central orientation: understanding consumers. Consumer demographics, social and psychological factors, the decision process, organizational consumers, developing a target market, and sales forecasting are detailed.

Parts Three through Six describe the components of the marketing mix (product, distribution, promotion, and price planning) and the decisions needed to carry out a marketing program in depth. Part Seven covers several topics that expand marketing's scope: international marketing, service and nonprofit marketing, and marketing and society. Part Eight considers the marketing management implications of the topics raised throughout the text and discusses how to integrate and analyze an overall marketing plan.

The text defines key terms, explains the significance of important concepts, studies the role of the marketing manager, and shows the scope of the field of marketing. In addition, numerous examples and illustrations of actual marketing practices by a variety of organizations and individuals are woven into the discussion of the framework of marketing and its components. Although topics such as organizational consumers, international marketing, service and nonprofit marketing, and marketing and society receive separate chapter coverage to highlight certain points, applications in these areas are presented throughout the text.

TABLE 1-1   Nike Versus Worlds of Wonder

Marketing Function	Nike	Worlds of Wonder
Environmental analysis and marketing research	Regular monitoring of environment and use of research	Limited monitoring of environment and use of research; overestimate of market
Consumer analysis	Precise definition of market—such as 15- to 22-year-olds and women	Vague definition of small market segment—upscale consumers
Product planning	Emphasis on performance, full lines, and good new products	Poorly focused by trying to develop 100–150 different new products; late introductions
Distribution planning	Advance dealer ordering required to reduce Nike's inventory levels	Deteriorating retailer relations due to late shipments, weak quality control, and the need for heavy discounting
Promotion planning	Superior use of advertising and celebrity endorsers; solid promotion budget	Drastic cutback in advertising because of cash-flow problems, leading to consumer indifference and lack of retailer support
Price planning	High performance image tied to high prices; good profit margins	Too slow to introduce inexpensive toys; heavy discounting to clear out excess inventory
Broadening the organization's scope	Good adaptation to special needs of foreign markets	Delivery delays and mechanical problems due to foreign suppliers
Marketing management	Coordinated planning, implementation, and control of marketing efforts	Disjointed planning, implementation, and control of marketing efforts

Summary

In this and every chapter in the text, the summary is linked to the objectives stated at the beginning of the chapter.

1. *To illustrate the exciting, dynamic, and influential nature of marketing*   Marketing influences us daily in our roles as goods and service providers and as consumers. As goods and service providers, we make such marketing-related decisions as choosing who our customers are, what goods and services to offer, where to sell our goods and services, what features to emphasize in advertising, and what prices to charge. As consumers, the marketing process affects the assortment of choices in the marketplace, where we shop, the availability of sales personnel, the prices that we pay, and other factors. Several examples show the dynamics of marketing.

2. *To define marketing and trace its evolution, with emphasis on the marketing concept*   The classical marketing definition focuses on the flow of goods and services from producer to consumer or user. In modern terms, marketing is defined as the anticipation, management, and satisfaction of demand through the exchange process.

While the evolution of marketing can be traced to people's earliest use of the exchange process, it has really developed since the Industrial Revolution, as mass production and improved transportation enabled more transactions to occur. For many companies, marketing has evolved through four eras: production, sales, marketing department, and marketing company.

The marketing concept requires an organization or individual to be consumer-oriented, have an integrated marketing program, and be goal-oriented. In contrast to a sales approach, a marketing approach is more involved with profit planning, analysis of trends, opportunities and threats, assessments of customer types and differences, and coordinated decision making.

3. *To show the importance of marketing as a field of study* The field of marketing is a crucial one for several reasons: it stimulates demand; marketing costs can be high; a large number of people are employed in marketing positions; it supports entire industries such as advertising and marketing research; all people are consumers in some situations; it is necessary to use scarce resources efficiently; it impacts on people's beliefs and lifestyles; and it influences the quality of our lives. The scope of marketing is quite broad and diversified.

4. *To describe the basic functions of marketing and those that perform these functions* The major marketing functions are environmental analysis and marketing research, consumer analysis, prod-uct planning (including goods, services, and ideas), distribution planning, promotion planning, price planning, broadening the organization's/individual's scope, and marketing management. The responsibility for performing these functions can be shifted and shared in several ways among manufacturers and service providers, wholesalers, retailers, marketing specialists, and consumers. One party usually does not perform all the functions. This is due to costs, assortment requirements, specialized abilities, company size, established methods of distribution, and consumer interests.

5. *To present and compare successful and unsuccessful approaches to marketing* Nike is doing so well because of its outstanding marketing job. Worlds of Wonder's inadequate marketing efforts have resulted in large losses and an uncertain future.

Key Terms

marketing (p. 9)
anticipation of demand (p. 9)
management of demand (p. 9)
satisfaction of demand (p. 10)
consumer demand (p. 11)

publics' demand (p. 11)
exchange (p. 11)
production era (p. 11)
sales era (p. 11)
marketing department era (p. 11)

marketing company era (p. 12)
marketing concept (p. 12)
marketing functions (p. 17)
marketing performers (p. 19)

Review Questions

1. How does marketing influence us in both our roles as providers of goods and services and as consumers?

2. What are the major differences between the classical (narrow) and modern (broad) definitions of marketing?

3. Explain the
   a. Anticipation of demand.
   b. Management of demand.
   c. Satisfaction of demand.
   d. Exchange process.

4. Distinguish between consumer and publics' demand.

5. Give an example of a good, service, organization, person, place, and idea that may be marketed.

6. Describe the four eras of marketing.

7. Define the marketing concept. How does your definition differ from that offered by McKitterick in 1957?

8. Describe at least five benefits of a marketing over a sales orientation.

9. What are basic functions performed by marketing?

10. Why do most consumers not buy products directly from manufacturers?

Discussion Questions

1. From a marketing perspective, evaluate these company actions (as noted in the text):
   a. Maaco's decision to expand via collision-repair work.
   b. Sony's introduction of the Video Walkman.
   c. Campbell's renewed use of the "M'm m'm good" slogan in ads.
   d. IBM's marketing management restructuring.

2. Does the presence of a marketing department mean a firm is following the marketing concept? Explain.

3. What would a nonmarketing major learn by studying marketing? Give examples for three distinct majors.

4. What marketing efforts must Nike engage in to maintain a steady sales growth?

5. Do you believe that Worlds of Wonder will be able to succeed in the future? Why or why not? What changes in its marketing practices should it enact to improve its chances for success?

Hints for Solving Cases

At the end of each chapter, from 2 through 24, two short cases are presented — a total of forty-six. These cases are intended to build on the material in the text, improve your reasoning skills, and stimulate class discussions. At the end of each part, one longer case is presented — a total of eight. These cases are intended to improve your reasoning skills, your ability to identify key points, and your ability to integrate multiple marketing concepts when making decisions.

The cases in *Marketing* describe actual marketing situations faced by a variety of organizations and individuals. The facts, circumstances, and people are all real. The questions following each case are designed to help identify the key issues encountered by the organization or individual, evaluate the responses to those issues, outline additional courses of action, and develop appropriate marketing strategies. The information necessary to answer the questions is contained within the case or the text chapter(s) to which the case relates.

These hints should be kept in mind when solving a case:

▶ Read all the material carefully. Underline important data and statements.
▶ List the key issues, problems, and organizational responses detailed in the case.
▶ Do not make unrealistic or unsupported assumptions.
▶ Read each question following the case. Be sure you understand the thrust of every question. Do not give the same (similar) answers for two distinct questions.
▶ Write up tentative answers in outline form. Cover as many aspects of each question as possible.
▶ Review relevant material in the appropriate chapter of the text. In particular, look for information pertaining to the case questions.
▶ Expand your tentative answers, substantiating them with data from the case and the chapter(s).
▶ Reread the case to be sure you have not omitted any important concepts in your answers.
▶ Make sure that your answers are clear and well written, and that their ramifications for the organization are considered.
▶ Reread your solutions at least one day after developing your answers. This ensures an objective review of your work.
▶ Make any necessary revisions.
▶ Be sure that your answers are not a summary ("rehash") of the case, but that you have presented a real analysis and recommendations.

CHAPTER 2

The Environment of Marketing

CHAPTER OBJECTIVES

1. To examine the environment within which marketing decisions are made and marketing activities are undertaken

2. To differentiate between those elements controlled by top management and those controlled by marketing, and to enumerate the controllable elements of a marketing plan

3. To enumerate the uncontrollable environmental elements that can affect a marketing plan and study their potential ramifications

4. To explain why feedback about and adaptation to the uncontrollable aspects of the environment are essential for a firm to attain its objectives

As the fifth anniversary of the AT&T divestiture rolled around on January 1, 1989, the great majority of the country's telephone customers, large and small, declared themselves satisfied with the service they receive. Despite predictions that AT&T would pummel its fledgling competitors, the industry has evolved into an entrepreneurial, freewheeling marketplace where customers and many shareholders reap big rewards.

Because environmental factors (such as the level of competition in an industry, government actions, and technological advances) have a key effect on a company's marketing efforts and overall performance, it is valuable for us to view some of the results of the largest corporate breakup in U.S. history. How has AT&T reacted to its new "playing field"?

In January 1982, AT&T and the U.S. Justice Department signed an agreement stipulating that pending government antitrust charges and a previous settlement barring AT&T from participating in new businesses would be dropped—in return, AT&T's local Bell divisions would become independent companies as of January 1, 1984. Thus, the agreement forced AT&T to divest itself of divisions accounting for three-quarters of its revenues and to participate in a newly competitive marketplace. As a public utility, AT&T often operated as a monopolist—free of competitors.

Now AT&T must engage more actively in marketing: "We're paying much more attention to outside forces, we're totally market driven, we know what the customer wants, what he's willing to pay, and what our competitors are offering." Let us examine AT&T's actions in four specific markets: long distance, telephone systems, business services, and computers.

AT&T's performance in long-distance telephone service, which contributes 80 per cent of its net income, is particularly strong. Despite competition from many firms, AT&T's hold on this market is impressive. Before its breakup, AT&T handled over 90 per cent of U.S. long-distance calls. Today, it still has two-thirds of the market; and long-distance operations are highly profitable. Since the divestiture, AT&T has reduced rates by 36 per cent.

The profits of its $10 billion consumer-products division, which sells phones and services to final consumers and small businesses, have improved. For example, AT&T offers 12 models in its consumer phone line (down from 54), and has cut production costs through overseas production and automation.

AT&T has innovatively expanded its business services. For example, a new 900 line allows corporate customers to shift the cost of incoming calls to their

Can anyone outperform the dazzling AT&T 6386 WorkGroup System?

Reprinted by permission.

consumers (if they decide not to allow toll-free 800 number calls). A consumer could dial a 900 number to get food recipes and be charged for the call.

AT&T has had a slow start with its computer division. This is partly because the operating system (Unix) used in some AT&T computers is incompatible with IBM's MS-DOS. Also, the initial sales strategy was not well conceived. Originally, AT&T had one sales force for computers, phone service, and phone equipment. Because phone-based systems were easier to sell, little time was devoted to computers. Today, AT&T has a specialized sales force and frequent communication with distributors.[1]

In this chapter, we will look at the complex environment in which marketing decisions are made. We will see that an organization's level of success (or failure) is related not only to its marketing efforts, but to the external environment in which it operates and to its ability to adapt to environmental changes.

[1] Kenneth Labich, "Was Breaking Up AT&T a Good Idea?" Fortune (January 2, 1989), pp. 82–87; John J. Keller et al., "AT&T: The Making of a Comeback," Business Week (January 18, 1988), pp. 58–62; and Paul Schreiber, "AT&T Breakup Causes Few Hangups," Newsday (December 12, 1988), pp. 106–107 ff.

Overview

*The **marketing environment** consists of controllable factors, uncontrollable factors, organizational performance, feedback, and adaptation.*

The environment within which marketing decisions are made and marketing activities are undertaken is depicted in Figure 2-1. The **marketing environment** consists of these five parts: controllable factors, uncontrollable factors, the organization's level of success or failure in reaching its objectives, feedback, and adaptation.

Controllable factors are those directed by the organization and its marketers. First, a number of basic interrelated decisions are made by top management. Then marketing managers make a number of decisions based on top management guidelines. In combination, these factors result in an overall marketing strategy or offering (A in Figure 2-1). The major uncontrollable factors are beyond the control of individual organizations, but they have an impact on how well the organization and its offering are accepted (B in Figure 2-1).

The interaction of controllable factors and uncontrollable factors determines the organization's level of success or failure in reaching its objectives. Feedback occurs when a firm makes an effort to monitor uncontrollable factors and assess its strengths and weaknesses. Adaptation refers to the changes in its marketing plan that an organization makes to comply with the uncontrollable environment. If a firm is unwilling to consider the entire environment in a systematic manner, it increases the likelihood that it will have a lack of direction and not attain proper results.

Failure to study the environment thoroughly may lead to poor results.

Throughout this chapter, the various parts of Figure 2-1 are described and drawn together so that the complex environment of marketing can be understood. In Chapter 3, the concept of strategic planning is presented. It establishes a formal process for developing, implementing, and evaluating marketing programs in conjunction with the goals of top management.

FIGURE 2-1
The Environment Within Which Marketing Operates

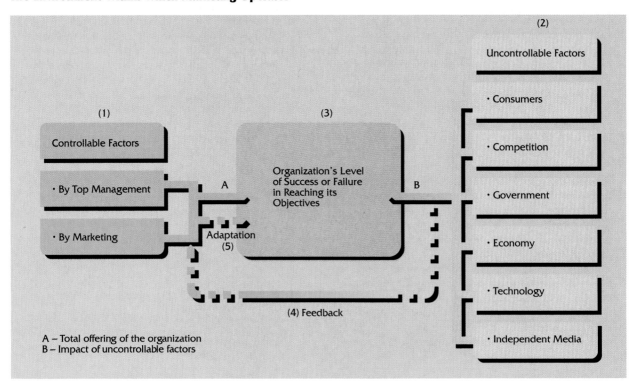

Controllable Factors

Controllable factors are directed by the organization and its marketers. Some of these factors are directed by top management; these are not controllable by marketers, who must develop plans to satisfy overall organizational goals. In situations involving small or medium-sized institutions, both broad policy and marketing decisions are often made by one person, usually the owner. Even in those cases, broad policy should be stated first and marketing plans must adjust to it. For example, a person could decide to open an office-supply store selling products to small business accounts (broad policy) and stress convenient hours, a good selection of items, quantity discounts, and superior customer service (marketing plan).

*The organization and its marketers can manage **controllable factors**.*

Factors Directed by Top Management

Although top management is responsible for numerous decisions, five basic ones are of extreme importance to marketers: the line of business, overall objectives, the role of marketing, the role of other business functions, and the corporate culture. These decisions have an impact on all aspects of marketing. Figure 2-2 shows the types of decisions that are required in these five areas.

The **line of business** refers to the general goods/service category, functions, geographic coverage, type of ownership, and specific business of a company. The general goods/service category is a broad definition of the kind of business a firm seeks to undertake. It may be energy, furniture, housing, education, or any number of others.

*A company's **line of business** consists of both its general and specific business category.*

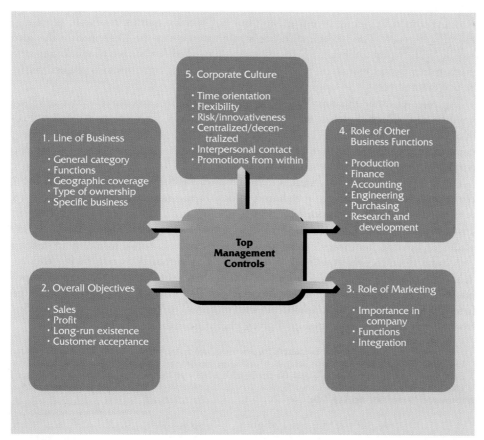

FIGURE 2-2
Factors Controlled by Top Management

The functions of the business outline a company's position in the marketing system — from supplier to manufacturer to wholesaler to retailer — and the tasks it seeks to undertake. It is important to note that a firm may want to undertake more than one of these functions. Geographic coverage can be neighborhood, city, county, state, regional, national, or international. The type of ownership ranges from a sole proprietorship, partnership, or franchise to a multiunit corporation. The specific business is a narrow definition of the firm, its functions, and its operations, such as Ed's Dry Cleaners (a local full-service dry cleaner specializing in outerwear).

Top management outlines ***overall objectives.***

Overall objectives are the broad, measurable goals set by top management. The success or failure of a firm may be determined by comparing these broad objectives with actual performance. Usually a combination of sales, profit, and other objectives is stated by management for short-run (one year or less) and long-run (more than one year) time periods. Most firms recognize that customer acceptance is an important goal that has a strong effect on sales, profit, and long-run existence.

*The **role of marketing** refers to its importance, functions, and level of integration.*

Management determines the ***role of marketing*** by noting its importance, outlining its functions, and integrating it into the overall operation of the firm. The importance of marketing in a firm is evident when marketing is given line (decision making) authority, the rank of the chief marketing officer is equal to that of other areas (usually vice-president), and adequate resources are provided. Marketing is not considered important by a firm that gives marketing staff (advisory) status, places marketing in a subordinate position (such as reporting to the production vice-president), equates marketing with sales, and withholds the resources needed for research, advertising, and other marketing activities.

The functions of marketing may be quite broad, including market research, new-product planning, inventory management, and many other marketing tasks; or they may be limited to selling or advertising but not include market research, planning, pricing, or credit. The larger marketing's role, the greater the likelihood of the firm having an integrated marketing organization. The smaller the role of marketing, the greater the possibility that the firm operates its marketing activities on a project, crisis, or fragmented basis.

Cooperation between marketing and other functions is necessary.

The roles of other business functions and their interrelationships with marketing need to be delineated clearly in order to avoid overlaps, jealousy, and conflict. Production, finance, accounting, engineering, purchasing, and research and development departments each have different perspectives, orientations, and goals. This is discussed further in Chapter 3.

Corporate culture *involves shared values, norms, and practices.*

Top management strongly influences the corporate culture adopted by a company. A ***corporate culture*** consists of the shared values, norms, and practices communicated to and followed by those working for a firm. A company's culture may be described in terms of its time orientation (Is the firm short-run or long-run oriented?); the flexibility of the job environment (dress code, ability to deviate from rules, formality in dealing with subordinates, etc.); the level of risk/innovation pursued (Is risk taking encouraged?); the use of a centralized/decentralized management structure (How much input into decisions is allowed of middle managers?); the level of interpersonal contact in the firm (Do employees freely communicate with one another?); and the use of promotions from within (Are internal personnel given preference when positions open up?).[2]

---

[2] For example, see Neil H. Snyder, Bernard A. Morin, and Marilyn A. Morgan, "Motivating People to Build Excellent Enterprises," *Business*, Vol. 38 (April-June 1988), pp. 14–19; Wendy Zellner, "Chrysler's Next Generation," *Business Week* (December 19, 1988), pp. 52–57; and Michael W. Miller and Paul B. Carroll, "Vaunted IBM Culture Yields to New Values: Openness, Efficiency," *Wall Street Journal* (November 11, 1988), pp. A1, A9.

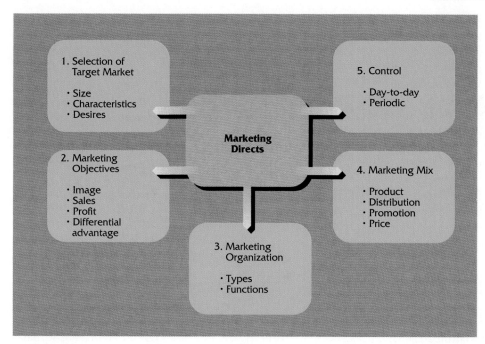

FIGURE 2-3
Factors Controlled by Marketing

Kellogg is a good example of how a progressive top management can establish a proper internal environment for marketing efforts. In the mature U.S. cereal industry, Kellogg has a 42 per cent market share (double that of second-place General Mills), with a goal to reach 50 per cent. Internationally, Kellogg's revenues are over $1 billion. Unlike its competitors, Kellogg concentrates on cereal products, which account for over 80 per cent of company sales. Top management encourages the introduction of new cereal products and believes in aggressive marketing efforts. In 1988, it allocated $865 million (20 per cent of company sales) for marketing. This philosophy, as stated by Kellogg's chief executive, shows the central role its top management places on marketing:

> You have to have enough muscle to bring to the marketplace value-added products that really do offer the consumer something better, and then you've got to be able to tell the consumer about them. You have to have strong [brand names] and continue to build on them.[3]

After top management sets company guidelines, the marketing area begins to develop the factors under its control.

Factors Directed by Marketing

The major factors controlled by marketing personnel are the selection of a target market, marketing objectives, the marketing organization, the marketing mix, and control of the marketing plan. See Figure 2-3.

One of an organization's/individual's most crucial marketing-related decisions involves the selection of a ***target market,*** which is the particular group(s) of customers the organization/individual proposes to serve, or whose needs it proposes to satisfy,

*A **target market** is the customer group to which an organization appeals.*

[3] Patricia Sellers, "How King Kellogg Beat the Blahs," *Fortune* (August 29, 1988), pp. 54–64.

FOR ADULTS

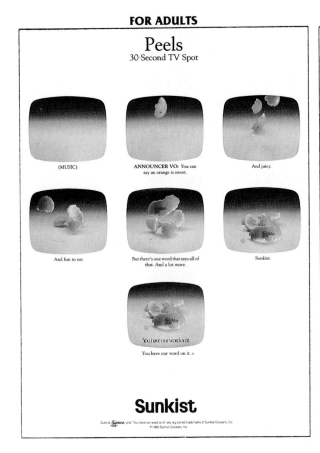

FOR CHILDREN

FIGURE 2-4
**Appealing to Two
Distinct Target Markets**
Reprinted by permission.

with a particular marketing program.[4] A firm can choose a very large target market or concentrate on a small customer group, or try to appeal to both with separate marketing programs for each. In general, these questions must be addressed before developing a marketing program: Who are our customers? What kinds of goods and services do they want? How can we attract them to our company?

When selecting a target market, the company usually engages in some form of **market segmentation,** which is

*Often, **market
segmentation** is used in
choosing a target market.*

> the process of subdividing a market into distinct subsets of customers, that behave in the same way or have similar needs.

> Each subset may conceivably be chosen as a target market to be reached with a distinct marketing strategy. The process begins with a basis of segmentation — a product-specific factor that reflects differences in customer requirements or responsiveness to marketing variables (possibilities are purchase behavior, usage, benefits sought, intentions, preference, or loyalty). Segment descriptors are then chosen, based on their ability to identify segments, to account for variance in the segmentation basis, and to suggest competitive strategy implications (examples of descriptors are demographics, geography, life-styles, customer size, and industry).[5]

See Figure 2-4.

[4] Peter D. Bennett (Editor), *Dictionary of Marketing Terms* (Chicago: American Marketing Association, 1988), p. 199.
[5] Ibid, p. 114.

At marketing-oriented firms, the choice of a target market has a large impact on all other marketing decisions. For example, a book publisher choosing to appeal to the high school science market would have a much different marketing program than a publisher choosing to appeal to the adult fiction market. The first firm would seek an image as a prestigious, well-established publisher; specialize its products offerings; make presentations to high school book selection committees; sell in large quantities; offer durable books with many photos and line drawings that could be used for several years; and so on. The second firm would capitalize on well-known authors' names or publish books on "hot" topics to establish an image; introduce books on a variety of subjects; place ads in newspapers and seek favorable book reviews; distribute through independent bookstores; sell in small quantities (except when large bookstore chains are involved); de-emphasize durability, photos, and line drawings and produce books as efficiently as possible; and so on.

Marketing objectives are more customer-oriented than those set by top management. For example, marketers are extremely interested in the image consumers hold of the company and specific products. Sales objectives reflect a concern for brand loyalty (repeat purchase behavior), growth through new product introductions, and appeal to unsatisfied market segments. Profit objectives are set in per unit or total-profit terms. Last and most important, marketers seek to create a ***differential advantage,*** the set of unique features in a company's marketing program that causes consumers to patronize the company and not its competitors. Without a differential advantage, a company adopts a "me-too" philosophy and offers the consumer no reasons to select its offerings over a competitor's. A differential advantage can be achieved through a distinctive image, new products or features, product quality, availability, customer service, low prices, and other characteristics.[6] See Figure 2-5.

A ***marketing organization*** is the structural arrangement for directing marketing functions. The organization outlines authority, responsibility, and tasks to be performed. Through the organization, functions are assigned and coordinated. An organization may be functional, with responsibility assigned on the basis of buying, selling, promotion, distribution, and other tasks; product-oriented, with product managers for each product category and brand managers for each individual brand in addition to functional categories; or market-oriented, with managers assigned on the basis of geographic markets and customer types in addition to functional categories. A single company may use a mixture of these forms. See Figure 2-6 for illustrations of functional, product-oriented, and market-oriented organizational forms.

The ***marketing mix*** describes the specific combination of marketing elements used to achieve an organization's/individual's objectives and satisfy the target market. The mix depends on a number of decisions with regard to four major variables: product, distribution, promotion, and price.

Product decisions involve determining what goods, services, and/or ideas to market, the level of quality, the number of items to sell, the innovativeness of the company, packaging, features (such as options and warranties), the level and timing of research, and when to drop existing offerings. Distribution decisions include whether to sell through intermediaries or directly to consumers, how many outlets to sell through,

Marketing objectives are highly consumer-oriented.

*A **differential advantage** consists of the firm's unique features that attract consumers.*

*A **marketing organization** may be functional, product-oriented, or market-oriented.*

*The **marketing mix** consists of four elements: product, distribution, promotion, and price.*

---

[6] See Kevin P. Coyne, "Sustainable Competitive Advantage — What It Is, What It Isn't," *Business Horizons*, Vol. 29 (January–February 1986), pp. 54–61; and Milind M. Lele and Jagdish N. Sheth, "The Four Fundamentals of Customer Satisfaction," *Business Marketing* (June 1988), pp. 80–94.

FIGURE 2-5
The Differential Advantages of Instant Quaker Oatmeal
This advertisement stresses a wide range of reasons for consumers to buy Quaker Instant Oatmeal. Reprinted by permission.

whether to control or cooperate with other channel members, what purchasing terms to negotiate, supplier selection, determining which functions to assign to others, and identifying competitors.

Promotion decisions include the selection of a combination of tools (advertising, publicity, personal selling, and sales promotion), whether to share promotions and their costs with others, how to measure effectiveness, the image to pursue, the level of customer service, the choice of media (such as newspaper, television, radio, magazine), the format of messages, and ad timing throughout the year or during peak periods. Price decisions include determining the overall level of prices (low, medium,

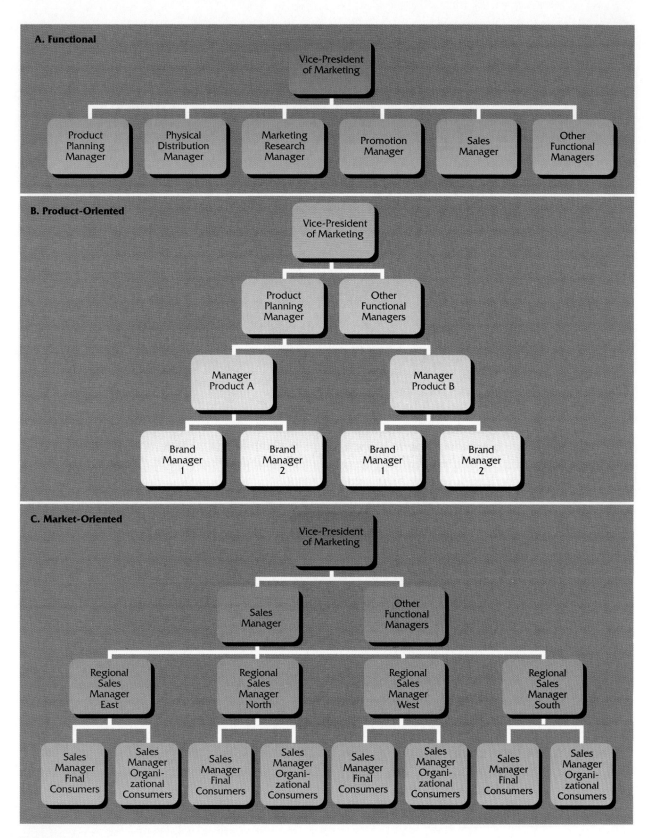

FIGURE 2-6
Illustrations of Marketing Organizations

You're the Marketer

How Can Polaroid Land on Top Again?

For decades, Polaroid's self-developing cameras were perceived as technological marvels. However in recent years, both self-developing photography and Polaroid have had difficulties. The popularity of 35mm cameras, one-hour photo-processing laboratories, and video cameras have hurt self-developing camera sales and profitability.

Polaroid's sales of self-developing cameras fell from a peak of 9.4 million units in 1978 to 3.5 million units in 1985, before stabilizing. Yet, as a former executive says, "Polaroid hasn't had a breakthrough product for years." Adds another observer, "the problem for many big companies is that they don't have an encore."

However, Polaroid insists that it now has a bright future:

▶ It is researching electronic imaging, a new stage of photography with important applications in publishing and medical diagnostic markets. Competitors (Kodak, Sony, and Matsushita) are also working on similar research.

▶ It is beginning to sell conventional film. Yet, although Polaroid's name and marketing expertise account for its being the leader in the videotape market, with a 12 per cent market share, Kodak has an 80 per cent market share and Fuji has an 8 to 10 per cent market share in the film market.

▶ Polaroid is the exclusive maker of self-developing film and cameras, having won a lawsuit against Kodak for patent infringement. It expects to receive a cash award of over $1 billion from Kodak as a result of its legal victory.

▶ It is increasing the emphasis on industrial products such as chemical coatings and employee photo-ID systems.

As Polaroid's marketing vice-president, what would you do to compete in this tough environment?

SOURCE: Based on material in Keith H. Hammonds, "Why Polaroid Must Remake Itself Instantly," *Business Week* (September 9, 1988), pp. 66–72; and Lawrence Ingrassia, "How Polaroid Fights to Regain Creativity After Its Long Slide," *Wall Street Journal* (August 12, 1988), pp. 1, 4.

or high), the range of prices (lowest to highest), the relationship between price and quality, the emphasis to place on price, how to react to competitors' prices, when to advertise prices, how prices are computed, and what billing terms to employ (such as a cash-only versus a credit policy).

When developing a marketing mix, product, distribution, promotion, and price decisions must be compatible with the desires of the selected target market and with each other; be compatible with the company's resource capabilities; be well coordinated; and communicate and deliver a clear differential advantage. These questions should all be considered:

▶ Are the target market segments precisely defined?
▶ Does the total program, as well as each element, meet the target market's needs?
▶ Are the elements consistent with one another?
▶ Do they add up to form a harmonious, integrated whole?

▶ Is each element being given its best use?

▶ Does the marketing mix build on the firm's cultural and tangible strengths? Does it imply a program to correct any weaknesses?

▶ Is a distinctive personality in the competitive marketplace created?

▶ Is the company protected from the most obvious competitive threats?[7]

Canon, a leading manufacturer of cameras and other products, is one of many firms that applies the marketing-mix concept well. Canon uses distinctive marketing mixes for different target markets, such as beginners, serious amateurs, and professional photographers. For beginners, Canon offers very simple cameras with automatic focus and a built-in flash. These cameras are sold through all types of retailers, including discounters and department stores. Advertising is concentrated on television and general magazines. These cameras retail for under $100. For serious amateur photographers, Canon offers relatively advanced cameras with superior features and a number of attachments. These cameras are sold via camera stores and finer department stores. Advertising is concentrated on specialty magazines, with some television advertising. These cameras retail for several hundred dollars. In sum, Canon markets the right products in the right stores, promotes them in the right media, and has the right prices for its various target markets.

The last, and extremely important, factor directed by marketing personnel involves *control:* monitoring and reviewing overall and specific marketing performance. Evaluations should be conducted at regular intervals. The external environment and internal company data should be reviewed continuously. In-depth research and analysis of performance (marketing audits) should be completed at least once or twice each year. Revisions need to be accomplished when the external environment changes or the company encounters difficulties.

Control involves monitoring and evaluating marketing performance.

Uncontrollable Factors

Uncontrollable factors are those elements affecting an organization's performance that cannot be directed by the organization and its marketers. It must be recognized that any marketing plan, no matter how well conceived, may fail if uncontrollable factors adversely influence it. Therefore, the external environment must be continually monitored and its effects incorporated into any marketing plan. Furthermore, contingency plans relating to uncontrollable variables should be an important part of a marketing plan. Uncontrollable variables that bear watching and anticipating are consumers, competition, government, the economy, technology, and independent media. See Figure 2-7.

Uncontrollable factors influence an organization and its marketers but are not directed by them.

Consumers

Although a marketer has control over the selection of a target market, he or she cannot control the characteristics of the population. Firms can react to, but not control, these consumer characteristics: age, income, marital status, occupation, race, education, and place and type of residence. For example, although Gerber could develop new baby foods, it could not stop the decline in U.S. births. To continue growing, Gerber has had to expand into other goods and services.

Organizations need to understand consumer characteristics, cultural and social factors, the decision process, and consumer groups.

[7] Benson P. Shapiro, "Rejuvenating the Marketing Mix," *Harvard Business Review*, Vol. 63 (September–October 1985), p. 34.

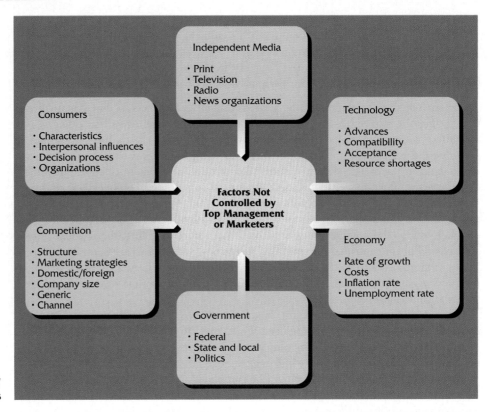

FIGURE 2-7
Uncontrollable Factors

A company must understand the interpersonal influences on consumer behavior. The purchases that consumers make are affected by their family, friends, religion, level of education, and personal standards and by the taboos, customs, and other factors that shape a culture and society. For instance, in some parts of the United States, stores are not allowed to open on Sundays, liquor sales are strictly regulated (as to prices, other goods that can be sold, and days open), and movies are closely rated. In other parts of the United States, stores are regularly open seven days a week, liquor is sold in many types of outlets, and any movie can be shown uncut.

Because consumers act differently in purchasing various types of goods and services, a company needs to comprehend the consumer's decision process. The decision process explains the steps a consumer goes through when buying a product. In the case of an automobile, the consumer carefully searches for information about a number of cars, ranks several alternatives, selects a favorite, negotiates terms, and finally completes the purchase. With a hamburger, the consumer looks at his or her watch, sees that it is lunchtime, and goes to a nearby fast-food outlet.

Today, consumer-rights groups and organizations speak out on behalf of consumers at public hearings, stockholder meetings, and before the media. To avoid negative consequences brought on by active consumer groups, a firm must communicate with consumers on relevant issues (such as a product recall), anticipate problems (such as delays in shipping ordered goods), respond to complaints (such as unsatisfactory customer service), and make sure that the company operates properly (such as sponsoring community projects).

Competition

The competitive environment frequently affects a firm's marketing efforts and its success in attracting a target market. Therefore, a company needs to analyze the competitive structure of the industry in which it operates and to examine competition on the basis of these characteristics: marketing strategy, domestic/foreign firms, company size, generic competition, and channel competition.

A company would operate under one of four possible competitive structures: monopoly, oligopoly, monopolistic competition, and pure competition. Table 2-1 shows the characteristics of each of these structures.

With a **monopoly,** just one firm sells a particular product. In the United States, this occurs if a firm has a patent (exclusive rights for seventeen years to a product it invented) or is a public utility, such as a local power company. Depending on the product, the market may be small or large. Consumer reactions to price changes depend on their need for the product. For example, people continue to use electricity no matter how high prices go.

One firm sells a product and has control over marketing in a **monopoly.**

A private-sector monopolist can totally control its marketing plan because of the unique nature of its product. Accordingly, the key marketing task is to maintain this uniqueness and not allow other firms to enter the market. As patents expire, competition generally increases. Public utilities are heavily regulated by government and must have their plans approved by it.

With an **oligopoly,** a few firms — generally large ones — comprise most of an industry's sales. The auto industry is a good illustration of this. General Motors, Ford, Chrysler, Honda, Toyota, and Nissan account for over 85 per cent of all automobiles sold in the United States. Other examples of oligopolistic industries are flat glass, cereal breakfast foods, turbines and turbine engines, household refrigerators and freezers, electric lamps, and cigarettes.

A limited number of large firms compete on nonprice factors in an **oligopoly.**

TABLE 2-1 Alternative Competitive Structures

	Structures			
Characteristics	**Monopoly**[a]	**Oligopoly**	**Monopolistic Competition**	**Pure Competition**
Number of firms	One	Few	Several	Many
Size of market for each firm	Small or large	Large	Small or large	Small
Control of marketing plan	Total control of price, distribution, promotion, and product	Some control of price, distribution, promotion, and product	Some control of price, distribution, promotion, and product	No control of price, ineffective control of distribution, promotion, and product
Ease of entry into industry	Difficult	Difficult	Easy	Easy
Differential advantage	Only source of product	Nonprice marketing factors	Any marketing factors	None
Key marketing task	Maintain unique product status	Differentiate product on nonprice factors	Differentiate product on any factors	Ensure supply of product at low prices and widespread distribution

[a] Characteristics of a private-sector monopolist (e.g., a firm with a patent for a product). A public-sector monopolist is more closely regulated.

The market is often quite large and contains various segments. Consumer demand for one firm's offering drops sharply if its prices are increased because other firms do not follow along; and demand increases only slightly if its prices are decreased because other firms also cut their prices. Because there are few firms, each is able to exert some control over its marketing plan. It is difficult for new firms to enter the market because capital (factory and equipment) costs are usually high. Oligopolistic firms seek to avoid price wars; instead, they try to distinguish their products on the basis of image, options, color, delivery, and other features. To be successful, oligopolistic firms need to convince consumers that their brands are distinctive. For instance, General Electric needs to persuade consumers that its refrigerators really are better than White-Westinghouse's.

*A number of firms offer a variety of marketing mixes in **monopolistic competition.***

Monopolistic competition occurs when there are several firms in an industry, each of which is trying to offer a unique marketing mix. In the United States, monopolistic competition is the most common competitive structure, followed by oligopoly. Service stations, garment makers, beauty salons, furniture makers, and shoe retailers are examples of companies operating under monopolistic competition. In each instance, a firm tries to attain a differential advantage through a marketing mix that is different from competitors and desirable to consumers.

Competition can be intense because a number of firms are making and/or selling essentially similar items. The size of the market depends on the necessity of the product. Control over price is based on how unique consumers view a particular brand or firm to be. A firm can charge a higher price than the industry average and not lose sales if its offering is viewed as distinct from the competition's. With a solid differential advantage, a firm is able to exert some control over its total marketing plan. However, in monopolistic competition, it is easy for new firms to enter the market because startup costs are relatively low. For continued success. a company must continually strive to differentiate itself from competitors.

*Numerous firms sell the same items, without a differential advantage, in **pure competition.***

Pure competition exists if there are many firms selling identical products. This situation occurs rarely in the United States and is most common for selected food items and commodities (and takes place only if there are a number of small firms competing with one another). The market for each firm is small. There is no control over price — because consumers are very sensitive to price changes; if a firm raises its prices, those consumers will purchase from competitors. And since standardized products are sold, there is little control over the other marketing variables. It is easy for new firms to enter the market.

With pure competition, no long-run differential advantage in the marketing mix is possible. It is essential that a firm develop a reputation for reliability, sell items at the lowest profitable prices, and convince as many distributors and retailers as possible to stock its products.

Competitor strategies need to be examined.

After analyzing the competitive structure of the industry in which it operates, a company should look at the marketing strategies of its competitors. Specifically, the firm should examine the target markets and marketing plans of competitors, the images of competitors, the differential advantages of competitors, which markets are saturated and which are unfulfilled, and the extent to which consumers are content with the level of service and quality provided by the competition.

The firm needs to study the level of both domestic and foreign competition. Most American industries are mature; and in these industries, the amount of domestic competition is relatively stable. In some industries, competition is increasing because of major innovations, such as personal computers. In other industries, competition is intensifying as a result of government deregulation. For example, Merrill Lynch now competes with Sears, Citicorp, American Express, and other firms as well as traditional brokerage companies for financial services business.

Foreign competitors have a major role in many industries. In the United States, foreign-based companies are capturing large market shares — over 30 per cent for automobiles, over 30 per cent for sporting goods and microwave ovens, 90 per cent for motorcycles, and almost 100 per cent for videocassette recorders. Also imported in large numbers are tires, calculators, televisions, watches, cameras, and a wide range of other products. At the same time, competition in overseas markets is more intense for U.S.-based firms than ever before. The success of foreign firms is often due to their ability to capitalize on innovations, better quality control than U.S. companies, relatively low labor costs, an emphasis on cost-cutting practices, and good distribution and promotion.

Foreign competition is intensifying.

In many industries, there has been a trend toward larger firms because of mergers and acquisitions as well as company sales growth. Some recent mergers and acquisitions involved consumer-products companies (Philip Morris acquiring Kraft), airlines (Texas Air acquiring Continental Airlines), retailers (Campeau acquiring Allied Stores and Federated Stores), and media companies (Capital Cities acquiring ABC). Internal sales growth has been great for such diverse firms as Boeing, Wal-Mart, Apple, and Federal Express, each of which has annual sales of several billion dollars. From a small-business perspective, personal service, an appeal to underserved market segments, an entrepreneurial drive, and flexibility are major differential advantages; and cooperative arrangements and franchising allow smaller firms to buy in quantity and operate more efficiently. From a large-business perspective, widespread distribution, economies of scale, well-known brands, mass media advertising, and low to moderate prices are competitive tactics.

Mergers and acquisitions are leading to larger competitors.

The firm should define its competition in generic terms, which means as broadly as possible. For instance, the competition for a movie theater is not just other movie theaters, but also movie-rental stores, television, sporting events, operas, plays, amusement parks, schools (continuing education programs), radio, bookstores, and restaurants. The theater owner needs to ask, "What can I do to compete with a whole variety of entertainment and recreation forms, in terms of movie selection, prices, hours, refreshments, parking, and the like?"

Competition should be defined generically—as widely as possible.

Finally, the firm should study the potential for competition with channel members (distribution intermediaries). First, each party in the distribution process has different objectives and each would like to maximize its control over the marketing mix. Second, many retailers carry their own brands in competition with the manufacturers' brands they handle. Third, in some cases, such as the supermarket industry, long-run relationships have been built up among manufacturers, wholesalers, and retailers. The relationships become assets as much as any raw materials or equipment. As a result, new firms may be unable to distribute products properly, while existing firms may find it easy to place even the most innovative of products. A great asset of a firm such as Procter & Gamble is its ability to place a new soap or detergent product into virtually every supermarket across the United States.

Government

For about 100 years, the U.S. Congress has enacted federal legislation affecting marketing practices, as highlighted in Table 2-2. This legislation can be divided into three

Marketing Controversy

Should Leveraged Buyouts and Corporate Mergers Be Allowed?

Kohlberg Kravis Roberts (KKR), an investment firm, is the current corporate takeover king. Through its acquisitions, KKR controls such major U.S. corporations as RJR Nabisco, Safeway, Beatrice, and Owens-Illinois. KKR acquires its companies via leveraged buyouts (LBOs), by which it finances the takeovers by "junk" bonds with high interest rates and bank loans—made possible because of the assets of the firms being acquired. Other recent LBOs, not involving KKR, include Borg Warner, Kraft, and Federated Department Stores.

Besides LBOs, between 1981 and 1988, there were over 11,000 corporate mergers—a record number. Fewer than 300 of them were challenged by the Justice Department for possible antitrust violations, despite the large number of mergers by firms in the same industry.

Many economists and marketing analysts are concerned about the level of LBO and merger activity, despite these potential advantages:

▶ Inefficient company practices are usually discontinued and costs cut through streamlining.

▶ Weak divisions and product lines are sold off.

▶ Cost savings can be passed on to consumers.

▶ Large U.S. firms should be better able to compete against giant firms from Japan, Germany, and Korea.

▶ Stockholder value is maximized.

Critics see these disadvantages:

▶ The high debts of leveraged companies can result in a preoccupation with short-run success at the cost of long-run opportunities.

▶ Innovativeness may be diminished because of a lack of resources.

▶ Marketing efforts may be cut back.

▶ Consumers may have fewer choices—with higher prices—if there are fewer competitors in the marketplace.

▶ There is a greater potential for bankruptcy due to larger debt obligations.

What do you think?

SOURCE: Based on material in John Paul Newport, Jr., "LBOs: Greed, Good Business—Or Both?" Fortune (January 2, 1989), pp. 66–68.

*Federal legislation involves interstate commerce. The **Federal Trade Commission** is most concerned with marketing.*

categories: antitrust, discriminatory pricing, and unfair trade practices; consumer protection; and deregulation.

In the first category are laws intended to protect smaller firms from anticompetitive actions by larger ones. These laws seek to maintain a "level playing field" for all competitors by prohibiting firms from using marketing practices that unfairly injure competitors. In the second category are laws geared toward helping the consumer deal with deceptive and unsafe company practices. These laws protect consumer rights and restrict certain marketing activities (such as banning cigarette advertising from television and radio). In the third category are laws deregulating various industries to stimulate a more competitive marketplace. These laws allow companies much greater flexibility in enacting their marketing mixes. For example, before 1978, airlines had to petition the federal government to change a flight route or prices; now, the airlines can

TABLE 2-2   Key Federal Legislation Affecting Marketers

Year	Legislation	Major Purpose
A. Antitrust, Discriminatory Pricing, and Unfair Trade Practices		
1890	Sherman Act	To eliminate monopolies and sustain competition
1914	Clayton Act	To prohibit specific anticompetitive practices, such as tie-in sales, exclusive dealing, and price discrimination
1914	Federal Trade Commission (FTC) Act	To establish an independent regulatory agency to eliminate monopolies and restraint of trade and to enforce rules against unfair methods of competition
1936	Robinson-Patman Act	To prohibit price discrimination against small distributors or retailers buying the same merchandise as large competitors
1937	Miller-Tydings Act (repealed by Consumer Goods Pricing Act of 1975)	To permit retail price maintenance (price fixing) in order to protect small retailers against large chains and discounters
1938	Wheeler-Lea Amendment	To revise the FTC Act of 1914 to include unfair or deceptive practices
1946	Lanham Trademark Act	To protect and regulate trademarks and brand names
1950	Celler-Kefauver Antimerger Act	To limit or prohibit the acquisition of competitors or their assets if the effects of the acquisition would lessen competition
B. Consumer Protection		
1906 1906	Food and Drug Act Meat Inspection Act	To prohibit adulteration and misbranding of food and drugs, create the Food and Drug Administration, and regulate meat packing and shipping
1914 1938	Federal Trade Commission Act Wheeler-Lea Amendment	To establish a commission and provisions for protecting consumer rights
1939 1951 1953 1958	Wool Products Labeling Act Fur Products Labeling Act Flammable Fabrics Act Textile Fiber Identification Act	To require wool products, fur products, and textile products to show contents and to prohibit sales of dangerous flammables
1958 1960 1962	Food Additives Amendment Federal Hazardous Substances Labeling Act Kefauver-Harris Drug Amendment	To prohibit food additives causing cancer, require the labeling of hazardous household products, and require drug manufacturers to demonstrate product effectiveness and safety
1966	Fair Packaging and Labeling Act	To require packages to be labeled honestly and reduce package size proliferation
1966	National Traffic and Motor Vehicle Safety Act	To set safety standards for automobiles and tires
1966 1969 1970 1972	Child Protection Act Child Protection and Toy Safety Act Poison Prevention Labeling Act Drug Listing Act	To ban hazardous products used by children, create standards for child-resistant packages for hazardous products, and provide drug information
1966 1970	Cigarette Labeling Act Public Health Smoking Act	To require health warnings on cigarette packages and ban cigarette advertising on radio and television
1967 1968	Wholesome Meat Act Wholesome Poultry Products Act	To mandate federal inspection standards
1968 1970	Consumer Credit Protection Act Fair Credit Reporting Act	To have full disclosure of credit and loan terms and rates and regulate reporting and use of credit information

TABLE 2-2 (Continued)

Year	Legislation	Major Purpose
1972	Consumer Product Safety Act	To create the Consumer Product Safety Commission and set safety standards
1975	Magnuson-Moss Consumer Product Warranty Act	To regulate warranties and set disclosure requirements
1975	Consumer Goods Pricing Act	To repeal the Miller-Tydings Act, which permitted retail price maintenance
1980	Fair Debt Collection Act	To eliminate the harassment of debtors and ban false statements to collect debts
1980	FTC Improvement Act	To reduce the power of the FTC to implement industrywide trade regulations (This Act reversed the trend toward increased federal government protection of consumers.)

C. Industry Deregulation

Year	Legislation	Major Purpose
1978	Natural Gas Policy Act	To make the natural gas, airline, trucking, railroad, and banking industries more competitive
1978	Airline Deregulation Act	
1980	Motor Carrier Act	
1980	Staggers Rail Act	
1981	Depository Institutions Deregulatory Committee Act	
1982	Depository Institutions Act	
1984	Drug Price Competition and Patent Term Restoration Act	To allow generic drugs to reach the market more quickly, while protecting innovators' patent rights

enact these changes as they see fit. The **Federal Trade Commission (FTC)** is the major federal regulatory agency that monitors restraint of trade and enforces rules against unfair methods of competition and deceptive business practices.

Every state and local government has regulations for firms.

In addition to federal legislation and agencies, each state and local government has its own legal environment for firms operating within its boundaries. Laws regulate where a firm may locate, the hours it may be open, the types of items that may be sold, whether it may operate door-to-door, if prices must be marked on every item sold, and how merchandise must be labeled or dated. To coordinate the legislative priorities of individual states, the National Association of Attorneys General (NAAG), with representatives from all fifty states, has developed guidelines for airline discount-fare advertising, prepared proposals for guidelines on car-rental price advertising, urged a federal judge to toughen restrictions on the sales of all-terrain vehicles, and begun a crackdown on telemarketing fraud.[8]

State and local governments also provide incentives for companies to operate. Recently, *Inc.* magazine rated each of the fifty states' attractiveness for small business on the basis of such factors as new jobs generated, new businesses founded, and young company growth. Arizona, New Hampshire, Maryland, Florida, Virginia, Georgia, Delaware, Nevada, California, and Tennessee ranked the highest.[9]

The political environment often signals legislation and government actions.

The political environment often affects legislation. Marketing issues such as these are almost always discussed and debated through the political process before legislation is enacted (or not enacted): Should mail-order sales to out-of-state customers be

---

[8] Richard L. Gordon, "Power Grabbers," *Advertising Age* (March 14, 1988), p. 12; and Jennifer Lawrence, "State Ad Rules Face Showdown," *Advertising Age* (November 28, 1988), pp. 4, 66.
[9] Joshua Hyatt, "Report on the States: 1988," *Inc.* (October 1988), pp. 79–81.

taxed? Should certain goods and services not be allowed to advertise on television? Should the minimum-wage rate be raised (which would have a significant effect on retailers)? Should state governments become more active in handling consumer complaints? Before legislation is passed, both companies and consumer-activist groups can have input into the process. Their goal is to market their positions to the relevant government officials. A strength of the American political system is its continuity, which enables organizations and individuals to develop marketing strategies for long periods of time.

The Economy

The rate of growth in a country's or region's economy can have a significant impact on a firm's marketing efforts. A high rate of growth means the economy in a country or region is usually strong and marketing potential large. Of prime significance to marketers are the perceptions of consumers regarding the economy. If they believe the economy will be favorable, they will increase spending. If they believe the economy will be poor, they will cut back on spending. See Figure 2-8.

FIGURE 2-8
Consumer Optimism/ Pessimism Affects the Economy
Reprinted by permission.

IF YOU'RE OPTIMISTIC ABOUT THE ECONOMIC FUTURE, TURN THIS PAGE UPSIDE DOWN.

Truth is, if enough people are optimistic, they'll turn the world rightside up.

At Drexel Burnham Lambert, we're optimists. But realists.

Which means we recognize the basic truth that it takes consumer confidence—and consumer spending—to fuel recovery, and to turn a bull market into a bullish economy.

In our view, the pieces of the puzzle of how to restore America's economic health are falling into place.

The next step? It's up to John Q.—and Joan P.—Public. If they believe the future is optimistic, they'll begin buying. Buying will, logically enough, lead business to expand. And more production will mean more jobs.

Drexel Burnham Lambert.

In a world that often seems upside down, we try to help you put things rightside up.

Drexel Burnham Lambert
Your bottom line is our top concern.

*Economic growth is measured by the **Gross National Product**.*

Nationally, economic growth may be studied by reviewing year-to-year changes in the **Gross National Product** (**GNP**), which is the total annual value of goods and services produced in a country. Personal consumption expenditures on durable goods, nondurable goods, and services account for about two-thirds of the GNP. When certain industries, such as automobile and housing, slow down, repercussions are often felt in other areas, such as insurance and home furnishings.

Forecasting the U.S. economy is difficult because of the uncertainty of many factors, particularly inflation, unemployment, and such outside factors as OPEC (Organization of Petroleum Exporting Countries) prices. To illustrate the complexity of predicting the economy, consider that between 1980 and 1989 the annual rate of inflation ranged between 1.1 and 13.5 per cent, the annual rate of unemployment ranged from 5.4 to 9.7 per cent, and the price of a barrel of oil ranged from $8 to $35. As a result, the annual real GNP growth fluctuated between -2.0 and $+6.5$ per cent over this period.

After going through a lengthy period of stagflation (a stagnant economy with high inflation), the United States is now in a stable period with much lower inflation, coupled with a slow-growth economy. The highest projection for real GNP growth in the United States over the next decade is about 3 to 4 per cent each year; but the rate could be lower if budget and trade deficits are not reduced. This growth rate is a strong improvement over that of the early 1980s.

Business costs affect marketing flexibility.

Several of the costs of doing business are generally beyond the control of the firm. These include raw materials, unionized labor wages, interest rates, machinery, and office (factory) rental. If costs rise by a large amount, marketing flexibility may be limited because a firm often cannot pass along all of the increase; it might have to cut back on marketing activities or be willing to accept lower profit margins. When costs are stable, marketing personnel have much greater opportunities to differentiate their offerings and expand sales because firms are more likely to invest in marketing activities.

*Inflation and unemployment affect purchases. **Real income** describes earnings adjusted for inflation.*

From a marketing perspective, what happens to the real income of consumers is of prime importance. While actual income is the amount of income earned by a consumer (or his/her family or household) in a given year, **real income** is the amount of income earned in a year adjusted by the rate of inflation. For example, if a person's actual income goes up by 4 per cent in a year (from $40,000 to $41,600) and the rate of inflation (which measures price changes for the same goods and services over time) is 4 per cent for the year, real income remains constant (($41,600) $-$ ($41,600/ 1.04) = $40,000). When actual income increases exceed the rate of inflation, real income rises; and consumers can buy more goods and services. When actual income increases are less than the rate of inflation, real income falls; and consumers must buy fewer goods and services.

A high rate of unemployment can adversely affect many firms because people cut back on nonnecessities where possible. Low unemployment leads to increased sales of large-ticket items, as buyers are optimistic and willing to spend their earnings.

Technology

Technology includes machinery, products, and processes.

Technology refers to the development and use of machinery, products, and processes. For several reasons, individual firms, especially smaller ones with limited capital, must usually adapt to technological advances (rather than control them).

Many firms are dependent on other companies to develop and perfect new technology, such as computer microchips, and only then can these firms use the new technology in their products, such as automated gasoline pumps at service stations, talking toys, or electronic sensors in smoke detectors for office buildings. And when a new technology is introduced, the inventor often secures patent protection, which excludes competitors from using that technology (unless the inventor licenses the rights to others for a fee).

In a number of areas, companies have been unable to achieve technological breakthroughs. For example, no company has been able to develop a cure for the common cold, a good-tasting nontobacco cigarette, a car powered by electricity, or a totally effective and safe diet pill.

When new technology first emerges, it may be expensive and in short supply both for companies using the technology in their products and for final consumers. The challenge is to mass produce and mass market the technology as efficiently as possible. For example, it took a decade for battery-operated pocket calculators to reach peak sales.

Technological advances may be costly and require employee training and retooling.

Some technological advances require employee training and consumer education before they can succeed in the marketplace. Company emphasis on user-friendliness can speed up the acceptance of new technology. That is why the current generation of personal computers focuses so much on ease of use, and personal selling (customer service) is so important.

Some technological advances may not be compatible with goods and services already on the market and/or require significant retooling by firms wanting to use them in their products. For instance, each time a firm buys new computer equipment to supplement existing equipment, it must determine whether the new equipment is compatible (Can it run all the computer programs used by the firm and "talk to" the firm's existing equipment?). And every time an auto maker introduces a significantly new car model, it must invest hundreds of millions of dollars to retool facilities.

To be successful, technological advances must be accepted by each firm along the distribution process (the manufacturer/service provider, the wholesaler, and the retailer). Should one of these firms not use a new technology, its benefits may be lost. For example, if a small retailer does not have electronic scanning equipment at its cash registers, its cashiers must ring up prices by hand, even though each package has been computer-coded by manufacturers.

A firm's technological abilities are also affected by the availability of scarce resources. During the past twenty years, sporadic shortages and volatile price changes have occurred for a variety of basic commodities such as home heating oil, other petroleum-based products, plastics, synthetic fibers, aluminum, chrome, silver, tungsten, nickel, steel, glass, grain, fertilizer, cotton, and wool. And despite efforts at conservation, some raw materials, processed materials, and component parts may remain or become scarce in the next decade.

Some resources may be scarce.

Resource shortages and/or rapid cost increases would require one of three actions by a company. First, substitute materials could be used in constructing products, requiring intensified research and product testing. Second, prices could be raised for products that cannot incorporate substitute materials. Third, companies could abandon products where resources are unavailable or used ineffectively and demarket others where demand is greater than it is able to satisfy.

Independent Media

Independent media affect perceptions of products and company image.

Independent media are communication vehicles (such as newspapers and television) that are not controlled by the firm; yet, they can influence the government's, consumers', and publics' perceptions of a company's products and overall image. The media can provide positive or negative coverage of a company when it produces a new product, pollutes the air, mislabels merchandise, contributes to charity, or otherwise performs a newsworthy activity. This coverage may be by print media, television, radio, or news organizations. In order to receive the best possible coverage, the company should willingly distribute information to the independent media and always try to get the company's position written or spoken about.

It is important to note that, although the independent media's coverage of information about a company or information released by a company is uncontrollable, paid advertising is controllable by the firm. Although the media may reject such advertising, if it is accepted it must be presented in the time interval and form stipulated by the firm.

Attainment of Objectives, Feedback, and Adaptation

Together, controllable and uncontrollable factors impact on success or failure.

The organization's level of success or failure in reaching its objectives depends on how well it directs and implements its controllable factors and the impact of uncontrollable factors on the marketing plan. As shown in Figure 2-1, it is the interaction of the organization's total offering and the uncontrollable environment that determines its success or failure.

Feedback provides information enabling a firm to adapt to its environment.

In order to improve its marketing effort and ensure its long-run existence, an organization needs to acquire **feedback** (information about the uncontrollable environment, the organization's performance, and how well the various aspects of the marketing plan are received). Feedback is obtained by measuring consumer satisfaction, looking at competitive trends, evaluating the relationship with government agencies, monitoring the economy and potential resource shortages, reading or viewing the independent media, analyzing sales and profit trends, talking with distribution intermediaries, and employing other methods of obtaining and assessing information.

After evaluating feedback, where necessary, the firm needs to engage in **adaptation,** thereby fine-tuning its marketing plan to be responsive to the surrounding environment while continuing to utilize its differential advantage(s). It is crucial that the firm continually look for opportunities that fit into its overall marketing plan and are attainable by the firm and respond to potential threats by revising marketing policies.

Marketing myopia is an inefficient, complacent marketing approach.

Marketing myopia, a shortsighted, narrow-minded view of marketing and its environment, must be avoided at all costs:

> [Good companies] have succeeded not primarily because of their product or research orientation but because they have been thoroughly customer-oriented also. It is constant watchfulness for opportunities to apply their technical know-how to the creation of customer-satisfying uses which accounts for their prodigious output of successful new products.[10]

---

[10] Theodore Levitt, ''Marketing Myopia,'' *Harvard Business Review*, Vol. 53 (September–October 1975), pp. 26–44, 173–181.

FIGURE 2-9
The Unique Appeal of Canfield's Diet Chocolate Fudge Soda
Canfield has a loyal customer following that has enabled it to succeed in a very competitive marketplace.
Reprinted by permission.

As an illustration, smaller soda manufacturers are in a tough struggle for their very survival, as the major firms have become more active marketers. Twenty-five years ago, Coca-Cola Co. sold two soft-drink products. Today, it offers about 20 in more than 100 packages (including bottles, cans, single-serving, 3-liter, etc.). As the strong and growing industry leaders, Coca-Cola and PepsiCo now account for 70 per cent of all U.S. soda sales. Due to their strength, smaller soda manufacturers have had a difficult time securing shelf space in grocery and convenience stores, restaurants, and vending machines. Typically, each new Coca-Cola product gets the same shelf space as that allotted to a small firm's entire soda line.

To exist in such an environment, smaller soda manufacturers have enacted a variety of adaptation strategies:

▶ Canfield Co. believes that "You can't win head on. You've got to seek out niches." Its most successful product is Diet Chocolate Fudge soda, which sold 30 million cans the year after it was introduced and received a "rave" review in the *Chicago Tribune.* See Figure 2-9.
▶ A&W markets the only nationally distributed brand of root beer and cream soda.
▶ Double Coke Co. has increased its sales overseas; there are growing markets in South America, the Middle East, Asia, and Africa.
▶ Carolina Beverages Corp. has cut prices, expanded its advertising budget, and placed 1,500 of its own vending machines in its geographic region.
▶ Dr Pepper features humor in its ads to create a distinctive image.[11]

---

[11] Nancy Giges, "Small Bottlers Get Fallout from Titans' Clash," *Advertising Age* (April 22, 1985), p. 44; Jennifer Lawrence, "Cola Wars Move In-Store," *Advertising Age* (November 9, 1987), p. 4; Pat Winters, "Cream of the Smaller Crop," *Advertising Age* (August 15, 1987), p. S-10; and Jennifer Lawrence, "Dr Pepper Bets on Big Laughs," *Advertising Age* (October 10, 1988), p. 71.

Summary

1. *To examine the environment within which marketing decisions are made and marketing activities are undertaken* The marketing environment consists of five parts: controllable factors, uncontrollable factors, the organization's level of success or failure in reaching its objectives, feedback, and adaptation.

2. *To differentiate between those elements controlled by top management and those controlled by marketing, and to enumerate the controllable elements of a marketing plan* Controllable factors are the elements of a strategy that are directed by the firm and its marketers. Top management decides on the line of business, overall objectives, the role of marketing, the role of other business functions, and the corporate culture. These decisions have an impact on all aspects of marketing.

   The major factors directed by marketing personnel are the selection of a target market, which is the particular group(s) of customers a company proposes to serve; marketing objectives, which are more customer-oriented than those set by top management; the marketing organizational structure; the marketing mix, which is a specific combination of product, distribution, promotion, and price decisions; and the control function, which involves monitoring and reviewing performance. It is especially important that marketing personnel strive to create a differential advantage, that set of unique factors in a company's marketing program that causes consumers to patronize that company and not its competitors.

3. *To enumerate the uncontrollable environmental elements that can affect a marketing plan and study their potential ramifications* Uncontrollable factors are the elements affecting an organization's performance that cannot be directed by the firm and its marketers. Any marketing plan, no matter how well conceived, may fail if uncontrollable factors adversely influence it.

   Among the most important uncontrollable variables are consumer characteristics, interpersonal influences on consumer behavior, the consumer's use of a decision process, and consumer-rights groups and organizations; the competitive structure of the industry in which a firm operates (monopoly, oligopoly, monopolistic competition, or pure competition) and such competitor characteristics as marketing strategy, country of origin, size, generic competition, and channel competition; government legislation and the political environment; the rate of economic growth (as measured by the GNP and real income) and the costs of doing business; technology, which refers to the development and use of machinery, products, and processes; and the independent media, which are communication vehicles not controlled by the firm.

4. *To explain why feedback about and adaptation to the uncontrollable aspects of the environment are essential for a firm to attain its objectives* An organization's level of success or failure in reaching its objectives depends on how well it directs and implements its controllable factors and the impact of uncontrollable factors on the marketing plan. When implementing a marketing strategy, a firm should obtain feedback (information about the uncontrollable environment and the firm's overall and marketing performance) and adapt the strategy so as to be responsive to the surrounding environment while continuing to utilize its differential advantage(s). Marketing myopia, a shortsighted, narrow-minded view of marketing and its environment, must be avoided.

Key Terms

marketing environment (p. 30)
controllable factors (p. 31)
line of business (p. 31)
overall objectives (p. 32)
role of marketing (p. 32)
corporate culture (p. 32)
target market (p. 33)
market segmentation (p. 34)
marketing objectives (p. 35)

differential advantage (p. 35)
marketing organization (p. 35)
marketing mix (p. 35)
control (p. 39)
uncontrollable factors (p. 39)
monopoly (p. 41)
oligopoly (p. 41)
monopolistic competition (p. 42)
pure competition (p. 42)

Federal Trade Commission
   (FTC) (p. 46)
Gross National Product (GNP) (p. 48)
real income (p. 48)
technology (p. 48)
independent media (p. 50)
feedback (p. 50)
adaptation (p. 50)
marketing myopia (p. 50)

Review Questions

1. Explain the environment of marketing.
2. Why are the factors controlled by top management usually considered uncontrollable by marketing personnel?
3. What criteria would you use to assess the role of marketing in a company?
4. Why should a firm select a target market *before* developing a specific marketing mix?
5. What is the most important marketing objective for an organization? Why?
6. What are the four forms of marketing organization from which a company may choose? Explain each in your answer.
7. Since companies can choose the target market to which they want their goods or services to appeal, why are consumers considered to be uncontrollable?
8. Why do some industries become oligopolistic and others result in monopolistic competition? What does this mean for firms in these industries?
9. What is the intent of each of these categories of federal legislation?
   a. Antitrust, discriminatory pricing, and unfair trade practices.
   b. Deregulation.
   c. Consumer protection.
10. How do the independent media affect a firm's marketing practices?

Discussion Questions

1. For each of the following, specify two to three top management objectives and two to three marketing objectives. How do they differ?
   a. Office furniture manufacturer.
   b. Real-estate firm.
   c. Florist.
   d. Public library.
2. What is the differential advantage for each of these? Explain your answers.
   a. Taco Bell restaurants.
   b. *People* magazine.
   c. A small commercial insurance company.
   d. Your college or university.
3. Distinguish between the marketing mixes used by Honda and Acura, two car lines of Honda.
4. Deregulation represents both opportunities and potential problems for companies. Offer several examples of both.
5. Comment on this statement: "By defining competition in generic terms, acquiring information about the uncontrollable environment, and modifying strategy when necessary, an organization will avoid marketing myopia and guarantee its long-term success."

◀ CASE 1 ▶

Airline Deregulation: Assessing the First Ten Years[*]

In 1978, Congress enacted the Airline Deregulation Act. This made it easier for new airlines to enter the industry. It also allowed existing airlines to determine and revise their routes and prices without the severe restrictions and time delays that had been imposed by the Civil Aeronautics Board (CAB). As of January 1, 1985, the CAB ceased to exist; today, airlines can fly anywhere in the United States and set any prices they would like.

[*] The data in this case are drawn from Christopher Power and Aaron Bernstein et al., "The Frenzied Skies," *Business Week* (December 9, 1988), pp. 70–73.

Through deregulation, Congress intended to increase competition, allow airlines to have more control over their marketing efforts, and stimulate lower prices for passengers (as a result of the greater competition and operating flexibility). By one standard, the first ten years since regulation were an unqualified success—passenger volume increased from 240 million trips in 1978 to 455 million trips in 1988. And such special incentives as frequent-flyer programs, which could not have been used in pre-deregulation years, were implemented. According to one U.S. Transportation Secretary, "deregulation turned out to be the most successful populist reform in the forty years since the war."

Yet, the overall impact of deregulation on the airline industry and on consumers has been mixed; and some former advocates are even calling for a return of some regulation. The mixed results can be seen by reviewing the change in the number of U.S. airlines, the total market shares of the major airlines and their market shares at their hub locations, and the airlines' evolving cost structures over the first ten years of deregulation.

In 1978, there were 30 airlines in the United States; by the early 1980s, there were 200 domestic carriers (many were commuter airlines). As of 1988, there were 125 airlines. Although these data seem to indicate that the industry has become more competitive, more than 125 airlines formed since deregulation have failed. Furthermore, because of mergers and consolidations, the total market share of the five largest U.S. airlines rose from 65 per cent in 1978 to 70 per cent in 1988. These air carriers (United, American, Delta, Northwest, and Texas Air's Continental/Eastern) were established well before deregulation.

Between 1978 and 1988, market competition fell even more at the major airlines' hub locations. For example, United Airlines' market share at its O'Hare (Chicago) hub increased from 29 per cent to 53 per cent; Northwest Airlines' share at its Minneapolis/St. Paul hub almost doubled to 82 per cent; and TWA soared to 82 per cent of the St. Louis market. In 1988, a single carrier controlled more than one-half of the passenger boardings at eighteen of the nation's busiest airports.

During the first ten years of airline deregulation, ticket prices dropped dramatically and the airlines' average ticket revenue per passenger mile decreased from 12.3 cents in 1978 to 9.8 cents in 1988 (adjusted for inflation). Thus, airlines became more interested in cost control measures. For example, airlines reduced labor expense from 40 per cent of total costs in the early 1980s to 35 per cent in 1988. Cost pressures also had the effect of lengthening the replacement schedules for planes. The average commercial plane is now 13 years old versus a little over 10 years old in 1979.

A recent survey of airline passengers found that 32 per cent felt airline deregulation was a good idea, 23 per cent felt it was a bad idea, 35 per cent thought it made little difference, and 10 per cent were not sure about its effects.

In summarizing the current state of the airline industry, one expert stated: "After years of struggle, the surviving big airlines face relative prosperity and stability. Now they don't have to worry about swarms of new competition. Instead, they have to make sure they don't become victims of their own success."

QUESTIONS

1. As the prospective owner of a new airline,
   a. Define your line of business.
   b. Explain your objectives.
   c. Define the role of marketing.
2. Describe and evaluate the marketing mix used by any one of the major five airlines cited in the case. (This question requires some library research).

3. What type of competitive structure exists in the airline industry? Explain your answer.
4. Should there be renewed regulation of the airline industry? Take the perspective of a small airline; then answer the question as a representative of a large airline.

◄ CASE 2 ►

Reacting to Consumer Perceptions About Inflation[†]

From 1979 to 1981, the prices of consumer goods and services in the United States rose between 10.4 and 13.5 per cent annually. As a result, many consumers were forced to cut back on purchases—particularly those involving nonnecessities. Consumer pessimism was at its highest level in years.

Then the level of annual price increases (the rate of inflation) came down considerably, through the joint efforts of business and government, and consumer purchases soared. Since 1983, yearly U.S. price increases have been between 3 and 6 per cent—with the exception of 1986, when the inflation rate was a shade over 1 per cent.

Now some economists believe a new consumer perception about price levels is prevalent: The yearly inflation rate has remained at the 3 to 6 per cent rate for so long that a lot of consumers are starting to accept annual price increases in that range as both normal and inevitable.

As a market analyst at First Boston Corporation says, "It's as if we have made 4 per cent inflation equal to zero inflation." The director of the University of Michigan's Survey Research Center adds, "People are judging their current situation against their historical memory of the late 70s and early 80s. They are saying 4 to 5 per cent inflation—that is not a big deal.'" In contrast, during 1971, President Nixon imposed government-mandated wage and price controls when prices rose beyond the 4 per cent annual rate.

According to the National Federation of Independent Business, a recent survey of its 2,000 member firms shows that only a handful consider inflation to be a problem or concern. And most consumers think that average price increases will remain in the 4 to 6 per cent range for the foreseeable future, according to the University of Michigan's Survey Research Center and the Conference Board.

This new consumer tolerance and acceptance for a moderate amount of inflation is helping a variety of companies to increase their per-unit profit; these firms now have more leeway in setting prices. For example, in 1988, Gillette successfully raised razor blade prices by 5 per cent. Similar Gillette price increases in 1985 and 1986 met with so much consumer resistance that it ended up using price discounts: "Now people are accepting 5 per cent increases as low. There is nothing low about it, but they are accepting such increases; they expect them."

Despite consumer acceptance of moderate inflation, manufacturers in very competitive markets are concerned about passing on cost increases in the form of higher prices. For instance, U.S. paper makers feel that "every time we think about raising prices, we have to keep an eye cocked on whether it will bring foreign products flooding into the market." To hold down costs, these firms have increased productivity by 35 per cent since 1980.

U.S. steel makers have increased productivity by 30 per cent since 1984. Although the steel industry is now operating at 90 per cent capacity, U.S. steel makers are aware that steel producers in countries around the world would gladly export their output to the United States if prices here rise.

[†] The data in this case are drawn from Louis S. Richman, "Why Inflation Is Not Inevitable," *Fortune* (September 12, 1988), pp. 117–124; and Louis Uchitelle, "Consumers Accepting 4 Per Cent Inflation," *New York Times* (October 11, 1988), pp. D1, D9.

QUESTIONS

1. Comment on this statement: "People are judging their current situation against their historical memory of the late 70s and early 80s. They are saying 4 to 5 per cent inflation—'that is not a big deal.'"
2. Does consumer acceptance of a moderate level of inflation make a firm's marketing efforts easier or harder to plan? Why?
3. With today's inflation rate, as a razor blade manufac-

turer, how would your company's pricing objectives and differential advantage differ from those of a steel producer?
4. After consulting with your economic forecasters, you have determined that inflation will reach 8 per cent annually within the next two years. How would this affect the factors controlled by your company's top management and those controlled by marketing?

CHAPTER *3*

Strategic Planning and Marketing

CHAPTER OBJECTIVES

1. To define strategic planning and consider its importance for marketing

2. To study the different types of marketing plans

3. To examine the relationships between marketing and the other functional areas in an organization

4. To thoroughly describe each of the steps in the strategic planning process: defining organizational mission, establishing strategic business units, setting marketing objectives, situation analysis, developing marketing strategy, implementing tactics, and monitoring results

5. To present examples of strategic plans in diverse companies

O ur outside comment is, "We believe we've made important progress." Our inside comment is, "There are still two to four companies ahead of us, depending on what measure you use." It is clearly our intent to be the best in those businesses in which we compete, so we've still got our work cut out for us. [recent observation by Philip Lippincott, chief executive officer, Scott Paper Company]

Reprinted by permission.

From the early 1900s through the early 1960s, Scott was the market leader in the paper-goods industry. But due to complacency, Scott's market share for products such as ScotTowels and ScotTissues eroded in the face of intense competition. Scott became a "fairly mediocre performer."

Then, under the new leadership of Kenneth Lippincott, Scott developed its first strategic plan. This "Strategic Plan of 1981" has been so successful that Scott is considered "a textbook example of how to turn around a company" via strategic planning. To us, good strategic planning means clearly outlining the direction a company will pursue in its chosen environment and setting guidelines for allocating resources and effort.

Today Scott regularly conducts situation analysis, in which it evaluates opportunities and potential problems. It uses portfolio analysis, in which every business unit is assessed and resources are assigned accordingly. It also uses a special form of portfolio analysis, the Boston Consulting Group matrix, to evaluate products in terms of market share and industry growth. Let us look at how Scott is actually applying these key strategic planning concepts.

On the basis of situation analysis, Scott feels that a strong opportunity exists in Europe where current per-capita consumption of tissue products is well below U.S. levels. Scott has a significant presence in Europe, which gives it advantages in terms of bargaining power, and production and distribution economies. And the reduction in European trade barriers by 1992 will further stimulate Scott's sales in this market.

Through portfolio analysis, Scott decides on resource levels for each of its business units based on their expected long-term growth and profitability. Poorly performing businesses ("bleeders and drain-ers"), such as a leisure furniture and lighting business, are sold. On the other hand, the firm is increasing its investment in attractive industry segments such as coated paper products.

Scott actively follows the strategy principles suggested by the Boston Consulting Group matrix. For example, a business unit with a high market share and industry growth rate is considered a "star," and efforts are geared to maintaining or increasing that unit's market position. One star business for Scott is its S.D. Warren subsidiary, the market-share leader in coated paper (used in producing magazines, corporate annual reports, and mail-order catalogs). S.D. Warren's annual growth rate is 16 per cent per year, compared to the industry average of 8 per cent. Accordingly, Scott has recently doubled production capacity. The star nature of S.D. Warren can be seen in its performance—it accounts for 27 per cent of company sales but contributes 54 per cent of total profits.[1]

In this chapter, we will study strategic planning from a marketing perspective and review, in depth, each of the steps in the strategic planning process. The concepts noted here (situation analysis, portfolio analysis, and the Boston Consulting Group matrix) will be discussed, as well as a number of other important strategic planning concepts.

[1] Frank Allen, "Once-Mediocre Scott Paper Excels from Make-Over," Wall Street Journal (October 4, 1988), p. A8; and Michael J. Milne, "Scott Paper Is on a Roll," Management Review (March 1988), pp. 37–42.

Overview

As described in Chapter 2, the environment within which marketing operates includes a number of factors directed by top management and others directed by marketing. In order to coordinate these factors and provide guidance for decision making, it is quite useful to employ a formal strategic planning process. From a marketing perspective, ***strategic planning*** outlines what marketing actions to undertake, why those actions are necessary, who is responsible for carrying them out, when and where they will be completed, and how they will be coordinated. It also "describes the direction [an organization] will pursue within its chosen environment and guides the allocation of resources and effort."[2]

A good strategic plan

> incorporates four distinguishing features: (1) an external orientation; (2) a process for formulating strategies; (3) methods for analysis of strategic situations and alternatives; and (4) a commitment to action.[3]

A discussion of strategic planning in marketing is presented early in the text for several reasons. One, a strategic plan gives direction to an organization's efforts and better enables it to understand the dimensions of marketing research, consumer analysis, product planning, distribution planning, promotion planning, and price planning. Strategic planning is a hierarchal process, moving from companywide guidelines down to specific marketing decisions:

> Strategic decisions are made at all levels of the company from the chief executive officer (CEO) to the individual salesperson. The CEO's strategic decisions determine how the company allocates capital to various divisions, while the salesperson's strategic decisions determine how the salesperson allocates his or her resource — selling time — to various customers.[4]

Two, a strategic plan makes sure that each division in an organization has clear objectives that are integrated with overall company objectives. Three, different functional areas are encouraged to coordinate their efforts. Four, strategic planning forces an organization to assess its strengths and weaknesses in terms of competitors and opportunities and threats in the environment. Five, alternative actions or combinations of actions that an organization can take are outlined. Six, a basis for allocating resources is established. Seven, the value of enacting a procedure for assessing performance can be demonstrated.

As the executive director of the Marketing Science Institute recently commented, it is necessary to

> integrate marketing into the strategic planning process. The business plan should stress market information, market-segment definition, and market targeting as key elements. All activities of the business should be built around the objective of creating the desired position with a well-defined set of customers. Separate market segments should be the subject of separate business plans that focus on the development of relationships with customers that emphasize the firm's distinctive competence.

---

[2] Peter D. Bennett (Editor), *Dictionary of Marketing Terms* (Chicago: American Marketing Association, 1988), p. 195.

[3] Ibid.

[4] Barton A. Weitz and Robin Wensley (Editors), *Readings in Strategic Marketing: Analysis, Planning, and Implementation* (Hinsdale, Ill.: Dryden, 1988), p. 4.

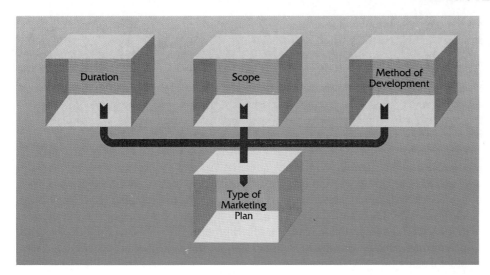

FIGURE 3-1
Categorizing Marketing Plans

[Marketing's] contribution to strategic planning and implementation begins with the analysis of market segments and the assessment of the firm's ability to satisfy customer needs. This includes the analysis of demand trends, competition, and, in industrial markets, the competitive conditions faced by firms in those segments. Marketing also plays a key role by working with top management to define business purpose in terms of customer-need satisfaction.

In this market-oriented view of the strategic planning process, financial goals are seen as results and rewards, not the fundamental purpose of business.[5]

Chapter 3 examines several types of marketing plans, the relationships between marketing and other functional areas in an organization, and the strategic planning process, and presents examples of strategic planning in marketing. Chapter 24, which concludes the text, considers how marketing plans are integrated and analyzed.

Types of Marketing Plans

Marketing plans can be categorized by duration, scope, and method of development. Plans range from short-run, specific, and department-generated to long-run, broad, and management-generated. See Figure 3-1.

Marketing plans may be short run (typically one year), moderate in length (two to five years), or long run (5 to 10 or even 15 years). Many firms rely on a combination of these plans. Short-run and moderate-length plans are more detailed and operational in nature than long-run plans. For example, a one-year plan might describe precise marketing objectives and strategies for every product offered by the firm, while a 15-year

Short-run plans are precise; long-run plans outline needs.

---

[5] Frederick E. Webster, Jr., "The Rediscovery of the Marketing Concept," *Business Horizons*, Vol. 31 (May-June 1988), pp. 37–38.

Consumer-products firms are most likely to use plans for each line.

plan might be confined to forecasting the environment during that period and determining the organization's long-term needs.[6]

The scope of marketing plans also varies. There may be separate marketing plans for each of the firm's major products; a single, integrated marketing plan encompassing all products; or a broad business plan with a section devoted to marketing. Separate marketing plans for each product line are most often used by consumer-goods manufacturers; a single, integrated marketing plan is most often used by service firms; and a broad business plan is most often used by industrial-goods manufacturers.[7]

Bottom-up plans foster employee input; top-down plans are set by management.

Last, marketing plans can be developed through either a bottom-up or top-down approach. In the bottom-up approach, information from salespeople, product managers, advertising personnel, and other marketing areas is used to establish objectives, budgets, forecasts, timetables, and marketing mixes. Bottom-up plans are realistic and good for morale. However, there may be difficulties in coordinating each bottom-up plan to attain one integrated plan and in incorporating different assumptions about the same concept, such as conflicting estimates about the impact of advertising on a new product's sales.

The problems of bottom-up plans are resolved in the top-down approach, which centrally directs and controls planning activities. A top-down plan can utilize complex assumptions about competition or other external factors and provide a uniform direction for the marketing effort. Nonetheless, input from lower-level managers is not actively sought and morale may be diminished. A combination of these two approaches could be used if top management sets overall objectives and policy, and if sales, advertising, product, and other personnel establish the plans for carrying out the policy.

Strengthening Relationships Between Marketing and Other Functional Areas in an Organization

The perspectives of marketing and other functional areas need to be reconciled.

Strategic planning efforts must accommodate the distinct needs of marketing as well as the other functional areas in an organization. This is not always simple, due to the different orientations of each area, as shown in Table 3-1. For example, marketing personnel may seek tailor-made products, flexible budgets, unique expenditures, a variety of product versions, frequent purchases, customer-driven new products, and aggressive actions against competitors. This may conflict with the goals of the other functional areas to seek mass production (production), well-established budgets (finance), routinized transactions (accounting), limited models (engineering), infrequent orders (purchasing), technology-driven new products (research and development), and passive actions against competitors (legal). Table 3-2 contains several illustrations of possible differences in perspectives between marketing and the production, finance, and engineering areas.

---

[6] David S. Hopkins, *The Marketing Plan* (New York: Conference Board, 1981), p. 10. See also Robert E. Linneman and Harold E. Klein, "Using Scenarios in Strategic Decision Making," *Business Horizons,* Vol. 28 (January-February 1985), pp. 64–74; and Ronald N. Paul and James W. Taylor, "The State of Strategic Planning," *Business,* Vol. 36 (January-March 1986), pp. 37–43.

[7] Ibid, p. 4.

TABLE 3-1   The Orientations of Different Functional Areas

Functional Area	Major Strategic Orientation
Marketing	To attract and retain a loyal group of consumers through a unique combination of product, distribution, promotion, and price factors
Production	To utilize full plant capacity, hold down per-unit production costs, and maximize quality control
Finance	To operate within well-established budgets, focus on profitable items, control credit, and minimize the costs of loans to the company
Accounting	To standardize reports, fully detail costs, and routinize transactions
Engineering	To develop and adhere to exact product specifications, limit models and options, and concentrate on quality improvements
Purchasing	To acquire materials through large, uniform orders at low prices and maintain low inventories
Research and development	To seek technological breakthroughs, improvements in product quality, and recognition for innovations
Legal	To ensure that the strategy is defensible against challenges from the government, competitors, channel members, and consumers

Top management's role is to make sure that each functional area understands management's desire for a balanced viewpoint in overall decision making and that each area has input into decisions. Although a certain degree of tension among departments is inevitable, conflict can be reduced by openly discussing differences and encouraging interfunctional contact; seeking employees who blend technical and marketing expertise; establishing interfunctional task forces, committees, and management-development programs; and setting objectives for each department which take into account other departments' goals.[8]

The Strategic Planning Process

The ***strategic planning process*** in marketing consists of seven interrelated steps: defining organizational mission, establishing strategic business units, setting marketing objectives, performing situation analysis, developing marketing strategy, implementing tactics, and monitoring results. The process is undertaken by a combination of both senior company executives and marketers. It is depicted in Figure 3-2.

This process is applicable for small and large firms, consumer-products and industrial-products firms, goods- and services-based firms, and profit-oriented and nonprofit-oriented organizations. While planning at each step in the process differs by type of organization, the use of a thorough strategic plan is beneficial for any organization.[9]

*The **strategic planning process** includes steps from defining a mission to monitoring results.*

[8] Benson P. Shapiro, "Can Marketing and Manufacturing Coexist?" *Harvard Business Review*, Vol. 55 (September-October 1977), pp. 104–114; J. Donald Weinrauch and Richard Anderson, "Conflicts Between Engineering and Marketing Units," *Industrial Marketing Management*, Vol. 11 (October 1982), pp. 291–301; and John R. Hauser and Don Clausing, "The House of Quality," *Harvard Business Review*, Vol. 66 (May-June 1988), pp. 63–73.

[9] See Richard G. Hamermesh, "Making Planning Strategic," *Harvard Business Review*, Vol. 64 (July-August 1986), pp. 115–120; Norman M. Scarborough and Thomas W. Zimmerer, "Strategic Planning for the Small Business," *Business*, Vol. 37 (April-June 1987), pp. 11–19; W. Keith Schilit, "How to Write a Winning Business Plan," *Business Horizons*, Vol. 30 (September-October 1987), pp. 13–22; and Bill Saporito, "Companies That Compete Best," *Fortune* (May 22, 1989), pp. 36–44.

TABLE 3-2   Illustrations of How Marketing, Production, Engineering, and Finance Can View One Another

Factor	Typical Marketing Comment	Typical Production Comment	Typical Finance Comment	Typical Engineering Comment
Technical service	"We need more engineering assistance on customer visits."	"Marketing has sold products for applications they were not designed to fulfill."	"Our technical service costs are higher than the industry average."	"Marketers don't need us as often as we're requested; they use us for credibility."
Promotion	"Our promotion is too technical."	"Product specifications and our quality control program should be stressed."	"Promotion should stress costs and benefits."	"Our promotion is not technical enough."
Design	"Design changes are too seldom."	"Design changes are too frequent."	"Design changes are generally very costly and therefore should be kept to a minimum."	"Design changes are too frequent."
Distributor selection	"We should select distributors based on their marketing savvy."	"We need distributors who can stock large inventory levels and provide steady orders."	"We should select distributors based on their financial resources."	"We need distributors who can provide high levels of technical service to clients."
Overseas markets	"Foreign markets represent excellent opportunities."	"Tailoring products to foreign needs and long lead times for shipments represent significant problems."	"While foreign markets represent excellent opportunities, we need to be concerned with foreign currency stability and nationalism."	"We must be careful not to give trade secrets to potential competitors."

Source: Adapted by the authors from Benson P. Shapiro, "Can Marketing and Manufacturing Coexist?" *Harvard Business Review*, Vol. 55 (September–October 1977), p. 105; and J. Donald Weinrauch and Richard Anderson, "Conflicts Between Engineering and Marketing Units," *Industrial Marketing Management*, Vol. 11 (October 1982), pp. 294–295.

The steps in the strategic planning process are discussed in the following sections.

Defining Organizational Mission

A firm commits to a place in the market through its ***organizational mission***.

Organizational mission refers to a long-term commitment to a type of business and a place in the market. It "describes the scope of the firm, and the dominant emphasis and values," based on the firm's history, current management preferences, environmental factors, company resources, and distinctive competencies.[10]

[10] Bennett, *Dictionary of Marketing Terms*, p. 46.

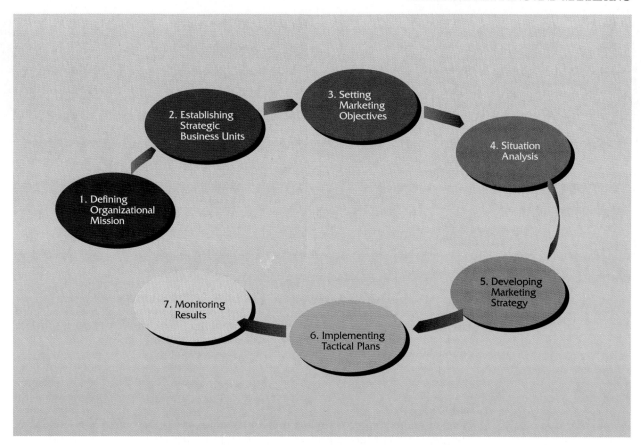

FIGURE 3-2
The Strategic Planning Process

An organizational mission can be defined in terms of the customer group(s) served, the goods and services offered, the functions performed, and the technologies utilized. It is more comprehensive and formal than the line of business concept described in Chapter 2. Organizational mission is considered implicitly whenever a company seeks a new customer group or abandons an existing one, introduces a new product (good or service) category or deletes an old one, makes an acquisition of another firm or sells one of its own businesses, performs more marketing functions (such as a manufacturer deciding to open its own retail stores) or performs fewer marketing functions (such as a small innovative computer software manufacturer deciding to license its inventions to an outside firm that would produce, distribute, and promote them), or shifts its technological focus (such as an accounting firm offering clients automated record-keeping services and placing less reliance on handwritten entries).

This is an illustration of a clear organizational mission:

> Hewlett-Packard Company designs, manufactures, and services electronic products and systems for measurement and computation. HP's basic business purpose is to provide the capabilities and support needed to help customers worldwide improve their personal and business effectiveness.[11]

---

[11] *Hewlett-Packard 1987 Annual Report.*

FIGURE 3-3 Hewlett-Packard: Adhering to a Focused Organizational Mission
One departmental computer such as the HP 300 can support from four to one hundred personal computers providing powerful data processing (left). Hewlett-Packard software makes information more useful because data are easy to access, analyze, and communicate (right).   Photos courtesy of Hewlett-Packard Company.

Overdiversification can result in a lack of organizational mission.

See Figure 3-3.

Organizations that diversify too much may not have a clear sense of mission. For example, General Mills had this organizational mission for a number of years:

> General Mills markets consumer goods and services in five principal business areas — Consumer Foods, Restaurants, Toys, Fashion, and Specialty Retailing. The company is committed to competitive excellence and to maintaining leadership among consumer goods companies through a strategy of balanced diversification, aggressive consumer marketing, and sound positioning within each industry group.[12]

However, due to poor results with toys and retailing, the firm decided to narrow its focus:

> [Now] our basic strategy is to be in only the most attractive segments of those businesses where our management is competitively superior and where our market position is strong. General Mills' structure, leading marketing positions, and aggressive investment plans will build the company's position as a premier performer in the best segments of the consumer foods and restaurant industries.[13]

Establishing Strategic Business Units

Strategic business units are separate operating entities within an organization.

After defining its mission, a company establishes strategic business units. Each **strategic business unit (SBU)** is a self-contained division, product line, or product department within an organization with a specific market focus and a manager with complete

[12] *General Mills Annual Report 1984.*
[13] *General Mills Annual Report 1988.*

responsibility for integrating all functions into a strategy.[14] An SBU may include all products with the same physical features or products that are bought for the same use by customers, depending on the mission of the organization.

SBUs are the basic building blocks of a strategic marketing plan, and each SBU has these general attributes: a specific orientation, a precise target market, a senior marketing executive in charge, control over its resources, its own strategy, clear-cut competitors, and a distinctive differential advantage.

The SBU concept was developed by McKinsey & Co. (the consulting firm) for General Electric in 1971 and has enabled General Electric and other firms to identify those business units with the greatest earnings potential and allocate to them the resources necessary for their growth. At General Electric, every SBU must have a unique purpose within the company, identifiable competitors, and all of its major business functions (manufacturing, finance, and marketing) within the control of that SBU's manager. Those units not performing up to expectations are constantly reviewed and, if necessary, sold or closed down.

The proper number of SBUs depends on the mission of an organization, its resources, and the willingness of top management to delegate authority. One study of U.S. service companies, manufacturers, and government agencies found that the typical company had from 6 to 48 SBUs.[15] A specialized firm can have as few as one SBU, a diversified one up to 100 or more.

Large firms can have dozens of SBUs.

Setting Marketing Objectives

Each strategic business unit in an organization needs to set its own objectives for marketing performance. Objectives are normally described in both quantitative terms (dollar sales, percentage profit growth, market share, etc.) and qualitative terms (image, level of innovativeness, industry leadership role, etc.).

Marketing objectives frequently encompass quantitative and qualitative measures.

There is an increasing tendency among organizations to integrate quantitative and qualitative goals. For instance, industry leadership may be evaluated on the basis of both market-share growth and innovativeness, assessed on the basis of the number of new patents registered. In this manner, qualitative objectives can be set without ambiguity.

Research has shown that, for industrial-goods manufacturers, the most important marketing objectives involve profit margins, field-sales effort, new-product development, sales to major accounts, and pricing policy. For consumer-goods manufacturers, objectives center on profit margins, sales promotion, new-product development, pricing policy, field-sales effort, and advertising expenditures. For service firms, objectives concentrate on field-sales effort, advertising themes, customer service, and sales promotion.[16]

---

[14] Subhash C. Jain, *Marketing Strategy and Planning,* Second Edition (Cincinnati: South-Western, 1985), pp. 17–20; and David G. Ratz, "Strategic Business Unit" in Walton Beacham, Richard T. Hise, and Hale N. Tongren (Editors), *Beacham's Marketing Reference* (Washington, D.C.: Research Publishing, 1986), pp. 936–941.

[15] Daniel H. Gray, "Uses and Misuses of Strategic Planning," *Harvard Business Review,* Vol. 64 (January-February 1986), p. 90.

[16] Hopkins, *The Marketing Plan,* pp. 23–24.

You're the Marketer

Where Does the Road Lead for Greyhound?

Between 1982 and 1987, Greyhound drastically changed its portfolio of businesses. The firm sold its Armour Food division in 1983 and its Greyhound Bus Lines (its former mainstay) in 1986, and greatly expanded its services and consumer-products businesses. In the latter two businesses, Greyhound is involved with airport restaurants, in-flight meals, Borax detergent, Dial Soap, Brillo scouring pads, and so on.

This is how Greyhound looked before and after its business portfolio was revamped:

▶ 1982 per cent of sales by business segment— food, 44; transportation, 19; services, 12; consumer products, 11; financial, 9; and bus manufacturing, 5.

▶ 1987 per cent of sales by business segment— food, 0; transportation, 0; services, 45; consumer products, 35; financial, 9; and bus manufacturing, 11.

Since its restructuring, Greyhound has done poorly in terms of sales performance (annual sales are now half of those in 1982) and earnings (which are only about 3 per cent of sales). Due to this, Wall Street brokers have given the firm the nickname "big dog."

Observers are concerned about the mix in Greyhound's current portfolio. For example, one expert believes that Greyhound's food outlets (including Burger King franchises, pizza parlors, the hotel operations at a national park, contract catering facilities, and ownership of Dobbs International Services, the nation's second-largest provider of in-flight meals) represent "an assortment of separate companies with no real connection."

As Greyhound's marketing vice-president, what would you do to improve its strategic plan?

SOURCE: Based on material in Frederick Rose, "Greyhound Strives to Meet Its Promises," *Wall Street Journal* (August 18, 1988), p. 6.

Situation Analysis

Situation analysis investigates a firm's strengths, weaknesses, opportunities, and threats.

In *situation analysis,* sometimes called SWOT analysis, an organization identifies its internal strengths (S) and weaknesses (W) as well as external opportunities (O) and threats (T). Situation analysis seeks answers to two general questions: Where is the firm now? In what direction is the firm headed? These questions are answered by recognizing both company strengths and weaknesses relative to competitors, searching the environment for potential opportunities and threats, assessing the organization's ability to capitalize on opportunities and to minimize or avoid threats, and anticipating competitors' responses to company strategies.

As an example, Whirlpool recently conducted a thorough situation analysis and reached these conclusions:

> The U.S. appliance market has limited growth opportunities, a high concentration of domestic competitors, and increasing foreign competition. Further, the United States represents only about 25 per cent of the worldwide potential for major appliance sales. Most importantly, our vision can no longer be limited to domestic borders because national borders no longer define market boundaries. The marketplace for goods and services is more global than ever before and growing more so every day.

Consumers in major industrialized countries are living increasingly similar life-styles and have increasingly similar expectations of what consumer products must do for them. As purchasing patterns become more alike, we think that companies that operate on a broad global scale can leverage their strengths better than those which only serve an individual market. Very likely, appliance manufacturing will always be done regionally. Yet the ability to leverage many of the strengths of a company on an international basis is possible only if that company operates globally.[17]

Accordingly, Whirlpool's long-run plans place great importance on expanding its international presence.

Sometimes situation analysis reveals weaknesses and/or threats that cannot be overcome, and a firm decides to drop a product line. In 1988, Firestone Inc. reached this difficult decision with its tire-making operations (a business that was the backbone of the company for more than eighty years) and sold controlling interest in that unit to Japan's Bridgestone. There were several reasons for Firestone's decision: radial tires (sold as original equipment on many vehicles) lasted two-and-a-half times longer than nonradial tires, reducing overall demand for tires; auto makers put great pressure on tire manufacturers to hold down prices; heavy competition led to frequent price cutting; investment costs were high; and Firestone saw better opportunities for its retail auto service centers and its building products, synthetic rubber materials, and other industrial products.[18]

Situation analysis may reveal insurmountable difficulties.

Developing Marketing Strategy

A **marketing strategy** outlines the manner in which the marketing mix is used to attract and satisfy the target market(s) and accomplish an organization's objectives. Marketing-mix decisions center on product, distribution, promotion, and price plans. A separate strategy is necessary for each SBU in an organization; these strategies must be coordinated. Every marketing strategy should be as explicit as possible to provide proper guidance.

*A good **marketing strategy** provides a framework for marketing activities.*

In planning its marketing strategy, a firm should consider four key factors for each SBU:

1. Organizational situation — What are the company's objectives, capabilities, and resources?

2. Product-market situation — Is the product category relatively new to the marketplace, growing, mature, or declining? What are the current size and expected future growth rate of the product category?

3. Competitive situation — How many competitors are there? What are their characteristics and marketing approaches? Can/should the firm be a market leader, a market challenger, a market follower, or a market nicher?

4. Environmental situation — What industrywide and company-specific environmental opportunities and threats are most important?[19]

---

[17] *Whirlpool Corporation Annual Report 1987.* See also Claudia H. Deutsch, "Whirlpool Is Gathering a Global Momentum," *New York Times* (April 23, 1989), Section 3, p. 10.

[18] Jonathan P. Hicks, "Firestone to Sell 75% of Tire Unit in $1 Billion Deal with Japanese," *New York Times* (February 17, 1988), pp. A1, D5.

[19] Adapted by the authors from David W. Cravens, "Strategic Forces Affecting Marketing Strategy," *Business Horizons,* Vol. 29 (September-October 1986), pp. 77–86.

FIGURE 3-4
The Product/Market Opportunity Matrix
SOURCE: Adapted from H. Igor Ansoff, "Strategies for Diversification," *Harvard Business Review,* Vol. 35 (September–October 1957), pp. 113–124.

Market

	Present	New
Present	Market Penetration Strategy	Market Development Strategy
New	Product Development Strategy	Diversification Strategy

Product

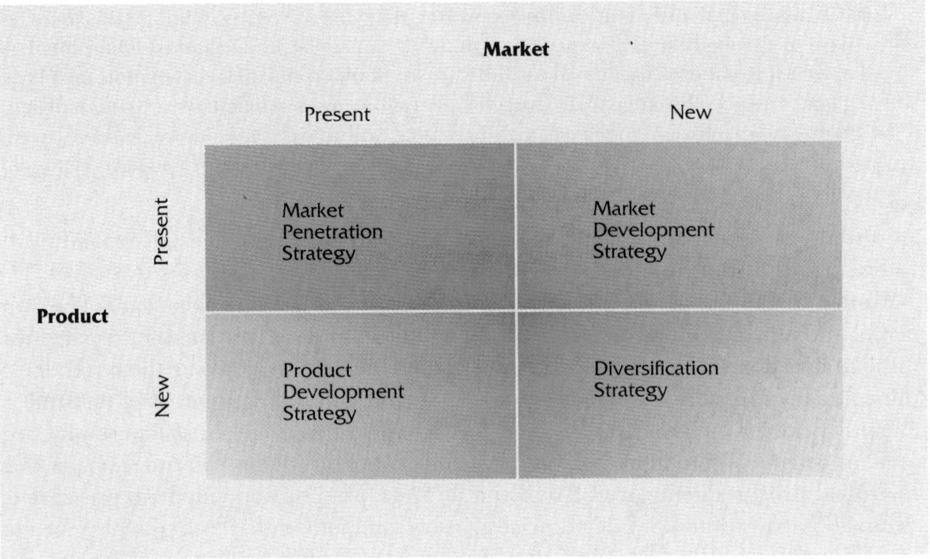

Portfolio analysis involves all of an organization's businesses and/or products.

Several systematic approaches to planning have been devised to enable organizations to develop better their marketing strategies. The approaches involve some form of *portfolio analysis,* by which an organization individually assesses and positions every business unit and/or product. Then, efforts and resources are allocated to each SBU and separate marketing mixes are aimed at their chosen target markets on the basis of these assessments. In this way, marketing plans can be adapted to the unique characteristics and needs of each business unit, consistent with its potential for short- and long-term growth and profitability.

Five approaches to strategy planning are presented in the next several subsections: the product/market opportunity matrix, the Boston Consulting Group matrix, Profit Impact of Market Strategy (PIMS), the General Electric business screen, and the Porter generic strategy model.

The Product/Market Opportunity Matrix

The product/market opportunity matrix explains market penetration, market development, product development, and diversification options.

The *product/market opportunity matrix* identifies four alternative marketing strategies that may be used to maintain and/or increase sales of business units and products: market penetration, market development, product development, and diversification.[20] See Figure 3-4. The choice of an alternative depends on the level of market saturation by the SBU or product and the firm's ability to introduce new products. Two or more of these alternatives may be combined.

Market penetration is effective for SBUs when the market is growing or not yet saturated. A firm seeks to expand the sales of its present products in its present markets through more intensive distribution, aggressive promotion, and competitive pricing. Sales are increased by attracting nonusers and competitors' customers and raising the usage rate among current customers.

[20] H. Igor Ansoff, "Strategies for Diversification," *Harvard Business Review,* Vol. 35 (September-October 1957), pp. 113–124.

Market development is effective when a local or regional business looks to widen its market, new market segments are emerging due to changes in consumer life-styles and demographics, and innovative uses are discovered for a mature product. A firm seeks greater sales of present products from new markets or new product uses. It can enter new geographic markets, appeal to market segments it is not yet satisfying, and reposition existing products. New distribution methods may be tried; promotion efforts are more descriptive.

Product development is effective when an SBU has a core of strong brands and a sizable consumer following. A firm develops new or modified products to appeal to present markets. It emphasizes new models, quality improvements, and other minor innovations closely related to established products and markets them to customers who are loyal to the company and its brands. Traditional distribution methods are used; and promotion stresses that the new product is made by a well-established firm.

Diversification is utilized so that an organization does not become overly dependent on one SBU or product line. A firm becomes involved with new products aimed at new markets. These products may be new to the industry or new only to the company. Distribution and promotion orientations are both different from those traditionally followed by the firm.

Table 3-3 applies the product/market opportunity matrix to Coca-Cola, which uses a combination of all four strategic approaches. The company's plan takes such factors as these into consideration: U.S. adults are increasing their soda consumption; in past years, Coca-Cola lost some ground to PepsiCo with the key 12- to 24-year-old market; there is heavy competition among soft-drink makers; consumer life-styles and tastes are changing; some markets are saturated; there are large overseas opportunities; the firm has strong assets in its well-known brands and in its distribution network; and it desires to be less dependent on soda for sales and profit growth.[21]

The Boston Consulting Group Matrix

The ***Boston Consulting Group matrix*** enables a company to classify each of its SBUs in terms of the SBU's market share relative to major competitors and the annual growth rate of the industry. By using the matrix, the firm can determine which of its SBUs are dominant, compared with competitors, and whether the industries in which it operates are growing, stable, or declining.[22]

The assumption is that the higher an SBU's market share, the better its long-run position in the marketplace due to its relatively low per-unit costs and high profitability. This is the result of economies of scale (larger firms can automate production,

*The **Boston Consulting Group matrix** uses market share and industry growth to describe **stars, cash cows, question marks,** and **dogs.***

[21] See Scott Ticer, "Coca-Cola: A Flexible Highflier," *Business Week* (October 5, 1987), p. 82; Jon Lafayette and Jo Beth McDaniel, "Admen Laud Coke Changes," *Advertising Age* (February 1, 1988), p. 77; and Michael J. McCarthy, "Coca-Cola Plans a New Ad Campaign in Its International Marketing Effort," *Wall Street Journal* (December 12, 1988), p. B5.

[22] See *Perspectives on Experience* (Boston: Boston Consulting Group, 1972); Bruce D. Henderson, "The Application and Misapplication of the Experience Curve," *Journal of Business Strategy*, Vol. 4 (Winter 1984), pp. 3–9; George S. Day, *Analysis for Strategic Market Decisions* (St. Paul, Mn.: West, 1986), pp. 167–190; and Christopher K. Bart, "Implementing 'Growth' and 'Harvest' Product Strategies," *California Management Review*, Vol. 29 (Summer 1987), pp. 139–156.

TABLE 3–3 The Product/Market Opportunity Matrix Applied to Coca-Cola

Market Penetration

More adults used in commercials; "You Can't Beat the Feeling" ad theme
New Coke ads aimed at core market of 12- to 24-year-olds
Price discounts and sales promotions (such as Fun Caps) directed at current consumers
Continuing domination of in-store soda-fountain market; increasing sales through fast-food
    chains
Greater promotion of non-Coke and diet brands
Strengthened bottler (distribution) network

Market Development

Company products marketed in 155 countries around the world
Greater emphasis placed on consumers in China, South America, Eastern Europe, Africa,
    and the Middle East
U.S. consumers encouraged to drink soda for breakfast
Diet Coke's appeal to male customers (as well as female customers)
Changing soda's image from children's drink to family beverage

Product Development

Improving product quality
Adding new brands and flavors (such as Minute Maid soda and cherry Coke, and decaffein-
    ated versions of Coke and Tab)
Introducing new container sizes (such as the 3-liter bottle)
Increasing the use of plastic bottles
Diet drinks reformulated with aspartame
Reintroducing Coke Classic

Diversification

Producing juice, coffee, tea, bottled water, and frozen foods
Manufacturing water-treatment and conditioning equipment
Acquiring and operating Columbia Pictures, Embassy Communications, and Merv Griffin
    Enterprises
Licensing company name for a clothing line by Murjani

advertising, and distribution), the experience curve (as projects and operations are repeated, the firm "learns" and becomes more effective), and improved bargaining power. However, at the same time, the industry growth rate indicates a firm's need to invest in each SBU. A high growth rate means that a large investment will be needed to maintain or expand the firm's position in a growing market.

The Boston Consulting Group matrix identifies four types of SBUs: star, cash cow, problem child (question mark), and dog, and suggests appropriate strategies for each. See Figure 3-5.

A *star* is a leading SBU (high market share) in an expanding industry (high growth). The major goal is to sustain the firm's differential advantage in the face of rapidly rising competition. A star can generate substantial profits but requires large amounts of resources to finance continued growth. Market share can be maintained or increased through more advertising, product introductions, greater distribution, and/ or price reductions. As industry growth slows, a star becomes a cash cow.

A *cash cow* is a leading SBU (high market share) in a relatively mature or declining industry (low growth). It usually has a loyal and established customer following, and it is difficult for competitors to woo consumers away. Because sales are relatively steady,

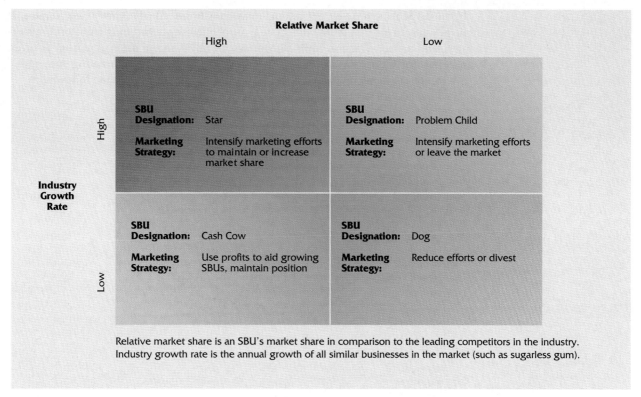

Relative Market Share

High | Low

Industry Growth Rate

High

SBU Designation: Star
Marketing Strategy: Intensify marketing efforts to maintain or increase market share

SBU Designation: Problem Child
Marketing Strategy: Intensify marketing efforts or leave the market

Low

SBU Designation: Cash Cow
Marketing Strategy: Use profits to aid growing SBUs, maintain position

SBU Designation: Dog
Marketing Strategy: Reduce efforts or divest

Relative market share is an SBU's market share in comparison to the leading competitors in the industry. Industry growth rate is the annual growth of all similar businesses in the market (such as sugarless gum).

FIGURE 3-5
The Boston Consulting Group Matrix
SOURCE: Adapted from Bruce D. Henderson, "The Experience Curve Reviewed: IV. The Growth Share Matrix of the Product Portfolio" (Boston: Boston Consulting Group, 1973), Perspectives No. 135.

without high marketing costs for product development, and the like, a cash cow generates more cash (profit) than is required to retain its market share. Profits support the growth of other company SBUs. The firm's marketing strategy is oriented toward reminder advertising, periodic price discounts, maintaining distribution channels, and offering new styles or options to encourage repurchases.

A **problem child** or **question mark** is an SBU that has made little impact in the marketplace (low market share) in an expanding industry (high growth). There is little current consumer support for the product, differential advantages are unclear, and competitors' products are market leaders. A problem child needs substantial marketing investment to maintain or increase market share in the face of such strong competition. The company must decide whether it is willing to increase its promotion budget, more aggressively pursue distributors, improve product attributes, and cut prices — or if it should abandon the market. The choice of strategy depends on whether the company believes the SBU can compete successfully with adequate support and what that support will cost.

A **dog** is an SBU with limited sales (low market share) in a mature or declining industry (low growth). Despite an adequate time in the marketplace, a dog is unable to attract a sizable customer following and is well behind its competition with regard to sales, image, cost structure, and so on. A dog usually has cost disadvantages and few growth opportunities. A company with such an SBU can attempt to appeal to a specialized market, harvest profits by cutting support services to a minimum, or leave the market.

General Mills, whose organizational mission was described earlier in the chapter, is one of many firms that follow the strategy principles suggested by the Boston Consulting Group matrix. General Mills categorizes its SBUs on the basis of market position and expected industry growth, and then develops appropriate marketing strategies.

A recent company analysis of several of its food lines revealed the following:

Established Product Categories	General Mills' 1988 Market Position	General Mills' 1988 Market Share	Categories' 1988 Share of Total General Mills' Revenues
Add-meat dinner mixes	1	64%	3.5%
Potatoes and side dish mixes	1	60%	2.3%
Flour and baking mixes	1	52%	5.0%
Dessert mixes	1	40%	8.6%
Ready-to-eat cereal	2	23%	25.3%

Growth Product Categories	General Mills' 1988 Market Position	General Mills' 1988 Market Share	Categories' 1988 Share of Total General Mills' Revenues
Fruit snacks	1	50%	3.0%
Frozen seafood	1	25%	4.6%
Yogurt	2	19%	4.2%
Microwave popcorn	2	18%	1.4%
Frozen novelties	3	6%	1.9%
Single-serving fruit drinks	New company product		

With its established product categories, General Mills maintains stable marketing efforts; it advertises regularly, introduces new product versions (such as Betty Crocker's MicroRave cake mixes), and strives to continue good relations with distribution intermediaries. Because the cereal line—which accounts for one-quarter of overall company sales—lags well behind Kellogg (which has almost double General Mills' market share), General Mills is more aggressive and has a larger marketing budget than for its other mature product categories. Said one outside analyst about its cereal efforts, "They are committed to significant new products and marketing support to regain what they've lost."

With its growth product categories, General Mills plans to spend increasing amounts on marketing to solidify its leading positions or achieve significant market breakthroughs. It uses relatively large advertising budgets, introduces many new brands (most using the powerful Betty Crocker name, such as Betty Crocker Brownie Sundae ice cream sandwiches and Betty Crocker Pop-Secret microwave popcorn), and is expanding distribution nationally and internationally: "General Mills has good growth and high return characteristics, combined with excellent internal reinvestment opportunities. We will emphasize businesses that build shareholder value and best fit our strengths."[23]

Profit Impact of Market Strategy (PIMS)

The *Profit Impact of Market Strategy* (*PIMS*) program, administered by the Strategic Planning Institute, provides individual firms with a data base summarizing the financial and market performance of over 2,800 business units representing several hundred firms. PIMS focuses on the links between various factors and profitability (ROI)/cash flow; and its data base includes successful companies and "real losers." By examining PIMS reports, a company can evaluate the potential effects of various marketing strategies on its performance — given the overall characteristics of relevant industries:

PIMS data describe the interaction between marketing factors, profitability, and cash flow.

> Each business can extract information about the experience of their "strategic peers" (i.e., businesses facing similar strategic positions but possibly in different industries). Three basic sets of variables have been found to account for 75 to 80 per cent of the variance in profitability and cash flow in the sample of businesses: (1) the competitive position of the business, as measured by market share and relative product quality; (2) the production structure, including investment intensity and productivity of operations; and (3) the relative attractiveness of the served market, comprising the growth rate and customers' characteristics.[24]

According to a recent book on PIMS by two senior executives with the Strategic Planning Institute, these are six of the most important recent PIMS findings regarding the linkages between strategy and performance:

1. In the long run, the most important single factor affecting a business unit's performance is the quality of its goods and services, relative to those of competitors.
2. Market share [relative to the three largest competitors] and profitability are strongly linked.
3. High-investment intensity acts as a powerful drag on profitability.
4. While market growth and relative share are linked to cash flows, many other factors also influence performance.
5. Vertical integration [ownership of other firms along a channel of distribution] is a powerful strategy for some kinds of businesses, but not for all. For small-share businesses, ROI is highest when the degree of vertical integration is low. But for businesses with average or above-average share positions, ROI is highest when vertical integration is either low or high, and lowest in the middle.
6. Most of the strategic factors that boost ROI also contribute to the long-term market value of the business.[25]

---

[23] *General Mills Annual Report 1988*; and Julie Liesse Erickson, "General Mills Refills Cereal Bowl," *Advertising Age* (October 10, 1988), p. 30.

[24] Bennett, *Dictionary of Marketing Definitions*, p. 145. See also Day, *Analysis for Strategic Market Decisions*, pp. 115–165.

[25] Robert D. Buzzell and Bradley T. Gale, *The PIMS Principles: Linking Strategy to Performance* (New York: Free Press, 1987), pp. 7–14.

TABLE 3-4   Industry Attractiveness and Company Business Strengths

Industry Attractiveness Depends on:	Company Business Strengths Depend on:
Market size, in units and dollars	Differential advantages
Market diversity	Market share, in units and dollars
Market growth, total and by segment	Sales volume and growth
Profitability, total and per unit	Breadth of product line
Stability of sales	Patent protection
Competitors	Sales/distribution effectiveness
Capital intensity	Promotion effectiveness
Economies of scale	Control over prices and margins
Technological breakthroughs	Economies of scale
Social/legal environment	Innovativeness

PIMS information is conveyed to participating firms through these major reports. The PAR report shows average return on investment and cash flow on the basis of market, competition, technology, and cost structure. The Look-Alikes report examines tactics of similar competitors, both successful and unsuccessful. The Strategy Analysis (sensitivity) report shows the effects of strategy changes on short-run and long-run return on investment and cash flow. The Optimum Strategy report suggests the strategy that will maximize results.

The General Electric Business Screen

*The **General Electric business screen** examines industry attractiveness and company business strengths.*

The **General Electric business screen** categorizes SBUs and product opportunities on the basis of an in-depth analysis of both industry attractiveness and company business strengths. The business screen incorporates many more variables than either the product/ market opportunity matrix or the Boston Consulting Group matrix, and it includes more qualitative factors than PIMS.[26] See Table 3-4.

For each SBU or product opportunity, a firm would assign weights (relative importance) to each industry and company attribute, rate the individual attributes, and derive overall ratings of industry attractiveness and company business strengths. An SBU may have high, medium, or low industry attractiveness as well as high, medium, or low company business strengths; and it would be positioned accordingly on the business screen shown in Figure 3-6.

SBUs shown in green in Figure 3-6 are investment/growth areas. These SBUs are in strong industries and are performing well in them. They are similar to stars in the Boston Consulting Group matrix. Full marketing resources are appropriate, and profitability is expected to be high. Innovations, product-line extensions, product and image advertising, distribution intensity, and solid price margins are sought.

SBUs shown in yellow in Figure 3-6 represent selectivity/earnings areas. These SBUs are not as well positioned as investment/growth ones. An SBU may have a strong position in a weak industry (similar to a cash cow), a moderate position in a somewhat attractive industry, or a weak position in an attractive industry (similar to a question mark). The firm wants to maintain the earnings and strength of cash cows, and uses marketing to retain customer loyalty and distribution support. For question marks, the

[26] See Derek F. Abell and John S. Hammond, *Strategic Market Planning* (Englewood Cliffs, N.J.: Prentice-Hall, 1979), pp. 211–227; and Day, *Analysis for Strategic Market Decisions,* pp. 193–216.

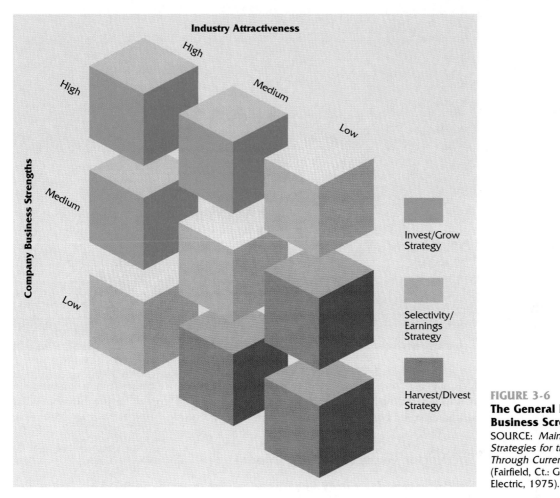

FIGURE 3-6
The General Electric Business Screen
SOURCE: *Maintaining Strategies for the Future Through Current Crises* (Fairfield, Ct.: General Electric, 1975).

company must determine whether to increase dramatically its marketing investment, focus on a specialized market niche, acquire a business in the industry, or trim product lines. The medium/medium SBU offers an opportunity for the firm to identify and appeal to underserved market segments, and invest in marketing on a selective basis.

SBUs shown in red in Figure 3-6 represent harvest/divest areas. These SBUs are similar to dogs in the Boston Consulting Group matrix. The company can minimize its marketing effort, concentrate on a few products rather than a product line, divest, or close down the SBU. Profits are harvested since investments are minimal.

On the basis of analysis using a version of the business screen, Boise Cascade has developed a three-part strategy. The first part of the strategy requires the firm to be increasingly efficient as a producer and distributor of paper and paper products, office products, and building products. The second part of the strategy calls for Boise Cascade to develop and maintain a distinctive competence by adding value to its goods and services, thus gaining a competitive edge. Depending on the business unit, its distinctive competence may be based on high-quality goods and services. Or it may be based on competitive prices. Or it may be achieved via new goods and services resulting from

FIGURE 3-7
Boise Cascade's High-Tech Approach to Innovation
Copyright Boise Cascade. Reprinted by permission.

technological innovation. Often, the distinctive competence comes from a combination of these. The third part of the strategy is a focus on growth in the high-potential segments of its businesses.[27] See Figure 3-7.

The Porter Generic Strategy Model

*The **Porter generic strategy model** distinguishes among cost leadership, differentiation, and focus strategies.*

The ***Porter generic strategy model*** examines two major marketing planning concepts and the alternatives available with each: competitive scope (broad target or narrow target) and competitive advantage (lower cost or differentiation).[28] By combining the two concepts, the Porter model identifies these basic strategies: cost leadership, differentiation, and focus. Figure 3-8 shows the Porter model.

With a cost leadership strategy, an SBU appeals to a broad market and produces goods and/or services in large quantities. Through economies of scale, the company is able to minimize per-unit costs and offer low prices. This allows the firm to have better profit margins than competitors, respond better to cost increases, and attract price-conscious consumers. Among the companies using cost leadership are Emerson Electric, DuPont, H.J. Heinz, and Chem Lawn.

With a differentiation strategy, an SBU aims at a large market by offering a product viewed as quite distinctive. The company makes a product that has a broad appeal, yet is perceived by consumers as unique by virtue of its design, features, availability,

---

[27] *Boise Cascade 1987 Annual Report.*

[28] Michael E. Porter, *Competitive Advantage: Creating and Sustaining Superior Performance* (New York: Free Press, 1985), pp. 11–26; and Michael E. Porter, *Competitive Strategy: Techniques for Analyzing Industries and Competitors* (New York: Free Press, 1980), pp. 34–46. See also William E. Fulmer and Jack Goodwin, "Differentiation: Begin With the Customer," *Business Horizons,* Vol. 31 (September-October 1988), pp. 55–63.

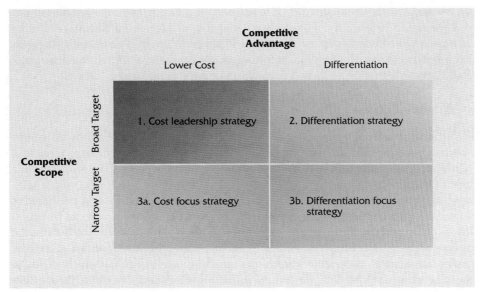

FIGURE 3-8
The Porter Generic Strategy Model
SOURCE: Michael E. Porter, *Competitive Advantage: Creating and Sustaining Superior Performance* (New York: Free Press, 1985), p. 12. Reprinted with the permission of The Free Press, a division of Macmillan, Inc. Copyright © 1985 by Michael E. Porter.

reliability, etc. As a result, price is not as important, and consumers become quite brand loyal. Among the firms using differentiation are Federal Express, Seiko, and Caterpillar Tractor.

With a focus strategy, an SBU seeks a narrow target segment through low prices or a unique offering. It is able to control costs by concentrating efforts on a few key products aimed at specific consumers, or build a specialized reputation and serve a market that may be unsatisfied by competitors. Martin-Brower is a low-cost food distributor servicing just a few fast-food chains. Porter Paint provides a unique combination of service, delivery, and quality paints for its market of professional painters.

According to the Porter model, the relationship between market share and profitability is U-shaped, as displayed in Figure 3-9. A firm with a low market share can succeed by developing a well-focused strategy. A firm with a high market share can succeed through cost leadership or a differentiated strategy. However, a company

The Porter model shows that small firms can succeed through a focused strategy.

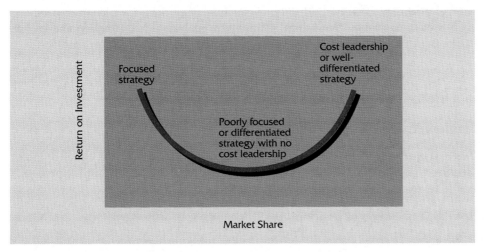

FIGURE 3-9
Relating Market Share and Return on Investment Via the Porter Generic Strategy Model
SOURCE: Adapted from Michael E. Porter, *Competitive Strategy: Techniques for Analyzing Industries and Competitors* (New York: Free Press, 1980), p. 43. Reprinted with the permission of The Free Press, a division of Macmillan, Inc. Copyright © 1980 by The Free Press.

can become "stuck in the middle" if it has neither a strong and unique offering nor cost leadership because it does not have a meaningful differential advantage. Unlike the Boston Consulting Group matrix and the PIMS program, the Porter model suggests that a small firm can profit by concentrating on one competitive niche, even though its total market share may be low. A firm does not have to be large to do well.

Evaluation of Strategic Planning Approaches

The strategic planning approaches discussed in the previous subsections, as well as other portfolio models, are used by many firms. One recent study of large industrial U.S. companies found that well over one-half of the respondents had introduced some form of portfolio planning.[29]

Strategic models have pros and cons, and should be only part of planning.

While an evaluation of each of the strategic planning approaches just presented is beyond the scope of this book, their common strengths and weaknesses can be noted. The major strengths of the approaches are that they allow a firm to describe and analyze each of its business units and products, study the ramifications of various strategy alternatives, determine which opportunities to emphasize and which threats to minimize or avoid (by modifying strategy or exiting a business), compute the marketing and other resources needed for each business unit and product, ascertain the best strategies for each business unit and product, focus on creating and sustaining meaningful differential advantages, compare performance against designated goals, and discover principles for improving performance. Competitors' actions and long-term trends can also be followed.

The major weaknesses of the strategic planning approaches are that they are sometimes difficult to implement (particularly by a small company), may be too simplistic and omit crucial factors, are somewhat arbitrary in defining SBUs and evaluative criteria (such as relative market share) — and these definitions can greatly affect a firm's analysis, may not be applicable to all company situations — assumptions are not always valid (for example, a dog SBU may actually be profitable and generate cash), do not adequately account for environmental conditions (such as the economy), have been inadequately researched, and are often used by staff planners rather than line managers.

The product/market opportunity matrix, Boston Consulting Group matrix, PIMS, General Electric business screen, and Porter generic strategy model should be viewed only as planning tools that aid decision making; they do not replace the need for executives to engage in "hands-on" planning by analyzing each situation and basing marketing strategies on the unique aspects of their industry, company, and SBUs:

> These methods and concepts can play an important role in supporting management judgment by simplifying and structuring complex situations. They are *not* substitutes for strategic thinking grounded in the realities of the particular situation.[30]

Implementing Tactical Plans

The marketing strategy is enacted through **tactical plans**.

Tactical plans specify the short-run actions (tactics) a firm would undertake in implementing a given marketing strategy. At this stage in the strategic planning process,

---

[29] Joel E. Ross, "Developing the Strategic Plan," *Industrial Marketing Management,* Vol. 16 (1987), p. 107.

[30] University of District of Columbia, "Strategic Planning and Marketing," class handout (1987), p. 2.

an action program is designed to meet strategic objective(s) using available resources and given existing constraints. It translates a strategic plan into operational terms. The action plan has three major components: (1) specific tasks—what will be done, including the specification of the marketing mix to be employed; (2) time horizon—when it will be done; and (3) resource allocation and budgeting—attaching a dollar figure to each income- and expense-related activity and allocating funds.[31]

The marketing mix (specific tasks) may range from a combination of high-quality, high-service, low-distribution intensity, personal-selling emphasis, and above-average prices to a combination of low-quality, low-service, high-distribution intensity, advertising emphasis, and low prices. There would be a distinct marketing mix for each SBU, based on its target market and strategic emphasis. The individual mix elements must be coordinated for each SBU and conflicts among SBUs minimized.

Proper timing (time horizon) may mean being the first to introduce a product, bringing out a product when the market is most receptive to it, or quickly reacting to a competitor's strategy to catch that firm off guard. The company must balance its desire to be an industry leader with a clear-cut competitive advantage against its concern about the risk of innovative actions. In any event, an organization must recognize that marketing opportunities exist for limited periods of time, and it needs to act accordingly. Firms need to plan carefully to capitalize on seasonal opportunities.

Opportunities exist only for specific periods.

Marketing investments (resource allocation) can be classified as order processing and order generating. ***Order-processing costs*** are expenses associated with filling out and handling orders, such as order forms, computer time, and merchandise handling. The goal is to minimize those costs subject to obtaining a given level of service. ***Order-generating costs,*** such as advertising and personal selling, are revenue producing. Reducing these costs may have a detrimental effect on a firm's sales and profits. Therefore, an organization needs to estimate revenues at various levels of costs and for various combinations of marketing functions. Maximum profit rarely occurs at the lowest level of expenditure on order-generating costs.

*There is a distinction between **order-processing** and **order-generating** costs.*

Tactical decisions differ from strategic decisions in several key ways. Tactical decisions have a short time horizon; strategic decisions are more concerned with obtaining a long-term sustainable competitive advantage. Tactical decisions require a considerably lower resource commitment; strategic decisions often involve a significant level of company resources, and these decisions are more important to the firm. Tactical decisions are made and adjusted on a regular basis—they center on internal factors; strategic decisions are made less frequently and are based more on external considerations. Tactical decisions are less complex and more structured; strategic decisions are more open-ended and more unique.[32]

As an example, Kodak is targeting quality service as a major aspect of its marketing strategy: "Selling good goods is not enough. Customers expect service, reliability, and responsiveness from their suppliers. The quality issue relates to how we respond to telephone inquiries, how well we service small accounts, how we respond to equipment users, how well we handle customer orders and billing." Accordingly, Kodak has enacted these tactical decisions to implement its quality-service strategy. Small business accounts are served by the Kodak Information Center through trained telephone representatives who are assigned specific customers, to ensure continuity. Via a

---

[31] Adapted by the authors from Bennett, *Dictionary of Marketing Definitions*, p. 92.
[32] Weitz and Wensley, *Readings in Strategic Marketing: Analysis, Planning, and Implementation*, pp. 3–4.

Marketing Controversy

Can Firms Overdo Being "Lean and Mean" in Marketing?

Today many companies are becoming more "lean and mean" in their marketing efforts by paying greater attention to trimming marketing costs. For example, IBM has reduced its advertising budgets; Xerox is intensively studying selling costs; and a number of firms are increasing their reliance on telephone sales calls (telemarketing) as an alternative to employing a field sales force in rural territories.

Although efficient marketing is an important and necessary activity in maintaining competitive advantages, a company must be very careful about the degree of cost-cutting. By attempting to cut out the "fat" in a marketing plan, a firm could easily cut too deeply and damage its marketing "muscle." Instead of a firm becoming more fit, it could, in fact, lose strength and resiliency.

There are several advantages to being lean and mean:

▶ Cost-cutting results in a more competitive and efficient organization.

▶ Funds saved as a result of cost-cutting can be deployed in other marketing areas, where they can be better used.

▶ Cost-cutting is particularly effective when order-processing costs are reduced. These reductions do not generally affect sales or customer-service levels.

But, there are disadvantages to being too lean and mean:

▶ A reduction in order-generating costs may affect customer service, and possibly a firm's long-term sales and profits.

▶ Cost-cutting may result in marketing practices such as inadequate coverage of sales territories or poor employee supervision.

▶ Cost-cutting activities may have a perspective that is too short-run.

It can be very difficult to be as efficient as possible without adversely affecting marketing performance.

What do you think?

SOURCE: Based on material in A. J. Magrath, "Are You Overdoing 'Lean and Mean'?" *Sales & Marketing Management* (January 1988), pp. 46–50.

direct telephone linkup between Kodak's computer system and their own personal computers, dealers and distributors can place orders, confirm bills, or ask questions. Customers in Australia, Asia, and Africa can obtain technical assistance through a telephone hotline. Kodak's Professional Products division has instituted a Kodachrome laboratory monitoring service to improve the quality of processed color slides.[33]

Monitoring Results

*Performance is evaluated by **monitoring results**.*

Monitoring results involves comparing the actual performance of a company, business unit, or product against planned performance for a specified time period. Budgets, timetables, sales and profit statistics, cost analyses, and image studies are just some of the measures that can be used to assess results. If actual performance lags behind plans, some corrective action should be taken (after problem areas are highlighted).

[33] *1987 Eastman Kodak Company Annual Report.*

In some cases, plans have to be revised because of the impact of uncontrollable variables on sales and costs. Many farsighted companies develop contingency plans that outline in advance their responses, should unfavorable conditions arise.

In Chapter 24, techniques for evaluating marketing effectiveness will be explained in depth. These techniques are covered in Chapter 24 so that the fundamental elements of marketing can be thoroughly explored first.

Examples of Strategic Planning in Marketing

Holiday Corporation and Westinghouse rely on strategic planning to guide marketing. Selected elements of their strategies are presented here. These firms have been chosen because they are in different industries, have different organizational missions, and utilize distinct marketing approaches.

Strategic-planning concepts are used by organizations in diverse industries.

Holiday Corporation[34]

Several years ago, a situation analysis showed Holiday Inns, Inc., that its traditional middle market for hotel facilities and services was saturated and that construction costs in desirable areas were too high for middle-priced hotel facilities. While Holiday Inns had strong brand recognition, it realized that a "middle-of-the-road" strategy would limit future growth.

On the basis of its situation analysis, Holiday Inns decided to launch new hotel chains, divest itself of more than thirty nonhospitality businesses, upgrade existing properties, and purchase/build hotels in all four important U.S. gambling centers. In 1985, it changed the corporate name to Holiday Corporation, to better reflect the firm's broader orientation.

Today the company has this organizational mission and strategic marketing focus (and nearly $2 billion in annual sales):

> Holiday Corporation is the world's largest hospitality company, operating in two businesses: hotels and hotel/casinos. We are a forward-looking, innovative industry leader with clearly defined goals, producing superior services and consistently high returns for our stockholders. With some 1,600 properties worldwide, the Holiday Inn hotel system is nearly three times the size of its nearest chain competitor. Three other hotel brands and a casino gaming company round out Holiday's diversified product portfolio. The other hotel brands are Embassy Suites, an all-suite, full-service hotel chain; Hampton Inn, a limited-service, moderately priced chain; and Homewood Suites, a new extended-stay hotel product introduced in early 1988. Together, the company's four hotel brands comprise more than 1,800 hotels and 353,000 rooms worldwide.
>
> Holiday's hotel/casino company, Harrah's, is the gaming industry's acknowledged leader, with properties in the four major U.S. gaming markets: Reno, Lake Tahoe, and Las Vegas, Nevada, and Atlantic City, New Jersey. A major Harrah's hotel/casino in what promises to be the fifth major gaming market in the U.S.—Laughlin, Nevada—was scheduled for fall 1988.

---

[34] "Holiday Inns Opens Doors for the Upscale Traveler," *Business Week* (April 25, 1983), pp. 100 ff.; Subrata N. Chakravarty and Anne McGrath, "Room at the Top?" *Forbes* (March 12, 1984), pp. 58–61; *Holiday Corporation 1987 Annual Report;* and Joe Agnew, "Hotel Industry Focusing on High-Quality Rooms," *Marketing News* (February 1, 1988), pp. 1, 24. Note: This section was written prior to the sale of Holiday Inn in late 1989.

FIGURE 3-10
Westinghouse: A Leader in Aircraft Radar Systems Westinghouse provides the airborne radar and other advanced electronics for the U.S. Air Force's Advanced Tactical Fighter. Shown here is a model undergoing testing in a research chamber near Baltimore. Reprinted by permission of Westinghouse.

Holiday Corporation monitors its strategic plan by analyzing sales by geographic market, sales by business and pleasure-traveler segments, traveler brand awareness, guest satisfaction, and room and facilities conditions.

Westinghouse[35]

Westinghouse

is a diversified, global, technology-based corporation. The principal business arenas are television and radio broadcasting, defense electronics, financial services, and the industrial, construction, and electric utility markets. Complementing these core businesses are operations serving selected "niche" markets such as vehicle transportation refrigeration equipment, community development, and beverage bottling.

In 1988, Westinghouse reorganized from four major operating groups with 23 strategic business units into seven major operating groups (broadcasting, defense electronics, financial services, industrial and construction, diversified markets, energy and utility, and international) containing 44 SBUs to better guide planning and implementation efforts. The SBUs include such businesses as satellite communications, aircraft electrical systems, corporate financing, Longines-Wittnauer watches, and municipal waste-to-energy systems. Some businesses are in market areas with strong outlooks, such as hazardous waste management, business communications, and defense electronics; others are in weak markets, such as nuclear power (because no new U.S. plants have been bought since the late 1970s). See Figure 3-10.

[35] "Operation Turnaround: How Westinghouse's New CEO Plans to Fire Up an Old-Line Company," *Business Week* (December 5, 1983), pp. 124–127 ff.; *1987 Westinghouse Annual Report* and *Form 10-K*; Walter Kiechel III, "Corporate Strategy for the 1990s," *Fortune* (February 29, 1988), p. 42; and Gregory Stricharchuk, "Westinghouse Readies First Big Ad Campaign in Years," *Wall Street Journal* (May 11, 1989), p. B6.

The company is placing less emphasis on mature businesses and greater effort on faster-growing businesses. It is also improving customer service, upgrading product quality, and emphasizing better worker productivity. It has developed and is applying a more sophisticated value-based strategic planning process. Tactics include utilizing a task force to examine ailing businesses, shifting from building U.S. nuclear plants to servicing existing ones and to foreign nuclear plant construction, establishing a quality control center in Pittsburgh, and inspecting all semiconductor products received from suppliers. A system for monitoring performance is in place.

Summary

1. *To define strategic planning and consider its importance for marketing* Strategic planning outlines what marketing actions to undertake; why those actions are necessary; who is responsible for carrying them out; when and where they will be completed; and how they will be coordinated. It provides guidance through a hierarchal process; clarifies objectives; encourages cooperation among departments; focuses on strengths and weaknesses, as well as opportunities and threats; examines alternatives; helps allocate resources; and points up the value of monitoring results.

2. *To study the different types of marketing plans* A firm's marketing plans may be short run, moderate in length, or long run. They may be for each major product, presented as one organizational marketing plan, or considered part of an overall business plan. A bottom-up or top-down management approach may be used.

3. *To examine the relationships between marketing and the other functional areas in an organization* The interests of marketing and other functional areas in an organization need to be accommodated in a strategic plan. Departmental conflict can be reduced by improving communications, by employing personnel with broad backgrounds, by establishing interdepartmental development programs, and by blending departmental objectives.

4. *To thoroughly describe each of the steps in the strategic planning process* First, a firm defines its organizational mission, its long-term commitment to a type of business and its place in the market. Second, the firm establishes strategic business units (SBUs), which are self-contained divisions, product lines, or product departments with specific market focuses and separate managers. Third, quantitative and qualitative marketing objectives are set. Fourth, through situation analysis, the company identifies its internal strengths and weaknesses, as well as external opportunities and threats.

Fifth, the firm develops a marketing strategy, which outlines the manner in which the marketing mix is used to attract and satisfy the target market(s) and accomplish organizational objectives. Each SBU has its own marketing mix. The approaches to strategy planning include the product/market opportunity matrix, the Boston Consulting Group matrix, PIMS (Profit Impact of Market Strategy), the General Electric business screen, and the Porter generic strategy model. All of these approaches involve some form of portfolio analysis, by which each of an organization's business units and/or products is individually assessed and positioned. Company resources can then be allocated and appropriate strategies developed. These approaches should be viewed as planning tools that aid decision making; they do not replace the need for executives to engage in hands-on planning for each situation.

Sixth, the firm uses tactical plans to specify the short-run actions necessary to implement a given marketing strategy. At this stage, specific tasks, a time horizon, and resource allocation are operationalized. Seventh, the company monitors results by comparing actual performance against planned performance. Adjustments in strategy are made as needed.

5. *To present examples of strategic planning in diverse companies* In different ways, Holiday Corporation (the world's largest hospitality company) and Westinghouse (a diversified, global, technology-based company) rely on strategic planning to guide their marketing efforts.

Key Terms

strategic planning (p. 58)
strategic planning process (p. 61)
organizational mission (p. 62)
strategic business unit (SBU) (p. 64)
situation analysis (p. 66)
marketing strategy (p. 67)
portfolio analysis (p. 68)
product/market opportunity
  matrix (p. 68)
market penetration (p. 68)

market development (p. 68)
product development (p. 68)
diversification (p. 68)
Boston Consulting Group
  matrix (p. 68)
star (p. 70)
cash cow (p. 70)
problem child (question
  mark) (p. 71)
dog (p. 71)

Profit Impact of Market Strategy
  (PIMS) (p. 73)
General Electric business
  screen (p. 74)
Porter generic strategy model (p. 76)
tactical plans (p. 78)
order-processing costs (p. 79)
order-generating costs (p. 79)
monitoring results (p. 80)

Review Questions

1. What are the benefits of strategic planning in marketing?

2. Distinguish between bottom-up and top-down marketing plans. What are the pros and cons of each?

3. Why are conflicts between marketing and other functional areas inevitable? How can these conflicts be reduced or avoided?

4. Under what circumstances should a company consider reappraising its organizational mission?

5. What is a strategic business unit? Why is this concept so important for strategic planning?

6. In situation analysis, what is the distinction between strengths and opportunities and between weaknesses and threats? How should a firm react to each of these factors?

7. In planning a marketing strategy, what are the four key factors a firm should consider for each of its SBUs?

8. Describe the product/market opportunity matrix and the General Electric business screen.

9. What are the basic strengths and weaknesses of the portfolio approaches to strategy planning?

10. Explain how tactical decisions differ from strategic decisions.

Discussion Questions

1. Comment on this statement: "In the market-oriented view of the strategic planning process, financial goals are seen as results and rewards, not the fundamental purpose of business."

2. What issues should a small bicycle manufacturer study during situation analysis? How could it react to them?

3. Give an example of a star, cash cow, question mark, and dog. Evaluate the current marketing strategy of each.

4. Develop a rating scale to analyze the industry attractiveness and company business strengths of a large insurance company, a medium-sized office supplies manufacturer, or a small auto-parts retailer.

5. Evaluate and compare the strategies of Holiday Corporation and Westinghouse.

◄ **CASE 1** ►

Mars: Examining the Marketing Strategy of a Leading Food Maker[*]

The fifty business units of Mars Inc. annually generate worldwide sales of well over $7.5 billion. Mars sells its candy (52 per cent of total sales), pet food (40 per cent of total sales), food (7 per cent of total sales), and electronics (1 per cent of total sales) products in more than twenty-five nations. According to various sources, the Mars family—which owns the privately held firm—is the richest family in the United States.

Mars is an especially powerful force in the candy market. As an example, four of the ten best-selling chocolate candies in the United States are Mars products. These are Snickers (the most popular chocolate bar), M&M's peanut and M&M's plain (the third and fourth best-selling chocolate-based products), and Milky Way (the seventh best-selling chocolate-based candy in the nation). Other popular Mars brands include Uncle Ben's converted rice and Kal Kan dog food. The firm spends more than $300 million each year to advertise its products in the United States and is among the thirty leading U.S. advertisers.

Nonetheless, in one recent twelve-month period, Mars' candy sales decreased by 0.4 per cent, while arch-rival Hershey's increased by 7.2 per cent. This disappointing performance is largely due to the limited success of Mars' new-product development efforts, its production rather than marketing orientation, and competitors having a much more vigorous acquisition policy.

In the early and mid-1980s, Mars' new-product development area was able to produce only two major new products: Kudos, a chocolate-covered granola bar (with $275 million in annual sales); and Skittles, a fruit candy (with yearly sales of $90 million). Mars had hoped that internal product-development efforts would lead to the introduction of at least one to two new products per year into the marketplace.

* The data in this case are drawn from Bill Saporito, "Uncovering Mars' Unknown Empire," *Fortune* (September 26, 1988), pp. 98–104; and Alix M. Freedman, "Mars Struggles to Reclaim Candy Crown," *Wall Street Journal* (March 29, 1989), p. B1.

Mars has functioned as a production-driven company. New products are chosen more on the basis of conformity with production equipment than on customer desires. For example, the firm's 3 Musketeers, Snickers, Milky Way, and Mars bars all are built around a common shape—and all are manufactured on machinery that runs 24 hours per day (to maximize production economies of scale). For a new product to use this machinery efficiently, it must have annual sales of $50 million; in contrast, competitors aim for new candies that can attain annual sales of $25 million.

Unlike its competitors, Mars has not pursued an aggressive external acquisition policy. For instance, the purchase of Cadbury Schweppes by Hershey means that firm now has a 44 per cent market share of the U.S. chocolate-bar market, versus Mars' 37 per cent share. Cadbury's brands (such as Peter Paul Almond Joy, Peter Paul Mounds, and York Peppermint Patties) have an 8 per cent market share in the United States. These brands give Hershey additional shelf space in stores, an important factor in the sale of self-service items such as candy.

As with its domestic candy line, Mars' pet food business has also suffered from the lack of new products and acquisitions. It was Quaker Oats' purchase of Gaines' Pet Foods in 1987 which gave that firm the number-two market-share position behind Ralston-Purina. Although Mars' Kal Kan is a leading brand, heavy spending on advertising and price-oriented promotions contributed to a loss of $49 million on sales of $460 million in 1987.

Mars' pet foods have been quite successful in Europe, where it was the first firm to market canned pet food. As recently as fifteen years ago, most Europeans fed their pets table scraps instead of pet food. For example, in France in 1975, only 21 per cent of dog owners purchased canned dog food; as of 1985, 60 per cent did. Mars' early market development has paid off well. Its market share in most European countries is at least 50 per cent.

In sum, "The Mars of the Seventies was fabulous. But now it must face the Nineties—or recede into them."

QUESTIONS

1. Describe an appropriate organizational mission for Mars.
2. Present a situation analysis for Mars. Outline several of the major opportunities and problems facing the firm.
3. Apply the product/market opportunity matrix to Mars. Specify appropriate strategies for each cell of this matrix.
4. Offer five recommendations for how Mars could apply strategic planning concepts.

◄ CASE 2 ►

Canon: Modifying a Successful Strategy[†]

Canon is a Japan-based manufacturer, with worldwide sales exceeding $8 billion (in U.S. dollars). Canon's well-known product lines include business machines, medical equipment, semiconductors, cameras, video equipment, and broadcast equipment. Business products account for 75 per cent of Canon's total annual sales, cameras represent 18 per cent of sales, and optical equipment and other products comprise 7 per cent of sales. In most of its markets throughout the world, Canon's major competitors are other Japan-based manufacturers, such as Sharp (which has a strong line of inexpensive photocopiers and other products aimed at the same small-business market that Canon often pursues), Minolta (Japan's largest camera manufacturer), and Nikon (known for its technologically advanced products). It also competes against such U.S. firms as Xerox, Kodak, and RCA. In 1985, Canon was the 125th largest firm in *Fortune's* ranking of industrial corporations outside the United States; today it is in the top 100.

Because it is highly committed toward maximizing its long-term performance (as are most Japanese companies), Canon has been re-evaluating its overall marketing approach and strategy—so that it may prepare properly for the future. In particular, Canon wants to address these two areas: its need to

be more market-oriented; and the need to maintain its strong level of foreign sales, particularly in North America and Europe.

Over the years, Canon has viewed itself as a technology-driven company. According to its corporate communications manager, "we aim to develop our own unique technologies, which can then form the basis of our products." As a result, Canon's new-product development has been considered a function of research and development, not marketing. But today, the firm realizes that this approach must be modified:

> Canon must change from a product-oriented company to a market-oriented one. Until now we have been more concerned with production and sales than marketing. We will be focusing more closely on the needs of different consumer groups in each country and less concerned with the traditional production-oriented way of thinking.

As part of the need to be more market-driven, Canon is considering restructuring from its present three product-based divisions (business machines, cameras, and optical equipment) to home, society, industry, and workplace divisions.

In giving marketing a greater role, Canon is also keeping this in mind: "As marketing is made stronger, there is the risk it will weaken the motivation of the engineers who both pilot the new technologies and develop the new products."

With regard to its international efforts, Canon relies on overseas markets for 70 per cent of its

[†] The data in this case are drawn from David Kilburn, "Canon Zooms in on Future Growth," *Advertising Age* (November 28, 1988), p. 28.

total annual sales; this is a much higher percentage than for its competitors. For example, North America and Europe are Canon's largest markets; each of these markets comprises 30 per cent of Canon's sales. Annually, the company spends about $200 million on media advertising, point-of-sale displays, and other promotion materials in North America and Europe.

To be more responsive to foreign-market needs, Canon introduced a global marketing system in 1988. This system allows Canon to have similar products and marketing approaches in various overseas markets while it better tailors business plans to the specialized needs of major market areas. For instance, Canon could develop a comput-er system with standardized hardware for all market areas, but with software that is tailored to each specialized market.

To reduce the impact of trade barriers (such as trade-protection laws restricting the sales of foreign products in domestic markets) and the high value of the Japanese yen relative to other currencies (thereby making Japanese products more expensive in other markets), Canon has begun opening more research-and-development and production facilities abroad. The objective of such a strategy "is to make Canon a company with no national identity and free from trade friction, keeping production facilities close to the place of consumption."

QUESTIONS

1. Describe the potential areas of conflict between the research-and-development department and the marketing department at Canon. How may potential conflicts be minimized?
2. Evaluate Canon's proposal to switch from product-based to market-based business units. What are the pros and cons of such an approach?
3. How could Canon use the Boston Consulting Group matrix in planning its marketing strategy?
4. Assess Canon's recent international marketing decisions.

CHAPTER *4*

Information for Marketing Decisions

CHAPTER OBJECTIVES

1. To consider why marketing information is needed

2. To define marketing research and its components

3. To examine the scope of marketing research

4. To describe the marketing research process: problem definition, examination of secondary data, generation of primary data (when necessary), analysis of data, recommendations, and implementation of findings

5. To explain the role and importance of the marketing information system

Information Resources Inc. (IRI)—the marketing research firm—knows what Paxton Blackwell of Williamsport, Pa., eats for breakfast. It monitors the television shows he watches. It tracks the coupons he uses, where he shops, the brands he buys. It even knows which newspapers he reads.

Today more than ever, companies are interested in having good information about their customers before making marketing decisions. As a result, marketing research firms such as IRI offer their corporate clients sophisticated techniques to analyze clients' marketing practices and to predict the success of their products and advertising campaigns. One exciting new technique involves single-source data collection, whereby the activities of individual consumer households are tracked from the programs they watch on television to the products they purchase at a store.

IRI monitors the television viewing habits and supermarket shopping behavior of 12,000 households in ten markets for such clients as Campbell, Searle, and Johnson & Johnson. Microcomputers are hooked to the participants' television sets and note all programs and commercials watched. Participants shop in supermarkets equipped with electronic scanning registers that provide printouts of purchases. When making purchases, consumers present the cashier with their Shoppers Hotline card, which resembles a credit card. The cashier enters each consumer's identification code, which is electronically associated with every item bought. Viewing and shopping behavior are then matched with consumer information, such as age and income, via computer analysis. Participants are not compensated; they are given an inexpensive annual gift which they select from a catalog.

In comparison, other marketing research techniques rely heavily on consumer memory (e.g., What did you purchase last week?) and usually do not track the same consumers (e.g., one consumer may respond anonymously to a shopping mall survey on attitudes toward specific television commercials, and another may have his or her in-store behavior observed). This makes it difficult to link marketing practices, such as advertising, with behavior.

Here are examples of how IRI's single-source data have been utilized by companies:

▶ Campbell discovered that the average viewer of *Guiding Light* consumed 40 per cent more of its V-8

Reprinted by permission of Information Resources Inc.

juice than the average viewer of *General Hospital*, despite the fact that *General Hospital* had a slightly higher per cent of viewers in the target market group of 25- to 54-year-old females.
▶ Searle was able to project correctly the first-year national sales of Equal artificial sweetener.
▶ Johnson & Johnson observed an upturn in Tylenol sales about a week after seven Chicago poisoning deaths were widely reported and publicized. At the same time, many marketing consultants were incorrectly commenting that Tylenol would never recover.

Despite its obvious advantages, these considerations should be kept in mind when using single-source data. Attitudes, as well as behavior, need to be analyzed to ensure the most accurate research results. Single-source data may concentrate on initial purchases; yet, it may take years to change consumers' behavior. Test results in small-town market areas may not be applicable to larger markets. Special circumstances in individual markets, such as couponing and special sales, may affect results.[1]

In this chapter, we will look at the value of marketing information, describe the marketing research process, and explain the role of a marketing information system (which gathers, stores, analyzes, and disseminates relevant marketing data). Single-source data are an important application of how information aids marketing decision making.

[1] Joanne Lipman, "Single-Source Ad Research Heralds Detailed Look at Household Habits," *Wall Street Journal* (February 16, 1988), p. 39; Claudia H. Deutsch, "The Battle to Wire the Consumer," *New York Times* (July 26, 1987), Section 3, pp. 1, 12–13; and Stephen P. Phelps, "Single Source: Proceed with Caution," *Journal of Advertising Research*, Vol. 27 (October–November 1987), pp. RC-8–RC-9.

Overview

Marketers make better decisions when they have good information.

It is essential that an organization (or an individual) obtain sufficient information before, while, and after making (and implementing) marketing decisions — if it is to assess accurately its strengths, weaknesses, opportunities, and threats; operate properly in the marketing environment; and maximize performance.[2] Many of the reasons why a firm should collect and analyze information with regard to its marketing plan or any of its elements are cited in Figure 4-1. Reliance on intuition, executive judgment, and past experience is not sufficient.

In this chapter, the two key aspects of marketing information are discussed in detail: marketing research and the marketing information system. Marketing research deals with the gathering and analysis of information related to specific marketing issues, whereas a marketing information system guides all of the firm's marketing-related information efforts — and stores and disseminates results — on a continuous basis.

Marketing Research Defined

Marketing research involves collecting, tabulating, and analyzing data about specific marketing issues.

Marketing research is the systematic gathering, recording, and analyzing of information about specific issues related to the marketing of goods, services, organizations, people, places, and ideas. Such research may be undertaken by an outside party or the firm itself.

Marketing research is

> the function which links the consumer [customer] and public to the marketer through information — information used to identify and define marketing opportunities and problems; generate, refine, and evaluate marketing actions; monitor marketing performance; and improve understanding of marketing as a process. It specifies the information required to address these issues; designs the method for collecting information; manages and implements the data collection process; analyzes the results; and communicates the findings and their implications.[3]

Several points about marketing research need to be emphasized. First, to be effective, it must be conducted in a systematic manner and not haphazardly or disjointedly. Second, marketing research involves a series of steps or a process. It is not a one-step activity; it includes data collection, recording, and analysis. Third, data may be available from different sources: the company itself, an impartial agency (such as the government), or a research specialist working for the company. Fourth, marketing research may be applied to any aspect of marketing that requires information to aid decision making. Fifth, research findings and their implications must be communicated to the appropriate decision maker.

---

[2] See Michael E. Porter and Victor E. Millar, "How Information Gives You Competitive Advantage," *Harvard Business Review*, Vol. 63 (July–August 1985), pp. 149–160; Andrew C. Gross, "The Information Vending Machine," *Business Horizons*, Vol. 31 (January–February 1988), pp. 24–33; and Frank E. Camacho and D. Matthew Knain, "Listening to Customers: The Market Research Function at Marriott," *Marketing Research*, Vol. 1 (March 1989), pp. 5–14.

[3] Peter D. Bennett (Editor), *A Dictionary of Marketing Terms* (Chicago: American Marketing Association, 1988), pp. 117–118.

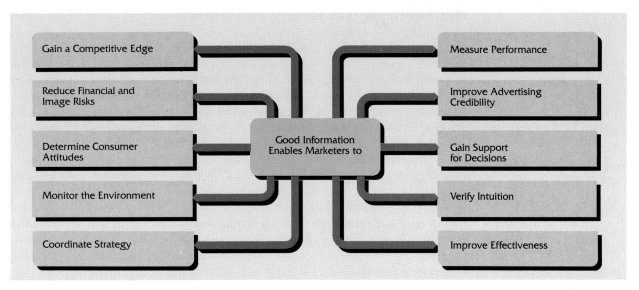

FIGURE 4-1   Reasons for Obtaining Information

When employing marketing research, the scientific method should be followed. The **scientific method** is based on objectivity, accuracy, and thoroughness.[4] Objectivity means that research is conducted in an unbiased, open-minded manner. Conclusions or opinions are not reached until after all data have been collected and analyzed. Accuracy refers to the use of research tools that are carefully constructed and utilized. Each aspect of research, such as the sample chosen, questionnaire format, interviewer selection and training, and tabulation of responses, needs to be carefully planned and implemented. For example, all questions in a survey should be pretested to ensure that the words are understood by prospective respondents. Thoroughness deals with the comprehensive nature of research. Mistaken conclusions may be reached if research does not probe deeply or widely enough.

*The **scientific method** requires objectivity, accuracy, and thoroughness.*

A company's decision to use marketing research does not mean that it must undertake extensive, expensive studies like test marketing and national consumer-attitude surveys.[5] The firm may obtain enough information through an analysis of internal sales data or informal meetings with sales personnel. What marketing research does require is a systematic approach and adherence to the principles of objectivity, accuracy, and thoroughness.

For each marketing issue studied, the amount and cost of marketing research depend upon the kinds of data needed to make informed decisions, the level of risk involved in making those decisions, the potential consequences of the decisions, the importance of the issue to the firm, the availability of existing data, the complexity of the research process for that issue, and other factors.

[4] Harper W. Boyd, Jr., Ralph Westfall, and Stanley F. Stasch, *Marketing Research: Text and Cases*, Seventh Edition (Homewood, Ill.: Richard D. Irwin, 1989), pp. 32–34.
[5] See Paul B. Brown, "On the Cheap," *Inc.* (February 1988), pp. 108–110.

The Scope of Marketing Research

Overall marketing research expenditures are high, yet they vary widely by type of company.

Companies annually spend about $5 billion worldwide (half in the United States) for information gathered by outside research firms.[6] This is in addition to the research sponsored by government and other institutions, and in addition to the research efforts of the companies themselves — which also run into the billions of dollars each year.

The use of marketing research varies widely by type of company. Although most firms use some form of marketing research, large companies are more likely to have research departments than small firms. Typically, firms with annual sales of $25 million and more spend about 3.5 per cent of their marketing budgets on marketing research; companies with sales less than $25 million spend about 1.5 per cent. On average, consumer-goods companies make greater expenditures in marketing research than industrial firms.[7]

There are many similarities in the marketing issues that different types of companies are apt to research. For example, typical U.S. consumer-goods, industrial, and service companies are most likely to engage in short-range forecasting (up to one year), long-range forecasting (over one year), measurement of market potential, sales analysis, pricing studies, new-product acceptance and potential studies, distribution-channel studies, and studies of ad effectiveness.[8]

Commercial data bases and new technology are growing, as is respondent dissatisfaction.

Three trends in marketing research are worthy of special discussion. These involve the growing availability of commercial data bases, the increasing use of new technology, and the declining image of survey research to many respondents and potential respondents.

Because they have recognized that companies need current, comprehensive, and relatively inexpensive information about the business and societal environment, a number of specialized research firms have developed commercial data bases that are sold to clients (usually for a relatively low fee). These data bases contain information on population characteristics, the business environment, economic forecasts, specialized bibliographies, and other material. For example, although IBM maintains 20 of its own data bases and adds 20,000 documents each year to its collection, it also buys data from seven research firms to supplement its information.

Generally, data bases are available in printed form, on computer diskettes, and via telephone hookup using a personal computer and a modem. Many libraries subscribe to one or more data bases and charge users a fee based on computer time. Among the leading data base services are ABI/Inform, Standard & Poors, Dow Jones, Funk & Scott (F & S), Predicasts, Dun & Bradstreet, and the Bureau of Labor Statistics. One firm, FIND/SVP (the Information Clearinghouse) services 1,400 corporate clients and maintains 1,500 data bases of publicly available information. FIND/SVP calls itself "an information retailer. We buy information, rearrange it, and sell it to you."[9] See Figure 4-2.

---

[6] Jack Honomichl, "Top Worldwide Research Companies," *Advertising Age* (December 5, 1988), p. S-1.

[7] A. Parasuraman, "Research's Place in the Marketing Budget," *Business Horizons*, Vol. 26 (March–April 1983), pp. 25–29; and George M. Zinkhan and Betsy D. Gelb, "Competitive Practices of Industrial Marketers," *Industrial Marketing Management*, Vol. 14 (1985), pp. 269–275.

[8] Dik Warren Twedt, *1983 Survey of Marketing Research* (Chicago: American Marketing Association, 1983).

[9] "Brokers Filling Businesses' Information Gaps," *Marketing News* (October 11, 1985), p. 3; FIND/SVP 1989 correspondence; and Mark Robichaux, " 'Competitor Intelligence': A Grapevine to Rivals' Secrets," *Wall Street Journal* (April 12, 1989), p. B2.

Over the past few years, significant technological innovations have been applied to marketing research, as these examples indicate:[10]

▶ Persoft, Inc. has developed a computer software program that enables direct-mail marketers to analyze their customers in terms of recency, frequency, and value of purchases. In this way, unprofitable mailings can be avoided.

▶ The Pretesting Company Inc. has introduced a PeopleReader to observe consumer responses to printed advertisements. The PeopleReader resembles a table lamp, with two cameras inside. One camera focuses on the reader's eyes, the other on each page of a magazine/newspaper. Respondent behavior is watched without him or her being aware of it.

▶ A.C. Nielsen has devised "people meters," which are used to note consumers' television viewing behavior. Each meter, which resembles a remote-control channel changer, has approximately eight number buttons (one per family member). At regular intervals, participants from 2,800 U.S. households punch in who is watching television. By computer, this information is linked to programming, channel switching, and so on. See Figure 4-3.

Many respondents and potential respondents now have a poor image of survey research. In the 1970s, 6 per cent of those responding to surveys found participation to be an unpleasant experience; but, by the mid-1980s this figure had risen to 12 per cent. And one recent analysis of the contacts made by marketing research firms with 1.4 million potential respondents found that 38 per cent refused to participate in surveys. The growing dissatisfaction with survey research is due to factors such as

[10] "Rifle Shot Marketing," *Forbes* (August 26, 1985), p. 123; Pretesting Company Inc., *The Hot Line*, Vol. 1, No. 7 (1988); and "People Meters to Be Sole Tool for '87 Nielsen TV Ratings," *Marketing News* (January 30, 1987), p. 1.

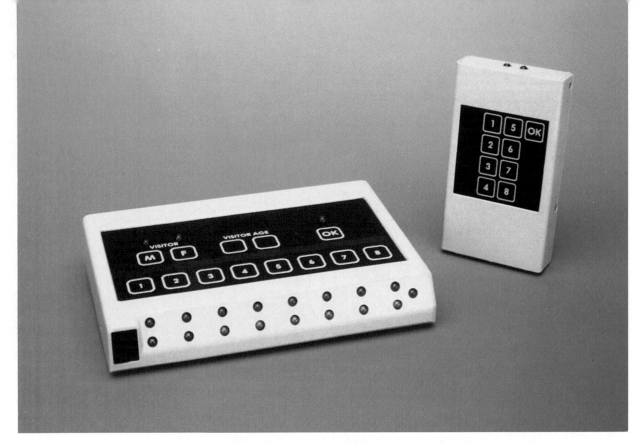

FIGURE 4-3 **A.C. Nielsen's "People Meter"** The "people meter" enables Nielsen to monitor the television viewing behavior of households across the United States. Reprinted by permission of Nielsen Media Research.

these: survey length, excessive contacts of the same persons by research companies, poor interviewing techniques, the invasion of privacy, the use of marketing research as a sales ploy, and the overly personal nature of some questions.[11] These issues need to be addressed if survey participation is to be high.

The Marketing Research Process

The ***marketing research process*** *consists of steps from issue definition to implementation of findings.*

The ***marketing research process*** is comprised of a series of activities: defining the issue or problem to be studied; examining secondary data (previously collected); generating primary data (new), if necessary; analyzing information; making recommendations; and implementing findings.

Figure 4-4 presents the complete marketing research process. Each step is undertaken in sequence. For example, secondary data are not examined until the firm states the issue or problem to be studied, and primary data are not generated until secondary data are thoroughly reviewed. The dashed line around primary data means that primary data do not always have to be collected. In many instances, a firm can obtain

---

[11] "Study Determines 38% Refuse to Participate in Research Surveys," *Marketing News* (February 28, 1986), pp. 1, 19; and George Gallup, Jr., "Survey Research: Current Problems and Future Opportunities," *Journal of Consumer Marketing*, Vol. 5 (Winter 1988), pp. 27–30.

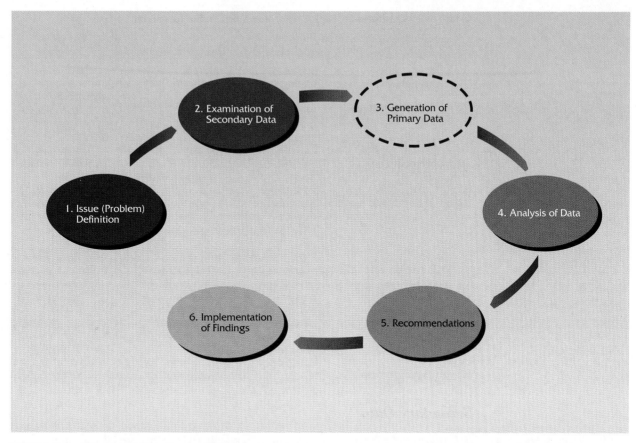

FIGURE 4-4 **The Marketing Research Process**

enough information internally or from published sources to make a marketing decision without gathering new data. Only when secondary data are insufficient should a firm generate primary data. The research process is described next.

Issue (Problem) Definition

Issue (problem) definition is a statement of the topic to be investigated via marketing research. Without a precise definition of the topic to be studied, a researcher may collect irrelevant and expensive data that confuses rather than clarifies issues. A good problem definition directs the research process toward the collection and analysis of appropriate information for the purpose of decision making.

When a researcher is uncertain about the precise topic to be investigated, ***exploratory research*** should be employed. The purpose of exploratory research is to develop a clear definition of the research issue or problem by utilizing informal analysis. After the problem definition is clarified, ***conclusive research*** should be used. Conclusive research is the structured collection and analysis of data pertaining to a specific issue or problem. Exploratory research techniques are not as structured as conclusive research. Table 4-1 contrasts exploratory and conclusive research.

*Research efforts are directed by the **issue definition**.*

__Exploratory research__ involves an uncertain topic; __conclusive research__ involves a well-defined study.

TABLE 4-1 Examples of Exploratory and Conclusive Research

Vague Research Topic	Exploratory Research	Precise Research Topic	Conclusive Research
1. Why are sales declining?	1. Discussions among key personnel to identify major cause	1. Why is turnover of sales personnel so high?	1. Survey sales personnel, interview sales managers
2. Is advertising effective?	2. Discussions among key advertising personnel to define effectiveness	2. Do adults recall an advertisement the day after it appears?	2. Survey customers and non-customers to gauge advertising recall
3. Will a reduction in price increase sales volume?	3. Discussions among key personnel to determine the level of a price reduction	3. Will a 10 per cent price reduction have a significant impact on sales?	3. Run an in-store experiment to determine effects

Secondary Data

Secondary data have been previously gathered for purposes other than the current research.

Secondary data consist of information "not gathered for the immediate study at hand but for some other purpose" that is available internally (within the organization) or externally.[12] Whether secondary data completely resolve a research issue or problem or not, their low cost and relatively fast availability require that primary data not be collected until a thorough search of secondary data is completed.

Next, the pros and cons as well as the sources of secondary data are presented.

Advantages and Disadvantages

Secondary data are usually inexpensive and quick to collect, and helpful in exploratory research.

Secondary data offer these general advantages:

▶ Many types are inexpensive because primary data collection is not involved.
▶ Data assembly is normally quick, especially for published or company materials.
▶ There are frequently several sources and perspectives available.
▶ A source (for example, government) may obtain information the firm would be unable to get itself.
▶ There is high credibility for data assembled by independent sources.
▶ They are helpful where exploratory research is needed.

[12] Bennett, *A Dictionary of Marketing Terms*, p. 182.

Secondary data may also offer these general disadvantages:

▶ Available data may not suit the current purpose of research, due to incompleteness, generalities, and so on.
▶ Information may be dated or obsolete.
▶ The methodology used in collecting the data (such as the sample size, date of the research, etc.) may be unknown.
▶ All the findings of a research study may not be made public.
▶ Conflicting results may exist.
▶ Because many research projects are not repeated, the reliability of data is not always proven.

Sources

There are two major forms of secondary data, internal and external. Internal secondary data are available within the company. External secondary data are available from sources outside the firm.

INTERNAL SECONDARY DATA.   Before spending time and money searching for external secondary data or collecting primary data, the researcher should look at the information contained inside his or her company. Internal sources include budgets, sales figures, profit-and-loss statements, customer billings, inventory records, prior research reports, and written reports.

At the beginning of the business year, most firms develop budgets for the following twelve months. These budgets, based on sales forecasts, outline planned expenditures for every good and service during the year. The budget and the company's performance in the attainment of budgetary goals (adherence to the outlined plan of expenditures) are good sources for secondary data.

Sales figures are frequently used as indicators of success. By examining the sales of each division, product line, item, geographic area, salesperson, time of day, day of week, and other factors and comparing these sales with prior time periods, a marketer can measure performance. An overdependence on sales data may be misleading because increased sales do not always reflect higher profits. Sales data should be used in conjunction with profit-and-loss statistics.

Profit-and-loss statements reveal a lot of information. Actual achievements can be measured against profit goals. Trends in company success over time can be determined. Profits can be analyzed by department, salesperson, and product. A detailed profit-and-loss breakdown can show strengths and weaknesses in the firm's marketing program and can lead to improvements.

Customer billings provide information about inventory movement, sales by region, peak selling seasons, sales volume, and sales by customer category. For example, credit customers can be examined by geographic area, size of outstanding balance, length of repayment time, products purchased, and demographic data.

Inventory records show the levels of merchandise bought, manufactured, stored, shipped, and sold throughout the year. Inventory planning is improved when the lead time for order processing is known and the proper level of safety stock (excess merchandise stored to avoid running out) is determined.

Prior research reports, containing the findings of past marketing research efforts, are often stored and retained for future use. When the report is used initially, it is primary data. Later reference to the report is secondary in nature because the report is

TABLE 4-2   Selected Sources of U.S. Government Information

American Statistical Index (Congressional Information Service), annual with monthly
    updates
Annual Survey of Manufactures (Bureau of Census), annual
Bureau of the Census Catalog and Guide (Bureau of Census), annual
Business Statistics (Bureau of Economic Analysis), biennial
Census of Manufactures (Bureau of Census), every five years ending in 2 and 7
Census of Population (Bureau of Census), every ten years ending in 0
*Census of Retail Trade, Wholesale Trade, and Selected Service
    Industries* (Bureau of Census), every five years ending in 2 and 7
Census of Transportation (Bureau of Census), every five years ending in 2 and 7
County and City Data Book (Bureau of Census), several times each decade
Federal Reserve Bulletin (Federal Reserve System), monthly
Monthly Labor Review (Bureau of Labor Statistics), monthly
Monthly Product Announcement (Bureau of Census), monthly
Monthly Vital Statistics Report (Health and Human Resources), monthly
Statistical Abstract of the United States (Bureau of Census), annual
Survey of Current Business (Bureau of Economic Analysis), monthly

no longer employed for its primary purpose. The currency of the report must be noted
in evaluating its worth.

Written reports (ongoing information stored by the company) may be compiled by
top management, marketing executives, sales personnel, and others. Among the information available from such reports are standards for marketing performance and
typical customer complaints.

*Government and
nongovernment sources
outside the firm make
available external
secondary data.*

EXTERNAL SECONDARY DATA.   If the research issue or problem is not resolved
through internal secondary data, a firm should utilize external secondary data sources.
External data are available from both government and nongovernment sources.[13]

All levels of government collect and distribute a wide range of statistics and descriptive materials. Table 4-2 shows selected U.S. government publications that should be
available in any medium-sized library. In addition to these, various U.S. government
agencies publish pamphlets on such diverse topics as franchising and deceptive sales
practices. These materials are usually distributed free of charge or sold for a nominal
fee. The *Monthly Catalog of United States Government Publications* contains a listing
of these items. When using government data, particularly census statistics, the date of
the project must be considered. In many cases, there is a lag before government data
are released.

There are three sources of nongovernment secondary data: regular publications;
books, monographs, and other nonregular publications; and commercial research
houses. Regular publications contain articles on various aspects of marketing and are
available in libraries or via subscriptions. Some are quite broad in scope (*Business
Week*); others are more specialized (*Journal of Advertising*). These periodicals are
published by professional or trade associations and regular publishing companies.
Table 4-3 contains a listing of selected periodicals.

[13] A valuable source for anyone involved with collecting marketing information is Jugoslav S. Milutinovich,
"Business Facts for Decision Makers: Where to Find Them," *Business Horizons*, Vol. 28 (March–April
1985), pp. 63–80. Regularly published reference guides include *Business Periodicals Index*, *Funk &
Scott*, *Monthly Catalog of United States Government Publications*, *Public Affairs Information Service
Index*, and *Readers' Guide to Periodical Literature*. Computer-generated bibliographic searches are also
available through many libraries and from firms such as Dun & Bradstreet.

TABLE 4-3 Selected Periodicals

Advertising Age, weekly
American Demographics, monthly
Business, quarterly
Business Horizons, bimonthly
Business Marketing, monthly
Business Week, weekly
California Management Review, quarterly
Chain Store Age Executive, monthly
Columbia Journal of World Business, quarterly
Editor & Publisher Market Guide, annually
Forbes, fortnightly
Fortune, semimonthly
Graphic Guide to Consumer Markets, annually
Harvard Business Review, bimonthly
Industrial Marketing Management, quarterly
Journal of the Academy of Marketing Science, quarterly
Journal of Advertising, quarterly
Journal of Advertising Research, bimonthly
Journal of Business, quarterly
Journal of Business Research, eight times a year

Journal of Business Strategy, bimonthly
Journal of Consumer Marketing, quarterly
Journal of Consumer Research, quarterly
Journal of Marketing, quarterly
Journal of Marketing Research, quarterly
Journal of Personal Selling & Sales Management, three times a year
Journal of Product Innovation Management, quarterly
Journal of Retailing, quarterly
Journal of Small Business Management, quarterly
Marketing & Media Decisions, monthly
Marketing Research, quarterly
Progressive Grocer, monthly
Rand McNally Commercial Atlas & Marketing Guide, annually
Sales & Marketing Management, monthly (annual *Survey of Buying Power*)
Standard Rate & Data Service, monthly
Stores, monthly
Wall Street Journal, daily

Other periodicals: Most trade associations distribute at least one regular publication.

Books, monographs, and other nonrecurring literature are also published by professional and trade associations and by conventional publishing companies. These materials deal with special topics in depth and are compiled on the basis of interest by the target audience.

Commercial research houses conduct periodic and ongoing studies and make the results of the studies available to many clients for a fee. The fee can be quite low or range into the tens of thousands of dollars, depending on the extent of the data. This kind of research is secondary when the firm purchasing the data acts as a subscriber and does not request specific studies pertaining only to itself. Several large commercial houses specialize in selling secondary data and provide a number of services at lower costs than the company would incur if the data were collected for its sole use. Among the leading research firms are A.C. Nielsen and IMS International (both owned by Dun & Bradstreet), Pergamon/AGB, SAMI/Burke, Arbitron, and Information Resources Inc. Figures 4-5 and 4-6 show two kinds of services provided by commercial research houses. A great many other such services are also available.

Primary Data

Primary data are information "collected specifically for the purpose of the investigation at hand."[14] Such data are necessary when a thorough analysis of secondary data does not provide satisfactory information for a marketing decision to be made.

Primary data study a specific marketing issue.

---

[14] Bennett, *A Dictionary of Marketing Terms*, p. 151.

FIGURE 4-5
**Selected Secondary Data
from Dun & Bradstreet**
Dun's Marketing Services Division serves
the needs of business-to-business clients
with printed directories and data bases
that can be accessed electronically.
Reprinted by permission.

FIGURE 4-6
**Retail Store Auditing by
Burke Marketing Services**
On a regular basis, Burke
Marketing Services
monitors the performance
of various types of retail
stores. Field auditors visit
a national sample of
stores, and provide clients
with information about
sales, inventories, brand
distribution, prices,
displays, and so on.
Reprinted by permission.

Marketing Controversy

Should a Marketing Research Firm Allow Its Name to Be Featured in Ads?

Recent Chrysler ads touting its cars as "Number 1 in quality" among U.S. car manufacturers, based on the results of a J.D. Power & Associates customer satisfaction survey, angered many competing auto makers. Although the information in the Chrysler ads was approved by Power (an independent marketing research firm), the survey cited was actually more related to dealer service than to a car's overall quality.

Furthermore, because virtually every car maker selling vehicles in the United States purchases some of the 200 reports annually produced by Power, a number of these firms feel that the research data should not be used for promotional purposes. As Nissan's U.S. consumer-research manager says, "I really dislike paying Power to do research that my competitors can use in their advertising against me."

The high profile of J.D. Power concerns many auto makers because potential car buyers may view the firm's results as a "Good Housekeeping Seal of Approval" or a brand endorsement. Those who feel that Power's research findings should not be promoted to final consumers contend that the data should be given only to the auto companies themselves to assess the quality of their dealer service or to detect problems with new models.

In contrast to Power's strategy of allowing subscribers to use survey data in advertising, Maritz, Inc. (its leading competitor), does not allow its findings to be used in ads or to be discussed with independent media. Although Maritz's annual billings for auto research are $14 million, versus Power's $10 million, few car buyers have ever heard of Maritz.

What do you think?

SOURCE: Based on material in Stewart Toy and James B. Treece, "When J.D. Power Talks, Car Makers Listen," *Business Week* (September 26, 1988), p. 134.

Next, the pros and cons of primary data as well as the elements of the research design used in collecting these data are presented.

Advantages and Disadvantages

Primary data offer these general advantages:

Primary data are precise, current, tailored, and private.

- They are collected to fit the precise purposes of the current research topic.
- Information is current.
- The methodology of data collection is controlled and known by the firm.
- All findings are available to the company, which can maintain secrecy from competitors.
- There are no conflicting data from different sources.
- Reliability can be determined (if desired).
- When secondary data do not resolve all questions, collecting and analyzing primary data are the only way to acquire information.

Primary data problems are collection time, expense, unavailability, and bias.

Primary data may also offer these general disadvantages:

▶ Collection may be time consuming.
▶ Costs may be high.
▶ Some types of information cannot be collected (e.g., census data).
▶ The company's perspective may be limited.
▶ The firm may be unable to collect primary data.

Research Design

*The **research design** outlines data collection.*

If the company decides that primary data are necessary, it must develop a research design. The **research design** is the "framework or plan for a study that guides the collection and analysis of the data,"[15] and includes the following decisions.

Internal or outside personnel can be used.

WHO COLLECTS THE DATA?   The company can collect the data itself or hire an outside research firm for a specific project. The advantages of an internal research department are the knowledge of company operations, total access to company personnel, ongoing assembly and storage of data, and high loyalty or commitment. The disadvantages of an internal department are the continuous costs, narrow perspective, and potentially excessive support of the views of top management. The strengths and weaknesses of an outside research firm are the opposite of those for the inside department.

WHAT INFORMATION SHOULD BE COLLECTED?   The kinds and amounts of information to be collected should be based on the issue (problem) definition formulated by the company. Exploratory research requires less data collection than conclusive research.

A study's population is the people or objects studied.

WHO OR WHAT SHOULD BE STUDIED?   First, the researcher must stipulate the people or objects to be studied. This is known as the population. People studies generally involve customers, company personnel, and/or channel members. Object studies usually center on company and/or product performance. Whether people or objects are analyzed, precise terms need to be employed:

Who or What Is to Be Investigated	Specifications
1. Target market of company	1. All single women in the Chicago area, ages 18 to 30
2. Product A	2. Model number 11, sales performance for 1990 calendar year by geographic region

***Sampling** the population saves time and money.*

Second, the manner in which people or objects are selected for investigation must be determined. Large and/or dispersed populations frequently are examined by sampling procedures. **Sampling** requires the analysis of selected people or objects in the designated population, rather than all of them. Sampling saves time and money; when used properly, the accuracy and representativeness of sampling can be measured.

The two approaches to sampling are probability and nonprobability. In a probability (random) sample, every member of the designated population has an equal or known

[15] Ibid, p. 172.

FIGURE 4-7
A Shopping Mall Interview
Personal surveys can often
be efficiently conducted at
shopping malls. The malls
are usually heavily trafficked
by a broad spectrum of
middle-class consumers
who are willing to spend
time in the mall.
Reprinted by permission of
Burke Marketing Services.

probability of being chosen for analysis. For example, a researcher may select every twenty-fifth person in a telephone directory. In a nonprobability sample, members of the population are chosen by the researcher or interviewer on the basis of convenience or judgment. For instance, a researcher may select the first 100 dormitory students entering the college cafeteria. A probability sample is more accurate; however, it is more costly and difficult than a nonprobability sample.

Third, the size of the sample to be investigated must be stated. Generally speaking, a large sample will yield greater accuracy and higher costs than a small sample. There are methods for assessing sample size in terms of costs and accuracy, but a description of them is beyond the scope of this text.[16]

WHAT TECHNIQUE OF DATA COLLECTION SHOULD BE USED?   There are four basic methods for primary data collection: survey, observation, experiment, and simulation.

A *survey* systematically gathers information from respondents by communicating with them. It can uncover data about attitudes, past purchases, and consumer characteristics. Yet, it is susceptible to incorrect or biased answers. With a survey, a questionnaire is used to record responses. A survey can be conducted in person, over the telephone, or by mail.

*A **survey** communicates in person, over the telephone, or by mail.*

A personal survey is conducted face-to-face, is flexible, elicits lengthy replies, and reduces ambiguity. It is expensive, however, and interviewer bias is possible because the interviewer may affect results by suggesting ideas to respondents or by creating a certain mood during the interview. A telephone survey is fast and relatively inexpensive, especially with the growth of discount telephone services. Responses are usually brief, and nonresponse may be a problem. It must be verified that the desired respondent is actually contacted. Some people do not have a phone or utilize unlisted numbers. The latter problem may now be overcome through computerized random digit-dialing devices. A mail survey can reach dispersed respondents, has no interviewer bias, and is relatively inexpensive. Nonresponse, slowness of returns, and participation by incorrect respondents are the major problems. The technique that is chosen depends on the objectives and needs of the specific research project. See Figure 4-7.

---

[16] See for example, Donald S. Tull and Del F. Hawkins, *Marketing Research: Measurement and Method,* Fourth Edition (New York: Macmillan, 1987), pp. 395–421.

A nondisguised survey reveals its purpose, whereas a disguised one does not.

A survey may be nondisguised or disguised. In a nondisguised survey, the respondent is told the real purpose of the study. In a disguised survey, the respondent is not told the real purpose of the study. The latter is used to probe indirectly attitudes or feelings and to avoid the respondent answering what he or she thinks the interviewer or researcher wants to hear or read. The left side of Figure 4-8 shows a nondisguised survey, which reveals the true intent of a study on sports car attitudes and behavior to respondents. The right side of Figure 4-8 shows how the survey can be disguised: By asking about sports car owners in general, the researcher is able to get more honest answers to personal questions than if he or she asks questions geared directly to the respondents. The real intent of the disguised study is to uncover the respondents' actual reasons for buying a sports car.

*The **semantic differential** uses bipolar adjectives.*

The **semantic differential** is a list of bipolar (opposite) adjective scales. It is a survey technique that employs rating scales instead of, or in addition to, questions. It may be disguised or nondisguised, depending on whether the respondent is told the true purpose of the study. Each adjective in the semantic differential is evaluated along a bipolar scale, and average ratings for all respondents are computed. An overall company or product profile is then developed. This profile may be compared with competitors' profiles and consumers' ideal ratings. An example of a completed semantic differential appears in Figure 4-9.

FIGURE 4-8
Nondisguised and Disguised Surveys

Nondisguised	Disguised
1. Why are you buying a sports car?	1. Why do you think people buy sports cars?
2. What factors are you considering in the purchase of a sports car?	2. What factors do people consider in the purchase of a sports car?
3. Is status important to you in a sports car purchase? ---- Yes ---- No	3. Are people who purchase sports cars status-conscious? ---- Yes ---- No
4. On the highway, I will drive my sports car ---- within the speed limit. ---- slightly over the speed limit. ---- well over the speed limit.	4. On the highway, sports car owners drive ---- within the speed limit. ---- slightly over the speed limit. ---- well over the speed limit.

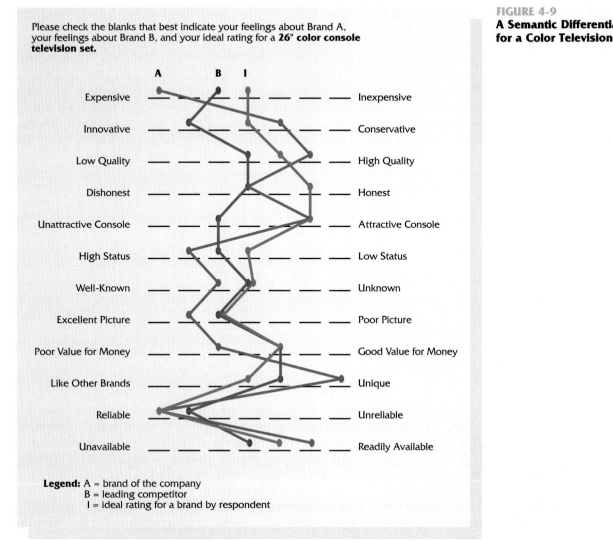

FIGURE 4-9
**A Semantic Differential
for a Color Television**

Please check the blanks that best indicate your feelings about Brand A, your feelings about Brand B, and your ideal rating for a **26" color console television set.**

| A | B | I |

Expensive — — — — — — — Inexpensive
Innovative — — — — — — — Conservative
Low Quality — — — — — — — High Quality
Dishonest — — — — — — — Honest
Unattractive Console — — — — — — — Attractive Console
High Status — — — — — — — Low Status
Well-Known — — — — — — — Unknown
Excellent Picture — — — — — — — Poor Picture
Poor Value for Money — — — — — — — Good Value for Money
Like Other Brands — — — — — — — Unique
Reliable — — — — — — — Unreliable
Unavailable — — — — — — — Readily Available

Legend: A = brand of the company
B = leading competitor
I = ideal rating for a brand by respondent

Multidimensional scaling is another popular survey research tool that may be disguised or nondisguised. With multidimensional scaling, respondents' attitudes are surveyed for many product and company attributes. Computer analysis then enables the firm to develop a single product or company rating, rather than a profile of several individual characteristics. A statistical description of the technique is beyond the scope of this text, but Figure 4-10 shows how it can be used to construct single overall ratings. In the figure, consumer attitudes about six brands of facial tissue and the consumers' ideal rating of facial tissue are depicted. Brand A most closely matches the consumers' ideal.

Observation is a research technique in which present behavior or the results of past behavior are observed and recorded. People are not questioned, and their cooperation is not necessary. Interviewer and question bias are minimized. Observation frequently is used in actual situations. The major disadvantages are that attitudes cannot be determined and observers may misinterpret behavior.

Multidimensional scaling develops overall ratings.

*In **observation,** behavior is viewed.*

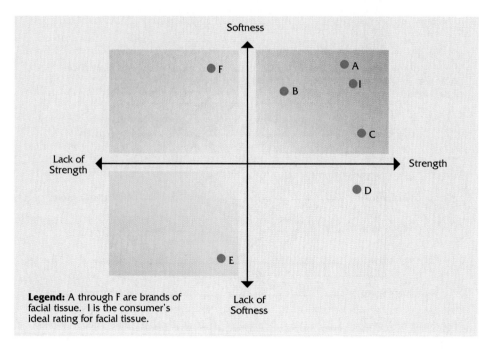

FIGURE 4-10
**Multidimensional
Scaling—Ratings for
Facial Tissues**

Legend: A through F are brands of facial tissue. I is the consumer's ideal rating for facial tissue.

In disguised observation, the consumer is not aware that he or she is being watched. A two-way mirror or hidden camera would be used. With nondisguised observation, the participant knows that he or she is being observed. Human observation is carried out by people; mechanical observation records behavior through electronic or other means, such as a movie camera filming in-store customer behavior or reactions to a sales presentation.

*An **experiment** varies marketing factors under controlled conditions.*

An **experiment** is a type of research in which one or more factors are manipulated under controlled conditions. A factor may be any element of marketing from package design to advertising media. In an experiment, just the factor under investigation is varied; all other factors remain constant. For example, in order to evaluate a new package design for a product, the manufacturer could send new packages to five retail outlets and old packages to five similar retail outlets. All marketing factors other than packaging would remain the same. After one month, sales of the new package through the five test outlets would be compared with sales of the old package through the five similar outlets.

The major advantage of an experiment is that it is able to show cause and effect — for example, a new package design increasing sales. It is also systematically structured and implemented. The major disadvantages are the high costs, frequent use of contrived settings, and inability to control all factors in or affecting the marketing plan. Under closely controlled conditions, a survey or observation could be used to determine the reactions to an experiment.

***Simulation** enables marketing factors to be analyzed through a computer model.*

Simulation is a computer-based technique that tests the potential effects of various marketing factors via a software program rather than through real-world applications. A model of the controllable and uncontrollable factors facing the firm is first constructed. Then different combinations of the factors are fed into a computer to deter-

TABLE 4-4 The Best Uses of Primary Data-Collection Techniques

Technique	Most Appropriate Uses
1. Survey	When determining consumer attitudes and motivations about marketing-mix factors, measuring purchase intentions, relating consumer characteristics to attitudes
2. Observation	When examining actual responses to marketing factors under realistic conditions, interest is in behavior not attitudes
3. Experiment	When controlling the research environment is essential, establishing a cause-and-effect relationship is important
4. Simulation	When deriving and analyzing many interrelationships among variables

mine their effects on the overall marketing strategy. Simulation requires no consumer cooperation and can handle many interrelated factors. However, it is complex and difficult to use and subject to the accuracy of the assumptions made.

Table 4-4 shows the most appropriate uses for each technique of primary data collection.

HOW MUCH WILL THE STUDY COST?   The overall and specific costs of the study must be clearly outlined. These costs include executive time, researcher time, support staff time, computer usage, respondents' incentives (if any), interviewers, printing, pretesting, special equipment, and marketing costs (such as advertising).

Research costs range from personnel time to marketing costs.

The costs of the study should be evaluated against the benefits to be derived. For example, suppose a firm realizes that a consumer survey costing $10,000 will enable it to improve the package design of a new product. With the changes suggested by research, the firm will increase its first-year profit by $30,000. Therefore, the net increase as a result of research is $20,000 ($30,000 profit less $10,000 in costs).

HOW WILL THE DATA BE COLLECTED?   The personnel necessary to collect the data outlined in the research design must be determined and the attributes, skills, and training of the data-collection force need to be specified. Too often this important phase is improperly planned, and data are collected by unqualified personnel.

Data collection can be administered by research personnel or be self-administered. With administered questionnaires, interviewers ask questions or observers note behavior; these personnel record answers or behavior and explain questions (if necessary) to respondents. In self-administered questionnaires, respondents read the questions and write their own answers. In the choice of these techniques, there is a trade-off between control and interviewer probing (administered) versus privacy and limited interviewer bias (self-administered).

Interviewers administer surveys or respondents fill them out.

HOW LONG WILL THE DATA COLLECTION PERIOD BE?   The researcher must stipulate the time frame within which data will be collected, or else a study can drag on. Too long a time frame may cause inconsistent responses and violations of secrecy. Short time frames are easy to set for personal and telephone surveys. Mail surveys, observation, and experiments often require substantially more time to implement. Nonetheless, time limits must be defined.

WHEN AND WHERE SHOULD INFORMATION BE COLLECTED?   The day and time of data collection must be specified. In addition, it must be decided whether the study is undertaken on the firm's premises or off them. The researcher has to weigh immediacy and convenience versus a desire to investigate hard-to-reach respondents at the proper time of the year.

You're the Marketer

Coffee, Tea, or Video?

Northwest Airlines, British Airways, and Qantas (the Australian airline) are testing the rental of three-inch color televisions to passengers on selected flights. For example, Northwest has installed 116 mini-televisions in the business and coach sections of a Boeing 747 jet used on a Detroit-to-Tokyo route. The airlines' cost of purchasing and installing mini-televisions averages $2,000 per unit. The televisions, permanently mounted on the seats in front of passengers, are being rented for between $4 and $8. However, the airlines have not yet determined the optimal price.

There are two major advantages that the mini-televisions have over the overhead screens that are prevalent: The mini-televisions are easier to see than the larger screens; and passengers can select from among six channels with options such as movies, news features, documentaries, music videos, cartoons, and programs in Japanese. No problems have been

reported with the televisions distracting adjacent passengers due to their light or their noise, because headphones must be used with the sets.

Marketing research conducted by Warner Brothers (which provides the programming for the mini-televisions) and Northwest Airlines indicates that 70 per cent of surveyed passengers prefer mini-televisions to overhead screens and that 70 per cent say they would be more likely to fly on airlines that install such televisions.

The developers see these TVs becoming part of a cabin management system in which passengers can also access hotels and car rental facilities from their plane seats.

As an airline's marketing research director, what kind of information would you collect before recommending the widespread purchase of mini-TVs?

SOURCE: Based on material in "Coffee, Tea, or Video? Airlines Testing Small TV's," *New York Times* (October 10, 1988), p. D12; and John Marcom, Jr., "Helping Time Fly," *Forbes* (March 6, 1989), pp. 149–150.

Data Collection

After all aspects of the research design are thoroughly detailed, the data are actually collected. It is important that the personnel responsible for data collection be adequately supervised and follow directions exactly. Responses and/or observations must be entered correctly.

Data Analysis

Data analysis consists of coding, tabulation, and analysis.

In *data analysis,* forms are first coded and tabulated and then analyzed. Coding is the process by which each completed data form is numbered and response categories are labeled. Tabulation is the calculation of summary data for each response category. Analysis is the evaluation of responses, usually by statistical techniques, as they pertain to the specific problem under investigation. The relationship of coding, tabulation, and analysis is shown in Figure 4-11.

Partial Questionnaire			Total responses
1. Do you drink coffee?	☐ Yes	01	375
	☐ No	02	125
2. Which of these brands have you heard of? Check all the answers that apply.	☐ Brim	03	195
	☐ Sanka	04	340
	☐ Savarin	05	212
	☐ None	06	63
3. Compared to tea, coffee is (check only **one** answer)	☐ more bitter	07	140
	☐ better for your health	08	12
	☐ more energizing	09	240
	☐ more expensive	10	108

Coding: Questionnaires numbered A001 to A500.
Each response labeled 01 to 10 (e.g., Sanka is 04. more energizing is 09).
Question 2 is a multiple-response question.

Tabulation: Total responses are shown above right.

Analysis: 75% drink coffee; Sanka is the most well-known brand; only 39% are familiar with Brim; coffee is viewed as energizing; yet compared to tea, it is not seen as better for health; high prices may be a problem.

Recommendations: The advertising of Brim must be increased and concentrated on stimulating brand awareness; emphasis should be placed on good taste, energizing qualities, and low price per serving.

Implementation of findings: A new advertising campaign will be developed and the annual media budget expanded. Other suggestions will be accepted as noted above.

FIGURE 4-11
Data Analysis, Recommendations, and Implementation of Findings for a Study on Brim Coffee

Recommendations

Recommendations are suggestions for future actions by a company, based on marketing research findings. These recommendations are generally presented in written (in some cases oral) form to marketing decision makers. The report must be written for the audience that will read it. For instance, any technical terminology must be defined. Figure 4-11 shows recommendations flowing from completed research.

Recommendations direct future actions.

Implementation of Findings

The research report represents feedback to marketing management, which is responsible for utilizing findings. If marketing decision makers ignore the findings, research has little value. If marketing management bases decisions on research results, then marketing research has great value and the organization benefits in the short and long run.

Marketing management determines how to respond to research.

109

Marketing managers are most likely to implement research findings when they have input into the research design, have broad control over marketing decisions, and have confidence that the results are accurate. Figure 4-11 provides an illustration of a how a company would implement research findings.

Marketing Information Systems

It is risky to gather marketing data haphazardly or infrequently.

A company should not approach marketing information collection as a haphazard, infrequent occurrence that is only necessary when the firm needs to generate data about a specific marketing topic. When marketing research is used in this manner, the firm faces several risks. Previous studies may not be stored in an easy-to-use format. There may be a lack of awareness about environmental changes and competitors' actions. Information collection may be disjointed. Time lags may result whenever a new research study is required. There may be no data to analyze over several comparable time periods. Marketing plans and decisions may not be effectively reviewed. Actions may be reactionary rather than anticipatory.

A marketing information system regularly gathers, stores, analyzes, and disseminates data.

Marketing research should be considered as just one part of an ongoing, integrated information process. It is essential that a firm develop and utilize a system for scanning the environment in a continuous manner and for storing data, so that they may be reviewed in the future. A *marketing information system* (*MIS*) can be defined as

> a set of procedures and methods designed to generate, store, analyze, and disseminate marketing decision information on a regular, continuous basis.[17]

Figure 4-12 presents a basic marketing information system. In this system, the firm begins with a statement of company objectives, which provide broad guidelines. These objectives are influenced by environmental factors, such as competition, government, and the economy. Marketing plans involve the controllable factors explained in Chapters 2 and 3, including the selection of the target market, marketing objectives, the type of marketing organization, the marketing mix (product, distribution, promotion, and price), and control.

A marketing intelligence network includes marketing research, continuous monitoring, and data storage.

After marketing plans are outlined, the total information needs of the marketing department can be specified and satisfied through a *marketing intelligence network,* which consists of marketing research, continuous monitoring, and data storage. *Marketing research* is used to obtain information to resolve particular marketing issues (problems). Information may be acquired from storage (internal secondary data) or by collecting external secondary data and/or primary data. *Continuous monitoring* is the procedure by which the changing environment is regularly viewed. Continuous monitoring can include subscriptions to business and trade publications, observing news reports, regularly obtaining information from employees and customers, attending industry meetings, and watching competitors' actions. *Data storage* involves the retention of all types of relevant company records (such as sales, costs, personnel performance, etc.), as well as the information collected through marketing research and continuous monitoring. These data aid decision making and are kept for future reference.

Depending on the resources of the firm and the complexity of its information needs, the marketing intelligence network may or may not be computerized. Small firms can

---

[17] Robert A. Peterson, *Marketing Research,* Second Edition (Dallas: Business Publications, 1988), p. 31.

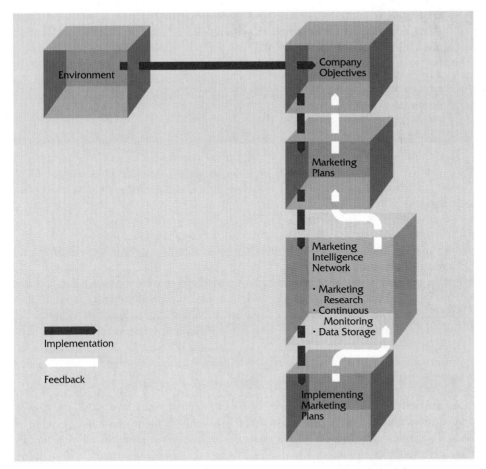

FIGURE 4-12
A Basic Marketing Information System

operate such systems very efficiently without computerization. In any system, information needs must be specified (in both quantitative and qualitative terms) and regularly reviewed, information sources must be identified and evaluated, company personnel must be assigned information tasks, storage and retrieval facilities must be set up, and data must be routed to the proper decision makers. The ingredients for a successful system are consistency, thoroughness, and a good filing technique.

Marketing plans should be implemented on the basis of the information obtained from the intelligence network. For example, by continuous monitoring, the firm may determine that the costs of its raw materials will be rising by 7 per cent during the following year. This would give the company time to explore its marketing options (e.g., switch to substitute materials, pass along cost increases, or absorb cost increases) and select one alternative to be implemented. If monitoring is not in effect, the firm might be caught by surprise and forced to absorb cost increases, without any choice.

In general, a marketing information system offers many advantages: organized data collection, broad perspective, retention of important data, avoidance of crises, coordination of the marketing plan, speed, quantifiable results, and cost-benefit analysis. However, developing a marketing information system may not be easy. Initial time and labor costs may be high, and setting up a system may be complex. Figures 4-13 and 4-14 show how marketing information systems can be used in planning marketing strategies.

MIS is being widely used by different types of firms.

Today, in greater numbers than ever before, companies utilize some form of MIS in their decision making; and this trend is expected to continue. One recent study on the use of marketing information systems by large U.S. industrial and service firms found that:

▶ More than three-quarters of the firms have a marketing information system. Of those that do, about 90 per cent are computer-based.

▶ Two-thirds of the companies have computer terminals available for personnel. Over half of marketing executives use a computer terminal daily, most often to retrieve or store data.

▶ Seventy per cent of the firms have in-house offices to collect customer data.

▶ Sixty per cent of the companies place more importance on internal accounting information (data storage) than on continuous monitoring of the environment or marketing research.

▶ Of those firms with computerized systems, 91 per cent store customer data, 33 per cent store competitive data, 25 per cent store data on potential customers and the national economy, and just 12 per cent store data on the federal government.

▶ Product decisions are most likely to rely on a marketing information system; promotion decisions are least likely.

▶ Top-management support for a marketing information system and its use in planning is growing.[18]

A study of various-sized mass merchandisers, department stores, specialty stores, and combination/grocery stores found that these retailers spend about one per cent of annual sales on MIS. Almost 90 per cent use computerized point-of-sale registers in their systems. These retailers also planned to spend considerable funds in developing or improving MIS capabilities in such areas as inventory control, merchandise planning, purchasing, and distribution during 1988 and 1989.[19]

Among the companies with well-structured marketing information systems are Ciba-Geigy, Clorox, Mrs. Fields Cookies, and Haworth. Each devotes considerable time and resources to its system. Examples follow of how these companies apply MIS.

Ciba-Geigy, a pharmaceutical firm, regularly acquires information about physicians from the American Medical Association and from survey results provided by an outside research company. These data are stored in Ciba-Geigy's computerized MIS and are distributed to the relevant marketing personnel, as necessary. The firm's sales representatives use portable laptop computers to access customer data and modify them to their own needs; the salespeople then can better develop weekly and monthly plans.[20]

---

[18] Raymond McLeod, Jr., and John Rogers, "Marketing Information Systems: Their Current Status in *Fortune* 1000 Companies," *Journal of Management Information Systems,* Vol. 1 (Spring 1985), pp. 57–75.

[19] "Retail MIS Field Reflects Technology Trends," *Chain Store Age Executive* (January 1988), pp. 100–102. See also "Survey Shows Increase in 1989 MIS Budgets," *Chain Store Age Executive* (August 1988), pp. 69–70.

[20] Thayer C. Taylor, "Marketers and the PC: Steady as She Goes," *Sales & Marketing Management* (August 1986), pp. 54–55.

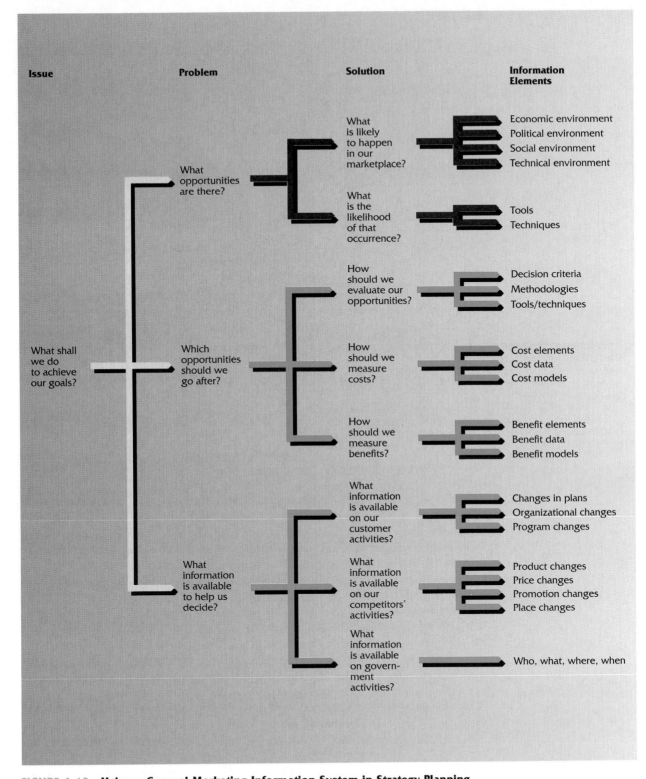

FIGURE 4-13 **Using a General Marketing Information System in Strategy Planning**
SOURCE: M. Edward Goretsky, "Frameworks of Strategic Marketing Information Needs," *Industrial Marketing Management,* Vol. 12 (February 1983), p. 11. Reprinted by permission of the publisher. Copyright 1983—by Elsevier Science Publishing Co., Inc.

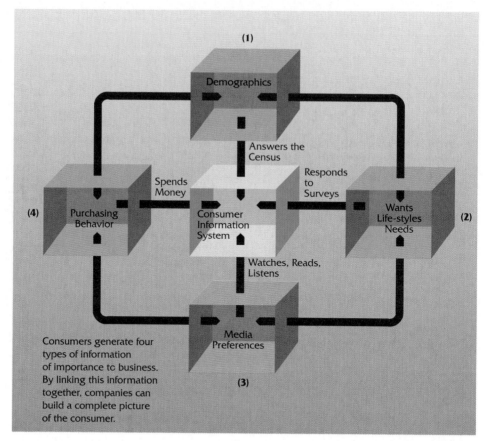

FIGURE 4-14
A Consumer-Based Marketing Information System to Aid Planning
SOURCE: Adapted from Peter K. Francese, "How to Manage Consumer Information," *American Demographics* (August 1985), p. 24. Reprinted by permission.

At Clorox, a consumer-goods company, a brand-management information system simplifies the firm's analysis of product tracking, market potential, sales, price, and competitive data. It combines statistics from various outside data bases into "meaningful market information," leading to "improved decision making." This system was quite helpful when Clorox recently introduced Kingsford with Mesquite charcoal (for barbeques) into specific geographic markets, guiding the firm in its advertising and distribution efforts.[21]

Mrs. Fields Cookies, a leading retail chain, uses a sophisticated marketing information system to plan and revise marketing strategies, communicate with individual stores, ensure consistent operations throughout the chain, and monitor trouble spots. For instance, at the beginning of a business day, each store manager enters the day of the week, etc., into his or her PC. Then, the computer compares data about the current day with the last three days most closely matched to it. Next, a day-planner and labor-scheduling software program instructs the store manager as to exactly how many and what kinds of cookies to sell in 15-minute intervals during the entire day. Every hour, updated information is entered into the PC. If sales are lower than expected, the

---

[21] "Marketing Information Systems: Hot Line to the Consumer," *Marketing Communications* (March 1987), pp. 85, 87.

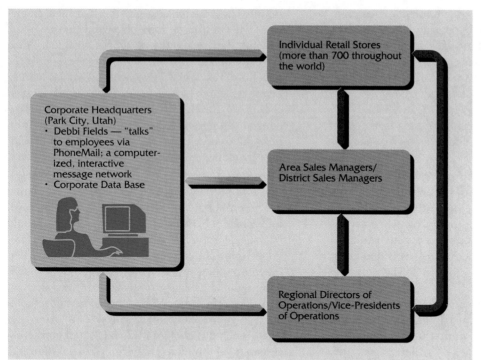

FIGURE 4-15
How Communication Flows in Mrs. Fields' MIS
SOURCE: Adapted by the authors from Tom Richman, "Mrs. Fields' Secret Ingredient," *Inc.* (October 1987), pp. 65–72.

computer makes suggestions (such as a change in the cookie assortment).[22] Figure 4-15 shows the communication flows in Mrs. Fields' marketing information system.

Haworth, Inc., an office-furniture firm, uses its MIS to track customer accounts and develop sales forecasts. For instance, in Dallas, all of its salespeople regularly provide data on their largest ten accounts via PC-based software. As the division manager commented:

> Rather than wade through 100 salesperson call reports, I pull one detailed weekly report that gives me the status on all the major accounts. [And], our monthly sales forecasts are faster and more accurate. Instead of preparing the forecasts manually, the sales reps ask their customers to look at computer printouts and help update expected orders.[23]

Summary

1. *To consider why marketing information is needed*
Marketing information enables a company to assess accurately its strengths, weaknesses, opportunities, and threats; operate properly in the marketing environment; and maximize performance. Reliance on intuition, judgment, and experience are not sufficient.

2. *To define marketing research and its components*
Marketing research is the systematic gathering, recording, and analyzing of data about specific issues related to the marketing of goods, services, organizations, people, places, and ideas. It may be conducted internally or externally. The scientific method requires objectivity, accuracy, and thoroughness in marketing research projects.

[22] "Mrs. Fields Automates the Way the Cookie Sells," *Chain Store Age Executive* (April 1988), pp. 73–76.
[23] Thayer C. Taylor, "Making Long-Term Sales Cycles Manageable," *Sales & Marketing Management* (August 1986), pp. 64–66.

3. *To examine the scope of marketing research* Expenditures on marketing research run into the billions of dollars annually. The use of marketing research varies by company. Large firms and consumer-goods companies are most likely to engage in marketing research. Three key trends are particularly noteworthy: the growing availability of commercial data bases, the increasing use of new technology, and the declining image of survey research.

4. *To describe the marketing research process* This process involves a series of activities: defining the issue or problem to be studied, examining secondary data, generating primary data (when necessary), analyzing data, making recommendations, and implementing findings. Many considerations and decisions are needed in each stage of the process.

   Exploratory research is used to develop a clear definition of the study topic. Conclusive research addresses specific issues in a structured manner. Secondary data — those not gathered for the immediate study at hand but for some other purpose — are available from internal and external (government, nongovernment, commercial) sources. Primary data — those collected specifically for the purpose of the investigation at hand — are available through surveys, observation, experiments, and simulation. Primary data collection requires a research design: the specified framework for controlling data collection and analysis. Primary data are gathered only if secondary data are insufficient. Costs must be weighed against the benefits of research. The concluding stages of marketing research are data analysis — consisting of coding, tabulating, and analysis stages; recommendations — suggestions for future actions based on research findings; and the implementation of findings by management.

5. *To explain the role and importance of the marketing information system* Marketing information collection should not be viewed as a haphazard, infrequent occurrence. Marketing research should be considered as just one part of an ongoing, integrated information process. Accordingly, a marketing information system involves a set of procedures and methods designed to generate, store, analyze, and disseminate marketing decision information on a regular, continuous basis. The marketing intelligence phase of an MIS consists of marketing research, continuous monitoring, and data storage. An MIS can be used by both small and large firms, and the applications of marketing information systems are spreading rapidly. Today many marketing executives participate in some form of computerized information system and have PCs in their offices.

Key Terms

marketing research (p. 90)
scientific method (p. 91)
marketing research process (p. 94)
issue (problem) definition (p. 95)
exploratory research (p. 95)
conclusive research (p. 95)
secondary data (p. 96)
primary data (p. 99)

research design (p. 102)
sampling (p. 102)
survey (p. 103)
semantic differential (p. 104)
multidimensional scaling (p. 105)
observation (p. 105)
experiment (p. 106)
simulation (p. 106)

data analysis (p. 108)
marketing information system (MIS) (p. 110)
marketing intelligence network (p. 110)
continuous monitoring (p. 110)
data storage (p. 110)

Review Questions

1. Why is marketing information necessary? What may result if managers rely exclusively on intuition?

2. What is the scientific method? Must it be used each time a firm engages in marketing research? Explain your answer.

3. How could a company reduce respondent dissatisfaction with surveys?

4. Differentiate between conclusive and exploratory research. Give an example of each.

5. What are the advantages and disadvantages of secondary data?

6. When is primary data collection necessary?

7. Outline the steps in a research design.

8. Under what circumstances should a firm use surveys to collect data? Observation? Explain your answers.

9. Distinguish between marketing research and a marketing information system. What is the proper role of each?

10. Describe the elements of a basic marketing information system.

Discussion Questions

1. A small savings bank wants to gather information about its customers. In particular, it wants to determine the average outstanding balances that customers keep in their various accounts, the incomes and occupations of customers, when in-bank traffic is heaviest and lightest, customer use of automatic teller machines, and customer satisfaction with bank services. Explain how the bank should obtain this information. In your answer, be sure to consider secondary versus primary data collection, and the responsibility for data collection.

2. 7-Eleven operates a national chain of convenience stores. Bob's 24-Hour Self-Serv is an independent neighborhood convenience store. Both retailers are interested in gathering information about their respective competitors' practices. How would the research design used by 7-Eleven differ from that of Bob's 24-Hour Self-Serv?

3. Develop a five-question disguised survey to determine attitudes toward energy prices in your area. Why use a disguised survey for this topic?

4. Comment on the ethics of disguised observation. Under which circumstances would you recommend its use?

5. How could a firm use the consumer-based marketing information system shown in Figure 4-14? Apply your answer to a firm marketing employee uniforms to the U.S. Postal Service.

═══════════ ◄ CASE 1 ► ═══════════

Marketing Research at Montgomery Ward *

Montgomery Ward is a Chicago-based retailer that was founded in 1872. Today the company operates well over 300 stores in about forty states; it also has a moderate-sized mail-order business. Originally Montgomery Ward was one of the two leading mail-order retailers in the United States, along with Sears Roebuck. The firm's annual sales of nearly $5 billion now rank it among the largest twenty-five U.S. retailers.

The firm operates a chain of department stores under the Montgomery Ward name, as well as several specialty-store chains, such as Electric Avenue (appliance and consumer electronics stores), Home Ideas (home furnishings stores), Auto Express (auto parts and service stores), and Gold 'N Gems (jewelry stores). These specialty chains focus on the product categories that Montgomery Ward wants to emphasize in the future.

* The data in this case are drawn from "Market Research Put to Creative Use," *Chain Store Age Executive* (May 1988), pp. 23–24, 26.

This is how Montgomery Ward views the role of marketing research in its decision making:

> It's almost become a way of life. We use research in a variety of ways. First, to determine what consumer segments we should focus on. Second, we use research to give us direct feedback on some of our latest concepts and merchandise programs. Third, we use research to make sure that the consumers are the judge of what they want, as opposed to ourselves. We don't want to become overly expert and rely on our intuition instead of our customers.

> We ask our target customer three questions. The first thing we do is measure the awareness of brands by our target customer. The second thing we ask is for our customer to rate the value of that merchandise. Then the third question we ask is "Do you expect to find that merchandise in our store?" We map it out and look for brands with high awareness, a high value reputation, and that the customer would expect to find in our store.

In its marketing research efforts, Montgomery Ward seeks to balance two opposing principles. On the one hand, it firmly believes that marketing research should emphasize asking consumers about their attitudes and preferences toward the firm, its products, and its customer service. What do its customers *think*? On the other hand, it also feels that retail executives can get a feel for consumer desires by visiting stores and observing consumer behavior. In this way, it may be able to "anticipate what the customer will like before a customer can articulate it." What are customers *doing*?

According to Montgomery Ward's senior vice-president of strategic planning and development, the company uses marketing research for specific topics and integrates research in an ongoing information system: "We typically don't undertake a strategic review of our business without a focused consumer research project" and a review of existing data and reports. As a result of such research, the firm recently adjusted its merchandise assortment.

To make marketing research a more integral part of the company's overall planning process, Montgomery Ward's marketing research director now reports directly to the senior vice-president of strategic planning.

Montgomery Ward is only one of the many retailers that use marketing research in planning. For example, Sears (the nation's largest retailer) has a full-time marketing research staff with about forty professionals. Since 1974, Sears has conducted its own national image studies, surveying 3,000 households each time, to determine its competitive positioning in relation to other retailers. Sears also annually tracks its market share for 600 different lines of merchandise. Recent research by Sears on whether the firm should add well-known manufacturer brands to its product mix (which primarily consisted of its own brands) convinced it to change the product strategy. Consumers especially desired manufacturer brands for consumer electronics.

QUESTIONS

1. When should Montgomery Ward rely on consumer attitude surveys to gather information? Observations of consumers? Explain your answers.
2. What are the advantages of the marketing research director reporting to the vice-president of strategic planning? The disadvantages?
3. Prepare a short questionnaire for Montgomery Ward to use in evaluating customer perceptions of its prices.
4. What could a small retailer learn from Montgomery Ward's and Sears' approach to marketing research?

◄ CASE 2 ►

The Many Uses of Customer Data Bases[†]

By developing and maintaining up-to-date customer data bases (including names and addresses and, if possible, other information such as purchase behavior, family status, and so on) in their marketing information systems, companies can greatly improve the effectiveness of their marketing strategies.

Firms can benefit from customer data bases in several ways. They can be used to improve the quality of marketing research. A large data base could enable a company to survey specifically a product's current users versus former users, and light users versus heavy users (categorized by degree of product usage)—instead of surveying a much broader group of people. With good data bases, companies can target promotions specifically to current users and minimize waste in advertising. This is especially

[†] Michael Finley, "Data-Base Marketing Alters Landscape," *Marketing News* (November 7, 1988), pp. 1, 2.

important in direct mail, where advertisers consider a 2 per cent return rate to be high. Also, tobacco-based companies have developed comprehensive data bases of smokers that they can use to contact consumers of tobacco products in the event that tobacco advertising is totally banned from print media in the future.

In many cases, companies have generated data bases that are quite large. For example, General Foods has a data base of 25-million customers and potential customers; and Ford has a 50-million name list.

These examples indicate how firms are developing and using customer data bases:

▷ American Express updates its data base by tracking credit slips (which indicate a retailer's merchandise grouping and its geographic location, as well as the amount of consumer purchases), analyzing computerized scanner data, and having questionnaires completed by consumers who have accepted premium offers. This allows American Express to target consumers better for future purchases of goods and services. For example, it can focus promotional efforts on such groups as those who make purchases in golf-pro shops, those who spend more than $500 per year in restaurants, and those who travel to Europe more than once a year.

▷ Merrill Lynch, the investment and brokerage firm, uses much of the material required by federal and state governments for tax-reporting purposes to develop data bases of its clients. Because certain information is required by the government, it is easier for Merrill Lynch to stay in contact with its clients than it is for some other companies. In addition to the required tax-reporting information, Merrill Lynch also acquires data on investment attitudes, age, and income; this allows it to plan special promotions targeted at selected groups for individual investment opportunities.

▷ R.J. Reynolds (RJR) uses special promotions to develop its data base. It recently ran a major promotion in which a free T-shirt was offered to all smokers who called an 800 toll-free number. This promotion gave RJR an additional 500,000 names to add to its data base. Through the effective use of promotions such as T-shirts, the RJR data base now contains 30 million names, about three-quarters of all smokers in the United States. This data base can be used not only to reach smokers if tobacco advertising in traditional media is further regulated, but also to entice users of competing brands to switch to RJR brands with special coupon or premium offers. For example, users of a competing brand may be offered a higher-value coupon as an incentive to try an RJR brand than current users of RJR products.

As one marketing expert concludes, "My sense is that the way we think of marketing research today is very different from what our senses of it will be in a few years. We're going to see an integration of internal and external data."

QUESTIONS

1. Discuss the advantages and disadvantages of a company's drawing a sample from its own large data base to conduct a major marketing research study instead of drawing a sample from the general population.
2. Develop a semantic differential for American Express to use in having its Gold Card customers rate the attributes of the Gold Card. Present a research design for gathering this information.
3. How should R.J. Reynolds categorize its 30-million name data base when storing and filing it in its marketing information system?
4. How could a small firm develop, maintain, and use a customer data base?

part 1 CASE

Appliance Control Technology: Anatomy of a Startup*

Introduction

In a business in which success has eluded the likes of Texas Instruments, National Semiconductor, and Motorola, Wallace Leyshon, the founder of two-year-old Appliance Control Technology Inc. (ACT), optimistically expects his company to succeed.

In an old-line industry in which potential customers — companies with familiar brand names such as Whirlpool, Tappan, and General Electric — usually take years to incorporate new product features, Leyshon brashly claims ACT can get its components designed into products within months.

In competition with rivals who do their manufacturing in Singapore and other low-wage locations, Leyshon confidently predicts that he'll beat their product quality, service, *and* prices by using stay-at-home U.S. labor.

Is Leyshon naive? Just hopeful? Or does he know something that the others don't?

ACT, Leyshon's first solo business venture, designs and manufactures microprocessor-based controls for major kitchen and laundry appliances — the electronic buttons and panels you use to make them work. The challenges confronting the company are prodigious. Its customers are the large, conservative U.S. and European corporations that manufacture the appliances, and persuading decision makers at such places to take

* Adapted by the authors from Tom Richman, "Made in the U.S.A.," *Inc.* (January 1989), pp. 47–53. Reprinted by permission. Copyright © Inc. Publishing Company, 38 Commercial Wharf, Boston, MA, 02110.

a little company's claims seriously is a major hurdle for Leyshon and his crew. And the almost revolutionary ambitiousness of those claims does not make clearing that hurdle any easier.

ACT, promises Leyshon, 39, who has education and experience in management and engineering, will be the low-cost producer of electronic controls. Aggressively reducing its price will not only assure his company's entry into the market, he says, it will greatly expand the size of the market by helping to make electronic controls price-competitive with old-style electromechanical knobs and dials. But at the same time that he touts his company's lower prices, Leyshon claims that ACT delivers measurably higher quality than the competition and demonstrably better service. And one other thing: Leyshon says that ACT will make the entire appliance industry more responsive to consumer demand by changing the working relationship between vendors and their appliance-manufacturing customers.

That's an awful lot of challenges for any company — but especially the youngest in the business — to take on all at once.

In 1986, Leyshon was running Motorola's electronic appliance-control business. When Motorola management decided to move the entire manufacturing operation to Taiwan, Leyshon took issue. The move offshore, along with his feeling that Motorola wasn't adequately funding his end of the business, precipitated his departure.

In December 1986, Leyshon incorporated ACT, headquartered in Addison, Ill., a western suburb of

Chicago. In March 1987, the Electrolux division that makes Tappan microwave ovens wrote a $3-million-plus purchase order to become ACT's first customer. In September of that year, ACT produced its first controls on a single, $1-million automated assembly line. Now, more than a year later, the company is operating two lines and contemplating a third.

ACT's Basic Strategies

Leyshon wooed Tappan with promises of lower prices, higher quality, and better service, the same line he uses on other prospective buyers. The issue is whether ACT can deliver.

Leyshon predicated his venture's early survival on its ability to drive the price of electronic controls down, thereby expanding the potential market and quickly building ACT's volume. Major appliance makers produce more than 45 million of the so-called white goods for the U.S. market annually. In 1986, maybe 15 per cent of those appliances incorporated electronic controls. But 60 per cent to 75 per cent of the unit volume in any appliance line, Leyshon's research revealed, is in the mid-price models, which electronics still hadn't penetrated. That's the market he wanted ACT to get into. By 1991, according to his projections, it will be worth some $750 million in the United States alone. There was also the European market, about the same size, to compete in.

To meet his objective, Leyshon elected to use three strategies. The first involved design and engineering; the second, manufacturing. And the third, maybe the riskiest, involved marketing.

Design and Engineering

Before and during Leyshon's management, Motorola's appliance-control group had concentrated on designing products that were proprietary to each of its customers. ACT's design, Leyshon decided, would aim for increased standardization. That doesn't mean that its controls will look alike to consumers who buy, say, different brands of microwave ovens incorporating the ACT product. They won't even look the same from model to model within the same brand. Higher-priced ovens will still have more features — a defrost cycle or a meat-temperature probe, for instance. But in the ACT design scheme, underneath the touch pad, there's the same chassis, same microprocessor, and the same components mounted on the same printed circuit board. The differences lie mainly in the software that's embedded in the microprocessor chip and in the panel face presented to the user. ACT's first product replaced 12 separate controls Tappan had been using on its family of microwave ovens with just 2 standard control models — one for domestic ovens and the other for export. The electronic ACT product was priced at $16.80, about 12 per cent less than the competitor's electronic control it replaced.

Standardizing its products within and even across appliance lines — from clothes washers to dishwashers, say — will reward ACT and its customers with substantial cost benefits. Instead of buying a million each of 10 different electronic components, for instance, ACT can buy 10 million of just one and get the higher volume price from the component maker. That's an important savings, since as much as 70 per cent of the cost of the control is in materials. But nearly as significant in the Leyshon scheme are the savings reaped from lower inventory costs and shorter lead times. ACT and its customers will have fewer different parts to inventory: and inventory demands will be easier to meet.

Manufacturing

If his design strategy breaches industry practice, Leyshon's manufacturing strategy violates all conventional wisdom. It's cheaper to manufacture in the United States, he insists, than to chase low-cost labor overseas. Cheaper in the high-wage United States? Yes, the way Leyshon figures costs.

He says, forget direct labor. It's not an issue. With automatic-insertion machines doing 70 per cent (and eventually more) of the assembly work on ACT's PC boards, direct labor constitutes less than 10 per cent of product cost. Anything the competition saves on direct labor overseas, says ACT engineering vice-president Althoff, they spend on duty, shipping, and airfreight: "It's a wash, we think."

But more important than these considerations, in the eyes of ACT's management, are the operational advantages to having engineering and manufacturing under the same roof. Those advantages, they argue, show up in product quality and service delivery.

Designer Jeff Krasnesky's computerized design system and manufacturing's assembly lines are separated by one wall and a few paces in ACT's headquarters and plant. "I can't tell you," says Leyshon, "how critical it is to have those people able to work closely together." Communications, says Althoff, "is the biggest advantage. Manufacturing can walk into Jeff's office and say, 'Here's a problem.' With Motorola's plant in Taiwan, they can't send their Jeff over every time they have a problem, so the design center may never hear things like 'This doesn't fit,' or 'We're having to insert this by hand.'"

If he has a problem on the line now, says quality vice-president Les Jones, he can take it right to engineering, "and instead of Band-Aiding it, we can fix it." More than a year into production, ACT estimates a field failure rate of 0.25 per cent on its controls, which is, according to Jones, "better than any other manufacturer." More impressive, the *actual* failure rate, Jones claims, is running 0.029 per cent.

Customer service is also easier to deliver from stateside. "In this business," says Bob van Dusen, vice-president of sales and marketing, "the next generation could be tomorrow, and customers want it yesterday. If you go overseas, you're 16 weeks on the boat. If you're on the East Coast and I'm in the Midwest, I'm 14 hours away . . . I've taken a truck to Atlanta in the afternoon and gotten it there for the 7:00 A.M. shift."

Marketing

ACT's domestic manufacturing strategy will lift skeptical eyebrows. But its protocol-defying marketing plan, in contrast, could irritate people who are important to the company's success. It's gutsy because it seeks efficiency at the expense of tradition.

Remember, ACT is not selling its product directly to consumers or even to retailers. It's simply a vendor to appliance manufacturers that may market their own brands or act as original equipment manufacturer (OEM) suppliers to such retailers as Sears, Roebuck & Co.

Traditionally, according to ACT's managers, vendors work from specifications. Sears, for instance, will tell Whirlpool's marketing people that it wants a new washer. The marketing people will generate ideas for product features based on Sears' suggestions, hand their ideas to the engineering department, which writes the specs and gives them to purchasing, which

puts them out to bid. So, maybe 8 or 12 months after Sears decides it wants a new washer, the control maker finally gets a look at what the OEM's marketing people think Sears wants.

Now maybe the vendor can make a control with the features Sears wants and for the price Sears wants to pay, or maybe it can't. And maybe it has a completely wrong-headed notion of what Sears wants, given the number of people the idea has passed through. Or maybe Sears would want something different if it knew what the new technology could do and what its costs were. The point, says Leyshon, is that the current process leads to "wholesale miscommunication" and takes entirely too long.

Instead, for key components, the manufacturer's marketing people and the vendor's marketing people and, if Sears is involved, its marketing people, too, should sit down in the same room at the outset. They could make all their trade-offs then, and everyone would be working with the same data. That, says Leyshon, is how the Japanese and Koreans do it.

And that's how ACT is trying to do it. "My target," says van Dusen, "is the marketing vice-president. He's the one guy you've got to sell. If you sell him, the VP of engineering is going to be predisposed to buy."

"We think it's important to American industry that everybody do this," says Althoff. "In Japan, they can work out design issues in a week. In the United States, it takes a year. The industry has to shorten the cycle."

But Leyshon and van Dusen have to persuade marketing VPs to talk to them, and they've got to assuage purchasing's hurt feelings. Whomever they talk to first, it's still purchasing that signs the purchase orders (POs).

Analyzing the Competition

In Leyshon's analysis of the competition his two-year-old startup will face, Far Eastern companies don't yet play a big role. Japanese and Korean microwave makers do supply controls for ovens manufactured in their own U.S. plants. And a couple of Asian firms have contracts to supply U.S. appliance makers. But except for microwaves, offshore appliance makers have found entry to the U.S. market tough for two reasons. Their own domestic appliances are very different from those sold here, so they can't practice in their home markets on designs that are saleable in the United States. Second, Leyshon's business plan points out, U.S. appliance manufacturers have kept their labor productivity quite high ($115,000 to $130,000 in sales per employee versus the U.S. manufacturing average of $64,000) and their costs low. Consequently, they don't provide the same wide price umbrella for imports that other industries — autos and machine tools, for instance — do.

Nor does Leyshon anticipate much competition from semiconductor makers. Texas Instruments and National Semiconductor tried and failed to capture significant shares of the appliance-control market. They never took the time, in Leyshon's view, to understand the old-line industry they were trying to sell to.

ACT's chief competition comes from two groups of firms: electromechanical-control makers trying to convert their products to the new technology and electronic-equipment makers.

The first group knows the market well, he concedes, but he holds that it is difficult for companies organized around one technology successfully to make their own products obsolete by converting to a new technology.

The second group he takes more seriously. Motorola, which was the market leader when Leyshon left the company two years ago, has fallen behind a relative upstart, Digital Appliance Controls Inc. DAC is headed by its founder, Peter W. Sognefest, the man who originally put Motorola into the appliance-control business in 1977. Sognefest left Motorola in 1984 when he was promoted out of the job he had and wanted to keep. Like Leyshon two years later, he launched his own company. With projected 1989 sales of $25 million, DAC claims it will hold the largest single share of the electronic-control market next year. But unlike ACT, DAC manufactures overseas, sells its products through OEM purchasing departments, and stresses proprietary design and quality over standardization and low pricing.

The total U.S. and European market for appliance controls of both types now runs some $2 billion a year, about equally split between each side of the Atlantic. By 1991, Leyshon projects, electronic controls will account for close to half this market, and ACT, his business plan predicts, will have grabbed about 12 per cent of the domestic market for electronic controls. It will also be competing in the European market, although just how European sales will be handled is still murky.

ACT's Current Status

Estimated sales for 1988 were $7.2 million, less than half the original business-plan projection, but not bad for a firm's first full production year. ACT lost an estimated $900,000 in 1988, down from its $1.2-million loss in 1987 — its first, partial operating year. Projections call for a $1.4-million profit in 1989, when sales, by the company's rosy predictions, will more than double. By 1991, Leyshon projects sales greater than $60 million, more than eight times 1988 revenues.

Besides the microwave controls sold to Tappan, ACT has added Maytag's Magic Chef division to its customer list. And it has development contracts in laundry and dishwasher products for Sears, Frigidaire, and White-Westinghouse.

One thing isn't working as planned. In his business plan, Leyshon said ACT would find eager customers among Japanese microwave-oven makers with U.S. plants in the United States. After all, he reasoned, having a domestic supplier would help satisfy those firms' just-in-time inventory demands. And the appreciated yen was making Asian-made controls expensive to install in U.S.-made products. But the Japanese weren't as eager as Leyshon thought they would be — or should be.

"It's a joke," he says, "I don't think they're the least bit serious about doing business with American companies. . . . The yen has appreciated 50 per cent in two years, and I'm still not doing business with them. The economics don't add up."

QUESTIONS

1. Is ACT a marketing-oriented firm? Explain your answer.
2. State several overall and marketing objectives for ACT to pursue and describe what it should do to achieve them.
3. What are ACT's major differential advantages? Its major differential disadvantages?
4. Evaluate the aspects of ACT's marketing strategy that are discussed in the case.
5. How would you characterize the level of competition ACT faces?
6. Present a long-term organizational mission for ACT.
7. What could ACT learn by studying the product/market opportunity matrix and the Boston Consulting Group matrix?
8. Do you think ACT will succeed in the future? Explain your answer.

part 2
UNDERSTANDING CONSUMERS

In Part 2, we explain why consumer analysis is necessary and discuss consumer profiles, characteristics, needs, and decision making — and how companies can develop marketing programs responsive to consumers.

5 **Consumer Demographics** This chapter is devoted to final consumer demographics, the objective and quantifiable characteristics that describe the population. We examine population size, gender, age, location, housing, mobility, income, expenditures, occupations, education, and marital status.

6 **Consumer Life-Styles and Decision Making** Here, we investigate final consumer life-styles and decision making, useful concepts in explaining why and how consumers act as they do. Life-styles are comprised of various social and psychological factors, which we note here. By studying the decision process, we see how consumers move from stimulus to purchase or nonpurchase.

7 **Organizational Consumers** In this chapter, we focus on the organizational consumers that purchase goods and services for further production, use in operations, or resale to other consumers. We look at their differences from final consumers, individual characteristics, buying objectives, buying structure, constraints on purchases, and decision process.

8 **Developing a Target Market Strategy** At this point, we are ready to examine consumer-demand patterns and segmentation bases; and to explain and contrast undifferentiated marketing (mass marketing), concentrated marketing, and differentiated marketing (multiple segmentation). We also consider the requirements for successful segmentation and the importance of positioning. We conclude with a discussion of sales forecasting.

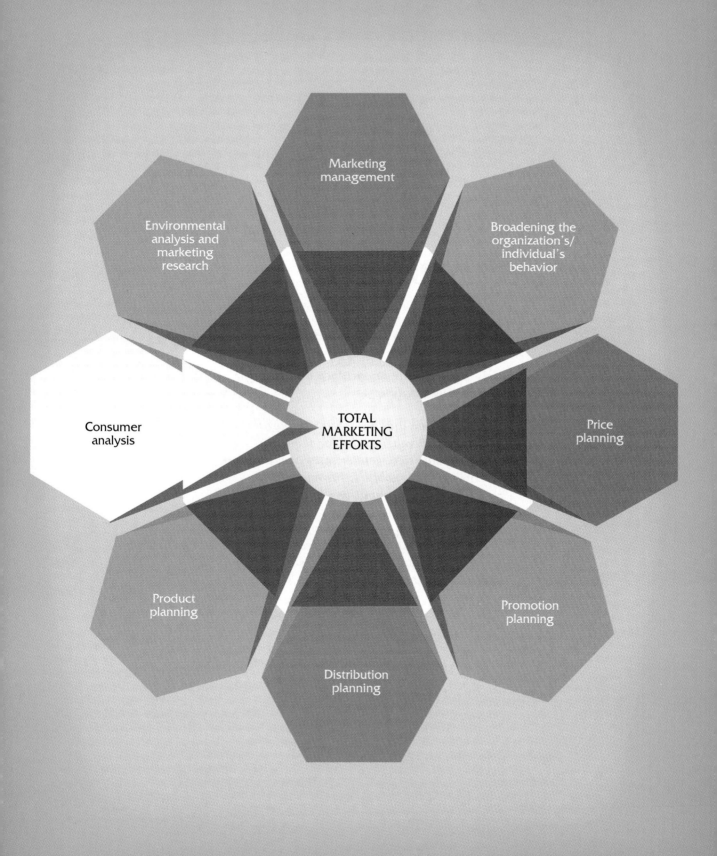

Consumer Demographics

B etween 1971 and 1980, blue jeans maker Levi Strauss & Co. saw earnings vault sevenfold to $224 million on sales of $2.8 billion. Then, just as spectacularly, it all came unbuttoned. Sales dropped so dramatically that the company had to close 22 plants and earnings crumbled to $41 million. A chagrined Chairman Peter Haas conceded: "The demographics have been against us."

The *demographics*? Here was a company with a top product, superior management, a solid balance sheet—everything it should have needed to preserve its success. But Haas had put his finger on the real problem: The company was first a beneficiary and then a victim of major shifts in the U.S. population, in this case the growth—and subsequent shrinkage—in the number of teenagers.

The difficulties faced by Levi Strauss illustrate why it is necessary for firms to understand the demographics of the marketplace (age, employment status, income, education, and so on), and develop appropriate marketing plans. Here, we will look at two key U.S. demographic trends—the aging of the population and the increase in working women—and show marketing approaches that address these trends.

Between now and the year 2000, the average age of the U.S. population is expected to go from 32 years to more than 36 years; and the proportion of the population ages 45 to 64 will go from about 19 per cent to 23 per cent. Also, although only about one-fifth of the U.S. population is currently 55 years of age or older, this age group controls over two-fifths of all consumer discretionary income (money left after paying for necessities such as food and shelter); and the population group over 65 presently controls over three-quarters of all financial assets.

What kinds of marketing responses should we have to the aging of the U.S. population? Here are some real-life examples. Campbell, Beech-Nut, and General Foods are developing specialized food products aimed at the nutritional needs of older persons. Wilson Sporting Goods offers a line of golf clubs with heads that are specifically weighted to compensate for changes in muscle strength that accompany aging.

More than fifty million adult U.S. women now work on either a full-time or part-time basis—up dramatically from prior decades. In a recent nationwide poll, 57 per cent of the women cited themselves as the individual in the household who has the most authority for making decisions about how money is spent or saved.

kay, tell me everything. You liked him and he didn't like you, or he liked you, but you couldn't stand him. Don't tell me. You're speechless because he is incredibly wonderful and you're running off with him to live in total bliss in Tahiti. And now we share one last Coors Light before you ride off into the sunset.

Okay, now I want the real story. What did you order for dinner, and did you bring any home for me?"

Coors Light. Just between friends.

The median yearly expenditures by working women on items such as apparel are far higher than those for nonworking women. And, because more than 50 per cent of married women with children are working, there is a growing interest in child care.

What kinds of marketing responses should we have to the increase in working women? Here are some real-life examples. Auto companies, such as Ford, and beer companies, such as Coors, are devoting more of their advertising efforts to women—in recognition of their greater role in purchases. Barney's, a clothing store that formerly catered to males, has a separate store-within-a-store for women (most of whom buy business attire). Kinder-Care and La Petite Academy offer licensed child-care centers for families with small children.[1]

At this point, we have reviewed just two of the many demographic trends taking place in the United States. In this chapter, we will focus on these and many other consumer demographic trends, and the related marketing implications.

[1] Joshua Mendes, "Profiting from a Changing America," *Fortune 1989 Investor's Guide* (Fall 1988), pp. 45–50; Charles D. Schewe, "Marketing to Our Aging Population: Responding to Physiological Changes," *Journal of Consumer Marketing*, Vol. 5 (Summer 1988), pp. 61–73; and Penny Gill, "Working Women, Where They Shop, How Much They Spend, On What," *Stores* (May 1988), pp. 42–43.

Overview

As noted in Chapters 1 and 2, the central focus of marketing is the consumer. In order to develop successful marketing plans, it is necessary to examine consumer characteristics and needs, life-styles, and purchase processes and structure marketing mix (product, distribution, promotion, and price) decisions accordingly. In this way, an individual company can identify and satisfy its target market(s), minimize consumer dissatisfaction, and remain ahead of competitors.

The scope of consumer analysis includes the study of who buys, what they buy, why they buy, how they buy, when they buy, where they buy, and how often they buy.[2] Table 5-1 shows the scope of consumer analysis for different types of goods and services.

Final consumers buy for personal, family, or household use; organizational consumers buy for production, operations, or resale.

In Chapters 5 through 8, the basic concepts necessary for understanding consumers, selecting target markets, and relating marketing strategy to consumer behavior are detailed. Chapters 5 and 6 examine final consumer demographics, social and psychological characteristics, and decision making. ***Final consumers*** purchase goods and services for personal, family, or household use. Chapter 7 centers on the characteristics and behavior of ***organizational consumers,*** who purchase goods and services for further production, usage in operating the organization, or resale to other consumers. Chapter 8 explains how to develop a target market and generate and use sales forecasts.

TABLE 5-1 Illustrating the Scope of Consumer Analysis

Who	What	Why	How	When	Where	How Often
Middle-aged male	Haircut	Messy hair	Use regular barber	Saturday morning	Regular shop	Every two months
Young female college graduate	Suit	Job interview	Read paper for sale, select conservatively	Next day	Store with low price and fast alterations	Once per year
Husband	Watch	Gift	Browse through a store	In two weeks	Local jeweler	Once
College student	College textbook	Required	Obtain book title from store list	By first class day	College store	Every term
Working woman, with husband	Auto	Transportation	Talk to friends, read ads, test drive, thoroughly evaluate	In two months	Nearby authorized dealer	Every four years
Hospital	Hospital beds	Replacement	See salespeople, set specifications, thoroughly evaluate	In three months	Regular supplier	Every seven years

---

[2] Adapted from Leon G. Schiffman and Leslie Lazar Kanuk, *Consumer Behavior*, Third Edition (Englewood Cliffs, N.J.: Prentice-Hall, 1987), p. 6.

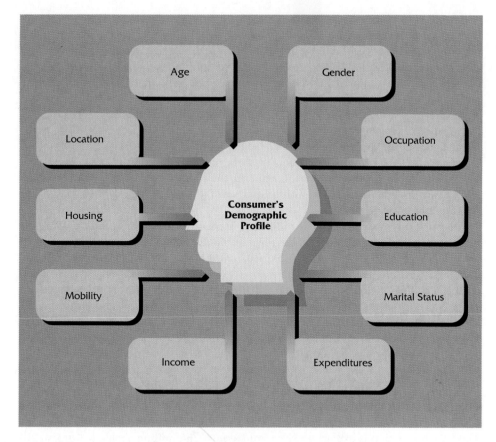

FIGURE 5-1
Factors Determining a Consumer's Demographic Profile

Demographics Defined and Enumerated[3]

Consumer demographics are objective and quantifiable population characteristics. They are easy to identify, group, measure, and analyze. The U.S. demographics discussed in this chapter are population size, gender, and age; location, housing, and mobility; income and expenditures; occupations and education; and marital status. By combining these demographics, a firm can establish consumer profiles that may pinpoint both attractive and declining market opportunities. See Figure 5-1.

For example, the number of U.S. households with annual incomes of $75,000 was expected to far exceed 6 million in 1990. And these households are far different from those with similar incomes in the past. Over half of married households do not have any dependent children; and most are comprised of dual-career married couples. More than two-thirds do not have one single household member earning $75,000 or more. Almost two-thirds of household heads have completed college. About two-thirds of the households live in the suburbs of large urban areas. Nearly 90 per cent own their own homes.[4] These households watch much less television than others, while they regularly read magazines. In terms of their purchases, upscale consumers are interested in convenience, high product quality, and self-improvement.

Consumer demographics are easily identifiable and measurable population characteristics.

---

[3] The data presented in this chapter are all from the U.S. Bureau of the Census, unless otherwise indicated.

[4] "Who the Affluent Are and Where They Live," *Wall Street Journal* (September 7, 1988), p. 29.

Demographic data are available from many secondary sources.

Several secondary sources provide a great amount of information about consumer demographics. The *Census of Population* is a federal government publication that presents a wide range of demographic data. In addition to providing total U.S. and statewide data, it breaks down geographic areas into blocks (about 200 households) and census tracts (about 1,200 households). A number of marketing research firms and state data centers offer the services of computer-based systems that arrange census data by zip code, provide forecasts, and update information. Since census data are gathered only once every 10 years, they can be supplemented by statistics from chambers of commerce, public utilities, and building departments.

American Demographics is a specialized magazine (published by Dow Jones) dealing exclusively with demographic information, the significance of demographic trends, and future projections. Each month a number of in-depth articles on various demographic topics are presented.

The *Survey of Buying Power* is published annually by *Sales & Marketing Management* magazine. It reports current data by metropolitan area and state. Many statistics not available from the *Census*, such as retail sales by merchandise category, personal disposable income, and five-year projections, are included. The *Survey* also measures each metropolitan area's sales potential through a buying power index (BPI) that weights the disposable income, retail sales, and population size of that area.

Other major secondary sources are *Editor & Publisher Market Guide*, *Rand McNally Commercial Atlas & Market Guide*, *Standard Rate & Data Service*, local newspapers, and regional planning boards.

Population Size, Gender, and Age

Population growth is slow, there are many firstborns, there are more women, and average age is rising.

The U.S. population is expected to rise from almost 250 million people in 1990 to 268 million people by the year 2000. As in recent years, the population will increase less than 1 per cent each year.

The annual number of births in the United States peaked at 4.3 million in 1957. During the 1990s, the annual birth rate is forecasted to be about 3.6 to 3.9 million. Unlike earlier decades, a large proportion of these births will be firstborns. Twenty-five per cent of all babies born in the 1960s were firstborns; this figure will exceed 40 per cent throughout the 1990s.

Females comprise about 51.3 per cent of the population, with males accounting for 48.7 per cent. The life expectancy for newborn females is about 78 years; it is about 71 years for newborn males. The median age of the U.S. population is about 32, and predicted to rise to 36.3 by the year 2000. Figure 5-2 shows the changing age distribution in the population from 1990 to 2000.

Marketing Implications

Companies need to focus efforts and appeal to more mature markets.

The large U.S. population offers a substantial market for all types of goods and services. However, the low annual rate of population growth indicates that companies need to focus on specific opportunities, such as firstborns, females, and expanding age segments. There will be heightened battles among firms for market share in current markets.

The rise in firstborns is significant because parents have many initial purchases to complete. They have large startup costs for the first child for items such as furniture,

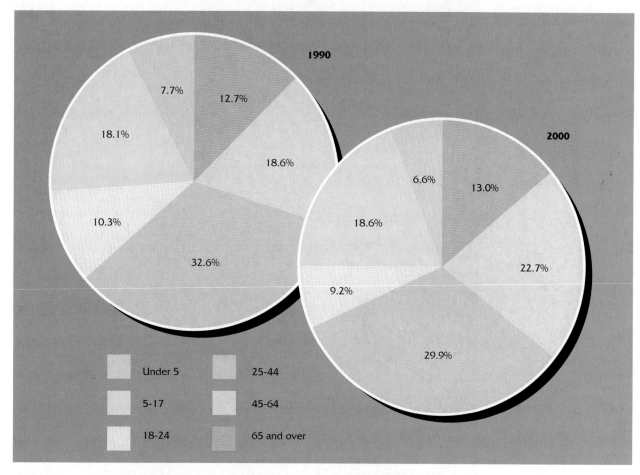

FIGURE 5-2 **The Age Distribution of the U.S. Population, 1990 and 2000**
SOURCE: U.S. Bureau of the Census, *Current Population Reports.* Based on middle series
projections.

clothing, and transportation (stroller, car seat, and so on). On average, parents spend
about $32,000 (including food, housing, health care, child care, and other items) to
raise a firstborn child to his or her fifth birthday, about 30 to 50 per cent more than on
each later child.[5]

There are over 6.5 million more females than males in the total population. This has
important implications for marketers of clothing, household services, appliances, cars,
and other items where there are differences in needs and buying behavior by gender.
Accordingly, more and more companies are gearing their appeals to women, as illustrated in Figure 5-3. Special interest should be paid to female senior citizens, who
substantially outnumber their male counterparts.

The shifting age distribution points up many opportunities. For example, colleges
and universities are increasing their recruitment of older, nontraditional students
because their prime market (18- to 24-year-olds) is declining. Sports and recreation

[5] "America Gives Birth to a 'New Baby Boom'," *Marketing Review* (June 1988), p. 21.

FIGURE 5-3
An Advertisement Oriented Toward Women
Reprinted by permission of the Lomas & Nettleton Financial Corporation.

companies are becoming more oriented toward the 45+ age group. The over-65 age group represents a growing market for food, medical care, utilities, vacation homes, travel, entertainment, and restaurants.

Location, Housing, and Mobility

The U.S. is highly urban, with 75 per cent of people in 16 per cent of land area.

During this century, there has been a major movement of the U.S. population to large urban areas and their surrounding suburbs. Today about 75 per cent of the total U.S. population resides in just 16 per cent of the land area. The Bureau of the Census

132

defines urban locales as Metropolitan Statistical Areas (MSAs), Consolidated Metropolitan Statistical Areas (CMSAs), and Primary Metropolitan Statistical Areas (PMSAs).[6]

A *Metropolitan Statistical Area* (*MSA*) is relatively freestanding and not closely associated with other metropolitan areas. An MSA contains either a city of at least 50,000 population or an urbanized area of 50,000 population (with a total population of at least 100,000). Its population can be over one million. There are 261 MSAs in the United States (excluding Consolidated Metropolitan Statistical Areas), such as Minneapolis-St. Paul, Minnesota-Wisconsin; Haven-Meriden, Connecticut; Spokane, Washington; Montgomery, Alabama; and Fargo, North Dakota.

Urban areas are classed as **Metropolitan Statistical Areas, Consolidated Metropolitan Statistical Areas,** *and* **Primary Metropolitan Statistical Areas.**

A *Consolidated Metropolitan Statistical Area* (*CMSA*) contains two or more overlapping and/or interlocking urban communities, known as Primary Metropolitan Statistical Areas, with a total population of at least one million. CMSAs comprise the twenty largest metropolitan areas in the United States. The biggest CMSA is New York-Northern New Jersey-Long Island, New York-New Jersey-Connecticut with a total population of 18 million and 12 component areas. A *Primary Metropolitan Statistical Area* (*PMSA*) is a large urbanized county or a cluster of counties that have strong economic and social links as well as ties to neighboring communities in its CMSA. Within the 20 CMSAs, there are 71 PMSAs. These are the 12 PMSAs in the New York-New Jersey-Connecticut CMSA: Bergen-Passaic, New Jersey; Bridgeport-Milford, Connecticut; Danbury, Connecticut; Jersey City, New Jersey; Middlesex-Somerset-Hunterdon, New Jersey; Monmouth-Ocean, New Jersey; Nassau-Suffolk, New York; New York City; Newark, New Jersey; Norwalk, Connecticut; Orange County, New York; and Stamford, Connecticut. Norwalk's population is about 128,000, while New York City's is well over 8 million.

The housing characteristics of the U.S. population are owner-oriented. About 60 per cent of American households reside in a home they own. Since 1960, there has been a change in the mix of housing. The proportion of households residing in multiple-unit structures has grown from one-fourth to more than one-third. It is not a paradox for ownership to be high and the percentage of single-unit housing to decline at the same time; this trend is explained by the growth in condominiums and cooperatives (the ownership of a single unit in a multiple-unit dwelling) and the increase in smaller households.

Most Americans live in their own homes.

The mobility of the U.S. population is quite high; about 15 to 20 per cent of all people move each year. To properly understand mobility, its different forms should be noted: local, statewide, regional, and foreign. For example, over 60 per cent of all residence changes are within the same county, over 80 per cent within the same state, and about 90 per cent within the same region. Less than 10 per cent of residence changes involve moves to a new region or abroad.

15 to 20 per cent of the population changes residences each year.

The mobility of the U.S. population varies by geographic region. Some regions are gaining in size, whereas others are declining. For the period from 1990 to 2000, the greatest growth will take place in the Mountain, Pacific, South Atlantic, and Southwest regions. Relative declines will occur in the Central Northeast, Central Southeast, Middle Atlantic, and Northern Midwest regions, as these areas account for lower percentages of total U.S. population (even though their actual populations will be rising).

---

[6] See James C. Douthit, "Whatever Happened to the SMSA System?" *Marketing News* (January 4, 1988), p. 48.

Marketing Implications

Urban areas are concentrated, with opportunities for home-related products, well-known brands, and growing regions.

The density of the U.S. population makes marketing programs more cost efficient and available to larger groups of consumers. Opportunities for mass distribution and advertising are plentiful. Suburban shopping is growing, leading to branch outlets in suburbs and improved transportation and delivery services.

The continuing interest in home ownership offers sales potential for furniture, appliances, carpeting, and so on. Specially modified products for apartment owners, such as space-efficient washers and dryers, are growing in importance. Because home purchases are affected by the economy, marketers need to monitor economic conditions carefully.

Population mobility provides opportunities for highly advertised national or regional brands, retail chains and franchises, and major credit cards. Their names are well known when consumers relocate and represent an assurance of quality. For example, Old Style, a Midwestern beer, is successful in Arizona because many Midwesterners spend the winter there. Macy's department stores prosper in Florida because a number of Northeasterners who were loyal customers have relocated there; yet, Macy's could not build a satisfactory customer following for its Missouri and Kansas stores and sold them off. MasterCard and Visa credit cards are accepted and popular throughout the United States.

As a result of the geographic growth of certain areas and the decline of others, marketing emphasis has shifted. The marketing efforts directed at consumers in states such as California, Texas, Florida, and Georgia have risen dramatically. Nevertheless, firms should be aware of the extensive competition in these states and the possibility of oversaturation. Regions that are being abandoned by some firms, such as the Central Northeast, should be reappraised by comparing population trends with the level of competition.

Income and Expenditures

1987 annual family income was almost $31,000, with many families earning $37,000 or more.

In 1987, median (average) annual family income was $30,853, up 4.7 per cent from 1986; and over 40 per cent of U.S. families had incomes of $37,000 or more. By comparison, during 1960, average family income was $21,587 (expressed in 1987 dollars) and less than one-fifth earned $37,000 or more. Most of this rise occurred in the 1960s and early 1970s. Between 1980 and 1982, real income actually declined — before increasing again after 1982. Figure 5-4 shows how actual and real (adjusted for inflation) income changed from 1960 to 1987.

The slowdown in real income growth occurred because percentage price increases (the rate of inflation) were high relative to income increases. This resulted in a higher cost of living, the total amount consumers annually pay for their goods and services. Over the past twenty years, the greatest price increases have been for medical care and housing; and the smallest increases have been for apparel and upkeep, and entertainment. Table 5-2 shows the prices for selected items in 1968, 1978, and 1988. Note how the change in family income compares with the price increases for each item over that period.

*The **Consumer Price Index** measures the cost of living.*

The federal government monitors the cost of living through the ***Consumer Price Index*** (***CPI***), which measures monthly and yearly price changes for a broad range of consumer goods and services, expressed in terms of a base period. At present, the base

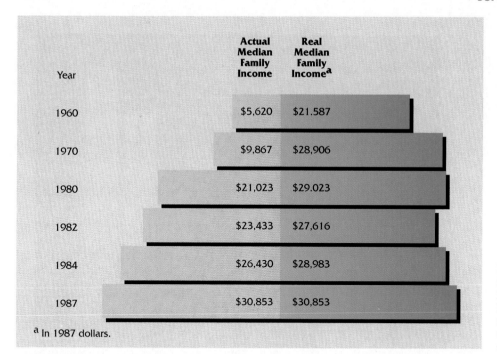

Year	Actual Median Family Income	Real Median Family Income[a]
1960	$5,620	$21.587
1970	$9,867	$28,906
1980	$21,023	$29.023
1982	$23,433	$27,616
1984	$26,430	$28,983
1987	$30,853	$30,853

[a] In 1987 dollars.

FIGURE 5-4
Median Annual Family Income of the U.S. Population, 1960–1987
SOURCE: U.S. Bureau of the Census, *Current Population Reports.*

TABLE 5-2   Typical Prices of Selected Goods and Services, 1968–88

Item	1968 Price	1978 Price	1988 Price	Per Cent Increase 1968-88
Barbie doll	$ 6.00	$ 8.00	$ 15.00	150
Best-selling novel (hardcover)	9.50	12.95	19.95	110
Broadway show orchestra ticket	15.00	25.00	50.00	233
Brooks Brothers cotton oxford shirt	9.50	20.00	42.00	342
Chanel No. 5 perfume (one oz.)	25.00	55.00	175.00	600
Huffy boy's bike (least expensive 20" model)	49.00	59.00	69.00	41
Lionel train set (six pieces)	35.00	55.00	100.00	186
Record album	4.50	7.50	8.50	89
Rolex men's watch (18-carat gold)	1,200.00	4,300.00	11,700.00	875
U.S. postage (mailing a one-oz. card or letter)	.06	.15	.25	317
Median family income (in actual dollars)[a]				235

[a] 1988 median family income estimated by the authors.

Source: Adapted by the authors from Teresa L. Petramala, "The Jingle of Holiday Spending," *New York Times* (December 25, 1988), Section 3, p. 4.

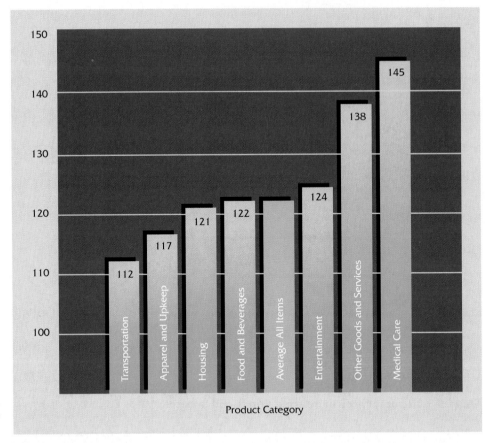

period is 1982–1984; and the price index for all items and individual items sold in 1982–1984 is 100. Changes are measured against this base. For example, if a family's typical monthly food costs were $300 in 1982–1984 and $366 in 1989, the 1989 CPI for food would be 122 [100 × ($366/$300)] — representing a 22 per cent rise in food prices from 1982–1984 to 1989. Since 1983, real family income has gone up slightly because the overall rise in the CPI has been kept to less than 6 per cent annually. Figure 5-5 shows the CPI for various goods and service categories as of 1989.

Over the past several years, U.S. consumption patterns have changed greatly. The percentage of their income that consumers spend on food, beverages, and tobacco, and on clothing, accessories, and jewelry has been declining. The percentage spent on housing, medical care, personal business, recreation, and, transportation has been increasing. From 1982 to 1988, total annual U.S. personal consumption expenditures rose from $2 trillion to well over $3 trillion. Today, both ***disposable income*** (after-tax income to be used for spending and/or savings) and ***discretionary income*** (earnings remaining for luxuries, such as a vacation or dining out, after necessities such as food, clothing, and shelter are bought) are rising as the result of increases in real family income.

*Consumption patterns reflect **disposable income** and **discretionary income**.*

Despite these overall favorable U.S. income trends, there has been a widening gap between the poorest and the richest people.[7] For example, in 1978, the bottom 20 per

---

[7] See Charles G. Burck, "Toward Two Societies?" *Fortune* (October 10, 1988), pp. 48–49.

cent of the U.S. population received 5.2 per cent of all income and the top 20 per cent of the population received 41.5 per cent. In 1988, the bottom fifth received 4.5 per cent of all income, while the top fifth received almost 44 per cent. And, as of 1988, about 13.5 per cent of the U.S. population was living on incomes considered to be at the level of poverty, up from 11.4 per cent in 1978.

By 1995, overall median real U.S. family income (in 1987 dollars) should be between $33,000 and $35,000. Yet, while real income is projected to rise throughout much of the 1990–2000 period, the growth rate will not approach that of the 1960s and early 1970s.

Marketing Implications

Two significant marketing implications can be drawn from the data on consumer income. First, many lower- and middle-income consumers are finding it difficult to keep pace with today's higher cost of living. For these people, increased earnings have

Trends have led to fewer purchases by some lower- and middle-income consumers; upper-income consumers are a prime market.

Marketing Controversy

Are We Better Off Today Than in 1980?

After the dramatic—and sometimes turbulent— changes in the U.S. economy during the 1980s, a demographic question frequently asked by consumers, business executives, and government officials alike is "Are we better off today than in 1980?" Although some Americans are clearly better off and some are clearly worse off, from an overall perspective, this question is a difficult one to answer.

Those who believe we are better off today than in 1980 cite data such as these:

▶ *America's misery index (the sum of the inflation rate and the unemployment rate) dropped from 17.9 per cent in January 1981 to 9.7 per cent in late 1988.*

▶ *Real per-capita personal income rose $1,500 from 1981 to 1988—to the highest level ever.*

▶ *Real family income has increased.*

▶ *Worker fringe benefits, such as health insurance and pension contributions (not counted*

as part of the hourly wage rate) are up 42 per cent since 1980.

Those who believe that we are not better off today than in 1980 cite data such as these:

▶ *The rise in family income is largely due to the increase in working women. For families where only one member works, real income has not gone up.*

▶ *For those ages 25 to 34, real median income dropped 5 per cent from 1981 to 1988; for the same period, real median income fell 12 per cent for 20- to 24-year-olds.*

▶ *From 1981 to 1988, the average hourly wage rate dropped 2.6 per cent, after taking inflation into account.*

▶ *Almost one million blue-collar factory jobs have disappeared since 1981.*

What do you think?

SOURCE: Louis S. Richman, "Are You Better Off Than in 1980?" Fortune (October 10, 1988), pp. 38–44; and Alan Murray, "Many Americans Fear U.S. Living Standards Have Stopped Rising," Wall Street Journal (May 1, 1989), pp. A1, A10.

been offset by rising prices; or, in many cases, earnings have not kept up with inflation. In great numbers, these consumers are holding on to durable products, such as automobiles and clothing, for longer periods; and it is hard for them to purchase a home. For example, in 1987, only 39 per cent of those under 35 years old with incomes under $30,000 were homeowners, down from 57 per cent in 1977. And the typical under-35-year-old had accumulated average outstanding debts of several thousand dollars (about 15 per cent of their income).[8] Appropriate marketing responses to the tight financial situation faced by many U.S. consumers include offering more basic models of products, developing less-expensive brands, providing flexible financing, selling do-it-yourself products, and building smaller homes on smaller lots.

Second, affluent consumers represent, on the other hand, a lucrative and expanding market. One-fifth of U.S. families have an annual income of at least $53,000; and there are well over 1.3 million millionaires. As one observer noted, "The class market is becoming the mass market." This means substantial possibilities for luxury autos, vacation homes, restaurants, and other items. For example, 63 per cent of U.S. families own two or more cars, 33 per cent have two or more stereos, 13 per cent own more than one home, and 38 per cent take two or more vacations each year.[9]

Occupations and Education

The trend toward white-collar and service occupations is continuing.

The labor force in the United States is continuing its steady movement toward white-collar and service occupations and away from blue-collar and farm occupations. Currently the total employed civilian labor force is over 115 million people. From 1960 to now, the percentage of those employed in professional, technical, and clerical white-collar jobs has risen substantially. The percentage of managers, administrators, and sales workers has remained relatively constant. Over the same period, the percentage of people employed as operatives (nonskilled workers) and nonfarm laborers has dropped substantially, while craft and kindred workers have been fairly constant. Only 3.5 million people have a farm-related occupation.

Women represent a large and growing percentage of the U.S. labor force.

Another important change in the U.S. labor force has been the increase in the number and percentage of working women. In 1960, 23 million women comprised 32 per cent of the total labor force. Today over 50 million women account for 45 per cent of the total labor force, and 54 per cent of all adult women are working. The growth in the number and percentage of married women in the labor force has been substantial. In 1960, 12 million married women (31 per cent of all married women) were employed. Today over 28 million married women (56 per cent of all married women) are in the labor force. The per cent of married women with children under 6 in the labor force has jumped from 19 per cent in 1960 to 53 per cent currently.

During 1981 and 1982, the U.S. labor force suffered the highest unemployment rates since the depression of 1932. At the end of 1982, the unemployment rate reached about 11 per cent, meaning that around one in nine people were out of work.

---

[8] National Association of Realtors, 1988.

[9] "Bruskin Draws Profile of the Multiple American," *Marketing Review* (November-December 1985), p. 29; R. H. Bruskin Associates, "Two Cars in Every . . . ," *Wall Street Journal* (March 26, 1986), p. 33; Sylvia Nasar, "Do We Live as Well as We Used To?" *Fortune* (September 14, 1987), pp. 32–46; and Thomas J. Stanley, "How to Sell to a Millionaire," *Sales & Marketing Management* (August 1988), pp. 62–66.

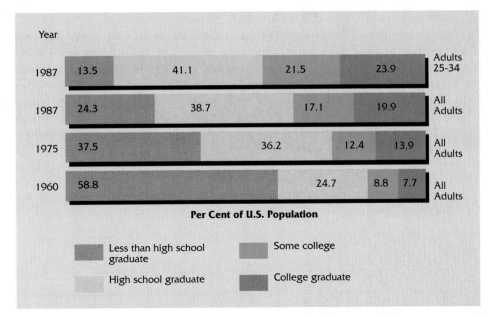

FIGURE 5-6
The Distribution of the U.S. Population by Educational Level, 1960–1987 (for persons 25 years old and over)
SOURCE: U.S. Bureau of the Census, *Census of Population* and *Current Population Reports.*

Some of the unemployment was temporary, due to domestic and worldwide economic conditions. But in other industries, such as automobile and steel, many job losses were permanent. Overall, this meant severe cutbacks in discretionary purchases until the unemployment rate was reduced. As of the end of 1988, the unemployment rate was under 5.5 per cent of the total available civilian labor force, about 6.6 million people.

The educational attainment of Americans has sustained its upward trend. As of 1960, 58.8 per cent of all adults 25 years old and older had not graduated from high school. This figure had dropped to 24.4 per cent in 1987. As of 1960, only 7.7 per cent of all adults 25 years old and older had graduated from college. This rose to 19.9 per cent in 1987. Of those adults aged 25 to 34 in 1987, 86.5 per cent had graduated high school and 23.9 per cent were college graduates. See Figure 5-6.

One-fifth of U.S. adults have graduated college; the figure is higher for young adults.

The sharp increase in working wives and increased educational attainment have contributed to the growing number of people in the upper-income brackets; the relatively high unemployment rate in some industries and a slow-growth economy have caused other families to have low incomes.

Marketing Implications

The occupations and education of the population have these marketing implications. A greater number and percentage of the total population are in the labor force than ever before. This large work force requires transportation, clothing, restaurants, and personal services. Stores have opportunities in major commercial centers. The market for job-oriented goods and services is growing and the shift in occupations means different needs and aspirations in consumer purchases.

Marketing opportunities exist for job-related and time-saving products, and longer store hours.

Working women have less time to spend in shopping and operating the home. They are often unable to shop during regular retail hours and require longer store hours and mail-order purchases. Such time-saving appliances as microwave ovens and food processors, prepared foods, prewrapped goods, and special services are also appealing to more working women. This convenience orientation is summed up by a Bloomingdale's clothing executive: "Women want quality, but they want to be able to dress quickly and look good without too much effort. These days, 30 seconds in the closet and 20 seconds in front of the mirror are enough."[10] Also, for working women, child-related services, such as daytime child care, are particularly important. Yet, only 5 per cent of U.S. companies help their employees in this area, leaving a prime opportunity for specialized firms to market these services.[11]

As the education level of the general population rises, marketers need to respond in terms of better information, better goods and services, enhanced safety and environmental controls, greater accuracy in generating and meeting consumer expectations, and improved consumer-complaint departments.

Marital Status

The percentage of married adults has been rather steady, with the age at first marriage rising.

Despite some publicity to the contrary, the data indicate that marriage and family remain important in the United States. Almost 2.5 million couples get married each year. Currently, about two-thirds of the population 18 and older (down slightly since 1960) are married. In 1960, the median age at first marriage was 23 years for males and 20 years for females. Today these figures are about 26 and 23, respectively. Therefore, in recent years, adults have been waiting somewhat longer to be married and to have children. As a result, the size of the average family has declined, from 3.7 members in 1960 to 3.2 now.

*A **family** has related persons residing together. A **household** has one or more persons who may not be related.*

A **family** is defined as a group of two or more persons residing together who are related by blood, marriage, or adoption. A **household** is defined as a person or group of persons occupying a housing unit, whether related or unrelated. In recent decades, there have been two important changes in family and marital status. First, the number of single-person households rose from 7.1 million in 1960 to 22.1 million in 1988. Almost one-quarter of all American households are now comprised of one-person units. Singles account for roughly 15 per cent of total consumer spending for goods and services. Figure 5-7 compares families and households.

Second, the size of the average household dropped from 3.3 in 1960 to 2.7 in 1988, as a result of later marriages, the greater number of widows and widowers, a high divorce rate, and many couples deciding to have fewer children. For example, from 1960 to 1988, the number of divorces jumped from 400,000 to 1.2 million annually (however, this number has remained stable since 1980).

Marketing Implications

Marital, family, and household trends offer diverse marketing opportunities.

Marriage and family are vital institutions in the United States, in spite of the high divorce level. The marketing implications of marital and family status include the following. There are opportunities for industries associated with weddings (such as

[10] Judith Graham, "Bloomingdale's Labors to Lure Working Women," *Advertising Age* (August 29, 1988), p. 58.
[11] "As the Pool of Young Workers Shrinks, Women Will Fill the Gap, and More Working Mothers Will Increase the Demand for Child Care," *Business Week* (September 19, 1988), pp. 112–113.

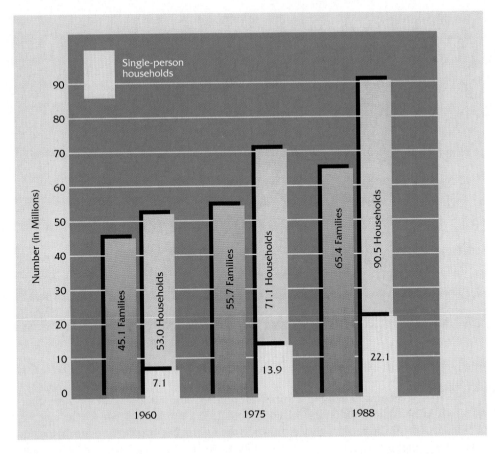

Number (in Millions)

Single-person households

45.1 Families | 53.0 Households | 7.1

55.7 Families | 71.1 Households | 13.9

65.4 Families | 90.5 Households | 22.1

1960   1975   1988

FIGURE 5-7
Families Versus Households, 1960–1988
SOURCE: U.S. Bureau of the Census, *Current Population Reports.*

caterers and travel agents), family life (such as financial services and full-sized automobiles), and divorce (such as attorneys).

Because marriage is occurring later in an individual's life, people have better financial resources and two-income families are prevalent. This presents opportunities for organizations involved with clothing, furniture, entertainment, and recreation.

The growth of single-person households provides opportunities for home and home furnishings industries and manufacturers who produce specialized products. These implications also apply to divorced and widowed persons. For example, as noted earlier in the chapter, smaller households have created a demand for smaller homes. In the 1960s, homes frequently occupied 2,000 square feet of living space; now townhouse units containing as little as 900 square feet are commonplace. Black & Decker, among other companies, has reacted to this trend by producing space-saving coffee makers, electric can openers, food processors, and so on. See Figure 5-8.

Uses of Demographic Data

After examining each of the demographics separately, a marketer would develop a ***consumer demographic profile*** that is a composite description of a consumer group based upon the most important demographics. Figure 5-9 recaps the demographic

*A **consumer demographic profile** combines individual demographic factors.*

141

FIGURE 5-8
Black & Decker Space-Saver Appliances
Reprinted by permission.

characteristics of U.S. consumers. In this section, several examples of demographic profiles are presented.

Figure 5-10 shows demographic profiles for 1985 and 2000, based on three characteristics: household units, age of household head, and annual household income. For each of the three age categories shown in the figure, the number of households and average annual income are expected to rise. However, the percentage of households headed by persons under 35 years old will fall from 29 to 22 per cent of all households. In contrast, the percentage of households headed by 35- to 49-year-olds will rise dramatically (from 28 to 34 per cent). In both 1985 and 2000, the average annual income of households headed by persons under 35 or by persons 50 and over will be much lower than households headed by persons 35 to 49. As a result, in the year 2000, the 35 to 49 age group will account for the greatest share of total household income, with the 50 and over group a close second.[12]

The increase in working women has greatly expanded the number of "two-earner" families. Today three-fifths of all married couples have each spouse working at least part-time; and two-earner families (with at least one spouse employed full-time) have annual incomes that are far greater than single-earner families. For these families, unemployment often has less impact because one of the earners is usually able to maintain his or her position during weak economic times. In comparison to single-earner families, two-earner families spend substantially more on transportation, child care, dry cleaning, clothing, home furnishings, convenience foods, and personal appliances.[13]

---

[12] *Baby Boomers in Midpassage* (New York: Conference Board, 1987).
[13] See Penny Gill, "The 'We' Decade: Marriage Is Back in Fashion; What It Means," *Stores* (May 1988), pp. 50–51.

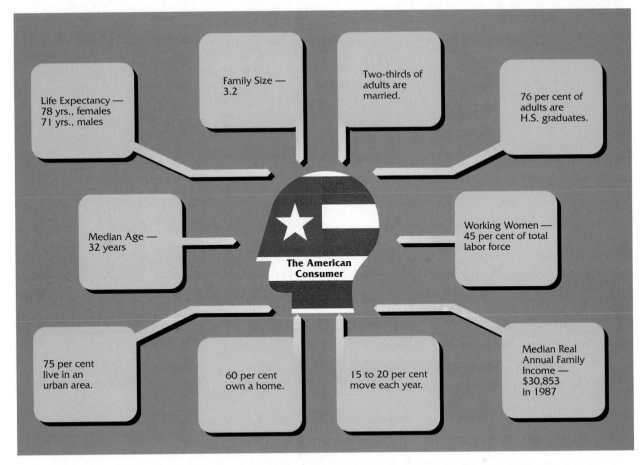

FIGURE 5-9
A Demographic Profile of the U.S. Consumer

Newspapers and magazines frequently collect and update demographic data about readers in order to attract advertising clients and set rates. For instance, *New Choices* (a national magazine for mature adults) recently described its audience in these terms. There are almost 1.5 million readers monthly. The readers' median age is 62. Average household income is $35,700, with about 2.1 people per household. Forty-six per cent of readers have attended or graduated college. Ninety-one per cent own their own home, over one-half with no outstanding mortgage. Ninety per cent have taken a domestic trip in the last year; 41 per cent have taken a foreign trip in the last three years. Ninety-seven per cent own at least one car.[14]

The average move-up house buyer (someone trading up to a bigger and more expensive home) is 38 years old, has an annual household income of $47,400, pays $110,000 for the house, makes a down payment equal to one-third of the purchase price, and makes monthly payments equal to 28 per cent of after-tax earnings.[15]

[14] "50 Plus Delivers the First-Class Segment of the Fastest-Growing Market," *Advertising Age* (March 30, 1988), p. 77.
[15] William Celis, III, "Emphasis in Housing Market Shifts Toward Costlier Trade-Up Homes," *Wall Street Journal* (March 10, 1986), p. 19.

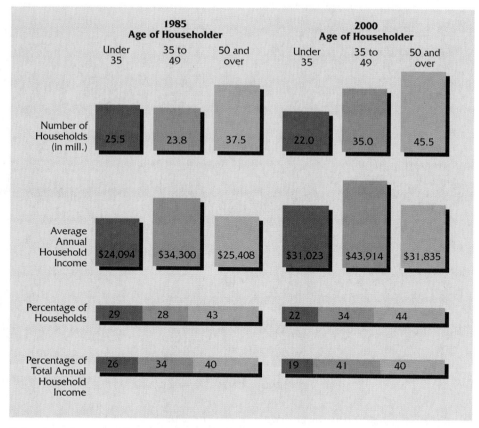

FIGURE 5-10
Household Units, Age of Householder, and Household Income, 1985 and 2000
SOURCE: Adapted by the authors from *Baby Boomers in Midpassage* (New York: Conference Board, 1987).

Limitations of Demographics

Demographic data may be dated, too general, require profile analysis, and not consider reasons for behavior.

When using demographic data, these limitations should be noted. One, demographic information may be dated. The national census is conducted only once every 10 years. And both decennial census data and regular statistical updates (provided by the Bureau of the Census, the Bureau of Labor Statistics, and others) normally have time lags — for example, 1990 census data will not be widely available until at least mid-1992. Two, summary data and trends may be too broad and hide opportunities and risks in small markets or specialized product categories.[16]

Three, single demographic statistics are often not very useful. A consumer demographic profile is needed. Four, demographic data do not consider the psychological or the social factors influencing consumers. They do not explain the decision process consumers utilize when making purchases. Most importantly, demographics do not delve into the reasons why consumers make particular decisions; demographics are descriptive in nature. For example, why do people with similar demographic profiles buy different products or brands? As one leading demographer noted, "We have a very elegant statistical apparatus, but we really don't have good ways of spotting changes in life-styles or tastes."[17] For these reasons, Chapter 6 examines the psychological and social factors affecting consumer behavior and the decision process consumers use.

[16] See William P. O'Hare, "How to Evaluate Population Estimates," *American Demographics* (January 1988), pp. 50, 52.

[17] Alan L. Otten, "Why Demographers Are Wrong Almost as Often as Economists," *Wall Street Journal* (January 29, 1985), p. 35.

You're the Marketer

How Do You Raise the Rate of Savings in the United States?

The average personal savings rate in the United States, about 3.7 per cent of disposable income in 1988, is the lowest of any major industrial nation in the world; and it is at the lowest level since the 1940s. Between 1980 and 1987, the total value of U.S. savings by individuals declined from $137 billion to $120 billion in actual dollars—if measured in deflated dollars, the decline would be even greater!

Many observers are concerned about the low savings rate because these funds provide the capital for business investments, reduce the need to borrow from foreign investors, and provide funds for the one-third of the population not having pensions.

The low savings rate is due to the high level of consumer interest in acquiring more goods and services, the increased prices of goods and services, interest rates on savings accounts not being attractive enough, and easy access to consumer credit (which means that fewer consumers save for a "rainy day").

There are a number of proposals to increase the savings rate, including these:

▶ *Allowing lower- and middle-income households to earn up to $1,000 of interest tax-free.*

▶ *Offering tax-deferred pension plans, which encourage consumers to reduce spending.*

▶ *Developing a consumption tax such as a national sales tax to reduce purchases.*

▶ *Limiting access to consumer credit by increasing the down-payment requirements for major purchases.*

▶ *Paying part of a worker's salary as a semi-annual bonus. In Japan, workers save a higher portion of their bonuses than of their regular wages.*

▶ *Developing a marketing campaign to show the American public the importance of savings to the individual and the overall economy.*

As a marketing consultant to the U.S. banking industry, what would you recommend?

SOURCE: Based on material in David Sylvester, "Is the Saving Rate Really That Bad?" *Fortune* (November 7, 1988), pp. 138–142.

Summary

1. *To show the importance and scope of consumer analysis* By analyzing consumers, a firm is able to determine the most appropriate audience to which to appeal and the combination of marketing factors that will satisfy this audience. The scope of consumer analysis includes who, what, why, how, when, where, and how often. This chapter examines consumer demographics. Chapters 6 to 8 focus on social and psychological factors affecting behavior, the consumer's decision process, organizational consumers, the development of a target market, and sales forecasting.

2. *To define and enumerate important consumer demographics for the U.S. population* Consumer demographics are objective and quantifiable population statistics. They include population size, gender, and age; population location, housing, and mobility; population income and expenditures; population occupations and education; and population marital status.

3. *To examine trends and projections of important demographics and study their marketing implications* The U.S. population now numbers almost 250 million people, increasing less than 1 per cent

each year. A large proportion of births is contributed by firstborns. There are slightly more women (who live longer) than men; both have life expectancies into the seventies.

The Bureau of the Census defines the urban areas that contain 75 per cent of the U.S. population as Metropolitan Statistical Areas (MSAs), Consolidated Metropolitan Statistical Areas (CMSAs), and Primary Metropolitan Statistical Areas (PMSAs). About three-fifths of the population reside in homes they own, with the number occupying multiple-unit dwellings going up. About 15 to 20 per cent of the population moves every year. Major growth is occurring in the Mountain, Pacific, South Atlantic, and Southwest regions.

Average annual real family income was almost $31,000 in 1987, up slightly since 1970. Over 40 per cent of families have incomes of $37,000 and higher. The rate of inflation and cost of living are measured through the Consumer Price Index (CPI). Total annual consumption exceeds $3 billion and can be categorized in terms of disposable income and discretionary income expenditures. There has been a widening gap between the poorest and the richest people.

The total employed U.S. labor force of over 115 million people continues its movement toward white-collar and service occupations. Women comprise a significant and rising portion of the labor force. In 1981 and 1982, U.S. unemployment reached 11 per cent before declining to less than 5.5 per cent by the end of 1988. Educational attainment has been improving, with a greater percentage of Americans graduating high school and attending college than ever before.

About two-thirds of adults 18 and older are married, while men and women are waiting until they are older for marriage. A family consists of relatives residing together. A household consists of a person or persons occupying a housing unit, related or not. Family and household size have declined, as single-person households have grown rapidly.

For each of these demographics, marketing implications are discussed in the chapter.

4. *To present examples of consumer demographic profiles* After examining each demographic separately, a marketer would develop a consumer demographic profile that is a composite description of a consumer group based upon the most important demographics. Several examples of such profiles are provided.

5. *To consider the limitations of consumer demographics* These limitations of demographics are noted: data may be obsolete; there may be hidden trends or implications; single demographic statistics are often not useful; and demographics do not explain the factors affecting behavior, consumer decision making, and motivation.

Key Terms

final consumers (p. 128)
organizational consumers (p. 128)
consumer demographics (p. 129)
Metropolitan Statistical Area
  (MSA) (p. 133)

Consolidated Metropolitan Statistical
  Area (CMSA) (p. 133)
Primary Metropolitan Statistical
  Area (PMSA) (p. 133)
Consumer Price Index (CPI) (p. 134)

disposable income (p. 136)
discretionary income (p. 136)
family (p. 140)
household (p. 140)
consumer demographic profile (p. 141)

Review Questions

1. How does the use of consumer demographics aid marketing decision making?
2. Compare final and organizational consumers.
3. What is the U.S. trend with regard to the birth of firstborns? Why is this meaningful to marketers?
4. How does a Metropolitan Statistical Area differ from a Primary Metropolitan Statistical Area?
5. Between 1960 and 1987, the actual median annual U.S. family income increased by almost 450 per cent, while real median annual U.S. family income rose by 43 per cent. Comment on this. What are the marketing implications?

6. Distinguish between disposable income and discretionary income. During inflationary times, what happens to each?
7. In addition to the examples cited in the text, what goods and services should grow as the number of working women and working mothers increases?
8. What is a household? Are U.S. households getting larger or smaller? Why?
9. What is the value of a consumer demographic profile?
10. Describe the major limitations of demographics.

Discussion Questions

1. Describe at least three ways Burger King could gather data to develop a demographic profile of its customers.

2. Develop a demographic profile of the people residing in your census tract, using the *Census of Population*. What are the marketing implications of this profile?

3. The biggest CMSA in the United States is New York-Northern New Jersey-Long Island, New York-New Jersey-Connecticut with 18 million people and 12 PMSAs. What are the pros and cons of marketing products there?

Recommend a marketing approach for a small dairy.

4. As the marketing vice-president for a lawn tool manufacturer, present a marketing plan that is based on the assumption that real income growth will be negative over the next five years.

5. As the owner of a prospective daytime child-care firm, what demographic factors would you study? Describe the demographic profile of your ideal consumer.

◀ CASE 1 ▶

How Gerber Uses Demographics in Marketing Planning*

Gerber has a market share amounting to about 70 per cent of the U.S. baby-food market. Its baby-food products range from Gerber First Foods for infants to Gerber Chunky Foods for toddlers. Despite its huge success with baby foods, Gerber is concerned about and is planning for the future—because this market is growing at only about two per cent per year.

In studying U.S. demographic trends, Gerber realizes that current birth rates (which are already lower than in the 1950s and 1960s) will plateau between 1990–1991 and then drop off in 1992. Because baby food comprises the bulk of Gerber's sales and profits, Gerber is especially sensitive to changes in this market. Under any circumstances, this is a tough business to master because of the turnover of customers (as babies get older). As one Gerber marketing executive notes, "we lose 10,000 customers each day because they outgrow our product. But just as we lose those 10,000, we've got another 10,000 coming into the market every day."

Gerber knows that it cannot survive on baby-food sales alone. The firm is intensifying its efforts in two distinct areas as a means of stimulating growth in

sales and profits: the marketing of general merchandise aimed at children and the development of a broad line of packaged foods targeted at a variety of age groups.

Gerber's line of general-merchandise products includes such well-known brands as Curity band-aids and Buster Brown shoes. It plans to introduce over fifty new items, such as feeding accessories and children's wear. Part of Gerber's marketing challenge in the general-merchandise business is for it to convince retailers that the space currently being used for competitive baby-food brands can be used more profitably for Gerber general merchandise (which would sit next to Gerber baby foods on store shelves).

The company also plans to market a varied line of packaged foods aimed at a broad grouping of ages. Gerber hopes to generate $200 million in annual sales for its new nonbaby foods business by 1994. Currently, Gerber estimates that about 10 per cent of its baby food, especially its desserts, is consumed by people other than babies. According to the firm's chairman, "there's still a lot of potential to grow in baby food. However, we really are a food-processing company. Our plant is not a baby-food plant but a food-processing plant in which we have chosen to process baby food." Gerber's strategy of appealing to a broader demographic group may benefit from the firm's image as a high-quality, nutritious marketer of foods. In the short run, it plans to limit its new product line to adult foods that are considered

* The data in this case are drawn from Richard Gibson, "Chief Wants Gerber to Grow Beyond Babies," *Wall Street Journal* (January 19, 1989), p. B12; "Gerber to Grow into Adult Market," *Advertising Age* (August 8, 1988), p. 12; and Wendy Zellner, "Gerber's New Chief Doesn't Take Baby Steps," *Business Week* (November 7, 1988), pp. 130, 132.

healthy. It is test marketing Fruit Classics, a single-serving fruit snack, and is studying whether to market fruit-based juices.

In attempting to generate a large adult-foods business, Gerber must overcome a number of hurdles. First, the firm was unsuccessful in its 1970s' attempt at selling adult-based foods. Second, some analysts question the timing of Gerber's plan. Because a new product roll-out can take up to two years, it may be very difficult to achieve a $200-million sales volume as of 1994. Third, the Gerber name still has a very high association with babies and a poor association with good-tasting food to many people.

To demonstrate the changing direction at Gerber, the "beaming tot" was removed from the cover of the firm's 1988 annual report in favor of a butterfly coming out of its cocoon.

QUESTIONS

1. What other demographic trends, aside from birth rates, would have a significant effect on Gerber's marketing planning? Explain their implications.
2. Evaluate Gerber's expansion into general merchandise and adult foods. Be sure to consider demographic trends in your analysis.
3. Why would a firm that has been so successful in the baby-food market not have been successful with the sale of adult foods? Isn't the marketing emphasis really the same? Explain your answer.
4. Comment on the statement, "Our plant is not a baby-food plant but a food-processing plant in which we have chosen to process baby food."

◄ CASE 2 ►

The Spending Patterns of Singles†

Because single households account for nearly one-quarter of all U.S. households, government and industry have intensively examined their spending. The U.S. Bureau of Labor Statistics' Consumer Expenditure Survey has separately computed expenditures for men and women.

The Bureau of Labor Statistics' survey indicates some key demographic and expenditure differences between single men and women. Here are a number of them:

▶ Although over half of single men are below 35, over half of single women are at least 55.
▶ Single men have much higher incomes than single women; the income gap is large for all age groups of singles—although it is greatest for men and women ages 45 to 54.
▶ Sources of income differ between male and female singles. Men receive 14 per cent of their income from social security, interest, dividends, and proceeds from property; one-third of women's income comes from these sources.
▶ On average, because of the income gap, single men annually spend about 36 per cent more on goods and services than do women.
▶ Single men allocate a greater proportion of their total expenditures to food consumed away from home, alcohol, transportation, entertainment, tobacco, cash contributions, and retirement, pension, and Social Security contributions than single women.
▶ Single women allocate a greater share of their total expenditures to food consumed at home, housing, apparel, health care, personal-care services, and reading material than men.
▶ Forty-one per cent of single women own a home, compared to 29 per cent of men.

Tables 1 and 2 show the 1985 spending patterns of single men and single women by age group. These are the latest data available on singles' spending.

---

† The data in this case are drawn from Stephanie Shipp, "How Singles Spend," *American Demographics* (April 1988), pp. 22–27.

TABLE 1 Average Annual Spending by Single Men (Selected Goods and Services)

Expenditure Category	All Single Men	Below Age 25	Age 25–34	Age 35–44	Age 45–54	Age 55–64	Age 65+
Total expenditures	$15,339	$10,172	$17,672	$20,024	$20,311	$16,866	$9,356
Food	2,288	1,711	2,451	2,735	2,958	2,554	1,758
Housing	4,503	2,355	5,307	6,128	6,141	4,823	3,216
Apparel and services	735	558	846	907	839	1,128	252
Transportation	3,006	2,335	4,208	3,382	3,292	2,372	1,381
Health care	483	242	316	412	791	765	948
Entertainment	815	688	1,004	1,002	1,010	755	243
Cash contributions	714	108	352	1,507	1,317	1,333	790
Personal insurance and pensions	1,275	470	1,531	2,255	2,009	1,597	228

SOURCE: U.S. Bureau of Labor Statistics, *Consumer Expenditure Survey.*

TABLE 2 Average Annual Spending by Single Women (Selected Goods and Services)

Expenditure Category	All Single Women	Below Age 25	Age 25–34	Age 35–44	Age 45–54	Age 55–64	Age 65+
Total expenditures	$11,102	$ 8,413	$15,051	$16,830	$13,830	$12,440	$8,814
Food	1,587	1,228	1,736	2,081	1,845	1,796	1,473
Housing	3,988	2,243	5,069	6,021	5,070	4,298	3,644
Apparel and services	657	751	1,075	1,159	882	682	340
Transportation	1,872	1,927	3,304	2,917	2,143	1,875	1,072
Health care	701	225	397	570	695	747	982
Entertainment	422	409	720	859	527	450	220
Cash contributions	402	29	199	434	484	512	561
Personal insurance and pensions	713	352	1,476	1,841	1,258	1,342	115

SOURCE: U.S. Bureau of Labor Statistics, *Consumer Expenditure Survey.*

QUESTIONS

1. In general, what goods and services represent the best opportunities for firms marketing to singles? The worst? Explain your answer.
2. Comment on the data contained in Tables 1 and 2, and discuss the marketing implications by gender and by age.
3. If the income gap between single men and women narrows, how would you expect their expenditures to change? Why? What are the marketing implications?
4. What other demographic data about the singles market should be reviewed before making marketing decisions? Explain your answer.

CHAPTER 6

Consumer Life-Styles and Decision Making

CHAPTER OBJECTIVES

1. To show why consumer demographic analysis is not sufficient in planning marketing programs

2. To define and describe consumer life-styles, examine selected life-styles, and present marketing implications of life-style analysis

3. To consider the limitations of consumer life-style analysis

4. To define and describe the consumer's decision process and present marketing implications

5. To consider the limitations of consumer decision-making analysis

W ant someone to fetch a meal from a local restaurant? In Austin, Texas, you can call Eat-OutIn. Plants need to be watered? In New York, you can call The Busy Body's Helper. Too busy to wrap and mail your packages? Stop by any one of the 72 outlets of Tender Sender, headquartered in Portland, Oregon. At Personalized Services in Chicago, "We'll find it, we'll do it, we'll wait for it." This means walking the dog, shuttling the kids to Little League, or waiting in line for theater tickets.

Reprinted by permission.

These and other "convenience peddlers" recognize that a lot of today's U.S. consumers have fast-paced life-styles, are unwilling to expend much effort in shopping, and are willing to pay for convenience. Let us look at each of these three factors.

First, according to the poverty-of-time concept, for some consumers, the quest for greater affluence means less free time because the alternatives competing for free time expand. Consumers often commute to work, have a second job, and so on; therefore they have little time to shop or do chores. Second, to some people, shopping is often socially and/or psychologically unimportant and unrewarding. They want to engage in ego-gratifying experiences rather than in tasks that they perceive as unrewarding. Third, over one-third of dual-earner families earn $50,000+ per year; they have enough money to pay for convenience-oriented goods and services.

Thus, many observers believe that convenience-oriented services will grow even more rapidly in the future. Among those areas with the highest forecasts for growth are delivered foods, service franchising, and mail-order retailing.

According to one expert, home delivery represents "the largest single opportunity for the restaurant industry." And, home delivery by restaurants is becoming more popular at both ends of the price spectrum. Better restaurants see it as a way of appealing to consumers with well-prepared meals eaten in the comfort of their own homes; mass-market food establishments, such as Domino's Pizza, see delivery as a way for consumers to enjoy convenience and to avoid driving, inclement weather, and changing into more stylish clothing—and to obtain quick service. Domino's promises delivery in 30 minutes or it will give a $3 rebate.

Customer convenience is a major differential advantage for a number of service-franchising businesses. In service franchising, a central owner (the franchisor) sells territorial rights to individual franchisees. For example, Molly Maid Inc., a home-cleaning chain, has franchise operators in over 25 states. Jiffy Lube, a chain of quick oil-change centers, and Chem Lawn, the lawn-care firm, are both national franchisors.

The high interest in convenience also means that mail-order sales will continue to rise. Mail-order firms enable shoppers to save time and minimize their effort. For example, Lands' End, a mail-order retailer of sporty clothing, encourages consumers to order through the mail or a toll-free 800 telephone number, accepts credit cards, delivers goods to the consumer's house in a few days, and has an unconditional money-back guarantee.[1]

By learning more about its customers than just their demographics (such as their interest in convenience), an organization can better pinpoint market needs, the reasons for purchases, and changing life-styles and purchase-behavior patterns. In this chapter, we will study the way consumers live and spend time and money—as well as how they make purchase decisions.

[1] Susan Benway et al., "Presto! The Convenience Industry: Making Life a Little Simpler," *Business Week* (April 27, 1987), pp. 86–94; and Raymond Serafin, "Making Domino's Deliver," *Advertising Age* (November 28, 1988), pp. 10, 56.

Overview

The collection and analysis of consumer demographic data are often not sufficient aids in planning marketing programs because these data do not address issues such as these:

- ▶ Why do consumers act as they do?
- ▶ Why do consumers with similar demographic characteristics act differently?
- ▶ Why do consumers become brand loyal or regularly switch brands?
- ▶ Why do some consumers act as innovators and buy products before others?
- ▶ Under what situations do families employ joint decision making?
- ▶ How do consumers behave when shopping for a product?
- ▶ Why does status play a large role in the purchase of some products and a small role in the purchase of others?
- ▶ How does risk affect consumer decisions?
- ▶ How do motives affect consumer decisions?
- ▶ How important is a purchase decision to a consumer?
- ▶ How long will it take for a consumer to reach a purchase decision?
- ▶ To whom does a consumer look for advice prior to purchasing?

In an attempt to answer these and other questions, marketers, in increasing numbers, are using demographic data in conjunction with and as part of consumer life-style and decision-making analysis. These topics are the focus of this chapter.

Social and psychological factors comprise a consumer's **life-style,** which is the pattern in which a person lives and spends time and money. A life-style combines the influences of personality and social values that have been internalized by an individual.[2] A person's demographic background has a strong influence on the life-style, or way of living, adopted.

The social aspects of life-style include culture, social class, social performance, reference groups, opinion leaders, the family life cycle, and time expenditures (activities). The psychological aspects of life-style include personality, attitudes (opinions), the level of class consciousness, motivation, perceived risk, innovativeness, and the importance of a purchase. Social and psychological factors overlap and complement each other; they are not independent or exclusive of one another.

Psychographics is the technique that classifies consumer life-styles by investigating how people live, what interests them, and what they like.[3] An AIO (activities, interests, and opinions) inventory is used in psychographic research to determine consumer life-styles. This inventory asks consumers to respond to a series of statements on their activities, interests, and opinions. Table 6-1 shows the range of topics covered in typical AIO inventories.

The consumer's decision process involves the steps a consumer goes through in purchasing a good or service: stimulus, problem awareness, information search, evaluation of alternatives, purchase, and postpurchase behavior. Demographic factors, social factors, and psychological factors affect the consumer's decision-making process.

---

[2] James F. Engel, Roger D. Blackwell, and Paul W. Miniard, *Consumer Behavior*, Fifth Edition (Hinsdale, Ill.: Dryden Press, 1986), p. 252.

[3] Peter D. Bennett (Editor), *Dictionary of Marketing Terms* (Chicago: American Marketing Association, 1988), p. 163.

TABLE 6-1 AIO Dimensions

Activities	Interests	Opinions
Work	Family	Themselves
Hobbies	Home	Social issues
Social events	Job	Politics
Vacation	Community	Business
Entertainment	Recreation	Economics
Club membership	Fashion	Education
Community	Food	Products
Shopping	Media	Future
Sports	Achievements	Culture

Source: Adapted by the authors from Joseph T. Plummer, "The Concept and Application of Life-Style Segmentation," *Journal of Marketing*, Vol. 38 (January 1974), p. 34. Reprinted by permission.

Consumer Life-Styles

The social and psychological characteristics that form consumer life-styles are described next.

Social Characteristics of Consumers

The social profile of a consumer is based on a combination of culture, social class, social performance, reference groups, opinion leaders, the family life cycle, and time expenditures (activities). See Figure 6-1.

A *culture* is a group of people sharing a distinctive heritage, such as Americans or Japanese. American culture places importance on achievement and success, activity, efficiency and practicality, progress, material comfort, individualism, freedom, external conformity, humanitarianism, youthfulness, and fitness and health.[4] Slower economic growth, the rising influence of foreign countries, and a maturing U.S. population may signal changes in some of these values. In Chapter 21, the American culture is contrasted with other cultures.

*American **culture** emphasizes success, materialism, freedom, and youthfulness.*

A *social class* system is the ranking of people within a culture. Social classes are based on income, occupation, education, and type of dwelling. Social class systems separate society into divisions, grouping people with similar values and life-styles. Each social class may represent a distinct target market for a company. See Table 6-2.

***Social class** separates society into divisions.*

Social performance is how a person carries out his or her roles as a worker, family member, citizen, and friend. At one extreme, a person may be a vice-president in a company, have a happy family life, be an active member of the community, and have many friends. At the other extreme, a person may never be promoted higher than assistant manager, be divorced, not participate in community affairs, and have few friends. It should be clear that many combinations of these performance criteria are possible — for example, vice-president and divorced. The advertisement shown in Figure 6-2 is oriented toward a person's interest in social performance.

***Social performance** describes how a person fulfills his or her roles.*

[4] Leon G. Schiffman and Leslie Lazar Kanuk, *Consumer Behavior*, Third Edition (Englewood Cliffs, N. J.: Prentice-Hall, 1987), pp. 491–503.

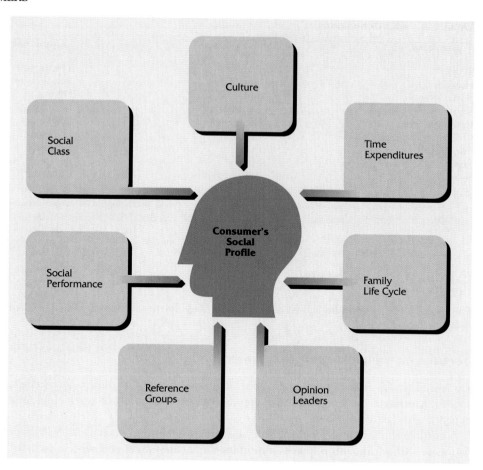

FIGURE 6-1
**Factors Determining a
Consumer's Social Profile**

*Reference groups influence
a person's thoughts and
behavior.*

A ***reference group*** is one that influences a person's thoughts or actions. For many goods and services, reference groups have an important impact on purchase behavior. A reference group may be aspirational, membership, or dissociative. An aspirational group is one to which a person does not belong but wishes to belong, such as a fraternity, professional society, or a social club. A membership group is one to which the person does belong, such as a family, union, or working women. A dissociative group is one to which the person does not want to belong, such as an unpopular social group, school dropouts, or a low-achievement group.

Those reference groups that are face-to-face, such as family or fraternity, have the most influence on a person. However, other — more general — reference groups also influence behavior and these are frequently appealed to when marketing products. By pinpointing the reference groups that affect consumers, marketing personnel can adapt their strategies. For example, commercials that show goods and services being used by college students, successful professionals, and pet owners often ask viewers to join the "group" in making a similar purchase. See Figure 6-3.

*Opinion leaders affect
other consumers through
face-to-face contact.*

Companies are quite interested in determining which persons in reference groups are ***opinion leaders***. These are people to whom other consumers turn for advice and information via face-to-face communication.[5] Opinion leaders tend to be expert about

---

[5] Bennett, *Dictionary of Marketing Terms*, p. 136.

TABLE 6-2 The Social Class Structure in the United States

Class	Size	Characteristics
Upper-upper	Less than 0.5%	Social elite; inherited wealth; exclusive neighborhood; summer home; children attend best schools; money not important in purchases; secure in status; "spending with good taste"
Lower-upper	Combined with upper-upper equals 1.5%	Highest income level; earned wealth; often professionals; social mobility; "nouveau riche"; college-educated but not at the best schools; seek the best for children; active in social affairs; value material possessions; not secure in position; "conspicuous consumption"; money not important in purchases
Upper-middle	12.5%	Career-oriented; successful professionals and businesspeople; no family status or unusual wealth; annual family earnings over $40,000; status based on occupation and earnings; most educated in society, not from prestige schools; active socially; demanding of children; careful but conspicuous; attractive home; nice clothing; "gracious living"
Lower-middle	32%	"Typical American;" respectable; conscientious; obedient; church going; conservative; home ownership sought; do-it-yourselfers; neat; work at shopping; price sensitive; variety of lower-level white-collar and highly-paid blue-collar occupations; incomes from $20,000 to $35,000; purchases related to income and occupation; college for children
Upper-lower	38%	"Family folk;" routine existence; blue-collar occupations; limited education; seek job security; income can overlap with lower-middle; child-oriented; impulsive for new purchases; brand loyal for regular items and "national brands"; little social contact; not status-oriented; protective against lower-lower
Lower-lower	16%	Present-oriented; impulsive; overpay; use credit; poor education; limited information; unemployed or work at most menial jobs; large market for food; poor housing; frustrated

Source: This table is derived from Richard P. Coleman, "The Continuing Significance of Social Class in Marketing," *Journal of Consumer Research*, Vol. 11 (December 1983), pp. 265–280; James F. Engel, Roger D. Blackwell, and Paul W. Miniard, *Consumer Behavior*, Fifth Edition (Hinsdale, Ill.: Dryden Press, 1986), pp. 344–348; Leon G. Schiffman and Leslie Lazar Kanuk, *Consumer Behavior*, Third Edition (Englewood Cliffs, N.J.: Prentice-Hall, 1987), p. 451; and Del I. Hawkins, Roger J. Best, and Kenneth A. Coney, *Consumer Behavior: Implications for Marketing Strategy*, Fourth Edition (Homewood, Ill.: Richard D. Irwin, 1989), pp. 135–141.

a product category, socially accepted, long-standing members of the community, gregarious, active, and trusted, and tend to seek approval from others. Opinion leaders normally have an impact over a narrow range of products; they are perceived as more credible than company-sponsored sources of information.

The *family life cycle* describes how a family evolves through various stages from bachelorhood to solitary retirement. At each stage, needs, experience, income, and family composition change. In addition, the use of *joint decision making* — the process whereby two or more consumers have input into purchases — changes throughout the cycle. The family life cycle is an excellent tool for market segmentation and for developing marketing campaigns. The number of people in different stages in the cycle can be obtained through a study of demographic data.

*The **family life cycle** describes family stages, which often use **joint decision making**.*

Table 6-3 shows the traditional family life cycle and its relevance for marketing. This cycle's stages include bachelor, newly married, full nest (children at home), empty nest, and sole survivor. However, when using family life-cycle analysis, marketers should note the growing numbers of people who do not follow the traditional pattern because they do not marry, do not have children, become divorced, belong to families with two working spouses even if there are small children, and so on. These people are

I acquired the painting of my dreams.
Only to discover it was a brilliant forgery.

I bought stocks like they were going out of style.
And they were.

I married for love.
Then found I was being married for money.

I bought myself a Waterman.

There are some decisions one never lives to regret.

Pens write. A Waterman pen expresses. For more than a century, this distinction has remained constant. The creation shown here, for example, has been crafted from sterling silver, painstakingly tooled and balanced to absolute precision. Those who desire such an instrument of expression will find Waterman pens in a breadth of styles, prices and lacquers.

WATERMAN
PARIS

© 1988 Waterman Pen Company

not reflected in Table 6-3 but may represent good marketing opportunities.[6] Table 6-4 shows the current status of families in the United States.

Time expenditures reflect the workweek, family care, and leisure.

Time expenditures refer to and involve the types of activities in which a person participates and the amount of time allocated to them. In recent decades, the average workweek for a full-time job has declined by about five hours per week, from roughly

---

[6] See, for example, Patrick E. Murphy and William A. Staples, "A Modernized Family Life Cycle," *Journal of Consumer Research*, Vol. 6 (June 1979), pp. 12–22; Cheryl Russell and Thomas Exter, "America at Mid-Decade," *American Demographics* (January 8, 1986), pp. 22–29; and John C. Mowen, *Consumer Behavior* (New York: Macmillan, 1987), pp. 404–407.

FIGURE 6-3
An American Express Request to Join a Successful Reference Group
Courtesy of American Express Travel Related Services Company, Inc. Copyright American Express.

40 hours per week to 35. Two other trends are worth noting: urban Americans are spending significantly less time in family care, and leisure-time activities are increasing substantially. Americans are quite active in picnicking, driving for pleasure, swimming, sightseeing, walking, attending outdoor spectator events, and playing outdoor games and sports.

Psychological Characteristics of Consumers

The psychological profile of a consumer combines personality, attitudes, class consciousness, motivation, perceived risk, innovativeness, and the importance of a purchase. See Figure 6-4.

A **personality** is the sum total of an individual's psychological traits that make that individual unique. Self-confidence, dominance, autonomy, sociability, defensiveness, adaptability, and emotional stability are selected personality traits. Personality has a strong impact on an individual's behavior. For example, a self-confident and sociable person often will not purchase the same goods and services as an inhibited and aloof person. It is necessary to remember that a personality is made up of many traits operating in conjunction with one another.

Personality describes the composite traits of a person.

157

TABLE 6-3 The Traditional Family Life Cycle

Stage in Cycle	Characteristics	Opportunities for Marketing
Bachelor, male or female	Independent; young; early stage of career; low earnings, low discretionary income	Clothing; automobile; stereo; travel; restaurants; entertainment; appeal to status
Newly married	Two incomes; relative independence; present- and future-oriented	Apartment furnishings; travel; clothing; durables; appeal to enjoyment and togetherness
Full nest I	Youngest child under 6; one to one-and-a-half incomes; limited independence; future-oriented	Goods and services geared to child; home; family-use items; practicality of items; durability; safety; pharmaceuticals; appeal to economy; child care
Full nest II	Youngest child over 6, but dependent; one-and-a-half to two incomes; one spouse established in career; future-oriented	Savings; home; education; family vacations; child-oriented products; some interest in luxuries; appeal to comfort and long-range enjoyment
Full nest III	Youngest child living at home, but independent; highest income levels; thoughts of retirement	Education; expensive durables for children; replacement and improvement of parents' durables; appeal to comfort and luxury
Empty nest I	No children at home; independent; good incomes; thoughts of self and retirement	Retirement home; travel; clothing; entertainment; luxuries; appeal to self-gratification
Empty nest II	Retirement; limited income and expenses; present-oriented	Travel; recreation; living in new home; pharmaceuticals and health items; little interest in luxuries; appeal to comfort at a low price
Sole survivor I	Only one spouse alive; actively employed; present-oriented; good income	Immersion in job and friends leading to interest in travel, clothing, health, and recreation areas; appeal to productive citizen
Sole survivor II	Only one person alive; retired; some feeling of futility; lower income	Travel; recreation; pharmaceuticals; security; appeal to economy and social activity

Attitudes can be positive, negative, or neutral.

Attitudes (opinions) are an individual's positive, neutral, or negative feelings about goods, services, companies, people, issues, and/or institutions. Attitudes are shaped by demographics, social factors, and personality. One role of marketing is to generate favorable attitudes; given the intensive competition in many industries, a firm cannot normally succeed without positive consumer attitudes.

When studying attitudes, two concepts should often be measured: the attitude itself and the purchase intent toward a firm's brand. For example:

Attitude Evaluation	Purchase Intention
1. Are you familiar with brand A?	1. Have you ever purchased brand A?
2. Do you like brand A?	2. Would you buy brand A in the future?
3. Do you prefer brand A above other brands?	3. Do you regularly buy brand A?
4. How does brand A compare with other brands?	4. Would you buy brand A if it were priced higher than other brands?

Class consciousness is low for inner-directed persons and high for outer-directed persons.

Class consciousness is the extent to which social status is desired and pursued by a person. Class consciousness helps determine a consumer's use of reference groups, a person's concern about social class mobility, and the importance of prestige purchases. An **inner-directed person** is interested in pleasing him- or herself. This type of person is generally attracted by do-it-yourself products, products that perform well functionally, and items that are challenging and can be used when the person is alone.

TABLE 6-4   The Current Status of U.S. Families

Family Status		Percentage of All U.S. Households
Single[a]		24.0
Age 15 to 24	1.4	
Age 25 to 44	7.4	
Age 45 to 64	5.5	
Age 65 and over	9.7	
Married couple, no children under age 18		30.0
Married couple, with children under age 18		27.0
Other type of family, with children under age 18[b]		15.0
Unmarried couple		2.7
With no children under age 18	1.9	
With children under age 18	0.8	
Other[c]		1.3
Total		100.0

[a] Includes people who have never married as well as those who are widowed, separated, and divorced.
[b] Includes one-parent families in which married couples are separated but not divorced, one-parent families headed by divorcees, one-parent families headed by widows and widowers, and one-parent families headed by never-married mothers and fathers.
[c] Includes roommates.

Source: U.S. Bureau of the Census, *Current Population Reports*.

The inner-directed person relies on his or her own judgment, is not involved with social mobility, and does not value prestige items. An ***outer-directed person*** is interested in pleasing the people around him or her. Approval by reference groups, upward social mobility, and the ownership of prestige items are sought. An outer-directed person is generally attracted by products that provide social visibility, well-known brands, and uniqueness. Functional performance may be less important.

Motivation is

> the driving force within individuals that impels them to action. This driving force is produced by a state of tension, which exists as the result of an unfulfilled need.[7]

Motivation is a drive-impelling action; it is caused by **motives**.

By identifying and appealing to a consumer's ***motives***, the reasons for behavior, a marketer can generate motivation. For example:

Motive	Marketing Actions That Motivate
Hunger	Television and radio commercials just before mealtime
Safety	Demonstration of a smoke detector
Sociability	Toothpaste and perfume commercials showing social success due to products
Achievement	Demonstration of knowledge obtained via a home computer
Economy	Newspaper coupons advertising sales

Each person has different motives for buying, and these change by situation and over time. Most consumers combine economic (price, durability) and emotional (status, self-esteem) motives when making a purchase.

[7] Schiffman and Kanuk, *Consumer Behavior*, p. 67.

FIGURE 6-4
**Factors Determining
a Consumer's
Psychological Profile**

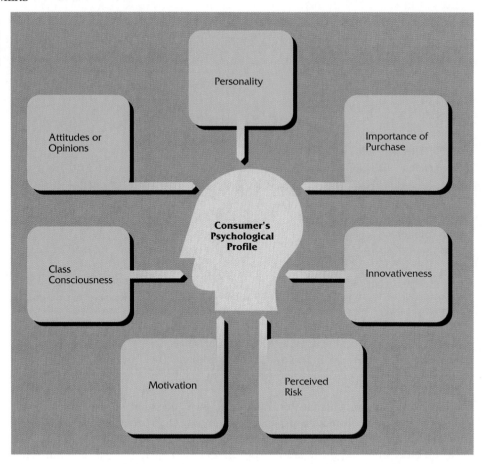

*Perceived risk is the
uncertainty felt by the
consumer.*

Perceived risk is the level of risk a consumer believes exists regarding the outcome of a purchase decision; this belief may or may not be correct. Perceived risk can be divided into six major types:

1. Functional — the risk that the product will not perform adequately.
2. Physical — the risk that the product will be harmful.
3. Financial — the risk that the product will not be worth its cost or time commitment.
4. Social — the risk that the product will cause embarrassment before others.
5. Psychological — the risk that one's ego will be bruised.
6. Time — the risk that the time spent making a purchase will be wasted if the product does not perform as expected.[8]

Companies must deal with perceived risk, even if consumers are incorrect in their beliefs, because a high level of perceived risk usually dampens customer motivation. Perceived risk can be reduced by avoiding controversial ingredients, offering money-back guarantees, providing greater information, and developing and maintaining a reputation for quality goods and services. See Figure 6-5.

[8] Ibid., pp. 214–215.

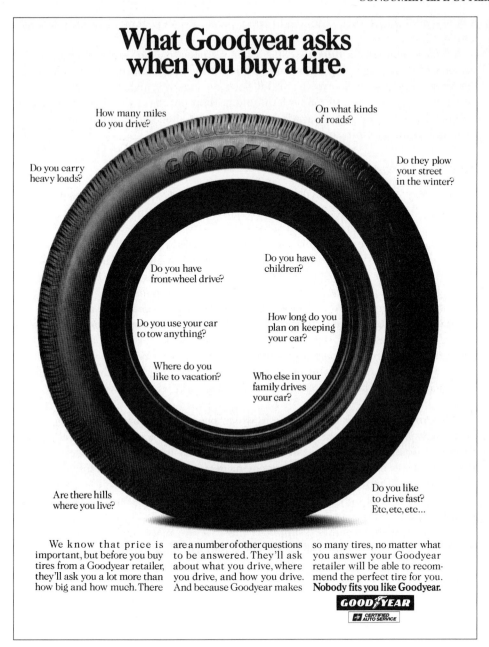

FIGURE 6-5
How Goodyear Reduces Perceived Risk
Reprinted by permission.

A consumer who is willing to try a new product that others perceive as having a high degree of risk is said to exhibit **innovativeness.** An innovator is likely to be well educated, literate, and have a high income and standard of living. This person is also apt to be knowledgeable, interested in change, achievement-motivated, open-minded, status-conscious, mobile, venturesome, and have aspirations for his or her children.[9]

Innovativeness is trying a new product others see as risky.

[9] Del I. Hawkins, Roger J. Best, and Kenneth A. Coney, *Consumer Behavior: Implications for Marketing Strategy,* Fourth Edition (Homewood, Ill.: Richard D. Irwin, 1989), pp. 199–203.

It is essential for marketers to identify and appeal to innovators when introducing a new good or service.

Importance of a purchase determines time, effort, and money spent.

The ***importance of a purchase*** has a major impact on the time and effort a consumer will spend shopping for a product and on the amount of money allocated. An important purchase will involve careful decision making, high perceived risk, and probably a large amount of money. An unimportant purchase will receive little decision-making time (the good or service may be avoided altogether), have little perceived risk, and probably be inexpensive.

Selected Consumer Life-Styles

Many distinct consumer life-styles are expected to continue. Five of these are discussed here: the "me" generation, voluntary simplicity, the blurring of gender roles, the poverty of time, and component life-styles.[10]

The "me" generation stresses self-expression and self-improvement.

For many consumers, there is an interest in a self-oriented life-style, that of the ***"me" generation.*** This life-style stresses being good to oneself. The me-generation concept is popular to some people because of the interest in free expression and self-expression. It places less emphasis on obligations, responsibilities, and loyalties. It involves less pressure to conform, as well as greater acceptance of diversity.

Consumers with this life-style are particularly interested in staying young and taking care of themselves. They stress nutrition, exercise, weight control, and grooming. Expensive cars and fur coats are bought, and full-service retailers are patronized. These consumers are more concerned with a product's appearance than its durability and place limited importance on conservation, especially if it will have a negative effect on their life-style.

Voluntary simplicity is based on self-reliance.

Voluntary simplicity is a life-style in which people seek material simplicity, have an ecological (environmental) awareness, strive for self-reliance, and purchase do-it-yourself products. It grew out of the 1960s and 1970s, when people first became aware that many natural resources were being depleted, and continued into the 1980s due to high inflation and unemployment. Although this life-style will be popular for some, it will expand only if Americans are again faced with resource shortages and rising prices.

Consumers with a voluntary-simplicity life-style are more likely to seek a frugal, simple life. They are conservative, cautious, and thrifty shoppers. They do not buy expensive cars and fur coats, they make gifts instead of purchase them, they grow their own vegetables and make their own clothes, and they patronize garage sales and flea markets. These consumers are more concerned with a product's durability than its

---

[10] See Ronald D. Michman, "New Directions for Life-Style Behavior Patterns," *Business Horizons,* Vol. 27 (July–August 1984), pp. 59–64; Arnold Mitchell, *The Nine American Life-Styles: Who We Are & Where We Are Going* (New York: Free Press, 1983); Lynn R. Kahle, Basil Poulos, and Ajay Sukdial, "Changes in Social Values in the United States During the Past Decade," *Journal of Advertising Research,* Vol. 28 (February–March 1988), pp. 35–41; Roy Goydon, "Doing Business with Mr. Mom," *Forbes* (January 13, 1986), p. 281; Ralph W. Jackson, Stephen W. McDaniel, and C. P. Rao, "Food Shopping and Preparation: Psychographic Differences of Working Wives and Housewives," *Journal of Consumer Research,* Vol. 12 (June 1985), pp. 110–113; Horst H. Stipp, "What Is a Working Woman?" *American Demographics* (July 1988), pp. 24–27, 59; and Bernd H. Schmitt, France LeClerc, and Laurette Dubé-Rioux, "Sex Typing and Consumer Behavior: A Test of Gender Schema Theory," *Journal of Consumer Research,* Vol. 15 (June 1988), pp. 122–128.

FIGURE 6-6
Blurring Gender Roles
With greater frequency,
males are becoming
regular patrons at super-
markets and drugstores,
such as the Medi Mart
unit shown here.
Reprinted by permission.

appearance and believe in conservation of scarce resources. There is also more attraction to rational appeals and no-frills retailing.

Because greater numbers of women have entered the labor force, more husbands
are assuming the traditional roles of their wives, thus **blurring gender roles.** These
husbands do chores in the home, and share the tasks of managing a household and
taking care of the family. In families with younger, better-educated, and more-affluent
husbands and wives, sharing is most likely. For example, one recent study of young
working parents found that males spend an average of 12 hours per week on home
chores and 15 hours per week on child care.[11] In general, these are the household
tasks men perform most frequently: taking out the garbage, washing dishes, cooking,
vacuuming, doing the laundry, and cleaning. Over 40 per cent of all food-shopping
dollars are spent by male consumers. These activities are expected to continue during
the next decade. See Figure 6-6.

Blurring gender roles
involves men and women
undertaking nontraditional
duties.

In many consumer households, the increase in working women, the long distances
between home and work, and the rise in people working at second jobs contribute to
less rather than more free time. The **poverty-of-time** concept states that for some
consumers the quest for greater affluence results in less free time because the alternatives competing for time expand. As the prices of houses, automobiles, food, and
other goods and services continue to go up in the future, even more households will
require two incomes and, perhaps, a second job for the main earner.

*A **poverty of time** exists*
when a quest for greater
affluence results in less free
time.

Their poverty of time leads these consumers to increased usage of time-saving goods

---

[11] Cathy Trost, "Men, Too, Wrestle with Career-Family Stress," *Wall Street Journal* (November 1, 1988),
p. B1.

Marketing Controversy

Store Hours: Is Later Better?

Retailers are well aware of consumer interest in long store hours during the hectic December shopping season. As a result, they typically increase store hours to twelve hours per day—or more—during the four weeks prior to Christmas. However, a number of retail analysts are beginning to wonder whether retailers understand the hours consumers would like them to be open over the rest of the year.

Some stores "open too early and close too early." With more working women available to shop after 6 P.M. and unavailable to shop at 10 A.M., some observers believe that stores should remain open later. They accuse stores of being unaware of consumer trends: "I can't believe that they don't realize it's not a Leave It to Beaver *family unit any more;" and "A greater number of stores could gain greater business by being open after office hours."*

Nonetheless, retailers that are fully aware of consumer trends may have good reasons for not extending store hours. Says the president of L.J. Hooker Retail Group (which includes Bonwit Teller and B. Altman), "Even in cities that have good downtown areas, you're still dealing with the tremendous commuter mentality." People want to return home after leaving work and do not want to stay downtown to shop.

Longer store hours may necessitate a larger staff. Yet, retailers already report difficulty in staffing for regular store hours, and employee unions are often opposed to increased evening hours. Not all business generated during extended store hours is new business; one estimate is that one-half of sales during extended hours would be made with an earlier closing.

What do you think?

SOURCE: Based on material in Leonard Sloane, "Store Hours: Is Later Better?" *New York Times* (November 11, 1988), p. 52.

---

and services such as convenience foods, disposable packages, microwave ovens, restaurants, and professional lawn and household care. For instance, currently, Americans annually purchase more than three million microwave ovens (up from 300,000 fifteen years ago) and two million food processors, and over 40 per cent eat out at least once a month.

*With **component life-styles**, consumer attitudes and behavior vary by situation.*

In increasing numbers, people are turning to **component life-styles,** whereby their attitudes and behavior depend on particular situations rather than an overall life-style philosophy. With component life-styles, consumers may belong to a health club (me generation), undertake their own plumbing repairs (voluntary simplicity), share household chores such as food shopping (blurring gender roles), and eat out a lot (poverty of time).

As the Roper Organization, a research specialist, notes:

> Consumer behavior is becoming more individualistic and less defined by reference to easily identified social groups. Americans are piecing together "component life-styles" for themselves, choosing goods and services that best express their growing sense of uniqueness. A consumer may own a BMW but fill it with self-service gasoline. Buy take-out fast food for lunch but good wine for dinner. Own sophisticated photographic equipment and low-priced home stereo equipment. Shop for socks at K mart and suits or dresses at Brooks Brothers.

This life-style fragmentation is most noticeable among affluent consumers. While they still seek social status and prestige, they feel less constrained by social custom and rigid standards. Instead, they are emphasizing *individual* style and taste — self-expression that combines class with the desire for convenience. But even less affluent people are behaving in less predictable ways. They, too, are pursuing greater choice and ways to express their individuality.

In the next few years, the trend is *away* from social conformity and *toward* the component life-style. New and surprising combinations of consumer interests, spending patterns, and buying habits will be the rule rather than the exception. This means that market research must pay closer attention to *actual* behavior and less to *presumed* psychographic categories. Successful selling tactics must recognize the product-specific and occasion-specific nature of the emerging consumer environment.[12]

Marketing Implications of Life-Style Analysis

During recent years, the analysis of the social and psychological characteristics of consumers has increased dramatically. In this section, both general and specific applications of life-style analysis in marketing are presented.

Several organizations are involved with defining and measuring consumer life-styles. They sell this information to client firms, which use it to improve their marketing efforts. These are three of the best-known services:

Information on life-styles is available from various sources.

▶ Yankelovich Monitor, which tracks over fifty social trends annually, including commitment to buy American, need for control, responsiveness to fantasy, and rejection of authority. Impermanent consumer profiles are developed, such as "successful adapters," "resistant adapters," and "traditional adapters" — which describe consumers in terms of their response to the changing environment.
▶ VALS (Values and Life-Styles), a research program sponsored by SRI International. SRI's VALS 2 classification, introduced in 1989, categorizes consumers in five basic life-style groups: strugglers, action-oriented, status-oriented, principle-oriented, and actualizers.
▶ PRIZM (Potential Rating Index by Zip Market), a program that relies on census data and examines consumer life-styles by zip code. It uses forty different neighborhood designations, such as blue blood ("old money") to describe life-styles.

These services have been used by firms marketing women's girdles, liquor, food, stock brokerage, automobiles, and other items.

Various studies of the life-styles of today's American consumers have been conducted. These are some of the findings that should be considered when a firm plans its marketing mix:

Many marketing opportunities can be determined from life-style analysis.

▶ The average person spends 7.9 hours per week eating, 5.7 hours shopping, 17.0 hours watching television, and 0.7-hour in gardening and pet care.
▶ One-hundred million people swim, 75 million bicycle, 37 million run or jog, and 85 million participate in exercise programs. Consumers spend over $1 billion annually on exercise equipment. And 59 per cent of adults exercise in some way daily.
▶ Do-it-yourself activities are increasing. Those activities are related to education, age, gender, and family type, but not as much to economic conditions.

---

[12] "31 Major Trends Shaping the Future of American Business," *The Public Pulse,* Vol. 2, No. 1 (1988), p. 1.

▶ Seventy-six per cent of U.S. consumers say they generally choose American-made clothing over foreign garments; yet more than 50 per cent of the clothing sold in the United States is foreign made. Fifty-two per cent say they "try a lot" to avoid eating too much sugar; yet per capita sugar consumption has increased steadily for more than twenty years.[13]

Perrier has used a distinctive, life-style-based marketing strategy since introducing its bottled water products in the United States. Its prime target market consists of upper-middle-class consumers, aged 25 to 45, college-educated, physically and socially active, health-oriented, and status conscious. At first, products were distributed mostly through expensive restaurants, hotels, and gourmet shops — before gradually being expanded to other outlets. Prices are higher than those of competitors. Promotion continues to be geared toward Perrier's natural ingredients, and it regularly sponsors events such as marathon races.[14]

A few years ago, Pfizer decided to shift the advertising emphasis for its Ben-Gay product. Until then, Ben-Gay was marketed as a pain-relieving ointment for older persons suffering from arthritis and back aches. But Pfizer recognized renewed interest in exercise and began promoting Ben-Gay for "sports-active" persons to apply to muscles before exerting themselves. It now runs campaigns featuring separate ads for arthritis suffering and exercise enthusiasts.[15]

Various marketing implications associated with the "me" generation, voluntary simplicity, the blurring of gender roles, the poverty of time, and component life-styles are shown in Table 6-5.

Limitations of Life-Style Analysis

Social and psychological factors can be difficult to measure.

Unlike demographics, many life-style factors are difficult to measure, somewhat subjective, usually based on the self-reports of consumers, and sometimes hidden from view (to avoid embarrassment, protect privacy, convey an image, and other reasons). In addition, there are still ongoing disputes over terminology, misuse of data, and reliability.

Several years ago, one of the pioneers of life-style analysis, William D. Wells, summarized the status of this research. His comments are just as valid today:

> From the speed with which psychographics have diffused through the marketing community, it seems obvious that they are perceived as meeting a keenly felt need. The problem now is not so much one of pioneering as it is one of sorting out the techniques that work best. As that process proceeds, it seems extremely likely that psychographic methods will gradually become more familiar and less controversial, and eventually will merge into the mainstream of marketing research.[16]

---

13 John P. Robinson, "Americans' Use of Time," *Wall Street Journal* (May 13, 1988), p. 6R; "Consumer Tastes," *Wall Street Journal* (April 21, 1986), p. 5D; Hank Gilman, "Clothing Shoppers Talk Domestic But Look First for Style, Savings," *Wall Street Journal* (October 15, 1985), p. 31; and Trish Hall, "Consumers Say They Avoid Sweet Drinks, So Why Do They Buy So Many of Them?" *Wall Street Journal* (July 3, 1985), p. 17.

14 Steven Greenhouse, "Perrier's New American Assault," *Wall Street Journal* (October 30, 1988), Section 3, pp. 1, 5.

15 Belinda Hulin-Salkin, "Pfizer's Ben-Gay Warms Up a Broader Market," *Advertising Age* (September 24, 1984), p. 54.

16 William D. Wells, "Psychographics: A Critical Review," *Journal of Marketing Research,* Vol. 12 (May 1975), p. 209.

TABLE 6-5   Selected Marketing Implications of Consumer Life-Styles

Life-Style Category	Marketing Implications
"Me" generation	Individuality in purchase decisions will gain greater acceptance. Luxuries will be desired. Nutritional themes will be important in food purchases. The interest in physical fitness will continue sales for health spas, bicycles, and exercise equipment. Health and beauty-aid products and personal-care retailing will grow. The concern for self-improvement will lead to more continuing education programs and the enrollment of adults in colleges.
Voluntary simplicity	Expansion will occur for do-it-yourself projects such as repair kits and "knock-down" furniture. There will be consumer interest in quality, durability, and simplicity (rational goals). No-frills retailing will grow. Environmentally safe products will be desired. Sales of insulation, solar energy, and energy-efficient products will continue.
Blurring of gender roles	Unisex goods, services, and stores will be popular. Shopping conditions will be favorable to joint husband and wife purchase behavior. Advertising will feature couples. There will be demand for goods and services that can be used jointly. Male and female stereotypes will no longer be applicable.
Poverty of time	Mail-order and telephone sales will grow. Service retailers will need to make and keep more accurate customer appointments. The sales of laborsaving devices will rise. One-stop shopping will be more important. Wardrobe consultants will save customers time. Well-known brands will facilitate shopping.
Component life-styles	Firms must understand the situations under which consumers follow different life-styles. Generalizations about consumers will be more difficult. Multiple themes may be needed in advertising campaigns (such as a sleek car design, the ease of do-it-yourself oil changes, *and* an appeal to both males and females). Research into consumer motives will be quite important.

The Consumer's Decision Process

The **consumer's decision process** is the procedure by which consumers collect and analyze information and make choices among alternative goods, services, organizations, people, places, and ideas.[17] It is comprised of two parts: the process itself and factors affecting the process. The decision process consists of six basic stages: stimulus, problem awareness, information search, evaluation of alternatives, purchase, and postpurchase behavior. Factors that affect the process are a consumer's demographic, social, and psychological characteristics. The total consumer decision-making process is shown in Figure 6-7.

When a consumer buys a good or service, decides to vote for a political candidate or donate to a charity, and so on, he or she goes through this decision process. In some situations, all six stages in the process are used; in others, only a few of the steps are

*The **consumer's decision process** has many stages and can be affected by various factors.*

[17] Bennett, *A Dictionary of Marketing Terms,* p. 53.

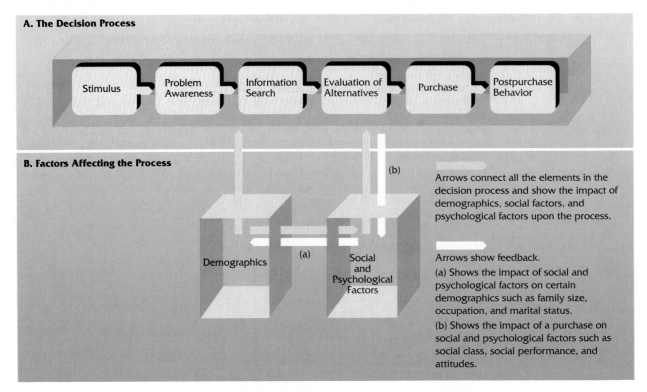

A. The Decision Process

Stimulus → Problem Awareness → Information Search → Evaluation of Alternatives → Purchase → Postpurchase Behavior

B. Factors Affecting the Process

(b)

Demographics   (a)   Social and Psychological Factors

Arrows connect all the elements in the decision process and show the impact of demographics, social factors, and psychological factors upon the process.

Arrows show feedback.

(a) Shows the impact of social and psychological factors on certain demographics such as family size, occupation, and marital status.

(b) Shows the impact of a purchase on social and psychological factors such as social class, social performance, and attitudes.

FIGURE 6-7 **The Consumer's Decision Process**

utilized. For example, the purchase of an expensive stereo requires more decision making than the purchase of a new tie.

The decision process outlined in Figure 6-7 assumes that the end result is the purchase of a good or service, a vote for a candidate, a charitable donation, and so on, by the consumer. However, it is important to realize that at *any* point in the process a potential consumer may decide not to buy, vote, or donate — and, thus, terminate the process. For example, a good or service may turn out to be unnecessary, unsatisfactory, or too expensive.

Stimulus

*A **stimulus** is a cue or drive intended to motivate a consumer.*

A **stimulus** is a cue (social, commercial, or noncommercial) or a drive (physical) meant to motivate or arouse a person to act. When one talks with friends, fellow employees, family members, and others, social cues are received. The distinguishing attribute of a social cue is that it comes from an interpersonal source not affiliated with the seller.

A second type of stimulus is a commercial cue, which is a message sponsored by a manufacturer, wholesaler, retailer, or other seller. The objective is to interest a consumer in a particular good, service, organization, person, place, or idea. See Figure 6-8. Ads, personal selling, and sales promotions are forms of commercial stimuli. These cues may not be regarded as highly as social cues, because consumers realize they are seller-controlled.

A third type of stimulus is a noncommercial cue, which is a message received from an impartial source such as *Consumer Reports* or the government. This cue has higher credibility because it is not affiliated with the seller.

A fourth type of stimulus is a physical drive. This occurs when a person's physical senses are affected. Thirst, cold, heat, pain, hunger, and fear cause physical drives.

A potential consumer may be exposed to any or all of these types of stimuli. If a person is sufficiently stimulated, he or she will go on to the next step in the decision

FIGURE 6-8
A Commercial Stimulus from Alba '77
Reprinted by permission.

process. If stimulation does not occur, the person will ignore the cue and delay or terminate the decision process for the given good, service, organization, person, place, or idea.

Problem Awareness

Problem awareness entails recognition of a shortage or an unfulfilled desire.

At the ***problem awareness*** stage, the consumer recognizes that the good, service, organization, person, place, or idea under consideration may solve a problem of shortage or unfulfilled desire.

Recognition of shortage occurs when a consumer becomes alerted to the fact that a repurchase is necessary. A product such as a suit may wear out. The consumer may run out of an item such as razor blades. A periodic service such as an eye examination may be needed. A political candidate supported by the consumer may be up for reelection. It may be time for a charity's annual fund-raising campaign. In each of these examples, the consumer recognizes a need to replenish a good, service, and so on.

Recognition of unfulfilled desire occurs when a consumer becomes aware of a good, service, organization, person, place, or idea that has not been patronized before. For instance, an item may improve self-image, status, appearance, living conditions, or knowledge in a manner that has not been tried before (luxury auto, cosmetic surgery, proposed zoning law, encyclopedia), or it may offer new performance characteristics not previously available (videotape camera, tobacco-free cigarettes). In either case, the consumer is aroused by a desire to try something new.

Many consumers are hesitant to react to unfulfilled desires because there are risks, and benefits may be hard to judge. There is less expertise with new items than with the replacement of a known product. Whether the consumer becomes aware of a problem of shortage or of unfulfilled desire, he or she will act only if the problem is perceived as worth solving.

Information Search

*An **information search** determines alternatives and their characteristics.*

After the consumer decides a shortage or unfulfilled desire is worth consideration, information is gathered. ***Information search*** requires listing alternatives that will solve the problem at hand and determining the characteristics of each.

The list of alternatives does not have to be written. It can be a group of items the consumer thinks about. The key is that the consumer considers various solutions to his or her problem. Normally, once there is a list of alternatives, items (brands, companies, people, and so on) not on the list do not receive further consideration.

This aspect of information search may be internal or external. Internal search occurs when the consumer has purchasing experience in the area under consideration and uses a memory search to list the alternatives to be considered. A consumer with minimal purchasing experience will usually undertake external search to list alternatives. This type of search can involve commercial sources, noncommercial sources, and/or social sources.

The second phase of information search deals with the characteristics of each alternative. This information is gathered in the same manner as the list of alternatives was generated, internally or externally, depending on the expertise of the consumer and the level of perceived risk. As risk increases, the information sought also increases.

Once the information search is completed, it must be determined whether the shortage or unfulfilled desire can be satisfied by any alternative. If one or more choices are satisfactory, the consumer moves to the next decision. The process is delayed or discontinued when no alternative provides satisfaction.

Evaluation of Alternatives

At this point, there is enough information to select one alternative from the list of choices. Sometimes this is easy, when one alternative is clearly superior to the others across all characteristics. A product with excellent quality and a low price will be an automatic choice over an average quality, expensive one. Often the choice is not that simple, and the consumer must carefully engage in an ***evaluation of alternatives*** before making a decision. If two or more alternatives are attractive, the consumer needs to determine what criteria (attributes) to evaluate and their relative importance. Then the alternatives are ranked and a choice made.

Evaluating alternatives consists of weighing features and selecting the most desired product.

Criteria for a decision are those features the consumer considers relevant. These may include price, color, style, options, quality, safety, durability, status, and warranty. The consumer sets standards for the features and develops an attitude toward each alternative according to its ability to meet the standards. In addition, the importance of each criterion is often determined because the multiple attributes of a given good, service, and so on, are usually of varying importance. For example, a consumer may consider shoe prices to be more important than style and act accordingly during a purchase by selecting inexpensive, nondistinctive shoes.

The consumer next ranks alternatives from most to least desirable and selects one from among all choices. In some cases, ranking is difficult because the alternatives may be technical, poorly labeled, new (the consumer has no experience in this area), or intangible (the consumer finds it hard to evaluate two political candidates). These alternatives are frequently ranked on the basis of brand name or price, which is used to indicate overall quality.

In situations where no alternative proves to be satisfactory, a decision to delay or not make the purchase is made.

Purchase

Following the selection of the best alternative, the consumer is ready for the ***purchase act:*** an exchange of money, a promise to pay, or support in return for ownership of a specific good, the performance of a specific service, and so on. Three important considerations remain: place of purchase, terms, and availability.

*The **purchase act** includes deciding where to buy, agreeing to terms, and seeing if the item is available.*

The place of purchase may be a store or nonstore location. The great majority of items are bought at stores. However, many items are purchased at school (books, stationery), work (health insurance), and home (mail, telephone, and door-to-door sales). The place of purchase is evaluated in the same manner as the product itself. Alternatives are noted, characteristics defined, and a ranking compiled. The most desirable locale is then chosen.

Purchase terms involve the price and method of payment. Generally, price is the total dollar amount (including interest, tax, and other charges) a consumer pays to achieve ownership or use of a good or service. It may also be a person's vote, time investment, and so on. The method of payment is the way the price is paid (cash, short-term credit, or long-term credit).

Availability refers to the timeliness with which a consumer receives a good or service that he or she purchases. It depends on stock-on-hand (service capacity if a service) and delivery. Stock-on-hand (service capacity) relates to the seller's ability to provide a good or service when requested by a consumer. For items that require delivery, the period from when an order is placed by the consumer until it is received and the ease with which an item is transported to its place of use are important.

The consumer will make a purchase if these elements are acceptable. However, dissatisfaction with any one may cause a consumer to delay or not buy, even though there is no problem with the good or service itself.

Postpurchase Behavior

Postpurchase behavior often embodies further buying and/or re-evaluation.

After making a purchase, the consumer frequently is involved with *postpurchase behavior,* in the form of further purchases and/or re-evaluation. In many cases, one purchase leads to others. For example, the purchase of a house leads to the acquisition of fire insurance. The purchase of a suit leads to the purchase of a matching tie. The purchase of a home videotape system leads to the acquisition of blank and movie cassettes.

The consumer may also re-evaluate a purchase. Are expectations matched by the actual performance of a good or service? Satisfaction usually results in repurchases when the good or service wears out, a charity launches its annual fund-raising campaign, and so on, and also leads to positive communication with other consumers interested in the same item. Dissatisfaction frequently results in brand switching and negative communications with other consumers.

Cognitive dissonance can be reduced by proper consumer aftercare.

Dissatisfaction is often the result of *cognitive dissonance* — doubt that the correct decision has been made. The consumer may regret making a purchase or wish another alternative was chosen. To overcome cognitive dissonance, the firm must realize that the decision process does not end with the purchase. Aftercare (follow-up telephone and service calls, advertisements aimed at purchasers, extended warranties) helps reassure consumers, particularly for important and expensive decisions with many alternatives. Coupling realistic promotion, so that expectations are not raised too high, with consumer aftercare should reduce or eliminate cognitive dissonance.

Factors Affecting the Consumer's Decision Process

The decision process is affected by consumer demographics and life-styles.

Demographic, social, and psychological factors have an impact on the way consumers utilize the decision process. These factors are not only helpful in developing consumer profiles and adapting marketing strategies to them, but they also aid in understanding how consumers use the decision process.

For example, a young male who is socially active and outgoing would use the decision process differently from a middle-aged male who is a homebody and introverted. The former would place heavy emphasis on social sources of information, whereas the latter would not. An affluent consumer would move through the process more quickly than a middle-income consumer because of less financial risk. A person under time pressure would also move through the process more quickly than one with sufficient time for shopping. An insecure consumer would spend more time making a decision than one who is secure.

By knowing how these factors affect decisions, a company can fine-tune its marketing strategies to cater to the target market and its purchase behavior, and answer these questions: Why do two or more consumers use the decision process in the same way? Why do two or more people use the process differently?

Types of Decision Processes

Each time a consumer buys a good or service, contributes to a charity, and so on, he or she uses the decision process. Often, it is used subconsciously and the consumer is not aware of its use. Some situations may allow the consumer to move through the process quickly and de-emphasize or skip certain steps; others may require the thorough use of each step in the process.

The consumer may use extended, limited, or routine decision making. This depends on the degree of search, level of prior experience, frequency of purchase, amount of perceived risk, and time pressure. See Figure 6-9.

Extended consumer decision making occurs when a consumer makes full use of the decision process shown in Figure 6-9. Considerable time is spent on information search and evaluation of alternatives. Expensive, complex items with which the consumer has had little or no experience require this form of decision making. Purchases are made quite infrequently. All kinds of perceived risk are usually high, and the purchase is quite important. The consumer has time available to make a choice. Delays in purchases often occur with extended decision making; and demographic, social, and psychological factors have their greatest impact. Extended decision making is usually required when choosing a college, a house, a first car, or a location for a wedding.

Extended consumer decision making is applied to expensive, unique items.

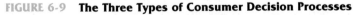

FIGURE 6-9 **The Three Types of Consumer Decision Processes**

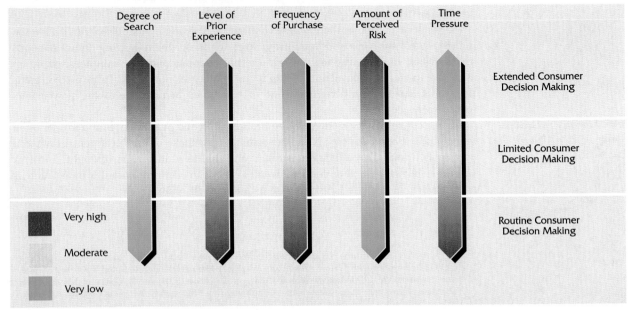

Limited consumer decision making is used for items purchased infrequently.

Limited consumer decision making takes place when a consumer uses each of the steps in the purchase process but does not spend a great deal of time on any of them. The consumer has previously purchased the good or service under consideration, but not regularly. Perceived risk is moderate, and the consumer is willing to spend some time shopping. The thoroughness with which the process is used depends mostly on the amount of prior experience, the importance of the purchase, and the time pressure facing the consumer. Emphasis is usually on evaluating a list of known alternatives, although an information search is undertaken by some consumers. The factors affecting the decision process have some impact on limited decision making. A second car, clothing, gifts, home furnishings, and a vacation are examples of items typically utilizing limited decision making.

Routine consumer decision making is used for regularly purchased items.

Routine consumer decision making occurs when the consumer buys out of habit and skips steps in the process. The consumer seeks to spend as little time as possible in shopping and often repurchases the same brands (or brands bought before). In this category are items with which the consumer has a great deal of experience. These goods and services are bought regularly and, as a result, have little or no perceived risk. They are relatively low in price. Once the consumer realizes a good or service is depleted, a repurchase is made. The time pressure to buy is high. Information search, evaluation of alternatives, and postpurchase behavior are normally omitted as long as the consumer is satisfied. Factors affecting the process have little impact on routine behavior because problem awareness almost always leads to a purchase. Examples of items routinely purchased are the daily newspaper, a haircut by a regular barber, and weekly grocery items.

Because consumers like to reduce the time spent shopping, the use of detailed decision making, and risk, most purchases are made through routine or limited decision making. Accordingly, consumers often engage in low-involvement purchasing and/or brand loyalty. With ***low-involvement purchasing,*** the consumer minimizes decision making for those goods and services perceived to be socially and/or psychologically unimportant. In these cases, consumers are passive about acquiring information, act quickly, and often evaluate products after (rather than before) purchases are made.[18]

Low-involvement purchases occur with unimportant products.

Marketers can respond to low-involvement purchasing by using repetitive advertising to create awareness and familiarity, stressing the problem-solving nature of goods and services, maintaining low prices, offering coupons and free samples, setting up attractive in-store displays, and selling items in all types of outlets. Table 6-6 contrasts the traditional high-involvement view of consumer behavior with the newer low-involvement view.

Brand loyalty reduces consumer time, thought, and risk.

After a consumer tries one or more brands of a good or service, brand loyalty often takes place. ***Brand loyalty*** is the consistent repurchase of and preference toward a particular brand. Through it, consumers are able to reduce time, thought, and risk whenever buying a good or service. Brand loyalty can occur for complex items such as automobiles, as well as for simple items such as gasoline.

---

[18] See Henry Assael, *Consumer Behavior and Marketing Action,* Third Edition (Boston: Kent, 1987), pp. 82–111; Richard Vaughn, "How Advertising Works: A Planning Model Revisited," *Journal of Advertising Research,* Vol. 26 (February–March 1986), pp. 57–66; and Richard L. Celsi and Jerry C. Olson, "The Role of Involvement in Attention and Comprehension Processes," *Journal of Consumer Research,* Vol. 15 (September 1988), pp. 210–224.

You're the Marketer

Sending E.T. Home: How Do You Make Video Buyers Out of Renters?

Most consumers who view prerecorded video-cassettes at home rent rather than own them. Because this situation enables video retailers to make money on rentals while video manufacturers do not, the latter are working hard to increase video sales. As a result, one researcher predicts that videocassette sales will increase from 87 million units in 1988 to 233 million units in 1993. To date, the best-selling video is E.T.: The Extra-Terrestrial, with sales of 12 million units.

To succeed in video sales, companies must convey the benefits of owning versus renting to consumers and convince retailers to devote more effort to selling videos. These are some of the marketing strategies being used:

▶ Marketing budgets are high for anticipated best-sellers. E.T. had a marketing budget of at least $25 million.

▶ More video makers set discount prices: "The magic price point seems to be $20, and more and more tapes are being sold at that level or lower." Such low prices also reduce the consumer's perceived risk of a purchase.

▶ Video tie-ins are aimed at low-involvement consumers to make purchases more worthwhile. With E.T., PepsiCo had a $5 rebate offer. These tie-ins help keep video prices down.

▶ Many videos are mass distributed. Video-rental chains are effective outlets for sales when they understand that such business is complementary and not competitive with rentals. These chains are cooperative when ad support is provided and prices are low. They are also afraid of losing business to K mart and others.

▶ There is an appeal to "collectors." After people purchase their first video, they typically purchase six or more additional videos over the following year.

As the marketing director for a video maker (you are a specialist on consumer life-styles and the consumer's decision process), what would you do to persuade consumers to buy your non-best-seller videos?

SOURCE: Based on material in Ronald Alsop, "Making Video Buyers Out of Renters," Wall Street Journal (September 23, 1988), p. 21.

In 1975, 77 per cent of those surveyed agreed that they "try to stick with well-known brands." In 1985, only 61 per cent of those surveyed agreed with the statement. Nonetheless, brand loyalty remains quite high for products that consumers purchase frequently. For example, today, at least 70 per cent of consumers are exclusive one-brand users for these products: antifreeze, table salt, nonstick cooking spray, powdered breakfast drinks, eye drops, baby powder, egg substitutes, oven cleaners, laxatives, spot removers, in-bowl toilet fresheners, and pet shampoos. Furthermore, brand loyalty tends to be high for items involving significant ego involvement on the part of the consumer. Items falling into this category are perfume, hair coloring, toothpaste, and 35mm film.

Among the low-involvement products with little brand loyalty are cat litter, paper towels, facial tissues, crackers, scouring powder, and hand lotion. These items are

TABLE 6-6   The Traditional High-Involvement View of Active Consumers Versus the Newer Low-Involvement View of Passive Consumers

Traditional High-Involvement View of Active Consumers	Newer Low-Involvement View of Passive Consumers
1. Consumers are information processors.	1. Consumers learn information at random.
2. Consumers are information seekers.	2. Consumers are information gatherers.
3. Consumers represent an active audience for advertising. As a result, the effect of advertising on the consumer is *weak*.	3. Consumers represent a passive audience for advertising. As a result, the effect of advertising on the consumer is *strong*.
4. Consumers evaluate brands before buying.	4. Consumers buy first. If they do evaluate brands, it is done after the purchase.
5. Consumers seek to maximize expected satisfaction. As a result, consumers compare brands to see which provide the most *benefits* related to needs and buy based on multiattribute comparisons of brands.	5. Consumers seek some acceptable level of satisfaction. As a result, consumers buy the brand least likely to give them *problems* and buy based on a few attributes. Familiarity is the key.
6. Personality and life-style characteristics are related to consumer behavior because the product is closely tied to the consumer's identity and belief system.	6. Personality and life-style characteristics are not related to consumer behavior because the product is not closely tied to the consumer's identity and belief system.
7. Reference groups influence consumer behavior because of the importance of the product to group norms and values.	7. Reference groups exert little influence on product choice because products are unlikely to be related to group norms and values.

Source: Henry Assael, *Consumer Behavior and Marketing Action,* Third Edition (Boston: Kent, 1987), p. 96. Reprinted by permission of PWS–Kent Publishing Company, a division of Wadsworth, Inc.

"designed to get boring tasks done as inexpensively as possible. Most consumers switch back and forth between brands with abandon, although some will pay for quality when they come across a brand that they believe does the job better than any other."[19]

Marketing Implications of the Consumer's Decision Process

The consumer's decision process has been examined in various settings.

Theories to explain the consumer's decision process began in the mid-1960s. The three leading theorists were Howard-Sheth, Engel-Kollat-Blackwell, and Nicosia.[20] Since that time, there has been considerable research on the marketing implications of the decision process. Today the applications span many elements of marketing, as these illustrations demonstrate:

▶ The average first-time home buyer looks at 14 houses and spends over four months before selecting a house. He or she spends 1.8 years saving for a down payment.[21]

[19] "Usage of Supermarket Products," *Progressive Grocer* (September 1988), pp. 137–138; and Thomas Exter, "Looking for Brand Loyalty," *American Demographics* (April 1986), pp. 32–33 ff.

[20] John A. Howard and Jagdish N. Sheth, *The Theory of Buyer Behavior* (New York: John Wiley, 1969); James F. Engel, David T. Kollat, and Roger D. Blackwell, *Consumer Behavior* (New York: Holt, 1968); and Francesco Nicosia, *Consumer Decision Processes* (Englewood Cliffs, N.J.: Prentice-Hall, 1966).

[21] Chicago Title Insurance Company, "Home-Buyer Profile," *Wall Street Journal* (April 22, 1985), p. 31.

▶ For major purchases, subscribers of *Consumer Reports* rely heavily on the magazine for information and recommendations. This helps to simplify choices.[22]

▶ In selecting stores at which to shop for clothing, consumers rate a broad selection and merchandise quality as more important purchase criteria than price, store location, and customer service. Half have no preference for any one store.[23]

▶ About 70 per cent of all adults visit a large shopping mall weekly. Yet, only one-quarter of them go to a mall to buy a specific preplanned item.[24]

▶ Most consumers view direct-mail advertisements as low-involvement purchases. Involvement (interest) can be increased by using premiums, sweepstakes, and flashy graphics.[25]

▶ Men are slightly less brand loyal than women. They also take less time to plan their shopping, use fewer coupons, and respond less to supermarket advertising. However, the behavior of working women is similar to that of men.[26]

▶ Satisfied new-car buyers discuss their experiences with eight people; dissatisfied buyers complain to an average of twenty-five people.[27]

Limitations of the Consumer's Decision Process

The limitations of the consumer's decision process for marketers lie in the hidden (unexpressed) nature of many elements of the process, the consumer's subconscious performance of the process or a number of its components, and the impact of demographic, social, and psychological factors on the process.

Much of purchase behavior is hidden or unconscious.

Summary

1. *To show why consumer demographic analysis is not sufficient in planning marketing programs* Because demographic data do not answer such questions as why consumers act as they do, why demographically similar consumers act differently, how risk and motives affect decisions, and how long it takes for consumers to reach purchase decisions, many firms now analyze consumer life-style and decision-making information in conjunction with demographics and then develop descriptive consumer profiles.

2. *To define and describe consumer life-styles, examine selected life-styles, and present marketing implications of life-style analysis* Social and psychological factors comprise consumer life-styles, which are the patterns in which people live and spend time and money. Psychographics is the technique by which life-styles are measured. Consumer social profiles are made up of several elements, including culture, social class, social performance, reference groups, opinion leaders, the family life cycle, and time expenditures. Psychological profiles are based on a combination of these attributes: personality, attitudes (opinions), level of class consciousness, motivation, perceived risk, innovativeness, and the importance of purchases.

These life-style types are expected to continue. The "me" generation stresses being good to one-

[22] Richard W. Olshavsky and Dennis L. Rosen, "Use of Product-Testing Organizations' Recommendations as a Strategy for Choice Simplification," *Journal of Consumer Affairs,* Vol. 19 (Summer 1985), pp. 118–139.

[23] Isadore Barmash, "Shoppers, in Survey, Say Service Is Not a Priority," *New York Times* (October 17, 1988), p. D6.

[24] Betsy Morris, "As a Favored Pastime, Shopping Ranks High With Most Americans," *Wall Street Journal* (July 30, 1987), pp. 1, 13.

[25] "Direct Mail Recipients Respond to Involvement," *Marketing News* (October 25, 1985), p. 32.

[26] Exter, "Looking for Brand Loyalty," p. 54.

[27] Raymond Serafin, "Auto Makers Stress Consumer Satisfaction," *Advertising Age* (February 23, 1987), p. S–12.

self, self-expression, and the acceptance of diversity. With voluntary simplicity, people seek material simplicity, have an ecological awareness, strive for self-reliance, and purchase do-it-yourself products. With blurring gender roles, more husbands are assuming the traditional roles of their wives. The poverty of time occurs for some consumers because the quest for greater affluence results in less free time as the alternatives competing for time expand. In component life-styles, consumer attitudes and behavior depend on particular situations rather than an overall life-style philosophy.

Several general and specific marketing implications relating to consumer life-styles are discussed.

3. *To consider the limitations of consumer life-style analysis* Many life-style concepts can be difficult to measure, somewhat subjective, based on self-reports by consumers, and sometimes hidden from view. There are disputes over terms, misuse of data, and reliability.

4. *To define and describe the consumer's decision process and present marketing implications* The consumer's decision process is the procedure by which consumers collect and analyze information and make choices among alternatives. It is composed of

the process itself and the factors affecting it (demographics, social factors, and psychological factors). It can be delayed or terminated by the consumer at any point.

The process consists of six steps: stimulus, problem awareness, information search, evaluation of alternatives, purchase, and postpurchase behavior. There are three types of consumer decision making: extended, limited, and routine. Consumers reduce shopping time, thought, and risk through low-involvement purchases (for goods and services perceived to be unimportant) and brand loyalty (the consistent repurchase of and preference toward a brand).

The marketing implications of the consumer's decision process have been detailed for over twenty years. Several of the current marketing applications are discussed.

5. *To consider the limitations of consumer decision-making analysis* The limitations of the decision process for marketers lie in the unexpressed nature of many parts of the process, the subconscious nature of many actions by consumers, and the impact of demographic, social, and psychological factors.

Key Terms

life-style (p. 152)
psychographics (p. 152)
culture (p. 153)
social class (p. 153)
social performance (p. 153)
reference group (p. 154)
opinion leaders (p. 154)
family life cycle (p. 155)
joint decision making (p. 155)
time expenditures (p. 156)
personality (p. 157)
attitudes (opinions) (p. 157)
class consciousness (p. 158)
inner-directed person (p. 158)

outer-directed person (p. 159)
motivation (p. 159)
motives (p. 159)
perceived risk (p. 160)
innovativeness (p. 161)
importance of a purchase (p. 162)
"me" generation (p. 162)
voluntary simplicity (p. 162)
blurring gender roles (p. 163)
poverty of time (p. 163)
component life-styles (p. 164)
consumer's decision process (p. 167)
stimulus (p. 168)
problem awareness (p. 170)

information search (p. 170)
evaluation of alternatives (p. 171)
purchase act (p. 171)
postpurchase behavior (p. 172)
cognitive dissonance (p. 172)
extended consumer decision
   making (p. 173)
limited consumer decision
   making (p. 174)
routine consumer decision
   making (p. 174)
low-involvement purchasing (p. 174)
brand loyalty (p. 174)

Review Questions

1. Why are demographic data alone frequently insufficient for marketing decisions?

2. How does social class affect an individual's life-style and purchases?

3. Describe the traditional family life cycle. What are its strengths and weaknesses?

4. When studying attitudes, which two concepts should usually be measured? Why?

5. How does class consciousness differ for inner-directed and outer-directed people? What does this signify for marketers?

6. Distinguish between actual risk and perceived risk. How may a firm reduce each type of perceived risk for a new cold remedy?

7. Differentiate among social, commercial, and noncommercial stimuli. Provide specific examples of each.

8. What causes cognitive dissonance? How may it be reduced?

9. Draw a flowchart showing the steps in routine behavior.

10. Define low-involvement purchasing and explain its use by consumers. Give an example.

Discussion Questions

1. American culture emphasizes achievement and success, activity, efficiency and practicality, progress, material comfort, individualism, freedom, external conformity, humanitarianism, youthfulness, and fitness and health. What are the implications of this for firms marketing the following goods and services?
   a. Vacation travel.
   b. Minivans.
   c. Entertainment.
   d. Televisions.

2. Give examples of current advertisements using a(n)
   a. Aspirational reference group.
   b. Membership reference group.
   c. Dissociative reference group.

3. How would a personal-selling approach aimed at self-confident, dominant consumers differ from one aimed at unsure, easily dominated consumers?

4. Several clothing manufacturers have hired you as a marketing consultant. They are particularly interested in learning more about the concept of component life-styles and developing appropriate responses.
   a. Explain the relevance of component life-styles for the clothing industry.
   b. Suggest a number of ways in which clothing manufacturers can appeal to component life-styles.

5. As a consumer, what criteria would you use to select from among three alternative colleges to attend? Three alternative apartments in which to live? Three savings banks at which to start an account? How would your decision process differ in selecting the best alternative for each of these items?

◄ CASE 1 ►

The Comeback of the Glitzy Automobile*

When the Arab oil embargo in 1973 reduced the availability of gasoline in the United States and led to significantly higher per-gallon gasoline prices, the life-styles of most U.S. consumers changed dramatically. Because many car owners worried that they might not be able to get sufficient fuel and that gas prices might make it too expensive to operate their vehicles, they began to drive a lot less and—in great numbers—turned from large "gas guzzlers" to compact "fuel-efficient" cars. Also, at the same time, the U.S. economy slowed down and many consumers could only afford to buy less expensive goods and services than before.

In response, auto makers downsized their cars,

improved fuel economy, and offered inexpensive models. By the mid-1980s, most full-sized Ford and General Motors cars were the same size as mid-sized vehicles a decade earlier, and Chrysler really had no full-sized car. And by 1988, the typical new car averaged over 25 miles per gallon of gasoline (about double the 1973 average).

Nonetheless, despite the trend toward the purchase of smaller, less powerful cars, many U.S. consumers were quite unhappy about this change in their life-styles; these people truly have a "love affair" with their cars—which represent status, a feeling of accomplishment, power, freedom, and so on. Cars play a central role in the lives of a large number of consumers. Some social scientists believe autos are really viewed as extensions of the office (due to the popularity of cellular phones) or the home (due to their poshness).

Accordingly, now, as consumer concerns about

* The data in this case are drawn from Jacob M. Schlesinger, "After an Era of Blandness, Big and Glitzy Autos Are Making a Comeback," *Wall Street Journal* (December 7, 1988), pp. A1, A8.

gasoline availability have disappeared, per-gallon prices are less than ten years ago, and the U.S. economy has bounced back, a large number of consumers are returning to their former automobile behavior patterns. For example,

> Five or six years ago, people were price shoppers. We'd sell the el strippo, basic cars. Today, people want the biggest motor they can get—they want something fancy.

> One customer recently walked in and unceremoniously dumped his stripped-down 1983 Volvo GL sedan for a new Celebrity Eurosport loaded to the gills with options. Another bid his gas-sipping, 1979 Toyota Celica farewell—and embraced a souped-up Monte Carlo Supersport with T-top. And yet another cast off her boxy 1984 Mercury Grand Marquis for a new red Camaro convertible.

These are some specific indicators of how "glitz," power, and styling are in—and "dull" is out—for automobile buyers:

> ▷ Cadillac will now spray a 24-carat gold covering over any model's regular trim for customers willing to pay an additional $395 or so.

And, beginning with the 1989 model year, Cadillac added nine inches to the length of the Sedan de Ville and also stretched its vertical tail-lights by six inches.

> ▷ The average horsepower per 100 pounds of car has increased steadily, from 3.4 in 1981 to more than 4.1 today. As an illustration, in 1986, the Toyota Camry had a 4-cylinder, 95-horsepower engine; now the car is available with an optional V-6 engine with 153 horsepower.

> ▷ Convertibles are popular once again. Yet, from 1977 to 1982, no major auto maker made convertibles (due in part to safety considerations and the popularity of sunroofs). Then in 1982, about 40,000 convertibles were sold. By 1988, annual sales of convertibles were over 200,000 units (almost 2 per cent of the total new-car market). Currently more than twenty different convertible models are available.

> ▷ Chevrolet officials are carefully considering "freshening" the style of their cars every two years, a strategy that is a throwback to the 1950s—when styles were changed annually.

QUESTIONS

1. What life-style factors (both social and psychological) do you think have the greatest impact on the purchase of a car? Explain your answer.
2. What kind of automobile would be most appealing to an inner-directed person? An outer-directed person? Why?
3. Explain how each type of perceived risk could affect the purchase of a new auto.
4. Relate automobile purchases to each of these life-style concepts:
   a. Voluntary simplicity.   c. The "me" generation.
   b. Blurring gender roles.   d. Component life-styles.

◀ **CASE 2** ▶

Brand Loyalty: A Powerful Marketing Tool[†]

Brand loyalty, that certain something that makes a consumer keep buying over and over again, is an elusive quality. When a branded product has been around a long time and is heavily advertised, it can pick up a lot of emotional freight; it can become part of a person's self-image or summon fond memories of days gone by.

Marketers battling to keep competitors from grabbing off customers complain that there just doesn't seem to be as much brand loyalty around as there used to be. Yet when Coca-Cola Co. dared to tamper with a 99-year formula to bring out "new" Coke, outraged U.S. consumers forced the red-faced company to bring back the old brand.

In 1988, R.H. Bruskin Associates, a marketing research firm, conducted a consumer survey to evaluate the relationship between brand discrimination (the perceived differences among competing

---

[†] The data in this case are drawn from Anne B. Fisher, "Coke's Brand Loyalty Lesson," *Fortune* (August 5, 1985), pp. 44–46; and R.H. Bruskin, "New Study on Brand Loyalty," *Marketing Review* (June 1988), p. 25.

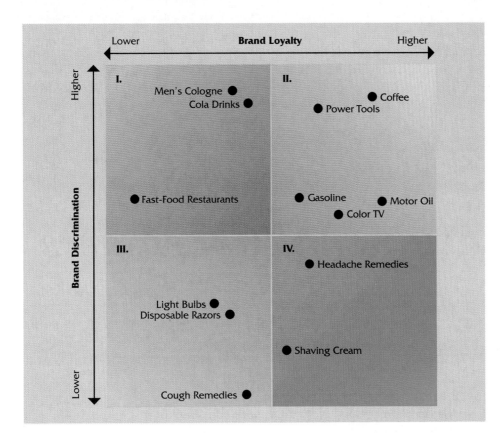

Lower **Brand Loyalty** Higher

Higher

I.
Men's Cologne ●
Cola Drinks ●

● Fast-Food Restaurants

II.
● Coffee
● Power Tools

● Gasoline   ● Motor Oil
   ● Color TV

Brand Discrimination

III.

Light Bulbs ●
Disposable Razors ●

Cough Remedies ●

IV.
● Headache Remedies

● Shaving Cream

Lower

FIGURE 1
The Relationship Between Brand Discrimination and Brand Loyalty
SOURCE: R.H. Bruskin, "New Study on Brand Loyalty," *Marketing Review* (June 1988), p. 25. Reprinted by permission.

brands) and brand loyalty. More than 2,000 adult respondents were asked these two questions for each of 13 product categories: (1) "Do you feel that all brands are pretty much alike except for price?" (brand discrimination) and (2) "Do you tend to buy just one brand, alternate between two or three brands that are acceptable to you, or do you switch around?" (brand loyalty)?

Figure 1 graphically summarizes the findings of the Bruskin study. Quadrant I contains product categories with high brand discrimination (consumers perceive large differences among brands) and low brand loyalty (consumers report that they often switch among brands). Quadrant II contains product categories with high brand discrimination and

high brand loyalty (consumers report that they rarely switch brands). Quadrant III contains products with low brand discrimination (consumers perceive small differences among brands) and low brand loyalty. Quadrant IV contains products with low brand discrimination but high brand loyalty.

In developing and implementing marketing strategies, companies should understand the implications of product categories being positioned in certain quadrants. For example, light bulbs and disposable razors are both positioned in Quadrant III. This suggests that firms need to differentiate products in a meaningful manner as well as stimulate target consumers to repurchase the same brand.

QUESTIONS

1. What factors can cause consumers to become brand loyal?
2. Why do you think that cola drinks are positioned in Quadrant I, while disposable razors are positioned in Quadrant III? What are the marketing implications of this?
3. What impact would the family life cycle and class consciousness have on brand loyalty?

4. As a new firm entering the power tool market,
   a. Would it be easy or difficult for you to succeed in this market (based on the position of power tools in Quadrant I)?
   b. What consumer life-style factors should you study?
   c. Describe your differential advantage in a way that would be appealing to consumers.

CHAPTER 7
Organizational Consumers

CHAPTER OBJECTIVES

1. *To introduce the concept of industrial marketing*

2. *To examine the characteristics of organizational consumers and show how they differ from final consumers*

3. *To describe the different types of organizational consumers and their buying objectives, buying structure, and purchase constraints*

4. *To explain the organizational consumer's decision process*

5. *To consider the marketing implications of appealing to organizational consumers*

The Standard Industrial Classification (SIC) system was developed by the federal government to facilitate the collection and dissemination of data pertaining to all business and industry activity in the United States. The two-digit level of detail, referred to as *Major Groups,* describes general manufacturing and nonmanufacturing categories. The four-digit SIC codes describe the various types of industrial activity related to each Major Group and are referred to as *Specific Industries.*

For firms marketing goods and services to organizational consumers (manufacturers, wholesalers, retailers, and government and other nonprofit institutions), the SIC system is extremely useful because commercial research houses, economists, the U.S. government, and others collect and distribute a great deal of information categorized by SIC code. Thus, SIC data can be used in determining a target market, analyzing industry prospects, and forecasting sales. As an illustration, a company marketing to ice-cream manufacturers could examine data relating to SIC 20 (representing food and kindred products firms) and SIC 2024 (representing ice-cream and frozen-dessert firms).

1987 was a milestone year for the SIC system because the federal government completed the first major revision in it since 1970. This revision provides us with insights into the evolving nature of U.S. industries. How? In the revision, growing industries are allocated additional four-digit codes to describe more accurately the nature of their expansion. In contrast, declining industries have been deleted or combined with adjacent industries because each of these industry groups alone may no longer be able to meet the "economic significance" standard of the SIC system. Let us look at some of these revised codes.

The most significant changes affect the computer and computer peripherals industries. Not surprisingly, the industry codes covering this industry have been greatly increased to respond to the breakneck growth of computers since 1970. Computer manufacturing, which previously was comprised of one four-digit industry (electronic computing equipment), is now broken down into five separate four-digit codes to reflect the diversity of computer types as well as the economic importance of each specific industry. As a result, firms marketing to computer companies are now able to obtain and analyze separate data for computer terminals, computer peripheral equipment, and recording media. In the past, these industry groups were consolidated under the four-digit electronic

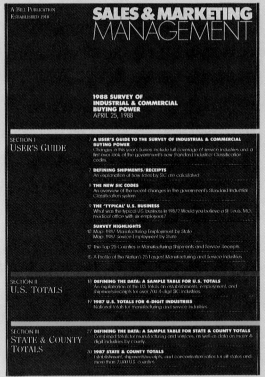

Reprinted by permission of *Sales & Marketing Management.* Copyright: *Survey of Commercial and Industrial Buying Power,* April 25, 1988.

computing-equipment code. Other new four-digit codes reflect the growth and importance of computer services (such as prepackaged computer software, computer rental and leasing, and computer maintenance and repair).

The revised codes also indicate the significant growth of the services sector of the economy. There is a new two-digit major group for selected professional and technical services. Management, consulting, and public relations (which was one four-digit grouping) are now subdivided into five categories. And new four-digit codes reflect the increased importance of such services as physical fitness, tax-return preparation, videotape rentals, and home health care.

On the other hand, anthracite mining has been deleted as a two-digit category. Its sales have declined too much for it to be considered a major group.[1]

In this chapter, we will study the characteristics and behavior of organizational consumers. Thus, the SIC classification will be an essential part of our discussion.

[1] "Defining the Data: A Sample Table for U.S. Totals," *Sales & Marketing Management* (April 25, 1988), p. 18; and Charles W. Stryker, "A User's Guide to the Survey of Industrial & Commercial Buying Power," *Sales & Marketing Management* (April 25, 1988), pp. 7–9.

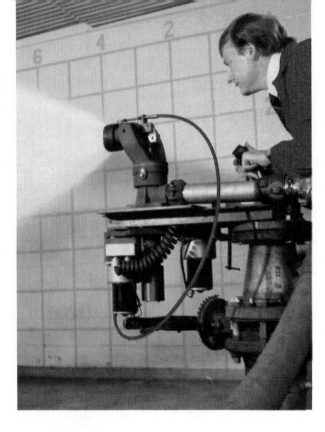

FIGURE 7-1
Premier: An Industrial Marketing Giant
Among the products distributed by Premier Industrial are a full line of fire-fighting equipment—ranging from nozzles, valves, and remote control products to portable fire-fighting systems. Its customers include fire departments, fire truck manufacturers, the military services, and industrial concerns.
Reprinted by permission.

Overview

*Companies involved with organizational consumers use **industrial marketing**.*

As defined in Chapter 5, organizational consumers purchase goods and services for further production, use in operations, or resale to others. In contrast, final consumers buy for personal, family, or household use. Organizational consumers are manufacturers, wholesalers, retailers, and government and other nonprofit institutions. When firms deal with organizational consumers, they engage in **industrial marketing,** as shown in these illustrations.

Premier Industrial Corporation of Cleveland, Ohio, is a "broad line distributor of electronic components used in the production and maintenance of equipment, a supplier of maintenance products for industrial, commercial, and institutional applications, and a manufacturer of high-performance fire-fighting accessories." To attract and keep customers, Premier offers the widest possible assortment; its electronic components catalog is 1,000+ pages and is distributed to almost one million industrial customers. Premier has a sophisticated computerized inventory management system to maximize customer service and satisfaction. A well-trained sales force is also employed; it specializes in identifying and solving customer problems in maintaining their buildings, vehicles, and equipment. Premier is quite innovative in developing fire-fighting products for 30,000 fire departments across the United States.[2] See Figure 7-1.

Sharp Electronics, Ricoh, and Canon are the three leading makers of facsimile ("fax") machines — one of the fastest-growing industrial product categories in recent

[2] *Premier Industrial Corporation 1988 Annual Report.*

years. Facsimile machines resemble small photocopiers and are attached to the telephones of a calling company and a receiving company, enabling the latter to quickly (about 20 seconds) reproduce printed documents from the sender. Sharp, Ricoh, Canon, and others market fax machines at prices ranging from about $700 to $12,000 and appeal to both large and small organizational consumers that are trying to improve their operating efficiency and speed the flow of information. Fax machines are distributed via stores as well as sold by field sales staffs. Newspaper and magazine advertising are plentiful. In 1990, fax sales are expected to approach $2.5 billion, up from $700 million in 1986.[3]

Major Leasing Inc. of Atlanta is a small service-based firm that leases vehicles, such as panel trucks. The company leases mostly to the independent dealers who sell Snap-On Tools at worksites and industrial parks (and use their leased trucks as mobile warehouses and showrooms). By leasing, the Snap-On dealers do not have to invest $45,000 or more in their vehicles; they receive personalized advice and follow-up service from Major Leasing; and they do not have to worry about trade-ins.[4]

In this chapter, organizational consumers are clearly differentiated from final consumers. The various types of organizational consumers are described. The special characteristics of organizational consumers are presented. The organizational consumer's decision process is outlined.

The Characteristics of Organizational Consumers

In undertaking industrial marketing, a company must recognize that organizational consumers differ from final consumers in several important ways. These differences are due to the nature of purchases and the nature of the market. See Table 7-1 and the discussion in the following subsections.

Differences from Final Consumers Due to the Nature of Purchases

Organizational and final consumers vary in the way they use goods and services and in the types of items purchased. Organizational consumers purchase capital equipment, raw materials, semifinished goods, and other products for use in further production or operations or for resale to others. Final consumers usually acquire finished items (and are not involved with million-dollar purchases of plant and equipment) for personal, family, or household use. Because of the nature of their purchases, organizational consumers are more likely to use specifications, multiple-buying decisions, value and vendor analysis, leased equipment, and competitive bidding and negotiation than are final consumers.

Many organizational consumers rely on product specifications in purchase decisions and do not consider alternatives unless they meet minimum standards, such as engineering and architectural guidelines, purity, horsepower, voltage, type of construction, and construction materials. Final consumers more often purchase on the basis of description, style, and color. See Figure 7-2.

---

[3] Susan M. Gelfond, "It's a Fax, Fax, Fax, Fax World," *Business Week* (March 21, 1988), p. 136; and "Fax Fixation," *Advertising Age* (August 15, 1988), pp. 3, 60.

[4] Stephen P. Galante, "Tiny Leasing Firm Beats a Giant with Focus on Market Segment," *Wall Street Journal* (August 31, 1987), p. 19.

TABLE 7-1   Major Differences Between Organizational and Final Consumers

Differences in Purchases

1. Organizational consumers acquire for further production, use in operations, or resale to other consumers. Final consumers acquire only for personal, family, or household use.
2. Organizational consumers commonly purchase installations, raw materials, and semifinished materials. Final consumers rarely purchase these goods.
3. Organizational consumers purchase on the basis of specifications and technical data. Final consumers frequently purchase on the basis of description, fashion, and style.
4. Organizational consumers utilize multiple-buying and team-based decisions more often than final consumers.
5. Organizational consumers are more likely to apply value and vendor analysis.
6. Organizational consumers more commonly lease equipment.
7. Organizational consumers more frequently employ competitive bidding and negotiation.

Differences in the Market

1. The demand of organizational consumers is derived from the demand of final consumers.
2. The demand of organizational consumers is more subject to cyclical fluctuations than final-consumer demand.
3. Organizational consumers are fewer in number and more geographically concentrated than final consumers.
4. Organizational consumers often employ buying specialists.
5. The distribution channel for organizational consumers is shorter than for final consumers.
6. Organizational consumers may require special services.
7. Organizational consumers are more likely than final consumers to be able to make goods and services as alternatives to purchasing them.

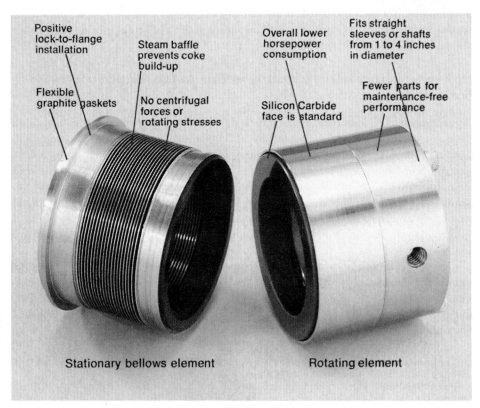

Positive lock-to-flange installation

Steam baffle prevents coke build-up

Overall lower horsepower consumption

Fits straight sleeves or shafts from 1 to 4 inches in diameter

Flexible graphite gaskets

No centrifugal forces or rotating stresses

Silicon Carbide face is standard

Fewer parts for maintenance-free performance

Stationary bellows element

Rotating element

FIGURE 7-2
A Mechanical Seal from Borg-Warner
In marketing this product, specifications are very important. Reprinted by permission.

FIGURE 7-3
Multiple-Buying Responsibility
Carter Hawley Hale, one of the largest retail chains in the United States, has a Market Services division with 130 professional and support personnel. This division works with buyers and merchants from store divisions to identify opportunities for private-label merchandise and to maximize order quantities in buying.
Reprinted by permission. © Paul Fusco, Magnum Photos.

Organizational consumers often utilize ***multiple-buying responsibility,*** in which two or more employees formally participate in complex or expensive purchase decisions. For example, a decision to buy computerized cash registers may involve input from computer personnel, marketing personnel, the operations manager, a systems consultant, and the controller. The firm's president might make the final choice about system characteristics and the supplier. Although final consumers use multiple-buying responsibility (joint decision making), they employ it less frequently and less formally. See Figure 7-3.

Multiple-buying responsibility may be shared by two or more employees.

Organizational consumers may apply value analysis and vendor analysis. With ***value analysis,*** these consumers systematically compare the costs versus the benefits of alternative materials, components, designs, or processes in order to reduce the cost/benefit ratio of purchases as much as possible.[5] They seek to answer such questions as these: What is the purpose of each good or service under purchase consideration? What are the short-run (purchase price) and long-run (operating costs) costs of each alternative? Is a purchase necessary? Are there substitute goods or services that could perform more efficiently? How long will the good or service last before it has to be replaced? Can uniform standards be set to ease reordering? In ***vendor analysis,***

Value analysis reduces costs; vendor analysis rates suppliers.

[5] Peter D. Bennett (Editor), *Dictionary of Marketing Terms* (Chicago: American Marketing Association, 1988), p. 209.

	Definitely Yes	Probably Yes	Uncertain	Probably No	Definitely No
· Can plastic pipe be substituted to reduce costs?	----------	----------	----------	----------	----------
· Can a standardized 1/3-horsepower motor be used?	----------	----------	----------	----------	----------
· Can an external float-triggered switch be used instead of an internal one?	----------	----------	----------	----------	----------
· Can a noncorrosive base replace the current base which is easily corroded?	----------	----------	----------	----------	----------
· Is a Westinghouse motor more reliable than a GE motor?	----------	----------	----------	----------	----------
· Is a 5-year warranty acceptable?	----------	----------	----------	----------	----------

FIGURE 7-4

Value Analysis by a Purchaser of an Electrical Pump

organizational consumers systematically assess the strengths and weaknesses of current or new suppliers in terms of such factors as merchandise quality, customer service, reliability, and price.[6] Satisfaction with the performance of current vendors often leads to customer loyalty. Figures 7-4 and 7-5 show examples of value analysis and vendor analysis.

Organizational consumers frequently lease major equipment. Yearly, firms spend almost $100 billion in leasing capital equipment, accounting for one-third of all such equipment acquired with external financing. Eight of every 10 U.S. firms, of all sizes, are regularly involved in leasing.[7] Final consumers are less involved with leasing; it is most common in apartment rentals.

Organizational consumers often utilize competitive bidding and negotiation in important (large) purchase situations. In **competitive bidding,** two or more sellers submit independent price quotations for specific goods and/or services to the buyer, who chooses the best offer. In **negotiation,** the buyer uses bargaining ability and order size to get the best possible prices from sellers. Bidding and negotiation are most applicable for complex, custom-made goods and services.

*In **competitive bidding,** sellers submit price bids; in **negotiation,** the buyer bargains to set prices.*

Differences from Final Consumers Due to the Nature of the Market

*Organizational consumers **derive demand** from final consumer demand.*

Derived demand occurs for organizational consumers because their purchases of goods and services are usually based on the anticipated demand of their final consumers for specific finished goods and services. For example, the demand for precision rivets used in aircraft construction is derived from the demand for new aircraft, which ultimately is derived from the demand for air travel. Manufacturers realize that unless

[6] Ibid., p. 210.
[7] Harvey Shapiro, "Equipment Leasing: Stronger Than Ever," *Forbes* (October 3, 1988), pp. A1–A5.

	Superior	Average	Inferior
· Speed of normal delivery	----------	----------	----------
· Speed of rush delivery	----------	----------	----------
· Distinctiveness of merchandise	----------	----------	----------
· Availability of styles and colors in all sizes	----------	----------	----------
· Handling of defective merchandise	----------	----------	----------
· Per cent of merchandise defective	----------	----------	----------
· Ability for organizational consumer to make a profit when reselling merchandise	----------	----------	----------
· Purchase terms	----------	----------	----------

FIGURE 7-5
Vendor Analysis of a Sweater Supplier by a Purchaser

demand is generated at the final consumer level, distribution pipelines become clogged quickly and channel members will not purchase fresh goods and services. For this reason, organizational consumers are less sensitive to price changes; as long as final consumers are willing to pay higher prices, organizational consumers will not object to price increases. On the other hand, low final consumer demand will result in reduced purchases by organizational consumers, even if prices are lowered. Figure 7-6 illustrates derived demand for major household appliances.

A good example of derived demand is the situation facing the U.S. beef industry. Since 1976, Americans have decreased their per capita consumption of beef by over 20 per cent. Today's consumer is more health conscious and eating more chicken products (up 50 per cent since 1976). As a result, supermarkets and restaurants are diversifying their offerings and placing less emphasis on beef items. This has adversely affected beef processors, who are placing fewer orders with cattle ranchers.[8]

*Through the **accelerator** **principle,** final consumer demand impacts on many organizational consumers.*

The demand of organizational consumers tends to be more volatile than that of final consumers. A small change in the final demand for highly processed goods and services can yield a large change in organizational consumers' demand. This is attributed to the **accelerator principle,** whereby final consumer demand affects several layers of organizational consumers. For example, a decline in automobile demand by final consumers reduces dealers' demand for automobiles, car manufacturers' demand for steel and other raw materials, and steel manufacturers' demand for iron ore. In addition, major purchases by organizational consumers (such as plant and equipment) are highly influenced by the economy.

Organizational consumers tend to be large and geographically concentrated.

Organizational consumers are fewer in number than final consumers. In the United States, there are about 360,000 manufacturing establishments, 420,000 wholesaling establishments, and 2 million retailing establishments, as compared with over 90 million final consumer households. In some industries, the largest firms dominate,

---

[8] Marj Charlier, "The U.S. Beef Industry Just Can't Seem to Get the Hang of Marketing," *Wall Street Journal* (January 4, 1989), pp. A1–A2.

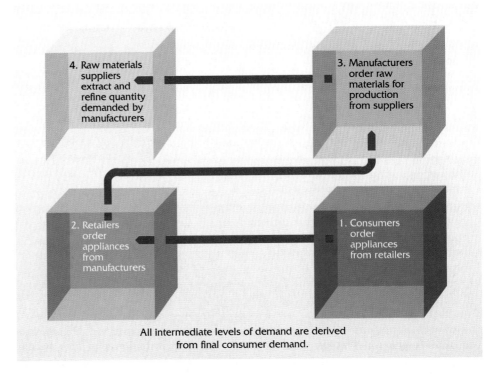

FIGURE 7-6
Derived Demand for Major Appliances

All intermediate levels of demand are derived from final consumer demand.

and their size gives them bargaining power in dealing with sellers. For example, when General Motors (GM) is displeased with suppliers, it drops them and selects others. This can severely affect those dropped. In 1988, as its tire operations were being acquired by Bridgestone, Firestone learned that GM planned to phase it out as a tire supplier. At the time, GM represented 20 per cent of Firestone's U.S. tire sales.[9]

Organizational consumers also are geographically concentrated. For example, eight states (California, New York, Illinois, Ohio, Pennsylvania, Michigan, Texas, and New Jersey) contain about half of the nation's manufacturing plants. Some industries (such as steel, petroleum, rubber, auto, and tobacco) are even more geographically concentrated.

Buying specialists negotiate with expertise.

Because of their size and the types of purchases, many organizational consumers use **buying specialists.** These employees often have technical backgrounds and are trained in supplier analysis and negotiating. Their full-time jobs are to purchase goods and services and analyze purchases. Expertise is high.

Because organizational consumers are large and geographically concentrated, purchase complex and custom-made goods and services, and use buying specialists, distribution channels tend to be shorter than those for final consumers. For example, a typewriter manufacturer would deal directly with a firm buying 100 typewriters, and a salesperson would call on that organization's purchasing agent. A company marketing typewriters to final consumers would distribute through retail stores and expect final consumers to visit those stores.

Organizational consumers may require special services, such as extended warran-

---

[9] Timothy D. Schellhardt, "GM to Drop Firestone as a Tire Supplier for North American Cars Within 2 Years," *Wall Street Journal* (April 25, 1988), p. 2.

You're the Marketer

Beware the Big Contract?

According to many marketing experts, small vendors need to be very careful when receiving a substantial contract from a large organizational customer, particularly if the customer would represent a major proportion of the vendors' overall sales and profits. These vendors need to look beyond their initial reactions of flattery and the promise of steady sales volume.

Here are some factors to consider in dealing with a large customer: the buyer is in a very powerful position; the loss of this client would be devastating to the seller; and the seller may may be forced to pay inadequate attention to other accounts. According to the director of one consulting firm, "Captives start losing their competitive edge. They stop using the street smarts and coping skills that got them rolling in the first place. They don't develop new products or internal systems or their own management talent. They become order takers."

The experience of Genex Corp., a small manufacturer of a critical ingredient in aspartame (Searle's popular artificial sweetener marketed under the Equal and Nutrasweet brand names), shows how problems can pop up. In 1983, one year after Genex agreed to manufacture this ingredient exclusively for Searle, the overall sales of Genex tripled from 1982 levels—and Searle's orders amounted to 76 per cent of Genex's overall revenues. However, after Searle decided to discontinue purchases from Genex as of July 1985, the firm did not have any other customers on hand to purchase the aspartame ingredient and could find no other means for using the manufacturing facilities. Genex lost $16 million in 1985, closed its factory, and had to begin to rebuild business.

As the owner of a small battery factory, what would you do if a large firm asks you to use your full plant capacity to make custom-designed batteries for it?

SOURCE: Based on material in Frank Allen, "Beware the Big Contract," *Wall Street Journal* (June 10, 1988), p. 36R.

---

ties, a liberal return policy, advertising support when reselling to final consumers, and free credit. Two other special services are systems selling and reciprocity. In **systems selling,** a combination of goods and services is provided to the buyer by a single source. This enables the buyer to have single-source accountability, one firm with which to negotiate, and an assurance of compatibility among various parts and components. Xerox employs systems selling for its main copiers, word processors, printers, typewriters, personal computers, and servicing. See Figure 7-7.

*Through **systems selling,** there is single-source accountability.*

Reciprocity is a procedure by which organizational consumers select suppliers who agree to purchase goods and services as well as sell them. The Justice Department and the Federal Trade Commission monitor reciprocity because of its potential lessening of competition. A legal example of reciprocity is the way that IBM has been experimenting with buying back used PCs from its dealers to encourage them (and their customers) to buy more new PCs: "IBM dealers are authorized to give trade-in allowances on old IBM PCs, XTs, and ATs when customers buy new PS/2s. IBM then buys back the old computers [from their authorized dealers]."[10]

*In **reciprocity,** suppliers purchase as well as sell.*

---

[10] Susan M. Gelfond, "Old PCs Don't Die, They Just Go Back to Market," *Business Week* (August 29, 1988), p. 52.

FIGURE 7-7
Systems Selling by Xerox
Reprinted by permission.

Last, organizational consumers may be able to produce goods and services themselves, if they find purchase terms, the way they are treated, or available choices unacceptable. Sometimes they may suggest to suppliers that they will make their own goods in order to improve their bargaining positions.

Types of Organizational Consumers

In developing a marketing plan aimed at organizational consumers, it is necessary to research their attributes: areas of specialization, size and resources, location, and goods and services purchased. As shown in Figure 7-8, organizational consumers may be placed into five broad major categories: manufacturers, wholesalers, retailers, government, and nonprofit.

*The **Standard Industrial Classification** provides information on organizational consumers.*

The ***Standard Industrial Classification (SIC)*** may be used to derive information about most types of organizational consumers. The SIC, compiled by the U.S. Office of Management and Budget, assigns organizations to eleven basic industrial classifications: agricultural, forestry, and fishing; mining; construction; manufacturing; transportation, communication, electric, gas, and sanitary services; wholesale trade; retail trade; finance, insurance, and real estate; services; public administration; and nonclassifiable establishments. There are also over 1,000 more specific industry classifications, such as computer programming services.

Substantial data by SIC code are available from various government and commercial publications. For example, the Bureau of Industrial Economics' *Industrial Outlooks, Standard & Poor's Register,* and *Dun & Bradstreet's Middle Market Directory* provide information by SIC code and geographic area. Information on government organizations is also available on a local, state, and federal level from sources such as the *Census of Governments.*

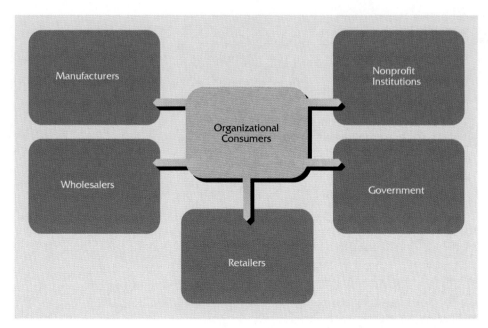

FIGURE 7-8
Types of Organizational Consumers

End-use analysis is one way in which SIC data can be employed. In end-use analysis, a seller determines the proportion of its sales that are made to organizational consumers in different industries. Table 7-2 shows end-use analysis for a glue manufacturer (in this example, the seller). First, the manufacturer ascertains the current relative importance of various categories of its customers—7-2(A). Then the firm applies end-use analysis to make an overall sales forecast by estimating the expected growth of each customer category in its geographic area—7-2(B).

In the following subsections, several characteristics of manufacturers, wholesalers, retailers, government, and nonprofit organizations as consumers are described.

*In **end-use analysis**, a seller studies sales made in different industries.*

Manufacturers as Consumers

Manufacturers produce products for resale to other consumers. The *Standard Industrial Classification Manual* lists twenty major two-digit industry groups in manufacturing. See Table 7-3. Each of the major industries is divided into three-digit groups; these are then broken down into four-digit subgroupings. For example, SIC 23 includes apparel and other textile products; 233, women's, misses', and juniors' outerwear; and 2331, women's, misses', and juniors' blouses and shirts.

__Manufacturers__ make items for resale to others.

In the United States, more than one-third of all manufacturers have twenty or more employees. The annual costs of materials to manufacturers far exceed $1 trillion. New capital expenditures for plant and equipment are over $150 billion each year. Manufacturers annually use 15 trillion BTUs of energy. Annual net sales are approaching $3 trillion, with the largest 500 U.S. industrial firms having sales of $2 trillion each year.[11]

[11] U.S. Bureau of Economic Analysis, *Survey of Current Business, Current Business Reports, Annual Survey of Manufactures;* and "The Fortune 500," *Fortune* (April 24, 1989), p. 372.

TABLE 7-2 End-Use Analysis for a Glue Manufacturer

(A) Simple End-Use Analysis

SIC Code	Industry Classification of Customers	Current Total Sales (in Per Cent)[a]
24	Lumber and wood products	25
25	Furniture and fixtures	20
27	Printing, publishing, and allied industries	17
30	Rubber and miscellaneous plastic products	15
31	Leather and leather products	10
39	Miscellaneous manufacturing industries	13
	Total	100

(B) Applying End-Use Analysis to Sales Forecasting

SIC Code	Industry Classification of Customers	Per Cent of Current Total Sales	Estimated Annual Percentage Growth Rate of Industry[b]	Overall Sales Growth for Glue Manufacturer[c]
24	Lumber and wood products	25	+10	+2.50
25	Furniture and fixtures	20	+12	+2.40
27	Printing, publishing, and allied industries	17	+ 7	+1.19
30	Rubber and miscellaneous plastic products	15	+ 3	+0.45
31	Leather and leather products	10	− 2	−0.20
39	Miscellaneous manufacturing industries	13	+ 5	+0.65
	Total estimated sales increase			+6.99

[a] Firm examines its sales receipts and categorizes them by SIC group.
[b] Firm estimates growth rate of each category of customer (in its geographic area) on the basis of trade association and government data.
[c] Firm multiplies per cent of current sales in each SIC group by expected growth rate in each industry to derive its own expected sales for the coming year. It expects sales to increase by 6.99 per cent during the next year.

By knowing where different industries are located, a firm can concentrate efforts and not worry about covering dispersed geographic markets. Because the purchasing decisions of manufacturers may be made centrally at headquarters, the seller must identify the location of the proper decision maker.

As consumers, manufacturers purchase many goods and services, including land and capital equipment, machinery, raw materials, component parts, trade publications, accounting services, supplies, insurance, advertising, and delivery services. For example, in a typical year, IBM buys goods and services from over 35,000 vendors (including thousands of small vendors that it has added in recent years) that sell it everything from graphics boards to mainframe computer parts to office furniture.[12]

Wholesalers as Consumers

Wholesalers buy or handle merchandise and its resale to nonfinal consumers.

Wholesalers buy or handle merchandise and its subsequent resale to organizational users, retailers, and other wholesalers. They do not sell significant volume to final users. Table 7-4 lists the major industry groups in wholesaling as well as related

[12] Udayan Gupta, "Technology Firms Act to Minimize the Risks of Their Ties to IBM," *Wall Street Journal* (July 10, 1986), pp. 1, 16.

TABLE 7-3   U.S. Manufacturing Industries

SIC Code	Industry Name	SIC Code	Industry Name
20	Food and kindred products	30	Rubber and miscellaneous plastic products
21	Tobacco products	31	Leather and leather products
22	Textile mill products	32	Stone, clay, glass, and concrete products
23	Apparel, other textile products	33	Primary metal industries
24	Lumber and wood products	34	Fabricated metal products
25	Furniture and fixtures	35	Industrial and commercial machinery, and computer equipment
26	Paper and allied products		
27	Printing, publishing, and allied industries	36	Electrical and electronic equipment
28	Chemicals and allied products	37	Transportation equipment
29	Petroleum refining and related industries	38	Instruments and related products
		39	Miscellaneous manufacturing

Source: *Standard Industrial Classification Manual 1987* (Washington, D.C.: Office of Management and Budget, 1987).

transportation industries. Chapter 13 contains a full and comprehensive discussion of wholesaling.

Wholesalers are most prominent in New York, California, Illinois, Texas, Ohio, Pennsylvania, and New Jersey. Total annual wholesaling and related sales (excluding agents and brokers) are well over $2 trillion. Sales are largest for groceries and related products; machinery, equipment, and supplies; motor vehicles and automotive parts and supplies; electrical goods; lumber and other construction materials; hardware, plumbing, and heating supplies; and paper and paper products.

As consumers, wholesalers purchase or handle many goods and services, including warehouse facilities, trucks, finished products, insurance, refrigerators, trade publications, accounting services, supplies, and spare parts. A major task in dealing with wholesalers is getting them to carry the selling firm's product line for further resale, thereby placing the items into the distribution system. For new sellers or those with new products, gaining wholesaler cooperation may be difficult.

Sometimes even well-established manufacturers can have problems with their wholesalers. For instance, after PepsiCo acquired the Seven-Up Co., the latter's relations with its outside wholesalers (bottlers) deteriorated. Philip Morris, "in its desire to build a soda company that could challenge the giants," treated the wholesalers "as mere distributors rather than partners." Today, under new ownership, Seven-Up realizes that "most of the great ideas in this industry come from some bottler somewhere. When the bottler gets excited, it's contagious."[13]

Retailers buy or handle goods and services for sale (resale) to the ultimate (final) consumer. They usually obtain their goods and services from a combination of man-

Retailers sell to the final consumer.

[13] Francis C. Brown, III, "Seven Up's Harford Courts His Bottlers," *Wall Street Journal* (April 16, 1987), p. 35.

TABLE 7-4   U.S. Wholesaling and Related Industries

SIC Code	Industry Name	SIC Code	Industry Name
40	Railroads	51	Nondurables
42	Trucking and warehousing		Paper and paper products
44	Water transportation		Drugs, proprietaries, and sundries
45	Air transportation		Apparel, piece goods, and notions
46	Pipelines, except natural gas		Groceries and related products
47	Transportation services		Farm-product raw materials
			Chemicals and allied products
50	Durables		Petroleum and allied products
	Motor vehicles and motor vehicle parts		Beer, wine, and distilled beverages
	Furniture and home furnishings		Miscellaneous nondurable goods
	Lumber and construction materials	73	Business services (such as)
	Sporting, recreational, and photographic goods		Advertising agencies
			Credit-reporting services
	Metals and minerals, except petroleum		Commerical photography
	Electrical goods		Building maintenance services
	Hardware, plumbing, and heating equipment		Equipment rental and leasing
			Computer-related services
	Machinery, equipment, and supplies		Security-systems firms

Source: Standard Industrial Classification Manual 1987 (Washington, D.C.: Office of Management and Budget, 1987).

TABLE 7-5   U.S. Retailing Industries

SIC Code	Industry Name	SIC Code	Industry Name
52	Building materials, hardware, garden supply, and mobile home dealers	70	Hotels, rooming houses, camps, and other lodging places
53	General merchandise stores	72	Personal services
54	Food stores	75	Automotive repair, services, and garages
55	Automotive dealers and gasoline service stations	76	Miscellaneous repair services
56	Apparel and accessory stores	78	Motion pictures
57	Furniture, home furnishings, and equipment stores	79	Amusement and recreation, except motion pictures
58	Eating and drinking places	80	Health services
59	Miscellaneous retail	81	Legal services
		82	Educational services
60	Banking	83	Social services
63	Insurance	84	Museums, art galleries, botanical and zoological gardens
65	Real estate		

Source: Standard Industrial Classification Manual 1987 (Washington, D.C.: Office of Management and Budget, 1987).

ufacturers and wholesalers. Table 7-5 lists the major industry groups in retailing. Chapter 14 has a thorough discussion of retailing.

U.S. retail store sales exceed $1.6 trillion annually. About 450,000 retail establishments involve franchising (contractual agreements between central owners and local operators). Chain retailers (those with two or more outlets) own more than one-fifth of all retail establishments, contributing over half of total retail sales. A large amount of retailing involves auto dealers, food stores, general merchandise group stores, eating and drinking places, gasoline service stations, furniture and home furnishings stores, and apparel stores.

As consumers, retailers purchase or handle a variety of goods and services, including store locations, physical plant, interior design, advertising, items for resale, insurance, and trucks. Typically they are more concerned about the composition and atmosphere of their physical facilities (stores) than are wholesalers, who are more involved with the resale items themselves. This is because final consumers usually shop at stores, whereas wholesalers often call on their customers. For that reason, retailers frequently buy fixtures, displays, and services to redecorate stores. As an example, in 1988, Seattle-based Ernst Home & Nursery (a home-center chain) spent over $11 million to renovate and remodel its seventy stores. In the remodelings, new signs and fixtures were bought. Many in-store departments were relocated and redesigned, and aisles were narrowed. Each aspect of the project was coordinated and executed by outside suppliers.[14]

Getting retailers to stock new items or continue handling current ones can be difficult because store space is limited and retailers have their own goals. For instance, New York-based Shoprite (a supermarket chain) recently charged an $86,000 slotting allowance — a fee set by the retailer for its providing shelf space — to stock $172,000 worth of new Old Capital microwave popcorn. Yet, Shoprite dropped the brand six weeks later when sales were low.[15] It took McCain Foods of Canada, a processor of Maine potatoes, eight years to win a favorable rating to be a supplier of french fries to Burger King. Until 1988, Burger King "did not believe that McCain could make french fries of consistent quality or that it had access to a sufficient supply of potatoes."[16] And automobile dealers now have greater power than ever before. There are half as many dealers today as in 1950, and a number are megadealers who operate large outlets featuring several manufacturers' models: "Detroit even worries that dealers may gain so much bargaining power that they could refuse to accept shipments of cars the makers want to push."[17]

Sometimes retailers (and wholesalers) insist that suppliers make items under the retailers' (wholesalers') names. For private-label manufacturers, the continued orders of these customers are essential. When Star-Lite (a major producer of automotive softgoods such as mats and slip covers for seats) and Easco (a tool maker) were phased out as suppliers by Sears, it took them several years to establish their own brand names.

---

[14] "Teamwork Inspires Ernst Remodel Program," *Chain Store Age Executive* (August 1988), pp. 96–98.

[15] Richard Gibson, "Supermarkets Demand Food Firms' Payments Just to Get on the Shelf," *Wall Street Journal* (November 1, 1988), pp. A1, A18.

[16] Allan R. Gold, "Fast-Food Deal Gives Maine Potato a Lift," *New York Times* (October 22, 1988), pp. 33, 45.

[17] Amal Nag, "Car Megadealers Loosen Detroit's Tight Rein," *Wall Street Journal* (July 1, 1985), p. 6; and William J. Hampton, "The New Super-Dealers," *Business Week* (June 2, 1986), pp. 60–66.

TABLE 7-6 Federal, State, and Local Government (Public Administration)

SIC Code	Industry Name
91	Executive, legislative, and general government, except finance
92	Justice, public order, and safety
93	Public finance, taxation, and monetary policy
94	Administration of human resource programs
95	Administration of environmental quality and housing programs
96	Administration of economic programs
97	National security and international affairs

Source: Standard Industrial Classification Manual 1987 (Washington, D.C.: Office of Management and Budget, 1987).

Government as Consumer

Government purchases and uses a variety of routine and complex products.

Government consumes goods and services in performing its duties and responsibilities. Federal (1), state (50), and local (86,000) units together account for the greatest volume of purchases of any consumer group in the United States. In total, all government branches spend hundreds of billions of dollars on goods and services each year (of their combined yearly budgets of nearly $2 trillion), half by the federal government. The greatest expenditures are on operations, capital outlays, military services, postal services, education, highways, public welfare, health, police, fire protection, sanitation, and natural resources. Statistics on state and local expenditures by item are annually reported in *Government Finances* and *City Government Finances*. Table 7-6 shows the major SIC codes for government.

Governmental consumers buy a wide range of goods and services, including food, military equipment, office buildings, subway cars, office supplies, clothing, and automobiles. Many purchases involve standard products offered to traditional consumers; others, such as highways, are specially made for a government customer. Although many big firms (such as Boeing and Lockheed) derive large percentages of their sales from government contracts, smaller sellers now account for one-third of federal purchases.[18]

Nonprofit Institutions as Consumers

Nonprofit institutions function in the public interest.

Nonprofit institutions operate in the public interest or to foster a cause and do not seek financial profits. Public hospitals, museums, most universities, political parties, civic organizations, and parks are examples of nonprofit institutions. They purchase goods and services in order to run their organizations and also buy items for resale to generate additional revenues to offset costs. Nonprofit institutions are discussed in detail in Chapter 22.

There are many national nonprofit institutions, such as the American Cancer Society, Democratic and Republican Parties, Boy and Girl Scouts, Chamber of Commerce, and the Red Cross. Hospitals, museums, and universities, because of their fixed locations, tend to be among the local nonprofit institutions. There no separate SIC code designations for nonprofit versus profit-oriented firms.

[18] See Don Hill, ''Who Says Uncle Sam's a Tough Sell?'' *Sales & Marketing Management* (July 1988), pp. 56–60.

Characteristics of Organizational Consumers

Organizational consumer behavior depends on buying objectives, buying structure, and purchase constraints.

Buying Objectives

Organizational consumers have several distinct objectives in purchasing goods and services. See Figure 7-9. In general, these ***organizational buying objectives*** are important: availability of items, reliability of sellers, consistency of quality, delivery, and price.

Availability means that a buyer is able to obtain items throughout the year or when-

Organizational buying objectives are related to availability, reliability, consistency, delivery, and price.

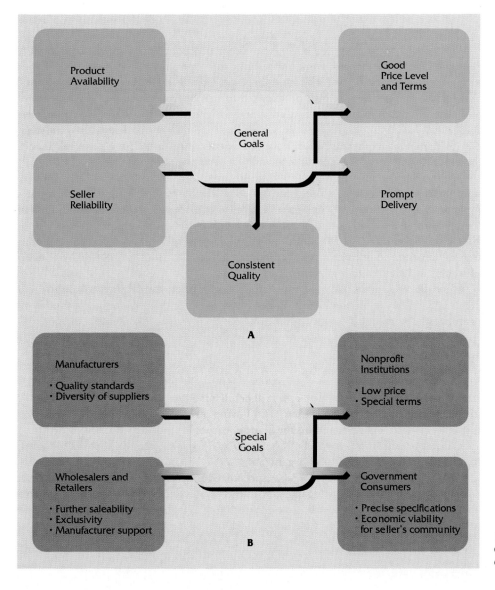

FIGURE 7-9
Goals of Organizational Consumers

ever necessary. An organization's production or resales are not possible if purchases are unavailable at the appropriate time. Seller reliability is based on the honesty in reporting bills or shipping orders, fairness to customers, responsiveness to special requests, ongoing relationships, and reputation. Consistency of quality refers to the buyer's goal of obtaining similar items on a continuous basis. For example, drill bits should have the same degree of hardness and employee uniforms the same color each time they are purchased. Delivery objectives include minimizing or stabilizing the length of time from the placing of an order to the receipt of items, minimizing the order size required by the supplier, having the seller maintain responsibility for shipments, minimizing costs, and adhering to an agreed-on schedule. Price considerations involve purchase price, discounts, availability of credit, and length of payment period.

Industrial marketers must recognize that price is only one consideration for organizational consumers, and many times it is less important than availability, quality, service, etc. As one observer noted: "The best buyers want value for the long term; they know that a short-term price often results in costly product problems and inefficiencies."[19]

With regard to more specific goals, manufacturers are concerned about quality standards for raw materials, component parts, and equipment. Some like to deal with a variety of suppliers to protect against shortages from a single supplier, to foster price and service competition, and to be exposed to new merchandise lines. Wholesalers and retailers consider further saleability as the highest priority. Where possible, they seek exclusive buying arrangements, which limit the number of distribution intermediaries that can carry goods and services in a geographic area. They also seek manufacturers' advertising, transportation, and warehousing support.

Saleability and exclusivity are keys for wholesalers and retailers.

Government consumers frequently require precise specifications for the products they purchase; and as large-volume buyers, they are able to secure these specifications. In some cases, government consumers may also consider the economic conditions in the geographic areas of potential sellers. As an illustration, Grumman Aerospace of New York often bids against McDonnell Douglas of California for government contracts. Sometimes contracts are awarded to the company that has the higher unemployment in its surrounding community.

Nonprofit consumers place the most emphasis on price, availability, reliability, and consistency. They sometimes seek special purchase terms in recognition of their nonprofit status.

Buying Structure

*The **buying structure of an organization** depends on its characteristics.*

The **buying structure of an organization** refers to the level of formality and specialization used in the purchase process. It depends on an organization's size, resources, diversity, and level of specialization. The buying structure is likely to be formalized (separate department or function) for a large, corporate, resourceful, diversified, and specialized organization. It will be less formalized for a small, independently owned, financially limited, and general organization.

Large manufacturers normally have specialized purchasing agents who work with engineers or the production department. Large wholesalers tend to have a single purchasing department or a general manager in charge of operations. Large retailers tend to be quite specialized and have buyers for each narrow product category. For instance,

[19] Clifton J. Reichard, "Industrial Selling: Beyond Price and Persistence," *Harvard Business Review*, Vol. 63 (March–April 1985), p. 127.

F.W. Woolworth's 59 buyers select the merchandise to be sold in its 1,130 U.S. variety stores.[20] Small manufacturers, wholesalers, and retailers have their buying functions completed by the owner-operator.

Each government unit (federal, state, and local) and division has a purchasing department. The General Services Administration (GSA) is the federal office responsible for centralized procurement and coordination of purchases. Each federal unit may purchase through the GSA's Bureau of Federal Supply or directly from suppliers; they must adhere to federal rules — which take up 45,000 pages of regulations, covering 4,000 different laws.[21] In a nonprofit organization, there is usually one purchasing department or a member of the operations staff performs buying functions.

Constraints on Purchases

For manufacturers, wholesalers, and retailers, derived demand is the major constraint on their purchase behavior. Without the demand of final consumers, production halts and sales drop as the backward chain of demand comes into play (final consumer → retailer → wholesaler → manufacturer).

Final demand is the major constraint on organizational purchases.

Manufacturers also are constrained by raw materials' availability and their ability to pay for large-ticket items. Wholesalers and retailers are limited by the finances available to make purchases and by the level of risk they are willing to take. In this case, risk is the probability that middlemen will be able to sell the merchandise they buy in a reasonable time period and at a satisfactory profit. Product categories such as fashion clothing have higher risks than staple merchandise such as disposable diapers.

Government consumers are constrained by the budget-setting process. Approval for categories of purchases must normally be secured well in advance, and deviations must be fully explained. Budgets must be certified by various legislative bodies. For many nonprofit consumers, cash flow (the timing of the money coming into the organization versus the money spent by it) is the major concern.

The Organizational Consumer's Decision Process

Organizational consumers use a decision-making procedure in much the same manner as final consumers. Figure 7-10 shows the **organizational consumer's decision process,** which has four major components: expectations, buying process, conflict resolution, and situational factors.[22]

*An **organizational consumer's decision process** is like a final consumer's.*

Expectations

Purchasing agents, engineers, and users bring a set of **organizational consumer expectations** to any buying situation:

> Expectations refer to the *perceived* potential of alternative suppliers and brands to satisfy a number of explicit and implicit objectives.[23]

Organizational consumer expectations are based on buyers' backgrounds, information, perception, and experience.

[20] Isadore Barmash, "Christmas Shopping a Year Early," *New York Times* (December 17, 1988), pp. 35, 37.
[21] Bob Davis, "'Convoluted' U.S. Purchasing System Is Blamed for Bad Habits of the $200 Billion-a-Year Buyer," *Wall Street Journal* (September 2, 1988), p. 34.
[22] The material in this section is drawn from Jagdish N. Sheth, "A Model of Industrial Buyer Behavior," *Journal of Marketing,* Vol. 37 (October 1973), pp. 50–56.
[23] Ibid., p. 52.

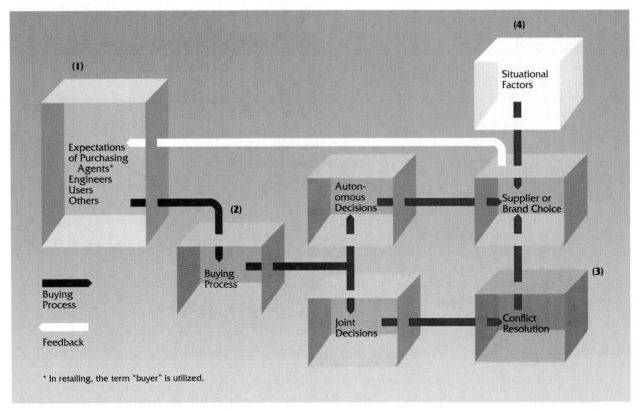

FIGURE 7-10
The Organizational Consumer's Decision Process
SOURCE: Adapted from Jagdish N. Sheth, "A Model of Industrial Buyer Behavior," *Journal of Marketing,* Vol. 37 (October 1973), p. 51. Reprinted by permission of the American Marketing Association.

In order for a purchase to be made, the buyer must have favorable expectations about such supplier attributes as product quality, availability, reliability, delivery time, and service. Expectations are based on the background of individuals, information sources, information search, perception, and satisfaction with past purchases.

The background of the buyer includes his or her educational training, job orientation, life-style, and personal objectives. Usually the background of a manufacturer's purchasing agent is different from a retail buyer's. For the former, emphasis is on technical training, knowledge of product specifications, interaction with engineers, and a conservative life-style. For the latter, emphasis is on marketing training, knowledge of final consumer demand, interaction with other buyers, and a contemporary life-style.

Information sources provide knowledge about suppliers and their offerings. Among the available sources are trade shows, direct mail, press releases, journal advertising, professional conferences, salespeople, trade newspapers, and others in the same business. In situations where there is not enough information, an organizational consumer will make an active search of information sources. This usually involves seeking answers to specific questions.

All information that is processed by organizational consumers is filtered by their perceptions, which are interpretations they place on that information. For example, a

Marketing Controversy

Should Buyer-Seller Relations Be More Collaborative?

Industrial marketing is undergoing a "quiet revolution" as organizational consumers are increasingly striving to establish closer relationships with suppliers. These relationships are collaborative, as buyers and sellers work together to reduce costs, improve quality, and exchange information. In the past, buyer-seller relationships were more adversarial; buyers bargained hard, used orders as rewards for low prices, and had little loyalty to any one supplier.

Among the organizational consumers that have collaborative relationships with their suppliers are General Motors, General Electric, Black & Decker, and Xerox. For example, today, Xerox has one-half the suppliers that it had in prior years, and it requires them to work with it on quality-improvement, research and development, and cost-reduction programs.

These are some benefits of collaborative relationships:

▶ *They accommodate a better and greater exchange of information. This allows inventory requirements to be reduced for both parties—saving warehousing costs, insurance,*

and ongoing interest expenses.

▶ *They reward supplier commitment and loyalty, and result in greater control over suppliers.*

▶ *Buyers can achieve many of the benefits of vertical integration (supplier ownership) without the necessary investment.*

▶ *Sellers have certainty about future orders and can anticipate derived demand better.*

These are some disadvantages of collaborative relationships:

▶ *Competition among multiple suppliers would assure buyers of the lowest-possible prices.*

▶ *The use of one or a few suppliers may result in too much dependence on each one. Errors in supplier choice are much more critical.*

▶ *Sellers may also become too dependent on one or a few buyers.*

▶ *By allocating purchases to multiple vendors, they could be kept "in line".*

What do you think?

SOURCE: Based on material in Robert E. Spekman, "Strategic Supplier Selection: Understanding Long-Term Buyer Relationships," *Business Horizons*, Vol. 31 (July-August 1988), pp. 75–81.

$20,000 computer software program may be perceived as economical and efficient by one buyer and cheap and too difficult to utilize by another.

Not all perceptions are positive. Sometimes buyers believe that suppliers oversell without regard to production and delivery capability, lack an understanding of the buyers' goals, do not give adequate follow-up service, and do not offer necessary promotional support. Sometimes suppliers believe that organizational consumers are preoccupied with holding out for the best price, lack decision-making autonomy, move too slowly in accepting promotional support, and refuse to cooperate for fear of being linked to one supplier. Through communications, these perceptions can be improved.

The level of satisfaction with past purchases also has an impact on the expectations that a supplier or brand will perform at the required level in the future. Satisfaction improves when the supplier provides customer aftercare.

Buying Process

During the buying process, a decision to consider making a purchase is initiated, information gathered, alternative suppliers evaluated, and conflicts among the different representatives of the buyer resolved. The process itself is similar to the final consumer buying process shown in Figure 6-7.

*Autonomous or joint decision making is based on **product-specific** and **company-specific buying factors**.*

The buying process may involve autonomous (independent) or joint decision making, depending on product-specific and company-specific factors. **Product-specific buying factors** are perceived risk, purchase frequency, and time pressure. Autonomous decisions occur with low perceived risk, routine products, and high time pressure. Joint decisions are the result of high perceived risk, unique or seldom-purchased products, and low time pressure for purchases. **Company-specific buying factors** are the firm's basic orientation, its size, and the level of decision-making centralization. Autonomous decisions occur in firms with a technology or production orientation, small size, and high centralization. Joint decision making is the result of a low technology or production orientation, large company size, and little centralization in decision making.

As noted earlier in the chapter, competitive bidding is frequently used with organizational consumers: potential sellers specify in writing all the terms and conditions of a purchase in addition to product attributes; then, the buyer selects the best bid. With open bidding, proposals can be seen by competing sellers. With closed bidding, contract terms are kept secret and sellers are asked to make their best presentation in their first bids. Bidding is most often used in government purchases in order to avoid charges of unfair negotiations or bias, and bids for government purchases are generally closed. Chapter 20 ("Applications of Pricing Techniques") contains an example of how competitive bidding is used.

Conflict Resolution

*Problem solving, persuasion, bargaining, and politicking lead to **conflict resolution**.*

Because of the different backgrounds and goals of purchasing agents, engineers, and users, joint decision making may result in conflicts. **Conflict resolution** is then necessary to make a decision.[24] Four methods of resolution are possible: problem solving, persuasion, bargaining, and politicking.

Problem solving occurs when the members of the purchasing team decide to acquire further information before making a decision. This is the best procedure for the company. Persuasion takes place when each member of the team presents his or her reasons why a particular supplier or brand should be selected. In theory, the most logical presentation should be chosen. However, the most dynamic speaker often persuades others to follow his or her lead.

Under bargaining, team members agree to support each other in different situations, regardless of merit. For example, one member is allowed to select the supplier of the current item. In return, another member chooses the vendor for the next item. The last, and least desirable, method of conflict resolution is politicking. With it, team members seek to persuade outside parties and superiors to back their positions and then seek to win at power plays.

---

[24] See also Ajay K. Kohli, "Measuring Multiple Buying Influences," *Industrial Marketing Management*, Vol. 17 (1988), pp. 197–204.

Situational Factors

A number of **situational factors** can interrupt the decision process and the actual selection of a supplier or brand. These include:

> temporary economic conditions such as price controls, recession, or foreign trade; internal strikes, walkouts, machine breakdowns, and other production-related events; organizational changes such as merger or acquisition; and ad hoc changes in the marketplace, such as promotional efforts, new-product introduction, price changes, and so on, in the supplier industries.[25]

Situational factors are variables that affect organizational consumer decisions.

Purchase and Feedback

After the decision process is complete and situational factors are taken into consideration, a purchase is made. The level of satisfaction with the purchase is fed back to the purchasing agent or team, and this information is stored for future use. To maintain customer satisfaction and ensure continued purchases, regular service and follow-up calls by sellers are essential:

> [Sellers] will find technological differentiation increasingly difficult to maintain in the years ahead because of the ever-higher costs of doing so. Differentiation will soon be prohibitively expensive for all but the largest firms. So [organizational] customers will not buy a specific brand because of what it does; all brands will be able to do the same thing. Rather they'll buy from a company they feel will support it and give maximum postsale satisfaction.[26]

Types of Purchases

A **new-task purchase process** is needed for an expensive product the firm has not bought before. Considerable decision making is undertaken, and perceived risk is high. This is similar to extended decision making for a final consumer. A **modified-rebuy purchase process** is employed for medium-priced products the firm has bought infrequently before. Moderate decision making is needed. This is similar to limited decision making for a final consumer. A **straight-rebuy purchase process** is used for inexpensive items bought on a regular basis. Reordering, not decision making, is applied because perceived risk is very low. This is similar to a routine final consumer purchase.

*Organizational buyers use a **new-task** process for unique items, **modified rebuys** for infrequent purchases, and **straight rebuys** for regular purchases.*

Marketing Implications

Although organizational and final consumers have substantial differences, as noted at the beginning of this chapter, they also have substantial similarities. Both can be described demographically, and statistical and descriptive data can be gathered and analyzed. Both have different categories of buyers, each of which has separate needs and requirements. Both can be defined by using social and psychological factors, such as operating style, buying structure, use of the purchase, expectations, perceived risk, and conflict resolution among buyers or purchasing agents. Both use a decision process, employ joint decision making, and face various kinds of purchase situations.

Accordingly, firms must develop marketing plans that reflect the similarities as well as the differences between organizational and final consumers. Furthermore, in their roles as sellers, manufacturers and wholesalers may need two marketing plans — one aimed at their intermediate buyers and another aimed at their final consumers.

There are many similarities, as well as differences, between organizational and final consumers.

[25] Sheth, "A Model of Industrial Buyer Behavior," p. 56.
[26] Milind M. Lele, "Product Service: How to Protect Your Unguarded Battlefield," *Business Marketing* (June 1983), p. 69.

Finally, it must be understood that organizational purchasing agents or buyers have personal as well as company goals. These buyers seek status, approval, promotions, bonuses, and other rewards. As noted in Figure 7-10, these individuals bring distinct backgrounds and expectations to each buying situation, as final consumers do.

Summary

1. *To introduce the concept of industrial marketing* When firms market goods and services to manufacturers, wholesalers, retailers, and government and other nonprofit institutions, they use industrial marketing.

2. *To examine the characteristics of organizational consumers and show how they differ from final consumers* Organizational consumers purchase goods and services for further production, for use in operations, or for resale to others; unlike final consumers, they do not buy for personal, family, or household use. These consumers are concerned with supplier reliability and consistency, and specific product attributes. Their demand is often derived from that of final consumers. Organizational consumers frequently use formal purchasing departments. They are more geographically concentrated, expect sellers to visit them, use joint decision making, make larger purchases, require personal attention, and look for favorable terms.

3. *To describe the different types of organizational consumers and their buying objectives, buying structure, and purchase constraints* Organizational consumers may be classified by area of specialization, size and resources, location, and goods and services purchased. As previously noted, the major types of organizational consumers are manufacturers, wholesalers, retailers, government, and nonprofit. The SIC system provides information on organizational consumers.

These consumers have general buying objectives, such as product availability, seller reliability, consistent quality, prompt delivery, and good prices. They also have specific objectives, depending on the type of firm involved. The buying structure of an organization refers to its level of formality and specialization in purchasing. Derived demand, availability, further saleability, and resources are leading purchase constraints.

4. *To explain the organizational consumer's decision process* This process includes buyer expectations, the buying process, conflict resolution, and situational factors. Important is whether the organization uses joint decision making and how. Bidding, open or closed, is often employed with organizational consumers (most often with government).

When conflicts arise under joint decision making, problem solving, persuasion, bargaining, or politicking is implemented to arrive at a decision. Situational factors can intervene between decision making and a purchase. These include strikes, economic conditions, and organizational changes.

New task, modified rebuy, and straight rebuy are the different purchase situations facing organizational consumers.

5. *To consider the marketing implications of appealing to organizational consumers* Organizational consumers and final consumers have many similarities and differences. It is important for firms to understand them and adapt marketing plans accordingly. Dual marketing campaigns may be necessary for manufacturers and wholesalers that sell to intermediate buyers and have their products resold to final consumers.

Purchasing agents and buyers have personal goals, such as status, promotion, and bonuses, which have a large impact on decision making.

Key Terms

industrial marketing (p. 184)
multiple-buying responsibility (p. 187)
value analysis (p. 187)
vendor analysis (p. 187)
competitive bidding (p. 188)
negotiation (p. 188)
derived demand (p. 188)

accelerator principle (p. 189)
buying specialists (p. 190)
systems selling (p. 191)
reciprocity (p. 191)
Standard Industrial Classification (SIC) (p. 192)
end-use analysis (p. 193)

manufacturers (p. 193)
wholesalers (p. 194)
retailers (p. 195)
government (p. 198)
nonprofit institutions (p. 198)
organizational buying objectives (p. 199)

Review Questions

1. Explain five important differences between organizational and final consumers of personal computers.
2. Compare competitive bidding and negotiation.
3. What is the relationship between derived demand and the accelerator principle?
4. What are the advantages of systems selling?
5. How is the Standard Industrial Classification a useful marketing tool?
6. What are the most important general organizational consumer-buying objectives?
7. For manufacturers, wholesalers, and retailers, what is the major constraint on their purchase behavior? Why?
8. On what basis are organizational consumer expectations formed?
9. How do product-specific and company-specific buying factors affect the use of autonomous or joint decision making?
10. Which is the worst form of conflict resolution? The best? Explain your answers.

Discussion Questions

1. As a government purchasing agent, what criteria would you consider in value analysis and vendor analysis for file cabinets?
2. A packaging firm knows that its current sales are allocated as follows: 30 per cent to pet food manufacturers (SIC code 2047), 10 per cent to chewing gum manufacturers (SIC code 2067), 40 per cent to soft drink manufacturers (SIC code 2086), and 20 per cent to coffee manufacturers (SIC code 2095). The firm expects next year's industry sales growth in these categories to rise as follows: pet food, 6 per cent; chewing gum, 2 per cent; soft drinks, 5 per cent; and coffee, 1 per cent. According to end-use analysis, by how much should the packaging firm's sales increase next year? Explain your answer.
3. Comment on this statement: "For new sellers or those with new products, gaining wholesaler cooperation may be difficult." What should be done?
4. Describe the organizational consumer's decision process for office staplers. Compare it with that for final consumers for the same product.
5. "It must be understood that organizational purchasing agents or buyers have personal as well as company goals." Comment on this statement.

◄ **CASE 1** ►

After Tough Times, the Re-Emergence of Caterpillar[*]

Caterpillar is a manufacturer of earth-moving, construction, and materials-handling machinery; and a wide variety of engines. For many decades, Caterpillar was

> as invincible as the mammoth yellow earth-moving machines it produced. Like its D10 tractor, standing 15 feet tall and weighing in at 73 tons, Cat could

push, crush, or roll over just about anything that got in its way. Competitors were too weak to be taken seriously. Customers were willing to pay fat premiums for Caterpillar quality and service.

At one point, the firm had fifty consecutive years of profits, with a very solid return on shareholder's equity.

Then came 1982! In that year, construction projects around the world fell off drastically as a result of a recession in the United States; a drop in

* The data in this case are drawn from Ronald Henkoff, "This Cat Is Acting Like a Tiger," *Fortune* (December 19, 1988), pp. 69–76.

oil prices, which created further economic difficulties in the Gulf States (causing companies in these states to cut back on construction and their purchase of related equipment); and the Latin American debt crisis (which meant that many of these countries could not afford heavy machinery). In the early 1980s, Caterpillar also saw the emergence of a major new competitor, Komatsu. Because of the high international value of the dollar at that time, Komatsu (a Japanese firm) was able to undercut Caterpillar's U.S. prices by as much as 40 per cent.

Caterpillar's response to the new economic and competitive environment has been to re-emphasize its commitment to productivity, focus on product quality, pay attention to markets it ignored in the past, and hold down price increases.

Caterpillar has reviewed every aspect of its tooling and manufacturing methods, with an eye toward improving efficiency. The PWAF ("Plant With A Future") project, begun in 1985, has resulted in the firm's reducing inventory costs alone by a cumulative $850 million. And by using such laborsaving strategies as changing plant layout, changing the reporting relationships among employees, and using cellular manufacturing (whereby workers handle multiple tasks, work in teams, and accept responsibility for their products' quality), Caterpillar has reduced its work force by 30,000 employees.

Although Caterpillar's management and employees always paid attention to product quality (unlike the "Big Three" U.S. auto makers), it was not until 1982 that it began to certify its major suppliers. Caterpillar machinists now visit suppliers' factories and assembly areas to aid them in maximizing those firms' overall quality performance. Caterpillar has certified 800 of its 4,000 major worldwide suppliers. In exchange for their high attention to product quality, certified suppliers get preferential treatment from Caterpillar. The rejection rate for parts purchased from certified suppliers is only 0.6 per cent versus 2.8 per cent for noncertified suppliers.

As part of its strategy to concentrate on new markets (which it may have ignored in better times), Caterpillar has developed a new group of "Century Line" excavators and tractors. These are usually purchased by small owner-operators that build houses, repair roads, and/or install sewers. For example, Caterpillar has been successful with its backhoe loader, a machine popular with small contractors.

When Komatsu began underselling it in the early 1980s, Caterpillar reduced its prices in markets throughout the world. Today, with the value of the Japanese yen high relative to the U.S. dollar (thus making U.S. products relatively less costly to produce), Caterpillar "hasn't made the mistake that Detroit (the auto industry) made of raising prices every time the dollar weakened." From 1986 to 1988, Caterpillar raised prices an average of only 5 per cent annually; over the same period, Komatsu implemented seven price increases.

Today, Caterpillar is a highly profitable and respected firm.

QUESTIONS

1. Explain how Caterpillar could use value analysis in evaluating the machinery, materials, and parts that it purchases.
2. Develop a vendor analysis system that would enable Caterpillar to appraise the quality of its suppliers. Why would it use noncertified suppliers?
3. Explain how the concept of derived demand affects Caterpillar. Draw an appropriate flowchart.
4. You are the purchasing agent for a mid-sized city that is considering the purchase of road-building equipment from Caterpillar. Describe how you would use the organizational consumer's decision process.

◀◀◀ **CASE 2** ▶▶▶

Boeing's 7J7 Jet: Having Difficulty Getting Off the Ground[†]

Boeing is the world's largest maker of aircraft, as well as the eighth largest defense contractor in the United States. Since Boeing introduced the 707 as the first commercially successful jet in 1958, its planes have been the industry standard. Worldwide, over one-half of the 11,000 to 12,000 jet aircraft that have ever been built or are on order (outside the Soviet Union) are Boeings. It has produced approximately 2,000 of its model 737 commercial aircraft—the most successful plane in commercial aviation history.

Despite its dominant position, over the last decade, Boeing has encountered intense competition from Airbus Industrie, a European manufacturer backed by several governments. During that period, Boeing's market share has fallen from 75 per cent to 55 per cent; today, Airbus has a 30 per cent market share, up from virtually zero a decade earlier.

Thus, to maintain its leadership role and market share, Boeing has been investing considerable resources and time to the development of its newest jet, code-named the 7J7. This jet would be the first in a prospective propfan jet series. Originally scheduled for widespread commercial introduction in the early to mid-1990s, the 7J7 is to use unducted fan engines (UDF), which burn two-thirds less fuel than current short-to-medium aircraft (such as Boeing's 727s) and one-third less fuel than the latest turbofan-powered engines (such as those used in the Airbus' A320).

Unfortunately, after a three-year, $100-million investment, in late 1987, Boeing announced an indefinite delay in the development of the 7J7. At that time, Boeing's management estimated that the 7J7 would have required a total investment of $4 billion to develop and market. And Boeing's airline customers expressed no real interest in the proposed new jet.

Although no airline questioned Boeing's fuel-savings claims or the sophistication of the aircraft's design and use of electronics, it had not received

† The data in this case are drawn from Howard Banks, "Mugged by $10 Oil," *Forbes* (August 11, 1986), pp. 30–33; and Katherine M. Hafner, Frank J. Comes, and Jonathan Kapstein, "Bright Smiles, Sweaty Palms," *Business Week* (December 1, 1988), pp. 22–23.

any orders for the 7J7 (while Airbus had almost 300 orders for its A320 jet, a plane that would compete with the 7J7). Market analysts and Boeing's management cite these reasons for the lack of airline interest in the 7J7:

- When Boeing began planning the 7J7 in the early 1980s, fuel costs were as high as 30 per cent of operating costs for airlines, with aviation fuel being $1.20 per gallon. Then fuel prices dropped to half that amount and remain at this level today. Airlines believe that fuel costs would have to rise to more than $1 per gallon for the 7J7's fuel efficiency to be an important factor in a purchase.
- The 7J7 would cost an estimated $30 million versus $12 million for a used 727. Even new Boeing 737 and Airbus A320 jets are considerably less expensive. The high price is a major deterrent to airlines, which are concerned with holding down costs because of airfare competition. As American Airlines' chairman stated, "All-new aircraft today are neither faster nor cheaper per seat, as used to happen with each new generation [of aircraft]. Airlines can't afford to buy only to meet growth."
- No consensus has developed among potential customers as to the plane's optimal size. For example, Scandinavian Airlines Systems wants a 130-seat configuration, whereas American Airlines prefers more than 175 seats. Other airlines want a much larger plane to enable them to increase the passenger load per flight.

Boeing's decision to delay development and production of the 7J7 means that it is quite possible that both Airbus and McDonnell Douglas will be able to market a propfan jet first. McDonnell Douglas also has cost advantages due to aircraft design features. And as one observer notes, "Boeing's next aircraft needs more than propulsion advances to set it apart and make it a success."

QUESTIONS

1. How should Boeing try to develop enthusiasm for the 7J7?
2. Evaluate American Airlines' statement about the purchase of a new-generation plane.
3. What criteria would be most important in an airline's decision to purchase a new jet?
4. Apply the organizational consumer's decision process to explain why the 7J7 has met with resistance from the airline market.

CHAPTER *8*

Developing a Target Market Strategy

CHAPTER OBJECTIVES

1. To describe the process of planning a target market strategy

2. To examine alternative demand patterns and segmentation bases

3. To explain and contrast undifferentiated marketing (mass marketing), concentrated marketing, and differentiated marketing (multiple segmentation)

4. To consider the requirements for successful segmentation and the limitations of segmentation

5. To show the importance of positioning in developing a marketing strategy

6. To discuss sales forecasting and its role in target marketing

In Atlanta, 91 per cent more consumers have video-cassette recorders than in Buffalo. Hispanic families in Houston show higher loyalty to retail grocers than Hispanic families in Chicago do. Cars made by foreign manufacturers, mostly Japanese, have fully half of the California market but account for only 15 per cent of sales in Michigan and less than 25 per cent in Ohio.

In planning their target market strategies, many companies are quite interested in determining the possible bases for segmenting the market. When they study regional differences, they are looking at geographic demographics—the basic identifiable traits of towns, cities, states, regions, and countries.

After studying regional differences, companies may decide to apply a differentiation strategy, whereby two or more geographic areas are considered to be distinct market segments and separate marketing plans are aimed at each segment. In regional marketing, companies concentrate on much smaller geographic groups than in traditional demographic segmentation. According to one regional marketing expert, "anyone who is not aware that regional markets—even segments of the same market—need different approaches is in marketing disarray." So, let us examine the concept of regional marketing in more detail.

Several factors account for the growing popularity of regional marketing. First, increasing market fragmentation, even within relatively small geographic areas, makes regional marketing economically feasible. Second, more firms want to pinpoint their differential advantages (and their resources) to specific groups, due to the overall high level of competition. Third, in-store scanning equipment at checkout counters allows companies to acquire sales data for small geographic areas. Fourth, there are now a number of powerful personal computer-based software programs that enable firms to interpret regional data.

However, regional marketing also has several important implications that firms must consider when deciding whether to use such a target market approach. In terms of promotional planning, a regional marketing strategy requires greater decentralization of decision making, more regional executive input, greater use of regional advertising agencies, and higher use of local media (and regional editions of national media). Regional marketing also requires greater product diversity (to cater to each regional market), decentralized distribution, and more marketing research.

Vons, a California-based supermarket chain, is a retailer that effectively practices regional marketing.

Reprinted by permission.

Each outlet's decor and product selection are matched to the demographics and purchase habits of local shoppers, who are divided into five categories: high Hispanic/low income, moderate to high Hispanic/moderate to high income, high Anglo-American/low income, high Anglo-American/moderate to high income, and average. Stores located as close as two miles from one another may have different product selections depending on their demographic makeup.

Frito-Lay, the snack maker, is a manufacturer that practices regional marketing. This gives Frito-Lay's six zone-marketing managers great autonomy. At present, the company is promoting two products geared to specific regions. For example, Frito-Lay is marketing its lighter Delta Gold potato chips in the Southeast and in the Illinois/Michigan area, and Lay's Salt & Vinegar flavored potato chips in the Northeast and in the Northwest.[1]

In this chapter, we will examine each of the steps involved in planning a target market strategy and the related topic of sales forecasting. A differentiation strategy, employing regional marketing, is only one of the many ways in which a company may appeal to a target market.

[1] Isadore Barmash, "Splintering of Markets: A Fine Art," *New York Times* (August 22, 1988), p. D9; Gregory Witcher, "Japanese Auto Makers Target Midwest," *Wall Street Journal* (December 19, 1988), p. B1; Brad Edmondson, "Hot Spots," *American Demographics* (January 1988), pp. 25–30; and Lynn G. Coleman, "Marketers Advised to 'Go Regional'," *Marketing News* (May 8, 1989), pp. 1, 8, 16. ,

Overview

A *market* consists of all possible consumers for a good or service. Through *market segmentation*, it can be subdivided.

After gathering information on consumer characteristics, desires, and decision making; company and industry attributes; and environmental factors; a firm is ready to select the target market(s) to which it will appeal and to develop an appropriate strategy. From a marketing perspective, the total *market* for a particular good or service consists of all the people and/or organizations who desire (or potentially desire) that good or service, have sufficient resources to make purchases, and are willing and able to buy. As noted in Chapter 2, in setting a target market strategy, firms often rely on *market segmentation,* dividing the market into distinct subsets of customers that behave in the same way or have similar needs. Each subset could be a possible target market.

In a *target market strategy,* a firm first studies consumer demand.

Developing a *target market strategy* involves three general phases: analyzing consumer demand, targeting the market, and developing the marketing strategy. This comprises the seven specific steps in Figure 8-1 and described in this chapter. First, the firm determines demand patterns that exist for a given good or service, establishes bases of segmentation, and identifies potential market segments. For example, do all potential consumers have similar needs and desires? Or, are there distinct clusters of demand, each with different needs and desires? Or, is consumer demand diffused, so that there is a great variety of needs and desires? Also, what consumer characteristics, desires, and behavior types can be used to describe market segments?

Next, a target market approach is chosen: *undifferentiated marketing, concentrated marketing,* or *differentiated marketing.*

Second, the firm targets the market. It chooses the best approach to use in appealing to the marketplace and selects its target market(s). A company can apply one of three market segmentation strategies: (1) *undifferentiated marketing (mass marketing)* — where the business attempts to appeal to the whole market with a single basic marketing strategy intended to have mass appeal; (2) *concentrated marketing* — where the business attempts to appeal to one well-defined market segment with one tailor-made marketing strategy; and (3) *differentiated marketing (multiple segmentation)* — where the business attempts to appeal to two or more well-defined segments of the market with a marketing strategy tailored to each segment.[2]

Then the marketing strategy is actually developed, with an emphasis on *product differentiation.*

Third, the firm positions its offering relative to competitors and outlines the appropriate marketing mix(es). Of particular importance at this phase is attaining *product differentiation,* whereby "a product offering is perceived by the consumer to differ from its competition on any physical or nonphysical product characteristic including price." When differentiation is favorable, it constitutes a differential advantage. Sometimes a company can achieve a key differential advantage by simply emphasizing how its offering satisfies existing consumer desires and needs better than competitors'. However, sometimes demand patterns must be modified for consumers to perceive the firm's product differentiation as worthwhile. For example, Tylenol is promoted as an alternative to aspirin for persons who cannot take aspirin (thus appealing to existing consumer needs), whereas Dove is marketed as a nonsoap cleanser with moisturizing qualities (thus modifying consumer perceptions of the role of soap). If targeted consumers cannot be persuaded that moisturizing is a meaningful product attribute for a cleanser to have, then they will probably not buy Dove — no matter how much better a job of moisturizing Dove does compared to competing soap products.[3]

---

[2] Peter D. Bennett (Editor), *Dictionary of Marketing Terms* (Chicago: American Marketing Association, 1988), pp. 114–115.

[3] Peter R. Dickson and James L. Ginter, "Market Segmentation, Product Differentiation, and Marketing Strategy," *Journal of Marketing,* Vol. 51 (April 1987), pp. 1–10.

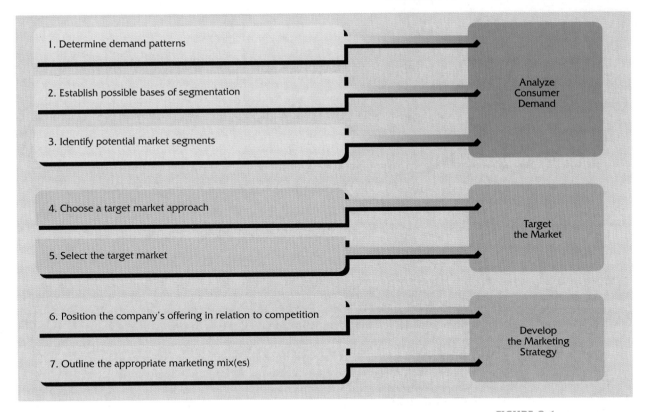

1. Determine demand patterns
2. Establish possible bases of segmentation
3. Identify potential market segments

Analyze Consumer Demand

4. Choose a target market approach
5. Select the target market

Target the Market

6. Position the company's offering in relation to competition
7. Outline the appropriate marketing mix(es)

Develop the Marketing Strategy

FIGURE 8-1
The Steps in Planning a Target Market Strategy

In this chapter, the steps in planning a target market strategy are presented in detail. Organizational consumer segmentation, the requirements for successful segmentation, and limitations of segmentation are also discussed. Sales forecasting and its role in developing a target market strategy are examined.

Analyzing Consumer Demand

The initial phase in planning a target market strategy (analyzing consumer demand) consists of three steps: determining demand patterns, establishing possible bases of segmentation, and identifying potential market segments.

Determining Demand Patterns

First, a firm must determine the demand patterns that it faces in the marketplace. *Demand patterns* indicate the uniformity or diversity of consumer needs and desires for particular categories of goods and services. The firm would face one of the three alternative demand patterns shown in Figure 8-2 and described here for each good or service category it markets.

When there is *homogeneous demand,* consumers have relatively uniform needs and desires for a good or service category. In this situation, a firm's marketing tasks are straightforward — to identify and satisfy the basic needs of consumers in a superior way. For instance, business customers in the express mail-delivery market are most

Demand patterns show how similar or different consumer desires are for a good or service.

Consumers may have homogeneous demand, clustered demand, or diffused demand.

213

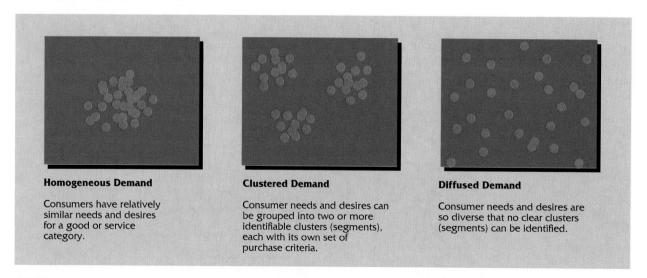

Homogeneous Demand

Consumers have relatively similar needs and desires for a good or service category.

Clustered Demand

Consumer needs and desires can be grouped into two or more identifiable clusters (segments), each with its own set of purchase criteria.

Diffused Demand

Consumer needs and desires are so diverse that no clear clusters (segments) can be identified.

FIGURE 8-2
Alternative Consumer Demand Patterns for a Good or Service Category

interested in these features: overnight delivery, reliability in delivery, and reasonable prices. A firm such as Federal Express appeals to customers by convincing them that it is doing a better job than competitors in these areas (product differentiation).[4] Usually, as competition intensifies, companies try to modify consumer demand patterns so that new product features become desirable and homogeneous demand turns to clustered demand, with only one or a few firms marketing the new feature.

In *clustered demand,* consumer needs and desires for a good or service category can be classified into two or more identifiable clusters (segments), with each having distinct purchase criteria. In this situation, the firm's marketing efforts must be geared toward identifying and satisfying the needs and desires of a particular cluster (or clusters) of consumers in a superior way. For example, in the passenger car market, consumers can be classified by their interest in price, car size, performance, styling, handling, sportiness, and other factors. Accordingly, auto makers offer luxury cars, economy cars, full-size family cars, high-performance vehicles, sports cars, and other vehicle categories — with each category appealing to a particular cluster of consumer needs and desires. Clustered demand is by far the most prevalent kind of demand pattern.

In *diffused demand,* consumer needs and desires for a good or service category are so diverse that clear clusters (segments) cannot be identified. In this case, the firm's marketing efforts are more difficult because product differentiation can be more costly and harder to communicate. For example, in the cosmetics market, consumers have very diverse preferences with regard to lipstick and nail polish color and shading; even the same customer may desire several colors and shades, to use on different occasions or to switch frequently to avoid boredom. That is why cosmetics companies offer hundreds of different colors and shades of lipstick and nail polish. It would be virtually impossible for a company to succeed in this market by marketing only one color for these products. In general, to make marketing strategies more efficient, companies frequently try to modify diffused consumer demand so that clusters of at least moderate size appear.

[4] Adapted by the authors from Dickson and Ginter, "Market Segmentation, Product Differentiation, and Marketing Strategy," p. 7.

TABLE 8-1   Possible Bases of Segmentation

Base	Examples of Possible Segments
Geographic demographics	
Population	
Location	North, South, East, West
Size	Small, medium, large
Density	Urban, suburban, rural
Transportation network	Mass transit, vehicular, pedestrian
Climate	Warm, cold
Type of commerce	Tourist, local worker, resident
Retail establishments	Downtown shopping district, shopping mall
Media	Local, regional, national
Competition	Underdeveloped, saturated
Growth pattern	Stable, negative, positive
Legislation	Stringent, lax
Cost of living	Low, moderate, high
Personal demographics	
Age	Child, teenager, adult, senior citizen
Gender	Male, female
Education	Less than high school, high school, college
Mobility	Same residence for 2 years, changed residence in last 2 years
Income	Low, middle, high
Occupation	Blue-collar, white-collar, professional
Marital status	Single, married, divorced, widowed
Family size	1, 2, 3, 4, 5, 6, or more
Nationality or race	European, Hispanic, American, Asian; black, white
Consumer life-styles	
Social class	Lower-lower to upper-upper
Family life cycle	Bachelor to solitary survivor
Usage rate	Light, medium, heavy
Usage experience	None, some, extensive
Brand loyalty	None, some, total
Personality	Introverted-extroverted, persuasible-nonpersuasible
Attitudes	Neutral, positive, negative
Class consciousness	Inner-directed, outer-directed
Motives	Benefit segmentation
Perceived risk	Low, moderate, high
Innovativeness	Innovator, laggard
Opinion leadership	None, some, a lot
Importance of purchase	Little, a great deal

Establishing Possible Bases of Segmentation

Next, the firm studies possible bases for segmenting the market for each of its product categories. Some segmentation bases describe consumer characteristics, such as gender and stage in the family life cycle. Other segmentation bases relate more specifically to consumer needs and desires, such as usage rates and brand loyalty. As shown in Table 8-1, the possible bases for segmenting the market can be placed into three broad categories: geographic demographics, personal demographics, and consumer lifestyles. The firm must decide which segmentation bases are most relevant for its particular situation.

Geographic Demographics

Geographic demographics *describe towns, cities, states, regions, and countries.*

Geographic demographics are the basic identifiable characteristics of towns, cities, states, regions, and countries. A company may use one or a combination of geographic demographics to describe its market. Segmentation strategies emphasize and cater to geographic differences. For example, it would be useful for food marketers to know that these are the leading geographic markets, in per-household consumption, for several products: bubble gum — Salt Lake City; cranberry juice — Boston; ketchup — Charlotte, North Carolina; pasta — Albany, New York; and canned spinach — Dallas. It would also be useful for firms to know that these are the geographic markets with the lowest per-household consumption for several products: frozen waffles — Shreveport, Louisiana; rice — Charleston, West Virginia; tea bags — Green Bay, Wisconsin; cider — Syracuse, New York; and pasta — Nashville, Tennessee.[5]

Geographic population traits include an area's location, population, and density. The locations of areas may reflect differences in income, culture, social values, and other consumer factors. For example, in the United States, Asian and Mexican restaurants are most popular in Western states, and Italian restaurants are most popular in the Middle Atlantic states.[6] Population size and density indicate whether an area has enough people to generate sales and the ease of mounting a marketing campaign. Figure 8-3 shows a demographic map of the United States.

An area's transportation network is its mass transit and highway mix. A locale with a limited mass transit system is likely to have different marketing needs from an area with an extensive system. For instance, in California, there are almost 21 million registered motor vehicles (with a population of 28 million), compared with about 10 million in New York (with a population of 18 million).[7]

A firm may segment on the basis of an area's climate. As an illustration, average annual U.S. per-capita consumption of ice cream is 15 quarts. However, in New England, consumption is 23 quarts (enough for a cone every other day). In comparison, Southeastern residents consume fewer than 12 quarts a year.[8]

An area's commerce mix involves its orientation toward tourists, workers, and residents. Tourist needs in New Orleans are distinct from worker needs in New Orleans and from resident needs in a New Orleans suburb. For example, tourists are attracted to restaurants, workers to fast-food outlets, and residents to supermarkets.

Central cities have downtown shopping districts, and suburbs have shopping centers. Each shopping district or center generally has its own distinctive image and combination of retailers. For instance, Reading, Pennsylvania, features a large factory-outlet shopping district, while Philadelphia contains the largest urban mall in the United States (the Gallery), anchored by Strawbridge & Clothier. The Gallery is an integral part of Philadelphia's redevelopment plan.

[5] Trish Hall, "What's the Hot Item in Town Depends on the Town," *New York Times* (January 13, 1988), pp. C1, C6.
[6] "Ethnic Eats," *American Demographics* (May 1988), p. 48.
[7] Federal Highway Administration.
[8] David Wessel, "To New Englanders, It's Never Too Cold for Eating Ice Cream," *Wall Street Journal* (January 1, 1985), pp. 1, 27; and Lisa H. Towle, "Fattening or Not, a National Passion," *New York Times* (July 17, 1988), Section 3, p. 13.

States	1987 Population Ranking	2000 Projected Population Ranking	1987 Per Capita Income Ranking	1987 Geographic Ranking	1980 Urbanization Ranking[a]
Alabama	22	24	44	29	36
Alaska	49	48	4	1	29
Arizona	25	15	29	6	9
Arkansas	33	32	47	27	42
California	1	1	7	3	1
Colorado	26	21	13	8	12
Connecticut	28	29	1	48	15
Delaware	47	49	11	49	20
Florida	4	3	19	22	8
Georgia	11	11	27	21	34
Hawaii	39	42	16	47	4
Idaho	42	39	43	13	39
Illinois	6	6	9	24	11
Indiana	14	14	31	38	30
Iowa	29	30	26	25	37
Kansas	32	34	21	14	27
Kentucky	23	25	41	37	43
Louisiana	20	19	46	31	22
Maine	38	41	33	39	45
Maryland	19	22	6	42	13
Massachusetts	13	16	3	45	9
Michigan	8	8	18	23	19
Minnesota	21	23	14	12	26
Mississippi	31	31	50	32	46
Missouri	15	20	24	19	23
Montana	44	44	40	4	40
Nebraska	36	38	25	15	32
Nevada	41	36	12	7	5
New Hampshire	40	40	8	44	41
New Jersey	9	9	2	46	2
New Mexico	37	37	45	5	18
New York	2	4	5	30	7
North Carolina	10	10	34	28	48
North Dakota	46	47	35	17	44
Ohio	7	7	23	35	17
Oklahoma	27	27	38	18	25
Oregon	30	26	30	10	24
Pennsylvania	5	5	20	33	21
Rhode Island	43	45	17	50	3
South Carolina	24	28	42	40	38
South Dakota	45	46	39	16	47
Tennessee	16	17	37	34	35
Texas	3	2	32	2	14
Utah	35	33	48	11	6
Vermont	48	50	28	43	50
Virginia	12	12	10	36	28
Washington	18	13	15	20	16
West Virginia	34	35	49	41	49
Wisconsin	17	18	22	26	30
Wyoming	50	43	36	9	33

[a] % of population living in urban areas.

FIGURE 8-3
A Demographic Map of the United States
SOURCES: Compiled by the authors from Bureau of the Census and Bureau of Economic Analysis data.

Media availability varies by area and has an important impact on a company's ability to segment. For example, Nebraska has 19 daily newspapers to serve a population of 1.6 million people, while Utah has 6 daily papers to serve a population of 1.7 million people.[9] This would make it more difficult for a firm seeking to reach a market segment in Utah. Many national publications now print regional issues to allow companies to advertise to selected audiences.

An area may be underdeveloped or saturated in competition for the sale of a particular product category. As a result, a firm may be able to succeed by entering smaller but underdeveloped markets. As an illustration, Ames Department Stores operates discount outlets in towns such as Ossipee, New Hampshire, and North Tonawanda, New York. In these cities, it is often the largest firm and faces limited competition.

The growth pattern of a region may be stable, negative, or positive, as discussed in Chapter 5. Often a company is likely to find an underdeveloped market in a growing area and a saturated market in a stable or declining area. However, growing areas quickly attract competitors and stable/declining areas may see an exodus of competitors (thus opening up the market). Accordingly, the opportunities in each market area should be studied carefully.

Legal restrictions vary by municipality and state. A firm may choose not to enter an area that restricts operations. If it does enter, it must abide by the requirements. For example, automobile emissions are more stringently controlled in California than elsewhere in the United States. Oregon also has strict environmental laws. In both of these states, firms offer modified products from those marketed in other states. Delaware is an attractive state for many firms because they do not have to charge sales tax; this draws shoppers from other states.

The cost of living can vary by area; and this can affect marketing strategy. For instance, in 1988, the cost of living in Boston was 7 per cent higher than in New York, 33 per cent higher than in San Diego, 65 per cent higher than in Birmingham (Alabama), and 81 per cent higher than in Columbia (Missouri).[10]

Personal Demographics

Personal demographics describe individual people.

Personal demographics are the basic identifiable characteristics of individual people and groups of people. They are often used as the basis for segmentation because groups of people with similar demographics may have similar needs and desires that are distinct from those with different backgrounds. Personal demographics may be viewed singly or in combinations.

Consumers can be divided into several age categories, such as child, teenager, adult, and senior citizen. Age is frequently used as a segmentation factor. In January 1989, Time Inc. introduced *Sports Illustrated for Kids,* aimed at the 13 million U.S. children ages 8 to 13; during the first year, Time expected circulation to reach 500,000 — a group of children having influence over billions of dollars of consumer expenditures. See Figure 8-4. The Young Americans Bank in Denver appeals to patrons ages 12 to 22 and offers savings accounts, checking accounts, and consumer loans (although those under 18 must have adult co-signers). John Hancock focuses its financial-services marketing efforts on people from their 20s to their 40s, and features advice on planning for children's college tuition bills, future retirement needs, and so on. Affinity is

---

[9] "Our Daily News," *American Demographics* (October 1988), p. 44.

[10] American Chamber of Commerce Researchers Association, *Inner-City Cost of Living Index* (Second Quarter 1988).

FIGURE 8-4
Sports Illustrated for Kids
Copyright Time Inc. Reprinted by
permission.

"the first shampoo created for hair over 40." *Modern Maturity,* the largest-circulation magazine in the United States, is targeted at readers 50 and older.[11]

Gender is a major segmentation variable for a number of goods and services, such as clothing, personal-care products, jewelry, and personal services. For example, Procter & Gamble now markets specially-designed Luvs Deluxe Diapers for Boys and Luvs Deluxe Diapers for Girls. See Figure 8-5. Whitman Chocolates and Godiva Chocolatier have separate Valentine's Day promotions aimed at men and women; in the past, all ads were oriented at gift-giving by men. Auto makers, financial-service firms, and others are placing greater emphasis on the female market. As a General Motors executive commented, "The auto market is more segmented than ever, and in the '90s we will accelerate our targeting of women."[12] On the other hand, since the 1970s, a countertrend has also developed: unisex goods and services — many hair stylists, clothing manufacturers, and others offer items that attract both men and women.[13]

[11] Ben Allen, "Her Baby, Now," *Advertising Age* (September 26, 1988), p. 78; Leonard Sloane, "Banks Children Can Call Their Own," *New York Times* (October 15, 1988), p. 38; David Wessel, "One Sure Fact: Baby Boomers Are Aging," *Wall Street Journal* (January 3, 1989), p. B1; Jon Lafayette and Lenore Skenazy, "How to Reach Seniors? Be Positive," *Advertising Age* (October 31, 1988), pp. 10, 49; and Ira Teinowitz, " 'Modern Maturity'—No Signs of Gray," *Advertising Age* (February 20, 1989), p. 12.

[12] Laurie Freeman, "P&G's Boy/Girl Diapers Roll in U.S.," *Advertising Age* (October 31, 1988), p. 51; Judann Dagnoli and Julie Liesse Erickson, "Valentine Candies Dress for Men," *Advertising Age* (January 25, 1988), p. 4; and Patrick Reilly, "What's a '90s Woman?" *Advertising Age* (December 5, 1988), p. 6.

[13] See Teri Agins, "More Women Are Finding Menswear Suits Them, Too," *Wall Street Journal* (September 14, 1988), p. 37.

219

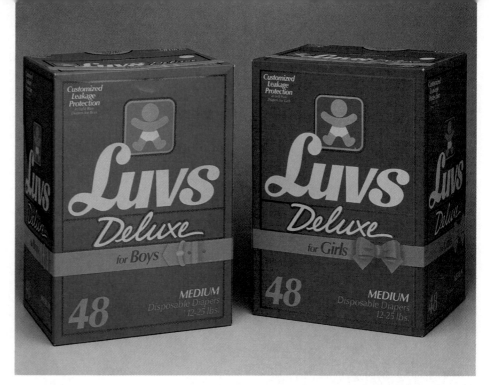

Educational level can be used to distinguish among market segments. A poorly educated consumer is likely to spend less time shopping, read less, and rely more on well-known brands than is a college-educated consumer. The latter is likely to comparison shop, read noncommercial sources of information, and purchase the product perceived as best, whether it is well known or not.

A person's mobility refers to the degree to which he or she changes residence. A mobile consumer relies on national brands and stores and nonpersonal information. A stationary consumer relies on an acquired knowledge of various brands and stores (national and local) and personal trust and information.

Consumers can be divided into low-, middle-, and high-income categories. And the income of a firm's target market can influence the marketing strategy used. At Dollar General, a discount department store chain, low-income consumers are attracted by low prices; many items are under $10. Dollar General locates in small Sunbelt communities, sells many irregulars and factory overruns, and has few employees in each store. On the other hand, American Express attracts very affluent consumers with its Platinum Card. These consumers pay a $300 annual fee and must charge $10,000 per year; in return, they get special services (such as a worldwide "valet service" to help them shop, plan trips, and so on) and a higher credit line.[14]

A consumer's occupation may affect purchases. For instance, a construction worker has different job-related needs and desires than a computer salesperson. Often the former wears flannel shirts, dungarees, and work shoes and brings lunch, while the latter wears a three-piece suit and wing-tip shoes and takes clients to restaurants.

Marital status and family size may provide bases for segmentation. Many firms have different offerings for single (sports car) and married (sedan) people. Hotels constantly advertise singles weekends and vacations for honeymooners. Family-size segmenta-

---

[14] Hank Gilman, "Retailers That Target Low Income Shoppers Are Growing Rapidly," *Wall Street Journal* (June 24, 1985), pp. 1, 12; and Jeffrey M. Laderman, "How Amex Is Revamping Its Big, Beautiful Money Machine," *Business Week* (June 13, 1988), pp. 90–92.

tion has resulted in different package sizes — such as single-serving and family size — and special offerings — such as discounts for large purchases.

Nationality or race represents another possible segmentation variable. For example, ethnic goods or services may be aimed at persons of Italian, German, and other backgrounds. As the black (12 per cent of the U.S. population) and Hispanic (8 per cent of the U.S. population) markets have grown, specialized newspapers, beauty-products firms, magazines, and other items have evolved to satisfy them.

Consumer Life-Styles

As defined in Chapter 6, life-styles are the patterns in which people live and spend time and money. By studying life-style factors, companies may be able to focus on distinct market segments. Table 8-1 shows a number of possible life-style segmentation bases.

Segments can be described on the basis of social and psychological factors.

Consumers may be segmented by social class and stage in the family life cycle. For example, posh hotels, such as San Francisco's Four Seasons Clift Hotel, appeal to upper-middle-class and upper-class guests with luxurious accommodations, whereas Holiday Corporation's Hampton Inn Hotels appeal to middle-class and lower-middle-class consumers with reasonable rates and limited services (such as no restaurant). To attract families with children, all Sheraton hotels in Hawaii have recently added extensive day-camp programs for children ages 4 to 12.[15]

Market segments may be based on usage rate, usage experience, and brand loyalty. Usage rate refers to the amount of a product consumed. A person may use very little, some, or a great deal. In the 1960s, Dik Warren Twedt coined the term **heavy-half** to describe the market segment accounting for a large proportion of an item's sales relative to the size of the market. Twedt found that, in some cases, less than 20 per cent of the market made 80+ per cent of purchases.[16]

*A **heavy-half** segment has a much larger share of sales than a light-half.*

Recent applications of the heavy-half theory include the following. Households headed by people ages 45 to 64 spend twice as much per week on gasoline as those headed by people under age 25. Nondieters consume 83 per cent of light beer, 59 per cent of sugar substitutes, and 61 per cent of diet soda. Less than 10 per cent of Visa and MasterCard holders use the cards more than twelve times per year; about 80 per cent use the cards six times or less per year.[17] Also see Figure 8-6. In some cases, the heavy-half segment may be attractive because of the volume it consumes; in other instances, the competition for consumers in that segment may make other opportunities more attractive.

Usage experience refers to the amount of prior exposure a consumer has had to a good or service. A consumer with no experience operates much differently from one with substantial experience. In addition, the firm should distinguish between nonusers, potential users (those evaluating a good or service for possible purchase), and regular users. Each segment has different needs.

---

[15] Ken Wells, "Hotels and Resorts Are Catering to Kids," *Wall Street Journal* (August 11, 1988), p. 29.

[16] Dik Warren Twedt, "How Important to Marketing Is the 'Heavy User'?" *Journal of Marketing*, Vol. 28 (January 1964), pp. 71–72.

[17] Caleb Solomon, "The Latest Gasoline Additive? Marketing," *Wall Street Journal* (December 15, 1988), p. B3; NPD Group, "I'm (Not) on a Diet," *Wall Street Journal* (December 11, 1985), p. 35; and Douglass K. Hawes, "Profiling Visa and MasterCard Holders: An Overview of Changes — 1973 to 1984, and Some Thoughts for Future Research," *Journal of the Academy of Marketing Science*, Vol. 15 (Spring 1987), p. 67.

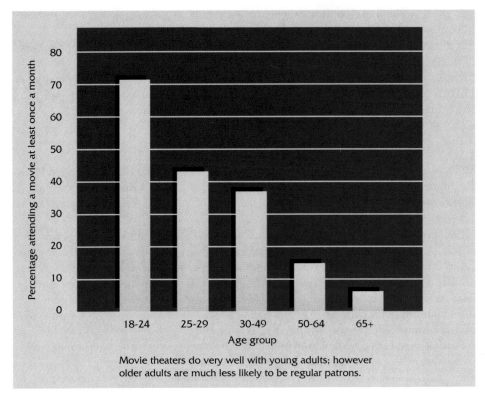

FIGURE 8-6
Applying the Heavy-Half
Theory to Movie
Attendance
SOURCE: Business Trend
Analysts, Inc., "Flick Figures,"
Wall Street Journal (January
16, 1987), p. 25.

Movie theaters do very well with young adults; however older adults are much less likely to be regular patrons.

Brand loyalty takes one of three forms: none, some, or total. If no loyalty exists, the consumer has no preference for a brand, is attracted by sales, switches brands frequently, and will try new products. If some loyalty exists, the consumer has a preference for a few brands, is attracted by discounts for those brands, switches brands infrequently, and is usually unwilling to try new brands. With total loyalty, the consumer insists on one brand, is not attracted by discounts for other brands, never switches brands, and will not try a new brand.

Consumers may be grouped by personality type, such as introverted-extroverted or persuasible-nonpersuasible. The introverted consumer will tend to be more conservative and systematic in purchasing behavior than an extroverted consumer. A nonpersuasible person will tend to react adversely to heavy personal sales efforts and be skeptical of advertising claims. A persuasible person may be convinced to buy an item through a strong sales pitch and be swayed by advertising.

Consumers may be categorized by their attitudes toward a firm, its offering, and/or a product category. Neutral attitudes ("I've heard of brand X, but I don't really know about it") require heavy informative and persuasive promotion. Positive attitudes ("Brand X is the best product on the market") require reinforcement through follow-up advertising and personal contacts with consumers. Negative attitudes ("Brand X is far inferior to brand Y") are difficult to change and require verified advertising claims, product improvements, an upgraded company image, and other tactics. It may be best for a firm to ignore this segment and concentrate on the first two; with segmentation, a firm does not have to please all groups.

Segmentation by class consciousness is possible for socially visible items such as clothing, automobiles, restaurants, travel, and real estate. Inner-directed consumers buy to satisfy themselves and are not impressed with fancy labels and high price tags. Outer-directed consumers seek social acceptance, regularly buy items with fancy labels, and pay higher prices. For example, single "social seekers" are restless and socially oriented. They "view themselves in terms of feelings about public image, fashion leadership, and nature and frequency of leisure activities."[18]

Consumer motives (reasons for purchases) may be broken down into benefit segments. **Benefit segmentation** "is the process of grouping consumers into markets on the basis of different benefits sought from the product."[19] This concept was popularized by Russell Haley in 1968 when he studied the toothpaste market and divided it into four groups. The sensory segment sought flavor and product appearance, had children, used spearmint toothpaste, favored brands like Colgate, had a degree of self-involvement, and was pleasure-oriented. The sociable segment sought bright teeth, was young, smoked, favored brands like Ultra Brite, and was sociable and active. The worrier segment sought decay prevention, had large families, used toothpaste heavily, favored Crest, had hypochondria, and was conservative. The independent segment sought low prices, was male, used toothpaste heavily, bought the brand on sale, and was autonomous and value-oriented.[20]

In a more recent study, Haley applied benefit segmentation to food consumption and uncovered five segments: child-oriented, diet concerned, meat and potatoes, sophisticated, and natural foods enthusiasts. Others have developed benefit segments for such product categories as VCRs and restaurant customers.[21] Figure 8-7 applies benefit segmentation to children's watches.

Consumers may be segmented on the basis of perceived risk. Risk takers are those who perceive various types of risk to be low; they would be attracted to new, distinctive items. Risk avoiders are those who perceive at least one type of risk (functional, physical, financial, social, psychological, or time) to be high; a firm that targets these consumers would have to reduce their perception of risk through such techniques as informative advertising, well-known brands, low introductory prices, trial package sizes, money-back guarantees, and in-store demonstrations.

Innovators have low perceived risk and are first to try new products. Laggards have high perceived risk and are last to try new products. They hold onto existing products for a long time and wait for new items to come down in price. Some innovators are opinion leaders who can influence fellow consumers. Others are not opinion leaders because they do not have the respect and confidence of their peers. As noted earlier, a person can be an opinion leader for one product and an opinion follower for another.

Purchase importance may also differ by consumer. For example, a suburban commuter would consider the purchase of an automobile more important than a city worker with access to mass transit. The purchase of a refrigerator would be more important for a family with a broken machine than one with a functioning model.

Benefit segmentation groups consumers on the basis of their reasons for using products.

[18] Barbara B. Stern, Stephen J. Gould, and Benny Barak, "Baby Boom Singles: The Social Seekers," *Journal of Consumer Marketing*, Vol. 4 (Fall 1987), pp. 5–22.

[19] Bennett, *Dictionary of Marketing Terms*, p. 14.

[20] Russell I. Haley, "Benefit Segmentation: A Decision-Oriented Research Tool," *Journal of Marketing*, Vol. 32 (July 1968), pp. 30–35.

[21] Russell I. Haley, "Benefit Segments: Backwards and Forwards," *Journal of Advertising Research*, Vol. 24 (February–March 1984), pp. 19–25; W. James Potter, Edward Forest, Barry S. Sapolsky, and William Ware, "Segmenting VCR Owners," *Journal of Advertising Research*, Vol. 28 (April–May 1988), pp. 29–39; and Kenneth D. Bahn and Kent L. Granzin, "Benefit Segmentation in the Restaurant Industry," *Journal of the Academy of Marketing Science*, Vol. 13 (Summer 1985), pp. 226–247.

FIGURE 8-7
**How Fisher-Price Uses
Benefit Segmentation for
Children's Watches**
Reprinted by permission.

Blending Demographic and Life-Style Factors

It is generally advisable to use a mix of demographic and life-style factors to establish possible bases of segmentation. A richer and more valuable analysis takes place when a variety of factors is reviewed.

VALS describes American market segments in terms of demographics and life-styles.

One extremely useful classification system for segmenting consumers in terms of a broad range of demographic and life-style factors is SRI's ***VALS (Values and Life-Styles) program,*** which divides Americans into various life-style categories.[22]

SRI introduced VALS 1 in 1978, when it identified nine major American consumer life-styles. An in-depth consumer study was conducted in 1980 to gain further insights into each of those life-style categories. Here are the highlights of that study:

▶ Need-driven
  (1) Survivors — Old, poor, mistrustful, removed from cultural mainstream, despairing, depressed. 4 per cent of population. Overrepresented in South, most over 65, 77 per cent female, lowest income, median 8th- to 9th-grade education.

---

[22] Arnold Mitchell, *The Nine American Life-Styles: Who We Are & Where We Are Going* (New York: Macmillan, 1983); and Nancy J. Olson, Keith G. Ricke, and Pamela Weisenberger, "Using VALS to Target Market Through Package Segmentation," *Journal of Direct Marketing Research*, Vol. 1 (Spring-Summer 1987), pp. 31-42.

(2) Sustainers — Angry, resentful, streetwise, poor, rebellious, dissatisfied. 7 per cent of population. Numerous in New England, 58 per cent under 35, 55 per cent female, below-average income, median 11th-grade education.

▶ Outer-directed

(3) Belongers — Aging, conventional, content, traditional Middle America, patriotic. 35 per cent of population. Numerous in South, median age of 52, 68 per cent female, average income, high school education.

(4) Emulators — Young, ambitious, hardworking, flashy, trying to break into the system. 10 per cent of population. Overrepresented in South Atlantic, median age of 27, 53 per cent male, average income, high school education plus.

(5) Achievers — Middle-aged, prosperous, self-assured, the leaders and builders of the American dream. 22 per cent of population. Overrepresented in Pacific region, median age of 43, 60 per cent male, well-above-average income, college graduate or more.

▶ Inner-directed

(6) I-am-me — Very young, impulsive, exhibitionist, self-centered. 5 per cent of population. Overrepresented in Atlantic and Northeast regions, 91 per cent under 25, 64 per cent male, below-average income, some college.

(7) Experiential — Youthful, seeking experience, oriented to inner growth, artistic. 7 per cent of population. Numerous in Pacific region, median age of 27, 55 per cent female, average income, 38 per cent college graduate or more.

(8) Societally conscious — Mission-oriented, mature, successful, out to change the world. 8 per cent of population. Numerous in New England and Pacific regions, median age of 39, 52 per cent male, above-average income, 58 per cent college graduate (39 per cent graduate school).

▶ Combined

(9) Integrated — Mature, tolerant, understanding, flexible, able to see "the big picture." 2 per cent of population. Most middle aged or older, slightly more males, above-average income, well educated. People combine the decisiveness of outer-direction (achievers) with the introspection of inner-direction (societally conscious).

Between 1978 and 1989, VALS 1 analysis was used by more than 150 leading corporate clients in devising and/or modifying their marketing strategies. Then, in 1989, SRI unveiled VALS 2, stating "When VALS 1 was introduced, values were closer to the surface and more reflective of people's behavior than they are now. But times have changed, and we're now living in an age of diminished expectations, when economic, educational, and other types of resources play a much more important role in how consumers act."

In VALS 2, there are eight life-style categories, which are based on such factors as education, income, health, energy level, self-confidence, and interest in consumer issues: (1) strugglers; action-oriented — (2) experiencers and (3) makers; status-oriented — (4) achievers and (5) strivers; principle-oriented — (6) fulfilleds and (7) believers; and (8) actualizers. SRI feels that VALS 2 is a good up-to-date predictor of consumer purchase behavior.[23]

A firm using VALS can determine the size of potential market segments, their characteristics and behavior, and product needs. Thus, it can maximize marketing

[23] Judith Graham, "New VALS 2 Takes Psychological Route," *Advertising Age* (February 13, 1989), p. 24.

efforts. Firms subscribe to the VALS data base to get comprehensive and current information about their target markets. Among the organizations that have used VALS data in their segmentation strategies are Merrill Lynch, Mercedes-Benz, Bell South, the Beef Industry Council, Dr Pepper, and Minnesota Mutual Life Insurance Company.

Organizational Consumer Segments

When segmenting, a firm should examine organizational consumers as well as final consumers.

A firm establishing possible bases of segmentation may be interested in appealing to organizational consumers instead of, or in addition to, final consumers. Accordingly, the distinctions between these two classes of consumers should be considered.

As noted in Chapter 7, organizational consumers require precise items, normally have strict price limits, frequently utilize joint decision making, buy in quantity, rate reliability and service very high, expect salespeople to visit them, and rely on trade publications. In contrast, final consumers frequently have flexibility in purchases, can vary price limits, often act alone, buy single units, may be relatively unconcerned about the future reliability of a vendor, usually go to a store, and rely on commercial media. The two markets often require different marketing approaches. For example, a firm selling vacuum cleaners to hospitals as well as to final consumers would need vastly different marketing plans for each.

When studying the organizational consumer market, a company would consider the same broad segmentation bases used with final consumers. Geographic demographics include the features of the area in which the organizational consumer resides. Personal demographics refer to the consuming organization and its personnel, including size, area of specialization, resources, existing contracts, past purchases, order size, and the demographics of decision maker(s). Life-style factors include the way in which the organization operates (centralized or decentralized), brand loyalty, reasons for purchases, and the social and psychological attributes of decision maker(s). These elements are all potential bases for segmentation.

The segmentation of organizational consumer markets may be applied to many different situations, as these examples demonstrate:

▶ The *Farm Journal* offers customized versions of its publications to its 900,000 subscribers. It services five kinds of farmers (cotton, dairy, beef, hog, and livestock) in six regions of the United States. Each version of the *Farm Journal* has a different combination of articles, ads, and various supplements.[24]

▶ The office computer market is segmented according to consumer needs, products offered, and price range. See Figure 8-8.

▶ The Ford Tractor division is actively seeking to attract women as customers for its farm tractors because many women use these products or have a major impact on decisions. Ford has redesigned its large tractors to make it easier for women to operate them, trained dealers to act more businesslike with women customers, and developed ads specifically directed at women.[25] See Figure 8-9.

▶ Atlanta's Bank South has a special program aimed at servicing the financial needs of companies with under $3 million in annual sales. Says its executive vice-president, "Most larger banks haven't touched this market in the past."[26]

[24] Dale E. Smith, "Data Base Harvest," *Direct Marketing* (October 1986), pp. 64–68.
[25] Jesse Snyder, "Ford Cultivating Larger Tractor Market," *Advertising Age* (February 27, 1984), p. 57.
[26] Roger Ricklefs, "Small Businesses Look Ever More Alluring to Big Banks," *Wall Street Journal* (December 13, 1988), p. B2.

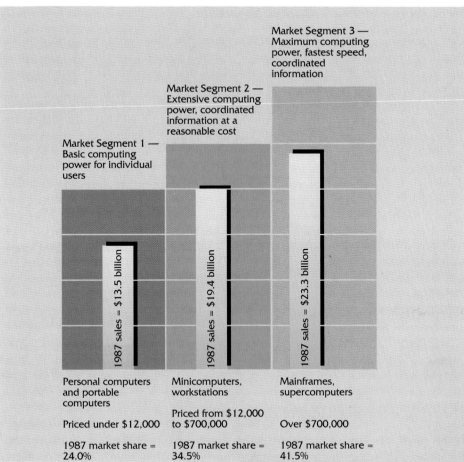

Market Segment 3 —
Maximum computing
power, fastest speed,
coordinated
information

Market Segment 2 —
Extensive computing
power, coordinated
information at a
reasonable cost

Market Segment 1 —
Basic computing
power for individual
users

1987 sales = $13.5 billion

1987 sales = $19.4 billion

1987 sales = $23.3 billion

Personal computers
and portable
computers

Minicomputers,
workstations

Mainframes,
supercomputers

Priced under $12,000

Priced from $12,000
to $700,000

Over $700,000

1987 market share =
24.0%

1987 market share =
34.5%

1987 market share =
41.5%

FIGURE 8-8
**Segmentation of the
Office Computer Market**
SOURCE: Adapted by the
authors from Stuart Gannes,
"Tremors from the Computer
Quake," *Fortune* (August 1,
1988), pp. 42–60.

FIGURE 8-9
Ford Tractor Targets Women Customers
Reprinted by permission of
Ford New Holland, Inc.

Identifying Potential Market Segments

Consumer profiles are used in identifying market segments.

After establishing the possible bases of segmentation, the firm is ready to develop consumer profiles. These profiles identify potential market segments by aggregating consumers with similar characteristics and needs and separating them from consumers with different characteristics and needs.

For example, a firm marketing gift items could identify potential market segments based on the consumer's place of residence, age, and income. Gift buying is highest for New Englanders who are ages 35 to 44 and have an annual household income greater than $50,000; it is lowest for Southwesterners who are under age 25 and have an annual household income under $15,000. A firm marketing financial services could identify such potential segments as speculators, entrepreneurs (business owners), retirement planners, and highbrows (status-conscious) based on income, age, occupation, investments as a percentage of income, and so on.[27] Table 8-2 identifies several of the potential market segments from which a maker of compact trucks may choose. A different marketing strategy would be appropriate for each of these segments.

Targeting the Market

The second phase in planning a target market strategy, targeting the market, consists of these steps: choosing a target market approach and selecting the target market(s).

Choosing a Target Market Approach

At this point, the firm must decide on the target market approach to pursue: undifferentiated marketing (mass marketing), concentrated marketing, or differentiated marketing (multiple segmentation). These three alternatives are contrasted in Figure 8-10 and Table 8-3 and discussed in the following subsections.

Undifferentiated Marketing (Mass Marketing)

With undifferentiated marketing, a company appeals to a broad range of consumers with one basic marketing plan.

An undifferentiated-marketing (mass-marketing) approach aims at a large, broad consumer market through one basic marketing plan. In this approach, the firm would believe that consumers have very similar desires regarding product attributes or it would choose to ignore the differences among market segments. An early practitioner of mass marketing was Henry Ford, who created and sold one standard automobile model at a reasonable price to many people. The original Model T had no options and came only in black.

Mass marketing was popular when large-scale production started, but the number of companies using a pure undifferentiated-marketing approach has declined rapidly in recent years. Among the factors contributing to its fall from use are that competition has grown, demand may be stimulated by an appeal to specific segments, improved

---

[27] "Christmas Shoppers Loosen Up (Barely)," *Wall Street Journal* (December 13, 1988), p. B1; and Thomas J. Stanley, George P. Moschis, and William D. Danko, "Financial Service Segments: The Seven Faces of the Affluent Market," *Journal of Advertising Research,* Vol. 27 (August–September 1987), pp. 52–67.

TABLE 8-2 Potential Market Segments for Compact Trucks

Segment Characteristics	Segment 1 — Compact Pickup Buyers, Domestic Vehicles	Segment 2 — Compact Pickup Buyers, Imported Vehicles	Segment 3 — Compact Sport Utility Buyers, Domestic Vehicles	Segment 4 — Compact Sport Utility Buyers, Imported Vehicles
Sex				
Male	92%	87%	72%	75%
Female	8%	13%	28%	25%
Median Age	39 years	34 years	38 years	34 years
Education				
Attended college or more	49%	62%	67%	74%
Occupation				
Professional/ manager	39%	45%	57%	63%
Blue collar	36%	32%	18%	22%
Median Household Income	$38,200	$38,000	$49,400	$46,700
Marital Status				
Married	73%	61%	74%	60%
Never married	18%	27%	16%	28%
Census Region				
Northeast	16%	14%	24%	17%
Midwest	32%	16%	23%	8%
South	38%	39%	33%	33%
West	14%	31%	20%	42%
Median Price	$10,500	$8,600	$16,100	$12,300
Example of vehicle appealing to this segment	Ford Ranger	Mazda B2000	Chevrolet S10 Blazer	Suzuki Samurai

Source: Jim Schwartz and Jim Stone, "Small Trucks, Big Bucks," *American Demographics* (January 1988), pp. 38–40. Based on *1987 Buyers of New Compact Trucks: A Research Report from Newsweek.* Reprinted by permission.

marketing research may be able to pinpoint the desires of different segments, and total production and marketing costs can be reduced by segmentation.

Before an organization undertakes undifferentiated marketing, it must examine several factors. Substantial total resources are needed to mass produce, mass distribute, and mass advertise. However, there may be per-unit production and marketing savings because limited products are offered, and different brand names are not employed. These savings may allow low competitive prices.

A major objective of undifferentiated marketing is to maximize sales — that is, a company attempts to sell as many units of an item as possible. National goals are usually set. Diversification is not undertaken.

Undifferentiated marketing seeks to maximize sales without diversifying.

For successful pure mass marketing, a large group of consumers must have a desire for the same product attributes (homogeneous demand), so that the company can use one basic marketing program. Or, consumer demand must be so diffused that it would not be worthwhile for the firm to aim marketing plans at specific segments; in this case, the company would try to make demand more homogeneous. Under undifferentiated marketing, different consumer groups are not identified and sought. As an

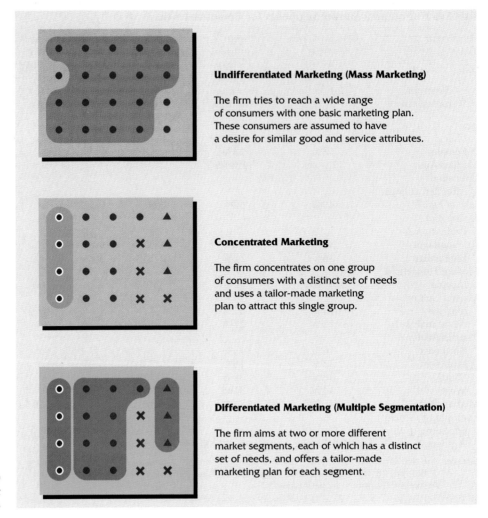

Undifferentiated Marketing (Mass Marketing)

The firm tries to reach a wide range
of consumers with one basic marketing plan.
These consumers are assumed to have
a desire for similar good and service attributes.

Concentrated Marketing

The firm concentrates on one group
of consumers with a distinct set of needs
and uses a tailor-made marketing
plan to attract this single group.

Differentiated Marketing (Multiple Segmentation)

The firm aims at two or more different
market segments, each of which has a distinct
set of needs, and offers a tailor-made
marketing plan for each segment.

FIGURE 8-10
**Contrasting Target
Market Approaches**

example, suppose all consumers buy Morton's salt because of its freshness, quality, storability, availability, and fair price. Then a pure mass-marketing strategy is appropriate. However, if some consumers want attractive decanters, low-sodium content, larger crystals, and smaller-sized packages, then Morton would be unable to appeal to all consumers through one basic marketing mix.

With undifferentiated marketing, a firm sells items through all possible outlets. Some channel members may not be pleased if the company's brand is sold at several nearby locations and may insist on carrying additional brands to fill out their product lines. It is very difficult to persuade them not to carry competing brands. The shelf space given to the company depends on the popularity of its brand and the promotional support given. Channel members often set final selling prices.

An undifferentiated marketing strategy should consider both total and long-run profits. Sometimes firms become too involved with sales and lose sight of profits. For example, for a number of years, the sales of A&P rose as the company continued its competition with Safeway for leadership in supermarket sales. Unfortunately, A&P

TABLE 8-3   Methods for Developing a Target Market

Marketing Approach	Undifferentiated Marketing	Concentrated Marketing	Differentiated Marketing
Target market	Broad range of consumers	One well-defined consumer group	Two or more well-defined consumer groups
Product	Limited number of products under one brand for many types of consumers	One brand tailored to one consumer group	Distinct brand for each consumer group
Distribution	All possible outlets	All suitable outlets	All suitable outlets—differs by segment
Promotion	Mass media	All suitable media	All suitable media—differs by segment
Price	One "popular" price range	One price range tailored to the consumer group	Distinct price range for each consumer group
Strategy emphasis	Appeal to various types of consumers through a uniform, broad-based marketing program	Appeal to one specific consumer group through a highly specialized, but uniform, marketing program	Appeal to two or more distinct market segments through different marketing plans catering to each segment

incurred large losses during that period. Only when A&P began to close some unprofitable stores and stop pursuing sales at any cost did it start to show profits.

A company can ensure a consistent, well-known image with a mass-marketing approach. Consumers have only one image when thinking of a firm, and it is retained for a number of years.

TV Guide magazine is an example of undifferentiated marketing in action. *TV Guide* is a weekly magazine that contains television program listings, descriptions, and evaluations as well as current events and articles on personalities, shows, and the industry. *TV Guide* sells about 17 million copies per week. It is advertised on television and in newspapers and stores. *TV Guide* is quite inexpensive and is available at several types of stores and newsstands. Many sales are through subscription. The product itself, the magazine, has undergone relatively few content changes (such as adding cable television listings and moving all feature stories to the front of the magazine) since its inception and is recognized as the standard in the field. Consumers of varying backgrounds buy *TV Guide* for the completeness of its listings and the interesting stories. Over 45 million people read it weekly.

Concentrated Marketing

With a concentrated-marketing approach, a firm would aim at a narrow, specific consumer group through one, specialized marketing plan that caters to the needs of that segment. This approach would be appropriate to consider if demand is clustered, or if diffused demand can be clustered by offering a unique marketing mix (product differentiation).

Concentrated marketing has emerged as a popular technique, especially for small firms. With it, a firm does not have to mass produce, mass distribute, or mass advertise. It can succeed with limited resources and abilities by concentrating efforts. This strategy does not normally maximize sales. Instead, the objective is efficiency—attract-

Via concentrated marketing, a firm can succeed by specializing. It appeals to one segment with a tailored marketing plan.

ing a large portion of one segment at controlled costs. The firm wants recognition as a specialist. It does not try to diversify.

If concentrated marketing is used, it is essential that the company do a better job of tailoring a marketing program for its segment than competitors. Areas of competitor strength should be avoided and weaknesses exploited. For instance, a new fast-food restaurant that sells hamburgers would have a more difficult time in distinguishing itself from competitors than a fast-food restaurant selling French onion soup and crepes.

If there are two or more attractive market segments from which the firm may choose, it should select the one offering the greatest opportunity; and it should be alert to two factors. One, the largest segment may not provide the best opportunity because of heavy competition or high consumer satisfaction with competitor offerings (for example, the cola segment of the soda market). A company entering this segment may regret it because of the **majority fallacy,** which causes some firms to fail when they go after the largest market segment because competition is intense. See Figure 8-11. Two, a potentially profitable segment may be one ignored by other firms. As an illustration, Frank Perdue is very successful in the poultry business. This has occurred because

*To avoid the **majority fallacy,** a company may enter a smaller but untapped segment.*

FIGURE 8-11
How the Majority Fallacy Occurs

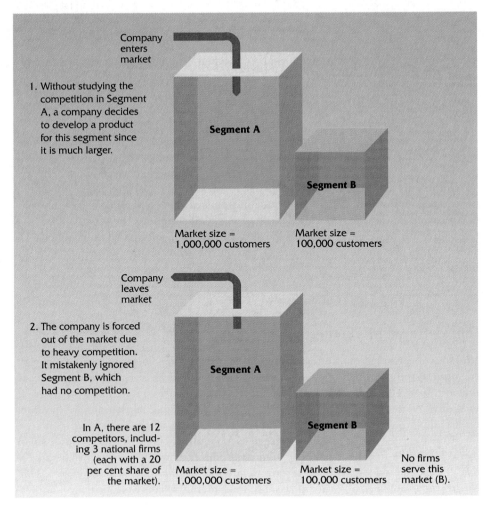

232

FIGURE 8-12
The Porsche 911
Carrera: A Class Appeal
Reprinted by permission.

Perdue was the first chicken producer to see a market segment that desired quality, an identifiable brand name, a guarantee, and would pay premium prices. Previously, chickens were sold as unlabeled commodities.

Concentrated marketing can enable a company to maximize per-unit profits but not total profits, because only one segment is sought. It also enables a firm with low resources to compete effectively with larger firms for specialized markets. For example, there are many regional producers that can effectively compete with national manufacturers in their region but that do not have the resources to compete on a national level. On the other hand, small shifts in population or consumer tastes can sharply affect a company engaging in concentrated marketing.

Through concentrated marketing, a firm may be able to carve out a distinct niche for a particular brand. This would encourage brand loyalty for the current offering and could be helpful if the company develops a product line under one name (such as Cuisinart). As long as the firm stays within its perceived area of expertise, the image of one product (food processors) will rub off on another (kitchen knives).

For example, Porsche aims at a very upscale market—"class appeal, not mass appeal." Its 1989 car models were priced from $40,000 to $75,000. Said its chief executive, "We're looking for exclusivity. We aren't fishing for volume."[28] See Figure 8-12.

Differentiated Marketing (Multiple Segmentation)

Under differentiated marketing (multiple segmentation), a company would appeal to two or more distinct market segments, with a different marketing plan for each segment. This approach combines the best attributes of undifferentiated marketing and

In differentiated marketing, two or more marketing plans are tailored to two or more consumer segments.

[28] Gail Schares and James B. Treece, "Porsche: Class Appeal, Not Mass Appeal," *Business Week* (December 12, 1988), p. 84.

Marketing Controversy

Can a Firm "Have It All?"

Businessland, a chain with stores in over thirty states, attained $600 million in annual revenues by selling PCs, computer networks, and computer software to large-scale organizational consumers. But, in 1988, Businessland decided it would also pursue final consumers and the home-office market. So, it purchased ComputerCraft, a chain primarily targeted to small businesses, professionals, and the home market.

Businessland has high hopes for Computer-Craft because of the quality of its sales force (in the largest stores, salespeople specialize in particular computer brands), the higher profit margins on sales to final consumers, and the high growth forecast for computer sales to home offices. There are four million home offices in the United States, but only 500,000 have personal computers.

Businessland plans to serve its major accounts and final consumers/small businesses with separate stores and to use both the Busi-

nessland and ComputerCraft names, so as not to confuse each chain's customers. By using a differentiated marketing approach, Businessland feels it can maintain separate identities for both chains, focus on the needs of different market segments, set distinct prices for each customer category, and maximize overall company sales and profit.

However, this approach could have important disadvantages. The separate identities' strategy does not result in economies due to shared advertising; separate nearby sales locations would have to be maintained (requiring separate personnel and inventory); controlling marketing efforts would be more complex; and some small businesses may be unsure as to which chain to patronize.

When asked "Why go into the home market at all?" Businessland's chief executive replied, "We need another vehicle to address an important, growing marketplace. We want it all." What do you think?

SOURCE: Based on material in Marc Beauchamp, "We Want It All," *Forbes* (June 27, 1988), pp. 58, 60.

concentrated marketing. As with differentiated marketing, a broad range of consumers may be sought; as with concentrated marketing, marketing efforts focus on satisfying identifiable consumer segments. Differentiated marketing is appropriate to consider if there are two or more significant demand clusters, or if diffused demand can be clustered into two or more segments and satisfied by offering unique marketing mixes to each.

Some firms, such as IBM, appeal to each segment in the market and achieve the same market coverage as with mass marketing. IBM markets products to all three office-computer segments shown in Figure 8-8 (as well as to final consumers). Other companies, such as Hewlett-Packard, appeal to two or more, but not all, potential market segments. Hewlett-Packard makes personal computers and minicomputers but does not produce mainframes.[29]

In some cases, companies use both mass marketing and concentrated marketing in their multiple-segmentation strategy. These firms have one or more major brands

[29] Stuart Gannes, "Tremors from the Computer Quake," *Fortune* (August 1, 1988), pp. 42–60.

aimed at a wide range of consumers (the mass market) and secondary brands geared toward specific segments. For example, Time Warner publishes *Time* and *People* for very broad audiences and *Fortune* and *Southern Living* for specialized segments. Coca-Cola markets Coke Classic to a broad spectrum of consumers, while Sprite, Mr. Pibb, and Mello Yello appeal to narrower groups of customers.

Multiple segmentation requires thorough analysis. Company resources and abilities must be able to produce and market two or more different sizes, brands, or products. This can be costly. Such is the case for computers. On the other hand, if a firm sells similar products under its own and retailer brands, added costs are small.

Differentiated marketing should enable the firm to achieve many company objectives. It is possible to maximize sales, when multiple segments are addressed. For example, Procter & Gamble has a 50+ per cent market share in the laundry and cleaning products field. This is made possible through a number of detergent brands such as Tide, Bold, Dash, Cheer, Gain, Oxydol, and Ivory Snow.

Recognition as a specialist can continue as long as the firm markets a narrow product line or uses different brand names for products aimed at different segments. For instance, Whirlpool maintains a distinct image under its own label; few consumers know it also makes products for Sears. Multiple segmentation also allows a firm to diversify and minimize its risks because all the emphasis is not placed on one segment. Gerber life insurance provides an excellent hedge against a drop in the sales of baby products for that company.

Differentiated marketing does not mean that a firm has to enter markets where competitors are strongest and be subjected to the majority fallacy. Its objectives, strengths, and weaknesses must be measured against competitors. The firm's philosophy should be to choose and develop only those segments that it can handle. The company should note that the majority fallacy also works in reverse. If the firm enters a market segment before a competitor, it may prevent the competitor from successfully entering that segment in the future.

Although differentiated marketing requires the existence of at least two sizable consumer segments (with distinctive desires by each), the more potential segments facing the firm, the greater the opportunity for multiple segmentation. In many cases, a firm that begins as a market segmenter is able to use multiple segmentation and pursue other segments after it becomes firmly established in one segment.

Chances are better for multiple segmentation when many unique segments exist.

Distribution intermediaries, such as wholesalers and retailers, usually find differentiated marketing on the part of their suppliers to be desirable. It enables them to reach different consumers, offers some brand exclusivity, allows orders to be concentrated with one seller, and encourages them to carry their own private brands. From the selling firm's perspective, several distribution benefits exist. Items can be sold to competing stores under different labels. Store shelf space would be provided to display various sizes, packages, or brands. Price differentials among brands can be maintained. Competition may be discouraged from entering the distribution channel. Overall, differentiated marketing places the seller in a good bargaining position.

Multiple segmentation can be extremely profitable because total profits should rise as the firm increases the number of segments it services. Per-unit profits should also be high, if the firm does a good job of developing a unique marketing plan for each segment. Then consumers in each segment are willing to pay a premium price for the tailor-made offering.

When a firm diversifies markets, risks from a decline in any segment are lessened. However, extra costs can be incurred by making product variations, selling through

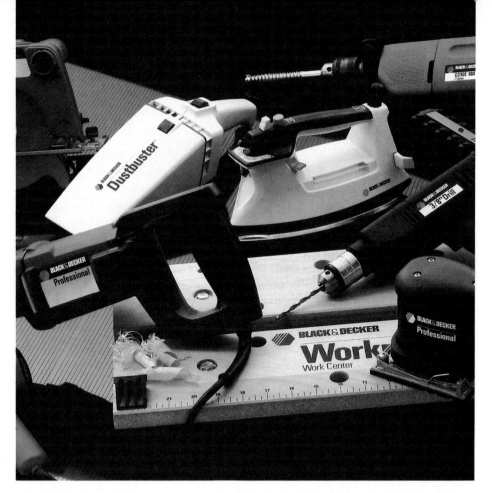

FIGURE 8-13
**Multiple Segmentation
by Black & Decker**
Reprinted by permission.

different channels, and promoting more brands. A firm must balance the revenues obtained from selling to multiple segments against the costs.

A company must be careful to maintain product distinctiveness in each consumer segment and guard its image. A firm's reputation can be hurt if it sells similar goods and services at different prices to different segments under separate brand names and consumers become aware of this. At one time, General Motors had a problem when a number of Oldsmobile and Buick customers discovered that their automobiles had engines from the less-expensive Chevrolet division.

Among other firms using multiple segmentation are Club Med, with separate resorts for couples only and families; the Clinique division of Estee Lauder, which makes skin-care products for women and for men; Oshkosh Truck, which makes rescue trucks for airports and all-terrain vehicles for the U.S. Army; and Black & Decker, which markets final and organizational consumer products. See Figure 8-13.

Selecting the Target Market(s)

The company now chooses which and how many segments to target.

At this point, a company has two decisions to make: Which segment(s) offer the greatest opportunities? How many segments should the firm pursue?

In deciding which segment(s) contain the greatest potential, a company should consider its objectives and strengths, competition, segment size, segment growth potential, distribution requirements, required expenditures, profit potential, company image, and its ability to develop and sustain a differential advantage. Figure 8-14 contains a rating form that could be applied by an industrial-goods manufacturer inter-

For each of the following factors, rate the three potential
market segments from 1 to 5, with 1 being excellent and 5 being poor.

Factor	Segment 1 — Basic Computing Power (Personal Computer)	Segment 2 — Extensive Computing Power (Minicomputer)	Segment 3 — Maximum Computing Power (Mainframe)
Consistency with company objectives	--------------	--------------	--------------
Match with company strengths	--------------	--------------	--------------
Level of competition	--------------	--------------	--------------
Size of segment	--------------	--------------	--------------
Segment growth potential	--------------	--------------	--------------
Match with present distribution channel	--------------	--------------	--------------
Level of required expenditures	--------------	--------------	--------------
Profit potential	--------------	--------------	--------------
Ability to develop a differential advantage	--------------	--------------	--------------
Ability to sustain a differential advantage	--------------	--------------	--------------
Overall Assessment	--------------	--------------	--------------

FIGURE 8-14
A Rating Form for Assessing the Market Segments for Office Computers, Selected Factors

ested in entering the office computer market, using the consumer segments shown in Figure 8-8.

Then, based on the target market approach it has chosen, the firm would decide whether to pursue one or more segments (or the mass market). Because of the high costs of entering the office computer market, and the existence of three well-defined demand clusters, it is most likely that a firm new to that industry would start with a concentrated-marketing effort. On the other hand, a new sweater manufacturer could easily use differentiated marketing and separately appeal to boys, girls, men, and women with its products.

Requirements for Successful Segmentation

For concentrated marketing and differentiated marketing plans to be successful, the selected market segment(s) have to meet five criteria:

1. There must be *differences* among consumers, or mass marketing would be an appropriate strategy.

Effectiveness requires segments that are distinct, homogeneous, measurable, large, and reachable.

237

2. Within each segment there must be enough consumer *similarities* to develop an appropriate marketing plan for the entire segment.

3. The firm must be able to *measure* the characteristics and needs of consumers in order to establish groups. This may be difficult for life-style factors.

4. A segment must be *large* enough to generate sales and cover costs.

5. The members of a segment must be *reachable* in an efficient manner. For example, young women can be reached through *Seventeen* magazine. It is efficient because males and older women do not read the magazine.

Limitations of Segmentation

The shortcomings of segmentation need to be considered.

Although segmentation is usually a consumer-oriented, efficient, and profitable marketing technique, it should not be abused. Firms may appeal to segments that are too small to be profitable, misinterpret consumer similarities and differences, become cost inefficient, spin off too many low-priced imitations of their original company brands, become short-run rather than long-run oriented, be unable to use certain media (due to the small size of individual segments), compete in too many disparate segments, confuse consumers, become locked into a declining market segment, and/or be too slow to seek out innovative opportunities for new goods and services.

Developing the Marketing Strategy

The third phase in planning a target market strategy, developing the marketing strategy, consists of these steps: positioning the company's offering in relation to competition and outlining the appropriate marketing mix(es).

Positioning the Company's Offering in Relation to Competition

The good or service must be carefully positioned against competitors.

Once a firm selects its target market(s), it must identify the attributes and images of each competitor and select a position for its own offering.

For example, a firm considering entry into the personal computer segment of the office market could describe the major strengths of a variety of its competitors as follows:

▶ IBM — Reliability, service, availability of software applications, product variety.
▶ Apple — User friendliness, graphics, desktop publishing capability, innovativeness.
▶ Compaq — Portability, good construction, quality of monitor, IBM compatibility.
▶ Tandy — Low prices, IBM compatibility, strong distribution network.

In positioning its offering against these competitors, the firm would need to present a combination of customer benefits that are not being offered by others and are desirable by a target market (product differentiation). Customers must be persuaded that there are clear reasons why to buy the new firm's computers rather than those of competitors. It would not be a good idea, in this case, for the firm to go head on against these large and well-positioned competitors. As one alternative, the company could consider focusing on small business customers and marketing fully configured computers; these computers would be installed by the seller, come with appropriate soft-

You're the Marketer

Bicycling to Success?

Americans spend over $8 billion annually on sports equipment. Yet 47 per cent of adults never play sports and most people who own sports equipment rarely use it. For example, 52 per cent of all bicycle owners never use their bikes, and only 8 per cent use them more than 60 days per year.

Bicycle owners can be divided into these three categories:

▶ *Actives—They participate in some form of sports (including biking) during 31 or more days per year. Of all U.S. adults ages 18 to 64, 27 per cent can be considered actives. They account for 49 per cent of the yearly U.S. purchases of sports equipment. About 40 per cent of this group owns bicycles.*

▶ *Low actives—They participate in some form of sports during 1 to 30 days per year. Of U.S. adults, 26 per cent can be considered*

low actives. They account for 31 per cent of yearly sports-equipment expenditures. About 25 per cent of this group owns bicycles.

▶ *Inactives—They do not participate in any sport during a year. As noted above, they represent 47 per cent of U.S. adults. They account for 20 per cent of annual sports-equipment purchases. About 7 per cent of this group owns bicycles.*

In choosing among these market segments, a bicycle maker would also consider the needs of each. For instance, high actives may be interested in upgrading their current bicycles; low actives may desire basic models; and inactives must be educated about the benefits of bicycling and then be persuaded to purchase bicycles.

As the marketing director for a medium-sized bike maker, what target market strategy would you use?

SOURCE: Based on material in Christine M. Brooks, ''Armchair Quarterbacks,'' *American Demographics* (March 1988), pp. 28–31.

ware libraries and customized programs included in the basic price, feature in-office training of employees, and so on. The positioning emphasis would be "to provide the best customer service possible to an underdeveloped market segment, small business owners."

Outlining the Appropriate Marketing Mix(es)

The last step in the target-marketing process is for the firm to develop its marketing mix(es) for each customer group to which it wants to appeal. The marketing-mix decisions relate to the product, distribution, promotion, and price.

The marketing mix must be attractive to the target market.

A logical marketing mix for the firm now entering the office personal-computer market and appealing to small business owners is the following:

▶ Product — State-of-the-art IBM clone with expansion capability; very user-friendly with a simple keyboard layout; high-resolution monitor; basic software library; customized software.
▶ Distribution — Direct calls at customers' places of business.
▶ Promotion — Emphasis on personal selling; hands-on on-site training programs; follow-up service calls; customer referrals.

▶ Price — Average to above average; customers directed to nonprice reasons for purchase; positioning linked to high value for the price relationship; price of computer, software, and service bundled together.

Sales Forecasting

*A **sales forecast** predicts company sales over a specified period.*

As a company develops a target market strategy, it should forecast the short-run and long-run sales of its offering to that market. A **sales forecast** outlines expected company sales for a specific good or service to a specific consumer group over a specific period of time under a well-defined marketing program. By accurately forecasting sales, the firm is able to develop a marketing budget, allocate marketing resources, measure success, analyze sales productivity, monitor the external environment and competition, and modify marketing plans.[30]

To estimate its sales, a firm should first look at industry forecasts, because they usually have a strong bearing on the sales of an individual company. Next, sales potential outlines the upper sales limit for the firm, based on its marketing and production capacity. Then a sales forecast details a firm's realistic sales level. This forecast is also based on the expected environment and the firm's performance. Figure 8-15 shows the sales-forecasting process.

A sales forecast should take into account demographics (such as per-capita income and the changing characteristics of the target market), economic conditions (such as the GNP and the rate of inflation), the competitive environment (such as price and advertising levels), the last year's sales, and other variables. When constructing a sales forecast, precision is required. The forecast should break sales down by specific good or service (model 123), specific consumer group (adult female), time period (January through March), and type of marketing plan (intensive advertising).

Data Sources

Data may be obtained from government, industry, and business publications.

A company has several available sources to generate the data needed for a sales forecast. The government collects information on national and local demographic trends, past sales by industry and product type, and economic conditions. Industry trade associations provide a variety of sales statistics. For example, the Conference Board publishes widely and maintains an extensive library for member firms. General business publications, such as *Business Week* and *Fortune*, offer forecasts on a regular basis.

The firm can also obtain data from present and future customers, executives, sales personnel, and internal records. This information will usually center on company rather than industry predictions.

Methods of Sales Forecasting

Sales forecasting methods range from simple to quite sophisticated. Among the simple methods are trend analysis, market share analysis, jury of executive or expert opinion, sales force surveys, and consumer surveys. Among the more complex methods are the chain-ratio method, market buildup method, and statistical analyses. At the end of this

---

[30] See F. William Barnett, "Four Steps to Forecast Total Market Demand," *Harvard Business Review*, Vol. 66 (July–August 1988), pp. 28–30 ff.; and "Special Section: Sales Forecasting and Decision Support Systems," *Journal of the Academy of Marketing Science*, Vol. 16 (Fall 1988), pp. 45–103.

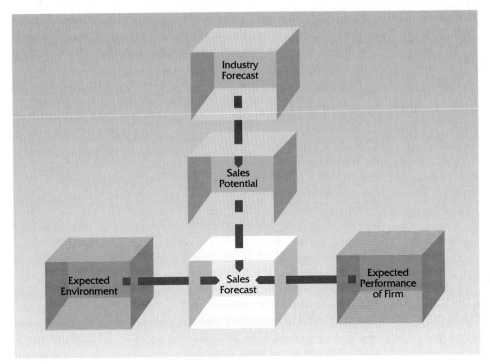

FIGURE 8-15
Developing a Sales Forecast

section, Table 8-4 contains illustrations of each of these. By combining two or more techniques, the firm can have a better sales forecast and minimize the weaknesses in any one technique.

With **simple trend analysis,** the firm forecasts sales on the basis of recent or current performance. For example, if a company's sales have increased an average of 10 per cent annually over the past five years, it forecasts next year's sales to be 10 per cent higher than this year's. While this technique is easiest to use, the problems with it are that past sales fluctuations, the economy, changing consumer tastes, changing competition, and market saturation are not considered. A firm's growth may be affected by these factors.

*In **simple trend analysis,** a firm extends past sales into the future.*

Market share analysis is similar to simple trend analysis, except that the company bases its forecast on the assumption that its share of industry sales will remain constant. However, all firms in an industry do not progress at the same rate. Although market share analysis has the same weaknesses as simple trend analysis, it does enable an aggressive or declining firm to adjust its forecast and marketing efforts; it relies more on industry data.

*In **market share analysis,** sales are related to market share.*

The **jury of executive or expert opinion** is used when the management of a company or other well-informed persons meet, discuss the future, and set sales estimates based on the group's experience and interaction. By itself, this method relies too heavily on informal analysis. In conjunction with other methods, it is effective because it enables experts to direct, interpret, and respond to concrete data. Because management establishes objectives, sets priorities, and guides an organization's destiny, its input is mandatory.

*The **jury of executive or expert opinion** has informed people estimate sales.*

A firm's employees most in touch with consumers and the environment are sales personnel. **Sales force surveys** enable a company to obtain input in a structured way. Salespeople are frequently able to pinpoint trends, strengths and weaknesses in a

Sales force surveys use input from those in touch with consumers.

company's offering, competitive strategies, customer resistance, and the traits of heavy users. They can also break sales forecasts down by product, customer type, and area. On the other hand, sales personnel can have a limited perspective, offer biased replies, and misinterpret consumer desires.

*Through **consumer surveys,** intentions are assessed.*

Many believe that the best indicators of future sales are consumer attitudes. By conducting **consumer surveys,** a company can obtain information on purchase intentions, future expectations, consumption rates, brand switching, time between purchases, and reasons for purchases. But consumers may not reply to surveys and may act differently from what they state.

*With the **chain-ratio method,** general data are broken down. The **market buildup method** adds segment data.*

In the **chain-ratio method,** a firm starts with general market information and then computes a series of more specific information. These combined data yield a sales forecast. For instance, general data could be an overall industry sales forecast for shoe sales, while more specific data would be the company's estimate of its sales accounted for by girls' shoes and the company's expected sales for its girls' shoes during the next three months. The chain-ratio method is only as accurate as the data plugged in for each market factor. Nonetheless, it is useful because it requires management to think through a forecast and obtain different information.

Opposite to the chain-ratio method is the **market buildup method** by which a firm gathers data from small, separate market segments and aggregates them. For example, the market buildup method enables a company operating in four metropolitan areas to develop a forecast by first estimating sales in each area and then adding the areas. When using this method, a marketer must note that consumer tastes, competition, population growth, and media differ by geographic area. Segments of equal size may offer entirely dissimilar sales opportunities. They should not be lumped together indiscriminately.

In test marketing, estimates are made from geographically limited sales.

Test marketing provides a form of market buildup analysis whereby a firm estimates a new product's total future sales based on a short-run, geographically limited test. In test marketing, the company usually introduces a new product into one or a few markets for a short time. The full marketing campaign of the firm is carried out during the test. Then the company forecasts total sales from test market sales. The firm must remember that test areas may not be representative of all locations. Furthermore, test market enthusiasm may not carry over into national distribution. Test marketing is discussed further in Chapter 10.

Detailed techniques use simulation, complex trend analysis, regression, and correlation.

A number of detailed statistical analyses are available for sales forecasting. Simulation allows a firm to enter market data into a computer-based model and forecast under varying conditions and marketing plans. With complex trend analysis, a firm includes past sales fluctuations, cyclical factors (such as economic conditions), and other factors when examining sales trends. Regression and correlation techniques explore the mathematical links between future sales and market factors, such as total family income. These methods depend on reliable data and the ability of personnel and management to use them correctly. A deeper discussion is beyond the scope of this text.

Additional Considerations

A forecast for a continuing product should be the most accurate.

The method and accuracy of sales forecasting depend a great deal on the newness of a firm's offering. A forecast for a continuing good or service could utilize trend analysis, market share analysis, executive and expert opinion, and sales force surveys. Barring major changes in the economy, competition, or consumer tastes, the sales forecast should be relatively accurate.

TABLE 8-4 Applying Sales Forecasting Techniques

Technique	Illustration	Selected Potential Shortcomings
Simple trend analysis	This year's sales = $2 million; company trend indicates 5 per cent growth per year; sales forecast = $2,100,000	Economic decline not considered
Market share analysis	Current market share = 18 per cent; company seeks stable market share; industry forecast = $10,000,000; company sales forecast = $1,800,000	New competitors and increased marketing efforts by current competition not considered
Jury of executive opinion	Three executives see strong growth and three see limited growth; they agree on a 6 per cent rise on this year's sales of $11 million; sales forecast = $11,660,000	Change in consumer attitudes not uncovered
Jury of expert opinion	Groups of wholesalers, retailers, and suppliers meet. Each group makes a forecast; top management utilizes each forecast in formulating one projection.	Each group has different assumptions about economic growth
Sales force survey	Sales personnel report a competitor's price drop of 10 per cent will cause company sales to decline 3 per cent from this year's $7 million; sales forecast = $6,790,000	Sales force unaware that competitor's price cut will be temporary
Consumer survey	85 per cent of current customers (1 million) say they will repurchase next year; 3 per cent of noncustomers (10 million) say they will purchase next year; sales forecast = 1,150,000 customers	Consumer intentions may not reflect actions
Chain-ratio method	Sales forecast (units) for introductory marketing text = number of students × per cent annually enrolled in marketing × per cent purchasing a new book × expected market share = $(10,000,000) \times (0.07) \times (0.87) \times (0.11) = 66,990$	Inaccurate estimate of enrollment in introductory marketing course
Market buildup method	Total forecast = region 1 forecast + region 2 forecast + region 3 forecast; sales = $2,000,000 + $7,000,000 + $13,000,000 = $22,000,000	Incorrect assumption that areas will behave similarly in the future
Test marketing	Total sales forecast = (sales in test market A + sales in test market B) × (25); sales forecast = ($1,000,000 + $1,200,000) × (25) = $55,000,000	Test markets not representative of all locations
Detailed statistical analyses	Simulation, complex trend analysis, regression, and correlation	Lack of understanding by management; not all factors affecting demand can be quantified

A sales forecast for an item new to the firm but continuing in the industry could use trade data, executive or expert opinion, sales force surveys, consumer surveys, the chain-ratio and market buildup methods, and test marketing. The first year's forecast should be somewhat accurate, the following years more accurate. It is hard to estimate first-year sales precisely because consumer acceptance and competition may be hard to gauge.

A forecast for a good or service new to both the firm and the industry should rely on consumer surveys, test marketing, sales force surveys, executive and expert opinion, and simulation. The forecast for the early years may be highly inaccurate because the speed of consumer acceptance is difficult to measure precisely. Later forecasts will be

TABLE 8-5 An Illustration of Sales Penetration and Diminishing Returns

Year 1	Year 2
Sales potential = $1,000,000	Sales potential = $1,000,000
Actual sales = $600,000 (60,000 units)	Actual sales = $700,000 (70,000 units)
Selling price = $10/unit	Selling price = $10/unit
Total marketing costs = $100,000	Total marketing costs = $150,000
Total production	Total production
costs (at $8/unit) = $480,000	costs (at $8/unit) = $560,000

$$\text{Sales penetration} = \frac{\$600,000}{\$1,000,000} = \underline{\underline{60\%}}$$

$$\text{Sales penetration} = \frac{\$700,000}{\$1,000,000} = \underline{\underline{70\%}}$$

Total profit = $600,000 −
   ($100,000 + $480,000)
   = $\underline{\underline{\$20,000}}$

Total profit = $700,000 −
   ($150,000 + $560,000)
   = $\underline{\underline{-\$10,000}}$

In year 1, sales penetration is 60 per cent and the firm earns a $20,000 profit. In year 2, the firm raises its marketing expenditures drastically in order to increase sales penetration to 70 per cent; as a result, it suffers diminishing returns — the additional $100,000 in actual sales is more than offset by a $130,000 rise in total costs (from $580,000 in year 1 to $710,000 in year 2).

more accurate. Even though the initial forecast may be inaccurate, it is necessary for budgeting, allocating resources, measuring success, monitoring the environment and competition, and setting market plans.

Sales penetration shows if a firm has reached its potential. Diminishing returns may result if it seeks nonconsumers.

A firm must consider **sales penetration,** the degree to which a company achieves its sales potential, when forecasting sales. It is expressed as:

Sales penetration = Actual sales/Sales potential

A firm with high sales penetration must realize that **diminishing returns** may occur if it attempts to convert remaining nonconsumers because the costs of attracting these people may outweigh revenues. Other products or segments may offer better opportunities. An illustration is shown in Table 8-5.

Again, a company must keep in mind that factors may change and cause a forecast to be inaccurate unless revised. These include economic conditions, industry conditions, company performance, competition, and consumer tastes.

Summary

1. *To describe the process of planning a target market strategy* After gathering information on consumers and environmental factors, a firm is ready to select the target market(s) to which it will appeal. A potential market contains people with similar needs, adequate resources, and a willingness and ability to buy.

   Developing a target market strategy consists of three general phases, comprising seven specific steps: analyzing consumer demand — determining demand patterns (1), establishing bases of segmentation (2), and identifying potential market segments (3); targeting the market — choosing a target market approach (4) and selecting the target market(s) (5); and developing the marketing strategy — positioning the company's offering relative to competitors (6) and outlining the appropriate marketing mix(es) (7). Of particular importance in this process is product differentiation, whereby a product offering is perceived by the consumer to differ from its competition on any physical or nonphysical product characteristic including price.

2. *To examine alternative demand patterns and segmentation bases* Demand patterns indicate the uniformity or diversity of consumer needs and desires for particular categories of goods and services. In homogeneous demand, consumers have relatively uniform needs and desires for a good or service category. In clustered demand, consumer needs and desires can be classified into two or more identifiable clusters (segments), with each having distinct purchase requirements. In diffused demand, consumer needs and desires are so diverse that clear clusters (segments) cannot be identified.

The possible bases for segmenting the market can be placed into three broad categories: geographic demographics — the basic identifiable characteristics of towns, cities, states, regions, and countries; personal demographics — the basic identifiable characteristics of individual people and groups of people; and life-styles — the patterns in which people live and spend time and money. It is generally advisable to use a mix of demographic and life-style factors to establish possible segmentation bases. Although the distinctions between organizational consumers and final consumers should be kept in mind, these three broad segmentation bases would be used in both cases.

After establishing possible segmentation bases, the company is now ready to develop consumer profiles. These profiles identify potential market segments by aggregating consumers with similar characteristics and needs.

3. *To explain and contrast undifferentiated marketing (mass marketing), concentrated marketing, and differentiated marketing (multiple segmentation)* An undifferentiated-marketing approach aims at a large, broad consumer market through one basic marketing plan. With a concentrated-marketing approach, a firm aims at a narrow, specific consumer group through one specialized marketing plan that caters to the needs of that segment. Under differentiated marketing, a company appeals to two or more distinct market segments, with a different marketing plan for each. When segmenting, a company must understand the majority fallacy — the largest consumer segment may not offer the best opportunity; it often has the greatest number of competitors.

In selecting its target market(s), a company should consider its objectives and strengths, competition, segment size, segment growth potential, distribution requirements, required expenditures, profit potential, company image, and its ability to develop and sustain a differential advantage.

4. *To consider the requirements for successful segmentation and the limitations of segmentation* Successful segmentation requires differences among segments, similarities within segments, measurable consumer traits and needs, large enough segments, and efficiency in reaching segments. Segmentation should not be abused by appealing to overly small groups, using marketing inefficiently, placing too much emphasis on imitations of original company brands, confusing consumers, and so on.

5. *To show the importance of positioning in developing a marketing strategy* In positioning its offering against competitors, the firm needs to present a combination of customer benefits that are not being offered by others and are desirable by the target market (product differentiation). Customers must be persuaded that there are clear reasons why to buy the firm's products rather than competitors'.

The last step in the target-marketing process is for the company to develop marketing mix(es) for each customer group to which it wants to appeal.

6. *To discuss sales forecasting and its role in target marketing* Short- and long-run sales should be forecast in conjunction with the development of a target market strategy. This helps a firm to compute budgets, allocate resources, measure success, analyze productivity, monitor the environment and competition, and adjust marketing plans. A sales forecast describes the expected company sales of a specific good or service to a specific consumer group over a specific time period under a well-defined marketing program.

A company can obtain sales-forecasting data from a variety of internal and external sources. Forecasting methods range from simple trend analysis to detailed statistical analyses. The best results are obtained when several methods and forecasts are combined. A sales forecast should consider the newness of the firm's offering, sales penetration, diminishing returns, and the changing nature of many variables.

Key Terms

market (p. 212)
market segmentation (p. 212)
target market strategy (p. 212)
undifferentiated marketing (mass marketing) (p. 212)
concentrated marketing (p. 212)
differentiated marketing (multiple segmentation) (p. 212)
product differentiation (p. 212)
demand patterns (p. 213)
homogeneous demand (p. 213)

clustered demand (p. 214)
diffused demand (p. 214)
geographic demographics (p. 216)
personal demographics (p. 218)
heavy-half (p. 221)
benefit segmentation (p. 223)
VALS (Values and Life-Styles) program (p. 224)
majority fallacy (p. 232)
sales forecast (p. 240)
simple trend analysis (p. 241)

market share analysis (p. 241)
jury of executive or expert opinion (p. 241)
sales force surveys (p. 241)
consumer surveys (p. 242)
chain-ratio method (p. 242)
market buildup method (p. 242)
sales penetration (p. 244)
diminishing returns (p. 244)

Review Questions

1. What are the three general phases in planning a target market strategy?
2. Explain this comment: "Sometimes a company can achieve a key differential advantage by simply emphasizing how its offering satisfies existing customer desires and needs better than competitors'. Sometimes demand patterns must be modified for consumers to perceive the firm's product differentiation as worthwhile."
3. Distinguish among homogeneous, clustered, and diffused consumer demand. What are the marketing implications?
4. Describe the heavy-half theory.

5. Why has the use of a pure undifferentiated-marketing approach declined? Does this mean there is no place for mass marketing? Explain your answer.
6. What is the majority fallacy? How may a firm avoid it?
7. Name the five key requirements for successful segmentation.
8. Why is sales forecasting important when developing a target market strategy?
9. Distinguish between the chain-ratio and market build-up methods of sales forecasting.
10. Why are long-run sales forecasts for new products more accurate than short-run forecasts?

Discussion Questions

1. How could a food marketer apply geographic-demographic segmentation?
2. Develop a personal-demographic profile of the students in your marketing class. For what goods and services would the class be a good market segment? A poor segment?
3. Describe several potential benefit segments for a firm marketing janitorial services to businesses.

4. Develop a marketing strategy for a truck manufacturer not currently making compact trucks to enable it to appeal to Segment 3 (compact sport utility buyers, domestic vehicles in Table 8–2) of the market.
5. A firm has a sales potential of $2,000,000 and attains actual sales of $850,000. What does this signify? What should the firm do next?

◄ CASE 1 ►

Marketing to College Students*

The college market is an important one for many companies. About thirteen million U.S. college students spend about $20 billion annually on discretionary purchases (approximately $130 per month per student), based on a recent study sponsored by the National Association of College Stores. One-fifth of college students have $250 or more to spend each month. Table 1 shows how college students spend their money. Another survey of college students examined their leisure-time activities. The highlights of this study are shown in Table 2.

Although the number of 18- to 24-year-olds in the U.S. population is expected to decline over the next several years, college enrollment should remain strong. A higher proportion of young adults in this age group will go to college, and more older

TABLE 1 How College Students Spend Their Money (As a Percentage of Discretionary Income)[1]

Expenditure Category	Per Cent of Discretionary Income
Clothing	14.6
Groceries and toiletries	14.3
Auto care	10.0
Restaurants	8.4
Bars and clubs	7.3
Gifts	6.3
Travel to visit family	4.6
Movies	4.0
Travel for vacation	2.7
Concerts/theater	2.5
Attending sporting events	2.2
Magazines/newspapers	1.9
Participation in sports	1.9
Cameras and equipment	1.2

[1] Total does not equal 100 per cent because not every college student purchases items from each category.

SOURCE: National Association of College Stores. Reprinted by permission.

* The data in this case are drawn from Joanne Levine, "Wealthy, Wise—Elusive," *Incentive Marketing* (March 1988), pp. 24–30.

TABLE 2 How College Students Spend Their Free Time (Mean Hours Per Week)

Activity	Hours Per Week
Listening to FM radio	13.0
Listening to records, tapes, and CDs	9.0
Watching television	7.2
Watching rented videotapes	4.8
Participating in sports	4.6
Going to fast-food restaurants	4.3
Reading newspapers	4.2
Shopping	3.6
Reading magazines	3.1
Going to the movies	3.1
Working on a hobby	3.0
Attending sports events	2.2
Playing musical instruments	1.5
Going to concerts	1.2
Using PCs at home	1.2

SOURCE: Teenage Research Unlimited. Reprinted by permission.

adults and other nontraditional students will be attending college.

Many firms have found that appealing to the college market is not a simple task. College students are somewhat of a paradox—students are "easy to find but hard to reach." For example, many college students may not be reached through traditional advertising media because they live on a unique time schedule and have little spare time. As indicated in Table 2, the typical college student spends just over seven hours per week watching television; the average U.S. adult ages 18 to 34 spends 28 hours per week.

One promotion executive recommends that firms seeking this market utilize on-campus advertising, promotions (such as contests), magazines targeted specifically to college students, and sports sponsorships. Word-of-mouth communication among students and displays in college stores also represent unique opportunities in this market. Word-of-mouth is crucial due to the close social interaction among college students. The college store represents an important opportunity due to the homogeneous nature of the college market: "The firm is guaranteed that walk-in traffic is the audience it wants to reach."

QUESTIONS

1. Do you agree with this statement: "The firm is guaranteed that walk-in traffic at a college store is the audience it wants to reach"? Why or why not?
2. How could a firm use a differentiated-marketing approach to appeal to marketing students?
3. Evaluate the college market from the perspective of the five requirements for successful segmentation discussed in this chapter.
4. Based on your analysis of the data in Tables 1 and 2, apply the heavy-half theory and benefit segmentation to the college market.

◀ CASE 2 ▶

Hotels: Targeting the Woman Business Traveler†

Women business travelers now account for 40 per cent of all U.S. business travel, up from 1 per cent in 1970; and it is predicted that this market segment will account for one-half of business travelers by the year 2000. Women now spend $23 billion annually on business travel, $10 billion of this on lodging alone.

Initial attempts by hoteliers to attract women business travelers met with limited success—the approaches were just too overt. Many women travelers felt ostracized when placed on single-gender floors or believed being located on separate floors was patronizing. Says a Ramada spokesperson, "They don't want to be treated like some dainty little thing who couldn't take care of herself. Women just want to be treated as professional business travelers."

As a consequence, a number of hotels have moved away from their past use of women-only floors and rooms with pink wallpaper. According to one consultant, "Hotels want to attract women without saying, 'We're doing this because we want you women.' If you tell women you're doing things for them, the defense mechanism goes up."

These are several illustrations of the practices being used to appeal to women business travelers:

▶ Increased security—Hilton, Hyatt, and Radisson hotels offer rooms on "club" floors for both women and men that require a special key to enter the floor from the passenger elevator. Rooms on these floors are priced at 20 per cent above those on traditional floors.
▶ Improved lighting—Econo Lodge is replacing dim incandescent lamps in its parking lots with high-intensity sodium lamps.
▶ Special dining accommodations—Marriott has "solo" dining tables in its restaurants, consisting of a table for one or two people with a reading lamp, notebook, writing instruments, and magazines. Marriott believes that women frequently dislike eating in their rooms, yet desire to eat alone. At the same time, some hotels have broadened their room service menus to include more lighter dishes such as quiche and chef's salad for women who do wish to dine in their rooms.
▶ Special amenities—Most hotels now equip at

† The data in this case are drawn from Michele Manges, "Hotels Change Pitch to Businesswomen," *Wall Street Journal* (October 14, 1988), p. B1.

least some rooms with makeup mirrors, hair dryers, terrycloth robes, shampoo, hair conditioner, and body lotion. Women often desire these amenities.

Many hotels report success with their special emphasis on women business travelers. For example, "Suites at the Radisson Plaza in Minneapolis are booked up faster than regular rooms," partly due to their appeal to women business travelers. And Marriott has had so much success with its "club" floors that it plans to feature them in every new hotel it builds.

However, there is some controversy about the value of hotel strategies specifically aimed at women. For instance, although some hotels find that women like suites so that they can have meet-ings in their rooms without the bed being visible, others find that women rarely hold business meetings in their rooms. They "tend to meet in the client's office, or in a coffee shop, cocktail lounge, or restaurant." Some hotel executives question whether special features designed to appeal to women are not important to men as well:

> Maybe I'm confused about what's different for a man and for a woman. Men use hair dryers and conditioners. I know some men who even use shower caps. (the sales manager at San Francisco's upscale Kensington Park)

> A lot of things hotels say they're doing for women business travelers they should be doing for all travelers. I don't like walking down long, dark hallways either. (the vice-president of marketing at the discount Motel 6 chain)

QUESTIONS

1. As a hotel executive, how would your marketing efforts differ if you decide to focus on business travelers rather than on pleasure travelers? Could you successfully appeal to both groups? Explain your answer.
2. Should hotels separate the business traveler market into two segments: men and women? Why or why not?
3. What other criteria (besides purpose of travel and gender) should hotels examine in developing their target market strategies?
4. How would you forecast the number of women business travelers who would visit an existing hotel during the next year? The number of women travelers visiting a new hotel over the next year?

part 2 CASE

How Do You Target Business Customers Effectively?*

Introduction

Buoyed by the success one of its projects achieved in-house and with a small group of outside customers, the financial services division of a large corporation decided to expand and offer its new service to a larger circle of corporate prospects.

However, four firms were already well-entrenched in the promising market segments identified by traditional demographic segmentation criteria such as location, company size, or industry. To succeed and avoid a chancy head-to-head battle, the new entrant had to find niches those leaders were not occupying. If it built its communications and sales strategies around demographic market data alone, the entrant likely would end up a "me-too" player.

The solution? In that real-world case, the financial services division ran its own research probing the "psychographic" dimension of corporate culture. It reasoned that companies' different operating styles—their corporate personalities—affect their buying behavior for the service in question, regardless of differences in their corporate demographics.

The division's study revealed three distinct types of corporate culture among different size companies in a broad array of industries. It dubbed the companies within each type "happy doers," "middle of the roaders," and "satisfaction seekers."

* Adapted by the authors from Tom Eisenhart, "How to Really Excite Your Prospects," *Business Marketing* (July 1988), pp. 44–45 ff. Copyright Crain Communications Inc. Reprinted by permission.

Within each group, members appeared to share common attitudes and motivations concerning the service in question, yet those behavioral characteristics differed among the groups. Satisfaction seekers looked like the most promising targets for the division's marketing communications and sales efforts, because they seemed to be the companies most willing to try new vendors. The new entrant could develop communications aimed at their cultural needs.

Business-Oriented Psychographic Research Emerges

A small but growing number of business marketers are finding that psychographic research can give them a strategic edge by helping them better understand what customers really want, and find the segments they can sell to best. Even business buyers are human; their psychological needs and personalities affect how they respond to mass and personal communications.

Hence AT&T Business Systems TV commercials conjure the fear of making the wrong decision and not buying from reliable Ma Bell. Advertising wags call the hardly subtle approach "slice of death."

IBM meanwhile uses well-liked characters recycled from the popular *M*A*S*H* TV series to sell the warmth of teamwork on PS/2 computers tied to corporate mainframes. And microcomputer challenger Apple Computer Inc. counters with the satisfaction of independence and one-upmanship achieved by desktop publishing system users making an end run around corporate data-processing departments.

Facing markets crowded with basically undifferentiated goods and services, and media increasingly cluttered with promotional noise, leading business-to-business marketers are understanding that emotional appeals invest extra value in their offerings, lifting them from "me-too" status in the customer's mind.

Choosing which appeals to aim at which targets "is done on the basis of building an additional wrapping of understanding," says John Mather, executive vice-president of research and information at Ketchum Communications Inc., Pittsburgh. Research and market segmentation begin with demographics and grow sequentially to encompass product usage, user benefits and needs, buyer motivations, life-styles, and emotional factors, he explains.

Hardly all business-to-business marketers need to reach beyond traditional demographics to segment markets properly, however. It depends upon the good or service category, the competitive landscape, the number and kind of buying influences involved in a purchase, and the breadth of customer heterogeneity, among many variables that come into play.

"Business marketers have to ask themselves whether it is worth spending the time and money in doing the additional wrapping," Mr. Mather adds, noting that studies probing buyer psychographics can approach the six-figure mark. Even a relatively simple one-shot focus group session can run anywhere from a low of about $4,000 to more than $10,000.

Business marketers face other limiting factors besides cost. Unlike the consumer world, it's difficult to find and contact the right business respondents for a thorough probe. Small samples can make findings unreliable. And communications and sales programs often cannot reach psychographically defined target segments efficiently.

Mounting a sophisticated segmentation study isn't an easy decision. The critical element, say knowledgeable marketers, is whether the insights will refine or confirm strategy, and whether segmentation criteria help explain buying behavior.

In his clients' product categories, "the differences between products are very small," says Steven Trygg, president of agency Anderson & Lembke Inc., Stamford, Conn. "But the emotional differences attached to those products are much more apparent."

He cites the Sperry IT microcomputer introduction $2\frac{1}{2}$ years ago. Although identical technically to the IBM AT, the Sperry (now Unisys) computer appealed to a different segment emotionally. It attracted more "change-oriented" prospects, Mr. Trygg says, buyers emotionally willing to assume risk in order to stay at the leading edge of technology. The AT inspired security-oriented buyers cherishing the notion that "you can't go wrong with the old standby."

For the most part, however, business marketers are not investing heavily in detailed psychographic research to dissect buyer attitudes with statistical precision. Instead of building quantitative models that link behavior to specific job functions or corporate cultures, marketers tend to rely more heavily on qualitative information such as focus group feedback or one-on-one interviews — seasoned by experience and intuition.

For instance, Anderson & Lembke's "crude" understanding of buying motivations, Mr. Trygg acknowledges, depends on a few in-depth customer interviews by creative people. Typically, they'll probe customers' immediate business concerns, what customers think are the most important functions of their jobs, and their receptivity to change.

In one investigation for a client making removable hard-disk computer drives, two groups were important: management information systems (MIS) managers and security managers. The MIS manager adapts to change; he wants his company to continue at the forefront of technology, Mr. Trygg says.

But security managers, charged with protecting sensitive data on disk drives, tend to take their jobs as second careers. Their perception of security is "no change." The client needs two ads to address each audience differently.

The Social Style Model

Building a framework to link emotional and behavioral style differences to job function is not a new idea. For the past 20 years, Wilson Learning Corp., Minneapolis, has used a "Social Style" model developed by Tracom Corp., Denver (a subsidiary of Cahners Publishing Co.), to describe typical need and behavior patterns among businesspeople.

The thinking is that social styles strongly influence how people react to various stimuli on and off the job, based on their "assertiveness" and "responsiveness." The approach, illustrated in Figure 1, groups individuals into one of four social styles: "analyticals," "drivers," "amiables," and "expressives."

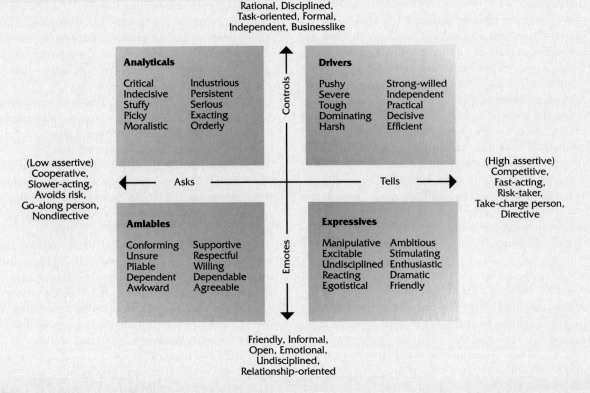

Rational, Disciplined,
Task-oriented, Formal,
Independent, Businesslike

Analyticals

Critical	Industrious
Indecisive	Persistent
Stuffy	Serious
Picky	Exacting
Moralistic	Orderly

Drivers

Pushy	Strong-willed
Severe	Independent
Tough	Practical
Dominating	Decisive
Harsh	Efficient

Controls

(Low assertive)
Cooperative,
Slower-acting,
Avoids risk,
Go-along person,
Nondirective

← Asks   Tells →

(High assertive)
Competitive,
Fast-acting,
Risk-taker,
Take-charge person,
Directive

Emotes

Amiables

Conforming	Supportive
Unsure	Respectful
Pliable	Willing
Dependent	Dependable
Awkward	Agreeable

Expressives

Manipulative	Ambitious
Excitable	Stimulating
Undisciplined	Enthusiastic
Reacting	Dramatic
Egotistical	Friendly

Friendly, Informal,
Open, Emotional,
Undisciplined,
Relationship-oriented

FIGURE 1
Social Style Model
SOURCES: Wilson Learning Corp. and The TRACOM Corp.

Understanding those styles, company founder Larry A. Wilson claims, helps to predict people's behavior. Then, for example, salespeople can tailor their delivery to the "psychological comfort zone" of their prospect. A "driver" salesperson trying to win over an "amiable" prospect, for instance, will have to adjust behavior to the prospect's relatively low-key style.

The model defines assertiveness as the degree to which one states opinions with assurance, confidence, and force, and the extent to which one tries to direct the actions of others. A less assertive person does more "asking," while a more assertive person does a lot of "telling." Less assertive people are cooperative, slower-acting, risk-avoiding, and nondirective, while high-assertives are competitive, fast-acting, take-charge individuals.

Responsiveness is the extent to which one reacts to appeals, influence, or stimulation. How one displays feelings, emotion, or impressions—maintaining control or emoting—also indicates responsiveness. Low-responsives are rational, disciplined, task-oriented, formal, independent, cool, and detached, the model says. High-responsives are friendly, informal, open, emotional, undisciplined, and relationship-oriented.

Based on varying degrees of those two behaviors, the model identifies four social style types:

➤ "Analyticals" are like the engineering-oriented managers who rate low in assertiveness and low in responsiveness. They keep themselves in control. As noted earlier, they tend to be rational and process-oriented.

➤ "Expressives" are highly assertive and highly responsive. The personality opposites of analyticals, expressives often are a company's social activists. They thrive on freedom from outside control and detail, they value varied interpersonal contact, and they prefer democratic supervisors. Because expressives seek approval for themselves, their departments, and companies, they favor appeals that make them feel like they've "made it" or have "arrived."

▶ "Drivers," low in responsiveness but highly assertive, are the prototypical hard-chargers seeking nonroutine challenges. Self-motivated, impatient workers who want to control their environment, they in turn want freedom from control, supervision, and details. Drivers are bottom-line oriented and are attracted to appeals that stress business benefits. That's because they want to build a string of highly visible financial success to move up the corporate ladder.

▶ "Amiables" are low-assertive, high-responsive individuals. They are team players: loyal, patient, empathetic, and good listeners. Amiables prefer dealing with people in low-pressure situations. And they also like to build long-term relationships. Establishing employee morale is one of their key concerns. Advertising appeals to them should stress interpersonal considerations: how the good or service will affect their employees, etc. In addition, marketers should stress security: the vendor's ability and willingness to provide personalized and frequent service.

Wilson Learning Corp. has categorized its managerial style data (based on client self- and peer assessments) by industry type, such as banking, computers and precision instruments, telecommunications, aerospace, pharmaceuticals, chemicals, utilities, and industrial and farm equipment. Analyticals predominate over the three other style types in all industries.

For example, among 9,857 chemical managers, 41 per cent were labeled analyticals, 24 per cent drivers, 19 per cent amiables, and 15 per cent expressives, according to 1984 Wilson data.

That implies that a business marketer selling to chemical industry managers should aim messages primarily at the analytical, generally engineering-oriented managers. They maintain high standards by logically defining, clarifying, criticizing, and testing decisions. They're more motivated by logic than emotion—at least when compared to more responsive types.

Appeals to them perhaps should acknowledge their technical expertise and respect their hard work in their specialty field. And because they're more concerned with the process than with output, it seems they will appreciate detailed specifications. Finally, because analyticals want to ensure that their equipment lasts for the long-term, advertising appeals probably should emphasize a product's durability and dependability.

VALS and the Business Customer[1]

Some business marketers attempt to learn more about their markets by applying final consumer research models, such as the well-known Values and Life-Styles (VALS) Classification System designed by SRI International, Menlo Park, Calif. VALS identifies a number of life-style types in the entire U.S. population based on shared values, attitudes, needs, wants, beliefs, and demographics.

While that typology has direct implications for consumer marketers, some of the VALS life-style types roughly reflect broad job function personalities. For example, Clarity, Coverdale Rueff Advertising Inc., Minneapolis, applied VALS characterizations to some extent in a program for former client Office Solutions Inc. (OSI), Madison, Wisconsin. Advertising for OSI's word-processing program had to appeal to two groups: MIS managers who work directly with the product and upper-level managers who make the purchasing decisions.

The agency identified MIS managers as "inner-directed" types, falling into VALS "societally conscious" and "experiential" life-style groups. According to VALS, inner-directed people focus on inner growth and turn to internal values to guide their behavior. They are considered self-expressive, person-centered, impassioned, individualistic, and diverse.

Experientials are the most inner-directed of the VALS life-styles. They want direct experience, vigorous involvement, and are often attracted to exotic, strange, and natural activities. They are also probably the most passionately involved with others and the most willing to try anything once, says the VALS model.

Societally conscious types are mature, prosperous, and highly educated. As the label implies, their psychological focus extends beyond the self and others to include society as a whole. They have a sense of societal responsibility which leads them to support causes such as conservation and environmentalism.

In contrast, OSI found its upper-level manager audience characterized as "outer-directed," people with VALS "achiever" life-styles.

---

[1] The discussion in this section is based on the original VALS typology, which was introduced in 1978 and used extensively through 1988. In 1989, an updated "VALS 2" typology was introduced—as discussed in Chapter 8.

Compared to inner-directed individuals, outer-directeds live in response to signals from others. Their consumption, activities, and attitudes are guided by what they think others may think. In general, outer-directeds are the most content of Americans. They are well attuned to the cultural mainstream.

Achievers, according to the VALS model, are part of the outer-directed category. Among this group are many leaders in business, the professions, and government. They are competent, self-reliant, and hardworking. Achievers also tend to be materialistic and oriented to fame and success. Also, achievers defend the economic status quo, satisfied with their rung in American society.

Because its budget did not allow separate campaigns for each target group, OSI and its agency attempted to attract both groups with the same ads. They ran long copy to satisfy the MIS managers who like thorough explanations. Because the agency expected that fast-paced achiever-type managers wouldn't want to waste time with fine print, the ads included bulleted information and subheads to capsulize key selling points.

"I think psychographics are very important, but they're harder to get at in business-to-business," says Rob Rueff, chief executive officer and marketing manager at the agency. He believes business marketers have to be content to take what descriptive information is available and make assumptions about the typical personality that will predominate in a buying group.

That's not always an effective solution, however. In terms of the VALS model, business marketers frequently find their targets clustered in the achiever and the related "emulator" life-style categories. The distinction usually isn't fine enough to guide business market segmentation.

What's Next in Targeting Business Customers?

Even the largest business-to-business advertisers tend to rely primarily on qualitative methods and intuition to develop emotionally potent communications. There are no mathematical formulas, yet.

AT&T Business Systems' current television campaign takes what the company calls a "progress through conflict approach." Originally, AT&T and its New York ad agency, Ogilvy and Mather Inc., ran focus groups, learning that executives in small business consider their phones their business lifelines.

Client and agency translated the idea into the "real-life" vignettes of businesspeople nervously regretting not having bought AT&T reliability. Unusual camera angles and a stark documentary feel added to the commercials' ability to unsettle viewers. AT&T's management has since adapted the emotionally laden approach to commercials for other products.

Max Blackston, an Ogilvy & Mather account planner, says the creative direction "didn't come from anything specific in the research" such as identifying small business executives' life-style factors. Rather, it was more of a creative leap from what was said in focus groups.

The advertising industry is making a start at better understanding the emotional side of business buying. The Advertising Research Foundation's Business Advertising Research Council (BARC), for example, has formed a Purchase Decision Committee which hopes to "get useful information that can be translated into creative action," says consultant Howard L. Gordon (a principal in George R. Frerichs Inc., Chicago), the committee's chairman.

The committee has pored through available literature and research, and plans to probe the few available psychographic business data bases for insights. The SMRB (Simmons Market Research Bureau) annual survey data base, to cite one, includes 6,000 heads of households with professional/managerial occupations. SMRB collects media and product-use data from each of them, and asks for their self-perceived values and styles via a VALS questionnaire.

Mr. Gordon says, however, that there are a few signals in those data about value differences by job category. Still, he feels the professional/managerial group needs to be divided into more specific job classes for differences to begin to appear in the numbers.

Could such a job-function behavioral model be operationally useful to marketers? Perhaps not, in part because self-perception ratings can be misleading. "There's so much measurement error in determining how people view themselves," says John Morton, vice-president and director of advanced statistical research at Total Research.

Mr. Morton cites a study his firm conducted for an upscale consumer publication. Out of nine variables predicting reading behavior, subscribers' self-perceptions placed last in accuracy.

Interestingly, a much better predictor turned out to be respondents' speculation about the magazine's typical reader. For instance, the magazine's actual readers didn't think of themselves as "sophisticated," but they attributed that quality to their perceived ideal reader.

Moreover, Wilson Learning says that in its communications training workshops, self-assessment is usually wrong 70 per cent of the time. That's why the firm developed special questionnaires on which participants are rated by their associates, to provide a more accurate picture.

Projective techniques such as used in the consumer magazine study are becoming more widespread and sophisticated in consumer marketing. However, sometimes they probe deeper than life-style and personality characteristics near the psyche's surface. Borrowed from clinical psychology, methods such as telling stories, drawing pictures, or acting out scenes are designed to overcome conscious response bias and reveal emotions.

A recent *Wall Street Journal* article, for instance, clucked admiringly over a roach spray product study. Projective techniques implied, the newspaper reported, that women equate roaches with men who've left them. Passive poisons don't kill roaches instantly, but the sprays do, making them the preferred product for women seeking revenge on men.

Probing the subconscious mind that thoroughly may not have operational value in business advertising, however. Buyers need to rationally justify decisions in reports to superiors. Neither may the comparatively simple models correlating behavioral styles and job functions, if they don't recognize the role of corporate culture. While a purchasing manager may have certain personality and self-image characteristics, his or her decisions are likely to be affected by the company's reward systems for doing things the company's way.

Whether focusing on company culture or a particular job function's normative behavior, psychographic research probably always will be an inexact science for marketers. Unlike behavioral science researchers content with accurately describing what people do, marketers have to use the information to find appropriate targets and move them to act. Lacking the certitude of demographic analysis, psychographic profiles of business buyers require judicious use in answering the central question: Will they make my communications and marketing more effective?

QUESTIONS

1. Why are more firms that market to organizational consumers turning to psychographics for better insights? Is this good or bad? Why?
2. What could industrial marketers learn by studying such final consumer concepts as perceived risk, low-involvement purchasing, and brand loyalty?
3. Explain the "Social Style" model shown in Figure 1. Give an example of a marketing appeal aimed at each of the four types of organizational buyers depicted in this figure.
4. How could the "Social Style" model be applied by firms that appeal to final consumers?
5. What are the pros and cons of business-to-business firms relying on VALS research?
6. Comment on this statement: "Whether focusing on company culture or a particular job function's normative behavior, psychographic research probably will always be an inexact science for marketers."
7. In developing a differentiated marketing strategy for air conditioners, how would your marketing mixes differ between large corporate customers and individual final consumers?
8. By using a combination of demographic and life-style data in developing a target market strategy, a company's sales forecasts become more accurate but also more difficult to construct. Why?

part 3
PRODUCT PLANNING

In order to adhere to the marketing concept, a firm needs to develop, implement, and monitor a systematic marketing plan. This plan centers on the four elements of the marketing mix: product, distribution, promotion, and price. We present these elements in Parts 3 through 6, with Part 3 concentrating on product planning.

9 **An Overview of Product Planning**   Here, we define tangible, augmented, and generic products and distinguish among different types of consumer and industrial products. We look at product mix strategies and product management organizations in detail. We also study product positioning and the product life cycle in depth.

10 **Conceiving, Developing, and Managing Products**   In this chapter, we look at products from their inception to their deletion. We discuss the types of new products, reasons for new-product failures, and the new-product planning process. We explain the growth of products in terms of the adoption and diffusion processes, and note several methods for extending the lives of mature products. We also offer product deletion strategies.

11 **Branding and Packaging**   Here, we look at the branding decisions that center on corporate symbols, branding philosophy, the choice of brand names, and the use of trademarks. We also consider the six basic functions of packaging: containment, usage, communication, market segmentation, channel cooperation, and new-product planning.

CHAPTER *9*

An Overview of Product Planning

CHAPTER OBJECTIVES

1. To define product planning and differentiate among tangible, augmented, and generic products

2. To examine the various types of products, product mixes, and product-management organization forms from which a firm may select

3. To discuss product positioning and its usefulness for marketers

4. To study the different types of product life cycles that a firm may encounter and the stages of the traditional product life cycle (introduction, growth, maturity, and decline)

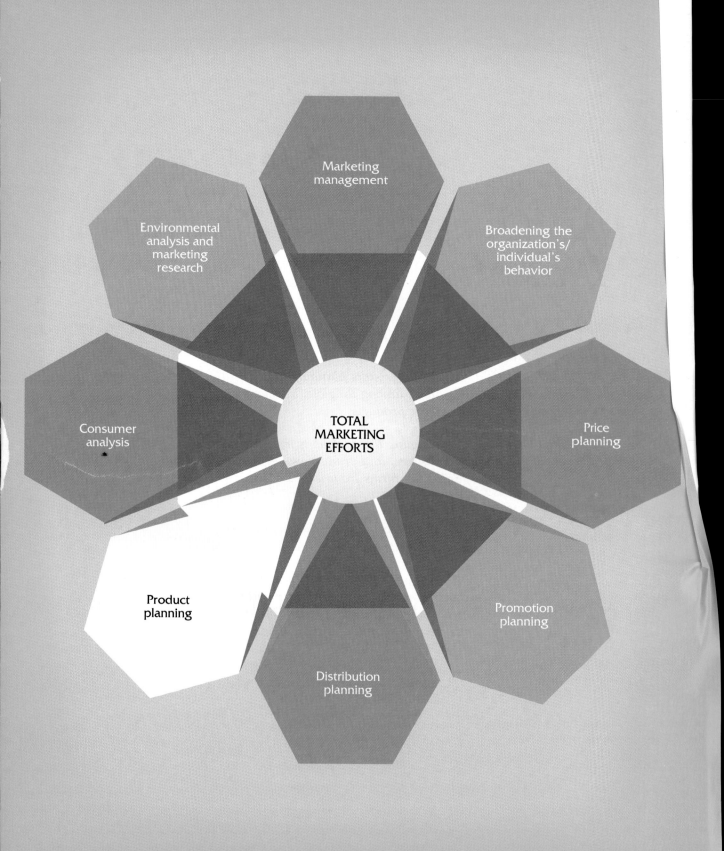

TOTAL
MARKETING
EFFORTS

Marketing
management

Environmental
analysis and
marketing
research

Broadening the
organization's/
individual's
behavior

Consumer
analysis

Price
planning

Product
planning

Promotion
planning

Distribution
planning

For four years, Bruce Miller spent most waking moments thinking about Crisco. "My whole life was Crisco," he says. From his small office at Procter & Gamble, he mulled over everything about the cooking fat—from its can size and label to the cents-off coupons offered at the nation's supermarkets. And he avidly watched competitors, especially his colleague down the hall handling P&G's Puritan brand.

That was the life of a brand manager, tapped to champion a single product and promised a fast-track rise at P&G if successful. But classic (product) brand management isn't working any longer, and P&G and its competitors are scrambling to overhaul the way they develop and sell products. The result: a revolution as they alter "the most sacred of sacred cows."

In product planning, one of the most important decisions a firm must make relates to the organization structure used to manage the efforts in this area. So let us take a closer look at Procter & Gamble's "classic" product-management system and its recent "revolutionary" changes in it.

P&G's classic system began in 1931, as a response to a problem with its new perfumed Camay soap. At that time, Camay did not have its own brand manager and trailed far behind Ivory soap, which was the firm's most successful and oldest brand; there was "too much Ivory thinking." So a young P&G advertising manager asked: "Why not pit the brands against one another?" His proposal? Each brand would have its own manager, who would compete against both P&G and non-P&G brands. Since then, some form of product (brand) management system has been implemented by virtually every U.S. consumer-products company and by many industrial-products firms.

But in 1987, P&G greatly revised its traditional organization, by adding a new level of "category" managers. The new approach does not abolish brand managers; it has them report to managers who oversee broader product lines, such as detergents. Each category manager is responsible and accountable for the sales, market share, and profit performance of all the brands within his or her product category.

Thus, the efforts of P&G's 80+ individual brand managers will be better coordinated by category managers: "By fostering internal competition among brand managers, the classic system established strong incentives to excel. But it also created conflicts and inefficiencies as brand managers squabbled over corporate resources, from ad spending to plant capacity. And it often meant not enough thought was given to how brands could work together."

Copyright The Procter & Gamble Company. Reprinted by permission.

With the new structure, advertising, product-development, finance, manufacturing, engineering, and sales-merchandising managers report to category managers (instead of division managers). The category managers report to the heads of the company's eight consumer-products divisions.

In this chapter, we will take a look at several basic product-planning decisions a firm must make, including the choice of organizational structure. While doing so, we will keep this in mind: "The smartest companies must tailor the organization of each of their business units to support their individual strategies."[1]

[1] Jolie Solomon and Carol Hymowitz, "P&G Makes Changes in the Way It Develops and Sells Its Products," *Wall Street Journal* (August 11, 1987), pp. 1, 12; and Zachary Schiller, "The Marketing Revolution at Procter & Gamble," *Business Week* (July 25, 1988), pp. 72–76.

Overview

Product planning involves developing and managing products that satisfy consumers.

Product planning is systematic decision making relating to all aspects of the development and management of a firm's products, including branding and packaging. Each **product** consists of a bundle of attributes (features, functions, benefits, and uses) capable of exchange or use, usually a mix of tangible and intangible forms. Thus,

> a product may be an idea, a physical entity (a good), or a service, or any combination of the three. It exists for the purpose of exchange in the satisfaction of individual and organizational objectives.[2]

A well-structured product plan enables a company to pinpoint opportunities, develop appropriate marketing programs, coordinate a mix of products, maintain successful products as long as possible, reappraise faltering products, and delete undesirable products.

A firm should define its products in three distinct ways: tangible, augmented, and generic. By considering all three definitions, the company is better able to identify consumer needs, competitive offerings, and distinctive product attributes. This is illustrated in Figure 9-1.

A tangible product has precise specifications.

A **tangible product** is the basic physical entity, service, or idea; it has precise specifications and is offered under a given description or model number. Heinz ketchup, an IBM business computer, a Nikon 35mm camera, a manicure, a seven-day European cruise on the QE2 (Queen Elizabeth 2), and cutting state income taxes by 3.5 per cent are examples of tangible products. Color, style, taste, size, weight, durability, quality of construction, and efficiency in use are some tangible features.

An augmented product includes image and service features.

An **augmented product** includes not only the tangible elements of a product, but also the accompanying cluster of image and service features. For example, one political candidate may receive more votes than another because of charisma, despite identical platform issues (tangible product). Rolex watches and Rolls-Royce autos are popular predominantly due to the image of luxury and status they convey. The augmented product for a computer includes software packages, instructions for users, maintenance, and promptness of service. Service features are often used to distinguish sellers of otherwise undifferentiated products.

A generic product centers on consumer benefits.

A **generic product** focuses on what a product means to the customer, not the seller. It is the broadest definition and is consistent with the marketing concept:

▶ "In the factory we make cosmetics, and in the drugstore we sell hope" (Charles Revson of Revlon).

▶ "One million quarter-inch drills were sold not because people wanted quarter-inch drills, but because they wanted quarter-inch holes" (Theodore Levitt, Harvard professor).

▶ "People no longer buy shoes to keep feet warm and dry. They buy because of how shoes make them feel—masculine, feminine, rugged, different, sophisticated, young, glamorous, in. Our business now is selling excitement rather than shoes" (President of Melville Corp., owner of Thom McAn).

▶ Sheaffer makes pens that "say it all" to consumers. See Figure 9-2.

---

[2] Peter D. Bennett (Editor), *Dictionary of Marketing Terms* (Chicago: American Marketing Association, 1988), p. 153. See also Roberto Friedmann and V. Parker Lessig, "Psychological Meaning of Products and Product Positioning," *Journal of Product Innovation Management*, Vol. 4 (December 1987), pp. 265–273.

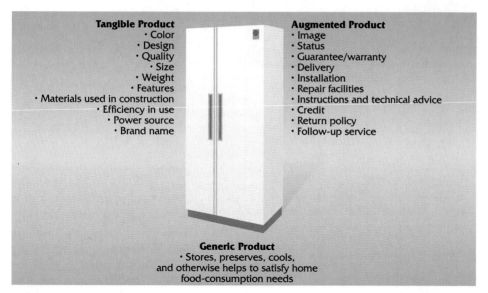

Tangible Product
· Color
· Design
· Quality
· Size
· Weight
· Features
· Materials used in construction
· Efficiency in use
· Power source
· Brand name

Augmented Product
· Image
· Status
· Guarantee/warranty
· Delivery
· Installation
· Repair facilities
· Instructions and technical advice
· Credit
· Return policy
· Follow-up service

Generic Product
· Stores, preserves, cools,
and otherwise helps to satisfy home
food-consumption needs

FIGURE 9-1
Illustrating the Three Product Definitions

This chapter provides an overview of product planning. It examines the basic areas in which a company must make decisions: product type(s), product mix, product management organization, and product positioning. It also describes the product life cycle and its marketing importance.

Chapter 10 presents an in-depth discussion of how to manage products over their lives, from finding new-product ideas to deleting faltering products. Chapter 11 concentrates on two specialized aspects of product planning: branding and packaging.

Types of Products

The initial product-planning decision is the choice of the type(s) of products to offer. Products can be categorized as goods or services and as consumer or industrial. Categorization is important because it focuses on the differences in the characteristics of products and the resulting marketing implications.

Distinctions Between Goods and Services

Goods marketing entails the sale of physical products. ***Durable goods*** are physical products that are used over an extended period of time, such as furniture and heavy machinery. ***Nondurable goods*** are physical products "that are (1) made from materials other than metals, hard plastics, and wood; (2) are rather quickly consumed or worn out; or (3) become dated, unfashionable, or in some other way no longer popular."[3] Examples are food and office supplies.

Service marketing encompasses the rental of goods, the alteration or repair of goods owned by consumers, and personal services. A ***rented-goods service*** involves the leasing of a good for a specified period of time. Examples include vehicle, hotel room, office building, and tuxedo rentals. An ***owned-goods service*** involves an alter-

*Goods marketing includes long-lasting **durable goods** and shorter-lasting **nondurable goods.***

*Service marketing includes **rented-goods, owned-goods,** and **nongoods services.***

[3] Bennett, *Dictionary of Marketing Terms*, pp. 63, 132.

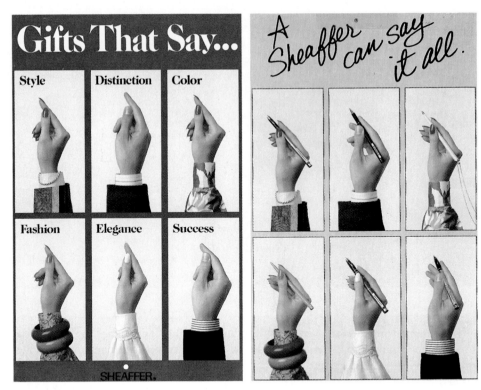

ation or repair of a good owned by the consumer. Examples include repair services (such as automobile, watch, and machinery), lawn care, car washing, equipment maintenance, and dry cleaning. A ***nongoods service*** involves personal service on the part of the seller; it does not involve a good. Examples include accounting, legal, and tutoring services.

Sometimes goods and services are confused. However,

> when we buy the use of a hotel room, we take nothing away with us but the experience of the night's stay. . . . Although a consultant's product may appear as a bound report, what the consumer bought was mental capability, not paper and ink.[4]

Generally, services have four characteristics that distinguish them from goods: intangibility, perishability, inseparability from the service provider, and variability in quality.[5] Table 9-1 contrasts these characteristics for services and goods.

*Services differ from goods in terms of their **intangibility, perishability, inseparability,** and **variability.***

The ***intangibility of services*** means they often cannot be displayed, transported, stored, packaged, or inspected before buying. This occurs for repair services and personal services. The service operator can only describe the benefits that can be derived from the service experience. The ***perishability of services*** means that many of them cannot be stored for future sale. For example, if a house painter who needs eight hours to paint a single house is idle on Monday, he or she will not be able to paint two houses on Tuesday. Monday's idle time is just lost. The service supplier must try to

---

[4] G. Lynn Shostack, "Designing Services That Deliver," *Harvard Business Review*, Vol. 62 (January–February 1984), p. 134.
[5] See Valarie A. Zeithaml, A. Parasuraman, and Leonard L. Berry, "Problems and Strategies in Service Marketing," *Journal of Marketing*, Vol. 49 (Spring 1985), pp. 33–46.

TABLE 9-1   Basic Differences Between Services and Goods

Services	Goods
1. *Services are often intangible.* They may involve acts, deeds, performances, efforts. Many services cannot be physically possessed. The value of a service may be based on an experience.	1. *Goods are tangible.* They are objects, things, materials. Value is based on ownership.
2. *Services are usually perishable.* Unused capacity cannot be stored or shifted from one time to another.	2. *Goods can be stored.* Surpluses in one period can be applied against shortages in another period.
3. *Services are frequently inseparable.* The quality of many services cannot be separated from the service provider.	3. *Goods can be manufactured by one firm and marketed by another.* The quality of a good can be differentiated from a distribution intermediary's quality.
4. *Services may vary in quality over time.* It is difficult to standardize some services because of their labor intensiveness and the involvement of the service user in diagnosing his or her service needs.	4. *Goods can be standardized.* Mass production and quality control can be used.

regulate consumer usage so there is consistent demand throughout various periods of the week, month, and/or year.

The ***inseparability of services*** means that the service provider and his or her services are sometimes inseparable. When this occurs, the service provider is virtually indispensible, and customer contact is often considered an integral part of the service experience. For example, the quality of machinery repair depends on the skill of the mechanic, and the quality of legal services depends on the skill of an attorney. ***Variability in service quality,*** differing service performance from one purchase experience to another, often occurs even if services are completed by the same operator. Variations may be due to the service firm's difficulty in diagnosing a problem (for repairs), an inability of the customer to verbalize service needs, and a lack of standardization and mass production for most services.

The impact of these characteristics is greatest for personal services. They are usually much more intangible, more perishable, and more inseparable from the service provider; and they have more quality variations than rented-goods services or owned-goods services.

Although services have different characteristics from goods, their sales are frequently connected. In goods marketing, goods dominate the offering and services augment them. For example, a tractor manufacturer may provide extended warranties, customer training, insurance, and financing. A clothing retailer may provide alterations and home delivery. In service marketing, services dominate the offering and goods augment them. For instance, the major cost of a haircut service is for the time of the operator, not the machinery used. Repair-service firms exist to install, modify, or fix all types of goods from televisions to plumbing. Other independent service firms aid consumers in their purchases, such as American Express and United Parcel Service offering credit and delivery respectively. In some instances, such as car leasing, an alternative to a purchase is provided.

Service marketing is more fully discussed in Chapter 22.

Consumer Products

Consumer products are goods and services destined for the final consumer for personal, family, or household use. The use of the good or service designates it as a consumer product. For example, a calculator, dinner at a restaurant, telephone ser-

Consumer products are final consumer goods and services.

TABLE 9-2 Characteristics of Consumer Products

Consumer Characteristics	Type of Product		
	Convenience	**Shopping**	**Specialty**
Knowledge prior to purchase	High	Low	High
Effort expended to acquire product	Minimal	Moderate to high	As much as necessary
Willingness to accept substitutes	High	Moderate	None
Frequency of purchase	High	Moderate or low	Varies
Information search	Low	High	Low
Major desire	Availability without effort	Comparison shopping to determine best choice	Brand loyalty regardless of price and availability
Examples	(a) Staple: cereal (b) Impulse: candy (c) Emergency: tire repair	(a) Attribute-based: name-brand clothes (b) Price-based: budget hotel	Hellman's mayonnaise

vice, a file cabinet, a vacuum cleaner, and an electric pencil sharpener are consumer products only if they are purchased for personal, family, or household use.

Consumer products were first classified almost seventy years ago by Melvin T. Copeland.[6] His three-category system of convenience, shopping, and specialty products is widely employed today. The system is based on shoppers' awareness of alternative products and their characteristics prior to the shopping trip and the degree of search shoppers will undertake. It is important to recognize that placing a product into one of these categories depends on shopper behavior. See Table 9-2.

Convenience products are those purchased with a minimum of effort because the buyer has knowledge of product characteristics prior to shopping. The consumer does not want to search for additional information (because the item has been bought before) and will accept a substitute (Libby's instead of Green Giant canned corn) rather than have to frequent more than one store.

*Convenience products are purchased with minimum effort and are categorized as **staples, impulse products,** and **emergency products.***

The tasks of marketing center on intensive distribution (all available outlets), convenient store locations, evening and weekend store hours, heavy use of mass advertising and in-store displays, well-designed store layouts, and self-service to minimize purchase time. Retailers often carry many brands.

Convenience products can be subdivided into staples, impulse products, and emergency products. *Staples* are low-priced items that are routinely purchased on a regular basis, such as detergent, mass transit, and cereal. *Impulse products* are items that the consumer does not plan to buy on a specific trip to a store, such as candy, a magazine, and a lottery ticket. There are four kinds of impulse purchase:

1. Pure—novelty or escape buying out of the normal routine.
2. Reminder—previous experience remembered.
3. Suggestion—an item seen and evaluated for the first time in the store.
4. Planned—purchase based on a sale or coupon offer.[7]

---

[6] Melvin T. Copeland, ''Relation of Consumers' Buying Habits to Marketing Methods,'' *Harvard Business Review,* Vol. 1 (April 1923), pp. 282–289. See also Patrick E. Murphy and Ben M. Enis, ''Classifying Products Strategically,'' *Journal of Marketing,* Vol. 50 (July 1986), pp. 24–42.

[7] Hawkins Stern, ''The Significance of Impulse Buying Today,'' *Journal of Marketing,* Vol. 26 (April 1962), pp. 59–62.

According to one study, 34 per cent of grocery store purchases are specifically planned, 13 per cent generally planned, and 53 per cent unplanned.[8] ***Emergency products*** are items purchased out of urgent need, such as tire repair to fix a flat, an umbrella during a rainstorm, and aspirin for a headache.

Shopping products are those for which consumers lack sufficient information about product alternatives and their attributes, and therefore must acquire further knowledge in order to make a purchase decision. The two major kinds of shopping products are attribute-based and price-based. For ***attribute-based shopping products,*** consumers get information about and then evaluate product features, warranty, performance, options, and other factors. The product with the best combination of attributes is purchased. Sony electronics and Calvin Klein clothes are marketed as attribute-based shopping products. With ***price-based shopping products,*** consumers judge product attributes to be similar and look around for the least expensive item/ store. Consumers will exert effort in searching for information because shopping products are bought infrequently or have a large purchase price. Budget hotels, electronics, and store-brand furniture are marketed as price-based shopping products.

Attribute-based shopping products and price-based shopping products require an information search.

The marketing emphasis for shopping products is on assortment (such as many colors and options), sales personnel, communicating competitive advantages, informative advertising, well-known brands (or stores or people), distributor enthusiasm, and customer warranties and follow-up service to reduce perceived risk. Shopping centers and business districts ease shopping by placing several stores in close proximity.

Specialty products are the particular brands, stores, and persons to which consumers are loyal. Consumers are fully aware of these products and their attributes prior to making a purchase decision. They are willing to make a significant effort to acquire the brand desired and will pay a higher price than competitive products, if necessary. For specialty products, consumers will not make purchases if their choice is not available. Substitutes are not acceptable.

*Consumers are loyal to **specialty products.***

The marketing emphasis for specialty products is on maintaining the product attributes that make the items so unique to loyal consumers, reminder advertising, distribution appropriate for the product (Hellman's mayonnaise and *Business Week* require different distribution to loyal customers: supermarkets versus home subscriptions), extension of the brand name to related products (such as Hellman's tartar sauce), product improvements, ongoing customer contact (such as *Friends* magazine, published for Chevrolet owners), and monitoring wholesalers' and retailers' performance.

The consumer-products classification recognizes that many customers view the same products differently. It is an excellent basis for segmentation. For example, Sure deodorant may be a convenience product for some consumers (who buy Ban or Right Guard if Sure is unavailable), a shopping product for others (who read ingredient labels before selecting a brand), and a specialty product for still others (who insist on Sure regardless of price or availability). Procter & Gamble, the maker of Sure, must understand how Sure fits into these different categories to plan its marketing strategy accordingly.

Industrial Products

Industrial products are goods and services purchased for use in the production of other goods or services, in the operation of a business, or for resale to other consumers. Industrial products include heavy machinery, raw materials, typewriters, janito-

Industrial products are organizational consumer goods and services.

[8] Judann Dagnoli, "Impulse Governs Shoppers," *Advertising Age* (October 5, 1987), p. 93.

TABLE 9-3 Characteristics of Industrial Products

Characteristics	Type of Product						
	Installations	Accessory Equipment	Raw Materials	Component Materials	Fabricated Parts	Supplies	Services
Degree of consumer decision making	High	Moderate	Low	Low	Low	Very low	Low to high
Per-unit costs	High	Moderate	Low	Low	Low	Very low	Low to moderate
Rapidity of consumption	Very low	Low	High	High	High	High	Low to high
Item becomes part of final product	No	No	Sometimes	Yes	Yes	No	Sometimes
Item undergoes changes in form	No	No	Yes	Yes	No	No	Sometimes
Major consumer desire	Long-term facilities	Modern equipment	Continuous, cost-efficient, graded materials	Continuous, cost-efficient, specified materials	Continuous, cost-efficient, fabricated materials	Continuous, cost-efficient supplies	Efficient, expert services
Examples	Production plant	Forklift truck	Coal	Steel	Thermostat	Light bulb	Machinery repair, accounting

rial services, and cash registers. A customer may be a manufacturer, wholesaler, retailer, or government or other nonprofit organization.

Industrial products may be categorized by the degree of decision making involved in a purchase, costs, rapidity of consumption, role in production, and change in form. Because industrial-products sellers normally seek out potential purchasers, store shopping behavior is often not involved. Installations, accessory equipment, raw materials, component materials, fabricated parts, business supplies, and business services are types of industrial products. Table 9-3 highlights these products.

Installations and accessory equipment are expensive and do not become part of the final product.

Installations and **accessory equipment** are capital goods. They are used in the production process and do not become part of the final product. Installations are nonportable goods involving a high degree of consumer decision making (usually by several upper-level executives), are very expensive, last many years, and do not change form. The major marketing tasks are direct selling from the manufacturer to the purchaser, lengthy negotiations about features and terms, providing complementary services such as maintenance and repair, tailoring products to buyers' desires, technical expertise, and team selling (in which various salespeople have different areas of expertise and interact with specialized executives of the buyer). Examples of installations are buildings, assembly lines, major equipment, large machine tools, and printing presses.

Accessory equipment are portable (movable) goods that require a moderate amount of consumer decision making, are less costly than installations, last a number of years, and do not become part of the final product or change its form. The major marketing tasks are tying sales to those of installations; providing a variety of choices in price, size, and capacity; employing a strong distribution or sales force; stressing durability and efficiency; and providing technical and maintenance support. Examples of accessory equipment are drill presses, motor trucks, vans, and lathes.

Raw materials, component materials, and *fabricated parts* are used up in production or become part of final products. They are expense rather than capital items. They require limited buyer decision making, are inexpensive on a per-unit basis, and are rapidly consumed. Raw materials are unprocessed primary materials from extractive and agricultural industries — minerals, petroleum, coal, crops, and iron ore, for example. Component materials are semimanufactured goods that undergo further changes in form — steel, cement, wire, textiles, and basic chemicals, for example. Fabricated parts are placed into products without further changes in form — electric motors, batteries, refrigerator thermostats, and microprocessors, for example.

Raw materials, component materials, and fabricated parts are consumed in production.

The major marketing tasks for materials and parts are to ensure continuity in shipments, quality items, and prompt delivery; actively pursue reorders; implement standardized pricing; employ aggressive distributors or sales personnel; seek long-term contracts; and satisfy specifications set by buyers.

Industrial supplies are convenience goods that are necessary for the daily operation of the firm. These goods can be maintenance supplies, such as light bulbs, cleaning materials, and paint; repair supplies, such as rivets, screws, nuts, and bolts; or operating supplies, such as stationery, pens, and business cards.

Industrial supplies are used daily.

Industrial supplies do not require extensive decision making by the buyer, are very inexpensive on a per-unit basis, are rapidly consumed, and do not become part of the finished product. Marketing emphasis is on availability, promptness, and ease of ordering.

Industrial services are of two general types: maintenance and repair, and business advisory. *Maintenance and repair services* include painting, machinery repair, and janitorial services. *Business advisory services* include management consulting, advertising agency services, accounting services, and legal services.

Industrial services are classified as maintenance and repair, and business advisory.

Maintenance and repair services usually involve a low degree of consumer decision making, are relatively inexpensive, and are consumed quickly. They may become part of the final product (for example, machinery repair) and undergo a change in form (for example, janitorial services). The major marketing thrust is on consistent, efficient service at a reasonable price. Business advisory services may involve a moderate to high level of consumer decision making when these service providers are first hired. Costs are generally low to moderate. The benefits of these services may be long-lasting. They do not become part of the final product, but they are receptive to consumer information requests. The major marketing emphasis is on presenting an image of expertise and clearly conveying the reasons for a client to use the service. Both types of industrial services are frequently purchased on a contract or retainer basis, and some firms may decide to undertake the services internally. A general principle is that services can be performed by others, but not eliminated.

Elements of a Product Mix

After determining the type(s) of products to offer, a firm needs to outline the variety and assortment of those products. A *product item* is a specific model, brand, or size of a product that a company sells, such as a college course on principles of marketing, a General Motors bus, or Maxell 3.5-inch floppy diskettes for personal computers. Usually a firm sells a group of closely related product items as part of a *product line.* In

A product item is a specific model; a product line has related items; a product mix is all a firm's lines.

FIGURE 9-3
Selected Brands in Campbell's Product Mix
Courtesy of Campbell Soup Company.

each product line, the items have some common characteristics, customers, and/or uses; they may also share technologies, distribution channels, prices, related services, and so on.[9] For example, Noxell markets Cover Girl lipstick, eye makeup, and other cosmetics. Caterpillar makes several different tractor models. Macmillan publishes a number of college textbooks in marketing. Many local lawn-care firms offer lawn mowing, landscaping, and tree-trimming services.

[9] Bennett, *Dictionary of Marketing Terms,* p. 156.

FIGURE 9-3
(Continued)

The **product mix** consists of all the different product lines a firm offers. For instance, Campbell markets soup, frozen foods, beverages, poultry, produce, baked goods, chocolate, and various other food products. Figure 9-3 shows selected brands in Campbell's product mix.

A product mix can be described in terms of its width, depth, and consistency. The **width of a product mix** is based on the number of different product lines a company offers. The **depth of a product mix** is based on the number of product items within each product line. The **consistency of a product mix** is based on the relationship

A product mix has levels of **width, depth,** *and* **consistency.**

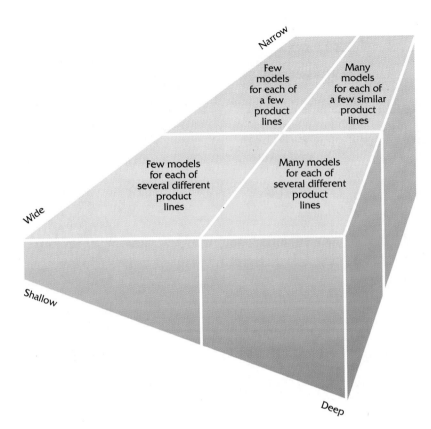

Narrow

Few
models
for each of
a few
product
lines

Many
models
for each of
a few similar
product
lines

Wide

Few models
for each of
several different
product
lines

Many models
for each of
several different
product
lines

Shallow

Deep

FIGURE 9-4
Product Mix Alternatives

among product lines in terms of their sharing a common end-use, distribution outlets, consumer group(s), and price range. Figure 9-4 shows product mix alternatives in terms of width and depth.

A wide mix enables a firm to diversify products, appeal to different consumer needs, and encourage one-stop shopping. It also requires resource investments and expertise in different product categories. A deep mix can satisfy the needs of several consumer segments for the same product, maximize shelf space, discourage competitors, cover a range of prices, and sustain dealer support. It also imposes higher costs for inventory, product alterations, and order processing. In addition, there may be difficulty in differentiating two similar product items. A consistent mix is generally easier to manage than an inconsistent one. It allows a firm to concentrate on marketing and production expertise, create a strong image, and generate solid distribution relations. However, excessive consistency may leave the firm vulnerable to environmental threats, sales fluctuations, or decreased growth potential because emphasis is on a limited product assortment. Figure 9-5 shows the wide/deep mix of Borden. Figure 9-6 shows part of Boeing's narrow/deep mix.

Product-mix decisions can have both positive and negative effects on companies, as these examples demonstrate:

▶ Wrigley's strategy has been to concentrate on chewing-gum products and not to market even closely related items such as hard candies: "If you are thinking of chewing gum, you are thinking Wrigley's." The company is so successful that it has a 47 per cent share of the U.S. market and its profits have increased 150 per cent since 1982.[10]

[10] Eric N. Berg, "Wrigley Stays True to Gum," *New York Times* (November 24, 1988), pp. D1, D4.

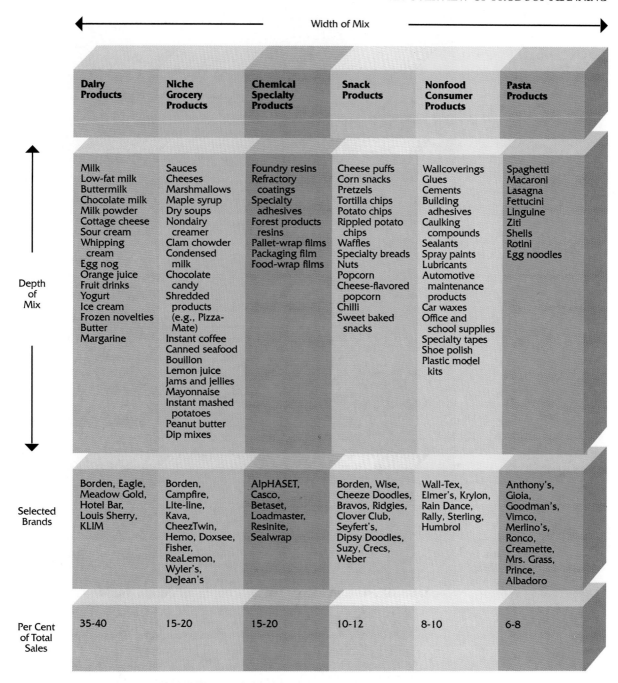

Width of Mix

Dairy Products	Niche Grocery Products	Chemical Specialty Products	Snack Products	Nonfood Consumer Products	Pasta Products
Milk Low-fat milk Buttermilk Chocolate milk Milk powder Cottage cheese Sour cream Whipping cream Egg nog Orange juice Fruit drinks Yogurt Ice cream Frozen novelties Butter Margarine	Sauces Cheeses Marshmallows Maple syrup Dry soups Nondairy creamer Clam chowder Condensed milk Chocolate candy Shredded products (e.g., Pizza-Mate) Instant coffee Canned seafood Bouillon Lemon juice Jams and jellies Mayonnaise Instant mashed potatoes Peanut butter Dip mixes	Foundry resins Refractory coatings Specialty adhesives Forest products resins Pallet-wrap films Packaging film Food-wrap films	Cheese puffs Corn snacks Pretzels Tortilla chips Potato chips Rippled potato chips Waffles Specialty breads Nuts Popcorn Cheese-flavored popcorn Chilli Sweet baked snacks	Wallcoverings Glues Cements Building adhesives Caulking compounds Sealants Spray paints Lubricants Automotive maintenance products Car waxes Office and school supplies Specialty tapes Shoe polish Plastic model kits	Spaghetti Macaroni Lasagna Fettucini Linguine Ziti Shells Rotini Egg noodles
Selected Brands Borden, Eagle, Meadow Gold, Hotel Bar, Louis Sherry, KLIM	Borden, Campfire, Lite-line, Kava, CheezTwin, Hemo, Doxsee, Fisher, ReaLemon, Wyler's, DeJean's	AlpHASET, Casco, Betaset, Loadmaster, Resinite, Sealwrap	Borden, Wise, Cheeze Doodles, Bravos, Ridgies, Clover Club, Seyfert's, Dipsy Doodles, Suzy, Crecs, Weber	Wall-Tex, Elmer's, Krylon, Rain Dance, Rally, Sterling, Humbrol	Anthony's, Gioia, Goodman's, Vimco, Merlino's, Ronco, Creamette, Mrs. Grass, Prince, Albadoro
Per Cent of Total Sales 35-40	15-20	15-20	10-12	8-10	6-8

Depth of Mix (left margin, with vertical arrow)

FIGURE 9-5 Borden's Product Mix, Selected Domestic and International Items and Brands
SOURCE: Figure developed by the authors based on data from Borden, Inc.

▶ H&R Block's strategy has been to add other service lines to its basic accounting and taxation services. Today the company operates CompuServe, a computer communications and information services subsidiary; Personnel Pool of America, a provider of supplemental personnel services; and Path Management Industries, a divi-

FIGURE 9-6
Selected Items in Boeing's Narrow/Deep Product Mix
Reprinted by permission.

sion offering various business-skills training seminars. These three service lines account for about 45 per cent of Block's annual sales.[11]

▶ In 1987, General Motors began a "deproliferation" strategy intended to reduce the number of car models marketed by its five divisions from 175 to 136 by 1992. This strategy is its response to weak sales for many General Motors cars; cost inefficiencies; and criticism from customers, industry analysts, and competitors about its look-alike autos.[12]

[11] *H&R Block, Inc. 1988 Annual Report.*
[12] Patricia Strnad, "New Chevies Lead GM Deproliferation," *Advertising Age* (January 12, 1987), p. 60.

TABLE 9-4 Comparing Product Management Organizations

| Organization | Characteristics | | |
	Staffing	Ideal Use	Permanency
Marketing-manager system	Key functional areas of marketing report to a manager with considerable authority.	A company makes one product line, has a dominant line, or uses category marketing managers.	The system is ongoing.
Product (brand) manager system	Each middle manager focuses on a single product or group of products.	A company makes many distinct products, each requiring expertise.	The system is ongoing.
Product-planning committee	Senior executives from various functional areas participate.	The committee should supplement another product organization.	The committee meets irregularly.
New-product manager system	Separate middle managers focus on new products and existing products.	A company makes several existing products and substantial time, resources, and expertise are needed for new products.	The system is ongoing, but new products are shifted to product managers after introduction.
Venture team	An independent group of company specialists guides all phases of a new product's development.	A company wants to create vastly different products than those currently offered and needs an autonomous structure to aid development.	The team disbands after a new product is introduced, turning responsibility over to a product manager.

Product Management Organizations

There are several organizational forms of product management from which a firm may choose: marketing manager, product manager, product-planning committee, new-product manager, and venture team.[13] See Table 9-4.

Under a ***marketing-manager system,*** an executive is responsible for designated marketing functions (such as marketing research, product and market planning, distribution, promotion, pricing, and customer services) and for coordinating with other departments that perform marketing-related activities (such as warehousing, order filling, shipping, credit, warranty fulfillment, and purchasing). This type of system works well for companies with a line of similar products or one dominant product line. It may be less successful when there are many product lines and each requires a different marketing mix — unless there are category marketing managers, with each responsible for a product line. Pepsi Cola USA, Purex, and Levi Strauss are companies using some form of marketing-manager system.

All marketing areas report to one manager with a ***marketing-manager system.***

With a ***product (brand) manager system,*** there is a middle manager who is responsible for the planning, coordination, and monitoring of the performance of a single product (brand) or a small group of products (brands). This type of manager handles new and existing products and is involved with everything from marketing research to package design to advertising. The product-manager system allows each product or brand to receive adequate attention. It works well when there are many

A manager handles new and existing products in a category in the ***product manager system.***

[13] The definitions in this section are drawn from Bennett, *Dictionary of Marketing Terms,* various pages.

distinct products or brands, each requiring individual expertise and marketing decisions. There are two problems with this system: lack of authority for the product manager and inadequate attention to new products. Procter & Gamble, RJR Nabisco, and Lehn & Fink are companies using product managers.

A product-planning committee has executives involved part-time.

A ***product-planning committee*** is staffed by high-level executives from various functional areas, including marketing, production, engineering, finance, and research and development (R&D). The committee handles product approval, evaluation, and development on a part-time basis. Once a product is introduced into the marketplace, the committee usually turns to other opportunities and gives that product over to a product manager. This system enables management to have a strong input into product decisions; however, it meets on an irregular basis and must pass projects on to line managers. The product-planning committee functions best as a supplement to other methods and is utilized by many large companies.

A new-product manager system has managers for new and for existing products.

A ***new-product manager system*** has product managers who supervise existing products and new-product managers who identify and develop new products. This system ensures adequate time, resources, enthusiasm, and expertise for new-product development. After a new product is introduced, it is turned over to the product manager. The new-product manager system can be costly, lead to conflicts, and cause discontinuity when the product is introduced. General Foods, General Electric, NCR, and Johnson & Johnson are among the companies that use new-product managers.

A venture team is an autonomous new-product department.

A ***venture team*** is a small, independent department within a firm that consists of a broad range of specialists, drawn from appropriate functional areas, who manage a specific new product's entire development process from idea generation to market introduction. Team members work on a new-product concept on a full-time basis and function as a separate unit within the company. The team disbands when the new product is introduced. A venture team provides adequate resources, a flexible environment, expertise, and continuity in new-product planning. It is quite valuable when a company wants to be more farsighted and reach out for truly new ideas. It is also expensive to establish and operate. Xerox, IBM, Polaroid, Monsanto, and 3M use venture teams.

The correct organizational form depends on the diversity of the firm's offerings, the number of new products introduced, the level of innovation, company resources, management expertise, and other factors.[14] A combination of forms may also be highly desirable. Among larger firms this is particularly common.

Furthermore, companies should keep the following in mind in setting up a product-management organizational structure:

> Successful companies are run by people who have their priorities straight, their values clear, their direction tight, and a strong grasp of culture.[15]

Entrepreneurship involves the ability and desire to recognize and pursue opportunity. The

---

[14] See Joel R. Evans and Kathryn V. Marinello, "Understanding the Impact of Overall Company Management Style on New Product Planning" in Robert F. Lusch et al. (Editors), *AMA Educators' Proceedings* (Chicago: American Marketing Association, 1985), pp. 302–307; P. L. Dawes and P. G. Patterson, "The Performance of Industrial and Consumer Product Managers," *Industrial Marketing Management*, Vol. 17 (1988), pp. 73–84; Erik W. Larson and David H. Gobeli, "Organizing for Product Development Projects," *Journal of Product Innovation Management*, Vol. 5 (September 1988), pp. 180–190; and Thomas Osborn, "Re-Organizing the Brand Management Structure," *Marketing Communications* (June 1987), pp. 41–56.

[15] Donald Clifford, Jr. and Richard E. Cavanagh, *The Winning Performance: How America's High-Growth Midsize Companies Succeed* (New York: Bantam Books, 1985).

pursuit of opportunity is distinguished from administrative tasks that involve managing resources. Some of the practices that contribute to the successful management of resources inhibit the pursuit of opportunity. Management must learn to achieve a balance in the interest of long-term survival.[16]

Product Positioning

In its product-planning efforts, of utmost importance to a firm is how the new and ongoing items in its product mix are perceived (positioned) in the marketplace. In particular, a company must work to ensure that each of its products is perceived as providing some combination of unique features (product differentiation) and that these features are desired by the target market (thus converting product differentiation to a differential advantage).

Distinctive and desirable product features must be communicated to the marketplace.

When a product is new, the firm must clearly communicate its attributes: What is it? What does it do? How is it better than the competition? Who should buy it? The firm's goal is to have consumers perceive the product's attributes as the company intends. When a product has an established niche in the market, the firm must continuously reinforce its image and focus on communicating the reasons for its success. Once consumer perceptions are formed, rightly or wrongly, they may be hard to change. It may also be difficult to later change a product's niche in the market (for instance, from low-price, low-quality to high-price, high-quality).

Through ***product positioning,*** a firm can map each of its products in terms of consumer perceptions and desires, competition, other company products, and environmental changes.[17] Consumer perceptions are the images consumers have of products, both a company's and competitors'. Consumer desires refer to the attributes consumers would like products to possess—that is, their ***ideal points.*** Whenever a group of consumers has a distinctive "ideal" for a product category, it represents a potential market segment. A firm will do well when the attributes of its products are perceived by consumers as being close to the ideal.

Product positioning *maps out consumer perceptions of product attributes.* ***Ideal points*** *show the most preferred attributes.*

Competitive product positioning refers to the perceptions consumers have of a firm relative to its competitors. The objective is for the firm's products to be perceived as "more ideal" than competitors'. Company product positioning shows a firm how consumers perceive the firm's different brands (items) within the same product line and the relationship of those brands (items) to each other. The objective here is that each of the firm's brands is positioned near an ideal point and that these brands are not too clustered near one another in the consumer's mind—the brands should appeal to different ideal points (market segments).

Both competitive and company product positioning are important.

A company must also monitor environmental changes that would alter the manner in which its products are perceived. These changes could include new products by competitors, changing consumer life-styles, new technology, negative publicity, and resource availability.

Product positioning is illustrated in Figure 9-7, which shows how a number of brands of ice cream are perceived by consumers on the basis of price and richness

---

[16] Howard H. Stevenson and Jose Carlos Jarrillo-Mossi, "Preserving Entrepreneurship as Companies Grow," *Journal of Business Strategy,* Vol. 7 (Summer 1986), p. 10.

[17] See Robert A. Kriegel, "Positioning Demystified," *Business Marketing* (May 1986), pp. 106–112; and Steven M. Shugan, "Estimating Brand Positioning Maps Using Supermarket Scanning Data," *Journal of Marketing Research,* Vol. 24 (February 1987), pp. 1–18.

You're the Marketer

At Lotus, How Do You Market Computer Software?

Marketing a new computer-software product such as the $395 Agenda (a personal information manager program) is a complex process even for Lotus, the number two software maker for personal computers in the United States. As Lotus' advertising manager says, "We have to tell people what a personal information manager is and why Agenda is the best personal information manager."

Agenda enables busy executives to store, sort, and recall information in their PCs on the basis of activity, date, destination, and priority. For example, Agenda can be used to sort information contained in electronic newswires, vendors' business cards, and correspondence.

To better position Agenda and gain early consumer acceptance, Lotus obtained input from various sources very early in Agenda's product-development process. Informal discussion groups watched a demonstration and made lists of what Agenda could do. A sample

of loyal Lotus users tried out applications for Agenda. 200 testers "had at" the software.

Lotus' confidence in Agenda's potential sales is evident from the $6 million marketing budget allocated to launching the product—an amount greater than the annual sales of most software programs. This is in recognition of how difficult it may be to communicate Agenda's features and to position the product in the minds of prospective consumers.

Lotus' initial marketing emphasis was on giving away thousands of free copies to "influential techies," on presenting demonstrations at over 100 seminars involving computer user groups, and on low-key advertising. At that time, the conceiver of Agenda said, "I'm eagerly awaiting the results from the marketplace. It could either be a big success or just a market presence."

As Agenda's marketing manager, what would you do now?

SOURCE: Based on material in William M. Bulkeley, "Selling Software That's Hard to Describe," *Wall Street Journal* (July 11, 1988), p. 21.

(level of butterfat content).[18] Godiva, Häagen-Dazs, Frusen Glädjé, and Alpen Zauber are perceived as expensive and very rich (high in butterfat content). Breyer's, Sealtest, Dolly Madison, and Louis Sherry are perceived as medium in price and richness. Weight Watcher's and Light 'n Lively are perceived as medium in price and not rich (low in butterfat content). Supermarket brands are perceived as low in price and moderate in richness.

Each of these brand groups has carved out a distinctive product position that matches an ideal point (market segment): I_1 — super premium, I_2 — regular, I_3 — low calorie, and I_4 — economy. There is no overlap among these categories. Demand is greatest for regular ice cream.

An examination of competitive product positioning reveals that the super-premium segment is relatively small and highly saturated. There is a lot of competition in the regular ice cream segment; however, the size of the segment merits this level of competition. The low-calorie and economy segments are medium in size and have fewer competitors.

[18] See Lawrence Ingrassia, "Ice Cream Makers' Rivalry Heating Up," *Wall Street Journal* (December 21, 1988), p. B1.

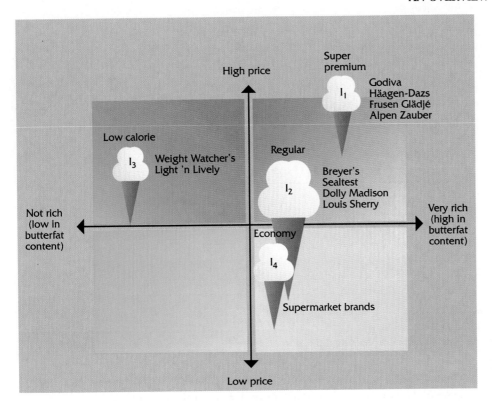

FIGURE 9-7
Product Positioning of Selected Ice Cream Brands

Frusen Glädjé, Breyer's, Sealtest, and Light 'n Lively are all marketed by Kraft. From an analysis of company product positioning, it is clear that Kraft well serves the customers in its markets. However, it must continue to differentiate carefully between Breyer's (the "all natural" ice cream) and Sealtest (the "ice-cream parlor" ice cream).

By undertaking product-positioning analysis, a company can learn a great deal and plan marketing efforts accordingly, which these examples show:

▶ Nuprin, Bristol-Myers' ibuprofen over-the-counter analgesic, has capitalized on its distinctive color to carve out a market niche—and a 30 per cent market share. At first, advertising focused on the product's strength for headache relief; but that appeal did not work. Then positioning efforts turned to Nuprin's yellow color (all the competitors' pills are white): "It is one way to dramatically and graphically show that Nuprin is different. You have to convince [consumers] that your product is different before they will believe the product is better. That Nuprin is yellow is superficial to the product superiority, yet it opens people's minds that this product is different."[19]

▶ As noted earlier in the chapter, General Motors is now striving to distinguish more clearly among its automobile product lines (company product positioning), which consumers have perceived as too similar. On the basis of thorough analysis, the company is concentrating on two product features—price and expressiveness—in its repositioning strategy. Figure 9-8 shows the product positions of General

---

[19] Patricia Winters, "Color Nuprin's Success Yellow," *Advertising Age* (October 31, 1988), p. 28.

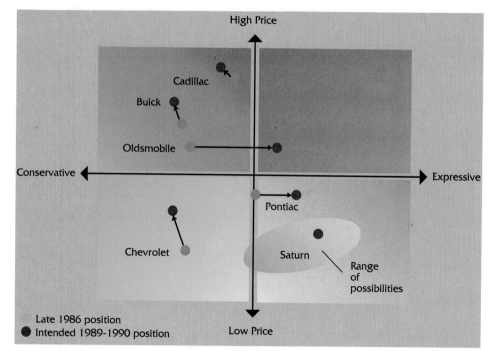

FIGURE 9-8

Applying Product Positioning to General Motors

SOURCE: Adapted by the authors from John C. Mowen, "Beyond Consumer Decision Making," *Journal of Consumer Marketing*, Vol. 5 (Winter 1988), pp. 22–23. Reprinted by permission.

Motors' car lines in late 1986 and its intended 1989–1990 positions. As of 1990, General Motors expects its new Saturn division to be operational.[20]

▶ Through a bold and consistent brand-identity program developed by Selame Design, Veryfine has become a recognized leader of natural fruit juices and other products. See Figure 9-9.

The Product Life Cycle

*The **product life cycle** describes each stage in its life.*

The **product life cycle** is a concept that attempts to describe a product's sales, profits, customers, competitors, and marketing emphasis from its beginning until it is removed from the market. The concept was popularized by Theodore Levitt in 1965.[21]

From a product-planning perspective, there is interest in the product life cycle for several reasons. One, some analysts have found that product lives are shorter now than previously. Two, new products are requiring increased marketing and other investments. Three, the product life cycle enables a firm to anticipate changes in consumer tastes, competition, and support from distribution intermediaries and to adjust the marketing plan accordingly. Four, the product life-cycle concept enables a company to consider the mix of products that it should offer; many firms seek to attain a **balanced product portfolio,** whereby a combination of new, growing, and mature products is maintained. (Portfolio analysis was explained in detail in Chapter 3.)

*Companies often desire a **balanced product portfolio**.*

The product life-cycle concept may be applied to a product class (watches), a product form (quartz watches), and a brand (Seiko quartz watches). However, product forms

---

[20] John C. Mowen, "Beyond Consumer Decision Making," *Journal of Consumer Marketing*, Vol. 5 (Winter 1988), pp. 15–25; and "Performance-Driven," *Advertising Age* (November 21, 1988), p. 31.

[21] Theodore Levitt, "Exploit the Product Life Cycle," *Harvard Business Review*, Vol. 43 (November–December 1965), pp. 81–94.

What has . . .
no sugar added . . .
no caffein . . .
no artificial flavor . . .
no chemical preservatives . . .
no carbonation . . .
. . . you guessed it!
The Veryfine Apple.
Veryfine
apple juice
natural
That's all there is in Veryfine Apple Juice.
natural
Look for the Veryfine Apple on the label.
Very
Very
Veryfine
Very, very, Veryfine . . . a taste worth looking for.
Veryfine
(Mother's voice) And it's all natural.

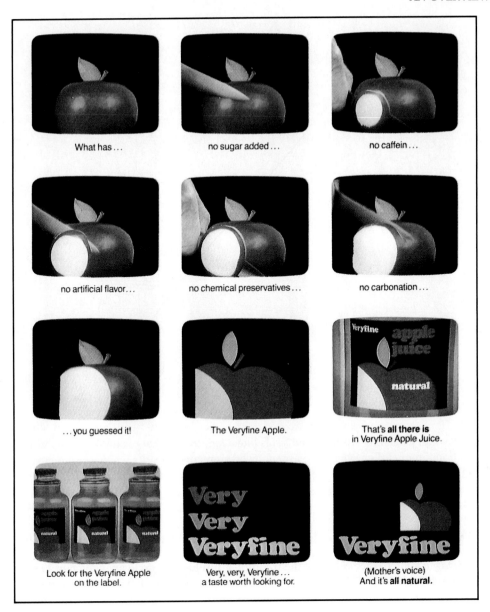

FIGURE 9-9
The All Natural Positioning of Veryfine Apple Juice
This ongoing program was developed by Selame Design, a unique visual marketing firm with full-service capabilities.
Reprinted by permission.

generally follow the traditional product life cycle more faithfully than product classes or brands.

Product life cycles may be traditional, boom, fad, extended fad, seasonal, revival, or bust.

Product life cycles vary a lot, both in length of time and shape,[22] as shown in Figure 9-10. The traditional curve contains distinct periods of introduction, growth, maturity, and decline. The boom or classic curve describes an extremely popular product that sells well over a long period. A fad curve represents a product with quick popularity

[22] See John E. Swan and David R. Rink, "Fitting Marketing Strategy to Varying Product Life Cycles," *Business Horizons,* Vol. 25 (January-February 1982), pp. 72-76; and Stanley R. Schultz and S. R. Rao, "Product Life Cycles of Durable Goods for the Home," *Journal of the Academy of Marketing Science,* Vol. 14 (Spring 1986), pp. 7-12.

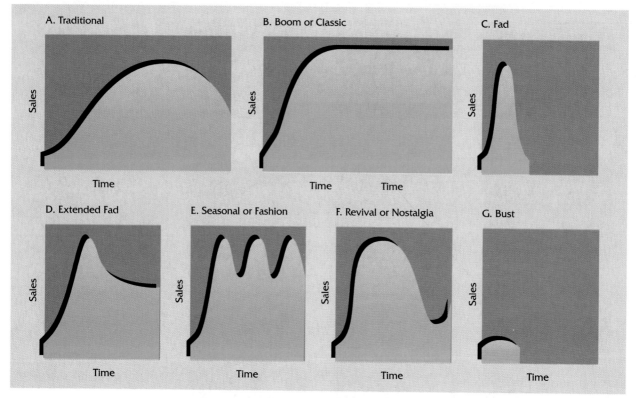

FIGURE 9-10
**Selected Product
Life-Cycle Patterns**

and a sudden decline. An extended fad is like a fad, except that residual sales continue at a fraction of earlier sales. A seasonal or fashion curve results when a product sells well during nonconsecutive periods. With a revival or nostalgia curve, a seemingly obsolete product achieves new popularity. A bust curve occurs for a product that fails.

The Stages of the Traditional Product Life Cycle

The stages and characteristics of the traditional product life cycle are shown in Figure 9-11 and Table 9-5, which refer to total industry performance during the cycle. The performance of an individual firm may vary from that of the industry, depending on its specific goals, resources, marketing plans, location, competitive environment, level of success, and stage of entry.

*In **introduction,** the goal is to establish a consumer market.*

During the ***introduction stage of the product life cycle,*** a new product is introduced into the marketplace and the objective is to generate customer interest. The rate of sales growth depends on the newness of the product as well as its desirability. Generally a product modification generates faster sales than a major innovation. At this stage, only one or two firms have entered the market and competition is limited. Losses are taken because of high production and marketing costs; and cash flow is poor. Initial customers are innovators who are willing to take risks, can afford to take them, and like the status of buying first. Because one or two firms dominate the market and costs are high, only one or two basic models of the product are sold. For a convenience item like a new cereal, distribution is extensive. For a luxury item like a new

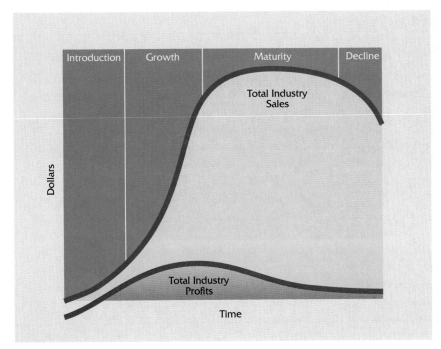

FIGURE 9-11
**The Traditional Product
Life Cycle**

boat, distribution is limited. Promotion must be informative, and free samples may be desirable. Depending on the product and choice of consumer market, the firm may start with a high status price or low mass-market price.

In the ***growth stage of the product life cycle,*** a new product gains wider consumer acceptance and the marketing objective is to expand distribution and the range of available product alternatives. Industry sales increase rapidly as a few more firms enter a highly profitable market that has substantial potential. Total and unit profits are high because an affluent mass market buys distinctive products from a limited

*During **growth,** firms enlarge the market and offer alternatives.*

TABLE 9-5   The Characteristics of the Traditional Product Life Cycle

Characteristics	Introduction	Growth	Maturity	Decline
	Stage in Life Cycle			
Marketing objective	Attract innovators and opinion leaders to new product	Expand distribution and product line	Maintain differential advantage as long as possible	(a) Cut back, (b) revive, or (c) terminate
Industry sales	Increasing	Rapidly increasing	Stable	Decreasing
Competition	None or small	Some	Substantial	Limited
Industry profits	Negative	Increasing	Decreasing	Decreasing
Customers	Innovators	Affluent mass market	Mass market	Laggards
Product mix	One or two basic models	Expanding line	Full product line	Best-sellers
Distribution	Depends on product	Rising number of outlets	Greatest number of outlets	Decreasing number of outlets
Promotion	Informative	Persuasive	Competitive	Informative
Pricing	Depends on product	Greater range of prices	Full line of prices	Selected prices

Marketing Controversy

Can (Should) Declining Product Life Cycles Be Reversed?

Sometimes companies are successful in rejuvenating declining products; sometimes intensive marketing efforts have little impact. For the latter, firms probably would be better off allocating the increased marketing expenditures to other products or to new-product development. Let us look at two attempts to revive declining products.

From 1945, when the ballpoint pen was introduced, until the mid-1980s, fountain-pen sales fell drastically. But, since then, their sales have risen at an annual rate of 20 to 25 per cent, making this the fastest-growing product in the industry. The revival of fountain pens can be attributed to the product's appeal to consumer individuality (an important concept today), the positioning of fountain pens as high-quality items, the creative use of advertising (such as the emphasis on fountain pens as gifts), and the higher advertising budgets devoted to this category by pen makers.

U.S. egg consumption (on a per-capita basis) is now at a record low level. Despite aggressive marketing actions, firms have been unable to reverse the steep decline—largely due to consumer concerns about the cholesterol content of eggs and the possibility of salmonella poisoning, as well as reduced in-home breakfast consumption. Even though all U.S. egg producers are participating in an industrywide campaign to increase consumption, many experts question whether the downward trend can ever be reversed. For example, ads aimed at young professionals who have low egg consumption and at heavy users (such as blacks, Orientals, and Hispanics) have both failed to increase egg consumption.

What do you think about trying to reverse declining product life cycles?

SOURCE: Based on material in Alison Fahey, "Don't Write Off Fountain-Pen Market," *Advertising Age* (November 28, 1988), p. 65; and Alix M. Freedman and Bruce Ingersoll, "Egg Producers Try to Halt Product's Slide," *Wall Street Journal* (November 11, 1988), p. B1.

group of firms and is willing to pay for them. To accommodate the growing market, modified versions of basic models are offered, distribution is expanded, persuasive mass advertising is utilized, and a range of prices is available.

*In **maturity,** companies work hard to sustain a differential advantage.*

During the ***maturity stage of the product life cycle,*** the product's sales growth plateaus and companies try to maintain a differential advantage (such as a lower price, improved product features, or extended warranty) for as long as possible. Industry sales stabilize as the market becomes saturated and many firms enter to capitalize on the still sizable demand. Competition is at its highest level. Therefore, total industry and unit profits decline because discounting becomes popular. At this stage, the average-income mass market makes its purchases. A full line of products is made available at many outlets and many price levels. Promotion becomes very competitive.

*In **decline,** firms reduce marketing, revive a product, or end it.*

In the ***decline stage of the product life cycle,*** a product's sales fall as substitutes enter the market or consumers become disinterested. Firms have three alternate courses of action. They can cut back on their marketing programs, thereby reducing the number of product items they make, the outlets they sell through, and the promotion they use; they can revive the product by repositioning, repackaging, or otherwise remarketing it; or they can terminate the product. At this stage, as industry sales decline, many firms leave the market because customers are fewer and they have less income to spend. The product mix concentrates on best-sellers, selected outlets and

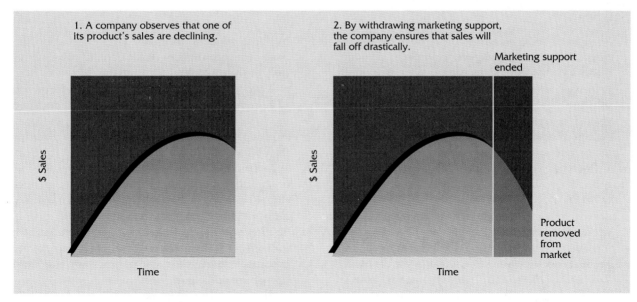

1. A company observes that one of its product's sales are declining.

2. By withdrawing marketing support, the company ensures that sales will fall off drastically.

Marketing support ended

Product removed from market

FIGURE 9-12   A Self-Fulfilling Prophecy

prices, and promotion that stresses, in an informative way, availability and price.

The pocket calculator is a good example of a product that has moved through the life cycle. It went from an exclusive, expensive item to a widespread, moderately priced item to a mass-marketed, inexpensive item in just a few years. Its characteristics during the life cycle closely paralleled the stages described in Table 9-5.

Evaluating the Product Life-Cycle Concept

As mentioned earlier, the product life cycle is an interesting and useful concept for marketers; but although it provides a good framework for product planning, it has not proven useful in forecasting.[23] In using the product life-cycle concept, these key points should be kept in mind:

1. The stages of the life cycle, the time span of the entire life cycle, and the shape of the cycle (such as flat, erratic, or sharply inclined) vary by product.

2. External factors such as the economy, the rate of inflation, and consumer life-styles may have a major impact on the performance of a product and shorten or lengthen its life cycle.

3. A company may not only be able to manage the product life cycle, it may also be able to extend it or reverse a decline. Effective marketing may attract a new market segment, find a new use for the product, or generate increased dealer support.

4. Some companies may engage in a ***self-fulfilling prophecy,*** whereby they predict that sales will decline and then ensure this will occur by reducing or removing marketing support. See Figure 9-12. With adequate support, these products might not fail.

*A **self-fulfilling prophecy** may occur when a firm reduces marketing.*

[23] Good synopses of the controversy surrounding the product life cycle are George Day, ''The Product Life Cycle: Analysis and Applications Issues,'' *Journal of Marketing,* Vol. 45 (Fall 1981), pp. 60–67; and Robert U. Ayres and Wilbur A. Steger, ''Rejuvenating the Life Cycle Concept,'' *Journal of Business Strategy,* Vol. 6 (Summer 1985), pp. 66–76.

Summary

1. *To define product planning and differentiate among tangible, extended, and generic products* Product planning is systematic decision making pertaining to all aspects of a firm's products. It allows the firm to spot opportunities, develop marketing programs, coordinate a product mix, maintain successful products, reappraise faltering ones, and delete undesirable ones.

   Products should be defined in a combination of ways. A tangible product is the basic physical entity, service, or idea; it is offered under a given description or model number. An augmented product includes tangible elements and the accompanying cluster of image and service features. A generic product focuses on the benefits a buyer desires.

2. *To examine the various types of products, product mixes, and product-management organization forms from which a firm may select* Goods marketing entails physical products, durables and/or nondurables. Service marketing encompasses the rental of goods, the alteration or repair of goods owned by consumers, and personal services. Goods and services often differ in terms of intangibility, perishability, inseparability from the service provider, and variability in quality.

   Consumer products are goods and services for the final consumer. They can be classified as convenience, shopping, and specialty items. These products are differentiated on the basis of consumer awareness of alternatives prior to the shopping trip and the degree of search and time spent shopping. Industrial products are goods and services used in the production of other goods or services, in the operation of a business, or for resale. Industrial products are divided into installations, accessory equipment, raw materials, component materials, fabricated parts, business supplies, and business services. They are differentiated on the basis of decision making, costs, rapidity of consumption, the role in production, and the change in form.

   A product item is a specific model, brand, or size of a product that the company sells. A product line is a group of closely related items sold by the firm. A product mix consists of all the product lines a firm offers.

   A firm may choose from or combine several organizations: marketing-manager system, product (brand) manager, product-planning committee, new-product manager system, and venture team.

3. *To discuss product positioning and its usefulness for marketers* A firm must ensure that each of its products is perceived as providing some combination of unique features and that these features are desired by the target market. Through product positioning, a firm can map its offerings in terms of consumer perceptions, consumer desires (ideal points), competition, its own products within the same line, and the changing environment.

4. *To study the different types of product life cycles that a firm may encounter and the stages of the traditional product life cycle* The product life cycle seeks to describe a product's sales, profits, customers, competitors, and marketing emphasis from inception until removal from the market. Many firms desire a balanced product portfolio, with products in various stages of the cycle. There are several derivations of the product life cycle, ranging from traditional to fad to bust. The traditional cycle consists of four stages: introduction, growth, maturity, and decline. During each stage, the marketing objective, industry sales, competition, industry profits, customers, and the marketing plan change. Although the life cycle is useful in planning, it should not be used as a forecasting tool.

Key Terms

product planning (p. 260)
product (p. 260)
tangible product (p. 260)
augmented product (p. 260)
generic product (p. 260)
goods marketing (p. 261)
durable goods (p. 261)
nondurable goods (p. 261)
service marketing (p. 261)

rented-goods service (p. 261)
owned-goods service (p. 261)
nongoods service (p. 262)
intangibility of services (p. 262)
perishability of services (p. 262)
inseparability of services (p. 263)
variability in service quality (p. 263)
consumer products (p. 263)
convenience products (p. 264)

staples (p. 264)
impulse products (p. 264)
emergency products (p. 265)
shopping products (p. 265)
attribute-based shopping products (p. 265)
price-based shopping products (p. 265)
specialty products (p. 265)

Review Questions

1. What are the four basic differences in the marketing of goods and services?

2. How are convenience and specialty products similar? How are they dissimilar?

3. How can one product be a convenience, shopping, *and* specialty good? What does this mean to marketers?

4. What are the similarities and differences between raw materials and fabricated parts?

5. Should a firm ever seek a wide/shallow product mix? Explain your answer.

6. Under what circumstances is a new-product manager system appropriate? A venture team?

7. What is the role of product positioning for a new product? A continuing product?

8. How do competitive positioning and company positioning differ? Give an example of each.

9. Explain the basic premise of the product life cycle. What is the value of this concept?

10. What is the key marketing objective during the growth stage of the product life cycle? Why?

Discussion Questions

1. For each of the following, describe the tangible, augmented, and generic product:
   a. Telephone.　　c. Lawn-care service.
   b. Contact lenses.　d. Tractor.

2. Develop a marketing plan for a firm making drill presses.

3. Evaluate the product mix for Borden, shown in Figure 9-5.

4. Evaluate General Motors' intended 1989–1990 product positioning for each of its car divisions, shown in Figure 9-8.

5. For personal stereos (e.g., the Sony Walkman), describe the consumer market and marketing plan during each stage of the product life cycle. What stage are they in now? Explain your answer.

> ◄ **CASE 1** ►

WD-40: How Does a One-Product Company Prosper?*

In the 1950s, a Rocket Chemical Company chemist invented WD-40 as a lubricant and rust and corrosion preventative that would be applied to the stain-

---

* The data in this case are drawn from Ellen Paris, "The One-Mystique Company," *Forbes* (April 26, 1982), p. 103; "WD-40 Tries Sight-of-Hand," *Sales & Marketing Management* (July 4, 1983), pp. 14, 16; and Joel Dreyfuss, "How to Be Happy in One Act," *Fortune* (December 19, 1988), p. 119.

less steel skins of the U.S. government's Atlas missiles. Soon thereafter, company employees began informally experimenting with WD-40 on their personal property. They used it on items such as squeaky chairs, engines, and rifles.

Then in the 1960s, cans of WD-40 were sold to an organization that sent gift packs to American soldiers in Vietnam. The soldiers rubbed WD-40 on their rifles, cooking utensils, and so on. Upon their return home, they quickly found new applications for it, such as lubricating and protecting tools, equipment, and home appliances; removing rust and tar; and loosening frozen screws and locks.

While WD-40 was gaining popularity in the late 1960s, John Barry became Rocket's chief executive and changed the company's name to WD-40. As of now, for over 25 straight years, sales have increased—to more than $82 million annually (yet the firm has only seventy employees).

Each dollar of WD-40's sales is divided approximately as follows: 44 cents for ingredients and packaging, 23 cents for overhead and advertising, 17 cents for earnings, and 16 cents for taxes. During the company's 1988 fiscal year, return on assets was 36 per cent; and return on stockholders' equity was 45 per cent—both extremely high figures.

WD-40 operates one manufacturing facility in San Diego, "where the secret ingredients are mixed in a single vat." The firm works with independent contractors who package the product in blue-and-yellow cans and bottles and send it to wholesalers and distributors. A large amount of sales are through mail orders. WD-40 is available in a variety of sizes, from a 2-ounce spray can to a 5-gallon pail.

A few years ago, WD-40 began broadening its market by distributing through supermarkets. Said one company executive: "We're trying to position the product to one that is found under the kitchen sink as well as in the garage and the workshop." The firm is also increasing efforts to expand in foreign markets. Already, 21 per cent of sales come from customers in Europe, Australia, and Asia.

WD-40 has prospered despite competition from firms such as DuPont, General Electric, and 3M. John Barry says that "a total of fourteen billion-dollar companies have come after us." But, all have been unsuccessful in the face of WD-40's competitive strengths: distribution expertise and intensive market coverage (WD-40 is sold in such diverse outlets as fishing tackle shops and auto supply stores), consumer awareness of the WD-40 brand, strong product positioning, and a clear focus on one product.

Since John Barry has been in charge, the firm has not developed or marketed products other than WD-40. When questioned, he replied: "We're already breaking all the Harvard Business School rules. You're not even supposed to have a one-product company. How can we follow this act?"

Nonetheless, Barry has stated that he never intended for the company to remain dependent on a single product for all its sales. He has just been unable to find the right new product. Under the proper circumstances, WD-40 would add another product: "We just don't want to dilute the name."

QUESTIONS

1. In positioning WD-40 as both a consumer product and an industrial product, how would your marketing efforts differ in appealing to each market segment?
2. How could WD-40 be perceived as a convenience product, as a shopping product, *and* as a specialty product? What are the marketing implications?
3. What are the marketing-related risks of being a one-product company? The benefits?
4. Present two possible products that WD-40 could consider adding to its product mix. Explain these choices.

◄ **CASE 2** ►

Colgate-Palmolive: Eliminating a Two-Year-Old Venture Group[†]

In 1986, Colgate-Palmolive (a maker of household, personal-care, and health-care products) formed

† The data in this case are drawn from Ronald Alsop, "Consumer-Product Giants Relying on 'Intrapreneurs' in New Ventures," *Wall Street Journal* (April 22, 1988), p. 35; and Laurie Freeman, "Colgate, Others Drop Inside Venture Groups," *Advertising Age* (October 24, 1988), p. 28.

the Colgate Venture Co. as an autonomous, internal venture group. Its goal was to develop innovative new products in an organizational setting that would minimize the effects of the firm's regimented bureaucracy. It was to be "an oasis for people with an entrepreneurial, risk-taking nature." As the venture group's president commented, "We move more quickly and we have the leeway to act on instinct, rather than wait for exhaustive market research. That's a very major change from the mainstream marketing culture at Colgate."

Colgate Venture Co. was given a sizable budget and had a total of 70 full-time employees. It specialized in developing new business categories that would be capable of attaining between $10 million and $90 million in yearly sales. Venture group members were given annual and long-term incentives that could be paid in either dollar bonuses or in equity (ownership) interests in ventures. Among the products the venture group worked on were a cleaning solution for teenagers' dental braces and retainers, a mail-order catalog featuring educational toys, and deodorizing pads for cat-litter boxes.

But two years after forming its venture group, Colgate-Palmolive announced (in late 1988) that it was eliminating the Colgate Venture Co. and getting out of many of the business areas it was developing. Although in principle, internal venture groups—such as the one at Colgate-Palmolive—offer employees high flexibility, an environment with less bureaucracy, and partnerlike rewards, this form of product management organization is often quite difficult to implement. Among the other consumer-products companies that have recently dropped internal venture groups are Gillette, Clorox, and S.C. Johnson. This is why some firms are abandoning their venture groups:

Senior company management is often hesitant to give venture groups sufficient latitude to accomplish desired objectives.

Results are normally quicker with other organizational formats.

The new products developed may have a poor fit with existing company product lines and/or business strengths.

Venture group efforts may be poorly commu-

nicated to senior management and/or poorly coordinated with other company projects.

Resource planning is more complex.

It is hard for employees to leave a bureaucratic environment one day and become entrepreneurial the next: "People just can't shake the corporate culture's baggage. They still want to do all that market research and testing."

Colgate's decision to drop its venture group coincided with the decision to concentrate on its core businesses and to have a solid cash position for external acquisitions. It also wanted to pursue opportunities such as entering the European bleach market. Among the products developed by its venture group, Colgate decided to keep Handi-wipes disposable cloths and Fresh Feliners (pads used to line cat-litter boxes). However, the responsibility for these products has been shifted to other company product managers.

Colgate is selling several other businesses that were started by the venture group, including:

Cleaning Dimensions—A chain of dry-cleaning stores based in Austin, Texas, that sold everything from basic detergents to chewing-gum remover. Customers visited the chain only for special problems and shopped elsewhere for routine cleaning supplies.

Maniac Fragrances—A cologne marketed to teenagers. According to market analysts, the lack of success of this product was based upon poor distribution in drugstores (and not the name!).

Teen Clean—A cleaning product for people wearing braces or retainers on their teeth. Colgate felt that teenagers would purchase this as an alternative to denture cleanser targeted to senior citizens; instead many preferred to use regular toothpaste.

QUESTIONS

1. Comment on Colgate's initial decision to set up an internal venture group.
2. Evaluate Colgate's decision to drop its internal venture group.
3. Now that the Colgate Venture Co. has been eliminated, how can Colgate encourage an entrepreneurial spirit?
4. Discuss the use of an internal venture group from the perspective of a balanced product portfolio.

CHAPTER 10

Conceiving, Developing, and Managing Products

CHAPTER OBJECTIVES

1. To examine the types of new-product opportunities available to a firm

2. To detail the importance of new products and describe why new products fail

3. To study the stages in the new-product planning process: idea generation, product screening, concept testing, business analysis, product development, test marketing, and commercialization

4. To analyze the growth and maturity of products, including the adoption process, the diffusion process, and extension strategies

5. To examine product deletion decisions and strategies

It's the week before Christmas, the biggest sales week of the year for most electronics, and camcorders, video games, and compact discs have been flying off the shelves. Cordless and cellular phones and radar systems for automobiles are also among this year's hot sellers. But television sales, the biggest segment in the industry, have been flat and the winners of Christmases past—microwave ovens and videocassette recorders—are selling more slowly this year since so many households now own them.

The dynamics in the consumer electronics industry illustrate the complexities in conceiving, developing, and managing products. Even when you're "up," as with cellular phones, you must be planning for the future so that you will not be "down," as with traditional VCRs. Let us look at selected events over the life cycle of VCRs to gain further insights.

The first videocassette recorder was marketed by Sony in 1975, when it introduced the Betamax model. In 1976, the Victor Company of Japan began marketing a VHS-format VCR. During 1976, about 30,000 VCRs were sold in the United States at well over $1,000 each. In 1980, 800,000 recorders were sold. And in 1987, a total of 14 million VCRs were sold in the United States, at an average price of less than $400. Although only 3 per cent of U.S. households owned a VCR in 1980, 56 per cent owned one as of mid-1988.

But in 1988, VCR sales were expected to drop by 5 per cent because of their high penetration of the market. The "go-go" days are over. So how are electronics manufacturers coping with the maturity of the VCR market? What are they doing to stimulate renewed consumer interest? Here are two examples, one involving a product in the growth stage of the product life cycle (camcorders) and the other in the introductory stage (the ultra-miniature VCR).

In 1985, the sales of camcorders (hand-held portable units that combine a VCR with a video camera) took off. Even though they were priced at $1,200 to $1,500 each, over 500,000 units were sold that year. By 1987, annual U.S. sales exceeded 1.5 million units, at an average price of over $1,000. During 1988, experts predicted that sales would reach two million units. Yet, sales should go even higher in the future—as of mid-1988, only 5 per cent of U.S. households owned one.

The newest VCR-related product is the ultra-miniature VCR with a built-in 3-inch flat screen television which retailed for $950 when introduced in late 1988.

Photo courtesy of Sony Corporation of America.

The mini-VCR, developed by Sony, uses 8mm tape (about the same size as a standard audiocassette). Up to four hours of video with sound can be contained on a single 8mm cassette. Sony expected to lower the price in the near future and to add new features, such as stereo. While some analysts feel that it will appeal to only small niche markets, such as salespeople giving presentations or business travelers, others see it as generating a high long-term sales level.[1]

Next, we will study how new products are developed, the factors causing rapid or slow growth for new products, how to manage mature products, and what to do when existing products falter. As with VCR manufacturers, our goal is to determine how to create and maintain consumer enthusiasm for goods and services as they move through their life cycle.

[1] Barnaby J. Feder, "For Electronic Retailers, a Replay," *New York Times* (December 18, 1988), Section 3, p. 4; and Larry Armstrong, "So You'd Like to Watch a Movie on the Subway," *Business Week* (October 3, 1988), pp. 135, 138.

Overview

Product planning involves new and existing products.

In this chapter, the conception and development of new products, the management of growing and mature products through their life cycle, and the termination of undesirable products are discussed.

As previously defined, a product combines tangible and intangible features to satisfy consumer needs. A *new product* involves a modification of an existing product or an innovation that the consumer perceives as meaningful. For a new product to succeed, it must have desirable attributes, be unique, and have its features communicated to consumers. Marketing support is necessary.

A new product may be a modification, a minor innovation, or a major innovation.

Modifications are alterations in a company's existing products and include new models, styles, colors, features, and brands. *Minor innovations* are items not previously sold by the firm that have been sold by others (such as blood-pressure instruments by Timex). *Major innovations* are items not previously sold by any firm (such as the first cellular telephone). If a company is involved with major innovations, the costs, risks, and time required for profitability all increase. Among large U.S. firms, 70 per cent of new products are modifications, 20 per cent minor innovations, and 10 per cent major innovations.[2]

New products may be conceived of and developed by the company itself or purchased from another firm. In the latter case, the company may buy a firm outright, purchase a specific product, or enter into a licensing agreement (whereby it pays the founder a royalty fee based on sales). Acquisitions may reduce risks and time requirements, but they rely on outside parties for innovations and may require large investments.

After introduction, products are managed from growth to decline.

During a product's life, there is usually a period of sales growth, as more consumers purchase and repurchase it. This is an exciting period. Next, the market becomes saturated, and competition intensifies. At this point, a company can maintain high sales by adding features that provide convenience and durability, using new materials in construction, emphasizing new packaging and product safety, offering a range of models, and adding customer services. It can also reposition the product, enter untapped geographic markets, demonstrate new uses, offer new brands, set lower prices, use new media, and appeal to new market segments. Then for the great majority of products, at some point down the road, the company must determine whether the product has outlived its usefulness and is a candidate for deletion.

The Importance of New Products

New products are vital for a company's long-run success.

A firm's product policy should look to the future and recognize that items, no matter how successful, are usually mortal — that is, they cannot sustain a peak level of sales and profits forever. Therefore, replacements need to be constantly planned and a balanced product portfolio pursued. This is true for both small and large firms, as these comments from the chairman of a small technology-based industrial-goods manufacturer indicate:

> If you are not developing something new, early in the current product's life cycle, you're living on borrowed time. If you wait until your line is mature, you're dead. The hardest

---

[2] *New Product Management for the 1980s* (New York: Booz, Allen & Hamilton, 1982), p. 9.

FIGURE 10-1
Perrier with a Twist
Reprinted by permission.

thing in all this is coming up with the idea for a new product. The second-hardest thing is to get people to accept the idea of life cycles and to get them thinking about the need to replace the existing line. The whole idea is to avoid crises. If you don't have a plan in place for introducing a new product, you'll have a major problem once what you are selling comes to the end of its life.[3]

The introduction of new products is important for many reasons. Desirable differential advantages can be fostered. Steelcase's new ergonomic office chairs are quite different from the traditional office chair — they have five legs to reduce the possibility of tip overs and feature variable reclining tension, seat height, and lap angle. Kodak's Ektar 25 film can be enlarged to poster size without the graininess of regular film. New Hershey's powdered chocolate mix is "more chocolatey and less sugary" than Nestle's Quik and comes in a plastic container with a wide mouth to accommodate larger spoons.[4] Often, new products enhance a firm's image and position it as an innovator.

New products offer differential advantages.

For some companies, new products are necessary for continued growth. This is why Perrier has added lemon-, lime-, and orange-flavored mineral water ("Perrier with a twist"), as shown in Figure 10-1; and Faberge has brought out a new men's cologne, deodorant, and shaving cream under the McGregor, Brut, and Cut Guard brands.[5] For

New products lead to sales growth or stability.

---

[3] Paul B. Brown, "The Eternal Second Act," *Inc.* (June 1988), pp. 119–120.

[4] Jeffrey A. Trachtenberg, "How Do We Confuse Thee? Let Us Count the Ways," *Forbes* (March 21, 1988), p. 160; "The Best New Products," *Business Week* (January 9, 1989), p. 118; and Dale M. Mazer, "Hershey Foods Plans Introduction of Powdered Chocolate Milk Mix," *Wall Street Journal* (September 2, 1988), p. 18.

[5] Steven Greenhouse, "Perrier's New American Assault," *New York Times* (October 30, 1988), Section 3, pp. 1, 5; and Pat Sloan, "Faberge Readies New-Product Push," *Advertising Age* (March 7, 1988), pp. 6, 79.

firms with cyclical or seasonal sales, new products can stabilize revenues and costs throughout the year. Union Carbide has diversified into such areas as medical-testing equipment to reduce its dependence on the cyclical chemicals business. Black & Decker, the world's largest maker of power tools, has cut back sharply on lawn mowers and hedge trimmers and looked for new opportunities in more traditional, stable product lines (such as acquiring the small appliance division of General Electric).

New products can take time.

Planning for growth must consider the time required for a new product to move from the idea stage to full commercialization. For instance, in 1971, Coca-Cola's business-development department determined that a soda-dispensing machine geared to small offices would be quite popular; there were more than one million offices around the United States with 45 or fewer employees that had no on-the-job access to soda. However, it was not until late 1988 that this "simple" machine (now called the Break-Mate) was introduced. In all, over 100 people worked on product development and there were at least six preliminary designs prepared. What took so long? It was not "simple" to "make all the parts small, yet keep the machine easy enough for office workers to operate and refill." Coca-Cola believes its efforts will pay off; by 1999, it expects twenty million gallons of syrup to flow through office soft-drink machines.[6]

New products can increase profits and control.

New products can lead to larger profits and allow a firm to gain control over marketing strategy. For example, when Coleco's Cabbage Patch Kids were introduced in late 1983, their sales soared — to a 1985 peak of nearly $600 million. This enabled Coleco to earn over $75 million in companywide profits in 1985 and gave it good clout in dealing with retailers. Unfortunately, Coleco has since been unable to develop other successful new products to compensate for the drop in Cabbage Patch Kids' sales (to $115 million in 1987); and in 1987, there was a companywide loss of $105 million. In 1988, without a new hit to sustain it, Coleco filed for bankruptcy protection.[7]

Risk may be lessened through diversity.

To limit risk, many firms seek to reduce dependence on one product or product line. Ocean Spray now makes a variety of beverages and fruit products; it no longer depends exclusively on cranberry products. Turtle Wax, the world's leading manufacturer of car-care products, has recently added shoe polish, rust inhibitors, and fabric protectors.[8] See Figure 10-2.

New products may improve distribution.

Some companies look to maximize the efficiency of their established distribution systems by introducing new products into them. This enables the firms to spread sales, advertising, and distribution costs among several products, obtain dealer support, and discourage potential competitors from entering the distribution network. Companies such as Microsoft (computer software and operating systems), Gallo, and Revlon are able to place new products in many outlets quickly and obtain dealer support.

Technology can be exploited.

Companies often seek technological breakthroughs. As an illustration, Sony has developed a filmless still-image camera, which records images on a magnetic disk for immediate viewing on a television set. Up to fifty images can be recorded on each reusable and erasable disk. However, due to the camera's high price, about $1,000, it is expected to take a while for explosive sales growth.[9] In some cases, firms try to find

---

[6] Mike Kennedy, "Office Soda Dispenser Nearly Fizzled," *USA Today* (January 4, 1989), Section B, pp. 1–2.

[7] Joseph Pereira, "Coleco Is Looking for Lettuce as Cabbage Patch Wilts," *Wall Street Journal* (March 18, 1988), p. 4.

[8] Barbara Buell, "How Ocean Spray Keeps Reinventing the Cranberry," *Business Week* (December 2, 1985), p. 142; and Scott Hume, "Turtle Wax Goes from Car to House," *Advertising Age* (June 22, 1987), p. 86.

[9] Peter Pae, "Sony Introduces Filmless Cameras for Mass Market," *Wall Street Journal* (December 16, 1988), p. B1.

FIGURE 10-2
Turtle Wax Diversifies into Shoe Polish
Reprinted by permission.

uses for waste materials from existing products. For example, the chicken industry has discovered that "we have four billion broilers, and the consumer generally doesn't want the necks and backs. What do we do? We grind it up into baloney and hot dogs and things like that."[10]

Firms introduce new products to respond to changing consumer demographics and life-styles. Henri's Salad Dressing to Go, Falbar's Wine in Glass, and ready-made Golden Grain spaghetti are for small families interested in convenience. Granola bars and soda with fruit juice are for health-conscious consumers. John Deere's new line of riding mowers appeals to older consumers, while cellular phones are for more active people (in business as well as in private life).[11]

New products respond to consumer needs.

Good long-run new-product planning requires systematic research and development, matching the requirements of new-product opportunities against company abilities, emphasis on consumers' perceived product attributes, sizable expenditures of time and money, and defensive as well as offensive planning. In addition, a firm must

[10] N. R. Kleinfield, "America Goes Chicken Crazy," *New York Times* (December 9, 1984), Section 3, p. 9.
[11] William Dunn, "Frozen Foods Heat Up," *American Demographics* (September 1985), pp. 38–41; Brian Dumaine, "America's Best Designs," *Fortune* (November 21, 1988), p. 129; and William M. Bulkeley, "Portable Phones Are Prompting Change in Business and Life-Styles," *Wall Street Journal* (January 1, 1988), p. 23.

Marketing Controversy

Revolution Versus Evolution in Product Planning?

Apple Computer has a product plan based on "line extensions." With this plan, it seeks to develop new computer models that fill gaps in its product lines but do not break new ground. In particular, Apple intends to exploit the growth possibilities of its Macintosh personal computers.

As Apple sees it, the major task is "fine-tuning" the Macintosh strategy: buying and writing software to make it work better in large computer networks, more effectively using the sales force, and increasing market share in the government and engineering sectors. Apple is also introducing a more compact version of the Macintosh II, a larger Macintosh II that can be used by several workers, and a Macintosh II laptop.

There is some question as to whether Apple's strategy of evolution (rather than revolution) will be sufficient to realize its 1993 objective of

$10 billion in annual sales. Apple would require a 25 per cent annual growth in sales to meet this objective; yet, many observers predict annual industrywide sales growth will be 15 per cent during this period. Some experts feel that although Apple's strategy will allow it to sell new Macintosh models to loyal users, it will not be strong enough to convert non-Mac users to Apple products.

Apple disagrees, believing that one of its major advantages is the "set of consistent, intuitive commands that work the same way on every program and on every size Macintosh—no matter how simple or complex the task on hand." This is an especially important competitive advantage to Apple's business customers, who now purchase about 70 per cent of all Macs.

What do you think?

SOURCE: Based on material in Maria Shao and Geoff Lewis, "Apple Turns from Revolution to Evolution," *Business Week* (January 23, 1989), pp. 90, 92; and Brian O'Reilly, "Apple Computer's Risky Revolution," *Fortune* (May 8, 1989), pp. 75–82.

be willing to accept that some new products may fail; a progressive firm will take risks. As Johnson & Johnson's chief executive once stated:

> Any successful company is riddled with failures, and there's just not any other way to do it. We love to win, but we also have to lose in order to grow.[12]

Figure 10-3 shows several of the new products Johnson & Johnson has introduced in the last few years.

Why New Products Fail

Despite better product-planning practices today than ever before, the failure rate for new products remains quite high. For example, while one major survey indicates that an average of 35 per cent of industrial and consumer products fail, others estimate that the failure rate may be still higher.[13]

---

[12] H. John Steinbreder, "Taking Chances at J&J," *Fortune* (June 6, 1988), p. 60.
[13] *New Product Management for the 1980s*, p. 7; and "Most New Products Start with a Bang, End Up as a Bomb," *Marketing News* (March 27, 1987), p. 36.

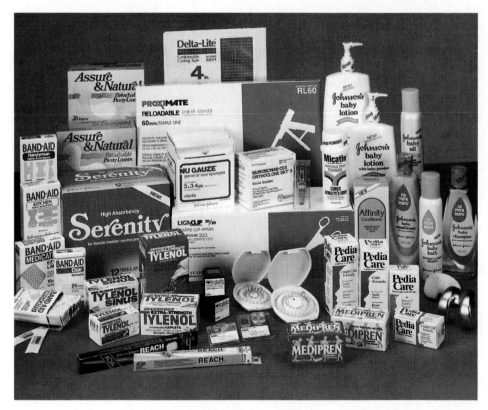

FIGURE 10-3
Johnson & Johnson's Aggressive New Product Strategy
These are just some of the hundreds of new products introduced by Johnson & Johnson in recent years. Twenty-five per cent of total company sales are from products that have been on the market for five years or less.
Reprinted by permission.

Product failure can be defined in absolute and relative terms. ***Absolute product failure*** occurs if a company is unable to regain its production and marketing costs. It incurs a financial loss. ***Relative product failure*** occurs if a company makes a profit on an item but a product does not reach profit objectives and/or adversely affects the firm's image. In computing profits and losses, the impact of the new product on the sales of other company items must be measured.

*Under **absolute product failure**, costs are not regained. Under **relative product failure**, goals are not met.*

Even firms with good new-product performance records have had failures along with their successes. These failures include McRib sandwiches (McDonald's), Mrs. Smith's frozen entrees (Kellogg), Oraflex (Eli Lilly), *TV-Cable Week* (Time Inc.), Real cigarettes (R.J. Reynolds), the Viewtron interactive cable-television shopping service (Knight-Ridder), the Lisa computer (Apple), Kodak instant cameras, and Johnson & Johnson disposable diapers.

There are a number of factors that may cause absolute or relative new-product failure.[14] Among the most important are lack of a differential advantage, poor planning, poor timing, and excessive enthusiasm by the product sponsor. Illustrations of weak product performance caused by these factors follow.

Leading to failure are lack of an advantage, poor planning and timing, and excess enthusiasm.

When Zap Mail was introduced, Federal Express expected it to revolutionize the

---

14 See John Stephen Davis, "New Product Success & Failure: Three Case Studies," *Industrial Marketing Management*, Vol. 17 (1988), pp. 103–109; R. G. Cooper and E. J. Kleinschmidt, "New Products: What Separates Winners from Losers?" *Journal of Product Innovation Management*, Vol. 4 (September 1987), pp. 169–184; and Peter L. Link, "Keys to New Product Success and Failure," *Industrial Marketing Management*, Vol. 16 (1987), pp. 109–118.

way business customers transmit messages. With it, customers could send documents almost anywhere in the United States in fewer than two hours. The sender called a Federal Express operator, who sent a courier to pick up a document from the firm, who took it to a Zap Mail location, which converted printed messages into electronic signals that were transmitted to a receiving Zap Mail site. Then the document was transported by truck and hand-delivered by courier. However, in only three years, Zap Mail was off the market. Although Federal Express felt that Zap Mail would have a clear differential advantage versus traditional overnight delivery services, the product failed for three reasons: computer modems enabled firms to communicate instantaneously and without an intermediary such as Federal Express; many customers were not convinced that two-hour service (at a higher price) was superior to overnight service (when they could send original documents at the close of one business day and have them delivered by 10:00 A.M. the next day); and as Zap Mail was being introduced, inexpensive facsimile machines began to flood the market.[15]

Anheuser-Busch, the world's leading beer manufacturer, has not done as well with some of its nonbeer ventures, such as its failed entries into wine coolers, soft drinks, and bottled water. In general, the company's failures have been due to Anheuser-Busch's poor planning. For instance, in the case of its Dewey Stevens wine cooler, it never adequately defined the target market; at various times, the cooler tried to appeal to women, calorie-conscious consumers, and sophisticated consumers. The company did not understand how to deal with supermarkets in a product category that it did not dominate: "Liquor stores may jump when A-B tells them to, but grocery stores didn't even return their calls." And when Babry's Champagne Cooler was introduced, its price was 75 per cent higher than wine-based coolers — in a very price-sensitive market.[16]

Procter & Gamble's failure with its Encaprin aspirin was mostly a result of poor timing. When it was introduced as an extra-strength arthritis pain reliever, it faced intense competition from two other new over-the-counter products — Advil (by American Home Products) and Nuprin (by Bristol-Myers). Between them, Advil and Nuprin had over $100 million in advertising support, thus drowning out Encaprin's message: "P&G's whole marketing push to arthritis sufferers was stepped on like 'Big Foot'." Accordingly, Encaprin could never reach more than a 1 per cent share of the analgesic market.[17]

Excessive enthusiasm caused RCA to lose almost $600 million on its videodisc player before phasing it out. Rather than drop the player when early sales did not meet expectations, RCA continued to believe that its high relative picture quality and low price would lead to large-scale success in the final consumer market. The firm underestimated VCR growth and the consumer's interest in recording programs (which the videodisc player could not do). Other firms, with more limited goals (such as NCR and Hitachi), have done well marketing videodisc players to organizational consumers as aids in sales training and point-of-purchase displays.[18]

---

[15] *Federal Express Corporation* and other reports.

[16] Scott Hume and Jennifer Pendleton, "Cooler Closeout," *Advertising Age* (November 23, 1987), pp. 3, 66; and Ira Teinowitz, "Why A-B's Waters Became Washouts," *Advertising Age* (March 14, 1988), p. 35.

[17] Laurie Freeman, "Encaprin Is Dissolved by Procter," *Advertising Age* (September 1, 1986), p. 3.

[18] Sandra Salmans, "RCA Defends Timing of Videodisc Canceling," *New York Times* (April 6, 1984), pp. D1, D15; and Marcia Watson, Jeff Kemph, and Judith Steele, "Marketing Muscle and the Videodisc," *Business Marketing* (June 1985), pp. 130–140.

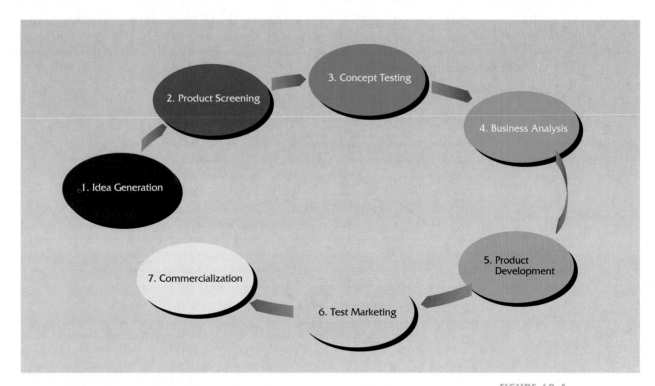

FIGURE 10-4
The New-Product Planning Process

New-Product Planning

The *new-product planning process* involves a series of steps from idea generation to commercialization. See Figure 10-4. During the process, the company generates potential opportunities, evaluates them, weeds out unattractive ones, obtains consumer perceptions, develops the product, tests it, and introduces it into the marketplace. The termination of an idea can occur at any point; costs increase the further into the process the company goes.[19]

According to one major study, it generally takes a firm an average of seven ideas to yield one commercially successful new product. But this number can be much higher. For example, in the pharmaceuticals industry, it may take up to 10,000 compounds in basic research to result in one drug that is approved by the Food and Drug Administration.[20]

In the new-product planning process, a firm needs to endeavor to balance competing goals such as these:

▶ A systematic process should be followed; however, there must be flexibility to adapt to each unique new-product opportunity.
▶ The process should be thorough, yet not unduly slow new-product introductions.
▶ True innovations should be pursued, yet finances must be considered.

*The **new-product planning** process moves from ideas to commercialization.*

[19] See R. G. Cooper and E. J. Kleinschmidt, "Resource Allocation in the New Product Process," *Industrial Marketing Management*, Vol. 17 (1988), pp. 249–262.
[20] *Product Management in the 1980s*, p. 6; and T. Erickson and L. Brenkus, *Healthcare R & D: Tools and Tactics* (Cambridge, Mass.: Arthur D. Little, October 1986), meeting notes.

▶ An early reading of consumer acceptance should be sought, but the firm must not give away too much information to potential competitors.

▶ There should be an interest in short-run profitability, but not at the expense of long-run growth.[21]

Idea Generation

Idea generation is the search for opportunities.

Idea generation is a continuous, systematic search for new-product opportunities. It involves delineating sources of new ideas and methods for generating them.

Sources of ideas may be employees, channel members, competitors, government, and others.[22] Market-oriented sources identify opportunities based on consumer needs and wants; then laboratory research is directed to satisfying these desires. Light beer, many recent ice cream flavors, roll-on deodorants, and easy-opening soda cans evolved from market-oriented sources. Laboratory-oriented sources identify opportunities based on pure research (which seeks to gain knowledge and indirectly leads to specific new-product ideas) or applied research (which uses existing scientific techniques to develop new-product ideas). Penicillin, antifreeze, and synthetic fibers evolved from laboratory sources.

Methods for generating ideas include brainstorming (small-group sessions that stimulate a wide range of ideas), analysis of existing products, and surveys. Many marketing analysts suggest that an open perspective is essential: the ideas of different people should be sought; a large number of ideas should be generated; and ideas should not be criticized, no matter how offbeat they first appear. See Figure 10-5.

For example, a 3M employee came up with the idea for note paper that could be stuck temporarily to telephones, desks, paper, and walls by a small adhesive strip on the back. The employee thought of the idea because his place mark kept falling out of his hymn book during choir practice.[23] Today annual sales of self-sticking Post-it note pads are $300 million. Figure 10-6 shows a typical Post-it ad.

Product Screening

Product screening weeds out undesirable ideas.

After a firm identifies potential products, it must screen them. In **product screening**, poor, unsuitable, or otherwise unattractive ideas are weeded out from further consideration. Today many companies use a new-product screening checklist for preliminary evaluation. In it, firms list the new-product attributes considered most important and compare each idea with those attributes. The checklist is standardized and allows ideas to be compared.

---

[21] See Yoram Wind and Vijay Mahajan, "New Product Development Process: A Perspective for Reexamination," *Journal of Product Innovation Management*, Vol. 5 (December 1988), pp. 304–310; Edward G. Krubasik, "Customize Your Product Development," *Harvard Business Review*, Vol. 66 (November–December 1986), pp. 46-52; and Milton D. Rosenau, Jr., "Speeding Your New Product to Market," *Journal of Consumer Marketing*, Vol. 5 (Spring 1988), pp. 23–36.

[22] See Tom W. White, "Use Variety of Internal, External Sources to Gather and Screen New Product Ideas," *Marketing News* (September 16, 1983), Section 2, p. 12; and Jeffrey Durgee, "New Product Ideas from Focus Groups," *Journal of Consumer Marketing*, Vol. 4 (Fall 1987), pp. 57–65.

[23] "Lessons from a Successful Intrapreneur," *Journal of Business Strategy*, Vol. 9 (March–April 1988), pp. 20–24; and Russell Mitchell, "Masters of Innovation," *Business Week* (April 10, 1989), pp. 58-63.

FIGURE 10-5
Keeping an Open Mind for New Ideas
Reprinted by permission.

FIGURE 10-6
Post-It Note Pads by 3M
Reprinted by permission.

Figure 10-7 illustrates a new-product screening checklist. It has three major categories: general characteristics, marketing characteristics, and production characteristics. Within each category, there are several product attributes to be assessed. They are scored on the basis of 1 (outstanding) to 10 (very poor) for every product idea. In addition, the importance of each attribute is weighted because the attributes vary in their impact on new-product success. This is an example of how a firm could develop overall ratings for two new-product ideas:

1. Product idea A receives an average rating of 2.5 on general characteristics, 2.9 on marketing characteristics, and 1.4 on production characteristics. Product idea B receives ratings of 2.8, 1.4, and 1.8, respectively.

2. The company assigns an importance weight of 4 to general characteristics, 5 to marketing characteristics, and 3 to production characteristics. The poorest possible overall average rating is 120 [(10 × 4) + (10 × 5) + (10 × 3)].

General Characteristics of New Products	Rating
Profit potential	- - - - - - - - - - - - - -
Existing competition	- - - - - - - - - - - - - -
Potential competition	- - - - - - - - - - - - - -
Size of market	- - - - - - - - - - - - - -
Level of investment	- - - - - - - - - - - - - -
Patentability	- - - - - - - - - - - - - -
Level of risk	- - - - - - - - - - - - - -
Marketing Characteristics of New Products	
Fit with marketing capabilities	- - - - - - - - - - - - - -
Effect on existing products (brands)	- - - - - - - - - - - - - -
Appeal to current consumer markets	- - - - - - - - - - - - - -
Potential length of product life cycle	- - - - - - - - - - - - - -
Existence of differential advantage	- - - - - - - - - - - - - -
Impact on image	- - - - - - - - - - - - - -
Resistance to seasonal factors	- - - - - - - - - - - - - -
Production Characteristics of New Products	
Fit with production capabilities	- - - - - - - - - - - - - -
Length of time to commercialization	- - - - - - - - - - - - - -
Ease of product manufacture	- - - - - - - - - - - - - -
Availability of labor and material resources	- - - - - - - - - - - - - -
Ability to produce at competitive prices	- - - - - - - - - - - - - -

FIGURE 10-7
A New-Product Screening Checklist

3. A obtains an overall rating of 28.7 [$(2.5 \times 4) + (2.9 \times 5) + (1.4 \times 3)$]. B obtains an overall rating of 23.6 [$(2.8 \times 4) + (1.4 \times 5) + (1.8 \times 3)$].

4. B's overall rating is better than that for A because of its better marketing evaluation (the characteristics judged most important by the firm).

*A **patent** gives exclusive selling rights for 17 years.*

During screening, patentability must be determined. A **patent** grants the inventor of a useful product or process exclusive selling rights for a period of 17 years (14 years for pharmaceutical products). An invention may be patented if it is a "useful, novel, and nonobvious process, machine, manufacture, or composition of matter" that has not already been patented by someone else. To secure a patent, plans for a working model must be provided to the U.S. Patent Office. When a patent is filed, information about it becomes public. A patent holder has the right to sell an invention, to receive licensing fees from it, and to sue those who infringe upon it.[24]

These are the kinds of patent questions a company should answer during the screening stage: Can the proposed new product be patented by the firm? Are competitive items patented? When do competitors' patents expire? Are patents on competitive items available under a licensing agreement? Would the firm be free of patent liability (infringement) if it introduces the proposed new product?

Concept Testing

Concept testing determines customer attitudes before product development.

Next, the firm needs to acquire consumer feedback about its new-product ideas. **Concept testing** presents the consumer with a proposed product and measures attitudes and intentions at an early stage of the new-product planning process.

Concept testing is a quick and inexpensive way of measuring consumer enthusiasm.

[24] Peter D. Bennett (Editor), *Dictionary of Marketing Terms* (Chicago: American Marketing Association, 1988), p. 141. See also Steven A. Meyerowitz, "Protection Through Patents," *Business Marketing* (July 1988), pp. 63–67; and Norm Alster, "New Profits from Patents," *Fortune* (April 25, 1988), pp. 185–190.

An air conditioner maker is developing a completely portable room model.
It is expected to weigh 8 pounds, operate on regular electrical current, be adaptable
to most home windows (the only tool needed being a screwdriver), and cool rooms
up to 12 x 20 feet. It can be moved from room to room and installed in five minutes.

**Would you please answer some questions to give us a better idea
of the air conditioner's marketability?**

1. React to the concept of a portable room air conditioner.

2. Under what circumstances would you consider buying a portable room air conditioner?

3. What would be a fair price for a portable room air conditioner?

4. Do you have any suggestions about the design or features of the air conditioner?

5. How likely would you be to buy a portable room air conditioner within the next year?
Check **one** answer.

Very likely   _____   _____   _____   _____   _____   Very unlikely

FIGURE 10-8
**A Brief Concept Test for
a Proposed Portable
Room Air Conditioner**

It asks potential consumers to react to a picture, written statement, or oral description of a product. This enables a firm to determine initial attitudes prior to expensive, time-consuming prototype development. Figure 10-8 shows a concept test for a proposed portable room air conditioner. Among the companies using concept testing are Kodak, Heinz, and Sony.

In general, concept testing should ask these types of questions of consumers:

▶ Is the idea easy to understand?
▶ Do you perceive distinct benefits for this product over those products currently on the market?
▶ Do you find the claims about this product believable?
▶ Would you buy the product?
▶ Would you replace your current brand with this new product?
▶ Would this product meet a real need?
▶ What improvements can you suggest in various attributes of the concept?
▶ How frequently would you buy the product?
▶ Who would use it?[25]

[25] Adapted from Philip Kotler, *Marketing Management: Analysis, Planning, and Control,* Sixth Edition (Englewood Cliffs, N.J.: Prentice-Hall, 1988), pp. 419–420. See also Kirk Brady, "Concept Testing Should Measure More Than the Intent to Purchase," *Marketing News* (January 31, 1986), pp. 63, 70; and Susan L. Holak, "Determinants of Innovative Durables Adoption: An Empirical Study with Implications for Early Product Screening," *Journal of Product Innovation Management,* Vol. 5 (March 1988), pp. 50–69.

Business Analysis

Business analysis looks at demand, costs, competition, etc.

At this point, the firm undertakes business analysis for the new-product concepts that have thus far been deemed attractive. **Business analysis** involves the detailed review and projection of relevant market factors, revenues, costs, and trends for a proposed new product. It is much more detailed than product screening.

Here are some of the criteria considered at this planning stage:

Criteria	Considerations
Demand projections	Price/sales relationship; short- and long-run sales potential; speed of sales growth; seasonality; rate of repurchases; distribution intensity
Cost projections	Total and per-unit costs; use of existing facilities and resources; startup vs. continuing costs; estimates of future raw materials and other costs; economies of scale; channel needs; break-even point
Competition	Short-run and long-run market shares of company and competitors; strengths and weaknesses of competitors; potential competitors; likely competitive strategies in response to new product by firm
Required investment	Product planning (engineering, patent search, product development, testing); promotion; production; distribution
Profitability	Time to recoup initial costs; short- and long-run total and per-unit profits; needs of distribution intermediaries; control over price; return on investment (ROI); risk

Because the next step is expensive and time-consuming product development, critical use of business analysis is essential to eliminate marginal items.

Product Development

Product development focuses on manufacturing and marketing strategy.

During **product development,** an idea for a new product is converted into a tangible form and a basic marketing strategy is identified. This stage in the planning process involves product construction, packaging, branding, product positioning, and consumer attitude and usage testing.

Product-construction decisions include the type and quality of materials comprising the product, the method of production, costs and production-time requirements per unit, plant capacity, alternative sizes and colors, and the time needed to move from development to commercialization. Packaging decisions include the materials used, the functions performed (such as promotion and storage), costs, and alternative sizes and colors. Branding decisions include the choice of a new or existing name, exclusivity, trademark protection, and the image sought. Product positioning involves selecting a market segment and positioning the new item against competitors and other company offerings. Attitude and usage testing center on consumer perceptions of and satisfaction with a new product.

When a modification is involved, product-development costs may be relatively low. However, an innovation may be quite costly—up to several million dollars or more. For example, DuPont invested several years and $700 million to develop and set up production for Kevlar, a super-tough aramid fiber that is a "lightweight miracle five times stronger than steel." Today, Kevlar is used in military helmets, bullet-resistant vests, cut- and heat-resistant gloves, composite aircraft structures, telecom-

FIGURE 10-9 **DuPont's Kevlar in Action**
Today, in some of the most important, competitive commercial fishing areas in the world, nets made with Kevlar aramid fibers are producing significant results in a key industry. Through the use of Kevlar, improvements in catch size, reduced fuel consumption, and net repairability are being realized.   Reprinted by permission.

munications cables, tennis equipment, commercial fishing nets, and many other products.[26] See Figure 10-9.

In addition to being costly, product development can be very difficult. For instance, in the early 1970s, Upjohn scientists discovered that its minoxidil prescription drug tablets, taken by consumers to relieve hypertension, caused an unexpected side effect — excessive hair growth. So Upjohn began investigating whether the drug could be converted to liquid or cream form and applied externally to scalps as a cure for baldness. The firm recognized that external applications would be far safer than internal consumption.

It took until 1985 to develop a relatively satisfactory product. Even then, testing showed hair growth for only one-third of those using minoxidil, light fuzz growth for another one-third, and no growth for the others. At that point, Upjohn was eager to file for Food and Drug Administration (FDA) approval, a procedure that would take nearly three years to complete. Finally, in October 1988, just a few months after securing FDA approval, Upjohn began marketing the product — now called Rogaine.

Is Rogaine worth Upjohn's effort? Sales for 1989 were projected at up to $100 million; and many analysts believe that Rogaine's annual sales will grow rapidly because there is a potential target market of forty million people in the United States alone.[27]

[26] Laurie Hays, "DuPont's Difficulties in Selling Kevlar Show Hurdles of Innovation," *Wall Street Journal* (September 29, 1987), pp. 1, 24; and DuPont 1989 correspondence.
[27] John Crudele, "Hair Growth Drug Seen as a Wonder for Upjohn," *New York Times* (May 28, 1985), pp. D1, D11; and Laurie Freeman, "Rogaine Ads Get Head Start as Sales Falter," *Advertising Age* (December 12, 1988), p. 62.

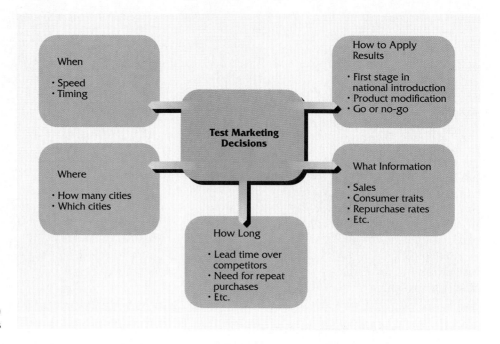

FIGURE 10-10
Test Marketing Decisions

Test Marketing

Test marketing occurs in selected areas and observes performance.

Test marketing involves placing a fully developed new product for sale in one or more selected areas (cities) and observing its actual performance under a proposed marketing plan. The purpose is to evaluate the product and pretest marketing efforts in a real setting prior to a full-scale introduction. Rather than inquire about intentions, test marketing allows a company to observe actual consumer behavior. A firm can also learn about competitive reactions and the responsiveness of wholesalers and/or retailers. On the basis of testing, a firm could decide to go ahead with its plans on a larger scale, modify the product and then expand its effort, modify the marketing plan and then expand its effort, or drop the product. Procter & Gamble, Time Inc., Levi Strauss, and McDonald's are among the companies that use test marketing. Consumer-products firms are more apt to engage in test marketing than industrial-products firms.

The test-marketing process requires several decisions: when, where, how long, what information to acquire, and how to apply results. See Figure 10-10. When a test is conducted depends on speed and timing. In a competitive environment, companies bring a product into test marketing as quickly as possible. For seasonal items, timing is more important than speed. For example, summer fashions would not test well in New York during December.

Where to test market consists of how many and which cities in which to introduce a product. Usually companies test market in two or three cities. A two-city test can cost up to $250,000 or more, depending on its length and the firm's marketing emphasis (such as high expenditures for samples and/or advertising). The choice of which city to use depends on its representativeness relative to the national market, the degree of retailer cooperation, costs, the level of competition, and a firm's ability to control and measure its marketing program. Among the most popular U.S. test market cities are

Minneapolis-St. Paul, Minnesota; Portland, Oregon; Columbus, Ohio; Syracuse, New York; and Kansas City, Missouri.[28]

The length of a test could range from about two months to two years. This depends on the company's lead time over competitors, the complexity of the test, the product's rate of repurchase, the revisions the company must make before the product and/or its marketing strategy are ready for a full introduction, and the desire for secrecy. The test should show sales after initial enthusiasm has worn off. For frequently purchased items, a six-month test is normally adequate.

A firm must decide what information it wants to seek and measure results against goals. Information can be gained about sales, consumers, purchase rates, distribution strengths and weaknesses, dealer enthusiasm, market share potential, the impact of a new item on other company products, competitive responses, marketing effectiveness, and product positioning.

Last, a firm must consider how to use test results. Some firms only use testing to gain consumer acceptance and as a first step in national introduction. Others use it to determine necessary modifications in product and marketing plans. Still others use test marketing for final go or no-go decisions; they drop products not performing up to company expectations before commercialization.

Although test marketing has been beneficial in many cases, some companies now question its effectiveness and downplay or skip this stage in new-product planning. Dissatisfaction with test marketing arises from its costs, the time delays before full introduction, information being provided to competitors, an inability to predict national results based on one or two test market cities, and the impact of external factors, such as the economy and competition, on test results. Test marketing frequently allows nontesting competitors to catch up with the innovative firm by the time the product is ready for national distribution. Procter & Gamble claimed that competitors copied its Duncan Hines cookies after seeing how successful they were in tests.[29]

There are limitations to test marketing.

Commercialization

After testing is successfully completed, the company is ready to introduce a new product to its full target market. This is known as ***commercialization*** and corresponds to the introductory stage of the product life cycle. Commercialization involves implementing a total marketing plan and full production.

Commercialization involves a major marketing commitment.

Among the factors to be considered in the commercialization stage are the speed of acceptance by consumers and distribution intermediaries, the intensity of distribution (how many outlets), production capabilities, the promotional mix, prices, competition, the time period until profitability occurs, and commercialization costs.

The commercialization stage often requires considerable expenditures and a long-term commitment. For example, when Kodak entered the U.S. battery market in mid-1986, it allocated $15 million for advertising during just the last four months of that year. But, together, the leading competitors, Eveready and Duracell, spent more than $60 million in advertising in calendar 1986. In 1987 and again in 1988, Kodak, Eveready, and Duracell spent a total of about $75 million on advertising. Despite its

[28] Saatchi & Saatchi DFS Compton, "The Most Popular Test Markets," *Wall Street Journal* (January 26, 1988), p. 42.

[29] Eleanor Johnson Tracy, "Testing Time for Test Marketing," *Fortune* (October 29, 1984), pp. 75–76; and Rich Glass, "Telescoping the Test Period: Shorter Is Better," *Sales & Marketing Management* (March 10, 1986), pp. 94 ff.

heavy spending, after two years on the market, Kodak batteries had only a 6 to 8 per cent market share, while Eveready and Duracell each had about 45 per cent.[30]

Sometimes commercialization of a new product must overcome consumer and distributor reluctance because of ineffective prior company offerings. This occurred with Texas Instruments in the business computer market, after it bowed out of the home computer market. Atari and Timex are other firms that have found that previous difficulties have negatively affected the commercialization of new products.

Growing Products

Once a new product is commercialized, the firm's objective is for consumer acceptance and company sales to rise as rapidly as possible. This occurs in some instances; in others, it may take a while. To a large extent, the growth rate and total sales level of new products rely heavily on two related consumer behavior concepts: the adoption process and the diffusion process.[31] In managing its growing products, a firm must understand these concepts and plan its marketing efforts accordingly.

*The **adoption process** explains the new-product purchase behavior of individual consumers.*

The ***adoption process*** is the mental and behavioral procedure an individual consumer goes through when learning about and purchasing a new product. The process consists of these stages:

1. Knowledge—A person (organization) learns of a product's existence and gains some understanding of how it functions.
2. Persuasion—A person (organization) forms a favorable or unfavorable attitude about a product.
3. Decision—A person (organization) engages in actions that lead to a choice to adopt or reject a product.
4. Implementation—A person (organization) uses a product.
5. Confirmation—A person (organization) seeks reinforcement and may reverse a decision if exposed to conflicting messages.[32]

The rate (speed) of adoption depends on consumer traits, the product, and the firm's marketing effort. Adoption will be faster if consumers have high discretionary income (resources) and are willing to try new offerings; the product presents little physical, social, functional, or financial risk; the product has an advantage over other items already on the market; the product is a modification of an existing idea and not a major innovation; the product is compatible with current consumer life-styles or ways of operating a business; the attributes of the product can be easily communicated; the importance of the product is low; the product can be tried in small quantities; the product is consumed quickly; the product is easy to use; mass advertising and distribution are used; and the marketing mix responds to the changing needs of the consumer as the person (organization) moves through the adoption process.

---

[30] Julie Liesse Erickson, "Eveready Loses Power in Market," *Advertising Age* (July 11, 1988), p. 4; and Richard Gibson and Robert Johnson, "Kraft to Sell Its Duracell Unit to KKR for an Unexpectedly High $1.8 Billion," *Wall Street Journal* (May 6, 1988), p. 3.

[31] See Hubert Gatignon and Thomas S. Robertson, "A Propositional Inventory for New Diffusion Research," *Journal of Consumer Research,* Vol. 11 (March 1985), pp. 849–867.

[32] Everett M. Rogers, *Diffusion of Innovations,* Third Edition (New York: Free Press, 1982), pp. 164–175.

You're the Marketer

How Quickly Will Consumers Buy Disposable Contact Lenses?

The most innovative development in the vision-correction field since Bausch & Lomb introduced contact lenses in 1971 involves the new disposable contact lenses being marketed nationally by both Bausch & Lomb and Johnson & Johnson.

Disposable lenses can be thrown away after one to two weeks of wear and eliminate the extensive care required for regular soft contacts. Disposables are praised by many opthalmologists because they eliminate infections caused from lengthy wear and/or improper cleaning of traditional soft contacts, and from allergic reactions to disinfecting solutions: "People won't be wearing dirty lenses."

However, the purchase price of disposable contacts is high—$500 per year (including doctor visits) for weekly replacement. Regular soft lenses cost as little as $100 per year (plus lens maintenance) and traditional eyeglasses (which last as long as three to five years or

more) usually cost from $50 to $200 (depending upon the frame).

Disposable lenses are packaged in inexpensive plastic-and-aluminum foil casings and are sold in cartridges containing a three- or six-month supply. In contrast, traditional long-life soft lenses are packaged in hard plastic cases or glass vials designed to last for the life of the lenses.

The potential sales for disposable lenses are estimated to be as high as $500 million per year, about half the 1988 sales of traditional contacts. Disposables can only be used by nearsighted individuals, who comprise 26 per cent of the 140 million people in the United States who need vision correction. At present, about 24 million people wear some type of contact lenses.

As Bausch & Lomb's marketing director, what would you do to stimulate rapid growth and long maturity for disposable lenses?

SOURCE: Based on material in Constance Mitchell, "Bausch & Lomb Aims at a New Market as It Prepares to Test Disposable Lenses," *Wall Street Journal* (July 20, 1988), p. 18; and Patricia Winters, "Sights Set on Disposable Lenses," *Advertising Age* (July 20, 1988), pp. 2, 101.

The **diffusion process** describes the manner in which different members of the target market often accept and purchase a product. It spans the time from product introduction through market saturation and affects the total sales level of a product as it moves through the life cycle:

*The **diffusion process** describes when different segments are likely to purchase.*

1. Innovators are the first consumers to buy a new product. They are venturesome, willing to accept risk, socially aggressive, communicative, and cosmopolitan. It is necessary to determine which innovators are opinion leaders—those who influence others to buy. This group represents 2.5 per cent of the target market.

2. Early adopters are the next consumers to buy a new product. They enjoy the leadership, prestige, and respect that early purchases bring. These consumers tend to be opinion leaders. They adopt new ideas but use discretion. This group represents 13.5 per cent of the market.

3. The early majority is the first part of the mass market to buy a product. They have status in their social class and are outgoing, communicative, and attentive to information cues. This group represents 34 per cent of the target market.

4. The late majority is the second part of the mass market to buy a product. They are less cosmopolitan and responsive to change. The late majority includes people with lower economic and social status, those past middle age, and skeptics. This group represents 34 per cent of the market.

5. Laggards are last to purchase. They are price-conscious, suspicious of change, low in income and status, tradition bound, and conservative. Laggards do not adopt a product until it reaches maturity. Some firms ignore them because it can be difficult to market a product to this small group. However, a market segmenter may do well by concentrating on products for laggards. This group represents 16 per cent of the market.[33]

The adoption and diffusion processes operate slowly for major innovations.

Growth for a major innovation often starts slowly because there is an extended adoption process and the early majority may be hesitant to purchase. It may then rise quickly. As an illustration, the home computer was first marketed in 1977; yet, by the end of 1981, less than 2 per cent of U.S. households owned one. Consumers had been hesitant to make a purchase because of high initial prices, the perceived difficulty of mastering the home computer, its early image as a game console, and the limited software. Then sales grew dramatically, going from two million units in 1982 to over five million in 1984, as inexpensive models entered the market, models became more user-friendly, the product lost its game image, and software applications became widely available. As of early 1989, 21 per cent of U.S. households (more than 19 million homes) owned a personal computer. However, the expected continued growth in home computer sales has slowed. Many consumers are now confused by the existence of noncompatible computer systems; a number of firms, such as Apple, are devoting more attention to the business market; the industry is not doing a good job in communicating product features to those who have not yet bought a home computer; and so on.[34]

The compact disc (CD) player, another major innovation, succeeded more quickly than home computers, although sales penetration was not immediate. See Figure 10-11. In 1983, only 30,000 units were sold, with CD player prices averaging almost $1,000. But sales of CD players reached 200,000 in 1984, as prices fell to an average of $400 to $500. By 1988, annual sales of CD players had reached nearly five million units — and well over 100 million compact discs were sold. As of the end of 1988, CD players were in about 15 per cent of U.S. households. These are some of the factors behind the rapid growth in CD player sales:

▶ A single technical standard is used, so that all discs can be played on any machine.

▶ An industry trade association was formed to outline technical specifications, print a catalog of compact disc titles, and maintain a toll-free telephone number for consumer inquiries. Now that diffusion is well under way, the association plans to disband.

▶ A price war helped stimulate demand. Between 1983 and 1988, retail prices fell by over 80 per cent. Today a CD player is no more expensive than a good record changer.

---

[33] Rogers, *Diffusion of Innovations,* pp. 246-261.

[34] Electronic Industries Association, *Consumer Electronics U.S. Sales* (Washington, D.C.: January 1989); and Michael W. Miller, "Confusing Days for Personal Computers," *Wall Street Journal* (September 13, 1988), p. 39.

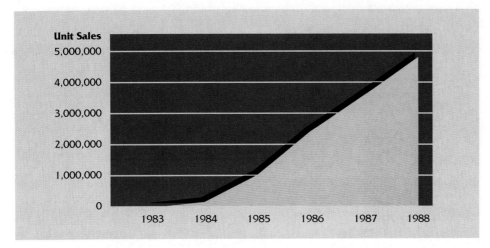

FIGURE 10-11
The Growth of CD Player Sales in the United States
SOURCE: Electronic Industries Association, *Consumer Electronics U.S. Sales* (Washington, D.C.: January 1989).

▶ A stream of product refinements is being introduced, such as CD players for automobiles.[35]

For minor innovations or product modifications, growth is even faster. As an example, in late 1985, McDonald's introduced the McD.L.T. sandwich (a quarter-pound hamburger with tomatoes and lettuce) on a national basis. See Figure 10-12. The McD.L.T.'s basic difference from its competitors is a styrofoam container that keeps the hamburger separate from the lettuce and tomatoes — "the hot and cool of it." During its first year on the market, McDonald's expected McD.L.T. to account for about $700 million in annual revenues.[36] And sales have been very strong since then.

These are among the many products now in the growth stage of the product life cycle. They represent good opportunities for firms skilled in marketing: minivans, laptop computers, solar-powered products, cellular phones, men's hair-coloring products, generic drugs, facsimile machines, stereo televisions, financial services, microwave oven foods, and adult education.

Mature Products

When products reach the late majority and laggard markets, they are in the maturity stage of the life cycle. Goals turn from growth to maintenance. Because new products are so costly and risky, more firms are placing marketing emphasis on mature products that offer steady sales and profits with minimal risk.

Proper marketing can enable mature products to maintain high sales.

In managing mature products, a company should consider factors such as these: the size of the existing market and its characteristics and needs, untapped market segments, competition, product modifications, the availability of a new product to replace a mature one, profit margins, the marketing effort necessary for each sale, wholesaler

[35] Barnaby J. Feder, "For Electronics Retailers, a Replay," *New York Times* (December 18, 1988), Section 3, p. 4; and Paul Duke, Jr., and Karen Blumenthal, "CD Recorder Poses Upset for Industry," *Wall Street Journal* (April 26, 1988), p. 6.
[36] Robert A. Bennett, "Whoever Dreamed That Up?" *New York Times* (December 29, 1985), Section 3, pp. 1, 25.

FIGURE 10-12
The McD.L.T.: "The Hot and Cool of It"
As a product modification, the McD.L.T. quickly captured a large and loyal consumer following.
SOURCE: McDonald's. Reprinted by permission.

Popular mature brands offer several benefits for companies.

and retailer satisfaction, the promotional mix, the importance of the products in the overall product line, the products' effects on company image, the number of remaining years for the products, and the management effort needed.

When a firm has a popular brand in a mature product category, there are many possible benefits. First, the product life cycle may be extended almost indefinitely. For example, Ivory soap, Lipton tea, Goodyear tires, Sherwin-Williams paints, Life Savers mints, Quaker Oats oatmeal, and Coke are all market leaders; each is at least 75 years old. See Figure 10-13. Second, the product provides the company with a large, loyal group of customers and a stable, profitable position in the market. Third, the risk of low consumer demand is greatly reduced; this is a real risk for new products. Fourth, the company's overall image and consumer recognition are enhanced. This may allow the firm to extend a popular name to other products. Fifth, there is more control over marketing efforts and more precision in sales forecasting. Sixth, mature products can be used as cash cows to support investments in new company products. However, marketing support must be continued if the mature product is to remain popular.

Successful companies and industries generate products that remain in maturity for long periods, as the following illustrate:

▶ Until about twenty years ago, Arm & Hammer baking soda (developed in 1846) was marketed simply as a baking soda to be used in cooking. But then, changing consumer life-styles — few people were interested in baking a cake from scratch — resulted in stagnant sales for the product. As a result, intensive advertising was begun as the baking soda was repositioned to include new (more modern) product uses: refrigerator freshener, kitchen drain deodorizer, bath water additive, plaque remover for dental plates, cat litter deodorizer, and so on. And over the last twenty years, a number of new Arm & Hammer baking soda-based products have been introduced, including detergent, deodorizing spray, carpet freshener, and tooth-

FIGURE 10-13
**Quaker Oats:
Staying on Top**
By periodically updating
Quaker Oats oatmeal, its
namesake company has
been able to maintain a
strong leadership position.
Courtesy of the Quaker Oats
Company.

paste. In 1988, Arm & Hammer baking soda-based products had their highest sales ever.[37]

▶ The first Corvette was marketed in 1953, at a price of $3,500; and it quickly appealed to a loyal group of customers with "an image of adventure, excitement, with-it-ness, virility." Except for a brief period during and after the 1973 oil embargo, the 1970s were strong years for the Corvette (with sales of nearly 50,000 cars per year). However, when the U.S. auto industry declined in 1981 and 1982, the Corvette also declined (1982 sales were 23,000 units). Then General Motors redesigned the Corvette and introduced a new $22,000 model. Reviewers called it the "most advanced production car on the planet," "an authentic American hero," and "one of the supercars of the world."[38] Since 1983, annual sales have averaged 30,000 units, with a car now priced at $35,000.

▶ The telephone was invented by Alexander Graham Bell in the 1870s. However, until 1977, telephones could be manufactured and sold only by AT&T. At that time, the Federal Communications Commission ruled that any company could make and sell phones. As a result, more than 100 firms entered this mature market and developed a wide assortment of products, from designer phones to hand-held phones, to stimulate sales. Between 1982 and 1984, annual sales rose from 5.7 million to 30 million units. Since then, yearly telephone sales have remained at well over 25 million units.[39]

---

[37] Ronald Alsop, "Arm & Hammer Baking Soda Going in Toothpaste as Well as Refrigerator," *Wall Street Journal* (June 24, 1988), p. 24.

[38] Bernice Kanner, "Betting on the 'Vette," *New Yorker* (May 16, 1983), pp. 18 ff.; and N. R. Kleinfield, "Exploring the Curious Cult of the Corvette," *New York Times* (July 19, 1987), Section 3, pp. 1, 29.

[39] Meryl Gordon, "What's New in Telephones," *New York Times* (October 20, 1985), Section 3, p. 17; and Electronic Industries Association, *Consumer Electronics U.S. Sales.*

TABLE 10-1 Strategies for Extending the Mature Stage of the Product Life Cycle

Strategy	Examples
1. Develop new uses for the product	Jell-O used in garden salads
	Arm & Hammer baking soda used as a refrigerator deodorant
2. Develop new product features and refinements	Zoom lenses for 35mm cameras
	Battery-powered televisions
3. Increase market segmentation	Family and individual sizes for food products
	Regional editions of major magazines
4. Find new classes of consumers for the present product	Nylon carpeting for institutional markets
	Johnson & Johnson's baby shampoo used by adults
5. Find new classes of consumers for the modified product	Industrial power tools altered for the do-it-yourself market
	Inexpensive copy machines for home offices
6. Increase product usage among current users	Multiple packages for soda and beer
	Jeans promoted for wear at social gatherings
7. Change marketing strategy	Hosiery sold in supermarkets
	Magazine subscriptions advertised on television

There are many strategies available for extending the mature stage of the product life cycle. Table 10-1 presents seven such strategies and provides examples of each.

Not all mature products can be revitalized or extended. The consumer's need may disappear, as occurred when frozen orange juice replaced orange juice squeezers. Better, cheaper, and more convenient products may be developed, such as VCRs and camcorders to replace movie projectors and plastic furniture moldings to replace wooden ones. Competitors may secure a strategic advantage, such as Polaroid maintaining patent protection for state-of-the-art self-developing cameras. Finally, the market may be saturated and additional marketing efforts may be unable to generate sufficient sales to justify time and cost expenditures, which is why IBM has drastically reduced its presence in the office-photocopier market.

Product Deletion

Products need to be deleted if they have consistently poor sales, tie up resources, and cannot be revived.

When products offer limited sales and profit potential, involve large amounts of management time, tie up resources that could be used for other opportunities, create wholesaler and retailer dissatisfaction due to low turnover, reflect poorly on the company, and divert attention from long-term goals, these products should be deleted from the firm's offerings.

However, there are a number of factors to consider before deleting a product. As a product matures, it blends in with existing items and becomes part of the total product line (mix). Customers and distribution intermediaries may be hurt if an item is withdrawn. A firm may not want competitors to have the only product for customers. Poor current sales and profits may be only temporary. The marketing strategy, not the product, may be the cause of poor results.

Ralph S. Alexander, the first marketer to write in depth about product deletion, proposed a systematic, four-step procedure to handle faltering products: (1) select products that are candidates for deletion, (2) gather and analyze information about these products, (3) make deletion decisions, and (4) remove the products from the line.[40]

Low-profit or rapidly declining products are often dropped or de-emphasized, as these 1988 examples show:

▶ Sony, which had popularized the videocassette recorder in the mid-1970s using the Beta format, announced that it would finally begin offering VHS-format recorders and de-emphasize its Beta line. At the time, only 10 per cent of worldwide video-cassette recorder sales were contributed by Beta-format models.[41]

▶ Rusty Jones — once the leading firm in its industry — decided to leave the new-car rustproofing business. In 1987, auto makers had extended their corrosion-protection warranties on new vehicles to up to 100,000 miles, thus discouraging consumers from paying $200 or more for extra protection from firms such as Rusty Jones.[42]

▶ Kodak suspended production of its declining disc camera line, which had sold thirty million units since its 1982 introduction. Industry observers attributed Kodak's action to picture-quality problems and the growing popularity of inexpensive easy-to-use 35mm cameras.[43]

▶ *Newsweek on Campus* and *Business Week Careers*, two magazines targeted to college students, were both discontinued. There was not enough reader interest or advertising support. Competition was just too intense.[44]

When discontinuing a product, the firm must be sure to consider replacement parts, notification time for customers and distribution members, and the honoring of warranties/guarantees. For example, a company planning to delete its line of office typewriters must resolve these questions: Replacement parts — Who will make them? How long will they be made? Notification time — How soon before the actual deletion will an announcement be made? Will distributors be alerted early enough so that they can line up alternate suppliers? Warranties — How will warranties be honored? After warranties expire, how will repairs be handled?

During deletion, customer and distributor needs must be considered.

[40] Ralph S. Alexander, "The Death and Burial of 'Sick' Products," *Journal of Marketing*, Vol. 28 (April 1964), pp. 1–7. See also George J. Avlonitis, "Advisors and Decision-Makers in Product Eliminations," *Industrial Marketing Management*, Vol. 14 (1985), pp. 17–26; and James P. Neelankavil and Elmer E. Waters, "New Product Abandonment Decisions" in Roger J. Calantone and Eugene E. Teeple (Editors), *Marketing in a Dynamic Environment* (Mid-Atlantic Marketing Association, 1984), pp. 94–100.
[41] Jeffrey A. Tannenbaum, "Sony to Begin Selling VCRs in VHS Format," *Wall Street Journal* (January 12, 1988), p. 39.
[42] "Rusty Jones Inc. Appears to Quit Rustproofing Field," *Wall Street Journal* (August 2, 1988), p. 13.
[43] Clare Ansberry, "Kodak Suspends Its Production of Disk Camera," *Wall Street Journal* (February 2, 1988), p. 4.
[44] "Owners Discontinue Some College Magazines," *Marketing News* (July 4, 1988), p. 6.

Summary

1. *To examine the types of new-product opportunities available to a firm* Product management involves creating and supervising products over their life. New products are modifications or innovations the consumer perceives as substantive. Modifications are alterations to existing products. Minor innovations are items not previously sold by the firm but sold by others. Major innovations are items new to the firm and not sold by others.

2. *To detail the importance of new products and describe why new products fail* New products are important because they may foster differential advantages, sustain sales growth for a firm, require considerable time for development, generate large profits, enable a company to diversify, make distribution more efficient, lead to technological breakthroughs, and respond to changing consumers.

   When a firm suffers a financial loss, a product is an absolute failure. When it makes a profit but does not attain its objectives, a product is a relative failure. Failures occur because of a lack of a significant differential advantage, poor planning, poor timing, and excessive enthusiasm by the product sponsor.

3. *To study the stages in the new-product planning process* New-product planning involves a comprehensive, seven-step process. During idea generation, new-product opportunities are sought. In product screening, unattractive ideas are weeded out through a new-product screening checklist. At concept testing, the consumer reacts to a proposed idea. Business analysis requires a detailed evaluation of demand, costs, competition, investment, and profits. Product development converts an idea into a physical form and outlines a marketing strategy. Test marketing, a much-disputed technique, involves placing a product for sale in selected areas and observing performance under actual conditions. Commercialization is the sale of a product to the full target market. A new product can be aborted or modified at any point in the process.

4. *To analyze the growth and maturity of products, including the adoption process, the diffusion process, and extension strategies* Once a new product is commercialized, the firm's objective is for consumer acceptance and company sales to rise as rapidly as possible. However, the growth rate and level for a new product are highly dependent on the adoption process—which describes how a single consumer learns about and purchases a product—and the diffusion process—which describes how different members of the target market learn about and purchase a product. These processes are faster for certain consumers, products, and marketing strategies.

   When products mature, company goals turn from growth to maintenance. Mature products can provide stable sales and profits and loyal consumers. They do not require the risks and costs of new products. There are several factors to consider and alternative strategies from which to choose when planning to sustain mature products. It may not be possible to retain aging products if consumer needs disappear, new products make them obsolete, competitors exhibit too much strength, or the market becomes too saturated.

5. *To examine product deletion decisions and strategies* At some point, a firm may have to determine whether to continue a faltering product. Product deletion may be difficult because of the interrelation of products, the impact on customers and distribution members, and other factors. It should be conducted in a structured manner; and replacement parts, notification time, and warranties should all be considered in a deletion plan.

Key Terms

new product (p. 290)
modifications (p. 290)
minor innovations (p. 290)
major innovations (p. 290)
absolute product failure (p. 295)
relative product failure (p. 295)

new-product planning process (p. 297)
idea generation (p. 298)
product screening (p. 298)
patent (p. 300)
concept testing (p. 300)
business analysis (p. 302)

product development (p. 302)
test marketing (p. 304)
commercialization (p. 305)
adoption process (p. 306)
diffusion process (p. 307)

Review Questions

1. Distinguish among a product modification, a minor innovation, and a major innovation. Present an example of each.
2. Give four reasons why new products are important to a company.
3. Explain the new-product planning process.
4. How does product screening differ from business analysis?
5. What are the major tasks during product development?
6. What are the pros and cons of test marketing?
7. How can a firm speed a product's growth?
8. Is the maturity stage a good or bad position for a product to occupy? Why?
9. Cite five ways in which a firm could extend the mature stage of the product life cycle. Provide an example of each.
10. Why is a product deletion decision so difficult?

Discussion Questions

1. Comment on this statement: "We never worry about relative product failures because we make a profit on them. We only worry about absolute product failures."
2. Develop a 10-item new-product screening checklist for a proposed miniature stereo television. How would you weight each item?
3. Construct a 50-word concept test for a product that reduces the need for weekly lawn cutting by slowing down grass growth. What would you expect to learn from this test?
4. Differentiate between the commercialization strategies for a product modification and a major innovation. Relate your answers to the adoption process and the diffusion process.
5. Select a product that has been in existence for ten or more years and explain why it cannot be rejuvenated.

◄ CASE 1 ►

McCaw Cellular Communications: Cellular Phones Come of Age*

The cellular (mobile) phone business is one of the fastest-growing, and potentially most lucrative, new industries in the United States. In 1989, U.S. sales of cellular phones were expected to reach 1.6 million units, nearly four times the number in 1986. It was also estimated that the cellular phone industry would reach 3.3 million subscribers during 1989—up from 125,000 in 1984—who would spend about $3.2 billion on cellular phone calls. For 1990, cellular phone calls are forecast to bring in revenues of over $6 billion.

This is how cellular phones work:

A cellular network is a honeycomb of cells, each with a low-power transmitter. As a caller travels from one cell area to the next, the transmitters feed a call in progress into the regular phone network and thence to the caller on the other end.

As of now, most cellular phones are used in automobiles and other vehicles (including aircraft).

In 1984, when the cellular phone business was just starting, most industry experts predicted that the carrier end of the business would be controlled by the "Baby Bells"—the seven phone companies spun off during AT&T's divestiture—because AT&T, but not the Baby Bells, was prevented from selling mobile phone service. Instead, the current market-share leader in cellular phone service is McCaw Cellular Communications, which originated at the same

---

* The data in this case are drawn from Jonathan B. Levine, "Craig McCaw's High-Risk Empire," *Business Week* (December 5, 1988), pp. 140–151.

time cellular phones became commercially viable. In 1984, McCaw's sales were close to zero.

At present, McCaw offers cellular phone service in 127 cities; and these geographic areas have a total potential base of 48 million customers, 70 per cent more than Pacific Telesis Group (the second-largest firm in the industry and one of the Baby Bells). By 1991, McCaw plans to be serving 825,000 customers and have $1.1 billion in revenues—both figures are about four times its 1988 levels. McCaw's overall marketing strategy is to provide high-quality service, set premium rates, achieve high market growth, and develop an efficient telephone calling network.

According to market observers, McCaw's chairman (Craig McCaw) has a "fetish for quality." It is not unusual for him to test a local cellular system himself on an unannounced basis. He is also concerned about growing so fast so that his firm will not be able to properly handle billing, accounting, and voice transmissions. Because cellular phone rates are unregulated, McCaw wants to be able to charge premium rates for high-quality service.

Despite Craig McCaw's concern about quality control, the firm is committed to a very fast growth rate through market expansion. It is actively seeking to enter new territories as well as to increase market penetration in current territories. McCaw believes that the number of subscribers will grow considerably in the future as manufacturers' prices of cellular phones further decline (for example, General Electric phone prices now begin at under $200) and as the number of mass retailers selling cellular phones "off-the-shelf" engage in price competition.

McCaw Cellular Communications has an efficient service network in the Northwest, Southeast, and Northern California. Yet in many other areas, its network is too dispersed; and the firm has poor market coverage in several major cities. For example, only 38 per cent of McCaw's potential customers are in the nation's biggest markets. In contrast, Pacific Telesis has 83 per cent of its potential customers in the largest, most densely populated markets and the other Baby Bells average 60 per cent. Some industry analysts believe McCaw should offer to trade market areas with Pacific Telesis, Southwestern Bell, and possibly Bell South to increase efficiency.

QUESTIONS

1. Comment on this statement: "Nothing is certain in the cellular business. Demand for service still isn't predictable. Prices for phones are still high, and there's always a chance that state regulators could cap the prices for cellular phone service."

2. Develop a concept test to use with consumers who have not yet heard of cellular phone service.

3. Describe how McCaw can use the concept of the diffusion process in developing its marketing strategy for the next five years.

4. How long do you think it will take cellular phone service to reach the maturity stage of the product life cycle? Why?

CASE 2

DuPont: Extending Teflon's Life Cycle†

1988 marked the fiftieth anniversary for DuPont's Teflon coating resin, an event duly noted in the firm's annual report:

† The data in this case are drawn from Laurie Hays, "DuPont Will Update Teflon's Image and Use the Coating on New Products," *Wall Street Journal* (April 7, 1988), p. 34.

This year the company is celebrating the fiftieth anniversary of two research breakthroughs—nylon and "Teflon" fluorocarbon resins. Since 1938, man-made materials have dramatically enriched the quality of life in many areas, including clothing, the home, recreation, electronics, communications, transportation, construction, and health care.

Over the years, DuPont has developed and sustained a group of strong core businesses to provide earnings and cash flow for dividends and to fund our thrusts into new, high-growth-potential markets. A key to DuPont's future is our ability to continue to make the most of existing businesses, working as closely as possible with customers.

Throughout its long life, Teflon has been very successful for DuPont. As an example, it still has a 50+ per cent share of the world market for wire and cable coatings. Telfon-coated nonstick cookware was first introduced in 1962. Overall, DuPont has produced more than 2.4 billion pounds of Teflon since 1938; and, annual Teflon sales are now over $300 million per year—their highest level ever.

DuPont does not want Teflon to become another mature product with only average sales and profit growth. It wants Teflon to remain a superstar performer. Yet, although Teflon continues in high demand because of its inert, slippery, and superior insulating properties, its annual sales growth rate has dropped from a high of 25 per cent per year to between 6 and 8 per cent per year. And recent profit performance has also been average.

To stimulate Teflon's sales, DuPont is taking aggressive actions. In the final consumer market, DuPont is working hard to increase consumer awareness of Teflon, which competes directly with 3M's Scotchgard products (they have a higher degree of brand recognition than Teflon in the consumer market), and to develop new uses for Teflon. In the industrial market, which is the biggest segment for Teflon, DuPont is interested in increasing Teflon's market share in its strongest applications, reducing production costs, and finding new uses for

Teflon. Says one DuPont executive, "you need a lot of ideas to keep a 50-year-old invention alive."

Finding new uses for Teflon has been an ongoing responsibility for generations of DuPont executives. Here are some of the newer applications:

- Teflon is now available in a spray can. In this way, it can be used to repel food stains, as well as to spray walls and switchplates to prevent fingerprints from marring surfaces. This strategy goes head on against Scotchgard.
- Teflon is being demonstrated at ski shows. When Teflon is sprayed on clothes, the clothes remain dry, despite direct exposure to snow.
- Teflon is good for automobile upholstery. For example, Mr. Goodwrench service centers sell Teflon as protection for car upholstery.
- Teflon-coated cookware is being revived. DuPont is reintroducing Teflon 2, inexpensive cookware that was taken off the market in 1980. DuPont's aim is to recapture the low-price market that has shifted to competitive products. It also wants Teflon 2 to attract consumers buying their first pots and pans in the hope that these customers will later on trade up to SilverStone and SilverStone Supra cookware, two other DuPont brands.
- Teflon-treated wallpaper and fabrics are scrubbable, and so durable that "you'd have to shoot them to kill them." For the first time, DuPont is advertising in such decorator-inspired magazines as *House Beautiful* and *Metropolitan Home.*

DuPont expects its efforts to lead to annual sales growth of 10 to 12 per cent for Teflon.

QUESTIONS

1. How would you explain the long life cycle for Teflon?
2. Evaluate DuPont's efforts at extending the maturity stage of Teflon's life cycle.
3. Present other strategies for stimulating Teflon's sales.

Refer to Table 10-1 in this chapter in your answer.
4. Where should DuPont allocate more of its future marketing resources for Teflon: on the industrial market or the final consumer market? Why?

CHAPTER *11*

Branding and Packaging

CHAPTER OBJECTIVES

1. To define and distinguish among branding terms and to examine the importance of branding

2. To study the key branding decisions that must be made regarding corporate symbols, the branding philosophy, the choice of brand names, and the use of trademarks

3. To define and distinguish among packaging terms and to examine the importance of packaging

4. To study the basic functions of packaging, key factors in packaging decisions, and criticisms of packaging

I n today's market, the greatest rewards will flow into the hands of those who honestly and rigorously dedicate themselves to building strong brands. And capitalizing on the strengths of existing brands is the name of today's marketing game.

We're not talking about adding some new flavors of taco dinners either; today's marketers are making brands jump across whole categories. Sun Maid's familiar logo and red packaging appears on the bread shelf as well as in the dried-fruit section. Häagen Dazs also is a liqueur, and Turtle Wax products will clean your home, not just your car. Household names like Dole, Tropicana, and Nestle's abound in new categories such as frozen novelties, where the "Dove Bar" may be the lone original brand name.

The increasing recognition of the value of existing brand names and the related use of brand-extension strategies are largely due to two factors: the long-term market leadership of popular brands and the high costs associated with developing new brand names. Brand extension is used whenever a company applies an existing name to a new product. Let us look further at the value of strong brands.

The Boston Consulting Group studied the market-leading brands in 30 product categories and found that 27 of the 30 leaders in 1920 were still the market-share leaders in 1988. Among these long-run leaders are Ivory soap, Campbell's soup, and Gold Medal flour.

In another study, Landor Associates (a firm specializing in image consulting) surveyed 1,000 consumers to measure their brand recognition and their level of regard for each of 672 corporate and consumer brands. Based on the responses of consumers, Landor then developed a list of the "10 most powerful brands" in the United States. They are (in order of overall power): Coca-Cola, Campbell, Pepsi-Cola, AT&T, McDonald's, American Express, Kellogg, IBM, Levi Strauss, and Sears. McDonald's is the newest of the power brands, and it started in the mid-1950s; Levi Strauss, Coca-Cola, and Campbell's are among the oldest (these firms began in 1873, 1886, and 1898, respectively).

As one expert notes, "with an established brand name, the product keeps selling itself through thick and thin. You can't kill a strong franchise."

The costs of developing new brands is getting higher all the time. For example, one marketing expert estimates that a brand-extension strategy generally costs one-half to one-third as much as developing a new brand. Savings are in the form of lower costs in package design, product-naming expenses, advertising (both to channel members and consumers), and other promotional costs.

Thus, making better use of existing brand names has been the single most common strategy among consumer companies (and many industrial marketers, as well) in recent years. Examples of brand extensions include the use of the Coca-Cola brand (once confined to one flavor) with diet, caffeine-free, cherry, and new Coke flavors, as well as with clothing. The Jell-O name once reserved for gelatin desserts is now also used on puddings and other products.[1]

Next, we will study various aspects of both branding and packaging. We will see how firms make such decisions as what corporate symbols to use, what emphasis to place on manufacturer versus dealer brands, and the basic functions of packaging—and of course, we will look further at the the role of brand extension in a marketing strategy.

[1] Norman C. Berry, "Revitalizing Brands," *Journal of Consumer Marketing*, Vol. 5 (Summer 1988), pp. 15–20; Heather Evans, "What's in a Brand Name?" *Management Review* (June 1988), pp. 33–35; and Richard W. Stevenson, "The Brands with the Billion-Dollar Names," *New York Times* (October 28, 1988), pp. A1, D21.

Overview

When conceiving, developing, and managing its products, a firm needs to make and enact a variety of decisions regarding the brand and package used with each item. A *brand* is a name, term, design, symbol, or any other feature that identifies the goods and services of one seller from those of other sellers. A *package* is a container used to protect, promote, transport, and/or identify a product.[2] It may consist of a product's physical container, an outer label, and/or inserts.

In this chapter, the various types of brand designations, key branding decisions, the basic functions of packaging, key packaging decisions, and selected criticisms of packaging are discussed.

Branding

An important part of product planning is *branding,* the procedure a firm follows in researching, developing, and implementing its brand(s). As already noted, a brand is a name, term, design, or symbol (or combination of these) that identifies the products of a seller or group of sellers. By establishing well-known brands, companies are usually able to obtain acceptance, extensive distribution, and higher prices.

There are four types of brand designation:

1. A *brand name* is a word, letter (number), group of words, or letters (numbers) that can be spoken. Examples are Charmin and Lipton Cup-a-Soup.
2. A *brand mark* is a symbol, design, or distinctive coloring or lettering that cannot be spoken. Examples are Ralston-Purina's checkerboard and Prudential's rock.
3. A *trade character* is a brand mark that is personified. Examples are Ronald McDonald and Morton Salt's umbrella girl.
4. A *trademark* is a brand name, brand mark, or trade character or combination thereof that is given legal protection. When it is used, a registered trademark is followed by ®. Examples are Scotch® Brand tape and MasterCard®.

Brand names, brand marks, and trade characters are marketing designations that do not offer legal protection against use by competitors, unless they are registered as trademarks (which all of the preceding examples have been). Trademarks ensure exclusivity for trademark owners or those securing their permission and provide legal remedies against firms using "confusingly similar" names, designs, or symbols. Trademarks are discussed more fully later in the chapter.

Branding started during the Middle Ages, when craft and merchant guilds required that each producer mark goods so that output could be restricted and inferior goods traced to the producer. The marks also served as standards for quality because items were sold outside the local markets in which the guilds operated. The earliest and most aggressive promoters of brands in the United States were patent medicine manufacturers. Examples of current U.S. brands that started more than one hundred years ago are Borden's Eagle Brand Condensed Milk, Quaker Oats, Vaseline, Pillsbury's Best Flour, and Ivory Soap. See Figure 11-1.

In the United States, there are now several hundred thousand brand names in circulation. Each year, the top hundred advertisers spend about $30 billion advertising

---

[2] Peter D. Bennett (Editor), *Dictionary of Marketing Terms* (Chicago: American Marketing Association, 1988), pp. 18, 140.

FIGURE 11-1
Borden's Long-Running Condensed Milk
Reprinted by permission.

their brands. Permanent media expenditures (such as a company logo, stationery, brochures, business forms and cards, and vehicular and building signs) for brands are another major marketing cost.

A major goal of companies is to develop brand loyalty, allowing them to maximize sales and maintain a strong brand image. Brand loyalty for supermarket products is particularly high. The majority of consumers are "exclusive one-brand users" of products such as light bulbs, razor blades, mouthwash, hair spray, cough syrups, salt, vinegar, dinner rolls, popcorn, waxed paper, oven cleaners, yogurt, and doughnuts.[3]

The use of popular brands can speed up public acceptance and gain dealer cooperation for new products. For instance, Castle & Cooke is now "less commodity-driven;" it realizes that its premier asset is the Dole brand, which it had not been emphasizing for over a decade.[4] Today the Dole name is associated with such newer products as Dole Fruit 'N Juice Bars, which obtained distribution in 80 per cent of all U.S. supermarkets and convenience stores less than two years after introduction.

Maintaining brand recognition is often a top priority for companies. As an example, in 1978, MEM (a personal-care products company) received permission from Hartmarx (the clothing firm) to use the name Racquet Club — Hartmarx owned the rights to the name — for a men's cologne. Soon Racquet Club cologne became quite successful for MEM. Then, in 1987, Hartmarx decided to revoke permission for MEM to call its cologne Racquet Club. Because of its low price, "the men's fragrance had become incompatible with Hartmarx's Racquet Club apparel." As a result, MEM stopped selling the product for a year, before reintroducing it in late 1988 as Classic Form; and

Product acceptance is improved by popularizing brand names.

---

[3] *Progressive Grocer,* various issues.
[4] Aimee L. Stern, "New Payoff from Old Brand Names," *Dun's Business Month* (April 1985), pp. 42–44.

FIGURE 11-2
Maintaining Brand Recognition
A three-step process was used by consultants Gerstman & Meyers to create a transition from Chix brand of baby products to the Dundee name, which became increasingly more prominent. Dundee is a registered trademark of Dundee Mills.
Reprinted by permission.

Branding creates identities, assures quality, and performs other functions.

MEM was not allowed to advertise that Classic Form was formerly known as Racquet Club. One marketing expert summed up MEM's situation thusly: "If you love a name so much and another company controls that trademark, you ought to negotiate a license that will last as long as you want to market your product."[5]

When Dundee Mills (a manufacturer of towels, rugs, health-care items, and baby products) acquired the Chix line of baby bedding and diapering accessories, it was given permission to use the Chix name for only five years. As a result, a three-stage transition was used to allow Dundee to retain loyal final consumers and retailers, while creating its own brand image, called Dundee.[6] See Figure 11-2.

These reasons summarize why branding is important:

▶ Product identification is eased. A customer can order a product by name instead of description.
▶ Customers are assured that a good or service has a certain level of quality and that they will obtain comparable quality if the same brand is reordered.
▶ The firm responsible for the product is known. The producer of unbranded items cannot be directly identified.
▶ Price comparisons are reduced when customers perceive distinct brands. This is especially true when special characteristics are attributed to different brands.

---

[5] Ronald Alsop, "The Smell's Familiar, But the Name?" *Wall Street Journal* (August 18, 1988), p. 23.
[6] "Three-Step Name Change Lets Firm Retain Brand Loyalty," *Marketing News* (August 17, 1984), p. 3.

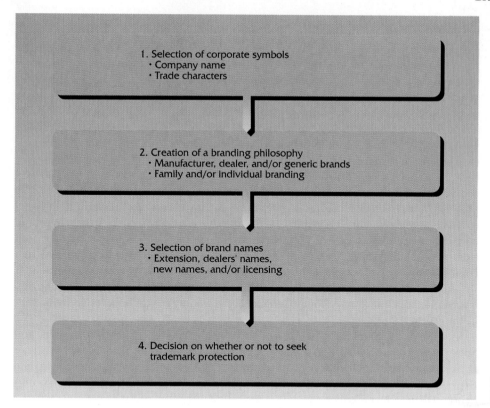

1. Selection of corporate symbols
   • Company name
   • Trade characters

2. Creation of a branding philosophy
   • Manufacturer, dealer, and/or generic brands
   • Family and/or individual branding

3. Selection of brand names
   • Extension, dealers' names,
     new names, and/or licensing

4. Decision on whether or not to seek
   trademark protection

FIGURE 11-3
Branding Decisions

▶ A firm is able to advertise (position) its products and associate each brand and its characteristics in the buyer's mind. This aids the consumer in forming a ***brand image,*** which is the perception a person has of a particular brand. It is "a mirror reflection (though perhaps inaccurate) of the brand personality or product being. It is what people believe about a brand—their thoughts, feelings, expectations."[7]

Brand images are the perceptions that consumers have of particular brands.

▶ Product prestige is increased, as social visibility becomes meaningful.

▶ Consumers feel less risk when purchasing a brand with which they are familiar and toward which they have a favorable attitude.

▶ Branding helps segment markets and create distinctive images. By using multiple brands, different market segments are attracted.

▶ Cooperation from distribution intermediaries is greater for well-known brands. A strong brand also may enable the producer to exert more control in the distribution channel.

▶ A brand may be used to sell an entire line of products, such as Polaroid cameras.

▶ A brand may be used to enter a new product category, such as Tylenol Extra-Strength Antacid.

There are four branding decisions a firm must undertake. These involve corporate symbols, branding philosophy, choosing a brand name, and using trademarks. See Figure 11-3.

[7] Bennett, *Dictionary of Marketing Terms,* p. 19.

Corporate Symbols

*Corporate symbols help
establish an overall image.*

Corporate symbols are a firm's name, logo, and trade characters. They are significant parts of overall company image. When a firm begins a business; merges with another company; drastically reduces or expands product lines; seeks new geographic markets; or finds its name to be unwieldy, nondistinctive, or confusing, it needs to evaluate and possibly change its corporate symbols. In 1988, almost 1,900 existing U.S. firms adopted new names — 52 per cent because of mergers, 23 per cent because of downsizing or restructuring, and 25 per cent for other reasons.[8] Following are illustrations of the role of corporate symbols in situations involving a new business, mergers, revised product lines, new geographic markets, and unwieldy, nondistinctive, and confusing names.

In 1982, a new manufacturer of portable computers hired a consultant to devise a company name. It wanted a name that "would be memorable and at the same time take command of the idea of portableness; something that would distinguish itself from all the other IBM PC compatibles." The consultant recommended a name that combined two syllables representing "communications" and "small but important."[9] By 1987, Compaq had annual sales exceeding $1 billion, the fastest that any company has reached that milestone. Today Compaq is the leading maker of portable computers in the world.

As a result of mergers, these firms have new corporate names: Burroughs and Sperry are now Unisys. The Bank of Virginia and Maryland's Union Trust are Signet Bank. Standard Oil, which was acquired by British Petroleum, is BP America. People Express and Continental Airlines, both acquired by Texas Air, are known as Continental Airlines.

If the nature of its business is altered, a company often changes its name. Thus, today International Harvester is Navistar International, after selling its farm-equipment business; and Zenith Radio is Zenith Electronics because it believed the old name was too restrictive. When making this type of name change, many firms retain parts of their original names (Walt Disney Productions becoming Walt Disney Co.) or develop acronyms from their former names (General Shoe Corporation becoming Genesco). This allows them to be more flexible in representing their product lines, as well as to retain their identities with loyal customers.

Because it expanded into new geographic markets, Allegheny Airlines changed its name to US Air; the old name suggested a small regional airline. See Figure 11-4. The Exxon name was developed because the company's regional brands, such as Esso and Humble, could not be used nationwide and others had unfortunate foreign connotations (for example, Enco means "stalled car" in Japanese).

The National Railroad Passenger Corporation was an unwieldly name; it became Amtrak. Consolidated Foods was a nondistinctive name; it became the Sara Lee Corporation, based on its leading brand (today, Sara Lee has an 87 per cent recognition rate, compared with 7 per cent for the Consolidated Foods name). See Figure 11-5. The United Biscuit Company of America changed its name to Keebler to avoid confusion with the Nabisco name.[10]

---

[8] Anspach Grossman Portugal Inc., 1988 survey of company name changes.
[9] Robert A. Mamis, "Name-Calling," *Inc.* (July 1984), pp. 67–74.
[10] Hal Goodman, "Name-Dropping," *Across the Board* (May 1983), pp. 35–39; Walter McQuade, "Cosmetic Surgery for the Company Name," *Fortune* (April 30, 1984), pp. 249–250; "Disney Proposes to Change Name to Walt Disney Co.," *Wall Street Journal* (January 3, 1986), p. 2; and Randall Rothenberg, "Company-Name Consultants Battle Over Poll," *New York Times* (July 4, 1988), p. 33.

SARA LEE CORPORATION

Developing and maintaining appropriate corporate symbols are not easy tasks. For example, the individual "Baby Bells" (Ameritech, Bell Atlantic, BellSouth, Nynex, Pacific Telesis, Southwestern Bell, and US West) are still not nearly as well known as AT&T — six years after being established as independent companies. And when Nissan Motor Corporation changed the name of its U.S. car division from Datsun to Nissan, its sales fell dramatically despite a major ad campaign; it took six years for the Nissan name to reach the level of brand awareness that Datsun had attained. Along the way, Nissan had numerous clashes with dealers that did not want the name change.[11]

Branding Philosophy

When developing a brand strategy, a company needs to determine its branding philosophy. This philosophy outlines the use of manufacturer, dealer, and/or generic brands, as well as the use of family or individual branding.

Manufacturer, Dealer, and Generic Brands

Manufacturer brands are well known and heavily promoted.

Manufacturer (national) brands contain the names of manufacturers and obtain the vast majority of sales for most product categories, such as 80+ per cent in food items, all automobiles, three-quarters of major appliances, and more than 80 per cent of gasoline. They appeal to a wide range of consumers who desire low risk of poor product performance, good quality, routinized purchase behavior, status, and convenience shopping. Manufacturer brands are well known and trusted because quality control is strictly maintained. These brand names are identifiable and present distinctive images to shoppers. Manufacturers normally produce a number of product alternatives under their brands.

Manufacturer brands are often sold through many competing retailers. For individual retailers, purchases (and inventory investments) may be low. In addition, the presold nature of these brands makes turnover high. Manufacturers spend large sums promoting their brands and frequently run cooperative advertisements with dealers, so that costs are shared. Prices are the highest of the three brands, with the bulk going to the manufacturer (who also receives the greatest profit). The major marketing focus for manufacturer brands is to attract and retain consumers who are loyal to the firm's offering and to control the marketing effort for the brands.

Dealer brands enable wholesalers and retailers to get loyal customers.

Dealer (private) brands contain names designated by wholesalers or retailers and account for significant levels of sales in many product categories, such as 50 per cent in shoes, about one-third of tires, 15 per cent of food items, and one-quarter of appliance sales. Also, many retailers, such as The Limited and McDonald's, generate the majority of sales from their own brands. Dealer brands often appeal to value-conscious consumers who compare prices and ingredients with manufacturer brands. When they believe dealer brands offer good quality at a lower price, they purchase them. They are willing to accept some risk regarding quality, but store loyalty causes these consumers to believe the products are reliable. Usually dealer brands are similar in quality to manufacturer brands, although packaging is less important. In some cases, these brands are made to dealer specifications. Assortments are less and the brands are unknown to shoppers who do not patronize the store.

---

[11] Julie Amparano, "Identity Problems Plague the Baby Bells," *Wall Street Journal* (May 10, 1988), p. 41; and John Holusha, "Can Nissan Stage a U.S. Comeback?" *New York Times* (December 4, 1988), Section 3, p. 4.

Dealers secure exclusive rights for their brands and are responsible for their distribution. Dealer brands require large total investments and purchases by their sponsors. Inventory turnover is generally lower than that of manufacturer brands. Promotion is also the responsibility of the dealer and prices are more controlled by the distributor/retailer. Because per-unit packaging and promotion costs are less for dealer brands, wholesalers and retailers are able to sell these items at lower prices and still obtain higher per-unit profits (their share of the final selling price is higher than for manufacturer brands). The marketing focus of dealer brands is to attract and retain customers who are loyal to the store and to exert control over the marketing plan for these brands. Large wholesalers and retailers now advertise their brands extensively. Some, such as Sears' Kenmore brand, have become as well known as manufacturer brands. Furthermore, some firms (for example, Sherwin-Williams) operate as both manufacturers and retailers.

Generic brands emphasize the names of the products themselves and not manufacturer or dealer names. They started in the drug industry as low-cost alternatives to expensive, heavily promoted manufacturer brands. Today generics have expanded into cigarettes, coffee, flashlight batteries, tennis shoes, underwear, beer, Scotch, motor oil, and other product categories. Nationally, generics represent nearly 30 per cent of prescription drug sales and 2 to 4 per cent of grocery sales; 85 per cent of U.S. supermarkets currently stock generics. Generics appeal to price-conscious, careful shoppers, who perceive them as representing "a solid, basic value for their purchasing dollar,"[12] are sometimes willing to accept lower quality, and often purchase for large families.

> *Generic brands* are low-priced goods that receive little advertising.

Generic brands are seldom advertised and receive secondary shelf space (for example, floor level). Consumers must search out these brands. Prices are less than other brands by anywhere from 10 to 50 per cent, due to quality, packaging, assortment, distribution, and promotion economies. The major marketing goal is to offer low-priced, lower-quality items to consumers interested in price savings. Table 11-1 compares the three types of brands.

Many manufacturers, wholesalers, and retailers employ a ***mixed-brand strategy***, whereby they sell a combination of manufacturer and dealer brands (and sometimes generic brands). This strategy provides benefits for both manufacturers and wholesalers/retailers. There is control over the brand bearing each seller's name. Exclusive rights to a brand can be obtained. Two or more market segments can be reached. Brand and store loyalty are encouraged, shelf space and locations coordinated, cooperation in the distribution channel improved, and assortments increased. Production is stabilized and excess capacity utilized. Sales are maximized and profits equitably shared. Long-run planning is coordinated.

> A ***mixed-brand strategy*** combines manufacturer and dealer brands.

Manufacturer, dealer, and generic brands also frequently engage in a ***battle of the brands***, in which each attempts to gain a greater share of the consumer's dollar, control over marketing strategy, consumer loyalty, product distinctiveness, maximum shelf space and locations, and a large share of profits. These are some indications of the extent of the battle:

> In the ***battle of the brands***, the three brand types compete.

▶ Several leading manufacturers have introduced their own lower-priced brands to complement their premium brands. One such brand is Procter & Gamble's Banner

---

[12] David M. Szymanski and Paul S. Busch, "Identifying the Generics-Prone Consumer: A Meta-Analysis," *Journal of Marketing Research*, Vol. 24 (November 1987), p. 430.

TABLE 11-1 Manufacturer, Dealer, and Generic Brands

Characteristic	Manufacturer Brand	Dealer Brand	Generic Brand
Target market	Risk avoider, quality-conscious, brand loyal, status-conscious, quick shopper	Value-conscious, comparison shopper, quality-conscious, moderate risk taker, store loyal	Price-conscious, careful shopper, willing to accept lower quality, large family
Product	Well known, trusted, best quality control, clearly identifiable, deep product line	Same overall quality as manufacturer, less emphasis on packaging, less assortment, not known to nonstore shoppers	Usually less overall quality than manufacturer, little emphasis on packaging, very limited assortment, not well known
Distribution	Usually sold at many competing retailers	Usually only available in the outlets of a single retailer	Varies
Promotion	Manufacturer-sponsored advertisements, cooperative advertisements	Dealer-sponsored advertisements	Few advertisements, secondary shelf space
Price	Highest, usually controlled by manufacturer	Moderate, usually controlled by dealer	Lowest, usually controlled by dealer
Marketing focus	To generate brand loyalty and manufacturer control	To generate store loyalty and control	To offer a low-priced, lesser-quality item to those desiring it

toilet tissue, which sells for almost 25 per cent less than the firm's Charmin and White Cloud brands. Banner has annual sales of more than $50 million.[13]

▶ A number of department-store chains have increased their emphasis on dealer brands in order to combat discounters selling national brands, improve their image, and increase store loyalty. These dealer brands are in product categories ranging from clothing to housewares.[14]

▶ In the prescription drug category, the market share of generic brands is expected to almost double between 1988 and 1993: "The engines of the expansion are the growing consumer acceptance of substitutes for brand names, a wave of opportunities stemming from the expirations of patents on most of the top 100 prescription medicines, and the expected passage of a bill in Congress that could mandate the use of generic pharmaceuticals for Medicare patients."[15]

Family and Individual Branding

Family branding uses a single name for many products.

Under *family (blanket) branding,* one name is used for two or more individual products. Many firms selling industrial products, such as Boeing and Xerox, utilize family branding for their entire product mixes. Other firms employ a family brand for each category of products. For example, Sears has Kenmore appliances and Craftsman tools. Family branding can be applied to both manufacturer and dealer brands.

Family branding is most effective for specialized firms or those with specialized product lines. Companies capitalize on a uniform, well-known image and promote the same name continually, which keeps promotion costs down. The major disadvantages are that differentiated-marketing efforts may be minimized (if only one brand name is

---

[13] Amy Dunkin, "No-Frills Products: An Idea Whose Time Has Come," *Business Week* (June 17, 1985), pp. 64–65.

[14] Muriel J. Adams, "Private Labels: Now Trump," *Stores* (June 1988), pp. 12–24.

[15] Phillip H. Wiggins, "Big Gains Seen in Generic Drugs," *New York Times* (March 23, 1988), p. D6.

You're the Marketer

Should There Be a New Coke?

When new Coke was introduced in April 1985, Coca-Cola Company thought it would be so successful that the 99-year-old Coke formula was removed and replaced with new Coke. In the month after new Coke's introduction, shipments to bottlers rose by the highest percentage in five years.

However, by May 1985, Coca-Cola executives began to sense a major problem as new Coke rapidly lost popularity in its weekly consumer surveys. Then, sales fell sharply. On June 6, 1985, the company decided to bring back old Coke, renamed "Coke Classic." Although the firm wanted new Coke to be its flagship brand, three months after Coke Classic was re-introduced it was outselling new Coke in 70 per cent of all markets.

As of March 1989, sales of new Coke accounted for 1.4 per cent of the total soft-drink market; Coke Classic accounted for 19 per cent. Yet Coca-Cola maintains that new Coke sales are stable, and it has changed the product's packaging "to maximize shelf impact."

Some industry observers say Coca-Cola should drop new Coke. They feel

▶ *The product is lost in the marketplace. It does not have a clear niche or a strong customer following, despite its high initial level of marketing support.*

▶ *The low sales level does not justify the need for bottlers to produce and distribute two sugar-based colas.*

▶ *New Coke may crowd out other more successful Coca-Cola brands in the fight for shelf space in supermarkets and in restaurant distribution.*

New Coke supporters feel it should be kept, stating that

▶ *A withdrawal would be embarrassing to Coca-Cola.*

▶ *It is successful in certain regional markets. Even a market share of 1.4 per cent represents hundreds of millions of dollars in annual sales.*

▶ *Some new Coke users would switch to brands of competitors.*

As the president of Coca-Cola Company, what would you do?

SOURCE: Based on material in Scott Ticer, "The Cola Superpowers' Outrageous New Arsenals," Business Week (March 20, 1989), pp. 162, 166.

used to appeal to all of a firm's customers), a company's image may be adversely affected when widely different products (such as luxury and economy watches or men's and women's cologne) carry one name, and innovativeness may not be projected to consumers.

One particularly effective use of family branding is ***brand extension,*** a strategy by which an established brand name is applied to new products. Relatively quick customer acceptance may be gained because people are already familiar with existing products bearing the same name, a favorable brand image (and the associated good will) can be carried over to a new product, and the risk of a new-product failure is reduced. As one new-product consultant notes: "At a time when breakthrough products are few and far between, smart marketers recognize that they can have a bigger

Brand extension gains quick acceptance.

total business through intelligent brand extensions. There is little question that brand extension is a good idea. The question is, 'How can it be done wisely?' "[16] Almost one-half of new consumer products utilize some form of brand extension.

There are seven situations in which a brand-extension strategy is most effective:

1. Same product in a different form — example, Jell-O Pudding Pops.
2. Distinctive taste/ingredient/component in a new item — example, Oreo cookies-and-cream ice cream.
3. New companion product — example, Colgate Plus toothbrush.
4. Same customer franchise for a new product (a different product for the same target market) — example, Visa traveler's checks aimed at Visa credit-card customers.
5. Expertise conveyed to new product — example, Canon copy machines.
6. Benefit/attribute/feature conveyed to new product — example, Ivory shampoo (which connotes mildness).
7. Designer image/status conveyed to new product — example, Pierre Cardin sunglasses.[17]

Individual branding uses distinct brands.

With ***individual (multiple) branding,*** separate brands are used for different items or product lines sold by the firm. As an example, in Hershey's deep line of candy bars are Hershey Bar, Mr. Goodbar, Kit Kat, Skor, Take Five, and New Trail. Ralston-Purina markets separate product lines with brands such as Purina Dog Chow, Bran Chex cereal, Eveready batteries, and Chicken of the Sea tuna. These brands have distinct images and appeals and are marketed differently. Ralston-Purina is careful not to confuse pet and human products.

Through individual branding, a firm can create multiple product positions (separate brand images), attract various market segments, increase sales and marketing control, and offer both premium and low-priced brands. Also, individual branding enables manufacturers to secure greater shelf space in retail stores. However, each brand requires its own promotion costs and there may be a loss of continuity (such as a slower diffusion process). Economies due to mass production are lessened. New products do not benefit from an established identity.

To obtain the advantages of family and individual branding, many firms combine the two. For example, Dodge is a family brand used by Chrysler to designate one product line with several automobile and truck models. The division has an overall image and appeals to a specific target market. New models benefit from the Dodge label, and there is an interrelationship among the models. Individual brands are also used with each model so that product differences can be identified and highlighted. Among the Dodge models are Shadow, Daytona, Caravan, Aries, and Ramcharger.

Choosing a Brand Name

*Brand sources range from existing names to **licensing agreements.***

When a firm chooses brand names, there are several potential sources:

1. Under a brand-extension policy, an existing name is applied to a new product (Cracker Jacks popcorn, *Ghostbusters II*).
2. For a dealer's brand, the dealer specifies the name (Outback Red — a sportswear brand of The Limited).

---

[16] Chester L. Kane, "How to Increase the Odds for Successful Brand Extension," *Journal of Product Innovation Management,* Vol. 4 (September 1987), p. 203.

[17] Edward M. Tauber, "Expanding Your Brand," *Advertising Age* (December 7, 1987), p. 18.

3. When a new name is sought, these alternatives are available:

- ▶ Initials (*PC Magazine*, A&W root beer).
- ▶ Invented name (Kleenex, Exxon).
- ▶ Numbers (Chanel No. 5, Century 21).
- ▶ Mythological character (Atlas tires, Samsonite luggage).
- ▶ Personal name (Lipton, Ford).
- ▶ Geographical name (Pittsburgh paints, Utica sheets).
- ▶ Dictionary word (Check-Up toothpaste, Whirlpool appliances).
- ▶ Foreign word (Nestlé, Lux).
- ▶ Combination of words (Head and Shoulders shampoo).

4. With a ***licensing agreement***, a company pays a fee to use a name whose trademark rights are held by another firm. Because of the high consumer recognition of many trademarks, company sales for a new product may be facilitated by paying a royalty fee to use one. Examples of names being used in licensing agreements are Jeep, Roger Rabbit, Coca-Cola, Sesame Street, Mickey Mouse, Smurf, and McKids (Sears' children's clothing line based on the McDonald's name). Licensed names and characters annually account for $60 billion to $70 billion in retail sales.

A good brand name suggests something about a product's use, benefits, or attributes (Beauty Rest mattress, Wash 'n Dry, Budget Rent-a-Car); is easy to spell and remember, and pronounceable in only one way (Bic, Tang, *Time* magazine); can be applied to a whole line of products (Gerber baby foods, Calvin Klein clothing, General Electric appliances); is capable of legal protection from use by others (Mr. Coffee, Big Mac, Equal artificial sweetener); and has a pleasant or at least neutral meaning in international markets (Exxon, Kodak, IBM).

Brand names should be suggestive, easy to remember, and flexible.

The process of developing a new brand name can be complex. At IBM, an eight-person branding department now devises names for a number of the 1,000 new products the company introduces each year. These are a few user-friendly names it has developed: InfoWindow, a touch-sensitive screen; Easystrike, a computer ribbon; and JetPrinter, a speedy color printer. Each of these products also uses the IBM family name.[18]

In choosing a brand name, it is essential that a firm understand and plan for the consumer's ***brand decision process,*** shown in Figure 11-6. For a new brand, a consumer begins with nonrecognition of the name, and the seller must make the consumer aware of the brand. Then the consumer moves to recognition, wherein the brand and its attributes are known, and the seller emphasizes persuasion. Next, the consumer develops a preference (or dislike) for the brand and purchases it (or chooses not to buy); the seller's task is to achieve brand loyalty. Last, some consumers exhibit an insistence (or aversion) for the brand and become loyal to it; the seller's role is to maintain this loyalty. In many cases, consumers develop preferences toward several brands but do not buy or insist upon one brand exclusively.

*The **brand decision process** moves from nonrecognition to insistence (or aversion).*

By using brand extension, a new company product would begin at the recognition, preference, or insistence stage of the brand decision process because of the carryover effect of the established name. However, consumers who dislike the existing product line would be unlikely to try a new product under the same name; but they might try another company product under a different brand. Also, some consumers may feel that brand extension is inappropriate if the new product category is too different.

[18] David Kalish, "Big Blue Joins Computer Name Game," *Newsday* (January 1, 1989), pp. 102, 100.

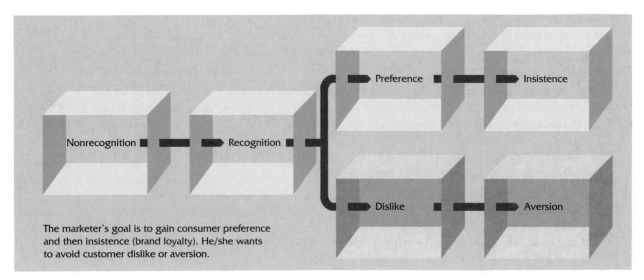

The marketer's goal is to gain consumer preference and then insistence (brand loyalty). He/she wants to avoid customer dislike or aversion.

FIGURE 11-6 The Consumer's Brand Decision Process

The Use of Trademarks

Trademark protection grants exclusive use of a brand for as long as it is marketed.

Finally, a firm must decide whether or not to apply for trademark protection under either the federal Lanham Act of 1946 or state law. A trademark gives the firm the exclusive use of a "word, symbol, combination of letters or numbers, or other devices such as distinctive packaging used to identify the goods of one company and to distinguish them from other companies" for as long as they are marketed. A service mark performs the same function for services (such as Weight Watchers).[19] Each year, 70,000 new-product names are registered with the U.S. government for trademark protection.

Trademarks are voluntary and require a registration procedure that can be time consuming, complex, and expensive (a successful challenge of a competitor may necessitate high legal fees and many years in court). A multinational firm must register trademarks in every country in which it operates. In order for a trademark to be legally protected, it must have a distinctive meaning that does not describe an entire product category, not be confusingly similar to other trademarks, be used in interstate commerce (for federal protection), and not imply characteristics that the product does not possess. A surname by itself cannot be registered because anyone can do business under his or her name. However, a surname can be registered if used to describe a specific business (for example, Roy Rogers' Restaurants).[20]

When brands become too popular or descriptive of a product category, they run the risk of becoming public property. Then a firm loses its trademark position. Brands that are fighting to remain exclusive trademarks include Xerox, Levi's, Frigidaire, Formica, Kleenex, and Teflon. Former trademarks that are now considered generic — and thus public property — are cellophane, aspirin, shredded wheat, kerosene, cola, linoleum, and monopoly.

[19] Thomas M. S. Hemnes, "How Can You Find a Safe Trademark?" *Harvard Business Review,* Vol. 63 (March-April 1985), pp. 36-37 ff.; and William M. Borchard, "Judge Takes a 'Functional' Look at Trademarks," *Advertising Age* (April 21, 1986), p. 52.

[20] Dorothy Cohen, "Trademark Strategy," *Journal of Marketing,* Vol. 50 (January 1986), pp. 61-74.

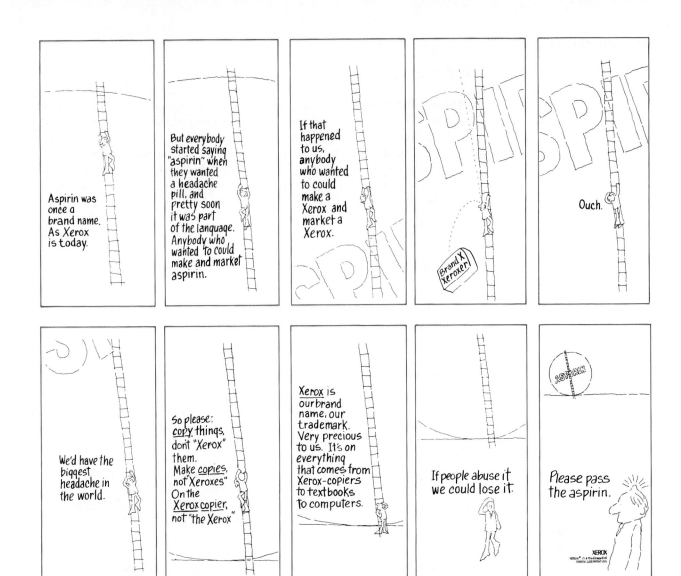

FIGURE 11-7
Trademark Protection by Xerox
Reprinted by permission.

DuPont has used careful research to retain a trademark for Teflon. A company survey showed that 68 per cent of the consumers questioned identified Teflon as a brand name. This enabled DuPont to win a court case against a Japanese firm using the name Eflon. On the other hand, the U.S. Supreme Court ruled that "Monopoly" was a generic term that could be used by any game maker. Similarly, a federal court ruled that Miller could not trademark the single word Lite for its lower-calorie beer.[21]

Trademark protection is essential to many firms because the exclusive use of brands and symbols enables them to maintain long-established images and market shares. For example, Xerox vigorously polices its brands. It realizes that a loss of brand recognition would be extremely harmful. See Figure 11-7.

In late 1988, the U.S. Congress passed legislation strengthening the rights of trademark holders.

[21] Ibid., p. 63; and Richard L. Gordon, "Monopoly Game Doesn't Pass Go," *Advertising Age* (February 28, 1983), pp. 3, 69.

Packaging

Packaging is that part of product planning in which a company researches, designs, and produces its package(s). As noted at the beginning of the chapter, a package consists of a product's physical container, label, and inserts.

The physical container may be a cardboard, metal, plastic, or wooden box; a cellophane or waxpaper wrapper; a glass, aluminum, or plastic jar or can; a paper bag; styrofoam; some other material; or a combination of these. Products frequently have more than one physical container. For example, cereal is individually packaged in small cardboard boxes, with an inner waxpaper wrapping, and shipped in large corrugated boxes. Watches are usually covered in inner cloth linings and shipped in plastic boxes.

A label indicates the product's brand name, the company logo, ingredients, promotional messages, inventory control codes, and/or instructions for use. Inserts are (1) detailed instructions and safety information that are carried in drug, toy, and other packages or (2) coupons, prizes, or recipe booklets. They are used as appropriate.

Prior to the advent of the modern supermarket and department store, manufacturers shipped merchandise in bulk containers, such as cracker barrels, sugar sacks, and butter tubs. Retail merchants repackaged the contents into smaller, more convenient units to meet customer needs. With the growth of mass merchants and self-service, manufacturers came to realize the value of packaging as a marketing tool. Today it is a vital part of a firm's product-development strategy; a package may even be an integral part of the product itself (such as the aerosol can for shaving cream).

It is estimated that up to $75 billion is annually spent on packaging, about 10 per cent of a typical product's retail price. The amount is higher for such products as cosmetics (up to 40 per cent and more). The complete package redesign of a major product might cost several million dollars for machinery and production. Packaging decisions must serve both channel member and final consumer needs. Plans are often made in conjunction with production, logistics, and legal personnel. Errors in packaging can be quite costly.

For these and other reasons, many firms exert a large effort in package design. As an example, Coca-Cola rejected 150 package designs for its new diet Coke before selecting a package with red lettering on a white-striped and silver-reflective background. Among the package colors turned down by Coca-Cola executives were blue (associated with Pepsi), silver (associated with Diet Rite), and a red background (too confusing due to its similarity to Coke's design). The packaging of diet Coke was so important because no other new product had ever used the Coke name in the firm's first 95 years of existence.[22]

Package redesign frequently occurs when a company's current packaging becomes too expensive or receives a poor response from channel members and customers; the company seeks a new market segment, reformulates a product, or changes product positioning; or new technology becomes available. For instance, demographic changes and increasing competition convinced Nabisco Brands that 50-year-old Ritz Crackers needed modified packaging. The new package is redder and trimmed with a thin band of gold: "We tried to make Ritz look ritzier. We want to speak to young, affluent consumers."[23] See Figure 11-8.

[22] Nancy Giges, "After 150 Tries Comes a Winning Design," *Advertising Age* (October 18, 1982), pp. M-4–M-5.
[23] "Putting New Glitz on the Ritz (Box)," *Advertising Age* (May 12, 1986), p. 52.

BEFORE   **AFTER**

FIGURE 11-8
Package Redesign for Ritz Crackers
Reprinted by permission.

The basic functions of packaging, factors considered when making packaging decisions, and criticisms of packaging are described next.

Basic Packaging Functions

There are six key *packaging functions:* containment and protection, usage, communication, segmentation, channel cooperation, and new-product planning.

For liquid, granular, and other divisible products, containment is needed to secure the items in a given quantity and form. A package also creates protection for a product while it is shipped, stored, and handled. In all cases, a package must protect a product against the effects of light, infestation, shock, vibration, breakage, evaporation, and spilling.

A package must facilitate product usage. Multiple packaging and larger sizes encourage greater product usage. Product dispensement may be eased through a no-drip spout, self-applicator, flip-top, squeeze tube, boil bag, oven-ready container, or other package design. For divisible products, the package needs to accommodate storage after the item is initially used. For example, a plastic margarine container with a snap-on lid makes continued storage simple. Finally, some firms offer packages that are reusable once a product is depleted (such as a soft-soap dispenser).

A package is an important method of communication with the customer. It identifies the brand, provides ingredients and directions, presents an image, and displays the product. A package differentiates a product from competitors by its design, color, shape, and materials. It serves as a promotional tool and is the final form of promotion the consumer sees prior to making a purchase decision. Packaging is particularly valuable for firms with self-service operations and those concentrating on impulse goods, such as candy. A package also serves as a reminder after a purchase is made.

Packaging functions range from containment and protection to product planning.

335

Marketing Controversy

How Radical Should a Package Redesign Be?

Firms redesigning their packages need to consider how dramatic a change is optimal. Package redesign is like walking a tightrope: a firm wants to attract new customers with updated packaging while not alienating any of its current customers.

When Coors changed the labels on its flagship beer from "Banquet Beer" to "Original Draft" to stimulate sales, it was surprised that the new labels were resisted in two of its most loyal markets: Southern California and West Texas. Despite attempts to convince consumers in these markets that only the label had been changed (and not the beer), consumers there returned to Coors only after cans with the old label were reintroduced. To appeal to old and new customers, Coors decided to distribute its beer in two different packages, each with a distinct label but the same beer, to about 20 of its 600 distributors. Retailers in these areas would stock both the old and new-style packages; in other locales, just the new packages would be shipped. But after further problems, the new label was totally scrapped.

When McCormick, a seasoning-and-flavoring manufacturer, decided to repackage its entire product line, it switched to plastic bottles from its old familiar red-and-white tins. The new packaging allows consumers to see product freshness. To further differentiate McCormick from dealer brands, the labels also have a new typeface and corporate logo. Because McCormick traditionally used a red color on packages, the firm uses red caps and labels on its new packages. Nonetheless, initially many shoppers did not associate the new bottles with McCormick. Its pepper sales dropped so much that it was forced to reintroduce its old tin-can package for that product. On its other products, the company is enlarging the type and adding shelf labels. Overall, the plastic bottles have been successful in attracting customers.

What do you think about package redesign?

SOURCE: Based on material in Marj Charlier, "Beer Drinkers in Texas, California Don't Swallow Change in Coors Label," *Wall Street Journal* (December 29, 1988), p. B4; and Rachel L. Swarns, "McCormick Is Repackaging Its Spices," *Wall Street Journal* (August 10, 1988), p. 22.

Packaging can be used to segment the market because a package can be tailor-made for a specific market group. For example, gift boxes appeal to shoppers buying presents. Single-serving containers attract one-person households. Unusual packages are sought by status seekers. When a company offers two or more package shapes, sizes, colors, or designs, it may employ differentiated marketing.

A firm must consider the needs of the wholesalers and retailers in its distribution channel — and use packaging that makes a product easy to ship, handle, and store. Packages should also be durable, allow their contents to have a reasonable shelf life, fit into pre-existing dealer facilities and displays, provide a convenient place for the price, make inventory control easier by including computer codes on labels, and make shoplifting more difficult. As an example, Veryfine juice bottles are placed in sturdy corrugated cartons and wrapped in form-fitting plastic to prevent damage in transport and to make it easier for wholesalers and retailers to store and display merchandise. See Figure 11-9.

Finally, packaging can be a major element of new-product planning. Some of the products successfully modified and presented as new as a result of packaging inno-

FIGURE 11-9
**Transporting and Storing
Veryfine Juices**
Veryfine packaging makes it convenient
for channel members to receive
merchandise, store it, and display it.
Packages also contain UPC codes to
facilitate inventory management.
Reprinted by permission.

vations are aerosol cans for shaving cream, deodorants, and hair sprays; disposable
containers for milk, soda, and beer; microwavable containers for frozen dinners; pop-
up tissues; self-sealing food packages; see-through meat packages; toothpaste with
pump dispensers; vacuum-packed tennis balls; and child-proof medicine bottles.

Factors Considered in Packaging Decisions

Several key factors must be weighed in making packaging decisions. A discussion of
each follows.

Package design affects the image a firm seeks for its products. Color, shape, and   *What image is sought?*
material all influence perceptions of a firm and its products. For example,

> the black-and-yellow box holding Sandoz Nutrition Corp.'s Screaming Yellow Zonkers
> shattered the taboo against using the color black in packaging. Since that revolution in the

late '60s, marketers found that everything from ice cream to orange juice jumped from store shelves when dressed in black. But the craze is fading, and so are colors. Black is on its way to becoming passé, and pastels — even stark white — are the rage.[24]

As noted previously, plain packaging fosters a lower-quality image for generics. Figure 11-10 shows the creative packaging used by ReaLemon.

Should family packaging be used?

In family packaging, a firm uses a common element on each package in a product line. It parallels family branding. Campbell has virtually identical packages for its traditional soups, distinguished only by flavor or content identification. American Home Products, the maker of Advil and Anacin over-the-counter analgesics, does not use family packaging and has different packages for each brand to attract different segments.

Should standard packages be used worldwide?

An international firm must determine whether a standardized package can be used throughout the world (with only a language change on the label). Standardization increases worldwide recognition. For this reason, Coke and Pepsi utilize standard packages wherever possible. Nonetheless some colors, symbols, and shapes have negative connotations in certain countries. For example, white can represent purity or mourning, two vastly different images.

What should costs be?

Package costs must be considered on a total and per-unit basis. As cited earlier, total costs can run into the millions of dollars; and per-unit costs can go as high as 40 per cent of a product's retail price — depending on the purpose and extent of packaging.

---

[24] Julie A. Doherty, "No Longer Black, It's White," *Advertising Age* (December 12, 1988), p. S-3.

CAN YOU SAY AS MUCH FOR YOUR SHAMPOO?

*no fillers,
no thickeners,
no colorants,
no heavy
perfumes,
no harsh
detergents,
no build-up,
lathers quickly,
rinses out faster,
milder on hair,
lasts longer...*

WELLA *So fine*®
Shampoo Mist

The Wella Corporation, Englewood, N.J. 07631 ©1988

FIGURE 11-11
**Wella's So Fine
Shampoo Mist**
Reprinted by permission.

*What materials and
innovations are right?*

A firm has a number of packaging materials from which to choose, such as paperboard, plastic, metal, glass, styrofoam, and cellophane. In the selection, trade-offs are probably necessary. For instance, cellophane allows products to be attractively displayed, but it is highly susceptible to tearing; paperboard is relatively inexpensive, but it is difficult to open. Also, a company must determine how innovative it wants its packaging to be. For example, Wella recently introduced So Fine Shampoo Mist, which features a self-pressurized pump that allows the product to be dispensed from any position (including upside down) and in the exact quantity (to avoid waste). Because of the packaging's technical nature, Wella sponsored informative ads, placed an instructional hang tag on the container, and promoted a toll-free 800-telephone number.[25] See Figure 11-11.

[25] "Wella Shampoo Container Employs High-Tech, Self-Pressurized System," *Marketing News* (February 1, 1988), p. 18.

FIGURE 11-12
The L'eggs Mystique:
Blending a Memorable
Brand Name and
a Distinctive
Package Shape
Reprinted by permission of
Sara Lee Corporation.

*What features should the
package incorporate?*

There is a wide range of package features from which to choose, depending on the product. These features include pour spouts, hinged lids, screw-on tops, pop-tops, see-through bags, tuck- or seal-end cartons, carry handles, product testers (for items like batteries), freshness dating, and blister cards (products are placed under a plastic dome mounted on a card with a hole in it and hung on a metal rack). These features may provide a firm with a differential advantage.

*What size(s), color(s), and
shape(s) are used?*

Next, a firm selects the size(s), color(s), and shape(s) of its packages. In selecting the package size, shelf life (how long a product retains its freshness), convenience, tradition, and competition must be considered. In the food industry, new and larger sizes have captured high sales. The choice of package color depends on the image sought for the brand. Mello Yello, a citrus soft drink by Coca-Cola, has bright orange and green lettering on a lemon-yellow background for its label. Package shape also affects a product's image. Hanes (a division of Sara Lee Corporation) created a mystique for L'eggs pantyhose by creating the egg-shaped package. See Figure 11-12. The number of packages used with any one product depends on competition and the company's use of differentiated marketing. By selling small, medium, and large sizes, an existing firm may ensure maximum shelf space, appeal to different consumers, and make it difficult and expensive for a new one to gain wholesaler and retailer support.

*How should the label and
inserts appear?*

The placement, content, size, and prominence of the label must be determined. Both company and brand names need to appear on the label. Package inserts range from recipes to directions for use to safety tips to coupons for future purchases, and their inclusion should be noted on the label. Sometimes a redesigned label may be confusing to customers and hurt the product's sales. For example, in early 1989, only six months after Coors changed its beer label from "Banquet Beer" to "Original Draft" to capitalize on the growing interest in draft beer, it had to reintroduce the old label nationwide and scrap the new one. Even though the beer had not been modified at all, loyal Coors' customers were upset—they perceived that the beer had been changed.[26]

[26] Marj Charlier, "And So It's Back to Drawing Board for Original Draft," *Wall Street Journal* (January 20, 1989), p. B4.

Multiple packaging couples two or more product items in one container. It may involve the same product (such as razor blades or soda) or a combination of different products (such as a comb and a brush or a first-aid kit). The goals of multiple packaging are to increase consumption (hoarding may be a problem), get the consumer to buy an assortment of items, or have the consumer try a new item (such as a new automatic pencil packaged with an established ball-point pen). Most multiple packs, like cereal, are versatile because they can be sold as they are shipped or broken into single units.

Should multiple packaging be used?

Individually wrapping portions of a divisible product may offer a competitive advantage. It may also be quite costly. Kraft has done well with its individually wrapped cheese slices. Alka-Seltzer sells its tablets in individually wrapped tin-foil containers, as well as in a bottle without wrapping.

Should items be individually wrapped?

For certain items, preprinted prices are desired by some dealers. These include T-shirts, magazines, watches, and candy. The dealers have the option of charging those prices or adhering their own labels. Some retailers prefer only a space for the price on the package and insert their own price labels automatically. Because of the growing use of computer technology by wholesalers and retailers in monitoring inventory levels, more of them are insisting on premarked inventory codes on packages. In 1987, the National Retail Merchants Association endorsed the Universal Product Code as the voluntary vendor marking standard.

Should a package have a preprinted price and use the UPC?

With the **Universal Product Code (UPC),** manufacturers premark items with a series of thick and thin vertical lines. Price and inventory data codes are represented by these lines, which appear on outer package labels — but are not readable by employees and customers. These lines may be "read" by computerized optical scanning equipment at the checkout counter. In these instances, the cashier does not have to ring up a transaction manually and inventory data are instantly transmitted to the main computer of the retailer (or the manufacturer). In the UPC system, human-readable prices must still be marked on merchandise, either by the manufacturer, the wholesaler, or the retailer.[27] The UPC's role is discussed further in Chapter 12.

Last, a company must be sure that the package design fits in with the rest of its marketing mix.[28] A well-known brand of perfume may be extravagantly packaged, distributed in select stores, advertised in upscale magazines, and sold at a high price. In contrast, a firm making perfumes that imitate leading brands has more basic packaging, distributes in discount stores, does not advertise, and uses low prices. Although the two perfume brands may cost an identical amount to make, the imitator would spend only a fraction as much on packaging.

How does the package interrelate with other marketing variables?

Criticisms of Packaging

The packaging practices of some industries and firms have been heavily criticized and regulated in recent years because of their impact (or potential impact) on the environment and scarce resources, high expenditures on packaging, questions about the honesty of labels and the confusion caused by inconsistent designations of package sizes (e.g., large, family, super), and critics' perception of inadequate package safety.

Packaging is faulted for waste, misleading labels, etc.

[27] See Barry Berman and Joel R. Evans, *Retail Management: A Strategic Approach,* 4th Edition (New York: Macmillan, 1989), pp. 200–202.
[28] See Richard T. Hise and James U. McNeal, "Effective Packaging Management," *Business Horizons,* Vol. 31 (January–February 1988), pp. 47–51.

Yet, consumers (as well as business) must bear part of the responsibility for the negative results of packaging. For example, throwaway bottles (highly preferred by consumers) use almost three times the energy of returnable bottles. And shoplifting annually adds to packaging costs by causing firms to add security tags and otherwise alter packages.

In planning their packaging programs, companies need to weigh the short-term and long-term benefits and costs of providing environmentally safer, less confusing, and more tamper-resistant packages. Generally, firms are responding quite positively to the criticisms raised here. These issues will be examined further in Chapter 23.

Summary

1. *To define and distinguish among branding terms and to examine the importance of branding* Branding is the procedure a firm follows in planning and marketing its brand(s). A brand is a name, term, design, or symbol (or combination of these) that identifies a good or service. A brand name is a word, letter (number), or group of words or letters (numbers) that can be spoken. A brand mark is a symbol, design, or distinctive coloring or lettering. A trade character is a personified brand mark. A trademark is a brand given legal protection.

In the United States, there are several hundred thousand brand names now circulating. Advertising expenditures on them are billions of dollars annually. Through strong brands, brand loyalty can be secured. Popular brands also speed up the acceptance of new products. Maintaining brand recognition is a top priority. Overall, branding benefits all parties: manufacturers, wholesalers and retailers, and consumers.

2. *To study the key branding decisions that must be made* Four fundamental decisions are necessary in branding. First, corporate symbols are determined and, if applicable, revised. The company's name, logo, and trade characters set its overall image. Second, a branding philosophy is set, which includes the proper use of manufacturer, dealer, and/or generic brands as well as family and/or individual branding. In addition, at this stage, a mixed-brand strategy, the battle of the brands, and brand extension are assessed.

Third, a brand name is chosen from one of several sources, including brand extension from existing names, dealer brands, and licensing a name from another company. With a new brand, the consumer's brand decision process moves from non-recognition to recognition to preference (dislike) to insistence (aversion). With a continuing name applied to a new product, the brand decision process would begin at recognition, preference (dislike), or insistence (aversion). Fourth, the use of trademarks is evaluated and planned.

3. *To define and distinguish among packaging terms and to examine the importance of packaging* Packaging is the procedure a firm follows in planning and marketing product package(s). A package consists of a physical container, label, and inserts. Today packaging is an integral part of a firm's new-product planning strategy.

$75 billion is spent annually on packaging. Package redesign can be quite expensive. Wholesaler, retailer, and final consumer needs must be taken into consideration. Errors can be quite costly.

4. *To study the basic functions of packaging, key factors in packaging decisions, and criticisms of packaging* There are six basic packaging functions: containment and protection, usage, communication, market segmentation, channel cooperation, and new-product planning.

Packaging decisions involve image; family packaging; standardization; package costs; packaging materials and innovativeness; package features; package size(s), color(s), and shape(s); the label and package inserts; multiple packaging; individual wrapping; preprinted prices and inventory codes (such as the Universal Product Code); and integration with the marketing plan.

Packaging has been criticized on the basis of environmental, safety, and other issues. Both business and consumers must assume some responsibility for unsatisfactory packaging practices.

Key Terms

brand (p. 320)
package (p. 320)
branding (p. 320)
brand name (p. 320)
brand mark (p. 320)
trade character (p. 320)
trademark (p. 320)
brand image (p. 323)

corporate symbols (p. 324)
manufacturer (national)
  brands (p. 326)
dealer (private) brands (p. 326)
generic brands (p. 327)
mixed-brand strategy (p. 327)
battle of the brands (p. 327)
family (blanket) branding (p. 328)

brand extension (p. 329)
individual (multiple) branding
  (p. 330)
licensing agreement (p. 331)
brand decision process (p. 331)
packaging (p. 334)
packaging functions (p. 335)
Universal Product Code (UPC)
  (p. 341)

Review Questions

1. Differentiate among these terms: brand mark, trade character, brand name, and trademark.
2. Why do manufacturer brands have such a large percentage of sales in so many product categories? Will private brands and generic brands eventually displace manufacturer brands? Explain your answer.
3. Contrast a mixed-brand strategy with the battle of the brands.
4. Under what circumstances is brand extension most effective?

5. "Even though a company wants a brand to be popular, it must not be used to describe an entire product category." Explain this.
6. What are the three components of a package?
7. Describe the six major functions of packaging.
8. Compare family packaging and standardized packaging.
9. What are the major goals of multiple packaging? The major problem?
10. How does the Universal Product Code (UPC) assist retailers?

Discussion Questions

1. The Michigan Seamless Tube Company changed its name to Quanex (an abbreviation for quality and nexus). Why do you think this name change was necessary? Do you think this is a good name? Explain your answer.
2. Present two unsuccessful examples of brand extension. Discuss why brand extension did not work.
3. How would you protect Xerox or Levi's from losing its trademark status? What would you recommend if either brand does become a generic term?

4. Evaluate the recent package redesigns of three products. Base your analysis on several specific concepts covered in this chapter.
5. Comment on this statement: "In planning their packaging programs, companies need to weigh the short-term and long-term benefits and costs of providing environmentally safer, less confusing, and more tamper-resistant packages."

◄ CASE 1 ►

The Battle of the Brands in the Prescription Drug Market*

In 1984, the makers of generic brands of prescription drugs received a significant marketing victory when the U.S. Congress simplified the Food and

* The data in this case are drawn from Reginald Rhein, Joseph Weber, and Michael Oneal, "Drugs: What's in a Name Brand? Less and Less," *Business Week* (December 5, 1988), pp. 172, 176.

Drug Administration's process for approving the production and marketing of generics. Since then, generic drugs have gained market share at the expense of manufacturer brands. In 1988, the sales of generic pharmaceuticals totaled $6.8 billion—29 per cent of the total prescription drug market.

This battle has traditional prescription-drug manufacturers concerned—and vulnerable. Their profit margins have been as high as 40 per cent of sales, versus the 5 to 6 per cent margins used by generics makers. The traditional firms argue that they need high margins to cover the millions of dollars used to finance the research and development of new products. In contrast, generics manufacturers have virtually no research and development costs; they basically copy the formulas of branded drugs after their patents expire.

These are some reasons why the sales of generic pharmaceuticals are expected to keep booming:

- As of June 1990, patents will expire on 80 per cent of the best-selling U.S. prescription drugs in 1988; and many other best-sellers will lose their patents within the next few years. In each case, it will then be legal for any firm to make low-priced generic equivalents.

- The Medicare Catastrophic Coverage Act of 1988 becomes effective in 1991. This act requires all U.S. pharmacies to dispense generic prescription drugs to medicare patients unless a physician insists on a manufacturer's brand.

- The West German government is close to passing a health reform bill that would base insurance reimbursements for most prescription drugs on the prices of generics. If this bill is enacted, U.S. makers of branded prescription drugs fear that when trade barriers are eliminated within European Community countries in 1992, the prices of all branded prescription drugs sold in Europe may fall to the level of the lowest-priced generic equivalents.

In the past, most makers of generic pharmaceuticals were small firms (many with annual sales of less than $1 million per year). But now, in self-defense, many large traditional manufacturers are getting into the production and marketing of generics. Among the latter are Warner-Lambert, Ciba-Geigy, American Cyanamid, and American Home Products. Yet, as a Ciba-Geigy executive noted, "as generics come of age and play an increasing role in the marketplace, there's always the opportunity of becoming the leading generic against your own brand."

One approach that holds great promise for prescription-drug patent holders is for them to produce and market generic equivalents of their own products through company subsidiaries prior to patent expiration. For example, Ciba-Geigy is considering letting its Cord Laboratories' subsidiary reformulate and market several major prescription drugs in generic form, even though the drugs are still under patent protection. Because it takes the Food and Drug Administration three years to approve a reformulated drug, this strategy would give Cord a three-year lead-time advantage over competitors. The president of American Cyanamid's Lederle Division thinks that such a strategy will become popular at that firm because generics "represent a solid business" for Cyanamid. "That it produces lower margins" than drugs still on patent "doesn't bother us."

At the same time, generic drug makers are being equally aggressive. Some are increasing their research expenditures; others are forming joint ventures with research institutions to develop new drug products or to obtain licenses to sell new drugs. For example, Bolar Pharmaceuticals and Mylan Laboratories—two major generic drug manufacturers—have jointly acquired Somerset Pharmaceuticals, a research company with exclusive marketing rights to a drug sold in Europe for the treatment of Parkinson's disease.

QUESTIONS

1. Contrast the marketing of generic-branded food products with the marketing of generic prescription drugs.

2. As a maker of branded prescription drugs, how would you attempt to win the marketing battle of the brands? As a maker of generic pharmaceuticals, how would you attempt to win?

3. Evaluate Ciba-Geigy's proposed strategy of giving its Cord Laboratories' division a head start in marketing products that are soon to lose their patents.

4. As a maker of branded prescription drugs, would you license the names of your drugs to other firms? Why or why not?

CASE 2

Can Consumer Acceptance Be Achieved for Nonrefrigerated Milk?[†]

Unlike conventional milk that must be refrigerated and has a very short shelf life, Ultra High Temperature (UHT) milk that is packaged in special containers can stay fresh for six months without refrigeration. Yet, despite its long life and ease of storing, Americans have thus far largely ignored UHT milk. At present, it has a market share of less than 1/2 of 1 per cent of the $24 billion U.S. annual milk market; and it has been an unprofitable product for its producers, who want to increase their market share to 2 per cent.

In processing, UHT milk is heated to between 275 and 300 degrees Fahrenheit for two to eight seconds; pasteurized milk is heated to 161 degrees for 16 seconds. The high temperatures used in UHT processing kill all bacteria. Unlike regular pasteurized milk, which is packaged in glass or paper-based containers, UHT milk is placed in aseptic containers (although these are quart-sized, they are similar to those used to package single-servings of fruit and vegetable juices). The inside surfaces of these cardboard aseptic containers are sterilized and then hermetically sealed to guard against bacteria. Lastly, UHT milk is packaged in the most sterile environment possible.

Food scientists are seeking ways to further extend the shelf life of UHT milk and improve its taste. Although UHT milk is currently safe for consumption beyond a six-month period, a gel or curd forms on its surface after six months: "It's clear that consumers won't accept UHT milk with the curd on it because they assume it has gone bad, even though it hasn't." Research to extend the milk's shelf life is being funded by U.S. dairy farmers who are required to pay 15 cents to the National Dairy Board for every 100 pounds of milk they produce.

UHT milk is more expensive than conventional pasteurized milk—for example, about $1.07 per quart for UHT milk and $0.65 per quart for regular milk in New York. However, it has advantages in terms of lower storage costs, greater flexibility in usage and storage, and lower transportation costs (as refrigerated transportation vehicles are not required). For example, supermarkets do not have to store the product in a refrigerated unit and parents can place it in a child's lunch box without worrying about spoilage. Nonetheless, despite the fact that UHT milk has been marketed by a major producer for nearly 40 years, sales remain disappointing. Moreover, only three U.S. producers now package UHT milk: Dairyman Inc. (based in Louisville, Kentucky), Real Fresh (based in Visalia, California), and Gossner Foods (based in Logan, Utah).

The makers of UHT milk want to increase consumption in the general marketplace as well as in specialty markets—such as campers, the airline industry, and government food assistance programs. But their major difficulty is in overcoming consumer resistance to a nonrefrigerated milk product. Says a spokesperson for a cooperative milk producer, "our biggest obstacle has been the fact that consumers have become so regimented to buying milk out of the refrigerated case that it's extremely difficult to get them to think differently." Today most of the sales of UHT milk are to markets that are either far from milk production or where refrigeration is not possible (such as military bases and schools in the Pacific).

[†] The data in this case are drawn from Calvin Sims, "Building a Wider Market for Unrefrigerated Milk," *New York Times* (March 9, 1988), p. D6.

QUESTIONS

1. Evaluate UHT milk from the perspective of the six basic packaging functions described in this chapter.
2. Should UHT milk be packaged like conventional pasteurized milk in quart and half-gallon containers or in single-serving packages and multiple packaging arrangements similar to fruit and vegetable juices and drinks? Explain your answer.
3. What additional market segments should UHT milk producers pursue to increase their market penetration? Explain your choice of segments.
4. Develop a marketing strategy to improve overall consumer perceptions (and purchases) of UHT milk.

part 3 CASE

Winning by Being the First to Market? Or Second?*

Introduction

A pioneering company is one that is the first to create a previously nonexistent market. Such companies build entirely new product categories. Well-known examples include Apple (personal computer), Dole (fruit juice bars), 3M (Post-it note pads), Federal Express (overnight delivery), Walt Disney (theme parks), BirdsEye (frozen vegetables), and McDonald's (fast food). Many pioneering companies achieve lasting fortune and fame.

There is also another, often equally successful road, one that is used much more commonly, but with less fanfare: a prudent follower strategy. IBM in personal computers, Texas Instruments in transistors, Matsushita in video recorders, UPS in overnight delivery, Domino's in pizza, and Pepsi in colas, all entered and prospered as prudent followers. Given the enormous investment in creating new product categories, many large companies often wait for other companies to open up the market and then enter with the expectation that their financial, marketing, and technological resources will enable them to dominate the pioneer. This is especially so in low-technology areas. It must also be realized that a company can be a successful follower in another category.

A problem arises, however, when companies try to answer the question: "Is a follower strategy better than a pioneering strategy for *my* firm?"

* Adapted by the authors from Daniel W. Haines, Rajan Chandran, and Arvind Parkhe, "Winning by Being the First to Market . . . Or Second?" *Journal of Consumer Marketing*, Vol. 6 (Winter 1989), pp. 63-69. Reprinted by permission.

Advantages of a Pioneering Strategy

Pioneering is associated with many advantages.

An Entrenched Position in Consumers' Minds

Consumers are more receptive to the advertising messages of a new product if they are received in the absence of competing messages from rival brands. For example, Perrier was able to establish itself as the leader in the premium bottled water market relatively easily given the fact that there was no competition to contend with. Consumers will generally try a pioneering brand if it promises to meet an existing, unmet need or want.

Through consumption or experience, consumers acquire information about the brand, including their perceived satisfaction from its use. But consumers have no comparable experience with follow-on brands, and the satisfaction to be derived from these brands is still uncertain. The risk-averse nature of most consumers causes them to avoid the perhaps lower satisfaction of the follower brands. In other words, the pioneering brand usually becomes the gold standard.

Even if the consumer is exposed to an advertising message for a newer brand, such information does not readily substitute for experience. And even if a follower brand has the same expected level of satisfaction as the pioneer, most consumers will choose the latter if they have had positive experiences with it, because doing so reduces their risk. This reluctance to switch results in a positive advantage to the first entrant into a market.

Higher Thresholds for Later Entrants

To overcome the advantage of the market pioneer and achieve an equal or better share, later entrants are forced to provide noticeable product advantages, more advertising and distribution support, and a reduced risk of initial trial. Kimberly-Clark had to do all these to overcome P&G's advantage with its pioneering Pampers brand. Product advantages can be intangible, in which case an even greater amount of advertising dollars are required to establish the product in the consumer's mind.

Followers must sometimes be satisfied with a diverse or geographically dispersed segment of potential consumers, making for difficult and expensive advertising and distribution. Reducing the risk of initial trial may require couponing, free samples, or other consumer or trade deals, all of which pose additional financial hurdles to successful entry.

Long-Term Market Share Advantages

There is generally a significant market share penalty for late entry. For example, one study led to the following statistics:[1]

	Average Market Share
Pioneer firm	29 per cent
Early follower firms	17 per cent
Late entrant firms	12 per cent

That is, pioneers generally had a sustained market share advantage over other firms in a category. Similar results were obtained in another study, which reported that, other things being equal, relative market share declines with the order of brand entry.[2] And if the later entrants' positioning or advertising support are inferior to the pioneer's, their market shares will be even lower.

Cost and Experience Barriers for Later Entrants

Market leadership is usually best seized at the outset, when experience quickly doubles and costs fall rapidly (e.g., Texas Instruments in calculators). Later, as accumulated industry volume increases and competition enters, costs fall much more slowly. The pioneering firm can thus build a significant cost advantage and gain lasting price leadership.

The pioneering firm can further strengthen its position and discourage competitive entries by increasing advertising and cutting prices. And being the first entrant, a pioneer can pre-empt the most lucrative product positioning and market segments.

Image/Reputation Benefits

Pioneering can firmly establish a brand name in the public's mind and associate it with innovative, state-of-the-art products (e.g., Sony through its Walkman and other such products). The company can even become synonymous with the product category (e.g., Xerox copiers).

This is a significant advantage for the pioneering firm, because it allows that firm to maintain a stable or growing market position while spending fewer advertising dollars per unit sold. When this "image advantage" (often expressed as consumer brand loyalty) exists on a large scale, later entrants may find it extremely difficult, even with heavy advertising expenditures, to challenge the pioneer's position.

Disadvantages of a Pioneering Strategy

Pioneering can be risky in terms of proper identification of market demand and choice of appropriate technology to meet that demand.

Seemingly promising markets can quickly disappear, along with invested cash, management time, and other corporate resources. The demand for CB radios disappeared in this manner, and Exxon suffered huge losses when, after investing hundreds of millions of dollars in shale oil technology, it saw the market vanish. The technology or product design that eventually will dominate the market is often unclear during the embryonic stage of development. The pioneer's entry may fail in the marketplace but provide valuable les-

[1] William T. Robinson, "Sources of Market Pioneer Advantages in Consumer and Industrial Goods Industries," paper presented at the Business Strategy and Life Cycle Concept workshop of the Marketing Science Institute (Boston: December 12, 1985).
[2] Glen L. Urban, Theresa Carter, Steven Gaskin, and Zofia Mucha, "Market Share Rewards to Pioneering Brands: An Empirical Analysis and Strategic Implications," *Management Science*, Vol. 32 (June 1986), pp. 645-659.

sons to later entrants. And the pioneer must always educate and persuade first-time buyers to purchase— usually an expensive proposition.

The technological risk in pioneering arises from the fact that several technologies are normally vying for supremacy during a product's infancy. One of these technologies usually will win out over the others and become the industry standard. This was clearly the case in the VCR market, where VHS technology got the nod over Beta technology. A pioneering firm that championed a side-tracked technology is likely to lose its investment.

Advantages of a Follower Strategy

The advantages of a prudent follower strategy center on the lower costs and risks which it entails.

Knowing the Market Is Really There

Some firms appear to operate under the premise that it is best to conserve their resources and keep their options open while allowing a competitor to take the expensive pioneering plunge. The follower's entry costs and risk of failure are reduced because the pioneer has demonstrated the viability of the market. The pioneer in effect sells the attractiveness and potential profitability of the market to those who follow.

Many firms hold back until the merits of the market become clearer. For example, IBM entered mainframe computers after Sperry, and personal computers after Apple, but built commanding leads over both groundbreaking pioneers. Coca-Cola initially held back in the caffeine-free, juice-added, and cherry-flavored segments of the cola market but now has dominant shares in all three segments.

Learning from the Pioneer's Experience

A pioneering firm's trials and tribulations, as it sails in uncharted waters, may teach valuable lessons to subsequent entrants.

For instance, RCA committed early to color TV. Potential followers observed from RCA's experience that demand for color TV sets was some years away and avoided premature entry. Learning can take place in a variety of ways. Companies often discover what they *should do* watching others demonstrate what they should *not* do.

Introducing Superior Manufacturing Techniques

A firm with experience in allied areas, or the ability to capitalize on forward or backward integration, may be able to enter the market soon after the pioneer and dominate the market with low-cost production and aggressive pricing. A follower can utilize newer manufacturing technologies to leapfrog over a pioneer in terms of manufacturing costs. It may also have access to the accumulated knowledge and experience of customers and suppliers of the pioneering firm.

For example, Texas Instruments was able to swamp Bowmar, the pioneer in hand-held calculators, by capitalizing on superior manufacturing technologies, forward integration, and cost efficiencies that were not available to Bowmar.

Introducing Products with Superior Design Attributes

If the pioneering firm correctly understands the needs of the market *and* designs its products to meet them, then it probably has pre-empted the "best positioning." Later entrants will then have lower market shares because, if they want to differentiate, they must adopt "inferior positions." If, however, market needs and the pioneering firm's product do not fit hand-in-glove, then the next entrant can gain an immediate advantage by redesigning its product attributes to better satisfy these current consumer needs (e.g., Matsushita in video recorders).

For instance, one segment of the U.S. automobile market was dominated by small-car pioneer Volkswagen (VW). Toyota knew that success in this market hinged on challenging and displacing VW. Japanese producers typically study the most successful competitor firm to learn the reasons for its success; accordingly, Toyota commissioned an American marketing research firm to interview VW owners and determine what they liked and disliked about their cars. VW owners wished that their cars heated up better in the winter, had more room in the back seat, and had more attractive interiors. The Japanese firm then went to the drawing board and designed small cars that offered all the perceived advantages of the VW with none of the perceived disadvantages. To clinch small-car segment leadership, Toyota put a lower price tag on its cars, spent more on advertising, and gave larger commissions to its dealers than did VW. Not surprisingly, Toyota moved into the top spot at VW's expense.

Fine-Tuning the Marketing Mix

A follower firm may succeed by modifying the marketing mix — product, price, distribution, and promotion — to wean customers away from the pioneer. Bartles and Jaymes (B&J) wine coolers provide a good example.

In 1981, California Cooler owned 75 per cent of the wine cooler market. The introduction of B&J caused California Cooler to lose 20 share points in just one year, and in 1986 B&J moved into the top position. It did this by identifying a discontinuity between the market as it was and as it might be. Instead of beer-type packaging, B&J designed a more sophisticated, wine-type package. It also removed all the fruit sediment and made the product look and taste more like wine. By maintaining the same price, it eliminated the chance that consumers might treat B&J as a premium niche product. These creative modifications gave the new entrant a more sophisticated look and positioning which appealed to a larger target audience, propelling B&J into market leadership. In short, a follower with creative imagination can modify a pioneer's idea to build a more profitable business.

Disadvantages of a Follower Strategy

A follower may find that the pioneer's position in the market is unassailable, even if the follower spends heavily on R&D, product improvement, and marketing. In some growth markets, later entrants have never been able to capture more than a fraction of the initial leader's position.

In low-calorie beers, for example, even a world-class company like Anheuser-Busch has been unable to crack Miller Lite's pioneering position, even with massive advertising expenditures to support its entries. Similarly, powerful later entrants with expertise in closely allied areas — such as Burger King — have been unable to make significant inroads in the fast-food market pioneered by McDonald's.

Considerations in Choosing a Strategy

It has been shown that both pioneering and follower strategies can lead to success (or failure). What are some considerations in choosing between these two strategies? We will consider both general and firm-specific criteria.

General Criteria

Perhaps the most important consideration in deciding to be a pioneer in a product category is a strong and unshakable conviction that there is an unmet want or need *and* that the potential size of the market justifies the costs and risks required to satisfy that need. Frederick Smith of Federal Express had such an unshakable conviction about overnight delivery, as did Art Fry of 3M about "Post-it" note pads.

Recent studies have revealed some common elements of pioneering success. These include superior product quality, superior service, lower direct costs, and lower selling prices, all relative to actual and potential competition. A firm incapable of exploiting these key variables technologically, financially, and managerially should not consider pioneering.

In some industries, there may be distinct disadvantages to pioneering. In electronics, for example, it seems better to wait and undercut pioneering entrants on capabilities and/or costs. Those who pioneer in this industry must bear the burden of having later entrants leapfrog one or more cycles of high-technology product and manufacturing research and development.

Firm-Specific Criteria

The choice between pioneering and following also depends on two other factors: sustainability of product/market leadership positions and institutionalization of first-mover advantages.

Pioneering is favored if product/market leadership can be sustained, either because competitors cannot easily duplicate the product or because the firm can continue to innovate as fast or faster than any competitor. Of course, the rate of technology diffusion depends on the industry. A firm can partially control (slow down) the rate of technology diffusion by means of (1) patents, (2) trade secrets, (3) in-house development of product prototypes and production equipment, (4) vertical integration into competitor-sensitive areas, and (5) enlightened personnel policies and innovative reward systems. Pioneers must always strongly challenge patent infringement. Pioneers such as IBM, Michelin, P&G, DuPont, and Kodak are well-known for closely safeguarding their technology. It is equally important that pioneers present a moving target. Gillette has kept leadership in the low-technology shaving market with continual innovative product introductions and creative avoidance of cannibalization.

Another important factor in the decision to be first-in is the firm's skill in identifying the characteristics of those who are likely to be early adopters of the pioneering brand. Only if potential consumers' socioeconomic life-styles and their attitudinal and behavioral characteristics can be correctly identified can the firm efficiently and effectively target its communications to them.

Pioneering firms can influence the rate of adoption of an innovation by enhancing the benefits offered by the product, its compatibility with existing life-styles, and the ease with which potential users can find out about and try the product. To the extent that a firm is skillful at encouraging adoption by large numbers of consumers, pioneering is an attractive strategy.

Pioneering is strategically desirable also when simply being the first allows the market leader to define the rules of the game and establish sustainable competitive advantages. These advantages include (1) reputation for quality and service, which translates to long-term image benefits and brand loyalty; (2) preemptive position in attractive product or market segments, which may force competitors to settle for other, less desirable segments; (3) higher share of voice, which has a chicken-egg relationship with higher share of market; (4) freedom of choice in channel selection, which allows the first mover to pick the best brokers, distributors, and retailers; (5) greater cumulative production experience, which may result in a permanent cost advantage; and (6) de facto definition of category/standards against which later entrants are judged. Rather than relying solely on what may be short-lived superiority, many successful pioneers vigorously pursue these first-mover prerogatives to define the competitive rules of the game in their favor.

Following in the footsteps of a pioneer can be advantageous and profitable too. It must be borne in mind that the pioneer spent a great deal of money to educate consumers and create the market. With this already accomplished, the follower firm can now concentrate on allocating its funds to building consumer recognition for its brand. Through marketing research, the follower can identify weaknesses and gaps in the pioneer's product and marketing strategy. Coupling this with better environmental and competitive analysis enables the follower firm to fine-tune its product and marketing mix to ensure success. In some industries, it is relatively easy to be a follower, because there is no patent protection, capital requirements are small, and existing products are easily copied. In others, lengthy reverse R&D and product redesign are required, and a follower strategy may indeed be a risky proposition.

A follower firm must ensure that its decision is consistent with the skills and resources it can bring to bear. In the case of Bartles & Jaymes, cited earlier, Gallo successfully brought together the elements of product development, advertising, packaging, pricing, and distribution—areas in which the company was confident it possessed considerable strengths.

For followers, awareness of changing societal trends that impact on consumer behavior is important. An example is the impact of the fitness movement on food selection. Heinz's Weight Watchers, the pioneering brand, focused on a narrow segment: women who wanted to diet. Stouffer's Lean Cuisine, the current market leader, recognized that low-calorie meant more than just weight loss. To many people, weight maintenance and low-calorie food are means of taking control of one's diet—with its contribution to overall health and well-being—without compromising on taste or convenience. Thus, a better reading of an underlying societal trend permitted the follower to surpass the pioneer. Quick reaction time and good execution skills were both necessary elements of this successful follower strategy.

Conclusions

The appropriate choice of strategy depends fundamentally upon the industry's characteristics, the firm's specific skills and strengths, and the caliber of current and potential competition.

QUESTIONS

1. Describe the basic advantages and disadvantages of pioneering and follower product strategies.
2. Under what circumstances would you recommend a pioneering strategy? A follower strategy? Why?
3. For a pioneering company, what type of product management organization would be most appropriate? Explain your answer.
4. How would product positioning goals differ for pioneering products and later competitors?
5. Should a pioneering firm use all the steps in the new-product planning process? A follower firm? Explain your answers.
6. How should a pioneering firm define absolute new-product failure and relative new-product failure? A follower firm?
7. Recommend several ways for a pioneering firm to speed up the diffusion process.
8. Should a pioneering firm use a brand-extension strategy? Why or why not?

part 4
DISTRIBUTION PLANNING

Part 4 deals with the second major element of the marketing mix, distribution.

12 **An Overview of Distribution Planning and Physical Distribution** Here, we study distribution planning, which involves the physical movement and transfer of ownership of a product from producer to consumer. We explore the functions of distribution, types of channels, supplier/middleman contracts, channel cooperation and conflict, and the industrial channel. We also look at physical distribution, in particular transportation and inventory management considerations.

13 **Wholesaling** In this chapter, we examine wholesaling, which encompasses the buying or handling of merchandise and its subsequent resale to organizational users, retailers, and/or other wholesalers. We show the impact of wholesaling on the economy, its functions, and its relationships with suppliers and customers. We describe the major types of company-owned and independent wholesalers and note recent trends in wholesaling.

14 **Retailing** Here, we concentrate on retailing, which consists of those business activities involved with the sale of goods and services to the final consumer. We show the impact of retailing on the economy, its functions in distribution, and its relationship with suppliers. We categorize retailers by ownership, store strategy mix, and nonstore operations. We describe several retail planning considerations and note recent trends in retailing.

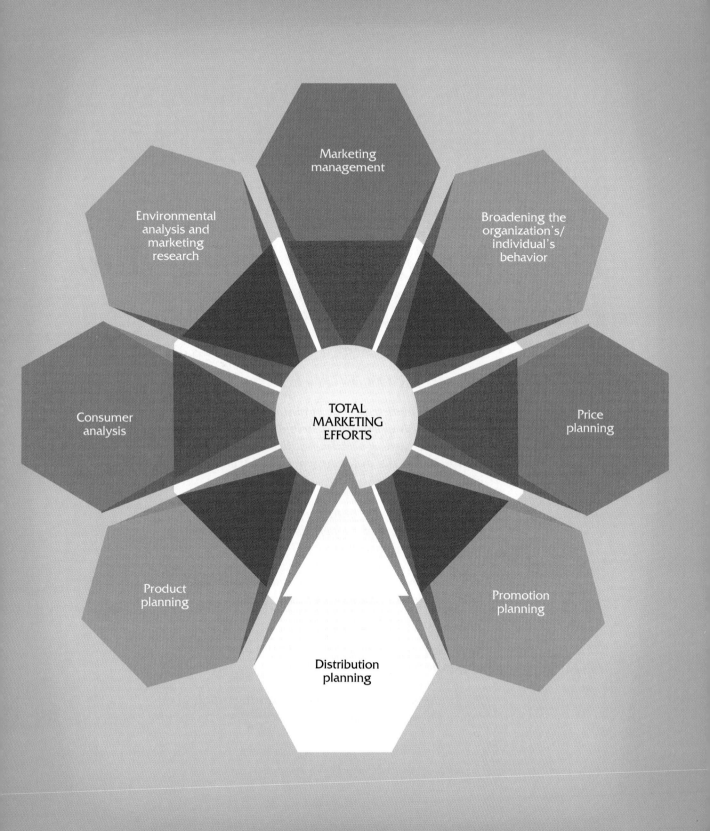

Marketing
management

Environmental
analysis and
marketing
research

Broadening the
organization's/
individual's
behavior

Consumer
analysis

TOTAL
MARKETING
EFFORTS

Price
planning

Product
planning

Promotion
planning

Distribution
planning

CHAPTER 12

An Overview of Distribution Planning and Physical Distribution

CHAPTER OBJECTIVES

1. To define distribution planning and to examine its importance, distribution functions, the factors used in selecting a distribution channel, and the different types of distribution channels

2. To describe the nature of supplier/middleman contracts, and cooperation and conflict in a channel of distribution

3. To show the special considerations relating to a distribution channel for industrial products

4. To define physical distribution and to demonstrate its importance

5. To discuss transportation alternatives and inventory management issues

Reprinted by permission.

A s a Yale undergraduate in 1965, Frederick W. Smith wrote an economics paper criticizing the slow, unreliable cargo services available then and proposing an independent air-service system for key documents, lightweight components, and spare parts. His professor, believing the idea futile, gave the paper a "C" grade.

Despite the lack of enthusiasm by his economics professor, in April 1973—after military service and a job selling corporate jets—Smith used his $4 million inheritance and $80 million contributed by private investors to launch his new air-delivery service. During the first month, the firm had 14 planes—yet it delivered only twenty packages. And business grew slowly for the first few years.

But today, Federal Express is the worldwide leader in air-express delivery and Frederick Smith has certainly demonstrated that he had an A+ idea. Federal Express dominates the overnight delivery market with a greater than 45 per cent market share in the United States. With its 1989 purchase of Flying Tigers, Federal Express has also increased its international presence. Its overall annual sales are several billion dollars. The firm handles a daily average of more than a million packages, serves all 335 major U.S. markets, offers guaranteed service to more than 40,000 communities, and delivers in 110 countries.

Why has Federal Express done so well? Frederick Smith is credited with inventing the physical distribution system for managing overnight air-express mail and package delivery, and with satisfying customer desires for fast, reliable service of important documents.

Federal Express' physical distribution strategy is based upon a hub-and-spoke distribution network system and the use of computers. Its hub-and-spoke system uses Memphis, Tennessee; Newark, New Jersey; and Oakland, California, as regional distribution facilities (hubs) at which packages are consolidated from various locations around the United States and then sent to local airports (spokes) for final delivery. A hub-and-spoke distribution system allows small market areas to be efficiently served through the spokes yet allows mechanization and automation at the hubs. Computers are extensively utilized by Federal Express. Hand-held scanners are used by drivers to track pack-

age pickups, to route packages, and to help drivers spot slow-paying accounts. Computers are also used to re-sort packages for the correct region and city at the hubs.

The firm has been innovative in anticipating and being responsive to consumer needs: The rapid expansion of the service economy has increased the number of documents shipped as well as the number of high-value small packages. The development of just-in-time inventory systems (whereby firms seek to minimize their inventory on hand through more frequent ordering) makes next-morning delivery of vital parts more important. Business customers believe that overnight express packages and letters have a high impact on the receiver—by showing that the sender cares about customer service or is communicating an important message.

As an example of its customer-service efforts, Federal Express now warehouses parts for IBM workstations at its Memphis hub facilities. By relying on Federal Express for deliveries, IBM has been able to close many of its parts depots around the country without negatively affecting customer service levels.[1]

In this chapter, we will learn more about the decisions made in distribution planning and the activities involved in physical distribution. Transportation and customer-service issues form an integral part of our discussion.

---

[1] Larry Reibstein, "Federal Express Faces Challenges to Its Grip on Overnight Delivery," *Wall Street Journal* (January 8, 1988), pp. 1, 10; and Dean Foust et al., "Mr. Smith Goes Global," *Business Week* (February 13, 1989), pp. 66–72.

Overview

Distribution planning is systematic decision making regarding the physical movement of goods and services from producer to consumer as well as the related transfer of ownership (or rental) of them. It encompasses such diverse functions as transportation, inventory management, and customer transactions.

Distribution activities are carried out through a ***channel of distribution,*** which is comprised of all the organizations or people involved in the distribution process. Those who participate in the distribution process are known as ***channel members*** and may include manufacturers, service providers, wholesalers, retailers, marketing specialists, and/or consumers. When the term ***middlemen*** is used, it refers to wholesalers, retailers, and marketing specialists (such as transportation firms) that are acting in their roles as intermediaries between manufacturers/service providers and their consumers. A middleman is an "independent business concern that operates as a link between producers and ultimate consumers or industrial users."[2]

This chapter presents an in-depth overview of distribution planning and examines the role of physical distribution. Chapter 13 discusses wholesaling's part in the distribution process. Chapter 14 covers the area of retailing.

Distribution Planning

A channel of distribution can be simple or complex. It can be based on a verbal agreement between a small manufacturer and a local retailer or require detailed written contracts among a number of manufacturers, wholesalers, and retailers. Many firms are interested in widespread distribution and need independent retailers to carry their merchandise and improve their cash flow. Others desire direct contact with consumers and do not use independent channel members. Industrial channels of distribution usually have more direct contact between manufacturers and customers than do final consumer channels.

The importance of distribution planning, the range of functions performed in the distribution process, the criteria to consider in selecting a channel of distribution, supplier/middleman contracts, channel cooperation and conflict, and the industrial channel of distribution are discussed next.

The Importance of Distribution Planning

Distribution decisions have a broad impact on the marketing program used by a firm. Because middlemen can provide a wide variety of marketing functions, the firm's marketing plan will differ if it sells direct rather than through intermediaries. Similarly, a decision to sell through retail stores rather than through the mail requires a different marketing orientation and tasks.

Often the choice of its channel of distribution is the most important one a firm will make. Good relations with wholesalers and retailers may take a long time to develop. Where established relationships exist among channel members, it may be hard for a new firm to enter. Furthermore, once a firm generates good channel relationships,

----

[2] Peter D. Bennett (Editor), *Dictionary of Marketing Terms* (Chicago: American Marketing Association, 1988), p. 123.

suitable new products are usually easier to place into distribution. Channel members need to plan and implement strategies in a coordinated manner. Strong distributors enhance manufacturers' marketing capabilities. Consumers like to purchase products in the same manner over time.

Costs as well as profits are affected by the selection of a particular type of distribution channel. A firm undertaking all functions must pay for them itself; in return, it reaps whatever profits are earned. A firm that uses independent wholesalers and retailers reduces its per-unit distribution costs; however, it also reduces its per-unit profits because these companies receive their share. With the latter type of channel, a firm's total profits would rise if middlemen help bring in significantly higher sales than it could accomplish itself.

Channel-of-distribution formats tend to be traditional in a number of product categories. For example, in the beverage and food industry, manufacturers normally sell through wholesalers that then deal with retailers. Automobile makers sell through franchised dealers. Mail-order firms line up product suppliers, print their catalogs, and sell directly to consumers. Often, firms must conform to the channel patterns in their industries.

In many instances, the size and nature of a firm's market are influenced by the location and number, geographic penetration, image, product selection, services provided, and overall marketing programs of the wholesalers, retailers, and marketing specialists with which it deals. In evaluating its distribution options, a firm should keep in mind that the more middlemen it employs, the less customer contact it achieves and the lower its control over a product's marketing mix.

These examples show the scope and importance of distribution planning:

▶ Sherwin-Williams, the world's largest paint producer, distributes its paints through more than 1,800 company-owned stores, as well as through independent paint stores, mass merchandisers, and wholesale distributors. It also employs a direct sales force for some industrial markets. The firm's retail stores operate in a very fragmented market with many competitors, while its direct sales force faces only a handful of major competitors for chemical coatings.[3] See Figure 12-1.

▶ Super Food Services is a wholesaler of food, health and beauty aids, general merchandise, and related nonfood items. It serves about 850 food stores in Michigan, Ohio, Kentucky, Indiana, and Florida. For those stores so desiring, Super Foods provides advertising, sales promotion, administrative, and other services. It operates seven warehouses, owns 500 trailer-trucks, and handles both manufacturer and dealer brands—representing over 18,000 different items.[4] Without Super Food, its retailers would see a steady stream of manufacturers' salespeople, receive small orders, and have much more complex inventory management.

▶ "Not everyone can whip down to New Orleans for a heap of cajun food or over to Memphis for a quick slab of ribs. And let's face it, most people just can't jet over to Boston for a clam bash. Some of the most popular restaurants are realizing this and have created what may be the ultimate in long-distance dining. K-Paul's, Rendezvous, and Legal Sea Foods are among a growing number of restaurants that ship their delicacies overnight to hungry customers across the country."[5]

▶ After Philip Morris acquired the Seven-Up Company in 1978, it promoted the

---

[3] *Sherwin-Williams Co. 1988 Annual Report.*
[4] *Super Food Services, Inc., 1988 Annual Report.*
[5] Cyndee Miller, "New Meaning for 'Box Lunch,'" *Marketing News* (August 15, 1988), p. 10.

FIGURE 12-1
**Sherwin-Williams: From
Manufacturing to Final
Consumers**
This photo depicts one of
the retail stores owned by
Sherwin-Williams, the
largest paint manufacturer
in the world.
Reprinted by permission.

soda's unique and healthful (no caffeine) attributes and sales rose. But this upturn was short-lived. Distributors became dissatisfied, because Seven-Up was too slow in matching competitors' price cuts and did not provide sufficient marketing and advertising support. The distributors were also loyal to Coke and Pepsi, and discouraged Seven-Up from introducing cola products. When it did, Like caffeine-free cola failed. Finally, in 1986, Philip Morris sold Seven-Up to Hicks & Haas, owner of Dr Pepper and A&W root beer.[6]

Channel Functions and the Role of Middlemen

Middlemen can perform
channel functions *and
reduce costs, provide
expertise, open markets,
and lower risks.*

For the great majority of goods and services, the ***channel functions*** shown in Figure 12-2 and described below must be undertaken. These functions must be completed by some member of the distribution channel and responsibility for them assigned.

Wholesalers and retailers can play a vital role in marketing research. Due to their closeness to the market, they have good insights into the characteristics and needs of customers.

In buying merchandise, middlemen sometimes pay when items are received; at other times, they accept items on consignment and do not pay for them until after a sale has been made. Furthermore, purchase terms may range from net cash (payment due immediately) to net sixty days (payment not due for sixty days) or longer. When middlemen do not pay manufacturers for merchandise until after resale, the manufactur-

---

[6] "Weak Bottler Ties Hurt 7-Up in Fight for Share," *New York Times* (January 20, 1986), pp. D1, D3; and Francis C. Brown III, "Seven-Up's Harford Courts His Bottlers," *Wall Street Journal* (April 16, 1987), p. 35.

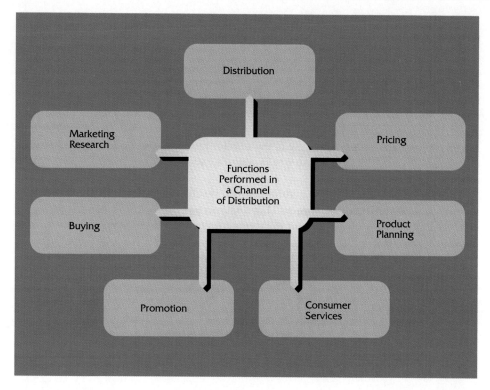

FIGURE 12-2
Channel Functions

ers risk poor cash flow, high merchandise returns, product obsolescence, spoilage, multiple transactions with wholesalers and retailers, and potentially low customer sales.

In assigning promotion responsibility, manufacturers usually take care of national advertising. Wholesalers help coordinate local promotion among retailers, and sometimes motivate and train retailer sales staffs. Retailers undertake local advertising, personal selling, and special events.

Consumer services include delivery, credit, in-home purchases, warranties and guarantees, and return policies. Again, these services can be provided by one channel member or a combination of channel members.

Middlemen can contribute to product planning in several ways. They often provide advice on new and existing products. Test marketing requires their cooperation. And middlemen can be quite helpful in properly positioning products against competitors and suggesting which products to delete.

Wholesalers and retailers usually have strong input into pricing decisions. They stipulate their required markups and generally prefer to price mark merchandise (or to specify how it should be marked). Court decisions have restricted manufacturers' ability to control final prices. Therefore, middlemen have great flexibility in setting final prices.

Distribution incorporates three major factors: transporting, inventory management, and customer contact. Somehow merchandise must be shipped from a manufacturer to its consumers; middlemen often provide this service. Because production capabilities and customer demand frequently differ, inventory levels need to be properly managed (and items may have to be stored in a warehouse before being sold). Last, the selling of goods and services to consumers may require a store or seller location, long

*The **sorting process** coordinates the goals of manufacturers and consumers.*

hours of operation, sales personnel, and store fixtures (such as cash registers and dressing rooms).

Middlemen can assist manufacturers in distribution by participating in the **sorting process,** which consists of accumulation, allocation, sorting, and assorting functions.[7] Accumulation is the wholesaler function of collecting small shipments from several manufacturers so they can be transported economically. Allocation is the wholesaler/ retailer function of distributing items to various consumer markets; it apportions goods. Sorting is the wholesaler/retailer function of separating merchandise into grades, colors, and sizes. Assorting is the retailer function of acquiring a broad range of merchandise so that the consumer is able to choose from different brands, price ranges, and models.

Through the sorting process, middlemen can resolve the differences in the goals of manufacturers and final consumers. For instance, manufacturers generally like to produce a limited variety of an item in large quantity and make as few transactions as possible to sell their entire output. However, final consumers like a variety of brands, colors, sizes, and qualities from which to choose and want to buy a small amount at a time. In addition, manufacturers prefer to sell merchandise from the factory, maintain 9-to-5 hours and spartan fixtures, and have a limited sales force. Yet, the final consumer wants to shop at a nearby location and be able to visit a store on weekends and evenings, appreciates store atmosphere, and frequently desires sales help. With the sorting process, wholesalers and retailers address these issues.

Selecting a Channel of Distribution

Channel choice depends on consumers, the company, the product, competition, existing channels, and legalities.

In selecting a distribution channel, a firm must consider several key factors:

▶ The consumer.
  Characteristics — number, concentration, average purchase size.
  Needs — store locations and hours, assortment, sales help, credit.
  Segments — size, purchase behavior.
▶ The company.
  Goals — control, sales, profit, timing.
  Resources — level, flexibility, service needs.
  Expertise — functions, specialization, efficiency.
  Experience — distribution methods, channel relationships.
▶ The product.
  Value — price per unit.
  Complexity — technical nature.
  Perishability — shelf life, frequency of shipments.
  Bulk — weight per unit, divisibility.
▶ The competition.
  Characteristics — number, concentration, assortment, customers.
  Tactics — distribution methods, channel relationships.
▶ Distribution channels.
  Alternatives — direct, indirect.
  Characteristics — number, functions performed, tradition.
  Availability — exclusive arrangements, territorial restrictions.
▶ Legalities — current laws, pending laws.

[7] Wroe Alderson, *Marketing Behavior and Executive Action* (Homewood, Ill.: Richard D. Irwin, 1957), Chapter 7.

While assessing these factors, the firm makes decisions about the type of channel employed, contractual arrangements or administered channels, channel length and width, channel intensity, and the use of dual channels.

There are two basic types of channel of distribution: direct and indirect. A ***direct channel of distribution*** involves the movement of goods and services from producer to consumer without the use of independent middlemen. An ***indirect channel of distribution*** involves the movement of goods and services from producer to independent middleman to consumer. Figure 12-3 shows the transactions in the sale of 200,000 men's umbrellas under direct and indirect channels. Figure 12-4 shows the most common indirect channels for final consumer and organizational consumer products.

*In a **direct channel,** the manufacturer performs all functions. An **indirect channel** uses independents.*

When a manufacturer or service provider sells to consumers through company-owned outlets (for example, Exxon-owned gas stations), this is a direct channel. With an indirect channel, a manufacturer may employ several layers of independent wholesalers (for example, regional, state, and local) and sell through different kinds of retailers (such as discount, department, and specialty stores).

A direct channel is most frequently used by firms that want to control their entire marketing program, desire close customer contact, and have limited target markets. An indirect channel is usually utilized by firms that want to enlarge their markets, increase sales volume, give up many distribution functions and costs, and are willing to relinquish some channel control and customer contact.

Because an indirect channel has independent members, a procedure for developing an overall marketing plan and assigning responsibilities is needed. With a ***contractual channel arrangement,*** all the terms regarding distribution functions, prices, and other factors are clearly specified in writing for each member. For example, a manufacturer and a retailer would sign an agreement stating delivery dates, payment terms, promotional support, and merchandise handling, marking, and displays. In an ***administered channel arrangement,*** the dominant firm in the distribution process plans the marketing program and itemizes and coordinates the responsibilities of each member. Depending on their relative strength, a manufacturer, wholesaler, or retailer could be the channel leader. For example, a manufacturer of a strong national brand would set its image, price range, and method of selling.

*A **contractual arrangement** or **administered arrangement** is used to set policy.*

In distribution, ***channel length*** refers to the levels of independent members along a channel. In Figure 12-3, *A* represents a short channel, while *B* shows a long channel. When a firm shortens its channel by acquiring a company at another stage, such as a manufacturer merging with a wholesaler, it is involved with ***vertical integration.*** This may enable a firm to be more self-sufficient, ensure supply, lower middleman costs, control channel members, and coordinate timing through the channel. Critics of vertical integration believe it limits competition, fosters inefficiency, and does not result in lower consumer prices.

ersion. ***Channel length*** *describes the levels of independents; it can be reduced by **vertical integration.***

Channel width refers to the number of independent members at any stage of distribution. A narrow channel is one in which the manufacturer sells through few wholesalers or retailers; in a wide channel, it sells through many. When a company wants to strengthen its position at its stage of the channel, it may engage in ***horizontal integration*** and acquire other businesses like itself. For example, one radio manufacturer could merge with another. Horizontal integration or expansion enables a company to increase its size and share of the market, improve bargaining power with outside channel members, enlarge its consumer market, and utilize mass media and distribution techniques more efficiently. Critics feel horizontal integration can greatly reduce competition and consumer choices.

Channel width *refers to the independents at one level. **Horizontal integration** adds strength.*

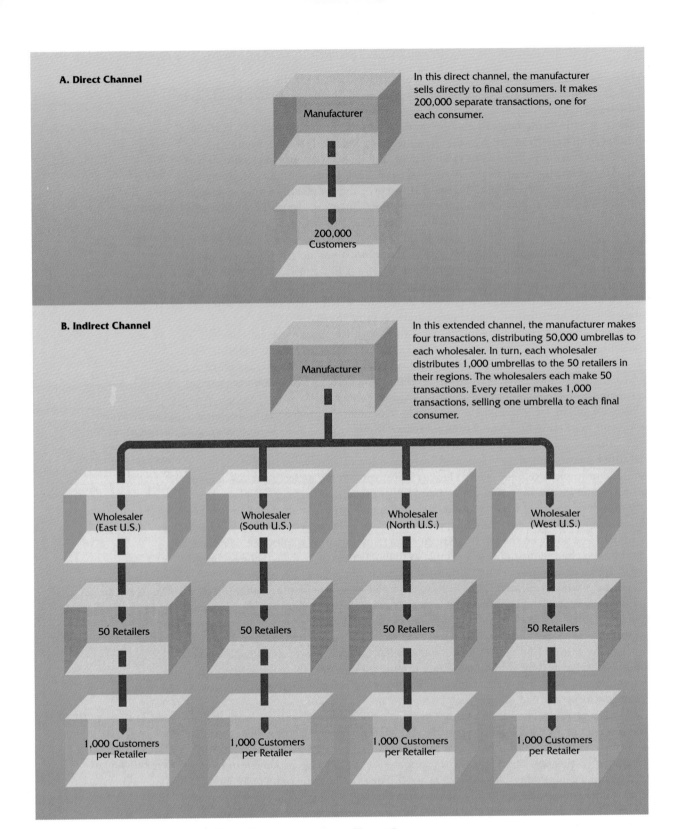

A. Direct Channel

Manufacturer

In this direct channel, the manufacturer sells directly to final consumers. It makes 200,000 separate transactions, one for each consumer.

200,000 Customers

B. Indirect Channel

Manufacturer

In this extended channel, the manufacturer makes four transactions, distributing 50,000 umbrellas to each wholesaler. In turn, each wholesaler distributes 1,000 umbrellas to the 50 retailers in their regions. The wholesalers each make 50 transactions. Every retailer makes 1,000 transactions, selling one umbrella to each final consumer.

Wholesaler (East U.S.)   Wholesaler (South U.S.)   Wholesaler (North U.S.)   Wholesaler (West U.S.)

50 Retailers   50 Retailers   50 Retailers   50 Retailers

1,000 Customers per Retailer   1,000 Customers per Retailer   1,000 Customers per Retailer   1,000 Customers per Retailer

FIGURE 12-3   **Transactions in a Direct Versus an Indirect Channel**

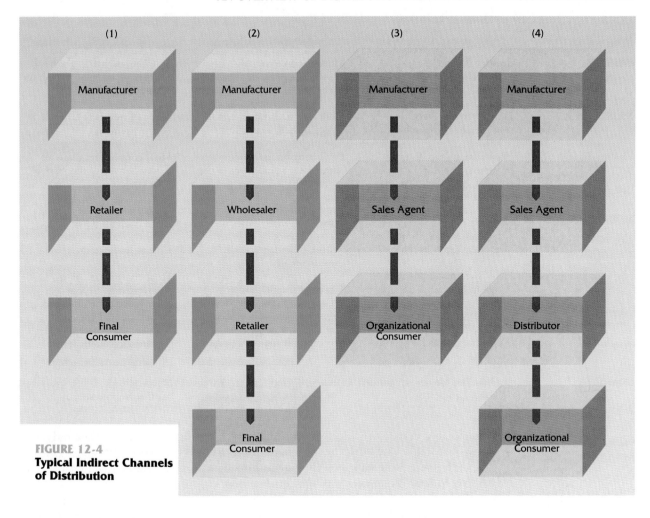

FIGURE 12-4
Typical Indirect Channels of Distribution

In choosing a distribution channel, a firm would determine the intensity of its channel coverage. Under *exclusive distribution,* a firm severely limits the number of middlemen (wholesalers and/or retailers) it utilizes in a geographic area, perhaps employing only one or two middlemen within a specific shopping district. It seeks a prestige image, channel control, and high profit margins and is willing to accept lower total sales than in another type of distribution. With *selective distribution,* a firm employs a moderate number of wholesalers and/or retailers. It tries to combine some channel control and a solid image with good sales volume and profits. In *intensive distribution,* a firm uses a large number of wholesalers and/or retailers. Its objectives are to obtain widespread market coverage, channel acceptance, and high sales volume and profits. Per-unit profits are low. It is a strategy aimed at the greatest number of consumers. See Table 12-1.

Some additional factors are important in selecting a channel. First, a firm may use a *dual channel of distribution,* whereby it appeals to different market segments or diversifies business by selling through two or more different channels.[8] For example, a

*Using **exclusive, selective,** or **intensive distribution** depends on objectives, middlemen, customers, and marketing.*

*A **dual channel** allows a company to reach different segments or to diversify.*

[8] See John A. Quelch, ''Why Not Exploit Dual Marketing?'' *Business Horizons,* Vol. 30 (January–February 1987), pp. 52–60.

TABLE 12-1 Intensity of Channel Coverage

Characteristics	Exclusive Distribution	Selective Distribution	Intensive Distribution
Objectives	Prestige image, channel control and loyalty, price stability and high profit margins	Moderate market coverage, solid image, some channel control and loyalty, good sales and profits	Widespread market coverage, channel acceptance, volume sales and profits
Middlemen	Few in number, well-established, reputable firms (outlets)	Moderate in number, well-established, better firms (outlets)	Many in number, all types of firms (outlets)
Customers	Final consumers: fewer in number, trend setters, willing to travel to store, brand loyal	Final consumers: moderate in number, brand conscious, somewhat willing to travel to store	Final consumers: many in number, convenience-oriented
	Organizational consumers: focus on major accounts, service expected from manufacturer	Organizational consumers: focus on many types of accounts, service expected from manufacturer or middleman	Organizational consumers: focus on all types of accounts, service expected from middleman
Marketing emphasis	Final consumers: personal selling, pleasant shopping conditions, good service	Final consumers: promotional mix, pleasant shopping conditions, good service	Final consumers: mass advertising, nearby location, items in stock
	Organizational consumers: availability, regular communications, superior service	Organizational consumers: availability, regular communications, superior service	Organizational consumers: availability, periodic communications, good service
Major disadvantage	Limited sales potential	May be hard to carve a niche	Limited channel control
Examples	Automobiles, designer clothes, capital equipment	Furniture, clothing, mechanics' tools	Household products, groceries, office supplies

manufacturer may use selective distribution for a prestige brand of watches and intensive distribution for a discount brand, or use both direct and indirect channels (such as an office-supplies company selling items directly to large business accounts and indirectly to final consumers through retail stores).

Second, a firm may move from exclusive to selective to intensive distribution as a product passes through its life cycle. However, it would be extremely difficult to go from intensive to selective to exclusive distribution. As an example, designer jeans moved rapidly from prestige stores to better stores to all types of outlets. This process would not have worked in reverse. Third, a company may distribute its products in a new way and achieve considerable success. L'eggs, a division of Hanes, revolutionized the sale of women's hosiery by placing the product in supermarkets.

Supplier/Middleman Contracts

Supplier/middleman contracts cover prices, sales conditions, territories, responsibilities, timing, and termination.

Supplier/middleman contracts focus on price policy, conditions of sale, territorial rights, the services/responsibility mix, and contract length and conditions of termination. The highlights of a basic supplier/middleman contract follow.

Price policy largely deals with the discounts provided to middlemen for performing trade functions, quantity purchases, and cash payments and with commission rates. Trade (functional) discounts are deductions from list prices given to wholesalers and retailers for performing storage, transportation, selling, and other activities. Quantity discounts are deductions for large-volume purchases. Cash discounts are deductions for immediate or early payment. Sometimes commissions are paid to middlemen (such as agents and brokers) for performing functions.

Conditions of sale cover price and quality guarantees, payment and shipping terms, reimbursement for unsaleable merchandise, and return allowances. Of particular importance is the guarantee against a price decline. It protects a wholesaler or retailer from paying a high price for an item that is then offered to other firms at a lower price; if prices are reduced, the original buyer receives a rebate so that the cost of its merchandise is similar to that of competitors. Otherwise it could not meet the prices competitors charge customers. Sometimes suppliers (manufacturers) employ full-line forcing, whereby middlemen are required to carry an entire line of products. This is legal as long as they are not prevented from purchasing competitive products from other suppliers.

Territorial rights outline the geographic areas (such as greater San Diego) in which channel intermediaries may operate and/or the target markets (such as small business accounts) that may be contacted by these firms. In some cases, they receive exclusive territories, such as McDonald's franchisees; in others, many competitive firms are given territorial rights for the same areas, such as retailers selling Sharp calculators.

The services/responsibility mix describes the role of the supplier and each middleman. It outlines such factors as who trains the sales force, delivers goods, writes advertising copy, stores inventory, and sets up displays; and it establishes performance standards. When included, a hold-harmless agreement protects middlemen in product-liability cases. Under it, manufacturers assume responsibility for legal suits arising from poor product design or negligence in production.

The length of the contract and conditions of termination protect a channel intermediary against a supplier (manufacturer) prematurely bypassing it after a territory has been built up. The supplier is protected by limiting the duration of the contract and specifying the factors leading to termination.

Not all relationships among channel members are this formal. Some firms operate with handshake agreements. However, without a contract, the danger exists that there will be misunderstandings regarding objectives, compensation, services to be provided, and the length of the agreement. The one constraint of a written contract may be its inflexibility under changing market conditions.

Channel Cooperation and Conflict

All the firms in a distribution channel have the same general goals: profitability, access to goods and services, efficiency in distribution, and customer loyalty. However, the way these and other objectives are accomplished frequently leads to differing views. For example: How are profits allocated along the channel? How can manufacturers sell products through many competing retailers and expect the retailers not to carry other brands? Who coordinates channel decisions? To whom are consumers loyal — manufacturers, wholesalers, or retailers?

Channel member goals need to be balanced.

It should be recognized that there are natural differences among the companies in a distribution channel by virtue of their positions in the channel, the functions performed, and the desire of every firm to maximize its own profits and control its strategy. A successful channel will be able to maximize cooperation and minimize conflict. Table 12-2 shows several potential causes of channel conflict. Table 12-3 shows how channel cooperation can reduce conflict.

In the past, manufacturers tended to dominate channels because they had national market coverage and recognition, and retailers were small and localized. Now, with the growth of large national (and international) retail chains, the purchase volume

Retailers are becoming more powerful and demanding.

You're the Marketer

How Can Honda's Distribution Network Become a Legend?

Despite the enormous success of Honda's Acura Legend—in terms of consumer sales and the car's reputation for luxury and quality—many Acura dealers have not been happy. Why? By the end of 1988, three years after Acuras were introduced into the U.S. market, nearly one-half of Acura dealers were losing money or making only a marginal profit. This is what happened.

Following the lead of luxury auto makers such as Mercedes-Benz and BMW, Honda decided to set up a separate dealer network to sell its Acura luxury autos. The separate dealer network enabled Honda to establish a distinctive upscale image for Acura, distinguish its Acura and Honda brands, and motivate Acura dealers to give proper emphasis to the new-car line.

However, the new Acura dealer network encountered unanticipated problems. Although used-car sales and car-maintenance and repair services typically produce one-half of car dealer

profits, Acura dealers did little business in these areas. They were unable to obtain a sufficient number of used cars because their models were too new. Likewise, Acuras were so new and so reliable (research studies show that Acura customers are more satisfied than customers of any other brand) that dealer service bays were frequently idle. As the general manager of an Acura dealership reported, "My service manager is the loneliest guy in the world." In addition, the separate Acura dealer network alienated many dealers who wanted to offer a better selection of brands to increase customer traffic.

In 1989, Honda planned to spend $60 million in advertising Acura models, an increase of 20 per cent from 1988. Acura accounted for two-thirds of Honda's total advertising budget, but only one-fifth of its unit sales.

As the vice-president of marketing for Acura, what would you do to improve the situation for your dealers?

SOURCE: Based on material in Stewart Toy, "This Isn't the Legend Acura Dealers Had in Mind," *Business Week* (November 28, 1988), pp. 106, 110.

accounted for by them, and the popularity of private-label merchandise, the balance of power has shifted somewhat toward retailers. As an example,

> It was called Project Nemo, and it was supposed to be Hasbro Inc.'s answer to Nintendo, the $100 home video-game system that has captivated kids for the past two years. Hasbro poured $20 million into it. Yet after one look at the Nemo player and game tapes, Toys "R" Us executives deemed it a dud. At $250 to $300 for the basic unit, they called Nemo too expensive — and not as exciting as Nintendo. The criticism from the world's largest toy retailer did not go unheeded. Hasbro canceled Nemo and took a $10 million pre-tax writeoff.[9]

If conflicts are not resolved cooperatively, they may lead to confrontations. Then a manufacturer may ship late, refuse to deal with certain middlemen, limit financing, withdraw promotional support, and use other tactics. Similarly, a wholesaler or retailer may make late payments, provide poor shelf space, refuse to carry items, return

[9] Amy Dunkin, Keith H. Hammonds, and Mark Maremont, "How Toys "R" Us Controls the Game Board," *Business Week* (December 19, 1988), pp. 58–60; and Brent H. Felgner, "Retailers Grab Power, Control Marketplace," *Marketing News* (January 16, 1989), pp. 1–2.

TABLE 12-2   Potential Causes of Channel Conflict

Factor	Manufacturer's Goal	Wholesaler's/Retailer's Goal
Pricing	To establish final price consistent with product image	To establish final price consistent with wholesaler's/retailer's image
Purchase terms	To ensure prompt, accurate payments and minimize discounts	To defer payments as long as possible and secure discounts
Shelf space	To obtain plentiful shelf space with good visibility in order to maximize brand sales	To allocate shelf space among many brands in order to maximize total product sales
Exclusivity	To hold down the number of competing brands each middleman stocks while selling through many middlemen	To hold down the number of competing wholesalers/retailers carrying the same brands while selling different brands itself
Delivery	To receive adequate notice before deliveries are required	To obtain quick service
Advertising support	To secure advertising support from middlemen	To secure advertising support from manufacturers
Profitability	To maintain adequate profit margins	To maintain adequate profit margins
Continuity	To receive orders on a regular basis	To receive shipments on a regular basis
Order size	To maximize order size	To have order size conform with consumer demand to minimize inventory investment
Assortment	To standardize production	To secure a full variety
Risk	To have middlemen assume risks	To have manufacturers assume risks
Branding	To sell products under the manufacturer's label	To sell products under dealer labels as well as manufacturer labels
Channel access	To be able to distribute items wherever desired by manufacturer	To carry only those items desired by middleman
Importance of account	To not allow any single middleman to dominate	To not allow any single manufacturer to dominate
Consumer loyalty	To have consumers loyal to the manufacturer	To have consumers loyal to the wholesaler or retailer
Channel control	To make the key channel decisions	To make the key channel decisions

TABLE 12-3   Methods of Channel Cooperation

Factor	Manufacturer's Action	Wholesaler's/Retailer's Action
New-product introduction	Thorough testing, adequate promotional support	Good shelf location and space, enthusiasm for product, assistance in test marketing
Delivery	Prompt filling of orders, adherence to scheduled dates	Proper time allowed for delivery, shipments immediately checked for accuracy
Marketing research	Data provided to wholesalers and retailers	Data provided to manufacturers
Pricing	Prices to middlemen enable them to achieve reasonable profits, wholesaler/retailer flexibility encouraged	Infrequent sales from regular prices, maintenance of proper image
Promotion	Training of wholesaler's/retailer's sales force, sales force incentives, development of national advertising campaign, cooperative advertising programs	Attractive in-store displays, knowledgeable salespeople, participation in cooperative programs
Financing	Liberal financial terms	Adherence to financial terms
Product quality	Product guarantees	Proper installation and servicing of products for customers
Channel control	Shared and specified decision making	Shared and specified decision making

IT'S IN THERE!™

It's causing a stir in *Bon Appetit* and *People.*
Spicing up interest in *Ladies' Home Journal* and *1001 Home Ideas.*
Whetting hearty appetites in *Sports Illustrated.*
And tempting the readers of *Sunset* and *Southern Living.*
It's the new print campaign for *Prego®* and *Prego Plus,®*
the spaghetti sauces with the homemade taste.
Beginning in October and continuing throughout the year,
the plan will generate and build awareness in these influential publications.
The kind of awareness that boosts sales.
The Beef & Onion ad we'll be featuring is the first
of six dramatic executions for Prego sauces.
Stock up on *Prego* and *Prego Plus,*
the spaghetti sauces that have it all.
Great taste. Great advertising support. And a consumer following
that will really get your sales and profits cooking.

PREGO & PREGO PLUS PRINT CAMPAIGN BREAKING IN OCTOBER & NOVEMBER

MAGAZINE	CIRCULATION	ISSUE DATE*	ON SALE DATE
Bon Appetit	1,300,887	October	September 25th
People	2,695,431	October 14th	October 7th
Sports Illustrated	1,312,500	October 14th	October 7th
Sunset	1,395,882	October	September 20th
Southern Living	2,253,569	October	September 25th
Ladies' Home Journal	5,058,538	November	October 15th
1,001 Home Ideas	1,546,497	November	October 15th

*See media flow chart for year long media plan.

IT'S IN THERE!™

Homemade taste. It's in there!™

FIGURE 12-5
A Pushing Strategy for Prego Spaghetti Sauce
Reprinted by permission.

many products, and apply other tactics. A channel cannot function well within a confrontational framework.

Following are some recent examples of channel conflict:

▶ Small publishers can no longer sell their books directly to B. Dalton Bookseller, the second-largest bookstore chain in the United States, with nearly 800 outlets. If a publisher's annual volume with the chain is less than $10,000 annually, it must "piggyback onto a larger publisher's distribution or work through a wholesaler. The effect on small publishers will be to reduce their chances of making the leap from obscurity to success."[10]

▶ Burger King franchise operators became so dissatisfied with their treatment from Pillsbury (their franchisor) that they thwarted Pillsbury's efforts to stop Grand Metropolitan PLC's (a British conglomerate) takeover of the entire company. According to three franchisees: "Burger King is a strong restaurant concept that has survived in spite of itself, in spite of bad promotions, poor marketing strategies, inconsistent operations, and shoddy management." "For years, Burger King has been under pressure from Pillsbury to produce profits at the expense of our own bottom lines." "I don't think Pillsbury ever had the long-term interests of Burger King in mind."[11]

▶ In a recent survey, 60 per cent of the responding supermarket executives reported that they are at most marginally satisfied with the quality of manufacturer-provided in-store displays. These are among the reasons for their displeasure: racks are often ineffective for inventory control; the displays use space poorly; the consumer is not

---

[10] Cynthia Crossen, "B. Dalton Plans to Shut Out Small Publishers," *Wall Street Journal* (April 22, 1988), p. 35.
[11] Eric N. Berg, "Burger King's Angry Franchisees," *New York Times* (November 14, 1988), pp. D1, D4.

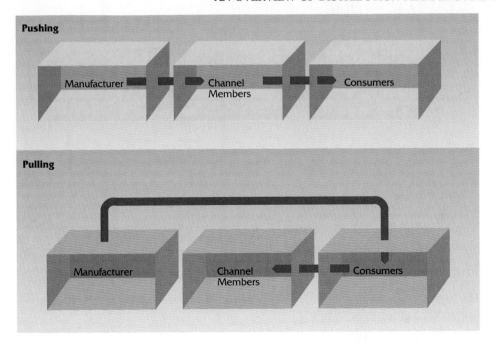

Pushing

Manufacturer → Channel Members → Consumers

Pulling

Manufacturer   Channel Members ← Consumers

FIGURE 12-6
Pushing Versus Pulling Strategies

aided in shopping; many racks are unattractive; and, many times, displays do not fit in with the stores' decor.[12]

A successful, existing manufacturer is frequently able to secure dealer support and enthusiasm when introducing a new product and in continuing existing ones. This occurs because the dealer knows the manufacturer's past track record, the type of promotional support that will be provided, and the manufacturer's reliability in future deliveries. Accordingly, a ***pushing strategy*** is used, whereby the various firms in a distribution channel cooperate in the marketing efforts for a product. Figure 12-5 shows a pushing strategy geared to retailers to alert them to a strong ad campaign for Prego.

Typically it is more difficult for a new manufacturer to break into an existing channel. Dealers will be unfamiliar with the company, be unable to gauge its sales potential, and wonder about its support and future deliveries. Because of these factors, the new firm would need to embark on a ***pulling strategy,*** whereby it first generates consumer demand and then secures dealer support. This requires heavy promotional expenses, paid entirely by the manufacturer; frequently it must offer dealers guarantees of minimum sales or profits (and make up any shortfalls). Figure 12-6 contrasts pushing and pulling strategies.[13]

In today's highly competitive environment, with so many new domestic and foreign products entering the marketplace each year, even market-leading firms must sometimes use pulling strategies to combat dealer resistance. They must convince their wholesalers and retailers that consumer demand exists for these products, before the middlemen agree to tie up scarce shelf space.

*In a **pushing strategy,** there is middleman cooperation. In **pulling,** a manufacturer generates demand before gaining channel support.*

---

[12] "Retailers Unhappy with Displays from Manufacturers," *Marketing News* (October 10, 1988), p. 21.

[13] See Alvin A. Achenbaum and F. Kent Mitchel, "Pulling Away from Push Marketing," *Harvard Business Review,* Vol. 65 (May–June 1987), pp. 38–40; and Robert J. Kopp and Stephen A. Greyser, "Packaged Goods Marketing — 'Pull' Companies Look to Improved 'Push,' " *Journal of Consumer Marketing,* Vol. 4 (Spring 1987), pp. 13–22.

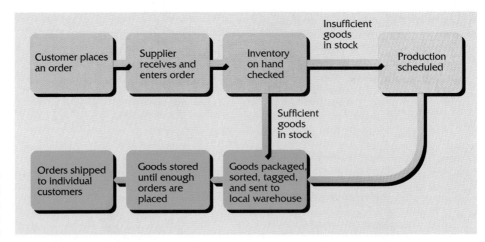

FIGURE 12-7
**Selected Physical
Distribution Activities
Involved in a Typical
Order Cycle**

The Industrial Channel of Distribution

*An industrial channel has
unique characteristics.*

The distribution channel for industrial products differs from that for consumer products in the following key ways:

1. Retailers are usually not utilized.
2. Direct channels are more readily used.
3. Transactions are fewer and orders are larger.
4. Specification selling is more prevalent.
5. Independent channel-member firms are more knowledgeable.
6. Team selling (two or more salespeople) may be necessary.
7. Distinct channel-member firms specialize in industrial products.
8. Leasing, rather then selling, may be required.
9. Customer information needs are more technical.

Physical Distribution

*Physical distribution
involves the location,
timing, and condition of
deliveries.*

Physical distribution encompasses the broad range of activities concerned with efficiently delivering raw materials, parts, semifinished items, and finished products to designated places, at designated times, and in proper condition. It may be undertaken by any member of a channel, from producer to consumer.

Physical distribution may involve such functions as customer service, warehousing, shipping, inventory control, private trucking fleet operations, packaging, receiving, materials handling, and plant, warehouse, and store location planning. The physical distribution activities involved in a typical *order cycle* — the period of time that spans a customer's placing an order and its receipt — are illustrated in Figure 12-7.

*An **order cycle** covers
many activities.*

Here is how an order cycle works at highly efficient The Limited, Inc., one of the world's leading apparel retailers:

> From point-of-sale computers, daily reports on what is selling well flow into headquarters of The Limited in Columbus, Ohio. To restock, the company sends orders by satellite to plants in the U.S., Hong Kong, South Korea, Singapore, and Sri Lanka. The goods are hustled back to Columbus from Hong Kong aboard a chartered Boeing 747 that makes

four flights a week. At a highly automated distribution center in Columbus, apparel is sorted, priced, and prepared for shipment—all within 48 hours. By truck and plane, the apparel moves out to The Limited's 3,200 stores, including Express and Victoria's Secret outlets. Within 60 days of the order, the apparel goes on sale. Most competitors still place orders six months or more in advance.[14]

The Importance of Physical Distribution

Physical distribution is important for a number of reasons: its costs, the value of customer service, and its relationship with other functional areas.

Costs

Physical distribution costs amount to 12 to 15 per cent of the U.S. GNP, with transportation (freight) accounting for over one-half of the total. To contain these costs, firms are working hard to improve efficiency. Today "the system is moving goods at lower cost, faster, and with fewer people" than a decade ago. As an example, because of improved transportation, companies have reduced the inventory levels they maintain by $100 billion, thus saving on other types of distribution costs (such as warehousing and interest expenses).[15]

Cost control is a major goal.

Distribution costs vary widely by industry and type of firm. At individual companies, total physical distribution costs depend on such factors as the nature of the business, the geographical area of operations, and the weight/value ratio of the products or materials involved. For instance, department stores and specialty stores spend about 2 per cent of sales on transportation from vendors and receiving, marking, storing, and distributing goods. Manufacturers spend about 9 per cent of sales on physical distribution activities. Printing and publishing firms, apparel manufacturers, and machinery manufacturers spend 4 to 5 per cent of sales on inbound and outbound transportation; petroleum refiners spend almost one-quarter of sales.[16]

It is essential for firms to identify the symptoms of a costly distribution system and strive to become more efficient. As an illustration, up to one-fifth of the perishable products carried by retail grocers, such as fish and dairy items, are lost to spoilage due to breakdowns in transportation or storage. To reduce losses, many grocers now insist on smaller, more frequent deliveries and are upgrading their own storage facilities. Table 12-4 shows many cost ramifications associated with poor distribution.

Customer Service

A major consideration in a firm's physical distribution program is the level of customer service it should provide. Decisions involve delivery frequency, speed, and consistency; emergency shipment policies; whether to accept small customer orders; warehous-

---

[14] Jeremy Main, "The Winning Organization," *Fortune* (September 26, 1988), p. 56.

[15] Daniel Machalaba, "Shippers' Market," *Wall Street Journal* (December 18, 1985), pp. 1, 18; and Ronald H. Ballou, *Business Logistics Management: Planning and Control,* Second Edition (Englewood Cliffs, N.J.: Prentice-Hall, 1985), pp. 13–20.

[16] Donald J. Bowersox, David J. Closs, and Omar K. Helferich, *Logistical Management,* Third Edition (New York: Macmillan, 1986), pp. 4–5; Lewis A. Spalding, "Kanban," *Stores* (April 1984), p. 59; J. R. Davis, "Physical Distribution Costs: The 1982 Distribution/Service Data Base" (Annual Proceedings, National Council of Physical Distribution Management, 1982), p. 55; and David L. Anderson, "Your Company's Logistics Management: An Asset or Liability in the 1980s?" *Transportation Review* (Winter 1983), p. 119.

TABLE 12-4 Selected Symptoms of a Poor Physical Distribution System

Symptom	Cost Ramifications
1. Slow-turning and/or too-high inventory	Excessive capital is tied up in inventory. The firm must bear high insurance costs, interest expenses, and high risks of pilferage and product obsolescence. Merchandise may not be fresh.
2. Inefficient customer service	Costs are high compared with the value of shipments; warehouses are poorly situated; inventory levels are not tied to customer demand.
3. A large number of interwarehouse shipments	Merchandise transfers increase physical distribution costs because items must be handled (packed, unpacked, stored, and verified) at each warehouse.
4. Frequent use of emergency shipments	Extra charges add significantly to physical distribution costs.
5. Peripheral hauls and/or limited backhauling	The firm uses its own trucking facilities; however, many hauls are too spread out and trucks may only be full one way.
6. A large number of small orders	Small orders often are unprofitable. Many distribution costs are fixed.

Distribution standards are needed.

ing; coordinating assortments; whether to provide order progress reports; and so on. Poor performance in these areas may result in lost customers.

Accordingly, ***distribution standards*** — clear and measurable goals regarding service levels in physical distribution — must be developed. Examples are filling 90 per cent of orders from existing inventory, responding to customer requests for order information within three hours, filling orders with 99 per cent accuracy, and limiting merchandise damaged in transit to 3 per cent or less.

*The **total-cost approach** considers both costs and opportunities.*

One way to determine the optimal customer service level is through the ***total-cost approach,*** whereby the distribution service level with the lowest total costs — including freight (shipping), warehousing, and the cost of lost business — is the optimal service level. An ideal system seeks a balance between low expenditures on distribution and high opportunities for sales. Seldom will balance be achieved at the lowest level of distribution expenditures; lost sales will be too great. Figure 12-8 illustrates the total-cost approach.

By offering a high level of customer service, a firm may be able to generate a significant competitive advantage. For instance, Frito-Lay has over 10,000 salespeople

FIGURE 12-8 An Illustration of the Total-Cost Approach in Distribution

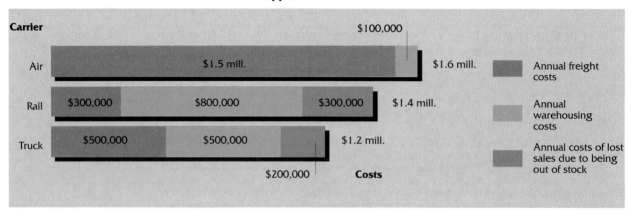

Marketing Controversy

How Can Customer Service and Inventory Investment Be Balanced?

Manufacturers, wholesalers, and retailers all want to have the proper level of products available (in stock) to satisfy consumer demand and, thus, provide superior customer service. Yet, if firms make too many products available, inventory-investment and inventory-holding costs (such as warehousing) may be too high.

The goal is to balance availability and inventory costs. Each firm must answer this question: "At what point do we risk not having a product in stock when a customer asks for it because it is too expensive to carry more than a certain quantity of that item?"

This is not easy to resolve, and there are many factors to consider. Here are a few examples:

▶ *One retailer says it is "running a service business, which means having to deliver to the expectations of the customer. The customer wants a frequent flow of goods. So, we have to run our business so that it is maximizing the customer's business and not maximizing ours, which is expense control." This*

means reducing the turnaround time for suppliers to fill orders, not having less merchandise available.

▶ *In a study of comparable discounters, it was determined that there are significant differences in inventory turnover rates. Although the average rate of the firms was 3.4, the range was from 2.4 to 5.0. The firms with the highest rates make fewer products available; those with the lowest rates have more products available. The rates are tied to the firms' customer-service and inventory-investment goals.*

▶ *With regard to warehousing, a consultant wonders which approach is best: "Do I want small regional distribution centers? Do I want one massive center? Do I put consolidation centers in New York and Los Angeles and then drop ship to local stores?"*

What do you think?

SOURCE: Based on material in Jules Abend, "Faster Flow-Through," *Stores* (August 1988), pp. 52–62.

who make more than 400,000 retailer calls weekly. They set up, stock, and arrange displays and take back "stales" (most products have a shelf life of only 35 days). Frito-Lay lives up to its pledge of guaranteed freshness and sells $4 billion of snack-food items doing so.[17] See Figure 12-9.

Physical Distribution and Other Functional Areas

Physical distribution interacts with every aspect of marketing as well as other functional areas within the company, as the following indicate.

Product assortment — variations in color, size, features, quality, and style — imposes a burden on a firm's distribution facilities. Greater variety means lower volume per item, which increases unit shipping and warehousing costs. The stocking of a broader range of replacement parts also becomes necessary.

Physical distribution must be coordinated with other areas.

[17] Steven E. Prokesch, "It's All in the Delivery," *New York Times* (December 2, 1985), pp. D1, D4; and *PepsiCo, Inc. 1988 Annual Report.*

FIGURE 12-9
A Frito-Lay Salesperson
Servicing a Retail
Account
Reprinted by permission.

Physical distribution is related to overall channel strategy. A firm seeking extensive distribution needs dispersed warehouses. One involved with perishables needs to be sure that most of a product's selling life is not spent in transit.

Because promotion campaigns are often planned weeks in advance, it is essential that distribution to middlemen be carried out at the proper times to ensure ample stocks of goods. Wholesalers and/or retailers may receive consumer complaints for not having sufficient quantities of the items they advertise, even though the manufacturer is really at fault. Some new products fail due to poor initial distribution.

Physical distribution also plays an important part in pricing decisions. A firm with quick, reliable delivery and an ample supply of replacement parts that will ship small orders and provide emergency shipments may be able to charge higher prices than a company that provides less service.

A distribution strategy has a major link with production and financial functions. For example, meat processors can reduce transportation costs by centralizing cutting operations because less waste is shipped to each store. High transportation costs encourage firms to locate plants closer to markets. Low average inventories in stock enable companies to reduce finance charges. Warehouse receipts may be used as collateral for loans.

A physical distribution strategy involves transportation, inventory, and facilities.

There are many decisions to be made and coordinated in the development of a **physical distribution strategy:** the transportation form(s) to be used, inventory levels and warehouse form(s), and the number and locations of plants, warehouses, and retail locations. A strategy can be fairly simple. A firm can have one plant, focus attention on one geographic market, and ship directly to customers without the use of decentralized warehouses. At the other extreme, a strategy can include multiple plants, assembly locations in each geographic market, thousands of customer locations, and integrating many transportation forms.

TABLE 12-5 The Relative Share of Shipping Mileage and Revenue by Transportation Form (Per Cent)

Transportation Form	Share of Ton Miles Shipped	Share of Shipping Revenue
Railroads	36%	14%
Motor carriers	25	75
Waterways	16	6
Pipelines	23	3
Airways	less than 0.3	2

Source: Adapted by the authors from Charles A. Taff, *Management of Physical Distribution and Transportation,* Seventh Edition (Homewood, Ill.: Richard D. Irwin, 1984), pp. 113–115; and *Statistical Abstract of the United States, 1988.*

The remainder of this chapter deals with the two central components of physical distribution strategy: transportation and inventory management (which includes warehousing).

Transportation

There are five basic transportation forms: railroads, motor carriers, waterways, pipelines, and airways. Table 12-5 shows the share of mileage and revenue contributed by each. Table 12-6 ranks them on the basis of seven operating characteristics.

Transportation is rated on speed, availability, dependability, capability, frequency, losses, and cost.

Over the last several years, the deregulation of transportation industries has greatly expanded the competition in and among these industries. In general, deregulation allows carriers greater flexibility in entering new markets, expanding their businesses, the products they carry, price setting, and the functions they perform. It also provides greater choices for those shipping.[18]

Each transportation form and such transportation services as parcel post are studied next.

Railroads

Railroads usually carry heavy, bulky items that are low in value (relative to their weight) over long distances. Railroads ship items too heavy for trucks.

Railroads transport mostly heavy items over long distances.

Despite their dominant position in ton miles shipped, railroads have been beset by a variety of problems in recent years. Fixed costs are high because of investments in facilities. Shippers face railroad car shortages during high-demand months for agricultural goods. Some tracks and railroad cars are in serious need of repair. Trucks are faster, more flexible, and are packed more easily. In response to these difficulties, railroads are relying on three solutions to improve performance: new shipping techniques, operating flexibility due to deregulation, and mergers to improve efficiency.

Motor Carriers

Motor carriers predominantly transport small shipments over short distances. They handle about 80 per cent of the country's shipments of less than 500 or 1,000 pounds. Seventy per cent of all motor carriers are used for local deliveries and 50 per cent of

Motor carriers handle small shipments over short distances.

[18] Lewis M. Schneider, "New Era in Transportation Strategy," *Harvard Business Review,* Vol. 63 (March–April 1985), pp. 118–126.

TABLE 12-6   The Relative Operating Characteristics of Five Transportation Forms

| Operating Characteristics | Ranking by Transportation Form[a] | | | | |
	Railroads	Motor Carriers	Waterways	Pipelines	Airways
Delivery speed	3	2	4	5	1
Number of locations served	2	1	4	5	3
On-time dependability	3	2	5	1	4
Range of products carried	1	2	3	5	4
Frequency of shipments	4	2	5	1	3
Losses and damages	5	4	2	1	3
Cost per ton mile	3	4	1	2	5

[a] 1=highest ranking.

Sources: Adapted by the authors from Donald J. Bowersox, David J. Closs, and Omar K. Helferich, *Logistical Management*, Third Edition (New York: Macmillan, 1986), p. 166; and Ronald A. Ballou, *Business Logistics Management: Planning and Control*, Second Edition (Englewood Cliffs, N.J.: Prentice-Hall, 1985), p. 194.

total truck miles are local. It is for these reasons that motor carriers account for such a large share of shipping revenue.

Motor carriers are more flexible than rail because they can pick up packages at a factory or warehouse and deliver them to the customer's door. They are also often used to supplement rail, air, and other forms that cannot deliver direct to customers. In addition, trucks are faster than rail for short distances. Like railroads, the trucking industry has been deregulated since 1980.

Waterways

Waterways specialize in low-value, high-bulk items.

Waterways involve the movement of goods on barges via inland rivers and on tankers and general-merchandise freighters through the Great Lakes, intercoastal shipping, and the St. Lawrence Seaway. Waterways are used primarily for transporting low-value, high-bulk freight (such as coal, iron ore, gravel, grain, and cement). Although this transportation is slow, and may be closed by ice during the winter, the rates are extremely low.

Various improvements in vessel design have recently occurred. For example, many "supervessels" are now operating on the Great Lakes. These supervessels can each carry more than 60,000 gross tons of iron-bearing rock in one trip. Their conveyor systems are twice as efficient as the ones on older boats. Navigation is usually computer-controlled.

Pipelines

Pipelines center on liquids, gases, and semiliquids.

Within **pipelines,** there is continuous movement and there are no interruptions, inventories (except those held by a carrier), and intermediate storage locations. Thus, handling and labor costs are minimized. Even though pipelines are very reliable, only certain commodities can be moved through them. In the past, emphasis was on gas and petroleum-based products. Recently, pipelines have been modified to accept coal and wood chips, which are transported in a semiliquid state. Nonetheless, lack of flexibility limits the potential of pipelines.

Some pipelines are enormous in size. For example, the proposed Alaska Highway natural gas pipeline would eventually cover 4,800 miles and deliver 900 billion cubic feet of natural gas annually to the lower 48 states. It is estimated that this pipeline will ultimately cost more than $10 billion to construct and will not be completed until at least the mid-1990s.[19]

Airways

Airways are the fastest, most expensive form of transportation. As a result, high-value, perishable, and emergency goods dominate air shipments. Even though air transit is costly, it may lower other costs, such as the need for outlying or even regional warehouses. The costs of packing, unpacking, and preparing goods for shipping are lower than for other transportation forms.

Airways stress valuable, perishable, and emergency items.

Airfreight has been deregulated since late 1977. As a result, many firms have stepped up cargo operations. A number of carriers now employ wide-bodied jets that can handle large containers. In addition, modern communications and sorting equipment have been added to airfreight operations. Firms specializing in air shipments have done well by emphasizing fast, guaranteed service at reasonable prices.

Transportation Services

Transportation service companies are marketing specialists that predominantly handle the shipments of small and moderate-sized packages. Some pick up packages from the sender's office and deliver direct to the addressee. Others require packages to be brought to a service company outlet. The three major kinds of service companies are government parcel post, private parcel, and express.

*These **transportation service companies** ship packages: government parcel post, private parcel, and express.*

Government parcel post operates out of post offices and utilizes rates based on postal zones, of which there are eight. Parcel post can be insured or sent COD (collect on delivery). Regular service is usually completed within a few days. Special handling is available to expedite shipments. Express mail is available for next-day service from a post office to an addressee.

Private parcel services specialize in small-package delivery, usually less than 50-pound shipments. Most services ship from manufacturers, wholesalers, distributors, and retailers to their customers within a several-state area. Regular service usually completes deliveries in two to three days. More expensive next-day service is also available from many carriers. The largest private firm is United Parcel Service (UPS), a multibillion-dollar, international company.

Specialized express companies, such as Federal Express and Emery Air Freight, generally provide guaranteed nationwide delivery of small packages for the morning-after pickup. The average express delivery is about 10 pounds.

[19] Alan Bayless, "Alaska Pipeline's Cost Projections Are Cut Sharply," *Wall Street Journal* (June 7, 1988), p. 24.

Coordinating Transportation

Because a single shipment may involve a combination of transportation forms, coordination is necessary. Two major innovations that improve a company's ability to coordinate shipments are containerization and freight forwarding.

Under **containerization,** goods are placed in sturdy containers that can be loaded on trains, trucks, ships, or planes. These marked containers are sealed until delivered, thereby reducing damage and pilferage. Their progress and destination are frequently monitored. The containers serve as mobile warehouses that can be moved from manufacturing plants to receiving docks, where they remain until the contents are needed.

In *freight forwarding,* specialized firms (known as freight forwarders) consolidate small shipments (usually less than 500 pounds each) from several companies. They pick up merchandise at each shipper's place of business and arrange for delivery at buyers' doors. Freight forwarders prosper because less than carload (lcl) shipping rates are sharply higher than carload (cl) rates. Freight forwarders also provide traffic management services, such as selecting the best transportation form at the most reasonable rate.

The Legal Status of Transportation Firms

*Carriers are classified as
**common, contract,
exempt,** or **private.***

Transportation firms are categorized as common, contract, exempt, or private carriers. **Common carriers** must transport the goods of any firm interested in their services; they cannot refuse any shipments unless the carrier's rules are broken (such as packing requirements). Common carriers provide service on a fixed and publicized schedule between designated points. A regular fee schedule is also published. All railroads and petroleum pipelines and some air, motor-vehicle, and water transporters are common carriers.

Contract carriers provide one or a few shippers with transportation services based on individual agreements. Contract carriers are not required to maintain fixed routes or schedules, and rates may be negotiated. Many motor-vehicle, inland-waterway, and airfreight transporters are contract carriers.

Exempt carriers are excused from legal regulations and must only comply with safety requirements. Exempt carriers are specified by law. Some commodities moved by water, such as coal, and most agricultural goods are exempt from economic restrictions.

Private carriers are shippers who possess their own transportation facilities. They are subject to safety rules. In the United States, there are 100,000+ private carriers.

Inventory Management

*Inventory management
deals with the flow and
allocation of products.*

The intent of **inventory management** is to provide a continuous flow of goods and to match the quantity of goods kept in inventory as closely as possible with sales demand. When production or consumption is seasonal or erratic, this can be quite difficult.

Therefore, inventory management (including warehousing) has broad implications. For example, a producer cannot afford to run out of a crucial item that could put a halt to production. However, inventory on hand should not be too large because the costs of storing raw materials, parts, and/or finished products for a year (such as floor space, insurance, supervision, and credit) can be substantial. In situations where models change yearly, as with automobiles, large inventories can adversely affect new-product sales. Also, excessive inventories may result in stale goods, cause a firm to mark down prices due to product obsolescence, and tie up working capital.

In order to improve their inventory management procedures, a number of firms are now applying either or both of two complementary concepts: a just-in-time inventory system and electronic data interchange. With a *just-in-time (JIT) inventory system,* the purchasing company reduces the amount of inventory it keeps on hand by ordering more frequently and in lower quantity. This requires better planning and information on the part of the purchaser, geographically closer sellers, improved buyer-seller relationships and stability, and better production and distribution facilities. Among retailers, a JIT system is often known as a *quick response (QR) inventory system,* which is a cooperative effort between retailers and their suppliers aimed at reducing retail inventory while providing a merchandise supply that more closely addresses the actual buying patterns of consumers.[20]

JIT and QR inventory systems closely monitor inventory levels.

JIT systems are being used by automobile firms, Hewlett-Packard, Levi Strauss, The Limited, Wal-Mart, J.C. Penney, Motorola, General Electric, Deere, Black & Decker, and many other manufacturers, wholesalers, and retailers. Figure 12-10 describes the Whirlpool JIT system, in use for many decades. As one observer noted,

> Just-in-time is not a fad, but a growing part of the world business scene, because it has demonstrated its ability to reduce inventories. JIT permits the manufacturer or merchant to offer faster response to customers, to operate with shorter lead times, to reduce the incidence of stockouts, and to reduce waste and scrap.[21]

Through *electronic data interchange (EDI),* suppliers and their manufacturers, wholesalers, and/or retailers exchange information via computer linkups. Electronic data interchange "is simply the electronic replacement of paper, providing direct computer-to-computer transmission of data."[22] This is how EDI works in conjunction with a just-in-time or quick response inventory system:

With EDI, computers are used to exchange information between suppliers and their customers.

> A man goes into a Belk store in Charlotte, N.C., and buys a pair of gray polyester-and-cotton twill pants with a 32-inch waist and a 30-inch inseam. The store normally stocks three pairs of these pants in that size, style, and color, and this purchase brings its inventory down to one. When the store's computer shows that only one pair remains in stock, it automatically sends an electronic reorder to the Haggar Company, which manufactures the pants. Haggar takes the pants from its stock and ships them to the store for arrival no later than 10 days after the customer has made his purchase.[23]

In order for EDI to work effectively, each of the firms in a distribution channel needs to use the Universal Product Code, because this standardized coding makes data processing much easier for all parties. According to one recent study, about 40 per cent of the domestic manufacturers of general merchandise currently use the UPC on their

---

[20] See Richard C. Walleigh, "What's Your Excuse for Not Using JIT?" *Harvard Business Review,* Vol. 64 (March–April 1986), pp. 38–54; "EDI and QR: A Lot More Than Alphabet Soup," *Chain Store Age Executive* (January 1988), pp. 89–90; Larry C. Giunipero and Charles O'Neal, "Obstacles to JIT Procurement," *Industrial Marketing Management,* Vol. 17 (1988), pp. 35–41; and Joseph L. Bower and Thomas M. Hout, "Fast-Cycle Capability for Competitive Power," *Harvard Business Review,* Vol. 66 (November–December 1988), pp. 110–118.

[21] Ken Ackerman, "Just-in-Time's American Practitioners," *Management Review* (June 1988), p. 57.

[22] Gene R. Tyndall, "Supply-Chain Management Innovations Spur Long-Term Strategic Retail Alliances," *Marketing News* (December 19, 1988), p. 10.

[23] Leonard Sloane, "From Dacron to Men's Pants," *New York Times* (October 1, 1988), p. 56.

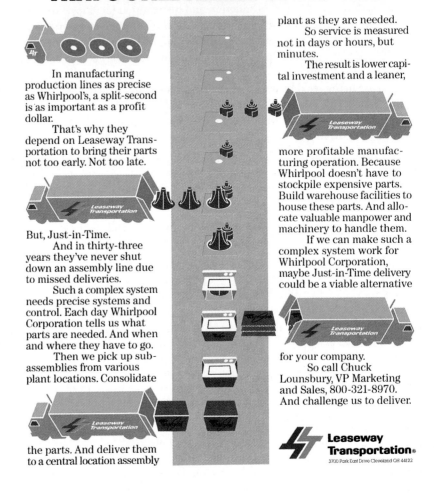

YEARS AGO, WHIRLPOOL CORPORATION CREATED A PRODUCTION SYSTEM THAT'S STILL AHEAD OF ITS TIME.

In manufacturing production lines as precise as Whirlpool's, a split-second is as important as a profit dollar.

That's why they depend on Leaseway Transportation to bring their parts not too early. Not too late.

But, Just-in-Time.

And in thirty-three years they've never shut down an assembly line due to missed deliveries.

Such a complex system needs precise systems and control. Each day Whirlpool Corporation tells us what parts are needed. And when and where they have to go.

Then we pick up subassemblies from various plant locations. Consolidate the parts. And deliver them to a central location assembly

plant as they are needed.

So service is measured not in days or hours, but minutes.

The result is lower capital investment and a leaner, more profitable manufacturing operation. Because Whirlpool doesn't have to stockpile expensive parts. Build warehouse facilities to house these parts. And allocate valuable manpower and machinery to handle them.

If we can make such a complex system work for Whirlpool Corporation, maybe Just-in-Time delivery could be a viable alternative for your company.

So call Chuck Lounsbury, VP Marketing and Sales, 800-321-8970. And challenge us to deliver.

Leaseway Transportation®
3700 Park East Drive Cleveland OH 44122

FIGURE 12-10
Whirlpool's Just-in-Time Inventory System
Reprinted by permission.

products; all major food makers use the UPC. And more firms are expected to begin using the UPC throughout the 1990s. At the corporate headquarters of Toys "R" Us, there is already a sign reading "No UPC, no purchase."[24]

Four specific aspects of inventory management are examined in the following subsections: stock turnover, when to reorder, how much to reorder, and warehousing.

[24] "Vendors Slow to Implement Quick Response," *Chain Store Age Executive* (January 1989), pp. 107–111.

Stock Turnover

The relationship between a firm's sales and the inventory level it maintains is expressed by **stock turnover,** which is the number of times during a stated period (usually one year) that average inventory on hand is sold. Stock turnover is calculated in units or dollars:

Stock turnover shows the ratio between sales and average inventory.

$$\begin{matrix} \text{Annual rate of} \\ \text{stock turnover} \\ \text{(in units)} \end{matrix} = \frac{\text{Number of units sold during year}}{\text{Average inventory on hand (in units)}}$$

$$\begin{matrix} \text{Annual rate of} \\ \text{stock turnover} \\ \text{(in dollars)} \end{matrix} = \frac{\text{Net yearly sales (in retail dollars)}}{\text{Average inventory on hand (in retail dollars)}}$$

For example, in retailing, average annual stock turnover ranges from 2.4 in jewelry stores to 28 in gasoline service stations.

There are various advantages to a high inventory turnover rate: inventory investments are productive, merchandise is fresh, losses from changes in styles and fashion are reduced, and the costs of maintaining inventory (such as insurance, breakage, warehousing, and credit) are lessened. Accordingly, the turnover rate can be improved by reducing assortments, eliminating slow-selling items, maintaining minimal inventories for some items, and purchasing from suppliers who deliver on time.

Nonetheless, too high a turnover rate may negatively affect a firm for several reasons. Small-quantity purchases may cause the loss of volume discounts. Low product assortment may reduce sales volume if consumers are unable to compare brands or related items are not carried. Low prices may be necessary to stimulate sufficient sales. The chances of running out of stock increase when average inventory size is lowered. As a purchasing chief at Pfizer once commented: "If you have too much inventory, you get yelled at; if you shut the plant because you don't have it, you get fired."[25] Figure 12-11 shows ways customers can react if a firm runs out of stock.

Knowing when to reorder merchandise helps protect against stockouts while minimizing inventory investments.

When to Reorder

By having a clear **reorder point** for each of its products (or raw materials or parts), a company establishes the inventory levels at which new orders must be placed. The reorder point depends on order lead time, the usage rate, and safety stock. Order lead time is the period from the date an order is placed until the date a product or part is ready for sale or use (received, checked, and altered, if needed). The usage rate refers to the average sales in units per day (for a wholesaler or retailer) or the rate at which a product is used in a production process (for a manufacturer). Safety stock is the extra inventory kept on hand to protect against out-of-stock conditions resulting from unexpectedly high demand, greater-than-anticipated production volume, and delivery delays. Safety stock must take into consideration the firm's policy toward running out of merchandise (or raw materials or parts).

*The **reorder point** is based on lead time, usage, and safety stock.*

---

[25] Richard F. Janssen and John Koten, "Leaner Inventories Than in Prior Slumps Could Lessen Severity of This Recession," *Wall Street Journal* (May 23, 1980), p. 48.

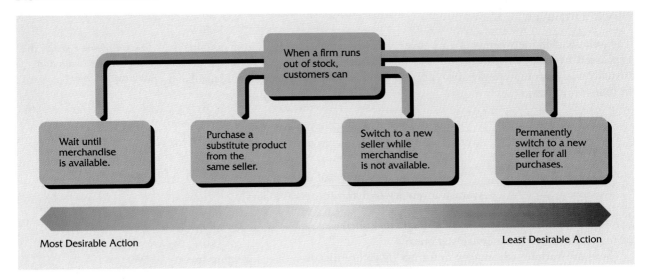

Most Desirable Action   Least Desirable Action

FIGURE 12-11
**What Happens When a
Firm Has Stock Shortages**

The reorder point formula is

Reorder point = (Order lead time × Usage rate) + (Safety stock)

For instance, a wholesaler that needs four days for its purchase orders to be placed and received, sells 10 items per day, and wants to have 10 extra items on hand in case of a supplier's delivery delay of one day has a reorder point of 50 [(4 × 10) + (10)]. Without the safety stock, the company would lose 10 sales if it orders when inventory is 40 items and the order is completed in 5 days. Figure 12-12 shows reorder points and their implications under four very different situations.

How Much to Reorder

Order size depends on discounts, resources, turnover, and costs.

Firms must determine their *order size,* the appropriate amount of merchandise, parts, and so on, to purchase at one time. Order size depends on several factors, including the availability of quantity discounts, the resources of the firm, the inventory turnover rate, the costs of processing each order, and the costs of maintaining goods in inventory. When a firm has large orders, quantity discounts are usually available, a large portion of its finances are tied up in inventory, its stock turnover rate is relatively low, per-order processing costs are reduced, and inventory costs are generally high. The firm is also less likely to run out of goods. The opposite is true for small orders.

The economic order quantity balances ordering and inventory costs.

Many companies seek to balance their order-processing costs (such as filling out purchase orders, computer utilization, and merchandise handling) and their inventory-holding costs (such as warehouse expenses, interest charges, insurance, deterioration, and pilferage). Processing costs per unit decline as orders get bigger, while inventory costs rise. The *economic order quantity (EOQ)* is the order volume corresponding to the lowest sum of order-processing and inventory-holding costs.

Table 12-7 demonstrates three ways to compute EOQ. In this illustration, a firm has an annual demand of 3,000 units for a product; the cost of each unit is $1; order-processing costs are $3 per order; and inventory-holding costs equal 20 per cent of each item's cost. As shown in the table, the economic order quantity is 300 units. Thus, the retailer should place orders of 300 units and have 10 orders per year.

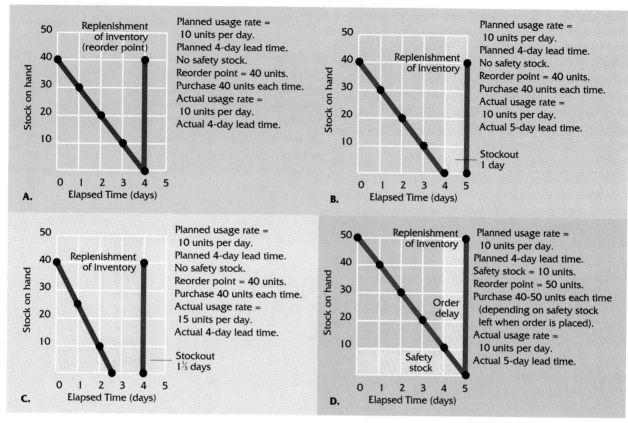

FIGURE 12-12 Reorder Points under Different Assumptions

Warehousing

Warehousing involves the physical facilities used primarily for the storage of goods held in anticipation of sales and transfers within a distribution channel.[26] Warehouses receive, identify, and sort merchandise. They store goods, implement product-recall programs, select goods for shipment, coordinate shipments, and dispatch orders.

Private warehouses are owned and operated by firms that store and distribute their own products. They are most likely to be used by companies with stable inventory levels and long-run expectations to serve the same geographic markets.

Public warehouses provide storage and related physical distribution services to any interested firm or individual on a rental basis. They are used by small firms that do not have the resources or desire to have their own facilities, larger firms that require additional storage space (because their private warehouses are filled), or any size of firm entering new geographic markets (where test marketing or preopening space is needed). If a product needs to be recalled, a public warehouse can be utilized as a collection point, where products are segregated, disposed of, and/or salvaged.

Public warehouses can provide transportation economies for users by allowing carload shipments to be made to such warehouses in local markets; then short-distance, smaller shipments are made from the warehouses to individual customers. Firms can also reduce their capital investments in facilities and maximize flexibility by using public warehouses, which are adapted easily to new or expanding markets. Public

Warehousing involves storing and dispatching goods.

[26] Bennett, *Dictionary of Marketing Terms*, p. 213.

383

TABLE 12-7 Computing an Economic Order Quantity

A.

	Order Quantity (Units)	Average Inventory Maintained (Units)[a]	Annual Order-Processing Costs[b]	Annual Inventory-Holding Costs[c]	Annual Total Costs
	100	50	$90	$10	$100
	200	100	45	20	65
EOQ ⟶	300	150	30	30	60
	400	200	24	40	64
	500	250	18	50	68

B.

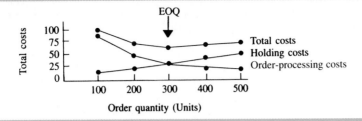

C.

$$EOQ = \sqrt{\frac{2DS}{IC}} = \sqrt{\frac{2\,(3,000)\,(\$3)}{0.20\,(\$1)}} = 300$$

where EOQ = Order quantity (units)   S = Costs to place an order ($)   I = Annual holding costs (as a % of unit costs)
D = Annual demand (units)   C = Unit cost of an item ($)

[a] The average inventory on hand = 1/2 × Order quantity
[b] Order-processing costs = Number of annual orders × Costs to place an order. Number of orders = Annual demand/Order quantity
[c] Inventory-holding costs = Annual holding costs as a per cent of unit cost × Unit cost × Average inventory

---

*With **bonded warehousing**, imported or taxable goods are stored. **Field warehousing** provides receipts.*

warehouses are available in major urban areas and in many smaller cities; there are about 15,000 public warehouses in the United States.

Bonded warehousing and field warehousing are also available through public warehouses. In **bonded warehousing**, imported or taxable merchandise is stored and can be released for sale only after the appropriate taxes are paid. A bonded warehouse allows firms to postpone tax payments until they are ready to make deliveries to customers. Cigarettes, liquor, and various other products are often stored in a bonded warehouse.

With **field warehousing**, a receipt is issued by a public warehouse for goods stored in a private warehouse or in transit to consumers. These goods are usually placed in a special area, and the field warehouser takes responsibility for the merchandise. A firm may use field warehousing because the warehouse receipt serves as collateral for a loan.

For many firms, a combination of private and public warehouses may be optimal. This enables the private warehouse to be full at almost all times and the public warehouse to stock items for peak seasons, bonded goods, and merchandise for geographic areas with low concentrations of customers.

Summary

1. *To define distribution planning and to examine its importance, distribution functions, the factors used in selecting a distribution channel, and the different types of distribution channels* Distribution planning is systematic decision making relating to the physical movement of goods and services from producer to consumer, as well as the related transfer of ownership (or rental) of them. A channel of distribution consists of the organizations or people involved with the movement and exchange of goods and services. Participants are known as channel members or middlemen.

Distribution decisions often have an impact on the company's marketing program. For many firms, the choice of a channel of distribution is the most important one that they make. Both costs and profits are affected by the distribution channel selected. Firms may have to conform to existing channel patterns; and their markets' size and nature are also influenced by the channel employed.

Regardless of who performs them, channel functions include marketing research, buying, promotion, customer services, product planning, pricing, and distribution. Independent channel-member firms can play an important role by performing various functions and resolving the differences between manufacturers' and consumers' goals. They are involved in the sorting process.

In selecting a method of distribution, these are among the key factors to be considered: the consumer, the company, the product, the competition, the distribution channels themselves, and legal requirements.

A direct channel requires one party to perform all distribution functions, while in an indirect channel these activities are carried out by both the producer and independent middlemen. In comparing the two methods, the firm must balance its costs and abilities against control and total sales. An indirect channel may use a contractual arrangement or an administered agreement.

A long channel has a number of levels of independent middlemen; a wide channel has a large number of firms at any stage in the channel. A distribution channel may be exclusive, selective, or intensive, depending on the firm's goals, middle-men, customers, and marketing emphasis. A dual channel allows a company to operate through two or more distribution methods.

2. *To describe the nature of supplier/middleman contracts, and cooperation and conflict in a channel of distribution* In contracts between suppliers and other channel-member firms, price policy, the conditions of sale, territorial rights, the services/responsibility mix, and contract length and termination conditions are specified.

Cooperation and conflict may both occur in a distribution channel. Conflicts need to be settled fairly because confrontation can lead to hostility and negative actions by all parties. Frequently, a pushing strategy — based on channel cooperation — can be utilized by established, successful firms. However, a pulling strategy — based on proving the existence of consumer demand prior to wholesaler or retailer support or acceptance — must be used by many new companies.

3. *To show the special considerations relating to a distribution channel for industrial products* The channel of distribution for industrial products normally does not use retailers but tends to be direct, involve few transactions and large orders, require specification selling and knowledgeable channel members, utilize team selling and distinct channel-member firms, include leasing arrangements, and provide more technical information.

4. *To define physical distribution and to demonstrate its importance* Physical distribution is involved with efficiently getting products delivered to designated places, at designated times, and in proper condition. It may be undertaken by any member of a channel, from producer to consumer.

There are a number of reasons for studying physical distribution: its costs, the value of customer service, and its relationship with other functional areas of the organization. Through the total-cost approach, the distribution service level with the lowest total cost (including freight, warehousing, and the cost of lost business) is the optimal level. In a physical distribution strategy, decisions are made regarding transportation, inventory levels, warehousing, and location of facilities.

5. *To discuss transportation alternatives and inventory management issues* Railroads typically carry

goods for long distances and ship bulky items. Motor carriers dominate in transporting small shipments over short distances. Waterways are used primarily for the shipment of low-value freight. Pipelines provide continuous movement of liquid, gaseous, and semiliquid products. Airways offer fast, expensive movement of perishables and high-value items. Transportation service companies are marketing specialists that mostly handle small and medium-sized packages. Transportation methods can be better coordinated through containerization and freight forwarding. There are common, contract, exempt, and private carriers.

Inventory management is needed to provide a continuous flow of goods and to match the quantity of goods kept in inventory as closely as possible with sales demand. With a just-in-time or quick response system, the purchasing firm reduces the amount of inventory it keeps on hand by ordering more frequently and in lower quantity. Through electronic data interchange, suppliers and customers exchange information via computer linkups.

The relationship between a firm's sales and the inventory level it maintains is expressed by stock turnover, which is the number of times during a year that the average inventory on hand is sold. A reorder point shows a pre-established minimum inventory level when merchandise must be reordered. The economic order quantity formula determines the optimal quantity of goods to order based on total order-processing and inventory-holding costs. Warehousing decisions include selecting a private or public warehouse and examining the availability of public warehouse services.

Key Terms

distribution planning (p. 356)
channel of distribution (p. 356)
channel members (p. 356)
middlemen (p. 356)
channel functions (p. 358)
sorting process (p. 360)
direct channel of distribution
    (p. 361)
indirect channel of distribution
    (p. 361)
contractual channel arrangement
    (p. 361)
administered channel
    arrangement (p. 361)
channel length (p. 361)
vertical integration (p. 361)
channel width (p. 361)
horizontal integration (p. 361)
exclusive distribution (p. 363)
selective distribution (p. 363)

intensive distribution (p. 363)
dual channel of distribution (p. 363)
supplier/middleman contracts
    (p. 364)
pushing strategy (p. 369)
pulling strategy (p. 369)
physical distribution (p. 370)
order cycle (p. 370)
distribution standards (p. 372)
total-cost approach (p. 372)
physical distribution strategy
    (p. 374)
railroads (p. 375)
motor carriers (p. 375)
waterways (p. 376)
pipelines (p. 376)
airways (p. 377)
transportation service companies
    (p. 377)
containerization (p. 378)

freight forwarding (p. 378)
common carriers (p. 378)
contract carriers (p. 378)
exempt carriers (p. 378)
private carriers (p. 378)
inventory management (p. 378)
just-in-time (JIT) inventory
    system (p. 379)
quick response (QR) inventory
    system (p. 379)
electronic data interchange (EDI)
    (p. 379)
stock turnover (p. 381)
reorder point (p. 381)
order size (p. 382)
economic order quantity (EOQ)
    (p. 382)
warehousing (p. 383)
bonded warehousing (p. 384)
field warehousing (p. 384)

Review Questions

1. Distinguish between these two terms: channel members and middlemen.

2. Explain the sorting process. Provide an example in your answer.

3. What factors influence the selection of a distribution channel?

4. Under what circumstances should a company engage in direct distribution? Indirect distribution?

5. Distinguish between vertical integration and horizontal integration. What is the goal of each?

6. Explain how a product could move from exclusive to selective to intensive distribution.

7. Compare railroad and airfreight deliveries on the basis of the total-cost approach.

8. The average stock turnover rate in grocery stores is 16. What does this mean? How could a grocery store raise its turnover rate?

9. Two wholesalers sell identical merchandise. Yet, one plans a safety stock equal to 10 per cent of expected sales, while the other plans no safety stock. Explain this difference.

10. Why would a firm use both private and public warehouses?

Discussion Questions

1. What distribution decisions would a new manufacturer of women's hosiery have to make?

2. AT&T distributes its telephones through its own stores and through independently operated stores. Evaluate this approach.

3. Devise distribution channels for the sale of a daily newspaper, office furniture, and fur coats.

4. Develop a list of distribution standards for a firm delivering floral products to florists and other retailers.

5. Are there any disadvantages to a JIT system? Explain your answer.

◀ CASE 1 ▶

Tandy Corporation: Revamping Its Distribution Channels*

Tandy Corporation makes over 1,200 electronic and computer products, stores merchandise in its own warehouses, ships items via its own trucks, and sells through various retailers (many of whom are company-owned). About one-third of U.S. households own at least one Tandy product. Overall, Tandy is one of the largest, most successful, and most complex vertically integrated corporations in the world.

At the manufacturing level, Tandy has nearly thirty factories in the United States, Asia, and the United Kingdom. These factories make, assemble, or package products under Tandy's brands (such as Radio Shack, Realistic, and Tandy) that contribute more than one-half of company sales.

At the wholesaling level, Tandy operates regional end-product warehouses, a computer product warehouse, and a "parts & pieces" distribution cen-

ter. Its computerized operating system facilitates communications among stores, warehouses, and the home office. This system provides reports and monitors advertised merchandise in order to allocate "hot" items among stores.

At the consumer level, Tandy is revamping its distribution channels. Now, three-quarters of sales are through company-owned stores. Its goal is to get a "50–50 ratio in the next five or six years." Here are selected elements of Tandy's company-owned distribution channels for consumers:

▷ There are 7,000 full-line Radio Shack stores carrying 2,750 items, ranging from telephones to security devices and small computer systems. About 75 per cent of these stores are owned by Tandy; the others are operated by dealers and franchisees.

▷ Tandy owns 300 Radio Shack Computer Center stores that specialize in computer and office products.

▷ Over 60 new Tandy-owned Grid Systems stores (converted from Radio Shack Computer

* The data in this case are drawn from Paul Duke, "Tandy Corp. Fights Hard to Shake Radio Shack Image," *Wall Street Journal* (December 8, 1988), p. B4; and Karen Blumenthal, "Tandy Realigns Computer Sales to Big Customers," *Wall Street Journal* (February 15, 1989), p. B7.

Centers) handle computer sales to government organizations and to companies with either 200 employees or $100 million and up in annual sales.

Among the new, independently-owned distribution channels that Tandy is now using to sell its personal computers are these: Wal-Mart stores, direct marketing through American Express and J.C. Penney, and traditional computer stores. To limit competition with current Radio Shack stores, Tandy is supplying Wal-Mart with older-model computers. It also contends that American Express and J.C. Penney flyer-based direct-marketing sales will attract a segment that does not nor will not shop in a Radio Shack store.

In the organizational market, it plans to sell through such distributors as office-products stores (as well as Grid Systems stores). In the past, Radio Shack salespeople had difficulty selling computers to large corporate users. Tandy feels that the addition of outside dealers will help it increase its share of the business market against such firms such as IBM, Compaq, and Apple Computer. Tandy will also

make some personal computers under the DEC name for Digital Equipment Corporation (DEC).

Tandy cites many reasons for its emerging dual-distribution strategy. One, it feels that sales of its less expensive line of personal computers have suffered due to the heavy reliance on company-owned stores. Two, it realizes that opportunities for new Radio Shack locations are limited. Three, the sale of computers through Grid Systems stores and other computer stores may help the firm shed its old image as a "low-budget supplier of wires and electronic parts." Tandy's goal was to sell over 100,000 IBM-compatible computers in non-Radio Shack stores during 1989. The firm sold 400,000 computers (almost entirely sold through Radio Shack stores) in fiscal 1988.

Tandy does face potential problems with its dual-distribution strategy. For example, existing Radio Shack franchisees may become disenchanted with the firm if they perceive the new channel members to be competing directly against them. Consumers may be confused as to which Tandy product to purchase at which outlet. Physical distribution efforts must be coordinated.

QUESTIONS

1. What are the pros and cons of Tandy's decision to increase its use of dual distribution and to place greater emphasis on sales through noncompany-owned stores?
2. How should a distribution channel for final consumers differ from that for large business accounts? Why?
3. Outline a strategy for Tandy to minimize conflict in its distribution channels.
4. What other distribution options should Tandy consider? Explain your answer.

<CASE 2>

Hygrade Furniture Transport: Providing Distribution Functions for Retailers[†]

Because apparel and related items are now such a large part of the merchandise mix of department stores, the stores require more room on both the selling floor and in the warehouse for these items. Thus, they need to carefully allocate their floor space for items such as furniture.

† The data in this case are drawn from "Store and Delivery: Retailers Rely on Hygrade," *Chain Store Age Executive* (May 1988), pp. 273–274.

Some department stores are using their floor space more efficiently by either placing the furniture department at a separate store location or eliminating certain slow-moving or marginally profitable furniture categories. Others are reducing their storage space needs for furniture by having distribution functions, such as warehousing and transportation, performed by outside specialists. For example, The Broadway, Abraham & Straus, Rich's, and G. Fox are just some of the retailers that use Hygrade Furniture Transport for the warehousing and distribution of furniture (as well as electronics and bedding).

Hygrade performs both warehousing and distribution functions for retailers that have annual sales of at least $6 million annually. It receives the furniture from manufacturers, stores it, and makes deliveries to the final consumers specified by its retailers. Hygrade takes total responsibility for customer deliveries, including setting up appointments, verifying that customers will be home, transportation from the warehouse to customers, and setting up furniture (such as installing mirrors on chests). It operates in New York, Atlanta, and California.

Each retailer is charged for Hygrade's services on the basis of merchandise costs, how much volume the retailer generates, and the space used in its warehouse. In some cases, Hygrade's charges may be less than the costs a retailer would incur if it performed storage and delivery services itself. Hygrade benefits from cost economies due to computerization and bar coding, multiple deliveries to a given city (due to its serving multiple retailers), and the scale of its operations.

For example, because of computerization, Hygrade's rate of error in the warehouse is only 1 to 2 per cent. One of its warehouses is 350,000 square feet, can process 500 pieces of merchandise daily, and can hold up to 60,000 pieces of furniture. The firm estimates that its costs are 20 to 40 per cent less than if a retailer undertakes distribution, warehousing, delivery, and customer service functions itself.

This is why Hygrade's distribution system works so well:

▷ Products are identified through the use of UPC tags, which record the description, stockkeeping number, and warehouse location of each item. When deliveries are scheduled, warehouse pickers are given the location, description, and truck number designated for each item. Portable scanners are used by the pickers to reduce errors in merchandise selection and trucking.

▷ The company is always able to determine the number of items in stock, the location of these items, and merchandise condition—and to quickly convey this information to retailers. For example, each item is coded 1 to 6 (with 1 indicating that the item is still in the vendor's packaging and has not been checked, and 6 indicating that the item is defective). On the basis of this information, retailers can choose to order more goods, reduce order quantities, or transfer stock to another warehouse.

▷ All items are double-checked using bar codes before being loaded on a delivery truck. This reduces possible errors.

▷ Hygrade has a backup system with a complete duplicate data set, in case the original invoice is missing or has evidence of tampering.

▷ Hygrade can deliver goods within three days of their arrival at its warehouse.

As an employee incentive, Hygrade pays its drivers a percentage of a retailer's delivery charges. Drivers are not paid for items that are delivered incorrectly or for delivering damaged items.

QUESTIONS

1. State several distribution standards that Hygrade Furniture Transport could set and how you would measure its success in achieving each standard.
2. Explain why a retailer should use Hygrade Furniture Transport rather than its own warehouse and trucking operation. Discuss the total-cost approach in your answer.
3. Is just-in-time inventory management possible with items such as furniture? Why or why not?
4. "Because of the carry-away nature of most apparel items, Hygrade does not plan to branch out into this area." Comment on this.

CHAPTER 13

Wholesaling

CHAPTER OBJECTIVES

1. To define wholesaling and show its importance

2. To describe the three broad categories of wholesaling (manufacturer wholesaling, merchant wholesaling, and agents and brokers) and the specific types of firms within each category

3. To examine recent trends in wholesaling

Reprinted by permission.

N ot long ago, salespeople from McKesson, as well as those from other wholesalers, would drop by drugstores to take orders for cough syrup, aspirin, penicillin, and Valium. When the store ran short between sales visits, clerks would read new orders over the phone to tape recorders at McKesson's warehouse.

Today a clerk can walk the aisles once a week with a McKesson-supplied computer in his or her palm. If the store is low on, say, bottles of cough syrup, the clerk waves a scanner over a McKesson-provided label stuck to the shelf. The computer takes note, and when the clerk is finished, transmits the order to McKesson, whose computers also print price stickers and tell store managers how profitable each of their departments is.

Because of the broad range of activities they perform, full-service wholesalers such as McKesson—which buy goods from manufacturers and provide a host of functions for their channel-member customers—now dominate many industries. For example, four pharmaceutical wholesalers have a 60 per cent market share in their industry. Let us see why.

In competing against limited-service wholesalers (which often emphasize low prices), full-service wholesalers have been steadily broadening their service capability. At McKesson, its increased competitiveness is largely based on its sophisticated computer system. At Spartan Stores, a regional food wholesaler, its competitive strategy is keyed to closer communication with member retailers and higher-quality services.

In the mid-1970s, McKesson had 800 salespeople selling about $915 million a year in merchandise to independent stores. At that time, it viewed its performance as so poor that McKesson considered dropping out of drugstore wholesaling. But it was able to turn the situation around. Now McKesson has fewer than 400 salespeople who sell $3 billion worth of merchandise annually; and drugstore distribution is the firm's biggest business.

According to a McKesson senior vice-president, "Everything we've been able to do has been driven by getting the customer on computers." Adds an outside analyst, "Computer links to drugstores not only cut costs and increase productivity, but also make customers so dependent on McKesson they rarely switch distributors."

Spartan Stores is a full-service, retailer-owned wholesale food cooperative with members based in Michigan, Indiana, and Ohio. In western Michigan, the company's strongest market, Spartan's members have a 60 per cent market share of the area's retail food business.

During the past few years, Spartan has enhanced its competitive strength by having better communication with members; upgrading warehousing and distribution systems; and recruiting specialists for distribution, human-resource, and management-information systems departments. For example, the appointment of a customer service director demonstrates "to the members that their interests are the first priority, and that Spartan management would not be isolated from them in any way."

Although Spartan has sold most of the 22 retail food stores it owned directly, it has kept three units: "We will use those stores for research and development purposes—for example, format and merchandising program development."[1]

In this chapter, we will examine the different types of firms that perform wholesaling activities and the strategies they use to compete in the marketplace. We will further draw the distinctions between full-service wholesalers and other firms engaging in wholesaling functions.

[1] David Wessel, "Computer Finds a Role in Buying and Selling, Reshaping Businesses," *Wall Street Journal* (March 18, 1987), pp. 1, 10; and Richard De Santa, "Renewing the Spartan Philosophy," *Progressive Grocer* (January 1988), pp. 28–29 ff.

Overview

Wholesaling is the buying/handling of merchandise and its resale to organizational buyers.

As noted in Chapter 12, wholesaling undertakes many functions in a distribution channel, particularly those in the sorting process. **Wholesaling** involves the buying or handling of merchandise and its subsequent resale to organizational users, retailers, and/or other wholesalers but not the sale of significant volume to final consumers.[2]

Sometimes, manufacturers serve as their own wholesalers; other times, independent middlemen are employed. The independents may or may not take title to or physical possession of goods, depending on the type of wholesaling performed. Some independents perform limited functions, such as contacting retailers or employing a personal sales force. Others perform a full range of distribution functions, including buying and transporting. Wholesaling does not include sales made at the retail level.

Industrial, commercial, and government institutions are the leading customers for wholesalers, followed closely by retailers. Sales from one wholesaler to another also represent a significant proportion of wholesaling activity. The following show the diversity of transactions considered as wholesaling:

▶ Sales to manufacturers, mines, oil companies, fisheries, railroads, public utilities, and government departments.

▶ Sales of office or laboratory equipment and supplies to professionals such as doctors and dentists.

▶ Sales of building materials to contractors, except when they buy on behalf of homeowners.

▶ All purchases of farm products for resale to other than individual consumers, regardless of whether such purchases are made directly from farmers or from middlemen.

▶ All sales by supply houses, as long as purchases are not by final consumers.

▶ Sales to grocery stores, restaurants, hotels, clothing stores, shoe-repair firms, and all other retailers.

▶ Sales by manufacturers to wholesalers, and wholesalers to other wholesalers.[3]

In this chapter, the importance of wholesaling, the different types of wholesaling, and recent trends in wholesaling are all discussed in depth.

The Importance of Wholesaling

Wholesaling is an important aspect of distribution because of its impact on the economy, its functions in the distribution channel, and its relationships with suppliers and customers.

Wholesaling's Impact on the Economy

Wholesale sales are high; and wholesalers greatly affect final prices.

In the United States, there are about 420,000 wholesale establishments (including manufacturers having wholesale operations) with total annual sales well above $2 trillion. Although wholesale revenues are much higher than those in retailing, there are about five times as many retail establishments as wholesale.

---

[2] Adapted from the U.S. Bureau of the Census.
[3] Adapted from C. Glenn Walters and Blaise J. Bergiel, *Marketing Channels,* Second Edition (Hinsdale, Ill.: Scott, Foresman, 1982), p. 108.

TABLE 13-1   Selected Performance Data for Wholesalers by Product Category[1]

Product Category of Wholesaler	Gross Profit (As Per Cent of Sales)[a]	Operating Expenses (As Per Cent of Sales)	All Other Expenses (As Per Cent of Sales)	Profit Before Taxes (As Per Cent of Sales)
Building materials	25.4	22.3	0.2	2.8
Chemicals and allied products	27.4	24.9	0.3	2.2
Coffee, tea, and spices	24.3	21.5	0.5	2.4
Cotton	12.3	10.8	0.2	1.4
Drug proprietaries and druggists' supplies	28.9	24.9	0.6	3.4
Electronic parts and equipment	29.3	26.9	0.7	1.7
Fish and seafoods	15.3	13.1	1.1	1.1
Flowers, nursery stock, and florists' supplies	38.3	33.6	1.2	3.5
General groceries	18.0	16.7	0.2	1.1
General merchandise	34.8	30.9	0.9	3.0
Hardware and paints	30.5	27.4	0.7	2.4
Jewelry	29.6	25.7	0.9	3.1
Motor vehicle supplies and new parts	31.7	29.0	0.5	2.2
Petroleum bulk stations and terminals	15.0	14.0	0.0	1.0
Wine, liquor, and beer	23.1	20.6	0.5	2.0

[1] In interpreting these data, RMA cautions that the Studies be regarded only as a general guideline and not as an absolute industry norm. This is due to limited samples within categories, the categorization of companies by their primary Standard Industrial Classification (SIC) number only, and different methods of operations by companies within the same industry. For these reasons, RMA recommends that the figures be used only as general guidelines in addition to other methods of financial analysis.

[a] Total costs of wholesaling, which include expenses and profit. Columns may not add across due to rounding.

Source: Adapted from *'88 Annual Statement Studies* (Philadelphia: Robert Morris Associates, 1988). © 1988, Robert Morris Associates; reprinted by permission.

High wholesale sales occur because they involve any purchases made by organizational consumers. In addition, some products move through several levels of wholesalers; there is only one level of retailing. Therefore, an item can be sold twice or more at the wholesale level (e. g., regionally, then locally), yet just once at the retail level. There are more retailers because they service small and geographically dispersed final consumer groups; wholesalers deal with fewer, larger, more geographically concentrated customers.

From a cost perspective, wholesalers have a significant impact on the price of merchandise. Table 13-1 shows the per cent of wholesale selling prices that go to selected wholesalers to cover their operating expenses and pre-tax profits. For example, 30.5 per cent of the price a hardware and paints wholesaler charges its retailers covers the wholesaler's operating and other expenses (28.1 per cent) and pre-tax profit (2.4 per cent). Operating costs include inventory charges, sales force salaries, advertising, and rent.

Wholesaler costs and profits depend on the rate of inventory turnover, the dollar value of products, the functions performed, efficiency, and the level of competition.

The Functions of Wholesalers

Wholesalers provide functions ranging from distribution to risk taking.

Among the important functions typically performed by wholesalers are the following. Wholesalers can

- ▶ Enable manufacturers to distribute locally without making customer contacts.
- ▶ Provide a trained sales force.
- ▶ Provide marketing and research assistance for manufacturers and retail or institutional consumers.
- ▶ Gather assortments for customers, letting them make few transactions.
- ▶ Purchase large quantities, thus reducing total physical distribution costs.
- ▶ Provide warehousing and delivery facilities.
- ▶ Offer financing for manufacturers (by paying for goods when they are shipped, not when they are sold) and retail or institutional consumers (by granting credit).
- ▶ Handle financial records.
- ▶ Handle returns and make adjustments for defective merchandise.
- ▶ Take risks by being responsible for the theft, deterioration, and obsolescence of inventory.[4]

Those wholesalers that take title to and possession of goods usually perform several or all of these functions. Those that facilitate sales, but do not take title or possession, are agents and brokers that generally concentrate on the first four functions.

The use of independent wholesalers varies by industry. For example, most consumer products, food items, replacement parts, and office supplies are funneled through independents. In other industries, including heavy equipment, mainframe computers, and gasoline, many manufacturers bypass independent wholesalers and retailers.

Without independent wholesalers, organizational consumers would have to develop supplier contacts, deal with a number of suppliers and coordinate shipments, perform more distribution functions, stock greater quantities, and place more emphasis on an internal purchasing agent or department. In addition, many small retailers and other businesses might be avoided as customers because they would not be profitably reached by a manufacturer/supplier; and these institutions might not be able to purchase necessary items elsewhere.

To illustrate wholesaling's importance, in the auto parts industry there used to be thousands of firms producing a wide range of products and marketing them through a multitude of selling organizations. Customers, mostly specialty stores and service stations, were constantly interrupted by salespeople. Sales costs were high for manufacturers. A smoother, less costly system exists today with the organized use of a moderate number of independent distributors.

Wholesalers' Relationships with Suppliers and Customers

Wholesalers have obligations to their suppliers and to their customers.

Independent wholesalers are very much "in the middle," not fully knowing whether their allegiance should be to the manufacturer/supplier or their own customer. These comments show the dilemma faced by many wholesalers:

---

[4] Adapted from Walters and Bergiel, *Marketing Channels,* p. 109; and Louis W. Stern and Adel L. El-Ansary, *Marketing Channels,* Third Edition (Englewood Cliffs, N.J.: Prentice-Hall, 1988), pp. 112–119.

You're the Marketer

How Can Huffy Succeed at Wholesaling?

Huffy Corporation, the largest U.S. bicycle manufacturer, has a 25 to 30 per cent share of the market; and bicycles account for about 70 per cent of total company sales. The firm also produces juvenile products, such as backpacks for infants, and is becoming more involved in wholesaling.

Huffy very much wants to be less dependent on manufacturing bicycles. It is concerned that industrywide U.S. sales of bikes declined by 25 per cent between 1987 and 1988, and that the firm's bike revenues dropped by 20 per cent from 1987 to 1988. Accordingly, in 1988, Huffy sold its Raleigh Cycle of America unit because it was unable to increase Raleigh's bicycle sales satisfactorily—despite newly introduced models that used technology similar to that in Olympic racing bicycles.

In an effort to diversify its business, Huffy purchased Washington Inventory Service, an independent wholesaling firm that counts inventories for retail stores, in late 1988. Huffy wants its wholesaling service business to grow to $100 million in annual sales by 1990–1991.

It believes that Washington's business can be expanded by investing in additional computer-based equipment and by increasing its emphasis on mass merchandisers (a market segment where Huffy has successfully sold its bicycles). At present, Washington is a heavy employer of part-time workers and does most of its business with drugstores and grocery stores.

Huffy's other wholesale service subsidiary is its YLC Enterprises Inc. unit, which assembles bicycles and performs other services for retailers. Unlike the Washington Inventory Service unit, YLC already has strong ties to mass merchandisers.

As one marketing analyst commented, Huffy needs to consider the following in expanding its wholesaling efforts:

> *I'd prefer to see them add more brand-name products that they could sell through mass merchandisers. They know manufacturing. However, the next best thing is a service that they can sell to mass merchandisers.*

As vice-president of Huffy's wholesaling division, what would you do?

SOURCE: Based on material in Ralph E. Winter, "Huffy Aims to Cut Reliance on Bicycles with Move to Retail-Inventory Control," *Wall Street Journal* (October 27, 1988), p. B5.

Ironically, a manufacturers' representative is almost doomed to failure. If he does a poor job, the businesses he represents will either replace him or conclude the territory is too weak to justify any sales support, and he will be dropped anyway. If he does well, and the territory grows, he may still be replaced; this time by a full-time captive salesperson on the payroll or the manufacturer whose products the manufacturers' representative did so well selling.[5]

Many wholesalers feel that they receive inadequate support from manufacturers/suppliers. They desire training, technical assistance, product literature, and advertising. Wholesalers dislike it when vendors alter territory assignments, shrink territory

---

[5] John J. Withey, "Realities of Channel Dynamics: A Wholesaling Example," *Journal of the Academy of Marketing Science,* Vol. 13 (Summer 1985), p. 73. See also Allan J. Magrath and Kenneth G. Hardy, "Avoiding the Pitfalls in Managing Distribution Channels," *Business Horizons,* Vol. 30 (September–October 1987), pp. 29–33.

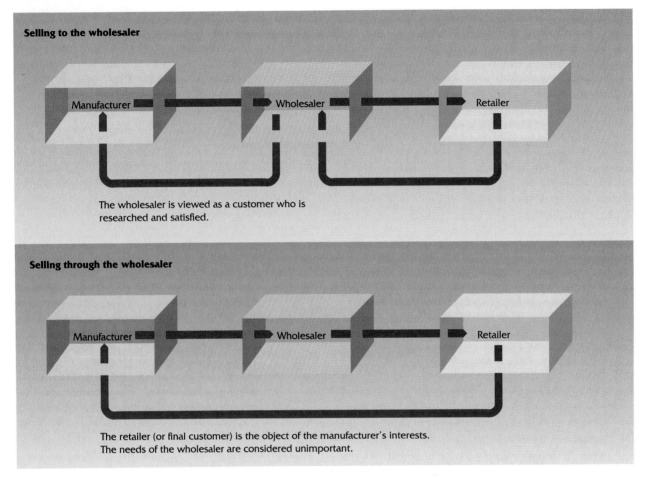

Selling to the wholesaler

Manufacturer → Wholesaler → Retailer

The wholesaler is viewed as a customer who is researched and satisfied.

Selling through the wholesaler

Manufacturer → Wholesaler → Retailer

The retailer (or final customer) is the object of the manufacturer's interests. The needs of the wholesaler are considered unimportant.

FIGURE 13-1
Selling To Vs. Selling Through the Wholesaler

size, add new distributors to cover an existing geographic area, or decide to change to a direct channel and perform wholesale functions themselves. Wholesalers want manufacturers/suppliers to sell to them and not through them. Selling to the wholesaler means the distributor is viewed as a customer who must be researched and satisfied. Selling through the wholesaler means the retailer or final consumer is the object of the manufacturer's/supplier's interest and that the needs of the wholesaler are less important.[6] See Figure 13-1.

These actions, involving the Coca-Cola Co. and the independent wholesalers (bottlers) that distribute its beverage products, illustrate how fragile manufacturer/wholesaler relationships can be:

▶ When Coca-Cola gave all bottlers the same commercials for local advertising (in order to improve efficiency and reinforce a single national image), many bottlers viewed these ads as inappropriate for their markets. Today bottlers can select commercials and promotions for their areas.

▶ Coca-Cola implemented a program that provided bottlers with a $100 contribution

[6] See James A. Narus and James C. Anderson, "Turn Your Industrial Distributors into Partners," *Harvard Business Review*, Vol. 64 (March–April 1986), pp. 66–71; and Robert F. McCarthy, "IBM Muscles the Distribution Channel—Again," *Business Marketing* (August 1988), pp. 49–57.

toward their advertising efforts for each new display rack they placed in stores. The bottlers felt the racks were unnecessary.

▶ For a long time, the bottlers believed that Coca-Cola was less interested in U.S. operations than in overseas markets. Domestic operations are now more valued; and Coca-Cola field representatives meet regularly with the bottlers and are aided by computer routing and other systems.

▶ During the past decade, Coca-Cola has used "its powers of persuasion and plenty of cash" to replace the majority of its existing distributors with new ones interested in "intelligent risk-taking and no-holds-barred marketing." Currently, Coca-Cola is satisfied with its bottler network.

▶ Coca-Cola has a large ownership interest in Coca-Cola Enterprises, the largest distributor of its products.

▶ Coca-Cola has been in a protracted and expensive battle with Pernod, a French wholesaler, over distribution rights in France.[7]

Types of Wholesaling

The three broad categories of wholesaling are outlined in Figures 13-2 and 13-3: manufacturer wholesaling, merchant wholesaling, and agents and brokers. Table 13-2 contains detailed descriptions of each type of independent wholesaler and shows their functions and special features.

Manufacturer Wholesaling

With **manufacturer wholesaling,** a producer undertakes all wholesaling functions itself. This occurs when a firm believes that it is able to reach its retailers or other organizational customers most effectively by assuming responsibility for wholesaling tasks. Manufacturer wholesaling accounts for almost one-third of total wholesale revenues and 10 per cent of establishments. Examples of firms engaged in manufacturer wholesaling are General Motors, IBM, Frito-Lay, Procter & Gamble, and Continental Baking. See Figure 13-4.

*In **manufacturer wholesaling,** a firm acts via its own **sales** or **branch** offices.*

Wholesale activities by a manufacturer may be conducted in either a sales office or branch office. A **manufacturer's sales office** is located at the company's production facilities or a site close to the market. No inventory is carried at the sales office. In contrast, a **manufacturer's branch office** includes facilities for warehousing goods as well as for selling them.

Manufacturer wholesaling is most likely when no independent middlemen are available, the available middlemen are unacceptable to the manufacturer, the manufacturer wants control over its marketing efforts, customers are few in number and each is a major account, customers desire a high level of personal service from the producer, customers are near to the manufacturer or they are geographically clustered, a computerized-ordering system links a manufacturer with its customers, and/or legal restrictions (particularly those in foreign markets) limit arrangements with independent middlemen.

---

[7] "Coke's New Program to Placate Bottlers," *Business Week* (October 12, 1981), p. 48; Thomas E. Ricks, "Coca-Cola Celebrates New Success After Restructuring Its Bottlers," *Wall Street Journal* (June 28, 1984), p. 31; Timothy K. Smith and Robert Johnson, "Coca-Cola to Buy Bottling Operations from Beatrice Cos. for About $1 Billion," *Wall Street Journal* (June 17, 1986), p. 3; and John Rossant and Scott Ticer, "Why Pernod Didn't Go Better with Coke," *Business Week* (June 20, 1988), p. 64.

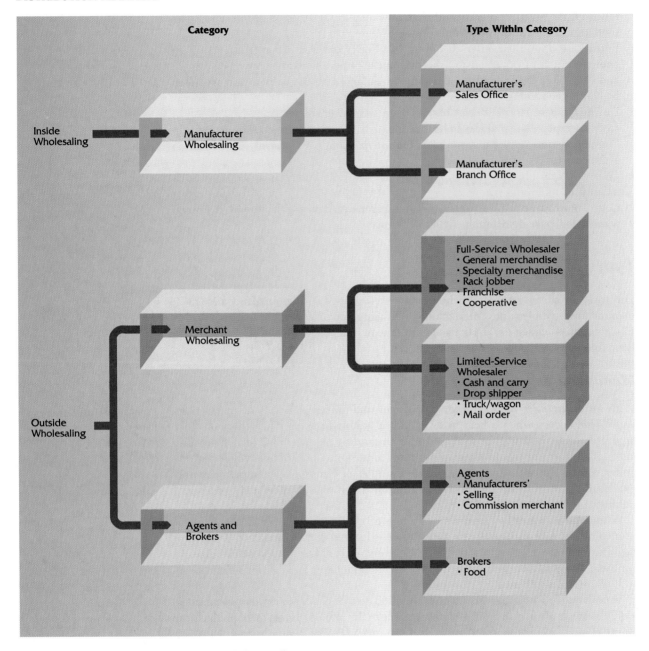

Category

Type Within Category

FIGURE 13-2 **The Broad Categories of Wholesaling**

Merchant Wholesaling

*Merchant wholesalers buy products and are **full** or **limited service.***

Merchant wholesalers buy, take title, and take possession of products for further resale. They represent the largest category of wholesalers in terms of sales — almost 60 per cent of the total — and establishments — more than 80 per cent of the total.

For example, Wetterau is a merchant wholesaler in the food industry. It handles thousands of products for its 2,400+ retailer customers, which are located in almost

Factors	Manufacturer Wholesaling	Merchant Wholesaling	Agents and Brokers
Control/ Functions	• The manufacturer controls wholesaling and performs all functions.	• The wholesaler controls wholesaling and performs many or all functions.	• The manufacturer and wholesaler each have some control and perform some functions.
Ownership	• The manufacturer owns products until they are bought by retailers or other organizational consumers.	• The wholesaler buys products from the manufacturer and resells them.	• The manufacturer owns the products and pays the wholesaler a fee/ commission.
Cash Flow	• The manufacturer does not receive payment until the retailer or other customer buys products.	• The manufacturer is paid when the wholesaler purchases products.	• The manufacturer does not receive payment until products are sold.
Best Use(s)	• The manufacturer deals with a small group of large and geographically concentrated customers; rapid expansion is not a goal.	• The manufacturer has a large product line that is sold through many small and geographically dispersed customers; expansion is a goal.	• The manufacturer is small, has little marketing expertise, and is relatively unknown to potential customers; expansion is a goal.

30 states. It helps these retailers design their stores, trains employees, provides credit, offers insurance coverage, installs computerized-inventory systems, and offers private-label items.[8] Figure 13-5 shows Wetterau's automated distribution warehouse in Pennsylvania, one of the twenty warehouses in its distribution network.

Merchant wholesalers may be full service or limited service. Both buy and take title to merchandise. *Full-service merchant wholesalers* perform a full range of distribution functions. They assemble an assortment of products in a given place. They provide trade credit, store and deliver merchandise, offer merchandising and promotion assistance, provide a personal sales force, and offer research and planning support. Information is passed along to suppliers and customers. Installation and repair services are given. Full-service merchant wholesalers act like the sales arms of their

FIGURE 13-3
Contrasting Manufacturer Wholesaling, Merchant Wholesaling, and Agents and Brokers

---

[8] *Wetterau Incorporated 1988 Annual Report.*

TABLE 13-2   Characteristics of Independent Wholesalers

Wholesaler Type	Major Functions						Special Features
	Provides Credit	Stores and Delivers Goods	Takes Title to Goods	Provides Merchandising and Promotion Assistance	Provides Personal Sales Force	Performs Research and Planning	
I. Merchant wholesaler							
A. Full service							
1. General merchandise	Yes	Yes	Yes	Yes	Yes	Yes	Carries nearly all the items normally needed by a customer
2. Specialty merchandise	Yes	Yes	Yes	Yes	Yes	Yes	Specializes in a narrow range of products, extensive assortment
3. Rack jobber	Yes	Yes	Yes	Yes	Yes	Yes	Furnishes racks and shelves, consignment sales
4. Franchise	Yes	Yes	Yes	Yes	Yes	Yes	Use of common business format, extensive management services
5. Cooperative							
a. Producer-owned	Yes	Yes	Yes	Yes	Yes	Yes	Farmer controlled, profits divided among members
b. Retailer-owned	Yes	Yes	Yes	Yes	Yes	Yes	Wholesaler owned by several retailers
B. Limited service							
1. Cash and carry	No	Stores, no delivery	Yes	No	No	No	No outside sales force, wholesale store for business needs
2. Drop shipper	Yes	Delivers, no storage	Yes	No	Yes	Sometimes	Ships items without physically handling them
3. Truck/wagon	Rarely	Yes	Yes	Yes	Yes	Sometimes	Sales and delivery on same call
4. Mail order	Rarely	Yes	Yes	No	No	Sometimes	Catalogs used as sole promotion tool
II. Agents and brokers							
A. Agents							
1. Manufacturers'	No	Sometimes	No	Yes	Yes	Sometimes	Sells selected goods for several manufacturers
2. Selling	Sometimes	Yes	No	Yes	Yes	Yes	Markets all the goods of a manufacturer
3. Commission (factor) merchants	Sometimes	Yes	No	No	Yes	Yes	Handles goods on a consignment basis
B. Brokers							
1. Food	No	Sometimes	No	Yes	Yes	Yes	Brings together buyers and sellers

FIGURE 13-4
Manufacturer Wholesaling by Continental Baking
The Continental Baking Company manufactures and distributes a line of high-quality bread and cake products under brand names such as Wonder and Hostess. Continental salespeople deliver products daily through more than 7,000 individual routes to major retailers.
Reprinted by permission.

FIGURE 13-5 Mechanized Food Distribution at Wetterau Wetterau, a large food wholesaler, operates its own automated distribution warehouse in Reading, Pennsylvania. Because it is so efficient, Wetterau's supermarket customers pay less for delivered merchandise. Reprinted by permission.

manufacturers. They are prevalent for grocery products, tobacco, alcoholic beverages, hardware, plumbing equipment, and drugs.

Limited-service merchant wholesalers do not perform all the functions of full-service merchant wholesalers. For example, they may not provide credit, merchandising assistance, or marketing research data. Limited-service merchant wholesalers are popular for construction materials, coal, lumber, perishables, and specialty foods.

On the average, full-service merchant wholesalers require higher compensation than limited-service merchant wholesalers, because they perform greater functions. Table 13-3 contrasts the marketing strategies of the two kinds of merchant wholesalers for medical supplies.

Full-Service Merchant Wholesalers

Full-service merchant wholesalers can be divided into general merchandise, specialty merchandise, rack jobber, franchise, and cooperative types.

General-merchandise (full-line) wholesalers carry a wide assortment of products, nearly all the items needed by the customers to which they cater. For example, general-merchandise hardware, drug, and clothing wholesalers stock many items for their retailers, but not much depth within any specific product line. They seek to sell their retailers or other organizational customers all or most of their products and develop strong loyalty and exclusivity with them.

Specialty-merchandise (limited-line) wholesalers concentrate efforts on a relatively narrow range of products and have an extensive assortment within that range. They offer expertise and many sizes, colors, and models in their product categories. Specialty wholesalers provide functions similar to general-merchandise and other full-service merchant wholesalers. Specialty wholesaling is popular for health foods, seafood, retailers' store displays, and frozen foods.

Rack jobbers furnish the racks or shelves on which merchandise is displayed. They own the merchandise on these racks, selling items on a consignment basis, so that their customers pay after goods are resold. Unsold merchandise is taken back. Jobbers set up displays, refill shelves, price mark merchandise, maintain inventory records, and compute the amount due from their customers. Heavily advertised, branded merchandise that is sold on a self-service basis is most frequently handled. Included are health and beauty aids, drugs, cosmetics, magazines, hand tools, toys, housewares, and stationery.

Rack jobbing came into being after World War II. General-merchandise wholesalers would not sell nonfood items to supermarkets because of potential conflicts with their regular drugstore and hardware store customers and their inability to stock a wide range of nonfood items for supermarkets. Over time, rack jobbers started to serve drugstores, hardware stores, variety stores, service stations, and restaurants, in addition to supermarkets. Recently some large retail chains have begun to bypass rack jobbers and assume their functions in order to increase profit margins.

In ***franchise wholesaling,*** independent retailers affiliate with an existing wholesaler in order to use a standardized storefront design, business format, name, and purchase system. In many instances, suppliers produce goods according to specifications set by the franchise wholesaler. This form of wholesaling is utilized for hardware, auto parts, and groceries.

Major franchise wholesalers include Independent Grocers Affiliate (IGA), Ben Franklin Stores, Western Auto, Walgreen, and Super Valu Stores. As an illustration,

General-merchandise wholesalers sell a range of items.

Specialty-merchandise wholesalers concentrate on a narrow line.

Rack jobbers set up displays, mark items, are paid after sales, and take returns.

With franchise wholesaling, retailers join with a wholesaler.

TABLE 13-3 Contrasting the Strategies of Full-Service and Limited-Service Medical-Supply Merchant Wholesalers

Full-Service Medical-Supply Wholesaler

Provides special services for physicians, such as frequent sales calls, emergency and small-order delivery, and liberal credit terms

Guarantees zero out-of-stock policy for key health-care items through an inventory-control system

Prepares an ideal inventory model for accounts and agrees to manage inventory to maintain appropriate stock levels

Uses a sales contract or prime vendor contract whereby the hospital agrees to do the majority of its purchasing through the contracting wholesaler

Maintains an inventory of 8,000–10,000+ items

Is paid, on average, every 50 days

Limited-Service Medical-Supply Wholesaler

Offers the lowest market price as the primary means of generating sales; gross profit margin is 10% of sales, compared with the industry average of 20%

Uses multiyear supply contracts with hospitals, reducing the need for field sales support; average selling costs as a per cent of new sales are 2.0%, compared with the industry average of 5.5%

Seeks sales contracts only from the largest-volume hospitals

Deals only in high-volume medical commodities

Uses high levels of computer cost controls and accounting controls

Maintains an inventory of 1,500–3,000 items

Is paid, on average, in fewer than 30 days

Source: Adapted from P. Ronald Stephenson, "Wholesale Distribution: An Analysis of Structure, Strategy and Profit Performance" in Arch G. Woodside et al. (Editors), *Foundations of Marketing Channels* (Austin, Tex.: Lone Star Publishers, 1978), pp. 103–107. © Lone Star Publishers, 1978; reprinted by permission.

retailers affiliated with IGA are supplied with a variety of food and nonfood services, such as site selection, store engineering, interior design, and merchandising assistance (furnishing advertising formats and point-of-sale promotion materials).

A ***wholesale cooperative*** is owned by its member firms to economize functions and offer broad support. Producer-owned wholesale cooperatives are popular in farming. For example, Land O'Lakes has 350,000 farm member firms and annual sales of $2.2 billion. It handles food products and farm commodities, and provides agricultural services. Cooperatives annually market 30 per cent of all U.S. agricultural commodities, 40 per cent of all raisins, 70 per cent of all milk, and over 90 per cent of all cranberries.[9] Producer cooperatives not only market, transport, and process farm products; they also manufacture and distribute farm supplies. In many cases, cooperatives sell to supermarkets under their own names, such as Ocean Spray, Land O'Lakes, Sunkist, Blue Diamond, and Welch's. Figures 13-6 and 13-7 show several Land O'Lakes and Sunkist products.

*Producers or retailers can establish a **wholesale cooperative.***

Retailer-owned wholesale cooperatives appear when independent retailers form associations that purchase, lease, or build wholesale facilities. The cooperative takes title to merchandise, handles cooperative advertising, and negotiates with suppliers. Retailer-owned cooperatives are used by hardware and grocery stores.

[9] James Cook, "Dreams of Glory," *Forbes* (September 12, 1983), pp. 92, 94; and Corie Brown, Mary Pitzer, and Teresa Carson, "Why Farm Co-Ops Need Extra Seed Money," *Business Week* (March 21, 1988), p. 96.

FIGURE 13-6
Selected Land O'Lakes Products
Reprinted by permission.

Limited-Service Merchant Wholesalers

Limited-service merchant wholesalers can be divided into cash-and-carry, drop shipper, truck/wagon, and mail-order types.

In cash-and-carry wholesaling, the customer drives to a wholesaler.

With ***cash-and-carry wholesaling,*** a small businessperson is able to drive to a wholesaler, order products, and take them back to the store or business. It emerged in the 1920s and 1930s as a result of the growing threat of chain stores against independent retailers. Cash-and-carry wholesalers offer no credit or delivery, provide no merchandising and promotion assistance, have no outside sales force, and do not aid in marketing research or planning. They are important for fill-in items, have low prices, and allow immediate product availability. Cash-and-carry wholesalers are common for construction materials, electrical supplies, office supplies, auto supplies, hardware products, and groceries.

Drop shippers buy goods but do not take possession.

Drop shippers (desk jobbers) purchase goods from manufacturers or suppliers and arrange for their shipment to retailers or industrial users. While they have legal ownership of products, they do not take physical possession of them and have no facilities for storing them. Drop shippers buy items, leave them at manufacturers' plants, contact customers by telephone, set up and coordinate carload shipments from manufacturers directly to their customers, and assume responsibility for items that cannot be sold. Trade credit, a personal sales force, and some research and planning assistance are provided; merchandising and promotional support are not. Drop shippers are often used for coal, coke, and building materials. These goods have high freight costs in relation to their unit value, because of their weight. Therefore, direct shipments from suppliers to customers are needed.

Truck/wagon wholesalers offer goods on a sales route.

Truck/wagon wholesalers generally have a regular sales route, offer items from the truck or wagon, and deliver goods at the same time they are sold. They also provide merchandising and promotion support. This wholesaler is considered to offer limited service because it usually does not extend credit and offers little research and planning help. Operating costs are high because of the personalized services performed and low average sales. These wholesalers often deal with goods requiring special handling or those that are perishable. These include bakery products, tobacco, meat, candy, potato chips, and dairy products.

Mail-order wholesalers sell through catalogs.

Mail-order wholesalers utilize catalogs, instead of a personal sales force, to promote products and communicate with their customers. They do not generally provide

Sunkist and Sunkist are registered trademarks of Sunkist Growers, Inc. © 1989 Sunkist Growers, Inc.

FIGURE 13-7
Selected Sunkist Products
Reprinted by permission.

credit or merchandising and promotion support. They do store and deliver goods and offer some research and planning assistance. Mail-order wholesaling is found with jewelry, cosmetics, auto parts, specialty food product lines, business supplies, and small office equipment.

Agents and Brokers

Agents and *brokers* provide various wholesale functions, but they do not take title to goods. Unlike merchant wholesalers, who receive profits from the sales of goods they own, agents and brokers work for commissions or fees as payment for their services. Roughly 10 per cent of wholesale sales and 8 to 10 per cent of wholesale establishments are comprised by agents and brokers. The principal difference between agents and brokers is that agents are more likely to be used on a permanent basis, whereas brokers are employed on a temporary basis.

Agents and brokers offer these major advantages: they allow a manufacturer or supplier to expand sales despite limited resources; their selling costs are a predetermined per cent of sales; and they provide a trained sales force.[10]

Agents are comprised of manufacturers' agents, selling agents, and commission (factor) merchants. *Manufacturers' agents* work for several manufacturers and carry noncompetitive, complementary products in exclusive territories. By selling noncompetitive items, agents are able to eliminate conflict-of-interest situations. By selling complementary goods, agents are able to stock a fairly complete line of products for their market areas. They do not offer credit but at times store and deliver products and provide research and planning aid. Merchandising and promotion support are given.

Manufacturers' agents may supplement the sales efforts of producers, help introduce new products, enter geographically dispersed markets, and sell products with low average sales. They often carry only a portion of a manufacturer's products. A manufacturer may employ many agents, each with a unique product-territorial mix. Larger firms might use a different agent for every major product line. Agents have limited input into the manufacturer's marketing program and price structure. They

Agents and *brokers* do not take title to goods.

Manufacturers' agents work for many firms and carry noncompeting items.

[10] See "The Use of Sales Reps," *Small Business Report* (December 1986), pp. 72–78.

405

Marketing Controversy

When Should a Company Use Manufacturers' Agents?

A firm's decision whether to utilize outside manufacturers' agents (reps) or an internal sales force can be a tough one.

These are some advantages of using reps:

▶ A firm has low or nonexistent fixed costs with reps. Because they are paid when sales are made, the firm's selling expenses (commissions) are variable costs. In contrast, a company sales force requires fixed expenditures for office space, sales management, and so on. Thus, at low sales volumes, the overall selling costs (variable and fixed) associated with reps are usually lower.

▶ Reps enable a firm to get widespread geographic coverage. This is particularly important for a small firm, with a narrow product line and limited resources that could not manage or afford its own regional or national sales force. Reps make it easier for such a firm to enter a new market.

▶ Reps often have contacts with accounts that a company sales force may not.

▶ Because reps handle the noncompetitive products of several manufacturers, they allow their customers to minimize the number of salespeople they must see.

Some disadvantages of using reps are:

▶ A firm has greater control over its sales force, which consists of employees. Reps are independent distributors.

▶ A company sales force has total commitment to the firm's product line. Reps have divided loyalties.

▶ Under high-volume conditions, a company sales force generally has an overall cost advantage.

▶ Customer feedback may be greater with a company sales force.

A decision to switch from reps to a company sales force may be difficult because of ethical and legal considerations. For example, should a firm use reps to build up territories and then switch to a company sales force?
What do you think?

SOURCE: Based on material in Thomas L. Powers, "Switching From Reps to Direct Salespeople," *Industrial Marketing Management*, Vol. 16 (1987), pp. 169–172.

generally earn commissions of 5 to 10 per cent of sales, and are major wholesalers of automotive products, iron, steel, footwear, and textile products.

Selling agents market all the products of a manufacturer.

Selling agents assume responsibility for marketing the entire output of a manufacturer under a contractual agreement. In effect, they become the marketing departments for their manufacturers/suppliers and are empowered to negotiate price and other conditions of sale, such as credit and delivery. They perform all wholesale functions except taking title to merchandise. While a manufacturer may use several manufacturers' agents, it may employ only one sales agent.

Selling agents are more likely to work for small manufacturers than large ones. These agents are common for textile manufacturing, canned foods, metals, home furnishings, apparel, lumber, and metal products. Because they perform more functions, they usually receive a higher commission rate than manufacturers' representatives.

Commission merchants assemble goods from local markets.

Commission (factor) merchants receive goods on consignment from producers, accumulate them from local markets, and arrange for their sale in a central market location. These merchants sometimes offer credit, store and deliver goods, provide a

FIGURE 13-8 **How Clorox Uses Food Brokers** Clorox region sales managers and food brokers play key roles in new-product introductions by ensuring the product is readily available and prominently displayed. Region Sales Manager Kevin Eichele (left) and Bob Guetersloh, Account Executive with the Carey-Ahrens food brokerage company in Oakland, check a Hidden Valley Ranch display in a large Oakland-area supermarket. Carey-Ahrens handles distribution and displays for Hidden Valley Ranch bottled salad dressing at more than 1,200 Northern California stores.
Reprinted by permission.

sales force, and offer research and planning help. They normally do not assist in merchandising and promotion.

Commission merchants can negotiate prices with buyers, provided that the prices are not below the seller's stated minimums. They may operate in an auction setting. The merchants deduct their commission, freight charges, and other expenses after the products are sold. The balance is sent to the producer or supplier. These wholesalers are used for agricultural and seafood products, furniture, and art.

Brokers are very common in the food industry. ***Food brokers*** introduce buyers and sellers of food and related general-merchandise items to one another and bring them together to complete a sale. They are well informed about market conditions, terms of sale, sources of credit, price setting, potential buyers, and the art of negotiating. They do not actually provide credit but sometimes store and deliver goods. Brokers also do not take title to goods and usually are not allowed to complete a transaction without formal approval. Brokers generally represent the seller, who pays their commission. See Figure 13-8.

Food brokers, like manufacturers' agents, operate in specific geographic locations and work for a limited number of food producers within these areas. Their sales forces

Food brokers *unite buyers and sellers to conclude sales.*

call on chain-store buyers, store managers, and institutional purchasing agents. Brokers work closely with advertising agencies. The average commission for food brokers is 5 per cent of sales.

Recent Trends in Wholesaling

During recent years, and continuing to the present, wholesaling has been changing dramatically as independent wholesalers try to protect their place in the distribution channel. Among the most prominent trends are those dealing with the evolving wholesaler mix, wholesaler size, productivity, service, and target markets.

Merchant wholesaling is growing, and firms are becoming larger.

Over the past several years, merchant wholesaling as a per cent of wholesale revenues has risen substantially, while manufacturer wholesaling and agents and brokers have seen their shares decline: "Both U.S. and foreign manufacturers who distribute goods in this country are increasingly dependent" on merchant wholesalers. On average, each of these wholesalers buys from over 130 suppliers and sells to more than 530 consumers.[11]

While many independent wholesalers are relatively small, family-owned businesses, these wholesalers are being squeezed by their larger competitors. In 1983, 42 per cent of all merchant wholesalers had annual sales of less than $20 million; this figure fell to 33 per cent in 1985 and is expected to drop to 22 per cent as of 1990. And, from 1985 to 1990, the total number of independent wholesalers in the United States was projected to drop by more than 10 per cent: "Wholesalers of everything from drugs to doors, from floor tiles to fabric, are merging."[12]

Wholesalers are emphasizing productivity and service.

Because wholesalers' profit margins are so small (e.g., about 1 per cent of sales for food wholesalers and 3–5 per cent of sales for durable-goods wholesalers), they are constantly seeking gains in productivity. For example, Vonnegut Industrial Products Corp. has installed an automated storage and retrieval system to reduce personnel costs: "One man operates the system, which stores 9,000 different products. By contrast, in an older part of the warehouse, six men are needed to manage 15,000 other items." Vonnegut has also automated its record-keeping functions and is working with large customers in a quick response (QR) ordering system.[13]

Wholesalers have learned that service is extremely important in securing a competitive advantage, developing customer loyalty, and attaining acceptable profit margins. In the steel industry, independent service centers are no longer just warehouses for their mills. Today they buy steel from domestic and foreign mills, which are concentrating on fewer products and higher-volume production runs. By assembling a vast variety of steel products, the centers have become "supermarkets for metal." And it is the service centers that most often finish processing the steel according to industrial customer needs. In addition, the centers greatly facilitate just-in-time inventory management for both mills and customers. While their prices "will always be higher than buying from mills, the total cost of getting the metal into the system is lower."[14]

---

[11] N. R. Kleinfield, "For Wholesalers, A New Look," *New York Times* (August 26, 1984), Section 3, p. 4.

[12] National Association of Wholesalers-Distributors; and Joseph Weber, "Mom and Pop Move Out of Wholesaling," *Business Week* (January 9, 1989), p. 91.

[13] Steven P. Galante, "Distributors Switch Strategies to Survive Coming Shakeout," *Wall Street Journal* (July 20, 1987), p. 21.

[14] Daniel F. Cuff, "Steel Service Centers: Oases in a Profit Desert," *New York Times* (March 17, 1985), Section 3, p. 6; and Rick Wartzman, "For Inland, Moving Steel Is Almost as Big as Making It," *Wall Street Journal* (March 23, 1989), p. A18.

In large numbers, wholesalers are diversifying the markets they serve or the products they carry, as these examples show. Farm and garden machinery wholesalers now sell to florists, hardware dealers, and garden supply stores. Plumbing wholesalers have added industrial accounts, contractors, and builders to their markets. Grocery wholesalers deal with hotels, airlines, hospitals, schools, and restaurants. Some food wholesalers have moved into apparel retailing and opened auto-parts stores.

Target market strategies are more complex.

Yet, some wholesalers are taking the opposite approach and seeking to appeal to one customer niche or need. For instance, the Ingram Book Company concentrates most of its efforts on 15,000 independent bookstore and library customers. Ingram makes large purchases from over 400 publishers, stores 100,000 titles through a sophisticated warehouse system, accepts small orders from customers, can process and deliver orders in fewer than 48 hours, and keeps prices reasonable. As one bookstore owner stated: "Thank God for Ingram. Without it, we could never compete against the chains, but now at least we have a fighting chance." As a result, Ingram distributes about 50 million books annually, roughly 6 per cent of all general-interest books sold.[15]

Summary

1. *To define wholesaling and show its importance* Wholesaling involves the buying or handling of merchandise and its resale to organizational users, retailers, and/or other wholesalers but not the sale of significant volume to final consumers. Approximately 420,000 wholesalers distribute over $2 trillion of merchandise annually.

   Wholesale functions encompass distribution, personal selling, marketing and research assistance, gathering assortments, cost reductions, warehousing, financing, returns, and risk taking. These functions may be assumed by the manufacturer or shared with an independent wholesaler. Wholesalers are sometimes in a precarious position because they are located between manufacturers/suppliers and customers and must determine their responsibilities to each.

2. *To describe the three broad categories of wholesaling (manufacturer wholesaling, merchant wholesaling, and agents and brokers) and the specific types of firms within each category* In manufacturer wholesaling, a producer undertakes all wholesaling functions itself. Manufacturer wholesaling can be conducted through sales or branch offices. The sales office carries no inventory.

   Merchant wholesalers buy, take title, and possess products for their own accounts. Full-service merchant wholesalers assemble an assortment of products, provide trade credit, store and deliver merchandise, offer merchandising and promotion assistance, provide a personal sales force, offer research and planning support, and complete other functions as well. Full-service merchant wholesalers fall into general merchandise, specialty merchandise, rack jobber, franchise, and cooperative types. Limited-service merchant wholesalers take title to merchandise but do not provide all wholesale functions. Limited-service merchant wholesalers are divided into cash-and-carry, drop shipper, truck/wagon, and mail-order types.

   Agents and brokers provide various wholesale functions, such as negotiating purchases and expediting sales; but they do not take title to goods. They are paid commissions or fees. Agents are used on a more permanent basis than brokers. Types of agents are manufacturers' agents, selling agents, and commission (factor) merchants. Food brokers dominate brokerage.

3. *To examine recent trends in wholesaling* The nature of wholesaling has changed over the last several years. Trends involve the evolving wholesaler mix, wholesaler size, productivity, service, and target markets.

[15] Edwin McDowell, "The Book Industry's Best-Selling Middleman," *New York Times* (July 8, 1984), Section 3, pp. 8–9; and Edwin McDowell, "Bookstores Look to Instant Ordering," *New York Times* (January 2, 1989), p. 33.

Key Terms

wholesaling (p. 392)
manufacturer wholesaling (p. 397)
manufacturer's sales office (p. 397)
manufacturer's branch office (p. 397)
merchant wholesalers (p. 398)
full-service merchant
 wholesalers (p. 399)
limited-service merchant
 wholesalers (p. 402)

general-merchandise (full-line)
 wholesalers (p. 402)
specialty-merchandise (limited-line)
 wholesalers (p. 402)
rack jobbers (p. 402)
franchise wholesaling (p. 402)
wholesale cooperative (p. 403)
cash-and-carry wholesaling (p. 404)
drop shippers (desk jobbers) (p. 404)

truck/wagon wholesalers (p. 404)
mail-order wholesalers (p. 404)
agents (p. 405)
brokers (p. 405)
manufacturers' agents (p. 405)
selling agents (p. 406)
commission (factor)
 merchants (p. 406)
food brokers (p. 407)

Review Questions

1. Why does wholesale sales volume exceed retail sales volume?
2. Differentiate between selling to a wholesaler and selling though a wholesaler.
3. Under what circumstances should a firm undertake manufacturer wholesaling?
4. Distinguish between a manufacturer's branch office and a manufacturer's sales office.
5. Which wholesaling functions are performed by merchant wholesalers? Which are performed by agents and brokers?

6. Distinguish between franchise wholesaling and wholesale cooperatives.
7. What are the unique features of cash-and-carry and mail-order merchant wholesalers?
8. Why are drop shippers frequently used for coal, coke, and building materials?
9. How do manufacturers' agents and selling agents differ from one another?
10. What is the role of the food broker?

Discussion Questions

1. "Wholesalers are very much in the middle, often not fully knowing whether their first allegiance should be to the manufacturer/supplier or the customer." Comment on this statement. Can they rectify this situation? Why or why not?
2. The marketing vice-president of a large hardware manufacturer has asked you to outline a support program to improve relations with its wholesalers. Prepare this outline.

3. As a rack jobber, how would you determine which retail outlets should stock your magazines?
4. Develop a short checklist a manufacturer could use to evaluate independent wholesalers.
5. How does a wholesaler such as Ingram Books earn a profit if it deals with so many small orders from customers, while other wholesalers make far fewer (and more efficient) transactions?

◄ CASE 1 ►

Audiovox: The Evolution of an Electronics Wholesaler*

In 1960, Audiovox Corporation was founded as an importer of leisure goods (such as baseball gloves and fishing reels) and porcelain china. Then, in 1965, the firm mistakenly received a car radio in a package

---

* The data in this case are drawn from Fleming Meeks, "Trouble on the Line," *Forbes* (July 11, 1988), pp. 84–85.

from a Japanese supplier. Audiovox realized immediately the potential market for car radios, and within months of receiving that incorrect shipment, the firm began to concentrate on selling car radios (and later on stereos and tape decks) to new-car dealers. It got out of its original business altogether.

 Prior to 1965, most new-car dealers purchased

automobiles with radios installed by car manufacturers. Then, as a result of good timing, Audiovox became one of the first wholesalers to benefit from a change in the distribution channel for auto radios. With this indirect channel arrangement, new-car dealers would purchase new cars without radios; the dealers would purchase the radios from Audiovox and other independent suppliers; and the dealers would install the radios.

These were some of the advantages of the revised distribution channel for new-car dealers and their customers:

> The dealers were able to purchase radios from Audiovox for 20 to 30 per cent less than a comparable radio bought from a new-car manufacturer.
> Dealers could offer car buyers a larger selection of radios because they were not bound to the selection of one manufacturer.
> Inventory problems were minimized. Under the old system, dealers often had to remove a manufacturer-supplied radio from a new car and replace it with an upgraded model to satisfy customer desires.
> If the dealer refused to substitute the radio, it would risk losing a car sale. Thus, dealers often had to switch radios from car to car or stock autos with different radio configurations.
> Dealers could view the car radio business as a profit center. Radios could be sold along with other dealer-installed options, such as rustproofing, undercoating, and alarms.

As a result, by 1983, the annual sales at Audiovox exceeded $100 million.

Then, in 1984, Audiovox sensed the tremendous potential for cellular car phones—believing their sales would grow at a much faster rate than car stereos—and became the exclusive distributor for Toshiba, a leading Japanese manufacturer of mobile phones. Audiovox quickly became the dominant firm in the cellular phone market. It currently has a 15 to 20 per cent market share, and cellular phones now account for about one-half of total sales for Audiovox. The company's yearly revenues are nearly $250 million.

Despite the expectation that cellular phone sales at Audiovox will continue to boom over the next several years, however, the firm must deal with each of these issues relating to its cellular phone business:

> Customer interest in cellular phones is tempered by the high prices of them. Cellular phones require very large financial commitments by consumers—the phones carried by Audiovox can wholesale for as much as $1,200 versus as little as $55 for car stereos.
> The wholesaler's profit margins for cellular phones average 20 per cent versus 30 per cent for car radios.
> The popularity of cellular phones will encourage new firms to enter the marketplace. Many of these new entrants will probably be major electronic firms with greater brand recognition than Audiovox.
> In July 1987, after a scandal in which Toshiba was accused of illegally selling classified military equipment to the Soviet Union, Audiovox overordered cellular phones from Toshiba. It feared that its supply of Toshiba-built phones would be cut off. But, the supply cut-off did not occur; and, at the same time, the prices of cellular phones dropped by 25 per cent as industrywide production was stepped up. These two events reduced the value of Audiovox's inventory, of its accounts receivable (as many dealers refused to pay their bills in full), and negatively affected its dealer relations.

QUESTIONS

1. As a merchant wholesaler, what functions should Audiovox perform for its manufacturers? For its new-car dealers?

2. As a manufacturer, what factors would you consider in deciding which wholesaler should distribute your brand of cellular phones?

3. As a new-car dealer, what factors would you consider in choosing the wholesaler to patronize when buying cellular phones?

4. What should Audiovox do next to sustain long-term sales growth and profits?

⟨ CASE 2 ⟩

Super Valu: Assessing the Marketing Strategy of a Grocery Wholesaler[†]

Super Valu is the largest food wholesaler in the United States, with 1988 sales of $8 billion (from its wholesaling business alone). Companywide sales and profit—including retailing—were $9.4 billion and $112 million, respectively. It has 18 retail support divisions providing a range of wholesaling functions and serving 3,000 independently owned retail food stores in 32 states. Although Super Valu is a merchant wholesaler, it would rather be called "a retail support company that has a total commitment to serving customers more effectively than anyone else could serve them."

Super Valu also owns retail food operations—such as Cub Stores (of its 52 stores in 1988, 33 were franchised and 19 were corporate owned) and Food Giant (an Atlanta-based chain)—and retail general-merchandise operations—such as Shopko (with 75 mass merchandise stores in 1988). However, retailing accounts for only 15 per cent of total company sales.

In 1978, there were about 1,400 U.S. grocery wholesalers; today, there are only 300 such wholesalers left. One competitor, Fleming, is close to Super Valu in size. However, the other major grocery wholesalers are significantly smaller than Super Valu (for example, Sysco and Wetterau each had total company sales below $5 billion in 1988). Moreover, Super Valu's five-year return on equity of 21.2 per cent is among the highest in the industry (and significantly above Fleming's 14.2 per cent, Sysco's 17.5 per cent, and Wetterau's 16.8 per cent).

While Super Valu has done quite well in expanding its wholesale business, some of its acquisitions of nonwholesaling companies have done poorly. According to its chief executive, "The only areas where we've had problems have been when we bought into situations that weren't typical wholesale opportunities."

An example of this was its purchase of Food Giant, a troubled 57-store supermarket chain that was Super Valu's biggest customer. Since its acquisition, Super Valu has had to close 16 Food Giant stores and has sold 33 others to retail food chains. The remaining units are still not profitable, in part due to oversaturation of the Atlanta market. Since 1987, competitors have added one million feet of new supermarket space in the Atlanta area.

These are some of the elements of Super Valu's very successful strategy as a "retail support" wholesaler:

▶ It is a full-service merchant wholesaler. Among the services provided to retailers are merchandising support, advertising programs, training seminars, operations advice, location planning, store design, and store engineering.

▶ It strives to provide strong leadership in initiating new store formats and in assisting its retailers in developing new formats.

▶ It works closely with retailers to help them achieve and maintain strong positions, to maximize Super Valu's support capability, and to identify and capitalize on new opportunities to grow.

▶ It uses decentralized management, so that each of its 18 divisions can determine how best to serve retailers and final consumers. Most of the divisions are divided along geographic lines, but Super Valu also has a few functionally oriented divisions, such as Risk Planners, Inc. The company believes that no one marketing approach can effectively serve small and large communities, and consumers with varied life-styles and ethnic heritages.

▶ It is actively promoting the Uniform Communication Standard (UCS), which is keyed to the Universal Product Code (UPC) and enables information to be transmitted from its computers to retailers' computers. Super Valu also works with its retailers in sharing and interpreting important accounting, financial, and sales

[†] The data in this case are drawn from Jan Parr, "Leader of the Pack," *Forbes* (February 8, 1988), pp. 35–36; and *Super Valu 1988 Annual Report.*

data by product category and product item.

► It is a leader in innovation. Super Valu developed dual temperature trailers, the use of 48-foot trailers (instead of using two trailers), and a reserve locator system (to enable a forklift operator to verify a transaction and quickly locate a product in a warehouse). Energy management systems (which control heating, air conditioning, and lighting systems) are used at each affiliated store.

QUESTIONS

1. Comment on this statement: "Our independent retailers are healthy and competitive, and it is our mission to keep them that way."

2. How could a limited-service wholesaler compete against Super Valu?

3. Evaluate Super Valu's decision to function as a retailer as well as a wholesaler.

4. As a food manufacturer, could you bypass Super Valu and sell directly to its supermarkets? Explain your answer.

CHAPTER 14

Retailing

CHAPTER OBJECTIVES

1. To define retailing and show its importance

2. To discuss the different types of retailers, in terms of ownership, store strategy mix, and nonstore operations

3. To explore five major aspects of retail planning: store location, atmosphere, scrambled merchandising, the wheel of retailing, and technological advances

4. To examine recent trends in retailing

When entrepreneur Ray Kroc opened his first restaurant in Des Plaines, Illinois, on Friday, April 15, 1955, his cash register rang up $366.12. He noted in his ledger, now part of the McDonald's complex at the site, "It rained."

A total of 22 million people now eat at one of McDonald's more than 10,000 outlets around the world each day, and average daily sales are over $4,000 per store. Let us look at the McDonald's story.

In 1954, Ray Kroc (who owned exclusive rights to the Prince Castle multimixer, a machine that could mix six milk shakes at once) received an order for eight multimixers from a single restaurant. He was so startled by the size of the order, that he flew to San Bernardino, California, to meet the buyers. When Kroc arrived at the McDonald brothers' hamburger business, he saw more people waiting in line under their golden arches than he could imagine.

Kroc talked the brothers into letting him franchise their outlets nationwide. In the next five years, a chain of 228 McDonald's was organized. Kroc recognized the potential of the chain and bought out the brothers in 1961.

Although the Singer Sewing Machine Company is recognized as the first firm in the United States to franchise its dealers, McDonald's is considered by many to be the firm to perfect the concept of mass-distribution franchising. In mass-distribution franchising, a franchisor seeks to maximize market coverage by attracting enough good franchisees (investors who operate individual outlets) to saturate the marketplace. There are two cornerstones to McDonald's successful strategy: it supports franchisees in all facets of their business, and it is never complacent.

Ray Kroc believed that the major flaw of franchising in the 1950s was that many franchisors behaved poorly. Some franchisors required franchisees to buy equipment or supplies from them and then sent items that were overpriced or of poor quality. Sometimes franchisees had territories that were too small for them to make a profit. As a result, many franchisees were forced out of business or gave up their franchise affiliation and converted their outlets to independent stores.

As author John Love explains in *McDonald's: Behind the Arches*, "the essence of Kroc's unique but amazingly simple franchising philosophy was that a franchising company should not live off the sweat of its franchisees, but should succeed by helping its franchisees succeed."

McDonald's has never been complacent; it wants to continue to generate record earnings—as of mid-1988, McDonald's had achieved higher profits for 92 consecutive sales quarters. To accomplish this, McDonald's is always looking for opportunities to open new stores. It figures that "any time one McDonald's is more than a five-minute drive from another," there is room for a new outlet. Because traditional locations in the United States are often occupied, McDonald's has been focusing on nontraditional and international sites. It has newer outlets in office buildings, hospitals, military bases, and zoos; and it is opening restaurants in some Sears' stores. About 40 per cent of new stores are being opened outside the United States—including twenty restaurants in the Soviet Union.[1]

In this chapter, we will examine various aspects of retailing—including franchising and the use of nontraditional locations—and consider their ramifications.

[1] Penny Moser, "The McDonald's Mystique," *Fortune* (July 4, 1988), pp. 112–116; and Kathleen Deveney, "Meet Mike Quinlan, Big Mac's Attack CEO," *Business Week* (May 9, 1988), pp. 92, 96–97.

Overview

Retailing encompasses those business activities involved with the sale of goods and services to the final consumer for personal, family, or household use. It is the final stage in a channel of distribution. Manufacturers, importers, and wholesalers act as retailers when they sell products directly to the final consumer.

The average retail sale is small, about $30.00 each for both department stores and specialty stores. Convenience stores, such as 7-Eleven, have average sales of about $3.00 (not including gasoline). Chain supermarkets average $16.00 per customer transaction.[2] Accordingly, retailers try to increase their sales volume by using one-stop shopping appeals, broadening merchandise assortments, increasing customer shopping frequency, and encouraging more family members to go shopping. Inventory controls, automated merchandise handling, and electronic cash registers enable retailers to reduce their transaction costs.

Despite the low average size of customer transactions, the majority of sales for retailers such as department stores and specialty stores involves some form of customer credit. This means these retailers must pay a percentage of each transaction to a bank or other credit-card service company or absorb the costs of their own credit programs—in return for increased sales. For example, Sears and J.C. Penney have a combined total of more than 65 million holders of their own credit cards; these people buy billions of dollars in goods and services every year.

Whereas salespeople regularly visit organizational consumers to initiate and conclude transactions, most final consumers patronize stores. This makes the location of the store, product assortment, store hours, store fixtures, sales personnel, delivery, and other factors critical tools in drawing customers to the store. See Figure 14-1.

Final consumers make many unplanned purchases. In contrast, those that buy for resale or use in manufacturing (or operating a business) are more systematic in their purchasing. Therefore, retailers need to place impulse items in high-traffic locations, organize store layout, train sales personnel in suggestion selling, place related items next to each other, and sponsor special events to stimulate consumers.

In this chapter, the importance of retailing, the various types of retailers, considerations in retail planning, and recent trends in retailing are all discussed in detail.

The Importance of Retailing

Retailing is an important aspect of distribution because of its impact on the economy, its functions in the distribution channel, and its relationships with suppliers.

Retailing's Impact on the Economy

Retail sales and employment comprise substantial amounts of total U.S. sales and employment. Annual retail store sales volume is well over $1.6 trillion; this does not include most vending machine, direct selling, and direct marketing sales or many retail services. See Table 14-1 for data on selected leading retailers.

Retailing is also a major source of employment. According to the Department of

[2] Authors' estimates, based on data from *Stores* and *Progressive Grocer*.

FIGURE 14-1 **The Personal Touch at Best Products** At Best (a retail catalog showroom chain), customers receive personal assistance in several key departments and encounter courteous well-trained sales counselors. Service does not stop at the store exit as customers purchasing large items simply drive to the front of the store where they are assisted by a Best employee. Reprinted by permission.

Labor, about one-sixth of the nation's total nonagricultural work force is employed in 2 million retail establishments in the United States. A wide range of retailing career opportunities is available, including store management, merchandising, and owning one's own retail business.[3]

From a cost perspective, retailing is a significant field. For example, on the average, about 40 cents of every dollar a consumer spends in a department store or a specialty goes to it as compensation for the functions it performs. The corresponding figure is 20

[3] A discussion of careers in retailing can be found in Barry Berman and Joel R. Evans, *Retail Management: A Strategic Approach*, 4th Edition (New York: Macmillan, 1989), pp. 627-639.

TABLE 14-1   Sales and Income Data on Selected Retailers, 1988

Name	Sales ($ Million)	Net Income ($ Million)	Net Income (As a Percentage of Sales)
A. Food Retailers			
Kroger	19,053	35	0.2
American	18,478	98	0.5
Safeway	13,612	31	0.2
Great Atlantic & Pacific (A&P)	9,532	103	1.1
Winn-Dixie	9,008	117	1.3
Albertson's	6,773	163	2.4
Publix	4,804	102	2.1
Stop & Shop	4,770	(22)	(0.5)
Vons	3,917	(24)	(0.6)
Food Lion	3,815	112	2.9
B. Nonfood Retailers			
Sears	50,251	1,454	2.9
K mart	27,301	803	2.9
Wal-Mart	20,649	837	4.1
J.C. Penney	14,833	807	5.4
Dayton Hudson	12,204	287	2.4
May Department Stores	11,921	534	4.5
F.W. Woolworth	8,088	288	3.6
Melville	6,780	355	5.2
Montgomery Ward	5,371	139	2.6
Walgreen	4,884	129	2.6

Source: Adapted by the authors from "The Largest 50 Retailing Companies," *Fortune* (June 5, 1989), pp. 378–379.

cents for a supermarket.[4] This compensation — known as gross margin — is for rent, taxes, fuel, advertising, management, personnel, and other retail costs, as well as profits.

Retailing Functions in Distribution

Retailers gather assortments, provide information, handle goods, and complete exchanges.

In general, retailers perform four distinct functions. They participate in the sorting process by collecting an assortment of goods and services from a wide variety of suppliers and offering them for sale; width and depth of assortment depend on the individual retailer's strategy. They provide information to consumers through advertising, displays and signs, and sales personnel; marketing research support is given to other channel members. They store merchandise, mark prices on it, place items on the selling floor, and otherwise handle products; usually, they pay suppliers for items before selling them to final consumers. They complete transactions by using appropriate store locations and hours, credit policies, and other services (for example, delivery). Figure 14-2 summarizes the functions that are typically performed at the retail stage in a distribution channel.

[4] Authors' estimates, based on data from *Stores* and *Progressive Grocer*.

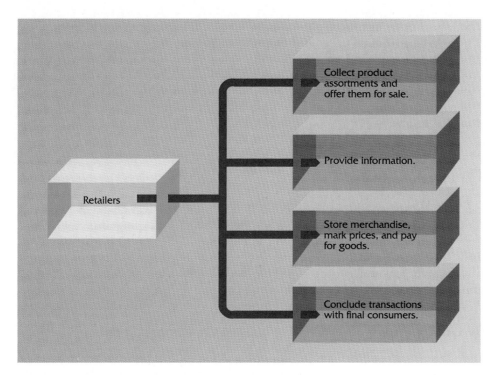

- Collect product assortments and offer them for sale.
- Provide information.
- Store merchandise, mark prices, and pay for goods.
- Conclude transactions with final consumers.

Retailers

FIGURE 14-2
Key Retailing Functions

The Relationship of Retailers and Suppliers

Retailers deal with two broad categories of suppliers: those selling goods or services for use by the retailers and those selling goods or services that are resold by the retailers. Examples of goods and services purchased by retailers for their use are store fixtures, data-processing equipment, management consulting, and insurance. Resale purchases depend on the lines sold by the retailer.

Suppliers must have knowledge of their retailers' goals, strategies, and methods of business operation in order to sell and service accounts effectively. Frequently, retailers and their suppliers have divergent viewpoints, which must be reconciled:

▶ At one time, retailers believed that Procter & Gamble acted in an arrogant manner, and that it "didn't care what the retailers wanted or needed." Today P&G works hard at retailer relations: "We are at least as anxious to listen to you as we are to offer the kinds of merchandising programs for our brands that you like and want."

▶ Winn-Dixie, a leading U.S. supermarket chain and a number of its suppliers (including Campbell, General Mills, and Quaker Oats) have been embroiled in a long-running dispute over the discounts that the suppliers offer Winn-Dixie for promotional activities. Winn-Dixie wants a uniform discount program for all of its stores; the suppliers want to provide the discounts on a market-by-market basis. For a short time, Winn-Dixie actually refused to restock the products of some manufacturers. As one neutral observer noted: "Eventually, Winn-Dixie'll have to gracefully back away from forcing the issue with marketers but not before it gets its point across."

▶ Imported merchandise such as cameras, watches, and cars is usually sold to retailers through authorized U.S. distributors. However, some U.S. retailers have chosen

Retailers have suppliers for products they use and for those they resell.

419

to bypass these distributors and purchase goods from international dealers; they import the goods into the United States on their own. These "gray-market" products are then marketed to final consumers at low prices, but without the guarantees of U.S. distributors. Both authorized distributors and the retailers who buy from them are troubled because of lost sales and the loss in goodwill when they refuse to honor manufacturers' guarantees. They want manufacturers to not allow gray-market goods.[5]

Types of Retailers

Retailers can be categorized by ownership, store strategy mix, and nonstore operations. See Figure 14-3. The categories are overlapping; that is, a retailer can be correctly placed in more than one grouping. For example, 7-Eleven can be classified as a chain, a franchise, and a convenience store. An examination of retailers by category provides information about their attributes, relative sizes and importance, different strategies, and the impact of environmental factors.

By Ownership

*An **independent retailer** has one outlet and offers service and location.*

An **independent retailer** operates only one outlet and offers personal service, a convenient location, and close customer contact. Over three-quarters of all U.S. retailers are independents, including many barber shops, dry cleaners, furniture stores, service stations, and neighborhood stores. This large number is due to the ease of entry in retailing because many kinds of retailing require low investments and little technical knowledge. Therefore, competition is plentiful. Many retailers do not succeed because of the ease of entry, their own poor management skills, and inadequate resources. Annually, several thousand firms fail—about one-third of new retailers do not last one full year and two-thirds not not make it past the first three years.[6]

*In a **chain,** one firm has multiple outlets and serves broad markets.*

A **retail chain** involves the common ownership of multiple units (outlets). It usually engages in centralized purchasing and decision making. While independents typically have simple organizations, chains often rely on specialization, standardization, and elaborate control systems. As a result, chains are able to serve a large, dispersed target market and maintain a well-known company name. Although chains operate less than one-quarter of all U.S. retail outlets, they account for well over one-half of total retail store sales. Only a few hundred chains operate 100 or more units, yet they are responsible for over 30 per cent of total U.S. store sales. Chains are widespread for supermarkets, department stores, variety stores, and fast-food restaurants, among others. Examples of large chains are Sears, K mart, and Kroger.

Retail franchising employs an established name and operates under certain rules.

Retail franchising is a contractual arrangement between a franchisor (which may be a manufacturer, wholesaler, or service sponsor) and a retail franchisee, which allows the franchisee to conduct a certain form of business under an established name and according to a specific set of rules. It is a form of chain ownership that allows a small businessperson to benefit from the experience, buying capabilities, and image of

---

[5] Jennifer Pendleton, "Dealing with No. 1," *Advertising Age* (August 20, 1987), p. 122; Julie Liesse Erickson, "Grocery Chain Dumps Major Package Goods," *Advertising Age* (October 10, 1988), pp. 1, 75; and Dale F. Duhan and Mary Jane Sheffet, "Gray Markets and the Legal Status of Parallel Importation," *Journal of Marketing*, (July 1988), pp. 75–83.

[6] Thomas Petzinger, Jr., "So You Want to Get Rich?" *Wall Street Journal* (May 15, 1987), p. 15D.

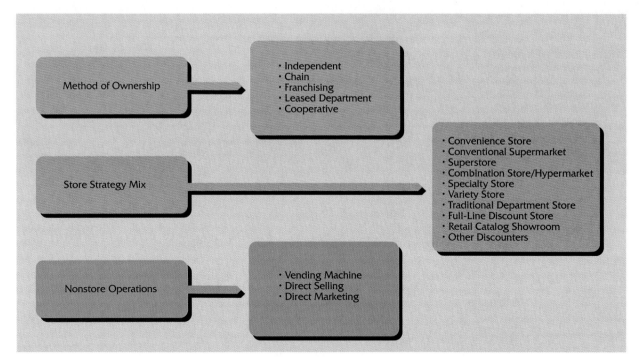

FIGURE 14-3
Categorizing Retailers

a large multiunit retailer. Usually the franchisee also receives management training, participates in cooperative buying and advertising, and acquires a well-established company name. The franchisor benefits by obtaining franchise fees and royalties, faster payments, strict controls over operations, consistency among outlets, and motivated owner-operators. Retail franchises annually account for more than $550 billion in U.S. sales through about 450,000 establishments.[7] Franchising is particularly popular for auto and truck dealers, gasoline service stations, fast-food outlets, hotels and motels, service firms, and convenience-foods stores. Examples of leading retail franchises are Chevrolet dealers, McDonald's, and H&R Block.

A *leased department* is a department in a retail store (usually a department, discount, or specialty store) that is rented to an outside party. The manager of a leased department is responsible for all aspects of its operation and pays a percentage of sales as rent; and the retailer places strict rules on the leased department operator. Lessors benefit because of the expertise of department operators, reduced risk and inventory investment, lucrative lease terms, increased store traffic, and an appeal to one-stop shopping convenience. Lessees benefit from the existence of an established location, the prestige of the lessor's name, the store traffic generated by the lessor, the one-stop customers attracted by the store as a whole, and whatever services (advertising, accounting, etc.) the lessor provides by mutual agreement. Leased departments are popular for beauty salons, jewelry, photographic studios, shoe repairs, and cosmetics. In U.S. department stores, leased departments yield $11+ billion in annual sales.

A cooperative may be operated by retailers or consumers. In a *retail cooperative,* independent retailers share purchases, storage and shipping facilities, advertising, planning, and other functions. The individual stores retain their independence but

*A **leased department** is rented to an outside party that provides expertise.*

*With a **retail cooperative,** stores organize to share costs.*

---

[7] See Andrew Kostecka, *Franchising in the Economy: 1986–1988* (Washington, D.C.: U.S. Department of Commerce, 1988).

421

FIGURE 14-4
Recreational Equipment Inc.: A Consumer Cooperative
REI has annual sales of $175 million and 1.9 million consumer members. Profits from REI's twenty stores are distributed to members in the form of price discounts.
Reprinted by permission.

agree on broad, common policies. These cooperatives are growing in response to the domination of independents by chains. They are common for liquor stores, hardware stores, and grocery stores. Ace Hardware, Associated Food Stores, and Certified Grocers are retail cooperatives.

*With a **consumer cooperative,** consumers operate a retail firm.*

In a ***consumer cooperative,*** a retail firm is owned by consumer members who invest, receive stock certificates, elect officers, manage operations, and share profits or savings. The goal is to offer reduced prices to members. Cooperatives have been most prevalent with food products, particularly produce items. However, they represent less than 1 per cent of total U.S. supermarket sales. They have not grown because they involve a lot of initiative, profits have been low, and consumer expertise in retailing has been lacking. One of the largest cooperatives is Recreational Equipment Inc., headquartered in Seattle, Washington. See Figure 14-4.

Table 14-2 compares the retail ownership forms.

By Store Strategy Mix

*A **retail store strategy mix** combines the hours and products, etc., offered.*

Retailers can be classified by the ***retail store strategy mix*** that they undertake. The typical retail store strategy mix consists of an integrated combination of hours, location, assortment, service, price levels, and other factors retailers employ. Store strategy mixes vary widely, as the following indicate.

*A **convenience store** has a good locale and fill-in items.*

A ***convenience store*** is usually a well-situated, food-oriented store with long hours and a limited number of items. In the United States, these stores have annual sales of $60 billion, including gasoline, and account for 7 per cent of total grocery sales. The average store has yearly sales that are about one-sixth those of a conventional supermarket.[8] Consumers use a convenience store for fill-in merchandise, often at off-

---

[8] Teresa Carson and Todd Vogel, "Karl Eller's Big Thirst for Convenience Stores," *Business Week* (June 13, 1988), pp. 86, 88; and "55th Annual Report of the Grocery Industry," *Progressive Grocer* (April 1988), p. 8.

TABLE 14-2 Key Characteristics of Retail Ownership Forms

| Ownership Form | Characteristics | | |
	Distinguishing Features	Major Advantages	Major Disadvantages
Independent	Operates one outlet, easy entry	Personal service, convenient location, customer contact	Much competition, poor management skills, limited resources
Retail chain	Common ownership of multiple units	Central purchasing, strong management, specialization of tasks, larger market	Inflexibility, high investment costs, less entrepreneurial
Retail franchising	Contractual arrangement between central management (franchisor) and independent businesspersons (franchisees) to operate a specified form of business	To franchisor: investments from franchisees, faster growth, entrepreneurial spirit of franchisees To franchisee: established name, training, experience of franchisor, cooperative ads	To franchisor: some loss of control, franchisees not employees, harder to maintain uniformity To franchisee: strict rules, limited decision-making ability, payments to franchisors
Leased department	Space in a store leased to an outside operator	To lessor: expertise of lessee, little risk, diversification To lessee: less investment in store fixtures, customer traffic, store image	To lessor: some loss of control, poor performance reflects on store To lessee: strict rules, limited decision-making ability, payments to store
Cooperative			
Retail	Purchases, advertising, planning, and other functions shared by independent retailers	Independence maintained, efficiency improved, enhances competitiveness with chains	Different objectives of participants, hard to control members, some autonomy lost
Consumer	Purchases, advertising, planning, and other functions shared by consumer owners	Savings to members, social experience, improves consumer leverage	Difficult to organize, member turnover, dwindling interest in performing functions

hours. Bread, milk, ice cream, newspapers, and gasoline are popular items (with gasoline contributing 40 per cent of all sales). 7-Eleven, Circle K, and Arco operate convenience stores. See Figure 14-5.

A ***conventional supermarket*** is a departmentalized food store with minimum annual sales of $2 million; it emphasizes a wide range of food and related products — sales of general merchandise are limited. It originated in the 1930s, when food retailers realized that a large-scale operation would enable them to combine volume sales, self-service, low prices, impulse buying, and one-stop grocery shopping. The automobile and refrigerator contributed to the supermarket's success by lowering travel costs and adding to the life span of perishable items. Today conventional supermarkets account for about 50 per cent of total U.S. supermarket sales (which are over $230 billion annually).[9] Safeway, Kroger, and A&P are among the large chains operating conventional supermarkets. Figure 14-6 shows some of the major distinctions between independent and chain supermarkets.

*A **conventional supermarket** is a large, self-service food store.*

[9] Berman and Evans, *Retail Management: A Strategic Approach*, pp. 101–105; and "55th Annual Report of the Grocery Industry," p. 8.

FIGURE 14-5
A Typical 7-Eleven
Convenience Store
Reprinted by permission.

*A **superstore** stocks food and other products to attract one-stop shoppers.*

A **superstore** is a diversified supermarket that sells a broad range of food and nonfood items. The latter account for 20 to 30 per cent of store sales. A superstore typically carries garden supplies, televisions, clothing, wine, boutique items, bakery products, and household appliances—in addition to a full line of supermarket items. While a conventional U.S. supermarket occupies about 15,000 to 20,000 square feet of space and has annual sales of $5.5 million, a superstore occupies 25,000 to 50,000 square feet of space and has annual sales of $13 million. Just 5,000 superstores account for nearly 30 per cent of all supermarket sales. Several factors are causing a number of conventional supermarkets to switch to superstores: an interest in one-stop shopping by consumers, the leveling off of food sales as a result of population stability and competition from restaurants and fast-food stores, improved transportation networks, and the higher margins on general merchandise (more than double those of food items). Among many larger food chains, the superstore is now the preferred supermarket format.[10] Figure 14-7 shows one of A&P's superstores.

*A **combination store** offers a large assortment of general merchandise as well as food items. One type is a **hypermarket**.*

A **combination store** combines food/grocery and general merchandise sales in one facility, with general merchandise providing 30 to 40 per cent of overall sales. It goes even further than a superstore in appealing to one-stop shopping by consumers, and occupies from 30,000 to 200,000 square feet or more of space. It enables the retailer to operate quite efficiently, increase the number of consumers drawn to a store, increase impulse purchases and the size of the average customer transaction, sell both high-turnover/low-profit food items and lower-turnover/high-profit general merchandise, and offer reasonable prices to consumers. A **hypermarket** is a special kind of combination store that integrates an economy supermarket with a discount department store; it is at least 60,000 square feet in size. In the United States, there are about

[10] Ibid.

FIGURE 14-6
Independent Versus Chain Supermarkets*
SOURCE: Computed by the authors from "55th Annual Report of the Grocery Industry," *Progressive Grocer* (April 1988), various pages.

Factor	Independent	Chain
Average annual sales per outlet	$5.3 million	$9.3 million
Average number of items stocked	13,000	16,500
Per cent of supermarket outlets	45	55
Per cent of supermarket sales	32	68
Per cent open Sundays	90	98
Per cent of stores using scanners	48	62

*Both categories include conventional supermarkets, superstores, and hypermarkets.

FIGURE 14-7
Constructing an A&P Superstore
Reprinted by permission.

Marketing Controversy

Will Hypermarkets Make It in the United States?

A hypermarket is a huge store that can carry as many as 70,000 food and nonfood items, have 60 checkout counters, and handle 15,000 customers daily.

Yet, although Europe already has 2,000 hypermarkets, retailers such as Wal-Mart, K mart, and Carrefour are only now beginning to introduce this store format here. And there is a considerable difference of opinion as to whether hypermarkets will do well.

Proponents of hypermarkets are optimistic for these reasons:

▶ *Hypermarkets are responsive to the consumer's growing interest in one-stop shopping.*

▶ *Successful stores are expected to draw customers from as far away as 50 miles (or more).*

▶ *There are many operating efficiencies due to the volume handled by hypermarkets.*

▶ *Sam Walton, referring to Wal-Mart's Texas hypermarket, has stated, "I'm more excited about this than anything in the history of our company." The store is expected to have annual sales of over $100 million.*

Critics of hypermarkets are pessimistic for these reasons:

▶ *Heavy customer traffic and a very high sales volume are needed for hypermarkets to turn a profit because of the amount of merchandise carried, employees needed, and so on. And it may take quite a while to generate adequate customer traffic. During its initial year, Bigg's (the nation's first hypermarket) lost $7 million.*

▶ *Many retailing experts are "not convinced that the American shopper wants to buy clothes and other fashion soft goods—things that are not necessities—along with food items."*

▶ *The United States has so many discount stores that hypermarkets will have a difficult time attracting loyal customers.*

▶ *Hypermarkets are having difficulties in obtaining zoning clearances in local communities due to their required size and the traffic congestion they would create.*

What do you think?

SOURCE: Based on material in "How Much Hype in Hypermarkets?" *Sales & Marketing Management* (April 1988), pp. 51–55; "Is U.S. Hypermarket-Ready? Carrefour Is Not So Sure," *Chain Store Age Executive* (January 1989), pp. 49–50; and Bob Geiger, "Going 'Hyper' in a Hypermarket," *Advertising Age* (May 8, 1989), pp. S-21–S-22.

1,000 combination stores (including hypermarkets), that account for about 6 per cent of supermarket sales. Among the companies operating combination stores are Wal-Mart, Jewel, Albertson's, and Bigg's.[11]

*A **specialty store** emphasizes one type of merchandise.*

A **specialty store** concentrates on the sale of one merchandise or service line, such as high-fidelity equipment or hair-care services. Consumers like specialty stores because they are not confronted with racks of merchandise, do not have to walk or search through several departments, are likely to find knowledgeable salespeople, are able to select from tailored assortments, and usually avoid crowds. Specialty stores are most successful in the apparel, gourmet food, appliance, toy, electronics, and sports product lines. For instance, U.S. specialty apparel-store sales exceed $80 billion annu-

[11] Ibid.

FIGURE 14-8 **Casual Corner: A Specialty-Store Chain Targeted to Career Women**
Reprinted by permission.

ally. Successful specialty stores include The Limited, Toys "R" Us, and Radio Shack. See Figure 14-8.

A ***variety store*** sells a wide assortment of inexpensive and popularly priced merchandise. It features stationery, gift items, women's accessories, toilet articles, light hardware, toys, housewares, and confectionaries. U.S. variety-store sales are about $9 billion per year. With the growth of other retail store strategy mixes, U.S. variety stores have stagnated in recent years. F.W. Woolworth, with more than $2 billion in annual U.S. variety-store sales, dominates the category; and Woolworth is now placing greater emphasis on its specialty-store divisions (such as Kinney, Foot Locker, and Athletic X-Press shoe stores).[12]

*A **variety store** sells an assortment of lower-priced merchandise.*

A ***department store*** employs at least 25 people and usually sells a general line of apparel for the family, household linens and dry goods, and furniture, home furnishings, appliances, radios, and television sets. It is organized into separate departments for purposes of buying, promotion, service, and control. There are two types of department store: the traditional department store and the full-line discount store.

*A **department store** offers the broadest assortment of goods and services.*

A ***traditional department store*** is a department store that has the greatest assortment of any retailer, provides many customer services, is a fashion leader, and dominates the stores around it. Prices are average to above average. These department stores have high name recognition and utilize all forms of media in advertising. In recent years, traditional department stores have set up many boutiques, theme displays, and designer departments to compete with other retailers. They face intense

*A **traditional department store** is a fashion leader with many customer services.*

---

[12] *F.W. Woolworth Co. 1988 Annual Report.*

TABLE 14-3   Key Characteristics of Retail Strategy Mixes

Retailer	Convenience of Hours	Convenience of Location	Width of Assortment	Depth of Assortment	Service[b]	Level of Advertising	Level of Prices
			Strategy Mix Ratings[a]				
Convenience store	1	1	3	5	4	4	3
Conventional supermarket	1	1	2	1	4	2	2
Superstore	1	3	1	1	4	2	2
Combination store	1	4	1	1	4	2	2
Specialty store	3	3	5	1	1	3	varies
Variety store	3	3	3	2	3	4	3
Traditional department store	2	3	1	1	2	1	3
Full-line discount store	2	4	2	2	4	3	2
Retail catalog showroom	3	4	3	3	5	4	2
Other discounters	4	5	varies	varies	5	5	1

[a] 1, outstanding; 3, average; 5, poor.
[b] Includes availability of sales personnel, delivery, custom orders, etc.

competition from specialty stores and discounters. Annual total U.S. sales for traditional department stores, including mail order, are over $60 billion. Examples of department store chains are Dayton Hudson, May, and R.H. Macy.

*A **full-line discount store** has self-service and popular brands.*

A ***full-line discount store*** is a department store with low prices, a relatively broad merchandise assortment, a low-rent location, self-service, brand-name merchandise, wide aisles, shopping carts, and most merchandise displayed on the selling floor. It relies much less on credit sales than does a traditional department store. U.S. full-line discount stores annually sell over $90 billion in goods and services. These stores are among the largest retailers of linens, toys and games, housewares, gifts, small electric appliances, and jewelry. About 30 per cent of their sales are from apparel. Together, K mart, Wal-Mart, and Target account for over one-half of all U.S. full-line discount store sales.[13]

*In a **retail catalog showroom,** consumers shop at a warehouse store.*

Another type of discount retailer is a ***retail catalog showroom,*** in which consumers select merchandise from a catalog and shop at a warehouse-style location. Customers frequently write up their own orders, products are usually stocked in a back room, and there are limited displays. Catalog showrooms specialize in national brands; and jewelry, electronics, housewares, gifts, and watches account for 70 per cent of their revenues. Annual U.S. sales have dropped from a high of $11 billion to about $7 billion at present. Catalog showrooms are being hurt by other, more flexible, discounters.[14] Best Products, Service Merchandise, and Consumers Distributing are among the largest catalog showrooms.

During recent years, various other forms of low-price retailing have grown rapidly. These include limited-line and warehouse food stores, off-price chains, discount drugstore chains, factory outlet stores, and flea markets. These retailers hold down their prices by limiting inventory on hand, using plain store fixtures, locating at inexpensive

[13] "Discounters and Specialists Win Merchandise Battle," *Chain Store Age Executive* (November 1988), pp. 64–66.
[14] Authors' estimate, based on data in *Discount Store News*.

TABLE 14-4   Typical Retail Strategy Mixes—A Discount Store Versus a Traditional Department Store

Discount-Store Strategy	Department-Store Strategy
1. Inexpensive rental location—low level of pedestrian traffic (Note: full-line discount stores are increasingly using more expensive locations).	1. Expensive rental location in shopping center or district—high level of pedestrian traffic.
2. Simple fixtures, linoleum floor, centralized dressing room, few interior or window displays.	2. Elaborate fixtures, carpeted floor, individual dressing rooms, many interior and exterior displays.
3. Promotional emphasis on price. Some discounters do not advertise brand names, but state "famous brand."	3. Promotional emphasis on full service, quality brands, and fashion leadership.
4. No alterations, telephone orders, delivery, or gift wrapping; limited credit.	4. Alterations included in clothing prices, telephone orders, and home delivery at little or no fee; credit available.
5. Reliance on self-service, dump-bin displays (plain cases with piles of merchandise), and rack displays; all merchandise visible.	5. Extensive sales force assistance, attractive merchandise displays, most storage in back room.
6. Emphasis on branded merchandise. Selection probably not complete; featuring "seconds," removal of labels from merchandise if required by manufacturer, and stocking of low-price nonbranded items.	6. Emphasis on a full selection of branded and privately branded first-quality merchandise; will not stock close-outs, discontinued lines, or seconds.
7. Year-round use of low prices.	7. Sales limited to end-of-season clearance and special events.

sites, and offering few customer services. They appeal to the large number of price-sensitive consumers in the United States.[15]

Table 14-3 highlights a number of the key aspects of retail strategy mixes, while Table 14-4 shows the differences between many discount-store and traditional department-store strategies.

By Nonstore Operations

Nonstore retailing occurs when a firm uses a strategy mix that is not store-based to reach consumers and complete transactions. A nonstore retailer does not utilize conventional store facilities. See Figure 14-3.

Nonstore retailing is nontraditional.

A *vending machine* uses coin- or card-operated machinery to dispense goods (such as beverages) or services (such as life insurance policies at airports). It eliminates the need for sales personnel, allows around-the-clock sales, and can be placed outside rather than inside a store.

Vending machines eliminate a sales force and allow 24-hour sales.

Vending-machine sales are concentrated in a narrow product line, with beverages, food items, and cigarettes representing 97 per cent of the U.S. total. Machines may require intensive servicing because of breakdowns, stock-outs, and vandalism. Improved technology now allows vending machines to make change for dollar bills, "talk" to consumers, use video screens to display merchandise, brew fresh coffee, and so on. Annual sales are over $20 billion.[16]

---

[15] See Kevin T. Higgins, "Megaretailing: Message to Marketers Is Mixed," *Marketing News* (January 31, 1986), pp. 13, 16; Elaine Sherman, Kevin F. McCrohan, and James D. Smith, "Informal Retailing: An Analysis of Products, Attitudes, and Expectations" in Elizabeth Hirschman and Morris Holbrook (Editors), *Advances in Consumer Research*, Vol. 12 (Provo, Utah: Association for Consumer Research, 1985), pp. 204–208; and Cathryn Jakobson, "They Get It for You Wholesale," *New York Times Business World Magazine* (December 4, 1988), pp. 24–25 ff.

[16] *Vending and Foodservice Management* (Chicago: National Automatic Merchandising Association, 1988); " 'Upscale' Vending Machine Designed for One-Stop Shopping," *Marketing News* (June 20, 1988), pp. 1–2; and Jonathan P. Hicks, "New Vending Machines to Elevate Snacking," *New York Times* (October 5, 1988), p. D9.

You're the Marketer

Is There More for Your Life at Sears?

In late 1988, Sears decided to convert from traditional department stores into full-line discount stores to turn around its sagging retail performance. To focus attention on this new strategy, Sears closed all of its 800+ stores from 6:00 P.M. on Monday February 27, 1989, to Wednesday March 1, 1989 at 12:00 noon—and marked lower prices on more than 50,000 items in each store. Prices were reduced by up to 50 per cent.

Sears now features "Everyday Low Prices" (EDLP) and will match any price advertised in a newspaper by a competitor. It is also adding 1,000 more brand-name products. Sears will continue to charge prediscount prices on certain strong-selling products, such as Craftsman tools (a Sears brand not available elsewhere).

Some observers are quite positive about Sears' new approach, citing these factors:

▶ A recent Gallop poll found Americans think of Sears as a company associated with high quality.

▶ Sears has had success with its new Brand Central national-appliance and consumer electronics departments in stores in Indiana and Kentucky.

▶ Research shows 75 per cent of Americans visit a Sears store at least once each year.

However, critics of Sears' EDLP strategy cite these factors:

▶ Sears has high overhead expenses. Its selling and administrative expenses are 30 per cent of sales versus 24 per cent at J.C. Penney and K mart. Its distribution costs are 8 per cent of sales versus 3 per cent at Wal-Mart and K mart.

▶ Sears' inventory management system needs improvement. Goods are frequently out-of-stock.

▶ Sears needs to be careful so as not to alienate existing customers and suppliers while attempting to satisfy new customers and new suppliers. EDLP retailers typically have plain fixtures, less desirable store locations, and few salespeople.

Said one neutral observer, "Long-term success will depend on how good Sears is in convincing customers that it is competitively priced."

As a Sears vice-president, what would you do next?

SOURCE: Based on material in Patricia Sellers, "Why Bigger Is Badder at Sears," *Fortune* (December 15, 1988), pp. 79–84; and James E. Ellis, Brian Bremner, and Michael Oneal, "Will the Big Markdown Get the Big Store Moving Again?" *Business Week* (March 13, 1989), pp. 110, 114.

Direct selling encompasses personal contacts with consumers in nonstore settings.

Direct selling involves both personal contact with consumers in their homes (and other nonstore locations) and telephone solicitations that are initiated by the retailer. Cosmetics, vacuum cleaners, household goods and services (such as carpet cleaning), encyclopedias, dairy products, and magazines and newspapers are among the items that some firms market via direct selling.

This form of retailing can be either on a cold canvass (Electrolux), referral (Avon), or party (Tupperware) basis. In a cold canvass, the salesperson goes through an area and telephones each resident or knocks on each door in search of customers. With a referral system, past buyers recommend friends to the salesperson. In the party method, one consumer acts as the host and invites friends and acquaintances to a sales demonstration in his or her home. For some consumers, direct selling has a poor

FIGURE 14-9
The Many Faces of Spiegel Catalogs
Reprinted by permission. Copyright Spiegel, Inc., Oak Brook, Il. All rights reserved.

image. In addition, sales force turnover is high and more consumers than ever are not at home during the day (because they are working). To increase direct selling business, salespeople at firms such as Avon now also aim at working women via office presentations during breaks and lunch hours. It is estimated that direct selling generates revenues of about $8 to $10 billion per year.[17]

Direct marketing occurs when a consumer is first exposed to a good or service through a nonpersonal medium (such as direct mail, television, radio, magazine, or newspaper) and then orders by mail or telephone. More than one-half of U.S. households make such purchases annually — mostly because of availability and convenience. The popularity of manufacturer brands (and consumer confidence in them), the large number of working women, and the acceptance of direct marketing as a mainstream way of shopping are all contributing to the rapid growth of this form of retailing.

Direct marketing is undertaken by both specialized direct-marketing firms and conventional store retailers that use it to supplement their regular business. The most popular direct-marketing items are gifts; books, records, and tapes; clothing; magazines; sports equipment; and home accessories. Yearly sales are about $175 billion. Direct marketing offers convenience for consumers, low operating costs, coverage of a wide geographic area, and new market segments. Large direct-marketing firms include Spiegel, L.L. Bean, and Sears (the leader).[18] See Figure 14-9.

*With **direct marketing**, a seller first communicates with consumers via nonpersonal media.*

---

[17] See "Fuller Brush Man Uses Soft Sell, Humor to Boost Sales," *Marketing News* (January 18, 1988), p. 3; Kerry Hannon, "Party Animal," *Forbes* (November 16, 1987), pp. 262–270; and Kate Ballen, "Get Ready for Shopping at Work," *Fortune* (February 15, 1988), pp. 95–98.

[18] *Direct Marketing in the Year 2000* (New York: Yankelovich, Skelly and White/Clancy, Shulman, Inc., 1987); Rebecca Fannin, "In Search of Safe Ground," *Marketing & Media Decisions* (August 1988), pp. 107–110; and "Direct Marketing," *Advertising Age* (August 1, 1988), pp. S-1—S-12.

Considerations in Retail Planning

There are many factors for retailers to consider when developing and implementing their marketing plans. Five of the most important ones are store location, atmosphere, scrambled merchandising, the wheel of retailing, and technological advances.

Store Location

Store location is important to retailers because it helps determine the customer mix and competition. Once selected, it is also highly inflexible. These are the basic forms of store location: the isolated store, the unplanned business district, and the planned shopping center.

*An **isolated store** is a freestanding outlet on a highway or side street.*

An **isolated store** is a freestanding retail outlet located on a highway or side street. Although there are no adjacent stores with which the firm competes, there are also no stores to help draw consumer traffic. The difficulty of attracting consumers is why large retailers are usually best suited for an isolated location. Customers are hesitant to travel to an isolated store that does not have a good product assortment and an established reputation. This type of location is sometimes used by discount stores because of low rent and manufacturers' desires for them to be far enough away from traditional stores that sell goods at full prices.

*In an **unplanned business district,** stores locate together with no planning.*

An **unplanned business district** exists where two or more stores are located close to one another without the use of prior planning as to the number and composition of stores. There are four kinds of unplanned district: the central business district, the secondary business district, the neighborhood business district, and the string.

A central business district (CBD) is the hub of retailing in a city and is synonymous with the term "downtown." It contains the largest commercial and shopping facilities in a city. Cultural, employment, and entertainment facilities surround it. There is at least one major department store and a broad grouping of specialty and convenience stores. CBDs have had some problems with crowding, lack of parking, older buildings, limited pedestrian traffic when offices close, nonstandardized store hours, crime, and other elements. However, in many urban areas, CBD sales remain strong. Among the innovations used to strengthen CBDs are closing streets to vehicular traffic, modernizing storefronts and equipment, developing strong merchant associations, planting trees to make areas more attractive, improving transportation, and integrating the commercial and residential environment.

A secondary business district (SBD) is a shopping area that is usually bounded by the intersection of two major streets. Cities generally have several SBDs, each having at least one junior department store, a variety store, and several small service shops. In comparison with the CBD, the SBD has less merchandise assortment, a smaller trading area (the geographic area from which a store draws its customers), and sells more convenience items.

A neighborhood business district (NBD) satisfies the convenience shopping needs of a neighborhood. The NBD contains a number of small stores, with the major retailer being a supermarket or variety store. An NBD is located on the major street in a residential area.

A string is usually composed of a group of stores with similar or compatible product lines that situate along a street or highway. However, because this location is unplanned, various store combinations are possible. Car dealers, antique stores, and clothing stores are retailers that frequently locate in a string.

A *planned shopping center* is centrally owned or managed, planned and operated as an entity, surrounded by parking, and based on balanced tenancy. *Balanced tenancy* means that the number and composition of stores within a planned shopping center are related to the overall needs of the surrounding population. The various stores complement each other in the variety and quality of merchandise. To ensure balance, a center may limit the merchandise lines any store carries. Planned centers account for approximately one-half of total U.S. retail store sales; unplanned business districts and isolated stores also account for one-half. The three types of planned center are regional, community, and neighborhood.

A regional shopping center sells mostly shopping goods to a geographically dispersed market. A regional center has at least one or two department stores and up to one hundred or more small retailers. Customers are willing to drive up to a half hour to reach a regional center. As in the case of central business districts, many regional shopping centers (especially those built 25 years ago or earlier) require renovation. Among the improvements being undertaken are enclosing malls, redesigning storefronts, erecting new store directories, adding more trees and plants, and replacing concrete in parking lots.

A community shopping center has a variety store and/or small department store as its major retailer, with several smaller stores. This center sells both convenience and shopping items. A neighborhood shopping center sells mostly convenience products. The largest store is a supermarket and/or drugstore, with a few smaller stores.

*A **planned shopping center** is centrally planned and has **balanced tenancy**.*

Atmosphere

Atmosphere is the sum total of the physical characteristics of a retail store or group of stores that are used to develop an image and draw customers. It influences the target market attracted, the customer's shopping mood and time spent in the store, the level of impulse purchases, and the long-term positioning of the store; and it is closely related to the strategy mix a retailer selects. For example, as was shown in Table 14-4, a discount store would have simple fixtures, linoleum floors, crowded displays, and centrally located dressing rooms. A traditional department store would have elaborate fixtures, carpeted floors, attractive displays, and several dressing rooms.

Atmosphere consists of a store's exterior, general interior, layout, and displays.

There are four basic components of a store's atmosphere:

▶ Exterior — includes such elements as the storefront, marquee, entrances, display windows, store visibility, store uniqueness, surrounding area, and traffic congestion.
▶ General interior — includes such elements as flooring, colors, scents, lighting, fixtures, wall textures, temperature, aisle width, dressing facilities, vertical transportation, personnel, cash register placement, and overall cleanliness.
▶ Store layout — includes such elements as floor space allotted for customers, selling, and storage; product groupings; and department locations.
▶ Interior (point-of-sale) displays — includes such elements as merchandise cases and racks, mobiles, in-store ads, posters, and mannequins.

The West Edmonton Mall in Canada — the largest planned shopping center in the world — uses its innovative atmosphere to draw several million people annually, some from 750 miles away and farther. It has 11 department stores, 800+ other shops, a mile-long concourse, and 58 entrances. Its size is equal to that of 115 football fields. The mall also contains an amusement park (complete with a submarine ride and

FIGURE 14-10
The Exciting Atmosphere
of the West
Edmonton Mall
Reprinted by permission.

Siberian tigers), an ice-skating rink, a miniature golf course, and other indoor attractions. It has parking for 20,000 vehicles. Total construction costs have already exceeded $700 million.[19] It is clear that "the entertainment component" of retailing is becoming more important. See Figure 14-10.

Scrambled Merchandising

*In **scrambled** merchandising, a retailer adds items to obtain one-stop shopping, higher margins, and impulse purchases.*

Scrambled merchandising occurs when a retailer adds products or product lines that are unrelated to each other and the retailer's original business. Examples are Sears department stores offering insurance (Allstate), real-estate brokerage (Coldwell Banker), and stock brokerage (Dean Witter); and supermarkets adding videocassette rentals.

There are several reasons for the popularity of scrambled merchandising: retailers seek to convert their stores to one-stop shopping centers; scrambled merchandise is often fast selling, generates store traffic, and yields high profit margins; impulse purchasing is increased; different target markets can be attracted; and the effects of seasonality and competition may be lessened. For example, convenience stores have added self-service food counters (with items such as frozen fountain drinks, hot beverages,

[19] Triple Five Corporation Ltd. 1988 press release.

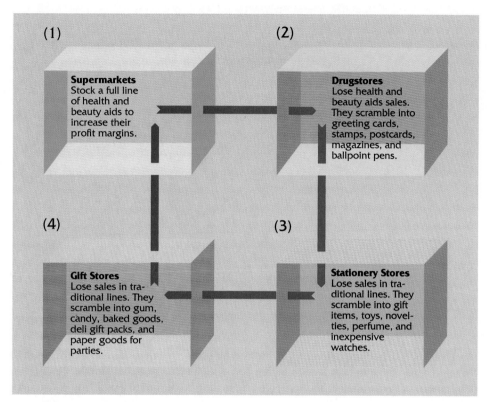

(1) Supermarkets
Stock a full line of health and beauty aids to increase their profit margins.

(2) Drugstores
Lose health and beauty aids sales. They scramble into greeting cards, stamps, postcards, magazines, and ballpoint pens.

(4) Gift Stores
Lose sales in traditional lines. They scramble into gum, candy, baked goods, deli gift packs, and paper goods for parties.

(3) Stationery Stores
Lose sales in traditional lines. They scramble into gift items, toys, novelties, perfume, and inexpensive watches.

FIGURE 14-11
The Self-Perpetuating Nature of Scrambled Merchandising

hot sandwiches, and other fast foods). These counters often have the highest profit margins of any of the product categories sold in these stores.

Scrambled merchandising frequently spreads quickly and leads to competition among unrelated retailers. For example, when supermarkets branched into nonfood personal-care items, they created a decline in drugstore sales. Drugstores were then forced to scramble into stationery and other product lines. This had an impact on specialty store sales, and so on. This is illustrated in Figure 14-11.

There are limits to how far a retailer should go with scrambled merchandising, especially if the addition of unrelated items would reduce buying, selling, and servicing expertise. Furthermore, a low rate of inventory turnover might occur for certain product lines, should the retailer expand into too many diverse product categories. Finally, because of its use of scrambled merchandising, a retailer's image may become fuzzy to consumers.

The Wheel of Retailing

The **wheel of retailing** describes how low-end (discount) strategies can evolve into high-end (full service, high price) strategies and thus provide opportunities for new firms to enter as discounters. According to the wheel, retail innovators often first appear as low-price operators with low profit-margin requirements and low costs.

As time passes, these innovators look to increase their sales and customer base. They upgrade product offerings, facilities, and services and develop into more traditional retailers. They may expand sales force support, utilize a more attractive store

*The **wheel of retailing** shows how strategies change, leaving opportunities for new firms.*

435

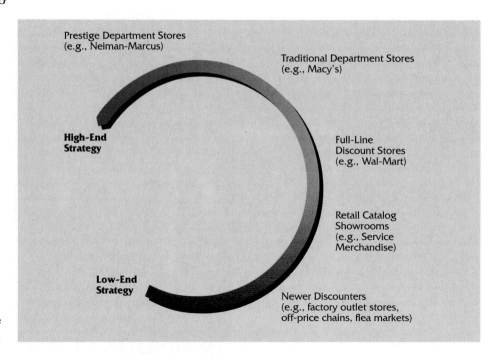

FIGURE 14-12
The Wheel of
Retailing in Action

location, and introduce delivery, credit, and alterations. These improvements lead to higher costs, which in turn lead to higher prices. This creates opportunities for another generation of new retailers to emerge by appealing to the price-conscious consumers who are left behind as existing firms move along the wheel.[20] Figure 14-12 shows the wheel of retailing in action.

Technological Advances

During the past several years, a number of technological advances have emerged in retailing. The most important advances involve the computerized-checkout system, video-shopping services, electronic banking, and operating efficiency.

A computerized-checkout system provides retailers with information and improves service.

With a **computerized-checkout (electronic point-of-sale) system,** a cashier manually rings up a sale or passes an item over or past an optical scanner; then a computerized register instantly records and displays a sale. The customer is given a receipt, and all inventory information is stored in the computer's memory bank. Such a system may lower costs by reducing checkout time and employee training, decreasing misrings, and reducing the need for price marking on merchandise. In addition, it generates a current listing of the types and quantities of merchandise in stock without taking a physical inventory, improves inventory control, reduces spoilage, and improves ordering.

The system is also able to verify and change transactions, provide instantaneous sales and profit reports, compute discounts, determine the prices of items with missing tags, and be part of a marketing information system. The major obstacles to computerized checkouts are their high purchase costs and consumers' insistence that price tags be adhered to each item.

[20] See Stephen Brown, "The Wheel of the Wheel of Retailing," *International Journal of Retailing*, Vol. 3 (1988), pp. 16–37.

FIGURE 14-13
Shopping with "Silent Sam"
Service Merchandise is one of the largest retail catalog showroom firms in the U.S., with 300+ outlets. To assist shoppers, many of these outlets utilize "Silent Sam," an in-store merchandise ordering system.
Reprinted by permission.

Video-shopping services allow retailers to efficiently, conveniently, and promptly present information, receive orders, and process customer transactions. These services can be divided into two basic categories: merchandise catalogs on videodiscs and videocassettes, and in-store and in-home ordering systems.

Video-shopping services include video catalogs and ordering systems.

Video catalogs (shown on special monitors or via disc players/ VCRs using conventional television sets) enable consumers to view prerecorded merchandise and sales presentations in store and nonstore settings without the seller having to set up costly and space consuming displays or invest in inventory. The catalogs are also useful in showing merchandise assortments, providing information, and reducing personnel costs. With these catalogs, supermarkets can market appliances, airport kiosks can market watches and accessories, department stores can market gourmet foods, and so on. By the early 1990s, it is expected that 70,000 video displays will generate $5 billion to $10 billion in annual U.S. sales.[21]

Video-ordering systems rely on information that is fed into and displayed on a computer monitor or is available on cable television programs. Some firms use their video merchandise catalogs in conjunction with in-store ordering systems. With an in-store system, a consumer orders merchandise by entering data into a self-prompting computer, which processes the order. After placing the order, the consumer goes to a checkout area where the item can be picked up and an invoice received. Then the consumer pays a cashier. Such a system is used by Service Merchandise. See Figure 14-13.

[21] Judith Graham, "Kiosks Gain Stature with Retailers," *Advertising Age* (July 25, 1988), p. 55; and Warren Berger, "Holiday Shopping by Touching a Screen," *New York Times* (November 27, 1988), Section 3, p. 11.

With an in-home shopping system, products are listed or displayed and then consumers order directly via special toll-free 800 telephone numbers or via their computers. Thus far, most in-home ordering has been from consumer telephone responses to cable and commercial television shows offered by companies such as the Home Shopping Network. Annual U.S. in-home television shopping revenues are about $5 billion.[22]

These factors are contributing to the unexpectedly slow growth in consumer demand for in-home computerized shopping services: Consumers are reluctant to pay for the services, which often require subscription fees and special terminals. To use the services, consumers must have both cable television and a home computer. Some consumers do not like buying by description or picture. They want to actually feel or try on merchandise. Many consumers enjoy shopping. A number of consumers believe the services to be overly complex to use. Nonetheless, Sears is now actively testing an in-home shopping system, named Prodigy.[23]

Electronic banking offers a wide variety of financial services and convenience.

Electronic banking involves the utilization of automatic teller machines (ATMs) and the instant processing of retail purchases. It provides centralized record keeping and enables customers to conduct transactions 24 hours a day, seven days a week at many bank and nonbank locations (such as supermarkets). Deposits, withdrawals, and other banking and retailing transactions can be completed.

At present, there are over 75,000 automatic teller machines operating in banks, shopping centers, airports, and other high-traffic sites. This figure is expected to continue rising for many years. By 1995, U.S. consumers will possess 250 million ATM access cards, up from 150 million in 1985. To allow customers to make financial transactions over wider geographic areas, a number of banks have formed automatic teller machine networks. There are now about 175 local and regional networks and about half a dozen national systems. For example, the Cirrus System enables customers to make transactions at 23,000 ATMs nationwide.[24]

As electronic banking spreads, more firms will employ a debit-only transfer system. In this arrangement, when a purchase is made, the amount is immediately charged against the buyer's account; no delayed billing is permitted without an interest charge. The debit-only plan is quite different from current credit-card policy whereby consumers are sent end-of-month bills and then remit payment. In the future, debit cards will receive wide acceptance as a substitute for checks. For example, Florida's Honor system already has several million debit-card holders and processes thousands of debit transactions each day through bank and retail store ATMs.

Technological advances aid operating efficiency.

Technological advances are also leading to greater retailer efficiency by

▶ Increasing the use of self-service operations by firms marketing gasoline, airline tickets, and rental cars, and for hotel registrations and payment.

▶ Providing data banks for real-estate brokers, who are better able to match buyers and sellers and secure mortgage sources for buyers.

▶ Linking manufacturers, warehouses, and transportation firms.

▶ Introducing antishoplifting tags that are attached to merchandise and set off an alarm if not properly removed by employees.

---

[22] Touche Ross, "Electronic Shopping Outlook: 1988–1992," *Chain Store Age Executive* (July 1988), p. 15.

[23] Kathleen A. Hughes, "IBM-Sears Computer-Services Venture Shows Promise, But a Lot of Kinks Remain," *Wall Street Journal* (February 8, 1989), p. B1.

[24] Jan Parr, "Contests Punch Up ATMs," *Advertising Age* (November 14, 1988), pp. S-4—S-5.

FIGURE 14-14
**Wendy's at a
Nontraditional Location:
The Columbus, Ohio Zoo**
This was the first
quick-service restaurant
at a zoo location in the
United States. © Wendy's
International.
Reprinted by permission.

▶ Automating energy-control systems that carefully monitor store temperature and
  reduce fuel costs.
▶ Computerizing site-selection programs that are able to evaluate the characteristics
  of many potential store locations.

Recent Trends in Retailing

During recent years, and continuing to the present, the nature of retailing has been
changing dramatically as firms try to protect their positions in the marketplace.[25]
Among the most prominent trends are those dealing with consumer demographics and
life-styles, competitive forces, operating costs, and the labor force.

The aging U.S. population, geographic population shifts, and the saturation of many
prime markets have resulted in various innovative retailing strategies. For example,
Limited Inc., which began by appealing to young, fashion-conscious women, now
operates Lane Bryant and Roaman's for older, full-size women. Macy's has stores in
Florida and California, to reduce the emphasis on its Northeast base. Nontraditional
locations, which have been underserved, are now being used — Baskin-Robbins has
outlets in U.S. Navy exchanges and Wendy's has an outlet in the Columbus, Ohio Zoo.
See Figure 14-14.

*Demographic and life-style
trends are being adapted to
by retailers.*

Retailers are adapting to the shopping needs and time constraints of working
women, and the increased consumer interest in quality and service. Many are stocking
labor-saving devices, such as microwave ovens and ready-to-eat foods; lengthening
store hours and opening additional days; expanding catalog sales efforts; re-empha-

[25] See "A Decade of Change," *Chain Store Age Executive* (November 1988), pp. 55–78; and Susan Cam-
initi, "What Ails Retailing," *Fortune* (January 30, 1989), pp. 61, 64.

sizing personal selling efforts; prewrapping gift items to eliminate waiting lines; setting up comprehensive specialty boutiques to minimize the number of departments a consumer must visit; adding special services, such as fashion coordinators; introducing high-quality dealer brands; and setting up more attractive displays.

Retail competition causes firms to modify strategies.

The intense, and growing, competition in retailing has resulted in various company responses. These are several illustrations:

▶ Montgomery Ward has greatly de-emphasized mail-order retailing to concentrate on store retailing.
▶ Dayton Hudson is opening a number of new Target and Mervyn's discount stores, but no new department store outlets.
▶ Toys Plus operates stores in small markets to avoid competing head-on with Toys "R" Us.
▶ Sears has been been opening a number of 14,000-square-foot stores (compared with its regular stores of 100,000+ square feet) in towns with populations of 5,000 to 20,000. These locales have less competition than more populated areas.
▶ To compete with shopping centers, more discounters are now situating in discount malls, whereby a variety of low-price retailers locate together. These malls enable retailers to share some costs, reduce customer gasoline consumption, encourage one-stop shopping, and expand the trading area of each retailer.
▶ Many store chains have merged.[26]

Retailers are more cost conscious.

Because of high inflation during the late 1970s and early 1980s, retailers are more concerned with cost control than ever before. For example,

▶ PepsiCo has been testing a fast-food format whereby a Kentucky Fried outlet, a Pizza Hut outlet, and a Taco Bell outlet share the same building. All of these fast-food chains are owned by PepsiCo. This new format allows common costs (and some employees) to be shared.
▶ Most small hardware stores participate in buying cooperatives that enable them to secure quantity discounts and "buy smarter."
▶ Many supermarkets are increasing use of bulk selling, by which consumers select exact quantities of items such as candy and dried fruit from open displays. Prices are reduced by up to one-third.[27]

There has been a labor shortage for many retailers.

In recent years, many U.S. retailers have had difficulty in attracting and retaining a quality labor force. According to one survey, retailers rank the labor shortage as one of the three most important issues for them to address.[28] These are among the reasons why the shortage exists: the number of available young people has declined; full-time career opportunities in other industries have attracted a number of part-time retail workers; many retail workers are inexperienced and have overly high job expectations, leading to employee dissatisfaction and turnover; hours can be long and irregular;

[26] "Department Stores 'Specialize' in Competitive Maneuvers," *Marketing News* (February 15, 1988), p. 14; *Dayton Hudson 1988 Annual Report*; Anthony Ramirez, "Can Anyone Compete with Toys "R" Us?" *Fortune* (October 28, 1985), pp. 71–75; Norman Miller, "Rural Retailing: The Last Frontier," *Chain Store Age Executive* (March 1986), pp. 18–22; and "Department Stores Face Tough Year," *Chain Store Age Executive* (August 1988), pp. 23–24.

[27] Douglas C. McGill, "The Fast-Food Market's New Lure," *New York Times* (January 19, 1989), pp. D1, D8; Jo Ellen Davis, "Hardware Wars: The Big Boys Might Lose This One," *Business Week* (October 14, 1985), pp. 84 ff.; and "Good News/Bad News About Bulk Foods," *Progressive Grocer* (February 1985), pp. 43–46.

[28] "Retailer Poll: Labor Concerns Rising," *Chain Store Age Executive* (October 1988), pp. 19–22.

some people do not like the pressure of interacting with customers on a regular basis; and the pay in other industries has been relatively higher.

These are a few of the actions that retailers are taking to resolve the labor shortage: recruiting at high schools and colleges, recruiting retired persons, offering child-care services for working mothers, raising starting salaries (sometimes to double the minimum wage or more), rotating employees among tasks to lessen boredom, rewarding good performance with bonuses, and encouraging the best employees to pursue full-time career paths in retailing.

Summary

1. *To define retailing and show its importance* Retailing encompasses those business activities involved with the sale of goods and services to the final consumer for personal, family, or household use. It is the final stage in a distribution channel. Average retail sales are small, yet the use of credit is widespread. Final consumers generally visit a retail store to make a purchase and they also make many unplanned purchases.

Retailing has an impact on the economy because of its total sales and the number of people employed. Retailers provide a variety of functions, including gathering a product assortment, providing information, handling merchandise, and completing transactions. Retailers deal with suppliers that sell products the retailers use in operating their businesses as well as suppliers selling items the retailers will resell.

2. *To discuss the different types of retailers, in terms of ownership, store strategy mix, and nonstore operations* Retailers may be categorized in several ways. The basic ownership formats are independent—a retailer operating only one outlet; chain—a retailer operating two or more outlets; franchise—a contractual arrangement between a franchisor and a franchisee to conduct a certain business; leased department—a department in a store that is leased to an outside party; and cooperative—an enterprise shared by retail or consumer owners. The ease of entry into retailing fosters competition and results in many new companies failing.

Different store strategy mixes are used by convenience stores—well-situated, food-oriented retailers; conventional supermarkets—departmentalized food stores with minimum annual sales of $2 million; superstores—diversified supermarkets that sell a broad range of food and nonfood items;

combination stores—outlets that go further than superstores in carrying both food and general merchandise; specialty stores—outlets that concentrate on the sale of one merchandise or service line; variety stores—outlets selling a wide assortment of inexpensive and popularly priced merchandise; traditional department stores—outlets that have the greatest assortment of any retailer, provide customer services, are fashion leaders, dominate surrounding stores, and have average to above average prices; full-line discount stores—department stores with a low-price, low-service orientation; retail catalog showrooms—stores in which the consumers select items from catalogs and shop in austere surroundings; and other discounters—including limited-line stores, warehouse stores, and others.

Nonstore retailing occurs when a firm uses a strategy mix that is not store-based. Vending machines use coin- or card-operated machinery to dispense goods and services. Direct selling involves both personal contact with consumers in their homes (or other places) and telephone solicitations initiated by retailers. Direct marketing occurs when consumers are exposed to goods and services through nonpersonal media, and then order via mail and telephone.

3. *To explore five aspects of retail planning: store location, atmosphere, scrambled merchandising, the wheel of retailing, and technological advances* A retailer may select from among three forms of store location: the isolated store, a free-standing outlet located on a highway or side street; the unplanned business district, in which two or more stores locate close to one another without prior planning as to the number and composition of stores; and the planned shopping center, which is centrally managed as well as planned and oper-

ated as an entity. Only planned shopping centers utilize balanced tenancy, thus relating the store mix to consumer needs.

A retailer's atmosphere is the sum total of a store's physical characteristics that help develop an image and attract customers. It depends on the store's exterior, general interior, layout, and interior displays.

Scrambled merchandising occurs when a retailer adds products unrelated to its original business. The goals of scrambled merchandising are to encourage customer one-stop shopping, increase sales of high-profit items and impulse purchases, attract different target markets, and balance sales throughout the year.

The wheel of retailing explains low-end and high-end retail strategies and how they emerge. As low-cost, low-price innovators move along the wheel, they leave opportunities for newer, more cost-conscious firms to enter the marketplace.

A number of technological advances have emerged over the past several years. These include the use of computerized checkouts, video-shopping services, electronic banking, and techniques to improve operating efficiency.

4. *To examine recent trends in retailing* The nature of retailing has changed dramatically in recent years. Among the key trends are those dealing with consumer demographics and life-styles, competitive forces, operating costs, and the labor force.

Key Terms

retailing (p. 416)
independent retailer (p. 420)
retail chain (p. 420)
retail franchising (p. 420)
leased department (p. 421)
retail cooperative (p. 421)
consumer cooperative (p. 422)
retail store strategy mix (p. 422)
convenience store (p. 422)
conventional supermarket (p. 423)
superstore (p. 424)
combination store (p. 424)

hypermarket (p. 424)
specialty store (p. 426)
variety store (p. 427)
department store (p. 427)
traditional department store (p. 427)
full-line discount store (p. 428)
retail catalog showroom (p. 428)
nonstore retailing (p. 429)
vending machine (p. 429)
direct selling (p. 430)
direct marketing (p. 431)

isolated store (p. 432)
unplanned business district (p. 432)
planned shopping center (p. 433)
balanced tenancy (p. 433)
atmosphere (p. 433)
scrambled merchandising (p. 434)
wheel of retailing (p. 435)
computerized-checkout (electronic point-of-sale) system (p. 436)
video-shopping services (p. 437)
electronic banking (p. 438)

Review Questions

1. Describe the four basic functions that are performed by retailers.
2. What are the advantages of an independent retailer in competing with retail chains?
3. What are the benefits of retail franchising to the franchisee? To the franchisor?
4. Why have consumer cooperatives not become a more important factor in food retailing?
5. Compare the strategies of convenience stores, supermarkets, and superstores.
6. Distinguish between direct marketing and direct selling. Which has greater sales? Why?
7. What are the pros and cons of scrambled merchandising?
8. Explain the wheel of retailing from the perspective of the battle between traditional department stores and full-line discount stores for market share.
9. Why have in-home computerized shopping services not grown as quickly as expected? How can this be overcome?
10. Why is attracting and retaining a quality labor force so difficult for many U.S. retailers?

Discussion Questions

1. Table 14-1 shows net income as a per cent of sales for 20 leading retailers. How can the percentages be so low if 40 cents of every customer dollar spent in department stores and 20 cents of every customer dollar spent in supermarkets go to the retailers?
2. At one time most of McDonald's outlets operated under franchise agreements. Today one-quarter of all McDonald's outlets are owned by the firm itself.
   a. Why was franchising a correct strategy for McDonald's in its early years?
   b. Why would McDonald's want to operate its own outlets now?
3. Develop a discount-store strategy for high-fidelity equipment. How would it compete with a high-priced specialty store?
4. Select a planned shopping center near your college or university and evaluate it.
5. Describe the atmosphere of a retail catalog showroom. Does it lend itself to the selling of fine jewelry? Explain your answer.

CASE 1

Selecting an Ice Cream Franchise*

Mary and John Cutler, both in their mid-twenties, have been married since graduating from college four years ago. At present, Mary is a manager at a small bookstore and John is a manager at a Baskin-Robbins outlet; but they want to open their own retail business.

The Cutlers have investigated franchise opportunities in a variety of fields and are most interested in the possibility of owning an ice cream and/or frozen yogurt shop. There are various reasons for this decision. First, both Cutlers have a lot of experience with

regard to retail store operations and personnel management; John Cutler has worked at Baskin-Robbins for six years (going back to his days as an undergraduate college student). Second, the initial investment required by most ice cream/frozen yogurt franchisors is quite reasonable—a fraction of the investment required by hamburger-based operations. Table 1 shows relevant data for the five leading franchise chains that the Cutlers are evaluating. Third, overall U.S. ice cream/frozen yogurt franchising has been experiencing rapid growth. See Table 2.

The Cutlers desire a franchised outlet rather than an independent store. Why? Ice-cream franchisors generally provide such services as site planning, store planning, equipment financing, promotional assistance, and store troubleshooting. The Cutlers also believe that new franchised outlets have an

* The data in this case are drawn from Mike Connelly, "Ice Cream Glut Spurs Questions on Operations," *Wall Street Journal* (December 2, 1988), pp. B1–B2; and Andrew Kostecka, *Franchising in the Economy: 1986–1988* (Washington, D.C.: U.S. Department of Commerce, 1988).

TABLE 1 Selected Financial and Operating Data for Ice Cream/Frozen Yogurt Franchises

Company	Initial Franchise Fee	Total Estimated Investment Required	Royalty and Advertising Fund (as % of Sales)	Total Stores in Chain	Franchised Stores in Chain
Baskin-Robbins	$ 0	$ 80,000–140,000	2%	2,500	2,438
Ben & Jerry's	15,600	125,000–150,000	4	80	75
Bresler's	10,000	125,000–145,000	9	300	300
International Dairy Queen	30,000	445,000–675,000	7–9	5,005	5,000
TCBY (The Country's Best Yogurt)	20,000	93,000–155,000	7	1,075	972

SOURCE: Mike Connelly, "Ice Cream Glut Spurs Questions on Franchising," *Wall Street Journal* (December 21, 1988), p. B2. Reprinted by permission. © Dow Jones & Company. All Rights Reserved Worldwide.

TABLE 2   Selected Data on U.S. Company-Owned and Franchised Ice Cream/Frozen Yogurt Stores

Year	Total Sales ($000)	Company-Owned Store Sales ($000)	Franchisee-Owned Store Sales ($000)	Total Stores	Company-Owned Stores	Franchisee-Owned Stores
1986	1,446,210	140,827	1,305,383	8,473	287	8,186
1987	1,610,666	150,688	1,459,978	9,272	320	8,952
1988	1,880,191	171,574	1,708,517	10,586	372	10,214

SOURCE: Andrew Kostecka, *Franchising in the Economy: 1986–1988* (Washington, D.C.: U.S. Department of Commerce, 1988), p. 19.

immediate customer following: "When you buy a franchise, you have a built-in customer base. That's really what you're buying when you buy a franchise. When you own your business, you have to develop your own customer base. That's one of the toughest things to do these days." Other important advan-

tages of a franchise operation include access to better locations (many property owners will not lease good locations to independents), and lower possible equipment costs due to quantity discounts and bargaining-power advantages.

QUESTIONS

1. Evaluate the ice cream/frozen yogurt franchise data in Tables 1 and 2.
2. What are the pros and cons of the Cutlers owning an independent outlet versus a franchised ice cream/frozen yogurt shop?
3. What additional information should the Cutlers obtain prior to deciding on a franchise? What are the sources of this information?
4. State several criteria for the Cutlers to use in rating the various franchising opportunities available to them.

◄ CASE 2 ►

Will Specialty Car-Care Malls Dominate the Marketplace?[†]

According to the International Council of Shopping Centers, of the 1,850 planned shopping centers built in the United States in 1988, only about one per cent were large regional shopping centers (versus 5 to 8 per cent throughout the 1960s and 1970s). Today about 85 per cent of all planned shopping centers being built in the United States are 100,000 square feet or smaller in size. One interesting trend in this area involves the growth of specialty shopping centers, which focus on one product category.

The car-care mall is a type of specialty shopping center that caters to the needs of automobile owners. This mall typically includes a car wash, a tire-

service store, a muffler-repair shop, and a quick-oil-change outlet. As of 1988, there were 600 car-care malls, a number expected to increase to 2,500 by 1992.

An example of a car-care mall is the 54,000-square-foot Route 34 Auto Mall in Naperville, Illinois (a suburb of Chicago). It features a cellular phone retailer, a muffler shop, an auto-glass replacement shop, a radiator installer, a quick-oil-change retailer, a foreign car mechanic, and an electronics specialist.

The popularity of the car-care mall is tied to four key concepts: the scarcity of modern facilities for car repair; its appeal to females; the low rent paid by repair shops; and the convenience of one-stop shopping.

According to one market analyst, there was a 60

[†] The data in this case are drawn from Rhonda Razzano, "Growth of Car-Care Malls Accelerates," *Chain Store Age Executive* (January 1989), pp. 33, 37.

per cent decline in the number of full-service gasoline stations between 1972 and 1986. This analyst estimates that, by the end of 1990, 67 per cent of neighborhood gasoline stations will not offer routine servicing of any kind. In contrast to the declining number of gasoline stations offering maintenance and repair services, consumer demand for these services has been increasing because of the longer life of automobiles. In 1970, the average age of a car on U.S. roads was 4.9 years; now, it is 7 years.

A recent *Automotive Week* study found that three-quarters of U.S. women are responsible for the car care in their households. Yet, female customers often feel uncomfortable in traditional garages. Many traditional garages do not have clean waiting rooms, separate bathrooms for females, or general-interest magazines for females to read. In contrast, Route 34 Auto Mall has several lounge areas that offer reading material and coffee, and a dance studio where customers can take lessons while their car is being repaired: "The key is to make the center upscale, so that women feel comfortable bringing their cars there."

Car-care malls can locate away from other retailers and thus offer low-rent possibilities for their tenants. Because many consumers view them as destination shopping centers, customers are willing to drive to car-care malls. Therefore, these malls do not have to worry as much about such location attributes as high traffic counts and visibility from major roads.

Lastly, car-care malls offer shoppers the convenience of one-stop shopping. This is important when a car owner seeks multiple services on a single trip—such as a car wash, quick oil change, and a tune-up. The potential time savings is especially important to households where both the husband and wife work.

A major developer of car-care malls is Auto Spa. That firm currently operates dozens of centers, whose average size is 12,000 to 15,000 square feet. According to Auto Spa's chairman, two factors are crucial in operating car-care malls. First, each mall requires an anchor tenant (such as a car wash or quick-oil-change service retailer) to generate a high volume of customer traffic. A local service station would not be a good anchor because it could not attract enough traffic. Second, tenants must be able to service cars both quickly and sequentially.

Questions

1. Evaluate the car-care mall concept as a type of planned shopping center.
2. What impact will specialty shopping centers such as car-care malls have on these existing retailers: local service station, central business district stores, and regional shopping center stores? Explain your answers.
3. Comment on the atmosphere created by a traditional garage and a car-care mall.
4. Compare regional shopping centers and specialty shopping centers on the basis of their use of scrambled merchandising.

part 4 CASE

Will Wal-Mart Take Over the World?*

Introduction

In just a couple of years, Wal-Mart Stores may be the largest retailer in the U.S. The only companies in its way are K mart and the floundering giant, Sears, and the gap is closing fast. Wal-Mart's 1,300 or so discount stores sell over $20 billion worth of goods a year — clothes, shoes, small appliances, cosmetics, and 50,000 other items. Even so, you may never have shopped in a Wal-Mart because the company is really just getting started. Early on, Sam Walton focused on the small-town markets ignored by national discounters, and though the company now operates Wal-Marts in such cities as Dallas, Houston, St. Louis, and Kansas City, its trade area still includes only 25 states.

The Wal-Mart Touch

This year, like last year, Wal-Mart will open 150 or so new stores. David Glass, the company's 53-year-old chief executive who assumed all but the role of corporate inspirational leader from Chairman Sam Walton last year, says there is no state he wouldn't enter. So sooner or later, there's bound to be a Wal-Mart in your future. When you do step into one, don't get rattled when someone — probably an elderly retiree type — approaches you with a smile and welcomes you to the store. This is the "people greeter," and every Wal-Mart has one because, it's the friendly thing to do, and one of the hourly associates suggested it and the idea worked its way up through the system and Sam liked it.

* Adapted by the authors from John Huey, "Wal-Mart: Will It Take Over the World?" *Fortune* (January 30, 1989), pp. 52–61. Reprinted by permission of Time Inc. All rights reserved.

If all this hospitality makes you think your company might like to sell something to Wal-Mart, a word of caution: Don't expect a greeter, and don't expect friendly. Plan on a tough trip over the river and through the woods and across the rock pile to a low-slung warehouse building in a town of 10,000 people. And even if you're a big deal at your company and have an appointment, don't be surprised if you're kept waiting an hour or two in a lobby filled with 150 molded-plastic chairs and mounted giant fish.

Unless you like cafeteria food, eat before you come, because Wal-Mart won't let you buy lunch or dinner or anything else for the buyer. And once you are ushered into one of the spartan little buyers' rooms, expect a steely eye across the table and be prepared to cut your price. "They are very, very focused people, and they use their buying power more forcefully than anybody else in America," says the marketing vice-president of a major vendor.

A High-Tech Approach

Come now to Wal-Mart's headquarters in Bentonville, Arkansas, where it is a Friday morning just before Christmas. Some 100 of the company's top managers — senior executives, divisional managers, regional managers — have flown back from visiting stores and are assembled for a weekly, no-holds-barred session with the sole agenda of moving merchandise. Most folks are clutching a thick printout that lists the inventory levels and rates of sale for key items that Wal-Mart stocks. The energy is high, for this is the playoff season of retailing.

For three hours, the managers pore over the printout. One is concerned that Wal-Mart has priced children's corduroy jeans at $3, while K mart is promoting them at two for $5; this is corrected. CEO Glass worries that a certain video game isn't moving in stores he has visited this week, and he wants orders cut off; the buyers have beaten him to it. Then a discussion ensues over knives, which the printout shows are heavily stocked in Wal-Mart's distribution centers. Quickly, a senior manager orders a Christmas gift knife display. Glass sees that only 500,000 sets of cookware are stocked in the stores, while he thinks 600,000 can be sold. Get them out there.

Word on the knives and cookware will reach all store managers by Monday, probably by phone. In more urgent cases, an executive can broadcast the message on TV from Bentonville to all stores over the company's six-channel satellite system, which also gathers store data for the master computer, handles credit-card approval transmission in five seconds, and tracks the company's complex distribution system. With the satellite, Glass says, "we can talk to every store at the same time as many times a day as we want, and we've dramatically reduced our phone costs. We train by satellite. But the biggest advantage is the sharing of merchandising information. A buyer can get on and say, 'These are the new items in department 16. Here's how you should display them.' "

The satellite is for efficiency and speed; management of this company is anything but remote control. Almost everyone at the meeting spends Monday through Thursday flying around to stores on one of Wal-Mart's eleven planes — mostly turboprops — then returns to share findings in Friday and Saturday meetings. This is a practice with deep roots in tradition. Sam Walton pilots his own plane, and at one time visited every store at least once a year.

Distribution Management

Nowhere is the technology of Wal-Mart more evident than at its fourteen distribution centers, most within a day's drive of the stores they serve. "Our distribution facilities are one of the keys to our success," says Glass. "If we do anything better than other folks, that's it. But the truth is, we were driven to a lot of this technology because the things we needed didn't exist in small-town America." In the early days of discounting, retailers paid distributors a cut, say 15 per cent, to supply merchandise and stock shelves. But there were no distributors available to Wal-Mart in such places as

Idabel, Oklahoma, or Van Buren, Arkansas, so it developed its own system, ordering directly from manufacturers and using its own fleet of trucks for delivery.

Consider 35-year-old Jimmy Wright's job as general manager of the 1.2-million-square-foot Cullman, Alabama, distribution center. He oversees 1,042 associates, all working under one 28-acre roof. They load 150 outbound Wal-Mart trailers a day and unload 160. They deliver to each of the center's 165 stores almost every day. Laser scanners route the goods along 11 miles of conveyor belts, which on a heavy day will handle 190,000 cases of goods. Says Wright: "The technology we use is standard — mechanized conveyors, bar coding, computerized inventory. A lot of companies use it. But no one runs it as hard as we do, and no one is as in touch with their business as we are."

"Better People"

Every Wal-Mart associate — from Sam Walton to a cashier named Janet at the Wal-Mart on Highway 50 in Ocoee, Florida — will tell you that "better people" are what really make the difference at the company. How Sam Walton and his top managers have motivated 215,000 employees — many of them unskilled workers with starting pay of less than $5 an hour — to work as partners in the process is the most oft-told, least understood chapter of the Wal-Mart saga.

As well as anyone can remember, it all began in the late 1960s when Sam and his brother Bud's private company had about twenty Wal-Marts. A union tried to organize two stores in Missouri, and Sam enlisted the help of labor lawyer John Tate, now an executive vice-president of Wal-Mart. "I told him, 'You can approach this one of two ways,' " Tate recalls. "Hold people down, and pay me or some other lawyer to make it work. Or devote time and attention to proving to people that you care.' " Sam chose the latter, and soon after held his first management seminar, entitled "We Care."

Subsequently, everyone at Wal-Mart became an "associate." "We," "us," and "our" became the operative words. Wal-Mart department heads, hourly associates who look after one or more of thirty-some departments ranging from sporting goods to electronics, see figures that many companies never show general managers: costs, freight charges, profit margins. The company sets a profit goal for each store, and if the store exceeds it, then the hourly associates share part of the additional profit. To control losses from theft and damage—also known as shrinkage, the bugaboo of all big merchants—Sam instituted the shrinkage bonus in 1980. If a store holds shrinkage below the corporate goal, every associate in that store receives up to $200. Wal-Mart's shrinkage is just above 1 per cent, vs. an industry average of 2 per cent.

The company's profit-sharing plan is invested principally in Wal-Mart stock. Truck drivers sipping coffee in company lounges don't mind telling you they've built considerable net worth from stock they've bought beyond the plan. Some store managers earn more than $100,000 a year in salary and bonuses, and some hourly associates retire with $150,000 in profit-sharing distributions.

Fighting Conventional Wisdom

According to Sam Walton, "If people believe in themselves, it's truly amazing what they can accomplish." And his story makes this point about as strongly as it can be made. The son of a Depression-era farm-mortgage banker, he grew up in the same four-state heartland where he is today (Arkansas, Missouri, Oklahoma, and Kansas all come together near Bentonville). He graduated from the University of Missouri in 1940 with an economics degree and hired on as a trainee at J.C. Penney. After World War II Army service, he opened a small Ben Franklin five-and-dime in Arkansas and eventually became the company's largest franchisee.

The former president of Ben Franklin recalls the first time he met Walton: "Sam said, 'Hey, there's some people putting some things on the street called discount stores, and I think they fit in rural markets as much as they do in the major metropolitan areas. I think you should franchise them, and I'll be your guinea pig.' " Ben Franklin said no thanks.

The conventional wisdom, which everybody told Sam over and over, was that a discount store could work only in an area with 50,000 or more people. But in 1962, Walton opened the first Wal-Mart in tiny Rogers, Arkansas, near Bentonville.

So how did Sam Walton get to be America's most admired retailer? He is an old-fashioned promoter in the P.T. Barnum style. But he is more than that. He's a little bit Jimmy Stewart, handsome with halting, "aw shucks" charm. He's a little bit Billy Graham, with a charisma and a persuasiveness that heartland folks find hard to resist. And he's more than a little bit Henry Ford, a business genius who sees how all parts of the economic puzzle relate to his business. Overlaying everything is a lot of the old yard rooster who is tough, loves a good fight, and protects his territory.

Sam Walton in Action

Sam still comes to Saturday Morning Meeting, a whoop-it-up 7:30 A.M. sales pep rally for 300 managers, complete with Wal-Mart cheers, awards, and occasional appearances by such groups as the singing truck drivers. In November, with the Christmas season approaching, Wal-Mart associates across the country arrived at work to find Sam—wearing his ubiquitous mesh ball cap—waiting to "visit with" them by satellite on a subject he said he was "totally obsessed with:" aggressive hospitality to the customers. This isn't just a sales pitch; it's a self-improvement video that Dale Carnegie would have envied.

"I don't think any other retail company in the world could do what I'm going to propose to you," he says. "It's simple. It won't cost us anything. And I believe it would just work magic, absolute magic on our customers, and our sales would escalate, and I think we'd just shoot past our K mart friends in a year or two and probably Sears as well." He proposes that whenever customers approach, the associates should look them in the eye, greet them, and ask to help. Sam understands that some associates are shy, but if they do what he suggests, "it would, I'm sure, help you become a leader, it would help your personality develop, you would become more outgoing, and in time you might become manager of that store, you might become a department manager, you might become a district manager, or whatever you choose to be in the company. It will do wonders for you." He guarantees it.

Then, just to make sure, Sam asks the associates to raise their right hands and execute a pledge, keeping in mind that "a promise we make is a promise we keep." The pledge: "From this day forward, I solemnly promise and declare that every customer that comes within ten feet of me, I will smile, look them in the eye, and greet them, so help me Sam."

You city slickers laugh all you want. This is one of the keys to the magic formula. The same principles apply to Sam's "Bring It Home to the USA" program to replace foreign goods in Wal-Mart with domestic goods. First, the program has created thousands of manufacturing jobs in the U.S. Second, it's a great sales promotion. Finally, every worker in a Wal-Mart-created job becomes a loyal Wal-Mart shopper. "It's the best thing that ever happened to Brinkley, Arkansas, and the best thing that every happened to me," says Farris Burroughs, an apparel manufacturer whose life changed one day in 1984 when Sam asked him to make 50,000 dozen flannel shirts. "Today we're making two million Wal-Mart shirts, we've got 275 employees, we're adding 70 more next year, and everybody knows what they're getting from the company for Christmas: $25 gift certificates to the Wal-Mart."

Missteps Along the Way

Not everyone shares Burroughs' love of Wal-Mart. Many small-town merchants have been trampled out of business by the company's "Everyday Low Prices" philosophy. And manufacturers' representatives have been largely shut out of the buying process at Wal-Mart. Some vendors find the company extremely difficult, and a high-ranking marketer for a big consumer-goods firm calls Wal-Mart "the rudest account in America." Bill Fields, Wal-Mart's executive vice-president of merchandise and sales, concedes, "We want to win at everything we do, and it has been ingrained in our buyers that we want to buy as well as possible." With some major manufacturers, though — Procter & Gamble, Rubbermaid, General Electric — Wal-Mart is trying a nonadversarial approach in which it shares sales projection data through computer links, hoping the vendor can anticipate its needs.

Not everything Wal-Mart does works well. The company tried a do-it-yourself building supplies concept that failed, and executives admit they would like to sell a small discount-drug chain they own. Other experiments have been more successful. Sam's Wholesale Clubs — 102 low-margin, high-volume operations geared to small-business owners or anyone else who wants to buy in bulk — are profitable in a competitive market. Its three Hypermart USA stores — huge, five-acre "malls without walls" — are believed to be in the black despite the tremendous volume required. "We will continue to experiment with concepts that are compatible with our core business," says Al Johnson, vice-chairman in charge of special divisions.

What Does the Future Hold?

In examining this gargantuan retailing amoeba, three questions naturally arise: How does Wal-Mart keep growing? How can it continue to manage such growth? And what happens after Sam Walton is gone?

"When we were doing $400 million," says Glass, "people said to me, 'Wait till you get to a billion. Things change. You can't do it the way you're doing it now.' So we worked real hard to make sure nothing bad happened at a billion. Then they said $5 billion was the number where everything would fall apart, then $10 billion. Then they said, 'Well, when you move into a new territory you'll have trouble.' So we do all these crazy things to make sure we can still communicate, regardless of our size." Like McDonald's, Wal-Mart has reduced the logistics of growth to a science. The strategy is basically to spread out and fill in. Wal-Mart opens a few stores in a new state or territory, then goes back and saturates that territory, working from a master book of potential sites. The real estate is largely self-financing because institutional investors snap up the stores in sale-leasebacks.

And what of Wal-Mart without Sam? "There's no transition to make," says Glass, "because the principles and the basic values he used in founding this company were so sound and so universally accepted." As for the future, Glass says, "there's more opportunity ahead of us than behind us. We're good students of retailing and we've studied the mistakes that others have made. We'll make our own mistakes, but we won't repeat theirs. The only thing constant at Wal-Mart is change. We'll be fine as long as we never lose our responsiveness to the customer."

QUESTIONS

1. Do you believe that Wal-Mart will overtake Sears and K mart to become the largest retailer in the United States? Explain your answer.
2. Evaluate Wal-Mart's decision to concentrate on smaller markets. For example, at present, it does not have stores in either California or New York.
3. Comment on Wal-Mart's relations with its suppliers. If you represented a firm selling to Wal-Mart, what pitfalls would you try to avoid?
4. As an apparel manufacturer selling to K mart, state at least seven key distribution standards that you would work hard to achieve.
5. Wal-Mart utilizes a just-in-time inventory system and electronic data interchange in managing its merchandise. How does this affect its stock turnover rate, reorder points, and economic order quantities?
6. Discuss the pros and cons of Wal-Mart's having its own warehouses.
7. What could other retailers learn by studying Wal-Mart's philosophy toward its employees?
8. What could Wal-Mart learn by studying the concepts of the wheel of retailing and scrambled merchandising?

part 5
PROMOTION PLANNING

Part 5 covers the third major element of the marketing mix, promotion.

15 **An Overview of Promotion Planning** Here, we broadly discuss promotion planning, which involves all communication used to inform, persuade, and/or remind people about an organization's or individual's goods, services, image, ideas, community involvement, or impact on society. We describe the basic types of promotion and the stages in a channel of communication. Next we present the steps in developing an overall promotion plan. We conclude the chapter with the legal environment and criticisms of promotion.

16 **Advertising and Publicity** In this chapter, we examine the two mass communication forms of promotion: advertising and publicity. We define advertising as the paid, nonpersonal communication of goods, services, organizations, people, places, and ideas by identified sponsors; and publicity as the nonpaid, nonpersonal communication of goods, services, organizations, people, places, and ideas by independent sources. We detail the scope of advertising and publicity and their attributes. We discuss the development of advertising and publicity plans in depth.

17 **Personal Selling and Sales Promotion** Here, we focus on the two other key elements of a promotion mix: personal selling and sales promotion. We define personal selling as oral communication with one or more prospective buyers by paid representatives for the purpose of making sales; and sales promotion as the paid marketing communication activities (other than advertising, publicity, or personal selling) that stimulate consumer purchases and dealer effectiveness. We describe the scope, characteristics, and stages in planning for both personal selling and sales promotion.

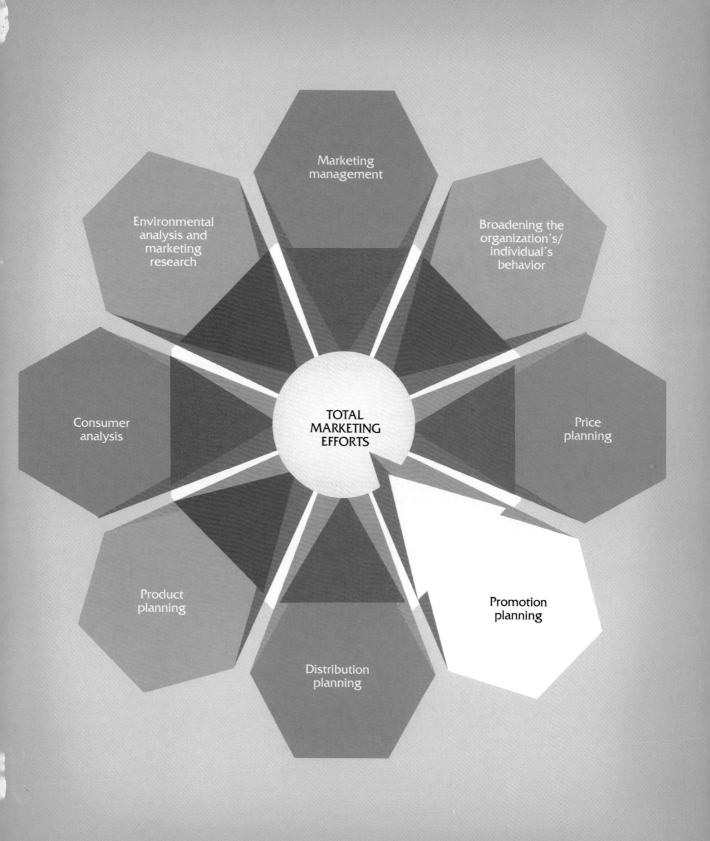

CHAPTER *15*

An Overview of Promotion Planning

CHAPTER OBJECTIVES

1. To define promotion planning and show its importance

2. To describe the general characteristics of advertising, publicity, personal selling, and sales promotion

3. To explain the channel of communication and how it functions

4. To examine the components of a promotion plan: objectives, budgeting, and the promotion mix

5. To discuss the legal environment and the criticisms and defenses of promotion

Lee Iacocca may have reached the end of the road as Chrysler Corp. spokesman. The man who told U.S. car buyers "If you can find a better car, buy it!" and put public confidence behind a failing Chrysler says he wants to retire from his role as pitchman. The Chrysler chairman says the long hours of filming and his feeling that he has become overexposed are contributing factors. "I think people are tired of me coming into their living rooms."

But what a long and profitable road Lee Iacocca has driven! He is undoubtedly the most successful corporate spokesperson in U.S. history. Let us see why.

During 1979-1980, Chrysler's major promotional objective was to assure the public that it would not go bankrupt and would be able to replace parts and honor service warranties. Its advertising agency developed the theme, "Trust us, support us, and we'll be around."

At that time, the agency sought to hire Walter Cronkite, then the CBS television news anchorman as a celebrity spokesperson; however, he would not accept a Chrysler offer. Instead, a reluctant Lee Iacocca was used in ads as a company spokesperson, saying only "I'm not asking you to buy any car on faith. I'm asking you to compare" or "If you buy any car without considering Chrysler, that'll be too bad for both of us."

After Chrysler received federal loan guarantees in January 1980, its advertising agency decided to use Iacocca more prominently in commercials. As Iacocca noted, he gave the ads tremendous credibility: "If people saw somebody on TV who, after making certain promises, would go back and make the cars, sales might not erode." Since then, Chrysler's sales and profits have steadily increased and Iacocca has been honored as Adman of the Year by *Advertising Age*.

According to one professor of communications, Iacocca's role at Chrysler has been a classic example of "icon making"—using a person or image to represent an entire company. Other experts believe that "his tough veneer and one-liners" have made him popular with the U.S. consumer.

Despite Lee Iacocca's high degree of recognition, over the years Chrysler has tried to limit his use in commercials. For example, he did not appear every time a

Reprinted by permission.

new car model was introduced and usually did not appear in retail incentive spots (such as factory-sponsored rebates). Chrysler has tried to avoid making Iacocca "the Cheryl Tiegs or Arnold Palmer of the auto industry." Nonetheless, as of early 1988, he had appeared in a total of 46 television commercials over the years.

Iacocca's decision to retire as company spokesperson came at a time when his overall ratings were extremely high. According to research by Chrysler's advertising agency, 87 per cent of the people who watched Iacocca in 1988 ads responded positively to those ads.

During late 1988 (several months after announcing his "retirement" as corporate spokesman), Lee Iacocca surprised observers by appearing in television commercials detailing Chrysler's new "Car Buyer's Bill of Rights."[1] As of this writing, these commercials continue to air. What does this mean? Lee Iacocca is still the king of the road.

In this chapter, we will study the many dimensions of promotion planning. Our discussion will include how the channel of communication works and the role of such sources in the channel as company spokespeople.

[1] "Last Pitch?" *Advertising Age* (February 29, 1988), p. 26; and Raymound Serafin, "Iacocca's Back With New Pitch in Chrysler Ads," *Advertising Age* (September 5, 1988), pp. 3, 56.

Overview

Promotion planning focuses on the total promotion effort— informing, persuading, and reminding.

Promotion is any form of communication used to inform, persuade, and/or remind people about an organization's or individual's goods, services, image, ideas, community involvement, or impact on society. ***Promotion planning*** is systematic decision making relating to all aspects of an organization's or individual's communications efforts.

Communication occurs through brand names, packaging, store marquees and displays, personal selling, trade shows, sweepstakes, messages in mass media (newspapers, television, radio, direct mail, billboards, magazines, and transit), and so on. It can be company sponsored or controlled by independent media. Messages may emphasize information, persuasion, fear, sociability, product performance, humor, and/or comparisons with competitors.

In Chapter 15, an overview of promotion planning is provided. Included are discussions on the importance of promotion, the basic types of promotion, the channel of communication, promotion planning, the legal environment, and general criticisms and defenses of promotion. Chapter 16 covers advertising and publicity—the paid and nonpaid forms of mass communication. Chapter 17 deals with personal selling and sales promotion—the individual and supplemental forms of communication.

The Importance of Promotion

Promotion is a vital part of marketing.

Promotion is a key element of the marketing mix for several reasons. With new products, customers must be informed about the items and their attributes before developing favorable attitudes toward them. For products that have a level of consumer awareness, the promotional thrust is on persuasion—converting product knowledge to product liking. For well-entrenched products, emphasis is on reminder promotion—reinforcing existing consumer beliefs.

The people to whom a firm's promotional effort is addressed may fall into several categories: consumers, stockholders, consumer organizations and lobbies, government, channel members, employees, and the general public. It is essential to realize that communication often goes on between a firm and each of these categories, not just with consumers. In addition, communication with each will be different because they have distinct goals, knowledge, and needs.

Word-of-mouth communication occurs when people state opinions to others.

Within an audience category (such as consumers), a firm should identify and appeal to opinion leaders—those individuals who influence their friends, neighbors, and so on. It also needs to understand the mechanisms of ***word-of-mouth communication***, the process by which people express their opinions and product-related experiences to one another. Without sustained positive word-of-mouth, it is difficult for a company to succeed.[2]

A firm's promotional plan usually stresses individual goods and services, with the objective of moving consumers from awareness to purchase. However, a company may also seek to communicate its overall image (industry innovator), views on ideas (nuclear energy), community involvement (funding of a new hospital), or impact on society

---

[2] See Barry L. Bayus, "Word of Mouth: The Indirect Effects of Marketing Efforts," *Journal of Advertising Research*, Vol. 25 (June–July 1985), pp. 31–39.

TABLE 15-1 The Value of Promotion

Promotion

► Establishes an image — such as prestige, discount, or innovative — for the company and its goods and services.
► Communicates features of goods and services.
► Creates awareness for new goods and services.
► Keeps existing goods and services popular.
► Can reposition the images or uses of faltering goods and services.
► Generates enthusiasm from channel members.
► Explains where goods and services can be purchased.
► Can persuade consumers to trade up from one good or service to a more expensive one.
► Alerts consumers to sales.
► Justifies the prices of goods and services.
► Answers consumer questions.
► Closes transactions.
► Provides afterservice for consumers.
► Places the company and its goods and services in a favorable light, relative to competitors.

(the number of workers employed). Table 15-1 shows some of the valuable functions performed by promotion.

A good promotion plan complements the product, distribution, and price components of marketing. For example, a manufacturer of quality stereo equipment would distribute merchandise through finer specialty stores and maintain high prices (avoiding discounting). It would advertise in magazines such as *Stereo Review* and expect its retailers to provide a significant level of personal selling. Ads would be full color and emphasize product features.

Promotion complements other marketing functions.

These are two illustrations of well-conceived promotion plans:

► For over 30 years, Pepsi has communicated the ''Pepsi generation'' message to its customers. Although the themes used by Pepsi have changed over the years, the general message has remained the same, for example: ''So young at heart'' (1958-1961); ''Come alive. You're in the Pepsi generation'' (1963-1968); ''Join the Pepsi people, feelin' free'' (1974-1976); ''Catch that Pepsi spirit! Drink it in'' (1980-1983); ''Pepsi. The choice of a new generation'' (1984-1988); and ''Pepsi. Generations ahead'' (1988-present). These themes have appeared in advertisements, sales promotions, and in-store displays. They provide Pepsi with a well-defined and stable image, and have contributed to the soda's strong second position, just behind Coke. For 1988, Pepsi ranked first in advertising awareness among all U.S. advertisers according to a poll by *Advertising Age.*[3] See Figure 15-1.
► Inmac is a direct marketer (and direct-sales firm) of computer-related products and supplies; it generates annual sales of nearly $200 million. Inmac uses a highly developed mailing list of two million names and sends out thirty million catalogs each year. The catalogs are easy to read and colorful, and convey a personal touch. They are published in six languages (one-half of Inmac's sales are in Europe) and present a classy company image — as well as generate sales. Inmac spends about one-half of one per cent of its sales on print ads encouraging consumers to write in

[3] James P. Forkan, ''Pepsi Generation Bridges Two Decades,'' *Advertising Age* (May 5, 1980), pp. 41–43; Amy Dunkin, ''Pepsi's Marketing Magic: Why Nobody Does It Better,'' *Business Week* (February 10, 1986), pp. 52–53 ff.; and Scott Hume, ''Pepsi Rises to Top Ad-Recall Spot,'' *Advertising Age* (January 30, 1989), p. 12.

FIGURE 15-1
Pepsi. Generations Ahead
A series of commercials have featured the popular and well-known Michael J. Fox.
Reprinted by permission.

FIGURE 15-2
Inmac: A Leading Direct Marketer
Reprinted by permission.

for a catalog; it does not use television or radio ads. It also has an 800-toll-free telephone number for customer inquiries and a staff of salespeople to call on corporate accounts.[4] See Figure 15-2.

The importance of promotion is also evident from the U.S. expenditures and employment of people in this area, as these data indicate. The "Big 3" U.S. auto

[4] David Kalish, "Eldred's Afterlife," *Marketing & Media Decisions* (March 1988), pp. 85–88.

makers spend over $2.3 billion annually, the leading five U.S. retailers $2.1 billion, and the major U.S. industrial-materials firms $110 million on media advertising for magazines, newspapers, outdoor, radio, and television. About 14 million people are employed as salespersons. Over 225 billion coupons are annually distributed. Each year, more than $200 million in sweepstakes prizes are given out to middlemen and consumers.[5]

Types of Promotion

In their communications programs, companies can be involved with one or more than one of the four basic types of promotion:

▶ *Advertising* is paid, nonpersonal communication regarding goods, services, organizations, people, places, and ideas that is transmitted through various media by business firms, nonprofit organizations, and individuals who are in some way identified in the advertising message as the sponsor. The message is generally controlled by the sponsor.

▶ *Publicity* is nonpersonal communication regarding goods, services, organizations, people, places, and ideas that is transmitted through various media but not paid for by an identified sponsor. The message is generally controlled by the media.

▶ *Personal selling* involves oral communication with one or more prospective buyers by paid representatives for the purpose of making sales.

▶ *Sales promotion* involves paid marketing communication activities (other than advertising, publicity, or personal selling) that stimulate consumer purchases and dealer effectiveness. Included are trade shows, premiums, incentives, giveaways, demonstrations, and various other limited-time selling efforts not in the ordinary promotion routine.[6]

Advertising and publicity are nonpersonal. Personal selling involves one-to-one contact. Sales promotion includes supplemental techniques.

The general characteristics of each type of promotion are shown in Table 15-2. As discussed later in the chapter, many firms somehow combine these four types in an integrated promotional blend. This enables them to reach their entire target market, present both persuasive and believable messages, have personal contact with customers, sponsor special events, and balance the promotional budget.

The Channel of Communication

To develop a proper promotion mix and interact effectively with consumers, the **channel of communication (communication process)** shown in Figure 15-3 must be understood. Through such a channel, a source develops a message, transmits it to an audience via some form of medium, and obtains feedback from the audience. The components of a communication channel are discussed next.

A message is sent to an audience through a channel of communication.

---

[5] "100 Leading National Advertisers," *Advertising Age* (September 28, 1988), pp. 152, 156; U.S. Department of Labor, Bureau of Labor Statistics; Alison Fahey, "Red Letter Cut from Coupon War," *Advertising Age* (April 3, 1989), p. 38; and Incentive Marketing, "The Incentive Field at a Glance," *Advertising Age* (May 2, 1989), p. S-2.

[6] Adapted by the authors from Peter D. Bennett (Editor), *Dictionary of Marketing Terms* (Chicago: American Marketing Association, 1988), pp. 4, 144, 164, and 179.

Marketing Controversy

Should Firms Use Advertorials and Ambush Marketing?

Advertorials are special advertising sections inserted into newspapers and magazines that resemble the articles in those publications. Many media executives now accept advertorials because they are under pressure to offer their advertisers a controlled, uncluttered environment for ads; and they understand that the best environment for some advertisers is created through advertorials.

Although advertisers believe they have the right to control their messages, particularly because they are paying for them, there are many critics of advertorials. They feel advertorials blur the distinction between advertising and editorial (article) content, and can confuse readers.

The American Society of Magazine Editors (ASME) has guidelines for special advertising sections. These state that the sections must be labeled as advertising, use different type than the editorial content, and not be listed on the magazine's cover or in its table of contents.

Ambush marketing occurs when a nonspon-sor of an event tries to associate itself with the event to obtain the prestige of a sponsor without the accompanying expense. For example, a company can ambush an official sponsor by purchasing commercial time during Olympic broadcasts or by supporting individual Olympic teams or athletes.

In 1988, McDonald's was an official sponsor of the Olympics. Yet, Wendy's advertised itself as a "proud sponsor of ABC's television coverage of the 1988 Winter Olympics." Wendy's could not display the five-ringed Olympic symbol, so it featured the nearly identical ABC symbol. As a Wendy's vice-president commented, "We found a way of getting the job done at considerably less expense."

Sponsors and Olympics officials are concerned that ambush marketing misrepresents firms' actual participation in events and diminishes the value of sponsorships—which can be sold to companies such as McDonald's for millions of dollars.

What do you think?

SOURCE: Based on material in Cynthia Crossen, "Proliferation of 'Advertorials' Blurs Distinction Between News and Ads," *Wall Street Journal* (April 21, 1988), p. 33; and Alan Bayless, " 'Ambush' Marketing Is Becoming Popular Event at Olympic Games," *Wall Street Journal* (February 8, 1988), p. 27.

The Source

*A **source** presents a message.*

The **source** of communication is usually a company, an independent institution, or an opinion leader that seeks to present a message to an audience. A company communicates through a(n) spokesperson, celebrity, actor playing a role, representative consumer, and/or salesperson.

Company sources range from spokepersons to salespersons.

A company spokesperson is typically a high-ranking employee of the firm who represents it in advertisements. The spokesperson provides an aura of sincerity, commitment, and expertise. Chrysler's Lee Iacocca, Remington's Victor Kiam, and Frank Perdue (the chicken processor) have been particularly effective. See Figure 15-4.

A celebrity is used when the goal is to gain the attention of the audience and improve product awareness. Problems can arise if consumers perceive the celebrity as insincere or unknowledgeable. Among the most popular celebrity sources are Michael J. Fox for Diet Pepsi, Bill Cosby for Jell-O Pudding Pops, Lynn Redgrave for Weight

TABLE 15-2 Characteristics of Promotional Types

Factor	Advertising	Publicity	Personal Selling	Sales Promotion
Audience	Mass	Mass	Small (one-to-one)	Varies
Message	Uniform	Uniform	Specific	Varies
Cost	Low per viewer or reader	None for media space and time; can be moderate costs for press releases and publicity materials	High per customer	Moderate per customer
Sponsor	Company	No formal sponsor in that media are not paid	Company	Company
Flexibility	Low	Low	High	Moderate
Control over content and placement	High	None (controlled by media)	High	High
Credibility	Moderate	High	Moderate	Moderate
Major goal	To appeal to a mass audience at a reasonable cost, and create awareness and favorable attitudes	To reach a mass audience with an independently reported message	To deal with individual consumers, to resolve questions, to close sales	To stimulate short-run sales, to increase impulse purchases
Example	Television ad for a Sony video camera	Newspaper article reporting on the unique features of a Sony video camera	Retail sales personnel explaining how a Sony video camera works	A Sony video camera displayed at consumer photography shows

Watchers, Snoopy and the other Peanuts characters for Metropolitan Life Insurance, and Michael Jordan for Nike.

Many advertisements use actors playing roles rather than celebrity spokespeople. In these commercials, emphasis is placed on presenting a message about a good, service, or idea—rather than on the consumer recognizing a celebrity. The hope is that the consumer will learn more about product attributes.

A representative consumer is one who likes a product and recommends it in an advertisement. This person is shown with his or her name and general address. The intent is to show a real consumer in an actual situation. A hidden camera or blind taste test is often used with the representative consumer. Today a number of viewers are skeptical about how "representative" the endorser is.

Finally, a company may be represented by a salesperson who communicates with consumers. Many salespeople are knowledgeable, assertive, and persuasive. However, consumers sometimes question their objectivity and tactics. Car salespeople rate particularly low in consumer surveys.

An independent institution is not controlled by the firms on which it reports. It presents information on company operations and products in a professional, nonpaid (by the companies) manner. Consumers Union and a local newspaper food critic are examples of independent sources. They usually have great credibility for their readers because they point out both good and bad points, but large segments of the population may not be exposed to these sources. The information presented may differ from that contained in a firm's commercials.

An independent institution is not paid by the firm on which it reports.

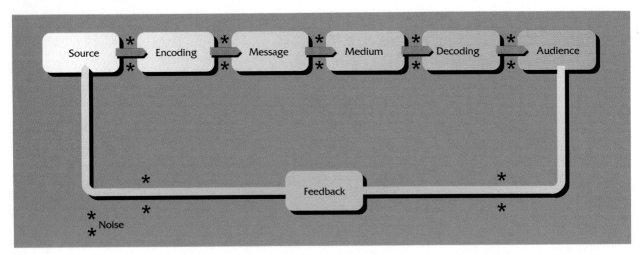

FIGURE 15-3   A Channel of Communication

*Opinion leaders participate in a **two-step flow of communication;** they are also influenced in a **multistep flow.***

Opinion leaders are people who have face-to-face contact with and influence other potential consumers. Because they deal on a personal level, opinion leaders usually have strong persuasive impact and believability. They are able to offer social acceptance for followers. Therefore, firms often address initial messages to opinion leaders, who then provide word-of-mouth communication to other consumers. This is the ***two-step flow of communication*** (company to opinion leader to target market). Marketers further believe that opinion leaders not only influence but also are influenced by the general public (opinion receivers); they need approval for their decisions. This is the ***multistep flow of communication.***

In assessing a source, these questions are most critical: Is he/she believable? Is he/she convincing? Does he/she present an image consistent with the firm? Do consumers value the message of the source? Is he/she perceived as knowledgeable? Does the source complement the product he/she communicates about or does the source overwhelm it? Do significant parts of the market dislike the source?

Encoding

*In **encoding,** a source translates a thought into a message.*

Encoding is the process whereby a thought or idea is translated into a message by the source. At this stage, preliminary decisions are made regarding message content, such as the use of symbolism and wording. It is vital that the thought or idea be translated exactly as the source intends. For example, a firm wanting to stress the prestige of its product would include the concepts of status, exclusive ownership, and special features in a message. It would not emphasize a price lower then competitors, availability in discount stores, or the millions of people who have already purchased it.

The Message

*A **message** combines words and symbols.*

A ***message*** is a combination of words and symbols transmitted to an audience. The focus of message content depends on whether the firm's goal is to inform, persuade, or remind its audience. This is examined later in the chapter.

Almost all messages include information on the company name, the good/service name, the desired image, the differential advantage, and good/service attributes and

FIGURE 15-4
Frank Perdue: "It Takes a Tough Man to Make a Tender Chicken"
Reprinted by permission.

benefits. Additionally, a firm would provide information about availability and price somewhere in the communication process.

Most communication involves ***one-sided messages,*** in which only the benefits of a good, service, or idea are mentioned. Fewer firms use ***two-sided messages,*** in which both benefits and limitations are discussed. Companies are not anxious to point out their own shortcomings, even though consumer perceptions of honesty may be improved through two-sided messages. For example, a television commercial for Volkswagen's Karmann Ghia showed it racing across a desert and then unable to break though a white sheet hung over the road, with the slogan, "Karmann Ghia. The most economical car you can buy. It's just not the most powerful." Because the auto's buyers thought they were purchasing a sports car, the ad was quickly withdrawn.[7]

*With **one-sided messages,** benefits are mentioned; **two-sided messages** also note limitations.*

Many messages use symbolism and try to relate safety, social acceptance, or sexual appeal to a purchase. For example, in commercials, life insurance provides safety for family members; clothing styles offer acceptance by peers; and toothpaste brightens teeth and makes a person more sexually attractive. With symbolic messages, the firm stresses psychological benefits rather than tangible product performance, such as miles per gallon.

Symbolism uses product safety, social value, or sexual appeals.

One type of symbolism, the use of fear appeals, has had mixed results. Although consumers respond to moderate fear appeals, strong messages may not yield favorable responses. For example, the National Highway Traffic Safety Administration found that a commercial for safety belts showing mangled cars and broken bones was too

[7] "VW Had Some Clinkers Among Classics," *Advertising Age* (September 9, 1985), p. 48.

You're the Marketer

What's Next for Miller Lite?

Although Miller Lite is by far the best-selling light beer in the United States, its recent growth has been slowed by such competitors as Bud Light and Coors Light. Between 1985 and 1988, Miller Lite's sales rose only 1 per cent annually versus 7 per cent annually for all light beers.

As a result, in late 1988, Miller Brewing decided to phase out its fifteen-year-old promotional campaign featuring retired athletes and sports celebrities and the "Tastes great, less filling" slogan. That campaign was to be replaced nationally by the "Lite Brigade" campaign. In addition, Miller began experimenting with regional advertising in Texas.

The new national campaign was to reposition Miller Lite as the only light beer that's not a "watered-down version" of a regular beer. The "Join the Lite Brigade" commercials featured five humorous characters in comic situations. For example, in one commercial, the Lite Brigade entered a lounge with a sign saying

Watered Down Bar & Grill. So the brigade provided its own Miller Lite Beer.

In its regional advertising experiment, Miller spent about $3 million to develop and run a new Miller Lite commercial every month for a year-and-a-half in the Texas market. The company wanted to study the impact of regionally targeted promotion efforts on sales, and the Texas market represents about one-fifth of total Miller Lite sales.

The Texas advertising experiment was scheduled to run until late 1989, when a further decision was to be made about regional promotions. However, in early 1989, Miller decided not to go ahead with the "Lite Brigade" campaign: "We tested across the country and we think there are some tremendous strengths in the new campaign. [Yet] we still feel like the best thing to do is to continue with our classic advertising."

As the product manager for Miller Lite, what would you do?

SOURCE: Based on material in Lisa Belkin, "A Texas-Size Bet in Advertising," *New York Times* (January 8, 1989), Section 3, pp. 1, 11; and "Miller 'Lite Brigade' Retreats," *Advertising Age* (February 27, 1989), p. 8.

---

overpowering for people, causing them to avoid viewing it. A subsequent campaign, based on "If you love me, you'll show me," sent out the same message but in a milder way. Detergents, telephone services, and dandruff shampoo are among the many goods and services that have successfully used moderate fear appeals based on social factors, rather than physical ones. But as one observer noted: "Anxiety may be a powerful appeal in communications, but it is very dangerous to use. If anxiety becomes too strong, it can lead the audience to 'turn off.' "[8]

Humor can attract attention but should not detract from image.

Humor is sometimes used to gain audience attention and retain it. Some examples of humor are the fictitious Ernest P. Worrell (a "repugnant redneck") who pesters his friend Vern in commercials for pizza, cars, furniture, and so on; the Bud Light beer commercials with bolts of fire or beams of light when a patron mistakenly asks for only a "light" and not a "Bud Light;" and Maytag's ads with its "lonely" repairman who never has any service calls because Maytag appliances are made so well. Also see Figure 15-5. However, a firm needs to be careful to get across the intended message

[8] Lynn Coleman, "Advertisers Put Fear into the Hearts of Their Prospects," *Marketing News* (August 15, 1988), p. 1.

Cream good enough for Colombian Coffee
isn't exactly easy to find.

100% Colombian Coffee

The richest coffee in the world."

FIGURE 15-5
An Eye-Catching Humorous Message for Colombian Coffee
Courtesy of The National Federation of Coffee Growers of Colombia. Reprinted by permission.

when using humor—which should not make fun of the company, its goods, or its services; and humor should never dominate the message so that the brand name or product's attributes go unnoticed. Many observers have criticized Burger King's highly unsuccessful (and expensive) "Herb the Nerd" ads: "This campaign remains a popular example of what can go wrong in marketing. Rather than think Herb had *never been* to Burger King, consumers associated the negative character with the chain."[9]

Comparative messages implicitly or explicitly contrast the firm's offerings with those of competitors. Implicit comparative messages use a brand X or leading brand campaign (such as "Our fabric softener is more effective than other leading brands"). Explicit comparative messages utilize direct comparisons (such as an Uncle Ben's rice television commercial stating, "Uncle Ben's is separate, not sticky. And it's whole, not broken like Minute Rice"). In recent years, the use of comparative messages has substantially increased. They now account for about one-third of all television commercials and about one-quarter of the ads in *Business Week* and *Fortune*.[10] Furthermore, salespeople frequently compare the characteristics of their products with those of competitors.

The content of a message must be presented in a desirable, exclusive, and believable manner. The good, service, or idea needs to be perceived by the audience as something worth purchasing or accepting. It also needs to be considered unique to the firm—that

Comparative messages position the firm's offerings versus competitors'.

A good message is desirable, exclusive, and believable.

---

[9] "Oops!" *Advertising Age* (February 13, 1989), p. 3.

[10] Christy Fisher and Judann Dagnoli, "Battle in the Rice Field," *Advertising Age* (February 6, 1989), p. 3; and Linda E. Swayne and Thomas H. Stevenson, "Comparative Advertising in Horizontal Business Publications," *Industrial Marketing Management,* Vol. 16 (1987), pp. 71–76.

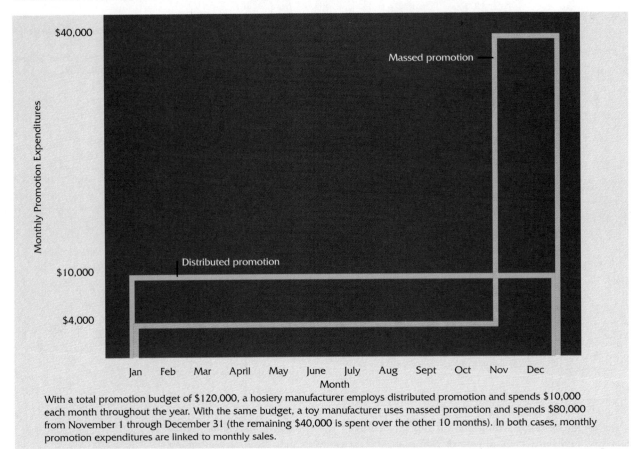

With a total promotion budget of $120,000, a hosiery manufacturer employs distributed promotion and spends $10,000 each month throughout the year. With the same budget, a toy manufacturer uses massed promotion and spends $80,000 from November 1 through December 31 (the remaining $40,000 is spent over the other 10 months). In both cases, monthly promotion expenditures are linked to monthly sales.

FIGURE 15-6 **Massed Versus Distributed Promotion**

Massed or distributed promotion and wearout rate must be carefully planned.

is, it cannot be obtained elsewhere. Finally, the message must contain believable statements and claims.

The timing of messages must be carefully planned. First, during what periods in the year should the firm advertise, add salespeople, or run sales promotions? With **massed promotion,** communication efforts are concentrated in peak periods, like holidays. With **distributed promotion,** communication efforts are spread throughout the year. Figure 15-6 compares massed and distributed promotion.

Second, the **wearout rate**—the time it takes for a message to lose its effectiveness—must be determined. Some messages wear out quickly, while others may last for months or years. The wearout rate depends on the frequency of communications, the quality of the message, the number of messages used by the company, and other factors. For example, some variation of Wisk's "ring around the collar" message was around from 1967 to 1989; and as the slogan's author once noted:

> It would be fair to call that commercial a screeching commercial, an abrasive commercial, an intrusive commercial. But the one thing you can't call it is a bad commercial because the purpose of a commercial is to do a commercial job.[11]

[11] Bill Abrams, " 'Ring Around the Collar' Ads Irritate Many Yet Get Results," *Wall Street Journal* (November 4, 1982), p. 33.

The Medium

The **medium** is the personal or nonpersonal means used to send a message. Personal media are company salespeople and other representatives, as well as opinion leaders. Nonpersonal media include newspapers, television, radio, direct mail, billboards, magazines, and transit.

Personal media offer one-to-one contact with the audience. They are flexible, able to adapt messages to individual needs, and can answer questions. They also appeal to a small audience and work best with a concentrated target market.

Nonpersonal (mass) media provide a large audience and low per-customer costs. They are inflexible and not as dynamic as one-to-one presentations. They work best with a dispersed target market.

When deciding between personal and nonpersonal media, a firm should consider both total and per-unit costs, product complexity, audience attributes, and communication goals. The two types of media work well together because nonpersonal media generate consumer interest and personal media help close sales.

*A **medium** is a personal or nonpersonal channel for a message.*

Decoding

Decoding is the process by which a message sent by a source is interpreted by the audience. This interpretation is based on the audience's background and the clarity of the message. For example, a housewife and a working woman might have different interpretations of a message on the value of child-care centers. An upper-class consumer would view Cadillac commercials differently from a lower-middle-class consumer. Usually, as symbolism increases, clarity decreases. "Nissan: Built for the human race" is not as understandable a message as "Ford: Quality is Job 1." As noted earlier, it is essential that a message be decoded in the manner intended by the source (encoding = decoding).

*In **decoding**, the audience translates the message sent by the source.*

Subliminal advertising is a highly controversial type of promotion because it does not enable a consumer consciously to decode a message. With it, visual or verbal messages are presented so quickly that consumers do not see, hear, or remember them. Yet they are expected to buy goods and services because of subconscious impulses. Ads of this type stress symbolism and sometimes sexual themes. The overwhelming evidence shows that subliminal advertising cannot get consumers to buy products they do not want. In addition, subliminal ads are often misinterpreted; and clear, well-labeled ads are much more effective.[12] In the United States, self-regulation by advertising associations (such as the National Association of Broadcasters) has all but eliminated subliminal ads.

***Subliminal advertising** aims at a consumer's subconscious.*

The Audience

The **audience** is the object of a source's message. In most marketing situations, the audience is the target market. However, a source may also want to communicate an idea, build an image, or provide information to stockholders, consumer groups, independent media, the public, or government officials.

*The **audience** is usually the target market, but it can also be others.*

---

[12] See Timothy E. Moore, "Subliminal Advertising: What You See Is What You Get," *Journal of Marketing,* Vol. 46 (Spring 1982), pp. 37–47; Jack Haberstroh, "Can't Ignore Subliminal Ad Charges," *Advertising Age* (September 17, 1984), pp. 3, 42, 44; and John Lofflin, "What's New in Subliminal Messages," *New York Times* (March 20, 1988), Section 3, p. 17.

The type(s) of communication channel used by a firm depend on the size and dispersion of the audience, demographic and life-style audience traits, and the availability of media appropriate for the audience. The communication process must be keyed to the audience, as these illustrations show. Adults are likely to respond favorably to other adults serving as spokespersons, models, or sales personnel; younger models may not be as effective for this group. The backgrounds of women determine how they react to promotion featuring homemakers or career women. Simple action-oriented commercials are successful with 5- to 6-year-old children, while "quieter" approaches rate poorly.[13]

One survey of the American public found that

▶ 30 per cent feel ads generally present an honest picture of the products mentioned.

▶ 72 per cent believe products do not work well as promotion claims indicate.

▶ 81 per cent feel a lot of ads are clever or funny.

▶ 92 per cent believe there are too many commercials in a row on television.[14]

Feedback

Feedback consists of purchase, attitude, or nonpurchase responses to a message.

Feedback is the response the audience makes to a message. It may take one of three forms: purchase, attitude change, or nonpurchase. A company must understand that each of these three alternative responses is possible and develop a procedure for monitoring them.

The most desirable kind of feedback occurs when a consumer purchases a good or service after communications with or from the firm. This means that the message is effective enough to stimulate a transaction.

A second type of feedback takes place when a firm determines that its promotional efforts have elicited a favorable attitude change toward the company or its offerings by the audience. With new goods or services, favorable attitudes must usually be created prior to consumer purchases (awareness→favorable attitude→purchase). With existing products, consumers may have bought a competing brand before the message was received or be temporarily out of funds. Generating favorable attitudes in these consumers may lead to future purchases.

The least desirable feedback is when the audience neither purchases an item nor develops a favorable attitude. This may happen for one of several reasons: no recall of message, contentment with present product, message not believed, or no differential advantage shown.

Following are selected techniques for monitoring or obtaining feedback. Several of these techniques may be combined:

▶ Pretest/posttest — Measures sales or attitudes before and after a promotion effort. Example — Prior to ad, 68 per cent liked product; after ad, 75 per cent liked product; favorable attitude increase: 7 per cent.

▶ Aided recall — Consumers asked multiple-choice questions or to select the ads seen

---

[13] Benny Barak and Barbara Stern, "Women's Age in Advertising: An Examination of Two Consumer Age Profiles," *Journal of Advertising Research*, Vol. 25 (December 1985 – January 1986), pp. 38 – 47; Thomas E. Barry, Mary C. Gilley, and Lindley E. Doran, "Advertising to Women with Different Career Orientations," *Journal of Advertising Research*, Vol. 25 (April – May 1985), pp. 26 – 35; and James P. Neelankavil, John V. O'Brien, and Richard Tashjian, "Techniques to Obtain Market-Related Information from Very Young Children," *Journal of Advertising Research*, Vol. 25 (June – July 1985), pp. 41 – 47.

[14] Ogilvy & Mather, *Listening Post* newsletter, 1985.

from a list. This method inflates recall but approximates actual shopping experience. Example—Which of these did you see advertised in yesterday's paper? (a) *Reader's Digest*, (b) Honda Accord, (c) Crest toothpaste.

▶ Unaided recall—Consumers asked open-ended questions. This method measures true recall but places too much emphasis on unaided memory. Example—Which products did you see advertised in yesterday's paper?

▶ Physiological test—Measures reactions to promotional efforts, such as skin responses and eye movements, through mechanical observation. Example—Consumer is hooked by electrode to a television monitor and watches a commercial; physical responses are tracked.

▶ Monadic test—Single commercial or sales presentation evaluated. Example—Consumer is shown an ad of a brand of shoes and asked to comment on it.

▶ Comparison test—Two or more commercials or sales presentations evaluated at the same time. Example—Consumer listens to the sales presentations of both Bob and Liz and is then asked to comment on them.

Noise

Noise is interference at any stage along a channel of communication. Because of noise, messages are sometimes encoded or decoded incorrectly or weak responses are made. Examples of noise are

Noise may interfere with the communication process at any stage.

▶ A telephone call interrupting the company's marketing manager while he or she is developing a promotional theme.

▶ A salesperson misidentifying a product and giving incorrect information.

▶ An impatient customer interrupting a sales presentation.

▶ Conversation between two consumers during a television commercial.

▶ A direct-mail ad being opened by the wrong person.

▶ A consumer seeing a sale on a competitor's item while waiting at a supermarket checkout counter.

Promotion Planning

After a firm gains an understanding of the communication process, it is ready to develop an overall promotion plan. Such a plan consists of three parts: objectives, budgeting, and the promotion mix.

Objectives

The objectives of promotion can be divided into two general categories: stimulating demand and enhancing company image.

In setting demand objectives, the ***hierarchy-of-effects model*** needs to be considered. This model outlines the intermediate and long-term promotional objectives the firm should pursue: awareness, knowledge, liking, preference, conviction, and purchase.[15] Obtaining a consumer purchase is often based on achieving each of the steps

*The **hierarchy-of-effects model** outlines demand objectives.*

---

[15] Robert J. Lavidge and Gary A. Steiner, "A Model for Predictive Measurements of Advertising Effectiveness," *Journal of Marketing*, Vol. 25 (October 1961), pp. 59–62. See also Robert E. Smith and William R. Swinyard, "Information Response Models: An Integrated Approach," *Journal of Marketing*, Vol. 46 (Winter 1982), pp. 81–93; and Stan Rapp and Tom Collins, "MaxiMarketing," *Journal of Direct Marketing*, Vol. 1 (Winter 1987), pp. 65–75.

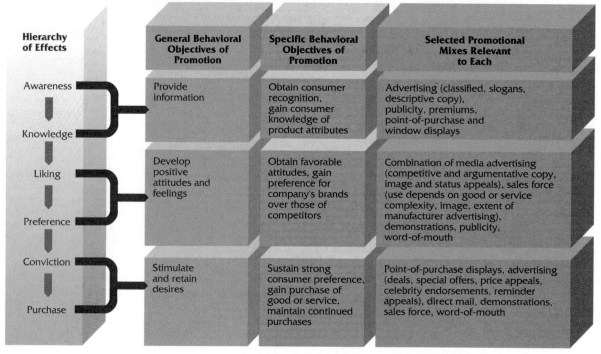

FIGURE 15-7 **Promotion and the Hierarchy-of-Effects Model**
SOURCE: Adapted by the authors from Robert Lavidge and Gary A. Steiner, "A Model for Predictive Measurements of Advertising Effectiveness," *Journal of Marketing,* Vol. 25 (October 1961), p. 61. Reprinted by permission of the American Marketing Association.

before it. Figure 15-7 shows the hierarchy-of-effects model and relates it to promotional objectives and tools.

By applying the hierarchy-of-effects model (or the adoption process described in Chapter 10), a firm can move from informing to persuading and then to reminding consumers about its offerings. At the early stages of the model, when a good or service is little known, ***primary demand*** should be sought. This is consumer demand for a product category, such as dietetic candy. At later stages, when preference is the goal, ***selective demand*** should be sought. This is consumer demand for a particular brand of a product. Sometimes, organizations use the hierarchy-of-effects model to revitalize interest in mature products. As an example, the Beef Industry Council regularly sponsors advertisements to generate primary demand for beef. See Figure 15-8.

Institutional advertising is used when the promotional objective is enhancing company image—and not selling goods or services. A great many of the large companies in the United States annually engage in some form of institutional advertising. Here are three illustrations of why they do so:

▶ In a study on corporate image, IBM, General Electric, Merck, Ford, and Chrysler were rated highest: "They convey the definite impression that their management has a clear vision of the firm's future and a plan to make it a reality. Because they are communicating vision and what they stand for, they're seen as winners and are enjoying the payoffs of a winning reputation."[16]

---

[16] " 'Winning!' Study Reveals '88 Corporate Image Leaders," *Marketing News* (November 21, 1988), p. 11.

Primary demand is for a product category; selective demand is for a brand.

Institutional advertising is involved with image objectives.

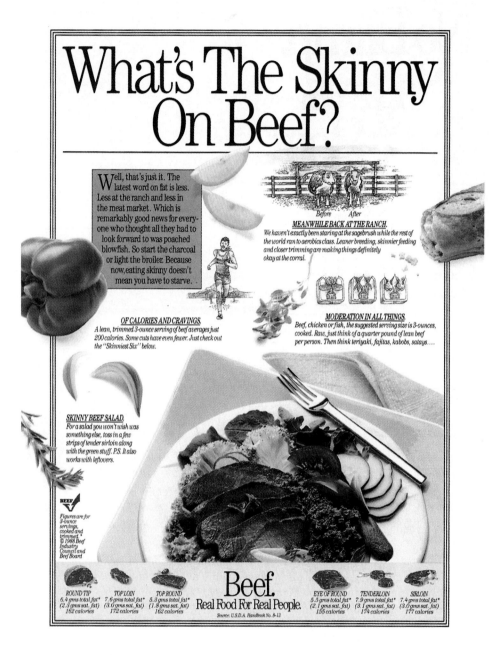

FIGURE 15-8
Generating Primary Demand for a Mature Product
Reprinted by permission.

▶ The U.S. Postal Service spent over $6 million on a television advertising campaign to improve its image in the eyes of customers and the general public. The lyrics of its theme song were, "We deliver through the rain and the sleet and the snow. Like we've always done, we deliver. Because the eagle flies higher and surer than anyone. We deliver, we deliver. It's the reason you trust us, you know that we're going to come through."[17]

[17] Janet Meyers, "Postal Service Ads to Help Image," *Advertising Age* (November 21, 1988), p. 12.

▶ From 1870 to 1986, B.F. Goodrich was in the tire-making business; then it decided to exit tires and concentrate on specialty chemicals, plastics, and aerospace products. Yet, two years later, people still believed that Goodrich was a tire maker, as a survey of executives at large firms indicated. At that time, Goodrich's spokesperson said, "We haven't met anybody who knows we're out of the tire business." As a result, in 1988-1989, Goodrich sponsored its first-ever institutional ads: "No Blimp. No Tires. Know How."[18] See Figure 15-9.

Budgeting

There are five alternative techniques for setting a total promotion budget: all you can afford, incremental, competitive parity, percentage of sales, and objective and task. The selection of a technique depends on the requirements and constraints of the individual firm. Promotional budgets often range from 1 to 5 per cent for some industrial-goods firms up to 20 to 30 per cent for some consumer-goods firms. Table 15-3 illustrates each budgeting method.

Budgeting techniques are all you can afford, incremental, competitive parity, percentage of sales, and objective and task.

In the **all-you-can-afford technique**, the firm first allocates funds for every element of marketing except promotion; whatever funds are left over are placed in a promotion budget. This method is the weakest of the five and is used most frequently by small, production-oriented companies. Its shortcomings are the little importance given to promotion, expenditures not being linked to objectives, and the risk of having no promotion budget if no funds are left over.

With the **incremental technique**, the company bases its new budget on previous expenditures. A percentage is either added to or subtracted from this year's budget in

---

[18] Gregory Stricharchuk, "Just Read Our Lips: No Blimps, No Tires, No Blimps, No Tires, No ...," *Wall Street Journal* (September 30, 1988), p. 29.

TABLE 15-3 Illustrations of Promotional Budgeting Techniques

Technique	Illustration
All you can afford	The firm has a $110,000 marketing budget: $50,000 is allocated for distribution costs, $40,000 for product testing, and $8,000 for consumer surveys. The remaining $12,000 is left for advertising, personal selling, and sales promotions.
Incremental	The current year's promotion budget is $30,000. Next year is expected to be a good year; therefore, 10 per cent is added to the budget. The new budget is $33,000.
Competitive parity	The current year's promotion budget is $50,000. The leading competitor is expected to increase its promotion budget by 2 per cent. The firm follows this strategy and establishes a budget of $51,000 for next year.
Percentage of sales	The promotion-to-sales ratio is 20 per cent (one dollar of promotion for every five dollars of sales). Next year's sales are forecast to be $1 million. The promotion budget will be $200,000.
Objective and task	The firm has three goals for next year: increase sales of brand A by 5 per cent, introduce brand B and attain recognition by 15 per cent of the target market, and improve the public's positive rating of the company from 60 to 75 per cent (based on a standardized attitude measure). The promotional tasks and tools needed to achieve these goals will result in a budget of $73,000.

order to determine next year's budget. This technique is also used by small firms. It offers these advantages: a reference point, a budget based on a firm's feelings about past successes and future trends, and easy calculations. Important disadvantages do exist: budget size is rarely tied to objectives, "gut feelings" are overemphasized, and there is difficulty in evaluating success or failure.

In the *competitive parity technique*, the company's promotion budget is raised or lowered according to the actions of competitors. It is useful to both large and small firms. The benefits of this method are that it is keyed to a reference point, it is market-oriented, and it is conservative. The shortcomings are that it is a following and not a leadership approach, it is difficult to obtain competitors' promotion data, and there is the assumption of a similarity between the firm and its competitors (in terms of years in business, goods or services, image, prices, and so on). The last point is particularly important; firms usually have basic differences from competitors.

With the *percentage-of-sales technique*, the company ties the promotion budget to sales revenue. In the first year, a promotion-to-sales ratio is established. During succeeding years, the per cent of promotion to sales dollars remains constant. The benefits of this procedure are the use of sales as a base, its adaptability, and the interrelationship of sales and promotion. The weaknesses are that there is no relationship to objectives, promotion is used as a sales follower and not a sales leader, and automatic promotion decreases are likely in poor sales periods (when increases could be beneficial). This technique provides too large a budget during high sales periods and too small a budget during low sales periods.

Under the *objective-and-task technique*, the firm outlines its promotional objectives, determines the tasks needed to satisfy those objectives, and then establishes the appropriate budget. It is the best of the five methods. The advantages are that objectives are clearly stated, expenditures are related to goal-oriented tasks, it offers adaptability, and it is relatively easy to evaluate success or failure. The major weakness is the complexity of setting goals and specific tasks, especially for small companies. Among the largest final consumer-products firms and the largest industrial-products firms, over 60 per cent use some form of the objective-and-task technique.[19]

[19] Vincent J. Blasko and Charles H. Patti, "The Advertising Budgeting Practices of Industrial Marketers," *Journal of Marketing*, Vol. 48 (Fall 1984), pp. 106-107.

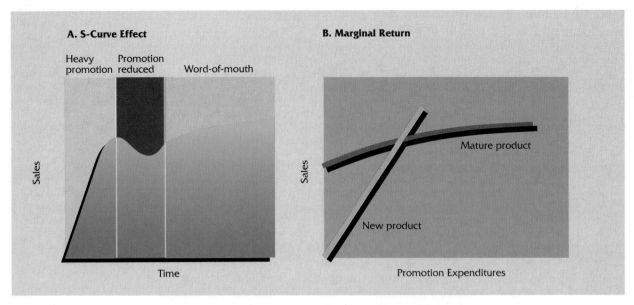

FIGURE 15-10 **The S-Curve Effect and Marginal Return**

*The **S-curve effect** and **marginal return** should be understood.*

While a promotion budget is being developed, the firm should consider the S-curve effect and marginal return. The **S-curve effect** occurs if the sales of a product rise sharply after it is introduced because of a heavy initial promotion effort (ads, coupons, samples, etc.), drop slightly as promotional support is reduced, and then rise again as positive word-of-mouth communication takes place. A more balanced budget may be able to minimize the S-curve effect. The **marginal return** is the amount of sales each increment of promotion will generate. When a product is new, the marginal return is high because the market is expanding. As a product becomes established, the marginal return is lower because each additional increment of promotion will have less of an impact on sales (the target market is saturated). See Figure 15-10.

The Promotion Mix

*A **promotion mix** combines advertising, publicity, selling, and/or sales promotion.*

After establishing a total promotion budget, the company must determine its **promotion mix**. This is the overall and specific communication program of the company, including its involvement with advertising, publicity, personal selling, and/or sales promotion.

It is rare for a company to use only one type of promotion—for example, a mail-order firm relying on advertising, a hospital on publicity, or a flea-market vendor on personal selling. In most cases, a mix of promotion types is used. For example, Frito-Lay has a sales force that visits every supermarket in which its products are stocked, advertises in a large number of newspapers and magazines and on television, and distributes cents-off coupons. IBM has a large technical sales force, advertises heavily in business and trade publications, and sends representatives to trade shows.

It is important to remember that each type of promotion serves a different function, and therefore complements the other types. Advertisements appeal to large audiences and create awareness; without them, the personal sales effort is much more difficult, time consuming, and expensive. Publicity provides credible information to a wide audience, but its content and timing cannot be controlled by the firm. Personal selling

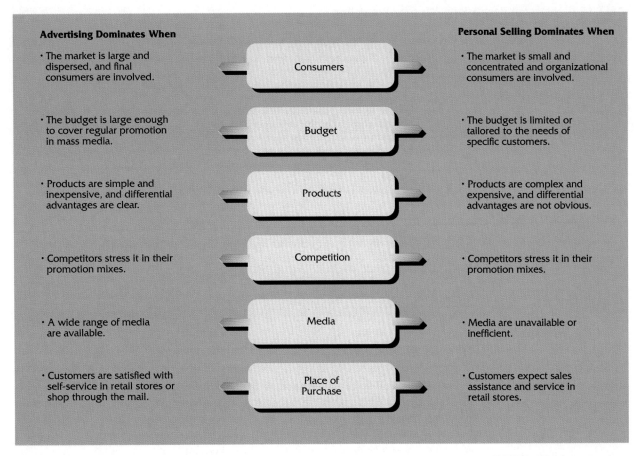

Advertising Dominates When

· The market is large and dispersed, and final consumers are involved.

· The budget is large enough to cover regular promotion in mass media.

· Products are simple and inexpensive, and differential advantages are clear.

· Competitors stress it in their promotion mixes.

· A wide range of media are available.

· Customers are satisfied with self-service in retail stores or shop through the mail.

Consumers

Budget

Products

Competition

Media

Place of Purchase

Personal Selling Dominates When

· The market is small and concentrated and organizational consumers are involved.

· The budget is limited or tailored to the needs of specific customers.

· Products are complex and expensive, and differential advantages are not obvious.

· Competitors stress it in their promotion mixes.

· Media are unavailable or inefficient.

· Customers expect sales assistance and service in retail stores.

FIGURE 15-11
Contrasting Promotion Mixes

offers one-to-one contact, flexibility, and the ability to close sales; without it, the initial interest caused by ads would be wasted. Sales promotion stimulates short-run sales and supplements advertising and selling.

The selection of a promotion mix also depends on company characteristics, the product life cycle, access to media, and middleman support. A small firm is restricted in the kinds of ads it can afford or use efficiently; it may have to rely on personal selling. A large firm covering a sizable geographic area could stress advertising as well as personal selling. As products move through the life cycle, promotional emphasis shifts from information to persuasion to reinforcement; and a different combination of media and messages is needed at each stage. Some media may not be accessible (no cigarette ads on television) or require excessive lead time (Yellow Pages). Middlemen may demand special promotions or sales support, or desire cooperative advertising allowances.

It is the responsibility of the company's marketing director (or vice-president) to establish a promotion budget and a promotion mix and then allocate resources and effort to each aspect of promotion. In large firms, there are often separate managers for advertising, personal selling, and sales promotion. They report to and have their efforts coordinated by the marketing director.

Figure 15-11 contrasts promotion mixes in which advertising and personal selling would dominate.

TABLE 15-4   Selected Regulations Affecting Promotion

Factor	Legal Environment
Access to media	Cigarettes, liquor, and billboards have restricted access. Legal, medical, and other professions have been given the right to advertise.
Deception	It is illegal to use messages that would mislead reasonable consumers and potentially harm them.
Bait-and-switch	It is illegal to lure a customer to a store with an advertisement for a low-priced item and then, after the customer is in the store, to use a strong sales pitch intended to switch the shopper to a more expensive item.
Door-to-door selling	Many locales restrict door-to-door sales practices. A cooling-off period allows a consumer to cancel an in-home sale up to three days after an agreement is reached.
Promotional allowances	These allowances must be available to channel members in a fair and equitable manner.
Comparative advertisements	Claims must be substantiated. The Federal Trade Commission favors naming competitors in ads (not citing a competitor as brand X).
Testimonials or endorsements	The celebrity or expert endorser must actually use the product if ads make such a claim.

The Legal Environment of Promotion[20]

Federal, state, and local governmental agencies have enacted a variety of laws and rules that affect a firm's promotional efforts. These regulations range from prohibiting billboards in many locations to requiring celebrity endorsers to use products if they claim to do so. See Table 15-4. The major federal agencies involved with promotion are the Federal Trade Commission (FTC) and the Federal Communications Commission (FCC).

Full disclosure, substantiation, cease-and-desist orders, corrective advertising, and fines are major governmental limits on promotion activities.

There are five key enforcement tools to protect consumers and competing firms against unsatisfactory promotion practices: full disclosure, substantiation, cease-and-desist orders, corrective advertising, and fines.

Full disclosure requires that all data necessary for a consumer to make a safe and informed decision be provided in a promotion message. For example, Alka Seltzer must mention that its regular version contains aspirin, and diet products must note how many calories they contain. In this way, consumers are able to assess the overall benefits and risks of a purchase.

Substantiation requires a firm to be able to prove all the claims it makes in promotion messages. This means thorough testing and evidence of performance are needed prior to making claims. For example, a tire company that says its brand will last for 70,000 miles must be able to prove this assertion with test results.

---

[20] For example, see Dorothy Cohen, *Advertising* (Glenview, Ill.: Scott, Foresman, 1988), pp. 596–620; Joshua Honigwachs, "Is It Safe to Call Something Safe? The Law of Puffing in Advertising," *Journal of Public Policy & Marketing,* Vol. 6 (1987), pp. 157–170; Eric J. Zanot, "Unseen But Effective Advertising Regulation: The Clearance Process," *Journal of Advertising,* Vol. 14 (Number 4, 1985), pp. 44–51 ff.; and Daniel Kahn, "Why Advertisers Like Censorship," *Newsday* (October 24, 1988), Business section, p. 7.

Under a ***cease-and-desist order,*** a firm is required to discontinue a promotion practice that is considered deceptive and to modify its promotion messages accordingly. The firm is often not forced to admit guilt or pay fines, as long as it obeys the cease-and-desist order. For example, Sears has agreed not to use bait-and-switch practices (whereby sales personnel try to pressure consumers to buy high-priced goods instead of heavily advertised low-priced items) to sell large home appliances.

Corrective advertising requires a firm to run new advertisements to correct the false impressions left by previous ones. For example, Listerine was told to spend $10.2 million on advertising to correct prior messages claiming that the product was a cold remedy. Listerine decided to run the ads (with the phrase "Listerine will not help prevent colds or sore throats or lessen their severity") after learning that it would not otherwise be permitted to continue any advertising.

The last major remedy is ***fines,*** which are dollar penalties levied on a firm for deceptive promotion. A company may be required to pay a large sum to the government, as in the case of STP, or forced to provide consumer refunds, as in the case of mail-order firms that do not meet delivery dates. STP was fined $700,000 for misrepresenting the effectiveness of this additive in raising auto gas mileage.

In recent years, the FTC has made two significant changes in the way it regulates promotion. First, it is now easier for firms to substantiate claims made in ads and sales presentations because less evidence is required in some cases. Second, today the definition of deceptive advertising includes only promotional claims that would mislead a "reasonable" consumer and result in "injury" (physical, financial, or other).

In addition to government restrictions, the media have their own voluntary standards regarding promotion practices. For example, the National Association of Broadcasters monitors the ads placed on television and radio. General industry groups, such as the Better Business Bureau and the American Association of Advertising Agencies, also participate in the self-regulation of promotion.

Criticisms and Defenses of Promotion

Promotion is probably the most heavily criticized area of marketing. Following are a number of these criticisms and the defenses of marketing professionals to them:

Promotion controversies center on materialism, honesty, prices, symbolism, and expectations.

Detractors Feel That Promotion	Marketing Professionals Answer That Promotion
Creates an obsession with material possessions.	Responds to consumer desires for material possessions. In an affluent society, these items are plentiful and paid for with discretionary earnings.
Is basically dishonest.	Is basically honest. The great majority of companies abide by all laws and set strict self-regulations. A few dishonest firms give a bad name to all.
Raises the prices of goods and services.	Holds down prices. By increasing consumer demand, promotion enables manufacturers to utilize mass production and reduce per-unit costs. Employment is high when demand is stimulated.
Overemphasizes symbolism and status.	Differentiates goods and services through symbolic and status appeals. Consumers desire distinctiveness and product benefits.
Causes excessively high expectations.	Keeps expectations high; it thereby sustains consumer motivation and worker productivity in order to satisfy expectations.

FIGURE 15-12

A Strong Defense of Promotion by the American Association of Advertising Agencies
Reprinted by permission.

A few years ago, the American Association of Advertising Agencies began a campaign to "change consumer perceptions that 'advertising makes people buy things they don't want, increases the costs of goods, and helps sell inferior products.' "[21] See Figure 15-12.

Summary

1. *To define promotion planning and show its importance* Promotion involves any communication that informs, persuades, and/or reminds people about an organization's or individual's goods, services, ideas, community involvement, or impact on society. Promotion planning is systematic deci-

---

[21] See Nancy Millman, "Four A's Tackles Ad Image with Ads," *Advertising Age* (March 12, 1984), pp. 1, 62; and Kevin T. Higgins, "4As Plans Acceleration of Image-Building Campaign," *Marketing News* (March 28, 1986), p. 8.

sion making relating to all aspects of a firm's communications efforts.

Promotion efforts are needed for both new products and existing ones. The audience for promotion may be consumers, stockholders, consumer organizations, government, channel members, employees, and the general public. Through word-of-mouth communication, people express their opinions and product-related experiences to one another. A firm may seek to communicate an image, views on ideas, community involvement, or impact on society—as well as persuade consumers to buy products. A good promotion plan complements the other marketing-mix elements.

2. *To describe the general characteristics of advertising, publicity, personal selling, and sales promotion*   Advertising is paid, nonpersonal communication that is transmitted through various media by organizations and individuals who are in some way identified in the advertising message as the sponsor. Publicity is nonpersonal communication that is transmitted through various media but not paid for by an identified sponsor. Personal selling involves oral communication with one or more prospective buyers by paid representatives for the purpose of making sales. Sales promotion involves paid marketing activities that stimulate consumer purchases and dealer effectiveness.

3. *To explain the channel of communication and how it functions*   Through a channel of communication, a source sends a message to its audience. A channel consists of the source, encoding, the message, the medium, decoding, the audience, feedback, and noise.

A source is a company, an independent institution, or an opinion leader that seeks to present a message to an audience. Encoding is the process by which a thought or an idea is translated into a message by the source. A message is a combination of words and symbols transmitted to the audience. A medium is a personal or nonpersonal channel used to convey a message. Decoding is the process through which the message sent by the source is translated by the audience. The audience is the object of the source's message. Feedback is the response the audience makes to the firm's message: purchase, attitude change, or nonpurchase. Noise is the interference at any stage along the channel of communication.

4. *To examine the components of a promotion plan: objectives, budgeting, and the promotion mix*   Promotion objectives may be demand- or image-oriented. Demand objectives should parallel the hierarchy-of-effects model, moving the consumer from awareness to purchase. Primary demand is total consumer demand for a product category; selective demand refers to consumer interest in a particular firm's brand. Institutional advertising is used to enhance company image.

There are five methods for setting a promotion budget: all you can afford, incremental, competitive parity, percentage of sales, and objective and task. The weakest is the all-you-can-afford technique. The best is the objective-and-task technique. The S-curve effect and marginal return should be considered when budgeting.

The promotion mix is the overall and specific communication program of the firm, including its use of advertising, publicity, personal selling, and/or sales promotion. Many factors need to be considered in developing a promotion mix.

5. *To discuss the legal environment and the criticisms and defenses of promotion*   There are many laws and rules affecting promotion. The major ways unsatisfactory promotion is guarded against are full disclosure, substantiation, cease-and-desist orders, corrective advertising, and fines.

Critics are strong in their complaints about promotion practices and their effects. Marketing professionals are equally firm in their defenses.

Key Terms

promotion (p. 454)
promotion planning (p. 454)
word-of-mouth communication (p. 454)

advertising (p. 457)
publicity (p. 457)
personal selling (p. 457)
sales promotion (p. 457)

channel of communication (communication process) (p. 457)
source (p. 458)
two-step flow of communication (p. 460)

multistep flow of communication
  (p. 460)
encoding (p. 460)
message (p. 460)
one-sided messages (p. 461)
two-sided messages (p. 461)
comparative messages (p. 463)
massed promotion (p. 464)
distributed promotion (p. 464)
wearout rate (p. 464)
medium (p. 465)

decoding (p. 465)
subliminal advertising (p. 465)
audience (p. 465)
feedback (p. 466)
noise (p. 467)
hierarchy-of-effects model (p. 467)
primary demand (p. 468)
selective demand (p. 468)
institutional advertising (p. 468)
all-you-can-afford technique (p. 470)
incremental technique (p. 470)

competitive parity technique (p. 471)
percentage-of-sales technique (p. 471)
objective-and-task technique (p. 471)
S-curve effect (p. 472)
marginal return (p. 472)
promotion mix (p. 472)
full disclosure (p. 474)
substantiation (p. 474)
cease-and-desist order (p. 475)
corrective advertising (p. 475)
fines (p. 475)

Review Questions

1. Why is promotion planning important?
2. Distinguish among advertising, publicity, personal selling, and sales promotion.
3. Differentiate between the multistep flow and two-step flow of communication.
4. What is a two-sided message? Why do relatively few companies use such messages?
5. What should be the relationship between encoding and decoding messages? Why?

6. A consumer listens to a sales presentation but does not make a purchase. Has the presentation failed? Explain your answer.
7. Explain the hierarchy-of-effects model. How is it related to demand objectives?
8. What is the best method of promotional budgeting? The worst method? Explain your answers.
9. When should personal selling dominate the promotion mix?
10. State the basic criticisms and defenses of promotion.

Discussion Questions

1. Give a current example of a comparative message and evaluate it.
2. What are the advantages and disadvantages of a firm's using the same message (theme) for an extended period of time?
3. Why are many companies likely to reduce promotion expenditures after a new product is introduced successfully? Is this a proper approach? Explain your answer.

4. Develop a promotion mix for
   a. A local movie theater.
   b. Kentucky Fried Chicken.
   c. Canon (office-products division).
   d. Revlon (cosmetic products).
5. Comment on this statement: "Full disclosure confuses consumers by giving them too much information. It also raises costs."

◄ CASE 1 ►

Is Using Multiple Celebrity Endorsers a Good Idea?*

In recent years, there has been a dramatic rise in the use of multiple celebrity endorsers in company promotion campaigns. For example, in 1988-1989, the Beef Industry Council had a $30 million television-based campaign "featuring celebrity-studded commercials."

---

* The data in this case are drawn from Julie Liesse Erickson, "Star-Studded Cast Flavors New Beef Ads," *Advertising Age* (September 12, 1988), pp. 3, 110; Gary Levin, "Marketers Turn to Multiple Celebrities," *Advertising Age* (September 12, 1988), p. 110; and Alix M. Freedman, "Marriages Between Celebrities and Their Firms Can Be Risky Ventures," *Wall Street Journal* (January 22, 1988), p. 29.

The Beef Industry Council's major goal was to increase the consumption of beef products by light beef users—those eating beef fewer than six times in any two-week period. In its campaign, the Council used eight different celebrities in separate 15-second television commercials. It often paired two related commercials to give them more dramatic effect.

In one Council ad, Julia Louis Dreyfus talked about how she "always gets stuck in these trendy restaurants" when she wants to order a burger. "I ask myself, 'What would Lauren Bacall do?'" In a companion spot, which would run one to two minutes afterward, Bacall replied: "When I get a taste for a burger, and they tell me it's not on the menu, I glare at the waiter and say 'Improvise.'" The Council also paired Larry Bird and Michael Cooper (basketball stars); actor Timothy Busfield (of *thirtysomething*) and model Kim Alexis; and country singer Reba McIntire and actress Madeline Kahn in sequential messages.

Although the sales impact of this campaign would be very difficult to measure, follow-up research indicated that it generated awareness among potential consumers and improved perceptions of beef's nutritional value, convenience, and taste.

There are various reasons why organizations such as the Beef Industry Council and General Motors (which featured more than a dozen celebrities and their children in its 1988-1989 Oldsmobile campaign) are turning to multiple celebrity endorsers instead of continuing the traditional use of one or two celebrities. These firms want to avoid embarrassment when a celebrity does not or cannot use the product, or when a celebrity gets negative publicity. They also want to avoid having their messages dominated by one person.

For the Beef Industry Council, the present use of multiple celebrities is largely a result of recent experiences with James Garner and Cybill Shepherd. While a Council spokesperson, Garner—a popular celebrity who also endorsed Mazda—underwent heart surgery; this made him less attractive as a spokesperson because of the perceived association between beef consumption and high cholesterol. Also, while a Council spokesperson, Shepherd told a reporter that she did not like to eat beef.

Using multiple celebrities can also minimize a company's embarrassment if a celebrity gets into trouble. As one advertising agency executive noted, "When the person personifying your brand gets in trouble, the brand indirectly gets in trouble." For example, Bruce Willis was the centerpiece of Seagram's wine-cooler advertising campaign as it moved ahead of Bartles & Jaymes. But when Seagram saw the negative publicity that occurred because of Willis' flamboyant personal life-style, his contract as a celebrity endorser was not renewed.

With multiple celebrities, a company also lowers the risk that a promotion campaign will be dominated by one person. This occurred in the early 1980s, when actor Orson Welles delivered the now-famous message "We will sell no wine before its time" for Paul Masson. Wells was so well-known that he overshadowed the product: "He was a 'video vampire'—he stole the show. The product was secondary to the man."

If firms are concerned about potential embarrassment from their celebrities, they may use these celebrities sparingly and/or carefully investigate them before featuring them in promotional messages. For instance, Miller Brewing Company carefully interviewed former teammates and others before signing retired athletes for its long-running Miller Lite advertising campaign.

QUESTIONS

1. Describe the difficulties that could be involved with the use of multiple celebrities from the perspective of the channel of communication.
2. What are the pros and cons of the Beef Industry Council's using multiple celebrities versus company spokespersons or representative consumers as sources?
3. Should the Beef Council use two-sided messages? Explain your answer.
4. Discuss how the Beef Council should determine its promotional budget.

Institutional Advertising by Banks[†]

U.S. banks are increasingly running image-oriented ads portraying them as "caring institutions that deliver impeccable services." They want to overcome consumer perceptions that they are cold and insensitive. Says one advertising agency executive, "Banks have all done market research and found general dissatisfaction among consumers. Now they want to seem more human and empathetic."

Among the banks that use institutional advertising are Irving Trust (New York), First Chicago (Illinois), and Gibraltar Savings (Texas):

▶ With regard to one of Irving Trust's recent ads, its advertising agency stated: "We wanted to try a sophisticated documentary approach and spend most of the time in the commercial setting up a very New York scene." The marketing focus of this ad was not initially easy to discern—and did not become clear until the end of the message. The beginning of the commercial focused on two women. Both the images and dialogue seemed ambiguous. At the end of the commercial, one woman said, "My friends are always complaining about their banks. I don't know what they are talking about." Then the words "The personal banker. Irving Trust" appeared on the screen.

▶ During each First Chicago commercial (or documonial, as the bank prefers to call them), an actor playing a customer role relates a personal story. In one advertisement, a women chatted in her kitchen about her decision to bank at First Chicago: "But hey, who thinks about changing checking accounts? You know, it's one of those things you do and you forget about, like getting married." According to First Chicago's advertising agency, "We're trying to humanize the monolith without simply saying we're caring folks. That kind of talk falls on deaf ears."

▶ Gibraltar Savings has been using "Stand by

Me" as its theme song. One recent ad showed a Gibraltar customer 45+ years ago as a World War II bomber pilot and today at a seminar. The tag line is, "Gibraltar Savings. Like Good Friends, We'll Stand By You." Said Gibraltar's advertising agency, "The song really had stopping power and created a warm, good feeling among the people in our consumer research studies."

Banks are stepping up their use of image-oriented advertisements at the same time that customers are demanding better service. In fact, some consumer surveys show that bank customers now consider quality service to be more important than a convenient location in choosing a bank.

There are numerous critics regarding banks' use of institutional advertising. These critics generally comment on the lack of believability in bank ads and on the lack of differentiation among bank slogans. For instance, one advertising agency executive feels that it is quite hard to get consumers to accept or believe a humanistic approach by their bank: "You're swimming upstream when you talk about being the friendly banker. It's almost as believable as saying you're a painless dentist."

Some critics assert that too many bank ads sound the same. As an example, these slogans are very similar: "We hear you" (First Pennsylvania Bank); "We put you first" (First National Bank of Chicago); and "The last thing I ever want to do is intimidate a customer, I'm an investor. I invest in people" (Trustcorp Bank, Toledo, Ohio). And how about these? Banc One (Columbus, Ohio) says that it employs "18,000 people who care," and the First National Bank of Louisville states that "there are more than 1,900 of us . . . who have pledged to work harder for you."

An illustration of a totally different promotional approach, one that still deals with company image, is National Westminster Bank's service guarantee at its New York branches. The bank promises to give $5 to each customer who is not treated courteously, and $50 to anyone whose loan request is not answered within the time period promised.

[†] The data in this case are drawn from Ronald Alsop, "Banks Aim New Image Ads at Consumers," *Wall Street Journal* (October 11, 1988), p. B1.

QUESTIONS

1. Should banks use humor in advertising? Comparative advertising? Why or why not?
2. Should banks use massed or distributed promotion? Explain your answer.
3. Evaluate the use of institutional advertisements by banks from the perspective of primary demand generation. From the perspective of selective demand generation.
4. Comment on the difficulties of promoting a bank service versus promoting a tangible good.

CHAPTER *16*
Advertising and Publicity

CHAPTER OBJECTIVES

1. To examine the scope, importance, and characteristics of advertising

2. To study the elements in an advertising plan: objectives, responsibility, budgeting, themes, media, advertisements, timing, cooperative efforts, and evaluating success or failure

3. To examine the scope, importance, and characteristics of publicity

4. To study the elements in a publicity plan: objectives, responsibility, publicity types, media, publicity messages, timing, and evaluating success or failure

Although the last Volkswagen Beetle made for American consumption spun off the production line more than a decade ago, the advertising extolling this homely cultural icon still commands awe more than a generation after the campaign's creation. When *Advertising Age* polled its readers in 1988, asking them to select the "most powerful advertising campaign" in U.S. history, Doyle Dane Bernbach's brilliant 1960s' work for the VW won by a country kilometer in a survey that produced nominations for more than 50 campaigns from A (Alka-Seltzer) to W (Wendy's).

What made the Beetle ads so popular and so enduring? *Advertising Age* readers lauded the campaign for its use of minimal copy (text) and its "incredible success in convincing Americans to purchase an import at a time when U.S. car makers dominated the market." Some readers commented that the Volkswagen ads "generated product awareness," "convinced people that a goofy-looking car was practical and fun," and "proved humor could be employed effectively without insulting the consumer's intelligence."

According to the same *Advertising Age* survey, the "second most powerful campaign" involved "Marlboro Country," a theme developed by the Leo Burnett advertising agency. The "rugged cowboy in the great outdoors approach" was credited for "transforming a lackluster women's cigarette into the dominant brand in the world" and "taking a cigarette originally geared to women and repositioning it as 'macho.'" The campaign's more than thirty-year longevity was also mentioned as evidence of its success. Yet, as in the case of the Volkswagen ads, the Marlboro campaign has not been run for a number of years (in this case due to restrictions on cigarette ads).

Other campaigns that received strong reader support included Alka-Seltzer's "I Can't Believe I Ate the Whole Thing," Miller Lite's "Tastes Great, Less Filling," and Coca-Cola's "It's The Real Thing."

How do current advertising campaigns rate? Video Storyboard Tests Inc. annually conducts a study of America's most popular television commercials, as judged by nearly 25,000 consumers. The five most popular television commercials of 1988, in order of their ranking (followed by their 1988 television advertising budgets—in millions), involved the California raisins ($6.8 million), Pepsi/Diet Pepsi ($106.4 million), McDonald's ($385.9 million), Bud Light ($57.4 million), and Isuzu ($30.0 million). For example, in the California raisin commercials, animated raisins danced to a Motown beat; the success of this campaign is espe-

Think small.

Reprinted by permission.

cially notable in that it had the second smallest budget of the top 25 commercials of 1988.

Of the top five television commercials of 1988, all but one was in the top five of 1987 (Isuzu ranked eighth). In 1988, the Partnership for a Drug-Free America's public-service television commercial showing an egg frying in a pan as an illustration of a "brain on drugs" ranked eleventh. Although media time for these commercials was donated, the estimated value of the time was $82.5 million.

Yet some observers question the validity of awareness or popularity studies of commercials. As one executive commented: "It's good to know people are at least paying attention to your message. But I've developed a healthy skepticism about how well memorable ads relate to what consumers buy."[1]

In this chapter, we will study both advertising and publicity aspects of promotion and seek to learn more about what makes a "good" ad or publicity campaign.

[1] Robert Goldsborough, "The Golden Lemon," *Advertising Age* (November 9, 1988), p. 170; and Ronald Alsop, "In '88, There Were No Ads Like Old Ads," *Wall Street Journal* (February 23, 1989), p. B1).

Overview

Chapter 16 examines the two mass communication forms of promotion: advertising and publicity. As defined in Chapter 15, advertising is paid, nonpersonal communication regarding goods, services, organizations, people, places, and ideas; it is transmitted through various media by business firms, nonprofit organizations, and individuals who are in some way identified in the advertising message as the sponsor. The distinguishing features of advertising are that the firm pays for its message, a set format is delivered to the entire audience through mass media, the name of the sponsor is clearly presented, and the company controls the message.

In contrast, publicity is nonpersonal communication regarding goods, services, organizations, people, places, and ideas; it is transmitted through various media but is not paid for by an identified sponsor. Its unique features are that the firm does not pay for media time or space, a set format is delivered to the entire audience through mass media, the message is presented by a source not affiliated with the company, and the independent source controls the message.

The differences between advertising and publicity are in part revealed by this statement: "Advertising is paid for, publicity is prayed for."

The scope and importance, characteristics, and planning considerations are covered in this chapter for both advertising and publicity.

The Scope and Importance of Advertising

The leading media are newspapers, television, and direct mail.

It was estimated that over $125 billion would be spent on advertising in the United States in 1989, an increase of about 6 per cent from 1988 and 33 per cent from 1985. Table 16-1 shows advertising expenditures by medium and the changing emphasis since 1960.

The leading medium throughout this period has been newspapers; however, newspapers' share of advertising has dropped substantially since 1960 (from 30.8 to 26.2 per cent). The second-leading medium is now television, whose relative size has grown

TABLE 16-1   U.S. Advertising Expenditures, 1960–1989, by Medium (in Billions)

Medium	1960 $	1960 %	1970 $	1970 %	1980 $	1980 %	1989[a] $	1989[a] %
Newspapers	3.69	30.8	5.70	29.2	15.62	28.5	32.91	26.2
Magazines	0.91	7.6	1.29	6.6	3.23	5.9	6.41	5.1
Farm publications	0.07	0.6	0.06	0.3	0.14	0.3	0.25	0.2
Television	1.63	13.6	3.60	18.4	11.33	20.7	27.38	21.8
Radio	0.69	5.8	1.31	6.7	3.69	6.7	8.29	6.6
Direct mail	1.83	15.3	2.77	14.2	7.65	14.0	22.60	18.0
Business publications	0.61	5.1	0.74	3.8	1.69	3.1	2.89	2.3
Outdoor	0.20	1.7	0.23	1.2	0.61	1.1	1.13	0.9
Miscellaneous	2.34	19.5	3.85	19.7	10.79	19.7	23.74	18.9
Total	11.96[b]	100.0	19.55	100.0[b]	54.75	100.0	125.60	100.0

[a] Estimated.
[b] Rounding error.

Source: Adapted by the authors from McCann-Erickson, Inc., and *Advertising Age* data.

TABLE 16-2 Advertising in Selected Industries, 1988

Industry	Advertising as Per Cent of Sales	Industry	Advertising as Per Cent of Sales
Games and toys	18.4	Security brokers	3.2
Perfume	10.2	Paper mills	2.9
Beverages	9.5	Lumber	2.2
Food products	7.3	Mainframe computers	1.3
Hospitals	5.8	Floor-covering mills	1.1
Adhesives and sealants	4.4	Food stores	0.6
Books	3.8	Advertising agencies	0.1

Source: Derived from Schonfeld & Associates, "Advertising-to-Sales Ratios, 1988 Estimates (By Industry)," *Advertising Age* (October 24, 1988), p. 49.

TABLE 16-3 The Ten Leading U.S. Advertisers, 1987

Company	U.S. Advertising Expenditures	Advertising as Per Cent of Sales
Philip Morris	$1,557,846,000	8.5
Procter & Gamble	$1,386,710,000	11.2
General Motors	$1,024,852,000	1.2
Sears	$ 886,529,000	2.0[a]
RJR Nabisco	$ 839,589,000	7.2
PepsiCo	$ 703,973,000	7.4
Kodak	$ 658,221,000	8.2
McDonald's	$ 649,493,000	6.1
Ford	$ 639,510,000	1.2
Anheuser-Busch	$ 635,067,000	7.5[a]

[a] Authors' estimate.

Source: "Top 100 Advertisers by Primary Business," *Advertising Age* (September 28, 1988), p. 152. Reprinted by permission of *Advertising Age*. Copyright 1988 by Crain Communications Inc.

significantly since 1960 (from 13.6 to 21.8 per cent). After a fall in advertising share between 1960 and 1980, direct-mail expenditures have risen significantly since 1980 (from 14.0 to 18.0 per cent). Radio's share of advertising has remained constant since 1970, up slightly from 1960 (6.6 per cent in 1989). Magazines, business publications, outdoor ads, and farm publications have all declined in relative importance since 1960. Miscellaneous advertising continues to represent nearly one-fifth of spending.

Advertising as a per cent of sales varies by industry and company. This is shown in Tables 16-2 and 16-3, which present 1988 data for selected industries and the 10 leading national advertisers in 1987. In general, advertising as a per cent of sales is quite low. For example, during 1988, in 40 per cent of U.S. industries, average advertising expenditures were less than 2.0 per cent of sales; in 35 per cent of U.S. industries, the average was between 2.0 and 4.0 per cent of sales; and in only one-quarter of U.S. industries, was the average above 4.0 per cent of sales.[2]

Firms usually spend less than 4 per cent of sales on advertising.

[2] Schonfeld & Associates, "Advertising-to-Sales Ratios, 1988 Estimates (By Industry)," *Advertising Age* (October 24, 1988), p. 49.

A strong emphasis on advertising is most likely when products are standardized, have easily communicated features, appeal to a large target market, are low in price, are sold through independent channel members, and/or are new. Leading brands usually receive large advertising expenditures to maintain their position. These are some of the findings from a recent survey of leading advertisers:

▶ 83 per cent feel that the role of advertising is to create brand awareness and to maintain strong brand names.
▶ 80 per cent feel that a cut in advertising expenditures would have a serious effect on long-term sales; 49 per cent say that short-run sales would be affected by such a cut.
▶ 72 per cent feel that their companies do not spend enough on advertising.
▶ 56 per cent feel that advertising is more important today than in the past.[3]

An advertising research study involving 20,000 consumers, and conducted over a three-year period, found that

▶ Behavior is easier to change than attitudes.
▶ Recall is a weak measure of advertising effectiveness.
▶ One ad can have a strong effect on brand awareness.
▶ It is easier to improve the favorable rating for a little-known product by advertising than a well-known product.
▶ Advertising effectiveness grows during extended campaigns.[4]

The Characteristics of Advertising

On the positive side, advertising attracts a large and geographically dispersed market; and, for print media, circulation is supplemented by the passing of a copy from one reader to another. The costs per viewer or listener are low. For example, a single television ad may cost $150,000 to air and reach 30 million viewers—a cost of $0.005 per watcher (this figure includes media time only and not commercial production costs). A broad range of media is available: from national television to local newspapers. Therefore, the objectives of a firm and its resources may be matched with the most appropriate medium. Figure 16-1 shows a few of the many media in which Nike advertises.

The sponsor has control over message content, graphics, timing, and size or length, as well as over the demographics of the audience. In addition, a uniform message is delivered to all members of the audience. And, with print media, consumers can study and restudy messages. Editorial content (a news story or segment of a television show) often surrounds an advertisement. This can increase readership or viewing, enhance image, and create the proper mood for an ad. It is for these reasons that firms may seek specialized media or sections of media (such as the sports section of a newspaper for a men's clothing ad).

Ads ease the way for personal selling by obtaining audience awareness and liking for a firm's brands. They also enable self-service retailers to operate, and they sustain an

---

[3] Graham Phillips, "Brands: A Case for the Balance Sheets," *Advertising Age* (November 9, 1988), p. 14.
[4] Stuart Emmrich, "Major Study Details Ads' Effect on Sales," *Advertising Age* (June 21, 1982), pp. 1, 80.

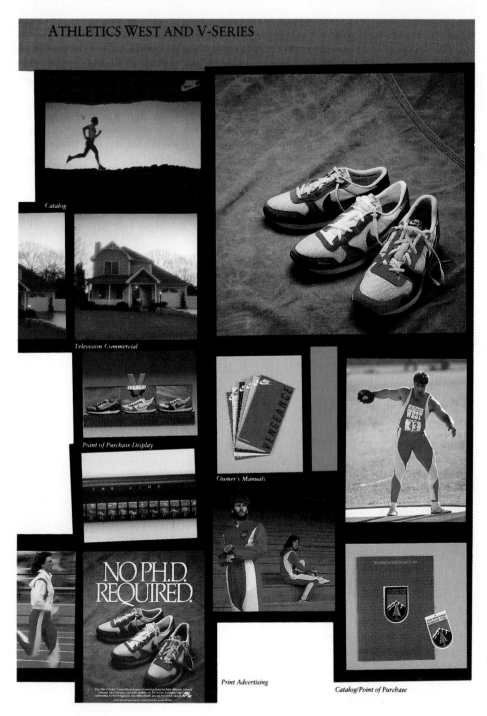

Catalog

Television Commercial

Point of Purchase Display

Owner's Manuals

NO PH.D. REQUIRED.

Print Advertising

Catalog/Point of Purchase

FIGURE 16-1
Selected Media
Used by Nike
Reprinted by permission.

entire industry—mail order. With a pulling strategy, advertising enables a firm to show its channel members that consumer demand exists.

On the negative side, because advertising messages are standardized, they are inflexible and not responsive to consumer questions. This makes it difficult to satisfy the needs of a diverse audience. Furthermore, because many media appeal to broad audiences, a large portion of viewers or readers may be wasted for the sponsor. For

Advertising is inflexible and can be wasteful, costly, and limit information and feedback.

487

example, a single-unit health spa or a roofing-materials company distributing locally might find that only one-half of a newspaper's readers live within its selling area. Or, a maker of clothes designed for 15- to 18-year-old females might find only magazines appealing to 13- to 25-year-old females.

Some types of advertising require high total expenditures, even though costs per viewer or reader are low. This may preclude smaller firms from utilizing certain media. In the example at the beginning of this section, it was stated that a television ad could cost only $0.005 per viewer. Nonetheless, the ad would cost $150,000 for media time alone — and this is for one ad placed once. Also, because high costs lead to brief messages, the majority of ads do not provide the audience with much information. In particular, television commercials are short, averaging 30 seconds or less; today, few are as long as one minute. And because ads are impersonal, feedback is difficult to obtain and usually not immediately available.

Mass media attract many people who do not view or listen to ads. They watch television, read print media, and so on, but they do not pay attention to advertising and discard direct-mail pieces. Of growing concern to television advertisers is "zapping," the process by which a viewer uses his or her remote-control device to switch programs when an ad comes on.

Developing an Advertising Plan

FIGURE 16-2
Developing an Advertising Plan

The development of an advertising plan consists of the nine steps shown in Figure 16-2. These steps are highlighted in the following subsections.

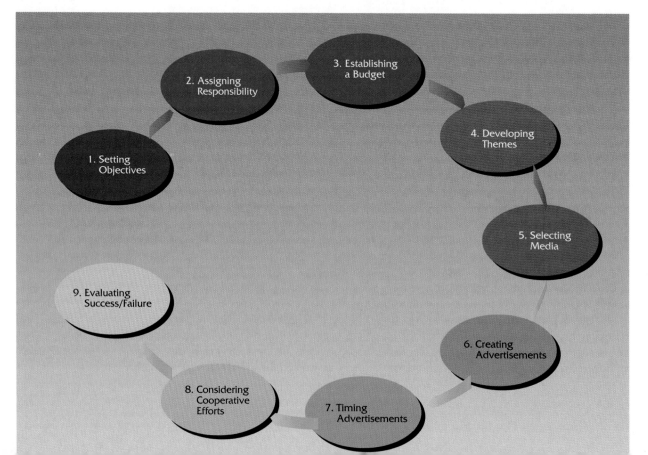

TABLE 16-4 Illustrations of Specific Advertising Objectives

Type of Objective	Illustrations
Demand-Oriented	
Information	To create brand awareness of a new product by the target market
	To acquaint consumers with new store hours
	To reduce the time it takes for salespeople to answer basic questions
Persuasion	To gain brand preference
	To increase store traffic
	To achieve brand loyalty
Reminding (retention)	To stabilize sales
	To maintain brand loyalty
	To sustain brand recognition and image
Image-Oriented	
Industry	To develop and maintain a favorable industry image
	To generate primary demand
Company	To develop and maintain a favorable company image
	To generate selective demand

Setting Objectives

The advertising objectives set by a firm can be divided into demand and image types, as described in Chapter 15. Table 16-4 outlines several specific objectives in each category. Usually a number of these are combined and pursued through an advertising plan.

Whirlpool, the appliance maker, is an example of a firm with clear advertising objectives. Its current advertising campaign is being used "to attack a growing perception among consumers that all major appliances in a category are alike." This campaign positions Whirlpool-branded products as the leaders in innovation, featuring the slogan: "Quality you can count on . . . today."[5]

Assigning Responsibility

In assigning advertising responsibility, a firm can rely on the internal personnel involved with its marketing functions, use a specialized in-house department, or hire an outside agency. Although many firms use internal personnel or have in-house departments, most involved with advertising on a continuous or sizable basis employ outside agencies (some in addition to their own personnel or departments). Diversified firms frequently employ a different advertising agency for each product line.

[5] Patricia Strnad, "Whirlpool Hawks Innovation," *Advertising Age* (December 26, 1988), p. 16.

*An **advertising agency** may work with a firm to develop its advertising plan, conduct research, or provide other services.*

An ***advertising agency*** is an organization that provides a variety of advertising-related services to its client firms.[6] It often works with client firms in developing their advertising plans — including themes, media selection, copywriting, and other tasks. A large agency would also offer market research, product planning, consumer research, public relations, and other services.

As an example, the Young & Rubicam advertising agency has the U.S. Army as a client. In addition to creating ads for the Army's annual $90-million advertising campaign for new recruits, Young & Rubicam writes solicitation letters to high school students, prepares brochures, creates posters, and sends out socks and T-shirts with the Army logo. The advertising agency has about 200 full- and part-time employees working on the Army account.[7] Figure 16-3 shows a recent Young & Rubicam recruiting ad for the U.S. Army.

For many years, most advertising agencies received 15 per cent of their clients' advertising media expenditures as payment for performing basic functions; they added charges for other services. However, new compensation arrangements have developed over the last several years because of the rapid increases in media costs, advertising companies' desire to link the actual functions performed (or time spent) by their agencies to compensation, and advertisers' determination to have more control over agency fees. Today only about one-third of all advertisers compensate their agencies via the 15 per cent commission rate; the others set standard fees for specific services (not tied to advertising expenditures), negotiate commission rates, and/or insist on a combination commission and bonus system keyed to performance.[8]

A firm's decision to use an outside advertising agency depends on its own expertise and resources, and the role of advertising for the firm.

Establishing a Budget

After determining the overall expenditures to be allocated to advertising by the all-you-can-afford, incremental, competitive parity, percentage-of-sales, or objective-and-task method, the firm establishes a detailed advertising budget. It must delineate the funds for each type of advertising (such as product and institutional messages) and each medium (such as newspapers and radio).

For example, this is what a typical retailer in these categories expected to spend on advertising in 1989: department-store chain, $16 million; supermarket chain, $11 million; discount-store chain, $7 million; home-center chain, $5.5 million; drugstore chain, $4.5 million; and apparel-specialty chain, $3.5 million. On average, U.S. retailers allocate 55 per cent of their budgets for newspapers, 14.8 per cent for direct mail, 10.8 per cent for conventional television, 9.7 per cent for radio, 4.5 per cent for magazines, and 5.2 per cent for other (cable television, outdoor, and so on).[9]

---

[6] Peter D. Bennett (Editor), *Dictionary of Marketing Terms* (Chicago: American Marketing Association, 1988), p. 4. See also Michael G. Harvey and J. Paul Rupert, "Selecting an Industrial Advertising Agency," *Industrial Marketing Management*, Vol. 17 (1988), pp. 119–127.

[7] Joanne Lipman, "Ad Firms Falter on One-Stop Shopping," *Wall Street Journal* (December 1, 1988), p. B1.

[8] Walecia Konrad, "A Word from the Sponsor: Get Results—Or Else," *Business Week* (July 4, 1988), p. 13; and Laurie Freeman, "P&G Seeks New Creative Thrust," *Advertising Age* (February 20, 1989), pp. 3, 74.

[9] "New Store Competition Drives Ad Budgets," *Chain Store Age Executive* (December 1987), pp. 16–17; and Judith Graham, "Modest Ad Gains," *Advertising Age* (February 6, 1989), p. 57.

The Army can teach you a lot. Because the Army gives you an education you can't get anywhere else. In the Army, you'll learn a valuable skill. You'll learn to work as part of a team.

And you'll learn about confidence. Determination. Self-discipline. And character.

Plus, the Montgomery GI Bill and Army College Fund give you the opportunity to learn even more. If you qualify, you can earn as much as $25,200 to help pay for your college education. To find out more, call toll-free 1-800-USA-ARMY.

With your college diploma and your Army experience, you'll have something that most other young people don't: an edge on life.

ARMY. BE ALL YOU CAN BE.

FIGURE 16-3
Young & Rubicam and the U.S. Army
"Dear Dad" advertisement by Young & Rubicam New York for the United States Army Recruiting Command. Copy: Brad Justus. Art: Mel Hioki. Reprinted by permission.

As another illustration, Table 16-5 shows the 1987 advertising budgets of Dow Chemical and FTD (Florists' Transworld Delivery Association), two vastly different companies. Dow makes chemical products, pharmaceuticals, and consumer products such as package wraps and deodorizers. FTD is a member-owned, nonprofit cooperative that processes consumer floral delivery requests, designs promotions and new products for members, and produces supplies for members. Figure 16-4 shows a recent FTD ad featuring Merlin Olsen, the sportscaster/actor.

Several points should be considered in budgeting. What are the costs for different alternatives (a 30-second national television spot versus a full-page magazine ad)? How many placements of an ad are necessary for it to be effective (if four telecasts of a single

TABLE 16-5   Dow Chemical's and FTD's 1987 U.S. Advertising Budgets

Media	Dow Chemical $	Dow Chemical %	FTD $	FTD %
Newspapers	599,000	0.4	2,860,000	8.6
Magazines	17,237,000	12.7	853,000	2.6
Farm publications	1,488,000	1.1	0	0
Cable television	2,132,000	1.6	223,000	0.7
Commercial television	70,355,000	51.8	16,038,000	48.5
Radio	6,856,000	5.1	6,141,000	18.5
Business publications	3,974,000	2.9	0	0
Outdoor	49,000	0.1	0	0
Other[a]	33,000,000	24.3	7,000,000	21.1
Total	$135,690,000	100.0	$33,115,000	100.0
Advertising as a percentage of U.S. sales		2.3		27.8

[a] Includes direct mail, coupons, product sampling, premiums, point-of-sale promotions, special events, and trade shows.

Source: "Dow Chemical Co.," *Advertising Age* (September 28, 1988), p. 66; and "Florists' Transworld Delivery Assn.," *Advertising Age* (November 23, 1988), p. S-13. Reprinted by permission of *Advertising Age.* Copyright 1988 by Crain Communications Inc.

FIGURE 16-4
An FTD Ad: "What Am I Looking For?"
Reprinted by permission.

TABLE 16-6 Advertising Themes

Theme	Example
Good or Service Related	
Dominant features described	Maytag washers emphasize dependability and durability.
Competitive advantages cited	Apple stresses how user friendly its computers are versus competitors' computers.
Price used as dominant feature	Suave beauty products advertise low prices.
News or information domination	New-model cars point out improvements in gas mileage.
Size of market detailed	Hertz emphasizes its leading position in car rentals.
Primary demand sought	Grapes are advertised.
Consumer Related	
Good or service uses explained	Pillsbury ads show cake recipes.
Cost benefits of good or service shown	Owens-Corning shows how consumers reduce heating bills with fiberglass insulation.
Emphasis on how good or service helps consumer improve	Listerine advertises that it eliminates bad breath.
Threatening situation displayed	American Express points out the risks of carrying cash.
Incentives given to encourage purchases	An ad mentions $1 off the purchase as an introductory offer for a new brand of coffee.
Institutional Related	
Favorable image sought	Exxon shows how it is searching for new energy sources.
Growth, profits, and potential described to attract investors	Full-page ads are taken in business sections of major newspapers.

television ad are needed to make an impact, the budget must provide for four placements)? How have media prices risen in recent years? How should a company react during an industry sales slump (firms that maintain advertising usually do better than those that do not)? Which channel member is assigned promotional tasks? Do channel members require contributions toward their advertising? What does it cost to produce an ad?[10]

Because demand-oriented advertising generates sales, firms should be very careful about reducing their budgets. A better campaign, not a lower budget, may be the answer if performance does not reach goals.

Developing Themes

A firm next develops *advertising themes*, the overall appeals for its campaign. A good or service appeal centers on the item and its attributes. A consumer appeal describes the good or service in terms of consumer benefits rather than product characteristics. An institutional appeal deals with corporate image.[11] Table 16-6 presents the full range of advertising themes from which a firm may select.

*The basic **advertising themes** are the product, consumer, and/or institutional appeals.*

[10] See Bob Donath, "How Much Should You Advertise?" *Business Marketing* (April 1988), pp. 78–86; and McCann-Erickson, "Media Price Trends," *Advertising Age* (November 28, 1988), p. S-18.
[11] This classification method was developed by William M. Weilbacher, *Advertising*, Second Edition (New York: Macmillan, 1984), pp. 198–213.

TABLE 16-7 Advertising Media (Continued)

Medium	Market Coverage	Best Uses	Advantages	Disadvantages
Daily newspaper	Entire metropolitan area; local editions sometimes used	Large retailers	Short lead time, concentrated market, flexible, passalongs, surrounded by content	General audience, heavy ad competition, limited color, limited creativity
Weekly newspaper	One community	Local retailers	Same as daily	Heavy ad competition, limited color, limited creativity, small market
Commercial television	Regional or national	Regional manufacturers and large retailers; national, large manufacturers and largest retailers	Reach, low cost per viewer, persuasive impact, creative options, flexible, surrounded by programs	High minimum total costs, general audience, lead time, short message, limited availability
Cable television	Local, regional, or national	Local, regional, and national manufacturers and retailers	More precise audience and more creative than commercial television	Limited number of consumers hooked up; ads not yet fully accepted on programs
Direct mail	Advertiser selects market	New products, book clubs, financial services, catalog sales	Precise audience, flexible, personal approach, no clutter from other messages	High throwaway rate, receipt by wrong person, low credibility
Magazines	National (most with regional editions) or local	National manufacturers; local service retailers and mail-order firms	Color, creative options, affluent audience, permanence of message, passalongs, flexible, surrounded by content	Long lead time, clutter, poor frequency, ad clutter, geographically dispersed audience
Radio	Entire metropolitan area	Local or regional retailers	Low costs, selective market, high frequency, immediacy of messages, surrounded by content	No visual impact, commercial clutter, channel switching, consumer distractions
Business publications	National or regional	Corporate advertising, industrial firms	Selective market, high readability, surrounded by content, permanence of message, passalongs	Restricted product applications, not final consumer oriented

TABLE 16-7   Advertising Media   (Continued)

Medium	Market Coverage	Best Uses	Advantages	Disadvantages
Outdoor	Entire metropolitan area or one location	Brand-name products, nearby retailers, reminder ads	Large size, color, creative options, frequency, no clutter of competing messages, permanence of message	Legal restrictions, consumer distractions, general audience, inflexible, limited content
Transit	Urban community with a transit system	Firms located along transit route	Concentrated market, permanence of messages, frequency, action orientation, color, creative options	Clutter of ads, consumer distractions, limited audience
Telephone directories	Entire metropolitan area (with local supplements)	All types of retailers, professionals, service companies	Low costs, permanence of message, coverage of market, specialized listings, action oriented	Clutter of ads, limited creativity, long lead time, low appeal to passive consumers
Flyers	Single neighborhood	Local retailers	Low cost, market coverage, little waste, flexible	High throwaway rate, poor image

Selecting Media

There is a wide variety of media from which to choose, as described in Table 16-7. When selecting media, these are several factors that should be considered: costs, reach, waste, narrowcasting, frequency, message permanence, persuasive impact, clutter, lead time, and media innovations. See Figure 16-5.

Advertising media costs are expenditures involved with placing messages in media and are related to the length or size of an ad as well as the characteristics of the chosen media. They should be assessed in two ways. First, the total costs to place each ad in a particular medium are calculated — for example, $30,000 for a full-page color ad in a national magazine. Second, per reader or viewer costs are computed. Costs are expressed on a per thousand basis, except by newspapers which use a cost per million base. If a $30,000 ad is placed in a magazine with a circulation of 500,000, the cost per thousand is $60.

Advertising media costs are total and per person.

Reach refers to the number of viewers or readers in a medium's audience. For television and radio, reach is the total number of people exposed to an advertisement. For print media, reach has two components, circulation and passalong rate. Circulation is the number of copies sold or distributed to consumers. Passalong rate is the number of times each copy is placed with another reader. For example, each copy of *Newsweek* is read by about six people. The passalong rate for magazines is much higher than that for daily newspapers.

Reach includes circulation and passalongs.

FIGURE 16-5
**Advertising Media
Selection**

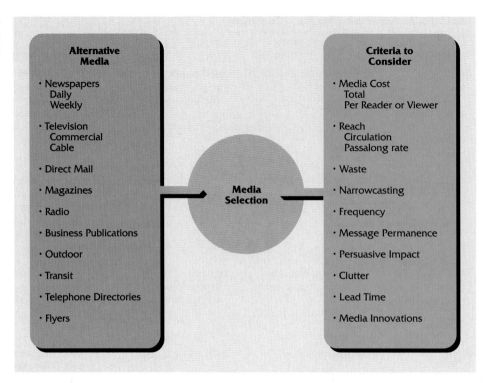

*Waste is the audience
segment not in the target
market.*

Waste is the portion of a medium's audience that is not in a firm's target market. Because media appeal to mass audiences, waste can be a significant factor in advertising. This is demonstrated by continuing the magazine illustration already noted in the discussion on media costs. Because the publication involved is a special-interest magazine for amateur photographers, a film manufacturer knows that 450,000 readers will have an interest in a new fast-speed film; 50,000 will have no interest. The latter represents the wasted audience for an ad on that film. Therefore, the real cost is $66.67 ($30,000/450,000 × 1,000 = $66.67) per thousand circulation. The firm is also aware that a general-interest magazine runs ads for film. This magazine has a circulation of one million and the cost of a full-page ad is $40,000, $40 per thousand. However, the film manufacturer knows that only 200,000 people have an interest in photography. Therefore, the real cost is $200 ($40,000/200,000 × 1,000 = $200) per thousand circulation. See Figure 16-6.

*Through **narrowcasting**,
advertisers seek to reduce
waste.*

One way of reducing the audience waste present with traditional mass media is to focus on **narrowcasting,** which presents advertising messages to relatively limited and well-defined audiences. This may be done through direct mail, local cable television shows, specialty magazines, and other targeted media. With narrowcasting, a firm is willing to have a smaller reach in return for better efficiency in reaching customers (less waste). Now that about 55 per cent of U.S. homes receive cable television programming, this medium has great potential for local narrowcasting.[12]

---

[12] "Cable Continues to Grow in Importance," *Advertising Age* (February 20, 1989), p. Cable-6.

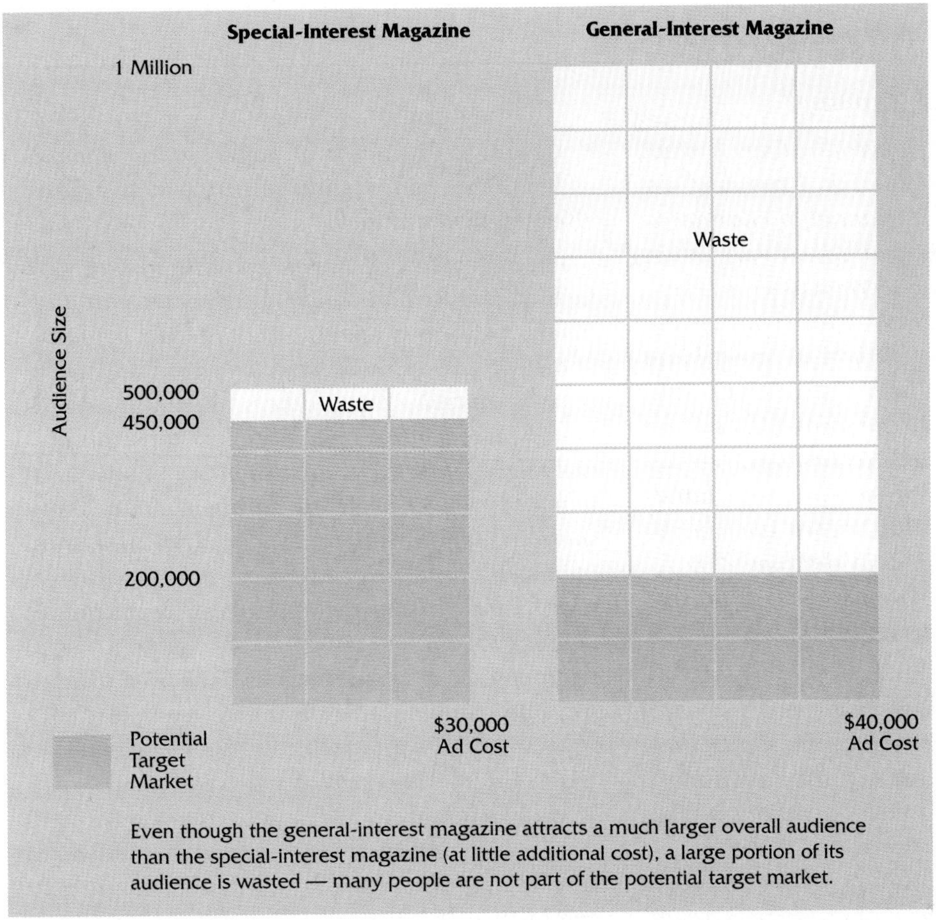
Special-Interest Magazine
General-Interest Magazine
1 Million
Audience Size
500,000
450,000
200,000
Waste
Waste
$30,000
Ad Cost
$40,000
Ad Cost
Potential
Target
Market
Even though the general-interest magazine attracts a much larger overall audience than the special-interest magazine (at little additional cost), a large portion of its audience is wasted — many people are not part of the potential target market.

FIGURE 16-6
Waste in Advertising

Frequency is how often a medium can be used. It is greatest for newspapers, radio, and television, where ads may appear daily and advertising strategy may be easily changed. Telephone directories, outdoor ads, and magazines have the poorest frequency. A Yellow Pages ad may be placed or changed only once per year.

Frequency is highest for daily media.

Message permanence refers to the number of exposures one advertisement generates and how long it remains available to the audience. Outdoor ads, transit ads, and telephone directories yield many exposures per message. In addition, many magazines are retained by consumers for long periods of time. On the other hand, radio and television commercials last only 5 to 60 seconds and are over.

*Exposures per ad involve **message permanence**.*

Persuasive impact is the ability of a medium to stimulate consumers. Television often has the highest persuasive impact because it is able to combine audio, video, color, animation, and other appeals. Magazines also have high persuasive impact. Many newspapers are improving their technology in order to feature color ads and increase their persuasive impact. According to one study of affluent consumers, television is the most authoritative, believable, exciting, and influential advertising medium.[13]

***Persuasive impact** is highest for television.*

13 R.H. Bruskin Associates, "Affluent Consumers' Image of Advertising in Major Media," *Advertising Age* (October 19, 1987), p. S-24.

You're the Marketer

How Do You Reduce Zapping?

According to a new television-ratings system developed by R.D. Percy & Co., "zapping"—a viewer's switching from channel to channel to avoid commercials—is more common than many advertising experts previously believed. In the past, research on television-viewing behavior focused on six-minute or one-minute time intervals; but the Percy system can evaluate television viewing by the second. Its system relies on state-of-the-art technology, which combines computers, heat sensors, and hand-held "people meters" (that record answers to such questions as "Who is in the room?").

Percy used its system to study viewers in New York City, the largest television market in the United States. It found that

▶ *Over all time slots, television ads have 17 per cent fewer viewers than the shows they accompany. Two-thirds of this amount is due to people leaving their televisions on but unwatched; the balance is due to zapping.*

▶ *Zapping reduces a prime-time television advertising audience by at least 10 per cent. Earlier research estimated zapping reduced that audience by between 2 and 4 per cent.*

▶ *Almost 20 per cent of participating households are heavy zappers (at least one zap every two minutes).*

The high level of zapping is due to various factors. Households now have access to an average of twenty television channels. One-half of all U.S. households have television sets with remote controls; many others have VCRs that add remote-control capabilities to their standard television sets. VCRs also allow "zipping," whereby viewers can zip through ads at fast speed during the playback of a show. Also, the increasing number of television ads (as advertisers turn to shorter messages) encourages viewers to zap.

Among the ways advertisers have tried to discourage zapping are to make commercials appear like programming, to use eye-catching ads, and to use special celebrities—such as Michael Jackson.

As a vice-president of an advertising agency specializing in television commercials, what would you do?

SOURCE: Based on material in Dennis Kneale, " 'Zapping' of TV Ads Appears Pervasive," *Wall Street Journal* (April 25, 1988), p. 29.

Clutter occurs when there are many ads.

Clutter involves the number of ads that are contained in a single program, issue, and so on of a medium. Clutter is low when a limited number of ads is presented, such as Hallmark placing a few scattered commercials on its television specials. Clutter is high when many ads are presented, such as the large number of supermarket ads in the Wednesday issue of a newspaper. And, overall, magazines have the highest level of clutter. Television networks are increasingly being criticized for permitting too much clutter, particularly in allowing companies to sponsor very brief commercials (e. g., 15 seconds or shorter). Today almost 40 per cent of all television ads are 15-second spots.[14] Figure 16-7 illustrates the problem of clutter.

[14] "New Index Tracks Ad Clutter," *Advertising Age* (August 29, 1988), p. 48; and Television Bureau of Advertising, "15-Second Spots on the Rise," *Advertising Age* (June 12, 1989), p. 54.

Every message is at the mercy of its environment.

Every ad is affected by two forces: the other messages surrounding it, and the editorial environment it appears in.

This editorial and advertising rub-off, separately and together, has the ability to add quality, credibility and integrity to a message. Or subtract from it.

Which is why these times demand The Times. Its editorial environment contrib-utes to every message it carries. Elevating it, framing it, separating it from the crowd.

The other messages sharing this environment do the same. For among them, they represent the finest products and services in the world.

So maybe, after all these years, McLuhan *was* right. The medium *is* the message.

These times demand The Times.

The New York Times

FIGURE 16-7
Clutter in Advertising
Copyright © by The New York Times Company. Reprinted by permission.

Lead time is needed for placing an ad.

Lead time is the period required by a medium for placing an advertisement. It is shortest for newspapers and longest for telephone directories and magazines. A long lead time means a firm must place its ads up to six months or more in advance and risk incorrect messages in a changing environment. Popular television shows may also require a long lead time because the number of ads they can carry is limited.

In recent years, there have been many media innovations. These include regional editions and special one-sponsor issues (''advertorials'') to revive magazines; newspapers improving their computer skills in placing ads; advertising on cable television; televised commercials in supermarkets, movie theaters, and airplanes; specialized Yellow Pages; more radio stations handling ads in stereo; better quality in outdoor signs; full-length advertising programs on television (such as a one-half program promoting a skin-care system); and a 3-D television ad on the 1989 Super Bowl by Coca-Cola.

Creating Advertisements

Creating advertisements involves content, scheduling, media placement, and variations.

Four fundamental decisions are involved in creating advertisements:

1. Determine message content and devise an ad. Each ad needs a headline or opening that creates consumer interest and copy that presents the message. Content decisions also involve the use of color and illustrations, ad size or length, the source, and the use of symbolism. The role of these factors depends on the firm's goals and resources.[15] Figure 16-8 shows a recent full-page color ad from Häagen-Dazs.
2. Outline a promotion schedule. This should allow for all copy and artwork and be based on the lead time needed for the chosen medium.
3. Specify the location of an ad in a broadcast program or print medium. For men, newspaper placement in the sports section increases readership. Women read the entertainment and food sections more frequently. As costs have risen, more and more companies have become concerned about improved ad placement.[16]
4. Choose how many variations of a basic message to utilize. This depends on the frequency of presentation and the quality of ads.

Multiunit advertising combines two or more products in one ad.

Because of the rising costs of advertising, and firms' interest in maximizing efficiency, it is expected that **multiunit advertising**, whereby two or more company products are included in a single ad, will continue to rise. Multiunit advertising can be used with any type of medium.

Timing Advertisements

Timing involves how often an ad is shown and when to advertise during the year.

Timing advertisements requires two major decisions: how often a particular ad is shown and when to advertise during the year. In the first decision, a firm must balance audience awareness and knowledge versus irritation if it places an ad a number of times in a short period. For example, McDonald's runs its ads repeatedly, but changes them very often.

---

[15] See Jeffrey F. Durgee, ''Understanding Brand Personality,'' *Journal of Consumer Marketing*, Vol. 5 (Summer 1988), pp. 21–25; and Julia M. Collins, ''Image and Advertising,'' *Harvard Business Review*, Vol. 67 (January–February 1989), pp. 93–97.

[16] Ronald Alsop, ''Advertisers See Big Gains in Odd Layouts,'' *Wall Street Journal* (June 29, 1988), p. 25; and Patrick Reilly, ''It's a Fight for Position Among Magazine Ads,'' *Advertising Age* (September 5, 1988), pp. 3, 57.

Here's some uplifting news from the finest ice cream in the world. There's a light way to enjoy the rich pleasures of Häagen-Dazs.

Sorbet & Cream—magical blends of refreshingly light fruit sorbets, gently folded into our creamy Vanilla.

Try Raspberry & Cream. Key Lime & Cream. Orange & Cream. Or our newest creation, Blueberry & Cream, made with wild Maine blueberries. And remember, each of these sweet celebrations has a third fewer calories than our other ice creams. So give yourself a lift today.

Look for Häagen-Dazs Sorbet & Cream at participating Häagen-Dazs Ice Cream Shoppes and at your favorite grocery.

FIGURE 16-8
Message Content
Reprinted by permission.

Second, a firm decides whether to advertise throughout the year or in concentrated periods.[17] Distributed advertising maintains brand recognition, balances sales, and increases sales in nonpeak periods. It is used by most manufacturers and general-merchandise retailers. Massed advertising is concentrated during peak periods, generates short-run consumer enthusiasm, and ignores sales in nonpeak periods. Specialty manufacturers and retailers use this method.

[17] See Andrea Rothman, "Timing Techniques Can Make Small Ad Budgets Seem Bigger," *Wall Street Journal* (February 3, 1989), p. B5.

We're making light of lamb.

American lamb and Sunkist® lemons have come to light.

191 light calories, to be exact. In a 3 oz. serving. A serving that's every bit as succulent, tender and juicy as it is light, healthy, and nutritious.

So, if you'd like to try a whole new way of preparing lamb, using fresh American lamb and fresh Sunkist lemons, try our new tangy Lemon Lamb Marinade.

You'll enhance your dinner table. Without enhancing your waistline.

LEMON LAMB MARINADE
Grated peel and juice of 1 Sunkist lemon
2 tbsp. vegetable oil
1 tbsp. grated onion
1 med. clove garlic, minced
1 tsp. dry rosemary leaves
1 tsp. dry tarragon leaves
1/4 tsp. coarse black pepper
1 boneless American lamb sirloin roast (1-1/4 to 2 lbs.)
1/2 cup chicken broth
2 tsp. cornstarch

In large bowl, combine lemon peel, juice, oil, onion, garlic, herbs and pepper. Add lamb and coat with marinade. Cover; refrigerate 2 hrs. or longer. Turn lamb occasionally. Reserve marinade; roast lamb on rack in shallow baking pan at 350°F for 30-35 min. per lb. or until meat thermometer reads 140-145°F for medium rare. In small saucepan, combine remaining marinade, broth and cornstarch. Cook over low heat; stir until thickened. Pour over sliced lamb. 5 to 8 servings lamb (163 cal/3 oz. serving). 2/3 c. sauce (28 cal/tbsp.).

Sunkist Lemons

©American Lamb Council, Inc. and Sunkist Growers, Inc. 1985. Sunkist and Sunkist, are registered trademarks of Sunkist Growers, Inc.

FIGURE 16-9
A Horizontal Cooperative Advertisement
This ad features Sunkist lemons and fresh American lamb. It is a cooperative effort of Sunkist and the American Lamb Council.
Reprinted by permission.

Other timing considerations include when to advertise new products, when to stop advertising existing products, how to coordinate advertising and other promotional tools, when to change basic themes, and how to space messages throughout the hierarchy-of-effects process.

Considering Cooperative Efforts

To stimulate advertising by channel members and/or to hold down its own advertising budget, a company should consider cooperative efforts. With **cooperative advertising,** two or more companies share the costs of some aspects of advertising.

In a vertical cooperative-advertising agreement, companies at different stages in a distribution channel (such as a manufacturer and a retailer) share costs. In a horizontal cooperative-advertising agreement, two or more independent firms at the same stage in a distribution channel share costs (for example, two retailers). Figure 16-9 shows a horizontal cooperative ad.

Good cooperative agreements state the share of costs paid by each party, the functions and responsibilities of each party, advertisements to be covered, and the basis for termination. They also benefit each participant.

It is estimated that $10 to $12 billion in vertical-cooperative advertising support is made available by manufacturers in the United States annually. However, retailers actually use only about 60 per cent of this amount.[18] The nonuse of cooperative advertising by so many retailers is due to their perceptions of manufacturer inflexibility involving messages and media, the costs of cooperative advertising to retailers, restrictive provisions (such as high minimum purchases to be eligible), and the emphasis on the manufacturer's name in ads. To remedy this, a number of manufacturers are now more flexible in the messages and media they will support, paying for a larger share of advertising costs, easing restrictive provisions, and featuring retailer names more prominently in ads.

*In **cooperative advertising**, costs are shared by channel members.*

Evaluating Success or Failure

A firm should select one or a combination of the general methods for evaluating promotion that were detailed in Chapter 15, remembering that the success or failure of advertising depends on how well it helps the company achieve promotion objectives. Creating customer awareness and increasing sales are two distinct goals; success or failure in attaining them must be measured differently. Furthermore, advertising is extremely difficult to isolate as the single factor leading to a certain image or sales level.

Since 1982, the largest advertising agencies in the United States have voluntarily adhered to several basic principles in measuring the effectiveness of advertising messages. *PACT* (Positioning Advertising Copy Testing) outlines these principles: Only data relevant to the objectives of the advertising under consideration are studied. There must be agreement about how results will be used before analysis is conducted. A combination of measurement methods is desirable because single methods are generally inadequate. Testing is keyed to the consumer's decision process, particularly receiving a stimulus, comprehending a message, and behavior response. The use of repetitious advertising is monitored. When comparing alternative messages, each requires the same degree of support. Biases are to be avoided. Audience sampling is to be carefully specified. Good tests are valid (accurate) and can be repeated with similar results (reliable).

Evaluation must relate results to goals.

---

[18] Leslie Brennan, ''How Retailers Are Putting It All Together,'' *Sales & Marketing Management* (May 1988), pp. 62–64.

Following are a variety of examples dealing with the evaluation of advertising success or failure:

▶ The typical U.S. consumer is bombarded with 5,000 advertising messages each day (via traditional advertising media as well as brief messages on parking meters, piped-in radio music at work, and so on). Yet, according to one study, consumers remember only 1 to 3 per cent of these messages when surveyed with unaided recall.[19]

▶ "Popular advertisements — the ads that are well-liked by the ad industry, hailed in the press, and recalled most frequently in audience surveys — don't always work. They may provoke smiles and laughter or warm memories of wonderfully human moments, but they frequently do not increase sales. It is an important lesson for the corporate executive who is reviewing the latest efforts from the company's advertising agency."[20]

▶ Research shows that 15-second television commercials are about 70 to 75 per cent as effective as 30-second commercials in getting a basic message across to the audience. However, they are not as effective for new products, complex messages, and setting moods or imagery.[21]

▶ In measuring the effectiveness of its industrial advertising, IBM employs an in-house research department. It uses a detailed "campaign research measurement model" that includes a mix of pretests and posttests. IBM also monitors the advertising of more than 300 competitors in about 20 business areas. All data are filed in a marketing information system.[22]

▶ Among women, the most popular newspaper ads involve restaurants, shoes and apparel, supermarkets, furniture, and jewelry. Among men, the most popular newspaper ads involve restaurants, tires and batteries, sporting goods, apparel, and financial services.[23]

The Scope and Importance of Publicity

Publicity can have a major impact on a firm.

Every company would like to receive favorable publicity about its offerings or the company itself, such as "This television reporter rates Panasonic portable color televisions as a superior effort" or "State Farm Insurance is considered one of the five best homeowners' insurance firms by this magazine." In some cases, such as restaurant reviews, publicity can greatly increase sales or virtually put a firm out of business. As one restaurant owner noted: "Do you know how many restaurants there are in New York? Someone has to justify your existence."[24]

Accordingly, the competition for publicity is intense. After all, there are only four national television networks (ABC, CBS, NBC, and PBS) and a few national periodi-

---

[19] Alison Leigh Cowan, "Ad Clutter: Even in Restrooms Now," *New York Times* (February 18, 1988), pp. D1, D19.

[20] Edward F. Cone, "Terrific! I Hate It," *Forbes* (June 27, 1988), p. 130.

[21] Verne Gay, "Premiums on :15s Attacked," *Advertising Age* (December 5, 1988), pp. 3, 63.

[22] Byron G. Quahn, "How IBM Assesses Its Business-to-Business Advertising," *Business Marketing* (January 1985), pp. 106–112.

[23] Leo Bogart and B. Stuart Tolley, "The Search for Information in Newspaper Advertising," *Journal of Advertising Research,* Vol. 28 (April–May 1988), p. 10.

[24] Trish Hall, "Who Matters Most to Any Restaurant? Hint: Not the Chef," *Wall Street Journal* (April 10, 1985), p. 23.

TABLE 16-8 Publicity-Related Situations and How a Firm Could Respond to Them

Situation	Poor Response	Good Response
Fire breaks out in a company plant	Requests for information by media are ignored.	Company spokesperson explains the cause of the fire and company precautions to avoid it and answers questions.
New product introduced	Advertising is used without publicity.	Preintroduction news releases, product samples, and testimonials are used.
News story about product defects	Requests for information by media are ignored, blanket denials are issued, hostility is exhibited toward reporter of story.	Company spokesperson states that tests are being conducted on products, describes procedure for handling defects, and answers questions.
Competitor introduces new product	The advertising campaign is stepped up.	Extensive news releases, statistics, and spokespeople are made available to media to present company's competitive features.
High profits reported	Profits are rationalized and positive effects on the economy are cited.	Profitability is explained, data (historical and current) are provided, uses of profits are detailed: such as research and community development.
Overall view of publicity	There is an infrequent need for publicity; crisis fighting is used when bad reports are circulated.	There is an ongoing need for publicity, strong planning, and contingency plans to counter bad reports.

cals. It is difficult to make the network news. However, there are numerous opportunities for publicity because there are nearly 5,000 AM radio stations, over 4,000 FM radio stations, 1,300 conventional television stations, 9,000 newspapers, and 11,000 periodicals located throughout the United States.[25] In addition, the number of cable television stations is rising rapidly.

Unfortunately many firms have poor or ineffective policies for dealing with the independent media or developing a sustained publicity campaign. Table 16-8 shows a variety of publicity-related situations and the alternative ways a firm could deal with them. From this table, it should be clear that unfavorable as well as favorable publicity can occur and the firm must be prepared to handle it in the best way possible. Negative publicity can happen to any company, but the successful one will have a contingency plan to handle it.[26]

---

[25] *Statistical Abstract of the United States,* 1988.
[26] See R. Eric Reidenbach and Dan L. Sherrell, "Negative Press: Is Your Company Prepared?" *Business,* Vol. 36 (January–March 1986), pp. 3–10; Tina Beaudoin, "Bad P.R. 101," *Management Review* (December 1988), pp. 44–48; Minda Zetlin, "Meet the Press—and Survive," *Management Review* (December 1988), pp. 35–40; and Stratford P. Sherman, "Smart Ways to Handle the Press," *Fortune* (June 19, 1989), pp. 69–75.

Public relations is image-directed—paid or nonpaid. Publicity is nonpaid and may be demand- or image-oriented.

It is important for the relationship of advertising, public relations, and publicity to be understood. Advertising is paid mass communication that is demand- or image-directed. *Public relations* is mass and personal communication that is image-directed. Such communication may be paid or nonpaid. Public relations efforts include institutional advertising, publicity, and personal appearances (which may be classified as either personal selling or sales promotion, depending on the situation) to enhance a firm's image. Publicity is nonpaid mass communication that is demand- or image-directed. Figure 16-10 contains examples of the three concepts.

The Characteristics of Publicity

Publicity has no time costs, a large audience, high credibility, and attentiveness.

Publicity offers several benefits. There are no costs for message time or space. An ad in prime-time television may cost $250,000 to $500,000 or more per minute for media time, whereas a five-minute report on a network newscast would not cost anything for media time. However, there are costs for news releases, a publicity department, and other items. As with advertising, publicity reaches a mass audience. Within a short time, new products or company policies are widely known.

Credibility about messages is generally high because they are reported in independent media. A newspaper review of a movie has more believability than an ad in the same paper because the reader associates independence with objectivity. Similarly, people are more likely to pay attention to news reports than to ads. For example, *Women's Wear Daily* has both fashion reports and advertisements. Readers spend

FIGURE 16-10 **The Relationship of Advertising, Public Relations, and Publicity**

Concept	Examples	
Advertising	An ad for Goodyear tires (paid, demand-directed)	
	An ad showing the growth of the Goodyear Tire & Rubber Company (paid, image-directed)	The same ad may be both advertising and public relations.
Public relations	An ad showing the growth of the Goodyear Tire & Rubber Company (paid, image-directed)	
	A speech at a local college by a representative of the Goodyear Tire & Rubber Company (personal contact, image-directed)	
	A report on the local news about the success of the Goodyear Tire & Rubber Company (nonpaid, image-directed)	The same news story may be both public relations and publicity.
Publicity	A report on the local news about the success of the Goodyear Tire & Rubber Company (nonpaid, image-directed)	
	A newspaper article on the durability of Goodyear tires (nonpaid, demand-directed)	

Marketing Controversy

What Should the Roles of Business and the Media Be to One Another?

Often the relationship between business and the media is adversarial. Companies are interested in receiving favorable publicity. Thus they would like the media to print or air their publicity releases as written; and they may refuse to comment (or say as little as possible) when situations that could receive negative publicity arise. Yet the media want to control the information in the stories they cover and to attract a sizable audience. Hence they may interview company critics (as well as advocates) and focus on sensational issues.

Nonetheless there are benefits for business, the media, and the general public if a more cooperative relationship between business and the media can be fostered. Such a relationship could give a firm more exposure, result in more accurate reporting by the media, and lead to more information for the general public. Business and the media need to understand each other better for greater cooperation to occur.

The media would like companies to

▶ *Answer questions in a clear, honest manner.*
▶ *Provide informed spokespersons.*
▶ *Not make unreasonable demands, such as holding up publication, omitting relevant data, or allowing company personnel to review and edit stories prior to publication.*

Companies would like the media to:

▶ *Train reporters and editors regarding their responsibilities to business (such as the need to provide sufficient notice for an interview and to verify data prior to publication).*
▶ *Give reporters sufficient time in their assignments so that they can develop two-way relationships with important businesspeople.*
▶ *Use factual data in stories and avoid data from unreliable sources and rumors.*
▶ *Allow businesses to present rebuttals to stories in the media.*
▶ *Encourage reporters to check all sides of a story prior to publication.*

What do you think?

SOURCE: Based on material in David Crawley, ''Business and the Media: Allies or Adversaries?'' *Management Review* (December 1988), pp. 32–34.

---

time reading the stories, but they flip through the ads. Furthermore, there may be 10 to 20 commercials during a half-hour television program or hundreds of ads in a magazine. Feature stories are much fewer in number and stand out more clearly.

Publicity also has some significant limitations compared to other promotional forms. A firm has less control over messages, their timing, their placement, and their coverage by a given medium. It may issue detailed news releases and find only portions cited by the media; and media have the ability to be much more critical than a firm would like. Media often find disasters (fires, car crashes, product side effects) more newsworthy than routine statements distributed by the firm.

Publicity cannot be controlled or timed accurately by the firm.

For example, in 1982, Procter & Gamble (P&G) faced a substantial publicity problem over the meaning of its 123-year-old company logo. A few ministers and other private citizens believed that the symbol was sacrilegious. These beliefs were covered extensively by the media and resulted in the firm receiving 15,000 phone calls about the rumor in June alone. To combat this negative publicity, P&G issued news releases featuring prominent clergy (such as Jerry Falwell) that refuted the rumors, threatened to sue those people spreading the stories, and had a spokesperson appear on *Good Morning America.* The media cooperated with the company and the false rumors were temporarily put to rest. However, in 1985, negative publicity became so disruptive that Procter & Gamble decided to remove the logo from its products.[27]

A firm may want publicity during certain periods, such as when a new product is introduced or a new store opened, but the media may not cover the introduction or opening until after the time it would aid the firm. Similarly, media determine the placement of a story; it may follow a report on crime or sports. Finally, the media ascertain whether to cover a story at all and the amount of coverage to be devoted to it. A company-sponsored jobs program might go unreported or receive three-sentence coverage in a local newspaper.

Sometimes it is difficult to plan publicity in advance because newsworthy happenings take can place quickly and unexpectedly. Therefore, short-run and long-run plans should be quite different in their specificity. Also, publicity needs to be viewed as complementary to advertising and not a substitute for it. The characteristics of each (credibility and low costs for publicity, control and coverage for advertising) are needed for an effective communications program.

To improve their control over the publicity they receive, more and more firms are now enacting well-conceived plans to manage their efforts in this area. For example, at many companies

Many firms now have plans to manage publicity efforts.

▶ Public relations/publicity personnel have access to senior executives and meet with them on a regular basis.
▶ The publicity value of annual reports is recognized.
▶ Written, oral, video, and/or other types of company communications are professionally prepared (with the same care used in writing ad copy) and given to the media on a continuous basis.
▶ Contacts between internal personnel and media personnel are encouraged.
▶ Public-service events are planned to obtain maximum media coverage.
▶ A portion of the promotion budget is allocated to publicity-generating activities.
▶ There is a better understanding of the kinds of stories that the media are likely to cover and how to present appropriate stories to the media.

Developing a Publicity Plan

Developing a publicity plan is much like developing an advertising plan. It involves the steps shown in Figure 16-11 and described in the following subsections.

Setting Objectives

The objectives of publicity are the same as those for advertising — they are demand-oriented (information, persuasion, reminding) and image-oriented (industry, company). The choice of objectives guides the entire publicity plan.

These are some of the publicity objectives that could be sought:

[27] Laurie Freeman, "After Devil of Fight, P&G Gives Up," *Advertising Age* (April 29, 1985), pp. 3, 100; and R. Eric Reidenbach, Troy A. Festervand, and Michael MacWilliam, "Effective Corporate Response to Negative Publicity," *Business,* Vol. 37 (October–December 1987), pp. 9–17.

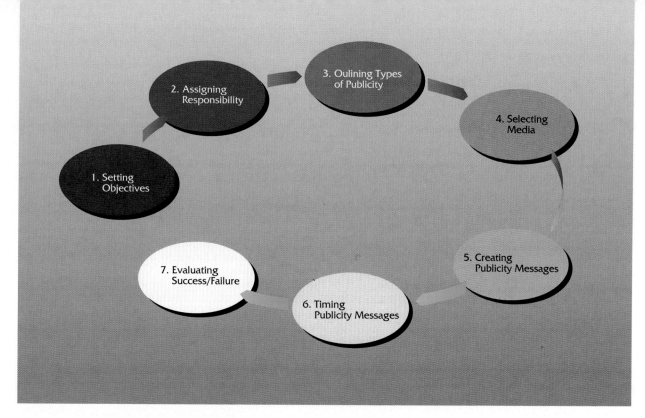

FIGURE 16-11 **Developing a Publicity Plan**

▶ To gain placement for news releases and company spokespersons in a variety of media.
▶ To have media report on the company in a favorable light.
▶ To have the company's position presented when controversy arises.
▶ To coordinate publicity with advertising.
▶ To gain more media coverage than competitors.
▶ To sustain favorable publicity as long as possible.

Assigning Responsibility

A firm has three options for assigning publicity responsibility: it may use its existing marketing personnel, employ an in-house public relations department, or employ an in-house publicity department to enact the entire publicity plan; it may have its outside advertising agency handle publicity; or it may hire a specialized public relations or publicity firm. Internal personnel or an in-house department ensure greater secrecy until releases are distributed. The outside firm has better contacts and expertise. Each approach is popular; and they may be combined.

A firm can use an in-house department, hire an outside ad agency, or hire a specialist.

For example, Procter & Gamble employs an in-house publicity department as well as several outside public relations agencies. On the other hand, smaller firms can rely on the services of specialists, such as Emergency PR Subscriber Service which handles emergency situations for clients for an annual fee of about $1,000 (this provides ten hours of consultation).[28]

[28] Laurie Freeman and Nancy Giges, "P&G Licking Its Wounds with PR Revamp," *Advertising Age* (September 16, 1985), p. 28; and Laurie Freeman, "Service Fielding PR Alarms," *Advertising Age* (October 8, 1984), p. 82.

TABLE 16-9 Types of Publicity

Publicity Type	Example
News publicity	Sears describes its decision to emphasize everyday low pricing throughout its stores, a radical change in strategy.
Business feature article	Kodak explains its goals and objectives for the 1990s.
Service feature article	A trade association offers 10 tips on how to reduce home heating costs.
Finance release	E.F. Hutton distributes quarterly financial data about the company.
Product release	Fuji announces its new fast-speed film.
Pictorial release	IBM distributes photos showing all of its personal computer products and related software.
Background editorial release	The Limited presents a biography of its president and her rise through the company.
Emergency publicity	The Red Cross makes a request for aid to tornado victims.

Outlining the Types of Publicity to Be Used

Publicity types involve news, features, releases, background material, and emergency information.

There are several general **publicity types** available to a firm, as shown in Table 16-9.[29] Each of the types can play a role in a good, well-integrated publicity program. News publicity deals with events of national, regional, or local interest. Planned news releases are those prepared and distributed by the firm on a regular basis.

Business feature articles are detailed stories about the company or its offerings that are distributed to business media. Service feature articles are lighter stories that focus on personal care, household items, and recipes and are distributed to newspapers and magazines. Finance releases are stories aimed at the business sections of newspapers and magazines. Product releases deal with new products and product improvements. They are aimed at all forms of media.

Pictorial releases are illustrations or pictures supplied to media. Background editorial material is extra information provided to media writers and editors; it enhances standard releases and provides filler for stories (such as the biography of the chief executive of the company). Emergency publicity consists of special spontaneous news releases keyed to disasters or serious problems.

Selecting the Media for Publicity to Appear

The firm next considers the media to which to target its publicity-generating efforts. It would generally choose from among newspapers, television, magazines, radio, and business publications. But, because of the infrequent nature of many magazines and some business publications, publicity-seeking efforts are often aimed at those media that appear daily or weekly.

A recent survey of public relations executives' attitudes regarding media found that

▶ Newspapers and business publications are ranked highest.
▶ The *Wall Street Journal*, *New York Times*, and *USA Today* are the most desirable newspapers.
▶ *Business Week*, *Fortune*, and *Forbes* are the preferred business publications.

[29] H. Frazier Moore, *Public Relations: Principles, Cases, and Problems,* Eighth Edition (Homewood, Ill.: Richard D. Irwin, 1981), pp. 163–167.

▶ *Time*, *Newsweek*, and *U.S. News & World Report* are the preferred general news magazines.[30]

Creating Publicity Messages

Creating publicity messages involves the same factors as in advertising—message content, message variations, and a production schedule. Publicity messages can be conveyed in one or a combination of forms: news conference, press or news release, phone calls or personal contacts, press kit (a combination of materials about a story), special events (Macy's Thanksgiving Parade, an appearance on the *Today* show), or films.

Timing Publicity Messages

Publicity should precede the introduction of new products and generate excitement for them. For emergencies, press releases and spokespeople should be immediately available. For ongoing publicity, messages should be properly spaced throughout the year. As noted previously, a company may have difficulty anticipating both unexpected and planned publicity because the media control timing.

Evaluating Success or Failure

There are several straightforward methods for evaluating the success or failure of a publicity campaign. The firm can count the media covering each story, analyze the length and placement of coverage, correlate desired with actual timing, evaluate audience reactions to publicity (in terms of awareness, image, sales, and so on), and/or compute the cost of comparable advertising.

Several techniques exist for assessing publicity efforts.

For example, to generate substantial favorable publicity as a skin-care specialist, Westwood Pharmaceuticals (a division of Bristol-Myers and the maker of Keri skin-care products) undertook a multiyear effort to gather meaningful information that the media would cover extensively. It devised a landmark study, "The Keri Report: Confidence and the American Woman," and collected data from more than 1,000 people. In its 124-page report on this study, Westwood cited a number of key overall findings (such as the relation between age and confidence) as well as several relating to skin care—for instance, "there is a direct correlation between how people feel about their appearance and their overall sense of confidence. This includes using body lotion and facial moisturizers."

The Keri report was released at a press conference attended by over 80 media representatives and the leaders of various women's organizations. In addition, each major finding was distributed to the media as a separate news release, and a videocassette on women and confidence was distributed to television stations nationwide. As a result, articles appeared in hundreds of newspapers and magazines (including *Vogue*, *Working Woman*, and *Self*). Radio and television stories appeared in dozens of cities. A news short was shown in upscale movie theaters. Overall, within months of its release, millions of potential customers were familiar with the Keri report, thus "creating high brand awareness among consumers and establishing a solid foundation for the next several years."[31]

---

[30] Jack Bernstein, "PR Execs Pick Favored Media," *Advertising Age* (October 31, 1988), p. 12.
[31] David Finn, "Creative PR Can Help Position a Brand," *Marketing News* (December 5, 1988), p. 18.

511

Summary

1. *To examine the scope, importance, and characteristics of advertising*   Advertising is paid, nonpersonal communication transmitted through various media by identified sponsors. U.S. advertising expenditures annually exceed $125 billion through such media as newspapers, magazines, farm publications, television, radio, direct mail, business publications, and outdoor. In most industries, advertising is 4.0 per cent or less of sales.

   Advertising is most appropriate for standardized products and when features are easy to communicate, there is a large target market, prices are low, middlemen are used in distribution, and/or products are new. In general, behavior is easier to change than attitudes; recall is a weak measure of advertising effectiveness; one ad can have a strong impact; ads are more effective for little-known products; and effectiveness rises during extended campaigns.

   Among the advantages of advertising are its appeal to a large and geographically dispersed audience, the low per customer costs, the availability of a broad variety of media, the firm's control over all aspects of a message, the surrounding editorial content, and how it complements personal selling. Disadvantages include the inflexibility of messages, wasted viewers or readers, high media costs, limited information provided, difficulty in obtaining audience feedback, and low audience involvement.

2. *To study the elements in an advertising plan*   An advertising plan has these nine steps: setting objectives — which fall into demand and image types; assigning responsibility — internally and/or externally; establishing a budget; developing themes — which fall into good/service, consumer, and institutional categories; selecting media — based on costs, reach, waste, narrowcasting, frequency, message permanence, persuasive impact, clutter, and lead time; creating advertisements — including message content, placement, and variations; timing advertisements; considering cooperative efforts — both vertical and horizontal; and evaluating success or failure.

3. *To examine the scope, importance, and characteristics of publicity*   Publicity is nonpersonal communication transmitted through various media but not paid for by identified sponsors. Firms seek to obtain favorable publicity and avoid or minimize negative publicity. Competition is intense for publicity releases. Many firms have poor or ineffective policies for dealing with independent media or developing a sustained publicity campaign.

   Public relations is mass and personal communication that is image-directed, both paid and nonpaid. It consists of institutional advertising, publicity, and personal appearances used to enhance a firm's image.

   Among publicity's advantages are the absence of costs for message time and content, the mass audience, the high level of credibility, and audience attentiveness. The disadvantages of publicity compared with other forms of promotion include the lesser control by the firm, the media interest in negative events, and the difficulty of planning in advance.

4. *To study the elements in a publicity plan*   A publicity plan has these seven steps: setting objectives — demand and/or image; assigning responsibility — internally and/or externally; outlining types of publicity — categorized as news publicity, business and service feature articles, finance releases, product and pictorial releases, background editorial releases, and emergency publicity; selecting media — from among newspapers, television, magazines, radio, and business publications; creating publicity messages; timing publicity messages; and evaluating success/failure.

Key Terms

advertising agency (p. 490)
advertising themes (p. 493)
advertising media costs (p. 495)
reach (p. 495)
waste (p. 496)

narrowcasting (p. 496)
frequency (p. 497)
message permanence (p. 497)
persuasive impact (p. 497)
clutter (p. 498)

lead time (p. 500)
multiunit advertising (p. 500)
cooperative advertising (p. 503)
public relations (p. 506)
publicity types (p. 510)

Review Questions

1. Explain the statement "Advertising is paid for, publicity is prayed for."

2. Under what circumstances is advertising most likely to be used?

3. List five objectives of advertising and give an example of how each may be accomplished.

4. A firm has an overall annual budget of $50,000 for advertising. What specific decisions must it make in allocating the budget?

5. Describe the concept of narrowcasting and the trade-offs involved when using it.

6. What are the pros and cons of cooperative advertising?

7. Distinguish between publicity and public relations.

8. What is a service feature article?

9. According to public relations executives, which are the two most preferred media for receiving publicity?

10. State three ways for a firm to evaluate the success or failure of its publicity efforts.

Discussion Questions

1. Devise an advertising plan for generating primary demand for American automobiles.

2. A food-processor manufacturer has determined that a full-page ad in a general-interest magazine would cost $50,000; the magazine's total audience is 3 million, of which 750,000 are potential consumers of a food processor. A full-page ad in a food magazine would cost $25,000; its total audience is 400,000, of which 325,000 are potential consumers. Which magazine should be selected? Why?

3. Present and evaluate an example of a company using advertising, public relations, and publicity.

4. Why do you think so many firms handle publicity situations poorly?

5. How would you obtain publicity for a small company that has developed a safe noncaloric sweetener to compete with aspartame and saccharin?

◀ CASE 1 ▶

How the Furniture Industry Advertises*

According to critics, until recently both furniture manufacturers and retailers made unsatisfactory attempts to develop brand recognition and brand loyalty and to persuade consumers that furniture—like clothing—could go out of fashion. Too many ads by furniture makers could be classified as "me too" or "look-alike" in nature, and too many retailer ads featured price to the exclusion of style.

The president of the Home Furnishings Council, a trade association, believes that firms "in the furniture industry went to sleep fifty years ago." And the recently retired president of a leading furniture maker adds that, "We have been overplaying that business of furniture lasting a lifetime. Even though it might not be be worn out, furniture can be just as outdated as a Cadillac with high fins."

Because of ineffectual marketing efforts, the furniture industry faces these problems:

▷ Annual U.S. sales have been increasing slowly. For instance, 1988 revenues were up only 2.4 per cent from 1987.

▷ The share of Americans' disposable income that is spent on furniture has decreased since the 1960s.

▷ One recent marketing research study reported that most consumers consider furniture to be "dull and expensive," and that they could easily postpone the purchase of furniture.

▷ Another research study found that two-thirds of consumers believe that most furniture ads look alike.

▷ There is still poor brand recognition and differentiation of furniture.

---

* The data in this case are drawn from Ronald Alsop, "Furniture Marketers Pull at Heartstrings in New Ads," *Wall Street Journal* (January 3, 1989), pp. B1, B3.

In response, the U.S. furniture industry sees the current climate as an ideal one for changing its advertising emphasis. Baby boomers are entering their heavy spending years; and some research suggests that this group is spending more leisure time at home than ever before—due in part to home entertainment innovations (such as cable television, videocassette recorders, and compact disc players) and the increased number of female working women.

Several leading furniture makers are raising their advertising expenditures, developing more creative ads, and attempting to reposition furniture as a lifestyle purchase rather than a long-term investment or as a permanent fixture in the home. Furniture marketers hope to persuade people to redecorate their homes more often and to view home furnishings as a fashion item. "People need to feel they're creatively designing space when they buy furniture. People see furniture as something permanent they're stuck with. It doesn't allow for personal growth," said a cultural anthropologist.

Among the major furniture advertisers with a more enlightened view of advertising are La-Z-Boy Chair and Thomasville Furniture. La-Z-Boy Chair used to feature such chair construction components as hardwood frames and foam cushions in their advertisements. In one current ad, the company shows a young father pacing the floor at night humming a tune to his baby. The ad states: "Nobody has rocked more babies to sleep than we have." The La-Z-Boy name flashes on the screen, and the father whispers, "Night, night, angel." As the creative director for La-Z-Boy's advertising agency said, "We wanted to get away from a direct hard-hitting approach and just sell warm feelings." Thomasville Furniture claims to have developed the first national television campaign for a full-line furniture company. It has spent about $10 million to implement the campaign. While this amount may seem low in comparison to ad budgets in other industries, it is a high level considering that the entire furniture industry (both manufacturers and retailers) has been spending about $30 million yearly on advertising.

To complement the heightened marketing efforts in the furniture industry, one marketing analyst predicts that furniture stores will soon begin to accept used furniture in a manner similar to that whereby a car dealer accepts used cars as trade-ins toward new-car purchases: "To encourage consumers to buy new furniture, you have to create a perception of residual value in their existing furniture. How often would people trade in cars if they could only have Goodwill pick up their old ones?"

QUESTIONS

1. Develop a series of advertising objectives for La-Z-Boy Chair.
2. Evaluate Thomasville Furniture's planned $10 million advertising expenditure level.
3. What criteria should Thomasville utilize in selecting media for its advertising campaign? Explain your answer.
4. Should La-Z-Boy and Thomasville offer cooperative advertising to retailers? Why or why not?

◀ CASE 2 ▶

The Suzuki Samurai: Dealing With Negative Publicity†

The July 1988 issue of *Consumer Reports* stated that:

† The data in this case are drawn from Michael de Courcy Hinds, "Only a Price Cut Gave Samurai a Push," *New York Times* (December 12, 1988), p. 52; and Stewart Toy, "Will Samurai Marketing Work for Suzuki?" *Business Week* (July 27, 1988), pp. 33–34.

In our judgment, the *Suzuki Samurai* is so likely to roll over during a maneuver that could be demanded of any car at any time that it is unfit for its intended use. We therefore judge it Not Acceptable.

This conclusion was made public at a June 2, 1988, news conference by Consumers Union (CU), the publisher of *Consumer Reports*.

Consumers Union conducted road tests of the four best-selling sport utility vehicles in the United States: the Jeep Cherokee, Isuzu Trooper II, Jeep Wrangler, and Suzuki Samurai. Each had handling characteristics evaluated. During one stage of testing, the Samurai (smaller and lighter than the other vehicles tested) started to roll over when the driver dodged an obstruction. Then, on a slower, but more difficult, course the Samurai rolled over "enough times to know it wasn't a freak accident." As a result, the Samurai was the first vehicle in a decade to be rated not acceptable by CU. And, almost instantly, its findings were discussed on television and radio broadcasts and in print stories around the country.

American Suzuki Motor Corporation (a subsidiary of the parent Japanese firm) believed it had to defend its reputation against CU's charges, particularly with the Samurai being the mainstay of its business. However, it encountered difficulties in developing and implementing an appropriate strategy to deal with such intense negative publicity.

For example, Suzuki learned of CU's rating only 12 hours in advance of the CU press conference. No one on Suzuki's crisis-planning team knew what CU's charges would be. And, although Suzuki's general manager purchased advertising time on the major television networks' news shows the evening that CU released its findings and arranged a satellite hookup to communicate the company's response, the only network that accepted the advertising was ABC.

But Suzuki executives were not discouraged by these events; they simply stepped up their efforts to instill consumer faith in the Samurai:

▷ The company pulled its "Born to Be Wild" ads immediately following CU's public announcement and replaced them with a campaign titled "Quotes," focusing on positive statements about the Samurai that had been published in auto specialty magazines. Those ads, which appeared frequently over the ten-day period following CU's announcement, cost Suzuki about $1.5 million. This was in addition to its original advertising budget of $22 million: "It's expensive, but what choice is there?"

▷ Suzuki's advertising agency conducted weekly consumer surveys. Right after the CU news conference, about 40 per cent of respondents easily identified Suzuki as "an auto company with a safety problem." An additional 20 per cent identified the firm from a list of car manufacturers as having a safety problem. Suzuki planned to continue the special advertising campaign until its negative association with car safety subsided: "We're not going to sit back and hope this crisis will go away."

▷ To increase Samurai's sales, which slid from over 5,000 units per month prior to CU's announcement to 2,000 units in June 1988, Suzuki instituted a $2,000 rebate program. Although 18,500 Samurais were sold over the six-week period from mid-July through August, sales slowed to fewer than 1,000 cars per month when the rebate ended. Apparently a September finding by the National Highway Traffic Safety Administration that "the rollover crash involvement of the Samurai appears to be within the range of most other light utility vehicles" did not have any major positive effect on sales.

Despite Suzuki's aggressive marketing efforts, a senior analyst for an auto-based marketing research firm summarized the feelings held by many, "I'm confident the Samurai will be out of the market by the end of the 1991 model year, or sooner if sales do not pick up quickly."

QUESTIONS

1. Evaluate Suzuki's overall response to the negative publicity it received.
2. Cite and discuss at least two other approaches that Suzuki could have taken after Consumers Union presented its findings.
3. Develop a flowchart of activities that Suzuki should follow the next time it receives adverse publicity.
4. In responding to negative publicity, what are the proper roles for advertising, public relations, and company publicity releases?

CHAPTER *17*

Personal Selling and Sales Promotion

CHAPTER OBJECTIVES

1. To examine the scope, importance, and characteristics of personal selling

2. To study the elements in a personal selling plan: objectives, responsibility, budget, type(s) of sales positions, sales techniques, sales tasks, and implementation

3. To examine the scope, importance, and characteristics of sales promotion

4. To study the elements in a sales promotion plan: objectives, responsibility, overall plan, types of sales promotion, coordination, and evaluation of success or failure

Reprinted by permission.

When Alexander Graham Bell invented the telephone over 100 years ago, he could not possibly have envisioned the impact it would have on the business world today.

According to one telemarketing consultant, "You can sell almost anything by telemarketing if you set it up properly, get the right people, train them right, and have a good follow through."

Let us look at what telemarketing is and why it is growing in popularity. Telemarketing involves the use of a telephone to sell or solicit business or to set up an appointment for a salesperson to sell or solicit business. According to the American Telemarketing Association, U.S. sales from telemarketing have more than doubled since 1983 and there are now over three million telemarketing personnel.

There are many factors behind the growth in telemarketing: its efficiency, its ability to tailor presentations to accounts, its use in conjunction with salesperson visits, and the new computerized auto-dialers with prerecorded messages.

Telemarketing is an efficient means of reaching prospects with low sales potential, or those in rural areas. This is particularly important if we consider that the average cost of a single business-to-business sales visit is over $250, and that multiple visits may be needed to make a sale.

Unlike catalogs, which are also used by many marketers to reach small accounts or those in rural areas, telemarketing allows firms to answer questions and to tailor presentations for particular prospects.

Telemarketing can be used in conjunction with traditional salesperson visits. For example, a firm may use telemarketing to generate sales leads. Telemarketing consultants assert that while direct mail may bring in a response rate of between 1 to 2 per cent, the response rate for telemarketing can be as high as 10 to 20 per cent if telemarketing calls are followed up by salesperson visits.

Computerized auto-dialers with prerecorded messages allow telemarketers to reach a large number of households at a low cost. Furthermore, although telemarketing personnel often find it difficult to endure the boredom and rejection beyond four hours at a time on the telephone, computerized auto-dialers do not require rest and do not feel rejected.

Among the firms successfully using telemarketing are Citicorp, Dell Computer, and Tech America:

► When Citicorp introduced a new mortgage program in the Baltimore area, the firm realized that it was not well known outside of the New York area. Its telemarketing program enabled bank personnel to explain the complicated new program as well as respond to client questions.

► Dell Computer is a manufacturer that makes half of its sales to large firms; the balance is made to smaller companies and final consumers. It uses a field sales force for large accounts and relies on telephone orders from smaller accounts and final consumers. Dell also uses telemarketing to contact large accounts that have not placed recent orders.

► Tech America is a pharmaceuticals firm that uses telemarketing to introduce new diagnostic products to office-based veterinarians as well as to private and government laboratories.[1]

In this chapter, we will study both the personal selling and sales promotion aspects of promotion and see how these tools can be used effectively and efficiently. As a form of personal selling, telemarketing represents just one of the topics we will discuss in Chapter 17.

[1] Ernan Roman, "The Newest Member of the Media Mix," *Marketing Communications* (June 1987), pp. 72–75; Bill Kelley, "Is There *Anything* That Can't Be Sold by Phone?" *Sales & Marketing Management* (April 1989), pp. 60–64; and Joel Kotkin, "The Innovation Upstarts," *Inc.* (January 1989), pp. 70–76.

Overview

Personal selling uses one-to-one interaction with buyers. Sales promotion includes paid supplemental promotion efforts.

This chapter examines the two other major types of promotion, personal selling and sales promotion. As defined in Chapter 15, personal selling involves oral communication with one or more prospective buyers by paid representatives for the purpose of making sales. Unlike advertising and publicity, selling relies on personal contact. The goals of personal selling are similar to other promotion types: information, persuasion, and/or reminding.

Sales promotion involves the paid marketing communication activities (other than advertising, publicity, or personal selling) that stimulate consumer purchases and dealer effectiveness. Among the aspects of promotion that are classified as sales promotion are samples, coupons, contests, trading stamps, and trade shows.

The scope and importance, characteristics, and planning considerations are covered in this chapter for both personal selling and sales promotion.

The Scope and Importance of Personal Selling

Professional personnel build accounts; clerical personnel complete sales.

In the United States, about 14 million people are employed in the sales positions defined by the Bureau of Labor Statistics. Professional sales personnel generate customer accounts, ascertain needs, interact with consumers, emphasize knowledge as well as persuasion, and provide substantial service. Top salespeople can earn more than $100,000 per year. Examples of professional sales personnel are stockbrokers, manufacturer sales representatives, insurance agents, and real-estate brokers. Clerical sales personnel answer telephone inquiries, obtain stock from inventory, recommend the best brand in a product category, and complete transactions by receiving payments and packing products. Examples are retail, wholesale, and manufacturer sales clerks.

Yet, personal selling really goes far beyond the 14 million people identified in sales positions because every contact between a company representative and a current or potential customer entails some degree of personal interaction. For example, lawyers, plumbers, hairdressers, and cashiers are not defined as sales personnel. But, each occupation involves a great degree of customer contact. At Albertson's, the importance of customer contact is recognized. See Figure 17-1.

Selling is stressed when orders are large, consumers are concentrated, items are expensive, service is required, and so on.

In a variety of situations, a strong emphasis on personal selling is usually needed. Large-volume customers require special attention and handling. Geographically concentrated consumers may be more efficiently served by a sales force than through advertisements in mass media. Custom-made, expensive, and/or complex goods or services require detailed consumer information, demonstrations, and follow-up calls. Tangential sales services — such as gift wrapping, delivery, and installation — may be requested. If ads do not provide enough information, questions can be resolved only through personal selling. New products may require personal selling to gain middleman acceptance. Finally, organizational customers expect a high level of personal contact and service. In general, the decision to stress personal selling rather than other promotion tools should be based on such factors as costs, audience size, audience needs, and the desire for flexibility.

High selling costs have led to a concern for efficiency.

The costs of personal selling are much greater than advertising for many companies. For example, on average, automotive parts and accessories firms, office and equipment firms, and appliance makers spend two to three times as much or more on

FIGURE 17-1
**The Importance of
Customer Contact**
Albertson's places a high
value on all employee-
consumer contacts:
"Helpful friendly service
throughout the store,"
and "We go out of our
way for you."
Reprinted by permission.

personal selling as on advertising. A Fuller Brush salesperson earns commissions ranging up to 50 per cent of sales. The average cost of a single business-to-business field sales call is well over $250; and in some cases, it takes several visits to complete a sale.[2]

A number of strategies have been developed to keep selling costs down and improve sales force efficiency, as these examples show:

▶ Because such personal selling costs as transportation, hotel, and compensation are so high, many firms are emphasizing effective routing of sales personnel to minimize travel time and expenses. Some companies are also bypassing smaller customers in their personal selling efforts and/or specifying minimum order sizes for personalized service. This is creating opportunities for other sellers that are offering personal attention for small accounts.

▶ *Telemarketing* is an efficient manner of doing business whereby telephone communications (telecommunications) are used to sell or solicit business or to set up an appointment for a salesperson to sell or solicit business. Through telemarketing, sales personnel can contact seven to twelve final consumers or three to seven organizational consumers per hour, centralize operations and reduce expenses, effectively contact and screen prospects, process orders and arrange shipments, provide customer service and follow-ups, assist the field sales force, speed communications with customers, and increase repeat business. A number of firms now rely on telephone sales personnel to contact customers; their outside sales personnel are more involved with customer service and technical assistance. At present, 80,000 small and large firms use some form of telemarketing.

*In **telemarketing**, phone calls are used to initiate sales or set up salesperson appointments.*

---

[2] *Sales & Marketing Management's 1989 Survey of Selling Costs*; Schonfeld & Associates, "Advertising-to-Sales Ratios, 1988 Estimates (By Industry)," *Advertising Age* (October 24, 1988), p. 49; Ronald Alsop, "Direct-Selling Firms Scramble to Boost Morale, Productivity," *Wall Street Journal* (October 3, 1985), p. 33; and "Average Business-to-Business Sales Call Increases by 9.5%," *Marketing News* (September 12, 1988), p. 5.

FIGURE 17-2
**Computers and
the Sales Force**
At Colgate-Palmolive,
sales personnel are armed
with powerful tools to
move products in the
retail marketplace. For
example, the innovative
use of laptop computers
was a key factor in the
successful launch of
Palmolive shampoo in
Puerto Rico. With the
computer screen,
salespeople are able to
use lively animated
graphics to describe a
product, its benefits, and
Colgate-Palmolive's
supporting campaign.

Copyright Richard Alcorn.
Reprinted by permission.

▶ Computerization is improving the efficiency of both in-store and field sales personnel by providing them with detailed (and speedy) information, making customer
ordering easier, coordinating orders by various salespeople, and identifying the
most lucrative prospects and their characteristics (such as preferred brands, price
range, and so on, based on prior purchases). See Figure 17-2. As an RJR Nabisco
director of sales commented, "The store operator might say, 'O.K., you want me to
buy the coffee that's on special, but what about that order of batteries we're expect-
ing?' If the sales rep can communicate with the home office instantly, using his
[her] laptop computer, and find the status of an order, he [she] might be able to sell
his [her] promotion or at least build the relationship so he [she] can sell it the next
time."[3]

The Characteristics of Personal Selling

*Selling uses a **buyer-seller
dyad** and is flexible,
efficient, closes sales, and
provides feedback.*

On the positive side, personal selling provides individual attention for each consumer
and passes along a lot of information. There is a dynamic, rather than passive, interaction between buyer and seller. This enables a firm to utilize a **buyer-seller dyad**,
which is a two-way flow of communication between both parties.[4] See Figure 17-3.
This is not possible with advertising. As a result, personal selling approaches can be

---

[3] Doron P. Levin, "Moving Beyond Patter and Persistence," *New York Times* (January 1, 1989), Section 3,
p. 6.
[4] See F. Robert Dwyer, Paul H. Schurr, and Sejo Oh, "Developing Buyer-Seller Relationships," *Journal of
Marketing*, Vol. 51 (April 1987), pp. 11-27; and Harvey B. Mackay, "Humanize Your Selling Strategy,"
Harvard Business Review, Vol. 66 (March-April 1988), pp. 36-47.

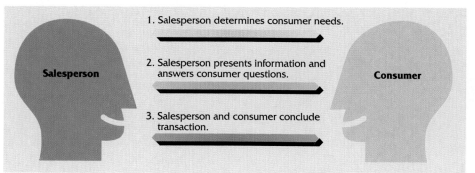

FIGURE 17-3
The Buyer-Seller Dyad

flexible and adapted to the needs of specific consumers. For example, a real-estate broker would use a different sales presentation for a couple buying a home for the first time than for a couple that has previously purchased a home. The salesperson can use as much persuasion as necessary and balance it against the need for information.

There is less waste with most forms of selling than with advertising. Personal selling centers on a more defined and concentrated target market. In addition, customers who walk into a store or who are contacted by a salesperson are more likely to purchase a product than those watching an advertisement on television. Because ads are intended to stimulate consumers, those who make it to the personal selling stage are often key members of the target market. Direct selling, when it is unsolicited, has the highest amount of wasted audience in personal selling.

Personal selling clinches sales and is usually the last stage in the consumer's decision process, taking place after an information search and exposure to advertisements. It holds on to repeat customers and those already convinced by advertising and resolves any doubts or concerns of undecided consumers. Personal selling answers any remaining questions about price, warranty, and other factors. It also settles service issues, such as delivery and installation. Feedback is immediate and clear-cut. Consumers may be asked about company policies or product attributes, or they may register complaints about the firm or its products. Salespeople may be able to determine the strengths and weaknesses of a marketing program, such as a new product's features.

On the negative side, personal selling is an ineffective tool for generating consumer awareness because sales personnel can accommodate only a limited number of consumers. For example, a retail furniture salesperson may be able to handle fewer than 20 consumers per day if the average length of a presentation is 15 minutes to a half hour. Sales personnel who call on customers can handle even fewer accounts, due to travel time. In addition, many consumers attracted by advertising desire self-service. This is discouraged by some aggressive salespeople.

Selling has a limited audience, high per customer costs, and a poor image.

Personal selling costs per customer can be very high. This is because of the one-on-one nature of selling. An in-store furniture salesperson who interacts with 20 customers per day might cost a company $6 per presentation ($120/day compensation divided by 20), an amount much higher than the cost per customer contact for advertising. For outside sales personnel, expenses associated with travel such as hotel, meals, and car rental can easily amount to more than $150 per day per salesperson, and compensation must be added to these costs.

Finally, personal selling, particularly on the retail level, has a poor image in the eyes

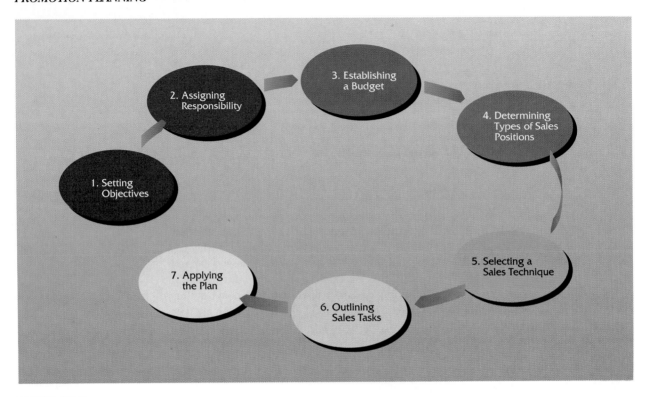

FIGURE 17-4
Developing a Personal Selling Plan

of a number of consumers. It is criticized for a lack of honesty, pressure sales pitches, and pushing consumers to make premature decisions. These criticisms may be overcome by improved sales force training and the use of modern marketing (consumer-oriented) rather than selling (seller-oriented) practices.

Developing a Personal Selling Plan

The development of a personal selling plan can be divided into the seven steps shown in Figure 17-4 and highlighted in the following subsections.

Setting Objectives

Personal selling objectives can be demand- and/or image-oriented. Illustrations of each type appear in Table 17-1. Although many firms have some interest in information, reminding, and image goals for personal selling, the major goal is persuasion: converting consumer interest into a sale.

Assigning Responsibility

A manager must oversee personal selling functions.

The personal selling function may be assigned to a marketing or sales manager who is involved with all aspects of selling, from planning to sales force management.[5] A small

---

[5] See Kevin F. Sullivan, Richard A. Bobbe, and Martin R. Strasmore, "Transforming the Salesforce in a Mature Industry," *Management Review* (June 1988), pp. 46–49.

TABLE 17-1   Specific Personal Selling Objectives

Type of Objective	Illustrations
Demand-Oriented	
Information	To explain fully all good and service attributes To answer any questions To probe for any further questions
Persuasion	To clearly distinguish good or service attributes from those of competitors To maximize the number of sales as a per cent of presentations To convert undecided consumers into buyers To sell complementary items, e.g., film with a camera To placate dissatisfied customers
Reminding	To ensure delivery, installation, etc. To follow up after a good or service has been purchased To follow up when a repurchase is near To reassure previous customers when making a new purchase
Image-Oriented	
Industry and company	To maintain a good appearance by all personnel in contact with consumers To follow acceptable sales practices

or specialized firm would have its marketing manager oversee personal selling or employ one general sales manager. A larger or diversified company usually has several sales managers, classified by geographic area, customer type, and/or product line.

These are the basic responsibilities of a sales manager:

▶ To understand the firm's objectives, strategies, market position, and basic marketing plan and to convey them to the sales force.
▶ To identify a sales philosophy, sales force characteristics, selling tasks, a sales organization, and methods of customer contact.
▶ To develop and update sales forecasts.
▶ To allocate selling resources based on sales forecasts and customer needs.
▶ To select, train, assign, compensate, and supervise sales personnel.
▶ To synchronize sales functions with advertising, product planning, distribution, marketing research, and production.
▶ To assess sales performance by salesperson, product, product line, customer, customer group, and geographic area.
▶ To monitor continuously competitors' actions.

Establishing a Budget

A *sales-expense budget* allocates selling expenditures among salespeople, products, customers, and geographic areas for a given period of time. A budget is usually based on a sales forecast and relates selling tasks to the achievement of sales goals. It should have some flexibility in the event the forecasted sales level is not reached or is exceeded.

A sales-expense budget apportions expenditures for a specific time.

These items should be covered in a sales-expense budget: projected sales, overhead (manager's compensation, office costs), sales force compensation, sales expenses (travel, lodging, meals, entertainment), sales meetings, selling aids, and sales management (employee selection and training) costs. Table 17-2 contains a sales-expense budgeting illustration for a small, specialized firm.

TABLE 17-2   A Sales Budget for a Small, Specialized Firm, 1990

Item	Estimated Annual Costs (Revenues)
Sales Forecast	$3,300,000
Overhead (1 sales manager, 1 office)	$ 90,000
Sales force compensation (2 salespeople)	80,000
Sales expenses	40,000
Sales meetings	3,000
Selling aids	5,000
Sales management costs	6,000
Total sales budget	$224,000
Personal selling as a percentage of sales forecast	6.8

The size of the sales-expense budget depends on many factors. It will be larger if customers are geographically dispersed and extensive travel is necessary. Complex goods and services require time-consuming sales presentations and result in fewer calls per salesperson. An expanding sales force needs expenditures for recruiting and training new salespeople.

Determining the Type(s) of Sales Positions

Salespeople can be broadly classified as order takers, order getters, or support personnel. Some companies utilize one type of salesperson, others a combination of all three.

*An **order taker** handles routine orders and sells items that are presold.*

An ***order taker*** processes routine orders and reorders. The job is more clerical than creative selling, usually involving goods or services that are presold. An order taker arranges displays, restocks items, answers simple questions, writes up orders, and completes transactions. He or she may work inside a store (retail clerk) or call on customers (a field salesperson dealing with liquor stores).

The order taker offers several advantages to an employer: compensation is low, little training is required, a variety of selling and nonselling functions are performed, and the sales force can be expanded or contracted quickly. However, they are not appropriate for goods and services requiring creative selling or extensive information for customers. Turnover of personnel is high. Enthusiasm is often limited because of the low salary and nature of routine tasks.

*An **order getter** obtains leads, provides information, persuades customers, and closes sales.*

An ***order getter*** is involved with generating customer leads, providing information, persuading customers, and closing sales. The order getter is the creative salesperson generally required for high-priced, complex, and/or new products. There is less emphasis on clerical work. Like the order taker, an order getter may be inside (automobile salesperson) or outside (Xerox salesperson). Figure 17-5 contrasts order takers and order getters. Table 17-3 presents the profile of an average order getter.

The order getter provides expertise and enthusiasm and expands company sales; the order taker maintains sales. The order getter is frequently able to convince undecided customers to make purchases or decided customers to add peripheral items, such as carpeting and appliances along with a new house. On the negative side, for many consumers, the image of the order getter is one of high pressure. The order getter may also require expensive and time-consuming training. Some nonsales functions such as filing reports may be avoided because they take away from the salesperson's time with

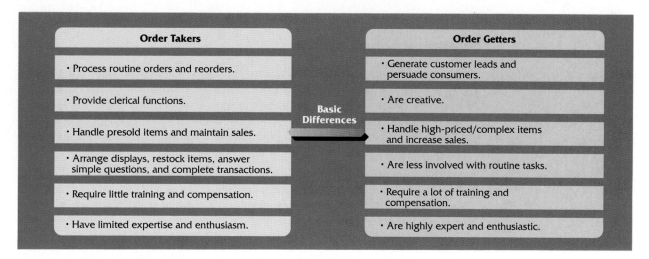

Order Takers		Order Getters
• Process routine orders and reorders.		• Generate customer leads and persuade consumers.
• Provide clerical functions.		• Are creative.
• Handle presold items and maintain sales.	**Basic Differences**	• Handle high-priced/complex items and increase sales.
• Arrange displays, restock items, answer simple questions, and complete transactions.		• Are less involved with routine tasks.
• Require little training and compensation.		• Require a lot of training and compensation.
• Have limited expertise and enthusiasm.		• Are highly expert and enthusiastic.

FIGURE 17-5   **Contrasting Order Takers and Order Getters**

customers and are seldom rewarded by the firm. Compensation can be very high for salespersons who are effective order getters.

Support personnel supplement the basic sales force by providing a variety of functions. A **missionary salesperson** is used to distribute information about new goods or services. The person does not sell but describes the attributes of new items, answers questions, and leaves written material. This paves the way for later sales and is most commonly used with pharmaceuticals and other medical products. A **sales engineer** may accompany an order getter when a highly technical or complex item is being sold. The person explains product specifications, alternatives, and long-range uses. An order getter initially contacts customers and closes sales for these products. A **service salesperson** usually interacts with customers after sales are completed. Delivery, installation, or other follow-up tasks are undertaken.

Missionary salespersons, sales engineers, and service salespersons are support personnel.

TABLE 17-3   The Profile of an Average Order-Getter Salesperson, 1988

Personal Characteristics

36 years of age
College graduate or some college education
7 years average length of service with the same company

Job Characteristics

Training costs (including compensation and training expenses) of $25,000–$30,000
Training period of 6 months
6 sales calls per day
5 calls needed to close a sale
15 hours per week in nonselling activities

Compensation

Trainee — $23,000 per year
Semiexperienced salesperson — $31,000 per year
Experienced salesperson — $40,000 per year
Sales manager — $50,000+ per year
Travel expenses and medical and life insurance paid by company

Source: Adapted by the authors from *Sales Force Compensation: Dartnell's 24th Biennial Survey* (Chicago: Dartnell Corporation, 1988). Copyright Dartnell Corporation. Reprinted by permission.

Selecting a Sales Technique

*The **canned sales
presentation** is a
memorized, nonadaptive
technique.*

There are two basic techniques for personal selling: the canned sales presentation and
the need-satisfaction approach. The ***canned sales presentation*** is a memorized, repetitive presentation given to all customers interested in a particular item. This approach
does not adapt to customer needs or traits but presumes that a general presentation
will appeal to all customers. Although the method has been criticized for its inflexibility and nonmarketing orientation, it retains some value:

> Logically, inexperienced salespeople who are lacking in selling instinct and confidence
> will benefit from the professionalism, anticipation of questions and objections, and other
> fail-safe mechanisms that are often inherent in a company-prepared memorized, audio-
> visual, or flip-chart presentation. Consequently, this method should be considered when
> qualified new salespeople are scarce and when brevity of training is essential.[6]

*The **need-satisfaction
approach** adapts to
individual consumers.*

The ***need-satisfaction approach*** is a higher-level selling method based on the principle that each customer has different characteristics and wants, and therefore the
sales presentation should be adapted to each individual consumer. With need satisfaction, the salesperson first asks such questions of the consumer as: What type of
product are you looking for? Have you ever purchased this product before? What price
range are you considering? Then the sales presentation can be more responsive to the
particular customer. Under this method, a new shopper would be treated quite differently from an experienced shopper. The need-satisfaction approach is the more
popular and customer-oriented technique; however, it requires better training and
skilled sales personnel. This approach includes

- ▶ Generating mutual respect.
- ▶ Listening aggressively.
- ▶ Making thoughtful presentations.
- ▶ Spending time on presales visit research.
- ▶ Exhibiting timeliness (and a willingness to leave when appointment
  time is over).
- ▶ Letting the customer talk.
- ▶ Showing competence.
- ▶ Admitting "I don't know, but I'll find out."
- ▶ Not wasting a prospect's time.[7]

The canned sales presentation works best with inexpensive, routine items that are
heavily advertised and usually presold. The need-satisfaction approach works best
with more expensive, more complex items that have moderate advertising and require
substantial additional information for consumers.

*The **selling process** consists
of seven steps.*

Outlining Sales Tasks

The tasks to be performed by the personal sales force need to be outlined. The ***selling
process*** involves prospecting for customer leads, approaching customers, determining

---

[6] Marvin A. Jolson, "The Underestimated Potential of the Canned Sales Presentation," *Journal of Marketing,* Vol. 39 (January 1975), p. 78.

[7] Kenneth A. Meyers, "The Selling Professional of the 1980s," *Business,* Vol. 32 (October–December
1982), pp. 44–46; Jeremy Main, "How to Sell by Listening," *Fortune* (February 4, 1985), pp. 52–54;
and James Lorenzen, "Needs Analysis Replacing Product Presentation," *Marketing News* (April 25,
1986), p. 8.

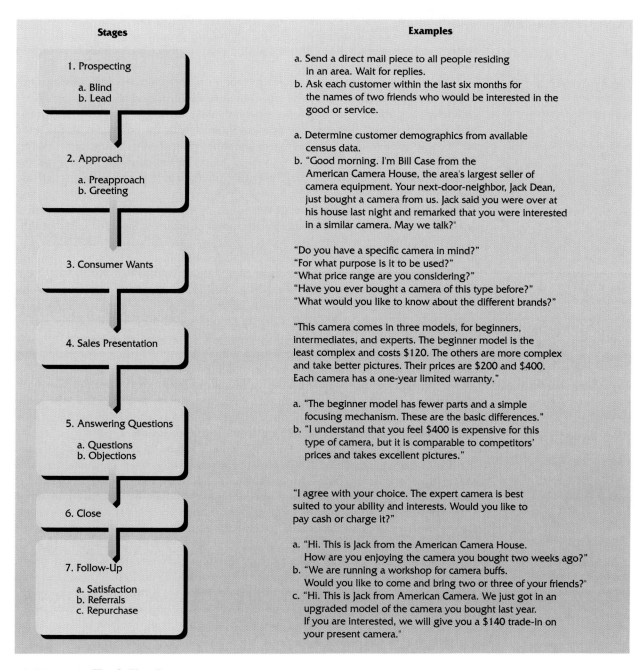

Stages	Examples
1. Prospecting a. Blind b. Lead	a. Send a direct mail piece to all people residing in an area. Wait for replies. b. Ask each customer within the last six months for the names of two friends who would be interested in the good or service.
2. Approach a. Preapproach b. Greeting	a. Determine customer demographics from available census data. b. "Good morning. I'm Bill Case from the American Camera House, the area's largest seller of camera equipment. Your next-door-neighbor, Jack Dean, just bought a camera from us. Jack said you were over at his house last night and remarked that you were interested in a similar camera. May we talk?"
3. Consumer Wants	"Do you have a specific camera in mind?" "For what purpose is it to be used?" "What price range are you considering?" "Have you ever bought a camera of this type before?" "What would you like to know about the different brands?"
4. Sales Presentation	"This camera comes in three models, for beginners, intermediates, and experts. The beginner model is the least complex and costs $120. The others are more complex and take better pictures. Their prices are $200 and $400. Each camera has a one-year limited warranty."
5. Answering Questions a. Questions b. Objections	a. "The beginner model has fewer parts and a simple focusing mechanism. These are the basic differences." b. "I understand that you feel $400 is expensive for this type of camera, but it is comparable to competitors' prices and takes excellent pictures."
6. Close	"I agree with your choice. The expert camera is best suited to your ability and interests. Would you like to pay cash or charge it?"
7. Follow-Up a. Satisfaction b. Referrals c. Repurchase	a. "Hi. This is Jack from the American Camera House. How are you enjoying the camera you bought two weeks ago?" b. "We are running a workshop for camera buffs. Would you like to come and bring two or three of your friends?" c. "Hi. This is Jack from American Camera. We just got in an upgraded model of the camera you bought last year. If you are interested, we will give you a $140 trade-in on your present camera."

FIGURE 17-6 **The Selling Process**

customer wants, giving a sales presentation, answering questions, closing the sale, and following up. See Figure 17-6.

Outside selling requires a procedure for generating a list of customer leads. This procedure is known as ***prospecting.*** Blind prospecting relies on telephone directories and other general listings of potential customers. With blind prospecting, a small percentage of the people contacted will be interested in the firm's offering. Lead prospecting depends on past customers and others for referrals. With lead prospecting, a greater percentage of people will be interested because of the referral from a person they know and respect. Inside selling usually does not involve prospecting because

Prospecting creates customer leads.

customers have already been drawn into the store or office as a result of advertisements or past purchase experience.

*The preapproach and greeting are each part of **approaching customers**.*

Approaching customers is a two-stage procedure: preapproach and greeting. During the preapproach, the salesperson tries to obtain information about the customer's characteristics from census and other secondary data, as well as from referrals. In this way, the salesperson is better equipped to interact with the customer. Inside retail salespeople are frequently unable to use a preapproach; therefore they know nothing about a consumer until he or she enters the store. In the greeting, the salesperson begins a conversation with the customer. The intention is to put the customer at ease and build a rapport.

The next step is to ascertain customer wants by asking the consumer a variety of questions regarding past experience, price, product features, intended uses, and the kinds of information still needed.

*The **sales presentation** converts an uncertain consumer.*

The **sales presentation** includes a verbal description of a product, its benefits, available options and models, price, associated services such as delivery and warranty, and a demonstration (if needed). As explained earlier, a sales presentation may involve a canned sales presentation or need-satisfaction method. The purpose of the sales presentation is to be thorough and convert an undecided person into a purchaser.

After the presentation, the salesperson usually must answer questions from the consumer. These questions are of two kinds: the first require further information, and the second raise objections that must be settled before a sale is made.

*The **closing** clinches a sale.*

Once questions have been answered, the salesperson is ready for the major goal: **closing the sale.** This involves getting the customer to agree to a purchase. The salesperson must be sure that no major questions remain before attempting to close a sale. In addition, the salesperson should not argue with the consumer.

Finally, for major purchases, salespeople should follow up after the sale to ensure that the customer is satisfied. This accomplishes three objectives: the customer gains short-run satisfaction; referrals are stimulated; and, in the long run, repurchases are more likely. "To keep buyers happy, vendors must maintain constructive interaction with purchasers—which includes keeping up on their complaints and future needs. Repeat orders will go to those sellers who have done the best job of nurturing these relationships."[8]

Sales personnel may be required to perform nonselling tasks.

Besides the tasks accomplished through the selling process, the firm must clearly delineate the nonselling tasks it wants sales personnel to perform. Among the nonselling tasks that may be carried out by the sales force are setting up displays, writing up information sheets, marking prices on merchandise, checking competitors' strategies, conducting such marketing research as test marketing analysis and consumer surveys, and training new employees.

Applying the Plan

Sales management tasks range from employee selection to supervision.

The application of the personal selling plan is accomplished through the firm's sales management structure. **Sales management** involves the planning, implementation, and control of the personal sales function. It covers employee selection, training, territory allocation, compensation, and supervision.

---

[8] Theodore Levitt, "After the Sale Is Over . . .," *Harvard Business Review,* Vol. 61 (September–October 1983), p. 87.

You're the Marketer

How Do You Negotiate with a Customer You Cannot Afford to Lose?

Sometimes a salesperson must deal with a key customer who requires a major concession before purchasing. Although the salesperson may think a simple compromise will accommodate the buyer, it may encourage the customer to expect similar results in the future.

According to an expert in customer relations, the best way for a salesperson to negotiate with a customer he or she cannot afford to lose is to "try to draw the customer into a creative partnership." This expert offers eight strategies for moving a customer away from a "hardball" mentality. A salesperson should

▶ *Know the lowest combination of price and terms acceptable to the seller. Emphasis should be placed on discussing the features that the salesperson and the customer have in common.*

▶ *Listen and obtain as much information from the customer as possible. The customer should be encouraged to continue talking.*

▶ *Keep track of the issues requiring discussion. Brief recaps can be used to reassure the customer that the salesperson is listening.*

▶ *Assert his or her company's needs and concentrate on problem-solving that satisfies the needs of both the buyer and the seller.*

▶ *Agree to a solution only after it is certain to work for both parties. The customer should help shape the proposal.*

▶ *Leave the hardest issues for last. Resolving easy issues shows the salesperson's interest in working with the customer.*

▶ *Start high and concede slowly. Concessions should be in small increments; the salesperson should gain something in return for concessions; and the salesperson needs to know the concession's value for both parties.*

▶ *Not be trapped by "emotional blackmail." He or she must remain calm and recognize that a customer may use emotion (such as anger) to push harder for concessions.*

As a salesperson negotiating with your most important customer, who says he (she) will buy from another company unless an additional 20 per cent price discount is offered, what would you do?

SOURCE: Based on material in Thomas C. Keiser, "Negotiating with a Customer You Can't Afford to Lose," Harvard Business Review, Vol. 66 (November–December 1988), pp. 30–34.

In selecting sales personnel, a combination of these personal attributes should be assessed: mental (intelligence, ability to plan), physical (appearance, speaking ability), experience (education, sales and business background), environmental (group memberships, social influences), personality (ambition, enthusiasm, tact, resourcefulness, stability), and willingness to be trained and to follow instructions.[9] Contrary to earlier beliefs, it is now generally accepted that good salespeople are not necessarily born; they are carefully selected and trained. Figure 17-7 shows a semantic differential comparing the traits of successful and unsuccessful salespeople, according to a study of sales managers at 71 manufacturing and wholesaling firms.

[9] Adapted from William J. Stanton, Richard H. Buskirk, and Stanley F. Stasch, *Management of the Sales Force,* Seventh Edition (Homewood, Ill.: Richard D. Irwin, 1989).

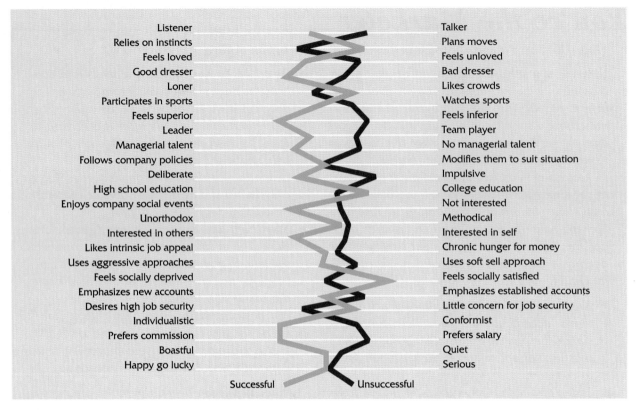

Successful		Unsuccessful
Listener		Talker
Relies on instincts		Plans moves
Feels loved		Feels unloved
Good dresser		Bad dresser
Loner		Likes crowds
Participates in sports		Watches sports
Feels superior		Feels inferior
Leader		Team player
Managerial talent		No managerial talent
Follows company policies		Modifies them to suit situation
Deliberate		Impulsive
High school education		College education
Enjoys company social events		Not interested
Unorthodox		Methodical
Interested in others		Interested in self
Likes intrinsic job appeal		Chronic hunger for money
Uses aggressive approaches		Uses soft sell approach
Feels socially deprived		Feels socially satisfied
Emphasizes new accounts		Emphasizes established accounts
Desires high job security		Little concern for job security
Individualistic		Conformist
Prefers commission		Prefers salary
Boastful		Quiet
Happy go lucky		Serious

FIGURE 17-7
Successful and Unsuccessful Salespeople Profiles
SOURCE: Bradley D. Lockeman and John H. Hallaq, "Who Are Your Successful Salespeople?" *Journal of the Academy of Marketing Science,* Vol. 10 (Fall 1982), p. 466. Reprinted by permission.

Training covers selling skills and company characteristics.

The traits of potential salespeople must also be matched with those of the customers with whom they interact and with the requirements of the good or service being sold. The buyer-seller dyad operates better when there are similarities in salesperson and customer characteristics: "The stronger the likeness/similarities between representatives of the buyer and seller organizations, the more source loyalty [loyalty to the seller] will characterize the relationship."[10] And some product categories require much different education, technical training, and sales activities than others (such as jewelry versus computers).

After these factors are studied, the firm would develop a formal selection procedure specifying the personal attributes sought, sources of employees (such as colleges and employment agencies), and methods for selection (such as interviews, application forms, and testing). This procedure would be based on the firm's overall sales program and needs.

The training of sales personnel may take one or a combination of forms. A formal program utilizes a trainer, classroom setting, lectures, and printed materials. This program may also include role playing (in which trainees act out parts) and case analysis. Field trips take trainees out on actual calls so they can observe skilled salespeople in action. On-the-job training places trainees in their own selling situations under the close supervision of the trainer or senior salesperson.

[10] Michael H. Morris and Jeanne L. Holman, "Source Loyalty in Organizational Markets: A Dyadic Perspective," *Journal of Business Research,* Vol. 16 (March 1988), p. 123.

Training often covers a wide range of topics. It should teach necessary selling skills and also include information about the company and its offerings, the industry, and employee responsibilities. In addition to initial training, many companies use continuous training or retraining of sales personnel in order to teach new techniques, explain new products, or improve performance. This is particularly important for highly technical goods and services.

Territory size and salesperson allocation are determined next. A **sales territory** consists of the geographic area, customers, and/or product lines assigned to a salesperson. When territories are assigned on the basis of customer type (such as large or small) or product type (such as computers or photocopiers), two or more salespeople may cover the same geographic area. Territory size depends on the geographic concentration of customers, order size, travel time and expenses, the time needed for each sales call, the number of yearly visits for each account, and the amount of hours per year each salesperson has available for selling tasks: "Each account should receive enough sales calls to meet current sales objectives and to develop future sales growth."[11]

*A **territory** contains the area, customers, and/or products assigned to a salesperson.*

The allocation of a salesperson to a specific territory depends on his or her ability, the buyer-seller dyad, the mix of selling and nonselling functions (for example, one salesperson may train new employees), and seniority. Proper territory size and allocation provide adequate coverage of customers, minimize territory overlap and salesperson conflict, recognize natural geographic boundaries, minimize travel expenses, encourage solicitation of new accounts, provide a large enough sales potential for a good salesperson to be well rewarded, and offer equity among salespeople in terms of territorial sales potential and workload.

Salesperson compensation can take one of three general formats: straight salary, straight commission, or a combination of salary and commission or bonus. Under a **straight-salary plan,** a salesperson is paid a flat fee per week, month, or year. Earnings are not tied to sales. The advantages are that both selling and nonselling tasks are specified and controlled, there is security for salespeople, and expenses are known in advance. The disadvantages are low sales force incentive to increase sales, expenses not tied to productivity, and continued costs even if there are low sales. Order takers are usually paid straight salaries.

*Sales compensation may be **straight salary, straight commission,** or a **combination** of the two.*

With a **straight-commission plan,** a salesperson's earnings are directly related to sales, profits, or some other performance measure. The commission rate is often keyed to a quota, which is a performance standard for the salesperson. A quota can be based on total sales, total profit, customers serviced, products sold, or some other criterion. The advantages of a straight-commission plan are motivated salespeople, no fixed salesperson compensation costs, and expenses tied to productivity. The disadvantages are lack of control over nonselling tasks performed, instability of a company's dollar expenses and employee earnings, and the risk to employees. Real-estate, insurance, and direct-selling order getters are often paid on a straight commission basis. For example, a real-estate salesperson might receive a 3 per cent commission of $3,900 for selling a $130,000 house.

To obtain the advantages of both salary- and commission-oriented approaches, many companies use elements of each in a **combination compensation plan.** Such plans balance company control, flexibility, and employee incentives. Sometimes

[11] Raymond W. LaForge and Clifford E. Young, "A Portfolio Model to Improve Sales Call Coverage," *Business*, Vol. 35 (April–June 1985), p. 11.

bonuses are stipulated for outstanding individual or company performance. All types of order getters work on a combination basis. According to one major study, almost 92 per cent of the responding firms compensate sales personnel through some form of combination plan. Just under 5 per cent use a straight-salary plan. About 3.5 per cent use a straight-commission plan.[12] On average, salespeople paid via a combination plan earn the most and those on a straight-salary plan the least.

Supervision involves motivation, performance measures, nonselling tasks, and modifying behavior.

Supervision incorporates four aspects of sales management: motivating the sales force, measuring performance, completing nonselling tasks, and initiating behavior changes. First, sales personnel must be motivated in their jobs. Motivation is related to such factors as the clarity of the salesperson's job (what functions must be performed), the salesperson's desire to achieve, the variety of functions performed, the incentives provided for undertaking each task (such as compensation), the style of the sales manager (such as all personnel being treated equitably and outstanding performance rewarded), flexibility, and recognition.

Second, performance must be measured. To do this, achievements must be gauged against objectives such as total sales and calls per day. This analysis should take into account territory size, travel time, experience, and other factors. Third, the sales manager must ensure that all nonselling tasks are completed, even when sales personnel are not rewarded for them. Fourth, if a salesperson's performance does not meet his or her manager's expectations, then some action may be needed to modify his or her behavior. For example, salespeople can go through career cycles similar to those of products — that is, at the maturity and decline stages, enthusiasm and productivity may fall. A sales manager should strive to maintain or rekindle salesperson enthusiasm through such tactics as increasing compensation, retraining, assigning new territories, adding responsibilities, and/or promoting the affected people.[13]

The Scope and Importance of Sales Promotion

Sales promotion efforts are greater now than ever before.

With the intensely competitive nature of so many industries, a number of companies are aggressively seeking every marketing edge possible. Thus, sales promotion activity in the United States is now at the highest level ever. Annual sales promotion expenditures are over $100 billion.[14]

The level of U.S. sales promotion activities can be shown through the following:

▶ Over 225 billion coupons are distributed annually (about 2,500 per household). During a typical year, 85 per cent of all American households use coupons, half on a regular basis. Nonetheless, only 3.3 per cent of the coupons distributed are actually redeemed by consumers.[15] Giant Food's new "Checkout Coupons" program is highlighted in Figure 17-8.

[12] A.S. Hansen, Inc., *Sales Compensation Survey 1986.*

[13] See Marvin A. Jolson, "The Salesman's Career Cycle," *Journal of Marketing,* Vol. 38 (July 1974), pp. 39–46; and William L. Cron, Alan J. Dubinsky, and Ronald E. Michaels, "The Influence of Career Stages on Components of Salesperson Motivation," *Journal of Marketing,* Vol. 52 (January 1988), pp. 78–92.

[14] Len Strazewski, "Promotion 'Carnival' Gets Serious," *Advertising Age* (May 2, 1988), pp. S-1–S-2 ff. Authors' note: There is some overlap in the expenditures reported for advertising and sales promotion because some sales promotion activities may be viewed as advertising.

[15] Manufacturers' Coupon Control Center, "Coupon Distribution and Redemption Show," *Progressive Grocer* (October 1988), p. 58; and Ira Teinowitz, "Coupons Gain Favor with U.S. Shoppers," *Advertising Age* (November 14, 1988), p. 64.

Checkout Coupons are issued based on the customers' actual purchase and are for the type of products they use.

During the year, we completed installation in all stores of an in-store couponing program, which we call "Checkout Coupons." This is the first electronic system to use checkout scanners for retail distribution of cents-off coupons. Tracking purchases as they are scanned, the system prints out coupons for products while the customer is at the checkout.

The coupons either complement the shopper's purchase or may be issued for a competing item. The value to the consumer is that savings are offered on the kinds of products he or she normally buys. All customers at Giant can benefit, not just those who receive newspapers or magazines, where the majority of coupons are offered.

FIGURE 17-8
"Checkout Coupons" from Giant Food
Reprinted by permission from *Giant Food Inc. 1988 Annual Report.*

▶ Each year approximately $400 million worth of trading stamps are given out. Roughly 8 per cent of U.S. supermarkets now handle trading stamps, down from a peak of 65 per cent.[16] Consumers have become more price-conscious and less interested in stamps.

▶ U.S. trade show attendance exceeds 35 million people per year; there are more than 9,000 shows containing 10 exhibits or more. The average attendee spends 7.8 hours at a show and visits 23 exhibits. Each year, more than 100,000 companies exhibit at the 150 largest trade shows alone, drawing over 3 million people.[17]

[16] Ann E. LaForge, "What's New in Trading Stamps," *New York Times* (August 16, 1987), Section 3, p. 19.
[17] Richard Kreisman, "Getting Ready for Show Time," *Inc.* (August 1986), pp. 87–88; Rayna Skolnik, "How to Get Them Where You Want Them," *Sales & Marketing Management* (February 3, 1986), pp. 68–72; and Jonathan M. Cox, Robert S. Ciok, and Ian K. Sequeira, "Trade Show Trends," *Business Marketing* (June 1986), pp. 142–148.

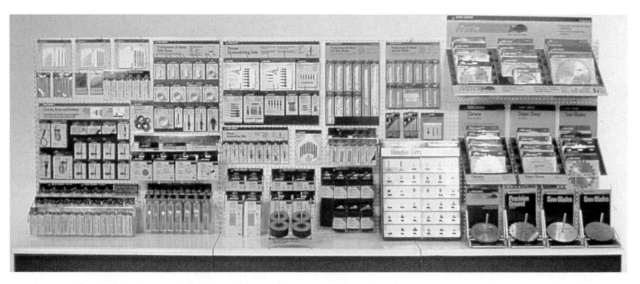

FIGURE 17-9   A Black & Decker Point-of-Purchase Display
Reprinted by permission.

▶ There are 1,000+ nationally advertised sweepstakes each year, awarding over $200 million in prizes. For example, Publishers Clearinghouse mails out about 90 million sweepstakes entries each year; and since 1986, its grand prize has been $10 million (payable over a number of years).[18]

▶ $12 billion to $15 billion per year is spent on point-of-purchase displays in retail stores. These displays stimulate impulse purchases and provide information. In addition to traditional cardboard, metal, and plastic displays, more and more stores are using digital electronic signs and video displays.[19] Attractive displays often lead to higher sales. Figure 17-9 shows a creative display by Black & Decker.

Several factors are contributing to the rapid growth of sales promotion as a marketing tool. As noted at the beginning of this section, many firms are looking for any competitive edge they can get and this increasingly involves some form of sales promotion. The various forms of sales promotions are now more acceptable to firms and consumers than in the past. Executives are better qualified to direct sales promotion efforts. Quick returns are possible, and many firms are seeking to improve short-run profits. Today more consumers look for sales promotions before buying, and channel members are putting more pressure on manufacturers for promotions. Because of rising costs, advertising and personal selling have become more expensive in relation to sales promotion. Advances in technology make many aspects of sales promotion, such as coupon redemption, easier to administer.[20]

Nowhere is the greater emphasis on sales promotion more evident than at Procter & Gamble:

[18] Mary Kuntz, "Taking a Chance on Sweepstakes," *Newsday* (June 21, 1987), pp. 76, 71.
[19] "P-O-P Spending Increases 10%," *Marketing News* (October 10, 1988), p. 22; and Lenore Skenasy, "Intel Brings Computer to Life," *Marketing News* (October 31, 1988), p. 54.
[20] See Joseph P. Flanagan, "Sales Promotion: The Emerging Alternative to Brand-Building Advertising," *Journal of Consumer Marketing*, Vol. 5 (Spring 1988), pp. 45–48; and Ajay Bhasin, Roger Dickinson, Christine G. Hauri, and William A. Robinson, "Promotion Investments That Keep Paying Off," *Journal of Consumer Marketing*, Vol. 6 (Winter 1989), pp. 31–36.

Marketing Controversy

Do Continuous Sales Promotions Destroy Brands?

Although many firms—of all types and sizes—offer sales promotions on a continuous basis, their long-term effect on consumer behavior is debatable. Some marketing experts believe that continuously running sales promotions can destroy brand and/or company reputations. Others believe such promotions are good and that they do not negatively affect their image.

These are some of the reasons critics feel continuous sales promotions can be detrimental:

▸ *They "train" or condition consumers to buy on the basis of a special offer. A lot of consumers avoid buying products when they are not promoted.*

▸ *They undermine the consumer's perception of value. The consumer infers that the real "price" is the advertised "sale" price, not the product's list price.*

▸ *They reduce the promotional funds available for image-related advertising.*

▸ *Brands are built by great advertising, not giveaways or special discounts.*

These are some reasons advocates feel con-tinuous sales promotions can be beneficial:

▸ *They can provide customer value and encourage repeat patronage. This occurs with coupons and trading stamps. Some retailers in highly competitive geographic and/or product areas require continuous promotions to generate store traffic.*

▸ *Brands such as Cracker Jack have offered in-box premiums for up to one-hundred years or more. Some consumers view these premiums as part of the product and would be disappointed not to receive them.*

▸ *Goods and services from major soda manu-facturers (such as Coca-Cola and PepsiCo), airlines, and car-rental firms are "on spe-cial" all-year long. Yet they all have strong brand images.*

▸ *A recent study of over 650 consumer house-holds found that only 3 per cent had unfa-vorable feelings toward brands receiving continuous promotional discounts.*

What do you think?

SOURCE: Based on material in W. E. Phillips and Bill Robinson, "Yes & No: Continuous Sales (Price) Promotion Destroys Brands," *Marketing News* (January 16, 1989), pp. 4, 8.

Visit a doctor's office and you're likely to find P&G displays and free product samples. On college campuses, P&G sponsors posters on trendy topics that carry ads for Crest. Its Tide detergent and Folgers coffee units sponsor racing cars; when they compete, P&G distrib-utes coupons or free samples at the speed tracks. And more samples of P&G products are appearing in mailboxes across the country.[21]

The Characteristics of Sales Promotion

Sales promotion has a number of advantages for a firm. It helps attract customer traffic and maintain brand or store loyalty. For example, new-product samples or trial offers draw customers. A manufacturer can retain brand loyalty through gifts to regular customers or coupons for its brands. A retailer can retain store loyalty by giving store

Sales promotion lures customers, maintains loyalty, creates excitement, is often keyed to patronage, and appeals to channel members.

[21] Alecia Swasy, "P&G Boosts Nontraditional Marketing," *Wall Street Journal* (November 25, 1988), p. 11.

trading stamps or store coupons. Quick results can be achieved. Some forms of sales promotion provide value to the consumer and are retained by them. They provide a reminder function. These include calendars, matchbooks, T-shirts, pens, and posters with the firm's name.

Impulse purchases can be increased through in-store displays. For example, an attractive display for batteries in a supermarket can significantly increase sales. In addition, a good display can lead to a larger-volume purchase than originally intended by the consumer. Excitement is created through certain short-run promotions involving gifts, contests, or sweepstakes. In particular, high-value items or high payoffs encourage consumers to participate. Contests offer the further benefit of customer involvement (through completion of a puzzle or some other skill-oriented activity).

Many types of sales promotion are keyed to customer patronage — with the awarding of coupons, trading stamps, referral gifts, and other promotions directly related to purchases. In these cases, the promotions can be a fixed percentage of sales and their costs not incurred until transactions are completed. Finally, middlemen are likely to cooperate better with manufacturers when sales-promotion support is provided in the form of displays, manufacturers' coupons, manufacturers' rebates, joint training of the retail sales force, and trade allowances.

Sales promotion may hurt image, cause consumers to wait for special offers, and shift the focus from the product.

There are also limitations to sales promotion.[22] The image of a firm may be diminished if it continuously runs promotions. Consumers may view discounts as representing a decline in product quality and believe the firm could not sell its offerings without them. When coupons, rebates, or other special deals are used frequently, consumers may not make purchases if the items are sold at regular prices; instead they will stock up each time there is a promotion. In addition, consumers may interpret the regular price as an increase for items heavily promoted.

Sometimes sales promotions shift the marketing focus away from the product itself onto secondary factors. Consumers may be attracted by calendars, coupons, or sweepstakes instead of by product quality, functions, and durability. In the short run, this generates consumer enthusiasm. In the long run, it may have adverse effects on a brand's image and on sales because a product-related differential advantage has not been developed. It must be remembered that sales promotion enhances, but does not replace, advertising, personal selling, and publicity.

Developing a Sales Promotion Plan

The development of a sales promotion plan consists of the steps shown in Figure 17-10 and explained in the following subsections.

Setting Objectives

Sales promotion objectives are almost always demand-oriented. These objectives may be related to channel-member firms or consumers.

Objectives pertaining to channel members include obtaining distribution, receiving adequate store shelf space, increasing dealer enthusiasm, increasing sales, and gaining cooperation in sales promotion expenditures.

---

[22] For a vigorous defense of sales promotion, see Paul W. Farris and John A. Quelch, "In Defense of Price Promotion," *Sloan Management Review,* Vol. 29 (Fall 1987), pp. 63–69.

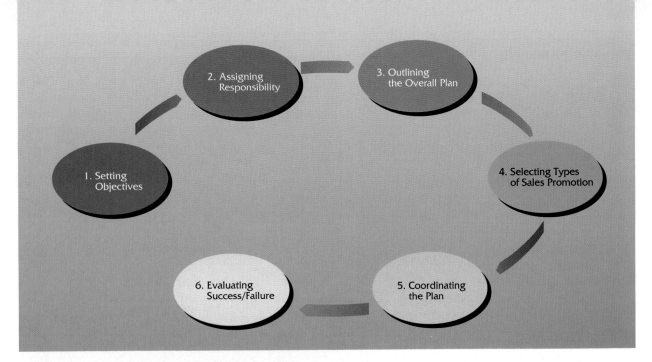

FIGURE 17-10 **Developing a Sales Promotion Plan**

Objectives pertaining to customers include increasing brand awareness, increasing trial of a good or service, increasing average purchases, stimulating repurchases, obtaining impulse sales, emphasizing novelty, and supplementing other promotional tools.

Assigning Responsibility

The responsibility for sales promotion is usually shared by advertising and sales managers. Each directs the promotions regarding his or her area. For example, the advertising manager would be involved with coupons, contests, trading stamps, matchbooks, calendars, and other mass-promotion tools. The sales manager would be involved with trade shows, trade allowances, cooperative promotions, special events, demonstrations, and other efforts requiring individualized attention directed at channel-member firms or final consumers.

In some cases, companies that utilize sales promotion employ specialized inside departments or outside sales promotion firms, such as Donnelley Marketing (a division of Dun & Bradstreet). Many outside sales-promotion firms tend to operate in narrow areas, such as coupons, stamps, or gifts, and generally are able to produce promotional items for less than the user company could. These firms offer expertise, fast service, flexibility, and, when requested, distribution.

Outlining the Overall Plan

The overall sales promotion plan should be outlined and include a budget, an orientation or theme, conditions, media, duration or timing, and cooperative efforts. When establishing a sales promotion budget, it is important to include all costs. For example, the average face value of a coupon is about 35 cents; in addition, manufacturers have to pay retailers an 8- to 10-cent handling charge for each coupon they redeem. Other coupon costs involve printing, mailing, advertising, and manufacturer handling.

Targeted to Channel Members   **Targeted to Final Consumers**

FIGURE 17-11   **A Fleischmann's Sales Promotion Targeted to Channel Members and to Final Consumers**
Reprinted by permission.

Sales promotion orientation may be toward middlemen and/or final consumers.

Sales promotion orientation refers to its focus — middlemen or consumers — and its theme. Sales promotions directed at middlemen should increase their product knowledge, provide sales support, offer rewards for their sales of the promoted product, and aim to increase their cooperation and productivity. Sales promotions directed at consumers should stimulate impulse and larger-volume sales, sustain brand-name recognition, and gain audience participation. The theme of sales promotion refers to its underlying middleman or consumer message, such as a special sale, store opening, new-product introduction, holiday celebration, or new-customer recruitment. Figure 17-11 shows how sales promotion can be oriented to both middlemen and consumers.

Sales promotion conditions specify eligibility requirements.

Sales promotion conditions are the requirements that middlemen or consumers must meet to be eligible for a specific sales promotion. These may include minimum purchases, performance provisions, and/or minimum age. For example, a middleman may have to stock a certain amount of merchandise and set up advertising displays in order to receive a free display case from a manufacturer. A final or organizational consumer may have to send in proofs of purchase in order to receive a refund or gift. In most situations, strict time limits are set that define the closing dates for participation in a sales promotion.

Without strict conditions, a sales promotion may backfire on a firm. This happened with a contest run by one consumer-products company because it did not place a limit on per-household winners and one consumer submitted 4,000 winning entries. The company canceled its contest and suffered much embarrassment.[23]

The media are the vehicles through which sales promotions reach middlemen or consumers. Media include direct mail, newspapers, television, the personal sales force, and group meetings.

The duration of a sales promotion may be short or long. Supermarket and fast-food coupons usually have quick closing dates. Trading stamps normally have no closing dates. The duration must be keyed to objectives. Coupons are used to increase store traffic, and trading stamps are used to maintain loyalty. As noted earlier, when sales promotions are lengthy or are offered frequently, consumers may come to expect them as part of the purchase. Some promotions are seasonal, and for these timing is crucial. They must be tied to the introduction of such seasonal activities as school openings or model or style changes.

Finally, the firm should determine the feasibility of shared sales promotions. With cooperative efforts, each participating channel-member firm pays part of the promotion cost and receives benefits. Cooperative sales promotions are frequently sponsored by industrial trade associations and by retail merchants via shopping-center associations. For example, a group of retailers may share the costs of operating a children's petting zoo located in a regional shopping center.

Selecting the Types of Sales Promotion

There is a wide range of sales promotion tools available to a firm. The characteristics of several sales-promotion tools oriented to channel-member firms are shown in Table 17-4. The characteristics of several consumer-oriented sales-promotion tools are displayed in Table 17-5. Examples for each tool are provided in these tables.

A variety of sales promotion tools can be offered.

In general, sales promotion budgets have been allocated as follows: meetings and conventions, 28 per cent; direct mail, 17 per cent; point-of-purchase displays, 14 per cent; premiums and incentives, 14 per cent; printing and audiovisuals, 9 per cent; promotion advertising space, 8 per cent; trade shows and exhibits, 6 per cent; and coupon redemption, 4 per cent.[24]

The selection of sales promotions should be based on factors such as the company image, company objectives, costs, participation requirements, and middleman or customer enthusiasm.

Coordinating the Plan

It is essential that sales promotion activities be well coordinated with other elements of the promotion mix. In particular,

Advertising and sales promotion should be integrated.

▶ Advertising and sales promotion plans should be integrated.
▶ The sales force should be notified of all promotions well in advance and trained to implement them.
▶ For special events, such as the appearance of a major celebrity, publicity should be generated.
▶ Sales promotions should be consistent with channel-member firm activities.

[23] Kevin T. Higgins, "Game Cancellation Demonstrates Promotions Need Greater Vigilance," *Marketing News* (January 17, 1986), pp. 1, 7.
[24] Russ Bowman, "Sales Promotion," *Marketing & Media Decisions* (July 1988), p. 150.

TABLE 17-4 Selected Types of Sales Promotion Directed at Middlemen

Type	Characteristics	Illustration
Trade shows or meetings	One or a group of manufacturers invites middlemen to attend sessions where products are displayed and explained.	The annual National Home Center Show attracts more than 1,000 exhibitors and tens of thousands of attendees.
Training	The manufacturer provides training for personnel of middlemen.	Apple trains retail salespeople how to operate and use its computers.
Trade allowances or special offers	Middlemen are given discounts or rebates for performing specified functions or purchasing during certain time periods.	A local distributor receives a discount for running its own promotion for GE light bulbs.
Point-of-purchase displays	The manufacturer or wholesaler gives the retailer a fully equipped display for its products and sets it up.	Coca-Cola provides refrigerators with its name on them to retailers carrying minimum quantities of Coca-Cola products.
Push money	Middlemen or their salespeople are given bonuses for pushing the brand of a particular manufacturer. Middlemen may not like this practice if sales-people shift their loyalty to the manufacturer.	A salesperson in a television store is paid an extra $50 for every console of a particular brand that is sold.
Sales contests	Prizes or bonuses are distributed if certain performance levels are met.	A wholesaler receives an extra $1,000 for selling 1,000 radios in a month.
Free merchandise	Discounts or allowances are provided in the form of merchandise.	A retailer gets one case of ballpoint pens free for every 10 cases purchased.
Demonstration models	A free item is given to the wholesaler or retailer for demonstration purposes.	A vacuum-cleaner manufacturer offers retailers a floor demonstrator.
Gifts	Middlemen are given gifts for carrying items or performing functions.	During one two-month period, Sherwood Medical Industries offered wholesalers purchasing a $6,000 syringe package a choice of a color television, microwave oven, or freezer filled with steaks.
Cooperative promotions	Two or more channel-member firms share the costs of a promotion.	A manufacturer and retailer each pay part of the costs for T-shirts with the manufacturer's and retailer's names embossed.

Evaluating Success or Failure

The success or failure of sales promotions is often simple to measure.

The success or failure of many types of sales promotion is relatively straightforward to measure because the promotions are so closely linked to performance or sales. By analyzing before-and-after data, the usefulness of these promotions should be quite clear.

For example, trade show effectiveness can be measured by counting the number of leads generated from a show, examining the sales from these leads and the cost per lead, getting customer feedback about a show from the sales force, and determining the amount of literature given out at a show.[25]

[25] Thomas V. Bonoma, "Get More Out of Your Trade Shows," *Harvard Business Review*, Vol. 61 (January–February 1983), p. 78; and E. Jane Lorimer, "Critical Data Can Measure Exhibits' Impact," *Marketing News* (May 10, 1985), p. 13.

TABLE 17-5 Selected Types of Sales Promotion Directed at Consumers

Type	Characteristics	Illustration
Coupons	Manufacturers or retailers advertise special discounts for customers who redeem coupons.	P&G mails consumers a 25-cents-off coupon for Sure deodorant, which can be redeemed at any supermarket.
Refunds or rebates	A consumer submits proof-of-purchase (usually to the manufacturer) and receives an extra discount.	First Alert fire alarms provides rebates to consumers submitting proof of purchase.
Samples	Free merchandise or services are given to consumers, generally for new items.	A computer service bureau offers a free one-month trial of its payroll software system to small businesses in the area.
Trading stamps	Consumers are given free stamps based on dollar purchases. Stamps are accumulated and exchanged for gifts or money.	Some A&P supermarkets distribute S&H trading stamps.
Contests or sweepstakes	Consumers compete for prizes by answering questions (contests) or filling out forms for random drawings of prizes (sweepstakes).	Publishers Clearinghouse sponsors annual sweepstakes and awards cash, automobiles, houses, and other prizes.
Bonuses or multipacks	Consumers receive discounts for purchasing in quantity.	An office-supply store runs a "buy one, get one free" sale on desk lamps.
Shows or exhibits	Many manufacturers cosponsor exhibitions for consumers.	The Auto Show is annually scheduled for the public in New York.
Point-of-purchase displays	In-store displays remind customers and generate impulse purchases.	Chewing gum sales in supermarkets are high because displays are placed at checkout counters.
Special events	Manufacturers or retailers sponsor celebrity appearances, fashion shows, and other activities.	Virtually every major league baseball team has an annual "Old Timers' Day," which attracts large crowds.
Gifts	Consumers are given gifts for making a purchase or opening a new account.	Savings banks offer a range of gifts for consumers opening new accounts or expanding existing ones.
Referral gifts	Existing customers are given gifts for referring their friends to the company.	Tupperware awards gifts to the woman hosting a Tupperware party in her home.
Demonstrations	Goods or services are shown in action.	The Evelyn Woods reading course technique is demonstrated in a complimentary lesson.

Similarly, companies can verify changes in their sales as a result of dealer-training programs. Firms using coupons can examine sales and compare redemption rates with industry averages. Attitudinal surveys of middlemen and consumers can indicate satisfaction with various kinds of promotions, suggestions for improvements, and the effect of promotions on image.

Some sales promotions, such as calendars, pens, and special events, are more difficult to evaluate because objectives are less definite.

Summary

1. *To examine the scope, importance, and characteristics of personal selling* Personal selling involves oral communication with one or more prospective buyers by paid representatives for the purpose of making sales. In the United States, about 14 million people are employed in personal-selling occupations. This number understates the value of personal selling because every contact between a company representative and a customer involves some amount of personal selling.

Personal selling is often emphasized with large-volume customers, geographically concentrated customers, expensive and/or complex products, and customers desiring sales services. Also, selling resolves questions and addresses other issues. Selling costs are higher than advertising costs for many companies. The average cost of one business-to-business sales call is well over $250.

Personal selling establishes a buyer-seller dyad (the two-way flow of communication between both parties), offers flexibility and adaptability, results in little waste in terms of audience, clinches sales, and provides immediate feedback. However, personal selling can handle only a limited number of customers, is relatively ineffective for creating consumer awareness, has high costs per customer, and has a very poor image for some consumers.

2. *To study the elements in a personal selling plan* A personal selling plan consists of these seven steps: setting objectives—demand- and/or image-related; assigning responsibility—to one marketing (or sales) manager or to several sales managers; establishing a budget—which allocates costs among salespeople, products, customers, and geographic areas; determining the type(s) of sales positions—order takers, order getters, and/or support salespeople; selecting a sales technique—the canned sales presentation or the need-satisfaction approach; outlining the sales tasks—including each of the relevant steps in the selling process and nonselling tasks; and applying the plan—which centers on sales management functions and execution.

3. *To examine the scope, importance, and characteristics of sales promotion* Sales promotion encompasses the paid marketing communication activities (other than advertising, publicity, and personal selling) that stimulate consumer purchases and dealer effectiveness. In the United States, sales promotion has annual expenditures exceeding $100 billion.

The rapid growth of sales promotion is the result of companies aggressively looking for a competitive edge, the greater acceptance of sales promotion tools by both firms and consumers, better management of the sales promotion effort, quick returns, the pressure by consumers and channel members for promotions, the high costs of other promotional forms, and technological advances.

Sales promotion helps attract customer traffic and loyalty, provides value to consumers and is sometimes retained by them, increases impulse purchases, creates excitement, is keyed to customer patronage, and improves middleman cooperation. However, sales promotion may hurt the firm's image, encourage consumers to wait for promotions before making purchases, and shift the focus away from product attributes. Sales promotion cannot replace other forms of promotion.

To study the elements in a sales promotion plan A sales promotion plan consists of these six steps: setting objectives—usually demand-oriented; assigning responsibility—to advertising and sales managers and/or outside specialists; outlining the overall plan—including the orientation, conditions, and other factors; selecting the types of sales promotion—such as trade shows, training, allowances, free merchandise, and cooperative promotions for middlemen and coupons, refunds, samples, stamps, and referral gifts for final consumers; coordinating the plan with the other elements of the promotion mix; and evaluating success or failure.

Key Terms

Review Questions

1. The Bureau of Labor Statistics lists 14 million people in sales positions in the United States. Why does this figure understate the importance of personal selling?
2. What is telemarketing? Why do firms use it?
3. Draw and explain the buyer-seller dyad.
4. Distinguish among order-taker, order-getter, and support sales personnel.
5. When is a canned sales presentation appropriate? When is it not appropriate?
6. Outline the steps in the selling process.
7. Why is sales promotion a rapidly growing marketing tool?
8. What are the limitations associated with sales promotion?
9. Differentiate between sales promotion orientation and conditions.
10. Why is the success or failure of many types of sales promotion relatively easy to measure?

Discussion Questions

1. How would you handle these objections raised at the end of a sales presentation?
   a. "The price is too high."
   b. "Your warranty period is much too short."
   c. "None of the alternatives you showed me is satisfactory."
2. How would you motivate a retail sales clerk? A life insurance salesperson?
3. Some observers believe that sales promotion is more important to a firm than advertising. Comment on this.
4. List several sales promotion techniques that would be appropriate for Cheerios cereal. List several that would not be appropriate. Explain your answer.
5. How could the effectiveness of a point-of-purchase display be determined?

▸ CASE 1 ▸

United Group: How an Insurance Agency Generates Sales Leads*

United Group is an insurance agency selling hospital protection plans to small businesses. Its customers are usually self-employed repairpeople, printers, electricians, and restaurant owners who have one to two employees (including themselves). United Group's yearly sales are $140 million.

Company sales agents sell United Group products exclusively and rely on a one-call close. To keep its sales force of 1,000+ agents busy, the firm needs to generate 750,000 qualified sales leads per year. Such leads are from two sources: one-third come from 15-million mail pieces, and two-thirds come from more than 10-million phone calls. United relies heavily on the lists of small businesses contained in such sources as the *Yellow Pages* and *Dun & Bradstreet New Business.*

The firm has set up a sophisticated system to determine the most responsive and profitable population groups contained in these lists. Responsive-

ness and profitability can be judged on the basis of such criteria as the number of sales made by the field sales force, the amount of business placed, lapses in insurance coverage (and nonrenewals), and claims experience.

Through an early mathematical model that it developed, United Group learned the following:

▸ Among occupational groups, gas station owners are highly profitable prospects; salespeople have sold $1,446 in premiums per 1,000 pieces mailed, 18 per cent above the average for all occupations. In contrast, although consultants have a high response rate, they have yielded only $554 of premiums per 1,000 pieces mailed.
▸ Among geographical areas, North Carolina residents have yielded an average of $2,080 in premiums per 1,000 pieces mailed (70 per cent above the national average), while Oregon residents have yielded only $940 in premiums per 1,000 mail pieces.

*The data in this case are drawn from Neal Kay, "Keeping the Sales Force Busy," *Direct Marketing* (January 1989), pp. 52–59.

This model gave United a sense of direction with its lead-generation process, but it needed to be further refined. For example, this model did not evaluate the relative value of each consumer characteristic (would North Carolina consultants generate greater premiums per 1,000 mail pieces than Oregon gas station owners?).

So United developed a second lead-generation model to study the relative importance of various consumer traits. A weighted score value was assigned to each lead characteristic that could be associated with the premiums generated. Then, the "perfect prospect" was assigned a value of 1,000; a worthless prospect was scored a zero.

Here are the score values assigned to selected occupational groups: auto sales and leasing, 0; food stores, 28; restaurants, 57; gas stations, 107; graphics services, 120; and home-care services, 178. Here are the score values assigned to selected non-occupational categories (note: a business may fall into two or more categories): individual ownership, 28; business owner known by name, 50; use of a post office box, 51; and prior response made to United Group, 90.

Each record (business) in United's master file has been scored by adding the value of various occupational and nonoccupational characteristics. The greater the score value, the better the prospect. This second model was tested via more than 300,000 mailings in which leads were placed into 13 groups based upon their total score value.

In this test, accounts with higher scores had a better quantity of leads for salespeople to call on—as well as better levels of premiums. For example, businesses with score values of 350 or more accounted for 21 per cent of United Group's data base and represented 27 per cent of its leads and 26 per cent of its sales. Businesses scoring 225 or higher accounted for 91 per cent of United's data base, and represented 92 per cent of its leads and 97 per cent of its total sales.

After seeing the results of this test, United decided to restrict future mailings to accounts with a minimum 225 total score. The firm estimates that it will save more than $238,000 in annual mailing costs through use of this model.

In the future, United plans to use two separate models: one for mail and one for telemarketing.

QUESTIONS

1. What other major sources of leads should United Group pursue?
2. What are the implications of United's lead-generation program with regard to the use of the canned sales presentation or the need-satisfaction approach?
3. How would United's lead-generation program be helpful throughout the selling process?
4. As a United sales manager, how would you allocate territories to salespeople? What criteria would you use to assess salesperson performance?

⟨ CASE 2 ⟩

Evaluating the Use of Trade Shows by Industrial Marketers[†]

Industrial firms spend billions of dollars annually to attend and participate in U.S. trade shows. Why? Trade shows enable companies to introduce themselves to new prospects, demonstrate new products to a focused audience, generate excitement about themselves, meet customers in a less pressured environment, motivate the firm's sales force, allow customers to conveniently compare the offerings of competitors, and/or to learn what competitors are doing.

† The data in this case are drawn from James Braham, "Trade Shows: The Agony of De-Feet," *Industry Week* (April 4, 1988), pp. 70–72.

These are among the emerging trade-show trends noted by an industry consultant:

▷ Attendees desire shorter presentations in more convenient formats.

▷ They are visiting fewer exhibits.

▷ They are paying greater attention to business discussions and less to image and awareness generation.

▷ Attendees are seeking out exhibits that demonstrate benefits, solutions, and applications.

▷ The days of "the Egyptian waterfalls and the free umbrellas," just to draw attendees into a booth, are largely passe.

Trade show experts cite Giddings & Lewis and CIMLINC as examples of industrial firms that have used trade shows well.

Gigglings & Lewis, a machine-tool manufacturer, wanted to promote itself as a technological leader in the plant automation-equipment industry. Rather than display its machinery at the International Machine Tool Show (in Chicago), the firm decided to develop a videotape of the machinery using computer-generated graphics, laser lighting effects, and music developed especially for the video. It rented a 2,500-seat theater, had 63 performances, and attracted over 23,000 visitors during the International Machine Tool Show: "You have individuals dedicated to your information for 15 solid minutes without any distractions, which are commonplace on an exhibition floor."

CIMLINC, a six-year-old computer software manufacturer with annual sales of $35 million, used its trade show exhibit at the Autofact show in Detroit to create awareness and develop a list of prospects. CIMLINC rented a 5,000-square-foot movie theater lobby for its booth and prominently featured its products on pedestals. Video demonstrations of all company products were presented at the booth entrance; at the rear of the booth, a video explained the firm. Through the trade show, CIMLINC generated over 650 customer leads and imparted an image as a large, growing company. It also won an award for the most attractive exhibit.

At the same time, some other industrial marketers are now evaluating their participation at trade shows. The firms question the effectiveness of trade shows and raise these points:

▷ There are nearly 10,000 industrial trade shows yearly in the United States alone. According to the manager of Hewlett-Packard's Technical Systems Sector Demonstration Centers, this number is expected to "multiply like rabbits." Companies must evaluate which trade shows they will exhibit at, as well as those they will attend.

▷ The costs of exhibiting at trade shows have risen rapidly. As one exhibitor notes, "Take all your salespeople and a lot of your engineers out of the field, and all your corporate people and stick them in hotels, on expense accounts, for three days. That's the big money."

▷ Many firms add to the costs of a trade show the lack of support given to existing customers while salespeople attend the show.

▷ Companies acknowledge that they often do not follow up on all customer inquiries or sales leads from trade shows. Says Hewlett-Packard's manager of Technical Systems Sector Demonstration Centers, "In many cases, fewer than two out of ten sales call requests are followed up over a 12-month period. That makes the CEO's or marketing manager's hair turn grayer."

▷ Because it may take months for an industrial-equipment sale to be made, linking sales results to trade shows can be difficult. In fact, some industry experts feel there is no reliable way to measure the effect of shows on long-term sales.

QUESTIONS

1. Present several trade show objectives for a firm marketing a new industrial service.

2. How should sales promotion orientation and sales promotion conditions apply to a company's participation in industrial trade shows?

3. Describe how Giddings & Lewis should coordinate its participation in trade shows with other elements of the promotion mix.

4. Cite at least five measures for CIMLINC to use in evaluating its trade show participation.

part 5 CASE

Carnival Cruise Lines: Aggressive Promotion Pays Off[*]

Introduction

Ocean-liner cruising has always conjured up lots of images, many of them worlds apart. There's the one of the grand poohbahs parading around the deck, directing the cartage of their Louis Vuitton luggage with one hand and holding the leash of an equally haughty wolf-hound with the other.

Then, of course, there's the other view. You know the one where "you sleep in steerage with 37 to a cabin," cracks Karine L. Armstrong, vice-president of marketing for Carnival Cruise Lines Inc. "There were a lot of preconceived notions." Indeed, one of Carnival's very real achievements is that it has been able to swab the deck clean of both those stereotypes and, as Armstrong says, "to put cruising into the hands of Middle America."

Carnival, with its unprecedented TV-advertising campaign and maybe some indirect help from the popularity of the TV series *Love Boat*, has made it clear that one doesn't need furs — be they mink or on a wolf-hound — to have fun, which was and is exactly what Carnival has been marketing for more than 10 years.

While some in the $4.5 billion industry have been trying to lure in a new cruise crowd with novelty-type cruises — trips to nowhere, "Great Chefs" eating extravaganzas, country-music hoe-downs, etc. — Carnival has successfully set sail with a "Fun Ships"

theme. The company enjoyed its biggest year ever in 1987, with net income of $152.8 million — 56 per cent higher than a year earlier — for the fiscal year ended Nov. 30, on revenues of $564.1 million. In 1988, net income reached $188.8 million on revenues of $595.1 million.[1]

The Carnival Story

Its success is well-deserved. Carnival's role in shaking up and changing the staid cruising industry is nothing short of remarkable. Up until about 20 years ago, people took ships simply to get from shore A to shore B. But the advent of airline travel put an end to that. Cruising had to become more than a mode of transportation and evolve into an adventure to be savored for its own merits. "Carnival was ahead of everyone else in marketing a cruise as a cruise-ship experience," says Richard S. Kahn, who is the president of RSK Travel Consultants.

While others also got the hang of that, the trouble was that they attracted a pretty narrow audience. Most of the cruise lines put the emphasis on luxury, sailed to faraway ports, took up to two weeks' time, and cost plenty. Naturally, this kind of trip attracted an older crowd, often of retired folk, who had the time and money to pay for all the coddling.

[*] Adapted by the authors from Paula Schnorbus, "Ain't We Got Fun!" *Marketing & Media Decisions* (March 1988), pp. 101–106. Reprinted by permission.

[1] Faye Rice, "How Carnival Stacks the Decks," *Fortune* (January 16, 1989), p. 114.

546

Carnival was in the forefront of changing the industry's image. It saw that only 5 per cent of the U.S. population had ever been on a vacation sail and so set about making the trips shorter, less expensive, and "more fun" in order to tap a wider audience. A Carnival cruise to the Caribbean lasts for a week and at base rate costs $995 to $1,995, including airfare.

Competition in the Cruise-Line Industry

Today, thanks to Carnival, more and more of the 34 North American members of the Cruise Lines International Association are defining themselves as "contemporary" sails rather than "traditionalists." Two of Carnival's main rivals, Norwegian Cruise Lines and Royal Caribbean Cruise Lines, offer similar packages. Norwegian's comparable seven-day sails run from $975 to $2,025, while Royal Caribbean's cost from $1,045 to $2,095.

A big difference is in the cruise ships' styles. Carnival doesn't compare itself to other cruise lines: it says it competes against land-based vacations, such as an excursion to Hawaii, and therefore what it sells (rather relentlessly) is fun. That means limbo contests and lots of gambling aboard ship, with Las Vegas-style revues to boot.

On the other hand, a Royal Caribbean cruise is better known for the fine food as well as subdued entertainment, such as solo violinists. And many of Norwegian's ships are smaller for more ambience, and its popular ship *Norway* (which is even pricier for a seven-day Caribbean jaunt) features star entertainment.

The other end of the scale, called traditional cruising, may be found in Cunard's *Sea Goddess*. Roaming the Caribbean for a week costs $4,600 without air fare, but all "rooms" are outside suites, and the smaller ship guarantees more personal attention. Geared to top executives, the Sea Goddess features financial- and stress-management lectures.

But the winner is still Carnival. Its folksiness has paid off in a big way. The cruise line has the greatest market share—almost 25 per cent—based on its passenger capacity. And its seven ships, which have about 8,448 berths at 100 per cent capacity, haven't had trouble getting filled for the past five years.

According to a November analysts' report from Alex. Brown & Sons Inc., Carnival's utilization never fell below 104 per cent in the years 1982–86 (over 100 per cent utilization assumes more than two passengers per cabin). Carnival boasts that it carried 552,774 passengers during 1987, an average occupancy level of 111.6 per cent, up 26 per cent from 1986's 438,399 passengers. As Harvey L. Katz, an analyst at Salomon Brothers Inc., puts it, "I think these guys run a very tight ship."

The Fun Ship is highly structured for a total vacation experience. The ports of call, which currently include the Bahamas, the Caribbean, and the Mexican Riviera, are the gravy. Says Dan Nesbett, marketing consultant, "Potential cruise people are worried about being cooped up on a ship. Carnival shows it's really fun, and there's a lot to do." He adds that other cruise lines may have as many activities, "but they don't advertise them like Carnival does."

Carnival's Advertising Approach

Actually, no one in the cruise business spends as much on advertising—well over $40 million annually—or gives over half its budget to television, which is what Carnival does. Robert Dickinson, Carnival's senior vice-president of marketing and sales, believes the key to his company's success is in sustained advertising. "It's like time-released aspirin," he finds.

Carnival's humble, even embarrassing, beginnings could hardly have foretold the success it is today. On its maiden voyage in 1972, the *Mardi Gras*, with 300 travel agents aboard, literally ran aground. The company remained beached until three years later, when Carnival chairman of the board Ted Arison, a founder of Norwegian Cruise Lines, bought out Carnival's parent AITS, Inc. Arison paid the Boston-based tour company one dollar and assumed Carnival's $5 million debt. A month later, the refurbished *Mardi Gras* showed a profit. And through 1975, it operated at more than 100 per cent capacity.

The turnaround came about as Carnival revamped its marketing program to go full-speed after first-time and younger cruisers. And in 1984, the company began offering three- and four-day "Fun Ship" cruises for newcomers to get the sea experience.

With its target audience and theme in place, Carnival launched a unique media assault. By 1984, Carnival had broken ranks with its competitors and moved away from the print standard to a mixed-media strategy. The company signed up agency McFarland & Drier to handle its broadcast work, and soon Carnival was practically drowning the public with spots of perky, semicelebrity Kathie Lee Gifford (formerly Johnson) belting out "Ain't We Got Fun" on a Carnival cruise.

Originally, the spots started out on morning and evening news programs, but they have since expanded to prime time. The placements also skew 50–50, says Geri Donnelly the agency's vice-president and media director, to both men and women on shows that run the gamut from *Miami Vice* to *Golden Girls*. Last September, in an effort to break through TV clutter, seven new 15- and 30-second commercials were developed featuring a game Gifford singing Carnival's version of "If My Friends Could See Me Now."

Carnival's Armstrong says that the majority of the remaining media dollars goes for newspaper advertising, with over 200 papers getting the business. Magazine ads run in trade and consumer travel books and everything from *Corporate Meetings and Incentives* to *Woman's Day*. Men's books aren't used, although Armstrong says that, surprisingly, men now are booking cruises as much or more than women. HMK Advertising Inc., Boston, provider of print advertising, has been a Carnival agency from day one.

Table 1 shows Carnival's 1988 advertising expenditures.

TABLE 1 Carnival Cruise Lines' 1988 Advertising Expenditures

Medium	1988 Expenditures	
	$	Per Cent of Total
Commercial television	23,714,000	56.520
Newspapers	16,102,400	38.378
Magazines	1,489,300	3.550
Cable television	619,900	1.476
Newspaper supplements	29,600	0.071
Outdoor	1,900	0.005
Radio	0,000	0.000
Total	41,957,100	100.000

Sources: Arbitron Ratings Company, Leading National Advertisers, Inc., Publishers Information Bureau, Inc., and Media Records, Inc.

Carnival's Relations with Travel Agents

One thing that a consumer will never find in a Carnival ad is a direct-response pitch. If people are interested in taking a Carnival cruise, they are instructed to call their local travel agents, who sell 99 per cent of Carnival cruises. "We've built up a reputation of being very supportive to the travel-agent community," states Armstrong. "We're probably the only travel entity selling a product that doesn't put 1-800 numbers on our consumer advertising, only in trade advertising so agents know where to contact us."

Armstrong also feels that, because Carnival identified theirs as the Fun Ships, it made the product easier to sell. It also makes its prices common rated for its cabin categories, meaning that pricing is equal across the board for the five ships that offer seven-day cruises and the two ships that have three- and four-day trips. For example, a veranda suite on the *Tropicale* going for a seven-day cruise to the Mexican Riviera costs the same—$1,995 base rate—as a veranda suite on the *Holiday* for a seven-day cruise to the Caribbean. To avoid confusion for the travel agent, sailing days never change.

Carnival also tries to appeal to a travel agent's busy schedule through a daily (9:00 A.M. to 8:00 P.M.) computerized reservation-and-ticketing system operated by about 170 in-house bookers. A travel agent should be able to book a cruise in about three minutes, Armstrong insists.

Meanwhile, Dickinson goes around the country telling travel agents how to do their jobs. On average, he lectures groups of 100 to 1,000 agents, telling them things like they should be motivating their salespeople with incentives based on productivity. Another of his pet peeves is that most travel agencies aren't open on Sunday, when most of the industry's ads run.

Still, the company goes to great lengths to keep agencies thinking Carnival. There's an agency-of-the-year competition, complete with dinners, prizes, and plaques; trade press ads stressing how profitable a Carnival cruise can be for the agency; and "thank you for the business" ads. Carnival also conducts a "Mystery Vacationer" promotion, where an employee poses as a prospective client at a travel agency. If a travel agent's first travel suggestion is a cruise, he or she is awarded $10. And if the agent first recommends a Carnival cruise, the cruise line hands over $1,000 on the spot. About $500,000 has been awarded since the program began in 1981.

What's on the Horizon for Carnival?

All of this wining and dining on Carnival's part makes sense when one looks out to the horizon and sees three more Fun Ships approaching. So sure of itself is Carnival these days that it is wading out into more traditional cruising water with the Tiffany Project. "We have such a humongous repeat factor," explains Armstrong, "that there are some people who have traveled on all of our ships. The natural evolution is to move up."

Furthermore, Dickinson boasts, "I'd like nothing better than to go in and show [the traditional cruise lines] just exactly how we think it should be done." Carnival's plan is to sell an upscale product at a mid-

level price. For example, Dickinson wants to have 350-cabin ships, as opposed to the 1,400-plus-berth Fun Ships, all with outside suites with private verandas. How would those be marketed? "If we can offer that particular product at a middle-of-the-road price, we won't have to do much marketing," he believes.

Carnival seems to have the deep pockets necessary for this scale venture, because it raised $397 million in its initial public offering in July, 1987. Though the stock took a hit in the October 1987 market thud, the shares have been recovering. "There was a general feeling that the timing was right, but it turned out to be better than we imagined," says Micky Arison, company president, CEO, and son of Ted. "We felt that if we were to maintain our market-dominant position, we would need the capital to be able to build at will the type and quantity of ships needed to keep that position." So far, at least, the coast looks remarkably clear for Carnival's marketing itinerary.

QUESTIONS

1. Discuss how Carnival uses the channel of communication. Refer to each of the stages in the channel in your answer.
2. Should Carnival use one-sided messages or two-sided messages? Fear appeals? Humor? Comparative messages? Explain your answers.
3. In its promotion efforts, should Carnival seek to increase primary demand or concentrate on selective demand? Why?
4. State at least five overall promotion goals that Carnival could set.
5. Comment on Carnival's heavy emphasis on television advertising.
6. How can Carnival generate positive publicity?
7. What is the proper role for personal selling in Carnival's promotion mix?
8. Carnival aims most of its sales promotions at travel agents; and 99 per cent of Carnival's business is through travel agents. What do you think of this strategy?

part 6
PRICE PLANNING

Part 6 covers the fourth and final major element of the marketing mix, pricing.

18 **An Overview of Price Planning**   In this chapter, we study the role of price in allocating goods and services among purchasers, its importance in transactions, and its relationship with other marketing variables. We contrast price and nonprice competition. We also look at each of the factors affecting price decisions in depth: consumers, costs, government, channel members, and competition.

19 **Developing a Pricing Strategy**   Here, we explain how to construct a pricing strategy. First, we distinguish among sales, profit, and status quo objectives. Next, we discuss the role of a broad price policy and introduce three approaches to pricing (cost-, demand-, and competition-based). Then, we examine a number of pricing tactics, such as customary and odd pricing. We conclude the chapter by noting different methods for adjusting prices.

20 **Applications of Pricing Techniques**   In this chapter, we show how cost-, demand-, and competition-based techniques of pricing may actually be applied; and we evaluate the attributes and variations of each technique. We use mathematical illustrations, based on the futuristic Phase III bicycle, to demonstrate the techniques. We also explain why cost-, demand-, and competition-based pricing methods must be integrated.

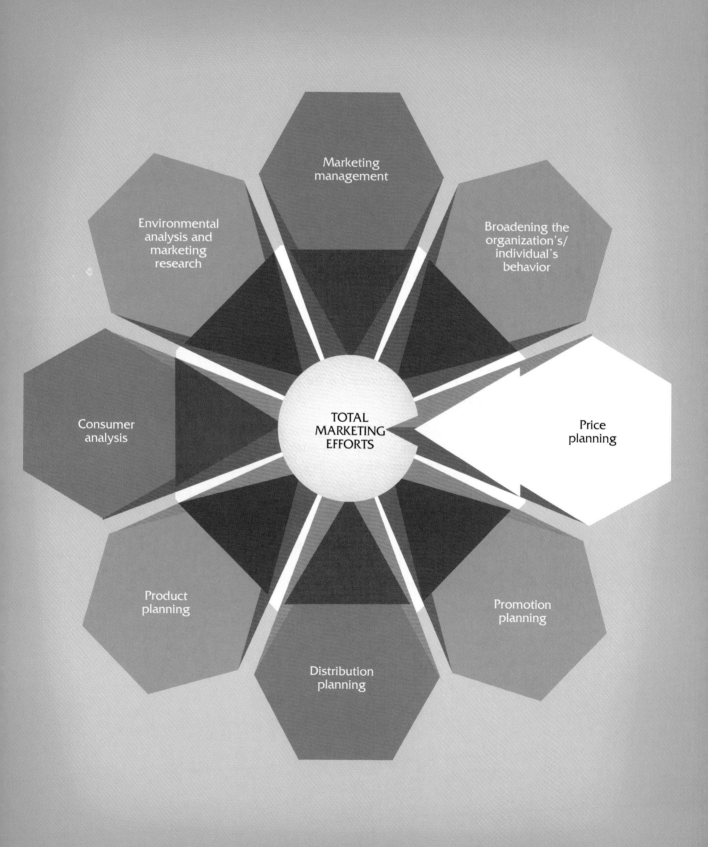

CHAPTER 18

An Overview of Price Planning

CHAPTER OBJECTIVES

1. To define the terms price and price planning

2. To demonstrate the importance of price and study its relationship with other marketing variables

3. To differentiate between price and nonprice competition

4. To examine the factors affecting pricing decisions: consumers, costs, government, channel members, and competition

The wholesale prices that manufacturers charge for fragrances headed for the United States often can be 25 per cent more than the wholesale prices in Europe. To guarantee that U.S. premium, perfume houses try to limit U.S. distribution through select [authorized] dealers to upscale stores. Yet gray marketers claim the industry's leaky distribution system tends to make perfume companies their own worst enemies.

For example, perfume houses ship huge quantities of their priciest essences to such unlikely playgrounds of the rich as Poland, Egypt, and Iran. French perfume exported directly to Panama, a major transshipment point of gray market goods to the United States, totals $40 million—theoretically making Panama's per-capita consumption of perfume 35 times that of the United States.

Gray market goods are foreign-made items that enter a country through distributors not authorized by the manufacturer for sale in that country. These goods are usually sold at retail prices below those of authorized dealers. U.S. gray market sales are estimated to be as high as $10 billion yearly. Let us look at this practice more closely.

In a landmark 1988 ruling, the U.S. Supreme Court decided that when a U.S. distributor and a foreign producer are affiliated, the U.S. trademark owner cannot prevent wholesalers and retailers from buying products overseas and selling them in the United States. This ruling is applicable even though certain products are not intended for the U.S. market.

About 90 per cent of gray market goods involve channels where an authorized U.S. distributor and a foreign producer are affiliated. Examples include Nikon cameras, Seiko watches, Cartier jewelry, and Duracell batteries. This means retailers such as K mart can legally buy many brands of cameras, watches, and jewelry overseas and sell them in the United States without the permission of the U.S. trademark owner.

The typical source of gray market goods is brokers who buy goods overseas, where wholesale prices are low. They bring goods into the United States and sell them to other wholesalers or to large retailers at prices considerably less than the manufacturers' officially-sanctioned wholesale prices.

In addition to being concerned about lost profits and the lack of channel control, many manufacturers are concerned about the quality of the gray market goods that bear their names when they are sold in the United States and the effect on the firms' image. For instance, Duracell worries about the shelf life for gray market batteries. Kodak worries about the heat and

humidity conditions of gray market film when it is shipped. And because warranty work on gray market products is not normally performed by authorized U.S. distributors, camera makers worry about the repair quality.

The 1988 Supreme Court decision has forced manufacturers to rethink their marketing strategies. Yet many firms are not finding decisions to be easy. Because the success of gray market goods is largely based on the price differentials between U.S. and overseas markets, manufacturers can reduce the differences to eliminate the basic advantage of gray marketers. However, this strategy might drastically reduce a firm's U.S. profitability or its competitiveness overseas.

Some manufacturers are more carefully monitoring sales to wholesale customers suspected of diverting products—with mixed results: "Sure you could trace diversion, but you would just antagonize your customer."[1]

In this chapter, we will learn more about the impact of consumers, costs, government, channel members, and competition on price planning.

---

[1] Pete Engardio et al., "There's Nothing Black-and-White About the Gray Market," *Business Week* (November 7, 1988), pp. 172–180; Bill Javetski and Peter Galuszka, "A Red-Letter Day for Gray Marketeers," *Business Week* (June 13, 1988), p. 30; and Larry S. Lowe and Kevin F. McCrohan, "Gray Markets in the United States," *Journal of Consumer Marketing*, Vol. 5 (Winter 1988), pp. 45–51.

Overview

*Through **price planning**, a **price** places a value on a good or service.*

A **price** represents the value of a good or service for both the seller and the buyer. **Price planning** is systematic decision making by an organization regarding all aspects of pricing.

The value of a good or service can involve both tangible and intangible marketing factors. An example of a tangible marketing factor is the cost savings obtained by the purchase of a new bottling machine by a soda manufacturer. An example of an intangible marketing factor is a consumer's pride in the ownership of a Porsche rather than another brand of car. For an exchange to take place, both the buyer and seller must feel that the price of a good or service provides an equitable value. To the buyer, the payment of a price reduces the purchasing power available for other items. To the seller, the receipt of a price is a source of revenue and an important determinant of sales and profit levels.

Exchange occurs only when there is satisfaction with the price.

Many words are substitutes for the term *price,* including: admission fee, membership fee, rate, tuition, service charge, donation, rent, salary, interest, retainer, and assessment. No matter what it is called, a price contains all the terms of purchase: monetary and nonmonetary charges, discounts, handling and shipping fees, credit charges and other forms of interest, and late-payment penalties.

A price can be in monetary or nonmonetary terms.

A nonprice exchange would be selling a new iron for 10 books of trading stamps or an airline offering tickets as payment for advertising space and time.[2] Monetary and nonmonetary exchange may be combined. This is common with automobiles, where the consumer gives the seller money plus a trade-in. This combination allows a reduction in the monetary price.

From a broader perspective, price is the mechanism for allocating goods and services among potential purchasers and for ensuring competition among sellers in an open market economy. If there is an excess of demand over supply, prices are usually bid up by consumers. If there is an excess of supply over demand, prices are usually reduced by sellers. See Figure 18-1.

In Chapter 18, the importance of price to any organization and its relationship to other marketing variables, price and nonprice competition, and the factors affecting price decisions are examined. Chapter 19 deals with the development and implementation of a price strategy. Chapter 20 concentrates on applying the techniques for setting prices.

The Importance of Price and Its Relationship to Other Marketing Variables

The value of price decisions has risen because more firms recognize their far-reaching impact, several industries have been deregulated, and other factors.

The importance of price decisions to marketing executives has risen substantially since the 1960s. In a 1964 study, executives ranked pricing as the sixth most important of 12 marketing factors, behind product planning, marketing research, sales management, advertising and sales promotion, and customer services. Half of the executives did not consider pricing to be one of the five most vital areas.[3] However, in a 1986

---

[2] See Arthur Bragg, "Bartering Comes of Age," *Sales & Marketing Management* (January 1988), pp. 61–63 ff.

[3] Jon G. Udell, "How Important Is Pricing in Competitive Strategy?" *Journal of Marketing,* Vol. 28 (January 1964), pp. 44–48.

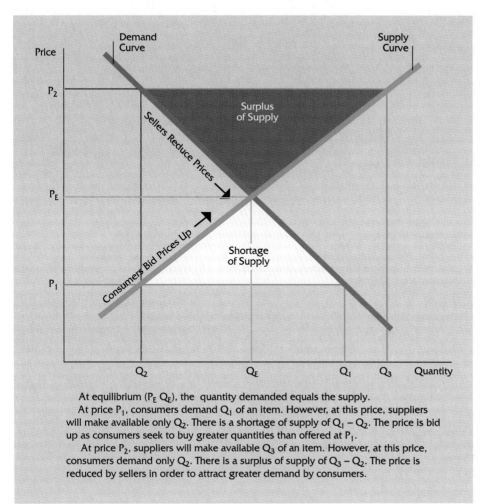

At equilibrium (P_E Q_E), the quantity demanded equals the supply.

At price P_1, consumers demand Q_1 of an item. However, at this price, suppliers will make available only Q_2. There is a shortage of supply of $Q_1 - Q_2$. The price is bid up as consumers seek to buy greater quantities than offered at P_1.

At price P_2, suppliers will make available Q_3 of an item. However, at this price, consumers demand only Q_2. There is a surplus of supply of $Q_3 - Q_2$. The price is reduced by sellers in order to attract greater demand by consumers.

FIGURE 18-1
The Role of Price in Balancing Supply and Demand

survey of executives, pricing was cited as the most critical "pressure point." It was rated ahead of new-product introductions, market segmentation, selling costs, and 14 other factors. And a 1987 survey of executives found that pricing was ranked second only to product planning among the 12 marketing factors analyzed.[4]

There are various reasons for this. First, because price in a monetary or nonmonetary form is a key component of exchange, it appears in every marketing transaction. And more companies now recognize the impact of price on image, sales, profit margins, and so on. Second, the deregulation of communications, banking, transportation, and other industries over the past fifteen years has resulted in greater price competition. Third, in the 1970s and early 1980s, costs and prices rose rapidly; this has led to both firms and consumers being more price conscious. Fourth, in the 1970s through the mid-1980s, a strong U.S. dollar with respect to foreign currencies gave many foreign competitors a price advantage in U.S. markets. Today a larger number of

[4] "Segmentation Strategies Create New Pressure Among Marketers," *Marketing News* (March 28, 1986), pp. 1, 19; and Saeed Samiee, "Pricing in Marketing Strategies of U.S.- and Foreign-Based Companies," *Journal of Business Research*, Vol. 15 (February 1987), pp. 17–30.

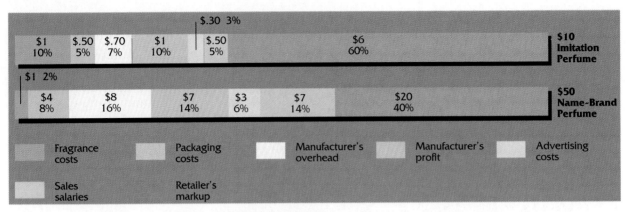

FIGURE 18-2 **Imitation Vs. Name-Brand Perfume Pricing**
SOURCE: Authors' estimates, based on "Breaking Down the Bottles," *Newsday* (April 1, 1985), Business, p. 1.

companies closely monitor international currency fluctuations and adapt their marketing strategies accordingly.

Pricing must be interrelated with product, distribution, and promotion decisions.

Because a price places a value on the overall combination of marketing variables offered to consumers (such as product features, image, store location, customer service, etc.), pricing decisions must be made in conjunction with product, distribution, and promotion plans. For example, Parfums de Coeur and other firms make imitations of expensive perfumes manufactured by Chanel, Estee Lauder, Giorgio, and so on, and sell them for one-third to one-fifth the price of those perfumes. The imitating firms use similar ingredients but save money on packaging, advertising, and sales salaries. They also distribute through mass merchandisers such as K mart. Their annual sales are about $200 million. Figure 18-2 compares the marketing costs of the imitators with those of brand-name companies. Figure 18-3 shows a recent ad by Parfums de Coeur.

Following are some of the basic ways in which pricing is related to other marketing and firm variables:

▶ Prices frequently vary over the life cycle of a product, from high prices to gain status-conscious innovators to low prices to attract the mass market.

▶ Customer service levels are affected by prices. Low prices are usually associated with little customer service.

▶ From a distribution perspective, the prices charged to channel members must adequately compensate them for their functions, yet be low enough to be competitive with other brands at the wholesale or retail level.

▶ There may be conflict in a distribution channel if a manufacturer tries to control or suggest final prices.

▶ Product lines with different features — and different prices — can attract different market segments.

▶ The personal sales force needs some flexibility in negotiating prices and terms.

▶ The efforts of marketing and finance personnel need to be coordinated. Marketers often begin with the prices that consumers are willing to pay and work backward to determine channel member prices and acceptable production costs. Finance people typically start with costs and add desired profits to come up with selling prices.

▶ When costs change, decisions must be made as to whether to pass these changes on to consumers, to absorb them, or to modify product features.

Price and Nonprice Competition

With *price competition,* sellers influence consumer demand primarily through changes in price levels. With *nonprice competition,* sellers minimize price as a factor in consumer demand by creating a distinctive good or service via promotion, packaging, delivery, customer service, availability, and other marketing factors. The more unique a product offering is perceived to be by consumers, the greater is the freedom of a firm to set prices above its competitors'. See Figure 18-4.

In price competition, sellers move along a demand curve by raising or lowering their prices. Price competition is a flexible marketing tool because prices can be adjusted quickly and easily to reflect demand, cost, or competitive factors. However, of all the controllable marketing variables, a pricing strategy is the easiest for a competitor to duplicate. This may result in a ''me-too'' strategy or even in a price war. Furthermore, the government may monitor anticompetitive aspects of price strategies.

In nonprice competition, sellers shift the demand curves of consumers by stressing the distinctive attributes of their products. This enables firms to increase unit sales at a given price or to sell their original supply at a higher price. The risk with a nonprice strategy is that consumers may not perceive the seller's attributes as better than the competition's. Then the consumer would buy the lower-priced item he or she believes is similar to the higher-priced item.

Price competition occurs when sellers stress low prices; nonprice competition emphasizes factors other than price.

557

You're the Marketer

How Do You Market $3,000 Luggage Sets?

Gedalio Grinberg and his family own 70 per cent of the North American Watch Corporation, which sold $128 million of Piaget, Corum, Concord, and Movado watches—priced from $195 to $500,000 each—during fiscal 1988. Grinberg is credited with making Americans more conscious of the status of watches, particularly gold watches. Now Grinberg wants to elevate the status of luggage.

Recently Grinberg purchased Wings Luggage, an upscale luggage maker that had fallen on hard times. When Grinberg bought Wings, annual sales were only $1 million; its factory, which once employed 125 workers, was down to only 25 employees.

This is how Grinberg plans to turn Wings around:

▶ *Wings' distinctive design will continue. Its water-repellant tan-and-brown diamond pattern in cotton jacquard with leather trim and 24 karat gold-plated brass hardware make the luggage highly visible.*

▶ *The luggage will be priced at $3,000 for a set of five matched pieces, versus $500 for traditional branded luggage sets. This is still significantly below the $9,000 for a compara-ble set of Louis Vuitton luggage or $40,000 for a set of Hermes luggage.*

▶ *Although he has had some legal difficulties stemming from his refusal to sell to discounters, Grinberg is determined to do everything possible to keep his products away from discounters.*

▶ *He plans to spend $1 million to advertise Wings in magazines such as* Town and Country, Vogue, *and* Travel & Leisure. *Each ad will bear the line "Impeccable design. Masterful craftsmanship. Made in America since 1912."*

There is some question as to whether Grinberg's formula will work with luggage. Comments an old-line luggage manufacturer: "You can wear a status watch literally everywhere, from the boardroom to the bedroom, but how much time are you really seen with your luggage?" And a fashion consultant is also not sure whether status can be successfully applied to luggage: "Who wants to give off those kinds of signals?"

As a marketing consultant for Gedalio Grinberg, what recommendations would you make regarding Wings?

SOURCE: Based on material in Phyllis Berman, "Is Traveling Well the Best Revenge?" *Forbes* (August 8, 1988), pp. 52–54.

These are examples of price- and nonprice-oriented strategies:

▶ Motel 6, Hampton Inns, Comfort Inn, and Red Roof Inns are all "no-frills" hotel chains that offer rooms at rates that are at least 20 to 50 per cent less than the rates charged by hotel chains such as Hilton. They appeal to travelers with feelings such as these: "We don't spend a whole lot of time in the hotel. Why spend $100 a night when you're getting the same benefit for $35 a night?"[5]

▶ At the Texas Heart Institute, a surgical organization founded by Dr. Denton A. Cooley (a noted heart surgeon), patients pay about $15,000 for standard heart

[5] Michael Totty, "No-Frills Motels Upgrade to Grab Business Travelers," *Wall Street Journal* (June 9, 1988), p. 33.

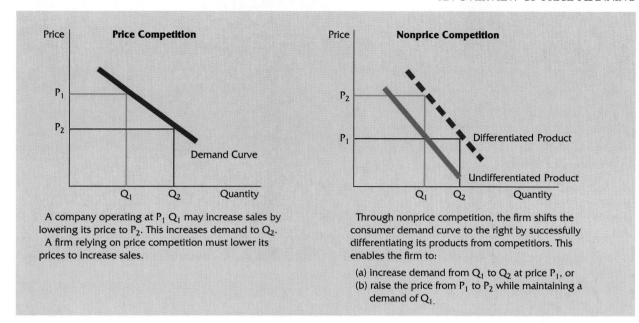

FIGURE 18-4 **Price and Nonprice Competition**

bypass surgery—about 40 per cent less than the national average. Patients pay one flat fee for everything, including the hospital stay, the surgeon, and other medical specialists. At other hospitals, they receive separate bills for each service that is provided.[6]

► Snap-On Tools makes a variety of tools that are sold primarily to service station mechanics and other professional repairpeople and technicians. Snap-On is able to charge prices 2.5 times those of its competitors because of superior quality and service. Its 4,300 distributors regularly visit customers in fully equipped vans; every six months they clean their customers' Snap-On tools, while showing new products.[7] See Figure 18-5.

► Curtis Mathes makes high-end televisions, stereos, and other consumer electronics. It features a free six-year buyer-protection plan that covers both parts and labor. The company's long-term goal is to increase its "base of brand-loyal customers by convincing consumers that the brand stands for value."[8]

Factors Affecting Pricing Decisions

Before a firm develops a pricing strategy (which will be described in Chapter 19), it should analyze the outside factors affecting decisions. Like distribution decisions, price decisions depend heavily on elements external to the firm. This contrasts with product and promotion decisions, which are more directly controlled by the firm.

Outside factors should be studied before enacting a price strategy.

[6] Mark Ivey, "Will Denton Cooley Make Medical History Again?" *Business Week* (March 27, 1989), pp. 56, 58.
[7] Geoffrey N. Smith, "Snap-On's Proprietary Ingredient," *Forbes* (October 6, 1986), pp. 156–162.
[8] Christy Fisher, "Curtis Mathes Does About-Face," *Advertising Age* (December 5, 1988), p. 36.

Sometimes the outside elements greatly influence the company's ability to set prices; in other instances, they have little impact. Figure 18-6 outlines the major factors, which are described next.

Consumers

*According to the **law of demand**, more is bought at low prices; **price elasticity** explains reactions to changes.*

It is essential for company personnel involved with pricing decisions to understand the relationship between price and consumer purchases and perceptions. This relationship is explained by two economic principles — the law of demand and the price elasticity of demand — and market segmentation.

The ***law of demand*** states that consumers usually purchase more units at a low price than at a high price. The ***price elasticity of demand*** shows the sensitivity of buyers to price changes in terms of the quantities they will purchase.[9]

Price elasticity is computed by dividing the percentage change in quantity demanded by the percentage change in price charged:

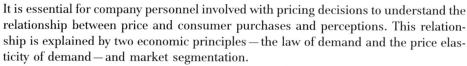

$$\text{Price elasticity} = \frac{\dfrac{\text{Quantity 1} - \text{Quantity 2}}{\text{Quantity 1} + \text{Quantity 2}}}{\dfrac{\text{Price 1} - \text{Price 2}}{\text{Price 1} + \text{Price 2}}}$$

This formula shows the percentage change in quantity demanded for each 1 per cent change in price. Because quantity demanded usually decreases as price increases, elasticity is a negative number. However, for purposes of simplicity, the elasticity calculations in this section are expressed as positive numbers.

*Demand may be **elastic**, **inelastic**, or **unitary**.*

Elastic demand occurs if relatively small changes in price result in large changes in quantity demanded. Numerically, price elasticity is greater than 1. With elastic

[9] See John Morton and Hugh J. Devine, Jr., "How Prices *Really* Affect Your Sales," *Business Marketing* (May 1987), pp. 90–103; and Gerard J. Tellis, "The Price Elasticity of Selective Demand: A Meta-Analysis of Econometric Models of Sales," *Journal of Marketing Research*, Vol. 25 (November 1988), pp. 331–341.

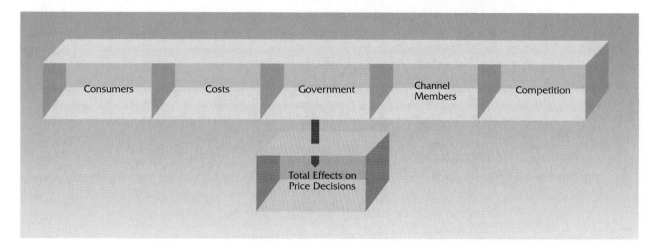

FIGURE 18-6
**Factors Affecting
Price Decisions**

demand, total revenue goes up when prices are decreased and goes down when prices rise. ***Inelastic demand*** takes place if price changes have little impact on quantity demanded. Price elasticity is less than 1. With inelastic demand, total revenue goes up when prices are raised and goes down when prices decline. ***Unitary demand*** exists if changes in price are exactly offset by changes in quantity demanded, so that total sales revenue remains constant. Price elasticity is 1.

The type of demand that exists is based on two criteria: availability of substitutes and urgency of need. When the consumer believes there are many similar goods or services from which to choose or there is no urgency to make a purchase, demand is elastic and highly influenced by price changes. A price increase will lead to the purchase of a substitute or a delayed purchase. A price decrease will expand sales as customers are drawn from competitors or move up the date of their purchases. For many customers, the airfare for a vacation is highly elastic. If prices go up, these consumers may travel by car or postpone a trip.

When the consumer believes a firm's offering is unique or there is an urgency to make a purchase, demand is inelastic and little influenced by price changes. Neither a price increase nor a price decline will have much impact on demand. For example, in most communities, if home heating oil prices are increased or decreased, demand remains relatively constant because there is often no viable substitute and people must have their homes properly heated. Brand loyalty also generates inelastic demand because consumers perceive their brand as distinctive and may not accept substitutes. Finally, emergency conditions increase demand inelasticity. A consumer with a flat tire would pay more for a replacement than a consumer with time to shop around. Figure 18-7 shows elastic and inelastic demand.

It should be noted that demand elasticity usually varies over a wide range of prices for the same good or service. At very high prices, even sales of essential items decline (transit ridership would drop dramatically if fares rose from $1 to $2; this would allow cars to become a more reasonable substitute). At very low prices, demand cannot be stimulated further, as market saturation is reached and consumers begin to perceive quality to be inferior.

Table 18-1 shows the price-elasticity calculations for an appliance repair service. There is a clear relationship between price and demand. At the lowest price, $16, demand is greatest: 11 service calls. At the highest price, $40, demand is least: 5

The type of demand depends on availability of substitutes and urgency of need.

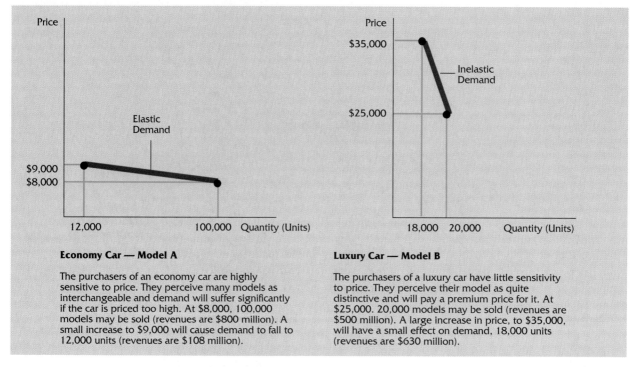

Economy Car — Model A

The purchasers of an economy car are highly sensitive to price. They perceive many models as interchangeable and demand will suffer significantly if the car is priced too high. At $8,000, 100,000 models may be sold (revenues are $800 million). A small increase to $9,000 will cause demand to fall to 12,000 units (revenues are $108 million).

Luxury Car — Model B

The purchasers of a luxury car have little sensitivity to price. They perceive their model as quite distinctive and will pay a premium price for it. At $25,000. 20,000 models may be sold (revenues are $500 million). A large increase in price, to $35,000, will have a small effect on demand, 18,000 units (revenues are $630 million).

FIGURE 18-7
Demand Elasticity for Two Models of Automobiles

service calls. Demand is inelastic between $16 and $28, and total revenue (price × quantity) increases as price increases. Demand is unitary between $28 and $32, and total revenue remains the same ($224). Demand is elastic between $32 and $40, and total revenue declines as the price rises within this range.

Although a fee of either $28 or $32 yields the highest total revenue, $224, other criteria must be evaluated before selecting a price. The appliance firm in Table 18-1 should consider costs per service call; total sales at each service call, including parts and additional labor; travel time; the percentage of satisfied customers at the different price levels, as expressed by repeat business; and the potential for referrals of new customers.

Consumers can be categorized on the basis of their price orientation.

It is also necessary to understand the importance of price to various market segments because all consumers are not equally price-conscious. For instance, consumers can be divided into segments such as these:

▶ Price shopper—This person is interested in the "best deal" for a product.
▶ Brand-loyal customer—This persons believes his/her current brand is superior to others and is willing to pay a "reasonable" price for a product.
▶ Status seeker—This person is interested in prestigious brands and product categories and willingly pays whatever price is set; higher prices signify greater status.
▶ Service/features shopper—This person places a high value on customer service and/or product features and is willing to pay for them.
▶ Convenience shopper—This person values nearby locations, long store hours, and so on, and is willing to pay above-average prices.

TABLE 18-1   Price Elasticity for an Appliance Repair Service

Price of Service Call	Service Calls Demanded per Day	Revenues from Service Calls	Price Elasticity of Demand[a]	Type of Demand
$16.00	11	$176.00		
			$E = \dfrac{(11 - 10)}{(11 + 10)} \Big/ \dfrac{(\$16 - \$20)}{(\$16 + \$20)} = 0.43$	Inelastic
$20.00	10	$200.00		
			$E = \dfrac{(10 - 9)}{(10 + 9)} \Big/ \dfrac{(\$20 - \$24)}{(\$20 + \$24)} = 0.58$	Inelastic
$24.00	9	$216.00		
			$E = \dfrac{(9 - 8)}{(9 + 8)} \Big/ \dfrac{(\$24 - \$28)}{(\$24 + \$28)} = 0.76$	Inelastic
$28.00	8	$224.00		
			$E = \dfrac{(8 - 7)}{(8 + 7)} \Big/ \dfrac{(\$28 - \$32)}{(\$28 + \$32)} = 1.00$	Unitary
$32.00	7	$224.00		
			$E = \dfrac{(7 - 6)}{(7 + 6)} \Big/ \dfrac{(\$32 - \$36)}{(\$32 + \$36)} = 1.31$	Elastic
$36.00	6	$216.00		
			$E = \dfrac{(6 - 5)}{(6 + 5)} \Big/ \dfrac{(\$36 - \$40)}{(\$36 + \$40)} = 1.73$	Elastic
$40.00	5	$200.00		

[a] Expressed as positive numbers.

The firm must determine which of these segments is represented by its target market and plan accordingly.

Research confirms that not all consumers use price as the dominant purchase determinant. One study found that more shoppers prefer traditional department stores than full-line discount stores. These shoppers are attracted by assortments, service, and return policies.[10] Another study determined that increased advertising reduces price sensitivity; demand becomes more inelastic due to greater brand preferences. Price-sensitive shoppers are most affected by ads.[11] A third study found that a consumer's perception of price as high or low, **subjective price,** may be more important than actual price.[12] For example, a consumer may believe that a low price represents a good buy or inferior quality — or that a high price represents status or poor value, depending on his/her perception.

The consumer's perception of a price level is the ***subjective price.***

Costs

The costs of raw materials, supplies, labor, advertising, transportation, and other items are frequently beyond the control of the firm. Yet, these costs have a great influence on company prices. In the United States, from the early 1970s through 1981, many costs rose rapidly and pushed prices to high levels, before leveling off in 1982. For example,

For a decade, costs increased dramatically in many areas, before leveling off in 1982.

[10] "Keying in on Convenience," *Chain Store Age Executive* (February 1986), pp. 11–15.
[11] Lakshman Krishnamurthi and S. P. Raj, "The Effect of Advertising on Consumer Price Sensitivity," *Journal of Marketing Research*, Vol. 22 (May 1985), pp. 119–129.
[12] Kent B. Monroe, "Buyers' Subjective Perceptions of Price," *Journal of Marketing Research*, Vol. 10 (February 1973), pp. 73–80; and Paul A. Scipione, "Perceived Value Gauged by Indexing Purchaser Response," *Marketing News* (April 11, 1986), p. 15.

▶ Fuel costs went up almost 500 per cent, before falling significantly in 1985 and 1986. This placed pressure on airlines, the trucking industry, and the automobile industry. Since 1988, fuel costs have increased moderately.

▶ Silver and gold prices were extremely volatile. Silver went from $6 per ounce to more than $50 per ounce, before dropping back to $6 – $10 per ounce. This created difficulties for the photography industry, which used silver as a prime ingredient in film. Gold went from $45 per ounce to about $1,000 per ounce, before settling at $350 – $500 per ounce. This had an effect on dentists and jewelers.

▶ The minimum wage rose from $1.60 per hour in 1970 to $3.35 per hour on January 1, 1981. This affected fast-food retailers and other firms who rely on unskilled labor. Congress is presently weighing legislation to phase in a higher per hour minimum wage.

▶ Mortgage interest rates more than doubled between 1977 and 1981, severely dampening the housing market, before starting to decline in 1983. They have fluctuated mildly since then.

▶ The cost of prime-time television commercials went up dramatically. As an illustration, a 30-second commercial on the 1972 Super Bowl cost $100,000. In 1989, the cost was $675,000.

Since 1982, overall cost increases have been relatively low. Although the 1980 inflation rate was 13.5 per cent, the 1989 rate was expected to be about 5 per cent or so. This has generally meant better cost control for marketers and more stable prices. However, unexpected events have still affected specific industries. For example, a 1988 drought led to higher costs in some food categories in 1989.[13]

When costs rise, companies pass along increases, alter products, or delete some items.

During periods of rapidly rising costs, companies can react in one or more ways. They can leave products unchanged and pass along all of their cost increases to consumers, leave products unchanged and pass along part of their increases and absorb part of them, modify products to hold down costs and maintain prices (by reducing size, offering fewer options, or using lesser-quality materials), modify products to gain consumer support for higher prices (by increasing size, offering more options, or using better-quality materials), and/or abandon unprofitable products.

Sometimes, despite a company's or an industry's best intentions, it may take several years to get runaway costs (and prices) under control. A good illustration is the automobile industry, where costs and prices have gone up drastically since 1970. At that time, an average U.S. automobile had a retail price of under $3,500; by 1988, the average price was over $14,000.[14] Among the costs auto executives have had to deal with are tens of billions of dollars in retooling from large to small cars; high fixed costs for plant, equipment, and unionized labor; hundreds of millions of dollars for anti-pollution devices and safety features; and investments of up to $1 billion or more to develop a single major new car model. As a result, pricing decisions have to be made well in advance; little flexibility is possible.

Cost decreases can have positive benefits for marketing strategies.

When cost declines occur, firms can lower selling prices or raise profit margins, as these illustrations show. The use of microprocessors in personal computers has reduced their costs significantly by requiring less wiring and assembly time during production, improving durability, and enlarging information-processing capability. Prices have been steadily lowered, thus expanding the market considerably. Low sugar

---

[13] Robert Johnson, "Effects of Drought Seen in Food Prices," *Wall Street Journal* (August 1, 1988), p. 19.

[14] U.S. Commerce Department data.

prices allow candy manufacturers to increase package size (and profits) without raising prices.

To assist companies in controlling costs, Polaroid has developed a computerized program for organizational consumers to deal with their suppliers. It is called zero base pricing (ZBP), and Polaroid is selling the program to interested firms. Under ZBP, a supplier provides a buyer with a breakdown of all unit costs, including materials, labor, and profit. The impact of these costs on each other is studied and forecasts are made. Then the buyer makes cost-cutting suggestions to the supplier. As Polaroid's purchasing director notes: "Our vendors are usually surprised to find out that we know as much about their businesses as they do."[15]

Suppliers also benefit from ZBP:

> For example, by encouraging a supplier of film rollers to substitute a plastic gear for a metal gear and to shift to reusable packaging, Polaroid helped the supplier knock nearly $600,000 a year out of production costs.[16]

Government

Government actions relating to pricing can be divided into the five major areas shown in Figure 18-8. They are discussed in the following subsections.

Price Fixing

The government places limitations on horizontal and vertical price fixing. **Horizontal price fixing** results from agreements among manufacturers, among wholesalers, or among retailers to set prices at a given stage in a channel of distribution. Such agreements are illegal according to the Sherman Antitrust Act and the Federal Trade Commission Act, regardless of how "reasonable" the price is.

Horizontal price fixing is illegal and results from agreements among companies at the same stage in a channel.

When violations are found, the penalties can be severe, as these illustrations show. The largest companies in the folding-carton industry were fined several hundred million dollars, and several executives were given jail sentences (or probation) for fixing the prices of corrugated cardboard boxes and cartons. A number of supermarket chains were fined a total of $1.5 million for agreeing to limit the use of double and triple coupons; with double or triple coupons, the retailers matched or exceeded manufacturer discounts with their own. And in an out-of-court settlement, six producers of chlorine and caustic soda agreed to pay almost $12 million to customers (such as the city of Philadelphia) that had accused them of horizontal price fixing.[17]

To avoid price-fixing charges, a company must be careful not to

▶ Coordinate discounts, credit terms, or conditions of sale with competitors;
▶ Discuss prices, markups, and costs at trade association meetings;
▶ Arrange with competitors to issue new price lists at the same date;
▶ Arrange with competitors to rotate low bids on contracts;

---

[15] Don Baum, "Polaroid Corp. Is Selling Its Technique for Limiting Supplier Price Increases," *Wall Street Journal* (February 13, 1985), p. 36; and Louis S. Richman, "Why Inflation Is Not Inevitable," *Fortune* (September 12, 1988), p. 122.

[16] Richman, "Why Inflation Is Not Inevitable," p. 122.

[17] Winston Williams, "Cardboard Makers to Pay $300 Million to End Pricing Suit," *New York Times* (May 2, 1979), pp. A1, D4; "Judge Fines Waldbaum and Stop & Shop Cos. on Antitrust Charges," *Wall Street Journal* (June 11, 1985), p. 46; and Lisa Lazorko, "Six Chlor-Alkali Producers Settle," *Chemical Week* (February 17, 1988), p. 8.

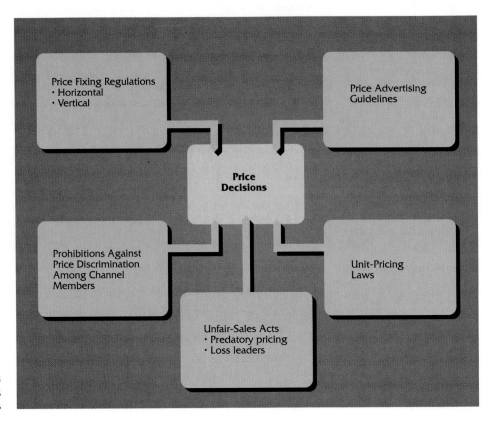

FIGURE 18-8
**Government Actions
Affecting Price Decisions**

▶ Agree with competitors to uniformly restrict production to maintain high prices; or

▶ Exchange information with competitors, even on an informal basis.[18]

*Under **vertical price fixing**, manufacturers or wholesalers try to control retail prices. Today this practice is limited.*

Vertical price fixing occurs when manufacturers or wholesalers are able to control the final selling prices of their goods or services. Until 1976, the Miller-Tydings Act (in conjunction with the McGuire Act) enabled these firms to strictly set and enforce retail prices if they desired. This practice was known as fair trade. It protected small retailers and maintained brand images by forcing all retailers within fair-trade states to charge the same price for affected products.

Fair trade was heavily criticized by consumer groups, many retailers, and a number of manufacturers for being noncompetitive, keeping prices artificially high, and rewarding retailer inefficiency. As a result, the Consumer Goods Pricing Act of 1975 terminated all interstate utilization of fair trade or resale price maintenance as of March 1976.

Today retailers cannot be required to adhere to list prices developed by manufacturers or wholesalers. In most cases, retailers are free to establish final selling prices. Manufacturers or wholesalers may control retail prices only through one of these methods:

▶ Manufacturer or wholesaler ownership of retail facilities.

---

[18] "Price Fixing: Crackdown Under Way," *Business Week* (June 2, 1975), pp. 42–48; and Steven Mitchell Sack, "Price Advice: Keep It Fair," *Sales & Marketing Management* (May 1986), pp. 53–55.

▶ Consignment selling, whereby the manufacturer or wholesaler owns items until they are sold and assumes costs normally associated with the retailer, such as advertising and selling.

▶ Careful screening of the retailers through which goods or services are sold. A supplier can bypass or drop individual distributors (if they are not performing up to the manufacturer's standards), as long as there is no collusion among the supplier and other distributors.

▶ Suggesting realistic retail list prices.

▶ Preprinting prices on products.

▶ Establishing a customary price (such as 25 cents for a newspaper) that is accepted by consumers.

In 1989, Panasonic agreed to pay consumers $16 million to avert court proceedings in New York on charges that it had fixed retail prices on electronics products. Nationwide, 665,000 consumers were eligible for rebates of $17 to $45. According to the New York State attorney general, Panasonic had threatened to cut off a number of retailers (including K mart and Dayton Hudson) unless they raised prices by 5 to 10 per cent: "If the scheme had not been stopped, the cost [to consumers] would have been monumental."[19]

Price Discrimination

The *Robinson-Patman Act* prohibits manufacturers and wholesalers from price discrimination in dealing with different channel-member purchasers of products of "like quality" if the effect of such discrimination is to injure competition. Covered by the act are prices, discounts, rebates, premiums, coupons, guarantees, delivery, warehousing, and credit policies. Terms and conditions of sale must be made available to all competing channel members on a proportionately equal basis.[20]

The Robinson-Patman Act was enacted in 1936 in order to protect small retailers from unfair price competition from large chains. It was feared that small retailers would be driven out of business due to the superior bargaining power of large chains with product suppliers. The act required price differences to be limited to a supplier's cost savings in dealing with different retailers. The act remains a major legal restriction on pricing.

There are some exceptions to the Robinson-Patman Act. Price discrimination within a channel is permissible if each buyer purchases products with substantial physical differences, if noncompeting buyers are involved, if prices do not injure competition, if price differences are justified by costs, if market conditions change (such as production costs rising), or if the seller reduces price to meet another supplier's bid.

Discounts are acceptable if the seller demonstrates that they are available to all competitive channel buyers on a proportionate basis, that they are sufficiently graduated so that small as well as large buyers can qualify, or that they are cost-justified. For example, the seller must prove that discounts for cumulative purchases (total volume

*The **Robinson-Patman Act** prohibits price discrimination when selling to channel members.*

---

[19] Ann Hagedorn, "Panasonic Plans Rebate to Avoid Pricing Charges," *Wall Street Journal* (January 19, 1989), pp. B1, B6.

[20] See Steven A. Meyerowitz, "Beware of Price-Discrimination Pitfalls," *Business Marketing* (June 1986), pp. 136–140; Norton E. Marks and Neely S. Inlow, "Price Discrimination and Its Impact on Small Business," *Journal of Consumer Marketing,* Vol. 5 (Winter 1988), pp. 31–38; and Rhonda Razzano, "FTC Decision May Affect Price-Breaks, Take-Backs," *Chain Store Age Executive* (February 1989), pp. 18, 20.

during the year) or multistore purchases by retail chains are based on cost savings.

Although the Robinson-Patman Act is oriented toward sellers, it provides specific liabilities for purchasing firms under Section 2(F):

> It shall be unlawful for any person engaged in commerce, in the course of such commerce, knowingly to induce or receive a discrimination in price which is prohibited in this section.

Channel members should attempt to obtain the lowest prices charged to any competitor in their class. Yet they should not bargain so hard that the discounts received cannot be explained by one of the acceptable exceptions to the act.

Minimum Prices

*Unfair-sales acts protect small firms from **predatory pricing** by large companies and limit the use of **loss leaders**.*

A number of states have enacted **unfair-sales acts (minimum price laws)** that prevent retailers from selling merchandise for less than the cost of the product plus a fixed percentage that covers overhead and profit. Approximately half the states have unfair-sales acts that cover all types of products and retail situations. About two-thirds of the states have laws that involve specific products, such as bread, dairy items, and liquor.[21] Unfair-sales acts are intended to protect small firms from predatory pricing by larger competitors and to limit the use of loss leaders by retailers.

Under **predatory pricing,** large companies cut prices on products below their cost in selected geographic areas in order to eliminate small local competitors. At the federal level, predatory pricing is banned by the Sherman and Clayton Acts. Manufacturers, wholesalers, and retailers are all subject to these acts. There is some evidence that predatory price enforcement is now being relaxed in terms of cost calculations and in the definitions of affected market areas.

Loss leaders, items priced below cost to attract customers to a seller — usually in a store setting, are also restricted by some unfair-sales acts. Sellers use loss leaders, typically well-known and heavily advertised brands, to increase overall company sales. They assume that customers who are drawn by loss leaders will also purchase nonsale items. Because consumers benefit from loss leaders, the laws pertaining to them are rarely enforced.

Unit Pricing

*With **unit pricing,** consumers can compare prices for different-sized packages.*

The lack of uniformity and consistency in package sizes has led to unit-pricing legislation in a number of states. **Unit pricing** enables consumers to compare price per quantity for competing brands and for various sizes of the same brand.

Food stores are affected most; and in many cases, they must express price per unit of measure as well as total price. For example, unit pricing would show that a 12-ounce can of soda selling for 30 cents is priced at 2.5 cents per ounce, whereas a 67.6-ounce (2-liter) bottle of the same brand of soda selling for $1.39 is priced at 2.1 cents per ounce. The larger size is cheaper than the smaller.

The costs of unit pricing to retailers include per-unit price computations, printing of shelf labels, and computer records. These costs are influenced by the number of stores in a chain, sales per store, the number of items under unit pricing, and the frequency of price changes.

---

[21] Louis W. Stern and Thomas L. Eovaldi, *Legal Aspects of Marketing Strategy* (Englewood Cliffs, N.J.: Prentice-Hall, 1984), p. 263.

When unit-pricing legislation was first enacted almost two decades ago, research showed it to be ineffective. Studies found that consumers in general did not use the information and that low-income consumers (for whom the laws were most intended) were least likely to use unit-price data. Accordingly, critics stated that the legislation was costly without providing consumer benefits.

More recent research shows unit pricing is effective and suggests that consumer learning about unit pricing and the resulting behavioral changes take time. However, urban residents (who have lower educational and income levels) are still less likely to use unit-pricing data than more upscale suburban residents.[22]

Price Advertising

Guidelines for price advertising have been developed by the Federal Trade Commission (FTC) and various trade associations, such as the Better Business Bureau. The FTC's guidelines specify standards of permissible conduct in five categories:

FTC guidelines establish standards for price ads.

▶ A company may not claim or imply that a price has been reduced from a former level unless the original price was offered to the public on a regular basis during a reasonable, recent period of time.

▶ A firm may not claim that its price is lower than that of competitors or the manufacturer's list price without verifying, through price comparisons involving large quantities of merchandise, that the price of an item at other outlets in the same trading area is in fact higher.

▶ A suggested list price or a premarked price cannot be advertised as a reference point for a sale or a comparison with other products unless the advertised product has actually been sold at the list or premarked price.

▶ Bargain offers such as "free," "buy one, get one free," "two-for-one sale," "half-price sale," and "1-cent sale" are frequently used by companies. These practices are considered deceptive if the terms of the offer are not disclosed at the beginning of a sales presentation or advertisement, the stated regular price of an item is inflated to create an impression of savings, or the quality or quantity of the merchandise is reduced without informing the consumer. A firm may not continuously advertise the same product as being on sale.

▶ **Bait-and-switch advertising** is an illegal procedure by which customers are lured to a seller that advertises items at exceptionally low prices and then told the items are out of stock or are of inferior quality. Sales personnel attempt to switch customers to more expensive substitutes, and there is no intention of selling the advertised item. Signs of bait-and-switch are a refusal to demonstrate requested products, the disparagement of sale items, an insufficient quantity of sale items to meet reasonable demand, a refusal to take orders, the demonstration of defective products, and a company compensation plan encouraging salespeople to engage in the practice.[23]

*Under **bait-and-switch advertising,** sellers illegally draw customers through deceptive pricing.*

These guidelines require careful record keeping and documentation.

---

[22] David A. Aaker and Gary T. Ford, "Unit Pricing Ten Years Later: A Replication," *Journal of Marketing,* Vol. 47 (Winter 1983), pp. 118–122.

[23] Earl W. Kintner, *A Primer on the Law of Deceptive Practices* (New York: Macmillan, 1978), pp. 213–230; and Stern and Eovaldi, *Legal Aspects of Marketing Strategy,* pp. 394–398.

Marketing Controversy

Are Price-Matching Policies Largely Promotional Ploys?

For years, various discount retailers have said that they will match or beat competitors' advertised prices—usually for 30 days after products are purchased from the retailers. But now, some traditional retailers are using price matching to reassure price-conscious consumers that their prices are fair. A price-matching pledge "amounts to an insurance policy that shoppers won't feel foolish."

In 1988, Montgomery Ward expanded its price-matching policy to all store items. In 1989, Sears began promoting its new price-matching policy as "a way to communicate to the customer the confidence that the prices are good throughout the store." Sears Tire America chain promises to refund 125 per cent of the price difference between its prices and lower-priced retailers for the same tires.

Retailers favoring a price-matching strategy cite the following:

▶ *Surveys indicate price matching is popular with consumers and helps sustain a value-for-the-price image.*

▶ *This strategy reduces perceived risk for shoppers because they know that they can get a refund if a product is advertised for less elsewhere.*

▶ *Price matching commits retailers to equal competitors' prices, not to beat them.*

▶ *Careful shoppers should be able to pay less than casual shoppers. For example, consumers who use coupons pay less than those who do not.*

Critics of price matching see these as the disadvantages:

▶ *This policy gives consumers the perception that regular prices are the lowest available. But if retailers really want to offer savings, they would set their everyday prices as low as possible.*

▶ *Although price matching lends itself to products such as branded appliances, it is difficult for consumers to use it with clothing or private-label merchandise.*

▶ *Retailers heavily promote price matching, yet realize that very few customers actually follow-up by bringing in competitors' ads after they make purchases.*

▶ *Consumers who do not carefully price shop (or who assume regular prices are already low) pay more than careful price comparison shoppers.*

What do you think?

SOURCE: Based on material in Francine Schwadel, "Are Price-Matching Policies Largely PR?" *Wall Street Journal* (March 16, 1989), p. B1.

Channel Members

Every channel member wants a role in setting prices.

Generally each channel member seeks to play a significant role in setting prices in order to generate sales volume, obtain adequate profit margins, derive a suitable image, ensure repeat purchases, and meet specific goals.

A manufacturer can gain greater control over price by using an exclusive distribution system or minimizing sales through price-cutting discounters, preticketing prices on merchandise, opening its own retail outlets, offering goods on consignment, providing adequate margins to channel members, and most importantly by developing strong national or regional brands that consumers have brand loyalty toward and for which they will pay premium prices.

A wholesaler or retailer can gain stronger control over price by stressing its importance as a customer to the manufacturer, linking resale support (displays, personal selling) to the profit margins allowed by the manufacturer, refusing to carry unprofitable products, stocking competitive items, developing strong dealer brands so that consumers are loyal to the seller and not the manufacturer, and purchasing outside traditional channels.

Wholesalers and retailers may engage in **selling against the brand,** whereby they stock well-known brands, place high prices on them, and then sell other brands for lower prices. This is often done to increase the sales of their own brands. The practice is disliked by manufacturers because the sales of their brands decline.

*To increase private-brand sales, some retailers **sell against the brand.***

Sometimes, when wholesalers and retailers go outside traditional distribution channels, they may purchase **gray market goods,** which are foreign-made products imported into the United States by distributors (suppliers) that are not authorized by the products' manufacturers. Personal stereos, videocassette recorders, car stereos, watches, and cameras are just some of the items handled in this manner. When wholesalers and retailers buy gray market goods, the purchase price is less than it would be otherwise, and they have greater control over their selling price. The result is often discounted prices for consumers, which may be upsetting to manufacturers and their authorized dealers.

Gray market goods enable channel members to pay lower prices by bypassing traditional channels.

To maximize channel-member cooperation regarding price decisions, the manufacturer needs to consider four factors: channel-member profit margins, price guarantees, special deals, and the impact of price increases. Wholesalers and retailers require appropriate profit margins in order to cover their costs (shipping, storage, credit, advertising, etc.) and earn reasonable profits. Therefore, the prices manufacturers charge their channel members must take these profit margins into account. An attempt by a manufacturer to reduce traditional margins for wholesalers or retailers may lose their cooperation and perhaps find them unwilling to carry a product. Pricing through the distribution channel is discussed further in Chapter 20.

Channel members may seek price guarantees to maintain inventory values and profit. As noted in Chapter 12, **price guarantees** assure wholesalers or retailers that the prices they pay are the lowest available. Any discount given to competitors will also be given to the original purchasers. Guarantees are most frequently requested for the new firms or the new products that want to gain entry into an established channel of distribution.

Price guarantees reassure channel members.

Often manufacturers present special deals, consisting of limited-time discounts and/ or free merchandise, to stimulate purchases by wholesalers and retailers. The deals may require channel members to pass their savings on to final consumers to increase the latter's demand. For example, soda bottlers normally give retailers large price discounts on new products to encourage the retailers to make purchases and to offer low introductory prices to consumers.

Finally, the effect of price increases on channel-member behavior should be evaluated. Usually when manufacturers raise prices to channel members, the increases are passed along to consumers. This practice is more difficult for items with customary prices, such as candy or newspapers, where small cost rises may be absorbed by the channel members. In any event, cooperation depends on an equitable distribution of costs and profit within the channel.

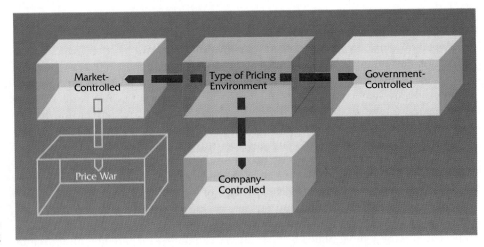

FIGURE 18-9
The Competitive Environments of Pricing

Competition

*A firm may face a **market-controlled**, **company-controlled**, or **government-controlled** price environment.*

Another factor contributing to the degree of control a firm has over prices is the competitive environment within which it operates. See Figure 18-9.

A ***market-controlled price environment*** is characterized by a high level of competition, similar goods and services, and little control over price by individual companies. Firms attempting to charge much more than the going competitive price would attract few customers because demand for any single firm is weak enough that customers would switch to a competitor. Similarly, a firm would gain little by selling for less because competitors would match price cuts.

A ***company-controlled price environment*** is characterized by moderate competition, well-differentiated goods and services, and strong control over price by individual firms. Companies may succeed with above-average prices because consumers view their offerings as unique. Differentiation may be based on brand image, features, associated services, assortment, or other factors. Discounters also can carve out a niche in this environment by attracting consumers interested in low prices. The choice of a price depends on the strategy and target market.

A ***government-controlled price environment*** is characterized by prices being set or strongly influenced by some level of government. Examples are public utilities, buses, taxis, and state universities. In each of these cases, government bodies determine prices after obtaining input from the affected firms, institutions, or industries as well as other interested parties (such as consumer groups).

Companies may have to adapt to changes in the competitive environment in their industry. For example, the price environment facing transportation (airlines, trucking, railroads, and intercity bus services), telecommunications (long-distance telephone services), and financial markets (banking and brokerage firms) has shifted from government-controlled to market-controlled — although some stronger firms in these industries have managed to develop a company-controlled price environment.

Price wars occur when competing firms frequently lower prices.

Because price strategies are relatively easy and quick to copy, the reaction of competition is predictable if the firm initiating price changes is successful. Accordingly, marketing decision makers should view price from both short-run and long-run perspectives. Excessive price competition may lead to long and costly ***price wars,*** in which various firms continually try to undercut each other's prices to draw customers.

These wars usually result in low profits or even losses for the participants and in some companies being forced out of business.

In recent years, price wars have been intense among car-rental firms, airlines, blank videocassette tape manufacturers, supermarkets, insurance companies, and others. For many, the experience has been similar to that voiced by one senior executive, "We've created a monster. The question is, have we created such a monster that we'll never be able to bring prices back up?"[24]

Summary

1. *To define the terms price and price planning* A price represents the value of a product for both the seller and the buyer. Price planning is systematic decision making relating to all aspects of pricing by a company; it involves both tangible and intangible factors, purchase terms, and the nonmonetary exchange of goods and services. Exchange does not take place unless both the buyer and seller agree that a price represents an equitable value. Price also balances supply and demand.

2. *To demonstrate the importance of price and study its relationship with other marketing variables* Since the 1960s, price decisions have become much more important to marketing executives. This is the result of price (monetary or nonmonetary) being part of every type of exchange, deregulation, cost rises in the 1970s and early 1980s, and foreign competition.

   Price decisions must be made in conjunction with other marketing-mix plans. And pricing is often related to the product life cycle, customer service levels, and other specific marketing and firm variables.

3. *To differentiate between price and nonprice competition* Under price competition, sellers influence consumer demand primarily through changes in price levels; they move consumers along a demand curve by raising or lowering prices. With nonprice competition, sellers minimize price as a sales tool and emphasize other marketing characteristics such as image, packaging, and features; they shift the demand curves of consumers by stressing product distinctiveness.

4. *To examine the factors affecting pricing decisions* Several factors affect a firm's pricing decisions: consumers, costs, government, channel members, and competition. The law of demand states that consumers usually purchase more units at a low price than at a high price. The price elasticity of demand explains the sensitivity of buyers to price changes in terms of the quantities they purchase. Demand may be elastic, inelastic, or unitary. It is influenced by the availability of substitutes and the urgency of need. Consumers can be divided into several market segments based on their level of price consciousness. Subjective price may be more important than actual price.

   The costs of raw materials, supplies, labor, advertising, transportation, and other items affect prices. Large cost increases often cause companies to raise prices to consumers, modify goods and services, and abandon some offerings. Cost declines can benefit marketing strategies by improving the firm's ability to plan prices.

   Government restrictions affect a broad variety of pricing areas. Price fixing, both horizontal and vertical, is subject to severe limitations. The Robinson-Patman Act bans most forms of price discrimination to channel members that are not justified by costs. Many states have unfair-sales acts (minimum price laws) to protect small firms against predatory pricing. Unit pricing requires specified retailers to post prices in terms of quantity. The Federal Trade Commission has a series of guidelines for price advertising.

   Often each channel member seeks a role in pricing. Manufacturers exert control through

---

[24] Betsy Morris, "Coke and Pepsi Step Up Bitter Price War," *Wall Street Journal* (October 10, 1988), p. B1.

573

exclusive distribution, preticketing, opening their own outlets, offering goods on consignment, providing adequate margins, and having strong brands. Wholesalers and retailers exert control by making large purchases, linking sales support to margins, refusing to carry items, stocking competitive brands, developing dealer brands, and purchasing outside traditional channels. Manufacturers need to consider channel-member profit margins, price guarantees, special deals, and the ramifications of price increases.

A market-controlled price environment has a high level of competition, similar products, and little control over price by individual firms. A company-controlled price environment has a moderate level of competition, well-differentiated products, and strong control over price by individual firms. In a government-controlled price environment, the government sets or influences prices. Some competitive actions may result in price wars, in which firms try to undercut each other's prices.

Key Terms

price (p. 554)
price planning (p. 554)
price competition (p. 557)
nonprice competition (p. 557)
law of demand (p. 560)
price elasticity of demand (p. 560)
elastic demand (p. 560)
inelastic demand (p. 561)
unitary demand (p. 561)
subjective price (p. 563)

horizontal price fixing (p. 565)
vertical price fixing (p. 566)
Robinson-Patman Act (p. 567)
unfair-sales acts (minimum price laws) (p. 568)
predatory pricing (p. 568)
loss leaders (p. 568)
unit pricing (p. 568)
bait-and-switch advertising (p. 569)
selling against the brand (p. 571)

gray market goods (p. 571)
price guarantees (p. 571)
market-controlled price environment (p. 572)
company-controlled price environment (p. 572)
government-controlled price environment (p. 572)
price wars (p. 572)

Review Questions

1. Cite at least three reasons why price decisions are more important today than in the 1960s.
2. Explain the role of price in balancing supply and demand. Refer to Figure 18-1.
3. What would be the risk with using a nonprice-oriented strategy?
4. Distinguish between elastic and inelastic demand. Why is it necessary for a company to understand these differences?
5. At a price of $30, a firm could sell 1,000 units. At a price of $20, it could sell 1,300 units. Calculate the elasticity of demand and state what price the firm should charge—and why.
6. If costs rise rapidly, how could a company react?
7. Is vertical price fixing always illegal? Explain your answer.
8. Does the buyer have any potential liability under the Robinson-Patman Act? Why or why not?
9. In what way are loss leaders different from bait-and-switch advertising?
10. How can a firm turn a market-controlled price environment into a company-controlled one?

Discussion Questions

1. How could a firm estimate price elasticity for a new product?
2. When would you pass along a cost decrease to consumers? When would you not pass the decrease along?
3. Present five examples of price advertising for a sporting-goods store that would violate FTC guidelines.
4. Under which circumstances could a manufacturer successfully decline to offer price guarantees to its retailers?
5. Describe several benefits and costs of a price war to the winner.

Big Steel: Betting the Future on Lower Costs*

During the turbulent 1979 to 1986 period, the U.S. steel industry was battered by imports—whose market share almost doubled to 26 per cent; and domestic steel prices fell by 30 per cent (to compete with imports). From 1982 to 1986, U.S. steel makers suffered cumulative losses of $11.7 billion.

Today, in contrast, the integrated operations of such steel companies as USX, LTV, Bethlehem, and Inland—all of which transform iron ore, limestone, and coal into steel—are considered among the best in the world. These companies "are the least vulnerable to foreign competition and an economic downturn because of their location and ongoing efforts to improve their productivity. They are by far the best plants in the U.S."

For example, the Gary Works, Indiana, plant of USX has operated at full capacity since early 1987. Gary Works is the nation's largest steel mill, with more than nine million tons of steel-making capacity. It lost $250 million per year in the early 1980s; today its annual operating profits exceed $300 million. Gary Works is considered "one of the most impressive plant turnarounds in the history of U.S. industry."

The present success of U.S. steel makers is due to several factors. The U.S. dollar's fall in value against the currencies of other countries has undercut the competitive position of foreign steel makers. For instance, the cost per ton of cold-rolled steel made in the United States is slightly less than that for steel made in Korea, Britain, and West Germany, and 20 per cent less than Japanese steel.

USX, LTV, Bethlehem, and Inland benefit by producing flat-rolled steel for auto makers, the industry's largest customers. Flat-rolled steel requires high quality control, which cannot be provided by minimills, and has steady demand.

By using continuous casting for 80 per cent of

finished U.S. steel, energy is saved and quality is improved. Inland's new continuous-casting process softens steel before rolling it a second time to temper it. This requires only four operators and one supervisor to process a coil of steel. Previously, Inland needed ten employees. Other improvements at Inland have also led to substantial cost decreases. A ton of steel is now made with just four hours of labor, compared with more than six hours at Japanese and German firms.

Steel workers at large U.S. steel firms accepted a $1.23 per hour wage cut in 1983. The reduction was supposed to be eliminated in 1986; but it was not restored by all firms. In addition, a 1987 contract between USX and its union reduced wages and benefits there by about $2.45 per hour (however, some of this reduction was given in exchange for profit sharing).

U.S. steel makers have closed their least efficient plants and focused attention on updating the newer plants that benefit from low transportation costs due to their access to the Great Lakes. The firms have devoted $2.9 billion (38 per cent of their total steel-related expenditures since 1981) toward upgrading these facilities and making them more competitive.

Although the cost picture for most large U.S. steel makers looks positive, there are three developments that could have a significant impact on them. First, because of past industry difficulties, union leaders were willing to accept wage reductions in return for job security. Now union leaders want their members to be rewarded for the industry turnaround. Second, the limitations on steel exports to the United States that were negotiated in the early 1980s are scheduled to expire shortly. Some analysts feel these limitations will not continue because of protests by domestic steel users or because of an international trade agreement. Third, the health of the U.S. steel industry could be affected by a recession or by a sudden rebound in the value of the dollar: "There are a lot of factors outside of the control of the steel makers."

---

* The data in this case are drawn from Julia Flynn Silver, " 'Big Steel' Bets the Future on Its Indiana Mills," *New York Times* (December 25, 1988), Section 3, p. 5; and Rick Wartzman, "Early Steel-Labor Contracts Anticipated," *Wall Street Journal* (May 3, 1989), p. A8.

QUESTIONS

1. Would you expect steel customers to have inelastic or elastic demand? Why? What are the consequences of this for steel makers?
2. Which cost advantages of U.S. steel producers would you view as permanent? Which are temporary? Explain your answer and its implications.
3. What other key cost factors for steel makers have not been noted in the case? Explain your answer.
4. Is the price environment for U.S. steel makers market-controlled, company-controlled, or government-controlled? Why?

◀ CASE 2 ▶

Art Dealers: The Furor Over Price Posting[†]

New York City, through its Department of Consumer Affairs, is now enforcing a 1971 "Truth in Pricing" law specifying that the prices for paintings and sculptures in art galleries must be clearly posted. According to the law, art dealers must mark the prices of all items for sale, either on the objects themselves or nearby. Fines for not posting prices range from $25 to $250 per object.

After randomly inspecting thirty galleries during fall 1987—and finding that none were displaying prices and most did not even have price lists available for inspection by customers, the Department of Consumer Affairs informed the galleries that they would be required to comply with the law by March 1, 1988, or face fines. On March 2, 1988, another 58 galleries were inspected at random and 17 were issued fines.

New York's Department of Consumer Affairs feels that it is as important for art galleries to post prices as it is for department stores, supermarkets, and appliance stores. Posting prices

- ▶ Reduces the possibility of consumer deception. Every consumer is entitled to know the price of an item and to use the same beginning point in bargaining. Art galleries do not have the right to raise the price of an item to an out-of-towner or to a consumer who "must have" a given painting.
- ▶ Helps educate consumers. Many works of art are unique. There are no list prices and no model number equivalents for art; thus judging

the value of art works is difficult for many consumers.

- ▶ Involves less wasted time for both shoppers and art galleries. Shoppers can concentrate on art that is within their price range; and salespeople spend less of their time being questioned about art that consumers would not consider buying.
- ▶ Leads to more price competition among dealers. Consumers are then able to more easily compare the price levels as well as the offerings of different art galleries.
- ▶ Leads to higher buyer confidence in purchases. The consumer has less doubt about whether the price charged for a piece of art is fair.
- ▶ Discourages the practice of art galleries whereby they exhibit important works to stimulate consumer attention but have no intention of selling these works.

Despite the preceding, the majority of art dealers do not like the concept of posting prices. Among the typical negative reactions to price-posting requirements are these: Posting prices affects the ability of dealers to effectively bargain with their customers; this is a right they should have.

Dealers do not want the general public (those who visit galleries just to look) to know the value of the works available in their galleries. They are concerned about the possible theft of and damages to expensive art.

Clearly posting prices encourages passersby to make verbal comments about the value of art pieces. Dealers are particularly concerned that cyn-

[†] The data in this case are drawn from Meg Cox, "What Effrontery! Art Dealers Are Told to Price Their Stuff," *Wall Street Journal* (March 17, 1988), pp. 1, 15.

ical or derogatory comments may be made in front of potential customers.

Dealers want to protect the privacy of their buyers. As one gallery director says, "You might see the price and then know what someone paid for it when you see it in his dining room."

By not posting prices, consumers who are interested in particular works of art are encouraged to inquire about them. This begins the dealer's process of communicating with customers, identifying their needs, and determining their price range. This is another right that dealers believe they should not have to give up.

Dealers say there are relatively few unscrupulous galleries that take advantage of consumers by unfair pricing methods. Thus, it is unreasonable to penalize all dealers by forcing them to incur the costs involved in posting and changing prices to reflect market conditions. These additional costs would have to be passed on to consumers.

QUESTIONS

1. Describe how an art gallery could utilize price and nonprice competition approaches.
2. Evaluate the arguments on both sides relating to the posting of prices on works of art.
3. As an art dealer, how would you handle New York's price-posting law? Why? Which laws discussed in this chapter also affect art galleries? How would you respond to them? Explain your answer.
4. Do you feel that art gallery prices in New York are market-controlled, company-controlled, or government-controlled? Why?

CHAPTER 19

Developing a Pricing Strategy

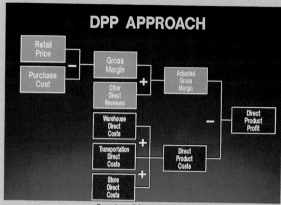

DPP APPROACH

Retail Price − Purchase Cost = Gross Margin

Gross Margin + Other Direct Revenues = Adjusted Gross Margin

Warehouse Direct Costs + Transportation Direct Costs + Store Direct Costs = Direct Product Costs

Adjusted Gross Margin − Direct Product Costs = Direct Product Profit

Reprinted by permission of Willard Bishop Consulting, Ltd.

A large, highly regarded consumer-goods manufacturer offers more than a dozen versions of one of its leading products. The numbers cranked out by the company's accounting system suggest that each version costs about the same to produce. Because the products are priced similarly, they apparently earn equivalent profit margins. But the company's top manufacturing executive knows otherwise. His gut tells him that some low-volume products are money losers. Says he: "We've been hiding the real picture from ourselves."

According to one accounting expert, "Many U.S. companies don't know where they are making money and where they are losing." The methods used to allocate costs among a firm's products have often been insufficient, resulting in prices that are too low for some products and too high for others.

Accordingly, a growing number of manufacturers, wholesalers, and retailers are insisting on better accounting data and are becoming more conscious of allocating all costs when making price decisions. These firms are refining their collection process for cost data and are better integrating cost analyses in pricing strategies. Let us look at some examples of this.

Among the industrial-goods manufacturers using more focused accounting data in price decision making are Rockwell International and IBM. In the past, Rockwell allocated overhead expenses in direct proportion to direct labor costs. As a consequence, a division making truck axles overcosted high-volume axles by 20 per cent and undercosted low-volume axles by as much as 40 per cent. Rockwell's practice of overpricing high-volume axles lured competitors into the marketplace, and the firm lost market share for one of its best-selling products. Said Rockwell's corporate cost-accounting director, "Competitors don't want your cats and dogs, they want the volume business." Rockwell is now one of thirty firms belonging to an organization called Computer Aided Manufacturing International, which is developing a framework to update cost management systems.

By refining its cost-accounting system, IBM today allocates overhead costs directly to specific products. For example, to better allow costs to be monitored, IBM uses self-contained production lines. At the Lexington, Kentucky plant, typewriters and computer keyboards have separate production lines. In the past, when these products shared production facilities, overhead costs had to be allocated arbitrarily.

Some wholesalers and retailers, by using a concept known as direct product profitability (DPP), are also better measuring the costs and profits associated with individual products. DPP allows these firms to assign direct costs (such as warehousing, transportation, handling, and selling) to individual items.

DPP looks at all of a wholesaler's or retailer's costs— from the time items are received to when they are placed in a customer's shopping bag or delivered to him/her. After costs are allotted, profit figures are calculated by item and the profitability of one item compared to another. The DPP framework allows firms to compute profits per unit based on cost analysis that was not typically considered in the past with gross margins. K mart, Kroger, and Neiman-Marcus are among the retailers using DPP spreadsheets to determine the costs and profits associated with individual items.[1]

In this chapter, we will look at the overall process of developing a pricing strategy—including the setting of pricing objectives, the use of various basic pricing approaches, how a pricing strategy is implemented, and how prices can be adjusted.

[1] Ford S. Worthy, "Accounting Bores You? Wake Up," *Fortune* (October 12, 1987), pp. 43-52; Gary Robins, "Focus on DPP: Not Only for Groceries," *Stores* (July 1988), pp. 48-52; and Priscilla Donegan, "DPP: Still Slow Going," *Progressive Grocer* (December 1988), pp. 39-45.

Overview

A pricing strategy includes objectives, broad policy, the strategy, implementation, and adjustments.

There are five stages in developing a pricing strategy: objectives, broad policy, strategy, implementation, and adjustments. See Figure 19-1. It is important to recognize that all these stages are affected by the external factors discussed in Chapter 18.

Like any planning activity, a pricing strategy begins with a clear statement of objectives and ends with an adaptive or corrective mechanism. It is essential that pricing decisions be integrated with the firm's overall marketing program. This is done in the broad price-policy phase shown in Figure 19-1.

The development of a pricing strategy is not a one-time occurrence. It needs to be reviewed when a new product is introduced, an existing product is revised, the competitive environment changes, a product moves through its life cycle, a competitor initiates a price change, costs rise, the firm's prices come under government scrutiny, and so on.

These are some indications that a pricing strategy may be performing poorly:

▶ Prices are changed too frequently.
▶ Pricing policy is difficult to explain to consumers.
▶ Channel members complain that profit margins are inadequate.
▶ Price decisions are made without adequate marketing research information.
▶ Too many different price options are available.
▶ Too much sales personnel time is spent in bargaining.
▶ Prices are inconsistent with the target market.
▶ A high proportion of goods are marked down or discounted late in the selling season in order to clear out surplus inventory.
▶ Too high a proportion of customers are price-sensitive and are attracted by competitors' discounts. Demand is elastic.
▶ The firm has major problems conforming with pricing legislation.

This chapter describes in detail each of the components of a pricing strategy shown in Figure 19-1.

Pricing Objectives

A pricing strategy should be consistent with and reflect overall company objectives. It is possible for different firms in the same industry to have dissimilar objectives and, therefore, different pricing strategies. For example, in the clothing industry, fashions are made and marketed by all kinds of firms. French designers seek a prestige image, control over prices, customer loyalty, and high per-unit profits. They produce expensive originals, appeal to upscale, status-conscious consumers, and use exclusive distribution (with virtually no promotion except for fashion shows). They sell a relatively small number of their products. In contrast, mass-production clothiers such as Gitano are low-cost manufacturers interested in volume sales and high total profits. They produce imitation versions of designer fashions, appeal to middle-class, bargain-hunting consumers, and use intensive distribution and print advertising.

Pricing objectives can be sales-, profit-, and/or status quo-based.

There are three general pricing objectives from which a firm may select: sales-based, profit-based, and status quo-based. With sales-based objectives, the firm is interested in sales growth and/or maximizing market share. With profit-based objectives, the firm is interested in maximizing profit, earning a satisfactory profit, optimizing the

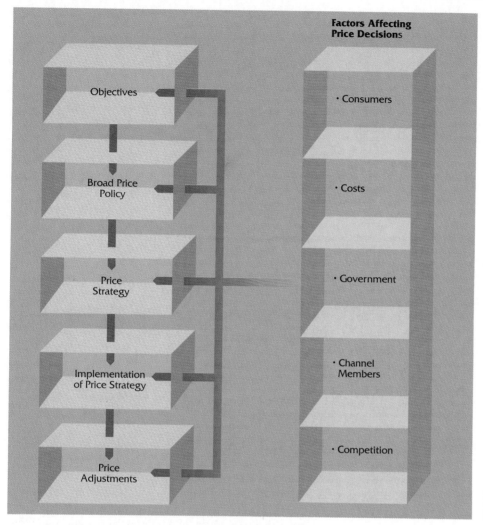

Objectives

Broad Price
Policy

Price
Strategy

Implementation
of Price Strategy

Price
Adjustments

· Consumers

· Costs

· Government

· Channel
Members

· Competition

FIGURE 19-1
**A Framework for
Developing a Pricing
Strategy**

return on investment, and/or securing an early recovery of cash. With status quo-based objectives, the firm seeks to avoid unfavorable government actions, minimize the effects of competitor actions, maintain good channel relations, discourage the entry of competitors, reduce demands from suppliers, and/or stabilize prices. See Figure 19-2.

A company with ***sales-based pricing objectives*** is oriented toward high sales volume and/or expanding its share of sales relative to its competitors'. A firm would focus on sales-based objectives for either (or all) of three reasons. One, it is interested in market saturation or sales growth as a major step leading to market control and sustained profits. Two, it seeks to maximize unit sales and is willing to trade low per-unit profits for larger total profits. Three, it assumes that higher sales will enable the firm to have lower per-unit costs.

A company with ***profit-based pricing objectives*** orients its strategy toward some type of profit goal. Profit-maximization objectives are used when a firm designates high dollar profit as a goal, such as $1 million before taxes. Satisfactory-profit objectives are used by a firm seeking stable profits over a period of time. Rather than maximize

*Sales-based objectives
seek high sales volume or
increased market share.*

*Profit-based objectives
range from maximization to
recovery of cash. Goals can
be per unit or total.*

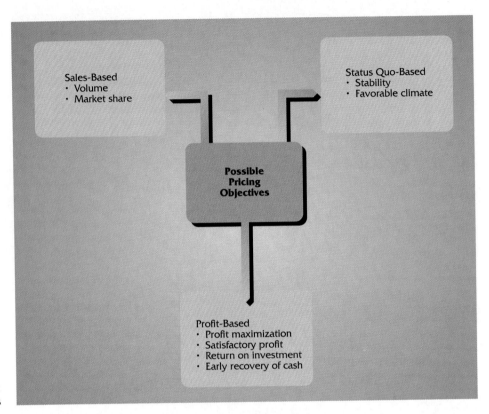

FIGURE 19-2
Pricing Objectives

profits in any given year, which could result in declines in nonpeak years, the firm sets a steady profit goal for a number of years, such as $700,000 per year for five years. With return-on-investment objectives, the firm states that profits must relate to investment costs. This objective is frequently used by regulated utilities as a means of justifying rate-increase requests. Early-recovery-of-cash objectives are used by firms that desire high initial profits because they are short of funds or uncertain about the future.

Profit may be expressed in per-unit or total terms. Per-unit profit equals the revenue a seller receives for one unit sold minus costs. An item such as designer clothing would have a high unit profit. Total profit equals the revenue a seller receives for all items sold minus costs. It is computed by multiplying per-unit profit times the number of units sold. An item such as Gitano clothing would have a low unit profit. Its profitability is based on the number of units that are sold (turnover). Products with high per-unit profits may have lower total profits than products with low per-unit profits because the lower prices of the latter could generate a much greater level of consumer demand. However, this depends on the elasticity of consumer demand.

Direct product profitability allots costs to products or product categories.

When using profit-based pricing objectives, firms need to allocate properly various general costs to each product or product category they market; otherwise they cannot determine if goals are being reached. One emerging technique for assigning costs is known as ***direct product profitability (DPP),*** whereby warehousing, transportation, handling, selling, and other costs are quantified and assigned to each product or product category.

Status quo-based pricing objectives are sought by a firm interested in stability or in continuing a favorable climate for its operations. Pricing strategy is oriented toward avoiding declines in sales and minimizing the impact of such outside parties as government, competitors, and channel members.

Status quo-based objectives seek stability and favorable business conditions.

It should not be inferred that status quo objectives require no effort on the part of the firm. For example, a manufacturer would have to instruct salespeople not to offer different terms to competing retailers, or else the government may accuse the company of a Robinson-Patman Act violation. To retain customers, a wholesaler may have to match the price cuts of its competitors. To maintain channel cooperation, a manufacturer may have to reduce its profit margins in the face of rising costs. A retailer may have to charge low prices to discourage competitors from stocking certain product lines.

A company may pursue more than one pricing objective at the same time, such as increasing sales by 5 to 10 per cent each year, achieving a 15 per cent return on capital investments, and keeping prices near those of competitors. A firm may also set distinct short-run and long-run objectives. For example, in the short run, it may seek high profit margins on new products; in the long run, those profit margins would drop to discourage potential competitors.

Broad Price Policy

A ***broad price policy*** sets the overall direction (and tone) for a firm's pricing efforts and makes sure that pricing decisions are coordinated with the firm's decisions regarding its target market, image, and other marketing-mix factors. Such a policy also incorporates short- and long-term pricing goals. For example, a high-income market segment purchasing status brands at prestigious stores would expect high prices. A moderate-income market segment purchasing private brands at discount stores would expect low prices.

*A **broad price policy** links prices with the target market, image, and other marketing elements.*

The two most popular broad price policies are penetration pricing and skimming pricing. These policies involve two opposing philosophies and are described here.

In order to achieve high sales volume, a penetration pricing policy is frequently used. ***Penetration pricing*** utilizes low prices to capture the mass market for a good or service. It is a proper strategy when customers are highly sensitive to price, low prices discourage actual and potential competitors, there are economies of scale (per-unit production and distribution costs decrease as sales increase), and a large consumer market exists. Penetration pricing also recognizes that a high price may leave a product vulnerable to competition. The penetration pricing policy used by Vivitar is shown in Figure 19-3.

Penetration pricing aims at the mass market.

Penetration pricing is also used by Lewis Galoob Toys, a San Francisco-based manufacturer. Galoob makes such toys as Micro Machines (a line of miniature cars)—which retail for about $4 each, and Bouncin' Babies dolls—which retail for under $10 each. As Galoob's president says, "With the volume we're doing, we're seeing very nice [profits]."[2]

In many cases, penetration pricing may tap markets that were not originally anticipated. For example, few people forecast that electronic hand-held calculators would

---

[2] Carrie Dolan, "Galoob 3rd-Period Net Rebounded on Strength in Low-Priced Toys," *Wall Street Journal* (October 27, 1988), p. B5.

FIGURE 19-3
A Subtle Use of Penetration Pricing
Reprinted by permission.

reach the sales volume attained during their peak. The market expanded rapidly after prices fell below $100. It grew again as new models were introduced for $20 and less.

Skimming pricing utilizes high prices to attract the market segment that is more concerned with product quality, uniqueness, or status than price. It is a proper policy if competition can be minimized (through patent protection, brand loyalty, raw material control, or high capital requirements), funds are needed for early recovery of cash or

Skimming pricing is aimed at the consumer segment interested in quality or status.

584

Marketing Controversy

Will $5 Perfume Be Successful in the United States?

Franc's Societe Bic has been quite successful in marketing low-priced, disposable products—such as nonrefillable ballpoint pens, cigarette lighters, and razors. Now it is mass marketing perfume, which it introduced in the United States in early 1989 (backed by a $22 million advertising budget).

Parfum Bic comes in four versions, two targeted to women and two to men. These products are priced at $5 each in the United States (versus $25 to $45 for leading designer brands and $8 to $10 for imitation brands). Unlike traditional fragrances that are sold at department stores and drugstores by cosmeticians, Parfum Bic is sold on a self-service basis via racks and checkout counters. According to the company, the perfume is following the "Bic heritage—high quality at affordable prices, convenient to purchase, and convenient to use."

Bic feels that $5 perfume will do well in the United States:

▸ *Parfum Bic fits into the firm's strong existing distribution network of drugstores, supermarkets, and other retailers.*

▸ *Young consumers will be attracted to Parfum Bic as their first perfume.*

▸ *The recent growth of "copy-cat" (designer-knockoff) fragrances to a $250 million per year business demonstrates the size of a price-sensitive market segment.*

▸ *Sales for Parfum Bic have been high in England.*

Those who do not feel that Parfum Bic will prosper offer these reasons:

▸ *Other attempts at marketing perfume at such low prices have failed. For example, Bristol-Myers' $5 fragrance called Savvy did not survive the test-marketing stage of the new-product planning process, due to poor sales performance.*

▸ *Women typically buy fragrances for their image and caché—and less for their price.*

▸ *Many price-conscious consumers would rather purchase a toilet water or cologne version of a well-known brand than a Bic brand of perfume.*

▸ *The sales of Parfum Bic in France have been less than 10 per cent of original projections.*

What do you think?

SOURCE: Based on material in Andrea Rothman, "France's Bic Bets U.S. Consumers Will Go for Perfume on the Cheap," *Wall Street Journal* (January 12, 1989), p. B4; and Pat Sloan, "$22 Million Campaign Urges: Spritz Your Bic," *Advertising Age* (February 20, 1989), pp. 3, 69.

further expansion, the market is insensitive to price or willing to pay a high initial price, and unit production and distribution costs remain equal or increase as sales increase (economies of scale are absent). The skimming price policy used by Xidex for its Dysan computer diskettes is shown in Figure 19-4.

Mercedes-Benz, a producer of automobiles and trucks, also employs skimming prices for the cars it markets in the United States. By establishing and retaining a luxury image for its vehicles, Mercedes-Benz is able to set high prices for them. The company earns at least a 20 per cent margin on these vehicles. It discourages discounting and sales. Advertising emphasizes styling, status, handling, and other product-related features; television commercials never mention prices. These were the U.S.

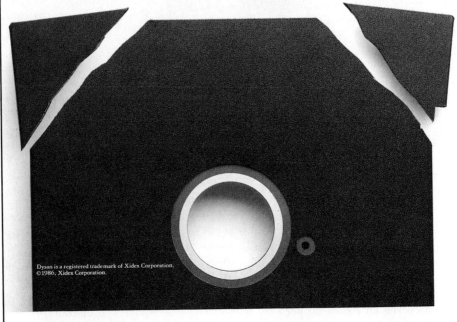

Are other diskette makers cutting more than prices?

Ever wonder why a less expensive diskette is less expensive?

Because it's less diskette.

True, most claim to be "certified 100% error-free." But 100% of what?

Most manufacturers only test 100% of the data tracks on their diskettes. But, unfortunately, they don't test between the tracks.

Dysan, on the other hand, tests 100% of the entire surface area. On every diskette we make.

Why? Because even the tiniest undetected error between tracks can render a diskette incapable of formatting or reading and writing data. And capable of suddenly and irreversibly losing all your data.

Here's another way other manufacturers take shortcuts. To determine the magnetic strength of their diskettes, they follow a standard set by the American National Standards Institute (A.N.S.I.).

But Dysan exceeds that standard by 88%. Because the stronger a diskette's magnetic signal, the longer it will record and retain your data.

Why don't other diskette makers go to the same extremes that we do? Quite simply, to save time and money.

But at Dysan, we think there's something much more important to save. Namely, your data.

Which is why we never cut corners.

For the name of the Dysan dealer nearest you, call toll free (800) 233-5099.

Dysan®

Somebody has to be better than everybody else.

Dysan is a registered trademark of Xidex Corporation.
©1986, Xidex Corporation.

FIGURE 19-4
The Skimming Price Strategy of Dysan Computer Diskettes
Reprinted by permission of Xidex Corporation.

base prices for selected 1989 models: 190E sedan, $31,590; 300E sedan, $44,850; and 500 SEC coupe, $79,840.[3]

In some situations, companies combine the two broad policies by first employing skimming pricing and then applying penetration pricing. There are several advantages to this approach. One, high prices are charged when competition is limited. Two, high prices help defray research-and-development and introductory advertising costs. Three, the first group of customers to purchase a new product is usually less sensitive to price than later groups. Four, high initial prices portray a high-quality image for a product. Five, raising initial prices often encounters market resistance; lowering prices is viewed favorably. Six, after the initial market segment is saturated, penetration pricing can be used to appeal to the mass market and expand total sales volume.

For example, Apple usually introduces new computers at relatively high prices and later lowers them to enlarge the market. In 1988, it dropped the price of the Macintosh Plus by 18 per cent. Apple's senior vice-president for marketing, in announcing the price cut, said that the reduction was intended to enable the Macintosh Plus "to reach the more value-conscious markets of home businesses and small businesses."[4]

Generally a company should outline its broad price policy by placing individual decisions into an integrated framework. The firm would decide on the interrelationship of prices for goods within a product line, how often special discounts are used, how prices compare to competition, the frequency of price changes, and the method for setting new-product prices. As one expert noted:

> Five factors define the range of a company's strategic pricing options: real costs and profits, value to the customer relative to competitor offerings, differences between market segments or customer demand factors, likely competitive reactions, and the company's marketing objectives.[5]

One useful technique for developing a broad price policy is the **multistage approach to pricing,** which divides price planning into six successive steps, with each placing constraints on the next step: identifying the target market, examining brand image, analyzing the other components of the marketing mix, outlining a broad price policy, determining a pricing strategy, and arriving at a specific price.[6] The first four steps concentrate on the enactment of a broad price policy; the last two steps center on the remaining aspects of pricing noted in Figure 19-1, which are discussed in the next several sections.

*The **multistage approach** can help set a broad price policy.*

Price Strategy

A price strategy may be cost-, demand-, and/or competition-based. See Figure 19-5. With a **cost-based price strategy,** a firm sets prices by computing merchandise, service, and overhead costs, and then adding the desired profit to these figures. Demand is not analyzed. For example, an item may cost $10 to manufacture and sell, and the firm may seek a $1 profit per unit. Selling price is then $11. Cost-based pricing

*Under a **cost-based strategy,** expenses are computed and a **price floor** set.*

---

[3] *Automotive News.*

[4] Brenton R. Schlender, "Apple Slashes Macintosh Plus Price 18% in Bid to Reposition Big-Selling Computer," *Wall Street Journal* (March 16, 1988), p. 6.

[5] "Panelists Offer Pricing Strategy Advice for Consumer and Industrial Products," *Marketing News* (February 1, 1985), p. 11.

[6] Alfred R. Oxenfeldt, "Multi-Stage Approach to Pricing," *Harvard Business Review,* Vol. 38 (July-August 1960), pp. 125–133.

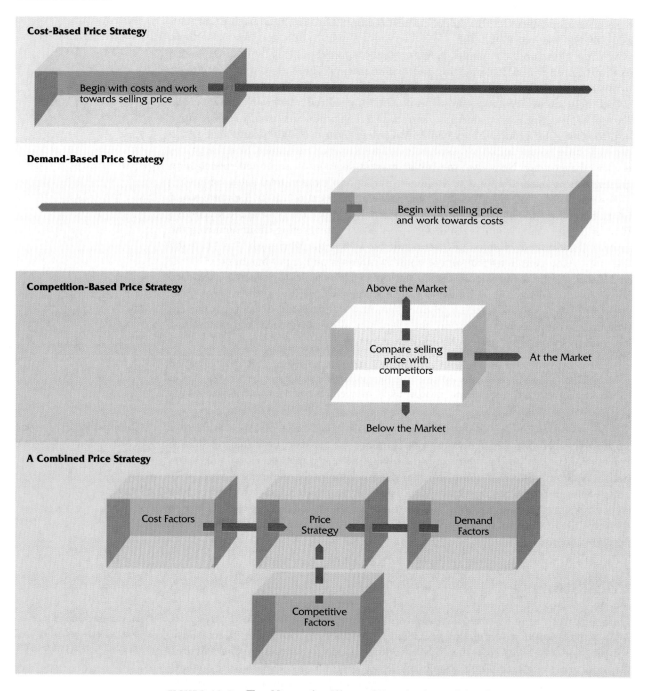

FIGURE 19-5 **The Alternative Ways of Developing a Price Strategy**

is often used by companies whose objectives are stated in terms of profit or return on investment. It sets the prices a firm must charge in order to attain its desired level of profitability. The ***price floor*** is the lowest acceptable price the firm can charge and attain its profit goal.

In a ***demand-based price strategy,*** the firm sets prices after researching consumer desires and ascertaining the range of prices acceptable to the target market. For example, if a manufacturer finds that its customers will pay $10 for an item and it needs a $3 margin to cover profit and selling expenses, production costs must not exceed $7. Demand-based pricing is used by companies that believe price is a key factor in consumer decision making. These companies identify the ***price ceiling,*** which is the maximum amount consumers will pay for a given good or service. If the ceiling is exceeded, consumers will not make purchases. Its level depends on the elasticity of demand (availability of substitutes and urgency of need).

Under a ***competition-based price strategy,*** the firm sets prices in relation to competitors. Its prices may be below the market, at the market, or above the market, depending on customer loyalty, services provided, image, real or perceived differences among brands or outlets, and the competitive environment. Competition-based pricing is applied by firms that encounter competitors selling similar items.

Elements of all three approaches should be combined when establishing a price strategy. They do not operate independently of one another. These questions demonstrate the interrelation of cost-, demand-, and competition-based methods of deriving prices. Will a given price level allow a firm to attain the desired profit (cost-based)? If prices are increased by 10 per cent, how much will unit sales decrease (demand-based)? What will competitors be likely to do if a company gives quantity discounts (competition-based)?

The attributes of cost, demand, and competitive pricing—and how they are calculated—are covered in greater depth in Chapter 20.

*Under a **demand-based strategy,** consumers are researched and a **price ceiling** set.*

*Setting prices in relation to other firms is a **competition-based strategy.***

Implementing a Price Strategy

Implementing a price strategy involves a wide variety of separate but related specific decisions in addition to the broader concepts discussed previously. The decisions involve whether and how to use customary versus variable pricing, a one-price policy versus flexible pricing, odd pricing, the price-quality association, leader pricing, multiple-unit pricing, price lining, price bundling, geographic pricing, and terms. In the following subsections, these concepts are described in detail.

Customary Versus Variable Pricing

Customary pricing occurs when a company sets good or service prices and seeks to maintain them over an extended period of time. Prices are not changed during this period. Customary pricing is used for items like candy, gum, magazines, restaurant food, and mass transit. Instead of modifying prices to reflect cost increases, organizations may reduce package size, change ingredients, or "impose a stricter transfer policy among bus lines." The assumption is that consumers prefer one of these modifications over a price hike.

Between 1971 and now, Wrigley has raised the price of its chewing gum only five times, from 10 to 15 cents, 15 to 20 cents, 20 to 25 cents, 25 to 30 cents, and 30 to 35 cents, despite steadily higher costs for sugar, gum base, and wrapping material. In order to minimize consumer resistance to the first increase from 10 to 15 cents, Wrigley changed the package size from five- to seven-stick packs. Wrigley could have

*With **customary pricing,** one price is maintained over an extended period.*

raised prices without changing package size and incurring the expense of modifying its wrapping machines, but it was concerned with consumer perceptions about value. For similar reasons, it reintroduced the five-stick pack for 25 cents in 1987.[7]

*Under **variable pricing**, prices reflect costs or differences in demand.*

With **variable pricing,** a firm intentionally alters prices to respond to cost fluctuations or differences in consumer demand. When costs fluctuate, prices are lowered or raised to reflect the changes; cost fluctuations are not absorbed and product quality is not modified in order to maintain customary prices. Through price discrimination, a company can offer distinct prices to appeal to different market segments. In this case, the prices charged to various consumers are not based on costs but on consumer sensitivity to price. Most firms use some form of variable pricing, which is examined further in Chapter 20.

It is also possible to combine customary and variable pricing. For example, a magazine may be priced at $2 per single copy and be available for $20 per year's subscription ($1.67 an issue). Under this strategy, two customary prices are charged; and the consumer selects the offer that he or she finds most attractive.

A One-Price Policy Versus Flexible Pricing

*All those buying the same product pay the same price under a **one-price policy**.*

With a **one-price policy,** a firm charges the same price to all customers who seek to purchase a good or service under similar conditions. Prices may vary according to the quantity purchased, time of purchase, and services obtained (such as delivery, installation, and an extended guarantee); but all consumers are given the opportunity to pay the same price for identical combinations of goods and services. A one-price policy builds consumer confidence, is easy to administer, eliminates bargaining, and permits self-service and catalog sales.

A one-price policy was first used over one-hundred years ago by John Wanamaker, who was also the first U.S. retailer to mark prices clearly on each item in stock. Today, throughout the United States, one-price policies are the rule for most retailers. In industrial marketing, a firm with a one-price policy would not permit its sales personnel to deviate from a published price list.

*With **flexible pricing**, different customers may pay different prices for the same product.*

Flexible pricing allows a firm to adjust prices based on the consumer's ability to negotiate or on the buying power of a large customer. For instance, consumers who are knowledgeable or who are good bargainers would pay lower prices than those who are not knowledgeable or who are poorer bargainers. Jewelry stores, automobile dealers, flea markets, real-estate brokers, antique shops, and many types of industrial marketers frequently use flexible pricing. In some cases, commissions are paid to sales personnel on the basis of the profitability of each order, which encourages them to solicit higher prices. Flexible prices to channel members are subject to the Robinson-Patman restrictions explained in Chapter 18.

One result of flexible pricing is the "free rider" phenomenon, whereby consumers gather product information from full-service sellers, shop around for the best available price, and then challenge discount sellers to "beat the lowest price."[8] This practice is detrimental to full-service companies and allows discounters to hold down their selling costs (and encourage further bargaining).

---

[7] Stephen Phillips, "The Sleepy Gum Giant Begins to Wake Up," *New York Times* (April 19, 1987), Section 3, p. 12; and "Wm. Wrigley Jr. Co.," *Advertising Age* (September 28, 1988), p. 149.

[8] Del I. Hawkins and Pamela Homer, " 'Free Riding:' The Nature of a Controversy" in Robert F. Lusch et al. (Editors), *1985 AMA Educators' Proceedings* (Chicago: American Marketing Association, 1985), pp. 82–85.

FIGURE 19-6
Odd-Pricing by Thayer Pharmacy
Reprinted by permission.

Odd Pricing

An **odd-pricing strategy** is used when selling prices are set at levels below even dollar values, such as 49 cents, $4.95, and $199. See Figure 19-6. Odd pricing has proven popular for several reasons. Consumers like receiving change. And because the cashier must make change, employers ensure that transactions are properly recorded and money is placed in the cash register. Consumers gain the impression that the firm thinks carefully about its prices and sets them as low as possible. Consumers may also believe that odd prices represent price reductions; a price of $8.95 may be viewed as a discount from $10.

*In an **odd-pricing strategy**, prices are set below even-dollar values.*

Odd prices that are one or two cents below the next even price (29 cents, $2.98) are common up to $4. Beyond that point and up to $50, five-cent reductions from the highest even price ($19.95, $49.95) are more usual. For expensive items, odd endings are in dollars ($499, $5,995).

Odd prices help many consumers to stay within their price limits and still buy the best items available. A shopper willing to spend "less than $10" for a tie will be attracted to a $9.95 tie and might be as likely to purchase it as a tie selling for $9 because it is within the defined price range. Yet the imposition of sales tax in over 45 states has the effect of raising odd prices into higher dollar levels and may reduce the effectiveness of odd pricing as a selling tool.

The Price-Quality Association

The **price-quality association** is a concept stating that consumers may believe high prices represent high quality and low prices represent low quality. When setting prices, a company should recognize that the price-quality association is usually most valid in situations where quality is difficult to judge on bases other than price, buyers

*The **price-quality association** deals with consumer perceptions.*

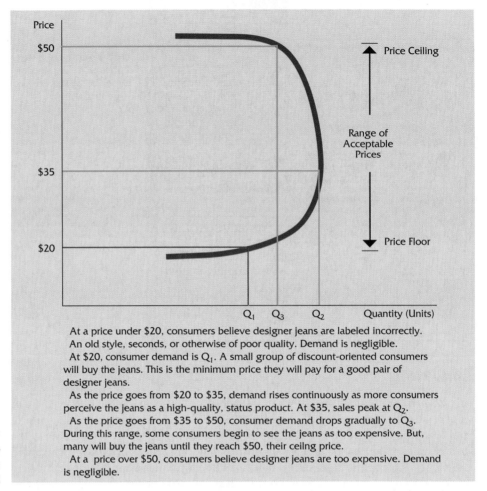

At a price under $20, consumers believe designer jeans are labeled incorrectly. An old style, seconds, or otherwise of poor quality. Demand is negligible.

At $20, consumer demand is Q_1. A small group of discount-oriented consumers will buy the jeans. This is the minimum price they will pay for a good pair of designer jeans.

As the price goes from $20 to $35, demand rises continuously as more consumers perceive the jeans as a high-quality, status product. At $35, sales peak at Q_2.

As the price goes from $35 to $50, consumer demand drops gradually to Q_3. During this range, some consumers begin to see the jeans as too expensive. But, many will buy the jeans until they reach $50, their ceilng price.

At a price over $50, consumers believe designer jeans are too expensive. Demand is negligible.

FIGURE 19-7
Demand for Designer Jeans under Prestige Pricing

perceive large differences in quality among brands, buyers have little experience or confidence in judging quality (as in the case of a new product), high prices exclude the mass market, brand names are unknown, or brand names require certain price levels to sustain their images.

However, if brand names are well known and/or consumers are confident of their ability to compare different brands in terms of nonprice factors, the price-quality association may be less valid. In these instances, many consumers may be more interested in the perceived value they receive for their money — and not believe that a higher price represents better quality. It is essential that prices properly reflect both the quality and the image the company seeks for its offerings.[9]

Prestige pricing indicates that consumers may not buy when a price is too low.

With **prestige pricing,** a theory drawn from the price-quality association, it is assumed that consumers do not buy goods or services at prices they consider to be too low. Most consumers set price floors and will not make purchases at prices below those floors — because they feel product quality and status would be inferior at

---

[9] See Valarie A. Zeithaml, "Consumer Perceptions of Price, Quality, and Value: A Means-End Model and Synthesis of Evidence," *Journal of Marketing,* Vol. 52 (July 1988), pp. 2–22; and Kent B. Monroe and William B. Dodds, "A Research Program for Establishing the Validity of the Price-Quality Relationship," *Journal of the Academy of Marketing Science,* Vol. 16 (Spring 1988), pp. 151–168.

extremely low prices. Most consumers also set upper limits for prices they consider acceptable for particular goods or services. Above the price ceilings, the items would be perceived as too expensive. For each good or service, a firm should set its price within the acceptable range between the floor and ceiling. See Figure 19-7.

When consumers are perceptually sensitive to certain prices and departures from these prices in either direction result in decreases in demand, they are responding to **psychological pricing.** Customary, odd, and prestige pricing are all forms of psychological pricing.

*In **psychological pricing,** certain prices are most effective.*

Leader Pricing

Under **leader pricing,** a firm advertises and sells key items in its product assortment at less than their usual profit margins. For a retailer, the objective of leader pricing is to increase customer traffic into a store. For a manufacturer, the objective is to gain greater consumer interest in its overall product line. In both cases, it is hoped that consumers will purchase regularly priced merchandise in addition to the specially priced items that draw them to the store or the manufacturer.

*Selling key items at low prices to attract customers is **leader pricing.***

Leader pricing is most often used with nationally branded, high-turnover, frequently purchased products. For example, in many drugstores, the best-selling items in terms of dollar sales are Kodak and Polaroid film. In order to stimulate customer traffic into these stores, film may be priced very low; in some cases, it is sold at close to cost. Film is a good item for leader pricing because consumers are able to detect low prices and they are attracted into a store by a discount on the item, which regularly sells for several dollars.

There are two kinds of leader pricing: loss leaders and prices higher than cost but lower than regular prices. As described in Chapter 18, the use of loss leaders is regulated or illegal in a number of states.

Multiple-Unit Pricing

Multiple-unit pricing is a practice whereby a company offers consumers discounts for buying in quantity in order to increase sales volume. For example, by offering items at two for 89 cents or six for $1.39, the firm attempts to sell more units than at 50 cents or 25 cents each.

*With **multiple-unit pricing,** quantity discounts are intended to result in higher sales volume.*

There are four major reasons for using multiple-unit pricing. First, customers may increase their immediate purchases if they believe a bargain is achieved through a multiple-unit purchase. Second, customers may increase their overall consumption if they make quantity purchases. For instance, the multiple-unit pricing of soda may encourage greater consumption. Third, competitors' customers may be attracted by the firm's discounts. Fourth, the firm may be able to clear out slow-moving and end-of-season merchandise.

Multiple-unit pricing will not achieve its goals if consumers merely shift their purchases and do not increase consumption of a company's brand. For example, multiple-unit pricing for Heinz ketchup will probably not result in consumers using more ketchup with their meals. Thus it will not raise total dollar sales; it will cause consumers to buy ketchup less frequently because it can be stored.

An extreme case of multiple-unit pricing exists in the computer software industry, where many software manufacturers offer site-licensing agreements to organizational consumers. Such an agreement allows a consumer to pay a flat fee for a computer software package and be able to make unlimited copies for employee use.

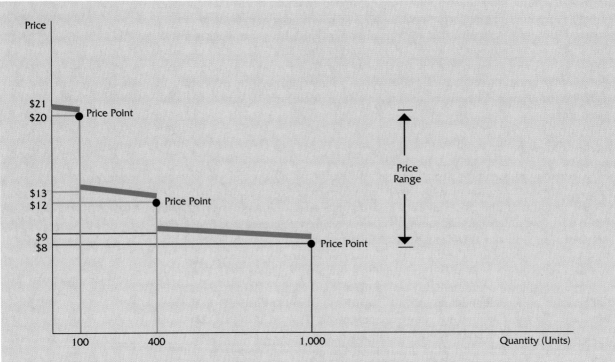

At $8, 1,000 radios can be sold. A price of $9 is perceived as substantially more expensive.

Between $9 and $12, demand remains at 400 radios, since consumers consider the prices within this range to be similar. Therefore, the price point should be $12, since this price provides the same unit sales as could be obtained at $9, $10, or $11 and total revenues are highest. A price of $13 is perceived as substantially more expensive.

Between $13 and $20, demand remains at 100 radios since consumers consider the prices within this range to be similar. Therefore, the price point should be $20, since the price provides the same unit sales and higher total revenues than any other price above $12. A price of $21 is perceived as substantially more expensive.

If the firm uses a price line of $8, $12, and $20, it will maximize total revenues. It will sell 100 radios at $20, 300 radios at $12, and 600 radios at $8. Total revenues are $10,400 (with only one price, $8, the same thousand radios would be sold, but revenues would be $8,000).

FIGURE 19-8 Price Lining for an Inexpensive Radio

Price Lining

Price lining establishes a range of selling prices and price points within that range.

Price lining involves selling products at a range of prices, with each price representing a distinct level of quality (or features). Instead of setting one price for a single version of a good or service, the firm sells two or more versions (with different levels of quality or features) at different prices. Price lining involves two decisions: defining the price range of the firm's offerings (floor and ceiling) and establishing specific price points within that range.

The price range may be defined as low, intermediate, or high. For example, inexpensive radios may be priced from $8 to $20, moderately priced radios from $22 to $50, and expensive radios from $55 to $120. After the range is determined, a limited number of price points is set. The price points must be distinct and not too close together. Inexpensive radios could be priced at $8, $12, and $20. They would not be priced at $8, $9, $10, $11, $12, $13, $14, $15, $16, $17, $18, $19, and $20. This

You're the Marketer

Should One-Price Stores Have More Than One Price?

At One Price Clothing Stores, the idea of selling all the merchandise in a store for the same price "is a very simplistic concept and is something every customer can understand." As of 1988, One Price Clothing—based in South Carolina—operated 98 stores and had annual sales of $41 million.

This is One Price Clothing's overall marketing strategy:

▶ *It carries pants, blouses, shirts, sweaters, and shorts, in a variety of sizes for juniors and misses.*

▶ *Each item sells for the same low price, which is under $10—except during special promotions when goods are discounted. Its gross profit margins are comparable to traditional specialty clothing stores.*

▶ *The chain's buyers look for special deals from manufacturers, such as when orders are canceled by other retailers or only incomplete size assortments are available.*

▶ *Inventory turns over ten times per year— about three times the turnover for a traditional specialty clothing store. Average sales*

per square foot are more than $200—comparable to a regular specialty clothing store.

▶ *It is a low-cost operator with low-rent locations, simple fixtures, and reduced merchandise-tagging expenses due to its one-price approach. Advertising is generally limited to grand opening announcements.*

Although the one-price approach is very popular among some consumers, many observers have reservations such as these: A one-price clothing store does not attract multiple consumer segments; it is difficult to maintain prices across-the-board when manufacturers raise prices on selected items; consumers may resist across-the-board increases (for example, going from $6 to $7 represents a 17 per cent price rise); consumers are not encouraged to trade up to higher-priced merchandise; price lining is not used; there is limited appeal to status; and there is too much focus on the gimmick of a one-price policy.

As a consultant to One Price Clothing Stores, which is embarking on a major store expansion program, what would you recommend regarding its price strategy?

SOURCE: Based on material in Alice Bredin, "One Price Clothing's Concept Adds Up," *Chain Store Age Executive* (April 1988), pp. 103–106.

would confuse consumers and be inefficient for the firm. Figure 19-8 illustrates price lining for inexpensive radios.

When developing a price line, the firm must consider the following factors. One, price points must be spaced far enough apart so that customers perceive quality differences among various versions — otherwise consumers might view the price floor as the price they should pay and believe that there is no difference among models. Two, price points should be spaced farther apart at higher prices because consumer demand becomes more inelastic. Three, the relationships among price points must be maintained when costs rise, so that clear differences are retained. For example, if radio costs rise 25 per cent, prices should be set at $10, $15, and $25.

Price lining offers benefits for both sellers and consumers. Sellers are able to offer an assortment of products, attract market segments, trade up consumers within a price range, control inventory by price point, reduce competition by carrying versions throughout the price range, and increase overall sales volume. Consumers are given an assortment from which to choose, confusion is minimized, comparisons may be made, and quality alternatives are available within the desired price range.

Price lining can also have several constraints. One, consumers may perceive the gaps between prices as too large. For example, a $25 handbag may be too inexpensive, whereas the next price point of $100 may be too expensive. Two, rising costs may put a squeeze on individual prices and make it difficult for a firm to maintain the proper relationship among prices. Three, markdowns or special sales may disrupt the balance in a price line, unless all items in the line are proportionately reduced in price.

Price Bundling

*A firm can use **bundled** or **unbundled pricing** in selling to consumers.*

A firm can use some form of price bundling in its strategy.[10] With **bundled pricing,** a firm offers a basic product, options, and customer service for one total price. For example, a full-service appliance store may have a single price for a refrigerator, its delivery, its installation, and a service contract. Individual items, such as the refrigerator, would not be sold separately.

With **unbundled pricing,** a firm breaks down prices by individual components and allows the consumer to decide what to purchase. For example, a discount appliance store may have separate prices for a refrigerator, its delivery, its installation, and a service contract.

Many companies choose to offer consumers both pricing options and allow a slight discount for bundled pricing. See Figure 19-9.

Geographic Pricing

*Geographic pricing alternatives are **FOB mill (factory), uniform delivered, zone,** and **base-point pricing.***

Geographic pricing outlines the responsibility for transportation charges. Often geographic pricing is not negotiated but depends on the traditional practices in the industry in which the firm operates; and all companies in that industry normally conform to the same pricing format. FOB mill (factory) pricing, uniform delivered pricing, zone pricing, and base-point pricing are the most common methods of geographic pricing.

With **FOB mill (factory) pricing,** the buyer selects the transportation form and pays all freight charges. The seller pays the costs of loading the goods (hence, "free on board"). The delivered price to the buyer depends on freight charges. Under **uniform delivered pricing,** all buyers pay the same delivered price for the same quantity of goods, regardless of their location. The seller pays for shipping. **Zone pricing** provides for a uniform delivered price to all buyers within a geographic zone. In a multiple-zone system, delivered prices vary by zone. In **base-point pricing,** firms in an industry establish basing points from which the costs of shipping are computed. The delivered price to a buyer reflects the cost of transporting goods from the basing point nearest to the buyer, regardless of the actual site of supply. These forms of pricing are summarized in Figure 19-10.

Terms

Terms outline all pricing provisions.

Terms are the provisions of price agreements, including discounts, the timing of payments, and credit arrangements. Discounts may be functional, cash, quantity, seasonal, or promotional. Payments may be made immediately, upon receipt of merchandise,

---

[10] See Joseph P. Guiltinan. "The Price Bundling of Services: A Normative Framework," *Journal of Marketing,* Vol. 51 (April 1987), pp. 74–85; and "AMA Cites 'Filtered Pricing' Move Toward Individualization," *Marketing News* (February 1, 1988), pp. 8, 30.

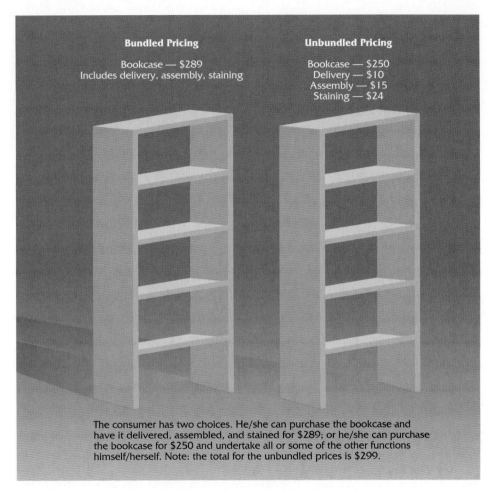

Bundled Pricing

Bookcase — $289
Includes delivery, assembly, staining

Unbundled Pricing

Bookcase — $250
Delivery — $10
Assembly — $15
Staining — $24

The consumer has two choices. He/she can purchase the bookcase and have it delivered, assembled, and stained for $289; or he/she can purchase the bookcase for $250 and undertake all or some of the other functions himself/herself. Note: the total for the unbundled prices is $299.

FIGURE 19-9
Price Bundling for a Bookcase

after a bill is received, or spread over time. The firm may insist on cash, allow open credit accounts, or accept revolving credit.

Discounts are reductions from final selling price that are available to channel members and final consumers for performing certain functions, paying cash, buying large quantities, purchasing in off-seasons, or enhancing promotions. For example, a wholesaler may purchase goods at 40 per cent off the manufacturer's suggested final list selling price. This 40 per cent would cover the wholesaler's expenses, profit, and discount to the retailer. The retailer would purchase goods for 25 per cent off list (the wholesaler would retain 15 per cent for its costs and profit).

Functional (trade) discounts are the traditional discounts provided to wholesalers and retailers to compensate them for the distribution tasks they perform. Cash discounts are reductions in invoice amounts that are given to stimulate immediate or early payments. Quantity discounts are price reductions related to efficiencies that result from large-volume purchases. Noncumulative quantity discounts are based on the size of individual orders. Cumulative quantity discounts are based on total purchases for a given period (usually one year).

Seasonal discounts are used to encourage off-peak purchases or advance orders. These purchases may receive forward dating, so that the customer does not pay for goods until after the order is received. The benefits to the seller are that storage costs

Discounts are reductions for performing functions, paying cash, and quantity and off-season buying.

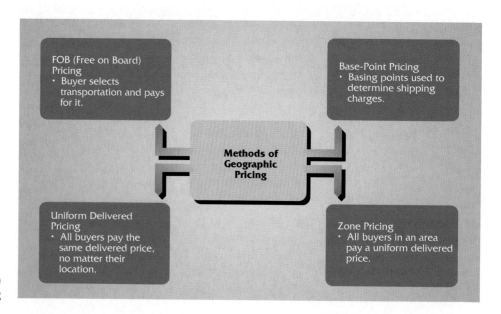

FIGURE 19-10
Geographic Pricing

are held down, risks are minimized, and production peaks can be eliminated. Promotional discounts reimburse channel members for promoting products. They may involve free merchandise, cash selling incentives, cooperative advertising allowances, or other methods for attaining channel cooperation. These discounts may be permanent or geared to specific promotions.

The total discounts a seller offers customers are often quoted in the form of a chain. Cash, quantity, seasonal, and promotional discounts are deducted after the functional or trade discount has been determined. Transportation costs are not discounted; they are added to the channel member's or consumer's purchase price. When providing discounts, the firm must be sure that they are proportionately available to all competing channel members to avoid violation of the Robinson-Patman Act.

The timing of payments needs to be specified in a purchase agreement. Final consumers may make payments immediately or after delivery of merchandise. In credit transactions, payments are not made until bills are received; they may be spread over time. Organizational consumers and channel members are also quite interested in the timing of payments and negotiate for the best terms. For example, terms of net 30 mean that goods do not have to be paid for until thirty days after receipt. At that point, they must be paid for in full. Terms of 2/10, net 30 mean that a buyer receives a 2 per cent discount if the full bill is paid within 10 days after receipt of merchandise. The buyer must pay the face value of the bill within 30 days after receipt of goods. Terms of 2/10 EOM, net 30 mean the buyer receives a 2 per cent discount if the full bill is paid within 10 days after the end of the month in which an order is processed or pays the face value within 30 days after the end of the month. A wide variety of time terms is available.

*A **credit account** may be open or revolving.*

A firm that allows credit purchases may use open accounts or revolving credit. With an ***open credit account,*** the buyer receives a monthly bill for goods and services bought during the preceding month. The account must be paid in full each month. With a ***revolving credit account,*** the buyer agrees to make minimum monthly payments during an extended period of time and pays interest on outstanding balances.

Today various types of companies (from John Deere to many colleges) offer some form of credit plan. And auto makers have been providing their own cut-rate financing programs to stimulate sales.

Price Adjustments

After a price strategy is implemented, it often requires continuous fine-tuning to reflect changes in costs, competitive conditions, and demand. Prices can be adjusted through changes in list prices, escalator clauses and surcharges, added markups, markdowns, and rebates. It is important that price planning be viewed as an adaptive mechanism.

When conditions change, prices must be modified.

List prices are the regularly quoted prices provided to customers. They may be preprinted on price tags, in catalogs, and in dealer purchase orders. Modifications in list prices are necessary if there are sustained changes in labor costs, raw material costs, and market segments and as a product moves through its life cycle. Because these events are long term in nature, they enable customary prices to be revised, new catalogs to be printed, and adjustments to be completed in an orderly fashion.

List prices, escalator clauses, surcharges, additional markups, markdowns, and rebates are key pricing tools.

Sometimes costs or economic conditions may be so volatile that revised list prices cannot be printed or distributed efficiently. Then escalator clauses or surcharges can be used. Each of these allows prices to be adjusted quickly. With an *escalator clause,* the firm is contractually allowed to raise the price of an item to reflect higher costs in the item's essential ingredients without changing printed list prices. Through an escalator clause, a company may be allowed to determine its selling prices at the time of delivery. *Surcharges* are across-the-board published price increases that supplement list prices. These are frequently used with catalogs because of their simplicity; an insert is distributed with the catalog.

When list prices are not involved, *additional markups* can be used to raise regular selling prices because demand is unexpectedly high or costs are rising. There is a risk to additional markups. For example, supermarkets have received adverse publicity for relabeling low-cost existing inventories at higher prices so that they match those of newer merchandise purchased at higher costs.

Markdowns are reductions from the original selling prices of items. All types of sellers use markdowns to meet the lower prices of competitors, counteract overstocking of merchandise, clear out shopworn merchandise, deplete assortments of odds and ends, and increase customer traffic.

Although manufacturers give discounts to wholesalers and retailers on a regular basis, they may periodically offer cash *rebates* to customers to stimulate consumption of an item or a group of items. Rebates are flexible, do not alter basic list prices, increase direct communication between consumers and manufacturers (because rebates are usually sent to consumers by manufacturers), and do not affect channel members' profits or inventory values (as permanent price reductions would). Price cuts by individual retailers do not generate the same kind of consumer enthusiasm. The recent popularity of rebates can be traced to their usage by the auto industry to help cut down on inventory surpluses. Rebates have also been used by Fedders, Gillette, Polaroid, Minolta, and a number of other companies, in addition to all the U.S. auto makers.

Whenever price adjustments are necessary, channel members should cooperatively determine their individual roles. Price hikes or cuts should not be unilaterally imposed.

Summary

1. *To present the overall process for developing a pricing strategy* A pricing strategy consists of five stages: objectives, broad policy, strategy, implementation, and adjustments. All are affected by the external factors noted in Chapter 18 and must be integrated with other elements of a marketing mix.

2. *To analyze sales-based, profit-based, and status quo-based pricing objectives* Sales objectives center on high volume and/or expanding market share. Profit objectives focus on profit maximization, satisfactory profits, optimizing return on investment, and/or early cash recovery. Profit can be expressed in unit or total dollar terms; and direct product profitability may be used to assign costs to each product or product category. Status quo objectives are geared to avoiding declines in business and minimizing the impact of outside parties. Two or more objectives may be combined.

3. *To describe the role of a broad price policy and to consider the alternative approaches to price strategy* A broad price policy sets the overall direction for a firm's pricing efforts and makes sure pricing decisions are coordinated with the firm's decisions regarding the target market, image, and other marketing-mix factors. With penetration pricing, a company uses low prices to capture a mass market. With skimming pricing, a firm intends to capture the market segment less concerned with price than quality or status. A firm may use a skimming and then a penetration pricing strategy. One useful technique for planning a broad policy is the multistage approach to pricing.

   With cost-based pricing, prices are computed by adding desired profits to production and selling costs. In demand-based pricing, final prices are based on consumer research. Under competition-based pricing, prices are set below, at, or higher than competitors. All three approaches should be integrated when establishing a price strategy.

4. *To discuss several specific decisions that need to be made in implementing a price strategy* Implementing a price strategy involves a variety of separate but interlocking specific decisions. Customary pricing is employed when a company maintains prices for an extended period of time. With variable pricing, a firm alters prices to coincide with fluctuations in costs or consumer demand.

   In a one-price policy, all consumers making purchases under similar conditions pay the same price. Flexible pricing allows a company to vary prices based on the consumer's ability to negotiate or the buying power of a large customer.

   An odd-price strategy is used when prices are set below even-dollar values. The price-quality association states that consumers may believe there is a correlation between price and quality. With prestige pricing, it is assumed that consumers do not buy products at prices that are considered too low. They set price floors as well as price ceilings.

   Under leader pricing, key items are sold at less than their usual profit margins in order to increase consumer traffic. Multiple-unit pricing is a practice in which a company offers consumers discounts for buying in quantity. Price lining is the sale of merchandise at a range of prices, with each price representing a distinct level of quality (or features). With bundled pricing, a firm offers a basic product, options, and customer service for one total price. Through unbundled pricing, a firm breaks down prices by individual components and allows the consumer to decide what to purchase.

   Geographic pricing outlines the responsibility for transportation. Terms are the provisions of price agreements, including discounts, timing of payments, and credit.

5. *To show the major ways that prices can be adjusted* After a price strategy is implemented, it usually requires regular fine tuning to reflect cost, competition, and demand changes. Prices can be adjusted by changing list prices, including escalator clauses and surcharges in contracts, marking prices up or down, and offering direct rebates.

Key Terms

sales-based pricing objectives (p. 581)
profit-based pricing objectives (p. 581)
direct product profitability (DPP) (p. 582)

status quo-based pricing
  objectives (p. 583)
broad price policy (p. 583)

penetration pricing (p. 583)
skimming pricing (p. 584)
multistage approach to pricing (p. 587)

cost-based price strategy (p. 587)
price floor (p. 588)
demand-based price strategy (p. 589)
price ceiling (p. 589)
competition-based price strategy
    (p. 589)
customary pricing (p. 589)
variable pricing (p. 590)
one-price policy (p. 590)
flexible pricing (p. 590)
odd-pricing strategy (p. 591)

price-quality association (p. 591)
prestige pricing (p. 592)
psychological pricing (p. 593)
leader pricing (p. 593)
multiple-unit pricing (p. 593)
price lining (p. 594)
bundled pricing (p. 596)
unbundled pricing (p. 596)
geographic pricing (p. 596)
FOB mill (factory) pricing (p. 596)
uniform delivered pricing (p. 596)

zone pricing (p. 596)
base-point pricing (p. 596)
terms (p. 596)
discounts (p. 597)
open credit account (p. 598)
revolving credit account (p. 598)
list prices (p. 599)
escalator clause (p. 599)
surcharges (p. 599)
additional markups (p. 599)
markdowns (p. 599)
rebates (p. 599)

Review Questions

1. State five indications that a company's pricing strategy may be performing poorly.
2. Explain this statement: "It should not be inferred that status quo objectives require no effort on the part of the firm."
3. When should a television manufacturer pursue penetration pricing? Skimming pricing?
4. Contrast customary pricing and variable pricing. How may the two techniques be combined?
5. Under what circumstances is the price-quality association most valid? Least valid?

6. When would multiple-unit pricing be a poor strategy?
7. How does price lining benefit manufacturers? Retailers? Consumers?
8. Distinguish between uniform delivered pricing and zone pricing.
9. Describe the major purposes of each of these types of discounts: functional, seasonal, and promotional.
10. Distinguish between escalator clauses and surcharges. When should each be used?

Discussion Questions

1. Discuss how several pricing objectives could be in conflict with each other.
2. Should Mercedes-Benz introduce a car priced at $100,000 or more? Cite the pros and cons of it doing so.
3. Why do you think that most U.S. firms apply a one-price policy? Should more companies utilize flexible pricing? Explain your answer.
4. Develop a price-lining strategy for each of these firms:
    a. A pizzeria.

    b. A janitorial service.
    c. An air-conditioner maker.

5. A manufacturer recently began marketing a new line of fashion watches priced at $49 each (to retailers). Its major suppliers have just announced a 10 per cent increase on key watch components and materials. Yet the initial response of consumers to the watches has been sluggish, and some retailers are selling the watches for $59 — about $26 less than the manufacturer's suggested list price. What should the manufacturer do next?

═══ CASE 1 ═══

Magazine Pricing: A Key to Long-Term Survival*

Magazine pricing can be quite complex: "Ask a publisher the price of his [her] magazine, and chances

---

* The data in this case are drawn from Cara S. Trager, "Right Price Reflects a Magazine's Health, Goals," *Advertising Age* (March 9, 1987), pp. S-8, S-12; and Albert Scardino, "Magazines Raise Reliance on Circulation," *New York Times* (May 8, 1989), p. D11.

are he [she] won't be able to give you a straight answer. Instead, he'll [she'll] offer at least four: newsstand, introductory subscription, subscription renewal, and test prices that vary from one market to another."

According to a recent study, consumer magazine purchases (circulation) account for more than one-half of total magazine revenues, up from 41 per cent in 1975; the remaining revenues are due to advertising. About two-thirds of consumer purchases involve subscriptions and the balance are single-copy sales.

Magazine pricing is further complicated because circulation (in terms of newsstand, initial subscription, and subscription renewal sales) is often price sensitive and magazine advertising rates are generally based on the level of circulation. Thus, although a low magazine price may reduce sales revenues from newsstand and subscription purchases, such a price would improve a magazine's circulation and enable it to charge higher rates for advertising space. Low subscription rates often result in the loss of single-copy newsstand sales; but advertisers are interested in loyal readers. So the magazine publisher's goal is to maximize the combined revenues from circulation and advertising.

Marketing experts are divided about whether a high magazine price is preferable to a low one. On the one hand, a high price increases a magazine's chances of surviving and growing: "Studies have been done that statistically prove that the higher the cover price, the better the chances of survival for the magazine."

A high magazine price also gives wholesalers (which receive a 20 per cent commission based on the newsstand price) a greater incentive to carry and to push a title. And a high price connotes high editorial quality and an upscale image to both readers and advertisers.

On the other hand, a low price encourages consumers to sample a magazine. When *Ladies Home Journal* lowered its cover price from $1.50 to $1.19 for several consecutive issues in various tests around the United States, it did so to get consumers to try the magazine. According to the *Journal's*

director of newsstand sales, the price reduction was its version of couponing. Based on the success of that experiment, the magazine lowered its cover price to $1.19 on a permanent basis in all its markets.

A low price also enables a magazine to meet or exceed its rate base (the circulation level guaranteed to its advertisers). If a magazine does not meet this rate base, it must reduce its advertising rates on a proportionate basis.

Magazines are increasingly conducting research when making price decisions: "In fact, few publishers will even consider raising their prices before testing them, no matter how much their own costs—in personnel, paper, ink, and production—have increased." For example, *Family Circle* engaged in significant research before raising its cover price from 95 cents to 99 cents: "Pretesting tells you how much the reader will tolerate, and right now 99 cents is a tolerable level of expense." However, even when research dictates that a new price level would be successful, many magazine executives do not want to be the first to change their price.

Today the average newsstand price for a magazine is more than $2, and the average price for a yearly magazine subscription exceeds $25. As a result, some industry analysts are concerned that high prices might cause consumers to purchase fewer magazines within a given category: "The way the selection process is going to occur is that instead of buying *Good Housekeeping* and *Better Homes and Gardens* both at $1.50, the reader, who is only interested in knowing about the home, might choose only one at $1.95. This could lead to added competition for market share among specialized publications or the growth of specialized publications at the expense of general-interest ones."

QUESTIONS

1. Develop appropriate pricing objectives relating to newsstand, introductory subscription, and subscription renewal rates.
2. Apply the multistage approach to the pricing of a magazine.
3. Why do most magazines utilize customary (versus variable) pricing for newsstand rates, yet use variable pricing for subscription sales?
4. Under what conditions should a magazine adjust its prices?

◄ CASE 2 ►

Waldenbooks: Testing a New Markdown Policy[†]

Pricing practices at bookstores differ from those at other retailers because bookstores are able to return unsold titles to their publishers for full credit, unlike the limited return privileges for most retailers. As a result, in the past, bookstores were reluctant to mark down slow-sellers. But in a significant strategy shift, in 1988, Waldenbooks—the nation's largest book chain—announced that it would gradually reduce the prices on some of its books until they were sold.

The firm decided to begin with a six- to twelve-month test involving 100 to 125 "bargain books," which could not be returned to publishers. Included were some former best-sellers, some children's books, and some art books. Because these books were not returnable, the publishers agreed to a lower than usual wholesale price in selling them to Waldenbooks.

In the test, Waldenbooks used an automatic markdown policy for setting discounted prices. The amount and timing of markdowns were controlled by the length of time that a book remained in stock. A three-stage discount program was developed: the first markdown occurred after a book was in a store for 60 days, the second after 90 days, and the third after 120 days. As prices were further reduced, the books would be moved from one location within a store to another, to stimulate attention.

Those who favor Waldenbooks' strategy believe it emulates the successful automatic markdown policy of such retailers as Filene's Basement, ensures fresh merchandise, maximizes inventory turnover, and generates excitement among consumers who

may make multiple (versus single) visits to a bookstore to shop for bargains among recently discounted titles. They feel that profitability is based on a combination of markups (profit margins) and inventory turnover, not just markups. Waldenbooks also hopes that this plan will increase impulse purchases: "While best-sellers will bring customers into the bookstores, discounts may increase the number of books each customer buys."

Those who feel that Waldenbooks' markdown plan is not a good idea think that low prices will not induce impulse sales. Said one bookstore owner: "I don't think that the public can be fooled, and if they don't want to buy a book, they won't regardless of price. If you don't want Sidney Sheldon at $17.95, you probably don't want it at $7.95 either."

These experts further believe that an automatic markdown plan would cause some customers to view early prices with skepticism, get some customers conditioned to waiting for price reductions, and get some consumers to question why all titles are not priced under the same markdown policy.

Still others state that an automatic markdown strategy can work selectively in increasing impulse sales. According to a vice-president at a regional bookstore chain, the best books for this strategy are specialty books that are too expensive for many readers but could be attractive at lower prices. On other titles, big discounts would have little impact in increasing impulse sales.

These are two other ideas: Waldenbooks could use an early markdown policy, whereby discounts are offered as soon as managers realize that titles are selling slowly (rather than wait 60 days). It could use storewide clearance sales for slow-selling titles on a periodic basis, such as twice a year.

[†] The data in this case are drawn from Cynthia Crossen, "Waldenbooks to Cut Some Book Prices in Stages in Test of New Selling Tactic," *Wall Street Journal* (March 29, 1988), p. 36.

QUESTIONS

1. Evaluate Waldenbooks' test markdown policy.
2. Should Waldenbooks use an automatic markdown policy with its popular titles? Explain your answer.
3. Assess the other markdown alternatives cited in the case that Waldenbooks could use instead of the automatic markdown policy it tested: an automatic dis-

count policy for specialty books, an early markdown policy, and storewide clearance sales.
4. Present several criteria that would enable Waldenbooks to measure the effectiveness of its markdown experiment.

Applications of Pricing Techniques

CHAPTER OBJECTIVES

1. *To examine and evaluate various cost-based pricing techniques and to present applications of them*

2. *To examine and evaluate various demand-based pricing techniques and to present applications of them*

3. *To examine and evaluate various competition-based pricing techniques and to present applications of them*

4. *To show why cost-, demand-, and competition-based pricing techniques should be integrated*

A sophisticated computer technique known as yield management pricing, long used in the airline industry as a way of getting the best possible price for each seat, is now being adapted to offer hotel discounts based on expectations of supply and demand.

Hotels know that when a certain day passes, they'll never fill that room. So they will adjust their rates to maximize their revenue. A hotel room is the most perishable commodity there is. If you're at 50 per cent capacity and someone walks in, you make a deal.

Yield management pricing is a form of demand-based price discrimination in which a firm determines the mix of price-quantity combinations leading to the greatest revenues for a given period. Prices reflect supply and demand conditions. Through yield management pricing, a firm tracks historical booking patterns and determines how many units (rooms, seats, and so on) to sell at discounted prices during each day. The number of discounted units can be changed to reflect up-to-date sales performance. Let us look at how yield management pricing may be applied.

For example, the number of hotel rooms and airline seats sold at various prices would be based on past sales patterns and current demand. At American Airlines, the goal "is to squeeze as many dollars as possible out of each seat and mile flown. This means trying to project just how many tickets to sell at a discount without running out of seats for the business traveler, who usually books at the last minute and pays full fare. It's a sophisticated guessing game. You don't want to sell a seat to a person for $69 when he or she is willing to pay $400."

American Airlines has dozens of yield managers who are linked by terminals to several IBM mainframe computers. They continuously monitor and adjust the fare mixes on thousands of flights involving 50 million passengers. Inventory management (the allocation of seats by fare category) begins 330 days prior to a flight's departure; full-fare coach seats are sold first. Computers alert yield managers if sales at a particular fare unexpectedly rise. All fare mixes are checked 180 days before a flight's departure. Later, more discount seats are placed on sale just before the advance purchase requirement expires.

AMR Corporation, the parent of American Airlines, is creating a yield management pricing program for the Hilton and Marriott hotel chains and Budget Rent A

Reprinted by permission of American Airlines.

Car that will be fully operational by 1991. This program will link price setting to such factors as anticipated occupancy, seasonality, and major events in town. Reservations personnel will be able to review inventory (unsold rooms or unrented cars) on a daily basis and change rates as often as necessary.

At present, there are two major distinctions in yield management pricing practices between airlines and hotels. First, although discounts of up to 70 per cent from full fares are not unusual for airlines, hotel rates are generally not reduced as much. Second, airlines more often impose restrictions on low-fare customers (such as length of stay, remaining at a destination over a Saturday evening, and nonrefundable tickets).[1]

In this chapter, we will look closely at various cost-based, demand-based (such as yield management pricing), and competition-based pricing techniques and see why these techniques should be integrated when setting prices.

[1] Leonard Sloane, "Hotels, Like Airlines, Offer Discounts," *New York Times* (September 3, 1988), p. 48; Eric Schmitt, "The Art of Devising Air Fares," *New York Times* (March 4, 1987), pp. D1, D2; and Peter S. Greenberg, "Playing the Hotel Room-Rate Game," *Newsday* (April 9, 1989), Travel, p. 3.

Overview

Chapter 20 examines in depth a number of specific techniques used in developing and applying cost-, demand-, and competition-based price strategies. Each technique is described and applications are shown.

As noted in Chapter 19, and again at the end of this chapter, it is very important to recognize that good price planning should include aspects of all three approaches: cost-, demand-, and competition-based. A company would be omitting crucial considerations if it does not relate its prices to costs, consumer demand, *and* competitors. The three techniques are treated separately for discussion purposes only.

Throughout the chapter, applications are tied to the fictitious Phase III bicycle. This is a futuristic, high-performance bicycle capable of speeds of 55 miles per hour, with three or more wheels and a fiberglass shell reinforced with crossbars for protection in accidents. It is streamlined to glide through the air. Although the technology is available to build this type of bicycle on a mass-production scale, bicycles such as Phase III have not yet been made commercial.

Cost-Based Pricing

Cost-based pricing is simple, based on relative certainty, and tied to a reasonable profit. It does not consider market conditions, plant capacity, and competitors.

With cost-based pricing, a firm determines prices by computing merchandise, service, and overhead costs and then adding an amount to cover the firm's profit goal.[2] These prices are relatively easy to derive because there is no need to estimate elasticity of demand or competitive reactions to price changes. There is also more certainty about costs than demand or competitor responses to prices. Finally, cost pricing seeks to attain reasonable profits because it is geared to covering all types of costs.

When used by itself, cost-based pricing does have some significant limitations. It does not consider market conditions, the existence of excess plant capacity, competitive prices, the product's phase in its life cycle, market-share goals, consumers' ability to pay, and other factors. For example, USX (formerly U.S. Steel) used to pass all cost increases on to consumers and thereby "kept prices high enough to allow [other] companies to take a substantial share of the market." From the mid-1950s to now, USX's industry market share has dropped from 34 to 17 per cent. As a result, its current prices are quite competitive because it is more vulnerable to the demands of its customers.[3]

In some situations, it is difficult to calculate how overhead costs such as rent, lighting, personnel, and other general expenses should be allocated to each product. These costs are often assigned on the basis of product sales or personnel time associated with each item. For instance, if product A accounts for 10 per cent of company sales, it might be allocated 10 per cent of overhead costs. If product B receives 20 per cent of personnel time, it might be allocated 20 per cent of overhead costs. Problems may arise because different methods for assigning costs may yield different results; how would costs be allocated if product A yields 10 per cent of sales and requires 20 per cent of personnel time?

---

[2] See Stewart A. Washburn, "Establishing Strategy and Determining Costs in the Pricing Decision," *Business Marketing* (July 1985), pp. 64–78; and John Y. Lee, "Developing a Pricing System for a Small Business," *Management Accounting* (March 1987), pp. 50–53.

[3] "Flexible Pricing," *Business Week* (December 12, 1977), p. 84; William Symonds et al., "The Toughest Job in Business," *Business Week* (February 25, 1985), pp. 50–56; and "USX Plans to Match Average 3% Price Rise Set by Competitors," *Wall Street Journal* (January 23, 1987), p. 14.

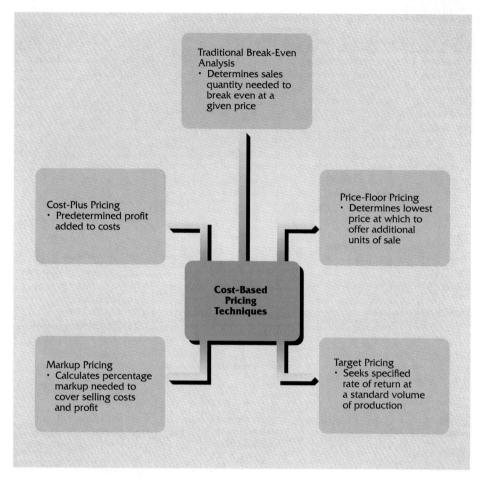

FIGURE 20-1
**Cost-Based Pricing
Techniques**

Next, the basic concepts surrounding cost-based pricing are described and five cost-based pricing techniques are discussed in detail: cost-plus, markup, target, price-floor, and traditional break-even analysis. See Figure 20-1.

Cost Concepts

Table 20-1 defines the key concepts in cost-based pricing and shows how they may be used with Phase III bicycles. Table 20-2 presents hypothetical cost data for Phase III bicycles for each of the concepts shown in Table 20-1.

Fixed, variable, and marginal costs are elements of cost-based pricing.

Several important cost relationships can be learned from Table 20-2:

1. Total fixed costs remain constant over the entire range of production. Average fixed costs fall as the quantity produced increases because overhead costs are spread over more units.
2. Total variable costs rise over the entire range of production. Average variable costs remain constant at $2,600 per unit produced.
3. Total costs rise over the entire production range, because total fixed costs are constant and total variable costs increase. Average total costs decline because aver-

607

TABLE 20-1   Key Cost Concepts and How They May Be Applied to Phase III Bicycles

Cost Concept	Definition	Examples[a]	Sources of Information	Method of Computation
Total fixed costs	Ongoing costs that are unrelated to volume. These costs are generally constant over a given range of output within a specified time.	Rent, administrative salaries, electricity, real-estate taxes, plant, and equipment.	Accounting data, bills, cost estimates.	Addition of all fixed cost components.
Total variable costs	Costs that change with increases or decreases in output (volume).	Bicycle parts (such as gears, fiberglass panels, wheels, brakes, tires), hourly employees who assemble bicycles, and sales commissions.	Cost data from suppliers, estimates of labor productivity, production estimates.	Addition of all variable cost components.
Total costs	Sum of total fixed and total variable costs.	See above.	See above.	Addition of all fixed and variable cost components.
Average fixed costs	Average fixed costs per unit.	See above under total fixed costs.	Total fixed costs and production estimates.	Total fixed costs/Quantity produced in units.
Average variable costs	Average variable costs per unit.	See above under total variable costs.	Total variable costs and production estimates.	Total variable costs/ Quantity produced in units.
Average total costs	Sum of average fixed costs and average variable costs.	See above under total fixed and total variable costs.	Total costs and production estimates.	Average fixed costs + Average variable costs or Total costs/Quantity produced in units.
Marginal costs	Costs of producing an additional unit.	See above under total fixed and total variable costs.	Accounting data, bills, cost estimates of labor and materials.	(Total costs of producing current quantity + one unit) − (Total costs of producing current quantity).

[a] Marketing costs, such as advertising and distribution, are often broken down into both fixed and variable components.

age fixed costs drop and average variable costs are constant, as production volume grows.

4. The marginal costs of producing additional bicycles are $2,600 (average variable costs) over the entire range of production because fixed costs remain constant throughout.

Cost-Plus Pricing

Cost-plus pricing is the easiest form of pricing, based on units produced, total costs, and profit.

With **cost-plus pricing,** prices are determined by adding a predetermined profit to costs. It is the simplest form of cost-based pricing.

In general, the steps for computing cost-plus prices are to estimate the number of units to be produced, calculate fixed and variable costs, and add a predetermined profit to costs. The formula for cost-plus pricing is

TABLE 20-2 Computing Key Cost Concepts for Phase III Bicycles (in Multiples of 100 Units)

Col. 1	Col. 2	Col. 3	Col. 4 = Col. 2 + Col. 3	Col. 5 = Col. 2/ Col. 1	Col. 6 = Col. 3/ Col. 1	Col. 7 = Col. 5 + Col. 6	Col. 8
Quantity Produced (in Units)	Total Fixed Costs	Total Variable Costs	Total Costs	Average Fixed Costs	Average Variable Costs	Average Total Costs	Marginal Costs (per Unit)[a]
100	$175,000	$ 260,000	$ 435,000	$1,750.00	$2,600	$4,350.00	
							$2,600
200	175,000	520,000	695,000	875.00	2,600	3,475.00	
							$2,600
300	175,000	780,000	955,000	583.33	2,600	3,183.33	
							$2,600
400	175,000	1,040,000	1,215,000	437.50	2,600	3,037.50	
							$2,600
500	175,000	1,300,000	1,475,000	350.00	2,600	2,950.00	
							$2,600
600	175,000	1,560,000	1,735,000	291.67	2,600	2,891.67	
							$2,600
700	175,000	1,820,000	1,995,000	250.00	2,600	2,850.00	
							$2,600
800	175,000	2,080,000	2,255,000	218.75	2,600	2,818.75	
							$2,600
900	175,000	2,340,000	2,515,000	194.44	2,600	2,794.44	
							$2,600
1,000	175,000	2,600,000	2,775,000	175.00	2,600	2,775.00	

[a] No increase in fixed costs is needed to produce quantities above 100 units. Therefore, for this example, marginal costs per unit equal average variable costs.

$$\text{Price} = \frac{\text{Total fixed costs} + \text{Total variable costs} + \text{Projected profit}}{\text{Units produced}}$$

As an illustration, if 300 Phase III bicycles are produced and the company desires a profit of $50,000, its per-unit selling price to retailers would be

$$\text{Price} = \frac{\$175,000 + \$780,000 + \$50,000}{300} = \$3,350$$

Although this method is easy to compute, it has shortcomings. Profit is not expressed as a per cent of sales but as a per cent of cost, and price is not tied to consumer demand. Adjustments for rising costs are poorly conceived, and there are no plans for using excess capacity. There is little incentive to improve efficiency to hold down costs, and marginal costs are rarely analyzed.

Cost-plus pricing is most effective when price fluctuations have little influence on sales and when a firm is able to control price. For example, the prices of custom-made furniture, ships, heavy machinery, and extracted minerals depend on the costs incurred in producing these items; firms set prices by determining costs and adding a reasonable profit. Often cost-plus pricing allows firms to receive consumer orders, produce items, and then derive prices after total costs are known. This protects the sellers.

Markup Pricing

Markup pricing considers per-unit product costs and the markups required to cover selling costs and profits.

In *markup pricing,* a firm sets its prices by calculating the per-unit costs of producing (buying) goods and/or services and then determining the markup percentages that are needed to cover selling costs and profit. Markup pricing is most commonly used by wholesalers and retailers. The formula for markup pricing is[4]

$$\text{Price} = \frac{\text{Product cost}}{(100 - \text{Markup per cent})/100}$$

For example, if a retailer pays \$3,350 for a Phase III bicycle and needs a 40 per cent markup to cover selling costs and profit, the final selling price is \$3,350/[(100 − 40)/100] = \$5,583.33. The retailer receives 40 per cent, or \$2,233.33, for its expenses and profit. Product costs are covered by \$3,350. As shown in this illustration, the markup percentage is usually expressed in terms of an item's selling price, not its cost.

Markups are expressed in terms of selling price rather than cost.

There are several reasons why markups are typically stated in terms of selling price instead of cost. First, expenses, markdowns, and profits are always computed as percentages of sales. When markups are per cents of sales, they aid in profit planning. Second, manufacturers quote their selling prices and trade discounts to channel members as percentage reductions from final list prices. Third, retail sales price information is more readily available than cost information. Fourth, profitability appears to be smaller if based on price rather than cost. This can be useful in avoiding criticism over high profits.

The size of a markup depends on traditional profit margins, wholesaler or retailer expenses, manufacturers' suggested list prices, inventory turnover, competition, the extent to which products must be altered or otherwise serviced, and the effort needed to complete sales. In order to respond to differences in selling costs among products, firms sometimes use a *variable markup policy,* whereby separate categories of goods and services receive different percentage markups. Variable markups recognize that some items require greater personal selling efforts, customer service, alterations, and end-of-season markdowns than others. For example, in a department store, expensive cosmetics utilize more personal selling than paperback books, a color console television needs more customer service than a black-and-white portable, men's suits need greater alterations than shirts, and fashion items are marked down more than traditional goods late in the selling season.

A variable markup policy responds to differences in selling costs among products by using distinct markups.

Markup pricing, while having many of the limitations of cost-plus pricing, remains very popular for wholesalers and retailers. It is fairly simple, especially for firms that use the same markup for a number of items. It offers channel members equitable profits. Price competition is reduced when retailers adhere to similar markups. Channel members are able to compare actual prices with manufacturers' suggested list prices. Price adjustments can be made when costs rise. Variable markups are responsive to selling cost differences among products or channel members.

---

[4] Markup can be calculated by transposing the formula above into

$$\text{Markup percentage} = \frac{\text{Selling price} - \text{Product cost}}{\text{Selling price}} \times 100$$

Target Pricing

In **target pricing,** prices are set to provide a particular rate of return on investment for a standard volume of production, which is the level of production a firm anticipates achieving. For example, in the paper industry, the standard volume of production is usually set at around 90 per cent of plant capacity.[5] For target pricing to operate properly, a company must sell its entire standard volume at specified prices.

Target pricing enables a rate of return on investment to be earned for a standard volume of production.

Target pricing is used by capital-intensive firms (such as auto makers) and public utilities (such as power and light companies). The prices charged by public utilities are based on fair rates of return on invested assets and must be approved by regulatory commissions. Mathematically, a target price is computed as

$$\text{Price} = \frac{\text{Investment costs} \times \text{Target return on investment (\%)}}{\text{Standard volume}}$$
$$+ \text{ Average total costs (at standard volume)}$$

A Phase III bicycle example demonstrates how target pricing works. If the firm must build a new factory at a cost of $2 million to mass produce bicycles, it might set target return on investment as a goal because investment costs represent such a large portion of expenses. Management projects the standard volume of production to be 700 units and desires a target return of 20 per cent. At this volume, average total costs are $2,850 (from Table 20-2). Selling price to retailers is then

$$\text{Price} = \frac{\$2,000,000 \times 0.20}{700} + \$2,850 = \$3421.43$$

Of this amount, $2,850 per unit goes for regular fixed and variable costs, and $571.43 per unit is used to pay off the capital investment. At a 20 per cent rate of return, this is accomplished in five years.

Target pricing has five major limitations. One, it is not useful for firms with low capital investments because it will understate selling price. Two, because prices are not keyed to demand, the entire standard volume may not be sold at the target price. Three, production problems may hamper output and the standard volume may not be attained. Four, price reductions to handle overstocked inventory are not planned under this approach. Fifth, if standard volume is lowered because of expected poor sales, an inappropriately high price would result under target pricing.

Price-Floor Pricing

In most instances, a firm's goal is to set unit prices that cover average fixed costs, average variable costs, and profit per unit. However, when a firm has excess (unused) capacity, it may use **price-floor pricing** to determine the lowest price at which it is worthwhile for the company to increase the amount of goods or services it makes available for sale. The general principle in price-floor pricing is that the sale of additional units can be used to increase profits or help pay for fixed costs (which exist whether or not these items are made) if marginal revenues are greater than marginal costs. Although a firm cannot survive in the long run unless its average total costs are

Price-floor pricing may be used when there is excess capacity.

---

[5] Stuart U. Rich, "Price Leadership in the Paper Industry," *Industrial Marketing Management*, Vol. 12 (April 1983), p. 101.

Marketing Controversy

Are Auto Insurance Rates Too High?

From 1984 to 1988, auto insurance premiums rose 76 per cent nationally. As a result, there were motorist complaints about rates and calls for cutbacks. For example, in California, a consumer group known as Voter Revolt got statewide voters to approve Proposition 103, which required a 20 per cent rate rollback. And Voter Revolt has been contacted by consumer groups in 44 other states who want to see their rates reduced.

The insurance industry insisted that the rate rollback in California was unconstitutional and appealed the matter to the California Supreme Court (where Proposition 103 was upheld). Just before the rollback vote, Travelers announced that it would stop selling auto insurance in California. After the vote, Aetna, State Farm, and Nationwide Mutual also decided to stop selling auto insurance there.

Motorists concerned about high auto insurance premiums feel that

▶ *Insurance companies readily underwrite drivers with unblemished records but are too quick to raise rates or refuse to renew policies once a driver has an accident or a moving violation.*

▶ *Rates should be based on driving records not the place of residence.*

▶ *Insurance companies have the right to rate increases, but should show the need for them by opening their financial records.*

▶ *Consumers should not place other policies with insurers that refuse to underwrite auto insurance in their state.*

Auto insurers state that

▶ *Automobile insurance is a money-losing venture. The overall industry lost four cents per premium dollar for auto insurance in 1985, two cents per premium dollar in 1986, and one cent per premium dollar in 1987.*

▶ *Many state regulations have already forced auto insurance premiums to be artificially low. Yet costs such as legal fees, medical bills, and car-repair expenses continue to escalate.*

▶ *They are being forced to sell auto insurance. In several states, insurers cannot sell other forms of insurance (such as homeowners' policies) if they withdraw from the auto insurance market.*

What do you think?

SOURCE: Based on material in Harry Hurt III, "Honk If You're for Proposition 103," *Newsweek* (March 27, 1989), p. 34; and Sonja Steptoe, "Auto Insurers Face Drive by Consumers for Rate Reductions," *Wall Street Journal* (November 22, 1988), pp. A1, A12.

covered by prices, it may enhance performance through price-floor pricing. The formula is

$$\text{Price-floor price} = \text{Marginal revenue per unit} > \text{Marginal cost per unit}$$

Price-floor pricing can be applied to Phase III bicycles. If the company's capacity is 1,000 units and it wants to operate at 100 per cent of that capacity, the firm would manufacture 1,000 bicycles. Its average total costs would be $2,775, average fixed costs would be $175, and average variable costs would be $2,600. Because the firm aims to be profitable, it might set a price of $3,000 to retailers. However, it is quite possible that the firm would receive orders for only 600 bicycles at that price and be forced to operate at 60 per cent of capacity, unless it re-evaluates its pricing strategy. Under price-floor pricing, the firm might be willing to sell 400 additional bicycles to retailers for just $2,700 each, even though its average total costs are not covered at that amount. The firm could do this by allowing retailers to buy two bikes at $2,700 each for every three bikes they buy at $3,000 each.

This is why the firm might consider price-floor pricing: With sales of 600 bicycles at $3,000 each, the company earns a profit of $65,000 [($3,000 × 600) − $1,735,000]. By selling an additional 400 units, profits are increased by $40,000 because marginal revenues ($2,700 × 400) exceed marginal costs ($2,600 × 400). Any price above $2,600 could be an acceptable price-floor price because marginal costs are covered. However the firm would have to be careful not to sell too many bicycles at the discounted amount.

Traditional Break-Even Analysis

Like target pricing, traditional break-even analysis examines the relationship among costs, revenues, and profits. While target pricing yields the price that results in a specified return on investment, ***traditional break-even analysis*** determines the sales quantity in units or dollars that is necessary for total revenues (price × units sold) to equal total costs (fixed and variable) at a given price. When sales exceed the break-even quantity, the firm earns a profit. When sales are less than the break-even quantity, the firm loses money. Traditional break-even analysis does not consider a firm's return on investment or the dollar value of investment. However, it can be extended to take profit planning into account, and it is used by all types of sellers.

Traditional break-even analysis computes the sales needed to break even at a specific price.

The break-even point can be computed in terms of units or sales dollars:

$$\text{Break-even point (units)} = \frac{\text{Total fixed costs}}{\text{Price} - \text{Variable costs (per unit)}}$$

$$\text{Break-even point (sales dollars)} = \frac{\text{Total fixed costs}}{1 - \dfrac{\text{Variable costs (per unit)}}{\text{Price}}}$$

These formulas are derived from the equation: Price × Quantity = Total fixed costs + (Variable costs per unit × Quantity).

Table 20-3 and Figure 20-2 show the costs, revenues, and profits for Phase III bicycles priced at $2,950 to retailers. At quantities below 500 units, the company would lose money. At quantities above 500 units, it would make a profit. At exactly 500 units, Phase III would break even. By using a break-even formula, the firm could find its break-even point without all the computations in Table 20-3 and Figure 20-2:

$$\text{Break-even point (units)} = \frac{\$175,000}{\$2,950 - \$2,600} = 500 \text{ units}$$

$$\text{Break-even point (sales dollars)} = \frac{\$175,000}{1 - \dfrac{(\$2,600)}{(\$2,950)}} = \$1,475,000$$

TABLE 20-3 Traditional Break-Even Analysis for Phase III Bicycles—Priced at $2,950 Each to Retailers

Col. 1	Col. 2	Col. 3	Col. 4 = Col. 2 + Col. 3	Col. 5	Col. 6 = Col. 1 × Col. 5	Col. 7 = Col. 6 − Col. 4	
Production Quantity (Units) (Q)	Total Fixed Costs	Total Variable Costs	Total Costs	Price per Unit (P)	Total Revenue (P × Q)	Total Profit (Loss)	
100	$175,000	$ 260,000	$ 435,000	$2,950	$ 295,000	$(140,000)	
200	175,000	520,000	695,000	2,950	590,000	(105,000)	
300	175,000	780,000	955,000	2,950	885,000	(70,000)	Loss
400	175,000	1,040,000	1,215,000	2,950	1,180,000	(35,000)	
500	175,000	1,300,000	1,475,000	2,950	1,475,000	0	Break-even point
600	175,000	1,560,000	1,735,000	2,950	1,770,000	35,000	
700	175,000	1,820,000	1,995,000	2,950	2,065,000	70,000	
800	175,000	2,080,000	2,255,000	2,950	2,360,000	105,000	Profit
900	175,000	2,340,000	2,515,000	2,950	2,655,000	140,000	
1,000	175,000	2,600,000	2,775,000	2,950	2,950,000	175,000	

Break-even analysis can be adjusted to take into account the profit sought by a firm:

$$\text{Break-even point (units)} = \frac{\text{Total fixed costs} + \text{Projected profit}}{\text{Price} - \text{Variable costs (per unit)}}$$

$$\text{Break-even point (sales dollars)} = \frac{\text{Total fixed costs} + \text{Projected profit}}{1 - \dfrac{\text{Variable costs (per unit)}}{\text{Price}}}$$

In the preceding Phase III example, if the company seeks a $100,000 profit, the break-even point is

$$\text{Break-even point (units)} = \frac{\$175,000 + \$100,000}{\$2,950 - \$2,600} = 785.71 \text{ units}^*$$

$$\text{Break-even point (sales dollars)} = \frac{\$275,000}{1 - \dfrac{(\$2,600)}{(\$2,950)}} = \$2,317,857^*$$

There are limitations to traditional break-even analysis. One, as with all forms of cost-based pricing, it does not consider demand. The assumption is that wide variations in quantity can be sold at the same price, and this is highly unlikely. Two, traditional break-even analysis assumes all costs can be divided into fixed and variable

* These numbers would be rounded off to 786 units and $2,318,700, because the firm could not sell part of a bicycle.

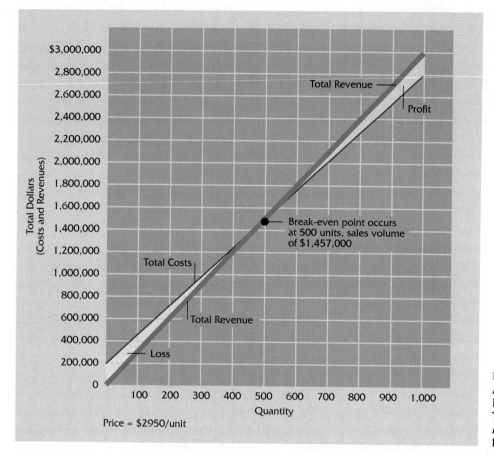

FIGURE 20-2
A Graphical Representation of Traditional Break-Even Analysis for Phase III Bicycles

categories. Yet some costs, like advertising, are difficult to define; advertising can be fixed or a per cent of sales. Three, traditional break-even formulas presume that variable costs per unit are constant over a range of quantities. However, discounts or overtime wages may alter these costs. Fourth, it is assumed that fixed costs remain constant; but increases in production may lead to higher costs for lighting, new employees, and other items.

By including demand considerations, each of the cost-based techniques can be improved. Demand-based pricing techniques are discussed next.

Demand-Based Pricing

With demand-based pricing, a firm determines the prices consumers and channel members will pay for goods and services, calculates the markups needed to cover selling expenses and profits, and then determines the maximum it can spend to produce (or buy) its offering. In this way, prices and costs are linked to consumer preferences and channel needs, and a specific product image is sought.

Demand-based techniques require some consumer research regarding the quantities that will be purchased at various prices, the elasticity of demand (sensitivity to price changes), the existence of market segments, and consumers' ability to pay.

Under demand-based pricing, prices are linked to consumer desires, channel needs, and product image.

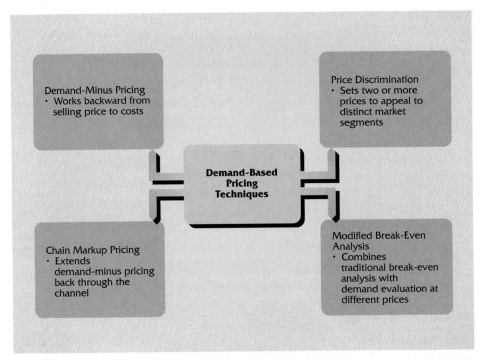

FIGURE 20-3
**Demand-Based
Pricing Techniques**

Demand estimates are usually less precise than cost estimates. Also firms that do inadequate research on costs and rely on demand-oriented data may end up losing money because they make unrealistically low assumptions about costs.

With demand-based pricing, highly competitive situations may result in small mark-ups and low prices because consumers will purchase substitutes. In these cases, it is necessary for costs to be held down or else prices will be too high — which might result under cost-based pricing. In noncompetitive situations, firms can achieve large mark-ups and high prices because demand is relatively inelastic. Companies could place little emphasis on costs when setting prices in these situations. Under cost-based pricing, the firm would be likely to set prices that are too low in noncompetitive markets.

Next, four demand-based pricing techniques are examined: demand-minus, chain-markup, modified break-even, and price discrimination. See Figure 20-3.

Demand-Minus Pricing

*In **demand-minus pricing,** final selling price, then markup, and finally maximum merchandise costs are computed.*

In **demand-minus (demand-backward) pricing,** the firm ascertains the appropriate final selling price and works backward to compute costs. This approach stipulates that price decisions revolve around consumer demand rather than internal company operations. It is used by companies that sell directly to consumers.

Demand-minus pricing consists of three steps. One, final selling price is determined through consumer surveys or other research. Two, the required markup percentage is derived from selling expenses and desired profits. Three, the maximum acceptable per-unit cost for producing or buying a product is computed. This formula is used:

$$\text{Maximum product cost} = \text{Price} \times [(100 - \text{Markup per cent})/100]$$

As noted, the product's cost is calculated after selling price and markup are set.

For example, a retailer for Phase III bicycles would first conduct a survey to measure consumer demand. Then it would compute selling expenses and desired profit. Finally, the maximum acceptable costs of a Phase III bicycle to the retailer would be derived. If the retailer finds that consumers would spend $6,000 for the bicycle and selling expenses plus profit are 40 per cent, then

$$\text{Maximum product cost} = \$6,000 \times [(100 - 40)/100] = \$3,600$$

At a per-unit cost of $3,600 or less, the retailer would stock Phase III. At a cost above $3,600, these bicycles would not be stocked because the retailer knows the higher cost could not be passed along to consumers and its profits would be too low.

The difficulty in demand-minus pricing is that marketing research may be time-consuming or complex, particularly if many items are involved. Also, new-product pricing research may be particularly inaccurate.

Chain-Markup Pricing

Chain-markup pricing extends demand-minus calculations all the way from middlemen back to their suppliers (manufacturers). With chain-markup pricing, final selling price is determined, markups for each channel member are examined, and the maximum acceptable costs to each member are computed.

Chain-markup pricing traces demand-minus calculations from middlemen to suppliers.

For example, in a traditional consumer-goods channel, the markup chain is composed of

1. Maximum selling price to retailer $=$ Final selling price $\times$ [(100 − Retailer's markup)/100]

2. Maximum selling price to wholesaler $=$ Selling price to retailer $\times$ [(100 − Wholesaler's markup)/100]

3. Maximum product cost to manufacturer $=$ Selling price to wholesaler $\times$ [(100 − Manufacturer's markup)/100]

If the manufacturer of Phase III bicycles decides to market the product through wholesalers and retailers, all three parties would share marketing costs and profits; and each would seek a markup of 20 per cent. Because they know the consumer will pay $6,000 for a Phase III bicycle, the chain markup is

1. Maximum selling price to retailer $= \$6,000 \times [(100 - 20)/100] = \$4,800$

2. Maximum selling price to wholesaler $= \$4,800 \times [(100 - 20)/100] = \$3,840$

3. Maximum product cost to manufacturer $= \$3,840 \times [(100 - 20)/100] = \$3,072$

Several conclusions can be drawn from this illustration. First, the selling prices of manufacturers, wholesalers, and retailers must be equal to or less than the amounts their respective customers are willing to pay. Second, cost increases need to be controlled. In this example, a manufacturing cost rise of $100 to $3,172 would result in a final selling price rise of $195.31 to $6,195.31, if each channel member maintains its 20 per cent markup. Third, by sharing cost increases, final prices can be stabilized. The price of $6,000 could be maintained, despite a manufacturing cost increase of $100, if the manufacturer, wholesaler, and retailer each reduce markup by less than 1 per cent. Fourth, changes in demand have a major impact on all channel members. For instance, if consumers would be willing to pay $6,500, there would be an extra $500 that could be allocated throughout the channel. This could cover higher costs or lead to higher profits.

Through chain-markup pricing, price decisions are related to consumer demand and each channel-member firm is able to see the effects of price changes on the total system. The interdependence of firms becomes clear; they cannot set prices independently of one another.

Modified Break-Even Analysis

Combining traditional break-even analysis with demand evaluation at various prices is **modified break-even analysis.**

Modified break-even analysis combines traditional break-even analysis with an evaluation of demand at various levels of price. Traditional analysis focuses on the sales needed to break even at a given price. It does not indicate the likely level of demand at that price, examine how demand responds to different levels of price, consider that the break-even point can vary greatly depending on the price the firm happens to select, or calculate the price that maximizes profits.

Modified analysis reveals the price-quantity mix that maximizes profits. It shows that profits do not necessarily rise as quantity sold increases because lower prices may be needed to increase demand. It also verifies that a firm should examine various price levels and select the one that maximizes profits. Finally, it relates demand to price, rather than assuming that the same volume could be sold at any price.[6]

Table 20-4 shows the quantities that Phase III would be able to sell under different retail prices from $4,500 to $7,000. This table assumes that sales are made from the manufacturer to the wholesaler to the retailer to the customer. Profits are maximized at a retail price-quantity mix of $6,000 and 300 units.

Price Discrimination

Setting distinct prices to reach different market segments is **price discrimination.**

Through a **price discrimination** approach, a firm sets two or more distinct prices for a product in order to appeal to different final consumer or organizational consumer market segments. In price discrimination, higher prices are offered to inelastic consumer segments and lower prices to elastic segments. Price discrimination can be customer-based, product-based, time-based, or place-based.

With customer-based price discrimination, prices differ by customer category for the same good or service. Price differentials may relate to a consumer's ability to pay (physicians, lawyers, and accountants partially set prices in this manner), negotiating ability (the final price of a new or used car is usually established by bargaining), or buying power (discounts are given for large purchases).

Under product-based price discrimination, a firm offers a number of features, styles, qualities, brands, or sizes of a product and sets a different price for each product version. Price differentials are greater than cost differentials for the various versions. For example, a dishwasher may be priced at $400 in white and $450 in brown, although the brown color costs the manufacturer only $10 more. There is inelastic demand by customers desiring the special color, and product versions are priced accordingly.

[6] See Michael H. Morris and Mary L. Joyce, "How Marketers Evaluate Price Sensitivity," *Industrial Marketing Management,* Vol. 17 (1988), pp. 169–176.

TABLE 20-4 Modified Break-Even Analysis for Phase III Bicycles—Priced from $4,500 to $7,000 at Retail

Col. 1	Col. 2	Col. 3	Col. 4 = Col. 2 × Col. 3	Col. 5	Col. 6 = Col. 4 − Col. 5	
Retail Selling Price	Quantity Demanded	Price Received by Manufacturer[a]	Manufacturer's Total Revenue	Manufacturer's Total Costs[b]	Manufacturer's Profit (Loss)	
$7,000	100	$4,480	$ 448,000	$ 435,000	$ 13,000	
6,500	200	4,160	832,000	695,000	137,000	
6,000	300	3,840	1,152,000	955,000	197,000	Maximum profit
5,500	400	3,520	1,408,000	1,215,000	193,000	
5,000	500	3,200	1,600,000	1,475,000	125,000	
4,500	600	2,880	1,728,000	1,735,000	(7,000)	

[a] The Phase III manufacturer receives 64 cents of every retail dollar ($1.00 × 0.8 × 0.8), using the traditional chain-markup involving the retailer, wholesaler, and manufacturer.
[b] From Table 20-2.

With time-based price discrimination, a company varies prices by day versus evening (movie theater tickets), time of day (telephone and utility rates), or season (hotel rates). Consumers who insist on prime time use pay higher prices than those who are willing to make their purchases during nonpeak times.

In place-based price discrimination, prices differ by seat location (sports and entertainment events), floor location (office buildings, hotels), or geographic location (resort cities). The demand for locations near the stage, elevators, or warm climates drives the prices of these locations up. General admission tickets, basement offices, and moderate-temperature resorts are priced lower in order to attract consumers to make otherwise less desirable purchases.

When a firm engages in price discrimination, it should use *yield management pricing*—whereby it determines the mix of price-quantity combinations that yields the highest level of revenues for a given period. A company would want to make sure that it gives itself every opportunity to sell as many goods and services at full price as possible, while also seeking to sell as many units as it can. It would not want to sell so many low-price items that it jeopardizes full-price sales. For example, a 1,000-seat theater that features first-run plays must determine how many tickets to sell as orchestra (at $40 each) and how many to sell as general admission (at $15 each). If it tries to sell too many orchestra tickets, there may be empty seats during a performance. If it tries to sell too many general admission tickets, the theater may be full but total revenues may be unsatisfactory.

Yield management pricing enables firms to optimize price discrimination efforts.

Figure 20-4 shows how a firm can benefit from a price discrimination strategy. It was established in Table 20-4 that Phase III's manufacturer would maximize profit for one model of bicycle if it sells 300 units at a retail price of $6,000 apiece. However, the firm could increase its profits from $197,000 to $263,000 by selling three different models of its bicycle—priced at $7,000, $6,500, and $6,000—and offering distinct features for each model (such as a leather seat, silver-plated handle bars, and chrome-plated wheel covers for the most expensive model).

Before employing price discrimination, a firm should consider these points. Are there distinct market segments? Do consumers communicate with each other about

FIGURE 20-4

Price Discrimination for Phase III Bicycles

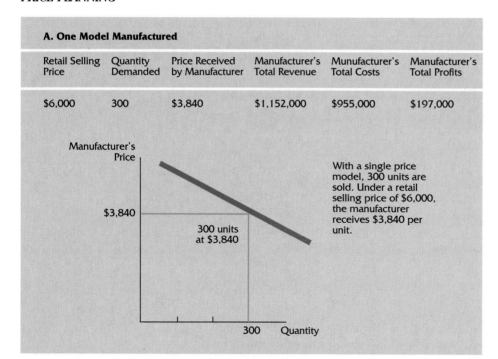

A. One Model Manufactured

Retail Selling Price	Quantity Demanded	Price Received by Manufacturer	Manufacturer's Total Revenue	Munufacturer's Total Costs	Manufacturer's Total Profits
$6,000	300	$3,840	$1,152,000	$955,000	$197,000

With a single price model, 300 units are sold. Under a retail selling price of $6,000, the manufacturer receives $3,840 per unit.

B. Three Models Manufactured

Model	Retail Selling Price	Quantity Demanded	Price Received by Mfr.	Mfr.'s Total Revenue	Mfr.'s Variable Costs*	Mfr.'s Total Costs†	Mfr.'s Total Costs	Mfr.'s Total Profit
AA	$7,000	100	$4,480.00	$448,000	$280,000	$58,333	$338,333	$109,667
BB	6,500	100	4,160.00	416,000	270,000	58,333	328,333	87,667
CC	6,500	100	3,840.00	384,000	260.000	58,333	318,333	65,667
Total		300		$1,248,000	$810,000	$175,000¹	$985,000¹	$263,000¹

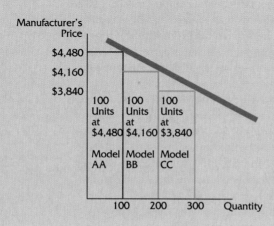

With three prices and models, three different market segments are attracted and 100 people buy each model. The manufacturer's revenue is increased by $96,000, while costs increase by only $30,000. Therefore, profits rise by $66,000.

* The materials for models AA and BB are upgraded by $200 and $100, respectively.

† The fixed costs of $175,000 are allocated to each model.

¹ Rounding errors.

You're the Marketer

What's Next for MCI?

The Federal Communications Commission (FCC) ended its practice of regulating AT&T's rate of return on long-distance telephone service in 1989. Until then, AT&T was allowed to earn a maximum return of 12.5 per cent on its investment. Now a price cap is used to limit AT&T's long-distance price increases, but there are no limits on its rate of return. Thus, if AT&T improves its productivity, it will be able to increase profits. AT&T can also file price changes with the FCC only 14 days in advance, versus the old 45-day rule.

Overall the FCC's rule changes give AT&T (with two-thirds of the market) more power to compete with such rivals as MCI (which has a 12 per cent market share). AT&T is encouraged to be more efficient because there are no longer constraints on profitability. It has greater flexibility in setting rates. In the past, competitors frequently challenged AT&T's rate applications to the FCC and delayed their introduction. In the interim, they introduced their own new rates. The burden to show that AT&T's prices violate FCC rules has shifted from AT&T to competitors.

MCI's 1970s' strategy was based on several factors. It was the first low-priced long-distance telephone service alternative to AT&T. MCI concentrated on a few potentially lucrative market segments, such as price-conscious businesses and final consumers. Costs were held down; its customers accepted poorer-quality service in return for huge price discounts. MCI gradually expanded its geographic coverage and upgraded service quality. Today MCI is a well-entrenched firm with loyal customers, high-quality service, and a positive company image. It is concentrating on large corporate and institutional customers and featuring service reliability, quality, and geographic coverage in its ads.

As an MCI vice-president, what short-run and long-run pricing actions would you recommend?

SOURCE: Based on material in Mary Lou Carnevale and Janet Guyon, "FCC Alters Long-Distance Regulation of AT&T, Aiding Its Competitive Clout," Wall Street Journal (March 17, 1989), pp. A3, A7; and Frances Seghers, "AT&T Unchained: Business May Be the Winner," Business Week (March 20, 1989), p. 42.

product features and prices? Can product versions be differentiated? Will some consumers choose low-priced models when they might otherwise buy high-priced models if they are the only ones available? How do marginal costs of creating additional product alternatives compare with marginal revenues? Will channel members stock all models? How difficult is it to explain product differences to consumers? Under what conditions is price discrimination legal (the firm would not want to violate the Robinson-Patman Act)?[7]

Competition-Based Pricing

In competition-based pricing, a firm uses competitors' prices rather than demand or cost considerations as its primary pricing guideposts. With this approach, the com-

Setting prices on the basis of competitors is competition-based pricing.

[7] See Michael H. Morris, "Separate Prices as a Marketing Tool," *Industrial Marketing Management*, Vol. 16 (1987), pp. 79–86.

pany may not respond to changes in demand or costs unless they also have an effect on competitors' prices. A company may set prices below the market, at the market, or above the market, depending on its customers, image, overall marketing mix, consumer loyalty, and other factors.

Competition-based pricing is popular for several reasons. It is simple, with no reliance on demand curves, price elasticity, or costs per unit. The ongoing market price level is assumed to be fair for both consumers and companies. Pricing at the market level does not disrupt competition and, therefore, does not lead to retaliations. However, it may lead to complacency; and different firms may not have the same demand and cost structures.

Two aspects of competition-based pricing are discussed in the following subsections: price leadership and competitive bidding.

Price Leadership

In price leadership, one or a few firms initiate price changes in an industry; they are effective when other firms follow.

Price leadership exists in situations where one firm (or a few firms) is usually the first to announce price changes and the other companies in the industry follow. The role of a price leader is to adapt prices to reflect market conditions, without disrupting the marketplace — by turning off consumers with price increases that are perceived as too large or by precipitating a price war with competitors through excessive price decreases.

Price leaders are generally firms that have significant market shares, well-established positions, respect from competitors, and the desire to initiate price changes. As an illustration, a frequent price leader in the newsprint industry is Abitibi-Price. It is the world's largest newsprint producer, has the greatest manufacturing capacity, and

TABLE 20-5 An Application of the Expected Profit Concept in Competitive Bidding for Government Machinery Contracts[1]

Company's Bid Amount	Costs of Fulfilling Contract	Profit (Loss)	Probability of Winning Bid[a]	Long-Run Average Expected Profit (Loss) at Each Bid Amount[b]	
$ 65,000	$75,000	$(10,000)	0.99	$(9,900)	
70,000	75,000	(5,000)	0.95	(4,750)	
75,000	75,000	0	0.85	0	
80,000	75,000	5,000	0.75	3,750	
85,000	75,000	10,000	0.60	6,000	
90,000	75,000	15,000	0.50	7,500	← —— Best average
95,000	75,000	20,000	0.30	6,000	long-run bid
100,000	75,000	25,000	0.15	3,750	
105,000	75,000	30,000	0.10	3,000	
110,000	75,000	35,000	0.05	1,750	

[1] The highest long-run average expected profit occurs at a bid amount of $90,000. The firm will earn $15,000 on each bid it wins, win half the contracts it bids on, and receive an average profit of $7,500 on all the contracts it bids on (0.5 × $15,000).

[a] The probability of having the winning (lowest) bid must be estimated by analyzing past bids, current competitive conditions, and the cost relationships of the company in contrast with its competitors.

[b] Average expected profit (loss) = Profit (loss) × Probability of winning bid.

has the dominant market share. Because over one-half of company sales are in newsprint, Abitibi-Price has a strong commitment to maintain the stability of its prices.

However, over the past several years, the role of price leaders has been substantially reduced in many industries — including steel, chemical, glass container, and newsprint — as many smaller firms have sought to implement their own independent strategies. Even Abitibi-Price has been affected by this trend. For example, in June 1988, Abitibi-Price announced it would raise newsprint prices by 6.9 per cent as of January 1, 1989. Yet, in November 1988, Abitibi-Price decided to rescind part of the increase and not enact the lower increase until February 1, 1989; its action was in response to competitors' not following its price leadership. As Abitibi-Price's senior vice-president of marketing remarked: "We are disappointed that our price announcement for the U.S. and Canada had to be modified, but we are obviously aware of the realities of the marketplace."[8]

Announcements of price changes by industry leaders must be communicated only through independent media or company publicity releases. It is illegal for firms in the same industry or in competing industries to confer with one another regarding the setting of prices.

Competitive Bidding

With competitive bidding, two or more companies independently submit prices to a customer for a specific good, project, and/or service.[9] Generally, sealed bids are offered in response to precise government or organizational consumer requests, and each seller has one chance to make its best offer.

Various mathematical models have been applied to competitive bidding. All of them utilize the **expected profit concept,** which states that as the bid price increases the profit to a firm increases but the probability of its winning the contract decreases. The long-run average expected profit (loss) at each bid amount equals a company's profit times its probability of obtaining the contract at this bid amount. Although a company's potential profit at a given bid amount can usually be estimated accurately, the probability of getting a contract (underbidding all other qualified competitors) can be difficult to determine.

*Competitive bids should be based on the **expected profit concept.***

Table 20-5 shows an application of the expected profit concept in the competitive bidding for government machinery contracts. A number of points can be drawn from this table. One, the costs of fulfilling a contract remain the same regardless of the bid. Two, a firm should study the impact of a wide range of bids (as done in Table 20-5). Three, long-run expected profit is the average yield for a bid amount used over a sustained period of time — not the actual profit on a single bid. Four, small errors in cost estimates or the probability of winning a bid may cause the firm to select a wrong bid. For example, if there is really a 40 per cent chance of winning contracts with a bid of $95,000, the long-run average expected profit at this amount would be $8,000 ($20,000 × 0.40).

[8] Peggy Berkowitz, "Abitibi-Price to Raise Cost of Newsprint 6.9% Jan. 1, First Increase in a Year," *Wall Street Journal* (June 20, 1988), p. 44; and Robert Melnbardis, "Abitibi-Price Reduces, Delays Paper Price Rise," *Wall Street Journal* (November 8, 1988), p. B7.

[9] See Paul D. Boughton, "The Competitive Bidding Process: Beyond Probability Models," *Industrial Marketing Management,* Vol. 16 (1987), pp. 87–94; and M. Edward Goretsky, "When to Bid for Government Contracts," *Industrial Marketing Management,* Vol. 16 (1987), pp. 25–33.

TABLE 20-6   Selected Issues to Consider When Integrating Pricing Techniques

Cost-Based

What profit margin does a price level allow?

Do markups allow for differences in product investments, installation and servicing, and selling effort and merchandising skills?

Are there accurate and timely cost data by good, service, project, process, and/or store?

Are cost changes monitored and prices adjusted accordingly?

Are there specific profit or return-on-investment goals?

What is the price floor for each good, service, project, process, and/or store?

What are the break-even points for each good, service, project, process, and/or store?

Demand-Based

What type of demand does each good, service, project, process, and/or store face?

Have price elasticities been estimated for various price levels?

Are demand-minus, chain-markup, and modified break-even analyses utilized?

Has price discrimination been considered?

How loyal are customers?

Competition-Based

How do prices compare with those of competitors?

Is price leadership used in the industry? By whom?

How do competitors react to price changes?

How are competitive bids determined?

Is the long-run expected profit concept used in competitive bidding?

Combining Techniques

It is essential that companies combine cost, demand, and competitive pricing techniques.

Although cost-, demand-, and competition-based pricing techniques have been discussed separately throughout this chapter, in practice aspects of the three approaches should be combined. A cost-based approach sets a price floor and outlines the various costs incurred in doing business. It establishes profit margins, target prices, and/or break-even quantities. A demand-based approach determines the prices consumers are willing to pay and the ceiling prices for each channel member. It develops the price-quantity mix that maximizes profits and allows a firm to reach different market segments. A competition-based approach examines the appropriate price level for the firm in relation to competitors.

Unless the techniques are combined, critical decisions are likely to be overlooked.[10] Table 20-6 provides a broad list of questions a firm should consider when setting prices; it expands on the questions presented in Chapter 19. Figure 20-5 shows a combined approach to pricing used by two successful Wetterau store chains: Save Mart and Shop 'N Save.

---

[10] See Eric Mitchell, ''Pricing Myths, Pitfalls to Avoid in 1989,'' *Marketing News* (February 13, 1989), p. 11.

FIGURE 20-5 Combining Pricing Techniques
Save Mart (left) and Shop 'N Save operate warehouse and super-warehouse stores that are cost efficient, demand-oriented, and competitive. Reprinted by permission.

Summary

1. *To examine and evaluate various cost-based pricing techniques and to present applications of them* With cost-based pricing, the firm computes merchandise, service, and overhead costs and then adds an amount to cover profit. Cost-based prices are relatively easy to implement, are founded on comparative certainty, and incorporate profitability. If used alone, they also disregard market conditions, plant capacity, competitive prices, a product's phase in its life cycle, market share, and the consumer's ability to pay. Overhead costs may be difficult to allocate.

When using cost-based techniques, it is necessary to understand several key cost concepts, including fixed costs, variable costs, total costs, average costs, and marginal costs.

Cost-plus pricing adds costs and a desired profit rate to set price. It is easy to compute but has several shortcomings — such as offering little incentive to improve efficiency. It is most effective when a firm is able to control selling price.

In markup pricing, a firm sets prices by calculating the per-unit costs of producing (buying) goods and/or services and then determining the markup percentages needed to cover selling costs and profit. Markup pricing is common among wholesalers and retailers. A variable markup policy allows a company to use different markups for distinct products.

In target pricing, prices are set to provide a specified rate of return on investment for a standard volume of production. It is used most often by capital-intensive firms and public utilities. Target pricing is relatively ineffective if a firm must use discounted prices to clear out slow-selling items.

When a firm has excess capacity, it may use price-floor pricing, in which prices are set at a level above variable costs rather than total costs. In the short-run, this would enable a company to sell additional units and use those revenues to increase profits or help pay for fixed costs. However, to survive in the long-run, the company would have to be sure that average total costs are covered by its prices.

Traditional break-even analysis determines the sales quantity at which total costs equal total revenues for a chosen price. It can be extended to include profit analysis. But it does not consider the actual level of consumer demand at the chosen price.

2. *To examine and evaluate various demand-based pricing techniques and to present applications of*

them For demand-based pricing, the company first determines the prices consumers and channel members will pay, then figures the markups needed to cover selling expenses and profits, and finally derives the maximum it can spend to produce (or buy) its offering. Prices are linked to consumer preferences, channel needs, and product image. Demand-based techniques require consumer research, may be predicated on imprecise data, and sometimes are not keyed to profitability.

In demand-minus pricing, the firm ascertains the appropriate final selling price and works backward to compute costs. It is used by firms that sell directly to consumers. Marketing research may be time-consuming or complex.

Chain-markup pricing extends demand-minus calculations all the way from middlemen back to their suppliers (manufacturers). Final selling price is determined; markups for each channel member are studied; and then maximum acceptable costs to each channel member are computed. This technique assures a proper final selling price and equitable markups throughout the channel.

Modified break-even analysis combines traditional break-even analysis with an evaluation of demand at various levels of price. It helps a firm select the price-quantity mix that optimizes its profit, and shows that profits do not necessarily rise as quantity sold increases — because lower prices may be needed to stimulate demand.

Price discrimination is a technique whereby a firm sets two or more distinct prices for a product in order to appeal to different market segments. It can be customer-, product-, time-, or place-based. By using yield management pricing, a company seeks to determine the mix of price-quantity combinations that yields the highest level of revenues for a given period.

3. *To examine and evaluate various competition-based pricing techniques and to present applications of them* In competition-based pricing, a firm uses competitors' prices as its main guideposts. Prices may be below, at, or above the market. It is simple, provides equity for customers and companies, and may minimize possible price confrontations.

A firm would determine whether it has the ability and the interest to be a price leader or price follower. Today the effectiveness of price leadership in many industries is less than it once was — due to competitive pressures.

Under competitive bidding, two or more companies independently submit prices in response to precise customer requests. They often rely on the expected profit concept in bidding.

4. *To show why cost-, demand-, and competition-based pricing techniques should be integrated* These three pricing techniques should be combined so that the firm includes all necessary factors in its pricing strategy. It is important for a company to consider cost-based price floors, the prices consumers are willing to pay, and the actions of competitors. Otherwise critical decisions are likely to be overlooked.

Key Terms

cost-plus pricing (p. 608)
markup pricing (p. 610)
variable markup policy (p. 610)
target pricing (p. 611)
price-floor pricing (p. 611)

traditional break-even analysis
  (p. 613)
demand-minus (demand-backward)
  pricing (p. 616)
chain-markup pricing (p. 617)

modified break-even analysis (p. 618)
price discrimination (p. 618)
yield management pricing (p. 619)
price leadership (p. 622)
expected profit concept (p. 623)

Review Questions

1. Why are overhead costs sometimes difficult to assign to specific goods and services?

2. What are the advantages and disadvantages of cost-plus pricing?

3. Why are markups usually computed on the basis of selling price?

4. When should a firm consider a variable markup policy?

5. A firm requires a 12 per cent return on a $500,000 investment in order to produce a new electric can opener. If the standard volume is 50,000 units, fixed costs are $200,000, and variable costs are $6.00 per unit, what is the target price?

6. What is the role of price-floor pricing?

7. A company making office desks has total fixed costs of $1 million per year and variable costs of $250 per desk. It sells the desks to retailers for $400 apiece. Compute the traditional break-even point in units and dollars.

8. Distinguish between demand-minus pricing and chain-markup pricing.

9. What is yield management pricing? Why is it important for sellers to understand this concept?

10. Compute the best average long-run competitive bid from among the following. The costs of fulfilling a contract are $7,000:

Bid Amount	Probability of Winning Bid
$10,000	0.90
11,000	0.80
12,000	0.70
13,000	0.60
14,000	0.50
15,000	0.40

Explain your answer.

Discussion Questions

1. A movie theater has weekly fixed costs (land, building, and equipment) of $3,000. Variable weekly costs (movie rental, electricity, ushers, etc.) are $2,000. From a price-floor pricing perspective, how much revenue must a movie generate during a slow week for it to be worthwhile to open the theater? Explain your answer.

2. A retailer determines that its customers are willing to spend $19.95 on a Julia Child cookbook. The publisher charges the retailer $15.00 for each copy. The retailer wants a 30 per cent markup. Comment on this.

3. A clock manufacturer knows consumers will pay $45 for a radio/alarm clock with a digital face and extra options. If the chain markup is 30, 30, 30, what is the maximum the clock can cost the manufacturer? What should be done if the clock costs less than the maximum amount?

4. a. An industrial wholesaler of small tools has fixed costs of $600,000, variable costs of $6 per tool, and faces this demand schedule from its hardware-store customers:

Price	Quantity Demanded
$15	100,000
$18	85,000
$21	65,000
$24	40,000

At what price is profit maximized?

b. If the company noted in Question 4a decides to sell 40,000 small tools at $24 and 25,000 of these tools at $21, what will its profit be? What are the risks of this approach?

5. Can a small firm become a price leader? Explain your answer.

<< CASE 1 >>

Pay-Per-View Television: Setting Prices for a New Service*

The number of U.S. homes equipped to receive pay-per-view television shows reached 10 million in 1988 and is expected to rise to 40 million as of 1996. Pay-per-view television's 1988 revenues from movies and events were less than $100 million, but some experts believe these revenues could reach $6 billion per year within the next decade. However, the long-run success of pay-per-view television will depend upon technological advances, the caliber of programs, and the prices charged to consumers.

* The data in this case are drawn from Laura Landro, "Hopes Rise Again for Pay-Per-View TV," *Wall Street Journal* (November 11, 1988), p. B1; and Andrew L. Yarrow, "Pay-Per-View Television Is Ready for Takeoff," *New York Times* (November 14, 1988), p. D9.

There are two different technologies by which homes can receive pay-per-view television. With addressable equipment, viewers must call their local cable companies prior to a program and arrange for them to unscramble the show for their homes. This often leads to cable operators being swamped with last-minute requests for a particular show that they cannot fulfill.

With a newer impulse technology, viewers select shows by pushing buttons on remote-control units in their homes; they can order a show at the last minute. Impulse technology generally results in a significantly larger number of orders than addressable technology. For example, at one pay-per-view company with impulse technology, viewers order five times more movies than the typical addressable-technology customer. At present, only 10 per cent of the homes equipped for pay-per-view television have access to impulse technology.

The popularity of pay-per-view television will be closely linked to the caliber of programs. Thus far, pay-per-view shows have concentrated on rock concerts, boxing and wrestling matches, Broadway plays, and movies. For example, the 1988 Mike Tyson-Michael Spinks heavyweight championship fight attracted 600,000 households at a price of $35 each. At present, on average, a film shown on pay-per-view television generates revenues of $250,000. Movie studios earned $36 million from pay-per-view rights in 1988 but feel earnings will go to $1 billion annually by 1997.

As the president of one pay-per-view network commented: "Pay-per-view can provide the program rights holder with the greatest revenue per exhibition. It's uniquely suited for the first televised exhibition of major events and movies."

Despite optimistic forecasts and the wide proportion of households equipped to accept pay-per-view, current usage is still low. Most consumers are not yet convinced that they should pay to see a movie in their own homes. For instance, why would a consumer pay $5 to watch a movie on pay-per-view when he or she could see a movie for free on HBO (assuming he or she already receives cable television shows)? This is the key question for pay-per-view companies: What is the appropriate price to charge for each show?

The majority of play-per-view shows are now priced between $1 and $10 (although prices for special events may range up to $40 or more) and pay-per-view revenues are less than 2 per cent of total cable television revenues. According to a recent study by Warner Communications, "most systems barely sell to 20 per cent of their total subscribers each month," generating average revenues equal to less than 80 cents per subscriber.

Pay-per-view operators have various other factors to consider in planning marketing strategies:

▶ AT&T has developed a new toll-free telephone service that enables pay-per-view companies to fill orders in as little as ten seconds. The initial cost of this system is about $10,000, and ongoing costs are 19 cents per order. This system gives cable operators with addressable converters the benefit of impulse technology.

▶ Opportunities exist in niche markets, such as opera fans. As the head of a pay-per-view company says, "With 20 million homes, even a 1 per cent buy rate for an opera, at $20, will bring in $4 million."

▶ Pay-per-view can be further extended at hotels and other commercial locales, giving business travelers and vacationers broader access to programs than otherwise available.

QUESTIONS

1. How would you overcome consumer resistance to paying for television shows in their own homes?
2. Develop a pricing strategy for a pay-per-view company specializing in movies.
3. How could a pay-per-view firm combine cost-, demand-, and competition-based pricing techniques in setting rates for events such as rock concerts and prize fights?
4. Apply these concepts to pay-per-view television companies: variable markup pricing, target pricing, chain-markup pricing, modified break-even analysis, and yield management pricing.

◄ CASE 2 ►

PC Clones: Aggressive Competitors†

Jim Carney is a 1989 college graduate who majored in computer science. Throughout his college years, Carney built personal computers (PCs), which he sold to friends and fellow students.

While a student, Carney took a marketing course and did research on PCs for his term paper. He is now using the data he gathered for that paper to develop a plan for making and marketing PC clones on a full-time basis. This is a summary of Carney's research on PCs:

▷ As recently as 1987, many predicted that small PC clone makers would be crowded out of the market. They cited factors such as IBM's new Personal System 2 models, new software standards, and reduced prices for IBM equipment. But to the surprise of IBM and others, this decline has not occurred.

▷ Clone makers have been able to cut their prices faster and more aggressively than IBM, IBM's old PC standard is still popular among consumers, and business customers have begun to feel more comfortable about buying clones. In fact, major organizations such as Raytheon, Eastman Kodak, GTE, and the U.S. Department of Transportation have purchased clones.

▷ There are three standards of clones: the XT (8088), AT (286), and 386 units. Generally the price of a clone in any of these categories—which are based on computing capabilities and speed—is roughly one-half that of a comparable IBM unit.

▷ Many mail-order clone firms are effective mass marketers. They heavily promote products (including their ratings in computer magazine reviews), have toll-free customer service centers, offer money-back guarantees and one-year warranties, and even pay for transportation costs if repairs are necessary.

---

† The data in this case are drawn from William M. Bulkeley, "Clone-Computer Business Is Booming," *Wall Street Journal* (October 7, 1988), p. B1.

▷ Many smaller clone makers compete with traditional PC manufacturers and "name-brand" clone makers on the basis of lower prices, home or office delivery, troubleshooting assistance, and word-of-mouth communication from satisfied users.

▷ Although firms such as Tandy produce "name-brand compatibles," their products often cannot accept many of the standardized peripherals (such as graphics boards, hard disks, and memory upgrades) that most "no-name" clones can accept.

Carney knows he must invest $20,000 in his business for machinery, test equipment, and so on. He also estimates that it would cost him $550 to $600 to build a basic IBM-compatible XT computer system (complete with a monochrome monitor, one floppy disk drive, one hard disk, and a keyboard). A comparable clone system currently sells for between $900 and $1,200 through the mail or at local retailers.

Jim initially plans to market computers through nearby office-equipment and college stores and to offer a one-year guarantee. The clones would be sold to the stores at a price enabling those stores to receive a 25 per cent markup at retail.

Although Jim has the expertise to build more complicated clones, he plans to start with just XTs. Because the XT is a basic entry system useful for applications such as word processing and spreadsheet analysis, it appeals to a large number of potential users. Also, XT customers typically desire a limited variety of configurations. Thus, Carney can limit his inventory investment.

Carney feels there are several reasons why consumers would buy his system. First, he will personally undertake all service calls at the customer's location. On-site service will save the customer the bother of mailing back parts and not having a computer until they arrive, and reduce the anxiety associated with repairs. Second, demonstrator units at stores will allow more sophisticated consumers to verify the compatibility of Carney's XT clone with computer software. Third, Jim will be available for technical service questions from both prospective buyers and actual purchasers. This service is especially important to first-time buyers.

QUESTIONS

1. Outline all the costs that Jim must consider in developing a pricing plan (beyond those stated in the case).
2. Compute Carney's selling price to retailers using target pricing. Assume a standard volume of 200 units per year and a target return on investment of 25 per cent. Comment on your answer.
3. What should be Carney's maximum selling price to college stores (assuming that the stores want a 25 per cent markup and Carney seeks a 20 per cent markup)? Comment on your answer.
4. How could Carney use modified break-even analysis in deciding on his selling price? Consider a range of retail prices of between $900 and $1,200. Explain your answer.

part 6 CASE

Tick Tock: Pricing in the Watch Industry*

Introduction

There are two indisputable elements in the watch business. One is that the dial-faced analog watch is clocking out electronic display digitals with the old one-two punch, causing even Casio to add analogs to its ranks. The renewed appeal of the analog points up another truth: Fashion is the buzzword that is setting off alarms in tick-tock land, and the once-popular digitals just don't make it in the fashion-flair category.

It comes as no surprise that Hong Kong, a giant digital-watch maker, which exports the most digitals at about $1 a piece, is increasing its output of analogs, whose export price is 10 times as high, according to *Modern Jeweler*. The American Watch Association says that 1987 imports totalled 191.7 million units, up 13 per cent from 1986, but that includes gray-market watches, counterfeits, and giveaways. (Almost all watches sold in the United States today are imported models.) The import value rose almost 11 per cent to nearly $1.3 billion.

Time has certainly been flying in the watch business. It was just 21 years ago that quartz was introduced into watch workings by the Swiss and quickly perfected by the Japanese. Quartz watches, which just need a battery to run, kicked the hand-wound mechanicals by the wayside. Then digital watches, which flash

the time in numerals, displaced the dial and time-telling hands of the traditional analog models. Then lo and behold—Swatch came along in 1983 and turned the business upside down. Not only did the hands of time regain popularity—Swatch watches are all battery-operated analogs—but so did multicolors and multiownership. Wearing several simultaneously became hip.

Since then, the Swatch watch that debuted at $19.95 has sent the industry scrambling. Fashion is what now makes the watch biz go and even Timex, which "takes a lickin' and keeps on tickin'," has swapped durability for design as its first priority.

Meanwhile, top-of-the-line luxe models have altered their marketing strategies to woo yuppie types into jewelry stores. Baume & Mercier, for example, has come out with less expensive watches, meaning $2,000 to $4,000 as opposed to $5,000 to $10,000. Cartier may call advertising an "accessory," but lately it has even bought space in *Elle*. North American Watch Co., distributor of luxury brands such as Piaget and Concord, now also markets Movado, which has a lower-priced line for status-seeking baby-boomers. And on the other wrist, mid-priced Citizen has moved upscale with its "Noblia" collection.

So take a look at your wristwatch. Is it a status symbol? Is it a fashion accessory? Is it a life-style statement? Can it be—just a wristwatch? Yes! It can be all that and more, say marketers.

The latest fashion trend is the retro, or antique, look. This may mean a simple analog with Arabic

* Adapted by the authors from Paula Schnorbus, "Tick Tock," *Marketing & Media Decisions* (October 1988), pp. 117–132. Reprinted by permission.

numbers on the dial and a honey-colored leather strap. It can also mean that there are more subdials than a submarine's control panel. You want high fashion? Get high technology. In an abbreviated list, there are moon phase indicators, tachymeters, stopwatches, alarms, day-and-date subdials, and dials to tell the time around the world. This is just on an analog watch. Casio likes to think of its digital watches as minicomputers. They boast data banks, calculators, auto telephone dialing, and currency conversion.

As many bells and whistles on one watch as a manufacturer can muster may be the ultimate, but that may not be what the masses will ante up for. Indeed, according to Mediamark Research Inc.'s spring 1988 data, most watch buyers are 18- to 34-year-olds, single, with a little above average income, and they spend under $50 on a timepiece.

In that category, Hong Kong digitals for a couple of bucks are big, but Timex still leads the way. Swatch may have been the industry catalyst, even getting Timex to come out with a "Watercolors" collection, but the Swiss-based concern has had its share of management problems.

Actually, digitals aren't totally dead yet, but they have been relegated to a sports-watch niche. Coming up is a battery-less watch, brought to you by Seiko, among others. And believe it or not, hand-wound watches may be making a comeback, however slight, with the revival of antique watches.

Packaged Facts Inc., a New York-based research company, reported last year that the wristwatch market is divided into three segments. There are the mass-market models, which list for under $75 at retail. This is where the real action is. These timepieces rack up a whopping 72 per cent of the market. The mid-market segment spans from a $75 to $300 ticket and holds 22 per cent of the market's business. Luxury watches, defined as costing over $300, make up a mere 6 per cent of the market.

In mass-market sales, Timex had an approximate 40 per cent market share; Casio and Swatch were both estimated at 10 per cent to 15 per cent; and Gluck, which makes Armitron, had a 10 per cent share.

Mid- and luxury-price market shares are often lumped together by company rather than brands within the company. Industry experts believe, however, that Seiko and Pulsar, both part of Hattori Seiko, as well as Citizen and Bulova are the mid-price mainstays. Luxury leaders are Rolex, Baume & Mercier, Cartier, and Omega.

Mass Market

Timex

The watch that "takes a lickin' and keeps on tickin' " is now fashion-conscious. Design is Timex's "number-one priority," as the push is on to capture the watch-as-fashion accessory market.

Swatch's style spurred Timex to issue fashion collections such as "Watercolors" for teenage girls. There is the fancier "Doubles" collection, women's watches with straps that wrap around the wrist twice, which Timex hopes to hawk through upscale retailers. There are also digital sport watches for everything from sail racing to skiing. There are, in fact, some 250 watches with the Timex name, and 15 per cent are digital.

In 1982, Timex started the introduction of "unique products" such as the sport watches. "There was some catch-up but also some go-ahead pieces such as the Victory yachting watch, which has a special countdown timing feature." That watch is $75, but the line's price range is generally between $9.95 and $69.95. By 1983, Swatch was on the horizon with its revolutionary positioning, and Timex eventually trotted out its own fashion-hued collection.

Timex is sold primarily by mass merchandisers, catalog showrooms, drugstores, and, to a lesser extent, department stores. With the new sport watches, specialty stores will become another option, such as ski shops for the Skiathlon.

Casio

With analog watches ruling the market, Casio has been expanding its collection to include watch faces other than digital. But that doesn't mean digitals are leaving Casio's line of more than 100 watches. Says company spokesperson, Gary E. Johnson, "Analogs will give people a choice."

Casio's target is primarily high-technology-oriented males and sportspeople. It targets mostly 18- to 34-year-old men and, as more of an afterthought, women. Prices range from as low as $6.95 to $150.

Casio sponsors the Olympic Regional Development

Authority and "tons and tons" of fun runs, races, and marathons. Casio is also the official timekeeper for the New York Yankees.

Swatch

The company that set off the alarms in the industry, signaling the coming of fun fashion watches, was actually founded on a technological concept. Swatch, says its makers, has fewer parts than a standard watch and they are welded together.

Swatch watches, which often look like anything but timepieces with their multicolored bands and dials, all have themes, such as "Love Field," which recalls early civil aviation. Steve Rechtenshaffner, who just returned to Swatch as its vice-president of advertising and promotion, claims that Swatches target more of a psychographic than a demographic market. ("My cat wears one, actually two. . . My grandmother likes the Pop Swatch because it is easier to tell the time.") Rechtenshaffner, who left the company because he thought it was becoming too traditional, says Swatch wearers live life to the fullest.

Swatch, which coined the concept of multiwatch buying and wearing, has about 246 styles currently, all analog. The company sold them for $19.95 in their debut year of 1983. Five years later, most of the watches carried a $35 tag.

Swatch has been known to set up its own separate counters in department stores and specialty stores. You won't find this mass-market watch in a drugstore or at a mass merchandiser.

Armitron

If Casio keeps time for the Yankees, Armitron does it for the New York Mets. And Mets catcher Gary Carter pitches Armitron All-Sport watches.

Owned by E. Gluck Corp., Armitron markets a myriad collection, ranging from prices of under $10 for a kid's watch to $225 for a grownup's diamond watch. There also is a Swatch knockoff called Awatch.

Armitron's advertising is extensively cooperative. If it wants to reach the young, female, fashion-conscious market, full-page ads with J.C. Penney, for example, will appear in *Seventeen*. Children's watches will be advertised on a cooperative basis at Christmas. The All-Sport is advertised in *Sports Illustrated, People, GQ,* and *Money.*

Mid-Price

Seiko

Seiko, which rules the mid-price range, came up with a new marketing tool two years ago to define its style. Four collections were developed to segment Seiko's 450 watches. The collections are divided into jewelry, status/sport ("a little more macho"), gentry ("for gentrified"), and boardroom, according to Hal Wilensky, executive vice-president of Seiko Time Corp. "Lifestyles have become very important," he explains.

Calling it a "mass class" brand, Wilensky says Seiko reaches just about all demographics. The average retail price is $210, but the range for a watch is from $75 to $450.

Seiko is sold through jewelry and department stores and catalog showrooms. A generic ad runs in magazines such as the *New Yorker, Vanity Fair, Elle,* and *Playbill.*

Citizen

This mid-priced watch company has been trying to move uptown with its Noblia collection, priced from $195 up to nearly $1,000. Noblia has come roaring in with its "Hanimal" advertising campaign by Lintas. The distinctive ads feature the wristwatches as animal collars on hands painted to resemble panthers, alligators, and race horses. The ads run in high-fashion magazines.

Laurence R. Grunstein, president of Citizen Watch Co. of America, says there are three product lines to go after the different demographic and psychographic markets. The basic $59 to $195 Citizen is for middle America; the $100 to $195 Elegance line "has the look of being much more expensive for people who can't afford the real thing;" and the more uptown Noblia goes after "the 5 per cent of the American population that can afford a watch in that price range."

There is some business with the Sharper Image catalog, but "we have to be careful with direct marketing so there isn't direct competition with retailers," warns Grunstein.

Pulsar

Pulsar "tosses the net far and wide" to attract "as many people as we possibly can," says Jonathan Nettelfield, senior general manager, advertising, for Pulsar Time. The demographic market is broad, targeting 25- to 49-year-olds with annual incomes of $30,000 and above.

Galileo is Pulsar's premier collection, with the "moondials and subwheels that are really a fashion look," says Nettelfield. Pulsar, which has 450 models, starts at $50 for a digital or a very basic analog watch and goes up to about $225 for one with diamonds. The watches are sold in jewelry and department stores as well as jewelry chains and some catalog showrooms.

The Pulsar collections aren't advertised separately, however. "We need to push the Pulsar name," says Nettelfield. "We will use fashion collections to represent Pulsar, but we won't advertise for the sake of a collection. It would fragment the budget too much."

Bulova

And now it's Bulova watch time, or as its current tagline goes, "It's America's time." And as one might expect, that translates into an emotional, traditional advertising pitch.

Robert Ryan, vice-president of marketing, says that the target audience is 18 to 45, but the psychographics are shifting. Bulova's older, blue-collar audience, with its traditional American values, is still intact. However, Bulova is upgrading the image in search of a broader, younger audience by bringing more of a sense of style and design to its watches, explains Ryan.

The majority of Bulova's watches are in the $100 to $300 price range. There are two 30-second television spots running at any given time. To catch the working couple or working single, they appear on early and late news or right after prime and prime access.

Luxury

Rolex

The Rolls-Royce of wristwatches, Rolex, gave us the first water-resistant watch in the 1920s and in 1931, the first self-winding watch activated by the "slightest movement of the wrist." Prices range from a little over $1,000 for a simple model to more than six figures for a fully-loaded timekeeper. But William Sullivan, vice-president, advertising, Rolex Watch U.S.A., says that while there is "obviously a level of affluence required, I would rather say it's an attitudinal demographic mar-

ket, people who want to wear a watch that is both durable and has a promised performance."

Rolex makes three lines of watches: Tudor, which has a lower price range; the Cellini line of 18-karat gold watches; and the Oyster, Rolex's pressure-proof, or water-resistant, watch. Oyster serves as Rolex's sports watch.

Rolex advertises mainly in magazines. Personalities such as intellectual, literary, musical, or sports figures pitch the products. "The ads stress the quality of the individual and the relevance of the watch to that individual's life-style," explains Sullivan.

Baume & Mercier

Baume & Mercier has been trying to reposition itself to the two-income household. Like everyone else, it wants to attract 30- to 45-year-old boomers with plenty of disposable income. B&M wants those who are "status-oriented," relates Steven Kaiser, director of sales and marketing. But, he admits, "We may have to go after an older audience. Younger people only have so much money to spend on luxury items."

The watch company has three core collections. Riviera, a sport-watch line started late in 1986, is the collection designed to appeal to the younger crowd. Price points are from $2,200 to $4,200. The collection for the older generation is the 18-karat, with $5,000 to $10,000 watches. "That one is a good growth area for us," says Kaiser. "Those who got hurt in the October 1987 stock market crash are the $2,000 to $4,000 buyers." A 14-karat line consists of diamond and non-diamond watches that fetch $1,000 to $5,000.

Baume & Mercier only advertises its Riviera and 18-karat lines. It strongly believes in image advertising.

Cartier

Cartier, which takes credit for inventing the modern wristwatch, also has been expanding its horizons and distributes its products outside of the Cartier boutiques. "More and more people have been developing a taste of luxury," says Thierry Chaunu, vice-president, marketing.

The Must Vermeil collection, which debuted in 1968, has the widest distribution of Cartier's 316 watches. There are also historical collections, "high jewelry" watches, the 18-karat Louis Cartier collection, the Pasha watch ("the ultimate watch, very big and extremely complicated"), the Panther, the Santos, and the 21—the last three of which are the steel-and-gold segment.

The Must products are distributed everywhere from duty-free shops to Macy's in New York, where they are currently being test marketed. The watches start at $895 and are geared to young professionals starting out in life. The 21, Santos, and Panther collections also start at $895 but a Panther with a diamond bezel goes for $116,000.

And Cartier's advertising? "It's an accessory," says Chaunu. "Cartier is built more on reputation. Cartier isn't a brand that's developed out of advertising."

Omega

Omega shot clear to the moon with Neil Armstrong in 1969, and the watch company continues to reach for the stars with its Constellation, Seamaster, and Symbole collections.

The company has been concentrating on those three recently as it cuts back on its profusion of brands.

Janet Cerutti, Omega's marketing service director, says the strategy is to link with more "brand identifiable products."

The Constellation and the Seamaster each have about 15 designs, and the Symbole, introduced last spring, has two. Prices range from $500 to $2,500, but it is possible to spend $37,000 if one so desires. The watches basically are 18-karat gold and/or stainless steel with a choice of onyx, lapis, or mother-of-pearl dials; diamonds; and other stones as the price climbs. The Constellation is dressier, while the Seamaster is more recreational. The Symbole's dial designs sport life symbols such as the sun.

Omega only sells its watches through retail jewelers and a few select department stores, aiming toward 25- to 44-year-old college-educated, business-oriented types with annual income of $55,000 and more. This is clarified in a two-year-old advertising campaign, "Significant Moments," which emphasizes achievement, ambition, and perseverance in the life-styles of professional people.

QUESTIONS

1. Differentiate among and comment on the basic marketing strategies used for mass-market, mid-price, and luxury watches.
2. Relate the concepts of the law of demand and price elasticity of demand to the watch market.
3. As a mass-market watch maker, how would you react to a cost increase in watch materials? How would you react as a luxury watch maker? Why?
4. As a luxury watch maker, how could you exert control over retail prices?
5. Cite three pricing objectives for Casio, three for Seiko, and three for Rolex.
6. Relate these concepts to the pricing of mass-market, mid-price, and luxury watches:
   a. Customary pricing.
   b. Flexible pricing.
   c. Odd pricing.
   d. Price lining.
   e. Price discrimination.
7. Should a watch maker use a variable markup policy? Explain your answer.
8. Show how a watch maker could combine cost-, demand-, and competition-based pricing techniques.

part 7
EXPANDING THE SCOPE OF MARKETING

In Part 7, we present an expanded perspective of marketing.

21 **International Marketing** In this chapter, we apply marketing principles to international situations and explore the factors behind the growth of international marketing. We assess cultural, economic, political and legal, and technological factors. We conclude by looking at the stages in the development of an international marketing strategy: company organization, degree of standardization, and product, distribution, promotion, and price planning.

22 **Service and Nonprofit Marketing** Here, we extend marketing to service and nonprofit organizations. First, we review the differences between services and goods marketing. And we discuss the use of marketing by service firms, special considerations for service marketers, how service firms can be classified, and the role of services in the economy. We then focus on nonprofit marketing and how it is distinct from profit-oriented marketing. And we discuss how nonprofit organizations can be classified, as well as the role of nonprofit marketing in the economy.

23 **Marketing and Society** In this chapter, we examine the interaction of marketing and society. We begin by exploring the concept of social responsibility and discussing the impact of company and consumer activities on natural resources, the landscape, environmental pollution, planned obsolescence, and ethics. We then turn to consumerism and consider the basic rights of consumers: to information, to safety, to choice in product selection, and to be heard. We also note the trend toward greater deregulation and the maturity of consumerism.

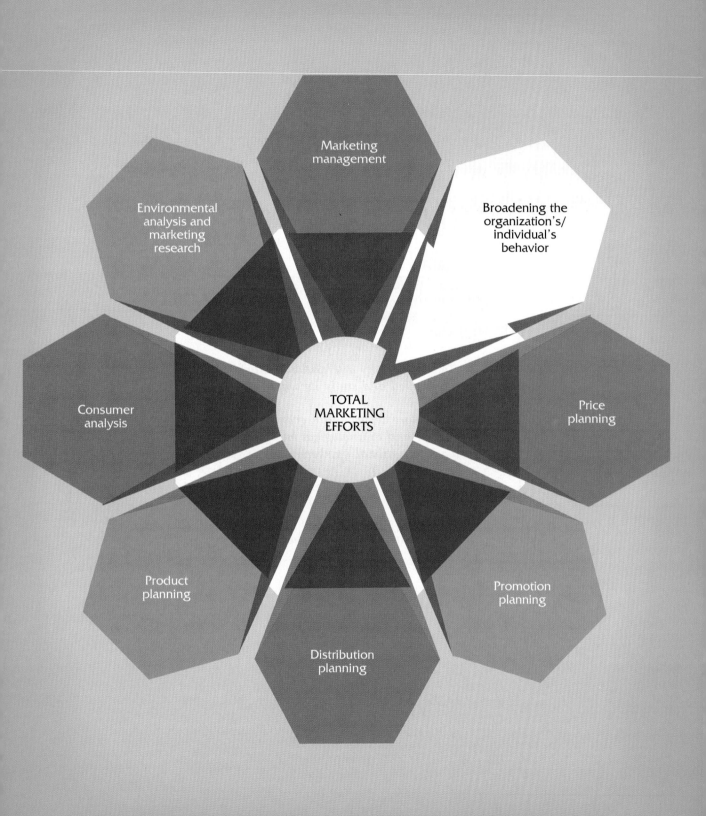

CHAPTER *21*
International Marketing

CHAPTER OBJECTIVES

1. To define international and multinational marketing

2. To explain why international marketing has developed and study its scope

3. To explore the cultural, economic, political and legal, and technological environments facing international marketers

4. To analyze the stages in the development of an international marketing strategy: company organization, degree of standardization, and product, distribution, promotion, and price planning

The European Community's drive to create a single market of 320 million free-spending consumers by the end of 1992 has become a potent engine of change. In a single pivotal decade, Europe will transform itself from a poky economic patchwork into a unified, fast-paced marketplace loaded with opportunities.

As incomes rise and tastes become more uniform, Europe will turn into a booming market for consumer goods from appliances to soft drinks. Deregulation will trigger growth. Businesses that have been held down by regulation and government monopolies, such as advertising and telecommunications, will grow far faster in Europe than in the United States. Foreign companies will be able to break into protected markets for the first time.

Up to now, the European Community (EC) has been a loose alliance of twelve West European nations with different customs and laws, some trade barriers among members, passport requirements when traveling between countries, and competing economic interests. But as of late 1992, the EC hopes to eliminate all internal borders and trade barriers among members and encourage economic policies stressing mutual interests. The EC will be the world's largest trading power, with over 20 per cent of global trade.

Accordingly, 1992 holds various opportunities and threats for companies dealing with the EC. Let us look at several of them:

▶ One estimate of the annual economic gain from a Europe without internal borders is $230 billion. This will result from greater economies of scale, increased competitiveness, and the removal of customs formalities. Until recently, for example, truckers crossing national borders needed to carry as many as 75 forms—resulting in massive traffic jams. Now only one administrative document is required.

▶ Uniform manufacturing standards are being developed for products distributed within the EC. For example, there are now common standards for oxygen tanks and machine tools.

▶ An agreement has been reached for jointly recognizing licenses for such professionals as pharmacists and accountants: "We once calculated that to qualify as an accountant in all twelve nations, you'd have to go to school for 50 years."

Die Karte.
Bequemlichkeit nur für Männer?

Ohne Risiko frei disponieren zu können und immer so viel Geld bei sich zu haben, wie man gerade be- Daß Sie mit der American Express Karte Deutschlands führendes Karten-System nutzen, macht sich sehr schnell

Reprinted by permission. © American Express.

▶ Some outsiders fear the possibility of trade protectionism against foreign goods: "What's important is that Europe not become free traders internally and protectionist externally. That's where the jury is out right now."

There are obstacles to the 1992 deadline for eliminating all economic barriers. First, France, Italy, and Spain want to preserve some trade barriers. Second, the twelve members have drastically different tax rates on products. For example, although prices must be equalized for free trade to develop, VCRs are now taxed at 28 per cent in France and 14 per cent in West Germany. In the future, the range of taxes is to be limited to 4 per cent to 19 per cent—yet even these differences will be obstacles to free trade.

Third, many major European food companies do business in just one or two countries. In the auto field, Peugeot, Renault, and Fiat do not have the market presence of General Motors or Ford. As one British executive says, "It can take years to combine skillfully companies with divergent cultures and management styles. We [Europeans] start from a disadvantage, and our problem is that we have to build an industrial structure quickly."[1]

In this chapter, we will explore the environment facing international marketers and see how to develop an international marketing strategy.

[1] Shawn Tully, "The Coming Boom in Europe," *Fortune* (April 10, 1989), pp. 108–114; Steven Greenhouse, "Making Europe a Mighty Market," *New York Times* (May 22, 1988), Section 3, pp. 1, 6; and Frank J. Comes, Jonathan Kapstein, John Templeman, and Elizabeth Weiner, "Reshaping Europe: 1992 and Beyond," *Business Week* (December 12, 1988), pp. 48–51.

Overview

*Marketing outside the firm's home country is **international marketing; multinational marketing** includes many foreign countries.*

International marketing involves the marketing of goods and services outside an organization's home country. ***Multinational marketing*** is a complex form of international marketing in which an organization engages in marketing operations in many foreign countries. Multinational firms include Nestlé, Unilever, Shell, Exxon, Coca-Cola, and ITT. These companies have brand names that are known throughout the world and have extensive worldwide operations. Large multinational organizations often allocate company resources without regard to national boundaries, even though they have a home country in terms of ownership and top management.

Nestlé, the world's largest food company, illustrates the multinational approach to marketing:

> While other food companies are just now starting to take baby steps toward operating on a global basis, Nestlé has long been a Colossus astride the globe. It has nearly 400 factories around the world, including a milk-powder plant in New Guinea and a cookie factory in Zimbabwe. Its home country [Switzerland] accounts for just 2 per cent of its sales, and its headquarters staff comes from 50 nations. Nestlé set up overseas subsidiaries early in its 122-year history, building its first American factory in 1900.[2]

International efforts vary widely. At one end, a small firm may limit itself to one or a few foreign markets, manufacture goods domestically, and market them to foreign countries with little or no adaptation of the domestic marketing plan. At the opposite end, a large multinational firm has a more global orientation, operates in many different countries, and uses foreign manufacturing and marketing subsidiaries to serve individual markets.

This chapter focuses on how to adapt the marketing principles discussed throughout the text to foreign markets. The chapter examines the development and scope of international marketing, its environment, and the components of an international marketing strategy.

Why International Marketing Takes Place

There are several reasons why countries and individual firms engage in international marketing. These are shown in Figure 21-1 and discussed in this section.

*Countries trade items in which they have a **comparative advantage.***

The concept of ***comparative advantage*** states that countries have different rates of productivity for different products because of their varying resources, specialization, mechanization, and/or climate. Therefore, countries can benefit by exchanging goods and services in which they have relative advantages for those in which they have relative disadvantages. For example, one of the greatest comparative advantages for U.S. firms involves their level of technological innovation: "We can't export common garden-variety products, such as hose that is round and black. We export specialty hose and fittings for refrigeration applications that don't let moisture get into the system or allow freon to get out, as standard hose and fittings might."[3]

---

[2] Steven Greenhouse, "Nestlé's Time to Swagger," *New York Times* (January 1, 1989), Section 3, p. 10.
[3] Ralph E. Winter, "U.S. Increases Its Exports, Despite Problems," *Wall Street Journal* (June 11, 1985), p. 6.

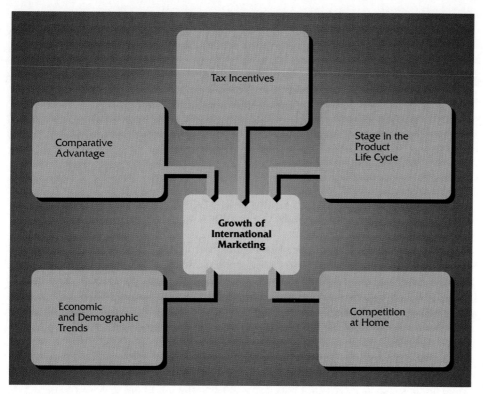

FIGURE 21-1
**Why International
Marketing Has Developed**

Economic and demographic trends vary by country. A firm in a country with adverse domestic conditions (such as high inflation or unemployment) and/or a small or stagnant population base can stabilize or increase sales by marketing goods and services in more favorable foreign markets. Because of these factors, the United States is an attractive market due to its low inflation and unemployment rates, and developing and less-developed countries are potentially attractive markets due to the growth of their populations. Over 90 per cent of world population growth is in developing and less-developed countries, and there is huge potential in those markets. As an illustration, "Heinz turned to developing [and less-developed] countries after discovering some years back that 85 per cent of the world's population had never been exposed to its brand."[4]

The domestic economy and demographics affect international efforts.

Competition in a firm's domestic market may become intense, thereby leading to international expansion, as these examples show:

Home competition may lead to international efforts.

▶ The U.S. market for express-delivery service is relatively saturated and dominated by Federal Express. In foreign markets, consumer demand is rising sharply and competition is more wide open because the market position of Federal Express is more vulnerable. As a result, the global market is a good one for U.S. express-delivery firms.

▶ In Japan, domestic automobile competition is so high that several of the nine Japanese auto makers are probably losing money; these firms make profits on their

[4] Louis Kraar, "How to Sell to Cashless Buyers," *Fortune* (November 7, 1988), p. 150.

foreign sales (mostly in the United States and Europe). Said one Japanese researcher, "The U.S. is a land of opportunity and Japan is a land of lack of opportunity. We close our market because opportunities are scarce and we don't want to share them with others."[5]

International marketing may extend the product life cycle or dispose of discontinued items.

In many instances, products are in different stages of the life cycle in different countries. Thus, exporting may provide situations for prolonging growth. For instance, foreign makers of small refrigerators found that those units could be sold in the United States for dens, dormitories, and studio apartments. In their home countries, they were used mainly as the major refrigerators for families. International marketing can also provide for the disposal of discontinued merchandise, seconds, and manufacturer remakes (products that have been repaired). These items can be sold abroad without spoiling the domestic market for full-price, first-quality merchandise. However, companies must be careful not to dump unsafe products on foreign markets. This creates ill will.

There may be tax gains.

There may be some tax advantages with international marketing. A number of countries entice new business from foreign companies by offering tax incentives in the form of reduced property, import, and income taxes for an initial period. In addition, multinational firms may adjust revenue reports so that the largest profits are recorded in the countries with the lowest tax rates.

The Scope of International Marketing

The United States accounts for 12 per cent of world exports.

The United States is the second-largest exporter in the world (after West Germany). In 1988, U.S. merchandise exports were approximately $322 billion, an amount equal to nearly 7 per cent of the overall U.S. GNP and about 12 per cent of total world exports. Among the leading U.S. exports are chemicals, aircraft, machinery, food grains, scientific instruments, and services such as management consulting and insurance.[6]

The involvement of U.S. firms in international marketing varies greatly. Although about 85 per cent of total U.S. exports have come from the top 250 U.S. multinational companies, 100,000 U.S. firms are engaged in some level of exporting: 86,500 are infrequent exporters, averaging nine foreign shipments per year; 9,900 are growing exporters, averaging 116 shipments; and 3,600 are frequent exporters, averaging 4,410 shipments.[7] During 1987, the 50 largest U.S. exporters accounted for $80 billion in foreign sales.[8] The latter figure is deceptively low because it does not include earnings on foreign investments and sales by foreign subsidiaries. Among major U.S. firms, exports range from 1.5 per cent of sales (Exxon) to 48.3 per cent of sales (Prime Computer). Table 21-1 shows the 10 largest U.S. exporters.

The United States is also the world's largest importer. In 1988, U.S. merchandise imports were $460 billion, accounting for over 16 per cent of total world imports.

[5] Rick Christie, "Battle Heats Up Over Global Air Delivery," *Wall Street Journal* (December 19, 1988), p. B1; and Karen Elliott House, "Though Rich, Japan Is Poor in Many Elements of Global Leadership," *Wall Street Journal* (January 30, 1989), p. A8.

[6] Office of Industry and Trade Information, U.S. Commerce Department, 1989.

[7] Hilary Stout, "Export Davids Sling Some Shots at Trade-Gap Goliath," *Wall Street Journal* (March 8, 1989), p. B2; and William J. Holstein and Brian Bremner, "The Little Guys Are Making It Big Overseas," *Business Week* (February 27, 1989), pp. 94–96.

[8] Edward C. Baig, "The 50 Leading Exporters," *Fortune* (July 18, 1988), pp. 70–71.

TABLE 21-1   The Ten Largest U.S. Exporters, 1987

1987 Rank	Company	Selected Products	Export Sales (Thousand $)	Total Company Sales (Thousand $)	Exports as Per Cent of Total Company Sales
1	General Motors	Motor vehicles and parts	8,731,300	101,781,900	8.6
2	Ford	Motor vehicles and parts	7,614,000	71,643,400	10.6
3	Boeing	Commercial and military aircraft	6,286,000	15,355,000	40.9
4	General Electric	Aircraft engines and medical systems	4,825,000	39,315,000	12.3
5	IBM	Computers and related products	3,994,000	54,217,000	7.4
6	DuPont	Specialty chemicals and energy products	3,526,000	30,468,000	11.6
7	McDonnell Douglas	Aerospace and information systems	3,243,400	13,146,100	24.7
8	Chrysler	Motor vehicles and parts	3,052,300	26,257,700	11.6
9	Eastman Kodak	Photographic equipment and supplies	2,255,000	13,305,000	16.9
10	Caterpillar	Heavy machinery, engines, and turbines	2,190,000	8,180,000	26.8

Source: "The 50 Leading Exporters," *Fortune* (July 18, 1988), p. 71. Reprinted by permission. © 1988 Time Inc. All rights reserved.

Among the leading U.S. imports are petroleum, motor vehicles, iron and steel, and clothing. Figure 21-2 shows selected imports' U.S. market shares for 1981 and 1985.

As a result of the high level of imports in 1988, the United States had a ***trade deficit*** of $138 billion, the amount by which the value of imports exceeded the value of exports. Trade deficits are relatively recent in the United States; from 1891 through 1970, the balance of trade showed a surplus each year. Since 1971, there has been a trade deficit in almost every year. The 1988 deficit represented a decline from the record amount of $170 billion in 1987.[9]

*In 1988, the U.S. had a large **trade deficit** because of the level of imports.*

The U.S. trade deficit is attributable to a variety of factors, including these:

▶ U.S. dependence on foreign natural resources.
▶ Increased competition in foreign markets.
▶ Less than optimal quality control for some U.S.-made products.
▶ High U.S. labor costs.
▶ Improving productivity by foreign companies.
▶ Trade restrictions in foreign markets.
▶ The decision of U.S. firms virtually to exit such markets as televisions and VCRs.
▶ Manufacturing products in the United States with imported parts and materials.
▶ The complacency of some U.S. firms in adapting their marketing strategies to the needs of foreign markets: "Spoiled by the breadth and plenty of the home market and ignorant of foreign languages and culture, U.S. executives as often as not have looked at foreign markets as dumping grounds for their surpluses and outdated

[9] Office of Industry and Trade Information, U.S. Commerce Department, 1989.

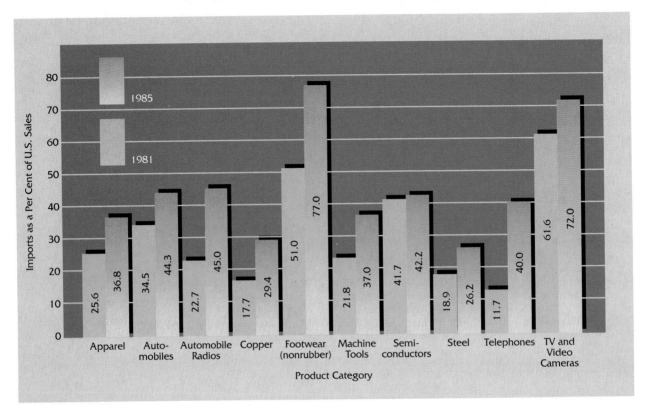

FIGURE 21-2
Selected Imports' U.S. Market Shares
SOURCE: U.S. International Trade Commission, 1985.

models. But exporting is also hard work. Language, time zones, regulations, customs inspections, laws, transportation systems, and business practices are only the most obvious obstacles."[10]

Furthermore, the U.S. market has been and remains a very lucrative one for foreign companies; its per-capita consumption is the highest of any country in the world for most goods and services. And U.S. firms often sacrifice market share for profit, while foreign competitors (such as the Japanese) try to keep their prices as stable as possible to maximize their market share—even if they must reduce profit margins to do so: "Since the dollar peaked in February 1985, foreign currencies have climbed nearly 70 per cent in value, but U.S. import prices have risen only 30 per cent. That means less than half of the currency swing was 'passed through' to prices."[11]

Because U.S. trade deficits have been so high over the past few years, many American companies have been improving the quality of their products, becoming more cost efficient, building overseas facilities, and so on. In addition, some U.S. firms have called for tighter controls on imports and more open access to restricted foreign markets. The U.S. government has been negotiating with foreign governments to improve the situation. For example, Japan has allowed the value of its yen to rise significantly against the U.S. dollar and has agreed to a number of trade provisions to improve its balance of trade with the United States. Yet, in 1988 alone, the United States had a

[10] Christopher Knowlton, "The New Export Entrepreneurs," *Fortune* (June 6, 1988), p. 90. See also Roger H. Hermanson and Woodrow C. Stillwagon, "The Foreign Deficit—Causes and Solutions," *Business,* Vol. 38 (January–March 1988), pp. 3–9.
[11] Paul Magnusson, Michael Mandel, Karen Pennar, and Mike McNamee, "Will We Ever Close the Trade Gap?" *Business Week* (February 27, 1989), p. 88.

trade deficit of more than $51 billion with Japan. Thus, Congress passed the Omnibus Trade & Competitiveness Act, which requires the U.S. president to press for more open foreign markets.[12] In 1989, Japan was cited for violating the act.

Many non-U.S. firms are becoming more active in international marketing. In 1964, for example, only 12 of the world's 50 largest industrial companies were non-American. By 1987, this figure had risen to 30. Among the largest non-U.S. companies are Royal Dutch/Shell Group, British Petroleum, Toyota, Daimler-Benz, Hitachi, and Unilever.[13]

Despite these trends, the United States remains a dominant force in international marketing. In 1987, of the world's 50 largest industrial firms, American companies comprised 20. Five of the top six were American, and these five had worldwide sales of over $355 billion.[14] A recent series on "World Leadership" by the *Wall Street Journal* reached this conclusion:

Of the six leading firms in the world, five are U.S.-based.

> Clearly, pessimism about America is in vogue. But as with many fashionable ideas, this one doesn't bear up well on closer scrutiny. In an effort to draw a reliable picture of the world that will develop in the next century, the *Journal* undertook an exhaustive survey: talks with several hundred leaders and laymen in America, Japan, Europe, China, and the Soviet Union, involving 100,000 miles of travel. The picture that emerges is clear, if surprising: whether America relishes the role or not, it is the pre-eminent power in the world today and will remain so for at least the next generation — and probably longer. This will not be the America of the postwar era, the lone Western power dictating a global agenda, but rather the America of this generation, a team captain cajoling and corralling others in the interests of global peace and prosperity.[15]

The Environment of International Marketing

Although the marketing principles described in this text apply to international marketing efforts, there are often significant environmental differences between domestic and foreign markets — and marketing practices may have to be adapted accordingly. Therefore each market should be evaluated separately. Only then can a company decide how much of its domestic marketing strategy can be used in foreign markets and what elements should be modified to fit the distinctive needs of given foreign markets.

As Victor Kiam, the chief executive of U.S.-based Remington, answered in response to the question "How do you go about getting a feel for a country?":

> Go there. Talk to the trade. Visit the stores. Talk to salespeople. Get reports on the market that are available through government agencies, advertising agencies, and other sources. Do an entire marketing plan for the country. Every country is different in some way. There are different nuances of distribution in Japan. There is a unique control factor of large companies in South America. You have to adapt your philosophy to the particular situation in which you find yourself.[16]

[12] Ibid., pp. 86–92; and Ann Reilly Dowd, "What to Do About Trade Policy," *Fortune* (May 8, 1989), pp. 106–112.

[13] Frederick Hiroshi Katayama and William Bellis, "The World's 50 Biggest Industrial Corporations," *Fortune* (August 11, 1988), pp. D1–D4.

[14] Ibid.

[15] Karen Elliott House, "For All Its Difficulties, U.S. Stands to Retain Its Global Leadership," *Wall Street Journal* (January 23, 1989), p. A1.

[16] "Growth Strategies at Remington," *Journal of Business Strategy*, Vol. 9 (January–February 1989), pp. 25–26.

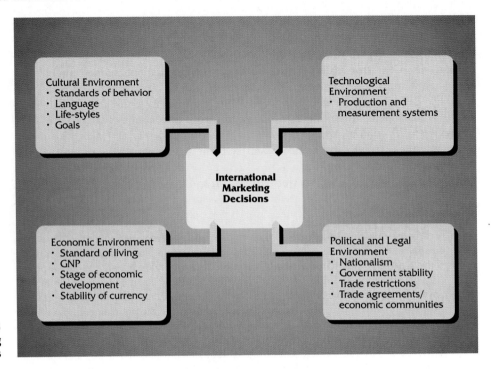

FIGURE 21-3
The Environment Facing International Marketers

The major cultural, economic, political and legal, and technological environments facing international marketers are discussed in the succeeding subsections. See Figure 21-3.

The Cultural Environment

International marketers need to be aware of each market's cultural environment. As defined in Chapter 6, culture refers to a group of people sharing a distinctive heritage. This heritage teaches behavior standards, language, life-styles, and goals. A culture is passed down from generation to generation and is not easily changed. Almost every country in the world has a different culture, and continental differences exist as well. A domestic firm unfamiliar with or insensitive to a foreign culture may try to market goods or services that are unacceptable to or misunderstood by that culture. For example, beef or pork products are rejected by some cultures.

Inadequate information about foreign cultures is a common cause of errors.

Table 21-2 illustrates the errors a firm engaged in international marketing may commit as a result of a lack of awareness about foreign cultures. In some cases, the firm may be at fault because it operates out of a domestic home office and receives little local foreign input. In other cases, such as marketing in less-developed countries, information may be limited because a low level of population data exists; and sometimes, mail and telephone service are poor. Thus, marketing research—which could determine the hidden meanings and the ease of pronunciation of brand names and slogans, the rate of product consumption, and reasons for purchases—cannot be fully utilized.

Cultural awareness can be improved by employing foreign personnel in key positions, hiring foreign marketing research specialists, locating company offices in each

TABLE 21-2   Illustrations of Errors in International Marketing Because of a Lack of Cultural Awareness

In Japan, Procter & Gamble discovered that low prices for its detergents and other products hurt the reputations of these items because price discounting is not a regular practice.

Pepsodent was unsuccessful in Southeast Asia because it promised white teeth to a culture where black or yellow teeth are symbols of prestige.

In Quebec, a canned-fish manufacturer tried to promote a product by showing a woman dressed in shorts, golfing with her husband, and planning to serve canned fish for dinner. These activities violated cultural norms.

Maxwell House advertised itself as the "great American coffee" in Germany. It found out that Germans have little respect for American coffee.

In Mexico, Braniff Airlines advertised that passengers could sit in comfortable leather seats; however, the phrase it used ("sentando en cuero") meant "sit naked."

In Brazil, Gerber could not convince mothers that baby food was a good alternative to food the mothers made themselves.

African men were upset by a commercial for men's deodorant that showed a happy male being chased by women. They thought the deodorant would make them weak and overrun by women.

Many U.S. franchisers have not reached expectations in setting up outlets in Britain: "Most of their problems appear to stem from their mistaken impression that what works at home will work in Britain. Even though they speak the same language, the British do business differently."

Sources: David A. Ricks, *Big Business Blunders* (Homewood, Ill.: Richard D. Irwin, 1983); Andrew Tanzer, "They Didn't Listen to Anybody," *Forbes* (December 15, 1986), pp. 168–169; Maureen Glabman, "Oops! Braniff's Ad Draws Hispanic Snickers," *Advertising Age* (February 9, 1987), p. 30; and Joann S. Lublin, "For U.S. Franchisers, a Common Tongue Isn't a Guarantee of Success in the U.K.," *Wall Street Journal* (August 16, 1988), p. 25.

TABLE 21-3   Examples of Cultural Opportunities for International Marketers

In Mexico, McDonald's is opening outlets geared to young, affluent consumers because its prices are too high for blue-collar workers and their families.

In China, the most popular color is red; it indicates happiness. Black with gold lettering also elicits a positive response because it denotes age and stability.

In France, chocolate is used in cooking. Italians serve chocolate as a snack for children, placing it between two slices of bread.

French Canadians consume more soft drinks, beer, and wine than do English-speaking Canadians.

Nigerians believe "good beer only comes in green bottles."

British consumers insist on cake mixes that require their adding fresh eggs, as reformulated Betty Crocker mixes sold there do.

Sources: William Stockton, "The Big Mac Goes to Mexico," *New York Times* (November 2, 1985), pp. 35–36; George Fields, "How to Scale the Cultural Fence," *Advertising Age* (December 13, 1982), pp. M-11–M-12; Charles M. Schaninger, Jacques C. Bourgeois, and W. Christian Buss, "French-English Canadian Subcultural Consumption Differences," *Journal of Marketing,* Vol. 49 (Spring 1985), pp. 82–92; James Brooke, "Of Ads and Elders: Selling to Nigerians," *New York Times* (April 20, 1987), p. D10; and Steven Greenhouse, "Building a Global Supermarket," *New York Times* (November 18, 1988), p. D4.

country of operations, actively studying cultural differences, and being responsive to cultural changes.[17] Table 21-3 shows several cultural opportunities.

[17] See David K. Tse, Kam-hon Lee, Ilan Vertinsky, and Donald A. Wehrung, "Does Culture Matter? A Cross-Cultural Study of Executives' Choice, Decisiveness, and Risk Adjustment in International Marketing," *Journal of Marketing,* Vol. 52 (October 1988), pp. 81–95.

The Economic Environment

A country's economic environment indicates its present and potential capacities for consuming goods and services. Measures of economic performance include the standard of living, Gross National Product (GNP), stage of economic development, and stability of currency.

*The quality of life in a country is measured by its **standard of living**.*

The **standard of living** refers to the average quantity and quality of goods and services consumed in a country. One way of measuring the standard of living is to determine the relative costs of various items — such as food, clothing, and transportation — in terms of the items' actual prices and the per-capita income in a country. Thus, the items' affordability is considered. According to United Nations data, the United States has the highest standard of living of any industrialized country in the world. Table 21-4 compares the standard of living in Washington, D.C., with that in Moscow (Soviet Union), Munich (West Germany), Paris (France), and London (Great Britain). The table shows the amount of work time required to pay for various items in these cities.

*The total value of goods and services produced in a country is its **Gross National Product**.*

The **Gross National Product (GNP)** indicates the total value of goods and services produced in a country each year. Total and per-capita GNP are the most frequently used measures of a country's wealth because they are regularly published and easy to calculate and compare with other countries. However, per-capita GNP figures may be misleading for two reasons. First, these figures represent means and not income distributions. A few wealthy citizens may boost the per-capita GNP even though the bulk of the population has low income. Second, incomes purchase different standards of living in each country; an annual income of $20,000 in the United States may represent the same standard of living as an annual income of $10,000 in another country where prices are much lower.

*Countries can be classified as **industrialized, developing,** and **less-developed**.*

Marketing opportunities often can be highlighted by looking at a country's stage of economic growth. One way of categorizing such growth is to divide nations into industrialized, developing, and less-developed classes. See Figure 21-4. **Industrialized countries** include the United States, Canada, Japan, the USSR, and nations in Oceania and Western Europe. These countries have high literacy, modern technology, and per-capita income of several thousand dollars. **Developing countries** include many Latin American nations. Education and technology are rising, and per-capita income is about $2,000. Developing countries have 20 per cent of the world's population and almost one-third of its income. **Less-developed countries** include a number of countries in Africa and South Asia. Literacy is low, technology is limited, and per-capita GNP is generally well below $1,000. Such countries have two-thirds of the world's population but less than 15 per cent of world income.

The greatest marketing opportunities generally occur in industrialized countries because of their higher discretionary income and standard of living. However, industrialized countries usually have stable population bases, and sales of some product categories may already be saturated. On the other hand, developing and less-developed countries have expanding population bases and currently purchase limited amounts of imports. There is long-run potential for international marketers in these nations: "Companies are going to India and Indonesia because of the potential they see 10 to 15 years out."[18]

[18] Louis Kraar, "How to Sell to Cashless Buyers," *Fortune* (November 7, 1988), p. 147.

TABLE 21-4 Comparing Standards of Living

Commodity[a]	Washington	Moscow	Munich	Paris	London
	Minutes of worktime (unless otherwise specified)				
Food and Beverages (Unit of measurement: 1 kilogram/2.2 pounds unless otherwise noted)					
White bread, unwrapped	6	17	25	20	11
Rice, polished, white	6	49	10	30	16
Chicken, fresh or frozen	18	189	17	31	20
Hamburger meat, beef	30	72	60	75	38
Steak, sirloin	83	195	93	109	123
Sausages, frankfurters	30	145	74	75	70
Cod, frozen	76	33	77	124	80
Tuna	36	183	40	129	50
Potatoes	9	11	5	9	3
Beans, packaged or frozen	9	84	17	29	17
Apples, eating	18	28	16	16	14
Ice cream, vanilla, l/qt	13	107	17	21	11
Milk, fresh, l/qt	4	20	6	8	6
Eggs, 10, cheapest	5	50	9	17	10
Cheese, fresh, Gouda-type	81	167	53	59	45
Sugar, white, granulated	6	52	8	11	8
Butter	40	195	37	63	38
Orange juice, l/qt	7	151	7	18	9
Cola, l/qt	7	58	7	21	5
Transportation					
Car, medium (months)	9	84	12	15	15
Gasoline, regular, 10 l/2.5 gal	17	167	47	66	64
Bicycle, men's, cheapest (hours)	17	49	17	29	23
Taxi fare, 3 km/2 mi	25	34	29	20	31
Bus fare, 3 km/2 mi	7	3	7	5	9
Clothing					
Jeans (hours)	4	56	7	10	5
T-shirt, cotton, white	28	184	70	55	56
Panty hose, one pair	16	279	16	17	14
Men's shoes, black, office (hours)	6	37	11	8	6
Men's office suit, 2-piece, dacron (hours)	18	118	33	34	16
Household Items and Services					
Refrigerator, small, 120-liter (hours)	44	102	31	30	30
Washing machine, automatic cycle (hours)	46	177	49	61	52
Television, color, 61 cm (hours)	30	669	54	106	75
Rent, monthly, 50-sq. m, unfurnished, subsidized apartment (hours)	55	11	24	15	26
Telephone, monthly rent	20	139	126	287	95
Miscellaneous					
Toothpaste, 75 g	6	22	12	16	7
Aspirin, 100, cheapest	7	33	75	44	9
Deodorant, spray can, 200 ml	18	139	11	39	17
Baby-sitter, per hour, excluding fare	44	279	47	37	43
Haircut, men's, dry, no extras	62	34	75	92	61
Suburban movie, best seat	40	28	42	48	52

[a] l = liter; qt = quart; gal = gallon; km = kilometer; mi = mile; cm = centimeter; m = meter; g = gram; and ml = milliliter.

Source: Keith Bush, *Retail Prices in Moscow and Four Western Cities in October 1986.* Reprinted by permission. © NFIB Foundation.

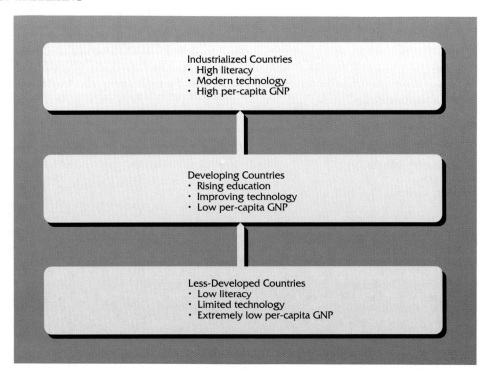

FIGURE 21-4
The Stages of Economic Development

Consumer demand can be estimated by studying product ownership.

By examining per-capita product ownership, a firm can obtain a good estimate of the current size of consumer demand in a country. Table 21-5 shows ownership and consumption of cars, televisions, steel, energy, and telephones for nine diverse countries. As already noted, there is usually long-run potential in countries where consumers presently have few goods and services. For example, Brazil has 70 automobiles per 1,000 population, Nigeria has 3 per 1,000, and India has fewer than 2 per 1,000. The one-billion-plus people of China own about 800,000 cars — fewer than those owned by people in Denmark, a country with just over five million people.

TABLE 21-5   Ownership and Consumption in Nine Countries

Country	Cars (per 100 People)	Televisions (per 100 People)	Steel (Kilograms per Year Used per Person)	Energy (Kilograms per Year Used per Person)	Telephones (per 100 People)
United States	57	60	448	9,563	70
Brazil	7	25	75	692	8
China	.07	7	63	693	.25
France	38	35	258	4,013	61
Great Britain	30	35	254	4,914	51
Italy	38	26	362	3,290	45
Japan	24	25	553	3,715	55
Soviet Union	4	29	NA[a]	6,131	11
West Germany	43	38	481	5,748	65

[a] NA=Not available.

Source: United Nations; and authors' estimates.

Currency stability is another economic factor a firm would consider in international marketing, because sales and profits could be affected if a foreign currency fluctuates widely in relation to the company's home currency. For example, from June 1988 to April 1989, the value of the Colombian peso against the U.S. dollar fell from 290 pesos per dollar to 361 pesos per dollar — in April 1989, a Colombian consumer had to spend 361 of his or her pesos to buy a $1 U.S. good.[19] This decline in the peso's value of nearly 25 per cent meant that Colombian goods became cheaper for consumers in other countries, while making it more expensive for Colombian consumers to purchase any foreign products. As a result, foreign firms had great difficulty exporting products to Colombia during this period because their prices were relatively high. In recent years, the currencies of industrialized countries have been much more stable than those of developing and less-developed countries.

Currency stability is important because it affects foreign sales and profit.

The Political and Legal Environment

In each country, a unique political and legal environment exists. Among the key political and legal factors for an international firm to examine are nationalism, government stability, trade restrictions, and trade agreements and economic communities.

Nationalism refers to a country's efforts to become self-reliant and raise its status in the eyes of the world community. Sometimes a high degree of nationalism may lead to tight restrictions on foreign companies and foster the development of domestic industry at their expense. In recent years, some countries have seized assets of multinational firms, revoked their licenses to operate, prevented the transfer of funds from one currency to another, increased taxes, and/or unilaterally changed contract terms.

Nationalism involves a host country's attempts to promote its interests.

Government stability needs to be examined on the basis of two factors: consistency of policies and orderliness in installing leaders. First, do government policies regarding taxes, company expansion, profits, and so on, remain relatively unchanged over time? Second, is there an orderly process for selecting and empowering new government leaders? Companies will probably be unable to function properly unless both of these factors are positive.

*For continued success in a foreign market, **government stability** is needed.*

For example, although food producers such as Nestlé and CPC International have made large investments in developing nations, many other food companies are staying away from some less-developed and developing countries. Said an executive of one U.S.-based food company:

> There's a long list of countries on the economic critical list, and another long list threatened with political upheaval. The risks you face as an investor are enormous.[20]

An international firm can protect itself against the adverse effects of nationalism and political instability. It can measure the potential for domestic instability (riots, government purges, excessive strikes), foreign conflict (diplomatic expulsions, military activity), the political climate (stability of political parties, manner of selecting government officials), and the economic climate (currency stability, economic strength, extent of government intervention) prior to entering a foreign market — and avoid countries deemed inappropriate.[21]

Investments can also be protected through insurance. The U.S. government's Over-

---

[19] Bankers Trust Co. data.

[20] Carol Hymowitz, "Heinz Sets Out to Expand in Africa and Asia, Seeking New Markets, Sources of Materials," *Wall Street Journal* (September 27, 1983), p. 37.

[21] See David A. Schmidt, "Analyzing Political Risk," *Business Horizons,* Vol. 29 (July–August 1986), pp. 43–50.

FIGURE 21-5
Foreign Investments May Be Protected by Insurance
Over the past decade, OPIC has provided $25 billion in insurance and financing support for more than 1,100 projects by U.S. investors in 85 developing and less-developed countries throughout the world.
Reprinted by permission.

YOU MAY JUST SEE ANOTHER TROPICAL RESORT. GREENLAW, INC. SAW THE PROFIT BEYOND.

Greenlaw saw the Dominican Republic's potential. And with OPIC's unique political risk insurance, they found it an ideal place for tropical fruit processing.

We're OPIC: The Overseas Investment Corporation.
And we can help make overseas expansion an economically successful move for you—and for the host country.
We specialize in political risk insurance. Insurance against loss due to war, revolution, insurrection, or civil strife. Expropriation, nationalization or confiscation. Or the inability to convert local currency into U.S. dollars—all on a long-term basis. We can help finance a venture through direct loans or loan guarantees. We can share in the cost of feasibility studies. And alert businessmen to specific

opportunities in certain countries.
We're business-oriented like you. And we're backed by our own substantial resources and by the full faith and credit of the United States. So if you've been thinking of overseas investment, we can help make your move both safe and profitable. We did it for Greenlaw, Inc. of Palmetto, Florida. We can do it for you.
Call toll free: 800-424-6742. Or write: OPIC, 1129 20th Street N.W., Washington D.C. 20527.

OPIC. We mean business all over the world.

© Dancer Fitzgerald Sample, Inc., NY, NY.

seas Private Investment Corporation (OPIC) insures investments in friendly underdeveloped countries against such perils as war damage and inconvertibility of earnings. In addition, private underwriters insure foreign investments.[22] See Figure 21-5.

Last, the risks of nationalism and political unrest can be reduced by taking on foreign partners, borrowing money from foreign governments or banks, and/or utilizing licensing, contract manufacturing, or management contracting. These are discussed later in this chapter.

Another aspect of the international political and legal environment encompasses trade restrictions. The most common form of restriction is a ***tariff,*** which is a tax placed on imported goods by a foreign government. The second major restriction is a ***trade quota,*** which sets limits on the amounts of goods that can be imported into a country. The strictest form of trade quota is an ***embargo,*** which disallows entry of specified products into a country. The third major regulation involves ***local content***

Tariffs, trade quotas, embargos, and local content laws are forms of trade restrictions.

[22] See Sue Kapp, "Uncle Sam's Marketing Man," *Business Marketing* (January 1989), pp. 8, 10, 14.

652

Marketing Controversy

How Should the United States Respond to Trade Barriers?

The 1988 Omnibus Trade & Competitiveness Act requires the Office of the U.S. Trade Representative to identify the foreign trade barriers that are most harmful to U.S. exports and to negotiate with the offending countries. Although the use of tariffs has decreased since World War II, nontariff protectionism has drastically increased.

U.S. beef producers lose $100 million in annual sales to Europe because they use growth hormones in cattle (to produce better beef). Although these hormones were declared safe by United Nations health authorities in 1987, U.S. beef cannot be sold in the European market.

Airbus Industrie competes with U.S. aircraft makers such as Boeing. When developing the model A320, Airbus received $3.4 billion in subsidies from Great Britain, France, West Germany, and Spain. Such subsidies allowed Airbus to undercut U.S. firms' prices for comparable aircraft, which resulted in $850 million in lost aircraft sales for those firms during 1988.

Japan's ban on rice imports costs U.S. producers $300 million in annual sales to this market—and results in higher prices for consumers. If only 10 per cent of this market were opened to U.S. rice makers, Japanese consumers could save $6 billion annually (because domestic firms would have to cut their prices).

In Argentina and Brazil, pharmaceutical sales by U.S. firms are impeded by these countries' failure to recognize U.S. patents. Thus, U.S. companies are at a cost disadvantage in these markets. The annual loss to U.S. firms is over $110 million.

Although the 1988 trade act enables the United States to retaliate with its own quotas, tariffs, and "voluntary" restraints, there is a question as to whether these actions would be beneficial. This policy could result in "you hurt your consumers, and we'll hurt ours." For example, U.S. quotas on imported textiles, autos, and steel cost U.S. consumers billions of dollars in higher prices, yet they have had little impact on foreign trade barriers.

What do you think?

SOURCE: Based on material in Rahul Jacob, "Export Barriers the U.S. Hates Most," *Fortune* (February 27, 1989), pp. 88–89.

laws, which require foreign-based manufacturers to establish local plants and use locally produced components; the goal of these laws is to promote domestic employment. These are examples of those trade restrictions:

▶ The United States imposes tariffs on imported clothing, ceramic tiles, rubber footwear, candy, trucks, and other goods. The tariffs raise the prices of the imports relative to domestic items.

▶ Many European countries have reached agreements with Japan setting voluntary quotas on certain goods exported by Japan to their countries. The agreements limit the sales of VCRs, automobiles, televisions, quartz watches, machine tools, and so on.

▶ To stimulate domestic production of computers, Brazil has placed an embargo on minicomputers and microcomputers. As a result, foreign firms such as IBM cannot export PCs to Brazil or produce small computers in their Brazilian subsidiaries.

▶ Until it was overruled by the European Court in 1987, West Germany had a local content law that effectively prohibited beer from other countries to be sold there.

*Trade agreements can reduce or eliminate trade barriers. GATT introduced the **most-favored nation principle**.*

In some cases, economic barriers among nations have been reduced through trade agreements and economic communities. In 1948, 23 nations, including the United States, accepted the idea of fostering multilateral agreements by signing the **General Agreement on Tariffs and Trade (GATT).** The main contribution of GATT is the **most-favored nation principle,** which allows every nation covered by the agreement to obtain the best contract terms received by any single nation. GATT members agree to meet every two years and to negotiate for tariff reductions. By 1989, 96 nations representing more than 80 per cent of the total volume of international trade were participating in GATT. The most notable nonmember has been the Soviet Union.

However, because of member countries' self-interests and many exceptions to the most-favored nation principle, GATT has not eliminated trade tensions. For instance, trade in services, agriculture, textiles, and investment and capital flows are not now covered by GATT — thus, it is estimated that the agreement covers only 5 to 7 per cent of global economic activity.[23] Another major exception to GATT allows member countries to participate in regional trade associations or economic communities that have fewer trade barriers among the nations involved in those associations or communities than with those that are not involved.

*The **European Community (EC)** joins 12 countries in trade and other agreements.*

The most important economic community is the **European Community (EC),** also known as the Common Market. EC members are Belgium, Denmark, France, Great Britain, Greece, Ireland, Italy, Luxembourg, the Netherlands, Portugal, Spain, and West Germany. The EC agreement calls for no tariffs or other trade restrictions among members as of 1992 and a uniform tariff with nonmember nations. In addition, the agreement encourages common standards for food additives, labeling requirements, and package sizes and a free flow of people and capital. The 1992 goal is for member countries to have an open marketplace, as exists among individual states in the United States. The combined GNP of Common Market members is about 85 per cent that of the United States; and the combined population is roughly 1.3 times that of the United States.[24]

Other significant economic communities include the Latin American Integration Association, the Andean Common Market, the Central American Common Market, the Caribbean Common Market, the European Free Trade Association (made up of Western European countries not in the European Community), the Council for Mutual Economic Assistance (made up of Eastern European countries), the Asian Common Market, the Association of South East Nations, the West African Economic Community, and the Economic Community of West African States. And in 1988, the United States and Canada reached agreement on a major mutual free-trade pact.[25]

The Technological Environment

International marketing may require adjustments in technology.

Technological factors such as these influence international marketing. Technology advances vary throughout the world. For example, outside the United States, the use of cable television is quite limited. Even in Western Europe, only 10 to 15 per cent of all

---

[23] Pat Choate and Juyne Linger, "Tailored Trade: Dealing with the World as It Is," *Harvard Business Review,* Vol. 66 (January–February 1988), p. 88.

[24] Karen Elliott House, "Europeans' Global Clout Is Limited by Divisions 1992 Can't Paper Over," *Wall Street Journal* (February 13, 1989), pp. A1, A10.

[25] See Subhash C. Jain, *International Marketing Management,* Second Edition (Boston: Kent, 1987), pp. 149–154; and Louis Kraar, "North America's New Trade Punch," *Fortune* (May 22, 1989), pp. 123–127.

households have cable television. Foreign workers must frequently be trained to operate and maintain equipment that is unfamiliar to them. Problems occur if maintenance standards or practices vary by country or adverse production conditions exist, such as high humidity, extreme hot or cold weather, or air pollution. Furthermore, the availability of electricity and electrical power needs may vary by country and require modifications in products. For example, U.S. appliances work on 110 volts; in Europe, appliances work on 220 volts.

Although the metric system has been adopted by most of the world, the United States still relies on ounces, pounds, inches, and feet:

> With the exception of the United States, Burma, and Brunei, 95 per cent of the world is being schooled in the metric system. Thus, it is difficult to convince a person in a developed or developing industrialized country that there is merit in selecting U.S.-made, English-measure products.[26]

Thus, auto makers, major tire manufacturers, all large soda and liquor bottlers, and other U.S. firms have recently converted or begun conversion to metric standards. As the United States converts to the metric system, the American market will have to be re-educated about measurement and learn the value of meters, liters, and other metric standards. This process will be a slow one.

Developing an International Marketing Strategy

In the following subsections, the vital parts of an international marketing strategy are explored: company organization, the degree of standardization, and product, distribution, promotion, and price planning.

Company Organization

There are three basic international organizational formats from which a company may choose: exporting, joint venture, and direct ownership. They are compared in Figure 21-6.

With **exporting,** a company reaches international markets by selling products made in its home country directly through its own sales force or indirectly through foreign merchants or agents. In direct selling, the firm situates its sales force in a home office or foreign branch offices. This technique is best when customers are easy to locate, concentrated, or come to the seller. In indirect selling, the firm hires outside specialists to search out and contact customers. These specialists may be based in the home or foreign country. In the United States, there are over 2,000 specialized export management firms that market products in foreign markets.[27] Indirect selling is applied in situations where customers are hard to locate, dispersed, the potential exporter has limited resources, and/or local customs are unique.

Exporting enables a firm to reach international markets without foreign production.

An exporting structure requires minimal investment in foreign facilities. There is no foreign production by the firm. The exporter may modify its packages, labels, or catalogs at its domestic facilities in response to foreign market needs. Exporting represents the lowest level of commitment to international marketing.

---

[26] Roger H. Hermanson and Woodrow C. Stillwagon, "The Foreign Trade Deficit — Causes and Solutions," *Business,* Vol. 38 (January–March 1988), pp. 3–4.
[27] Holstein and Bremner, "The Little Guys Are Making It Big Overseas," pp. 94–96.

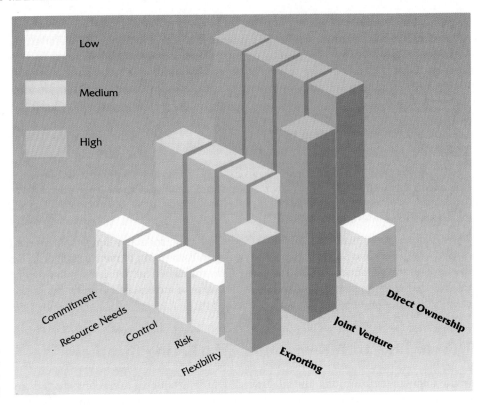

FIGURE 21-6
**Alternative Company
Organizations for
International Marketing**

As an illustration of exporting, Mead Corp. (a U.S. manufacturer) is investing $500 million on a new mill in Alabama that will be used to make coated paperboard for consumer packaging. It expects to sell $100 million of paperboard annually in Japan within five years: "The packaged goods are there, but the trees aren't." The paperboard will be sold through a large Japanese distributor to "pull the product through the user's end" by making customized boxes at the Alabama plant. Mead will not have production facilities in Japan, and can convert its U.S. plant to other uses if overseas sales do not meet its goals.[28]

*A **joint venture** can
be based on licensing,
contract manufacturing,
management contracting, or
joint ownership.*

In a ***joint venture,*** a firm agrees to combine some aspect of its manufacturing or marketing efforts with those of a foreign company in order to share expertise, costs, and/or connections with important persons. As one observer recently noted:

> Companies are just beginning to learn what nations have always known: in a complex, uncertain world filled with dangerous opponents, it is best not to go it alone. Great powers operating across broad theaters of engagement have traditionally made common cause with others whose interests ran parallel with their own. No shame in that. Entente — the striking of an alliance — is a responsible part of every good strategist's repertoire. In today's competitive environment, this is also true for corporate managers.[29]

One company that actively engages in joint ventures is N.V. Philips, a large Netherlands-based manufacturer. Philips is

[28] Knowlton, "The New Export Entrepreneurs," p. 90.
[29] Kenichi Ohmae, "The Global Logic of Strategic Alliances," *Harvard Business Review,* Vol. 67 (March–April 1989), p. 143.

▶ Manufacturing a version of the Victor Company of Japan's VHS videocassette recorder in Europe.

▶ Marketing AT&T's digital telephone-switching systems in Europe.

▶ A major owner of Grundig of West Germany, a leading electronics company. It also manages the firm.

▶ Cooperating with CIT-Alcatel of France to develop microwave transmission systems and other high-technology products.

▶ Manufacturing and marketing compact discs for prerecorded music with Sony around the world.

▶ Working with 28 other European firms to develop high-definition television (HDTV) sets.

▶ Marketing appliances in Europe with Whirlpool.[30]

A joint venture may result in reduced costs and favorable trade terms from a foreign government if products are produced locally and foreign ownership is established. For example, the number of joint ventures between Japanese and U.S. companies is growing because Japanese firms see them as reducing the possibility of U.S. trade restrictions (such as local content laws) and as a method of easing political tension. U.S. firms view these ventures as a means of opening up the Japanese market and as a way to monitor the operations of potential competitors.

A joint venture can take the form of licensing, contract manufacturing, management contracting, or joint ownership. Licensing gives a foreign firm the rights to a manufacturing process, trademark, patent, and/or trade secret in exchange for a commission, fee, or royalty. Coca-Cola and PepsiCo license their products in some countries. Under contract manufacturing, the firm agrees to have a foreign company make its products locally. The firm markets the products itself and provides management expertise. This arrangement is common in book publishing.

In management contracting, the firm acts as a consultant to foreign firms. Many hotel chains, such as Hilton International, engage in management contracting. With joint ownership, a firm agrees to manufacture and market products in partnership with a foreign company in order to reduce costs and spread risk. As an illustration, in 1988, Ford and Nissan decided that they would jointly produce and sell a new minivan. Their goal was to enter an attractive market "without all the expense" of developing and marketing the product on their own.[31] In some instances, a foreign government may require joint ownership with local businesses as a condition for entry. For example, in Canada, outsiders must use joint ownership arrangements with Canadian firms for new ventures.

Direct ownership involves the full undertaking and control of its international operations by a firm—which owns production, marketing, and other facilities in foreign countries without any partners. In some cases, international operations are organized into wholly owned subsidiaries. For example, in the United States, Pillsbury is now a wholly owned subsidiary of Grand Metropolitan of Britain and CBS Records is a wholly

Direct ownership involves total control of foreign operations and facilities by a firm.

---

[30] Howard V. Perlmutter and David A. Heenan, "Cooperate to Compete Globally," *Harvard Business Review,* Vol. 64 (March–April 1986), pp. 136–152; Johnnie L. Roberts, "N.V. Philips and Sony to Jointly Market Disk That Combines Music and Video," *Wall Street Journal* (February 13, 1987), p. 8; Norm Alster, "TV's High-Stakes, High-Tech Battle," *Fortune* (October 24, 1988), p. 166; and Robert Johnson and Matthew Winkler, "Venture Is Set by Whirlpool and N.V. Philips," *Wall Street Journal* (August 19, 1988), p. 3.

[31] John Holusha, "Ford and Nissan Take New Route," *New York Times* (September 22, 1988), p. D2.

FIGURE 21-7
Direct Ownership by Colgate-Palmolive
Through its Colgate-France subsidiary, Colgate-Palmolive operates a high-tech plant in Compiegne, France. The plant, with its 13 blow molding lines, makes 60 per cent of the bottle requirements for Colgate-France, including the brightly colored containers for Soupline fabric softener.
Copyright Richard Alcorn. Reprinted by permission.

owned subsidiary of Sony of Japan. Similarly, the foreign subsidiaries of U.S.-based companies annually generate sales revenues of hundreds of billions of dollars.[32] See Figure 21-7.

With direct ownership, a firm has all the benefits and risks associated with owning a foreign business. There are potential savings in labor, and marketing plans are more sensitive to local needs. Profit potential may be high, although investment costs may also be high. There is a possibility of nationalistic acts, and government restrictions are likely to be more stringent. This is the riskiest form of organization.

Companies frequently combine organizational formats. For instance, a firm could use an exporting organization in a country that has a history of taking over the assets of foreign firms and a direct ownership organization in a country that provides tax advantages for plant construction. In the case of McDonald's, international expansion is carried out by combining company-operated stores (718 in early 1988), franchisee-operated stores (988 in early 1988), and affiliate-operated stores (638 in early 1988). With affiliate-operated stores, the McDonald's Corporation usually owns 50 per cent or less of their assets; the rest are owned by resident nationals. Company stores are mostly in Canada, Great Britain, West Germany, and Australia; franchisee outlets are

---

[32] John J. Curran, "What Foreigners Will Buy Next," *Fortune* (February 13, 1989), pp. 94–97; and Louis Uchitelle, "Trade Barriers and Dollar Swings Raise Appeal of Factories Abroad," *New York Times* (March 26, 1989), Section 1, pp. 1, 23.

You're the Marketer

How Do You Manage Joint Ventures?

Although joint ventures between U.S.-based companies and foreign partners may be beneficial to each partner (due to shared research and development costs, better access to foreign markets, and a broadened product line), they also may involve considerable difficulties (due to exchanging trade secrets with a potential competitor if a venture disbands and coordination problems).

One U.S. company successfully involved in multiple joint ventures with foreign partners is Corning Glass Works. Corning obtains over one-half of its total profits from 23 different joint ventures, two-thirds of which are with foreign-based companies.

For example, when profits and sales dropped in Corning's glass-bulb business because fewer U.S. firms were producing television picture tubes, Corning decided to look for foreign partners. In its first joint venture in this market, Corning worked with Asahi Glass of Japan. Asahi received immediate access to Corning's plants in the United States and Mexico and to its technological know-how. Corning received immediate access to Japanese manufacturers that assembled televisions in the United States and to Asahi's improvements in Corning's

original technology—which were important in the production and marketing of large-screen televisions.

In another joint venture in the television glass-bulb market, Corning and Samsung of Korea are engaged in production in Korea. This joint venture is staffed entirely by Koreans from Samsung and is diversifying into producing materials for videotape recorders and integrated circuits.

Having two partners in glass-bulb production gives Corning valuable research advantages: "The technical synergy is remarkable, and we're the focal point of the relationship."

Corning likes to think of itself as a long-term stockholder in its joint ventures and often lets the partner "run the show," despite Corning's 50 per cent ownership. However, Corning insists that joint-venture partners have strong management teams that can operate a business without constant intervention from corporate parents.

As the marketing vice-president of Corning's joint venture with Asahi Glass, how would you respond to Corning's increasing involvement with Samsung?

SOURCE: Based on material in Louis Kraar, "Your Rivals Can Be Your Allies," *Fortune* (March 27, 1989), pp. 66–76.

concentrated in Canada and Western European countries; and affiliate restaurants are common in Japan and other Pacific countries. McDonald's first outlets were scheduled to open in the Soviet Union in 1989; these stores fall into the affiliate category.[33]

Standardizing Plans

A firm engaged in international marketing activities must determine the degree to which its plans should be standardized. Both standardized and nonstandardized plans have benefits and limitations.

[33] *McDonald's Corporation 1987 Annual Report;* and Peter Gumbel, "Golden Arches to Rise Near Kremlin as McDonald's Sets a Moscow Venture," *Wall Street Journal* (May 2, 1988), p. 21.

*Under a **standardized approach,** a common marketing plan is used in each country in which a firm operates. Under a **nonstandardized approach,** each country is given a separate marketing plan. A **mixed approach** is a combination strategy.*

With a ***standardized*** or ***global approach,*** a company utilizes a common marketing plan for all countries in which it operates. There are usually marketing and production economies because product design, assembly, advertising, packaging, and other costs are spread over a large product base. A uniform image is presented, training of foreign personnel is reduced, and centralized control is applied. It works best when foreign markets are similar to the home country and/or consumer demand patterns can be clustered across countries. However, this approach is not sensitive to individual market needs, and the input from foreign personnel is limited:

> When global marketing does work, it can save a company millions in manufacturing, packaging, and advertising costs. Colgate-Palmolive, for example, introduced its tartar-control toothpaste in over 40 countries, each of which could choose one of two ads. (The one in the U.S. featured little men building a wall of tartar on giant teeth.) It estimates that it saves $1 million to $2 million in production costs alone. Colgate has saved millions more by standardizing the look and packaging of certain brands, then consolidating the factories that make them.

> But such savings are quickly destroyed if a global strategy bombs. U.S. executives in search of global markets have found that the French don't drink orange juice for breakfast; that Middle Easterners prefer toothpaste that tastes spicy; that the Japanese like herbs in their cold medicines; and that laundry detergent is used to wash dishes in parts of Mexico.[34]

A ***nonstandardized approach*** assumes that each market is different and requires a distinct marketing plan. This strategy is sensitive to local needs and provides opportunities for the development of foreign managers. Decentralized control is undertaken. It works best when distinctive major foreign markets are involved and/or the company has many product lines. For instance, although Nestlé has several well-known ''global'' brands such as Nescafé coffee, it strongly believes in a decentralized strategy tailored to individual markets:

> In particular, Nestlé gets high marks for emphasizing local marketing. It has, for example, developed 200 different blends of Nescafé brand coffee to appeal to different palates from Arkansas to Sri Lanka. In Japan, where foreign companies often give up in frustration, Nestlé has cornered more than 70 per cent of the coffee market.

Says Nestlé's chief executive, ''You can't take the way of life of one country and try to impose that on the whole world, seeing yourself in control and everyone else as a satellite.''[35]

In recent years, more and more international firms (including Nestlé) have turned to a ***mixed approach*** for marketing planning. Under a mixed approach, a combination of standardized and nonstandardized efforts enable companies to maximize production efficiencies, maintain a consistent image, exercise some home-office control, and yet be sensitive and responsive to local needs. As an illustration, a Black & Decker marketing executive recently summarized his firm's mixed approach as follows:

> We make products in Europe similar to those in the United States, with changes for voltage and local electrical systems, of course. We don't have to reinvent the power tool in

---

[34] Joanne Lipman, "Marketers Turn Sour on Global Sales Pitch Harvard Guru Makes," *Wall Street Journal* (May 12, 1988), pp. 1, 4. See also James F. Bolt, "Global Competitors: Some Criteria for Success," *Business Horizons,* Vol. 31 (January–February 1988), pp. 34–41; and Damon Darlin, "Myth and Marketing in Japan," *Wall Street Journal* (April 6, 1989), p. B1.

[35] Greenhouse, "Nestlé's Time to Swagger," Section 3, p. 10.

every country, but rather, we have a common product and adapt it to individual markets. The product can be substantially the same, but features are changed for local tastes. Advertising and promotions are tailored to the needs of individual markets and end users. The products are marketed quite differently in some cases due to local customs.[36]

When determining a marketing approach, a firm should evaluate whether differences among countries are sufficiently great to warrant changes in marketing plans, which elements of marketing can be standardized, whether the size of each foreign market will result in profitable adaptation, and if modifications can be made on a regional rather than a country basis.

Product Planning

International product planning can be based on straight-extension, product-adaptation, backward-invention, and/or forward-invention strategies.[37]

In a ***straight-extension*** strategy, the company manufactures the same products for domestic and foreign sales. The firm is confident that successful products can be sold abroad without any modifications in the product, its brand name, package design, or ingredients. It is a simple, straightforward approach that allows costs to be minimized through economies of scale in production. However, it does not take into account differences in laws, customs, technology, and other factors. Soda companies, such as Coca-Cola and PepsiCo, often use a straight-extension strategy; and "both successfully cross multitudes of national, regional, and ethnic taste buds trained to a variety of deeply ingrained local preferences of taste, flavor, consistency, effervescence, and aftertaste."[38] Beer companies also apply straight-extension strategies. In fact, imported beer often has a higher status than domestic beer; and it is therefore advantageous to use a straight-extension strategy.

With a ***product-adaptation*** strategy, domestic products are modified to meet language needs, taste preferences, foreign conditions, electrical requirements, water conditions, or legal regulations. This is a relatively simple way to plan products for international markets because it is assumed that new products are not necessary and minor changes are sufficient. Product adaptation is the most frequently used strategy in international marketing. See Figure 21-8.

In some cases, a product's flavor is modified to satisfy local tastes, as occurred when Dunkin' Donuts decided to use local fruit fillings (such as papaya and guava) in its classically shaped donuts in Brazilian stores.[39] A product-adaptation strategy is also appropriate for gasoline formulations, which must vary according to a country's weather conditions; detergent formulations, which must be changed to satisfy a country's water hardness; and electrical appliances, which are changed to accommodate voltage requirements. Sometimes adaptation is needed because a product's function differs by country. For example, a consumer lawn mower would be modified if it were to be used as a commercial mower in a foreign country.

Straight extension, product adaptation, backward invention, and forward invention are the basic methods of international product planning.

---

[36] "Winning Turnaround Strategies at Black & Decker," *Journal of Business Strategy,* Vol. 9 (March–April 1989), p. 31.

[37] See Warren J. Keegan, *Multinational Marketing Management,* Third Edition (Englewood Cliffs, N.J.: Prentice-Hall, 1984), pp. 317–324.

[38] Theodore Levitt, "The Globalization of Markets," *Harvard Business Review,* Vol. 61 (May–June 1983), pp. 92–102.

[39] Laurel Wentz, "New Doughnut Snack Has Brazilians Confused," *Advertising Age* (March 25, 1983), p. 54.

This is how Boeing used a product-adaptation strategy in marketing its 737 jet in the Mideast, Africa, and South America:

> The runways in developing [and less-developed] countries were too short to accommodate the jet, and too soft, made of asphalt instead of concrete. Boeing's engineers redesigned the wings to allow shorter landings and added thrust to the engines for quicker takeoffs. Boeing also redesigned the landing gear and installed low-pressure tires so the plane would stick to the ground when it touched down.[40]

See Figure 21-9.

With *backward invention,* a firm appeals to developing and less-developed countries by making products that are less complex than the ones it sells in its domestic market. An example of backward invention is the sale of manual cash registers and nonelectric sewing machines in countries without widespread electricity. Singer markets nonelectric sewing machines in rural foreign communities throughout the world (such as Mexico).

In *forward invention,* a company develops new products for its international markets. This plan is riskier and more time-consuming and requires higher capital investments than the other strategies. It may also provide the firm with great profit potential and, in some situations, worldwide recognition for its beneficial practices. An illus-

[40] Andrew Kupfer, "How to Be a Global Manager," *Fortune* (March 14, 1988), p. 52.

tration of forward invention is Procter & Gamble's development of Ariel laundry detergent, which is marketed mostly in Europe where washload requirements differ from those in the United States. In West Germany, the typical washload is presoaked at a temperature of 95 degrees for an hour and then washed at 140 to 200 degrees (U.S. machines operate at 95 degrees) in front-load machines holding only 3.5 gallons of water (U.S. machines hold 17 gallons of water). Ariel is the top-selling powder detergent in Europe.[41]

Distribution Planning

International distribution planning encompasses the selection and use of channel members and the physical movement of products. As noted earlier in this chapter, a firm may sell products directly through its own sales force or hire outside middlemen to complete transactions. When making channel decisions, the company would examine traditional relationships, the availability of appropriate middlemen, differences in wholesaling and retailing patterns from those in the home country, government restrictions, and costs.

Channel members and physical distribution methods depend on customs, availability, costs, and other factors.

For example,

▶ In Brazil, PepsiCo distributes its soft drinks through the domestic Brahma beer and soda company because of Brahma's extensive distribution network.
▶ In Europe, Nike has had to adjust to a distribution system that centers on small, independently owned stores carrying little inventory.
▶ In 1985, after an 11-year absence, Kentucky Fried Chicken opened outlets in Hong Kong. It had previously failed because consumers were not yet ready for fast-food (which is now popular) and the lack of tables and chairs in restaurants.

[41] Dennis Kneale, "New Foreign Products Pour into U.S. in Increasing Numbers," *Wall Street Journal* (November 11, 1982), p. 22; and Dennis Chase, "A Global Comeback," *Advertising Age* (August 20, 1987), pp. 142–146 ff.

FIGURE 21-10
**A New Toys "R" Us Store
in West Germany**
Reprinted by permission.

▶ Because they are so busy, Japanese consumers are now beginning to buy through mail-order companies (which they formerly believed sold shoddy goods).

▶ In Europe, by the year 2000, Toys "R" Us plans to spend over $1.5 billion to build 300+ stores. These full-line stores will compete with "tens of thousands of mom-and-pop shops."[42] See Figure 21-10.

Physical distribution in international markets often requires special planning. The processing of marine insurance, government documents, and other papers may be time-consuming, and transportation modes may be unavailable or inefficient. For example, a foreign country may have inadequate docking facilities, poor highways, or too few motor vehicles; and distribution by ship is lengthy and subject to delays. Inventory management should take into account the value and availability of warehousing and the costs of shipping in small quantities.

Promotion Planning

International promotion planning depends on the overlap of audiences and languages and the availability of media.

Promotional campaigns can be standardized, nonstandardized, or mixed (as shown in Figure 21-11). For companies marketing in different European countries, some degree of standardization in promotion is often desirable because of the overlap of readership, listeners, and viewers in these nations. For instance, West German television broadcasts are received by a substantial percentage of Dutch homes with televisions. The

---

[42] Roger Cohen, "Pepsi Aims to Liberate Big Market in Brazil from Coke's Domination," *Wall Street Journal* (November 30, 1988), p. B6; "Nike Pins Hope for Growth on Foreign Sales and Apparel," *New York Times* (March 24, 1983), p. D5; Lynne Reaves, "KFC Back in Hong Kong After 10-Year Absence," *Advertising Age* (October 28, 1985), p. 58; Kathryn Graven, "Japanese Discover Mail-Order Buying in New-Found Burst of Consumerism," *Wall Street Journal* (December 17, 1986), p. 26; and Shawn Tully, "The Coming Boom in Europe," *Fortune* (April 10, 1989), p. 114.

BECAUSE
LIFE IS NOT
A SPECTATOR
SPORT.

La vita non è uno sport da spettatori. E Reebok è una scarpa d'azione. Hi-tops progettate per il massimo delle performances nell'esclusivo pellame Reebok. Per l'aerobica o anche solo per il piacere di indossarle.

FREESTYLE HI-TOP

EX-O-FIT HI-TOP

Reebok ⚑

AEROBICS • FITNESS • RUNNING • TENNIS

FIGURE 21-11

A Mixed Approach to Advertising in Foreign Countries
In this Reebok ad used in Italy, one of the firm's basic themes is stated in English while the text is in Italian.
Reprinted by permission.
© Reebok International Ltd.

magazine *Paris Match* has substantial readership in Belgium, Switzerland, Luxembourg, Germany, Italy, and Holland.

There are also reasons for utilizing more nonstandardized promotion tools. Many countries have cultural differences that are not satisfied through a single promotion campaign. These differences include customs, language, the meaning of colors and symbols, and the level of literacy. Media may be unavailable or inappropriate. In a number of countries, there are few televisions in operation, advertising is restricted or banned, or mailing lists are not current. Finally, national pride sometimes requires that individual promotions be used:

> The U.S. is a continent *united* by a language and a deep desire to "belong." Europe, to the contrary, is a grouping of countries and their inhabitants, speaking many languages and dialects, most of whom have at some time or another been at war with their neighboring country, sometimes for centuries.[43]

Through the EC, Europeans hope to reduce the impact of these differences.

---

[43] Anthony J. Rutigliano, "Global Vs. Local Advertising," *Management Review* (June 1986), p. 31.

Most companies combine standardized and nonstandardized tools into mixed promotion plans. As one advertising expert commented: "No global advertiser can take one ad and send it around the world in a plain brown envelope with the instructions: 'Take it, translate it, run it. Don't argue.'" For example, Exxon's tiger represents an internationally recognized symbol of power, speed, and leadership. It has appeared in some form in ads appearing in 32 countries.[44] However Exxon's specific commercials and messages are adapted to individual foreign markets.

In 1989, it was expected that total annual worldwide advertising expenditures — outside the United States — would be about $136 billion. The leaders in non-U.S. advertising are Unilever, Procter & Gamble, Nestlé, and Nissan. Each spends hundreds of millions of dollars each year on ads outside the United States. Although overall worldwide per-capita advertising expenditures average $55, U.S. expenditures are over $500 per resident and many European countries average over $100 per resident. The lowest per-capita expenditures are in Africa and Asia. They are about 10 cents per person in Ethiopia.[45]

Media patterns and costs vary by country. In the United States, 22 per cent of ad expenditures goes to television and 7 per cent to radio. In Colombia, 52 per cent goes to television and 25 per cent to radio. A 30-second television ad costs two to three times as much to make in the United States as in Spain.[46]

Price Planning

*Major decisions in international price planning involve standardization, levels, currency, and sales terms. **Dumping** is disliked by host countries.*

The basic considerations in international price planning are whether prices should be standardized, the level at which prices are set, the currency in which prices are quoted, and terms of sale.

Standardization of prices is difficult unless a firm operates within an economic community, such as the Common Market. Taxes, tariffs, and currency exchange charges are among the added costs a company incurs when engaged in international marketing. As an example, in Japan, domestic beers are priced much lower than Budweiser. The higher price is due to taxes and shipping costs.

When setting a price level, a firm would consider local economic conditions such as per-capita GNP. For this reason, many firms try to hold down prices in developing and less-developed countries by marketing simplified product versions or employing less-expensive local labor. On the other hand, prices in such industrialized countries as West Germany can reflect product quality and the added charges of international marketing.

Some firms set lower prices in foreign countries in order to enlarge the market or remove excess supply from the home market and preserve the home market's price structure. **Dumping** is involved when a firm sells a product in a foreign country at a price much lower than that prevailing in the exporter's home market, below the cost of production, or both. In the United States and other countries, duties may be levied on products that are dumped by foreign companies. For example, in late 1988, AT&T filed charges against twelve Far East makers of communications equipment for small

[44] Gordon L. Link, "Global Advertising: An Update," *Journal of Consumer Marketing,* Vol. 5 (Spring 1988), pp. 69–74.

[45] Julie Skur Hill, "Euro, Pacific Spending Spree," *Advertising Age* (April 10, 1989), pp. 4, 55; "Unilever Ranked No. 1 in Non-U.S. Advertising," *Advertising Age* (December 19, 1988), p. 26; and "Advertising's Bigger Than Ever," *Economist* (March 9, 1985), pp. 78–79.

[46] McCann-Erickson, Inc.; *Advertising Age;* and authors' estimates.

business with the U.S. Commerce Department and the International Trade Commission. AT&T stated that these firms were selling equipment in the United States at prices that were often less than half of those in the firms' home markets. If AT&T's position was supported, through a process that would take at least one year to complete, heavy tariffs could be imposed.[47]

A third fundamental pricing decision relates to the currency in which prices are quoted. If a firm sets prices on the basis of its own nation's currency, the risk of a foreign currency devaluation is passed on to the buyer and better control is maintained. However, this strategy also has limitations. For example, consumers may be confused or unable to convert the price into their currency, or a foreign government may insist that transactions be quoted and completed in its currency.

Finally, terms of sale need to be determined. This involves such judgments as to what middlemen discounts are needed, when ownership is transferred, what form of payment will be required, how much time customers will have to pay bills, and what constitutes an appropriate refund policy.

Summary

1. *To define international and multinational marketing* International marketing involves the marketing of goods and services outside an organization's home country. Multinational marketing engages an organization in operations in many nations. For international companies to succeed, it is vital that they research and understand the similarities and differences among countries and plan their strategies accordingly.

2. *To explain why international marketing has developed and study its scope* International marketing has developed for several reasons. Countries are interested in exchanging products with which they have comparative advantages for those with which they do not. Firms seek to minimize adverse economic conditions and attract growing markets, avoid intense domestic competition, extend the product life cycle and dispose of discontinued items, and utilize tax breaks.

   The United States accounts for 12 per cent of the world's exports. About 100,000 U.S. firms engage in some level of exporting. The United States also imports $460 billion in goods annually, causing a substantial trade deficit—$138 billion in 1988. The U.S. market is the most attractive one in the world for many foreign firms. Non-U.S. firms are increasing their role in international marketing.

3. *To explore the cultural, economic, political and legal, and technological environments facing international marketers* International firms work within several environments. The cultural environment includes the behavior standards, language, life-styles, and goals of a country's citizens. The economic environment incorporates a country's standard of living, Gross National Product, stage of economic development, and stability of currency. The political and legal environment encompasses nationalism, government stability, trade restrictions, and trade agreements and economic communities such as the European Community. The technological environment creates opportunities as well as problems and varies by country.

4. *To analyze the stages in the development of an international marketing strategy* In developing an international marketing strategy, a firm may emphasize exporting, engage in joint ventures, or directly own foreign subsidiaries. Each of these approaches entails a different level of commitment, resource needs, control, risk, and flexibility.

   A company may adopt a standardized, nonstandardized, or mixed approach to marketing. Its decision would depend on the differences among the countries it serves, which marketing elements can be standardized, the size of each foreign market,

[47] Janet Guyon, "AT&T to Charge Far East Firms in Pricing Case," *Wall Street Journal* (December 21, 1988), p. A4.

and the possibility of regional—rather than country by country—adaptation.

Product planning would extend existing products into foreign markets, modify existing products to local needs, produce less sophisticated items for developing nations, or invent new products specifically for foreign markets. Distribution planning would investigate channel relationships and establish a formal network for direct sales or middle-men. In addition, physical distribution features would be analyzed and the proper modifications made. Promotion planning would stress standardized, mixed, or nonstandardized campaigns. Mixed strategies combine the best standardized and nonstandardized promotion tools. Price planning would outline whether prices should be standardized, the level at which prices are set, the currency in which prices are quoted, and sale terms.

Key Terms

international marketing (p. 640)
multinational marketing (p. 640
comparative advantage (p. 640)
trade deficit (p. 643)
standard of living (p. 648)
Gross National Product (GNP)
  (p. 648)
industrialized countries (p. 648)
developing countries (p. 648)
less-developed countries (p. 648)
currency stability (p. 651)
nationalism (p. 651)

government stability (p. 651)
tariff (p. 652)
trade quota (p. 652)
embargo (p. 652)
local content laws (p. 653)
*General Agreement on Tariffs and
  Trade (GATT)* (p. 654)
most-favored nation principle
  (p. 654)
European Community (EC) (p. 654)
exporting (p. 655)
joint venture (p. 656)

direct ownership (p. 657)
standardized (global)
  approach (p. 660)
nonstandardized approach
  (p. 660)
mixed approach (p. 660)
straight extension (p. 661)
product adaptation (p. 661)
backward invention (p. 662)
forward invention (p. 662)
dumping (p. 666)

Review Questions

1. Explain the concept of comparative advantage.
2. Why has the United States had such large trade deficits? How can the annual deficit be reduced?
3. How can a firm improve its cultural awareness?
4. How can a country's GNP be a misleading indicator of marketing opportunities?
5. Distinguish among industrialized, developing, and less-developed countries.
6. If the value of the Colombian peso goes from 361 pesos per U.S. dollar to 400 pesos per U.S. dollar, will U.S. goods be more or less expensive in Colombia? Why?

7. Define each of the following:
   a. Embargo.
   b. Tariff.
   c. Quota.
8. What are the advantages and disadvantages of direct ownership?
9. Why would a firm use a standardized international marketing strategy? What are the potential risks of this strategy?
10. Distinguish among straight-extension, product-adaptation, backward-invention, and forward-invention product planning. When should each be used?

Discussion Questions

1. Cite three basic differences between marketing in the United States and in Canada.
2. In Italy, there are 45 telephones per 100 people, compared with 70 per 100 people in the U.S. What are the ramifications of this from a marketing perspective?
3. What are the advantages and disadvantages of a country belonging to an economic community such as the Common Market?
4. Develop a 10-question checklist by which a luggage manufacturer could determine its most effective overseas distribution system.
5. Provide a current example of an international ad combining standardized and nonstandardized elements. Evaluate the ad.

Procter & Gamble: A Multinational Power*

Procter & Gamble (P&G) markets 165 brands in 11 product categories in 140 countries. Many of its brands—such as Crest toothpaste, Head & Shoulders shampoo, and Pampers diapers—have high brand recognition throughout the world. In 1988, P&G had international sales of $6.5 billion, an 18 per cent increase from 1987. Although its U.S. sales were more than $12 billion in 1988, this was only a 1.7 per cent increase over 1987. Thirty per cent of P&G's total profit came from outside the United States in 1988.

In foreign markets, the company is making a concerted effort to increase its market shares in most major product categories from their current number two or number three positions. P&G is one of the largest advertisers in the United States and globally.

Among P&G's largest and most important international markets are Japan and Europe. And it has not always done well in these markets. For example, as P&G executives acknowledge, the firm has encountered various difficulties in the Japanese market. The Pampers diapers originally sold in Japan were the same version marketed in the United States. P&G did not understand that Japanese mothers desired cloth diapers and considered domestically made ones to be superior in both comfort and absorbency. P&G also made a mistake in Japan when initially promoting Cheer laundry detergent as effective in all water temperatures. The company did not realize that Japanese people typically wash clothes in cold water—so they had little or no interest in an all-temperature detergent.

But Procter & Gamble has worked hard to correct its missteps. Today in Japan, the firm markets an improved superabsorbent diaper and a reformulated Cheer (with "cold water" cleaning ability).

There is also more use of Japanese personnel, so that P&G can better read cultural values.

Pampers has a 23 per cent market share (versus 40 per cent for Japan's Kao Corporation, which offers consumers three different brands), and Cheer is one of the company's best-selling products in Japan. Nonetheless, Kao attracts one-half of the Japanese detergent market. Kao's Attack brand detergent is so concentrated that a small easy-to-carry package contains enough detergent to wash 60 loads. P&G is in the process of introducing Ariel, its leading European detergent brand, in Japan.

In Europe, P&G's great success with detergent is due to its building a strong brand image for Ariel powder detergent—an innovative product developed expressly for the European market—and then extending the Ariel brand to a liquid version. Because regular liquid detergents did not work in European washers, P&G engineers developed a "dosing ball" that is filled with detergent and placed in each load of wash. As a result, P&G has been able to maintain a 50 per cent share of the European liquid-detergent market. Many European consumers believe that Ariel's main liquid competitor, Wisk, moves through the washing machine without cleaning clothes.

In Great Britain, P&G is the leader in disposable diapers with a 20 per cent market share. And the firm is planning to use the well-established distribution channels of its Richardson-Vicks subsidiary to expand its Blendax toothpaste and shampoo sales into other parts of Europe. Blendax is a popular West German brand.

As it seeks to further expand in foreign markets, Procter & Gamble faces some other obstacles. For instance, in Japan and in other countries, Vicks cough drops are considered a drug and need to be registered. The Mexican government will not allow the firm to build a second plant unless P&G agrees to sell a majority interest in it to a Mexican company. In South Korea, P&G intends to get around some trade barriers by forming a joint venture with the South Korean government.

---

* The data in this case are drawn from Laurie Freeman and Laurel Wentz, "P&G on a Roll Overseas," *Advertising Age* (June 27, 1988), p. 30; and Alecia Swasy, "After Early Stumbles, P&G Is Making Inroads Overseas," *Wall Street Journal* (February 6, 1989), p. B1.

QUESTIONS

1. How can Procter & Gamble plan better to anticipate the potential problems and opportunities with foreign cultures?
2. In deciding whether to enter a new foreign market, what factors (besides culture) should P&G evaluate? Why?
3. Should P&G's international organizational format differ by country? Explain your answer.
4. What aspects of P&G's marketing strategy for diapers could be standardized? Which should not be standardized? Why?

<CASE 2>

China: Marketing Opportunities and Risks[†]

Since diplomatic relations between the United States and mainland China resumed in 1979, U.S. firms have looked to China as a major trading partner. In 1983, an additional impetus was provided when the the U.S. government shifted China's trade status to "friendly, nonaligned country"—thus giving China the same recognition as nations in Europe, Africa, and Asia. From 1979 to the present, U.S. companies have invested or signed commitments to invest $3 billion in China.

There is interest in China due to its high industrial growth rate—almost 20 per cent per year; its more than one billion population; its encouragement of ventures by foreign firms; and its regulations exempting wholly owned foreign subsidiaries from currency exchange restrictions. For example, the wholly owned operations of PepsiCo, W.R. Grace, and 3M are now allowed to send profits made in China back to the United States (as long as they balance the inflows and outflows of foreign exchange).

Yet, despite its high promise, foreign companies operating in China have faced—and continue to face—many difficulties doing business there. Most importantly, there is continuing uncertainty with

regard to the policies and stability of the Chinese government—particularly in light of the tragic events in 1989 when student protests led to violent government reactions. Foreign firms are unsure as to how favorable China's long-term political climate will be.

Firms operating in China must also deal with its multilevel bureaucracy. Johnson & Johnson had to negotiate for more than four years before reaching an agreement to produce its Band-Aids product in Shanghai. RJR Nabisco spent six years in negotiations for its Ritz crackers there.

Some other complications have also surfaced. First, inflation has been rampant; overall prices increased by 30 per cent in 1988. An August 1988 announcement that all price ceilings would be eliminated within a five-year period caused a consumer buying spree—and hoarding. Some food prices jumped by 60 per cent or more immediately following the announcement. As of September 1988, in an attempt to control inflation, the Chinese government canceled plans to decontrol additional prices, reimposed price ceilings, and increased tariffs on imported luxury goods.

Second, Western managers involved in joint ventures in China have experienced significant delays in getting paid by their Chinese customers. Some are worried that their Chinese partners may not be able to obtain much needed bank credit.

Third, rivalries among regions in China have intensified due to their different stages of economic development. In some cases, problems have been created by poorer provinces, which have been able

[†] The data in this case are drawn from Dinah Lee, "Beijing Opens the Door to Bubble Gum and Band-Aids," *Business Week* (August 8, 1988), p. 40; Susan Leshnower, "China's Opportunities for American Firms," *Management Review* (July 1988), pp. 48–51; Ford S. Worthy, "Why There's Still Promise in China," *Fortune* (February 27, 1989), pp. 95–101; and William Glasgall, "China: The Great Leap Backward," *Business Week* (June 19, 1989), pp. 28–33.

to keep important raw materials from reaching wealthy industrially based provinces.

Heinz and PepsiCo are among the foreign firms that have learned how to adapt to the Chinese environment. Heinz, which produces baby food and cereal in China, saw the price of rice quadruple in one eighteen-month period; and credit restrictions meant that some Heinz distributors paid their bills a week or two later than usual. Heinz convinced the Chinese government to allow it to import rice and prevailed on the government to loosen its credit restrictions on distributors of a "socially beneficial" product such as baby food.

While PepsiCo is allowed to sell soda concentrate to bottlers in China who pay with U.S. dollars, it also has a joint venture with a U.S.-based spice company to export spices to the United States. In this manner, PepsiCo is able to balance its currency flow with China.

As one foreign businessman says, in explaining why companies are willing to confront the complexities of dealing with China, "In a country with a billion-plus consumers, you have to ask yourself, 'What are the consequences if I'm not here and my competition is?'"

QUESTIONS

1. Cite several major opportunities and risks in doing business in China.
2. Develop a checklist for a television manufacturer to use in considering whether to open a plant in China.

3. What type of product planning strategy would be most appropriate in China?
4. Discuss the statement: "In a country with a billion-plus consumers, you have to ask yourself, 'What are the consequences if I'm not here and my competition is?'"

CHAPTER *22*

Service and Nonprofit Marketing

CHAPTER OBJECTIVES

1. To distinguish between the marketing of services and goods

2. To discuss the use of marketing by service firms, special considerations for service marketers, a classification system for service firms, the role of services in the U.S. economy, and applications of service marketing

3. To distinguish between nonprofit and profit-oriented marketing

4. To discuss a classification system for nonprofit marketing, the role of nonprofit marketing in the U.S. economy, and applications of nonprofit marketing

U ntil recently, locally rendered services particularly relied on the personalities performing the services, "the friendly mechanic, the family dentist, or the neighborhood hairdresser." In the past decade, however, these and many other services have been standardized to the point that convenience and/or quality and/or economy—as rendered or perceived—effectively substitute for the personal touch and help establish local businesses.

This has led to further routinization and specialization, in some industries to the extent of nationwide expansion, as chains have developed for services ranging from mufflers to teeth-cleaning to divorces.

The standardization of services—often called the industrialization of services—can be accomplished via automation (such as automatic car washes), systematic training of personnel (such as authorized service representatives for repairs), specialization (such as medical offices where only one ailment is treated), and/or substituting preplanned systems for individual services (such as preplanned vacation tours). Let us further examine this concept.

Service providers benefit from industrialization because they are better able to offer consistent service quality, expand business, simplify personnel training, establish personnel performance standards, reduce reliance on key personnel, and so on. Consumers benefit because of higher service reliability, reduced service-time requirements, and lower service costs.

Examples of industrialization include the use of computers by law offices, automatic teller machines (ATMs) by banks, personnel training by tax-preparation firms, and specialization in specific ailments by hospitals.

Law offices are industrializing by using computers instead of typewriters or pads. A single personal computer can store hundreds of common paragraphs used in wills and other legal documents, and call them up when needed. As a result, computers are doing away with the time-consuming need to clip and paste together pieces of old documents, make additions in long hand, and type multiple drafts.

ATMs enable banks to expand hours of operation, give customers 24-hour access to information on their accounts (even while traveling), allow customers to save time when tellers are busy, provide more consistent service quality than tellers, and reduce the banks' need to hire and train tellers.

Tax-preparation firms such as H&R Block are interested in reducing the variability of service quality. Block understands that customers want tax returns

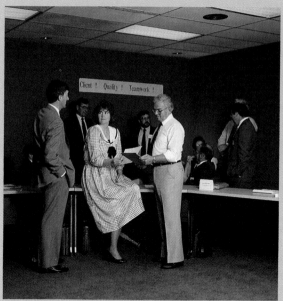

Reprinted by permission of H&R Block, Inc.

completed accurately. Yet, it is also aware of the potential for service quality variability due to its use of 40,000 seasonal employees at more than 8,700 tax-preparation offices. As a result, H&R Block has standardized services by developing a policy-and-procedures manual, using plan-ahead calendars (which tell managers when office space needs to be rented, furniture put in place, and employees hired), running yearly training programs for tax preparers, creating specialized forms for itemizing taxpayer sources of income and expenditures, and writing extensive tax-code manuals for employee use.

Hospitals are also industrializing their services. For instance, the Shouldice Hospital near Toronto specializes in hernia operations. Its physicians use only local anesthetics—allowing the length of an average hospital stay to be reduced and lessening the risk of medical complications associated with general anesthetics. The specialization in hernia surgery enables the hospital to have such high service quality that the remission rate at Shouldice is less than one-tenth that of the average North American hospital.[1]

In this chapter, we will study key concepts pertaining to service and nonprofit marketing—including the industrialization of services.

[1] " 'Standardized' Services Run Gamut From Mufflers to Wills," *Marketing News* (April 10, 1987), pp. 17, 43; "ATMs Not the Time Savers Some Bankers Expected," *Marketing News* (March 28, 1988), p. 8; James L. Heskett, "Lessons in the Service Sector," *Harvard Business Review*, Vol. 65 (March–April 1987), pp. 118–126; and "Taxman Henry Bloch," *Inc.* (December 1987), pp. 35–42.

Overview

Chapter 22 examines the marketing of services as well as the marketing activities of nonprofit organizations. Several aspects of service and nonprofit marketing are distinct and different from goods and profit-oriented marketing. Those differences require separate chapter coverage of these areas.

There is a substantial interaction between service and nonprofit marketing because many nonprofit organizations are involved with services. Examples are colleges and universities, health facilities, and libraries.

Service Marketing

Service marketing involves personal services and goods rental and repair. Intangibility, perishability, inseparability, and variability differentiate services from goods.

As defined in Chapter 9, **service marketing** encompasses the rental of goods, the alteration or repair of goods owned by consumers, and personal services. And typically, services have four characteristics that distinguish them from goods: the higher level of intangibility, the greater degree of perishability, the inseparability of the service from the service provider, and the greater variability in quality. The effect of these characteristics is greatest for personal services.

In the following sections, service marketing is examined in terms of the use of marketing by service firms, special considerations for service marketers, a classification system for service firms, and the extent of services in the economy. Three illustrations of service marketing are presented: marketing by hotels, marketing by car repair and servicing firms, and marketing by lawyers.

The Use of Marketing by Service Firms

The low use of marketing has been due to an emphasis on technical expertise, small firm size, limited competition, negative attitudes, and other factors.

Service firms have typically lagged behind manufacturing firms in developing and using marketing. This is explained by several factors. One, many service firms stress technical expertise. Often these firms were started because of specialized skills, such as repairing plumbing systems, preparing food, or having knowledge of the law. Two, most service firms are so small that marketing specialists cannot be used. Three, strict licensing provisions sometimes limit competition and the need for marketing. Four, consumers have held a variety of service professionals, particularly doctors and lawyers, in such high esteem that marketing has not been needed. Five, in the past, a number of associations prohibited advertising by their members. This was changed by Supreme Court rulings in the late 1970s that permitted advertising by professionals. Finally, there are still a number of service professionals who have a dislike for marketing, lack a full understanding of it, or question the use of marketing practices, such as advertising, in their fields.

Service firms' use of marketing practices is expected to increase in the future.

Over the next several years, it is expected that the use of marketing by service firms will increase significantly, as a result of many factors: a better understanding of the importance of consumer satisfaction in gaining new patrons and holding on to existing ones, deregulation in many industries (such as banking, transportation, and communication), growing competition among service providers (such as dental services in retail stores versus traditional dentists), the continued growth in the do-it-yourself market segment due to the rising costs of services, and the expanding number of service professionals with formal business training.

This shows how marketing practices can be utilized by consumer-oriented service firms:

> Lawyers brief new clients to reduce confusion about office procedures. Physicians and dentists take the trouble to check with their patients after treatment. Consultants and accountants scrutinize their billing procedures, knowing that such details affect how a client views their abilities.

> These actions exemplify the kind of postsale emphasis that brings success to leading marketers of professional services; they also offer useful lessons for all services marketers. The services marketers with the most difficult challenge in satisfying their buyers view marketing as a process that continues long after the buyer has made the commitment to purchase.[2]

Special Considerations for Service Marketers

In planning its marketing strategy, a service firm needs to consider how intangible its offering is, how perishable its services are, how inseparable service performance is from specific service providers, the potential variability of service quality, and the role of peripheral services. The firm's goal is to develop and enact a marketing strategy that enables consumers to perceive its offering in a tangible manner, that makes its services less perishable, that encourages consumers to seek it out but enables a number of employees to be viewed as competent, that makes service performance as efficient and consistent as possible, and that uses peripheral services to complement its core services.

The intangibility of services can make promotion decisions more difficult. Unlike goods promotion, which may stress tangible attributes and consumer analysis (such as touching, tasting, and so on) prior to a purchase, much service promotion must rely on performance attributes (such as how well a car handles following a tune-up), which can be measured only after a purchase. Nonetheless, there are several ways to use promotion to help consumers perceive a service in a more tangible manner. For instance, a firm can:

Intangibility makes promotion and pricing decisions more complex.

▶ Develop a tangible representation of its services. For example, a credit card, although not a financial service itself, still serves as a physical product with its own image and benefits.

▶ Associate an intangible service with a tangible object better understood by the customer, such as "You're in good *hands* with Allstate."

▶ Focus on the relationship between the company and its customers and away from the intangible service itself. It can sell the competence, skill, and concern of service representatives and other company employees to develop client relationships. See Figure 22-1.

▶ Offer a tangible benefit, such as American Express promoting an immediate replacement of lost or stolen traveler's checks.

▶ Establish a clear product position, such as a discount, no-frills hotel.

▶ Popularize its company name and use a family brand approach. In this way, consumers would develop a clear brand image: "Although a service vendor may have a

---

[2] Betsy D. Gelb, Samuel V. Smith, and Gabriel M. Gelb, "Service Marketing Lessons from the Professionals," *Business Horizons,* Vol. 31 (September–October 1988), p. 29.

FIGURE 22-1
Tangibly Promoting a Service
Reprinted by permission of American International Group of Companies.

variety of offerings—first class, business class, and coach; or checking accounts and loan services—consumers tend to perceive all of them as components of a single brand. Each conjures up an overall brand image."[3]

The intangibility of services can also make pricing decisions more difficult. For example, should an automobile mechanic set a price for the repair of a transmission on the basis of a standardized price list or place a value on his or her time and set a specific price after the transmission is repaired? How should the price be broken down into problem analysis and service components? Should prices vary among repairs

---

[3] James H. Donnelly, Jr., "Use Three Methods to Help Market Intangible Service," *Marketing News* (October 19, 1979), p. 5; Kathleen A. Krentler and Joseph P. Guiltinan, "Strategies for Tangibilizing Retail Services: An Assessment," *Journal of the Academy of Marketing Science,* Vol. 12 (Fall 1984), pp. 77–92; Judith Graham, "Traveler's Checks Tout Refunds," *Advertising Age* (April 3, 1989), p. 58; and Leonard L. Berry, Edwin F. Lefkowith, and Terry Clark, "In Services, What's in a Name?" *Harvard Business Review,* Vol. 66 (September–October 1988), pp. 28–30.

performed by the head mechanic and regular mechanics? In setting routine prices, what is covered in the basic service? Services that are equipment-based and routine in nature may be suited to cost-oriented pricing. Other services should rely on competitive and demand-based pricing.

For some services, only a small portion of the service mix is visible to the consumer. As an example, in-store repairs are normally not seen by consumers. Although the repairperson may spend two hours on a television and insert two parts priced at $6, the consumer sees a bill for $57 and does not realize the amount of service involved. Therefore, a firm must explain how much time is needed to render each service — and the functions performed — to make that service more tangible to customers.

Consumers may see only a small portion of the service mix.

Because of their perishability, services often cannot be stockpiled. For example, if a movie theater has 500 seats, it cannot admit more than 500 customers to a Saturday night showing even though a Wednesday matinee had 400 empty seats. Thus, to better match demand with supply, a service firm would have to alter the timing of consumer demand and/or exert better control over the supply of its service offering. It should avoid situations in which excess demand goes unsatisfied, as well as situations in which excess capacity leads to an unproductive use of resources. Following are a number of methods for matching demand with supply:

Services often cannot be stored for later sale; demand must be carefully matched with supply.

▶ Market similar services to consumer segments having different demand patterns.
▶ Market new services having countercyclical demand patterns from those of existing services.
▶ Market new services that complement existing service offerings.
▶ Market service "extras" during nonpeak periods.
▶ Market new services not affected by existing capacity constraints.
▶ Train personnel to perform multiple tasks.
▶ Hire part-time employees during peak periods.
▶ Educate consumers to use services during nonpeak periods.
▶ Offer incentives and price reductions in nonpeak periods.[4]

The existence of a close service provider-consumer relationship makes employee interpersonal skills important. The work force must be trained to interact well with consumers in such diverse situations as selling and performing services, processing payments, and delivering repaired goods. The importance of this relationship was confirmed in a study of several hundred retail and organizational salespeople: it found that more personal involvement, personal contact, and customer input are required to sell services than to sell goods.[5] See Figure 22-2.

Interpersonal skills are crucial.

In planning its service provider-consumer relationship, a company should also keep this in mind: Many customers of personal-service firms become loyal to a particular company employee rather than to the company. If that person leaves the firm, he or she may take a lot of customers with him or her. That is why it is important for a firm to demonstrate to its customers that multiple employees are equally capable of providing excellent service.

By their very nature, many services have the potential for great variability in their quality. For instance, it is hard for lawn-care firms to mow lawns in the exact same manner each week and for marketing consultants to make sales forecasts for their

---

[4] Leonard L. Berry, A. Parasuraman, and Valarie A. Zeithaml, "Synchronizing Demand and Supply in Service Businesses," *Business,* Vol. 34 (October–December 1984), pp. 36–37.
[5] William R. George and J. Patrick Kelly, "The Promotion and Selling of Services," *Business,* Vol. 33 (July–September 1983), pp. 14–20.

FIGURE 22-2
The Close Service Provider-Consumer Relationship
In the rental of tools by do-it-yourselfers, company personnel must explain which tools are best for which jobs, how to use various tools, and how to operate tools safely.
Reprinted by permission.

*The **industrialization of services** can lower inefficiency and excessive variability through **hard technologies**, **soft technologies**, or **hybrid technologies**.*

clients that are always accurate. But what service firms can do is endeavor to make their performance as efficient and consistent as possible.

One solution to the problem of high costs (inefficiency) and low reliability (excessive variability in performance) is the ***industrialization of services*** by using hard, soft, and hybrid technologies.[6] ***Hard technologies*** substitute machinery for people, such as the implementation of an electronic credit-authorization system instead of manual credit checks. Hard technologies cannot be readily applied to services requiring extensive personal skill and contact such as medical, legal, and hairstyling services.

Soft technologies substitute preplanned systems for individual services. For example, many travel agents sell prepackaged vacation tours. This standardizes transportation, accommodations, food, and sightseeing. ***Hybrid technologies*** combine both hard and soft technologies. Examples include computer-based truck routing and specialized low-priced repair facilities, such as muffler repair shops.

Service reliability can also be improved by setting higher-level standards and by tying employee pay, promotions, and retention to performance levels. As an example, American Airlines developed a series of standards that enabled the company to become one of the most preferred domestic airlines in the United States:

▶ Reservation phones must be answered within 20 seconds.
▶ 85 per cent of passengers should not have to stand in line more than 5 minutes.
▶ Flights must take off within 5 minutes of scheduled departure time.
▶ Cabins must have their proper supply of magazines.
▶ Flights should land within 15 minutes of scheduled arrival time.
▶ Doors are to be opened 70 seconds after the plane stops rolling.
▶ The last baggage should reach the terminal not more than 17 minutes after passengers begin to disembark from the plane.[7]

---

[6] Theodore Levitt, *The Marketing Imagination* (New York: Free Press, 1983), pp. 50–71.
[7] Jeremy Main, "Toward Service Without a Snarl," *Fortune* (March 23, 1981), p. 61; and Robert C. Lewis and Bernard H. Booms, "The Marketing Aspects of Service Quality" in Leonard L. Berry, G. Lynn Shostack, and Gregory D. Upah (Editors), *Emerging Perspectives on Services Marketing* (Chicago: American Marketing Association, 1983), pp. 100–102.

You're the Marketer

How Can Stock Brokers Lure Back Small Investors?

Stock brokers are suffering from a decline in small-investor business, partly caused by the stock market decline in October 1987 and the subsequent loss of investor confidence. Between 1983 and 1988, the trading of odd lots (transactions involving fewer than 100 shares of stock) fell dramatically at the New York Stock Exchange. And overall, the percentage of stock market volume now attributable to individual investors is about 10 per cent.

Discount brokers are particularly affected by the low activity of small investors. At a typical discount firm, commissions make up 60 per cent of revenues, with the balance coming from interest charges to customers. Discounters typically sell few equities and bonds, and do not manage mutual funds or receive management fees. As a result, because of the drop in small-investor transactions, their pre-tax return on equity fell from 50 per cent in 1986 to 20 per cent in 1987 to 6 per cent in early 1988.

The chairman of Schwab & Co., a major discount broker, says "It's the most difficult envi-

ronment for everyone since 1973-1974." Schwab is adjusting by reducing costs, changing its product/customer mix, and raising commissions. It has laid off 210 employees and reduced the pay of an additional 300. The firm is heavily promoting fixed-income securities (rather than stocks). More efforts are aimed at independent financial investment advisers; Schwab now serves more than 400 such advisers whose clients' accounts represent almost 20 per cent of all customer assets at Schwab. The company has raised its commissions, calling this a "catch-up" move because it had not raised commission rates for four years.

In contrast, Quick & Reilly—a Schwab competitor—has no plans to raise its commission rates, even though it has not done so in over seven years: "In times like this, when business is lousy, you don't raise rates because people notice."

As a consultant, retained by Schwab's president, what would you recommend that the firm do to lure back the small investor?

SOURCE: Based on material in Gary Weiss, Leah Nathans, and Kathleen A. Behof, "For Discount Brokers, the Crash Still Isn't Over," Business Week (December 5, 1988), pp. 154–155.

In planning marketing strategies, it is also important for firms to understand service quality from the perspective of customers. According to three prominent researchers,

Service firms need to know what quality means to consumers.

Customers assess service quality by comparing what they want or expect to what they actually get or perceive they are getting. To earn a reputation for quality, an organization must meet — or exceed — customer expectations. And what do service customers expect?

Our research suggests these expectations cover five areas:

- Tangibles — the physical facilities, equipment, appearance of personnel;
- Reliability — the ability to perform the desired service dependably, accurately, and consistently;
- Responsiveness — the willingness to provide prompt service and help customers;
- Assurance — employees' knowledge, courtesy, and ability to convey trust and confidence; and
- Empathy — the provision of caring, individualized attention to customers.[8]

[8] Leonard L. Berry, A. Parasuraman, and Valarie A. Zeithaml, "The Service-Quality Puzzle," *Business Horizons*, Vol. 31 (September–October 1988), p. 37.

*By adding **peripheral services** to their **core services**, firms can create a competitive advantage.*

Finally, in their marketing strategies, firms need to specify which are core services and which are peripheral — and the level of peripheral services to offer. ***Core services*** are the basic services that companies provide for their customers. In the case of Federal Express, core services involve picking up packages, transporting them overnight, and delivering them the next morning. ***Peripheral services*** are supplementary services that companies provide to their customers. For Federal Express, peripheral services include giving advice and information, taking telephone orders, making address labels and special packaging materials available, documenting shipments, and tracing packages in transit.[9]

Although peripheral services may increase a service firm's investment, may require additional employee and management skills, and may be time-consuming, they may also enable a company to create and sustain a competitive advantage: "Each firm should decide what the basis for its competitive strategy will be. When targeting a specific market segment, where will superior performance — or a service element not offered by competitors — yield a meaningful competitive edge? And where will it suffice simply to offer the industry standard of performance on a given service element?"[10]

Classifying Services

Services may be classified in terms of market, tangibility, skill, goals, regulation, labor intensity, and customer contact.

Figure 22-3 shows a detailed, seven-way classification system for services. This system is a useful way of showing the diversity of service marketing.[11]

In selecting a market segment, a firm should recognize that final and organizational consumers have similarities as well as differences, as detailed in Chapter 7. The same basic service (for example, carpet cleaning, typewriter repair, lawn care, and air travel) may be offered to each segment. Both use decision making to select a service, although buying influences may be different. Each can counter high prices or poor service levels by performing some tasks itself. The major differences between the segments are the reasons for the service, the quantity of service required, and the complexity of the service performed.

Services may differ significantly in terms of their tangibility. In general, the less tangible the service, the less service marketing resembles goods marketing. For nongoods services, performance can be judged only after the service is completed; and a consistent service level is difficult to maintain. Rentals and owned-goods services involve physical goods and are more tangible than nongoods services; thus they may be marketed in a manner similar to goods.

Services may be provided by persons of greatly varying skills. For services requiring high levels of skills, customers are quite selective in their choice of provider. That is why professionals often achieve customer loyalty. For services requiring low levels of skill, the range of acceptable substitutes is usually much greater.

Service companies may be profit or nonprofit-oriented. Nonprofit-service marketing may be undertaken by government or private organizations. Nonprofit marketing is discussed in depth in the second part of this chapter.

---

9 Christopher H. Lovelock, "Competitive Advantage Lies in Supplementary, Not Core, Services," *Marketing News* (January 30, 1989), p. 16.

10 Ibid.

11 For a more detailed discussion, see Christopher H. Lovelock, "Classifying Services to Gain Strategic Marketing Insights," *Journal of Marketing*, Vol. 47 (Summer 1983), pp. 9–20; and G. Lynn Shostack, "Service Positioning Through Structural Change," *Journal of Marketing*, Vol. 51 (January 1987), pp. 34–43.

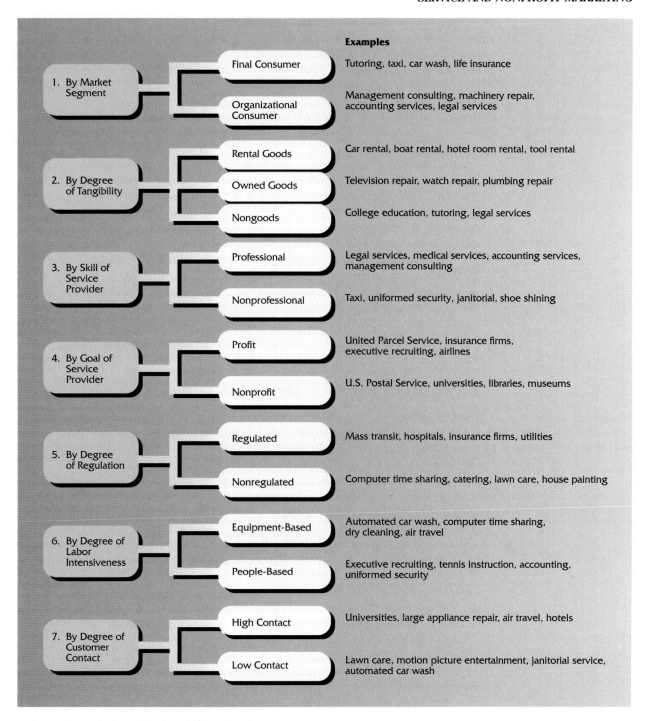

Examples

1. By Market Segment
   - Final Consumer — Tutoring, taxi, car wash, life insurance
   - Organizational Consumer — Management consulting, machinery repair, accounting services, legal services

2. By Degree of Tangibility
   - Rental Goods — Car rental, boat rental, hotel room rental, tool rental
   - Owned Goods — Television repair, watch repair, plumbing repair
   - Nongoods — College education, tutoring, legal services

3. By Skill of Service Provider
   - Professional — Legal services, medical services, accounting services, management consulting
   - Nonprofessional — Taxi, uniformed security, janitorial, shoe shining

4. By Goal of Service Provider
   - Profit — United Parcel Service, insurance firms, executive recruiting, airlines
   - Nonprofit — U.S. Postal Service, universities, libraries, museums

5. By Degree of Regulation
   - Regulated — Mass transit, hospitals, insurance firms, utilities
   - Nonregulated — Computer time sharing, catering, lawn care, house painting

6. By Degree of Labor Intensiveness
   - Equipment-Based — Automated car wash, computer time sharing, dry cleaning, air travel
   - People-Based — Executive recruiting, tennis instruction, accounting, uniformed security

7. By Degree of Customer Contact
   - High Contact — Universities, large appliance repair, air travel, hotels
   - Low Contact — Lawn care, motion picture entertainment, janitorial service, automated car wash

FIGURE 22-3 **A Classification System for Services**

Services may also be categorized by the extent of government regulation. Some firms, such as insurance companies, are highly regulated. Others, such as caterers and house painters, are subject to limited regulation.

The traditional view of services has been that they are something performed by one individual for another. However, this view is too narrow. Services do differ in their labor intensity — for example, an automated versus a manual car wash or teller-oriented versus automated bank services. Labor intensity increases when highly skilled personnel are involved and/or services must be provided at the customer's home or place of business (as a result of the inability to transport heavy equipment and the amount of time necessary for travel, the basic service, and follow-up). Some labor-intensive services may be performed by do-it-yourself consumers — for example, home repair.

Last, service firms may be classified by their degree of customer contact. As stated earlier, when customer contact is high, training personnel in interpersonal skills is essential. This is in addition to the technical training needed to properly perform a service. Such personnel as appliance repairpeople, car mechanics, and other service personnel may be the only contact a consumer has with the firm. When customer contact is low, technical skills are most essential.

It is important to note that an organization would normally be classified on the basis of a combination of the factors listed in Figure 22-3. For example, a firm that tutors students for college-board exams appeals to final consumers, offers an intangible service, requires skill by the service provider, is profit-oriented, is not regulated, employs many trainers, and has high customer contact. A company may also operate in more than one part of a category. For example, an accountant may deal with both final and organizational consumer markets.

The Extent of Services in the Economy

The average American family spends over one-half of its budget on services.

The United States has been described as the leading service economy in the world. In the private sector, 75 per cent of the labor force is now employed in a service capacity. During 1960, the typical family spent 40 per cent of its budget on services. By 1988, the figure was 53 per cent. Over this period, annual service expenditures rose from $131 billion to over $1.6 trillion for final consumers. Housing, medical care, personal services, and household operations account for almost 80 per cent of consumer service spending. In addition to final-consumer services, U.S. industrial-service firms account for well over $200 billion in annual revenues.[12]

Various reasons have been cited for the growth of final consumer-related services, such as the increased prosperity of the population, complex goods requiring specialized installation and repair, and the leisure orientation of U.S. society. In the industrial sector, these are among the service firms experiencing the greatest growth over the past decade: computer repair and training, management consulting, engineering, and equipment leasing. See Figure 22-4.

*The **hidden service sector** includes services offered by goods-oriented firms.*

Despite the sizable revenue figures noted at the beginning of this section, these data still underestimate the importance of services in the United States. They do not include the **hidden service sector,** which encompasses the delivery, installation, maintenance, training, repair, and other services provided by firms that emphasize goods sales. For example, although Apple and Xerox are classified as manufacturers, many of their employees are involved in dealer- and user-training programs, equipment maintenance, parts delivery, and warranty repairs.

The following illustrations show the scope of service marketing:

[12] Bureau of Economic Analysis, U.S. Commerce Department, 1988.

FIGURE 22-4
TRW's Equipment Repair
TRW is one of the leading repair-service firms in the United States, with over 100,000 corporate customers. When summoned to a customer site to fix electronic equipment, company field service personnel bring a proprietary electronic device that enables them to diagnose the source of a problem quickly and thoroughly. Here, the device is used to repair a computerized sales terminal at a Los Angeles store of Sherwin-Williams.
Reprinted by permission.

▶ There are over 270,000 certified public accountants (CPAs) in the United States. In 1988, their professional association—the American Institute of Certified Public Accountants—reversed an 80-year-old ban and now permits CPAs to sell securities, insurance, and other financial services. As one accountant noted, "It means that accountants will be able to sell stock, mutual funds, annuities, insurance products, collateral management, limited partnerships, and loan brokerage services in competition with other financial services professionals."[13]

▶ Twenty-four-hour service businesses are growing rapidly. Many of these businesses feature computerized vending machines that process videotape rentals, banking transactions, dry cleaning drop-off and pick-up, and so on. Says a videotape rental executive: "What we're selling is convenience and automation. Americans know how to use technology, and they're getting what they want when they want it." These services are often advertised in print media.[14]

▶ Together the four leading private profit-oriented U.S. child-care firms (Kinder-Care, La Petite Academy, Children's World, and Gerber) operate 2,500 centers nationally. They service hundreds of thousands of children each year, at weekly fees ranging up to $85 per child, and frequently rely on franchising to expand business.[15] See Figure 22-5.

▶ Business consulting firms now generate greater than $10 billion in annual U.S. revenues, and sales are growing by 20 per cent yearly. According to one consultant, the growth is due to this: "We're in the uncertainty-absorption business. The more

---

[13] Nina Andrews, "C.P.A. Group Votes to Allow Members to Sell Securities," *New York Times* (August 31, 1988), p. D2.

[14] Eric Asimov, "The Insomniac's Dream: All-Night Services Grow," *New York Times* (September 3, 1988), p. 48.

[15] Kenneth F. Englade, "The Bottom Line on Kinder-Care," *Inc.* (April 1988), pp. 44–53.

FIGURE 22-5
Child-Care Services by Kinder-Care
The largest chain of child-care centers in the United States is operated by Kinder-Care Learning Centers Inc. It provides a number of child-related services for working parents and has convenient hours and locations.
Copyright Kinder-Care Learning Centers, Inc. Reprinted by permission.

uncertainty there is, the more people are likely to look for outside help." Yet because competition among consulting firms is also more intense, they are marketing their services more aggressively than before (but not discounting prices).[16]

▶ Twenty per cent of U.S. new-automobile transactions involve leasing; and over one-quarter of all leases are with final consumers. Some dealers believe "the future is leasing" because leases make higher-priced vehicles more affordable, encourage more frequent trade-ins, and build customer loyalty. Therefore, in their selling and advertising programs, dealers are placing greater emphasis on leasing.[17]

Illustrations of Service Marketing

This section examines marketing by hotels, car repair and servicing firms, and lawyers. These three examples represent a rented-goods service, an owned-goods service, and a nongoods service. They differ by the degree of tangibility, the skill of the service provider, the degree of labor intensiveness, and the level of customer contact.

Hotels may appeal to one or more consumer segments from among business travelers, through tourists (who stay one night), regular tourists (who stay two or more nights), extended-stay residents (who stay up to several months or longer), and conventioneers. Each segment requires different services. The business traveler seeks

[16] Anne B. Fisher, "The Ever-Bigger Boom in Consulting," *Fortune* (April 24, 1989), pp. 113–134.
[17] James B. Treece, "How Leases Are Souping Up the Car Makers," *Business Week* (August 1, 1988), pp. 58–61.

efficient service, a desk in the room, and convenient meeting rooms. The through tourist seeks a convenient location, low prices, and fast food service. The regular tourist seeks a nice room, recreational facilities, and connections for sightseeing. The extended-stay resident seeks a homey atmosphere, in-room kitchen facilities, and other "apartment-like" facilities. Conventioneers seek large meeting rooms, preplanned sightseeing, and hospitality suites.[18]

To attract and retain customers, hotels have been adding new services and improving their marketing efforts. First-run movies that can be viewed in the room, frequent consumer bonuses, travel discounts, and casino gambling (where legal) are some of the services now offered. For example, Best Western, Hilton, Hyatt, Radisson, and Sheraton are just some of the hotels offering frequent-stay bonus plans for repeat customers.[19]

Marketing efforts involve greater reliance on research, publicity, television advertising, the use of well-conceived slogans, and greater personal attention for consumers. For instance, through research, it was determined that hotels located near hospitals often have high occupancy. And because of a creative positioning strategy (centering on a nineteenth-century Victorian theme), the ten-room Queen Anne Inn in Denver received publicity in the *New York Times, Inc., Elle,* and *Bridal Guide* (which rated it one of America's top ten wedding night sites).[20]

Hotels are also trying to resolve consumer complaints more effectively. For example, frequent business travelers are quite concerned about overbooking—even those with guaranteed reservations could get turned away, long waiting lines, late check-in times, and unresponsive or discourteous staffs. Hotels are responding by arranging for alternative accommodations if they are overbooked, computerizing check-in facilities, offering express checkouts (whereby bills are mailed to their guests' businesses or homes), serving free drinks and providing baggage handling if check-in times are late, and better training their staffs.

Automobile repairs and servicing are carried out through two basic formats: manufacturer-owned or sponsored dealerships and independent service centers. More than $80 billion is spent annually on auto repairs and servicing, about one-third through manufacturer dealerships and two-thirds through independents. About one-half of new-car buyers buy service contracts—priced from $200 to $800 and up per year—from manufacturer dealerships and insurance companies.[21]

For example, General Motors cars can be repaired and serviced through the company's "Mr. Goodwrench" program, which is available at approved GM dealerships. To qualify for the Mr. Goodwrench program, dealers must satisfy a number of specific quality standards. General Motors supports this program by spending several million dollars yearly on advertising, supervising dealers, and improving service techniques. According to one study, over 90 per cent of General Motors' car buyers are aware of the Mr. Goodwrench name.[22] See Figure 22-6.

[18] Mary Lu Carnevale, "Homey Atmosphere Helps Long-Stay Hotels Flourish," *Wall Street Journal* (March 2, 1989), p. B1.

[19] Michele Manges and Jonathan Dahl, "Hotels Gamble on 'Frequent-Stay' Plans," *Wall Street Journal* (February 27, 1989), p. B1.

[20] Patricia K. Guseman, "How to Pick the Best Location," *American Demographics* (August 1988), pp. 42–43; and Lynn Coleman, "Hotelier Uses 'Audacious PR' to Capture Media Attention," *Marketing News* (July 4, 1988), pp. 1–2.

[21] Bureau of Economic Analysis, U.S. Commerce Department, 1988; and authors' estimates.

[22] Raymond Serafin, "Mr. Goodwrench Gets 'Hands' on Aftermarket," *Advertising Age* (November 4, 1985), p. 45.

**FIGURE 22-6
"Mr. Goodwrench" by
General Motors**
Reprinted by permission of
General Motors Corporation.

GM vehicles can also be repaired and serviced through independent repair shops; tire, muffler, and battery outlets; mass merchandisers (such as Sears); and service stations. The independents handle a wide variety of makes and models. They emphasize a convenient location, personalized service, more flexible prices, faster service time, and longer hours. One of the largest independent service operations is Master-Care by Firestone, which has thousands of technicians at greater than 1,500 locations throughout the United States who handle 10 million customers per year. Firestone has invested in excess of $25 million in "MasterMind" equipment (a computerized diagnostic device) and $12 million in NCR computer terminals for order processing and inventory control. Annual revenues at MasterCare outlets are about $1 billion.[23]

[23] *Firestone Annual Report,* various years.

The growth in foreign car sales and the increased period of time that consumers hold on to their cars have resulted in more independent servicing of automobiles. Some firms specialize in foreign car work because of higher profit margins. Others accept imports only grudgingly — because of difficulties with getting parts, the metric system, and the relatively small working space under the hood. Long waiting lists at car dealers and relatively high repair prices have also shifted many car owners from dealer service centers to independent firms.

In an attempt to gain business back, more manufacturers have urged their dealers to accept credit cards, promote specials, stress quality control, extend service hours, and provide more accurate repair estimates. Extended warranties, such as Chrysler's 7 year/70,000 mile warranty, also encourage consumers to visit their dealers for repairs and maintenance. Further, computerized technology in newer cars is often better understood by service personnel at new-car dealers than at independent repair shops.[24]

In 1977, the U.S. Supreme Court ruled that attorneys could not be prohibited from advertising their services and fee structures.[25] Since then, legal services advertising has increased significantly and a number of marketing innovations have been implemented. Lawyers now advertise on television and radio and in newspapers and magazines; television advertising expenditures alone annually exceed $60 million. The great majority of attorneys advertise in the Yellow Pages and 75 per cent of medium-to-large law firms use brochures and 50 per cent send out newsletters. As one lawyer recently commented: "Marketing and advertising are areas of the legal profession that are evolving, and [lawyers are] experimenting with new techniques."[26]

Law clinics and franchised law firms have developed. These operations feature a large staff of attorneys, convenient locations (such as in shopping centers), standardized fees and services (such as $100 for a simple will), plain fixtures and furniture, and word-processing systems. The companies concentrate on routine legal services.

The two largest franchised law firms are Hyatt Legal Services — with 185 offices and 500 attorneys — and Jacoby & Meyers — with 150 offices and 300 attorneys. Jacoby & Meyers has the highest advertising budget of any U.S. law firm, spending $6.5 million annually. These are some of the characteristics of Hyatt Legal Services, which is not affiliated with the hotel chain. Hyatt

- ▶ Counsels more than 200,000 clients each year.
- ▶ Has very low prices (e.g., $375 for a divorce compared with $750 to $1,500 for traditional competitors).
- ▶ Spends $4 million per year on television advertising.
- ▶ Sets fees in advance and in writing.
- ▶ Pays new lawyers relatively low salaries.
- ▶ Provides prepaid legal services to workers in several labor unions and companies (such as PepsiCo). These workers pay about $140 per year. Included in this fee are the preparation of wills, deeds, mortgages, house closings, and so on.[27]

---

[24] See Joseph B. White, "Auto Mechanics Struggle to Cope with Technology in Today's Cars," *Wall Street Journal* (July 26, 1988), p. 37.

[25] Today all professionals are able to advertise their services.

[26] Lenore Skenazy, "Jury Is Still Out," *Advertising Age* (April 11, 1988), p. 76; and Tracy A. LaFlamme, "More Lawyers Turn to Marketing as Legal Competition Heats Up," *Marketing News* (September 26, 1988), p. 25.

[27] Patricia Bellew Gray, "Hyatt Legal Services' Fast Growth Leaves Trail of Management Woes," *Wall Street Journal* (May 6, 1987), p. 33; and Laurie P. Cohen, "PepsiCo Will Offer Legal Services to All Employees Through Hyatt," *Wall Street Journal* (January 13, 1989), p. B5.

The marketing of legal services has been met with resistance and objections from many attorneys. They criticize price advertising for stressing price at the expense of quality and mass-marketing techniques as eliminating personalized counseling. They also believe the public's confidence in the profession will decline, information in ads may not be accurate, and overly high consumer expectations will be created. Attorneys applying marketing techniques state that they are making legal services available to new groups of consumers and those who could not otherwise afford them. The majority of attorneys still do not advertise in mass media (except for the Yellow Pages); they rely on referrals.

Nonprofit Marketing

Nonprofit marketing serves the public interest and does not seek financial profits.

As defined in Chapter 7, **nonprofit marketing** is conducted by organizations and individuals which operate in the public interest or to foster a cause and do not seek financial profits. It may involve organizations (religious groups, labor unions, trade associations), people (political candidates), places (resorts, convention centers, industrial sites), and ideas ("stop smoking"), as well as goods and services.

Although nonprofit organizations conduct exchanges, they are not necessarily in the form of dollars for goods and services. Politicians request votes in exchange for promises of better and more effective government services. The U.S. Postal Service wants increased use of zip codes in exchange for improved service and lower rate hikes. The American Cancer Society seeks funds for cancer research and treatment programs.

Often the prices charged by nonprofit organizations have no relationship to the cost or value of services. For example, the Girl Scouts of America sells cookies to raise funds, but only part of the purchase price goes for the cookies. On the other hand, the price of a chest X-ray at a local health clinic may be below its cost or even free.

In the following sections, nonprofit marketing is examined in terms of a comparison with profit-oriented marketing, a classification system, and its extent in the economy. Three examples of nonprofit marketing are examined in depth: marketing by the U.S. Postal Service, marketing by colleges and universities, and marketing by public libraries.

Nonprofit Versus Profit-Oriented Marketing

Nonprofit marketing has both similarities with and distinctions from profit-oriented marketing.

It is important to recognize that there are a number of significant similarities between nonprofit and profit-oriented firms with regard to marketing, as well as many differences. In today's uncertain and competitive environment, it is becoming increasingly necessary for nonprofit organizations to learn and apply appropriate marketing concepts and strategies.[28]

With both nonprofit and profit-oriented marketing, consumers typically can choose among the offerings of competing companies; the benefits provided by competing organizations differ; consumer segments may have distinctive reasons for their choices; consumers are attracted by the most desirable marketing mix; and consumers

---

[28] See Fisher Howe, "What You Need to Know About Fund Raising," *Harvard Business Review*, Vol. 63 (March–April 1985), pp. 18, 22–25; Charles W. Lamb, "Public Sector Marketing Is Different," *Business Horizons*, Vol. 30 (July–August 1987), pp. 56–60; Bonnie S. Guy and Wesley E. Patton, "The Marketing of Altruistic Causes: Understanding Why People Help," *Journal of Consumer Marketing*, Vol. 6 (Winter 1989), pp. 19–30; Karen Schwartz, "Nonprofits' Bottom Line," *Marketing News* (February 13, 1989), pp. 1–2; and Barnaby J. Feder, "A Nonprofit Institution That Counts on Profits," *New York Times* (May 27, 1988), pp. D1, D5.

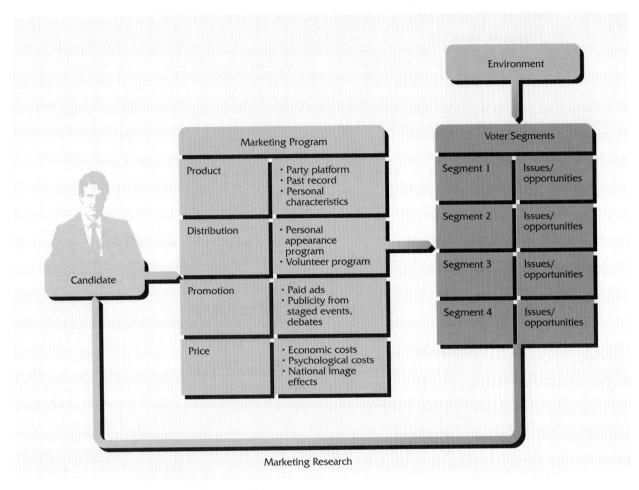

FIGURE 22-7 **The Political Marketing Process**
SOURCE: Adapted by the authors from Phillip B. Niffenegger, "Strategies for Success from the Political Marketers," *Journal of Consumer Marketing,* Vol. 6 (Winter 1989), p. 46. Reprinted by permission.

experience either satisfaction or dissatisfaction with performance. For example, Figure 22-7 shows how a political candidate could seek various target markets (voter segments) through a well-conceived marketing mix. This approach is like the one that a profit-oriented firm would use.

As the research manager for the Direct Marketing Association (DMA), a large nonprofit trade association, once stated:

> Running an association is just like running a commercial business; members are the customers, services are the products, and dues are the prices put on the services.[29]

The DMA is interested in determining the needs of member firms, developing appropriate new services, and improving the value of the association to members, the perceptions of members, and the awareness of the services it does provide. These goals are similar to those of profit-oriented marketers.

[29] Glenda Shasho, "Method May Vary, But Goals Don't When 'Nonprofits' Conduct Research," *Marketing News* (May 13, 1983), Section 2, p. 24.

TABLE 22-1   The Basic Differences Between Nonprofit and Profit-Oriented Marketing

Nonprofit Marketing	Profit-Oriented Marketing
1. Nonprofit marketing is concerned with organizations, people, places, and ideas, as well as goods and services.	1. Profit-oriented marketing is largely concerned with goods and services.
2. Exchanges can be in the form of votes in return for better government or the use of a zip code in return for improved service and lower rate increases.	2. Exchanges are generally in the form of dollars for goods and services.
3. Objectives are more complex because success or failure cannot be measured strictly in financial terms.	3. Objectives are generally stated in terms of sales, profits, and recovery of cash.
4. The benefits of nonprofit services are often not related to consumer payments.	4. The benefits of profit-oriented marketing are usually related to consumer payments.
5. Nonprofit organizations may be expected or required to serve economically unfeasible market segments.	5. Profit-oriented marketing seeks to serve only those market segments that are profitable.
6. Nonprofit organizations typically have two constituencies: clients and donors.	6. Profit-oriented marketing has one constituency: clients.

*Nonprofit marketing is broad in scope and is frequently involved with **social marketing**.*

There are also a number of basic differences in marketing between nonprofit and profit-oriented organizations. These differences are outlined in Table 22-1 and described in the following paragraphs.

Nonprofit marketing includes organizations, people, places, and ideas, as well as goods and services. It is much more likely to promote social programs and ideas than is profit-oriented marketing. Examples include recycling, highway safety, family planning, gun control, and energy conservation. The use of marketing to increase the acceptability of social ideas is referred to as ***social marketing***.

Table 22-2 contains illustrations of the exchange process for organizations, people, places, and ideas. Nonprofit marketing may not generate revenues in day-to-day exchanges. Instead, it may rely on infrequent fund-raising efforts. In addition, a successful marketing campaign may actually lose money if services or goods are provided at less than cost. It is necessary for operating budgets to be large enough to serve the number of anticipated clients, so that none are poorly treated or turned away.

Objectives are sometimes complex because success or failure cannot be measured strictly in financial terms. A nonprofit organization might have this combination of objectives: raise $300,000 from government grants, increase client usage, find a cure for a disease, change public attitudes, and raise $500,000 from private donors. Objectives must include the number of clients to be served, the amount of service to be rendered, and the quality of service to be provided.

Consumer benefits may not be related to their payments.

The benefits of nonprofit organizations are often not distributed on the basis of consumer payments. Only a small portion of the population contracts a disease, requires humanitarian services, visits a museum, uses a public library, or goes to a health clinic in a given year; yet the general public pays to find cures, support fellow citizens, or otherwise assist nonprofit organizations. In many cases, the group that would benefit most from a nonprofit organization's activities may be the one least prone to seek or use them. This occurs for libraries, health clinics, remedial programs, and other nonprofit organizations and activities. With profit-oriented organizations, benefits are usually distributed equitably, based on consumers' direct payments in exchange for goods or services.

TABLE 22-2   Illustrations of the Exchange Process for Organizations, People, Places, and Ideas

	Exchange Process	
Organizations		
College fraternities	Benefits to members: social experience, convenient place to live, assistance from upper classmen and graduates	Benefits to fraternities: membership dues, greater on-campus exposure, improved facilities
People		
Political candidates	Benefits to voters: efficient government, better services, election of candidates with similar views	Benefits to candidates: election, prestige, power
Places		
Major cities as sites for conventions	Benefits to attendees: central locations, cultural facilities, superior accommodations and transportation	Benefits to cities: revenues, prestige, lessening of tax burdens for residents
Ideas		
Nonsmoking campaigns	Benefits to smokers: improved health, better self-image, increased social acceptance	Benefits to nonsmokers: cleaner environment, longer life span for loved ones, lower costs for medical system

Nonprofit organizations are frequently expected, or even required, to serve market segments that profit-oriented organizations find uneconomical. For example, the U.S. Postal Service must maintain rural post offices and Amtrak must provide passenger rail service on routes across sparsely populated areas. This may give profit-oriented firms an advantage because they can concentrate their efforts on the most lucrative market segments.

Although profit-oriented firms have one primary constituency to which they offer goods and services and from which they receive payment, the typical nonprofit organization has two constituencies: *clients* — for whom it provides membership, elected officials, locations, ideas, goods, and services — and *donors* — from whom it receives resources (which may be time from volunteers or money from foundations and individuals). Often there is little overlap between clients and donors.

*Nonprofit organizations must satisfy **clients** and **donors**.*

Private nonprofit organizations have also been granted a number of legal advantages over their profit-oriented counterparts. These include tax-deductible contributions, exemptions from most sales and real-estate taxes, and special reduced postal rates.

Classifying Nonprofit Marketing

Nonprofit marketing may be classified on the basis of tangibility, organization structure, objectives, and constituency. This four-way classification is shown in Figure 22-8. As in the service-marketing classification, a nonprofit organization would be categorized by a combination of these factors. For example, postage stamps for collectors are tangible products, distributed by the federal government, intended to reduce the deficit of the Postal Service, and aimed at the general public.

The classification of nonprofit marketing may be based on tangibility, structure, objectives, and constituency.

As noted before, nonprofit marketing may involve organizations, people, places, ideas, goods, and services. For example, organizations include foundations, universities, religious institutions, and government; people include politicians and volunteers;

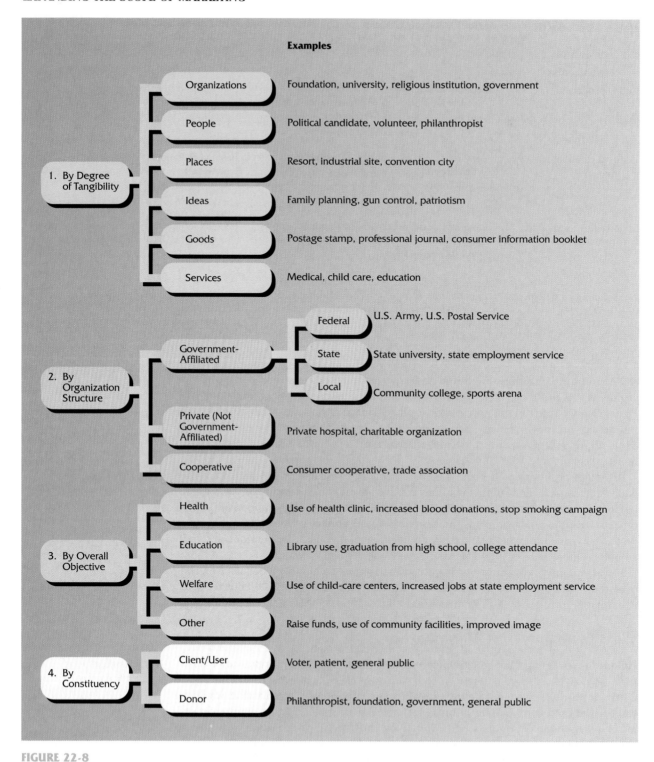

Examples

1. By Degree of Tangibility

- Organizations — Foundation, university, religious institution, government
- People — Political candidate, volunteer, philanthropist
- Places — Resort, industrial site, convention city
- Ideas — Family planning, gun control, patriotism
- Goods — Postage stamp, professional journal, consumer information booklet
- Services — Medical, child care, education

2. By Organization Structure

- Government-Affiliated
  - Federal — U.S. Army, U.S. Postal Service
  - State — State university, state employment service
  - Local — Community college, sports arena
- Private (Not Government-Affiliated) — Private hospital, charitable organization
- Cooperative — Consumer cooperative, trade association

3. By Overall Objective

- Health — Use of health clinic, increased blood donations, stop smoking campaign
- Education — Library use, graduation from high school, college attendance
- Welfare — Use of child-care centers, increased jobs at state employment service
- Other — Raise funds, use of community facilities, improved image

4. By Constituency

- Client/User — Voter, patient, general public
- Donor — Philanthropist, foundation, government, general public

FIGURE 22-8
A Classification System for Nonprofit Marketing

Marketing Controversy

Should Museum Shops Have Tax-Exempt Status?

New York's Metropolitan Museum of Art (the "Met") has shops in Short Hills, New Jersey; Stamford, Connecticut; and Macy's main store in Manhattan. These shops carry T-shirts, souvenirs, jewelry, educational tapes, and reproductions of artifacts. They also sell "museum collections" of sheets and fabrics, with the Met deriving royalties from manufacturers licensing its name.

A Met spokesperson says that income from retail shops is vital to its long-run existence—because earnings from its endowment fund do not cover operating costs. In 1967, endowment income covered 62 per cent of its annual budget; but in 1988, endowment income accounted for only 17 per cent of the budget. During 1988, earnings from retail operations contributed 8 per cent ($5 million) of the museum's budget. According to the Museum Store Association, the majority of its members' retail operations earn less than $150,000 per year.

The Coalition for Unfair Competition, representing twenty-seven industry trade associations, is concerned about nonprofit institutions such as the Met encroaching on retailing. It believes these institutions "are enjoying lower postal rates and avoiding business taxes at the expense of tax-paying enterprises." Others point out that profit-oriented retailers also sell educational items but have no tax-exempt status. For example, Nature Co. is a 19-store chain specializing in the sale of items relating to nature and wildlife.

The U.S. House Ways & Means Committee has been considering whether to tax nonprofit groups when the items they sell are unrelated to their major mission. One subcommittee proposal would tax museums when they sell reproductions and artifacts whose value exceeds $50, unless they are "educational materials." Royalty income not tied to a museum's educational efforts (such as the Met's earnings from sheets and fabrics), would also be subject to income tax. Earnings from the sale of items priced under $15 (such as souvenirs and T-shirts) would remain tax exempt.

What do you think?

SOURCE: Based on material in Teri Agins, "Growth of Museum Shops Stirs Debate on Tax Status," *Wall Street Journal* (February 27, 1989), p. B1, B4.

places include resort cities and industrial centers; ideas include family planning and patriotism; goods include postage stamps and professional journals; and services include medical care, child care, and education.

Nonprofit organizations may have one of three alternative structures: government-affiliated (federal, state, local), private, or cooperative. For example, the federal government markets military service to potential recruits, postal services, and various goods and services. State governments market universities and employment services. Local governments market colleges, libraries, and sports arenas. In addition, government marketing is often used to increase voter registration, secure approval of bonds, and obtain passage of school and library budgets. Private organizations market hospitals, charities, social services, and other goods and services. They also use marketing to increase membership and donations. Cooperative organizations (such as the Better Business Bureau) aid consumers and/or businesses. The success of cooperatives depends on their ability to attract and maintain a large membership base and on their efficiency in performing functions.

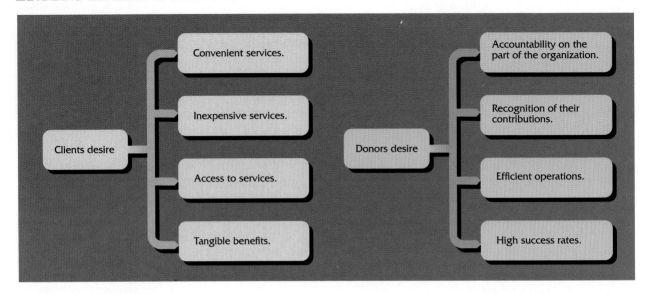

FIGURE 22-9   Clients Versus Donors

Overall nonprofit marketing objectives may be divided into health (increase the number of nonsmokers), education (increase usage of the local library), welfare (list more job openings at a state employment office), and other (increase membership in the Boy Scouts) components.

Last, nonprofit organizations must remember that they usually require the support of both clients/users and donors. Clients/users are interested in the direct benefits they obtain from participation in an organization, such as their improved health, education, or welfare. Donors are concerned about the efficiency of operations, success rates, the availability of goods and services, and the recognition of their contributions. For each constituency, an organization must correctly pinpoint its target market. As an example, the League of Women Voters might concentrate on unregistered voters during an enrollment drive and seek funds from corporate foundations. Figure 22-9 shows some of the differing interests between clients and donors.

The Extent of Nonprofit Marketing in the Economy

Nonprofit organizations are diverse in their focus and use of marketing.

Thousands of organizations and individuals engage in nonprofit marketing in the United States; and their efforts vary widely, as these examples show:

▶ The American Red Cross is the largest charitable organization in the United States, with annual revenues of $1 billion. It spends $76 million each year for fund raising and administration. The Red Cross is active in joint marketing promotions with firms such as Johnson & Johnson, Upjohn, Warner-Lambert, and Searle. These firms pay the Red Cross royalty fees for using its name and logo in "cause-related" promotions.[30]

▶ Labor unions have increased their involvement in image-oriented television commercials since the highly successful International Ladies Garment Workers Union

[30] Janice E. Simpson, "Some Charity Begins at the Cash Register," *Wall Street Journal* (November 24, 1987), p. 33.

Watch a scholar overcome a hurdle.™

FIGURE 22-10
Promoting Women's College Sports
Minneapolis/St. Paul firms have donated services and space to build awareness of women's sports at the University of Minnesota. This ad is used on billboards and bus shelters.
Reprinted by permission.

(ILGWU) ads began fifteen years ago. These ads featured workers singing, "Look for the union label." In 1987–1988, the United Auto Workers union spent $7 million on television commercials, while the AFL-CIO spent $13 million. The goals of the ads are to change the public's perception of unions. Said an AFL-CIO spokesperson, "Unfortunately, what you see on TV [news shows] is unions on strike."[31]

▶ At the University of Minnesota, the women's sports programs used a small yearly budget for marketing expenditures to improve the image of women's sports and increase attendance at events. To supplement this limited budget, a number of Minnesota businesses and local television stations donated media time; and an advertising agency donated creative services. One slogan was "watch a scholar," a reference to the high proportion of women athletes who graduate college.[32] See Figure 22-10.

[31] Associated Press, "Unions Turn to TV Ads to Boost Membership," *Marketing News* (December 19, 1988), p. 6.
[32] Kevin T. Higgins, "Gopher the Gold," *Marketing News* (February 14, 1986), pp. 1, 32.

▶ State lotteries generate billions of dollars in revenues each year. In such states as New York, Pennsylvania, Massachusetts, and Michigan, annual sales exceed $1 billion apiece. The surplus from these revenues (after deducting prize money and expenses) are allocated to education, highways, and so on. Many states use heavy television and radio advertising; some even use direct mail.[33]

▶ Amtrak, the federally sponsored rail service, carries 22 million passengers and has revenues exceeding $1.1 billion yearly. To stimulate business, it is wooing passengers from the airlines with "skiing packages, movies and phones on some trains, and even an experimental return of linen and china to dining cars."[34]

▶ In 1988, candidates for the U.S. Congress spent a total of $457 million on their campaigns. Of this amount, $256 million was spent by candidates for the House of Representatives and $201 million by Senate candidates.[35]

Illustrations of Nonprofit Marketing

This section examines marketing by three nonprofit organizations: the U.S. Postal Service, colleges and universities, and public libraries. The activities of these organizations differ because of their degree of tangibility, structure, objectives, and constituencies.

The Postal Reorganization Act of 1970 created the U.S. Postal Service as an independent federal agency and called on it to become a self-supporting enterprise. It was previously a traditional government agency with no mandate to improve its marketing efforts. Today the Postal Service has 750,000 employees, generates yearly revenues of $33 to $35 billion, and delivers 150 billion pieces of mail annually. Its competition is intense and the Postal Service must deliver all mail, no matter how uneconomical. Despite its best efforts, the Postal Service usually has a tough time breaking even; and all rate increases must be approved by a Board of Governors.[36]

To protect itself against competitors and stimulate consumer demand for its services, the Postal Service has enacted a strong marketing program that is comprised of a mix of continuing and new offerings and extensive advertising. For example, Express Mail delivers packages and letters to distant cities overnight; these items can be dropped at specially designated collection boxes (thus eliminating waiting lines). Express Mail produces over $500 million in yearly revenues. ZIP + 4 is an improved zip code service that offers cost savings for both the Postal Service and its business customers; however, it has not been widely used by customers and is considered a disappointment by the Postal Service.

Self-service stamp vending machines are available in shopping centers. A special commemorative stamp program was started in 1975; annual sales now exceed $200 million. Many post offices sell such items as inexpensive hand-held scales, padded envelopes for small packages, airmail markers, and a device for adhering stamps to envelopes.[37]

---

[33] Laura Loro, "Lotteries Sell Luck at Home," *Advertising Age* (September 26, 1988), p. 68E; and Paul Magnusson, "A National Lottery Is Not Such a Long Shot," *Business Week* (April 10, 1989), p. 57.

[34] William E. Schmidt, "Amtrak Rolls Up Records in Riders and Is Expanding," *New York Times* (March 13, 1989), pp. A1, B7.

[35] "Democrats Spent Most on Election," *New York Times* (February 26, 1989), p. 27.

[36] Authors' estimates.

[37] Kathleen Behof, "Postal Service Gets Serious About Selling," *Sales & Marketing Management* (July 1, 1985), pp. 64–65; Jeanne Saddler, "Postal Service Seeks to Dispel Bad Image," *Wall Street Journal* (May 27, 1987), p. 6; Joe Agnew, "Postal Service Gives Marketing Its Stamp of Approval," *Marketing News* (August 14, 1987), p. 17; and Laurie Baum, "Where You Can Study Postal Management 101," *Business Week* (April 11, 1988), pp. 84J–84K.

The Postal Service has an annual advertising budget of $40 to $45 million, with a large portion of this going to Express Mail, direct-mail ads for business accounts, and commemorative stamps. Young & Rubicam is its advertising agency.[38] Figure 22-11 shows recent Postal Service ads.

[38] "U.S. Government," *Advertising Age* (September 28, 1988), p. 141.

Colleges and universities are aware that the years of rapid growth in overall enroll-ments are over. Since 1977, the number of high school graduates has fallen steadily and will not level off until 1992 (when there will be 2.3 million high school graduates, compared to 3.2 million in 1977).[39] Accordingly, new markets are being sought and marketing strategies are being employed by more educational institutions than ever before.

Many schools are actively seeking nontraditional students. Today 43 per cent of all college students attend part-time; and by 1992, at least one-half of college students will be at least twenty-five years old.[40] Furthermore, the National Center for Educational Statistics estimates that about 20 million adults are now involved in some type of higher education program at colleges, universities, and private companies. The adult market requires class meeting times that do not infringe on work commitments and convenient locations (which may be at work, at a neighborhood library, or in a busi-ness district).

Traditional students are also being actively pursued. Many colleges and universities typically spend hundreds of dollars on recruitment efforts for each new student that enrolls. A large number of schools purchase direct-mailing lists of prospective stu-dents from the Educational Testing Service (the organization that administers college-board examinations). And hundreds of colleges now distribute recruiting films or videocassettes, costing up to $60,000 and more to produce, to high schools.

The growing use of marketing by colleges and universities is not confined to poor- or average-quality institutions. For example, the California Institute of Technology (Cal Tech) sponsors receptions and slide shows for accepted students in two dozen metro-politan areas and holds a "pre-frosh weekend" in April—complete with a faculty barbeque, a visit to the Magic Mountain amusement park, and a tour of the nearby Jet Propulsion Laboratories (which Cal Tech runs for the National Aeronautics Adminis-tration). Says Cal Tech's admissions director about the pre-frosh weekend, "We want to give a little Southern California feeling to the students."[41]

At Dartmouth College in New Hampshire, a prominent alumnus pays for 80 top student prospects to fly in from throughout the United States to participate in "Expe-rience Dartmouth Weekend." At Colby College in Maine, the admissions office has sent a 9-minute videocassette to high schools across the country; and its recruiters are covering a much wider geographic area. The school believes it is doing a better job "telling the Colby story."[42]

This is a crucial period for public libraries. Most U.S. adults visit a public library one or fewer times during a typical year. Juvenile use in many public libraries has declined significantly since the mid-1970s. U.S. demographic trends are also not favorable for long-run increases in the library's prime market because libraries have been most successful with children (a declining proportion of the population).

To respond to the changing composition and needs of the marketplace, as well as to satisfy donors (the local communities that fund them), many public libraries are becoming more marketing-oriented. Some are turning into multimedia centers, where

---

[39] National Center for Education Statistics, U.S. Department of Education.

[40] Edward B. Fiske, "Private Colleges Flourish Despite Forecasts That They Will Shrivel Away," *New York Times* (September 7, 1988), p. B8.

[41] Gary Putka, "With Applications Down, Top Colleges Get Friendlier," *Wall Street Journal* (April 7, 1989), p. B1.

[42] Ibid.; and Deirdre Carmody, "Admissions Boom at Top Colleges," *New York Times* (September 21, 1988), p. B9.

even tools, toys, and video games can be borrowed. Others are changing into community centers, by providing meeting rooms for neighborhood groups. Still other libraries are appealing to markets they have served poorly in the past by implementing literacy programs, offering specialized collections for minority groups, accommodating disabled persons, and reaching out to senior citizens. Some libraries are doing all of these things.[43]

More public libraries are beginning to utilize strategic marketing planning. For example, a number are using clear consumer-oriented mission statements that focus on promoting increased awareness, acceptance, and use of public libraries; securing and maintaining adequate funding; and providing the materials wanted by the most people in the service area. They also use marketing research during the planning process and regularly conduct satisfaction studies.

Summary

1. *To distinguish between the marketing of services and goods* Service marketing involves goods rental, goods alteration and repair, and personal services. In general, services are less tangible, more perishable, less separable from their provider, and more variable in quality than goods that are sold. The effect of these characteristics is greatest for personal services.

2. *To discuss the use of marketing by service firms, special considerations for service marketers, a classification system for service firms, the role of services in the U.S. economy, and applications of service marketing* Many service firms have lagged behind manufacturing firms in the use of marketing because of their technical emphasis, their small size, less competition, the lack of a need for marketing, the high esteem of consumers for certain service providers, past prohibitions on advertising, and a dislike of marketing by some service professionals.

There are often special considerations for service firms in planning their marketing strategies. They need to enact strategies that enable consumers to perceive their offerings more tangibly, that make their offerings less perishable, that encourage consumers to seek them out but enable a number of employees to be viewed as competent, that make performance as efficient and consistent as possible, and that use peripheral services to complement core services.

Services can be classified by the market served, the degree of tangibility, the skill of the service provider, the goal of the service provider, the degree of regulation, labor intensiveness, and the amount of customer contact. An organization would be classified on the basis of a combination of these factors.

The United States is the leading service economy in the world, with 75 per cent of the American private labor force employed in services. U.S. families spend 53 per cent of their income on services. Business services have also experienced significant growth in recent years.

In this chapter, marketing practices of hotels, car repair and servicing firms, and lawyers are examined.

3. *To distinguish between nonprofit and profit-oriented marketing* Nonprofit marketing is conducted by organizations and individuals which operate in the public interest or to foster a cause and do not seek financial profits. It has both similarities with and differences from profit-oriented marketing. These are some of the major differences. Nonprofit marketing is more likely to involve organizations, people, places, and ideas. Nonprofit firms' exchanges do not have to involve money, and their objectives can be difficult to formulate. The benefits of nonprofit firms are often distributed unequally, and economically unfeasible market segments may have to be served. Two

---

[43] See, for example, Bessie B. Moore and Carol Fraser Fisk, ''Improving Library Services to the Aging,'' *Library Journal* (April 15, 1988), pp. 46–47; and Jean Ann Tevis and Brenda Crawley, ''Reaching Out to Older Adults,'' *Library Journal* (May 1, 1988), pp. 37–40.

constituencies must be satisfied by nonprofit organizations: clients and donors.

4. *To discuss a classification system for nonprofit marketing, the role of nonprofit marketing in the U.S. economy, and applications of nonprofit marketing* Nonprofit marketing can be classified on the basis of tangibility, organization structure, objectives, and constituency. A nonprofit organization would be categorized by a combination of these factors.

Marketing efforts by nonprofit institutions vary widely but have increased greatly in a very short time. They play a key role in the U.S. economy.

In this chapter, the marketing practices of the U.S. Postal Service, colleges and universities, and public libraries are examined.

Key Terms

service marketing (p. 674)
industrialization of services (p. 678)
hard technologies (p. 678)
soft technologies (p. 678)

hybrid technologies (p. 678)
core services (p. 680)
peripheral services (p. 680)
hidden service sector (p. 682)

nonprofit marketing (p. 688)
social marketing (p. 690)
clients (p. 691)
donors (p. 691)

Review Questions

1. Why have service firms lagged behind manufacturers in the development and use of marketing?
2. How can promotion be used to make a service more tangible?
3. Why can't many services be stockpiled?
4. Describe how hard, soft, and hybrid technologies may be used to industrialize services.
5. What are peripheral services? Discuss their advantages and disadvantages from a marketing perspective.
6. What is the hidden service sector?
7. What are some of the similarities and differences involved in the marketing efforts used by nonprofit and profit-oriented organizations?
8. When is an organization engaged in social marketing?
9. Discuss the factors that may be used to classify nonprofit marketing.
10. How do the goals of clients and donors differ?

Discussion Questions

1. Present three ways a beauty salon can match demand and supply on days following holidays.
2. What peripheral services should be considered by an indoor tennis center? Why?
3. Classify an accounting service and an appliance-repair firm using the seven factors shown in Figure 22-3.
4. Present five objectives that could be used to evaluate the effectiveness of a state motor vehicle office.
5. Discuss several innovative fund-raising programs for the American Red Cross to use.

◄ CASE 1 ►

MasterCard: Is It Mastering the Possibilities?*

Although MasterCard's advertising has advised customers and potential customers to "Master the Possibilities," many observers say that MasterCard International has been unable to master its own possibilities. The company, which is controlled by about 150 large banks, has had a host of problem areas.

MasterCard incurred a loss of $5.3 million in 1987, when bad debts totaled 2.9 per cent of receivables (versus Visa's bad debts of 2.4 per cent). Because of this loss, MasterCard cut back on customer solicitations through mass mailings (which could have bad-debt rates exceeding 10 per cent).

It attracted criticism from retailers and others after announcing an increase in the fees that card-issuing banks would charge retailers for each customer transaction made with MasterCard. The rate increase was viewed as excessive by firms such as Wal-Mart and Toys "R" Us and had to be rolled back.

The fee rollback helped retailers, but it cost MasterCard in terms of lost profitability. The firm also suffered because the higher fee was intended to provide member banks with an incentive to push MasterCard rather than Visa. According to an executive at one of the largest card-issuing banks: "The fee was very important to us. If MasterCard had remained committed to the higher fee, we definitely would issue more MasterCards."

MasterCard has experienced a decline in market share. Until the late 1970s, it had the number one position in worldwide credit-card charge volume. However, in 1979, Visa passed MasterCard and became the market leader—which it remains today. The market share gap between Visa and MasterCard has steadily widened.

* The data in this case are drawn from Judith Graham, "Master-Card Readies $20 Million Ad Campaign," *Advertising Age* (March 31, 1989), p. 3, 73; Robert Guenther, "MasterCard Confronts Major Challenges," *Wall Street Journal* (November 16, 1988), p. A8; and Frederic Miller and Jonathan B. Levine, "Is MasterCard Mastering the Possibilities?" *Business Week* (October 10, 1988), p. 123.

The relatively new American Express Optima card (which—unlike American Express' other cards that require full payment each month—is a true credit card and allows customers to pay their bills over an extended time period) is encroaching on MasterCard's market share. In less than two years on the market, Optima became one of the top ten credit cards in the United States.

Both MasterCard and Visa are owned by member banks that support them with dues. Bankers are increasingly questioning the rationale of supporting two competing organizations. As one banker says, "The infighting between MasterCard and Visa is hurting us all. We should be fighting AmEx."

Although MasterCard developed the first premium bank credit card in 1983, Visa is pressing MasterCard with heavy promotion. In 1988, within six months after introducing its premium card, Visa was able to equal MasterCard in members.

In order to remedy this situation—and capitalize on its powerful name (one study found MasterCard to be the fourteenth most powerful brand name in the United States)—the company began a new advertising campaign with a $20 million budget and the theme of "Master the Moment" (to replace the "Master the Possibilities" slogan) in 1989. The new campaign's "strength is that it breaks through and defines MasterCard in a way people are not used to thinking about it."

For the first time, MasterCard's advertising now stresses the card's cash-advance features and the ability of a cardholder to obtain funds from Master-Card's nationwide Cirrus teller machine network. The new ads are also designed to change the public's perception of MasterCard as a "woman's shopping card."

As the editor of *Credit Card Management* observes, it is imperative for MasterCard to enhance its image: "Credit-card marketing now focuses on what the card can do for you. [Referring to American Express' "Membership Has Its Privileges Campaign" and Visa's aggressive comparative advertising.] But MasterCard has been out there with a very fuzzy image and neglected to explain what the card can actually do."

Part of MasterCard's fuzzy image has been due to its past practice of frequently changing advertising campaigns. For example, in 1988, MasterCard devoted part of its advertising budget to a short-lived fourth-quarter "Choose to Make a Difference" promotion.

QUESTIONS

1. Comment on the difficulties in marketing MasterCard because of its intangibility. How would you address this issue?
2. How should MasterCard position itself against Visa and American Express?
3. How can MasterCard industrialize its services?
4. Present a comprehensive marketing plan to increase MasterCard's market share.

◄ CASE 2 ►

Marketing Comes to Nonprofit Hospitals[†]

Health-care marketers cite service quality, physician referral systems, and focused health-care programs as three key factors affecting a nonprofit hospital's long-run success.

Service quality is viewed as the most important issue for nonprofit hospitals to address. Thus, health-care marketers are using new procedures to measure and quantify service quality. Among the tools being applied at a growing number of hospitals are "total quality" performance measures and customer-patient satisfaction measures. According to the president of the Academy for Health Services Marketing:

> Understanding how quality is produced, consumed, measured, and assured is of tremendous importance in health care today. It will be even more so in the future.

Despite differences in their size, location, management style, and ownership format, the University of Michigan's University Medical Center, Methodist Hospital Systems of Houston, and Boston University Medical Center's University Hospital are among the nonprofit hospitals emphasizing high service quality. As the director of planning and marketing at the University of Michigan's medical cen-

ter notes: "Without question, hospitals are rediscovering the position of quality as a differentiating value in marketing their services."

Methodist Hospital of Houston features such innovative services as helicopter transport for seriously ill patients and seeks to maintain a technological advantage over other hospitals. Boston University has used university-designed media inserts, distributed throughout the Northeast (including in the *New York Times*), to communicate its record of excellence in medical care. Some inserts focused on a new Atrium Pavilion as one means of differentiating Boston University's hospital from among the four medical schools and eleven teaching hospitals in Boston.

Physician referral systems are becoming more valued as nonprofit hospitals strive to generate and maintain a steady flow of patients. For example, at the University of Alabama in Birmingham, computer terminals have been installed in the offices of 100 physicians who make referrals to the university's hospital. These terminals provide instantaneous retrieval of hospital medical records and professional data bases. As a hospital administrator says, "We envision more patient self-referral in the 1990s, and we have to continue to develop better materials for MDs and patients."

Computer links enable physicians to get laboratory results more quickly and aid them in diagnosing patient symptoms. They also help in bonding

[†] The data in this case are drawn from Larry M. Strum, "Health Care Marketers Eye Hot Topics," *Marketing News* (February 27, 1989), pp. 1, 10.

doctors to specific hospitals. According to the vice-president of planning and marketing at Lutheran General Hospital, Park Ridge, Illinois, "Physician bonding means bonding to the hospital by making the physician feel very comfortable and making the services of the hospital very accessible to the doctor. We focus most of our energies on marketing to doctors."

University Hospital in Boston provides promotional materials to its staff of house physicians, as well as to frequent and important potential referrers. New York's Mount Sinai Medical Center has run ads in major daily newspapers to promote physician referrals.

Lastly, many nonprofit hospitals are targeting health-care programs at specific groups of patients and types of health conditions. Each program requires a marketing effort that concentrates on the special needs of a particular market segment. Focused offerings include:

▷ Gerontology programs dealing with older patients' sociological and mental condition—in addition to geriatric programs (covering medical and physical conditions).
▷ Community-oriented women's health-care centers promoting services such as public education classes and outdoor weekend health fairs.
▷ Well-publicized mobile mammography centers that travel through a hospital's service area on a scheduled basis.
▷ Drug and alcohol abuse treatment centers.

Hospitals' increasing focus on specific groups of patients and health conditions is causing them to rethink their marketing strategies. A number of nonprofit hospitals now devote less of their promotional budgets to overall image ads and more to targeted programs. These hospitals are also more likely to evaluate the success of a promotion campaign on the basis of facilities' use.

QUESTIONS

1. How should a nonprofit hospital deal with the intangibility and perishability of its offerings, the potential variability of service quality, and the use of peripheral services?
2. What do you think are the basic differences in the role of marketing at a nonprofit hospital versus a profit-oriented hospital? Explain your answer.
3. Cite several different constituencies for a nonprofit hospital. What would be the marketing goal in dealing with each one?
4. Comment on the marketing strategies identified in this case.

CHAPTER *23*

Marketing and Society

F ormal ethics codes are hot these days. Companies without them are scrambling to commit corporate values to paper. Companies that already have codes are rushing to update, disseminate, and interpret them.

But difficulties—and skeptics—abound. Some employees resist codes. They feel pressured to go along, and resent having their own values questioned. And ethics specialists say some codes are mere window dressing: They look good but aren't expected to interfere with the realities of the business world.

In 1987, the American Marketing Association (AMA)—the leading professional association in marketing—adopted a new code of ethics. This code deals with the responsibilities of marketers for the consequences of their actions; the honesty and fairness of marketers; the rights and duties of the parties in the marketing exchange process; and organizational relationships, such as dealings with employees, suppliers, and customers. Any AMA member found to violate the code could have his or her association membership suspended or revoked.

The AMA code has come at a very appropriate time for us as marketers. Why? As the director of the AMA task force that developed the code noted: "Our hope is to encourage businesses, institutions, and organizations to establish their own ethical policies that are widely communicated and enforced through standard control systems. We hope that the AMA will be a leader and catalyst in helping them to be more ethical."

Here are two illustrations of the use of ethics codes by companies. Johnson & Johnson's code of ethics is "a unifying force that keeps individual business units marching together." The code addresses both the need for the firm to make a sound profit and the need for it to respect employees as individuals, to make high-quality products, and to serve society. The firm's ethical code is credited with successfully guiding it through its two Tylenol product-tampering crises. To keep the code current and instill ethical values in its top managers, the company has executives attend meetings to discuss ethics. Recently, 1,200 managers (in groups of 25) attended a two-day seminar. "Challenge meetings" are also held twice each year for new top managers.

Code of Ethics

Members of the American Marketing Association (AMA) are committed to ethical professional conduct. They have joined together in subscribing to this Code of Ethics embracing the following topics:

Responsibilities of the Marketer

Marketers must accept responsibility for the consequence of their activities and make every effort to ensure that their decisions, recommendations, and actions function to identify, serve, and satisfy all relevant publics: customers, organizations and society.

Marketers' professional conduct must be guided by:

1. The basic rule of professional ethics: not knowingly to do harm;
2. The adherence to all applicable laws and regulations;
3. The accurate representation of their education, training and experience; and
4. The active support, practice and promotion of this Code Ethics.

Honesty and Fairness

Marketers shall uphold and advance the integrity,

■ Participa should be

1. Produc for the
2. Comm sevice
3. All par financ
4. Appro adjust cernin

It is unde is not lim. marketer:

In the are ment,
● disclos produc
● identifi tion th; impact
● identifi

In the are
● avoidal

Reprinted by permission of the American Marketing Association.

At Hertz, despite an ethics code and the requirement that employees sign a compliance statement, the company had a major scandal a few years ago. Car renters involved in accidents, and their insurers, were overcharged $13 million in repairs between 1978 and 1985. As much as 80 per cent of the overcharges were the result of Hertz billing the renters and their insurers for the retail costs of car repairs while Hertz received quantity discounts on the repairs. Hertz's senior management approved this practice on the advice of in-house counsel (who pointed out that Avis, Budget, and Alamo followed similar practices). However, unlike its competitors, Hertz did not disclose to customers that they would be billed for damages at "prevailing retail rates." Hertz subsequently fired 19 executives and refunded more than $3 million to customers and their insurers. Says Hertz's chairman, "If I catch one guy billing at something other than cost, I'll throw him out the window myself."[1]

In this chapter, we will examine several issues relating to the interaction of marketing with overall society as well as with consumers.

[1] Amanda Bennett, "Ethics Codes Spread Despite Skepticism," *Wall Street Journal* (July 15, 1988), p. 17; "AMA Adopts New Code of Ethics," *Marketing News* (September 11, 1987), pp. 1, 10; and John A. Byrne, "Businesses Are Signing Up for Ethics 101," *Business Week* (February 15, 1988), pp. 56–57.

Overview

Individually (at the company level) and collectively (at the industry level), the activities involved with the marketing of goods, services, organizations, people, places, and ideas can have a strong impact on society. Such marketing activities have the potential for both positive and negative consequences regarding factors such as

- ▶ The quality of life (standard of living).
- ▶ Consumer expectations and satisfaction with goods, services, and so on.
- ▶ Consumer choice.
- ▶ Product design and safety.
- ▶ Product durability.
- ▶ Product and distribution costs.
- ▶ Final prices.
- ▶ Competition.
- ▶ Natural resources, the landscape, and environmental pollution.
- ▶ Communications with consumers.
- ▶ Employment.
- ▶ Innovation.
- ▶ Deceptive actions.

For example, in the United States, marketing practices have made a wide variety of goods and services available at relatively low prices and through convenient locations. These include food products, transportation goods and services, clothing, entertainment, books, insurance, banking, television sets, furniture, and personal computers. On the other hand, marketing activities can sometimes create unrealistic consumer expectations, result in costly minor product design changes, or adversely affect the environment.

A large number of persons feel that marketing practices are not always satisfactory.

People's perceptions of marketing are mixed, at best. Over the years, studies by R.H. Bruskin, Simmons, and A.C. Nielsen have shown that many Americans feel cheated in their purchases due to deception, lack of proper information, high-pressure sales presentations, and so on. Others have reported that consumers may believe they are being "ripped off" when prices are increased. And waiting on store lines and poor customer service are two other key areas of consumer unhappiness.

Companies need to recognize that consumer dissatisfaction is not always transmitted to them. Consumers may just decide not to buy a product and privately complain to friends. Only a small percentage of disgruntled consumers usually take the time to write or call offending companies. The true level of consumer dissatisfaction may be "hidden." Yet a recent study found that just 9 per cent of those consumers who are dissatisfied, but do not complain, buy the product again. In contrast, over one-half of those who complain and have their complaint resolved buy again.[2]

In Chapter 23, the discussion of marketing and society is broken into two broad categories: social responsibility — which involves the general public, employees, channel members, stockholders, competitors, and others; and consumerism — which involves the consumers of a firm's offering.

---

[2] Patricia Sellers, "How to Handle Customers' Gripes," *Fortune* (October 24, 1988), p. 92.

Social Responsibility

Social responsibility involves a concern for "the consequences of a person's or institution's acts as they might affect the interests of others. Corporate social responsibility is seriously considering the impact of the company's actions and operating in a way that balances short-term profit needs with society's long-term needs; thus ensuring the company's survival in a healthy environment."[3]

Social responsibility requires that marketing actions not only seek to achieve a firm's sales and profit goals, but also seek to protect or enhance society's interests. This calls for both the company to be accountable to society for its actions and for consumers to act responsibly (such as disposing of trash properly and not being abusive to salespeople). Figure 23-1 shows some of the socially responsible activities of McDonald's.

From a marketing perspective, social responsibility also encompasses the ***socioecological view of marketing.*** This concept states that companies, their customers, and others should consider all the stages in a product's life span from raw materials to the junkpile in developing, selling, purchasing, using, and disposing of the product; and that they should incorporate the interests of all consumers who are influenced by the use of a good or service, including involuntary consumers who must share the consequences of someone else's consumption.[4] For instance, how much of a scarce resource should a firm use in making a product? What should be the rights and responsibilities of smokers and nonsmokers to one another?

There are times when social responsibility poses dilemmas for companies and/or their customers because various popular goods and services may have potential adverse effects on consumer or societal well-being. Examples of items that offer such dilemmas are tobacco products, no-return bottles, food with high taste appeal but low nutritional content, shoes with high heels, crash diet plans, and liquor.

Until the 1960s, it was accepted that marketing's role was limited to satisfying customers and generating profits. Environmental resources, such as air, water, energy, and paper, were viewed as limitless. Responsibility to the general public was rarely considered. Now many companies realize that they should be responsive to the general public, environmental issues, employees, channel members, stockholders, and competitors — as well as to their customers. Table 23-1 contains examples of how marketing can be socially responsible in these areas. As an American Express report on public responsibility recently noted:

> At American Express, we measure performance by profitability and return on investment. There is, however, another significant measure: How we fulfill our responsibility to the communities from which our profits are derived. Public responsibility is a fundamental corporate value at American Express. It is visible in everything we do — from marketing to philanthropy, from our hiring practices to our consumer education programs. Some might call our traditions of caring and involvement enlightened self-interest. We call

*Social responsibility benefits society. The **socioecological view of marketing** considers the environment and involuntary consumers.*

---

[3] Peter D. Bennett (Editor), *Dictionary of Marketing Terms* (Chicago: American Marketing Association, 1988), p. 189.

[4] Etienne Cracco and Jacques Restenne, "The Socio-ecological Product," *MSU Business Topics,* Vol. 19 (Summer 1971), pp. 27–34. See also James H. Leigh, Patrick E. Murphy, and Ben M. Enis, "A New Approach to Measuring Socially Responsible Consumption Tendencies," *Journal of Macromarketing,* Vol. 8 (Spring 1988), pp. 5–20.

FIGURE 23-1
Social Responsibility at McDonald's
Reprinted by permission.

it common sense. Contributing to the quality of life in our communities is just good business.[5]

Both company and consumer activities have a significant impact on natural resources, the landscape, pollution, planned obsolescence, and standards of ethics. Each of these areas is discussed in the following subsections.

[5] *American Express Public Responsibility: A Report of Recent Activities* (1987), p. 3.

TABLE 23-1   Examples of Socially Responsible Marketing Practices

Regarding the General Public and the Environment

Recycling of products
Elimination of offensive signs and billboards
Proper disposal of waste
Use of goods and services requiring low levels of environmental resources
Hiring of the hard-core unemployed
Involvement in the community
Donations to nonprofit organizations

Regarding Employees

Ample internal communications
Employee input into decisions
Employee training about social issues and the appropriate responses to them
No reprisals against employees who uncover questionable company policies
Recognition of socially responsible employees

Regarding Channel Members

Honoring verbal as well as written commitments
Fair distribution of scarce goods
Adherence to reasonable requests of channel members
Not forcing channel members to act irresponsibly
No coercion of channel members
Cooperative programs addressed to the general public and the environment

Regarding Stockholders

Honest reporting and financial disclosure
Publicity of company activities
Stockholder participation in setting socially responsible policy
Explanation of social issues affecting the company
Earning a responsible profit

Regarding Competitors

Adherence to high standards of performance
No illegal or unethical acts to hinder competitors
Cooperative programs for the general public and environment
No actions that would lead competitors to waste resources

Natural Resources

In the last several years, there has been a growing awareness that the supply of natural resources is not unlimited. Both consumers and marketing practices have contributed to some resource shortages.

Americans throw out more than 170 million tons of materials annually, about 1,400 pounds for every man, woman, and child. The United States has 5 per cent of the world's population but generates more than half of the world's trash. Included in the United States' annual refuse total are large amounts of aluminum, glass, paper, plastic, tires, appliances, copper, furniture, clothing, and food. For example,

> Each year Americans throw away 16 billion disposable diapers, 1.6 billion pens, 2 billion razors and blades, and 220 million tires. They discard enough aluminum to rebuild the entire U.S. commercial airline fleet every three months.[6]

[6] John Langone, "A Stinking Mess," *Time* (January 2, 1989), p. 45.

Americans spend $20 billion each year on garbage collection and disposal—yet only 10 per cent of U.S. garbage is recycled so that natural resources can be reused.[7]

Packaging materials alone use up millions of tons of natural resources. Since World War II, the use of these materials has increased several times faster than the population. And despite the billions of dollars firms spend on packaging, 90 per cent of total packaging is thrown away. Packaging in the United States now accounts for 30 to 40 per cent of all refuse.

Resource depletion can be slowed by reducing consumption, improving efficiency, limiting disposables, and lengthening products' lives.

In general, the depletion of natural resources can be reduced if the consumption of scarce materials is lessened and more efficient alternatives are chosen; fewer throwaway or disposable items such as soda bottles and cans, pens, cigarette lighters, and carbon typewriter ribbons are bought; products are given longer life spans; and styles are changed less frequently. Convenient recycling and repair facilities, better trade-in arrangements, common facilities such as apartments (which share electricity, water, and so on), and simpler packaging can also contribute to the more efficient use of resources. For example, it has been estimated that an effective returnable-container system could reduce U.S. consumption of glass by 40 to 45 per cent, of aluminum by 6 to 11 per cent, and of steel by 0.5 to 2 per cent.[8]

Progressive actions require cooperation among business, stockholders, government, employees, the general public, consumers, and others. They also involve changes in life-styles and values. For instance, more than 500 communities throughout the United States have adopted curbside recycling programs—some are mandatory and some require the sorting of different categories of throwaways (such as newspapers, cans, and bottles); and aluminum producers now derive 40 to 60 per cent of their output from recycling. See Figure 23-2.

The Landscape

Littering has become a major factor in marring the landscape. Various states have introduced regulations to lessen it.

Discarded no-deposit beverage containers and abandoned autos are examples of items that can mar the landscape. Thirty years ago virtually all beverage containers were recycled. Then no-return bottles and cans were developed. As a result, littering at roadsides and other areas became a major problem. In an attempt to reduce litter, several states, including Oregon, Vermont, Maine, Iowa, Connecticut, and Michigan, have enacted laws requiring beverage containers to have deposit fees that are refunded to consumers when they return empty containers. Many manufacturers and retailers believe these laws unfairly hold them responsible for the disposal of products because littering is done by consumers. Also, labor and recycling costs associated with container returns have caused beverage prices to rise slightly. As of now, beverage container laws have had limited effectiveness; consumers must be better educated as to the value of disposing of these containers in the proper manner.

Cars are frequently abandoned on highways and streets, where they are subsequently stripped of usable parts. One suggestion is to include an amount to cover the disposal of a car in its original price or in a transfer tax. For example, Maryland imposes a small fee on title transfers to aid in the removal of abandoned cars.

Other means of reducing the marring of the landscape include limits or bans on billboards and roadside signs, fines for littering, and better trade-ins for automobiles

---

[7] Hilary Stout, "The Economics of the Waste Crisis," *New York Times* (October 23, 1988), Sec. 3, p. 4; and George J. Church, "Garbage, Garbage, Everywhere," *Time* (September 5, 1988), pp. 81–82.
[8] W. Kent Moore and David L. Scott, "Beverage Container Deposit Laws: A Survey of the Issues and Results," *Journal of Consumer Affairs*, Vol. 17 (Summer 1983), pp. 60–61.

FIGURE 23-2
Recycling by Alcoa
In 1974, 14 per cent of Alcoa's can body sheet was produced from recycled aluminum beverage cans. Today, about 60 per cent of can sheet is from recycled cans, far above the industry average. Billions of cans are recycled each year, with can collectors receiving tens of millions of dollars for returning the used cans to Alcoa's 2,300 recycling centers. Reprinted by permission. Courtesy of Alcoa.

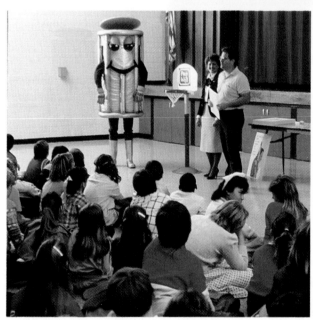

FIGURE 23-3
Consumer Education About Littering
Reprinted by permission of Waste Management, Inc.

and appliances. Neighborhood block associations, merchant self-regulation, area planning and zoning, and consumer education can also increase appreciation for the landscape. See Figure 23-3. Maintaining an attractive landscape is a cooperative effort. A merchant cleanup patrol cannot overcome pedestrians who throw litter on the street rather than in waste baskets.

Environmental Pollution

Dangerous pollutants need to be eliminated from the environment and safe substitutes found. The Environmental Protection Agency (EPA) is the major federal organization involved with pollution. Many state agencies are also quite active in this area.

Environmental pollution can be caused by fluorocarbon propellants (as were used in most U.S. spray cans, such as insecticide, deodorant, hairspray, and paint until the late 1970s), ocean dumping of industrial waste, lead from gasoline and paint, pesticides, sulfur oxide and other emissions, improper disposal of garbage, and so on. The EPA estimates that nearly 250 million tons of toxic, corrosive, ignitable, or explosive wastes must be disposed of by U.S. manufacturers each year; about 96 per cent of these wastes are taken care of at the plants where they are generated.[9]

Although greater attention is now being paid to it, environmental pollution will remain a major challenge for the foreseeable future. Here are examples of how communities and businesses are planning to meet this challenge.

In early 1989, a variety of Southern California government and regulatory officials offered a multiyear regional air-pollution control plan. If implemented in its proposed form, these are just a few of the product changes required by this plan:

▶ Items in aerosol cans and paints would have to be reformulated. Consumers would pay a surcharge for products not meeting the new standards.
▶ Restaurants using charcoal broilers would have to install special vents to lower emissions. Backyard barbeques could not be lit with starter fluid.
▶ Bias-ply tires, which propel more rubber particles into the air than do radial tires, would be banned.
▶ In bakeries, special devices would have to be placed on ovens to reduce emissions, modifying oven performance and resulting in poorer quality bread.
▶ Lawn mowers with gasoline engines would be banned.

The final Southern California plan will be important for marketers everywhere to study: "It's going to have an impact on the rest of the country because California is the role model."[10]

These are some of the activities being voluntarily undertaken by companies:

▶ Allied-Signal recycles waste by-products from chemical manufacturing into materials used in fluorine-based items, such as toothpaste.
▶ Dow Chemical has developed a product stewardship concept in which it anticipates and attempts to solve a product's environmental problems by performing toxicological studies.
▶ Poly-Tech is now marketing environmentally safe biodegradable garbage bags and diapers.
▶ Some supermarkets have NutriClean, a private testing lab, inspect their fruits and vegetables. Pesticide-free products get the NutriClean "seal of approval."[11]

[9] Jeremy Main, "Here Comes the Big New Cleanup," *Fortune* (November 21, 1988), pp. 102–118; and Stout, "The Economics of the Waste Crisis," Section 3, p. 4.

[10] Richard W. Stevenson, "Facing Up to a Clean-Air Plan," *New York Times* (April 3, 1989), pp. D1, D7.

[11] Steven J. Marcus, "The Recycling of Chemical Waste," *New York Times* (January 8, 1984), Section 3, p. 4; Claudia H. Deutsch, "Dow Chemical Wants to Be Your Friend," *New York Times* (November 22, 1987), Section 3, p. 6; Laurie Freeman, "Marketers Tout Biodegradable," *Advertising Age* (January 30, 1989), p. 32; and Alix M. Freedman, "Furor Over Rating of Store Produce," *Wall Street Journal* (June 23, 1988), p. 35.

Planned Obsolescence

Planned obsolescence is a marketing practice that capitalizes on short-run material wearout, style changes, and functional product changes. It is supported by marketers as a means of satisfying consumer demand and criticized by consumer advocates for increasing resource shortages, waste, and environmental pollution.

Planned obsolescence can involve materials, styles, and functions.

In material planned obsolescence, manufacturers choose materials and components that are subject to comparatively early breakage, wear, rot, or corrosion. For example, the makers of disposable lighters and razors use this form of planned obsolescence in a constructive manner by offering inexpensive, short-life convenient products. However, there is growing resistance to material planned obsolescence because of its effects on natural resources and the landscape.

In style planned obsolescence, a manufacturer makes some minor changes to differentiate clearly this year's model from last year's. Because some consumers — particularly in the United States — are style-conscious, they are willing to discard old items while they are still functional in order to acquire new items with more status. This is common with fashion items, automobiles, and so on.

With functional planned obsolescence, a manufacturer introduces new product features or improvements to generate consumer dissatisfaction with a currently owned product. These features or improvements may have been intentionally withheld from an earlier model in order to obtain faster repurchases. Companies using this approach risk competitors' introducing new features or improvements first. A change in style frequently accompanies a functional change in order to heighten the consumer's awareness of the "new" product.

Marketers reply to the criticisms of planned obsolescence with the following: it is a response to consumer demands regarding prices, styles, and features and is not coercive; without rapid product turnover, consumers would be disenchanted by the lack of choices; consumers like disposable items and frequently discard products before they lose their effectiveness; manufacturers use materials that hold down prices; competition requires companies to produce the best products they can, firms cannot hold back on improvements; and, for some products, such as clothing, consumers desire continuous style changes.

Ethics

In any marketing situation, ***ethical behavior*** based on honest and proper conduct ("what is right" and "what is wrong") should be followed.[12] Figure 23-4 outlines a general theory of marketing ethics. It consists of environmental and personal factors, a perceived ethical problem (a question as to whether a marketing practice is right or wrong), perceived alternatives, perceived consequences, evaluations about the rightness or wrongness of different alternatives, ethical judgments, intentions, behavior, situational constraints, and the actual consequences of carrying out a given act.[13]

Ethical behavior involves honest and proper conduct.

These two comments sum up the complexity of ethical issues for individuals and institutions:

> What are the canons [rules] of business? How do we assess economic behavior? Can we be both economically successful and ethical? Is the mark of greed an inherent part of

[12] Bennett, *Dictionary of Marketing Terms*, p. 115.
[13] Shelby D. Hunt and Scott Vitell, "A General Theory of Marketing Ethics," *Journal of Macromarketing*, Vol. 6 (Spring 1986), pp. 5–16.

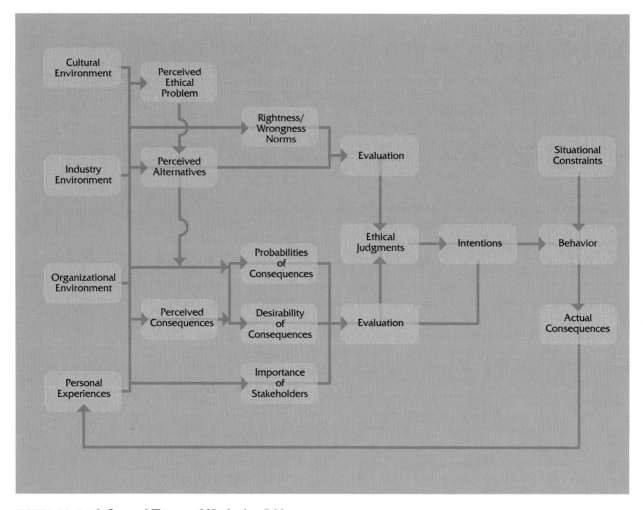

FIGURE 23-4 **A General Theory of Marketing Ethics**
SOURCE: Adapted by the authors from Shelby D. Hunt and Scott Vitell, "A General Theory of
Marketing Ethics," *Journal of Macromarketing,* Vol. 6 (Spring 1986), p. 8. Reprinted by permission.

business success? How do we assess our own economic behavior? That of others? Do we
judge the behavior of others by one standard? Ours by another? Is it perfectly proper for us
to buy low and sell high? For others? Is there but one standard for all, applicable to us as
well as others?[14]

The possibility that ethical and commercial considerations will conflict has always faced
those who run companies. It is not a new problem. The difference now is that a more
widespread and critical interest is being taken in our decisions and in the ethical judgments behind them. There is no simple, universal formula for solving ethical problems.
We have to choose from our own codes of conduct whichever rules are appropriate to the
case in hand; the outcome of those choices makes us who we are.[15]

[14] Harvey C. Burke, "Should We Teach Business Ethics?" *Business Horizons,* Vol. 31 (July–August 1988),
p. 3.
[15] Sir Adrian Cadbury, "Ethical Managers Make Their Own Rules," *Harvard Business Review,* Vol. 65
(September–October 1987), p. 69.

Marketing Controversy

Should the American Heart Association Give Food Products Its Seal of Approval?

The American Heart Association (AHA), a non-profit organization, has decided to begin allowing food products that meet its fat, cholesterol, and sodium levels to use its logo as an endorsement in ads. Many consumers will view this as the equivalent of a Good Housekeeping Seal of Approval. Each firm seeking the "seal" must pay the AHA a fee, used to fund product testing as well as consumer-education programs.

There are many critics of this approach. For example,

▶ *A General Foods spokesperson thinks that "it's simplistic to, in effect, stamp a smile or a frown on a food."*

▶ *Another food executive complains that the program could become a "costly nuisance for some companies, particularly smaller ones," because each company will want to obtain the seal once a competitor has obtained it.*

▶ *The AHA only plans to disclose the brands that receive its endorsement. "Bad brands" will not be disclosed.*

▶ *A U.S. Agriculture Department official says there "is no scientific evidence to show that a cookie or a cracker with, say, 10 grams of fat will reduce the risk of a heart attack any more readily than one with 12."*

▶ *A U.S. Food and Drug Administration spokesperson is concerned that using the seal in an ad may be interpreted as a health claim, implying that a food is useful in the prevention or treatment of a disease.*

▶ *The AHA will not allow its seal of approval to be used with all food categories, thus confusing consumers.*

The AHA's legal counsel disputes these criticisms. For example, he states that the program is in response to consumer requests and focuses on promoting a healthy diet—not specific brands: "The public is getting a clutter of information; they're looking for a way to help them buy foods that are better for them."

What do you think?

SOURCE: Based on material in Alix M. Freedman, "Heart Association to Put Seal of Approval on Foods—But Will Consumers Benefit?" Wall Street Journal (December 13, 1988), p. B1.

In marketing, ethical issues can be divided into two categories: process-related and product-related.[16] ***Process-related ethical issues*** "involve the unethical use of marketing strategies or tactics." Examples include bait-and-switch advertising, price fixing, selling products overseas that have been found unsafe in the United States, and bribing purchasing agents of large customers.

Product-related ethical issues involve "the ethical appropriateness of marketing certain products." For example, how should tobacco products, intimate personal hygiene items, sugar-coated cereals, political candidates, and nonprofit organizations be marketed? More specifically, should cigarettes be manufactured? Should there be restrictions on their sales? Should advertising for cigarettes be limited? Should taxes on cigarettes be raised to discourage use? Should cigarette smoking be banned in offices, restaurants, and planes?

Marketers need to consider process-related and product-related ethical issues.

[16] Gene R. Laczniak, Robert F. Lusch, and William A. Strang, "Ethical Marketing: Perceptions of Economic Goods and Social Problems," *Journal of Macromarketing*, Vol. 1 (Spring 1981), p. 49.

These examples show the varying responses to ethical issues: The Center for Science in the Public Interest (CSPI) and other organizations are calling for bans on alcohol ads on broadcast media, eliminating ads aimed at heavy drinkers and young people, warnings on alcoholic beverage labels, and restricting distribution channels for alcohol.[17] Seagram is one of a number of alcoholic beverage makers that are revising their ad messages to encourage moderation. See Figure 23-5.

In 1988, 7-Up became the first soda to be advertised on children's Saturday and after-school television programs. The firm's marketing vice-president said, "Establishing brand loyalty during the formative years of a child could give us a big advantage. We believe kids will tell mom to pick up 7-Up at the store and that they'll buy it for themselves with their own allowances." In response, the president of Action for Children's Television (a consumer group) stated: "After consumer protests about advertising other sugary products to kids, there was a kind of unspoken agreement that companies wouldn't sell sodas on Saturday morning TV. This is a further erosion of advertisers' concerns about the special vulnerability of children.[18]

General Mills "believes strongly in putting its half-century of food expertise to work to improve dietary habits, health, and nutrition." It provides nutrition information on food packages; prepares educational materials for use by health-care professionals, consumers, teachers, and children; and donates several million pounds of food to a nationwide food bank for the needy each year.[19]

"A business practice that would fall into the gray area of ethical/unethical was reported in the *Wall Street Journal:* The Best Western Hotel in Winter Park, Florida, charges guests daytime long-distance rates 24 hours a day without informing the guests; the hotel then pockets the difference between what the telephone company charges and what the guest pays. When the general manager was asked about the practice, his reply was, 'There's nothing in the Florida law that requires us to [inform the guests], so we don't.' However, most people would argue that the practice is unethical because the hotel does not inform the guests that it is charging daytime rates at all times."[20]

In order for a company to maintain the highest possible level of ethical conduct by its employees, the senior executives in that company must make a major commitment to ethics, clearly communicate standards of conduct to every employee (perhaps through a written code of ethics), reward ethical behavior, and discourage unethical behavior. The key "is for an organization to never let up on its vigilance to achieve ethical practices. Only then can an organization have a conscience."[21]

Ethical decisions should consider the consequences of actions and the public good.

When individuals make marketing decisions, they should consider these broad ethical questions:

▶ What are the probable consequences of alternative strategies?

▶ Which company policy will result in the greatest possible good for the greater number?

▶ Is a practice right? Is it just? Is it honest?

[17] Joe Agnew, " 'Lighter' Wares, Appeals Counter Negative Trends," *Marketing News* (January 30, 1987), pp. 1, 12.

[18] Ronald Alsop, "Seven-Up Ads on Children's TV Shows Risk Alienating Health-Conscious Parents," *Wall Street Journal* (December 9, 1988), p. B1.

[19] *General Mills Annual Report 1985*, p. 17; and *General Mills Annual Report 1988*, p. 16.

[20] Maynard M. Dolecheck and Carolyn C. Dolecheck, "Ethics: Take It from the Top," *Business,* Vol. 39 (January–March 1989), p. 13.

[21] Ibid., pp. 17–18.

Surprised?

We can understand if you are. It seems hard to believe that the alcohol content in the three groups of glasses above is, in fact, equal.

And so it's true that sometimes when you think you're drinking less, you may actually

THE HOUSE OF SEAGRAM

be drinking more. Because any alcoholic beverage should be used only in moderation, it's important that you know what you're drinking as well as how much. Remember, even though it may look light, it shouldn't be taken lightly.

FOR REPRINTS PLEASE WRITE ADVERTISING DEPT. CU-184, THE HOUSE OF SEAGRAM, 375 PARK AVE., N.Y., N.Y. 10152

FIGURE 23-5
A Socially Responsible Ad
Reprinted by permission.

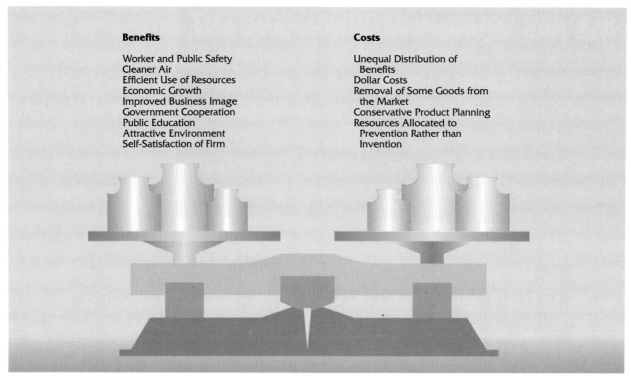

Benefits

Worker and Public Safety
Cleaner Air
Efficient Use of Resources
Economic Growth
Improved Business Image
Government Cooperation
Public Education
Attractive Environment
Self-Satisfaction of Firm

Costs

Unequal Distribution of
  Benefits
Dollar Costs
Removal of Some Goods from
  the Market
Conservative Product Planning
Resources Allocated to
  Prevention Rather than
  Invention

FIGURE 23-6 The Benefits and Costs of Social Responsibility

▶ Does a policy put people first?
▶ Does a proposed strategy or solution anticipate consequences in the larger environment as well as in the immediate situation?

The Benefits and Costs of Social Responsibility

Social responsibility has benefits as well as costs; these need to be balanced.

The performance of socially responsible actions has both benefits and costs. Among the benefits are improved worker and public safety, as reflected in fewer and less severe accidents, longer life spans, and less disease; cleaner air; more efficient use of resources; economic growth; a better image for business; government cooperation; public education; an attractive and safe environment; and self-satisfaction for a firm. Many of these benefits cannot be quantified. Furthermore, although costs are borne by all, the benefits of worker safety programs and many industrial environmental programs are enjoyed primarily by workers and their families. Nonetheless, a study by Johnson & Johnson showed that over a 30-year period those firms having a strong commitment to social responsibility had seen their profits grow at a rate more than two times greater than the Dow Jones Industrial Average.[22]

The costs of socially responsible actions vary. For instance, between 1980 and 1987, U.S. firms spent almost $70 billion on pollution-control devices; 52 per cent of this went for air devices, 36 per cent for water devices, and 12 per cent for solid-waste

[22] "J&J Shows Civic Service Pays," *Advertising Age* (February 13, 1984), p. 53.

devices.[23] Pollution control and worker safety programs now account for up to one-quarter of the capital budgets for some chemical, petroleum, nonferrous metals, steel, and paper firms. Various environmentally questionable products that are efficient have been removed from the marketplace or greatly modified, such as leaded gasoline. Because of various legal restrictions and fears of law suits, new-product planning tends to be more conservative; and resources are often allocated to prevention rather than invention. Figure 23-6 weighs the benefits and costs of social responsibility.

The twenty-year controversy over introducing automobile air bags offers a good illustration of the benefits and costs associated with social responsibility. Advocates of a passive restraint system (such as air bags that automatically inflate in an auto crash) stated that this system would save the country billions of dollars yearly in medical costs, insurance costs, and lost wages due to deaths and injuries. They believed the usefulness of air bags was proven long ago in various tests and through actual use (e.g., more than 20,000 Mercedes-Benz cars). Although air bags would cost $300 to $800 per car, depending on sales volume, insurance experts forecast that an average motorist would save an equivalent amount in premiums over a 10-year period. Critics of a passive restraint system argued that air bags were complex and relatively untested, could go off when they should not, did not work in all situations, had to be used in conjunction with seat belts, could injure riders not sitting normally, and were too expensive. In 1984, the Department of Transportation issued a ruling that required passive restraint systems (either air bags or automatic seat belts) in all new cars as of 1990. Finally, in 1988, Chrysler became the first U.S. auto maker to decide that all its 1990 model cars would be equipped with driver-side air bags. Ford and General Motors then announced that they would equip several of their 1990 cars — introduced in 1989 — with driver-side air bags.[24]

Consumerism

Whereas social responsibility involves the interface of marketing personnel with all of their publics, consumerism is limited to the relationship of marketers with their consumers. ***Consumerism*** can be defined as

> the wide range of activities of government, business, and independent organizations that are designed to protect people from practices that infringe upon their rights as consumers.

or

> the organized efforts of consumers seeking redress, restitution, and remedy for dissatisfaction they have accumulated in the acquisition of a standard of living.[25]

Consumerism has evolved through four distinct eras. The first era occurred in the early 1900s and concentrated on the need for a banking system, product purity, postal rates, antitrust, and product shortages. Emphasis was on business protection against unfair practices.

Consumerism protects consumers from practices that infringe upon their rights.

There have been four eras of consumerism.

---

[23] Bureau of Economic Analysis, U.S. Commerce Department, 1988.

[24] "Interview: Diane Steed," *Automotive News* (February 29, 1988), p. E6; Joseph B. White, "U.S. Auto Makers Decide Safety Sells," *Wall Street Journal* (August 24, 1988), p. 17; Henry Gilgoff, "The Great Air-Bag Battle," *Newsday Sunday Magazine* (February 5, 1989), pp. 8–13 ff.; and Philip E. Ross, "G.M. Plans Wider Use of Air Bags," *New York Times* (April 6, 1989), p. D5.

[25] Bennett, *Dictionary of Marketing Terms*, p. 42.

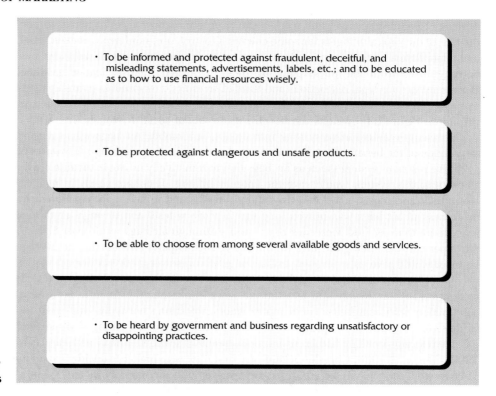

- To be informed and protected against fraudulent, deceitful, and misleading statements, advertisements, labels, etc.; and to be educated as to how to use financial resources wisely.

- To be protected against dangerous and unsafe products.

- To be able to choose from among several available goods and services.

- To be heard by government and business regarding unsatisfactory or disappointing practices.

FIGURE 23-7
Consumers' Basic Rights

The second era lasted from the 1930s to the 1950s. Important issues were product safety, bank failures, labeling, misrepresentation, performance standards, stock manipulation, deceptive advertising, credit, and consumer refunds. Consumer groups, such as Consumers Union and Consumers' Research, and government legislation grew. Issues were initiated but seldom resolved.

The third era began in the early 1960s and continued until 1980. It dealt with all areas of marketing and had a great impact on business. Two major events dominated the beginning of this era: President John Kennedy's announcement of a ***consumer bill of rights*** and publication of Ralph Nader's *Unsafe at Any Speed.* President Kennedy said that all consumers had four basic rights: to information, to safety, to choice in product selection, and to be heard. See Figure 23-7. *Unsafe at Any Speed,* released in 1965, was a detailed examination and critique of the automobile industry.[26]

President Kennedy stated a ***consumer bill of rights:*** *to information, to safety, to choice, and to be heard.*

Several other factors also contributed to the growth of the third era. Birth defects related to the use of thalidomide by pregnant females occurred in the 1960s. A number of books, including *Hidden Persuaders* by Vance Packard (about marketing's ability to influence people), *Silent Spring* by Rachel Carson (about marketing's contribution to a deteriorating environment), and *American Way of Death* by Jessica Mitford (about practices in the funeral industry), were published. Consumers became increasingly dissatisfied with product performance, companies' handling of complaints, and deceptive and unsafe business practices. In addition, consumers became more sophisticated and skeptical, and they set higher — and perhaps unrealistic — expectations. Product

---

[26] For a current synopsis of Ralph Nader's activities, see Douglas A. Harbrecht and Ronald Glover, "The Second Coming of Ralph Nader," *Business Week* (March 6, 1989), p. 28; and Thomas A. Stewart, "The Resurrection of Ralph Nader," *Fortune* (May 22, 1989), pp. 106–116.

scarcity occurred for some items. Self-service retailing and more complex products caused uncertainty for some customers. The media began to publicize poor business practices more frequently. Government intervention heightened; in particular, the Federal Trade Commission expanded its activities regarding consumer issues.

During the 1980s, a fourth era emerged. Consumerism entered a mature phase as a result of the dramatic gains of the 1960s and 1970s and an increased emphasis on business deregulation (and self-regulation). Today more companies take into account consumer issues when developing and implementing their marketing plans; far fewer firms ignore consumer input or publicly confront consumer groups. Cooperation between business and consumers is better; and confrontations are less likely.

In the following subsections, these key aspects of consumerism are examined: consumer information and education, consumer safety, consumer choice, consumers' right to be heard, the responses of business to consumer issues, and the future of consumerism.

Consumer Information and Education

The right to be informed includes protection against fraudulent, deceitful, or grossly misleading information, advertising, labeling, pricing, packaging, or other practices. A number of federal and state laws have been enacted in this area.

One example on the federal level is the Magnuson-Moss Consumer Product Warranty Act.[27] A **warranty** is an assurance given to consumers that a product will meet certain performance standards. An express (stated) warranty is one that is explicitly communicated to the consumer, such as a printed form showing the minimum mileage for truck tires. An implied (implicit) warranty does not have to be stated to be in effect; it stipulates that a product is fit for use, packaged and labeled properly, and conforms to promises made on the label. For the most part, the terms warranty and guarantee are synonymous. The major distinction is that the term guarantee is used more often in promotion, such as "satisfaction guaranteed" or "money-back guarantee."

*A **warranty** assures consumers that a product will meet performance standards.*

Through several provisions, Magnuson-Moss ensures that warranties are properly stated and enforced. Warranties must be made available prior to purchases, so that consumers may read them in advance. The FTC is empowered to require product-accompanying information regarding the identity and location of the warrantor, exceptions in warranty coverage, and how consumers may complain. A full warranty must cover all parts and labor for a specified period of time. A limited warranty may contain stipulations and exceptions, as well as a provision for labor charges. Implied warranties may not be disclaimed. Figure 23-8 describes the full warranty provided by Lands' End, a direct marketer.

Individual states have regulations relating to consumer information. As an illustration, cooling-off laws (allowing consumers to reconsider and, if they desire, cancel purchase commitments made in their homes with direct salespeople) are now in force in about forty states. Unit-pricing legislation, aimed at enabling consumers to compare prices of products that come in many sizes (such as small, medium, large, family, and economy), is also on a state-by-state basis. Food stores are most affected by unit pricing and, in many cases, these stores must express price per unit of measure as well as total package price.

---

[27] See Joshua Lyle Wiener, "An Evaluation of the Magnuson-Moss Warranty and Federal Trade Commission Improvement Act of 1975," *Journal of Public Policy & Marketing,* Vol. 7 (1988), pp. 65–82.

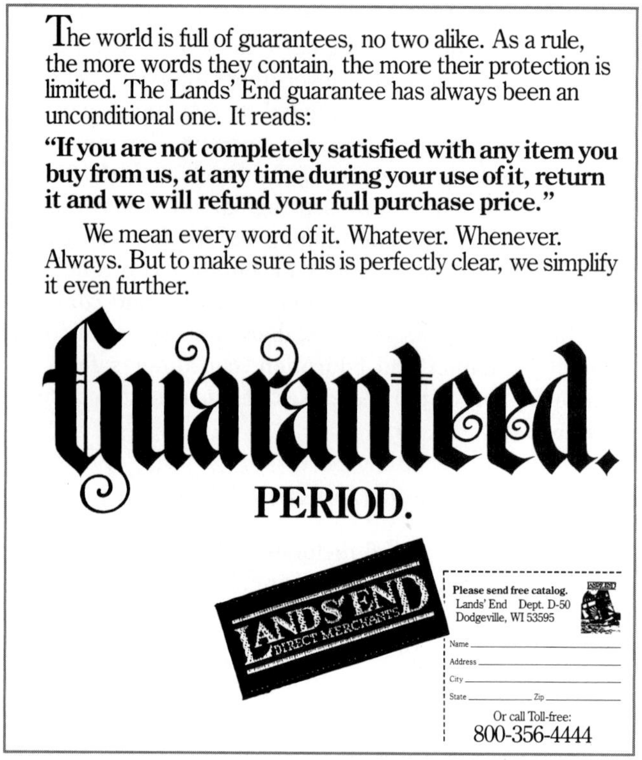

The world is full of guarantees, no two alike. As a rule, the more words they contain, the more their protection is limited. The Lands' End guarantee has always been an unconditional one. It reads:

"If you are not completely satisfied with any item you buy from us, at any time during your use of it, return it and we will refund your full purchase price."

We mean every word of it. Whatever. Whenever. Always. But to make sure this is perfectly clear, we simplify it even further.

Guaranteed.
PERIOD.

LANDS' END
DIRECT MERCHANTS

Please send free catalog.
Lands' End Dept. D-50
Dodgeville, WI 53595

Name _____
Address _____
City _____
State _____ Zip _____

Or call Toll-free:
800-356-4444

FIGURE 23-8
The Lands' End
Full Warranty
Reprinted by permission.

*Teaching consumers the wise use of financial resources in the marketplace is the goal of **consumer education**.*

Unfortunately the existence of information does not mean that all consumers will use it in their decision making. Studies have shown that consumer information is sometimes ignored or misunderstood, especially by those who need it most (such as the poor). As a result, consumer education is often necessary. ***Consumer education*** is defined as the "formalized teaching efforts to provide consumers with the skills and knowledge to allocate their resources wisely in the marketplace."[28]

The great majority of state departments of education have consumer education staffs. Some states, such as Illinois, Oregon, Wisconsin, Florida, Kentucky, and Hawaii, require all students in public secondary schools to take a course in consumer education. Hundreds of consumer-education programs are conducted by federal, state, and local governments, as well as private profit and nonprofit institutions. These programs typically cover how to wisely purchase goods and services; important features of credit agreements, contracts, and warranties; and consumer-protection laws.

Consumer Safety

There are millions of accidents yearly involving nonautomobile products.

In large part, the concern over consumer safety in the United States arises from the fact that annually millions of people are hurt, over 100,000 disabled, and more than 30,000 killed in incidents involving products other than automobiles. The yearly cost of product-related injuries is several billion dollars. Critics believe that up to 25 per cent of these injuries could be prevented if manufacturers produced safer, better-designed products.

[28] Bennett, *Dictionary of Marketing Terms*, p. 40.

You're the Marketer

How Would You Market Channel One*?*

In 1989, Whittle Communications ran a test of an innovative television program called Channel One at six junior highs and high schools throughout the United States. During the test, 10,000 students were shown a daily twelve-minute program via closed-circuit television. Channel One featured news and current affairs information, and contained two minutes of commercials for products such as shampoo, jeans, and candy. On the basis of the test, Whittle decided to introduce the program nationally.

In exchange for requiring that all students view Channel One every day, each participating school would receive $50,000 worth of video equipment (such as videocassette recorders, color televisions, and satellite dishes) that could be used for any educational purposes.

Channel One has encountered considerable criticism from leading educational associations, such as the National Education Association, the American Federation of Teachers, and the National Parent-Teachers Association, and the California schools superintendent. The groups are concerned about these issues:

▶ *While embarking on this project nationwide, Whittle is seeking to extend Channel One to 8,000 schools nationwide, representing one of the largest captive groups of teenagers ever assembled.*

▶ *At home, teenagers could "zap" commercials; at school, they are expected to sit and listen attentively.*

▶ *Schools cannot edit commercials or refuse to allow commercials for unhealthy products.*

▶ *Schools cannot preview or edit news coverage, which might be biased.*

Whittle defends Channel One on several grounds. First, by providing news programming to students, it ensures their exposure to important current events. Second, the program contains material to update textbooks. Third, because of commercial revenues, Whittle would be able to donate the latest video technology to schools, which they could not otherwise afford. Fourth, there have been virtually no objections to school policies requiring students to purchase newspapers or magazines that contain advertising. Fifth, the programming is aimed at teenagers, not at younger children who might have had less exposure to commercials.

As a Whittle marketing vice-president, what recommendations would you make?

SOURCE: Based on material in Deidre Carmody, "News Shows with Ads Are Tested in 6 Schools," *New York Times* (March 7, 1989), p. A16; and Bill Carter, "Whittle Plans School News Nationwide," *New York Times* (June 5, 1989), pp. D1, D14.

The ***Consumer Product Safety Commission (CPSC),*** established in 1972, is the federal agency with the major responsibility for product safety. It has jurisdiction over thousands of products — such as television sets, bicycles, lamps, ranges and ovens, toys, sporting goods, ladders, furniture, housewares, and lawn mowers. The CPSC also regulates structural items in homes such as stairs, retaining walls, and electrical wiring.

The only products over which the CPSC does not have jurisdiction are food, drugs, cosmetics, tobacco, automobiles, tires, firearms, boats, pesticides, and aircraft. Each of these products is regulated by other agencies. For example, the Environmental Protection Agency has the authority to recall cars not meeting emission standards. The

*The **Consumer Product Safety Commission** has a number of enforcement tools, including **product recall**.*

Food and Drug Administration oversees food, drugs, cosmetics, medical devices, radiation emissions, and so on.

The CPSC has extensive powers. It can

1. Require products to be marked with clear, understandable, and adequate warnings and instructions.
2. Issue mandatory standards pertaining to performance, construction, and packaging that may have the effect of forcing firms to redesign their products completely.
3. Require manufacturers, private labelers, distributors, and retailers to notify it immediately whenever they discover that a product manufactured or sold by them contains a defect that would create a substantial risk of injury. This covers defects in design, manufacture, or assembly.
4. Require manufacturers to conduct reasonable testing programs to make sure their products conform to established safety standards. After testing, manufacturers must supply distributors or retailers with certificates stating that all applicable consumer protection safety standards have been met.

If after an investigation the CPSC determines that a product hazard exists, it can issue orders compelling a manufacturer to bring the product into conformity with the provisions of the applicable safety rule or repair the defect in the product, exchange the product for a like or equivalent item that complies with safety requirements, or refund the purchase price of the product less a reasonable allowance for use. Firms found in violation of safety standards can be fined from $2,000 to $500,000 per violation; top executives can be fined up to $50,000 and imprisoned for up to one year. However, the primary enforcement tool used by the CPSC is ***product recall,*** whereby the Commission orders companies to recall and modify (or discontinue) unsafe products.

Since its inception, the CPSC has been responsible for initiating numerous product recalls. Sometimes a single product recall involves millions of units of a product. These were some of the products that the CPSC ordered recalled in 1988 and 1989:

▶ 6.5 million fixed-flame lighters — The flame might not go out.
▶ 2 million stomach exercise devices — A spring could break and injure the user.
▶ 420,000 whirlpool hot spas — Immersing the motor in a bathtub could electrocute the bather.
▶ 100,000 mobile home furnaces — They could leak deadly carbon monoxide gas.
▶ 40,000 deep-fat fryers — A wiring problem could cause serious shock.
▶ 30,000 crib gyms — The straps could injure or strangle a child.[29]

Over the years, the CPSC has also banned products such as flammable contact adhesives, easily overturned refuse bins, certain asbestos-treated products, and Tris (a flame retardant used in children's clothing that was linked to cancer).

The motor-vehicle industry, under the jurisdiction of the National Highway Traffic Safety Administration, has had a number of vehicles recalled for safety reasons. From 1977 through 1988, there were over 1,700 different recalls in the United States — involving millions of cars, trucks, and other vehicles (some of which were recalled more than once).[30] These were some of the major vehicle recalls during 1988 and 1989:

[29] *Consumer Reports,* various issues.
[30] Center for Auto Safety, 1988.

- ► 360,000 1985–1987 Honda Civics and 1986–1987 Acura Integras — The windshield wipers could fail.
- ► 104,000 1987–1989 Volkswagen Foxes — The steering wheel could come off.
- ► 60,000 1985 Chrysler and Dodge cars — The driver's seat frame could fail, allowing the seat to shift while driving.
- ► 57,000 1988 Ford light trucks — An optional sliding rear window could shatter into large fragments.
- ► 43,000 1986–1988 Harley-Davidson 1340cc motorcycles — The transmission could fail and cause the rear wheel to lock up.
- ► 13,000 1989 Pontiac Sunbirds, Buick Skyhawks, and Chevrolet Cavaliers, Corsicas, and Berettas — The fuel tank could leak, possibly causing a fire.
- ► 1,300 1987–1989 Winnebago and Itasca motor homes — The rear brakes could become ineffective, and an optional rear sway bar could fall off, affecting vehicle handling.[31]

In addition to these government activities, consumers have the right to sue the manufacturer or seller of an injurious product. A suit filed on behalf of many affected consumers is known as a ***class-action suit.*** Consumers can sue on the basis of negligence, breach of warranty, strict liability, or misinterpretation or misrepresentation. With negligence, consumers must prove that carelessness on the part of the seller resulted in injury. With breach of warranty, the seller is responsible for failures to abide by expressed or implied warranties. The most common implied warranty is that the product is safe, usable, and fit for its reasonably intended purpose. Under strict liability, the manufacturer is liable when an article placed on the market is proven to have a defect that causes injury. Carelessness does not have to be proven. Under misrepresentation, the seller is liable for falsities leading to consumer misuse of products.[32]

*A **class-action suit** can be based on a claim of negligence, breach of warranty, strict liability, or misrepresentation.*

A company can reduce the negative effects of product recalls and reduce the possibility of expensive class-action suits by enacting a systematic consumer communication program when it determines that a product is unsafe. This involves a broad announcement to affected consumers, identification of specific product models that are unsafe, a fair adjustment offer (repair, replacement, or refund), and prompt fulfillment of the adjustment offer.[33]

Consumer Choice

The right to choose means that consumers have available several products and brands from which to select. The government has taken various actions in this regard. Exclusive patent rights are limited to seventeen years. After this period, all firms can utilize the patents. Noncompetitive business practices such as unfair price cutting are restricted. Firms with strong trademarks, such as Borden's ReaLemon, are sometimes encouraged to license their products to competitors.

When consumers have several alternatives available to them, they are given the right to choose.

---

[31] *Consumer Reports,* various issues.

[32] See Dorothy Cohen, "Product Liability" in Victor P. Buell (Editor), *Handbook of Modern Marketing,* Second Edition (New York: McGraw-Hill, 1986) pp. 98-2–98-4.

[33] David L. Malickson, "Are You Ready for a Product Recall?" *Business Horizons,* Vol. 26 (January–February 1983), pp. 31–35; and George C. Jackson and Fred W. Morgan, "Responding to Recall Requests: A Strategy for Managing Goods Withdrawal," *Journal of Public Policy & Marketing,* Vol. 7 (1988), pp. 152–165.

FIGURE 23-9 **Do U.S. Consumers Have Too Many Choices?** Reprinted by permission of Stop & Shop Companies.

Government agencies are responsible for examining the potential impact of company mergers on consumer choice. In some cases, they have stopped proposed mergers or forced firms to divest themselves of certain subsidiaries if the product offerings in an industry would be lessened. Franchise restrictions requiring franchisees to purchase all goods and services from their franchisors have similarly been reduced.

Retailers are encouraged to carry wide ranges of product categories and different brands within each category. The media are monitored to ensure that advertising space or time is made available to small as well as large firms. Imports are allowed to compete with American-made items. Information standards are enforced. A number of industries, such as banking, airline, and railroad, have been deregulated to foster price competition and encourage new firms to enter the marketplace.

Today in the United States, consumer choice in many product categories is so extensive that some are wondering whether "there is such a thing as too much choice." Sixty-three per cent of the respondents to an American Express survey believe there are so many products available that consumers can become confused and unable to make a selection. Long-distance telephone services (several hundred competitors), prerecorded videocassettes (several thousand titles), hair mousse (almost 50 varieties), and lipstick shades (150+ offered just by Revlon) are a few of the categories in which consumers have extensive selections.[34] See Figure 23-9.

Consumers' Right to Be Heard

Although there is no general federal consumer agency, there are federal, state, and local agencies involved with consumers.

The right to be heard means that consumers should be able to voice their opinions (sometimes in the form of complaints) to business, government, and other parties. This gives consumers input into the decisions that affect them. As of this date, no overall federal consumer agency exists to represent consumer interests, although several federal agencies regulate various business practices pertaining to consumers. The

[34] Lisa Belkin, "Consumers Confused by Number of Choices," *New York Times* (August 8, 1985), pp. A1, C12; and authors' estimates.

726

addresses and phone numbers of these agencies, as well as those of trade associations, are listed in the *Consumer's Resource Handbook,* published by the U.S. Office of Consumer Affairs. Most states and municipalities have their own consumer affairs offices, as do many major corporations. Each encourages consumer input. During the last several years, these offices have been quite active.

In addition to government and industry consumer specialists, there are many consumer groups that act on behalf of the general public or specific consumer segments. These groups are quite motivated in their attempts to voice consumer complaints, represent consumers before government and industry hearings, and otherwise generate consumer input into the decision-making process of government and industry. Because a single consumer rarely has a significant impact, consumer groups frequently become the individual's voice.

The Responses of Business to Consumer Issues

Over the past 25 to 30 years, the U.S. business community has greatly increased its acceptance of the legitimacy and importance of consumer rights; today many firms have formal programs and real commitments to resolve consumer issues. Nonetheless, a number of companies have raised reasonable questions about the impact of consumerism on their operations. Following are some of these questions:

Companies have become much more responsive to consumers, yet questions remain about the effects of consumerism on firms.

▶ Why do different states and municipalities have dissimilar laws regarding business practices? How can a national company be expected to comply with each of these regulations?

▶ Do government rules cause unnecessary costs and time delays in the introduction of new products that outweigh the benefits of these rules?

▶ Is it the responsibility of business to ensure that consumers obey laws (such as not littering) and use products properly (such as wearing seat belts)?

▶ Is it the role of government or business to assure that the marketplace is responsive to consumer needs? Is self-regulation preferred over government regulation?

▶ Are multimillion dollar jury awards to injured consumers getting out of hand?

As an illustration, 30+ states now have mandatory auto seat-belt use laws. In most of these states, consumer compliance was relatively high shortly after the laws were enacted. Since then, compliance has fallen dramatically. Auto makers have wondered why they have to install passive safety devices (air bags or automatic seat belts) on new cars, if consumers are at fault because they refuse to "buckle up" with traditional seat belts.

Business responses to consumer issues can range from acts that are illegal to behavior that is quite supportive of consumer interests, as shown in Table 23-2. The remedial alternatives for protecting consumers against unacceptable marketing practices are explained in Table 23-3.

Selected responses to consumer issues by manufacturers, retailers, and trade associations are discussed next.

Manufacturers

A number of manufacturers have developed systematic programs to deal with consumer issues, as these examples show. In 1961, Maytag introduced Red Carpet Service to improve its appliance repair service. Zenith set up a customer relations depart-

TABLE 23-2 The Range of Business Responses to Consumer Issues

Response	Characteristics
Illegal behavior	Business practices that violate government statutes, such as price fixing, deceptive advertising, and price discrimination
Questionable behavior	Legal business practices that are highly criticized, such as advertising to children
Opportunistic behavior	Practices by which a firm capitalizes on the difficulties of a competitor, such as publicizing a product recall
Adaptive behavior	Actions that are taken after laws are enacted or court rulings are handed down
(a) Cooperative	(a) Complete compliance
(b) Noncooperative	(b) Circumvention efforts, such as withdrawing rather than modifying popular, but dangerous, products
Defensive behavior	Self-protective actions prior to government mandates
(a) Cooperative	(a) Voluntary improvements, such as unit pricing and nutritional labeling
(b) Noncooperative	(b) Increased conflict with government, such as attacks on federal agencies and lobbying
Supportive behavior	Voluntary efforts to improve practices taken at the initiative of business, such as labeling toys by the age of children

Source: Adapted by the authors from Paul N. Bloom and Nikhilesh Dholakia, "Marketer Behavior and Public Policy: Some Unexplored Territory," *Journal of Marketing,* Vol. 37 (October 1973), pp. 63–77.

TABLE 23-3 Remedial Alternatives for Consumer Protection

Alternative	Methods of Implementation
Prevention	Consumer abuses prevented through 1. Voluntary codes of conduct by firms or trade associations. 2. Laws mandating information disclosure, such as truth-in-packaging, truth-in-lending, and unit pricing. 3. Substantiation of advertising claims.
Restitution	Compensation to consumers for product-related losses, damages, or injuries through 1. Affirmative disclosure, requiring the firm to disclose both negative and positive points in its advertising. 2. Corrective advertising, requiring the firm to devote a proportion of future advertising to dispel past doubtful claims. 3. Refunds or replacement products. 4. Limitations on contracts, such as cooling-off laws, which give buyers the right to rescind certain direct-selling contracts. 5. Arbitration.
Punishment	Future misconduct deterred by inflicting losses on wrongdoers through 1. Fines. 2. Loss of profits. 3. Class-action suits on behalf of many consumers.

Source: Dorothy Cohen, "Remedies for Consumer Protection: Prevention, Restitution, or Punishment," *Journal of Marketing,* Vol. 39 (October 1975), pp. 24–31.

ment in 1968; Motorola created an Office of Consumer Affairs in 1970; and RCA implemented a consumer affairs office at the corporate level in 1972. Frigidaire presents an Award of Merit to the dealers and service units that meet rigid service standards.

General Electric operates the GE Answer Center, which handles consumer tele-

CHRYSLER MOTORS ANNOUNCES
THE CAR BUYER'S BILL OF RIGHTS.

1. EVERY AMERICAN HAS THE RIGHT TO A QUALITY CAR

You want a car that will start every morning.

You want a car that will age well. And give you years of satisfaction.

You want quality. It's your right. Undisputed right.

Quality is also the first commitment of the carmaker. Without it he becomes morally and fiscally bankrupt. Chrysler has no intentions of forsaking this commitment.

Since 1980, Chrysler–with new leadership and a new resolve–initiated **Five Key Quality Programs** involving every member of the work force, every level of management. Chrysler has completed 5 million hours of worker training, enrolled 26,000 employees in quality schools and put 583 quality teams in place.

The goal: top the quality of the imports. It's an ambitious goal, but results are already showing it is within reach. Corporate quality indicators show that, over the last 8 years, Chrysler-built car and truck quality has improved 43%.

Lowest recalls. During the same 8-year period, Government records show that Chrysler has the lowest average safety recall record of any American car company for passenger cars registered for the '80 through '87 model years.

And over the last 5 years, lower than such prominent imports as BMW, Porsche and Volvo.

2. EVERY AMERICAN HAS THE RIGHT TO LONG–TERM PROTECTION

Chrysler has consistently led the industry in long-term quality protection.

In 1980, Chrysler introduced the innovative 5/50 Protection Plan. In 1987, Chrysler extended this coverage substantially on the most important part of your car, the engine and powertrain, to 7 years or 70,000 miles. It's the **longest powertrain protection** in the industry. And you also get 7-year or 100,000-mile protection against outer body rust-through.* The plan covers every car, truck and minivan Chrysler builds in North America, and now it includes '89 Jeep vehicles. 7/70, unprecedented when introduced...unsurpassed today.

Now, Chrysler breaks new ground again. With its new **Crystal Key Owner Care Program** that comes with the Chrysler New Yorker. It is a remarkable warranty. It protects the entire car for 5 years or 50,000 miles. It covers engine, powertrain, air conditioning, steering, rust, suspension, electrical–everything right down to the door handles.* All you have to do is take care of normal maintenance, adjustments and wear items.

Not even Rolls or Mercedes match this warranty.

3. EVERY AMERICAN HAS THE RIGHT TO FRIENDLY TREATMENT, HONEST SERVICE AND COMPETENT REPAIRS

Dealer service is the key link–the most fragile link–between the car buyer and the carmaker. It can make or break a relationship.

Chrysler understands this, better than most. And (under the direction of Lee Iacocca) has taken specific action to strengthen and revitalize this relationship. Results are gratifying.

Highest satisfaction. Chrysler owners have the highest level of satisfaction of any buyers of American cars. Higher than GM owners. And significantly higher than Ford owners.**

As Lee Iacocca says, "The next great leap forward in the car industry isn't going to happen in Detroit. It's going to happen at the dealership." One telling example: In 1981, our dealer technicians received 184,000 hours of training. Last year, 542,184 hours. That's an increase of almost 300%.

Chrysler is also giving tangible rewards to the Dodge, Chrysler, Plymouth, Jeep and Eagle dealers and their technicians for improving customer service. Because when they do, we achieve one of the highest goals in the auto industry, a satisfied customer.

4. THE RIGHT TO A SAFE VEHICLE

Safety is a right we all desire, not just for ourselves, but for our families, too. That's why Chrysler has committed enormous resources and talents to building you a safe car. And that commitment has taken hold:

...Chrysler Motors is the first American car company to offer **air bags as standard equipment.** And by 1990, Chrysler will feature driver-side air bags on every car it builds in the United States.

...Every Chrysler-built passenger car has over 30 safety features standard for '88.

...By 1992, Chrysler will have spent 440 million dollars on testing to learn how to enhance your safety.

...Chrysler Motors has a **Safety Shield Program** from design through assembly. Safety components are identified by a safety shield, so everyone at the factory knows its importance to safety.

This program guards against the malfunction of critical items such as brakes, wipers, steering systems and starters. And is one of the prime reasons why Chrysler Motors has the lowest average percentage of safety-related recalls for any American car company.

5. THE RIGHT TO ADDRESS GRIEVANCES

If you have a warranty-related problem with your dealer, you have an impartial ear ready and willing to listen to your side of the story, and this comes at no cost to you: **The Customer Arbitration Board.**

This Arbitration Board consists of three voting members: a local customer advocate, a technical expert and a person from the general public. And not one of them is affiliated with Chrysler in any way.

All decisions made by the Board include the action to be taken by the dealer or Chrysler and the time by which the action must be taken.

All decisions are binding on the dealer and Chrysler, but not on you, unless you accept the decision. The whole process normally takes no longer than 40 days.

6. THE RIGHT TO SATISFACTION

Chrysler believes there's no secret to satisfying customers. Build them a quality product. A safe product. Protect it right–with the longest powertrain warranty in the business. Service it right. And treat them with respect. It's that simple.

And Chrysler is doing exactly that. The proof is coming from you, the customer.

J.D. Power and Associates, one of the most respected research organizations in the industry, surveyed over 25,000 owners of 1987 passenger cars for product quality and dealer service. The results: Chrysler Motors has the **highest customer satisfaction** of any American car company–**two years running**–for overall product quality and dealer service.**

As good as that is, it's not good enough. If we don't satisfy you better than the next guy...you have every right to go to the next guy. So, we're never going to stop improving present programs, and creating new ones.

Because Chrysler believes it's our job to satisfy your needs. We have the obligations...you have the rights.

"QUALITY IS YOUR RIGHT. AND WE INTEND TO SEE THAT YOU GET IT."

Lee Iacocca

⬥ **CHRYSLER MOTORS**

CHRYSLER·PLYMOUTH·DODGE
DODGE TRUCKS·JEEP·EAGLE

*See these limited warranties at dealer. Deductibles and some restrictions apply. **J.D. Power and Associates 1988 CSI Customer Satisfaction with Product Quality and Dealer Service for 1986 and 1987 domestic cars.

FIGURE 23-10
Chrysler's Car Buyer's Bill of Rights
Reprinted by permission.

phone inquiries 24 hours a day, seven days a week, via a toll-free number. It receives three million calls each year. The Center responds to questions from potential consumers and do-it-yourselfers and tries to resolve complaints from disgruntled customers. It also receives suggestions regarding company improvements. Through the Answer Center, GE can satisfy current customers and attract potential ones, gather information about consumer demographics, and gain insights about its marketing strategy.[35]

In 1988, Chrysler hired a vice-president of consumer affairs and announced a car buyers' bill of rights, shown in Figure 23-10. Said Chrysler's new vice-president, the firm "wants me to be the voice of the consumer. My value to the company is that I am unlike other executives: I'm not a car person, I'm a consumer person. I'm very different from any one of them."[36]

In the area of product recalls, manufacturers' actions have varied widely, as these two examples show:

▶ When tampering resulted in rat poison being discovered in a few capsules of Contac cold medicine, Smithkline Beckman (the product's manufacturer) immediately removed all Contac capsules from retail shelves across the United States. Contac was not sold for several months, while Smithkline Beckman developed a new sealed

---

[35] Sellers, "How to Handle Customers' Gripes," pp. 96, 100.
[36] Patricia Strnad, "Consumer Power," *Advertising Age* (November 14, 1988), p. 26.

capsule. Only then was Contac returned to stores. This strategy cost Smithkline Beckman $50 million — plus lost sales while Contac was off the market.[37]

▶ Audi, a Volkswagen subsidiary, agreed to recall its Audi 5000 models with automatic transmission only after heavy pressure from the National Highway Traffic Safety Administration. Data showed that 513 accidents, 271 injuries, and 5 deaths may have been caused by a sudden-acceleration problem that occurred as a person shifted from park into drive or reverse. At first, Audi blamed driver error, leading one expert to comment: "They're creating a lot of resentment among the group of people who would ordinarily be their best source of future sales."[38]

Now more and more companies are employing voluntary recalls when they become aware of product defects or unsafe product features.

Despite manufacturers' greater interest in consumer issues, there are still situations in which they do battle with consumer organizations. For example, *Consumer Reports* provides monthly evaluations of a wide variety of goods and services for its millions of readers. Since the magazine was founded in 1936, its publisher (Consumers Union) has vigorously fought to keep its ratings from being quoted in ads and brochures. With rare exceptions, firms have honored this policy. However, in the 1980s, Hobart appliances, Schrafft's ice cream, Remington electric razors, Regina vacuum cleaners, and a few others quoted from favorable *Consumer Reports* reviews in ads. Consumers Union filed legal suits against these companies, with little success. It does periodically inform readers of the violators:

> If you agree with us that *Consumer Reports* should be kept for the use of consumers, not for the use of advertisers, you may want to write to the handful of companies who have refused to cooperate with our no-commercialization policy. Here's the dishonor roll.[39]

Retailers

Various retailers have expressed a positive attitude regarding consumer issues, some for more than 50 years. For example, J.C. Penney adopted a consumer philosophy in 1913; Macy's established a Bureau of Standards to test merchandise in 1927; and Abraham & Straus recognized the need for merchandise labeling in 1937.

More recently, Sears developed an extensive education program and related literature; Hess Department Stores became heavily involved in community affairs and in 1977 introduced a "Consumer Expo," which demonstrates new products; and Giant Food, a large supermarket chain, developed its own consumer bill of rights over fifteen years ago:

▶ Right to safety — no phosphates, removal of certain pesticides, age-labeling of toys.

▶ Right to be informed — improved labeling, unit pricing, readable dating of perishable items, and nutritional labeling.

▶ Right to choose — continued sale of cigarettes and food with additives.

---

[37] Nancy Giges, "Aid from Rivals Helped to Hasten Contac's Return," *Advertising Age* (May 26, 1986), pp. 3, 90.

[38] Douglas R. Sease, "Audi Problems May Not Be Over, Despite Recent Recall," *Wall Street Journal* (January 20, 1987), p. 37.

[39] "We're Taking This Rental to Court," *Consumer Reports* (November 1985), p. 642.

► Right to be heard — dialogue with reputable consumer groups, in-house consumer advocate.

► Right to redress — money-back guarantee on all products.

► Right to service — availability of store services.[40]

In 1988, Vons (the largest supermarket chain in Southern California) removed all cigars and pipe and chewing tobacco from store shelves because manufacturers of these products would not place consumer warning labels on the products. And Northwest Airlines became the only U.S. airline to ban smoking on all North American flights.[41]

In one key area, retailers and consumer groups have opposing views. This involves *item price removal*, whereby prices are marked only on store shelves or aisle signs and not on individual items. Many retailers, particularly supermarkets, want to employ item price removal because computerized checkouts allow them to ring up prices through premarked codes on packages. Retailers state that this practice reduces labor costs significantly and that these reductions can be passed on to consumers. Consumer groups believe the practice is deceptive and will make it difficult for them to guard against misrings. Item price removal is banned in a number of states and local communities. Giant Food is one of the major users of item price removal; it passes cost savings along to consumers.

*With **item price removal**, prices are displayed only on shelves or signs.*

Trade Associations

Trade associations are organizations that represent groups of individual companies. Many of them have been quite responsive to consumer issues through a variety of activities, such as coordinating and distributing safety-related research findings, developing consumer and company education programs, developing product standards, and handling complaints.

The Major Appliance Consumer Action Panel (MACAP) is an effective educational and complaint-resolution program sponsored by the Association of Home Appliance Manufacturers. See Figure 23-11. The Bank Marketing Association stresses a Financial Advertising Code of Ethics (FACE) for member firms; the Direct Marketing Association sets industry guidelines and operates a consumer action line; and the National Retail Merchants Association has a Consumer Affairs Committee and provides information to the public.

The Better Business Bureau (BBB) is the largest and broadest business-operated trade association involved with consumer issues. The BBB publishes educational pamphlets and books, investigates complaints, supervises arbitration panels, has available a Consumer Affairs Audit, outlines ethical behavior, presents symposiums, publicizes unsatisfactory practices and names the firms involved, and has local offices throughout the country. It emphasizes self-regulation as an alternative to government legislation. Nationwide the BBB handles hundreds of thousands of arbitration cases each year. These cases — most of them involving auto complaints — are decided by an impartial

---

[40] Esther Peterson, "Consumerism as a Retailer's Asset," *Harvard Business Review*, Vol. 52 (May–June 1974), pp. 91–92 ff.; and Mary Johnson, "A Giant Step Toward Consumer Protection," *Progressive Grocer* (August 1983), p. 21.

[41] John R. Emshwiller, "Vons Stores Remove Tobacco Products That Lack Health Warning Labels," *Wall Street Journal* (October 5, 1988), p. B6; and Glenn Kramon, "Northwest Airlines Bans Smoking on Most Flights," *New York Times* (March 24, 1988), p. A20.

If you have a complaint about your

- Clothes Washer/Dryer
- Dehumidifier
- Dishwasher
- Food Waste Disposer
- Freezer
- Microwave Oven
- Range/Oven
- Refrigerator
- Room Air Conditioner
- Trash Compactor

You should . . .

1. Read the *Use and Care Booklet* that came with the appliance. Also *Check the Plug* as well as *Fuses, Pilots and Controls.* You may find the answer to your problem. If not,

2. Call your *Local Dealer* or the *Service Agency* authorized to fix the brand you own. They are trained and equipped to handle appliance service problems.

3. If you still aren't satisfied, contact the *Manufacturer* of your appliance. You will find the address and phone number in your use and care booklet.

4. Then, if your problem is not resolved to your satisfaction, write

MACAP
The Major Appliance
Consumer Action Panel
20 North Wacker Drive
Chicago, IL 60606

When writing MACAP, be sure to provide

- your name, address and a daytime phone number
- the type of appliance, brand, model and serial number
- the purchase date and price of your appliance
- the name, address and phone number of your dealer or repair service
- copies of all letters you have written or received about your complaint
- copies of all service receipts
- a clear description of your problem and what you think is a reasonable solution.

The Major Appliance Consumer Action Panel (MACAP)
is an independent, complaint mediation group. After your complaint reaches MACAP, it is immediately forwarded to the appliance company for one last reconsideration. If you are not satisfied with the company's response, the Panel reviews all available facts about your complaint and considers a specific recommendation to the manufacturer, which is not binding on either party. In some cases, the Panel may determine that the facts don't substantiate your complaint and then will make no recommendation to the company.

To be a satisfied appliance owner, MACAP recommends you

- Ask where you can get service when you buy your appliance and then make note of the agency's address and phone number.
- Follow directions given in the use and care booklets provided with your appliances.
- Make sure your house wiring is adequate for your appliances. Check gas lines for safety.
- Know what your warranties cover and who is authorized to service your appliance. (Contact your manufacturer for the authorized servicers in your area.)
- Try all the appliance features so any necessary repairs or adjustments can be made within the warranty. Report problems immediately because warranties are based on time, not usage.
- Keep all your appliance warranties, use and care booklets, purchase and service receipts in one place.
- Do not accept delivery of damaged appliances.
- Compare features on several models before purchase to ensure the selection most suitable to your needs.

MACAP is sponsored by:
Association of
Home Appliance Manufacturers
(AHAM)

FIGURE 23-11
The Major Appliance Consumer Action Panel
Reprinted by permission.

arbitrator within 10 days of a hearing (at no cost to the complainant). The rulings are usually binding on participating companies but not on consumers.

Sometimes trade associations vigorously oppose potential government regulation. For example, the Tobacco Institute (an association funded by tobacco companies) has lobbied against further restrictions on tobacco sales, promotion, distribution, and use.

The Current Role of Consumerism

In recent years, consumerism efforts have been less intense than in the 1960s and 1970s.

Consumerism is now in a period of maturity, as pointed out earlier in the chapter. As in the 1980s, the decade of the 1990s will see less activism than the 1960s and 1970s. This is due to several factors: the current level and quality of self-regulation, the success of consumerism, the increased conservatism of Congress and the American people, and the importance of other issues.

As described throughout the text, and particularly in this chapter, organizations are much more responsive to consumer issues today. Because many firms have consumer affairs departments, use voluntary product-recall programs, and conduct ongoing consumer surveys, there is less pressure for government agencies or consumer groups to intervene. Accordingly, there is a strong trend toward industry deregulation as a way of increasing competition, encouraging innovative marketing programs, and stimulating lower prices. For a lot of firms, deregulation is resulting in greater marketing flexibility, as well as in a more uncertain environment for them.

Consumerism activity is less necessary because of the successes of past actions. On the federal, state, and local levels, government protection for consumers has improved dramatically over the last 25 to 30 years. Class-action suits have won large settlements from firms, making it clear that unsafe practices are financially costly. Consumer groups and independent media have publicized negative company practices, so that firms are aware that such activities do not go unnoticed. The major goal for consumer rights advocates during the 1990s is to hold on to and consolidate the gains of the 1960s and 1970s.

Many members of Congress and sectors of the American public are now more conservative about the role of government in regulating business than in the 1960s and 1970s. They believe that government has become too big, impedes business practices, and causes unnecessary costs. As a result, some government agency activities have been limited and their budgets closely monitored. Congress passed the FTC Improvement Act of 1980, which restricted the agency's powers. Under this act, Congress was given veto power over industrywide trade regulations approved by the FTC.[42]

The FTC Improvement Act of 1980 gave Congress the ability to veto FTC trade regulations.

Finally, recently consumerism issues have not been as important to some people as a number of other factors. These include unemployment, interest rates, industrial productivity, the rate of inflation, product and resource shortages, the federal budget deficit, and the negative international balance of trade.

The comments made in this section are not intended to convey the impression that consumer issues will be unimportant in the 1990s. They are intended, rather, to stress that business, consumers, and government must and will continue working together to resolve consumer issues. As the director of customer satisfaction at Neiman-Marcus, the upscale retail chain, noted,

> We're not just looking for today's sale. We want a long-term relationship with our customers. If that means taking back a piece of Baccarat crystal that isn't from one of our stores, we'll do it. If you let profit protection or security rule the way you treat customers, satisfaction is bound to suffer.[43]

Summary

1. *To consider the impact of marketing on society* At the company and industry levels, marketing activities can have a strong impact on society. Such activities have the potential for both positive and negative consequences regarding such areas as the quality of life and consumer expectations. Various studies have shown that people's perceptions of marketing are mixed. And firms need to recognize

that many dissatisfied consumers do not complain; they simply do not buy the offending product again.

2. *To study social responsibility and consider its benefits and costs* Social responsibility involves a concern for the consequences of a person's or institution's acts as they might affect the interests of others. It requires that marketing actions seek to

---

[42] For a good overview of the current status of the Federal Trade Commission, see the *Journal of Public Policy & Marketing's* special issue on the FTC, Vol. 7 (1988).

[43] Sellers, "How to Handle Customers' Gripes," p. 92.

protect or enhance society's interests as well as to reach sales and profit goals. Social responsibility also encompasses the socioecological view of marketing, which looks at all the stages of a product's life from raw materials to junkpile and includes consumers and nonconsumers. Social responsibility can pose dilemmas because various popular goods and services may have potential adverse effects on consumer or societal well-being.

Both consumers and marketing practices have contributed to some resource shortages. To stem the depletion of natural resources, cooperative efforts among business, stockholders, government, employees, the general public, consumers, and others are needed.

Discarded beverage containers and abandoned autos are just two of the items that mar the landscape. As a result, several states have enacted legislation to rectify this situation.

Dangerous pollutants need to be eliminated from the environment and safe substitutes found to replace them. Environmental pollution will remain a challenge for the foreseeable future.

Product obsolescence is a heavily criticized marketing practice that encourages material wearout, style changes, and functional product changes. Marketers say that it is responsive to consumer demand, while critics say it increases resource shortages, is wasteful, and adds to environmental pollution.

Ethical behavior, based on honest and proper conduct, can be divided into two categories: process-related and product-related. When marketing decisions are being made, ethical considerations should focus on the consequences of actions, honesty, spin-off effects, and other factors.

Socially responsible actions have many benefits, such as worker and public safety, cleaner air, and a more efficient use of resources. These actions also have many costs, such as the unequal distribution of benefits, dollar expenditures, and conservative new-product planning. The benefits and costs need to be balanced.

3. *To explore consumerism and examine the consumer bill of rights* Consumerism deals with the relationship of marketers with their consumers. It is defined as the wide range of activities of government, business, and independent organizations that are designed to protect people from practices that infringe upon their rights as consumers.

Consumerism has progressed through four eras: early 1900s, 1930s to 1950s, 1960s to 1980, and 1980 to the present. The third era was the most important and began with President John Kennedy's announcement of a consumer bill of rights — to information, to safety, to choice in product selection, and to be heard. During the current era, consumerism has reached a mature phase and there is renewed interest in the deregulation of business.

The right to be informed includes consumer protection against fraudulent, deceitful, or grossly misleading information, advertising, labeling, pricing, packaging, or other practices. Consumer education involves teaching consumers to use their financial resources wisely.

The concern over the right to safety arises from the large numbers of people who are injured, disabled, or killed in product-related accidents. The Consumer Product Safety Commission has the power to order product recalls or modifications for a wide range of products, although other agencies oversee products such as automobiles and pharmaceuticals.

The right to choose stipulates that consumers should have several products and brands from which to select. In the United States, some observers wonder whether "there is such a thing as too much choice."

The right to be heard means that consumers should be able to voice their opinions to business, government, and other parties. A number of consumer groups and government agencies provide this voice.

4. *To discuss the responses of manufacturers, retailers, and trade associations to consumerism* Many individual firms and trade associations are reacting positively to consumer issues. This group is growing. A smaller number of organizations intentionally or unintentionally pursue unfair, misleading, or dangerous practices. There are remedies to correct these actions.

5. *To look at the current role of consumerism* As in the 1980s, the decade of the 1990s will see less activism than the 1960s and 1970s as a result of the current level and quality of self-regulation, the past accomplishments of consumerism, increased conservatism in the United States, and the importance of other issues. Nonetheless, business, consumers, and government will continue working together to resolve important consumer issues.

Key Terms

social responsibility (p. 707)
socioecological view of
    marketing (p. 707)
planned obsolescence (p. 713)
ethical behavior (p. 713)
process-related ethical issues
    (p. 715)

product-related ethical issues
    (p. 715)
consumerism (p. 719)
consumer bill of rights (p. 720)
warranty (p. 721)
consumer education (p. 722)

Consumer Product Safety
    Commission (CPSC) (p. 723)
product recall (p. 724)
class-action suit (p. 725)
item price removal (p. 731)

Review Questions

1. What are some of the areas in which marketing practices have the potential for both positive and negative consequences for society?

2. Define the term *social responsibility*. What are the implications for marketers?

3. Explain the responsibilities of the final consumer according to the socioecological view of marketing.

4. How can the depletion of natural resources be reduced?

5. Describe the pros and cons of planned obsolescence as a marketing practice.

6. What is ethical behavior? Distinguish between process-related and product-related ethical issues.

7. How does the concept of consumerism differ from social responsibility?

8. Explain the consumer bill of rights.

9. Why is item price removal a controversial practice?

10. Describe the current role of consumerism.

Discussion Questions

1. Comment on the statement, "Our firm looks for opportunities that will help the community. In the end, that helps us too."

2. Why are people's perceptions of marketing mixed? What can be done to improve these perceptions?

3. Evaluate the use of product recall as a tool for regulating product safety.

4. Do consumers in the United States have too many goods and services from which to choose? Why or why not?

5. From a manufacturer's perspective, what would be the advantages and disadvantages of an overall federal agency representing consumer interests?

◄ CASE 1 ►

Alcohol Advertising: Should It Be Further Restricted?*

The twelve members of the Workshop on Drunk Driving recently sent their recommendations about imposing further restrictions on alcohol advertising to the U.S. Surgeon General. The Surgeon General, after reviewing the recommendations as well as comments from the advertising community and beverage makers, was scheduled to make his own recommendations to Congress. Then it would be up to Congress to consider whether to make changes

in the laws relating to the use of advertising and sales promotion in marketing alcoholic beverages.

From its inception, the workshop panel—which contained no representatives from the advertising and alcohol marketing industries—faced controversy. For example, both the National Association of Broadcasters and the Association of National Advertisers declined invitations to participate. And although attendance at workshop sessions was originally scheduled to be on an invitation-only basis, the National Beer Wholesalers Association won a lawsuit requiring that meetings be open to

---

* The data in this case are drawn from Cyndee Miller, "Proposed Alcohol Ad Restrictions Cause Brew-Haha," *Marketing News* (February 13, 1989), pp. 2, 8.

the public and the media. As an *Advertising Age* editorial stated: "It's a pretty disastrous start for an issue that is so important to all parties."

After all meetings were held, the Workshop on Drunk Driving concluded that alcohol advertising "tends to glamorize alcohol use," yet does not provide users with adequate information about the implications of drinking. These were some of the panel's specific recommendations:

- There should be as much media time (space) for public health and safety messages as for alcohol-related advertising.
- Official sponsorships of athletic events, including the Olympics, by alcohol marketers should be banned.
- The tax deductibility of alcohol-related advertising and sales promotions by firms should be reduced.
- Warning labels should be placed in a clear and conspicuous manner in all alcohol advertising. Such warnings were required on alcohol beverage containers as of October 1989.
- Beer and wine excise taxes should be raised to the level for distilled spirits.
- There should be additional research into the effects of specific forms of advertising and sales promotion on alcohol consumption.
- The use of celebrities with a strong "youth appeal" should be banned from alcohol advertising and promotions.
- Alcohol advertising and promotions on college campuses should be discontinued.

The reactions to these recommendations from the Alcohol Beverage Legislative Council, the

National Beer Wholesalers Association, and the American Advertising Federation were all fast and furious—"few of the workshop participants could have expected the intensity of the fight put up by the alcohol and ad industries."

The Alcohol Beverage Legislative Council's president—referring to the lack of panel representation from the advertising and marketing industries—said it was "difficult to comment on a kangaroo court." The head of the government affairs division of the National Beer Wholesalers Association stated that, although the proposed excise tax on beer could result in a more than 1,000 per cent increase in the price of beer, it would not stop abusers from driving: "It's like increasing the tax on automobiles to cut down on drunken driving." He also cited data from the Centers of Disease Control in Atlanta showing that the number of alcohol-related driving accidents had declined by 17 per cent over the prior five years.

The American Advertising Federation's president called the recommendations "clearly unconstitutional, counterproductive, and discriminatory." He also found the panel's conclusions to be "based upon conjecture and anecdotal evidence with marked bias against alcohol and advertising." Before the workshop began, the federation had given the U.S. Surgeon General copies of two comprehensive research studies—one by the Federal Trade Commission, the other by the University of Texas—which found no relationship between alcohol advertising and alcohol usage. The federation recommended that all final actions relative to advertising regulation be postponed until additional conclusive research is conducted in this area.

QUESTIONS

1. Evaluate the issue of the advertising of alcoholic beverages from a social responsibility perspective.
2. Is the advertising of alcoholic beverages a product- or process-related ethical issue? Explain your answer.
3. Should the panel have included representatives from the advertising and marketing industries? Discuss the

pros and cons of not including such representatives.
4. Present a range of alternative laws for Congress to consider regarding the use of advertising and sales promotion for alcoholic beverages. Discuss the ramifications of each.

◄ CASE 2 ►

Doing Well by Doing Good?†

In cause-related marketing, profit-oriented firms contribute a specific amount to a given charity for each consumer purchase of certain goods and services. The term cause-related marketing was first popularized in 1983 when American Express agreed to contribute one cent to the restoration of the Statue of Liberty every time consumers used its credit cards.

Although cause-related marketing in the United States raised only $100 million for charities in 1988—versus $4.6 billion in conventional corporate giving, many charities are increasingly turning to cause-related marketing programs. For example, by 1993, the American Red Cross plans to raise $10 million annually (40 per cent of its national disaster relief budget) through this approach.

There are various ways in which cause-related marketing can be implemented. The American Red Cross is working on a licensing arrangement in which it would receive royalties from a Red Cross logo placed on a Clara Barton doll. Johnson & Johnson's Personal Products Co. contributes $1 million each year to Shelter Aid (a network of shelters and a national hotline for victims of domestic violence), based on special coupon redemptions. The March of Dimes Birth Defects Foundation received $150,000 from Campbell Soup, when the latter sponsored a walkathon.

Even small- and medium-sized firms have been using cause-related marketing. For instance, one Ohio retailer ran a promotion in which toy pandas were sold for $19.99 each, with the retailer donating $2 to the Toledo Zoo for every panda sold. The proceeds were used for the care of the zoo's real pandas.

Marketing personnel, hired by charities and other nonprofit organizations to expand cause-related marketing programs, usually study product season-

ality and traditional coupon redemption rates. Then they choose sponsors whose products are popular, who are willing to provide promotional support, and who are willing to make an appropriate contribution per good or service purchased or coupon redeemed.

Advocates of cause-related marketing feel it

▷ Generally results in increased, rather than decreased, direct corporate giving.
▷ Is used judiciously by nonprofit organizations, which usually have strict standards for choosing their partners. For example, many charities will not join forces with tobacco companies.
▷ Creates a "win-win" situation. Sponsors promote their products' usage, and nonprofit organizations gain funding. And each party gains visibility and prestige from the other.
▷ Helps differentiate company products from those of competitors.
▷ Can generate substantial revenues for charities. As an illustration, Big Brothers/Big Sisters relies on cause-related marketing for 15 to 20 per cent of its overall budget. The revenues obtained in this method are especially important to those charities facing reductions in government spending or in corporate philanthropy.

Despite the potential advantages of cause-related marketing to both parties, critics feel this practice

▷ Is contrary to traditional "no-strings attached" corporate giving. There are major philosophical differences between company contributions that are purely humanitarian and those based on indirect business gains.
▷ Supports well-established and noncontroversial charities and causes at the expense of newer and more controversial charities and causes. For example, MasterCard recently raised $3 million for six charities; the relative contributions to each charity were partially decided on the basis of a consumer poll.

---

† The data in this case are drawn from Mary Ann Linsen, "Charitable Contributions: Altruism or Good Business?" *Progressive Grocer* (November 1988), pp. 111–115; and Zachary Schiller, "Doing Well by Doing Good," *Business Week* (December 5, 1988), pp. 53, 57.

▶ Could result in negative publicity for the sponsor if there is mismanagement on the part of the charity.

▶ Could compromise a charity's neutrality and its broad-based appeal. For instance, the United Way, the largest fund-raiser for charities, suggests that its affiliate organizations show extreme caution in the use of cause-related marketing and in the selection of marketer/sponsors.

▶ May disproportionately benefit the sponsor in relation to the charity. Many charities do not fully realize the value of their name to a marketer/sponsor.

QUESTIONS

1. Evaluate the arguments for and against the use of cause-related marketing.
2. Set up a plan for a small firm to become involved in cause-related marketing.
3. Present several criteria for the Boy/Girl Scouts to use in considering the choice of a sponsor and marketing theme for a major fund-raising drive.
4. Comment on this statement: "American Express has avoided national cause-related marketing campaigns lately because it doesn't see any causes that would spark big enthusiasm."

part 7 CASE

Colgate-Palmolive: Fine-Tuning an International Marketing Strategy*

Introduction

To get some insight into the issue of global branding and segmentation, we will look at an example of a multinational company that has several global brands. Colgate-Palmolive is truly global in scope, with subsidiaries in 55 countries and an official presence in 120. The company's product mix includes several global brands — including the two parent brands, Colgate toothpaste and Palmolive soap. The former is sold in 53 countries and the latter in 43.

C-P's early experience in global branding was similar to that of many other packaged-goods companies that expanded their sales base in the early twentieth century. Basically, they took the key products that were successful in the United States and Europe and began to move them out across the developing countries. In many cases, the success of these brands appears to be due to the order-of-entry phenomenon. They often were the first entries into a country. They literally created the category and their names became synonymous with it. But were these truly "global" brands?

Evaluating the Global Nature of Brands

Colgate-Palmolive's Business Development Group was

* Adapted by the authors from Elana Hudak, "Global Branding and Segmentation: Are They Interdependent?" *Journal of Consumer Marketing,* Vol. 5 (Summer 1988), pp. 27–34. Reprinted by permission.

formed in 1980 and its mission was to assist the company in caring for people, their possessions, and their environment by supplying consumer goods and services of real value to the global marketplace.

One of the group's first projects was to review the company's global brands. As a result of their investigations, several startling facts were uncovered. For instance, although Palmolive soap was considered a global brand, it was sold in 9 different shapes, 22 different fragrances, and 17 different packages. Similar situations existed for Colgate toothpaste and Palmolive shampoo.

C-P decided that while these brands were being sold on a global basis, the company was not enjoying the benefits of global branding such as advertising and manufacturing efficiencies, capital expenditure savings, and so on. Therefore, C-P implemented a program to correct existing inconsistencies as well as to provide control for the growth of new global properties.

The Research Plan: Rudimentary Segmentation

One of the key elements of the program was the consumer research. It revolved around the identification and analysis of basic subgroups. In one respect, this is a kind of rudimentary segmentation, since the sample is split into self-defined groups which have certain commonalities (demographics, hair type, method of washing dishes, etc.). One analysis that has proved to be particularly useful was a basic user analysis, splitting respondents into various user groups based on their response to the following eight-point scale:

1. I have never heard of the brand
2. I only know the name
3. I have never used it and I would be interested in trying it
4. I have never used it and I would not be interested in trying it
5. I have used it in the past and did not like it
6. I have used it in the past and would be willing to use it again
7. I occasionally use it
8. I regularly use a product or products under this brand name

A comparison of loyal brand users to occasional and nonuser groups helped to identify areas of weakness and strength.

When this technique was used in several countries around the world, it was discovered that Palmolive soap clearly had two very different strategic positionings: as an all-family soap and as a cosmetic soap. It was also discovered that regardless of the positioning, the brand was generally viewed as traditional, wholesome, and a good value among the loyal users and as old-fashioned and for older people among the occasional and nonusers. The brand image was also less well developed among the younger consumers. On the basis of these data, it was decided to update the brand's image while globalizing its various product elements.

Globalizing Palmolive Soap

The relaunch was not easy, since the company was dealing with two very different strategies. Wherever possible, the changes selected worked well with either positioning. There wasn't always one viable solution, however, and this certainly became evident in the case of copy. In order to address the two distinct strategic positionings, two very different creative directions were taken. Eventually, two ads were selected. The first was directed at younger soap users and attempted to give the brand a more contemporary image. This commercial, called "Sensacion," started airing in 1984 and is now showing in 26 countries. In the majority of these markets, the brand has experienced strong share gains, and the lead markets are showing

signs of positive imagery shifts, particularly among the target audience.

For those markets, on the other hand, where the brand was seen as all-family, somewhat natural, and wholesome, a different ad was developed, called "Pure Soap." It first aired in 1986 and is running in several countries including the United Kingdom, the country of origin. Because of its use of British/or tongue-in-cheek humor, this commercial had a much more limited ability to transcend cultures. Though the ads are very different, each satisfied a particular set of brand marketing needs.

In terms of shapes, fragrances, and packages, the task of consolidation has also been successful. Today Palmolive soap has only 3 shapes (down from 9), 7 fragrances (rather than 22), and 3 packages (rather than 17) worldwide. One might say that this part of the program was driven by "mechanical" segmentation — taking all competitive packages, fragrances, and shapes and finding a combination that would make the product distinct.

Expanding the Plan to Other Products

A similar program for Palmolive shampoo involved broad-scale consumer research undertaken in 1983 and 1984 in Europe and South America, whose countries account for 70 per cent of Palmolive shampoo's worldwide sales. The studies included a segmentation analysis, and while the segments that were identified in each country were quite similar, they did differ in size. From the analysis, it also became apparent that none of these markets were developed to the point where a strong brand or even attitudinal segmentation existed. Although the segments did differ somewhat in what they desired in a shampoo and a conditioner, these differences were driven by the respondent's age or hair-care problems, such as oily or dry hair. Overall, the differences noted were not as major as one would expect in a country such as the United States.

Once again, it was a simple analysis of the various Palmolive user groups that proved to be particularly insightful. The results indicated that (1) it was possible to have a single strategy for the brand, and (2) the strategy should focus on the brand's strengths (all-family, traditional, practical, and casual) and correct its weaknesses (old-fashioned, ordinary, dull). A modernization program for the brand image and packaging were undertaken.

Subsequent to the study, the Palmolive strategy has been strengthened to include a natural ingredient story. The formulas have been designed to address the needs of specific hair types (normal, dry, and oily). Packaging has been updated to communicate the natural, wholesome positioning in a modern look. Advertising copy focuses on the shiny, healthy looking hair which comes from using new Palmolive.

In addition, it was decided that C-P could further enhance Palmolive's image by expanding the range of hair-care products offered under its trademark. The natural expansion was to launch conditioners, a category that is still developing in many countries where Palmolive shampoo is sold. Since it is likely that the first purchasers would be its shampoo users, the company planned on variants that correspond to the shampoo types and that feature the same fragrance. To date, the brand has been relaunched in ten countries with shampoo sales increasing 40 to 50 per cent during the first year and conditioner sales coming in about as forecast.

As the program of globalization of existing products got under way, the company turned its attention toward expanding and updating each category's portfolio. As with many of its global brands, it identified its next body-cleaning opportunity through analyzing a multicountry study of consumers' washing habits. This study identified a trend away from bar soaps toward gels and liquid bath/shower products.

C-P undertook a project to introduce a line of these products, with Europe as the lead division. In order to ensure that this was a Pan-European effort, a project marketing coordinator was appointed and assigned to a European office. Since one of the primary goals of the line extension was to contemporize the Palmolive brand image, the new design was to incorporate as many of the key elements of the bar soap as possible. The final line includes a cosmetic-looking pearlized bottle with a green cap and green liquid-shower gel matching the parent brand and a blue cap and blue liquid-bath foam extension. While the seashell insignia shown on these bottles was originally selected because of its cosmetic image, there has been some indication that consumers do not relate these products to the parent brand.

A program is currently underway to incorporate the bar soap graphics on these items in a consumer-acceptable way. Launch advertising uses the "Sensacion" ad mentioned earlier and features both the liquid products and the bar soap. This copy has proven to be quite effective in communicating the new products and contemporizing the brand's image.

Searches for the next generation of Colgate-Palmolive global products have involved various methods of getting closer to the consumer. For the dishwashing category, consumers were observed washing dishes in their homes. Using this method, a bright marketing manager was able to take a consumer need and turn it into a global marketing opportunity. Specifically, it was noticed that women in several third world countries who lacked hot water or, in some cases, indoor plumbing would place the leftover chips of their laundry detergent bar into a small bowl beside the sink and then add water, creating a thick soapy product with which they washed their dishes.

The marketing challenge was to produce a product that would allow these women to continue to wash dishes in this manner. It would have a formula created especially for dish cleaning, being more effective and longer lasting, thus representing a good value to these women. Axion dishwashing was Colgate-Palmolive's answer to the challenge. The product is a green paste with a lemon fragrance that is sold in a small tub. To date, this product has been introduced in 17 countries and has taken a lion's share of the market in most of them.

Consumer-Oriented Marketing on a Global Scale

Prior to the formation of the Business Development Group, Colgate-Palmolive's global focus on various categories had traditionally been formula- or product-driven. Management had forgotten the maxim that "People don't buy products, they buy solutions to problems." Its market research efforts had been largely product-oriented and generally had a narrow focus. In 1986, however, a large-scale household products research initiative was undertaken in the United States and several European countries. The objectives of the program centered on (1) updating C-P consumer knowledge on the current state of the home: the incidence of surfaces, appliances and their material composition, cleaning habits and practices, and consumer attitudes toward home maintenance; (2) providing a foundation for a consumer-driven new-products program; and (3) providing valuable direction for the marketing efforts of current C-P products.

The research action plan included both qualitative and quantitative phases. The qualitative phase took place in the respondent's home and included extensive photographing of all rooms. The quantitative phase utilized a modular questionnaire. The six modules were incidence and surface composition, cleaning habits and practices, importance of attributes for various cleaning tasks, consumer attitudes toward home maintenance, consumer perceptions of major household product segments, and demographics.

A wealth of consumer insight was generated by these studies, but one analysis in particular has proven quite exciting. Using a computer model and inputting information on the frequency of cleaning, the usage method, and the amount of the product used per application, it was possible to generate the relative volumetric usage of the full range of cleaning products. These data were then related to the six modules in the questionnaire. Each module's data could be added to the preceding one to give a truly complete picture of the cleaning experience.

In 1985, C-P decided to further consolidate its marketing efforts by selling a line of products under each global brand name. While the company is still in the early stages of this effort, it has made a good beginning by conducting a major brand image study in several key countries. The purpose of the study was to determine which of the corporate names most lend themselves to franchise management. On the basis of this research, several strategic platforms have been developed and tested, and new guidelines for advertising and packaging are being implemented.

A Basic Consumer Insight Tool Kit

Colgate-Palmolive believes in the basics of getting unique consumer insight by integrating and synthesizing its knowledge from formal and informal research. Jim Figura, Director of Corporate Research at Colgate-Palmolive, has challenged marketing and market research to use basic methods first before delving into elaborate research. The following is a description of what items a basic consumer tool kit should contain and how best to use them.

Use focus group interviews and in-depths better. People who have witnessed these "consumer encounters" were most likely out of sight, behind a one-way mirror. In the opinion of many people, these continue to be among the most powerful — yet misused — tools. There are, however, several ways to make them more useful and insightful. First, ask the right question. All too often people are brought in and asked only about the most obvious things. Observers seldom get a genuinely good, rich, feeling for the people. While the setting doesn't help, the real problem is a lack of focus on ideas. For instance, instead of asking people about product attributes and benefits and usage behavior for shampoos, why not focus on grooming rituals, perceptions of beauty, feelings about hair and femininity or masculinity, and so on. The right question is one that leads to a unique insight, which in turn leads to an idea about how to do things better. Also, observers must learn to listen and watch. Often the room behind the mirror is turned into a coffee klatch with little concern for what is happening on the other side. Observers must pay attention not only to what people say but to how they say it. They must listen as detached observers. They must watch for nonverbal responses as well as spoken ones.

Create ethnography. This is just a fancy term for the concept of management probes. At Colgate-Palmolive, these probes were meant to bring the manufacturer and consumer together. The ideal setting for this encounter is in the consumer's home, where their behavior can be observed. It's important to learn how people think and live. Today, with the use of video recorders, this can prove to be a rich and meaningful experience similar to the Axion Paste example mentioned previously.

Apply personal brand experience. This device is slightly contrived, but it makes one shift away from marketing expert to consumer. A business team is asked to use a product over a certain time period. They then meet to share their experiences and generate ideas. Simple, but how often do firms really use this technique?

Participate in the consumer's world. This too is very basic, but how many times in the past year have marketing executives done any of the following: Read the books and magazines aimed at their target market (not just looked at the ads)? Gone to their restaurants, shops, clubs, etc.? If they have done these things, have they really involved themselves or have they done them from a distance with their marketing hat on?

Describe who the consumer is in the first person. Try to write a story about the consumer. Marketers should try to relate the consumer and the product and the consumer/product experience to something they know and feel.

Bring the consumer to a company meeting. If marketers have done all of the above, consumers will be interested in buying products.

Conclusion

On the basis of Colgate-Palmolive's experience, it can be said that although global branding and segmentation have not been interdependent in the past, they may be in the future. But don't think of segmentation in complex terms. Keep it simple, using the tools on hand. There is still a lot of mileage in the most basic kinds of methods and analysis, especially when it comes to global research.

QUESTIONS

1. Evaluate Colgate-Palmolive's international marketing strategy.
2. What could other firms learn from Colgate-Palmolive?
3. How should Colgate-Palmolive's marketing efforts differ in industrialized, developing, and less-developed countries?
4. As Colgate-Palmolive seeks to expand internationally, should it be involved with joint ventures? Why or why not?
5. Would you view Colgate-Palmolive's international product planning to be aggressive or conservative? Explain your answer.
6. Comment on this statement: "Although global branding and segmentation have not been interdependent in the past, they may be in the future."
7. If Colgate-Palmolive decides to become a service marketer operating internationally, what special considerations would it face?
8. What social responsibility and ethical issues should Colgate-Palmolive keep in mind when engaged in international marketing?

part 8
MARKETING MANAGEMENT

In Part 8, we tie together the concepts introduced in Chapters 1 through 23 and discuss planning for the future.

24 **Integrating and Analyzing the Marketing Plan**   In this chapter, we examine each of the elements in a well-integrated marketing plan: a clear organizational mission, long-term competitive advantages, a precisely defined target market, compatible subplans, coordination among SBUs, coordination of the marketing mix, and stability over time. As an illustration, we look at the strategy of Kentucky Fried Chicken. Next, we study three types of marketing plan analysis: marketing cost analysis, sales analysis, and the marketing audit. These are important tools for evaluating the success or failure of marketing plans. We conclude with a look at how firms should anticipate and plan for the future.

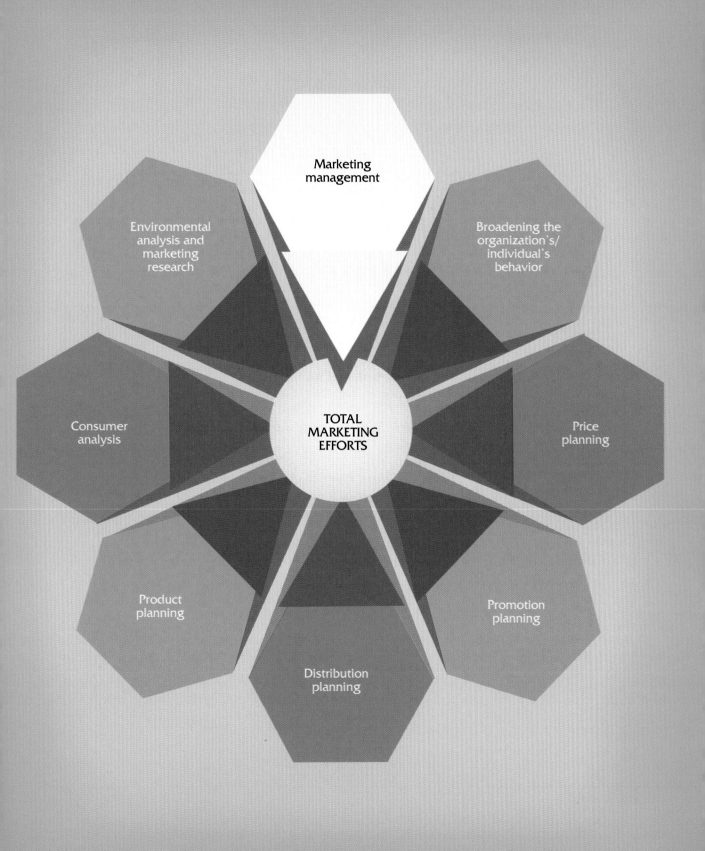

CHAPTER *24*

Integrating and Analyzing the Marketing Plan

CHAPTER OBJECTIVES

1. To show the value of an integrated marketing plan

2. To discuss the elements of a well-integrated marketing plan

3. To present three types of marketing plan analysis: marketing cost analysis, sales analysis, and the marketing audit

4. To demonstrate the importance of anticipating and planning for the future

Whom do America's top business leaders consider the most effective member of their brotherhood? When asked in the latest *Fortune 500/CNN Moneyline* CEO poll, executives mentioned more than 100 names. The winner, Ford Motor chief Donald E. Petersen, was a bit of a surprise, considering the vast amount of favorable publicity that has surrounded Detroit rival Lee A. Iacocca.

The selection of Petersen, who received votes from 25 per cent of the chief executives who participated in the poll, is largely due to Ford's recent performance. For example, in 1988, Ford's $5.3 billion profit was higher than General Motors'—although GM's sales were 31 per cent greater. And while General Motors' market share slipped slightly from 1987 to 1988 (despite the introduction of eight new models), Ford's market share (with only two new models) rose. Let us see why.

Ford's success is keyed to its utilization of an integrated marketing strategy. This strategy relies on marketing research, stylish design, employee participation, and a focus on quality.

Ford now uses extensive marketing research. According to Petersen, "We had made so many mistakes in the past following this or that trend, this or that competitor. Finally we realized that we should not be driven by other people's choices but by our customers. We've been going our own way ever since."

Ford regularly researches consumers to determine their reactions to proposed designs and features. For example, Ford chose not to use fender skirts and a hatchback design for a new model Thunderbird after hearing negative comments from consumers. It also decided to reinstate an old-style push-pull headlight switch because customers liked that version better than a modern rocker or rotary one. Ford is even considering giving a sample of consumers a peek at a model that will be available in five years.

Special emphasis is placed on styling via Ford's "Concept to Customer" program, which involves brainstorming on styling concepts and designers working closely with engineering. For instance, the popularity of Ford's Lincoln Continental and Ford Probe (with the same power train and platform as Mazda's MX-6, but outselling the MX-6 by four to one) are closely linked to attractive styling.

Petersen was among the first U.S. CEOs to give lower-level workers a prominent voice in decisions: "Anyone who has a legitimate reason, who will be affected by a decision, ought to have the feeling that people want to know how he or she feels."

Reprinted by permission.

Ford's "Quality is Job One" image has been heavily promoted. The firm takes pride in being viewed as a quality leader among U.S. car makers via high ratings from such impartial sources as J.D. Power & Associates.

The company also realizes that it must not be complacent if it wants to be successful in the future. Foreign competition is strong. General Motors is beginning to aggressively emerge from its extended slump. The overall U.S. auto industry may be up one year and down the next due to erratic consumer demand. Many consumers now wait for special financing incentives before buying. And Ford's emphasis on high quality must be maintained although some of its plants are operating at capacity, with workers there regularly on overtime; Ford knows that it must hold on to its reputation for quality to sustain long-run sales growth.[1]

In this chapter, we will study how a firm can integrate and analyze a marketing plan—and see the value of developing and implementing a clear, forward-looking, cohesive, and adaptable marketing strategy.

[1] Kate Ballen, "The No. 1 Leader Is Petersen of Ford," *Fortune* (October 24, 1988), pp. 69–70; Alex Taylor III, "Why Fords Sell Like Big Macs," *Fortune* (November 21, 1988), pp. 122–123; and James B. Treece and Wendy Zellner, "Detroit Tries to Rev Up," *Business Week* (June 12, 1989), pp. 78–82.

Overview

Chapters 1 and 2 in the text introduced basic marketing concepts and described the marketing environment. Chapter 3 presented the strategic planning process as it applies to marketing. Chapters 4 through 20 centered on the specific aspects of planning in marketing: marketing research and information systems, describing and selecting target markets, and the four basic aspects of the marketing mix (product, distribution, promotion, and pricing). Chapters 21 through 23 broadened the scope of marketing to include international marketing efforts, service and nonprofit marketing, and the societal implications of marketing.

Chapter 24 describes how a marketing plan can be integrated and evaluated. An integrated marketing effort is necessary if the individual components of marketing (particularly product, distribution, promotion, and pricing factors) are to be synchronized. Marketing analysis is necessary if an organization wants to appraise performance, capitalize on strengths, minimize weaknesses, and plan for the future.

Integrating the Marketing Plan

The many parts of a marketing plan should be unified, consistent, and coordinated.

An integrated marketing plan is one in which all of its various parts are unified, consistent, and coordinated. Although this appears to be a simple task, it is important to recall that a firm may have long-run, moderate-length, and short-run plans; the

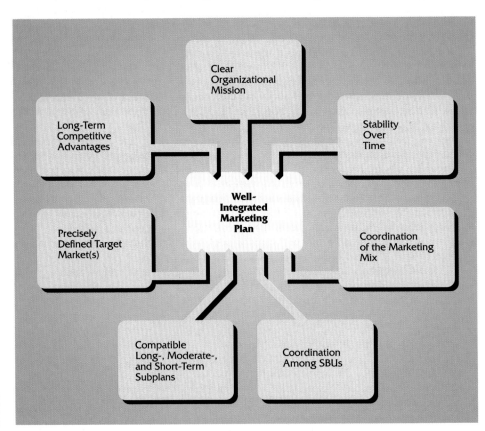

FIGURE 24-1
Elements Leading to a Well-Integrated Marketing Plan

different strategic business units in an organization may require separate marketing plans; and each aspect of the marketing mix requires planning. For example,

▶ An overall plan would be poorly integrated if short-run profits are earned at the expense of moderate- or long-term profits. This could occur if marketing research or new-product planning expenditures are reduced to raise profits temporarily. A firm could also encounter difficulties if plans are changed too frequently, leading to a blurred image for consumers and a lack of focus for executives.

▶ Resources need to be allocated among SBUs, so that funds are given to those with high potential. The target markets, product images, price levels, and so on, of each SBU must be distinctive — yet not in conflict with one another. Physical-distribution efforts and channel-member arrangements need to be timed so that the system is not strained by two or more SBUs making costly demands simultaneously.

▶ Even though a promotion plan primarily deals with one strategic element, it must also be integrated with product, distribution, and pricing plans. It must reflect the proper image for the company's products, encourage channel cooperation, and demonstrate that the products are worth the prices set.

In the next subsections, the elements of a well-integrated marketing plan are described, and the marketing plan of Kentucky Fried Chicken is examined in terms of its level of integration.

The Elements of a Well-Integrated Marketing Plan

A well-integrated marketing plan incorporates the elements shown in Figure 24-1 and explained in this subsection.[2]

A clear organizational mission outlines a firm's commitment to a type of business and a place in the market. Its organizational mission is involved whenever a company seeks new customer groups or abandons existing ones, adds or deletes product lines, acquires other firms or sells part of its own business, performs different marketing functions, and/or shifts technological focus (as noted in Chapter 3). Both top management and marketing personnel must be committed to an organizational mission for it to be achieved; and the mission must be communicated to all company employees. For example, Heinz has a directive — yet flexible — organizational mission:

The organizational mission should be clear and directive.

> [At Heinz,] we have had to think beyond traditions and transform ourselves from an old pickling-and-bottled-goods business into a resourceful, creative, and decisive food-processing-and-nutritional-services company. We have fashioned new strategies for growth, applied them to thriving market niches, and exploited opportunities which, with skillful nurturing, we have turned into substantial and profitable ventures.
>
> The process by which we have transformed ourselves and our markets can be outlined in three steps. First, we explore the niches that make up the nation, and even the world. We are alert to trends and attentive to tastes as we keep pace with the effects of culture, life-style, and technology on eating habits around the globe. Second, we devise a strategy to fill the niches. We plan for the long term, with patience and sometimes stealth. We target areas of growth and promise, looking for products, processing, or packaging that will match the needs of the market, whatever they might be. Finally, we seize opportunities. Through prudent, prescient acquisitions, we find products and companies best

---

[2] See Barry Berman and Joel R. Evans, "Integrating the Marketing Plan: Lessons from Marketing Management, Strategic Marketing, and Marketing Implementation" in Robert F. Lusch et al. (Editors), *1985 AMA Educators' Proceedings* (Chicago: American Marketing Association, 1985), pp. 269–274.

suited to each particular strategy. Through new-product development, we present consumers with processed foods of the highest quality, the greatest purity, and the most competitive price.[3]

Many experts believe that a firm should reappraise its organizational mission if it has values that do not fit a changing environment; its industry undergoes rapid changes; its performance is mediocre or worse; it is changing size (from small to large or large to small); or opportunities unrelated to its original mission arise.[4]

---

[3] Anthony J. F. O'Reilly, "Strategy & Opportunism: Companions to Business Success," remarks to the New York Society of Security Analysts (March 14, 1988), p. 11.

[4] Adapted by the authors from Bro Uttal, "The Corporate Culture Vultures," *Fortune* (October 17, 1983), p. 70.

Long-term competitive advantages are company and product attributes whose distinctiveness and appeal to consumers can be maintained over an extended period of time. A firm must capitalize on the product attributes that are most important to consumers and develop competitive advantages accordingly. For competitive advantages to be sustainable, consumers must perceive a consistent positive difference in key attributes between the company's offerings and those of competitors; that difference must be linked to a capability gap that competitors will have difficulty in closing (due to patents, superior marketing skills, customer loyalty, and so on); and the company's offerings must appeal to some enduring consumer need.[5]

> *Competitive advantages should center on company (product) attributes that have long-range distinctiveness.*

Here are three examples of firms that have developed successful long-term competitive advantages because they identified opportunities in the marketplace at a time when others did not — and seized upon them: Chem Lawn saw a fragmented lawn-care industry comprised of many small competitors. It enacted a strategy that offered consistent quality, responsive services, a trusted name, reasonable prices, and guaranteed results. Lens Crafters saw the potential for a chain of optical outlets because the eye-care industry was dominated by single-office optometrists. It opened a number of stores in convenient locations, offered eye exams and optical products at reasonable prices, and had one-hour service.[6] Club Med saw the opportunity for vacations that featured sports, relaxation, and social interaction in an informal setting. Today Club Med has all-inclusive vacation facilities around the world. It offers "the antidote for civilization." See Figure 24-2.

Because smaller firms often cannot compete on the basis of low prices, they may concentrate on other competitive advantages, such as

▶ Providing unique offerings through specialization. Firms can design innovative products, handle customized orders, or otherwise tailor items for individual customers. "Your best customers can sometimes be your best sources of information."

▶ Stressing product quality and reliability. "The more crucial the performance of the product to the customers' needs, the lower will be their concern with pricing."

▶ Making extra efforts to gain customer loyalty. These include making the purchase process easy, giving personal attention, and promising the long-term availability of goods and services. As one small-firm executive said, "We know our products are reliable and do not require visits. But when our clients see us physically inspecting our machines, sometimes merely dusting them off, they derive a sense of security and comfort."[7]

When implementing a marketing strategy, a firm should note that its competitive advantages may not apply in all situations. As an illustration, Domino's Pizza is the second largest fast-food pizza chain in the United States (behind Pizza Hut), with annual sales of more than $2 billion. Domino's has dominated its U.S. market niche because it was the first company to recognize consumers' interest in prompt and reliable home delivery; when it began, there was no major competitor. Domino's

---

[5] Kevin P. Coyne, "Sustainable Competitive Advantage — What It Is, What It Isn't," *Business Horizons*, Vol. 29 (January–February 1986), pp. 55–60. See also Patricia Sellers, "Getting Customers to Love You," *Fortune* (March 13, 1989), pp. 38–49.

[6] David W. Cravens, "Gaining Strategic Marketing Advantage," *Business Horizons*, Vol. 31 (September–October 1988), p. 53.

[7] Peter Wright, "Competitive Strategies for Small Business," *Collegiate Forum* (Spring 1983), pp. 3–4; and Steven P. Galante, "More Firms Quiz Customers for Clues about Competition," *Wall Street Journal* (March 3, 1986), p. 21.

Marketing Controversy

Is Big Beautiful?

One of the classic debates in marketing relates to the importance of company size in developing, integrating, and implementing strategies: Can small firms compete successfully against larger ones? Can a firm become so large that it is no longer responsive to the marketplace?

Those who advocate smallness make these points:

▶ *Small firms compete against larger ones on the basis of flexibility, niche marketing, personal service, quicker reactions to marketplace changes, and high product quality.*

▶ *Many new U.S. technological advances are generated by small firms. For example, "virtually every innovation in computation since the mainframe—the microprocessor, personal computer, minicomputer, workstation, and much software—has been started or commercialized by entrepreneurial firms."*

▶ *A Business Week study of the top 1,000 U.S. companies found that the largest companies were the most profitable in only 4 out of 67 industries.*

▶ *Small firms are instrumental in job creation. According to one economist, small firms have generated a majority of the more than twenty million new jobs that have been added to the U.S. economy since 1977.*

Those who favor bigness counter with these points:

▶ *Large firms benefit from economies of scale, bargaining power, name recognition, strong distribution networks, large promotion budgets, and employee specialization.*

▶ *Large firms can have the best of both worlds if they use organization structures that are responsive and entrepreneurial. For example, General Electric, Johnson & Johnson, and Hewlett-Packard have organized themselves into groups of smaller companies (SBUs).*

▶ *Large size is needed to compete against foreign firms that are often huge, subsidized, and sometimes even country-owned. According to one expert, "small companies can't survive against Japan's stable, concentrated, and protected alliances."*

▶ *The largest corporations account for almost 30 per cent of U.S. GNP and employ 80 per cent of the nation's scientists and engineers.*

As a marketing analyst, what do you think?

SOURCE: Based on material in John A. Byrne, "Is Your Company Too Big?" *Business Week* (March 27, 1989), pp. 84–94; and Walter Guzzardi, "Big Can Still Be Beautiful," *Fortune* (April 25, 1988), pp. 50–64.

---

features guaranteed 30-minute delivery service on telephone orders through its thousands of U.S. outlets, consistent quality, courteous employees, reasonable prices, and hot pizza.[8] About 85 per cent of Domino's U.S. sales involve delivery. However, in international markets, Domino's must sell the concept of home delivery; in most countries, this service has not been available to consumers before and they need to be persuaded of its benefit. Furthermore, transportation facilities in some countries make 30-minute delivery difficult.

The target market(s) should be identified precisely.

By precisely defining its target market(s), a firm identifies the specific consumers to be addressed in its marketing plans. This guides the firm's current marketing efforts

---

[8] Cravens, "Gaining Strategic Marketing Advantage," p. 53; and "Domino's Pizza," *Advertising Age* (November 21, 1988), p. S-13.

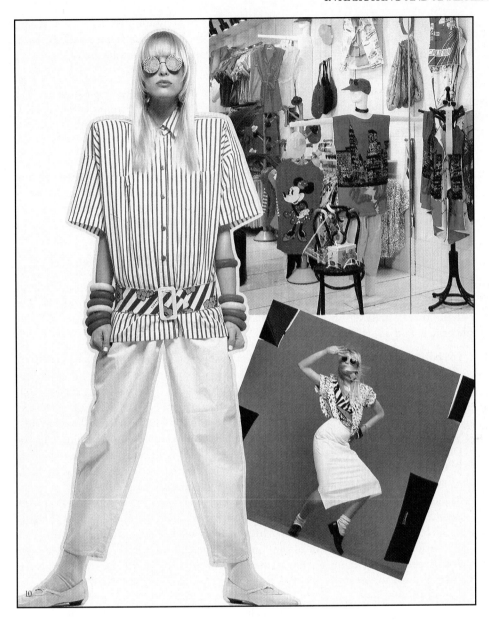

and future direction. When a company engages in differentiated marketing (multiple segmentation), it is essential that each segment be described fully. For example, Limited Inc. appeals to several distinct market segments and has separate stores (catalogs) for each, such as: Express stores for trendy younger women; The Limited stores for fashion-conscious women; Lerner stores for budget-conscious women; Lane Bryant and Roaman's stores for full-size women; Henri Bendel's store for upscale high-fashion women; and Victoria's Secret and Brylane's for women catalog shoppers.[9] Figure 24-3 highlights the Limited Inc.'s Express.

[9] *The Limited Inc. 1988 Annual Report;* and Carol Hymowitz, "Limited Inc., on New Tack, Pulls Ahead of Retail Gang," *Wall Street Journal* (February 24, 1989), pp. B1, B5.

Sometimes a firm's target market approach has to be fine-tuned because of changing demographics and life-styles — or declining sales. As an illustration, with the aging of the U.S. population, many companies are placing greater emphasis on older consumers:

> People in this market respond well to advertisers who show older people in happy, productive, and fun settings. Sales of General Foods Corp.'s Post Natural Bran flakes have gone up 10 per cent since GF began using ads with Lena Horne, Rue McClanahan of *Golden Girls*, and Steve Allen. Research also shows that older viewers like Coke Classic ads featuring Art Carney with a young boy who plays his grandson.[10]

Long-, moderate-, and short-term subplans should be compatible.

The long-, moderate-, and short-term marketing subplans of the company need to be compatible with one another. Long-term plans are the most general and set a broad framework for moderate-term plans. Short-term plans are the most specific; but they should be derived from both moderate- and long-term plans, as the following Dayton Hudson example shows.

Dayton Hudson is a retailer with stores in 36 states. It operates Target, an upscale discount-store chain; Mervyn's, a discount department-store chain; Dayton's and Hudson's, department-store chains; and Lechmere, a home-and-leisure-products-store chain. Dayton Hudson operates a total of 600+ stores and has annual sales exceeding $11 billion. Its marketing strategy is based on a compatible combination of long-, moderate-, and short-term plans:

▶ Executives meet regularly to discuss long-range plans. The overriding goal is to "achieve consistent earnings growth and a significant return on investment for our shareholders. We know that in order to achieve this goal we must balance our long-term investments and our near-term performance." As a result, in recent years, the firm has divested itself of B. Dalton Bookseller, the second-largest bookstore chain in the United States; Branden's, a household-goods chain; and the Dayton Hudson Jewelers' chain. See Figure 24-4. A decentralized management structure places great control in the hands of the executives at each of its store chains. Marketing research studies are conducted regularly.

▶ Moderate-term plans focus on changes in target customers, service-level requirements and projections, resource allocation, merchandise trends, and expansion. Between 1985 and 1990, Dayton Hudson planned to spend about $4 billion on expansion, with 90 per cent of that amount allocated to Target and Mervyn's. No department-store expansion was planned. Over the last decade, the relative importance of department stores has fallen sharply. They now account for less than 15 per cent of total sales.

▶ Short-term plans are geared toward achieving and maintaining dominance (having the best possible assortment of the merchandise categories carried), quality (in merchandise, management, service, and shopping environment), fashion (timeliness for wearing apparel, kitchen utensils, home furnishings, and so on), convenience (respect for the consumer's time), and price (competitive and fair value).[11]

[10] Walecia Konrad and Gail DeGeorge, "U.S. Companies Go for the Gray," *Business Week* (April 3, 1989), p. 67.

[11] Kenneth A. Macke, "Managing Change: How Dayton Hudson Meets the Challenge," *Journal of Business Strategy*, Vol. 4 (Summer 1983), pp. 78–81; *Dayton Hudson Corporation 1987 Annual Report;* and "Discounters and Specialists Win Merchandise Battle," *Chain Store Age Executive* (November 1988), pp. 64–71.

FIGURE 24-4
**B. Dalton Bookseller:
Not Fitting into Dayton
Hudson's Integrated
Marketing Strategy**
In late 1986, Dayton
Hudson announced that it
was selling the 777-unit
B. Dalton Bookseller
because it did not fit into
its long-term plans. Profits
were too low, stores were
too small, and discount
competition was too
intense.
Reprinted by permission.

Coordination among an organization's SBUs is enhanced when the functions, strategies, and resources allocated to each are described in long-term, moderate-term, and
short-term plans. For instance, at General Electric (GE), there are now fourteen
SBUs — down from dozens several years ago. GE's goal is to "attain competitive advantages that allow it to rank first or second in every market it serves." And its planning
and resource allocation are structured accordingly. In the United States, ten of General
Electric's SBUs rank first in the market: aircraft engines, broadcasting (NBC), circuit
breakers, electric motors, engineering plastics, industrial and power systems, lighting,
locomotives, major appliances, and medical diagnostic imaging. Crucial SBUs are
singled out for the special attention of top management, which coordinates the plans
and allocates resources. GE's management monitors strategy implementation to be
sure of conformity with overall company policy.[12]

Sometimes acquisitions make the coordination of SBUs especially difficult, as IBM
recently discovered. IBM was unable to make the telecommunications division that it
established in 1984, after acquiring Rolm, profitable and therefore sold most of it in
1988. The firm could not meld its telecommunications and computer divisions satisfactorily, did not have the same customer loyalty for telecommunications products as
for computers, and could not overcome the "cut-throat" competition in the telecommunications market.[13]

*SBUs should be
coordinated.*

---

[12] Stratford P. Sherman, "Inside the Mind of Jack Welch," *Fortune* (March 27, 1989), pp. 38–50.
[13] Paul B. Carroll, "IBM to Sell Much of Rolm to Siemens AG in a Retreat from Telecommunications,"
    Wall Street Journal (December 14, 1988), p. A3.

The marketing mix within each SBU should be coordinated.

The components of the marketing mix (product, distribution, promotion, and price) need to be coordinated and consistent with the firm's organizational mission. For example, until 1982, Tonka was known as the "sleepy little toy company that made trucks." The firm manufactured and marketed only a line of moderate-priced trucks, sold them at toy and other stores, and stressed durability in ads. Then Tonka diversified and became a multifaceted toy maker. In 1987, it acquired Kenner Parker Toys. Between 1982 and 1988, annual sales rose from $67 million to $900 million. Tonka's broadened organizational mission has resulted in this well-conceived marketing mix:

▶ Product—Tonka now makes Starting Lineup sports figures, Real Ghostbusters action figures, dolls, Pound Puppies and Care Bear plush animals, Play-Doh, Nerf balls, Monopoly and Clue board games, and many other items.
▶ Distribution—Its toys are carried by all types of stores, from specialized toy stores to discount chains. International sales account for 36 per cent of revenues.
▶ Promotion—Advertising expenditures have increased to $65 million annually. Tonka also participates in television cartoon series and full-length animated movies based on several of its toy characters.
▶ Price—Its toys are usually priced at $20 and less. This encourages multiple purchases and repeat buying.[14]

The stability of the plan should be maintained over time.

A marketing plan must have a certain degree of stability over time in order for it to be implemented and evaluated properly. This does not mean that a marketing plan should be inflexible and therefore unable to adjust to a dynamic environment. Rather, it means that a broad marketing plan, consistent with the firm's organizational mission, should guide long-term efforts and be fine-tuned regularly; the basic plan should remain in effect for a number of years. Short-run marketing plans can be much more flexible, as long as they conform to long-term goals and the organizational mission. For example, low prices might be part of a long-term marketing plan. However, in any particular year, prices might have to be raised in response to environmental forces.

One firm working hard to maintain a stable marketing effort is OshKosh B'Gosh Inc., the manufacturer of overalls and other clothing. Between 1981 and 1988, OshKosh's sales rose from $47 million to $253 million annually, as its children's clothing sales (including overalls, jeans, jumpers, shirts, and blouses) skyrocketed. See Figure 24-5. Because of its growth, OshKosh had to add 10 plants in the South to keep up with demand. As a result, it sometimes had problems in coordinating shipments and maintaining proper levels of inventory. The firm's executives worried that OshKosh would saturate the market too fast and then fade, like Izod. So a strategy to manage growth was devised. OshKosh has built a new distribution center and consolidated its raw-material warehousing efforts to better handle deliveries and inventory levels. It has a licensing agreement with Sears for the latter to make and market some of its mens' sportswear. Price-inelastic consumers are sought; prices are higher than those of Health-Tex and Carter. It is also stepping up efforts in geographic areas where it has not been strong, such as overseas.[15]

Next the marketing plan of Kentucky Fried Chicken is analyzed, on the basis of the elements identified in Figure 24-1.

[14] Mary J. Pitzer, "Why Tonka Needs Truckloads of Pay Dirt," *Business Week* (October 24, 1988), pp. 96–97.
[15] Andrew Patner, "At OshKosh B'Gosh, Childhood's Magic Days Are Past," *Wall Street Journal* (March 9, 1989), p. B2.

FIGURE 24-5
OshKosh B'Gosh's Popular Children's Clothing
Reprinted by permission.

Kentucky Fried Chicken: Turning to a Well-Integrated Marketing Strategy[16]

In the late 1970s, Kentucky Fried Chicken (KFC) — as of 1986 a subsidiary of Pepsi-Co — performed poorly. Sales declined at a level of 3 per cent per year, while pre-tax profits dropped at an annual rate of 26 per cent. In some ways, the company was its own worst enemy. Many restaurants were sloppy, and the food was unappetizing. Even founder Colonel Harland Sanders publicly complained that the chain served "the worst fried chicken I've ever seen," and that the gravy "resembled wallpaper paste."

Since then, the chain has turned the situation around by developing a thorough, systematic, and integrated marketing plan — based on sound research and analysis.

After some difficulties, Kentucky Fried Chicken devised a well-integrated marketing plan.

[16] Richard P. Mayer, "Chain's Fortunes Improved When It Rearticulated Its Mission and Strategic Plan," *Marketing News* (July 9, 1982), p. 14; Scott Hume, "KFC to Stick with What It's Finally Doing Right," *Advertising Age* (June 27, 1983), pp. 4, 74; Charles Bernstein, "The KFC Challenge: Fight Off McDonald's," *Nation's Restaurant Business* (November 14, 1988), p. F3; and "PepsiCo Inc.," *Advertising Age* (September 28, 1988), p. 119.

TABLE 24-1 Kentucky Fried Chicken's Well-Integrated Marketing Plan

Element of Marketing Plan	Kentucky Fried Chicken's Approach
Clarity of organizational mission	Concentrates on fried chicken and related items
Long-term competitive advantages	High market share, high store loyalty and name recognition, distribution strength, quality products
Precision with which target market is defined	Specific: Family-oriented, largely take-out, nutritional appeal
Compatibility of long-, moderate-, and short-term subplans	Menu, pricing, and expansion proposals based on long-term objectives; long-term gains no longer sacrificed for short-term profits
Coordination among SBUs	KFC a self-contained unit of PepsiCo with adequate resources and no conflicts with other SBUs
Coordination of marketing mix	Standardization of procedures, new locations carefully determined, variations of the "we do chicken right" theme, store remodeling, moderate prices
Stability of strategy over time	One consistent strategy in effect since the late 1970s, all future plans keyed to it

KFC's objective is to be the strongest, most profitable, and fastest-growing quick-service chicken restaurant chain in the world. It has certainly reached this goal.

Research was conducted on the firm's environment, competition, and available resources. Several company strengths were revealed: positioning in an attractive industry segment, a strong distribution network of several thousand restaurants, a leading market share in the chicken segment of the fast-food industry, and high potential consumer loyalty for a properly prepared product line.

An analysis of the research findings by KFC management led to a marketing plan featuring these elements:

▶ The firm concentrates on the chicken segment of the fast-food industry and does not offer menu items such as hamburgers or roast beef sandwiches.

▶ It attracts families and those interested in nutrition.

▶ Menus and prices are set on the basis of long-term instead of short-term implications. Prices are moderate.

▶ Advertising focuses on product attributes and quality, with such themes as "it's so nice to feel so good about a meal" and "we do chicken right." The firm spent over $120 million on advertising and sales promotion in 1988.

▶ Standardized chicken recipes and cooking procedures are used. Product quality is evaluated using "mystery shoppers." There is a systematic training program.

▶ Priority is given to new-store development and remodeling. Each year, hundreds of new stores are opened in the United States and abroad. By early 1989, there were nearly 8,000 restaurants worldwide. Over 90 per cent of company-owned outlets and over one-half of franchised stores have been remodeled over the last several years. Much of sales are take-out.

▶ Complementary new products, such as biscuits, Kentucky Nuggets, and chicken sandwiches, are regularly added.

The solid performance of Kentucky Fried Chicken is related to its superior marketing plan.

Because it has properly integrated its marketing strategy, KFC has been able to generate several years of real sales gains (after adjusting for price increases). In actual dollars, total annual systemwide sales have quadrupled and average yearly sales per company-owned store have more than doubled since the late 1970s. And despite intense competition, KFC currently has a 46 per cent share of worldwide fast-food chicken restaurant sales.

Table 24-1 highlights the elements of Kentucky Fried Chicken's marketing plan in terms of its level of integration.

Analyzing the Marketing Plan

Marketing plan analysis involves comparing actual performance with planned or expected performance for a specified period of time. If actual performance is unsatisfactory, corrective action may be necessary. Sometimes plans have to be revised because of the impact of uncontrollable variables.

Marketing plan analysis compares actual and planned achievements.

Three techniques used to analyze marketing plans are discussed in the following subsections: marketing cost analysis, sales analysis, and the marketing audit. While the discussion of these techniques is restricted to their utility in evaluating marketing plans, they may also be employed in the development and modification of these plans.

Marketing Cost Analysis

Marketing cost analysis is used to evaluate the cost effectiveness of various marketing factors, such as different product lines, order sizes, distribution methods, sales territories, channel members, salespersons, advertising media, and customer types. Although a company may be quite profitable, it is highly unlikely that all of its products, distribution methods, and so on, are equally cost effective (or profitable).

Cost effectiveness is measured through marketing cost analysis.

Through marketing cost analysis, a firm can determine which factors (classifications) are cost efficient and which are cost inefficient, and make appropriate adjustments. Marketing cost analysis can also provide information that may be needed to substantiate price compliance with the Robinson-Patman Act.

In order for this type of analysis to work properly, the firm needs to obtain and to use continuous and accurate cost data. Table 24-2 presents several examples of marketing cost analysis.

The procedure for utilizing marketing cost analysis consists of three stages: studying natural account expenses, reclassifying natural accounts into functional accounts, and allocating functional accounts by marketing classification.

Studying Natural Account Expenses

The first step in carrying out marketing cost analysis is to determine the level of expenses for all *natural accounts;* these accounts report costs by the names of the expenses and not by the expenditures' purposes. Natural-account expense categories include salaries, rent, advertising, supplies, insurance, and interest. These are the names most often entered in ledgers (bookkeeping records). Table 24-3 illustrates a natural-account expense classification.

Natural accounts are reported as salaries, rent, and insurance.

Reclassifying Natural Accounts into Functional Accounts

Natural accounts are then reclassified into *functional accounts,* which indicate the purposes or activities for which expenditures have been made. Included as functional expenses are marketing administration, personal selling, advertising, transportation, warehousing, marketing research, and general administration. Table 24-4 reclassifies the natural accounts of Table 24-3 into functional accounts.

Functional accounts denote the purpose or activity of expenditures.

TABLE 24-2   Examples of Marketing Cost Analysis

Marketing Factor	Strategy/Tactics Studied	Problem/Opportunity Discovered	Action Applied
Product	Should a manufacturer accept a retailer's proposal that the firm make 700,000 private-label sneakers?	Substantial excess capacity exists; the private label would require no additional fixed costs.	A contract is signed. Different features for private and manufacturer labels are planned.
Order size	What is the minimum order size a hardware manufacturer should accept?	Orders below $30 do not have positive profit margins; they are too costly to process.	Small orders are discouraged through surcharges and minimum order size.
Distribution	Should a men's suit manufacturer sell directly to consumers, as well as through normal channels?	Startup and personal selling costs would be high. Additional sales would be minimal.	Direct sales are not undertaken.
Personal selling	What are the costs of making a sale?	15 per cent of sales covers compensation and selling expenses, 2 per cent above the industry average.	Sales personnel are encouraged to phone customers before visiting them, to confirm appointments.
Advertising media	Which is more effective, television or magazine advertising?	Television advertising costs $0.05 for every potential customer reached; magazine advertising costs $0.07.	Television advertising is increased.
Customer type	What are the relative costs of selling X-rays to dentists, physicians, and hospitals?	Per-unit costs of hospital sales are lowest (as are prices); per-unit costs of dentist and physician sales are highest (as are prices).	Current efforts are maintained. Each customer is serviced.

TABLE 24-3   A Natural-Account Expense Classification

Net sales (after returns and discounts)		$1,000,000
Less: Cost of goods sold		450,000
Gross profit		$550,000
Less: Operating expenses (natural account expenses)		
Salaries and fringe benefits	220,000	
Rent	40,000	
Advertising	30,000	
Supplies	6,100	
Insurance	2,500	
Interest expense	1,400	
Total operating expenses		300,000
Net profit before taxes		$250,000

Once functional accounts are established, cost analysis becomes clearer. For instance, if salaries and fringe benefits increase by $25,000 over the prior year, natural-account analysis would be unable to allocate the rise to a functional area. Functional-account analysis would be able to pinpoint the areas of marketing having higher personnel costs.

TABLE 24-4   Reclassifying Natural Accounts into Functional Accounts

Natural Accounts	Total	Functional Accounts						
		Marketing Administration	Personal Selling	Advertising	Transpor- tation	Ware- housing	Marketing Research	General Administration
Salaries and fringe benefits	$220,000	$30,000	$50,000	$15,000	$10,000	$20,000	$30,000	$65,000
Rent	40,000	3,000	7,000	3,000	2,000	10,000	5,000	10,000
Advertising	30,000			30,000				
Supplies	6,100	500	1,000	500			1,100	3,000
Insurance	2,500		1,000			1,200		300
Interest expense	1,400							1,400
Total	$300,000	$33,500	$59,000	$48,500	$12,000	$31,200	$36,100	$79,700

TABLE 24-5   Allocating Functional Expenses by Product

	Total	Product A	Product B	Product C
Net sales	$1,000,000	$500,000	$300,000	$200,000
Less: Cost of goods sold	450,000	250,000	120,000	80,000
Gross profit	$550,000	$250,000	$180,000	$120,000
Less: Operating expenses (functional account expenses)				
Marketing administration	33,500	16,000	10,000	7,500
Personal selling	59,000	30,000	17,100	11,900
Advertising	48,500	20,000	18,000	10,500
Transportation	12,000	5,000	5,000	2,000
Warehousing	31,200	20,000	7,000	4,200
Marketing research	36,100	18,000	11,000	7,100
General administration	79,700	40,000	23,000	16,700
Total operating expenses	300,000	149,000	91,100	59,900
Net profit before taxes	$250,000	$101,000	$ 88,900	$ 60,100
Profit as per cent of sales	25.0	20.2	29.6	30.1

Allocating Functional Accounts by Marketing Classification

The third step in marketing cost analysis assigns functional costs by product, distribution method, customer, or other marketing classification. This develops each classification as a profit center.[17] Table 24-5 illustrates how costs can be distributed among different products, using the data from Tables 24-3 and 24-4. From Table 24-5, it can be determined that product A has the highest net sales and highest total net profit. However, product C has the greatest profit as a per cent of sales.

When allocating functional marketing costs, these two points should be kept in mind. First, assigning some costs—such as marketing administration—to different

Functional costs are assigned with each marketing classification becoming a profit center.

[17] See Robin Cooper and Robert S. Kaplan, "Measure Costs Right: Make the Right Decisions," *Harvard Business Review,* Vol. 66 (September-October 1988), pp. 96–103.

products, customers, or other classifications is usually somewhat arbitrary. Second, the elimination of a poorly performing classification would lead to overhead costs — such as general administration — being allotted among the remaining product or customer categories. This may actually result in lower overall total profit. Thus, the company should distinguish between those separable expenses that are directly associated with a given classification category and can be eliminated if the category is discontinued and those common expenses that are shared by various categories and cannot be eliminated if one is discontinued.

A company should also distinguish between order-generating and order-processing costs (described in Chapter 3) before making any strategic changes suggested by marketing cost analysis. The managers of Munsingwear learned that lesson the hard way:

> [They] set out to increase profits by cutting expenses. To do that, they changed the labels on the underwear boxes, making it difficult for retailers to find them in their storerooms. Even worse, they removed the distinctive waistbands encircled with Munsingwear's name. That saved a few cents in weaving costs for each brief, but neither shoppers nor retailers liked the blank waistbands.[18]

Those managers were soon replaced, and Munsingwear underwear was changed back to its former design.

Sales Analysis

*With **sales analysis**, sales data are evaluated to determine the effectiveness of a marketing strategy.*

Sales analysis is the detailed study of sales data for the purpose of appraising the appropriateness of a marketing strategy. Without adequate sales analysis, the importance of certain market segments and territories may be overlooked, sales effort may be poorly matched with market potential, fashion trends may be overlooked, or assistance for sales personnel may not be forthcoming. Sales analysis enables plans to be set in terms of sales by product, product line, salesperson, region, customer type, time period, price line, method of sale, and so on. It also compares actual sales against planned sales. More companies engage in sales analysis than marketing cost analysis.

*The **sales invoice** and **control units** are essential aspects of sales analysis.*

The main source of sales analysis data is the ***sales invoice***. It contains such information as the customer's name, the quantity ordered, the price paid, purchase terms, the geographic location of the purchaser, all the different items bought at the same time, the order date, shipping arrangements, and the salesperson. Summary data can be generated by adding invoices. The use of computerized marking and inventory systems speeds the recording and improves the accuracy of sales data.

In conducting sales analysis, proper control units must be selected. ***Control units*** are the sales categories for which data are gathered, such as boys', men's, girls', and women's clothing. Although a marketing executive can broaden a control system by summarizing several sales categories, wide categories cannot be broken down into components. Therefore, a narrow sales category is preferable to one that is too wide. It is also helpful to select control units that are consistent with other company, trade association, and government data. A stable classification system is necessary to compare data from different time periods.

7-Eleven is an example of a company that uses sales analysis. 7-Eleven knows that its best-selling products are gasoline, tobacco products, beverages, groceries, such

---

[18] Frank E. James, "Munsingwear Regains Order and Discipline But Faces a Tough Battle to Restore Profits," *Wall Street Journal* (September 6, 1983), p. 37.

food service as fast-food sandwiches, such nonfood items as disposable diapers and magazines, dairy products, and candy. 7-Eleven sells more candy bars and canned beer than any other U.S. retailer. Over one-half of its goods are consumed within 30 minutes after purchase. The typical customer is a young male.[19]

A key concept in undertaking sales analysis is that summary data such as overall current sales or market share are usually insufficient to diagnose a firm's areas of strength and weakness. More intensive investigation is necessary. Two sales analysis techniques that offer in-depth probing are the 80–20 principle and sales exception reporting.

According to the ***80–20 principle,*** in many organizations, a large proportion of total sales (profit) is likely to come from a small proportion of customers, products, or territories.[20] Thus, in order to function as efficiently as possible, firms need to determine sales and profit by customer, product, or territory. Then marketing efforts would be allocated accordingly. Firms err when they do not isolate and categorize data. Through faulty reasoning, they would place equal effort into each sale instead of concentrating on key accounts. These errors are due to a related phenomenon known as the ***iceberg principle,*** which states that superficial data are insufficient to make sound evaluations.

*The **80–20 principle** notes that a large part of total sales (profits) often comes from few customers, products, or territories. Analysis errors may be due to the **iceberg principle.***

This is how the 80–20 principle could be utilized in sales analysis:

> A company manufacturing pharmaceutical products may assign 30 per cent of its sales force to cover doctors located in towns of less than 10,000 people, because out of 20,000 accounts, this customer segment numbers 6,000. However, in terms of sales, these doctors may represent only 10 per cent of the company's sales and thus should be accorded only 10 per cent of the sales force. Therefore, a realignment of resources would be in order.[21]

Sales analysis can be further enhanced by using ***sales exception reporting,*** which lists situations where sales goals are not met or sales opportunities are present. A slow-selling item report lists products whose sales are below forecasts. It could also suggest corrective actions such as price reductions, promotions, and sales incentives to increase unit sales. A fast-selling item report lists items whose sales exceed forecasts. It points out sales opportunities and items that need more inventory on hand to prevent stockouts. Finally, sales exception reporting enables a firm to evaluate the validity of sales forecasts and make the proper modifications in them. Figure 24-6 presents examples of the 80–20 principle, the iceberg principle, and sales exception reporting.

Sales exception reporting *centers on unmet goals or special opportunities.*

Organizations also may use sales analysis to identify and monitor consumer buying patterns by answering questions such as these:

▶ Who purchases? Organizational vs. final consumer, geographic region, end use, purchase history, customer size, customer demographics

▶ What is purchased? Product line, price category, brand, country of origin, package size, options purchased

▶ How are items purchased? Form of payment, billing terms, delivery form, wrapping technique

▶ When are purchases heaviest and lightest? Season, day of week, time of day

---

[19] John Holusha, "7-Eleven Sells Convenience," *New York Times* (July 13, 1987), pp. D1, D6; and authors' estimates.

[20] See Richard T. Hise and Stanley H. Kratchman, "Developing and Managing a 20/80 Program," *Business Horizons,* Vol. 30 (September-October 1987), pp. 66–73.

[21] Ibid., p. 72.

80-20 Principle

	Annual Sales		Marketing Expenditures	
	$	%	$	%
Product A	1,000,000	50.0	200,000	44.4
Product B	750,000	37.5	150,000	33.3
Product C	250,000	12.5	100,000	22.2
Total	$2,000,000	100.0	$450,000	100.0*

*Rounding error.

Although a company gets only 12.5 per cent of total sales from Product C, it spends 22.2 per cent of its marketing budget on that product.

Sales Exception Reporting

SALES REPORT

	Expected Sales	Actual Sales
Product 1	$50,000	$100,000
Product 2	$50,000	$50,000
Product 3	$75,000	$75,000
Product 4	$75,000	$50,000

A review of the sales report indicates that Product 1 has done much better than expected, while Product 4 has done much worse.

Iceberg Principle Only the tip of the iceberg is seen with superficial analysis (aggregate data).

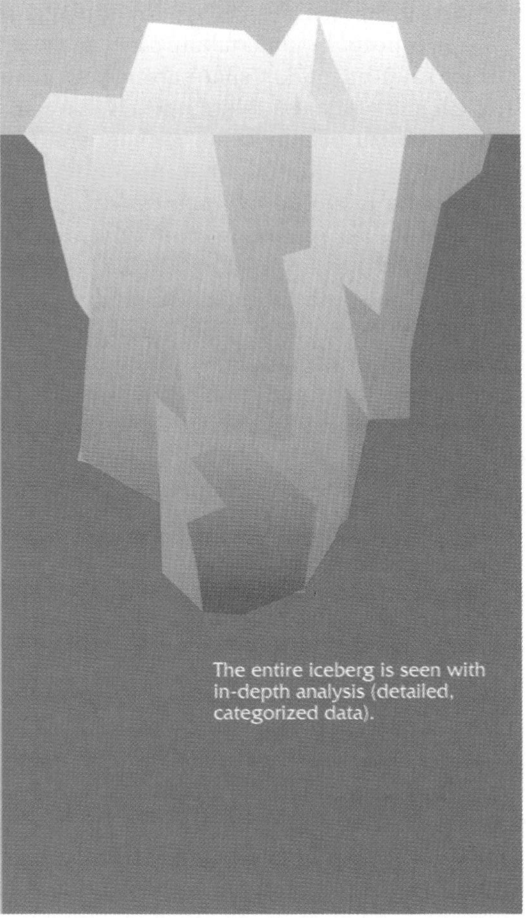

The entire iceberg is seen with in-depth analysis (detailed, categorized data).

FIGURE 24-6
Sales Analysis Concepts

▶ How much is purchased? Unit sales volume, dollar sales volume, profit margin
▶ Where are purchases made? Place of customer contact, purchase location, warehouse location

The Marketing Audit

A marketing audit examines a firm in a systematic, critical, and unbiased manner.

A **marketing audit** is

> a systematic, critical, and unbiased review and appraisal of the basic objectives and policies of the marketing function, and of the organization, methods, procedures, and personnel employed to implement those policies and to achieve those objectives. Clearly, not every evaluation of marketing personnel, organizations, or methods is a marketing audit; at best, most such evaluations can be regarded as parts of the audit.[22]

[22] Adapted by the authors from Abraham Schuchman, "The Marketing Audit: Its Nature, Purpose, and Problems," *Analyzing and Improving Marketing Performance,* Report No. 32 (New York: American Management Association, 1959), p. 13; and Alfred R. Oxenfeldt, *Executive Action in Marketing* (Belmont, Calif.: Wadsworth Publishing, 1966), p. 746.

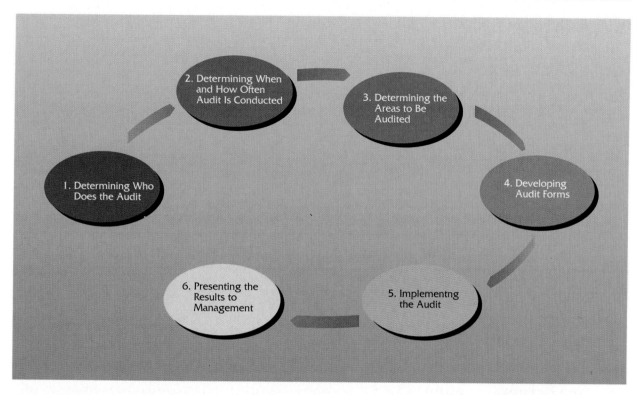

FIGURE 24-7
The Marketing Audit Process

The purpose of a marketing audit is to generate topics of discussion for future company planning and to identify the areas in which an organization needs to correct deficiencies. It includes an investigation of the firm's marketing objectives, strategy, implementation, and organization. An effective marketing audit is conducted on a regular basis, is comprehensive, is systematic, and is carried out in an independent manner.[23]

The marketing audit process consists of the six steps shown in Figure 24-7:

1. A marketing audit may be conducted by company specialists, by company division or department managers, or by outside specialists.

2. An audit may be undertaken at the end of a calendar year, at the end of a company's annual reporting year, or when conducting a physical inventory. An audit should be performed at least annually, although some companies prefer more frequent analysis. The audit should be completed during the same time period each year to allow comparisons. In some cases, unannounced audits are useful to keep employees alert and to ensure spontaneous answers.

3. A ***horizontal audit*** (often referred to as a marketing-mix audit) studies the overall marketing performance of the company with particular emphasis on the interrelationship of variables and their relative importance. A ***vertical audit*** is an in-depth analysis of one aspect of the firm's marketing strategy, such as product planning. The two audits should be used in conjunction with one another because the horizontal audit often reveals areas that need further investigation.

*A **horizontal audit** studies overall marketing performance; a **vertical audit** analyzes one aspect of marketing.*

[23] Adapted by the authors from Philip Kotler, *Marketing Management: Analysis, Planning, and Control,* Sixth Edition (Englewood Cliffs, N.J.: Prentice-Hall, 1988), p. 747.

Does Your Department, Division, or Firm...   Answer Yes or No to
                                                                   Each Question

Planning, Organization, and Control
  1. Have specific objectives?   --------------
  2. Devise objectives to meet changing conditions?   --------------
  3. Study customer needs, attitudes, and behavior?   --------------
  4. Organize marketing efforts in a systematic way?   --------------
  5. Have a market planning process?   --------------
  6. Engage in comprehensive sales forecasting?   --------------
  7. Integrate buyer behavior research in market planning?   --------------
  8. Have strategy and tactics within the marketing plan?   --------------
  9. Have clearly stated contingency plans?   --------------
 10. Monitor environmental changes?   --------------
 11. Incorporate social responsibility as a criterion for decision making? --------------
 12. Control activities through marketing cost analysis, sales analysis, and the marketing audit? --------------

Marketing Research
 13. Utilize marketing research for planning as well as problem solving? --------------
 14. Have a marketing information system?   --------------
 15. Give enough support to marketing research?   --------------
 16. Have adequate communication between marketing research and line executives? --------------

Products
 17. Utilize a systematic product-planning process?   --------------
 18. Plan product policy relative to the product life-cycle concept? --------------
 19. Have a procedure for developing new products?   --------------
 20. Periodically review all products?   --------------
 21. Monitor competitive developments in product planning?   --------------
 22. Revise mature products?   --------------
 23. Phase out weak products?   --------------

Distribution
 24. Motivate channel members?   --------------
 25. Have sufficient market coverage?   --------------
 26. Periodically evaluate channel members?   --------------
 27. Evaluate alternative shipping arrangements?   --------------
 28. Study warehouse and facility locations?   --------------
 29. Compute economic order quantities?   --------------
 30. Modify channel decisions as conditions warrant?   --------------

Promotion
 31. Have an overall promotion plan?   --------------
 32. Balance promotion components within the plan?   --------------
 33. Measure the effectiveness of advertising?   --------------
 34. Seek out favorable publicity?   --------------
 35. Have a procedure for recruiting and retaining sales personnel? --------------
 36. Analyze the sales force organization periodically?   --------------
 37. Moderate the use of sales promotions?   --------------

Prices
 38. Have a pricing strategy that is in compliance with government regulations? --------------
 39. Have a pricing strategy that satisfies channel members?   --------------
 40. Estimate demand and cost factors before setting prices?   --------------
 41. Plan for competitive developments?   --------------
 42. Set prices that are consistent with image?   --------------
 43. Seek to maximize total profits?   --------------

FIGURE 24-8
A Horizontal Marketing Audit Form

You're the Marketer

What's Your Recipe for Pillsbury?

Grand Metropolitan, the British conglomerate that acquired Pillsbury in late 1988, wants to be a "powerful global player" in three business sectors: alcoholic beverages, food, and restaurants. Its annual worldwide sales of wines and spirits are 90 million cases, making it the largest firm in the industry. It is the eighth-largest food processor in the world, with such popular Pillsbury brands as Green Giant vegetables, Totino's pizza, and Häagen-Dazs ice cream. Eighty-six per cent of Pillsbury's sales come from products that are either number one or number two in market share. In its restaurant businesses, which include Burger King in the United States and pubs and family-style restaurants in Britain, Grand Met is either number one or a strong number two.

As a result of Grand Met's purchase of Pillsbury, the firm has a number of complex issues to address:

▶ *To improve Pillsbury's performance, costs must be cut, strong brands must be revitalized, and new products must be developed. Pillsbury's costs as a percentage of sales are 1 to 2 per cent above the industry average.*

▶ *Pillsbury's pre-tax profit margins in its basic food division are 6 per cent, far below the industry average of 9 per cent—and less than one-half those of such top industry performers as Kellogg, Heinz, and Gerber.*

▶ *Pillsbury lags the industry in sales per employee.*

▶ *Pillsbury's market share for products such as microwave popcorn, Van de Kamp's seafood products, and Totino's frozen pizza have begun to slip.*

▶ *Pillsbury's Burger King unit has average per-store sales that are one-third lower than those at McDonald's. Burger King's operating profits were $165 million in 1988 versus $200 million in 1986.*

▶ *Although the performance of Häagen-Dazs has been strong, it is Pillsbury's only dairy product line. Grand Met may sell Häagen-Dazs and other businesses that do not fit with Pillsbury's main lines.*

As a consultant to Grand Met, what marketing recommendations would you make regarding Pillsbury's strategy?

SOURCE: Based on material in Richard I. Kirkland, Jr., "Grand Met's Recipe for Pillsbury," *Fortune* (March 13, 1989), pp. 61–68; and "What Grand Met Got," *Advertising Age* (December 26, 1988), pp. 1, 17.

4. Audit forms list the topics to be examined and the exact information required to evaluate each topic. The forms usually resemble questionnaires, and they are completed by the auditor. An illustration of a horizontal audit form is contained in Figure 24-8.

5. The decisions to be made at this stage involve the time duration of the audit, whether employees are to be aware of the audit, whether the audit is performed while the organization is open or closed, and how the final audit report is to be prepared.

6. The last step in an audit is to present the findings and recommendations to management. However, the auditing process is complete only after appropriate responses are taken by management. It is the responsibility of management, not the auditor, to determine these responses.

TABLE 24-6 Selected Marketing Implications of U.S. Demographic Trends

Trends	Implications
Stable U.S. population	Many domestic markets are saturated. Foreign markets may hold greater opportunities for growth.
Increase in middle-aged and retired persons	There is potential for differentiated marketing strategies. For example, AT&T offers special amplifiers for telephones. Beecham has introduced an easy-to-swallow liquid version of Sominex. Procter & Gamble is marketing disposable diapers for incontinent adults.
Strong home market	There will be demand for home-oriented goods and services. Luxury townhouses will be popular, especially those with large master bedrooms that make it easier for two working spouses to dress in the morning.
Shift to West and South regions	Some regions face continued outmigration of population and industry. Brands distributed nationally will prosper as consumers move about.
Rise in real income	There will be opportunities for discretionary goods and services, such as home furnishings and vacation travel.
Rise in white-collar jobs	There will be opportunities for clothing firms and computer makers.
Increase in working women	These women have little time for shopping or preparation of foods. Faster checkouts, expanded evening hours, one-stop shopping, and convenience goods will be needed. Expenditures in business clothing, luggage, and airline travel will rise.
Increase in education	Consumers will be more discerning and critical.
Stable percentage of married adults	Many two-income families will have children at later ages. Joint decision making will be high.
Growth of single-person households	Smaller homes and condominiums will be demanded, as will single-serving products.

Despite the merits, many firms still do not use formal marketing audits. Three factors account for this. First, success or failure is difficult to establish in marketing. A firm may have poor performance despite the best planning if environmental factors intervene. On the other hand, good results may be based on the firm's being at the right place at the right time. Second, when marketing audits are completed by company personnel, they may not be comprehensive enough to be considered audits. Third, the pressures of other activities often mean that only a small part of a firm is audited or that audits are done on a nonregular basis.

Anticipating and Planning for the Future

Over the next decade, there will be many opportunities and risks.

The decade of the 1990s promises to be a significant one for U.S. marketers as they try to anticipate trends and plan long-run strategies.[24] On the positive side, the next ten years should see increasing consumer affluence, improvements in technological capabilities, expanding worldwide markets, greater deregulation of industry, and other opportunities. On the negative side, the decade will probably witness some resource instability, greater competition from foreign companies, a relatively stagnant domestic market, and an uncertain economy among the potential problems.

[24] See Dale D. McConkey, "Planning in a Changing Environment," *Business Horizons,* Vol. 31 (September–October 1988), pp. 64–72; Walter Kiechel III, "Corporate Strategy for the 1990s," *Fortune* (February 29, 1989), pp. 34–42; Andrew Kupfer, "Managing Now for the 1990s," *Fortune* (September 26, 1988), pp. 44–47; and Gary Hector, "Yes, You *Can* Manage for the Long Term," *Fortune* (November 21, 1988), pp. 64–76.

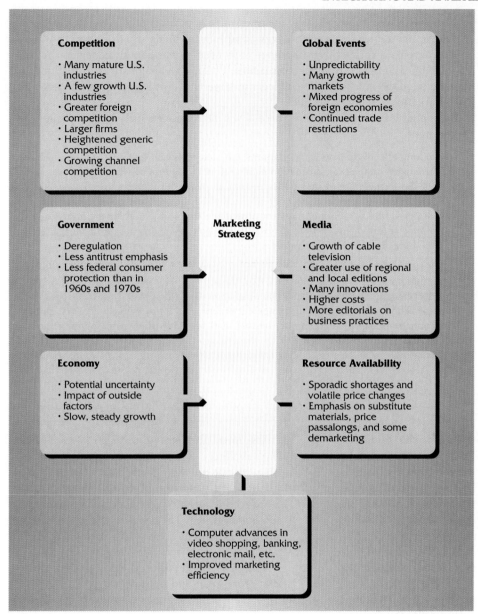

Competition
- Many mature U.S. industries
- A few growth U.S. industries
- Greater foreign competition
- Larger firms
- Heightened generic competition
- Growing channel competition

Global Events
- Unpredictability
- Many growth markets
- Mixed progress of foreign economies
- Continued trade restrictions

Government
- Deregulation
- Less antitrust emphasis
- Less federal consumer protection than in 1960s and 1970s

Marketing Strategy

Media
- Growth of cable television
- Greater use of regional and local editions
- Many innovations
- Higher costs
- More editorials on business practices

Economy
- Potential uncertainty
- Impact of outside factors
- Slow, steady growth

Resource Availability
- Sporadic shortages and volatile price changes
- Emphasis on substitute materials, price passalongs, and some demarketing

Technology
- Computer advances in video shopping, banking, electronic mail, etc.
- Improved marketing efficiency

FIGURE 24-9
The Impact of Environmental Trends on Marketing Strategy

Long-range plans must take into account both the external variables facing a firm and its capacity for change. Specifically, what variables will affect the firm? What trends are forecast for them? Is the firm able to respond to these trends (for example, does it have the necessary resources and lead time)? A company that does not anticipate and respond to future trends has a good possibility of falling into Levitt's marketing myopia trap and losing ground to more farsighted competitors.

Table 24-6 highlights the marketing implications of several expected U.S. demographic trends, while Figure 24-9 shows the impact of a number of anticipated environmental trends on marketing strategy.

According to one survey of chief executive officers and other top managers, 64 per

Planning efforts must consider external factors and company abilities.

769

cent believe that marketing is now the most important functional area for their firms: "Strategic marketing, market strategies, and market plans which help corporations hold or develop a competitive advantage have become paramount management challenges and major unresolved business issues."[25] Another major survey concludes that 58 per cent of the chief executive officers at large U.S. firms want their successors to have marketing/sales backgrounds.[26]

A company's chances of future success will be improved if these observations are kept in mind:

Firms need to be farsighted and adaptive in approaching the future.

> Planning effectively for change requires the collection and analysis of the information (particularly on the external environment) required to determine when changes are occurring; the formulation of major assumptions to make the future more manageable; the development of alternatives to help ensure that all major future possibilities have been considered; the selection of the most probable courses of action for the future; and the planning of contingency actions that will be implemented if the most probable plan proves to be unrealistic or not worthwhile.

> The real key to planning for uncertainty and change must be to accept the premise that the planning process is more important than the written plan, that the manager is continuously planning and does not stop planning when the written plan is finished. The written plan is only a snapshot as of the moment it is approved. If the manager is not planning on a continuous basis—planning, measuring, and revising—the written plan can become obsolete the day it is finished. This obsolescence becomes more of a certainty as the increasingly rapid rate of change makes the business environment more uncertain.[27]

Summary

1. *To show the value of an integrated marketing plan* An integrated marketing plan is one in which all of its various parts are unified, consistent, and coordinated. This may not be a simple task because of different-length subplans, the existence of several SBUs, and the planning needed to coordinate the marketing mix.

2. *To discuss the elements of a well-integrated marketing plan* There are several major elements in a properly integrated marketing plan. A clear organizational mission outlines a firm's commitment to a type of business and a place in the market. Long-term competitive advantages are company and product attributes whose distinctiveness and appeal to consumers can be maintained over an extended period of time. A precisely defined target market enables the firm to identify the specific consumers it addresses in a marketing plan.

The long-, moderate-, and short-term marketing subplans of the company need to be compatible with one another. Coordination among SBUs is enhanced when the functions, strategies, and resources of each are described and monitored by top management. The components of the marketing mix need to be coordinated within each SBU. The plan must have some stability over time.

Kentucky Fried Chicken has a well-integrated marketing plan and is prospering.

3. *To present three types of marketing plan analysis: marketing cost analysis, sales analysis, and the marketing audit* Marketing plan analysis compares a firm's actual performance with its planned or expected performance for a specified period of time. If actual performance is unsatisfactory, corrective action may be needed. Plans may have to be revised because of the impact of uncontrollable variables.

[25] Coopers & Lybrand, *Business Planning in the Eighties: The New Marketing Shape of American Corporations* (New York: 1985).

[26] "CEO Survey Finds Marketers Sought for Their Successors," *Marketing News* (January 30, 1987), p. 5.

[27] McConkey, "Planning in a Changing Environment," p. 72.

Marketing cost analysis evaluates the cost effectiveness of various marketing factors, such as different product lines, order sizes, distribution methods, sales territories, channel members, salespersons, advertising media, and customer types. Continuous and accurate cost data are needed. Marketing cost analysis involves studying natural account expenses, reclassifying natural accounts into functional accounts, and allocating accounts by marketing classification.

Sales analysis is the detailed study of sales data for the purpose of appraising the appropriateness of a marketing strategy. Sales analysis enables plans to be set in terms of sales by product, product line, salesperson, region, customer type, time period, price line, or method of sale. It also monitors actual sales against planned sales. More companies use sales analysis than marketing cost analysis. The main source of sales data is the sales invoice; control units must be specified. Sales analysis should take the 80–20 principle

and sales exception reporting into account.

The marketing audit is a systematic, critical, and unbiased review and appraisal of the firm's marketing objectives, strategy, implementation, and organization. It contains six steps: determining who does the audit, establishing when and how often the audit is conducted, deciding what the audit covers, developing audit forms, implementing the audit, and presenting the results. A horizontal audit studies the overall marketing performance of a company. A vertical audit is an in-depth analysis of one aspect of the marketing strategy.

4. *To demonstrate the importance of anticipating and planning for the future* Long-range plans must take into account both the external variables facing a firm and its capacity for change. A firm that does not anticipate and respond to future trends has a good chance of falling into Levitt's marketing myopia trap — something that should be avoided.

Key Terms

marketing plan analysis (p. 759)
marketing cost analysis (p. 759)
natural accounts (p. 759)
functional accounts (p. 759)
sales analysis (p. 762)

sales invoice (p. 762)
control units (p. 762)
80–20 principle (p. 763)
iceberg principle (p. 763)

sales exception reporting (p. 763)
marketing audit (p. 764)
horizontal audit (p. 765)
vertical audit (p. 765)

Review Questions

1. State the seven elements of a well-integrated marketing plan.
2. What competitive advantages may be offered by smaller firms?
3. Why is it important for a marketing plan to have stability over time?
4. What is marketing plan analysis?
5. Why is functional account cost analysis more useful than natural account analysis?

6. Distinguish between marketing cost analysis and sales analysis.
7. When conducting sales analysis, why is it necessary that control units not be too wide?
8. Explain the 80–20 principle.
9. Differentiate between a vertical and a horizontal marketing audit.
10. What are some of the positive and negative trends firms are likely to face in the 1990s?

Discussion Questions

1. Evaluate the level of integration of your college or university's marketing plan, using the elements outlined in Figure 24-1.
2. Develop a five-year marketing plan for Kentucky Fried Chicken. Include marketing objectives, the target market, and product, distribution, promotion, and price factors. Should Kentucky Fried Chicken add hamburgers? Explain your answer.
3. What information could a manufacturer obtain from a

monthly analysis of its sales to wholesalers? How could this information improve marketing plans?
4. Develop a vertical marketing audit for the U.S. Postal Service to assess the performance of its overnight express delivery service.
5. Why do you think the role of marketing in a company's strategic planning process is expected to increase in importance over the next decade?

◄ CASE 1 ►

Next: The Apple of Steve Jobs' Eye*

After losing a bitter power play with John Sculley, Steve Jobs—the young co-founder of Apple Computer—decided to leave the company he had created. Less than three years later, Steve Jobs' new firm—Next Inc.—had developed an innovative computer system designed for universities and businesses. As one observer noted: "Part of Steve wanted to prove to others and to himself that Apple wasn't luck. He wanted to prove that Sculley should never have let him go."

The $6,500-$10,000 Next computer system contains a number of important technological features. Its monitor is capable of the fine detail work required in such applications as molecular modeling. The computer can recreate such sounds as an orchestra and is able to transmit digitized recorded messages between computers.

Next is also the first personal computer to use higher-capacity erasable optical disk drives. The system's $50 removable disk-drive cartridges can hold 256 megabytes of data (ten times more than the usual capacity of personal-computer hard drives).

Included in the bundled price of a Next system are eight megabytes of internal memory (which are required to run certain programs) and extensive software programs (including a data-base program, word processing, a mathematics program, a standard dictionary, and Shakespeare's complete works).

The Next computer is designed to be easy to run and easy to program (to encourage commercial software developers to produce an extensive array of software). It is the first major personal-computer system to be based on object-oriented programming, which enables programmers to reuse elements from prior, more basic, programs. Next's software is so innovative that IBM has already paid at least $10 million to license its "graphic interface" (which makes the unit so easy to use) and its software tools (which make it easy to write applications programs).

Unlike at Apple, where Jobs assessed consumer needs himself, the Next computer was developed with considerable input from universities. Jobs and his marketing team visited several of them and created a 24-member advisory board to provide suggestions. Jobs was responsive to the advisory board in terms of product features and pricing.

Yet, despite its innovative use of technology, many analysts believe that Next computers will not have the same success as Jobs' Apple models:

▷ Development snags delayed volume shipments of Next computers by eighteen months—to mid-1989. This enabled some of Next's important differentiating features to be duplicated by competitors. For example, several computer makers planned to use the Motorola sound-producing signal chip (used in the Next machine) in their 1989 models.

▷ The higher-education market will be a difficult one for Next to penetrate. This market is currently dominated by Apple, IBM, Sun Microsystems, and Digital Equipment; all of these firms provide significant discounts to universities. Furthermore, the relatively high per-unit price of the Next system is beyond the budgets of most students.

▷ Next computers do not run either IBM or Apple software, and several commercial software developers have stated that they will not produce separate software versions for Next. To be successful, Next will have to emerge as a third software standard, alongside Apple and IBM.

Jobs strongly believes that he will have a major winner with the Next computer system. First, he has a loyal following among university administrators and professors due to his successes at Apple. Second, Jobs considers Next computers to be an excellent value for the money, given the capabilities and

---

* The data in this case are drawn from Katherine M. Hafner and Richard Brandt, "Steve Jobs: Can He Do It Again?" *Business Week* (October 24, 1988), pp. 74–80; and Richard Brandt and Maria Shao, "Steve Jobs Gets the Keys to the Office PC Market," *Business Week* (April 10, 1989), pp. 80–81.

software included in the base price. Third, Next is well-funded. In addition to Jobs' personal investment in this project, Next received $20 million from billionaire H. Ross Perot and $100 million from Canon. Together they own 30 per cent of Next. Fourth, in early 1989, Jobs reached an exclusive agreement with Businessland—a chain of computer stores—for it to buy a minimum of $100 million of Next computers over a twelve-month period. This gives Next entry into the $15 billion annual office PC market.

QUESTIONS

1. Assess the opportunities and threats now facing Next Inc.
2. Present a well-integrated marketing plan for Next Inc.
3. How should Next's organizational mission change over the next decade? Why?
4. What measures could Next use to determine its level of success during its first two years?

◄ CASE 2 ►

Rubbermaid: Can the Good Times Continue to Roll?[†]

Over the years, Rubbermaid—the manufacturer of plastic-based housewares—has expanded its product mix beyond the kitchen to include such goods as toys and insulated containers. The firm's diversification strategy has been quite successful. For example, net income increased steadily between 1981 and 1988; 1988's net income was about five times the 1978 level. Rubbermaid plans to reach an annual sales volume of $2 billion in 1992, double the revenues in 1988.

Prior to a major restructuring in 1980, Rubbermaid had eight major divisions. Yet, it derived 96 per cent of its income from just two of them: home products and commercial products. As its chief executive officer acknowledged, "It was obvious we could not carry six nonperformers."

So the firm decided to sell its U.S. auto accessories business and to acquire Little Tikes, a toy manufacturer; Con-Tact, a manufacturer of adhesive-covering materials; Gott, an insulated-container maker; Seco Industries, a floor-care products firm; and Micro-Computer Accessories, a supplier of personal computer-based accessories.

Although analysts generally agree that Rubbermaid's acquisitions have done well, they also mention that the Gott line has not been growing as fast as other divisions. The company is currently replacing the Gott name with the Rubbermaid name on some insulated containers to stimulate brand recognition and sales.

One of Rubbermaid's most successful acquisitions involves Little Tikes. This SBU, which was acquired in 1984, originally made toy boxes—shaped like frogs. Today Little Tikes is viewed as a maverick by many toy industry experts. The company is no longer a member of the Toy Manufacturers of America because it does not agree with the trade association's defense of advertising to children. And unlike many competitors that spend between 15 and 20 per cent of their revenues on advertising, Little Tikes spends less than 6 per cent of its sales on advertising. It advertises mostly in magazines oriented to parents (versus competitors' sponsoring child-oriented television programs) and by placing flyers inside toy cartons. Little Tikes' president says: "We rely on word of mouth. Mothers love to tell their friends about a good product."

Little Tikes concentrates on classic toys, such as doll houses and trucks, and avoids risky new products that may be fads. Its new products are usually line extensions, such as sturdier trucks and baby rattles. Little Tikes generates annual sales of more than $200 million.

One of Rubbermaid's current companywide ob-

[†] The data in this case are drawn from Alecia Swasy, "Rubbermaid's Acquisitions Take It Beyond the Kitchen," *Wall Street Journal* (February 3, 1989), p. B2.

jectives is to generate 30 per cent of each year's sales from products introduced within the previous five years. As such, the company has an aggressive product-development program in which existing lines are updated and new markets are entered. Rubbermaid aims to introduce a major new product every eighteen months.

Examples of recent new or updated products include ice-cube trays that enable homemakers to release the cubes more easily, garbage cans available in a range of colors, and a workshop organizer for tools. The popularity of these products is generally keyed to Rubbermaid's ability to obtain shelf space in retail stores, its premium pricing strategy, and its high level of brand recognition. Rubbermaid claims to have a 96 per cent brand awareness level among U.S. consumers. One independent observer says, "Rubbermaid has almost become a generic name."

Rubbermaid is expanding the distribution of its home- and toy-based products in Europe. It is also planning to begin selling office and commercial products in Europe. Although the company's efforts may be slowed by Europe's lack of appropriate retailers and by the low degree of brand recognition among Europeans, Rubbermaid hopes that international sales will eventually account for at least 25 per cent of overall earnings—up from the present 10 per cent.

Rubbermaid is concerned about future increases in the costs of petrochemical resins, the key ingredient in many of its products. In 1988, Rubbermaid spent $400 for resins—up from $250 million in 1987. Accordingly some of Rubbermaid's products now include mixtures of recycled plastic and fresh plastic. Rubbermaid's pet research project involves creating a line of products made from recycled tires and plastic soda bottles.

QUESTIONS

1. List and evaluate Rubbermaid's long-term competitive advantages.
2. Describe how Rubbermaid could use marketing cost analysis and sales analysis in assessing operations.
3. What factors should Rubbermaid study in a horizontal marketing audit? Explain your answer.
4. Develop a vertical product-planning audit form to evaluate Little Tikes.

part 8 CASE

Kodak: Beyond 1990*

Introduction

When your eye spots one of the myriad of green or amber bottles on grocery store shelves, what company produced that bottle polymer?

When you think about a well-made Japanese car, what company's high-speed, electronic motion analysis system has probably contributed to that Japanese quality effort?

When you see a traveler using a "lap-size" portable printer hooked to a miniature personal computer, what company is supplying this ink-jet technology?

When you need a series of blood test results within an hour at a physician's office, what company's analyzer can give quick turnaround and cost savings?

When you reach for a flashlight and you count on its working because a lithium battery is capable of ten years of shelf life, what company is delivering this reliable performance?

When you ski at a resort at the start or end of the season, what company is in the business of helping to make artificial snow?

When you want a cost-effective, electronic image management system, what company can give you such a system, to make information manageable, in ways people want it?

The title of this case answers each of those questions. And those answers make a strong point: East-man Kodak is currently embarking on a number of new directions for growth.

For years, Kodak's universal brand franchise has been the familiar yellow film box. To millions of consumers, Kodak is the film and easy-to-use camera company — the company still exploiting George Eastman's genius in creating a mass appeal for photography. Kodak of the 1990s, however, will be much more than photography. In fact, currently its photographic business accounts for only about 45 per cent of its total revenue. Moreover, it is working to become a world leader in other major markets not traditionally associated with Kodak brands.

One of Kodak's major strengths has been its international brand reputation. Other vital strengths include a century of imaging experience, a worldwide technology base, international channels of distribution and marketing, and a commitment to manufacturing and customer service. Kodak is re-examining and expanding those strengths as a base for growth into a "Kodak of tomorrow."

A New Group Structure

Over the years at Kodak, there have been a number of reorganizations. Two important recent ones should be noted.

First, about two and a half years ago, the large imaging segment was reorganized. The outdated functional organization was replaced by a series of business units focused on specific customers and markets. They are

* Adapted by the authors from Frank P. Strong, "Kodak: Beyond 1990," *Journal of Consumer Marketing*, Vol. 5 (Summer 1988), pp. 53–60. Reprinted by permission.

run by managers with worldwide responsibility for products, research, manufacturing, marketing—and also the financial performance of their units.

Second, last year, a new structure was created in order to link technology strategies with business strategies and to recognize the integral position of the $2.8 billion chemicals business within the corporation. This current structure consists of five major business groups, each with its own operating research labs: Photographic Products, Commercial and Information Systems, Diversified Technologies, Eastman Chemicals, and Life Sciences.

Obviously each of these groups starts at a different point on the business curve, but management believes each has the same approximate potential for success. And, again, each is being held accountable for its performance and growth.

Kodak sees this group structure as its organization for the future that will make it a world leader in all of these major sectors. It is working toward this position in several vital directions.

Quicker and More Effective Functioning

First, a leaner, more market-focused organization leads to better planning, better decision making, and better and quicker results. With these business units, Kodak is now a series of independent companies within a company. Each unit is closer to its customers. Each has all of the resources to compete effectively. Each is encouraging more "risk-calculated" growth.

An example of seizing a business opportunity and moving it forward with speed and entrepreneurial spirit is Ultra Technologies, one of the newest business units. This unit manufactures and markets a new 9-volt lithium battery and also markets a full line of "gold-tipped" alkaline batteries. Typical development time for this kind of marketing project would have been five to seven years. However, it took just over two years from the formation of this unit to the time when production began for a lithium battery with a total new power cell design.

Business units are also commercializing faster in more traditional areas. For instance, after design specifications were set, the Professional Photography Division brought Kodachrome 200 professional film to the market in just over a year.

Linking of Research and Business

A second important direction of the "the new Kodak" is strengthening the linkage between research, manufacturing, and marketing. With group laboratories, research can now be coupled with critical business strategies. Entire product systems can be moved from origin to market with greater speed.

Kodak's Diversified Technologies Group lab has initiated a series of strategic proposals for its business units. This exchange brings a two-way understanding: the lab learns first-hand about short-term business needs, and the units become partners in long-term technical strategies.

Promoting a Unified Image for a Wide Range of Products

A third direction to improve Kodak's responsiveness is new advertising to handle a broader base of products while keeping the Kodak image clearly in front of its customers.

A good example of this "new advertising" comes out of the Commercial/Information Systems and Diversified Technologies groups. Both have a full range of important nonconsumer product lines, from copier/duplicators to diagnostic imaging products to clinical blood analyzers to microfilmers to pre-press color proofing systems to electronic publishing and image management systems.

Kodak and its agency addressed two key questions. First, is Kodak viewed as a technology company? Second, is its nonconsumer advertising viewed as one company?

To answer those questions, twenty past print campaigns were assembled in the same room and a select management team was asked to review them, not only in terms of the creative approaches but in terms of the elements leading into this creativity, such as the appearance of the products themselves. The conclusion was clear: there was no consistent image, no uniform product color, and no image of a high-tech company. The customer could rightfully ask: "What is this company—it looks like twenty companies?"

Furthermore, business leaders surveyed in the United States, Japan, and Europe for the most part knew Kodak only from a narrow product perspective. Many decision makers were unaware of Kodak's capability and scope in the business and industrial marketplace. They did know Kodak as a photographic world leader and associated the name and famous "Kodak yellow" with quality, reliability, and excellent service.

The new communications campaign uses these strong, positive perceptions as it increases awareness of Kodak's broad business capabilities and gains a consistent look for many nonconsumer products.

The campaign's theme is "The New Vision of Kodak." Each ad has a big, bold headline which at first glance could be for a typical consumer photo product from Kodak. The visuals, however, are photographs of Kodak's business and industrial products and systems. A simple but contemporary signature graphic — a yellow stripe/corporate symbol treatment — will appear in all advertising and will carry through all promotional materials as well, as a further way of unifying all of these nonconsumer products.

A unified approach has also been developed for all business-to-business promotional activities, for Kodak exhibits worldwide, and for product and package design. This uniformity of image, message, and product positioning should help make Kodak business and industrial advertising more effective.

Moreover, just as Kodak is giving a number of diverse product lines a distinctive and unified identity in communications, it is using its major exhibits to demonstrate a Kodak "synergism" by combining its well-recognized technologies, like film and magnetics, with leading-edge technologies like electronics.

To illustrate this new effort, Kodak is redesigning its 11,000 square feet of space at the Dallas Infomart, which advertises itself as "the world's first information processing market center." Here it will demonstrate to sophisticated business audiences its long-term interest in image-intensive information systems. A special theater presentation will show visitors the "dimensions" of Kodak they may know little about. Relevant Kodak products and systems will be seen in the context of information management, printing and publishing, and general business communications.

Developing a Worldwide Brand Identity

Kodak is also working internationally to create a world brand for its well-known products such as film. The goal is not only to impact today's sales, but to build business for the future. The specific advertising task is to project Kodak film as a young, dynamic modern brand, while reaching the consumer in a highly impactful way.

Research has indicated that people everywhere want bright saturated colors in their prints. Kodak wants to make color synonymous with the Kodak brand. It also wants advertising that could travel across a number of different world markets. Each creative execution is dedicated to just one color. One commercial — one color. A campaign was launched in Japan and has been carried to Latin America and other parts of the world.

Thus, coherent, coordinated creative strategies are critical in making Kodak's marketing more effective. The goals are to inform customers of the broad scope of nonconsumer products, and to reinforce a worldwide brand identity for its universal consumer products.

An Expanding Product Portfolio Through Ventures

Eastman Technologies, a subsidiary of the Diversified Technologies Group, demonstrates how Kodak is moving beyond its core businesses to develop new product lines and to increase market participation. It is a true nurturing ground, operating a number of internal venture projects.

The venture program was established to develop ideas that don't fit current product strategies, to make them clearer, and to nurture them to a point where some of them can make a positive contribution to the growth of the company.

A venture often starts in one of the twenty Offices of Innovation throughout the company. Here anyone can take an idea and receive informal help that adds strength to that idea. Last year, more than 1,000 ideas were submitted for products, concepts, or processes to help the business grow.

Many of these ideas can be used within existing or traditional businesses. But for those promising ideas outside the mainstream, there is a modest seed grants program leading into business plans, and possible approval as independent business activities. Currently the areas of interest of operational venture businesses include machine vision systems, proprietary filters and membranes for gas and liquid separation applications, and semiconductor fabrication equipment.

Some of these ventures can quickly become producers. Ultra Technologies, mentioned earlier, started up as a venture in 1984, announced its first products in 1986, and now is gaining an increasing share of the consumer battery market.

Also Sayett Technology, created last year, has received immediate market acceptance for its Datashow system, a user-friendly, cost-effective interface between the personal computer and the overhead projector. Sayett Technology's rapid start is helped by the fact that it is using the established Motion Picture and Audiovisual Products Division as its marketing arm, so this venture has an in-place selling team, marketing to a known customer network for its first products.

In addition to their financial payback, these venture units are providing the favorable attributes of small business. Their contagious spirit, their instincts to challenge what exists, their eagerness to try something new, and their attitude of entrepreneurship are inspiring the entire Kodak enterprise.

In the past, Kodak has used a careful and conservative strategy—relying almost exclusively on its own resources for each product, and waiting until the product was pluperfect before introducing it. This strategy is no longer appropriate. Customers cannot be expected to wait when technology begins to offer attractive products. They also are not content with anything less than the best technology—regardless of its root source.

Kodak line-of-business managers now are impatient to develop new products and enter new markets at a record pace. So as a product or systems matrix is defined in a given nonconsumer market, they quickly determine what Kodak can do by itself and where there are "gaps" that may require external actions.

All of the companies Kodak has been acquiring recently—such as Atex, Datatape, Diconix, Verbatim, and BioImage—fit particular product matrix strategies or provide high-value technology or other long-term capabilities. And Kodak is getting this business value at less cost and quicker than it could provide it alone.

Delivering the Goods to the Customer

Kodak is also redefining quality in terms of customer expectations. For each new product or system, the company is determining the basis on which it can compete most effectively. This is not exactly a "new direc-

tion," but by looking hard at the principles of quality management, Kodak has developed a better understanding of the competitive importance of the whole supply system linking the manufacturing processes with the customers.

For example, Kodak's worldwide distribution network consists of global central distribution centers and regional centers serving multiple countries or marketplaces. This is a sophisticated network linked to nine factories in eight countries. It is a multichannel system, because they sell direct, go through several tiers of resellers, and also work with exclusive distributors and suppliers. However, given Kodak's extensive product portfolio and diverse customer base, it was at risk of falling into a trap: namely, with all of these facilities and the intense customer service focus, isn't it best to build up inventories to meet the sudden demands of world customers wherever they need the product?

Of course, the problem is these large inventories do little for return on investment. Every dollar tied up in inventory means one dollar less to invest in the business. For instance, if there is a target of 15 per cent ROI, then $100 million should be invested in inventory *only* if it contributes $115 million to the bottom line. So quality management focuses Kodak's efforts on becoming the low-cost provider. And "provider" encompasses not only production costs, but distribution performance, overhead expense, and the aggressive task of identifying and discontinuing unprofitable products.

One action course is product rationalization. A recent study indicates that 20 per cent of Kodak's products contribute over 90 per cent of its revenues.

Also, by applying quality management procedures, Kodak rediscovered ways to optimize its supply system. For example, making sure its manufacturing locations consistently transfer 25 per cent of their four-week period schedules each week enables Kodak to reduce its finished goods inventory and its period work-in-progress inventory at each plant.

As a result, Kodak is moving to a continuous flow in the supply chain with no sacrifice in the quality of customer service. It is also able to be more responsive in case of a product improvement, product change, or packaging change; with no large existing inventories, it can make such improvements quicker, at less cost.

At the same time, Kodak is shifting to a high degree of mechanization with an automatic warehouse planning system called SWIFT—Service With Improved Forward Technology. This is a conveyor system, controlled by software, permitting products to be selected, packed, and moved at the right times to the loading areas, where it tells how trucks should be loaded.

Moving into the Future with a New Optical Disk System

As Kodak moves into the next decade and beyond, more and more of its marketing focus is being directed at the business, government, health care, and industrial markets. The Mass Memory Division, created in 1985 within the Diversified Technologies Group, has the mission of establishing Kodak as a leader in the data recording and storage industry.

Mass Memory is presently one of the few suppliers in the world making and marketing both magnetic and optical media and hardware systems. This division is finding that many information managers are challenged in accessing stored information and putting it to constant use. There's a strong demand for systems that combine the benefits of mass storage and rapid access to very large data bases.

Mass Memory's optical disk 6800 System is the newest member of Kodak's family of image-intensive information systems. These systems combine image management with computer data and word processing, to capture, store, process, and display image-rich information in a variety of forms. Kodak's optical disk systems should help reshape the entire data storage industry. Optical technology offers a spectrum of performance options and some clear advantages over mature magnetic technology. For instance, it offers greater storage capacity, packing densities up to 100 times greater than their magnetic counterparts.

Kodak's 14-inch optical disk stores up to 6.8 gigabytes of information—the equivalent of documents filling 110 four-drawer file cabinets, or a stack of paper 92 stories high—higher than the Eiffel Tower.

This 14-inch optical technology brings up the challenge of standardization. Right now no single format dominates in the optical storage area. With some formats, such as 12-inch systems, a number of incompatible products do exist. So Kodak is working with other companies and with the American National Standards Institute to develop industrywide standards for 14-inch optical media.

Kodak's marketing decisions on its optical systems program reflect the new Kodak practices. Mass Memory will not market its System 6800 or its new optical disk library directly to end users. Instead, it will use both in-house and outside sources. Kodak will become a major vendor, distributing its optical disk systems through other Kodak business units, including the Business Imaging Systems Division, OEM customers, and a number of outside systems integrators. It will thus be able to serve a broad customer base while building capacity, increasing productivity, and reducing unit costs—meeting high performance standards at a price competitive with other media.

The unified communications campaign discussed earlier is being used for these optical disk products. Clearly Kodak is a company that is changing. The Kodak of the future can be seen in the methods of product introduction for its optical disks:

▷ Kodak is rapidly expanding its technology base, moving into a number of emerging technologies as represented by its optical disk systems.

▷ Such technologies are nontraditional for Kodak, but it knows its imaging experience is useful in creating many new systems of unique worth.

▷ A number of these innovative systems are entrepreneurial in nature, indicative of Kodak's willingness to take new risks and support new ideas anywhere in the company.

▷ By concentrating its resources and energies in business units, Kodak is compressing time lines from product design to commercialization, in order to compete more effectively.

▷ These new market directions represent many and varied—and for Kodak, different—channels of distribution, as it, for instance, markets these optical disk products through OEMs and other outside systems integrators, as well as in-house channels.

▷ And all of this change and timely product innovation "plays off" the new organization structure, a structure speeding up Kodak's decision making, moving it closer to the marketplace, and sharpening its focus on customer needs.

Continuing into New Directions

Kodak has headed into new directions to make it a more agile company, one ready to exploit more marketing opportunities in the demanding 1990s. There is still more to do, of course, to find even better ways to get the marketing task done. Founder George Eastman once said: "The person who thinks he's done everything he can do has simply stopped thinking." Like all

companies, Kodak must keep thinking about its marketing momentum, extending its traditional strengths into new areas.

QUESTIONS

1. Describe and evaluate Kodak's organizational mission.
2. Cite and assess several of Kodak's long-term competitive advantages.
3. State a number of short-term and long-term goals for Kodak to pursue. Which goals are most likely to be reached? Which are least likely to be reached? Why?
4. Comment on the changes in Kodak's organizational structure that are mentioned in the case.

5. What could Kodak learn from applying the 80-20 principle?
6. Present a vertical product-planning audit form for Kodak to use in assessing its marketing of batteries.
7. Do you think that Kodak is well-positioned for the future? Why or why not?
8. What environmental trends will have the most impact on Kodak? How should it deal with them? Explain your answers.

APPENDIX *A*

Careers in Marketing

Career opportunities in marketing are quite extensive and diversified. Many marketing positions give a considerable amount of responsibility to people early in their careers. For example, within six months to one year of being hired, assistant retail buyers are usually given budget authority for purchases involving hundreds of thousands of dollars. Beginning salespeople typically start to call on accounts within several weeks of being hired. Marketing research personnel actually develop preliminary questionnaires, determine sampling procedures, and interpret study results within a short time after their initial employment. A marketing career is excellent preparation for a path to top management positions in all types of organizations.

A number of marketing positions are highly visible. These include sales personnel, sales managers, retail buyers, brand managers, industrial traffic managers, credit managers, and advertising and public relations personnel. This allows effective persons to be recognized, promoted, and properly compensated. In fact, the compensation in sales positions is usually based on sales volume and/or profitability and is directly linked to an individual's own performance.

Marketing offers career opportunities for people with varying educational backgrounds. An associate's or a bachelor's degree is generally required for most management-training positions in retailing, inventory management, sales, public relations, and advertising. A master of business administration degree is increasingly necessary for marketing research, marketing consulting, brand management, senior management, and industrial sales positions. Frequently marketing consultants, marketing research directors, and marketing professors have earned Ph.D. degrees in marketing or related subjects.

A marketing background can also train a person to operate his or her own business. Among the entrepreneurial opportunities available are careers as retail store owners, manufacturers' agents, wholesalers, insurance and real-estate brokers, marketing consultants, marketing researchers, and free-lance advertising illustrators or copywriters.

Table 1 contains a detailed, but not exhaustive, listing of job titles in marketing. Table 2 shows the types of firms that employ people in marketing positions. Table 3 outlines the outlook for selected marketing careers through the year 2000.

TABLE 1   Selected Job Titles in Marketing

Job Title	Description
Account executive	Liaison person between an advertising agency and its clients. The individual is employed by the agency to study the clients' promotional objectives and create promotional programs (including messages, layout, media, and timing).
Advertising copywriter	Creator of headlines and content for advertisements.
Advertising layout person	Producer of illustrations or one who uses other artists' illustrations to formulate advertisements.
Advertising manager	Director of a firm's advertising program. He or she determines media, copy, budget size, advertising frequency, and the choice of an advertising agency.
Advertising production manager	Person who arranges to have an advertisement filmed (for television), recorded (for radio), or printed (for newspaper, magazine, etc.).
Advertising research director	Person who researches markets, evaluates alternative advertisements, assesses media, and tests advertisements.
Agent (broker)	Wholesaler who works for a commission or fee.
Catalog manager	Person who determines target market, products, copy, displays, pricing, and so on, for sales catalogs.
Commercial artist	Creator of advertisements for television, print media, and product packaging. This artist selects photographs and drawings and determines the layout and type of print to be used in newspaper and magazine advertisements. Sample scenes of television commercials are sketched for clients.
Consumer affairs specialist (customer relations specialist)	Company contact with consumers. This person handles consumer complaints and attempts to have the firm's policies reflect customer needs. Community programs, such as lectures on product safety, arise from the consumer affairs specialist.
Credit manager	Supervisor of the firm's credit process, including eligibility for credit, terms, late payments, consumer complaints, and control.
Customer service representative	Person responsible for order status inquiry, merchandise expediting, field sales support, and returns and claims processing.
Direct-to-home (or office) salesperson	Person who sells goods and services to consumers by personal contact at the consumer's home or office.
Display worker	Person who designs and sets up retail store displays.
Fashion designer	Designer of apparel, such as beachwear, hats, dresses, scarves, and shoes.
Franchisee	Person who leases or buys a business that has many outlets and a well-known name. The franchisee normally operates one outlet and participates in cooperative planning and advertising. The franchisor sets rules for operating all outlets.
Franchisor	Person who develops a company name and reputation and then leases or sells parts of the firm to independent businesspeople. The franchisor oversees the company, sets policy, and usually trains franchisees.
Freight forwarder	Wholesaler who consolidates small shipments from many companies.
Industrial designer	Designer who improves the appearance and function of machine-made products.
Industrial traffic manager	Arranger of transportation to and from firms and customers for raw materials, fabricated parts, finished goods, and equipment.
International marketer	Person who works overseas or in the international department of a domestic company and is involved with some aspect of marketing. International marketing positions are available in all areas of marketing.

TABLE 1 (Continued)

Job Title	Description
Inventory manager	Person who controls the level and allocation of merchandise throughout the year. This manager evaluates and balances inventory amounts against the costs of holding merchandise.
Life insurance agent (broker)	Person who advises clients on life insurance policy types available, relative to their needs. Policies provide life insurance and/or retirement income.
Manufacturers' representative (agent)	Salesperson who represents several, usually small, manufacturers that cannot afford their own sales force. The representative normally sells to wholesalers and retailers. He or she determines needs and then displays, demonstrates, and describes goods and services, often at the customer's place of business.
Marketing manager (vice-president of marketing)	Executive who plans, directs, and controls all of a company's marketing functions. The manager (vice-president) oversees all marketing decisions and personnel.
Marketing research project supervisor	Person who develops the research methodology, evaluates the accuracy of different sample sizes, analyzes data, and assesses statistical errors.
Media analyst	Person who evaluates the characteristics and costs of available media. The analyst examines audience size and traits, legal restrictions, types of messages used, and so on. The effectiveness of company messages is also measured.
Media director (space or time buyer)	Person who determines the day, time (for radio and television), media, location, and size of advertisements. The goal is to reach the largest desirable audience at the most efficient cost. The director (buyer) negotiates contracts for advertising space or air time.
Missionary salesperson	Support salesperson who provides information about new and existing products.
Order-fulfillment manager	Supervisor responsible for shipping merchandise. He or she verifies orders, checks availability of goods, oversees packing, and requests delivery.
Packaging specialist	Person responsible for package design, durability, safety, appeal, size, and cost. This specialist must be familiar with all related legislation.
Political consultant	Person who advises political candidates on media relations, political polls, fund raising, and overall campaign strategy.
Pricing economist	Specialist who studies sources of supply, consumer demand, government restrictions, competition, and costs and then offers short-run and long-run pricing recommendations.
Product manager (brand manager)	Person who supervises the marketing of a product or brand category. In some firms, there are product (brand) managers for existing items and new-product (brand) managers for new introductions. For a one-brand or one-product company, the product (brand) manager is actually the marketing manager.
Property and casualty insurance agent (broker)	Person who evaluates client risks from such perils as fire, burglary, and accidents; assesses coverage needs; and sells policies to indemnify losses.
Public relations director	Manager of a company's efforts to keep the public aware of its accomplishments and benefits to society and minimize negative reactions to company policies and activities. The director constantly measures public attitudes and seeks to maintain a favorable public opinion of the firm.
Purchasing agent	Buyer for a manufacturer, wholesaler, or retailer. The agent purchases items necessary for the operation of the firm and usually buys in bulk, seeks reliable suppliers, and sets precise specifications.
Real-estate agent (broker)	Liaison who brings together a buyer and a seller, lessor and lessee, or landlord and tenant. This salesperson receives a commission.
Retail buyer	Person responsible for purchasing items for resale. The buyer generally concentrates on a product area and develops a plan for proper styles, assortments, sizes, and amounts of the product. The buyer analyzes vendors on the basis of quality, style, availability, fit, flexibility, reliability, and price.

A3

TABLE 1 (Continued)

Job Title	Description
Retail department manager	Supervisor of one retail department, often at a branch store. The manager usually works with the buyer and is responsible for displaying merchandise, counting it, and reordering it. Department manager is often the first position a college graduate assumes after an initial training program.
Retail merchandise manager	Supervisor of several buyers. This manager sets the retailer's direction in terms of styles, product lines, image, pricing, and so on, and allocates budgets among buyers.
Retail salesperson	Salesperson for a retailer who deals with final consumers.
Retail store manager	Supervisor of the day-to-day operations of a store. All in-store personnel report to this manager.
Sales engineer	Support salesperson involved with technical goods or services.
Sales manager	Supervisor of the sales force; responsible for recruitment, selection, training, motivation, evaluation, compensation, and control.
Sales promotion director	Person involved with supplementary promotional activities, such as trading stamps, coupons, contests, giveaways, and free samples.
Salesperson	Company representative who interacts with consumers. A salesperson may require limited or extensive skills, deal with final or intermediate customers, work from an office or go out in the field, and be a career salesperson or progress in management.
Securities salesperson (commodities broker)	Salesperson involved with the buying and selling of stocks, bonds, government securities, mutual funds, and other financial transactions.
Traffic manager	Supervisor of the purchase and use of alternative methods of transportation. This manager routes shipments and monitors performance.
Warehouser	Person responsible for storage and movement of goods within a company's warehouse facilities. The warehouser maintains inventory records and makes sure older items are shipped out before newer ones (rotating stock).
Wholesale salesperson	Salesperson representing a wholesaler to retailers and other firms.

Jobs in marketing are growing at a much more rapid rate than those in other occupational categories—and this is expected to continue. For example, today there are about 25 million people working in U.S. retailing and wholesaling activities, representing over one-fifth of all civilian employees 16 years old and over.[1] And according to projections, U.S. retailing and wholesaling employment is expected to increase by 27 per cent between 1986 and 2000; in contrast, overall U.S. employment is expected to increase by 19 per cent over the same period.[2]

The strong demand for marketing personnel is based upon several factors. More service firms, nonprofit institutions, political candidates, and others are applying marketing principles. The deregulation of several major industries (such as banking, communication, and transportation) has encouraged companies in these industries to increase their marketing efforts. Although production can be mechanized and auto-

---

[1] *Statistical Abstract of the United States,* 1988 (Washington, D.C.: U.S. Bureau of the Census).
[2] *Occupational Outlook Handbook,* 1988-1989 Edition (Washington, D.C.: U.S. Government Printing Office, U.S. Department of Labor, April 1988), pp. 9-10.

TABLE 2   Selected Employers of Marketing Personnel

Advertising agencies	Franchisees	Public relations firms
Agents and brokers	Franchisors	Raw material extractors
Common carriers	Fund-raising organizations	Real-estate firms
Computer service bureaus	Government	Retailers
Consulting firms	Industrial firms	Self-employed
Credit bureaus	International firms	Service firms
Delivery firms	Manufacturers	Shopping centers
Direct-marketing businesses	Marketing research firms	Sports teams
Educational institutions	Marketing specialists	Transportation firms
Entertainment firms	Media	Warehousers
Exporters	Nonprofit institutions	Wholesalers
Financial institutions	Product-testing laboratories	

TABLE 3   The Outlook for Selected Marketing Careers through 2000

Job Classification	Employment Outlook
Advertising worker	Faster than average
Commercial artist	Faster than average
Credit analyst	Average
Financial services salesperson	Much faster than average
Industrial designer	Average
Industrial salesperson	Varies by industry
Insurance agent (broker)	Average
Manufacturer's salesperson	Varies by industry
Marketing manager	Faster than average
Marketing researcher	Faster than average
Public relations specialist	Faster than average
Purchasing agent	Faster than average
Real-estate agent (broker)	Much faster than average
Retail buyer	Slower than average
Retail salesperson	Faster than average
Sales manager	Faster than average
Securities salesperson	Much faster than average
Travel agent	Faster than average
Wholesale buyer	Slower than average
Wholesale salesperson	Faster than average

Sources: Occupational Outlook Handbook, 1988–1989 Edition (Washington, D.C.: U.S. Government Printing Office, Bureau of Labor, April 1988); and authors' estimates.

mated, many marketing activities require personal contact. The rise in foreign competition and the maturity of several market segments are causing U.S. firms to expand and upgrade their marketing programs.

New technologies such as electronic checkouts, marketing-based computer software, and single-source data collection techniques are creating marketing opportunities for companies. The changes in U.S. society (such as blurring gender roles, recreational activities, and the rise in single-person households) need to be monitored through marketing research and marketing information systems, and adapted to via careful marketing planning. As the chairman of DuPont notes, "While the world becomes more and more competitive, you have to sharpen all your tools. Knowing what's on the customer's mind is the most important thing we can do."[3]

These are several indications of the opportunities available to people pursuing careers in marketing:

► According to a recent survey, senior corporate executives believe that during the next decade marketing will have a more critical role in determining a company's success or failure than ever before. Said the survey's director, "Marketing will assume its rightful place in the executive suite, taking on the mantle of one of the determining factors—if not the key factor—in major corporate strategies and decisions."

► In the past, many jobs for marketing professionals were concentrated with consumer-goods firms. Now extensive competition among high-technology companies, banks, brokerage firms, airlines, retailers, and others is creating substantial additional career opportunities. As one Delta Airlines executive commented, "We do business 180 degrees differently than before deregulation. A lot more responsibility now falls on the marketing function."

► In a *Forbes* study of 785 chief executive officers, median compensation was ranked on the basis of the business backgrounds of those executives. Of the 14 business backgrounds analyzed, retailing was rated second highest, marketing fourth highest, and sales seventh highest in median compensation.

► An analysis of executive compensation at medium-sized firms found that the firms tend to pay their top marketing executives more than the heads of such other functional areas as manufacturing, finance, and research and development. At the companies studied, the chief executive officer earned a median annual salary of $139,000; the median salary of the top marketing officer was $90,000.

► There are significant career opportunities for women in marketing. The findings of one U.S. Bureau of Labor study show that 24 per cent of all managerial positions in marketing are filled by women. For example, Xerox reports that 18 of its 67 U.S. sales districts are managed by women. In 1988, females held nearly 44 per cent of all public relations positions (up from 10 per cent in 1980).

► Rapidly expanding areas of marketing, such as direct marketing, offer a wide variety of career opportunities. Among the positions available in direct-marketing firms are buyer, copywriter, art director, catalog manager, research/mail-list manager, and order fulfillment manager.[4]

The 1989 starting salaries for marketing personnel typically ranged from $12,000 to $20,000 for those with an associate's degree, $18,000 to $30,000 for those with a bachelor's degree, and $27,000 to $50,000+ for those with a master of business administration degree. In addition to salary, many marketing positions provide a com-

---

[3] Patricia Sellers, "Getting Customers to Love You," *Fortune* (March 13, 1989), p. 38.

[4] Elizabeth M. Fowler, "Marketing's Challenges and Rewards, *New York Times* (December 20, 1988), p. D9; Eric N. Berg, "A Very Special Time for Marketing Specialists," *New York Times Careers: 1986 National Employment Report* (October 13, 1985), p. 226; "Who Gets the Most Pay: Who Made What at the Top in U.S. Business," *Forbes* (June 3, 1985), pp. 114–117 ff.; "Marketing 2000: CEOs See Expanding Role for Marketing," *Marketing News* (January 2, 1989), p. 41; *Occupational Outlook Handbook,* 1988–1989 Edition, p. 37; Michael F. Kastre, "Pink Collar Ghetto, Adieu," *Managing Your Career* (Spring 1989), p. 10; Jan Greenberg, "Inside Public Relations," *Business Week Careers* (February 1988), p. 48; and Nicholas Basta, "Direct Marketing," *Business Week's Guide to Careers* (March 1986), pp. 51–53.

pany car, bonus, and/or expense account that are not common in other professions.

Table 4 outlines the compensation ranges for established personnel in selected marketing positions. Many of the positions shown have open-ended ranges because

TABLE 4 Annual Compensation for Personnel in Selected Marketing Positions[a]

Advertising Positions	*Compensation*
Assistant media planner	$ 12,000 – $ 30,000+
Copy/art trainee	$ 18,000 – $ 21,000+
Assistant account executive	$ 18,000 – $ 40,000+
Senior art director	$ 20,000 – $ 45,000+
Account executive	$ 25,000 – $ 40,000+
Account supervisor/group promotion manager	$ 40,000 – $ 70,000+

Marketing Research Positions	*Compensation*
Full-time interviewer	$ 12,000 – $ 16,000+
Field work director	$ 12,000 – $ 35,000+
Junior analyst	$ 15,000 – $ 23,000+
Analyst	$ 22,000 – $ 35,000+
Associate media research director	$ 35,000 – $ 50,000+
Senior analyst/project director	$ 40,000 – $ 60,000+
Associate research director	$ 50,000 – $ 65,000+
Media research director	$ 65,000 – $ 80,000+
Research director	$ 70,000 – $100,000+

Product Management Positions	*Compensation*
Marketing analyst	$ 15,000 – $ 30,000+
Senior marketing analyst	$ 17,000 – $ 35,000+
Assistant product manager	$ 30,000 – $ 45,000+
Product manager	$ 37,000 – $ 75,000+
Group product manager	$ 40,000 – $100,000+

Retailing Positions	*Compensation*
Executive trainee	$ 17,000 – $ 25,000+
Chain store manager	$ 18,000 – $ 90,000+
Assistant buyer	$ 20,000 – $ 30,000+
Buyer	$ 20,000 – $ 60,000+
Divisional merchandise manager	$ 23,000 – $ 80,000+
Department store manager	$ 25,000 – $ 70,000+
General merchandise manager	$ 40,000 – $100,000+

Sales Positions	*Compensation*
Travel agent	$ 12,000 – $ 50,000+
Sales trainee	$ 15,000 – $ 30,000+
Real-estate agent (broker)	$ 15,000 – $100,000+
Field sales trainee	$ 17,000 – $ 25,000+
Insurance agent (broker)	$ 17,000 – $100,000+
Manufacturers' representative (agent)	$ 20,000 – $ 60,000+
Field salesperson	$ 23,000 – $ 45,000+
Technical field salesperson	$ 24,000 – $ 40,000+
Sales manager	$ 31,000 – $ 75,000+
Senior field salesperson	$ 35,000 – $ 70,000+
Securities salesperson	$ 35,000 – $200,000+

TABLE 4 (Continued)

Miscellaneous Marketing Positions	*Compensation*
Display worker	$ 15,000–$ 30,000+
Graphic artist	$ 15,000–$ 30,000+
Customer service representative	$ 17,000–$ 35,000+
Industrial designer	$ 17,000–$ 50,000+
Purchasing agent	$ 20,000–$ 50,000+
Public relations specialist	$ 27,000–$ 70,000+
Customer service supervisor	$ 30,000–$ 50,000+
Sales promotion director	$ 40,000–$ 80,000+
International general sales executive	$ 42,000–$ 75,000+
Distribution executive	$ 42,000–$ 90,000+

Top Marketing Positions	*Compensation*
Senior public relations executive	$ 40,000–$ 60,000+
Senior sales executive	$ 50,000–$100,000+
Branch office manager, advertising agency	$ 50,000–$200,000+
Senior international executive	$ 60,000–$120,000+
Marketing director	$ 70,000–$110,000+
Executive vice-president, advertising agency	$ 75,000–$175,000+
Vice-president of marketing	$ 75,000–$700,000+
President, advertising agency	$100,000–$400,000+

[a]Includes bonus.

Sources: Nicholas Basta, "Sales Promotion Managers," *Business Week Careers* (Spring–Summer 1988), p. 22; Ben S. Cole and Matt Sizing, "Agency Pay: Performance Counts," *Advertising Age* (May 23, 1988), p. 34; Claudia H. Deutsch, "The Haves—and Have Nots—in Public Relations," *New York Times* (May 31, 1987), Section 3, p. 12; Connie Fletcher, "What I Do on the Job: Advertising Space Sales," *Business Week Careers* (December 1988), p. 41; Sandra Gillis, "On the Job: Product Manager," *Business Week Careers* (April–May 1988), p. 66; Tony Lee, "Salaries Stabilize Despite Healthy Hiring," *Managing Your Career* (Spring 1989), p. 38; Joe Mandese, "The Curtain Rises," *Marketing & Media Decisions* (April 1988), p. 44; "1989 Survey of Selling Costs: Compensation & Expenses," *Sales & Marketing Management* (February 20, 1989), pp. 15–16, 20–24; *Occupational Outlook Handbook,* 1988–1989 Edition (Washington, D.C.: U.S. Government Printing Office, Bureau of Labor, April 1988); "Retail Pay: Surprisingly Better," *Career Paths* (January 1988), pp. 8–9; "Where the Money Is," *Advertising Age* (November 21, 1988), p. 23; and authors' estimates.

commissions or bonuses depend on performance. As an example, one recent study of top advertising agency personnel found that 39 per cent of these executives earn bonuses. On average, the bonuses equal 19 per cent of the executives' base salaries.[5] The compensation amounts in Table 4 do not include expense accounts.

Figure 1 shows potential career paths for four selected areas of marketing. These career paths are general ones and are intended to give you a perspective about "moving up the ladder." Individual organizations have their own variations of the career paths illustrated in Figure 1. Also, please note that specialized career opportunities exist in each of the areas shown (such as sales training, support sales, final consumer versus organizational consumer sales, and so on in the sales area); and these are not revealed in Figure 1.

[5] Ben S. Cole and Matt Sizing, "Agency Pay, Performance Counts," *Advertising Age* (May 23, 1988), pp. 34–35.

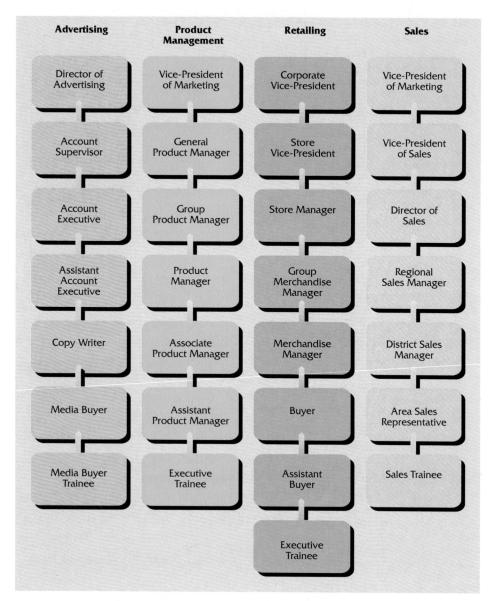

Advertising	Product Management	Retailing	Sales
Director of Advertising	Vice-President of Marketing	Corporate Vice-President	Vice-President of Marketing
Account Supervisor	General Product Manager	Store Vice-President	Vice-President of Sales
Account Executive	Group Product Manager	Store Manager	Director of Sales
Assistant Account Executive	Product Manager	Group Merchandise Manager	Regional Sales Manager
Copy Writer	Associate Product Manager	Merchandise Manager	District Sales Manager
Media Buyer	Assistant Product Manager	Buyer	Area Sales Representative
Media Buyer Trainee	Executive Trainee	Assistant Buyer	Sales Trainee
		Executive Trainee	

FIGURE 1
Selected Marketing Career Paths

The typical head of marketing for a *Fortune* 500 industrial or service firm is 47 years old and married. The chief marketing executive has been with his or her firm for 13 years and has held two other jobs since college. The executive is responsible for an annual marketing budget of $49.5 million.[6]

In the United States, marketing executives are frequently chosen as the chief executive officers (CEOs) of major industrial and nonindustrial corporations. Table 5 shows some of the U.S. companies that had CEOs with marketing backgrounds during 1989. The executives who are listed in this table each earn at least several hundred thousand dollars per year plus bonuses. According to a recent study of CEOs by a

[6] "Chief Marketing Executive Is Usually a Well-Paid Man," *Marketing News* (December 19, 1988), p. 5.

TABLE 5 Selected Companies Whose Chief Executive Officers Have Marketing Backgrounds, 1989

Amdahl	Dun & Bradstreet	Monsanto
American Medical	Engelhard	Nalco Chemical
American Stores	Federal Paper Board	Nordstrom
Apple Computer	Geico	Owens-Corning
Armstrong World Industries	General Mills	J.C. Penney
Avery International	Great A&P	Philip Morris
Baxter International	H.J. Heinz	Pittston
Brown-Forman	George A. Hormel	PPG Industries
Bruno's	IBM	Procter & Gamble
Brunswick	K mart	Quaker Oats
Campbell Soup	Kellogg	Ralston Purina
Carter Hawley Hale	Kroger	Reebok International
CBI Industries	Leslie Fay Companies	Reynolds Metals
Central Bancshares	Eli Lilly	Rubbermaid
Champion International	Limited	Sears
Circle K	Louisiana-Pacific	SmithKline Beckman
Clorox	Mattel	Snap-on Tools
Colgate-Palmolive	Maytag	Subaru of America
CPC International	McKesson	US Life
Crown Cork & Seal	Melville	Whirlpool
Dayton Hudson	Mercantile Stores	Xerox
Deere	Fred Meyer	Zayre

Source: "Corporate America's Most Powerful People," *Forbes* (May 29, 1989), pp. 192–195 ff.

TABLE 6 Selected Publications Dealing with Marketing Careers

Advertising Career Directory (Hawthorne, N.J.: Career Press, 1985).
American Marketing Association, *Careers in Marketing* (Chicago: 1985).
Business Week Careers, published occasionally.
Changing Times Annual Survey: Jobs for New College Grads.
Chemical Marketing Research Association, *Careers in Industrial Marketing Research* (New York: n.d.).
College Placement Council, *CPC Annual.*
Dow Chemical Company, *Finding That First Job in Public Relations* (Midland, Mich.: 1985).
Dow Jones & Co., *Managing Your Career,* published twice a year.
Lebhar-Friedman, Inc., *Careers in Retailing,* published annually.
Magazine Publishers Association, *Guide to Business Careers in Magazine Publishing* (New York: n.d.)
National Council of Physical Distribution Management, *Careers in Distribution* (Oak Brook, Ill.: 1983).
National Employment Business Weekly.
Peterson's Business & Management Jobs, published annually.
Public Relations Society of America, *Careers in Public Relations* (New York: n.d.).
U.S. Department of Labor, *Occupational Outlook Handbook* (Washington, D.C.: published biennially).
U.S. Department of Labor, *Occupational Projections and Training Data* (Washington, D.C.: published biennially).

management recruiting firm, more CEOs have had backgrounds in marketing or sales than any other functional area. Over 28 per cent of the CEOs have had a marketing or sales background versus 26 per cent for finance, 21 per cent for manufacturing or operations, 12 per cent for engineering and research, and 7 per cent for law.[7] Another study, by a major accounting firm, found that "there is a trend for more chief executives to have a marketing background."[8]

Table 6 cites selected publications that discuss marketing careers. Table 7 shows sources that may be contacted for more specific information.

[7] Fowler, "Marketing's Challenges and Rewards," p. D9.
[8] Ibid.

TABLE 7   Selected Sources of Additional Marketing Career Information

Career Opportunity	Sources
Advertising	American Advertising Federation 1400 K Street NW, Suite 1000 Washington, DC 20005
	American Association of Advertising Agencies 666 Third Avenue, 13th Floor New York, NY 10017
	Business Professional Advertising Association 205 East 42nd Street New York, NY 10017
Bank marketing	Bank Marketing Association 309 W. Washington Street Chicago, IL 60606
Buying (retail)	National Retail Merchants Association 100 West 31st Street New York, NY 10001
Consumer advocate	Consumer Federation of America 1424 16th Street NW, Suite 604 Washington, DC 20036
Customer service	International Customer Service Association 111 East Wacker Drive, Suite 600 Chicago, IL 60601
Direct marketing	The Direct Marketing Association 6 East 43rd Street New York, NY 10017
Direct selling	Direct Selling Association 1776 K Street NW, Suite 600 Washington, DC 20006
Industrial design	Industrial Designers Society of America 1142 E. Walker Road Great Falls, VA 22006
Life insurance sales	American Council of Life Insurance 1001 Pennsylvania Avenue NW Washington, DC 20004
	National Association of Life Underwriters 1922 F Street NW Washington, DC 20006

TABLE 7 (Continued)

Career Opportunity	Sources
Manufacturers' representation	Sales & Marketing Executives International Statler Office Towers, #458 Cleveland, OH 44115
Marketing	American Marketing Association 250 S. Wacker Drive, Suite 200 Chicago, IL 60606
	College Placement Annual 62 Highland Avenue Bethlehem, PA 18017
Marketing consulting	The Association of Management Consulting Firms 230 Park Avenue New York, NY 10169
	The Institute of Management Consultants 19 W. 44th Street New York, NY 10036
Marketing research	American Association for Public Opinion Research PO Box 17 Princeton, NJ 08542
	Chemical Marketing Research Association 139 Chestnut Avenue Staten Island, NY 10305
	Council of American Survey Research Companies 3 Upper Devon Belle Terre Port Jefferson, NY 11777
	Marketing Research Association 111 E. Wacker Drive, Suite 600 Chicago, IL 60601
Physical distribution	National Council of Logistics Management 2803 Butterfield Road, Suite 380 Oak Brook, IL 60521
Political consulting	American Association of Political Consultants 1211 Connecticut Avenue NW, Suite 506 Washington, DC 20036
Property and casualty insurance	Independent Insurance Agents of America 100 Church Street, Suite 1901 New York, NY 10007
	Insurance Information Institute 110 William Street New York, NY 10038
	Professional Insurance Agents 400 N. Washington Street Alexandria, VA 22314

Public relations	National Investor Relations Institute 1730 M Street NW Washington, D.C. 20036
	Public Relations Society of America, Inc. 33 Irving Place, 3rd Floor New York, NY 10003
Purchasing agents	National Association of Purchasing Management 2055 E. Centennial Circle PO Box 22160 Tempe, AZ 85282
	National Institute of Governmental Purchasing, Inc. 115 Hillwood Avenue Falls Church, VA 22046
Real-estate sales	National Association of Realtors 430 N. Michigan Avenue Chicago, IL 60611
Retailing	International Mass Retailing Institute 570 Seventh Avenue, Suite 900 New York, NY 10018
	National Retail Merchants Association 100 West 31st Street New York, NY 10001
Sales Promotion	Council of Sales Promotion Agencies 176 Madison Avenue New York, NY 10016
	Promotion Marketing Association of America, Inc. 322 Eighth Avenue, Suite 1201 New York, NY 10001
Securities sales	Securities Industry Association 120 Broadway New York, NY 10271
Supermarket industry	Food Marketing Institute 1750 K Street NW, Suite 700 Washington, DC 20006
	National Association of Retail Grocers of the U.S. 1825 Samuel Morse Drive Reston, VA 22090
Traffic management	American Society of Transportation and Logistics PO Box 33095 Louisville, KY 40232
Travel agents	American Society of Travel Agents 1101 King Street Alexandria, VA 22314
Wholesaling	National Association of Wholesaler-Distributors 1725 K Street NW Washington, DC 20006

APPENDIX B

Marketing Mathematics

To properly design, implement, and review marketing programs, it is necessary to understand basic business mathematics from a marketing perspective. Accordingly this appendix describes and illustrates the types of business mathematics with which marketers should be most familiar: the profit-and-loss statement, marketing performance ratios, pricing, and determining an optimal marketing mix.

The crucial role of marketing mathematics can be seen through the following:

▶ By properly utilizing marketing mathematics, a firm can evaluate monthly, quarterly, and annual reports; and study performance on a product, market, SBU, division, or overall company basis.

▶ Marketing plans for all types of channel members (manufacturers, wholesalers, and retailers) and all time periods (short term through long term) should be based on sound marketing mathematics.

▶ Both small and large, goods and services, and profit and nonprofit organizations need to rely on marketing mathematics in making decisions.

▶ Marketing mathematics provide a systematic basis for establishing standards of performance, reviewing that performance, and focusing attention on opportunities and problem areas.

▶ By understanding marketing mathematics, better pricing and marketing-mix decisions can be made.

▶ By using marketing mathematics, decision making with regard to entering or withdrawing from a market, budgeting expenditures, and the deployment of marketing personnel can be aided.

The Profit-and-Loss Statement

The ***profit-and-loss (income) statement*** presents a summary of the revenues and costs for an organization over a specific period of time. Such a statement is generally developed on a monthly, quarterly, and yearly basis. The profit-and-loss statement enables a marketer to examine overall and specific revenues and costs over similar time periods (for example, January 1, 1989 to December 31, 1989 versus January 1, 1988 to December 31, 1988), and analyze the organization's profitability. Monthly and quarterly statements enable the firm to monitor progress toward goals and revise performance estimates.

The profit-and-loss statement consists of these major components:

▶ *Gross sales*-The total revenues generated by the firm's goods and services.
▶ *Net sales*-The revenues received by the firm after subtracting returns and discounts (such as trade, quantity, cash, and special promotional allowances).
▶ *Cost of goods sold*-The cost of merchandise sold by the manufacturer, wholesaler, or retailer.
▶ *Gross margin (profit)*-The difference between net sales and the cost of goods sold; consists of operating expenses plus net profit.
▶ *Operating expenses*-The cost of running a business, including marketing.
▶ *Net profit before taxes*-The profit earned after all costs have been deducted.

When examining a profit-and-loss statement, it is important to recognize a key difference between manufacturers and wholesalers or retailers. For manufacturers, the cost of goods sold involves the cost of producing products (raw materials, labor, and overhead). For wholesalers or retailers, the cost of goods sold involves the cost of merchandise purchased for resale (purchase price plus freight charges).

Table 1 shows an annual profit-and-loss statement (in dollars) for a manufacturer, the General Toy Company. From this table, these observations can be made:

▶ Total company sales for 1989 were $1,000,000. However, the firm gave refunds worth $20,000 for returned merchandise and allowances. In addition, discounts of $50,000 were provided. This left the company with actual (net) sales of $930,000.
▶ As a manufacturer, General Toy computed its cost of goods sold by adding the cost value of the beginning inventory on hand (items left in stock from the previous period) and the merchandise manufactured during the time period (costs included raw materials, labor, and overhead), and then subtracting the cost value of the inventory remaining at the end of the period. For General Toy, this was $450,000 ($100,000 + $400,000 - $50,000).
▶ The gross margin was $480,000, calculated by subtracting the cost of goods sold from net sales. This sum was used for operating expenses, with the remainder accounting for net profit.
▶ Operating expenses involve all costs not considered in the cost of goods sold. Operating expenses for General Toy included sales force compensation, advertising, delivery, administration, rent, office supplies, and miscellaneous costs, a total of $370,000. Of this amount, $225,000 was directly allocated for marketing costs (sales force, advertising, delivery).
▶ General Toy's net profit before taxes was $110,000, computed by deducting operating expenses from gross margin. This amount would be used to cover federal and state taxes as well as company profits.

Performance Ratios

Performance ratios are used to measure the actual performance of a firm against company goals or industry standards. Comparative data can be obtained from trade

**TABLE 1 General Toy Company, Profit-and-Loss Statement for the Year
January 1, 1989 Through December 31, 1989 (in dollars)**

Gross sales		$1,000,000
Less: Returns and allowances	$ 20,000	
Discounts	50,000	
Total sales deductions		70,000
Net sales		$ 930,000
Less cost of goods sold:		
Beginning inventory (at cost)	$100,000	
New merchandise (at cost)[a]	400,000	
Merchandise available for sale	$500,000	
Ending inventory (at cost)	50,000	
Total cost of goods sold		450,000
Gross margin		480,000
Less operating expenses:		
Marketing expenses		
Sales force compensation	$125,000	
Advertising	75,000	
Delivery	25,000	
Total marketing expenses	$225,000	
General expenses		
Administration	$ 75,000	
Rent	30,000	
Office supplies	20,000	
Miscellaneous	20,000	
Total general expenses	145,000	
Total operating expenses		370,000
Net profit before taxes		$ 110,000

[a] For a manufacturer, new-merchandise costs refer to the raw materials, labor, and overhead costs incurred in the production of items for resale. For a wholesaler or retailer, new merchandise costs refer to the purchase costs of items (including freight) bought for resale.

associations, Dun & Bradstreet, Robert Morris Associates, and other sources. Among the most valuable performance ratios for marketers are the following:

(1) Sales efficiency ratio (percentage) $= \dfrac{\text{Net sales}}{\text{Gross sales}}$

The *sales efficiency ratio (percentage)* compares net sales against gross sales. The highest level of efficiency is 1.00; in that case, there would be no returns, allowances, or discounts. General Toy had a sales efficiency ratio of 93 per cent ($930,000/$1,000,000) in 1989. This is a very good ratio; anything better would mean General Toy was too conservative in making sales.

(2) Cost-of-goods-sold ratio (percentage) $= \dfrac{\text{Cost of goods sold}}{\text{Net sales}}$

The *cost-of-goods-sold ratio (percentage)* indicates the portion of net sales that is used to manufacture or purchase the goods sold. When the ratio is high, the firm has little revenue left to use for operating expenses and net profit. This could mean costs are too high or selling price is too low. In 1989, General Toy had a cost-of-goods-sold ratio of 48.4 per cent ($450,000/$930,000), a satisfactory figure.

$$\text{(3) Gross margin ratio (percentage)} = \frac{\text{Gross margin}}{\text{Net sales}}$$

The **gross margin ratio (percentage)** shows the proportion of net sales that are allocated to operating expenses and net profit. When the ratio is high, the company has substantial revenue left for these items. During 1989, General Toy had a gross margin ratio of 51.6 per cent ($480,000/$930,000), a satisfactory figure.

$$\text{(4) Operating expense ratio (percentage)} = \frac{\text{Operating expenses}}{\text{Net sales}}$$

The **operating expense ratio (percentage)** expresses these expenses in terms of net sales. When the ratio is high, the firm is spending a large amount on marketing and other operating costs. General Toy had an operating expense ratio of 39.8 per cent in 1989 ($370,000/$930,000), which meant that almost 40 cents of every sales dollar went for operations, a moderate amount.

$$\text{(5) Net profit ratio (percentage)} = \frac{\text{Net profit before taxes}}{\text{Net sales}}$$

The **net profit ratio (percentage)** indicates the portion of each sales dollar that goes for profits (after all costs have been deducted). The net profit ratio varies drastically by industry. For example, in the supermarket industry, net profits are just over 1 per cent of net sales; in the industrial chemical industry, net profits are about 6 per cent of net sales. The 1989 net profit for General Toy was 11.8 per cent of net sales ($110,000/$930,000), well above the industry average of 7 per cent.

$$\text{(6) Stock turnover ratio} = \frac{\text{Net sales (in units)}}{\text{Average inventory (in units)}}$$

or

$$\frac{\text{Net sales (in sales dollars)}}{\text{Average inventory (in sales dollars)}}$$

or

$$\frac{\text{Cost of goods sold}}{\text{Average inventory (at cost)}}$$

The **stock turnover ratio** shows the number of times during a specified period, usually one year, that the average inventory on hand is sold. It can be calculated on the basis of units or dollars (in selling price or at cost). In the case of General Toy, the 1989 stock turnover ratio can be calculated on a cost basis. The cost of goods sold during 1989 was $450,000. Average inventory at cost = (Beginning inventory at cost + Ending inventory at cost)/2 = ($100,000 + $50,000)/2 = $75,000. The stock turnover ratio was ($450,000/$75,000) = 6. This compared favorably with an industry average of 4 times. This meant General Toy sold its merchandise one and a half times more quickly than competitors.

(7) Return on investment $= \dfrac{\text{Net sales}}{\text{Investment}} \times \dfrac{\text{Net profit before taxes}}{\text{Net sales}}$

$= \dfrac{\text{Net profit before taxes}}{\text{Investment}}$

The **return on investment (ROI)** compares profitability with the investment necessary to manufacture or distribute merchandise. For a manufacturer, this investment includes land, plant, equipment, and inventory costs. For a wholesaler or retailer, it involves inventory, the costs of land, the outlet and its fixtures, and equipment. To determine the return on investment for General Toy, total investment costs would be determined from its **balance sheet,** which lists the assets and liabilities of a firm at a particular time.

There are two components to the return on investment measure — the investment turnover ratio and the net profit ratio (percentage):

$$\text{Investment turnover ratio} = \dfrac{\text{Net sales}}{\text{Investment}}$$

$$\dfrac{\text{Net profit ratio}}{\text{(percentage)}} = \dfrac{\text{Net profit before taxes}}{\text{Net sales}}$$

The investment turnover ratio computes the dollar sales generated per dollar of investment. The management at General Toy calculated that an overall investment of $550,000 was necessary to yield 1989 net sales of $930,000. Therefore, the firm's investment turnover ratio was 1.7 times ($930,000/$550,000). General Toy's net profit ratio was 11.8 per cent ($110,000/$930,000). Thus, the firm's return on investment equaled 20 per cent (1.7 × .118). This figure was above the industry norm.

Table 2 shows a percentage profit-and-loss (income) statement for the General Toy Company based on the same period as in Table 1. All figures in this table are computed on the basis of net sales equaling 100 per cent. This table allows a marketer to quickly observe such performance ratios as cost-of-goods sold (percentage), operating expense (percentage), and net profit (percentage).

TABLE 2   General Toy Company, Profit-and-Loss Statement for the Year January 1, 1989 Through December 31, 1989 (in per cent, with net sales = 100.0)

Net sales		100.0
Less cost of goods sold		48.4
Gross margin		51.6
Less operating expenses:		
Marketing expenses	24.2	
General expenses	15.6	
Total operating expenses		39.8
Net profit before taxes		11.8

Pricing

The material in this section expands upon the discussion in Chapters 18 through 20. Five specific aspects of pricing are examined: price elasticity, fixed versus variable costs, markups, markdowns, and profit planning using markups and markdowns.

Price Elasticity

As defined in Chapter 18, **price elasticity** refers to the sensitivity of buyers to price changes in terms of the quantities they will purchase. Elasticity is based on the availability of substitutes and the urgency of need. It is expressed as the percentage change in quantity demanded divided by the percentage change in price:

$$\text{Price elasticity} = \frac{\dfrac{\text{Quantity 1} - \text{Quantity 2}}{\text{Quantity 1} + \text{Quantity 2}}}{\dfrac{\text{Price 1} - \text{Price 2}}{\text{Price 1} + \text{Price 2}}}$$

For purposes of simplicity, price elasticity is often expressed as a positive number (as it will be here).

Table 3 shows a demand schedule for women's blouses at several different prices. When selling price is reduced by a small percentage from $40 to $35, the percentage change in quantity demanded rises significantly from 120 to 150 units. Maxine's Blouses gains a strong competitive advantage. Demand is highly elastic (very price sensitive):

$$\text{Price elasticity} = \frac{\dfrac{120 - 150}{120 + 150}}{\dfrac{\$40 - \$35}{\$40 + \$35}} = 1.7 \text{ (expressed as a positive number)}$$

As price is reduced, total revenues go up.

At a price of $25, the market becomes more saturated: the percentage change in price from $25 to $20 is directly offset by the percentage change in quantity demanded from 240 to 300 units:

$$\text{Price elasticity} = \frac{\dfrac{240 - 300}{240 + 300}}{\dfrac{\$25 - \$20}{\$25 + \$20}} = 1.0 \text{ (expressed as a positive number)}$$

Total revenues remain the same at a price of $25 or $20. This is known as unitary demand, whereby total revenues stay constant as price changes.

At a price of $20, the market becomes extremely saturated, and further price reductions have little impact on demand. A large percentage change in price from $20 to $15 results in a small percentage change in quantity demanded, from 300 to 350 units. Maxine is able to sell relatively few additional blouses. Demand is inelastic (insensitive to price changes):

TABLE 3   Maxine's Blouses, A Demand Schedule

Selling Price	Quantity Demanded	Elasticity[a]	Total Revenue[b]	
$40	120		$4,800	
		1.7		
35	150		5,250	
		1.5		
30	190		5,700	
		1.3		
25	240		6,000	← Maximum
		1.0		total
20	300		6,000	← revenue
		0.5		
15	350		5,250	
		0.3		
10	390		3,900	

[a] Expressed as positive numbers.
[b] Total revenue = Selling price × Quantity demanded.

$$\text{Price elasticity} = \frac{\dfrac{300 - 350}{300 + 350}}{\dfrac{\$20 - \$15}{\$20 + \$15}} = 0.5 \text{ (expressed as a positive number)}$$

Notice that total revenue falls as demand changes from elastic to inelastic; at this point, price cuts are not effective.

Total revenue is maximized at the price levels where price and demand changes directly offset each other (in this example, $25 and $20). How does a firm choose between those prices? It depends on marketing philosophy. At a price of $25, profit will probably be higher because the firm needs to produce and sell fewer products, thus reducing costs. At a price of $20, more units are sold; this may increase the customer base for other products the firm offers and thereby raise overall company sales and profits.

Figure 1 graphically shows the demand elasticity for Maxine's Blouses. This figure illustrates that a demand curve is not necessarily straight and that a single demand schedule has elastic, unitary, and inelastic ranges.

It is important to remember that price elasticity refers to percentage changes, not to absolute changes. For example, a demand shift from 120 to 150 units involves a greater percentage change than a demand shift from 300 to 350 units. Furthermore, each product or brand faces a different demand schedule. Milk and magazines have dissimilar demand schedules, despite similar price ranges, because of the different availability of substitutes and urgency of need.

Fixed Versus Variable Costs

When making pricing decisions, it is essential to distinguish between fixed and variable costs. **Fixed costs** are ongoing costs that are unrelated to production or sales volume; they are generally constant over a given range of output for a specific time

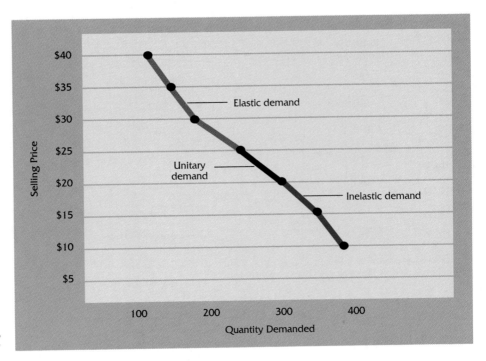

FIGURE 1
Maxine's Blouses, Demand Elasticity

period. In the short run, fixed costs cannot usually be changed. Examples of fixed costs are rent, full-time employee salaries, plant, equipment, real-estate taxes, and insurance.

Variable costs are directly related to production or sales volume. As volume increases, total variable costs increase; as volume declines, total variable costs decline. Per-unit variable costs frequently remain constant over a given range of volume (e.g., total sales commissions go up as sales rise, while sales commissions as a per cent of sales remain constant). Examples of variable costs are raw materials, sales commissions, parts, salaries of hourly employees, and product advertising.

Figure 2 graphically shows how fixed, variable, and total costs vary with production or sales volume for Eleanor's Cosmetics, a leased-department operator selling popular-priced cosmetics in a department store. In this figure, total fixed costs are $10,000. Variable costs are $5.00 per unit. Figure 2A depicts total costs: as volume increases, total fixed costs stay constant at $10,000, while total variable costs and total costs rise by $5.00 per unit. At 1,000 units, total fixed costs are $10,000, total variable costs are $5,000, and total costs are $15,000. At 5,000 units, total fixed costs are $10,000, total variable costs are $25,000, and total costs are $35,000.

Figure 2B depicts average costs: as volume increases, average fixed costs and average total costs decline (because fixed costs are spread over more units), while average variable costs remain the same. At 1,000 units, average fixed costs are $10.00, average variable costs are $5.00, and average total costs are $15.00. At 5,000 units, average fixed costs are $2.00 ($10,000/5,000 units), average variable costs are $5.00, and average total costs are $7.00.

By knowing the relationship between fixed and variable costs, marketers are better able to set prices. They recognize that average total costs usually decline as sales volume expands, which allows them to set skimming prices when volume is low and

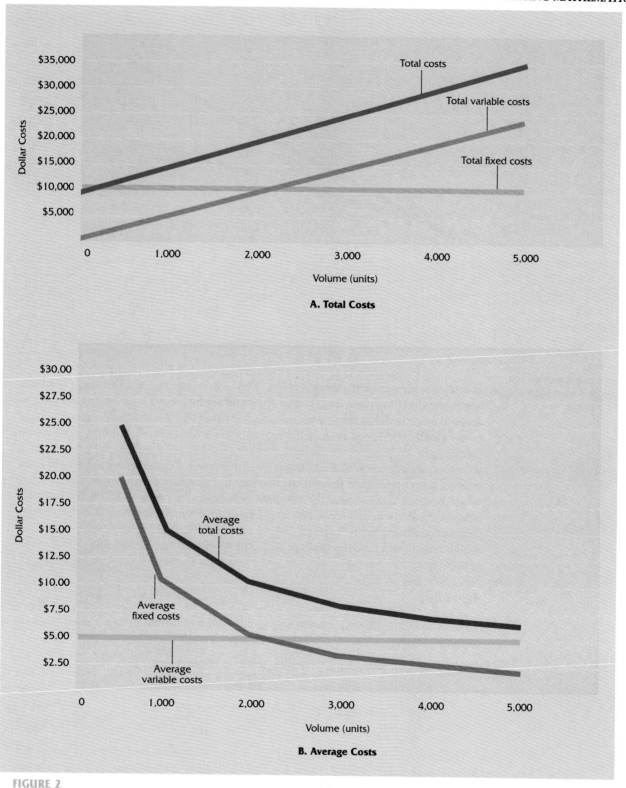

FIGURE 2

Fixed and Variable Costs for Eleanor's Cosmetics

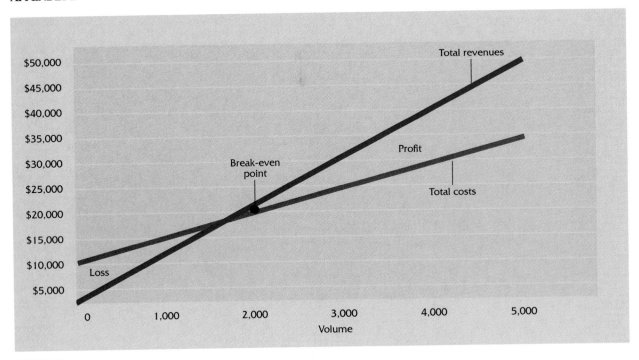

FIGURE 3
Break-Even Analysis for Eleanor's Cosmetics

penetration prices when volume is high. They also realize that the firm can reduce its losses with a selling price that is lower than average total costs — as long as the price is above average variable costs, a transaction will contribute toward the payment of fixed costs. Finally the break-even point can be shown on a total-cost curve graph. See Figure 3.

With a selling price of $10.00 per unit, Eleanor's Cosmetics would lose money unless 2,000 units could be sold. At that amount, the firm breaks even. For all sales volumes above 2,000 units, the company would earn a profit of $5.00 per unit, an amount equal to the difference between selling price and average variable costs (fixed costs are assumed to be "paid off" when sales reach 2,000 units). A sales volume of 5,000 units would return a profit of $15,000 (total revenues of $50,000 − total costs of $35,000).

Markups

A ***markup*** is the difference between product cost and selling price for each channel member. Markup is usually expressed as a percentage:

$$\text{Markup percentage (on selling price)} = \frac{\text{Selling price} - \text{Product cost}}{\text{Selling price}}$$

$$\text{Markup percentage (at cost)} = \frac{\text{Selling price} - \text{Product cost}}{\text{Product cost}}$$

Table 4 shows markup percentages on selling price and at cost for an item selling for $10.00 under varying costs. Because companies often consider a markup percentage as the equivalent of the gross margin percentage discussed earlier in this appendix,

TABLE 4   Markups on Selling Price and at Cost

Selling Price	Product Cost	Markup (% on Selling Price)	Markup (% at Cost)
$10.00	$9.00	10	11
10.00	8.00	20	25
10.00	7.00	30	43
10.00	6.00	40	67
10.00	5.00	50	100
10.00	4.00	60	150
10.00	3.00	70	233
10.00	2.00	80	400
10.00	1.00	90	900

Formulas to convert markup percentages:

$$\text{Markup percentage (on selling price)} = \frac{\text{Markup percentage (at cost)}}{100\% + \text{Markup percentage (at cost)}}$$

$$\text{Markup percentage (at cost)} = \frac{\text{Markup percentage (on selling price)}}{100\% - \text{Markup percentage (on selling price)}}$$

they use the markup percentage on selling price in their planning. As with gross margins, firms use their markups to cover operating expenses and net profit.

It is necessary for channel members to understand the discounts provided to them by vendors (suppliers). In addition to the markups they receive for providing regular marketing functions, they may also obtain quantity, cash, seasonal, and/or promotional discounts. Transportation costs are added to the final purchase price; they are not discounted.

Table 5 shows the calculation of a purchase price by a television retailer, based on a functional markup of 40 per cent and individual discounts of 10 (quantity), 2 (cash), 5 (seasonal), and 5 (promotional) per cent. The discounts do not total 62 per cent off final selling price. They total 52.2 per cent because the discounts are computed upon successive balances. For example, the 10 per cent quantity discount is computed on $165, which is the purchase price after deducting the functional markup allowed by the vendor.

Markdowns

One of the major price adjustments made by most firms is the ***markdown,*** which is a reduction in the original selling price of an item in order to sell it. Markdowns are caused by slow sales, model changes, and other factors.

Markdown percentages can be computed in either of two ways:

$$\text{Markdown percentage (off-original price)} = \frac{\text{Original selling price} - \text{Reduced selling price}}{\text{Original selling price}}$$

$$\text{Markdown percentage (off-sale price)} = \frac{\text{Original selling price} - \text{Reduced selling price}}{\text{Reduced selling price}}$$

For example, the off-original markdown percentage for an item that initially sold for $20 and has been marked down to $15 is ($20 − $15)/$20 = 25. The off-sale mark-

TABLE 5 A Television Retailer's Final Purchase Price, After Deducting All Discounts—Model 123

Discounts Offered by Manufacturer (in %)

Functional	40
Quantity	10
Cash	2
Seasonal	5
Promotional	5

Suggested Final Selling Price $275.00

Shipping Charges $ 15.30

Computation of Purchase Price Paid by Retailer

List price	$275.00
Less functional markup ($275.00 × 0.40)	110.00
Balance	$165.00
Less quantity discount ($165.00 × 0.10)	16.50
Balance	$148.50
Less cash discount ($148.50 × 0.02)	2.97
Balance	$145.53
Less seasonal discount ($145.53 × 0.05)	7.28
Balance	$138.25
Less promotional discount ($138.25 × 0.05)	6.91
Balance after all discounts	$131.34
Plus shipping charges	15.30
Price to channel member	$146.64

Total of Discounts $143.66

Total Discount % ($143.66/$275)   52.2

down percentage is ($20 − $15)/$15 = 33. While the off-original percentage is more accurate for price planning, the off-sale percentage indicates a larger price reduction to consumers and may generate increased interest.

Profit Planning Using Markups and Markdowns

Although lower markups (higher markdowns) generally result in higher unit sales and higher markups (lower markdowns) generally result in lower unit sales, it is important for marketers to determine the effect of a change in selling price on the firm's profitability. The impact of a price adjustment on total gross profit (also known as gross margin) can be determined through the use of this formula:

$$\begin{array}{l}\text{Unit sales required} \\ \text{to earn the same} \\ \text{total gross profit} \\ \text{with a price} \\ \text{adjustment}\end{array} = \frac{\text{Original markup (\%)}}{\text{Original markup (\%)} +/- \text{ Price change (\%)}} \times \begin{array}{l}\text{Expected unit} \\ \text{sales at original} \\ \text{price}\end{array}$$

For example, if a wholesaler that pays $7 to buy one unit of an item decides to reduce the selling price of that item by 10 per cent—from its original price of $10 to

$9, its markup on selling price decreases from 30 per cent ($3/$10) to 22.2 per cent ($2/$9). Because the wholesaler originally planned to sell 1,000 units at the $10 price, it must now sell 1,500 units at the $9 price to maintain the same gross profitability (30/20 × 1,000). Conversely, if the wholesaler decides to raise its price by 10 per cent — to $11, its new markup on selling price would be 36.4 per cent ($4/$11), and it would have to sell only 750 units to maintain the original gross profit level (30/40 × 1,000).

Determining an Optimal Marketing Mix

When developing, implementing, and assessing a marketing plan, it is necessary to consider the alternative marketing mixes available to the firm and determine the most effective one. Because many marketing costs (such as packaging, distribution, advertising, and personal selling) are both order generating and variable, marketing executives need to estimate and compare revenues for various combinations at various levels of costs. Table 6 shows how a company could set prices and allocate its $2 million annual marketing budget among product, distribution, advertising, and personal selling in a manner that maximizes profit. In this situation, the firm would choose an exclusive marketing mix that results in a skimming price, a high-quality product, limited distribution, and an emphasis on personal selling.

The concepts of opportunity cost and sales response curves provide valuable information in determining an optimal marketing mix. *Opportunity cost* measures the foregone revenues (profit) from not utilizing the optimal marketing mix. For example, it may be possible for a firm to sell an additional 55,000 units in a mass marketing strategy by increasing its advertising expenditures by $100,000 and reducing its distribution expenditures by $100,000. A firm that is unaware of this strategy would have an opportunity cost — in terms of profit — of $220,000:

$$\text{Opportunity cost} = (\text{Foregone unit sales} \times \text{Selling price}) - \text{Added costs}$$

$$= (55,000 \times \$10) - (55,000 \times \$6)$$

$$= \$220,000$$

At its optimal marketing strategy, a firm's opportunity cost would equal zero.

TABLE 6 Determining an Optimal Marketing Mix for a Company with a $2 Million Annual Marketing Budget

Alternative Marketing Mix	Selling Price	Unit Sales	Sales Revenue	Total Product Costs	Distribution Costs	Advertising Costs	Personal Selling Costs	Total Costs	Profit
Mass marketing	$10	1,000,000	$10,000,000	$6,000,000[a]	$850,000	$850,000	$ 300,000	$8,000,000	$2,000,000
Selective marketing	20	400,000	8,000,000	4,800,000[b]	600,000	750,000	650,000	6,800,000	1,200,000
Exclusive marketing	40	250,000	10,000,000	5,500,000[c]	500,000	400,000	1,100,000	7,500,000	2,500,000

[a] $6 per unit for labor, materials, and other production costs.
[b] $12 per unit for labor, materials, and other production costs.
[c] $22 per unit for labor, materials, and other production costs.

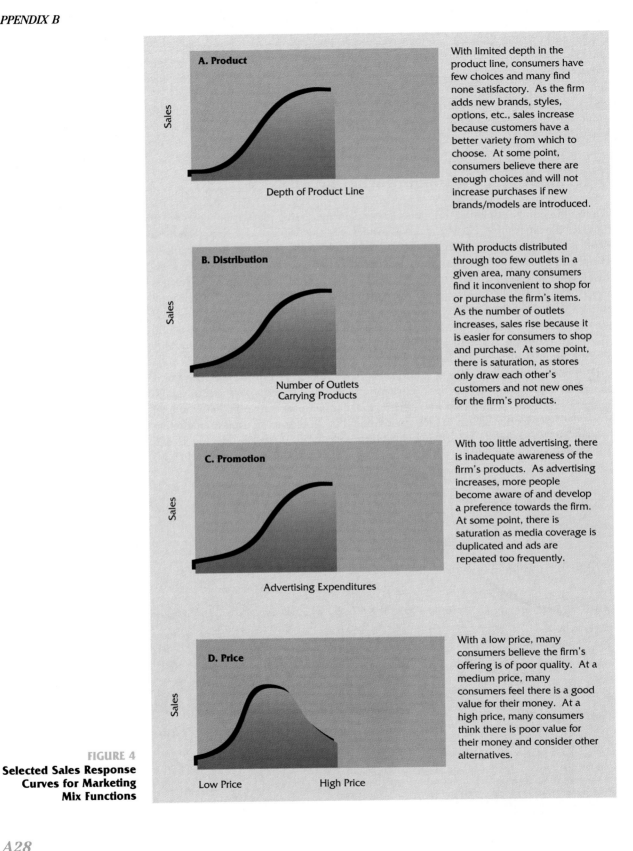

A. Product

Sales

Depth of Product Line

With limited depth in the product line, consumers have few choices and many find none satisfactory. As the firm adds new brands, styles, options, etc., sales increase because customers have a better variety from which to choose. At some point, consumers believe there are enough choices and will not increase purchases if new brands/models are introduced.

B. Distribution

Sales

Number of Outlets Carrying Products

With products distributed through too few outlets in a given area, many consumers find it inconvenient to shop for or purchase the firm's items. As the number of outlets increases, sales rise because it is easier for consumers to shop and purchase. At some point, there is saturation, as stores only draw each other's customers and not new ones for the firm's products.

C. Promotion

Sales

Advertising Expenditures

With too little advertising, there is inadequate awareness of the firm's products. As advertising increases, more people become aware of and develop a preference towards the firm. At some point, there is saturation as media coverage is duplicated and ads are repeated too frequently.

D. Price

Sales

Low Price   High Price

With a low price, many consumers believe the firm's offering is of poor quality. At a medium price, many consumers feel there is a good value for their money. At a high price, many consumers think there is poor value for their money and consider other alternatives.

FIGURE 4
Selected Sales Response Curves for Marketing Mix Functions

Sales response curves show the expected relationships between sales revenue and functional marketing efforts. These curves can be estimated on the basis of executives' judgment, surveys, industry data, and/or experimentation (whereby marketing-mix factors are systematically varied in a controlled environment).

Figure 4 shows sales response curves for a company considering four aspects of its marketing effort: depth of product line, number of outlets carrying products, advertising expenditures, and price level. For each of these factors, the impact of a strategy change on sales is shown; it is clear that different actions will result in different sales responses.

When using sales response curves, these considerations should be kept in mind:

▶ Sales responsiveness may vary by product and by market segment. For example, marketing expenditures have a much greater influence on new products/growing markets than on mature products/mature markets. See Figure 5.

▶ The range of efficient marketing efforts must be determined. At low levels, marketing activities may be insufficient to generate consumer interest. At high levels, these activities may be redundant and appeal to a saturated market. The range of marketing efforts having the greatest impact on sales is the appropriate one. See Figure 6.

▶ Sales response curves are related to the combination of marketing-mix factors employed by the firm. To determine its overall sales response curve, the company would combine all the individual curves shown in Figure 4 (or use all the data in Table 6).

▶ Sales response curves examine revenue fluctuations. Before making marketing decisions, profit response curves should also be studied.

▶ Sales response curves should be estimated under different conditions, such as good economy/poor economy or heavy competition/light competition.

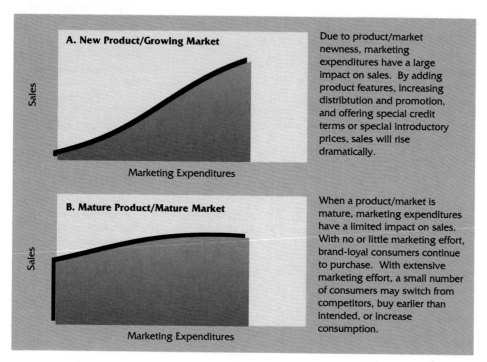

A. New Product/Growing Market

Sales

Marketing Expenditures

Due to product/market newness, marketing expenditures have a large impact on sales. By adding product features, increasing distribtution and promotion, and offering special credit terms or special introductory prices, sales will rise dramatically.

B. Mature Product/Mature Market

Sales

Marketing Expenditures

When a product/market is mature, marketing expenditures have a limited impact on sales. With no or little marketing effort, brand-loyal consumers continue to purchase. With extensive marketing effort, a small number of consumers may switch from competitors, buy earlier than intended, or increase consumption.

FIGURE 5
Sales Response Curves and Product/Market Maturity

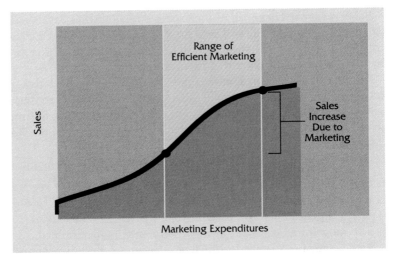

FIGURE 6
Optimal Marketing Expenditures

QUESTIONS

1. What information can a marketer obtain from a profit-and-loss statement (in dollars)?

2. Develop a profit-and-loss statement for The Deluxe Phone Center, a retail store, based on the following:

Beginning inventory (at cost)	$ 800,000
New merchandise (at cost)	600,000
Ending inventory (at cost)	550,000
Gross sales	2,000,000
Returns and allowances	300,000
Marketing expenses	350,000
General expenses	250,000

3. Using the profit-and-loss statement from Question 2, calculate:
   a. Return on investment. (Assume that investment equals $600,000 plus average inventory.)
   b. Stock turnover ratio.
   c. Net profit ratio (percentage).
   d. Operating expense ratio (percentage).
   e. Gross margin ratio (percentage).
   f. Cost-of-goods-sold ratio (percentage).
   g. Sales efficiency ratio (percentage).

4. How would The Deluxe Phone Center determine whether its performance ratios are satisfactory?

5. a. What is the impact on return on investment of a firm's increasing its investment turnover from three times to four times?
   b. List five ways for a firm to increase its investment turnover.

6. A wholesaler estimates that it can sell 10,000 compact-disc players at $115 or 6,000 at $150. The disc player costs the wholesaler $100.

   a. Calculate price elasticity between the $115 and $150 price levels.
   b. What factors should determine the price to be set?

7. A car wash has conducted research on its customers' sensitivity to price. These are the results:

Price	Number of Car Washes Demanded in Market Area per Year
$4.00	600,000
4.50	500,000
5.00	420,000
5.50	300,000
6.00	200,000
6.50	90,000

   a. Calculate price elasticity for all price levels.
   b. At what price is total revenue maximized?
   c. What price should be set? Why?
   d. What other information, not given in this question, is important in setting price?
   e. Which expenses for a car wash are fixed? Which expenses are variable?

8. The car wash in Question 7 can accommodate up to 300,000 cars per year with fixed costs of $600,000. Above 300,000 cars, fixed costs increase to $750,000. Variable costs are $1.00 per car wash.
   a. Compute average fixed costs, average variable costs, and average total costs for the car wash at each price.
   b. At what price is profit maximized?
   c. Why might the car wash set a price that does not maximize profit?

9. A tire manufacturer has fixed costs of $750,000 and variable costs of $35.00 per tire.
   a. Calculate total costs for volumes of 10,000, 25,000, and 50,000 tires.
   b. Calculate average total, fixed, and variable costs for the same volumes.
   c. At a volume of 25,000 tires, would the firm make a profit or loss with a wholesale selling price of $79.00? What is the total profit or loss?

10. A supermarket retailer sells medium-sized shaving-cream containers for $0.99; they are purchased for $0.59. Large-sized containers sell for $1.79; they are purchased for $1.29.
   a. For each size container, determine the markup percentage on selling price and at cost.
   b. Why would the company use a different markup percentage for medium containers from that for large containers?
   c. If a shaving cream manufacturer offers the supermarket a 30 per cent markup on selling price for medium-sized containers, as well as a cash discount of 8 per cent and a quantity discount of 5 per cent, what is the purchase price to the supermarket? What is the overall discount? There are no transportation costs.

11. A wholesaler requires a 50 per cent markup on selling price for profit projections to be met. The merchandise costs $17.00.
   a. What must the selling price be for the wholesaler to meet its markup goal?
   b. What would be the minimum selling price if the wholesaler has a markup goal of 40 per cent on selling price?

12. Convert the following markups from selling price to cost:
   a. 30 per cent markup on selling price.
   b. 40 per cent markup on selling price.
   c. 55 per cent markup on selling price.

13. Convert the following markups from cost to selling price:
   a. 100 per cent markup at cost.
   b. 150 per cent markup at cost.
   c. 175 per cent markup at cost.

14. An automobile parts distributor is offered the following discounts: functional markup, 40 per cent; quantity discount, 5 per cent; cash discount, 2 per cent; and seasonal discount, 3 per cent. If the suggested final selling price of the total order is $750 and shipping charges are $35.00, compute the total order cost to the firm.

15. A glove manufacturer originally sold suede gloves for $35 per pair. An end-of-season sale has reduced the price of these gloves to $25.
   a. Compute the off-original and off-sale markdown percentages.
   b. Why is there a difference in these calculations?

16. a. A firm expects to sell 1,000 personal computer systems yearly at a price of $1,000 per system (including monitor, keyboard, and graphics board). At the $1,000 price, the company's markup is 20 per cent. How many units would the firm need to sell to earn the same total gross profit at a selling price of $1,150 as it would at a selling price of $1,000?
   b. How many units would the firm need to sell to earn the same total gross profit at a selling price of $900 as it would at a selling price of $1,000?

17. A manufacturer estimates the following relationship between marketing expenses and sales:

Marketing Expenses	Unit Sales
$100,000	200,000
200,000	250,000
300,000	300,000
400,000	350,000
500,000	400,000

If a product has a gross profit of $3 per unit and general operating expenses are constant at $100,000, at what marketing expenditure level is profit maximized?

18. Calculate the opportunity cost associated with each marketing expenditure level in Question 17.

19. a. Why do most sales response curves have "S" shapes?
   b. Under what conditions would sales response curves have different shapes?
   c. Draw sales response curves based on the information in Table 6.

APPENDIX *C*

Computer-Based Marketing Exercises

This appendix and an accompanying computer diskette allow you to engage in marketing decision making under simulated conditions and to apply many of the concepts studied during an introduction to or survey of marketing course. To use *Computer-Based Marketing Exercises,* you need to purchase a blank computer diskette and make a personal copy of the master exercise diskette which is available to your instructor.

The exercises described in this appendix are designed to reinforce text material; to allow you to manipulate controllable marketing factors and to see their impact on costs, sales, and profits; to have you better understand the influence of uncontrollable factors; and to have you gain experience in using a computer to assess marketing opportunities and solve marketing problems. All fourteen exercises are designed to be handed in for class assignments or for your own use. The exercises are balanced in terms of subject and level.

These are among the features of *Computer-Based Marketing Exercises:*

▶ The exercises are linked to important concepts discussed throughout *Marketing,* 4th Edition. Text page references are provided for each exercise both on the computer diskette and in this appendix.
▶ Although each exercise closely parallels the text, it allows great flexibility in your data input. You are encouraged to manipulate data and compare the results attained under different assumptions. This provides you with ''hands-on'' experience.
▶ The format of the exercises is very user-friendly. All directions are contained on screens that introduce each exercise, and the exercises are self-prompting. No knowledge of computer programming or computers is required.
▶ There is a broad variety of applications. Exercises are included for each of the eight parts of *Marketing* and for Appendix B (''Marketing Mathematics'').
▶ All exercises are as realistic as possible.
▶ The quality of graphics is high (yet a graphics board is not required). Although some exercises contain spreadsheet-type analyses, Lotus or other spreadsheet software is not required.

► The software operates on either IBM personal computers or IBM compatibles, and with a color or monochrome monitor. The exercise diskette is available in 3 1/2 and 5 1/4 inch formats.

► After setting up your copy of the exercise diskette, your name will appear at the top of every screen and on any pages you print from the screen.

How To Use the Computer-Based Exercise Diskette

Setting Up Your Diskette

This section explains how to make your copy of the *Computer-Based Marketing Exercises* diskette from the master diskette supplied by your instructor or your college's computer center; and how to permanently place your name, class, and section on your diskette (so that assignments may be submitted with your name printed on them). NOTE: These directions assume that you are working with a two disk-drive computer with floppy disk drives designated as drive "A" and drive "B".

To make your copy from the master exercise diskette, insert a disk operating system (DOS) diskette in drive A (usually the left or bottom disk drive) and close the door. Turn the computer on. Should the drive light come on for the drive with the diskette, fine. Otherwise, place the DOS diskette into the drive with the light on; for the computer you are using, this is drive A.

If your DOS diskette is configured with date and time options, it will be necessary to press the return key once when the date prompt appears and press the return key again when the time prompt appears. When the screen displays "A>" (the A prompt), type "DISKCOPY A: B:" (without the quote marks), and then press the return key. In some computers, the disk copy program may be on a second DOS master diskette. If so, you must insert this diskette in drive A to start the disk copy program.

This message—or one similar to it—now appears: "Insert SOURCE diskette in drive A: Insert TARGET diskette in drive B: Strike any key when ready." Remove the DOS diskette from drive A, place the *Computer-Based Marketing Exercises* master diskette in drive A, place your blank diskette in drive B, close each disk drive door, and press any key.

When the copying process is complete, this message—or one similar to it—appears: "Copy complete. Copy another (Y/N)?" Type "N" (without the quote marks) and press the return key, if necessary (as prompted by the computer screen). The screen should display an "A>". Then remove both diskettes and turn off the computer. With a soft-tipped felt pen, mark your name on your copied diskette (the one from drive B). Return the master diskette to your instructor or the computer center operator.

At this point, you are ready to insert your name, class, and section on your copy of the exercise diskette; once you enter this information, it will appear on every computer screen and printout. Place a DOS diskette in drive A, close the door, and turn on the computer. When "A>" appears, remove the DOS diskette and place your copy of the exercise diskette in drive A. Close the disk drive door, type "CBME" (without the quote marks), and press the return key. The program on your exercise diskette will do the rest. At the screen prompts, enter your name, class, and section. This information becomes a permanent part of your exercise diskette. If you desire, you may now continue onto the exercise menu and do an exercise. After you finish, remove your diskette from drive A and turn off the computer.

Each subsequent time that you want to use the exercise diskette, simply place the DOS diskette in drive A, close the door, and turn on the computer. When "A>" appears, remove the DOS diskette and place your copy of the exercise diskette in drive A. Close the disk drive door, type "CBME" (without the quote marks), and press the return key. The program on your exercise diskette will do the rest and guide you to the main menu.

Some computers have hard disk drives. When they are turned on, a "C>" appears on the screen. Should that occur, type "A:" (without the quote marks) and press the return key. Then follow the instructions stated above.

How to Use the Main Menu

When using your diskette, all exercises can be accessed from the MAIN MENU screen. To run an exercise, enter the appropriate number (1–14) and press the return key. Entering "Q" (without the quote marks) will enable you to quit the program.

The menu is arranged in the same order as the topics appear in the text and shows text page references so that you may review concepts before (or while) doing an exercise:

Part 1:   **Introduction to Marketing**
  1. Boston Consulting Group Matrix (p. 69)
  2. Questionnaire Analysis (p. 108)

Part 2:   **Understanding Consumers**
  3. End-Use Analysis (p. 193)
  4. Segmentation Analysis (p. 228)

Part 3:   **Product Planning**
  5. Product Screening (p. 298)

Part 4:   **Distribution Planning**
  6. Total-Cost Approach (p. 372)
  7. Economic Order Quantity (p. 382)

Part 5:   **Promotion Planning**
  8. Advertising Budget (p. 490)

Part 6:   **Price Planning**
  9. Price Elasticity (p. 560)
  10. Key Cost Concepts (p. 607)

Part 7:   **Expanding Marketing Scope**
  11. Standardizing Marketing Plans (p. 659)

Part 8:   **Marketing Management**
  12. Allocating Functional Costs (p. 759)

Appendix B: Marketing Mathematics
  13. Performance Ratios (p. A16)
  14. Optimal Marketing Mix (p. A27)

After returning to DOS (Q on the menu screen), simply remove your diskette and store it carefully for future use. Always remember to turn off the computer when you conclude a session.

How to Print from the Exercise Diskette

While using the exercise diskette, you may print any screen for your own reference or for the submission of a class assignment. Simply turn on the printer (either dot-matrix, letter-quality, or laser) that is connected to the computer you are using. Then simultaneously press the shift key and the [PrtSc] key and the screen appearing on your computer monitor will automatically be printed—including your name, class, and section.

The Exercises

In the following sections, each exercise is discussed. For every exercise, we present objectives, a list of the relevant key terms and concepts from the text, an explanation of the exercise, and questions/assignments to be answered or completed.

Exercise 1: Boston Consulting Group Matrix

Objectives

1. To apply the Boston Consulting Group matrix to a firm's marketing planning activities
2. To see how a product category's relative market share and industry growth rate affect its placement as a star, cash cow, problem child, or dog
3. To consider the appropriate balance of stars, cash cows, problem children, and dogs for a firm

Key Terms and Concepts

strategic business unit (SBU)	*star*
portfolio analysis	*cash cow*
Boston Consulting Group	*problem child/question mark*
matrix	*dog*

Explanation of Exercise

As a marketing executive for the Ivory Paper Company, a table allows you to enter revised values for the relative market shares and industry growth rates for any or all of Ivory's product categories (SBUs). Then the products are displayed in a Boston Consulting Group matrix.

In this exercise, the dividing lines between high and low relative market shares, as well as high and low industry growth rates, are the average market share and the average industry growth rate for all of Ivory's product categories. The averages change when you vary relative market shares and industry growth rates for individual product categories.

When examining the Boston Consulting Group matrix, study the balance of products in each grouping. For example, are there enough cash cows to support problem children? Also consider the balance of products for future periods. For example, from where will future stars come?

The exercise is keyed to pages 69–73 in the text.

Questions/Assignments

1. Print and evaluate a Boston Consulting Group matrix with these current percentage values for Ivory Paper Company: Paper Towels—190 (share) and 10 (growth); Bathroom Tissues—80 (share) and 6 (growth); Disposable Mats—40 (share) and 15 (growth); Baby Wipes—70 (share) and 10 (growth); Facial Tissues—20 (share) and 3 (growth); Napkins—30 (share) and 5 (growth); Party Favors—150 (share) and 14 (growth); and Industry Aprons—100 (share) and 25 (growth).

2. Print and evaluate a Boston Consulting Group matrix with these 1995 projections for Ivory Paper Company: Paper Towels — 150 (share) and 8 (growth); Bathroom Tissues — 70 (share) and 4 (growth); Disposable Mats — 30 (share) and 15 (growth); Baby Wipes — 50 (share) and 6 (growth); Facial Tissues — 10 (share) and 3 (growth); Napkins — 20 (share) and 5 (growth); Party Favors — 210 (share) and 10 (growth); and Industry Aprons — 130 (share) and 15 (growth).

3. Compare the current and projected matrices. Will Ivory Paper Company be in a stronger, weaker, or equal position in 1995 than it is now? Why?

4. What should an ideal projected Boston Consulting Group matrix for Ivory Paper Company look like? Print the matrix and explain your answer.

5. What short-run and long-run recommendations would you make for Ivory?

Exercise 2: Questionnaire Analysis

Objectives

1. To implement a survey dealing with consumer attitudes, usage, and purchase behavior
2. To explore the differences between market segments via a survey
3. To see how coding, tabulation, and analysis are undertaken
4. To present recommendations based upon survey results

Key Terms and Concepts

survey	*tabulation*
data analysis	*analysis*
coding	*recommendations*

Explanation of Exercise

In this exercise, you are a market researcher who is requested to collect data for a consumer survey on coffee consumption. The exercise screens explain how blank copies of the survey may be printed as well as how the survey may be administered at the computer.

After interviewing the respondents, you input their answers into the computer and a summary of the responses is provided automatically — separated into coffee drinker and noncoffee drinker market segments. The questionnaire consists of several questions and varies slightly for the two segments. For the analysis to be meaningful, you should interview at least twenty respondents.

The exercise is keyed to pages 108–110 in the text.

Questions/Assignments

1. Prepare ten blank questionnaires for coffee drinkers and ten for noncoffee drinkers. Then interview ten adult coffee drinkers and ten adult noncoffee drinkers. Record their answers on the blank questionnaires (one per respondent) and enter these answers on your exercise diskette. Print a coffee questionnaire analysis screen summarizing the responses.

2. Analyze the data generated from question/assignment 1. Write a two-page report recapping the findings of your study. Make sure your analysis covers each question, brand, and market segment in the questionnaire.

3. Develop specific recommendations for the marketing of Maxwell House (a regular coffee) and Sanka (a decaffineated coffee) based upon your analysis in question/assignment 2.

4. Evaluate the questionnaire used in this exercise.
   a. Is the wording clear?
   b. What additional questions should be asked?
   c. How else could the attitudes/behavior of coffee versus noncoffee drinkers be studied?

Exercise 3: End-Use Analysis

Objectives

1. To show the value of the Standard Industrial Classification (SIC) for marketers
2. To apply end-use analysis for a firm marketing to organizational consumers
3. To forecast a company's overall sales based on customer growth projections by SIC code

Key Terms and Concepts

organizational consumer   *Standard Industrial Classification (SIC)*
derived demand   *end-use analysis*

Explanation of Exercise

As the director of marketing for a medium-sized glue manufacturer, a table allows you to enter revised values for the proportion of your company's sales that are made to various organizational consumers — which are classified by SIC code — as well as the growth of these consumers' industries. After you enter the new values, the computer screen shows the overall sales growth for the glue manufacturer. You may vary the values for any or all of the consumer groups by SIC category.

Mathematically, the company's overall projected sales growth is equal to the per cent of its sales accounted for by a customer category (SIC code) times the expected growth of that category's industry, summed for all customer categories. Customers accounting for a large proportion of the company's revenues have the greatest impact on the sales forecast.

The exercise is keyed to pages 193–194 in the text.

Questions/Assignments

1. The glue manufacturer in this exercise has prepared data to be used in forecasting sales for 3-, 5-, and 10-year periods:

SIC Code	3-Year Projections		5-Year Projections		10-Year Projections	
	% of Co. Sales	% Growth by Indus.	% of Co. Sales	% Growth by Indus.	% of Co. Sales	% Growth by Indus.
24	25	+10	27	+10	30	+8
25	17	+12	15	+10	13	+5
27	20	+ 5	21	+ 2	22	+2
30	12	+ 3	13	+ 6	14	+9
31	9	− 2	7	− 2	5	−2
39	17	0	17	+ 1	16	+1
	100		100		100	

Enter the data onto your computer diskette and print the end-use analyses for each of the three projections.

2. Analyze the projections in question/assignment 1, in terms of
   a. Overall company sales growth.
   b. The sales increases/decreases by SIC category.
   c. The relative importance of each customer group.
3. What are the marketing implications of the projections in question/assignment 1 with regard to product, distribution, promotion, and price planning?
4. What would be the impact of increasing the industry growth estimates for SIC code 27 by two per cent in each of the years projected? Print the revised end-use analyses and comment on the change in the sales forecast.
5. How would you alter the firm's marketing strategy based on the improved outlook for SIC code 27?

Exercise 4: Segmentation Analysis

Objectives

1. To better understand the alternatives for developing a target market strategy: undifferentiated marketing (mass marketing), concentrated marketing, and differentiated marketing (multiple segmentation)
2. To show how the choice of a target market approach and alternative marketing budget levels affect a firm's sales and profitability
3. To relate such concepts as product differentiation, demand patterns, the majority fallacy, sales penetration, and diminishing returns to marketing budget allocations

Key Terms and Concepts

market
market segmentation
target market strategy
undifferentiated marketing (mass marketing)
concentrated marketing

differentiated marketing (multiple segmentation)
product differentiation
demand patterns
majority fallacy
sales penetration
diminishing returns

Explanation of Exercise

A table allows you, the vice-president of marketing for a medium-sized local company, to allocate a $3-million annual marketing budget between two market segments. By varying the budget, unit sales, sales revenues, manufacturing costs, total costs, and profit are affected. Different levels of marketing expenditures are required to be successful in each market segment.

Segment A is large and very competitive. Consumers have many brands from which to choose. Segment B is much smaller and consumer needs have not been fulfilled; no firms serve this market.

The exercise is keyed to pages 228–238 in the text.

Questions/Assignments

1. At what marketing budget level would you be most profitable in segment A? Print your optimal budget level for this market and explain your answer.
2. At what marketing budget level would you be most profitable in segment B? Print your optimal budget level for this market and explain your answer.
3. Describe the basic differences between segment A and segment B in terms of the relationship among sales, profits, and marketing expenditures. What does this mean to marketers?
4. At what marketing budget allocation levels would your firm's total profits be maximized? Print your optimal budget allocation and explain your answer. NOTE: You may use a differentiated marketing approach.
5. Explain how these concepts relate to the exercise:
   a. Product differentiation.
   b. Demand patterns.
   c. Majority fallacy.
   d. Sales penetration.
   e. Diminishing returns.

Exercise 5: Product Screening

Objectives

1. To demonstrate the use of a new-product screening checklist as a product evaluation tool
2. To show how the importance of various product characteristics can be denoted
3. To illustrate how different assumptions regarding the importance of product characteristics and the ratings of individual attributes affect a product's overall rating
4. To consider what minimum overall evaluation score would be necessary for a product to successfully pass the product-screening stage of new-product planning

Key Terms and Concepts

modifications	*new-product planning process*
minor innovations	*product screening*
major innovations	*new-product screening checklist*

Explanation of Exercise

A new-product screening checklist lets you—acting as a marketing expert who specializes in new-product concepts—weight the importance of various general, marketing, and production characteristics; and then rate a new-product idea in terms of each of these characteristics. The computer program then computes separate indexes for general, marketing, and production factors—as well as an overall evaluation index.

Mathematically, every specific index equals the average of all its attributes' weights times their ratings. For example, the general characteristics index equals

$$\frac{\text{The sum of (Each attribute's weight} \times \text{That attribute's rating)}}{\text{The total weights assigned to general characteristics}}$$

The exercise is keyed to pages 298–300 in the text.

Questions/Assignments

1. As a new-product planning analyst at Colgate-Palmolive (C-P), you have been asked to explore the feasibility of a new toothpaste aimed at smokers. One major competitor already markets a product for this market segment. However, most toothpaste brands aim at segments that are more concerned with decay prevention, fresh breath, and plaque removal. C-P's proposed product is specifically formulated to restore teeth whiteness and to soften "smoker's breath." The company's marketing personnel believe that there will be no major production difficulties with the new product; but they are somewhat concerned about competitors being able to imitate the toothpaste's ingredients. C-P's tentative brand name is "Colgate-S for Smokers," and the product would be available in both tube and pump dispensers. Based on this information, use the computerized new-product screening checklist to evaluate Colgate-S. Print both the individual weights and ratings that you assign to the product, as well as the overall analysis screen.

2. a. Explain your choice of weights and ratings for each of the criteria in the new-product screening checklist for question/assignment 1.
   b. How should Colgate-Palmolive use concept testing with this product?
   c. Would you recommend that Colgate-S for Smokers skip test marketing? Why or not?

3. A manufacturer of high-fidelity components (receivers, speakers, and turntables) has been conducting marketing research for new products/markets over the past ten years. An unfulfilled market need which has been discovered through such research is for a high-quality FM home/office radio with one detachable speaker. The firm's research suggests that people have become increasingly dissatisfied with the quality of alarm-clock radios for even casual listening. Poor reception, a tinny sound, and poor controls (dials) are frequently cited complaints. Suggested locales for a high-quality FM radio are dormitories, bedrooms, and home offices. The firm proposes to make a radio with superior specifications regarding power and distortion. A 6-inch speaker would be built into the receiver, and a matching 6-inch detachable speaker would be available as an option. The basic radio would carry a retail list price of $150, and the optional speaker would list for $50. Although the price is considered low in terms of quality high-fidelity components, conventional clock radios often sell for as low as $15. The new radio would be distributed through the manufacturer's regular distribution channel. Use the com-

puterized new-product screening checklist to evaluate the proposed radio. Print both the individual weights and ratings that you assign to the product, as well as the overall analysis screen.

4. **a.** Explain your choice of weights and ratings for each of the criteria in the new-product screening checklist for question/assignment 3.

 b. Should the manufacturer proceed further with this product? Why or why not?

 c. Comment on the risks inherent in marketing the new FM radio. Compare these to the risks in Colgate-Palmolive's marketing a new toothpaste for smokers.

Exercise 6: Total-Cost Approach

Objectives

1. To apply the total-cost approach to distribution planning for rail, truck, and air transportation forms
2. To better understand the components of the total-cost approach: freight, warehousing, and lost sales
3. To analyze differences in the distribution strategies of durable and perishable goods
4. To determine optimal distribution strategies for durable and nondurable goods

Key Terms and Concepts

physical distribution   *railroads*
distribution standards   *motor carriers*
total-cost approach   *airways*

Explanation of Exercise

By answering several questions, you — as a distribution manager — are able to determine your company's total freight, warehouse, and lost sales costs for durable goods and for perishable goods, which can be shipped via rail, truck, and/or air. Bar charts show the results.

First, you indicate the type of goods to be analyzed (durable or perishable). Then, you assign the percentage of company transportation efforts to be allocated to rail and truck (air is recorded as 100 per cent minus the percentage allotted to rail and truck). The computer automatically calculates the various total costs and displays them. All the necessary data to make decisions are presented on the exercise diskette.

The exercise is keyed to pages 372 – 373 in the text.

Questions/Assignments

1. Explain the basic differences between durable goods and perishable goods for the various distribution cost components (freight, warehousing, and lost sales). Be sure to comment separately on each of the transportation forms as well as on the overall total costs.
2. If motor carriers (trucks) have the lowest total costs for durable goods and air shipments have the lowest total costs for perishable goods, why would a firm often use multiple forms of transportation?

3. a. Calculate the total transportation costs for durable goods when the company ships 20 per cent by rail, 40 per cent by truck, and 40 per cent by air. Print and assess the results.

   b. Calculate the total transportation costs for perishable goods when the company ships 20 per cent by rail, 40 per cent by truck, and 40 per cent by air. Print and assess the results.

4. a. For durable goods, print and compare these transportation mixes: Mix 1 — 20 per cent by rail, 40 per cent by truck, and 40 per cent by air; Mix 2 — 25 per cent by rail, 45 per cent by truck, and 30 per cent by air; and Mix 3 — 30 per cent by rail, 50 per cent by truck, and 20 per cent by air.

   b. For perishable goods, print and compare these transportation mixes: Mix 1 — 20 per cent by rail, 40 per cent by truck, and 40 per cent by air; Mix 2 — 25 per cent by rail, 45 per cent by truck, and 30 per cent by air; and Mix 3 — 30 per cent by rail, 50 per cent by truck, and 20 per cent by air.

Exercise 7: Economic Order Quantity

Objectives

1. To consider the overall ramifications of order size for a firm when it makes purchases
2. To examine the individual components of economic order quantity (EOQ): annual demand, wholesale unit costs, order-processing costs, and inventory-holding costs
3. To calculate economic order quantities
4. To see the impact of different assumptions on economic order quantity

Key Terms and Concepts

just-in-time (JIT) inventory   *order-processing costs*
   system   *inventory-holding costs*
stock turnover   *economic order quantity (EOQ)*
order size   *warehousing*

Explanation of Exercise

As the purchasing manager for a firm, you can determine its economic order quantity under various assumptions by answering questions about expected annual demand for a product, its unit cost at wholesale, order-processing costs, and inventory-holding costs (as a percentage of a unit's wholesale cost). The computer program uses the EOQ formula and a screen graphically displays the results.

Mathematically,

$$EOQ = \sqrt{\frac{2 \times \text{Annual demand} \times \text{Order-processing costs}}{\text{Inventory-holding costs \%} \times \text{Unit cost}}}$$

The exercise is keyed to pages 382–384 in the text.

Questions/Assignments

1. a. How can order-processing and inventory-holding costs be estimated by a company?
    b. How can a company reduce its order-processing costs? What are the pros and cons of this?
    c. How can a company reduce its inventory-holding costs? What are the pros and cons of this?
2. A mail-order retailer wishes to apply the EOQ concept to its purchases of key items to minimize the sum of its order-processing and inventory-holding costs. For example, it annually buys 900 units of one model of a transparency tape dispenser. The cost at wholesale is $1.50. Each order the retailer places with its supplier costs the retailer $7.50. Inventory-holding costs are 25 per cent of unit cost. Print and comment on the economic order quantity for the retailer.
3. Determine how each of the following (one at a time) impacts on the EOQ of the mail-order firm noted in question/assignment 2. Discuss these changes and print the relevant screens.
    a. Reduce annual demand from 900 to 600 units.
    b. Increase the cost at wholesale from $1.50 to $1.75.
    c. Reduce order-processing costs from $7.50 to $5.00.
    d. Raise inventory-holding costs from 25 per cent to 35 per cent.
4. Describe three situations in which the economic order quantity model would be inappropriate for the mail-order retailer.

Exercise 8: Advertising Budget

Objectives

1. To practice setting an advertising budget—using such concepts as reach, waste, cost per thousand, and effective cost per thousand
2. To examine the characteristics of alternative magazines as advertising media
3. To see how the allocation of an advertising budget among various magazines affects promotion effectiveness
4. To build upon the Part 5 case in the text ("Carnival Cruise Lines: Aggressive Promotion Pays Off")

Key Terms and Concepts

advertising media costs	*waste*	*message permanence*
reach	*effective cost per thousand*	*lead time*
cost per thousand	*narrowcasting*	*frequency*
		clutter

Explanation of Exercise

As the advertising director for Carnival Cruise Lines (see the Part 5 case on pages 546–549), one of your many responsibilities is to allocate the firm's ad budget among various magazines via a computerized-spreadsheet table. The maximum amount you have to spend on magazine ads is $2 million.

You make decisions with regard to the number of insertions (full-page ads) that Carnival should make in these magazines during the year and the per cent of each magazine's audience that would be wasted for Carnival. You are provided with the names of the magazines, their cost per full-page ad (equal to one insertion), and their reach. These data are from *Standard Rate and Data Service* and Simmons. Based on your decisions, the computer program calculates the budget allocated to each magazine, its cost per thousand, and the effective cost per thousand. For instance, the effective cost per thousand for a specific magazine equals

$$\frac{\text{Advertising budget for a magazine}}{\text{Reach for that magazine} \times (100 - \text{per cent waste})} \times 1{,}000$$

The program also derives company totals, using weighted averages. As an example, the total waste for Carnival's magazine advertising equals

> (% of magazine ad budget allocated to magazine A × % waste for magazine A) + (% of magazine ad budget allocated to magazine B × % waste for magazine B) + (other magazines, based on individual budgets and waste)

The exercise is keyed to pages 490–500 in the text.

Questions/Assignments

1. a. Evaluate each of the magazines shown on the computer screen for this exercise in terms of cost per 1-page ad and reach. These are the full titles of the magazines: *Cruise Travel, Modern Bride, Modern Maturity, People, Preferred Traveler, Travel & Leisure, TV Guide,* and *Woman's Day.*
   b. Estimate waste as a percentage of reach for each magazine and explain your answer.
   c. Allocate your $2 million advertising budget roughly equally among all the magazines. Print and comment upon the results.
2. Carnival's marketing vice-president has given you these guidelines in making your actual magazine budget expenditure decisions: You should spend as close to your entire $2 million magazine advertising budget as possible. You should use no fewer than five magazines. You should allocate no more than 35 per cent of the budget to any one magazine. The effective cost per thousand should be minimized.
   a. Develop an advertising budget that meets these guidelines.
   b. Print and explain your budget allocations.
   c. What is the role of reach in your decision making?
3. Carnival's marketing vice-president has decided to modify two of the guidelines stated in question/assignment 2. First, you may use as few magazines as you deem proper (you may even use just one magazine). Second, there are no restrictions on the maximum per cent of the budget that may be spent on any single magazine.
   a. Develop an advertising budget that meets these guidelines.
   b. Print and explain your budget allocations.
   c. What are the pros and cons of concentrating your budget on fewer magazines?
4. Explain how each of these factors would affect your magazine advertising budget decisions:
   a. Passalong rates (as a part of reach).
   b. Narrowcasting.
   c. Frequency.
   d. Clutter.
   e. Message permanence.
   f. Lead time.

Exercise 9: Price Elasticity

Objectives

1. To illustrate the law of demand
2. To distinguish among elastic, inelastic, and unitary demand
3. To see how a firm can estimate demand at different price levels
4. To further explore the interrelationship among price, demand, total revenue, and price elasticity

Key Terms and Concepts

law of demand   *inelastic demand*
price elasticity of demand   *unitary demand*
elastic demand   *subjective price*

Explanation of Exercise

As the owner-operator of a small appliance-repair firm, you are concerned about what price to charge for a basic service call. First, you answer a series of questions about the price range to be considered and the expected average amount of consumer demand (which may be expressed in hundredths) at various prices. Then, the computer program calculates the elasticity of demand for the various price intervals and graphically displays it.

Your answers affect the type of demand the firm would face at different prices. Demand may be elastic, inelastic, or unitary—based on the price elasticity formula discussed in the text.

The exercise is keyed to pages 560–563 in the text.

Questions/Assignments

1. You are contemplating the use of one of two service strategies: low-end and high-end. The low-end strategy involves 9:00 A.M. to 5 P.M. service hours during Monday through Friday, only cash or check payments, use of a telephone-answering machine for customer inquiries, no emergency service, and a 30-day guarantee on rebuilt parts. The minimum acceptable price for this strategy is $10 per call. The high-end strategy includes 24-hour-a-day service during seven days a week, acceptance of credit cards (as well as cash and checks), live operator assistance for customer inquiries, emergency service, and a 1-year guarantee on new factory-built parts. The minimum acceptable price for this strategy is $20 per call. Here is the estimated average service-call demand per day at various prices for each of the two strategies:

Price	Average Low-End Demand (Calls Per Day)	Average High-End Demand (Calls Per Day)
$10	15	15
$15	12	14
$20	8	12
$25	4	10
$30	1	7
$35	0	6
$40	0	3
$45	0	2
$50	0	1

Determine the price elasticities at the various prices for the two strategies. Print the computer-generated tables and assess them.

2. **a.** Could your firm utilize both a low-end and a high-end marketing strategy? Explain your answer.

   b. Based on the information provided for question/assignment 1, could you determine the most profitable price level for the firm? If yes, what is it? If no, why not?

   c. How could you improve your ability to estimate the demand at various price levels?

3. **a.** Present average customer demand levels so that price elasticity at every interval between $10 and $28 (at $3 intervals) is elastic. Print and discuss your answer.

   b. Present average customer demand levels so that price elasticity at every interval between $20 and $50 (at $5 intervals) is inelastic. Print and discuss your answer.

   c. Is it realistic that demand would always be elastic or always be inelastic over a broad price range? Explain your answer.

4. **a.** Under what conditions would the price elasticity of demand equal 0? Why?

   b. Under what conditions would the price elasticity of demand equal 1? Why?

   c. Print a demand curve screen showing both 0 and 1 price elasticities.

Exercise 10: Key Cost Concepts

Objectives

1. To study fixed and variable cost concepts in detail
2. To distinguish between total and average fixed costs and total and average variable costs
3. To show the effects of changes in fixed and variable costs on a variety of cost components
4. To see how fixed, variable, and total costs are related to the level of production

Key Terms and Concepts

total fixed costs

total variable costs

total costs

average fixed costs

average variable costs

average total costs

marginal costs

Explanation of Exercise

As a pricing consultant for Phase III bicycles, you answer questions about the fixed and variable costs of making the futuristic bicycle at various production levels. First, you set the total fixed costs at two different production levels. Next, you set the average (per-unit) variable costs at four different production levels. NOTE: You should reduce per-unit variable costs as the production volume increases.

After you enter your decisions, the computer program automatically generates a screen showing production levels; total fixed, variable, and overall costs; average fixed, variable, and overall costs; and the change in per-unit costs as volume increases.

The exercise is keyed to pages 607–609 in the text.

Questions/Assignments

1. You have been asked to prepare an analysis of bicycle production costs for the purpose of gathering background data to be used in the development and implementation of Phase III's pricing strategy. You estimate that fixed costs would be $160,000 if 100 to 499 units are produced and $190,000 if production involves 500 or more units. You further estimate that average (per-unit) variable costs would be $3,000 if 100 to 299 units are produced, $2,700 if 300 to 599 units are produced, $2,400 if 600 to 899 units are produced, and $2,200 if 900 or more units are produced. Print and analyze a key cost calculations screen based on these data.

2. Use the same variable costs as in question/assignment 1, but assume that fixed costs are $175,000 for all production levels. Print the key cost calculations screen based on these data and compare it to the one you generated for question/assignment 1.

3. Using all the data from question/assignment 1, what would be the price-floor price at each production level (100 units, 200 units, 300 units, etc.)? Would you be willing to sell your full production of 1,000 units at the price-floor price? Explain your answers.

4. How could you use the information from this exercise to undertake traditional break-even analysis? Modified break-even analysis? What additional data would be needed to complete these analyses?

Exercise 11: Standardizing Marketing Plans

Objectives

1. To see the dynamics of international marketing
2. To study several components of an international marketing strategy: brand name, product design, manufacturing adaptation, advertising, and packaging
3. To consider the conditions under which a standardized (global), a nonstandardized, or a mixed approach to international marketing is preferred
4. To demonstrate how specific changes in an international marketing strategy affect the overall level of standardization

Key Terms and Concepts

international marketing   *nonstandardized approach*
multinational marketing   *mixed approach*
standardized (global) approach

Explanation of Exercise

By answering a series of questions, you — as an international marketing consultant —
are able to make decisions regarding the level of standardization for five factors: a
product's brand name, its design, its manufacture, its advertising, and its packaging.
You can vary each factor from pure standardized (global) to mixed to pure nonstandardized.

Each time you change a factor's level of standardization the graph on the bottom of
the exercise screen automatically moves to reflect the overall degree of standardization
for your marketing strategy. All of the five factors are weighted equally. The graphic
scale has fifteen gradation points.

The exercise is keyed to pages 659–661 in the text.

Questions/Assignments

1. There are distinctions in the way Mercedes-Benz automobiles (from West
   Germany) are marketed in the United States and Europe as a result of legal and
   consumer taste differences between the two areas. For example, to be sold in the
   United States, the autos must have reinforced door panels and satisfy much stricter
   emission control requirements. Cars sold in the United States also have more
   available options due to the status appeal for customers. Determine Mercedes-
   Benz's level of standardization for each of the factors covered in this exercise. Print
   out and comment on your decisions.
2. You have been asked to develop a marketing strategy for a U.S.-based health-
   and-beauty-aids manufacturer which wants to begin selling products in three less-
   developed nations in Asia.
   a. What important questions regarding consumers, competition, distribution
      channels, and the legal and economic environment should you resolve prior to
      recommending a marketing strategy for the firm?
   b. Select an appropriate level of standardization for each of the factors covered in
      this exercise. Print out and comment on your decisions.
3. a. Under what conditions should a washing-machine manufacturer adopt a pure
      standardized marketing strategy? Why?
   b. Under what conditions should a washing-machine manufacturer adopt a pure
      nonstandardized marketing strategy? Why?
4. a. What problems would confront a computer manufacturer that utilizes a pure
      standardized approach in all of its markets? Explain your answer.
   b. What problems would confront a computer manufacturer that utilizes a pure
      nonstandardized approach in all of its markets? Explain your answer.

Exercise 12: Allocating Functional Costs

Objectives

1. To explain and apply marketing cost analysis
2. To analyze marketing costs by product category
3. To see how functional costs can be allocated on the basis of sales, gross profit, floor space, number of marketing personnel, and assigned percentages
4. To show how different bases of functional cost allocation can affect an individual product's profitability

Key Terms and Concepts

marketing plan analysis   *80-20 principle*
marketing cost analysis   *iceberg principle*
natural accounts   *marketing audit*
functional accounts

Explanation of Exercise

As a marketing consultant, you are quite interested in the ways in which various costs may be allocated. You realize that one allocation method may reveal dissimilar results regarding a product's performance than another method.

Through a series of tables on computer screens, you are able to observe how certain indirect (broad) functional costs — in this exercise, these are marketing administration, advertising, marketing research, and general administration expenses — may be allocated on the basis of sales, gross profit, floor space, and number of marketing personnel. You may also assign these functional costs by product as you see fit, and see the impact of your decisions on product profits. Direct variable costs such as personal selling, transportation, and warehousing do not change based on the allocation technique and per cent selected.

The exercise is keyed to pages 759–767 in the text.

Questions/Assignments

1. a. Print the profit-and-loss statements for products A, B, and C using these allocation methods: sales, gross profit, floor space, and personnel.
   b. Interpret the results of each allocation method and compare the findings from the different methods to one another.
2. a. Allocate indirect functional costs using the assigned method. Print the appropriate profit-and-loss screen and explain your decisions.
   b. Is the assigned method better or worse than the methods used in question/assignment 1? Why?
3. After conducting a thorough marketing cost analysis of products A, B, and C, what conclusions would you reach? What recommendations would you make for each product?
4. What additional information would you like to examine to do a better job of marketing cost analysis?

Exercise 13: Performance Ratios

Objectives

1. To evaluate company efficiency and effectiveness by using performance ratios
2. To apply several company performance ratios: sales efficiency, cost-of-goods sold, gross margin, operating expense, net profit, stock turnover, and return on investment
3. To show the relationship between profit-and-loss statement values and company performance ratios
4. To build on the Part 8 case in the text ("Kodak: Beyond 1990")

Key Terms and Concepts

profit-and-loss (income) statement

performance ratios

sales efficiency ratio (percentage)

cost-of-goods sold ratio (percentage)

gross margin ratio (percentage)

operating expense ratio (percentage)

net profit ratio (percentage)

stock turnover ratio

return on investment (ROI)

Explanation of Exercise

As an Eastman Kodak executive vice-president (see the Part 8 case on pages 775–780), you are quite interested in using performance ratios to measure your company's relative success or failure across several criteria. The pre-set data in this exercise (those programmed into the exercise diskette) are all real; they are drawn from Kodak's 1988 annual report.

By entering new data onto a profit-and-loss screen, you can see the impact of changes in Kodak's sales efficiency, cost of goods sold, gross margin, operating expenses, net profit, stock turnover, and return on investment on the company's related performance ratios. For example, what would happen to ROI if Kodak's assets rise by 5 per cent?

After you input the new data, the computer calculates revised performance ratios and shows a screen summarizing all the ratios. The screen also stipulates whether each ratio is excellent, good, or poor, based on criteria that you may access via the exercise diskette.

The exercise is keyed to pages A16–A19 in Appendix B ("Marketing Mathematics") of the text.

Questions/Assignments

1. a. Evaluate Kodak's performance on the basis of the pre-set data appearing on the exercise screens. Print the relevant screens.
   b. What recommendations would you make to Kodak?

2. Enter these revised data (all in millions) on the profit-and-loss screen: assets — $24,000; gross sales — $20,000; returns — $75; ending inventory — $1,000; and operating expenses — $5,500. The other data categories should retain the pre-set values. Print the relevant screens and comment on Kodak's performance. Compare your findings with those you reached in question/assignment 1.

3. Enter these revised data (all in millions) on the profit-and-loss screen: assets — $20,000; gross sales — $18,000; returns — $20; beginning inventory — $1,000; and operating expenses — $3,000. The other data categories should retain the pre-set values. Print the relevant screens and comment on Kodak's performance. Compare your findings with those you reached in questions/assignments 1 and 2.

4. Enter these revised data (all in millions) on the profit-and-loss screen: gross sales — $25,000; beginning inventory — $4,000; purchases — $12,000; and ending inventory — $2,000. The other data categories should retain the pre-set values. Print the relevant screens and comment on Kodak's performance. Compare your findings with those you reached in questions/assignments 1, 2, and 3.

Exercise 14: Optimal Marketing Mix

Objectives

1. To apply and compare mass marketing, selective marketing, and exclusive marketing strategies

2. To determine the impact of specific marketing-mix factors on mass, selective, and exclusive marketing strategies

3. To see how the optimal marketing mixes for mass, selective, and exclusive marketing strategies may be calculated

4. To demonstrate the value of sales response curves

Key Terms and Concepts

alternative marketing mixes   *opportunity cost*
optimal marketing mix   *sales response curves*

Explanation of Exercise

A table allows you — the marketing director for a small industrial manufacturer — to make decisions regarding your firm's $2 million annual marketing budget. You have the ability to make decisions regarding the expenditures for advertising, personal selling, and distribution and to set the price for your product for each of three strategy alternatives: mass marketing, selective marketing, and exclusive marketing. Thus, you are involved with two distinct areas of decision making: (1) For each strategy alternative (mass marketing, selective marketing, and exclusive marketing), what is the best marketing mix? (2) Which strategy alternative should your firm pursue?

In setting prices, you must use penetration pricing (a range of $7 to $15) with mass marketing and skimming pricing (a range of $35 to $99) with exclusive marketing. In allocating the $2 million marketing budget, you assign values to advertising and personal selling; the computer subtracts these figures from $2 million and displays the amount you want to spend on distribution. The costs of making the product depend on which strategy alternative is involved. For example, an exclusive-marketing strategy requires a much higher cost to make the product than a mass-marketing strategy.

Once you enter decisions, the computer program automatically calculates and displays unit sales, revenues, total product costs, total costs, and profit. The results will differ substantially for the three alternative strategies.

The exercise is keyed to pages A27–A30 in the text.

Questions/Assignments

1. For each strategy alternative (mass marketing, selective marketing, and exclusive marketing), what is the best marketing mix? Print the relevant table and explain it.
2. Which strategy alternative should your firm pursue? Why?
3. If you could reduce your product costs by 10 per cent, which strategy alternative would you choose? Why? NOTE: This question/assignment requires you to make some computations with a calculator and should be answered after you respond to questions/assignments 1 and 2.
4. a. Develop separate sales response curves for price, advertising, personal selling, and distribution under a mass-marketing strategy.
   b. Develop separate sales response curves for price, advertising, personal selling, and distribution under an exclusive-marketing strategy.
   c. Compare the curves in a and b.
   NOTE: In deriving each sales response curve, vary only the factor for which you are devising that response curve (for example, price). Otherwise, you will not be able to trace the response to the single factor you are studying.

APPENDIX *D*

Glossary

Absolute Product Failure Occurs if a company is unable to regain its production and marketing costs. The firm incurs a financial loss.

Accelerator Principle Final consumer demand affects several layers of organizational consumers.

Accessory Equipment Industrial capital items, which require a moderate amount of decision making, are less expensive than installations, last a number of years, and do not change in form or become part of the final product.

Adaptation A firm's responses to the surrounding environment, while it also continues to utilize its differential advantage(s), including looking for new opportunities and responding to threats.

Additional Markups Used to raise regular selling prices because demand is unexpectedly high or costs are rising.

Administered Channel Arrangement An indirect channel arrangement in which the dominant firm in the distribution process plans the marketing program and itemizes responsibilities.

Adoption Process The mental and behavioral procedure an individual goes through when learning about and purchasing a new product. The adoption process consists of five stages: knowledge, persuasion, decision, implementation, and confirmation.

Advertising Paid, nonpersonal communication regarding goods, services, organizations, people, places, and ideas that is transmitted through various media by business firms, nonprofit organizations, and individuals who are identified as the sponsor.

Advertising Agency An outside company that usually works with a firm in developing its advertising plan, including themes, media selection, copywriting, and other tasks.

Advertising Media Costs Expenditures involved with placing messages in media. They are related to the length or size of an ad as well as the characteristics of the chosen media.

Advertising Themes The overall appeals for a campaign. Themes can be good or service, consumer, or institutional.

Agents Wholesalers that do not take title to goods and are compensated through payment of a commission or a fee. They may be manufacturers' agents, selling agents, or commission (factor) merchants.

Airways The fastest, most expensive transporters. They are used for high-value, perishable, and emergency goods.

All-You-Can-Afford Technique A means of developing a promotional budget in which the firm first allocates funds for every element of marketing except promotion. Whatever funds are left over are placed in a promotion budget.

Anticipation of Demand Requires a firm to do consumer research on a regular basis so that it develops and introduces offerings that are desired by consumers.

Approaching Customers The stage in the selling process that consists of the preapproach and greeting.

Atmosphere The sum total of the physical characteristics of a retail store or a group of stores that are used to develop an image and draw customers.

Attitudes (Opinions) A person's positive, neutral, or negative feelings about goods, services, companies, people, issues, and/or institutions.

Attribute-Based Shopping Products Products for which consumers seek information about and then evaluate product features, warranty, performance, options, and other factors.

Audience The object of a source's message in a channel of communication.

Augmented Product Includes tangible elements of a product and also the accompanying cluster of image and service features.

Backward Invention An international product strategy in which a firm appeals to developing and less-developed countries by making products that are less complex than the ones it sells in its domestic market.

Bait-and-Switch Advertising An illegal procedure by which customers are lured to a seller by advertising items at exceptionally low prices and then told that the items are out of stock or are of inferior quality. The retailer has no intention of selling the advertised items.

Balanced Product Portfolio A strategy by which a firm maintains a combination of new, growing, and mature products.

Balanced Tenancy Relates the type and number of stores within any planned center to the overall needs of the surrounding population. To ensure balance, a shopping center may limit the merchandise lines any store carries.

Base-Point Pricing A form of geographic pricing in which firms in an industry establish basing points from which costs of shipping are computed. The delivered price to a buyer reflects the cost of transporting goods from the basing point nearest to the buyer, regardless of the actual site of supply.

Battle of the Brands Manufacturer, dealer, and generic brands each attempting to increase their market share, control marketing strategy, obtain consumer loyalty, maximize distribution, and obtain a larger share of profits.

Benefit Segmentation The process of grouping consumers into markets on the basis of different benefits sought from the product.

Blanket Branding *See* Family Branding.

Blurring Gender Roles Occurs when husbands (wives) assume a greater share of the traditional role of their wives (husbands).

Bonded Warehousing Allows for public storage of imported or taxable merchandise. Goods are released only after appropriate taxes are paid. Allows firms to postpone tax payments until goods are ready to be shipped to customers.

Boston Consulting Group Matrix A framework which enables a company to classify each of its strategic business units (SBUs) in terms of its market share relative to major competitors and the annual growth rate of the industry. The matrix identifies four types of products: star, cash cow, problem child (question mark), and dog, and suggests appropriate strategies for each.

Brand A name, term, design, symbol, or any other feature that identifies the goods and services of one seller from those of other sellers.

Brand Decision Process Consists of nonrecognition, recognition, preference (dislike), and insistence (aversion) stages that consumers pass through.

Brand Extension A strategy of applying an established brand name to new products.

Brand Image The perception a person has of a particular brand.

Brand Loyalty The consistent repurchase of and preference toward a particular brand. The consumer attempts to minimize time, thought, and risk.

Brand Mark A symbol, design, or distinctive coloring or lettering that cannot be spoken.

Brand Name A word, letter (number), or group of words or letters (numbers) that can be spoken.

Branding The procedure a firm follows in researching, developing, and implementing its brand(s).

Break-Even Analysis *See* Traditional Break-Even Analysis *and* Modified Break-Even Analysis.

Broad Price Policy Sets the overall direction for a firm's pricing efforts and makes sure that pricing decisions are coordinated with the firm's decisions regarding its target market, image, and other marketing-mix factors. It also incorporates short- and long-term pricing goals.

Brokers Temporary wholesalers, paid by a commission or fee, who introduce buyers and sellers and help complete transactions.

Bundled Pricing An offering of a basic product,

options, and service for one total price.

Business Advisory Services   Industrial services that include management consulting, advertising agency services, accounting services, and legal services.

Business Analysis   The stage in the new-product planning process which projects demand, costs, competition, investment requirements, and profits for new products.

Buyer-Seller Dyad   Two-way flow of communication between buyer and seller.

Buying Specialists   Employees of organizational consumers who have technical backgrounds and are trained in supplier analysis and negotiation.

Buying Structure of an Organization   Refers to the level of formality and specialization used in the purchase process. It depends on an organization's size, resources, diversity, and level of specialization.

Canned Sales Presentation   A memorized, repetitive sales presentation given to all customers interested in a particular item. This approach does not adapt to customer needs or traits but presumes that a general presentation will appeal to all customers.

Cash-and-Carry Wholesaling   A limited-service merchant wholesaler which enables a small businessperson to drive to a wholesaler, order products, and take them back to the store or business. No credit, delivery, merchandise, and promotional assistance are provided.

Cash Cow   A category in the Boston Consulting Group matrix which describes a leading strategic business unit (high market share) in a relatively mature or declining industry (low growth). A cash cow generates more cash (profit) than is required to retain its market share.

Cease-and-Desist Order   A form of consumer protection which legally requires a firm to discontinue deceptive practices and modify its promotion messages.

Chain-Markup Pricing   A form of demand-based pricing in which final selling price is determined, markups for each channel member are examined, and the maximum acceptable costs to each member are computed. Chain-markup pricing extends demand-minus calculations from middlemen all the way back to their suppliers.

Chain-Ratio Method   A sales forecasting technique in which a firm starts with general market information and then computes a series of more specific information. These combined data yield a sales forecast.

Channel Functions   The functions completed by some member of the channel: marketing research, buying, promotion, consumer services, product planning, pricing, and distribution.

Channel Length   Refers to the number of independent members along the channel.

Channel Members   Organizations or people who participate in the distribution process.

Channel of Communication (Communication Process)   The mechanism through which a source develops a message, transmits it to an audience via some form of medium, and obtains feedback from the audience.

Channel of Distribution   All the organizations or people involved in the distribution process.

Channel Width   Refers to the number of independent members at any stage of distribution.

Class-Action Suit   A law suit filed on behalf of many affected consumers.

Class Consciousness   The extent to which social status is desired and pursued by a person.

Clients   The constituency for which a nonprofit organization offers membership, elected officials, locations, ideas, goods, and services.

Closing the Sale   The stage in the sales process that involves getting the customer to agree to a purchase. The salesperson must be sure that no major questions remain before attempting to close a sale.

Clustered Demand   Demand pattern in which consumer needs and desires for a good or service category can be classified into two or more identifiable clusters (segments), with each having distinct purchase criteria.

Clutter   Involves the number of advertisements that are contained in a single program, issue, etc., of a medium.

CMSA   *See* Consolidated Metropolitan Statistical Area.

Cognitive Dissonance   Doubt that the correct purchase decision has been made. To overcome cognitive dissonance, the firm must realize that the purchase process does not end with the purchase.

Combination Compensation Plan   A sales compensation plan that combines salary and commission plans to provide control, flexibility, and employee incentives.

Combination Store Combines food/grocery and general merchandise sales in one facility, with general merchandise providing 30 to 40 per cent of overall sales.

Commercialization The final stage in the new-product planning process. The firm introduces the product to its full target market. This corresponds to the introductory stage of the product life cycle.

Commission (Factor) Merchants Agents who receive goods on consignment, accumulate them from local markets, and arrange for their sale in a central market location.

Common Carriers Companies that must transport the goods of any firm interested in their services; they cannot refuse any shipments unless their rules are broken. Common carriers provide service on a fixed and publicized schedule between designated points. A regular fee schedule is published.

Common Market *See* European Community (EC).

Communication Process *See* Channel of Communication.

Company-Controlled Price Environment Characterized by a moderate level of competition, well-differentiated goods and services, and strong control over price by individual firms.

Company-Specific Buying Factors Company-based variables which lead to either autonomous (independent) or joint decision making by organizational consumers. These variables include the degree of technology or production orientation, company size, and degree of centralization.

Comparative Advantage A concept in international marketing which states that countries have different rates of productivity for different products. Countries can benefit by exchanging goods and services in which they have relative advantages for those in which they have relative disadvantages.

Comparative Messages Implicitly or explicitly contrast the firm's offerings with those of competitors.

Competition-Based Price Strategy Prices set in accordance with competitors. Prices may be below the market, at the market, or above the market.

Competitive Bidding Sellers submit independent price quotations for specific goods and/or services.

Competitive Parity Technique A method in which the company's promotional budget is raised or lowered according to the actions of competitors.

Component Life-Styles Living patterns whereby the attitudes and behavior of people depend on particular situations rather than an overall life-style philosophy.

Component Materials Semimanufactured industrial goods that undergo further changes in form. Component materials are considered as expense rather than capital items.

Computerized-Checkout (Electronic Point-of-Sale) System A system in which a cashier manually rings up a sale or passes an item over or past an optical scanner; then a computerized register instantly records and displays a sale.

Concentrated Marketing A company's attempt to appeal to one well-defined market segment with one tailor-made marketing strategy.

Concept Testing Stage in the new-product planning process in which a consumer is presented with a description or picture of a proposed product. Attitudes and intentions are measured at an early stage of the process.

Conclusive Research Structured collection and analysis of data pertaining to a specific issue or problem.

Conflict Resolution A procedure in organizational buying for resolving disagreements in joint decision making. The methods of resolution are problem solving, persuasion, bargaining, and politicking.

Consistency of a Product Mix The relationship among product lines in terms of their sharing a common end use, distribution outlets, consumer group(s), and price range.

Consolidated Metropolitan Statistical Area (CMSA) A Bureau of Census designation which contains two or more overlapping and interlocking Primary Metropolitan Statistical Areas (PMSAs), with a total population of at least one million.

Consumer Bill of Rights A statement by President Kennedy saying that consumers have four basic rights: to information, to safety, to choice in product selection, and to be heard.

Consumer Cooperative A form of retailer that is owned and operated by consumer members.

Consumer Demand Refers to the characteristics and needs of final consumers, industrial consumers, wholesalers and retailers, government institutions, international markets, and nonprofit institutions.

Consumer Demographic Profile A composite description of a consumer group based upon the most important demographics.

Consumer Demographics Objective and quantifiable population characteristics that are easy to identify, collect, measure, and analyze.

Consumer Education A learning process whereby the consumer acquires the skills and knowledge to use his or her financial resources wisely in the marketplace.

Consumer Price Index (CPI) A federal government measure of the cost of living. Monitors the monthly and yearly price changes for selected consumer goods and services in different product categories, expressing the changes in terms of a base period.

Consumer Product Safety Commission (CPSC) The major federal agency responsible for product safety. It has jurisdiction over thousands of products.

Consumer Products Goods or services destined for the final consumer for personal, family, or household use.

Consumer Surveys A method of sales forecasting that obtains information about purchase intentions, future expectations, rates of consumption, brand switching, time between purchases, and reasons for purchases.

Consumerism The wide range of activities of government, business, and independent organizations that are designed to protect people from practices that infringe upon their rights as consumers.

Consumer's Decision Process Procedure by which consumers collect and analyze information and make choices among alternative goods, services, organizations, people, places, and ideas. It consists of six stages: stimulus, problem awareness, information search, evaluation of alternatives, purchase, and postpurchase behavior. Demographics, social factors, and psychological factors affect the consumer's decision process.

Containerization A coordinated transportation practice that allows goods to be placed in sturdy containers, which serve as mobile warehouses. Containers can be placed on trains, trucks, ships, and planes.

Continuous Monitoring The stage in a marketing information system by which a changing environment is regularly viewed.

Contract Carriers Companies that provide one or a few shippers with transportation services based on individual agreements. Contract carriers are not required to maintain routes or schedules and rates may be negotiated.

Contractual Channel Arrangement Specifies in writing all the terms regarding distribution functions, prices, and other factors for each channel member in an indirect channel.

Control The monitoring and reviewing of overall and specific marketing performance.

Control Units Sales categories for which data are gathered, such as boys', men's, girls', and women's clothing.

Controllable Factors Decision elements directed by the organization and its marketers. Some of these factors are directed by top management; others are directed by marketers.

Convenience Products Items purchased with a minimum of effort, where the buyer has knowledge of product characteristics prior to shopping. Types are staples, impulse, and emergency products.

Convenience Store A retail store featuring food items that is open long hours and carries a limited number of items. Consumers typically use a convenience store for fill-in merchandise, often at off-hours.

Conventional Supermarket A departmentalized food store with minimum annual sales of $2 million that emphasizes a wide range of food and related products.

Cooperative Advertising Allows expenses to be shared by two or more companies. It can be vertical or horizontal.

Core Services The basic services that companies provide for their customers.

Corporate Culture Consists of the shared values, norms, and practices communicated to and followed by those working for a firm.

Corporate Symbols A firm's name, logo, and trade characters that play a significant role in the creation of an overall company image.

Corrective Advertising A form of consumer protection which legally requires a firm to run new advertisements to correct the false impressions made by previous ones.

Cost-Based Price Strategy Sets prices by computing merchandise, service, and overhead costs and then adding the desired profit to these figures. Demand is not analyzed.

Cost-Plus Pricing A form of cost-based pricing in which prices are computed by adding a predetermined profit to costs. It is the simplest form of cost-based pricing:

$$\text{Price} = \frac{\text{Total costs} + \text{Projected profit}}{\text{Units produced}}$$

CPI *See* Consumer Price Index.

CPSC *See* Consumer Product Safety Commission.

Culture A group of people sharing a distinctive heritage.

Currency Stability An economic factor that could affect sales and profits if a foreign currency fluctuates widely in relation to the company's home currency.

Customary Pricing Occurs when a company sets good or service prices and seeks to maintain them for an extended period of time.

Data Analysis The coding, tabulation, and analysis of marketing research data.

Data Storage The stage in a marketing information system involving the retention of all types of relevant company records (such as sales, costs, personnel performance, etc.), as well as the information collected through marketing research and continuous monitoring.

Dealer (Private) Brands Items that contain the name of the wholesaler or retailer. Dealers secure exclusive rights for their brands and are responsible for their distribution.

Decline Stage of the Product Life Cycle Period during which industry sales decline and many firms leave the market because customers are fewer and they have less income to spend.

Decoding The process in a channel of communication by which a message sent by the source is interpreted by the audience.

Demand-Backward Pricing *See* Demand-Minus Pricing.

Demand-Based Price Strategy Prices set after researching consumer desires and ascertaining the ranges of prices acceptable to the target market.

Demand-Minus (Demand-Backward) Pricing A form of demand-based pricing whereby the firm ascertains the appropriate final selling price and works backward to compute costs. The formula used in demand-minus pricing is

$$\text{Maximum product cost} = \text{Price} \times \\ [(100 - \text{Markup per cent})/100]$$

Demand Patterns An indication of the uniformity or diversity of consumer needs and desires for particular categories of goods and services.

Department Store A retailer which employs 25+ people and usually sells a general line of apparel for the family, household linens and dry goods, and furniture, home furnishings, appliances, radios, and televisions. It is organized into separate departments for purposes of buying, promotion, service, and control.

Depth of a Product Mix The number of product items within each product line.

Derived Demand Occurs for organizational consumers because their purchases are usually based on the anticipated demand of their final consumers for specific finished goods and services.

Desk Jobbers *See* Drop Shippers.

Developing Countries Have rising education level and technology, but a per-capita income of about $2,000.

Differential Advantage The set of unique features in a company's marketing program that causes consumers to patronize the company and not its competitors.

Differentiated Marketing (Multiple Segmentation) A company's attempt to appeal to two or more well-defined segments of the market with a marketing strategy tailored to each segment.

Diffused Demand Demand pattern in which consumer needs and desires for a good or service category are so diverse that clear clusters (segments) cannot be identified.

Diffusion Process Describes the manner in which different members of the target market often accept and purchase a product. It spans the time from product introduction through market saturation.

Diminishing Returns Reduced productivity is possible if a firm attempts to attract nonconsumers when it has high sales penetration. In some cases, the costs of attracting additional consumers may outweigh the revenues.

Direct Channel of Distribution Involves the movement of goods and services from producer to consumer without the use of independent middlemen.

Direct Marketing Occurs when a consumer is first exposed to a good or service through a nonpersonal medium (such as direct mail, television, radio, magazine, or newspaper) and then orders by mail or telephone.

Direct Ownership A form of international marketing company organization that involves the full undertaking and control of all international operations.

Direct Product Profitability (DPP) A technique for assigning costs whereby warehousing, transportation, handling, selling, and other costs are quantified and assigned to each product or product category.

Direct Selling A nonstore retail operation which involves both personal contact with consumers in their homes and telephone solicitations.

Discounts Reductions from final selling prices that are available to channel members and final consumers for performing certain functions, paying in cash, buying large quantities, purchasing in off seasons, or enhancing promotions.

Discretionary Income Earnings remaining for luxuries after necessities are bought.

Disposable Income After-tax income to be used for spending and/or savings.

Distributed Promotion Communication efforts spread throughout the year.

Distribution Planning The systematic decision making regarding the physical movement and transfer of ownership of goods and services from producer to consumer. It includes transportation, inventory management, and customer transactions.

Distribution Standards Clear and measurable goals regarding customer service levels in physical distribution.

Diversification A product/market opportunity matrix strategy in which a firm markets new products aimed at new markets.

Dog A category in the Boston Consulting Group matrix which describes a low market-share strategic business unit (SBU) in a mature or declining industry. A dog usually has cost disadvantages and few growth opportunities.

Donors The constituency from which a nonprofit organization receives resources.

DPP *See* Direct Product Profitability.

Drop Shippers (Desk Jobbers) Limited-service merchant wholesalers that purchase goods from manufacturers/suppliers and arrange for their shipment to retailers or industrial users. While they have legal ownership of products, they do not take physical possession of them.

Dual Channel of Distribution A strategy whereby the firm appeals to different market segments or diversifies business by selling through two or more different channels.

Dumping Selling a product in a foreign country at a price lower than that prevailing in the exporter's home market, below the cost of production, or both.

Durable Goods Physical products that are used over an extended period of time.

EC *See* European Community.

Economic Order Quantity (EOQ) The order volume corresponding to the lowest sum of order-processing and inventory-holding costs.

EDI *See* Electronic Data Interchange.

80–20 Principle States that in many organizations a large proportion of total sales (profit) comes from a small proportion of customers, products, or territories.

Elastic Demand Occurs if relatively small changes in price result in large changes in quantity demanded.

Electronic Banking Provides centralized record keeping and enables customers to conduct transactions 24 hours a day, seven days a week (at many bank and nonbank locations) through the use of automatic teller machines and instant processing of retail purchases.

Electronic Data Interchange (EDI) Allows suppliers and their manufacturers, wholesalers, and/or retailers to exchange information via computer link-ups.

Electronic Point-of-Sale System *See* Computerized-Checkout System.

Embargo A form of trade restriction that prohibits specified products from entering a country.

Emergency Products Convenience items purchased out of urgent need.

Encoding The procedure in a channel of communication whereby a thought or idea is translated into a message by the source.

End-Use Analysis   A process by which a seller determines the proportion of its sales that are made to organizational consumers in different industries.

EOQ   *See* Economic Order Quantity.

Escalator Clause   A form of price adjustment that allows a firm to contractually raise the price of an item to reflect higher costs in the item's essential ingredients without changing printed list prices.

Ethical Behavior   Based on honest and proper conduct.

European Community (EC)   Also known as the Common Market. The EC calls for no tariffs among members and a uniform tariff with nonmember nations. In addition, the agreement encourages common standards for food additives, labeling requirements, and package sizes, and a free flow of people and capital.

Evaluation of Alternatives   A stage in the consumer's decision process in which criteria for a decision are set and alternatives ranked.

Exchange   The process by which consumers and publics give money, a promise to pay, or support for the offering of a firm, institution, person, place, or idea.

Exclusive Distribution   A policy in which a firm severely limits the number of middlemen it utilizes in a geographic area, perhaps employing only one or two middlemen within a specific shopping district.

Exempt Carriers   Transporters that are excused from legal regulations and must only comply with safety requirements. Exempt carriers are specified by law.

Expected Profit Concept   A mathematical calculation applied to competitive bidding which states that as the bid price increases the profit to a firm increases but the probability of its winning the contract decreases. The long-run average expected profit at each bid amount equals the company's profit times its probability of obtaining the contract at this bid amount.

Experiment   A type of research whereby one or more factors are manipulated under controlled conditions. Experiments are able to show cause and effect.

Exploratory Research   Used when the researcher is uncertain about the precise topic to be investigated. This technique develops a clear definition of the research problem by utilizing informal analysis.

Exporting   A form of international marketing company organization in which a firm reaches international markets by selling directly through its own sales force or indirectly through foreign merchants or agents. An exporting structure requires minimal investment in foreign facilities.

Extended Consumer Decision Making   Occurs when considerable time is spent on information search and the evaluation of alternatives before a purchase is made. Expensive, complex items with which the consumer has had little or no experience require this form of decision making.

Fabricated Parts   Industrial goods used in manufacturing without further changes in form. Fabricated parts are considered as expense rather than capital items.

Factor Merchants   *See* Commission Merchants.

Factory Pricing   *See* FOB Mill Pricing.

Family   A group of two or more persons residing together who are related by blood, marriage, or adoption.

Family (Blanket) Branding   A strategy in which one name is used for several products. It may be applied to manufacturer and dealer brands.

Family Life Cycle   Describes how a family evolves through various stages from bachelorhood to solitary retirement. At each stage in the cycle, needs, experience, income, and family composition change.

Federal Trade Commission (FTC)   The major federal regulatory agency that monitors restraint of trade and enforces rules against unfair methods of competition and deceptive business practices.

Feedback (Channel of Communication)   The response the audience makes to a message.

Feedback (Uncontrollable Environment)   Information about the uncontrollable environment, the organization's performance, and how well the various aspects of the marketing plan are received.

Field Warehousing   Situation in which a public warehouse issues a receipt for goods stored in a private warehouse or in transit to consumers. The field warehouse receipt can serve as collateral for a loan.

Final Consumers   Purchase goods and services for personal, family, or household use.

Fines A legal concept in consumer protection that levies a dollar penalty on a firm for a deceptive promotion.

Flexible Pricing Allows a firm to adjust prices based on the consumer's ability to negotiate or the buying power of a large customer.

FOB Mill (Factory) Pricing A form of geographic pricing in which the buyer selects the transportation form and pays all freight charges. The delivered price to the buyer depends on the freight charges.

Food Brokers Middlemen involved with food and related general merchandise items who introduce buyers and sellers to one another and bring them together to complete a sale.

Forward Invention An international product strategy in which a company develops new products for its international markets.

Franchise Wholesaling A full-service merchant-wholesaling format whereby independent retailers affiliate with an existing wholesaler in order to use a standardized storefront design, business format, name, and purchase system.

Freight Forwarding A transportation service which consolidates small shipments (usually less than 500 pounds each) from several companies, picks up merchandise at the shipper's place of business, and arranges for delivery at the buyer's door.

Frequency How often a medium can be used.

FTC *See* Federal Trade Commission.

Full Disclosure A consumer-protection legal concept requiring that all data necessary for a consumer to make a safe and informed decision be provided.

Full-Line Discount Store A retailer characterized by low prices, a broad merchandise assortment, low-rent location, self-service, brand-name merchandise, wide aisles, use of shopping carts, and most merchandise displayed on the selling floor.

Full-Line Wholesalers *See* General-Merchandise Wholesalers.

Full-Service Merchant Wholesalers Assemble an assortment of products, provide trade credit, store and deliver merchandise, offer merchandise and promotion assistance, provide a personal sales force, offer research and planning support, make information available, provide installation and repair services, and act as the sales arm for their manufacturers.

Functional Accounts Occur when natural account expenses are reclassified by function. These accounts indicate the purposes or activities for which expenditures have been made. Examples of functional accounts are marketing administration, transportation, and marketing research.

GATT *See* General Agreement on Tariffs and Trade.

General Agreement on Tariffs and Trade (GATT) A multilateral agreement that allows every nation covered to obtain the best contract terms received by a single nation. GATT members agree to meet every two years and to negotiate for tariff reductions.

General Electric Business Screen Categorizes strategic business units and product opportunities on the basis of an in-depth analysis of industry attractiveness and company business strengths.

General-Merchandise (Full-Line) Wholesalers Full-service merchant wholesalers which carry a wide assortment of products, nearly all the items needed by the customers to which they cater.

Generic Brands Items that emphasize the names of the products and not the manufacturer's or dealer's name.

Generic Product The broadest definition of a product which centers on customer need fulfillment. It focuses on what a product means to the customer, not the seller.

Geographic Demographics The basic identifiable characteristics of towns, cities, states, regions, and countries.

Geographic Pricing Outlines the responsibility for transportation charges. The basic forms of geographic pricing are FOB (free on board), uniform delivered pricing, zone pricing, and base-point pricing.

Global Approach *See* Standardized Approach.

GNP *See* Gross National Product.

Goods Marketing Entails the sale of physical products.

Government Uses goods and services in performing its duties and responsibilities. There are 1 federal, 50 state, and 80,000 local governmental units.

Government-Controlled Price Environment Characterized by prices set or strongly influenced by some level of government.

Government Stability Refers to the consistency of

political policies and the orderliness in installing leaders.

Gray Market Goods Foreign-made products that are imported into the United States by distributors (suppliers) that are not authorized by the products' manufacturers.

Gross National Product (GNP) The total value of goods and services produced in a country each year.

Growth Stage of the Product Life Cycle Period during which industry sales increase rapidly as a few more firms enter a highly profitable market that has substantial potential.

Hard Technologies The way some services are industrialized by substituting machinery for people.

Heavy-Half A market segment accounting for a large proportion of an item's sales relative to the size of the market.

Hidden Service Sector Encompasses the delivery, installation, maintenance, training, repair, and other services provided by firms that emphasize goods sales.

Hierarchy-of-Effects Model Outlines the intermediate and long-term promotional objectives the firm should pursue: awareness, knowledge, liking, preference, conviction, and purchase.

Homogeneous Demand Demand pattern in which consumers have relatively uniform needs and desires for a good or service category.

Horizontal Audit Studies the overall marketing performance of the company, with particular emphasis on the interrelationship of variables and their relative importance.

Horizontal Integration The practice of a firm acquiring other businesses like itself.

Horizontal Price Fixing Agreements among manufacturers, among wholesalers, or among retailers to set prices. Such agreements are illegal according to the Sherman Antitrust Act and the Federal Trade Commission Act, regardless of how ''reasonable'' the prices are.

Household A person or group of persons occupying a housing unit, whether related or unrelated.

Hybrid Technologies A technique for industrializing services that combines hard and soft technologies such as computer-based truck routing and specialized low-priced auto repair facilities.

Hypermarket A special kind of combination store that integrates an economy supermarket with a discount department store. It is at least 60,000 square feet in size.

Iceberg Principle States that superficial data are insufficient to make sound marketing evaluations.

Idea Generation The stage in the new-product planning process which involves the continuous, systematic search for opportunities. It involves delineating sources of new ideas and methods for generating them.

Ideal Points The combinations of attributes that consumers would like products to possess.

Importance of a Purchase Related to the degree of decision making, level of perceived risk, and amount of money to be spent/invested. The level of importance of a purchase has a major impact on the time and effort a consumer will spend shopping for a product and on the amount of money allocated.

Impulse Products Convenience items that the consumer does not plan to buy on a specific trip to a store.

Incremental Technique A promotional budget method in which the company bases its new budget on previous expenditures. A percentage is either added to or subtracted from this year's budget in order to determine next year's.

Independent Media Those not controlled by the firm; they can influence the government's, consumers', and publics' perceptions of a company's products and overall image.

Independent Retailer A retailer operating only one outlet.

Indirect Channel of Distribution Involves the movement of goods and services from producer to independent middleman to consumer.

Individual (Multiple) Branding Separate brands used for different items or product lines sold by the firm.

Industrial Marketing Occurs when a firm deals with organizational consumers.

Industrial Products Goods or services purchased for use in the production of other goods or services, in the operation of a business, or for resale to other consumers.

Industrial Services Include maintenance and repair, and business advisory services.

Industrial Supplies Convenience goods that are necessary for the daily operation of the firm.

Industrialization of Services Improves service efficiency by applying hard, soft, and hybrid technologies.

Industrialized Countries Have high literacy, modern technology, and high per-capita income.

Inelastic Demand Occurs when price changes have little impact on quantity demanded.

Information Search A stage in consumer's decision process that involves listing alternatives that will solve the problem at hand and determining the characteristics of each alternative. Information search may be either internal or external.

Inner-Directed Person One who is interested in pleasing him- or herself.

Innovativeness The willingness to try a new product that others perceive as having a high degree of risk.

Inseparability of Services Inability of many services to be separated from the service provider. Customer contact is considered an integral part of the service experience.

Installations Industrial goods capital items used in the production process that do not become part of the final product.

Institutional Advertising Used when the promotional objective is enhancement of company image and not sales of goods and services.

Intangibility of Services Inability of many services to be displayed, transported, stored, packaged, or inspected before buying.

Intensive Distribution A policy in which a firm uses a large number of wholesalers and retailers in order to obtain widespread market coverage, channel acceptance, and high-volume sales.

International Marketing Involves the marketing of goods and services outside the organization's home country.

Introduction Stage of the Product Life Cycle Period during which only one or two firms have entered the market and competition is limited. Initial consumers are innovators.

Inventory Management Concerned with providing a continuous flow of goods and matching the quantity of goods in inventory with sales demand.

Isolated Store A freestanding retail outlet located on a highway or side street.

Issue (Problem) Definition A statement of the topic to be investigated in marketing research. It directs the research process toward the collection and analysis of appropriate information for the purpose of decision making.

Item Price Removal A practice whereby prices are marked only on store shelves or aisle signs and not on individual items.

JIT *See* Just-in-Time Inventory System.

Joint Decision Making The process by which two or more consumers have input into purchases.

Joint Venture A form of international marketing company organization in which a firm combines some aspect of its manufacturing or marketing efforts with those of a foreign company in order to share expertise, costs, and connections with important persons.

Jury of Executive or Expert Opinion A sales forecasting method by which the management of a company or other well-informed persons meet, discuss the future, and set sales estimates based on the group's experience and interaction.

Just-in-Time (JIT) Inventory System A procedure by which the purchasing firm reduces the amount of inventory it keeps on hand by ordering more frequently and in lower quantity.

Law of Demand A theory stating that consumers usually purchase more units at a low price than at a high price.

Lead Time The time required by a medium for placing an advertisement.

Leader Pricing Advertising and selling key items in the product assortment at less than their usual profit margins. The objective of leader pricing is to increase store traffic or to gain greater consumer interest in an overall product line.

Leased Department A department in a retail store (usually a department, discount, or specialty store) that is rented to an outside party.

Less-Developed Countries Have low literacy, limited technology, and per-capita income generally well below $1,000.

Licensing Agreement Allows a company to pay a fee to use a name whose trademark rights are held by another firm.

Life-Style The pattern in which a person lives and spends time and money. The combination of personality and social values that has been internalized by an individual.

Limited Consumer Decision Making Occurs when a consumer uses each of the steps in the purchase process but does not spend a great deal of time on any of them. The consumer has previously purchased the good or service under consideration, but not regularly.

Limited-Line Wholesalers *See* Specialty-Merchandise Wholesalers.

Limited-Service Merchant Wholesalers Buy and take title to merchandise but do not perform all of the functions of a full-service merchant wholesaler. May not provide credit, merchandise assistance, or market research data.

Line of Business Refers to the general goods/service category, functions, geographic coverage, type of ownership, and specific business of a company.

List Prices Regularly quoted prices provided to customers. They may be preprinted on price tags, in catalogs, and in dealer purchase orders.

Local Content Laws Require foreign-based manufacturers to establish local plants and to use locally produced components. The goal of these laws is to promote domestic employment.

Loss Leaders Items priced below cost to attract customers to a seller — usually in a store setting.

Low-Involvement Purchasing Occurs when the consumer minimizes decision making for those goods and services perceived to be socially and/or psychologically unimportant.

Mail-Order Wholesalers Limited-service merchant wholesalers that use catalogs instead of a personal sales force to promote products and communicate with customers.

Maintenance and Repair Services Those industrial services that include painting, machinery repair, and janitorial services.

Major Innovations Items that have not been previously sold by any firm.

Majority Fallacy Concept stating that companies sometimes fail when they go after the largest market segment because competition is intense. A potentially profitable market segment may be one that is ignored by other firms.

Management of Demand Includes stimulation, facilitation, and regulation tasks.

Manufacturer (National) Brands Contain the names of manufacturers and obtain the vast majority of sales for most products. The major marketing focus for manufacturer brands is to attract and retain consumers who are loyal to a firm's offering and to control the marketing effort for the brands.

Manufacturer Wholesaling Occurs when the producer undertakes all wholesaling functions itself. Includes manufacturer's sales offices and manufacturer's branch offices.

Manufacturers Firms that produce products for resale to other consumers.

Manufacturers' Agents Agents who work for several manufacturers and carry noncompetitive, complementary products in exclusive territories. A manufacturer may employ many agents, each with a unique product-territorial mix.

Manufacturer's Branch Office A form of manufacturer wholesaling that assigns warehousing and selling tasks to a branch office.

Manufacturer's Sales Office A form of manufacturer wholesaling that assigns selling tasks to a sales office but maintains inventory only at production facilities.

Marginal Return The amount of sales each additional increment of promotion will generate.

Markdowns Reductions from the original selling prices of items to meet lower prices of competitors, counteract overstocking of merchandise, clear out shopworn merchandise, deplete assortments of odds and ends, and increase customer traffic.

Market Consists of all the people and/or organizations who desire (or potentially desire) a good or service, have sufficient resources to make a purchase, and the willingness and ability to buy.

Market Buildup Method A sales forecasting technique in which a firm gathers data from small, separate market segments and aggregates them.

Market-Controlled Price Environment Characterized by a high level of competition, similar goods and services, and little control over price by individual companies.

Market Development A product/market opportunity matrix strategy in which a firm seeks greater sales of present products from new markets or new product uses.

Market Penetration A product/market opportunity matrix strategy in which a firm seeks to expand the sales of its present products through more intensive distribution, aggressive promotion, and competitive pricing.

Market Segmentation The process of subdividing a market into distinct subsets of customers that behave in the same way or have similar needs.

Market Share Analysis A method of sales forecasting that is similar to simple trend analysis, except that a company bases its forecast on the assumption that its share of industry sales will remain constant.

Marketing The anticipation, management, and satisfaction of demand through the exchange process.

Marketing Audit A systematic, critical, and unbiased review and appraisal of the basic objectives of the marketing function and of the organization, methods, procedures, and personnel employed to implement these policies and to achieve these objectives.

Marketing Company Era Recognition of the central role of marketing. The marketing department becomes the equal of others in the firm. Company efforts are integrated and frequently re-evaluated.

Marketing Concept A consumer-oriented, integrated, goal-oriented philosophy for a firm, institution, or person.

Marketing Cost Analysis Evaluates the cost effectiveness of various marketing factors, such as different product lines, distribution methods, sales territories, channel members, salespersons, advertising media, and customer types.

Marketing Department Era Stage during which the marketing department participates in company decisions but remains in a subordinate or conflicting position to the production, engineering, and sales departments.

Marketing Environment Consists of controllable and uncontrollable factors, the organization's level of success or failure in reaching its objectives, feedback, and adaptation.

Marketing Functions Include environmental analysis and marketing research, consumer analysis, product planning, distribution planning, promotion planning, price planning, broadening the organization's/individual's scope, and marketing management.

Marketing Information System (MIS) A set of procedures and methods designed to generate, store, analyze, and disseminate marketing decision information on a regular, continuous basis.

Marketing Intelligence Network The part of a marketing information system that consists of marketing research, continuous monitoring, and data storage.

Marketing-Manager System A product-management organizational format under which an executive is responsible for designated marketing functions and for coordinating with other departments that perform marketing-related activities.

Marketing Mix Describes the specific combination of marketing elements used to achieve an organization's/individual's objectives and satisfy the target market. The mix depends on a number of decisions with regard to four major variables: product, distribution, promotion, and price.

Marketing Myopia A shortsighted, narrow-minded view of marketing and its environment.

Marketing Objectives More customer-oriented than the overall goals set by top management.

Marketing Organization The structural arrangement for directing marketing functions. The organization outlines authority, responsibility, and the tasks to be performed.

Marketing Performers Include manufacturers and service providers, wholesalers, retailers, marketing specialists, and organizational and final consumers.

Marketing Plan Analysis Involves comparing actual performance with planned or expected performance for a specified period of time.

Marketing Research The systematic gathering, recording, and analyzing of information about specific issues related to the marketing of goods, services, organizations, people, places, and ideas.

Marketing Research Process Consists of a series of activities: definition of the problem or issue to be studied, examination of secondary data, generation of primary data (if necessary), analysis of information, recommendations, and implementation of findings.

Marketing Strategy Outlines the manner in which the marketing mix is used to attract and satisfy the target market(s) and accomplish an organization's objectives.

Markup Pricing A form of cost-based pricing in which prices are set by calculating per-unit product costs and then determining the markup percentages that are needed to cover selling costs and profit. The formula for markup pricing is

$$\text{Price} = \frac{\text{Product cost}}{(100 - \text{Markup per cent})/100}$$

Mass Marketing *See* Undifferentiated Marketing.

Massed Promotion Communication concentrated in peak periods, like holidays.

Maturity Stage of the Product Life Cycle Period during which industry sales stabilize as the market becomes saturated and many firms enter to capitalize on the still sizable demand. Companies seek to maintain a differential advantage.

"Me" Generation A consumer life-style that stresses "being good to myself."

Medium The personal or nonpersonal means in a channel of communication used to send a message.

Merchant Wholesalers Buy, take title, and take possession of products for further resale. Merchant wholesalers may be full-service or limited-service.

Message The combination of words and symbols transmitted to the audience through a channel of communication.

Message Permanence Refers to the number of exposures one advertisement generates and how long it remains with the audience.

Metropolitan Statistical Area (MSA) A Bureau of Census designation which contains either a city of at least 50,000 population or an urbanized area of 50,000 population (with a total population of at least 100,000).

Middlemen Refers to wholesalers, retailers, and marketing specialists that are acting in their roles as intermediaries between manufacturers/service providers and their consumers.

Minimum Price Laws *See* Unfair-Sales Acts.

Minor Innovations Items that have not been previously sold by the firm but that have been sold by others.

MIS *See* Marketing Information System.

Missionary Salesperson Type of sales support person used to distribute information about new goods or services. This person does not sell, but describes the attributes of new items, answers questions, and leaves written material.

Mixed Approach to International Marketing An international marketing strategy which combines standardized and nonstandardized efforts to enable a company to maximize production efficiencies, maintain a consistent image, exercise home-office control, and yet be sensitive and responsive to local needs.

Mixed-Brand Strategy Occurs when a combination of manufacturer and dealer brands (and sometimes generic brands) are sold by manufacturers, wholesalers, and retailers.

Modifications New products involving alterations in a company's existing products. They can be new models, styles, colors, features, and/or brands.

Modified Break-Even Analysis Combines traditional break-even analysis with an evaluation of demand at various levels of price. Determines the price-quantity mix that maximizes profits.

Modified-Rebuy Purchase Process A moderate amount of decision making undertaken by organizational consumers in the purchase of medium-priced products that have been bought infrequently before.

Monitoring Results Involves the comparison of planned performance against actual performance for a specified time.

Monopolistic Competition A situation in which there are several competing firms, each trying to offer a unique marketing mix.

Monopoly A situation in which only one firm sells a particular product.

Most-Favored Nation Principle Allows every nation covered by the General Agreement on Tariffs and Trade to obtain the best contract terms received by any single nation.

Motivation The driving force within individuals that impels them to act.

Motives Reasons for behavior.

Motor Carriers Transporters of small shipments over short distances.

MSA *See* Metropolitan Statistical Area.

Multidimensional Scaling A survey research tool in which respondent attitudes are ascertained for many product and company attributes. Then computer analysis enables the firm to develop a single product or company rating, rather than a profile of several individual characteristics.

Multinational Marketing A complex form of international marketing that involves an organization engaged in marketing operations in many foreign countries.

Multiple Branding *See* Individual Branding.

Multiple-Buying Responsibility Two or more employees formally participating in complex or expensive purchase decisions.

Multiple Segmentation *See* Differentiated Marketing.

Multiple-Unit Pricing A practice by which a company offers consumers discounts for buying in quantity in order to increase sales volume.

Multistage Approach to Pricing A popular technique for developing a broad price policy. Divides price planning into six successive steps, with each placing constraints on the next step.

Multistep Flow of Communication The communication theory which suggests that opinion leaders not only influence but are influenced by the general public (opinion receivers).

Multiunit Advertising The practice of including two or more products in a single ad to reduce media costs.

Narrowcasting The presenting of advertising messages to relatively limited and well-defined audiences.

National Brands *See* Manufacturer Brands.

Nationalism Refers to a country's efforts to become self-reliant and raise its status in the eyes of the world community. Sometimes nationalism leads to tight restrictions for foreign companies and fosters the development of domestic industry at their expense.

Natural Accounts Costs which are reported by the names of the expenses and not the expenditures' purposes. Natural account expense categories include salaries, rent, and advertising.

Need-Satisfaction Approach A sales presentation method based on the principle that each customer has different characteristics and wants. The sales presentation is adapted to each customer.

Negotiation Situation in which the buyer uses bargaining ability and order size to set prices.

New Product A modification of an existing product or an innovation that the consumer perceives as meaningful.

New-Product Manager System A product management organization form which utilizes a product manager for existing products and a new-product manager for new products. After a new product is introduced, it is turned over to the product manager.

New-Product Planning Process A series of steps from idea generation to commercialization. The company generates potential opportunities, evaluates them, weeds out unattractive ones, obtains customer perceptions, develops the product, tests it, and introduces it into the marketplace.

New-Task Purchase Process A large amount of decision making undertaken by organizational consumers in the purchase of expensive products that have not been bought before.

Noise Interference at any stage along a channel of communication.

Nondurable Goods Physical products that are made from materials other than metals, hard plastics, and wood. They are rather quickly consumed or worn out; or become dated, unfashionable, or in some other way no longer popular.

Nongoods Service Involves personal service on the part of the seller. It does not involve a good.

Nonprice Competition Minimizes the role of price as a factor in consumer demand through the development of a unique product offering. This is accomplished by the creation of a distinctive good or service via promotion, packaging, delivery, customer service, availability, and other factors.

Nonprofit Institutions Operate in the public interest or to foster a cause and not seek financial profits.

Nonprofit Marketing Conducted by organizations and individuals that operate in the public interest or to foster a cause and do not seek financial profits. Nonprofit marketing may involve organizations, people, places, and ideas as well as goods and services.

Nonstandardized Approach An international marketing strategy that assumes each market (country) is different and requires a distinct marketing plan.

Nonstore Retailing Occurs when a firm uses a strategy mix that is not store-based to reach consumers and complete transactions.

Objective-and-Task Technique A promotional budget method in which the firm clearly outlines its promotional objectives and then establishes the appropriate budget.

Observation A research technique in which present behavior or the results of past behavior are observed and recorded. People are not questioned, and their cooperation is not necessary.

Odd-Pricing Strategy Used when selling prices are set at levels below even-dollar values, such as 49 cents, $4.95, and $199.

Oligopoly Situation in which there are few firms, generally large, that comprise most of an industry's sales.

One-Price Policy The same price charged to all customers who seek to purchase a good or service under similar conditions.

One-Sided Messages Communication in which the firm mentions only the benefits of its good, service, or idea.

Open Credit Account A credit purchase in which a buyer receives a monthly bill for goods and services bought during the preceding month. The account must be paid in full each month.

Opinion Leaders People to whom other consumers turn for advice and information via face-to-face communication. Opinion leaders normally have an impact over a narrow range of products.

Opinions *See* Attitudes.

Order Cycle The period of time that spans a customer's placing an order and its receipt.

Order-Generating Costs Costs that are revenue producing, such as advertising and personal selling.

Order Getter A type of salesperson who is involved with generating customer leads, providing information, persuading customers, and closing sales.

Order-Processing Costs Costs associated with filling out and handling orders such as order forms, computer time, and merchandise handling.

Order Size The appropriate amount of merchandise, parts, etc., to purchase at one time. Depends on the availability of quantity discounts, the resources of the firm, inventory turnover, the costs of processing each order, and the costs of maintaining goods in inventory.

Order Taker A type of salesperson who processes routine orders and reorders. The order taker usually handles goods and services that are presold.

Organizational Buying Objectives Include the availability of items, reliability of sellers, consistency of quality, delivery, and price.

Organizational Consumer Expectations The perceived potential of alternative suppliers and brands to satisfy a number of explicit and implicit objectives.

Organizational Consumers Purchase goods and services for further production, usage in operating the organization, or resale to other consumers.

Organizational Consumer's Decision Process Consists of expectations, the buying process, conflict resolution, and situational factors.

Organizational Mission A firm's long-term commitment to a type of business and a place in the market. Mission can be defined in terms of customer groups served, the goods and services offered, the functions performed, and technologies utilized.

Outer-Directed Person One who is interested in pleasing the people around him or her.

Overall Objectives The broad, measurable goals set by top management.

Owned-Goods Service Involves an alteration or repair of a good owned by the consumer.

Package A container used to protect, promote, transport, and/or identify a product.

Packaging The part of the planning process in which a company researches, designs, and produces its package(s).

Packaging Functions Consist of containment and protection, usage, communication, segmentation, channel cooperation, and new-product planning.

Patent Awards exclusive selling rights for 17 years to the inventor of a useful product or process.

Penetration Pricing Uses low pricing to capture the mass market for a good or service.

Perceived Risk The level of risk a consumer believes exists regarding the outcome of a purchase decision; this belief may or may not be correct. Perceived risk can be divided into six major types: functional, physical, financial, social, psychological, and time.

Percentage-of-Sales Technique A promotional budget method in which a company ties the promotion budget to sales revenue.

Peripheral Services Supplementary services that companies provide to their customers.

Perishability of Services Means that many services cannot be stored for future use. The service supplier must regulate consumer usage so that there is consistent demand throughout the week, month, or year.

Personal Demographics The basic identifiable characteristics of individual people and groups of people.

Personal Selling An oral communication with one or more prospective buyers by paid representatives for the purpose of making sales.

Personality The sum total of an individual's psychological traits that make the individual unique.

Persuasive Impact The ability of a medium to stimulate consumers.

Physical Distribution The broad range of activities concerned with efficiently delivering raw materials, parts, semifinished items, and finished products to designated places, at designated times, and in proper condition.

Physical Distribution Strategy Includes the transportation form(s) to be used, inventory levels and warehouse form(s), and the number and locations of plants, warehouses, and retail locations.

PIMS *See* Profit Impact of Market Strategy.

Pipelines A transportation form that involves continuous movement, with no interruptions, inventories, or intermediate storage locations.

Planned Obsolescence A practice that capitalizes on short-run material wearout, style changes, and functional product changes.

Planned Shopping Center A retail location that is centrally owned or managed, planned, and operated as an entity, surrounded by parking, and based on balanced tenancy. The types are regional, community, and neighborhood.

PMSA *See* Primary Metropolitan Statistical Area.

Porter Generic Strategy Model A model that examines two major marketing planning concepts and the alternatives available with each: competitive scope (broad or narrow target) and competitive advantage (lower cost or differentiation).

Portfolio Analysis A technique by which an organization individually assesses and positions every business unit and/or product. Company efforts and resources are allocated and separate marketing mixes are aimed at their chosen target markets on the basis of these assessments.

Postpurchase Behavior A stage in the consumer's decision process when further purchases or re-evaluation of the purchase are undertaken.

Poverty of Time A consumer life-style where greater affluence results in less free time because the alternatives competing for time expand.

Predatory Pricing An illegal practice in which large companies cut prices on products in selected geographic areas below their cost with the intention of eliminating small, local competitors.

Prestige Pricing Assumes that consumers do not buy goods or services at prices that are considered too low.

Price Represents the value of a good or service for both the seller and the buyer.

Price-Based Shopping Products Products for which consumers judge attributes to be similar and look around for the least expensive item/store.

Price Ceiling The maximum amount customers will pay for a given good or service.

Price Competition Demand influenced primarily through changes in price levels.

Price Discrimination A form of demand-based pricing in which the firm sets two or more distinct prices for a product in order to appeal to different final consumer or organizational consumer market segments. Price discrimination may be customer-, product-, time-, or place-based.

Price Elasticity of Demand Shows the sensitivity of buyers to price changes in terms of the quantities they will purchase. Price elasticity is computed by dividing the percentage change in quantity demanded by the percentage change in price charged.

Price Floor The lowest acceptable price the firm can charge and attain its profit goal.

Price-Floor Pricing The lowest price at which it is worthwhile for a company to increase the amount of goods or services it makes available for sale.

Price Guarantees Manufacturers' assurances to wholesalers or retailers that the prices they pay are the lowest available. Any discount given to competitors will also be given to the original purchasers.

Price Leadership A form of competition-based pricing in which one firm (or a few firms) is usually the first to announce price changes and the other companies in the industry follow.

Price Lining Involves the sale of merchandise at a range of prices, with each individual price representing a distinct level of quality.

Price Planning The systematic decision making pertaining to all aspects of pricing by the organization.

Price-Quality Association A concept stating that consumers believe high prices mean high quality and low prices mean low quality.

Price Wars Situations in which various firms continually try to undercut each other's prices to draw customers.

Primary Data Collected to solve the specific problem or issue under investigation.

Primary Demand Consumer demand for a product category. Important when the product is little known.

Primary Metropolitan Statistical Area (PMSA) A Bureau of Census designation which includes a large urbanized county or a cluster of counties that have strong economic and social links as well as ties to neighboring communities in its CMSA.

Private Brands   *See* Dealer Brands.

Private Carriers   Shippers possessing their own transportation facilities.

Problem Awareness   A stage in the consumer's decision process during which the consumer recognizes that the good, service, organization, person, place, or idea under consideration may solve a problem of shortage or unfulfilled desire.

Problem Child   A category in the Boston Consulting Group matrix which describes a low market-share strategic business unit (SBU) in an expanding industry. A problem child requires substantial marketing investments to maintain or increase market share in the face of strong competition.

Problem Definition   *See* Issue Definition.

Process-Related Ethical Issues   Involve the unethical use of marketing strategies or tactics.

Product   The combination of tangible and intangible features that seek to satisfy individual and organizational objectives.

Product-Adaptation Strategy   An international product-planning strategy in which domestic products are modified to meet language needs, taste preferences, foreign conditions, electrical requirements, water conditions, or legal regulations.

Product Development   A product/market opportunity matrix strategy in which a firm develops new or modified products to appeal to present markets.

Product-Development Stage of New-Product Planning   Converts a product idea into a physical form and identifies a basic marketing strategy.

Product Differentiation   Occurs when a product offering is perceived by the consumer to differ from its competition on any physical or nonphysical product characteristic including price.

Product Item   A specific model, brand, or size of a product that a company sells.

Product Life Cycle   A concept that attempts to describe a product's sales, profits, customers, competitors, and marketing emphasis from its beginning until it is removed from the market. It is divided into introduction, growth, maturity, and decline stages.

Product Line   A group of closely related items.

Product (Brand) Manager System   A product-management organization format under which a middle manager focuses on a single product or a small group of products. This manager handles new and existing products and is involved with everything from marketing research to package design to advertising.

Product/Market Opportunity Matrix   Identifies four alternative marketing strategies that may be used to maintain and/or increase sales of business units and products: market penetration, market development, product development, and diversification.

Product Mix   Consists of all the different product lines that a firm offers. *See also* Consistency of a Product Mix; Depth of a Product Mix; *and* Width of a Product Mix.

Product Planning   The systematic decision making relating to all aspects of the development and management of a firm's products, including branding and packaging.

Product-Planning Committee   A product-management organization staffed by executives from functional areas including marketing, production, engineering, finance, and research and development. It handles product approval, evaluation, and development on a part-time basis.

Product Positioning   Enables the firm to map its products in terms of consumer perceptions and desires, competition, other company products, and environmental changes.

Product Recall   The primary enforcement tool of the Consumer Product Safety Commission.

Product-Related Ethical Issues   Involve the ethical appropriateness of marketing certain products.

Product Screening   A stage in the new-product planning process when poor, unsuitable, or otherwise unattractive ideas are weeded out from further consideration.

Product-Specific Buying Factors   Product-based variables which lead to either autonomous (independent) or joint decision making by organizational consumers. These variables include the degree of perceived risk, routineness of decision, and degree of time pressure.

Production Era   Devotion to the physical distribution of goods and services due to high demand and low competition. Consumer research, product modifications, and adapting to consumer needs are not needed.

Profit-Based Pricing Objectives   Those that orient a firm's pricing strategy toward some type of profit goal: profit maximization, return on investment, and/or early recovery of cash.

Profit Impact of Market Strategy (PIMS)   A program

that provides individual firms with a data base summarizing the financial and market performance of over 2,800 business units representing several hundred firms. It focuses on links between various factors and profitability/cash flow.

Promotion Any form of communication used by an organization or individual to inform, persuade, or remind people about goods, services, image, ideas, community involvement, or impact on society.

Promotion Mix The overall and specific communication program of the firm, including its use of advertising, publicity, personal selling, and/or sales promotion.

Promotion Planning Systematic decision making pertaining to all aspects of a communications effort.

Prospecting The stage in a selling process which generates a list of customer leads. It is common with outside selling. Prospecting can be blind or lead in orientation.

Psychographics A technique by which life-styles can be classified. An AIO (activities, interests, and opinions) inventory is used in psychographic research to determine consumer life-styles.

Psychological Pricing Assumes consumers are perceptually sensitive to certain prices. Departures from these prices in either direction result in decreases in demand. Customary, odd, and prestige pricing are all forms of psychological pricing.

Public Relations Mass and personal communication that is image-directed.

Publicity Nonpersonal communication regarding goods, services, organizations, people, places, and ideas that is transmitted through various media but not paid for by an identified sponsor.

Publicity Types Consist of news publicity, business feature articles, service feature articles, finance releases, product releases, pictorial releases, background editorial releases, and emergency publicity.

Publics' Demand Refers to the characteristics and needs of employees, unions, stockholders, consumer groups, the general public, government agencies, and other internal and external forces that affect company operations.

Pulling Strategy Occurs when demand is first generated through direct advertising to customers; then dealer support is obtained.

Purchase Act An exchange of money, a promise to pay, or support in return for ownership of a specific good, the performance of a specific service, and so on.

Pure Competition Situation with many firms selling identical products.

Pushing Strategy Occurs when various firms in a distribution channel cooperate in the marketing efforts for a product.

QR Inventory System *See* Quick Response Inventory System.

Question Mark *See* Problem Child.

Quick Response (QR) Inventory System A cooperative effort between retailers and their suppliers aimed at reducing retail inventory while providing a merchandise supply that closely addresses actual buying patterns of consumers.

Rack Jobbers Full-service merchant wholesalers that furnish the racks or shelves on which merchandise is displayed. Rack jobbers own the merchandise on their racks, selling the items on a consignment basis.

Railroads Transporters of heavy, bulky items that are low in value (relative to their weight) over long distances.

Raw Materials Unprocessed primary industrial materials from extractive and agricultural industries. Raw materials are considered as expense rather than capital items.

Reach Refers to the number of viewers or readers in the audience. For television and radio, reach is the total number of people who are exposed to an advertisement. For print media, reach equals circulation times passalong rate.

Real Income The amount of income earned in a year adjusted by the rate of inflation.

Rebates A form of price adjustment in which cash refunds are given directly from the manufacturer to the customer in order to stimulate consumption of an item or group of items.

Reciprocity A procedure by which organizational consumers select suppliers who agree to purchase goods and services as well as sell them.

Reference Group A group that influences a person's thoughts or actions.

Relative Product Failure Occurs if a company is

able to make a profit on an item but the product does not reach profit objectives and/or adversely affects image.

Rented-Goods Service Involves the leasing of a good for a specified period of time.

Reorder Point Establishes an inventory level at which new orders must be placed. It depends on order lead time, usage rate, and safety stock. The reorder point formula is

$$\text{Reorder point} = \frac{(\text{Order lead time} \times \text{Usage}}{\text{rate}) + (\text{Safety stock})}$$

Research Design The framework or plan for a study used as a guide in collecting and analyzing data. A research design includes decisions relating to the person collecting data, data to be collected, group of people or objects studied, data-collection techniques employed, study costs, method of data collection, length of study period and time, and location of data collection.

Retail Catalog Showroom A discount retailer at which consumers select merchandise from a catalog and shop at a warehouse location. Customers frequently write up their own orders, products are usually stored in a back room, and there are limited displays.

Retail Chain Involves the common ownership of multiple units (outlets).

Retail Cooperative A format that allows independent retailers to share purchases, storage and shipping facilities, advertising, planning, and other functions.

Retail Franchising A contractual agreement between a franchisor who may be a manufacturer, wholesaler, or service sponsor and a retail franchisee, which allows the franchisee to conduct a certain form of business under an established name and according to a specific set of rules.

Retail Store Strategy Mix The combination of hours, location, assortment, service, price levels, and other factors a retailer employs.

Retailers Organizations or individuals who buy or handle goods and services for sale (resale) to the ultimate (final) consumer.

Retailing Encompasses those business activities involved with the sale of goods and services to the final consumer for personal, family, or household use. Retailing is the final stage in the channel of distribution.

Revolving Credit Account A credit purchase in which the buyer agrees to make minimum monthly payments during an extended period of time and pays interest on outstanding balances.

Robinson-Patman Act Prohibits manufacturers and wholesalers from price discrimination in dealing with different channel-member purchasers of products of ''like quality,'' if the effect of such discrimination is to injure competition.

Role of Marketing Determined by management, which notes its importance, outlines its functions, and integrates it into the overall operation of the firm.

Routine Consumer Decision Making Occurs when the consumer buys out of habit and skips steps in the decision process. In this category are items that are purchased regularly.

S-Curve Effect Occurs if the sales of a product rise sharply after it is introduced because of a heavy initial promotion effort (ads, coupons, samples, etc.), drop slightly as promotional support is reduced, and then rise again as positive word-of-mouth communication takes place.

Sales Analysis The detailed study of sales data for the purpose of appraising the appropriateness of a marketing strategy.

Sales-Based Pricing Objectives Those that orient a firm's pricing strategy toward high sales volume or expanding sales relative to competitors.

Sales Engineer Accompanies an order getter when a highly technical or complex item is being sold. This salesperson explains product specifications, alternatives, and long-range uses.

Sales Era Involves hiring a sales force and conducting advertising to sell merchandise, after production is maximized. The goal is to fit consumer desires to the attributes of the products being manufactured.

Sales Exception Reporting Lists situations where sales goals are not met or sales opportunities are present.

Sales-Expense Budget Allocates expenditures among salespeople, products, customers, and geographic areas for a given period of time.

Sales Force Surveys A method of sales forecasting that enables sales personnel to pinpoint trends, strengths and weaknesses in a company's offering, competitive strategies, customer resistance, and the traits of heavy users.

Sales Forecast Outlines expected company sales for a specific good or service to a specific consumer group over a specific period of time under a well-defined marketing program.

Sales Invoice The main source of sales analysis data. It contains information on customer name, quantity ordered, price paid, purchase terms, geographic location of purchaser, all different items bought at the same time, order date, shipping arrangements, and salesperson.

Sales Management The planning, implementation, and control of the personal sales function. It covers employee selection, training, territory allocation, compensation, and supervision.

Sales Penetration The degree to which a company achieves its sales potential:

$$\text{Sales penetration} = \frac{\text{Actual sales}}{\text{Sales potential}}$$

Sales Presentation Stage in the selling process that includes a verbal description of the product, its benefits, available options and models, price, associated services (such as delivery and warranty), and a demonstration (if necessary).

Sales Promotion Involves marketing activities — other than advertising, publicity, or personal selling — that stimulate consumer purchases and dealer effectiveness. Included are shows, demonstrations, and various nonrecurrent selling efforts not in the ordinary routine.

Sales Promotion Conditions The requirements that middlemen or consumers must meet to be eligible for a sales promotion.

Sales Promotion Orientation Refers to the focus of sales promotion toward middlemen or consumers and its theme.

Sales Territory Consists of the geographic area, customers, and/or product lines assigned to a salesperson.

Sampling Requires the analysis of selected people or objects in the designated population, rather than all of them.

Satisfaction of Demand Involves actual performance, safety, availability of options, after-sale service, and other factors.

SBU *See* Strategic Business Unit.

Scientific Method A philosophy for marketing research based on objectivity, accuracy, and thoroughness.

Scrambled Merchandising Occurs when a retailer adds products or product lines that are unrelated to each other and the retailer's original business.

Secondary Data Those data that have been previously gathered for purposes other than solving the current problem under investigation. The two types of secondary data are internal and external.

Selective Demand Consumer demand for a particular brand of a product.

Selective Distribution A policy by which the firm employs a moderate number of wholesalers and retailers.

Self-Fulfilling Prophecy A situation in which a company predicts that sales will decline and ensures this by removing marketing support.

Selling Against the Brand A practice used by wholesalers and retailers, whereby they stock well-known brands, place high prices on them, and then sell other brands for lower prices.

Selling Agents Those that assume responsibility for marketing the entire output of a manufacturer under a contractual agreement. They perform all wholesale functions except taking title to merchandise.

Selling Process Involves prospecting for customer leads, approaching customers, determining customer wants, giving a sales presentation, answering questions, closing the sale, and following up.

Semantic Differential A survey technique that uses rating scales of bipolar (opposite) adjectives. An overall company or product profile is then developed.

Service Marketing Encompasses the rental of goods, the alteration or repair of goods owned by consumers, and personal services.

Service Salesperson Usually interacts with customers after sales are completed. Delivery, installation, or other follow-up tasks are undertaken.

Shopping Products Items for which consumers lack sufficient information about product alternatives and their attributes prior to making a purchase decision. The two major kinds of shopping products are attribute-based and price-based.

SIC *See* Standard Industrial Classification.

Simple Trend Analysis A method of sales forecasting by which a firm forecasts future sales on the basis of recent or current performance.

Simulation A computer-based technique that tests the potential effects of various marketing factors via a software program rather than through real-world applications.

Situation Analysis The identification of an organization's internal strengths and weaknesses as well as external opportunities and threats. Situation analysis seeks answers to two general questions: Where is the firm now? In what direction is the firm headed?

Situational Factors Those that can interrupt the organizational consumer's decision process and the actual selection of a supplier or brand. They can include strikes, machine breakdowns, organizational changes, and so on.

Skimming Pricing Utilizes high prices intended to attract the market segment that is more concerned with product quality, uniqueness, or status than price.

Social Class The ranking of people within a culture. Social classes are based on income, occupation, education, and type of dwelling.

Social Marketing The use of marketing to increase the acceptability of social ideas.

Social Performance How a person carries out his or her roles as a worker, family member, citizen, and friend.

Social Responsibility Involves a concern for the consequences of a person's or institution's acts as they might affect the interests of others. Corporate social responsibility balances a company's short-term profit needs with society's long-term needs.

Socioecological View of Marketing Examines all the stages of a product's life span from raw materials to junkpile. The socioecological view incorporates the interests of all consumers who are influenced by the use of a good or service.

Soft Technologies A way to industrialize services by substituting preplanned systems such as prepackaged vacation tours for individual services.

Sorting Process The distribution activities of accumulation, allocation, sorting, and assorting necessary to resolve the differences in the goals of manufacturers and final consumers.

Source The company, independent institution, or opinion leader that seeks to present a message to an audience. Part of the channel of communication.

Specialty-Merchandise (Limited-Line) Wholesalers Full-service merchant wholesalers that concentrate their efforts on a relatively narrow range of products and have an extensive assortment within that range.

Specialty Products Items to which consumers are brand loyal. Consumers are fully aware of product attributes prior to making a purchase decision and are willing to make a significant purchase effort to acquire the brand desired.

Specialty Store A retailer that concentrates on the sale of one merchandise line.

Standard Industrial Classification (SIC) A coding system compiled by the U.S. Office of Management and Budget for which much data has been assembled. It assigns organizations to several basic industrial classifications.

Standard of Living The average quantity and quality of goods and services consumed in a country.

Standardized Approach An international marketing strategy in which a company utilizes a common marketing plan for all countries in which it operates.

Staples Low-priced convenience items that are routinely purchased.

Star A category in the Boston Consulting Group matrix that describes a high market-share strategic business unit (SBU) in an expanding industry. A star generates substantial profits but requires large amounts of resources to finance continued growth.

Status Quo-Based Pricing Objectives Those that orient a firm's pricing strategy toward stability or continuing a favorable climate for operations.

Stimulus A cue (social, commercial, or noncommercial) or a drive (physical) meant to motivate or arouse a person to act.

Stock Turnover Represents the number of times during a specific period (usually one year) that the average inventory on hand is sold. Stock turnover is calculated in units or dollars:

$$\text{Annual rate of stock turnover (units)} = \frac{\text{Number of units sold during year}}{\text{Average inventory on hand (in units)}}$$

$$\text{Annual rate of stock turnover (dollars)} = \frac{\text{Net yearly sales (in dollars)}}{\text{Average inventory on hand (in dollars)}}$$

Straight-Commission Plan   A sales compensation plan that ties a salesperson's earnings directly to sales, profits, or some other performance measure.

Straight Extension Strategy   An international product-planning strategy in which a company manufactures the same products for domestic and foreign sales.

Straight-Rebuy Purchase Process   Routine reordering by organizational consumers for the purchase of inexpensive items bought on a regular basis.

Straight-Salary Plan   A sales compensation plan that pays a salesperson a flat fee per week, month, or year.

Strategic Business Unit (SBU)   A self-contained division, product line, or product department within an organization with a specific market focus and a manager with complete responsibility for integrating all functions into a strategy.

Strategic Planning   Outlines what marketing actions to undertake, why those actions are necessary, who is responsible for carrying them out, when and where they will be completed, and how they will be coordinated.

Strategic Planning Process   Consists of seven interrelated steps: defining organizational mission, establishing strategic business units, setting marketing objectives, situation analysis, developing marketing strategy, implementing tactics, and monitoring results.

Strategy   *See* Marketing Strategy.

Subjective Price   The consumer's perception of a price as high or low.

Subliminal Advertising   A controversial type of promotion that does not enable a consumer to consciously decode a message.

Substantiation   A consumer protection legal concept which requires that a firm be able to prove all promotion claims it makes. This means thorough testing and evidence of performance are needed prior to making claims.

Superstore   A diversified supermarket that sells a broad range of food and nonfood items.

Supplier/Middleman Contracts   Focus on price policy, conditions of sale, territorial rights, the services/responsibility mix, and contract length and conditions of termination.

Surcharges   A form of price adjustment in which across-the-board price increases are published to supplement list prices. Frequently used with catalogs because of their simplicity; an insert is distributed with the catalog.

Survey   The systematic gathering of information from respondents by communicating with them in person, over the telephone, or by mail.

Systems Selling   A combination of goods and services sold by a single source. This enables the buyer to have single-source accountability, one firm with which to negotiate, and assurance of the compatibility of various parts and components.

Tactical Plans   Specify the short-run actions (tactics) a firm would undertake in implementing a given marketing strategy.

Tangible Product   The basic physical entity, service, or idea which has precise specifications and is offered under a given description or model number.

Target Market   The particular group(s) of customers that the organization/individual proposes to serve, or whose needs it proposes to satisfy, with a particular marketing program.

Target Market Strategy   Consists of three general phases: analyzing consumer demand, targeting the market, and developing the marketing strategy.

Target Pricing   A form of cost-based pricing in which prices are set to provide a particular rate of return on investment for a standard volume of production. Mathematically it is

Target price = [(Investment costs × Target return on investment %)/ Standard volume] + (Average total costs at standard volume)

Tariff   The most common form of trade restriction, in which a tax is placed on imported goods by a foreign government.

Technology   Refers to the development and use of machinery, products, and processes.

Telemarketing   An efficient manner of doing business whereby telephone communications are used to sell or solicit business or to set up an appointment for a salesperson to sell or solicit business.

Terms   The provisions of price agreements, including discounts, timing of payments, and credit arrangements.

Test Marketing   The stage in a new-product planning process in which a product is placed for sale in one or more selected areas and its actual sales performance under the proposed marketing plan is observed.

Time Expenditures Involve the types of activities in which a person participates and the amount of time allocated to them.

Total-Cost Approach Determines the distribution service level with the lowest total costs, including freight, warehousing, and the cost of lost business. The ideal system seeks a balance between low distribution costs and high opportunities for sales.

Trade Character A brand mark that is personified.

Trade Deficit Occurs when the value of imports exceeds the value of exports for a country.

Trade Quota A form of trade restriction in which limits are set on the amount of goods that may be imported into a country.

Trademark A brand name, brand mark, trade character, or combination thereof that is legally protected.

Traditional Break-Even Analysis Determines the sales quantity (in units or dollars) at which total costs equal total revenues at a given price:

$$\frac{\text{Break-even}}{\text{point}} = \frac{\text{Total fixed costs}}{\text{Price} - \frac{\text{Variable costs}}{\text{(per unit)}}}$$

$$\frac{\text{Break-even}}{\text{point}} = \frac{\text{Total fixed costs}}{1 - \frac{\text{Variable costs (per unit)}}{\text{Price}}}$$

Traditional Department Store A store that has the greatest assortment of any retailer, provides many customer services, is a fashion leader, and dominates the stores around it.

Transportation Service Companies Handle the shipments of small and moderate-sized packages. The three kinds of companies are government parcel post, private parcel service, and express service.

Truck/Wagon Wholesalers Limited-service merchant wholesalers which have regular sales routes, offer items from a truck or wagon, and deliver goods as they are sold.

Two-Sided Messages Communication in which a firm mentions both benefits and limitations of its good, service, or idea.

Two-Step Flow of Communication Theory stating that a message goes from the company to opinion leaders and then to the target market.

Unbundled Pricing A strategy that breaks down prices by individual components and allows consumers to decide what to purchase.

Uncontrollable Factors Those elements affecting an organization's performance that cannot be directed by the organization and its marketers. These include consumers, competition, government, the economy, technology, and independent media.

Undifferentiated Marketing (Mass Marketing) A company's strategy to appeal to the whole market with a single basic marketing strategy intended to have mass appeal.

Unfair-Sales Acts Legislation in several states preventing retailers from selling merchandise for less than the cost of the product plus a fixed percentage that covers overhead and profit.

Uniform Delivered Pricing A form of geographic pricing in which all buyers pay the same delivered price for the same quantity of goods, regardless of their location. The seller pays for shipping.

Unit Pricing Prices expressed per unit of measure as well as by total value. Enables consumers to compare price per quantity for competing brands and for various sizes of the same brand.

Unitary Demand Exists if changes in price are exactly offset by changes in quantity demanded, so that total sales revenue remains constant.

Universal Product Code (UPC) Requires manufacturers to pre-mark items with a series of thick and thin vertical lines; price and inventory data are contained but are not readable by employees and customers.

Unplanned Business District A retail location form in which a group of stores is located close to one another without the use of prior planning. There are four types of unplanned business districts: central business district, secondary business district, neighborhood business district, and string.

UPC *See* Universal Product Code.

VALS (Values and Life-Styles) Program A classification system for segmenting consumers in terms of a broad range of demographic and life-style factors. The VALS program divides American life-styles into various categories.

Value Analysis A comparison of the costs versus the benefits of alternative materials, components, designs, or processes in order to reduce the cost/

benefit ratio of purchases as much as possible.

Variability in Service Quality Due to the difficulty of diagnosing a problem (for repairs), the inability of the customer to verbalize his or her service needs, and the lack of standardization and mass production for most services.

Variable Markup Policy A form of cost-based markup pricing whereby separate categories of goods and services receive different percentage markups. Variable markups recognize differences in personal selling efforts, customer service, alterations, and end-of-season markdown requirements.

Variable Pricing A firm's intentional altering of prices to respond to cost fluctuations or differences in consumer demand.

Variety Store A retailer which sells a wide assortment of low and popularly priced merchandise.

Vending Machine A nonstore retail operation which uses coin- or card-operated machinery, eliminates the use of sales personnel, allows around-the-clock sales, and can be placed outside rather than inside a store.

Vendor Analysis The assessment of the strengths and weaknesses of current or new suppliers in terms of such factors as merchandise quality, customer service, reliability, and price.

Venture Team A product-management organization form in which a small, independent department consisting of a broad range of specialists manages a new product's entire development process from idea generation to market introduction. Team members work on a full-time basis and function as a separate unit within the company.

Vertical Audit An in-depth analysis of one aspect of the firm's marketing strategy.

Vertical Integration When a firm shortens its channel by acquiring a company at another stage in the channel.

Vertical Price Fixing Occurs when manufacturers or wholesalers can control the final selling prices of their goods or services.

Video-Shopping Services Allow retailers to efficiently, conveniently, and promptly present information, receive orders, and process customer transactions. Its two basic categories are merchandise catalogs on videodiscs and videocassettes, and in-store and in-home ordering systems.

Voluntary Simplicity A consumer life-style in which people seek material simplicity, have an ecological

awareness, strive for self-reliance, and purchase do-it-yourself products.

Warehousing Involves the physical facilities used primarily for the storage of goods held in anticipation of sales and transfers within a distribution channel.

Warranty An assurance given to consumers that a product will meet certain performance standards.

Waste The portion of a medium's audience that is not in the firm's target market.

Waterways Transporters of goods on barges via inland rivers and on tankers and general merchandise freighters through Great Lakes, intercoastal shipping, and the St. Lawrence Seaway.

Wearout Rate The time it takes for a message to lose its effectiveness.

Wheel of Retailing A concept describing how low-end (discount) strategies can turn into high-end (high price) strategies and thus provide opportunities for new firms to enter as discounters.

Wholesale Cooperative A full-service merchant wholesaler owned by member firms which seeks to economize functions and offer broad support. There are producer-owned and retailer-owned wholesale cooperatives.

Wholesalers Organizations or individuals who buy or handle merchandise and its subsequent resale to organizational users, retailers, and other wholesalers.

Wholesaling Involves the buying and handling of merchandise and its resale to organizational users, retailers, and/or other wholesalers but not the sale of significant volume to final consumers.

Width of a Product Mix The number of different product lines a company offers.

Word-of-Mouth Communication The process by which people express their opinions and product-related experiences to one another.

Yield Management Pricing A form of demand-based pricing whereby a firm determines the mix of price-quantity combinations that yields the highest level of revenues for a given period.

Zone Pricing A form of geographic pricing which provides for a uniform delivered price to all buyers within a geographic zone. In a multiple-zone system, delivered prices vary by zone.

Company Index

Name Index

Subject Index

*Absolute product failure, 295
*Accelerator principle, organizational consumer's demand and, 189
*Accessory equipment, 266–267
Account executive, A2, A7, A9
Account supervisor, A7, A9
Accounting, marketing and, 61
Accumulation, in sorting process, 360
Acquisitions, 43
Actor playing a role, as source of communication, 459
*Adaptation, organization's attainment of, 30, 50, 51
*Additional markup, 599
*Administered channel, 361
*Administered questionnaires, for data collection, 107
*Adoption process, of new product, 306–307
*Advertising, 454, 459, 472
  bait-and-switch, 474, 475, 569
  careers in, A1, A2, A5, A7, A8, A9, A11
  characteristics of, 486–488
  comparative, 474
  cooperative, 502, 503
  corrective, 475
  costs of, 495
  deceptive, 474
  definition, 457, 484
  distributed, 501
  expenditures, 15
  full disclosure, 474
  institutional, 468–470
  legal aspects of, 474–475
  massed, 501
  multiunit, 500
  personal selling and, 473, 521
  plan for, 488–504
    advertisement creation in, 500, 501
    advertisement timing in, 500–502

*denotes listing of term in Glossary.

advertising themes in, 493
budget in, 490–493
cooperative advertising in, 502, 503
evaluation in, 502–503
media selection in, 494–500
objectives set in, 489
responsibility for advertising in, 489–490
price, 569
in promotion mix, 472–473
public relations distinguished from, 506
publicity distinguished from, 484, 506
scope and importance of, 484–486
subliminal, 465
*Advertising agency, 490
Advertising copywriter, A2
Advertising layout person, A2
Advertising manager, A2
*Advertising media costs, 495
Advertising production manager, A2
Advertising research director, A2
*Advertising themes, 493
Advertorials, advertising in, 458, 500
Age
  consumer demographics considering, 130, 131–132
  as segmentation factor, 218–220
*Agent (broker), A2
  see also Wholesaling
Aided recall, feedback obtained or monitored with, 467
AIO inventories, life-styles classified by, 152, 153
Airline Deregulation Act, 46
*Airways, as transportation form, 375, 376, 377
*All-you-can-afford technique, of promotional budgeting, 470, 471

Allocation, in sorting process, 360
Ambush marketing, 458
American Demographics, 130
American Way of Death (Mitford), 720
Andean Common Market, 654
*Anticipation of demand, 9
Antitrust, legislation on, 44, 45
*Approaching customers, in selling process, 528
Art director, A7
Asian Common Market, 654
Aspirational group, 154
Assistant account executive, A7
Association of South East Nations, 654
Assorting, in sorting process, 360
*Atmosphere, as retailing consideration, 433–434
*Attitudes, 157
  change in as feedback form, 466
  in consumer's psychological profile, 157–158
  product development and, 302
  segmentation based on, 219
*Attribute-based shopping products, 265
*Audience, in communication process, 465–466
*Augmented product, 260, 261
Automatic teller machines (ATMs), 438, 673
Autonomous decision making, by organizational consumer, 204
Availability
  as organizational buying objective, 199–200
  as purchase act consideration, 172
Average fixed costs, 607, 608, 609
Average total costs, 607, 608, 609
Average variable costs, 607, 608, 609

Background editorial release, as publicity type, 510